CRIMINAL LAW

Oxford University Press, the world's leading academic publisher, offers you a tailored teaching and learning solution with this custom text which contains chapters selected from OUP texts.

This custom text has been compiled for De Montfort University

Please bear in mind that any cross-references will apply to chapters in the original book rather than to chapters within this custom text. If you would like to follow up on any of these references, please consult the original work in which the chapter appears. See **www.oup.com** for the full catalogue of OUP books.

Each page in this custom text has two sets of page numbers for ease of use. The page numbering of the original books is included to enable correct citation and reference back to the book from which the chapter is taken. There is also consecutive page numbering throughout this custom text in a shaded band at the bottom of each page.

The authors included in this custom text are responsible only for the ideas expressed in their own writing and not for any views that might be expressed by authors of other chapters.

CRIMINAL LAW

3rd Edition

COMPILED FROM

Smith & Hogan's Essentials of Criminal Law
2nd edition
John Child and David Ormerod

Smith & Hogan's Criminal Law
15th edition
David Ormerod and Karl Laird

OXFORD
UNIVERSITY PRESS

OXFORD
UNIVERSITY PRESS

Great Clarendon Street, Oxford, OX2 6DP,
United Kingdom

Oxford University Press is a department of the University of Oxford.
It furthers the University's objective of excellence in research, scholarship,
and education by publishing worldwide. Oxford is a registered trade mark of
Oxford University Press in the UK and in certain other countries

This custom text © Oxford University Press 2018

The moral rights of the authors have been asserted

Impression: 1

Public sector information reproduced under Open Government Licence v3.0
(http://www.nationalarchives.gov.uk/doc/open-government-licence/open-government-licence.htm)

Published in the United States of America by Oxford University Press
198 Madison Avenue, New York, NY 10016, United States of America

British Library Cataloguing in Publication Data
Data available

ISBN 978–0–19–883473–1

Printed in Great Britain by
Ashford Colour Press Ltd, Gosport, Hampshire

Compiled from:

Smith, Hogan, & Ormerod's Essentials of Criminal Law 2e
By John Child and David Ormerod
ISBN: 9780198788683
© Oxford University Press 2017

Smith & Hogan's Criminal Law 15e
By David Ormerod and Karl Laird
ISBN: 9780198807094
© Oxford University Press 2018

CONTENTS

Foreword   vii

1. **Introduction**   1
   (Chapter 1 from Child & Ormerod: *Smith & Hogan's Essentials of
   Criminal Law* 2nd edn)

2. ***Actus reus***   37
   (Chapter 2 from Child & Ormerod: *Smith & Hogan's Essentials of
   Criminal Law* 2nd edn)

3. ***Mens rea***   82
   (Chapter 3 from Child & Ormerod: *Smith & Hogan's Essentials of
   Criminal Law* 2nd edn)

4. **Interaction of *actus reus* and *mens rea***   126
   (Chapter 4 from Child & Ormerod: *Smith & Hogan's Essentials of
   Criminal Law* 2nd edn)

5. **Murder**   145
   (Chapter 5 from Child & Ormerod: *Smith & Hogan's Essentials of
   Criminal Law* 2nd edn)

6. **Manslaughter**   162
   (Chapter 6 from Child & Ormerod: *Smith & Hogan's Essentials of
   Criminal Law* 2nd edn)

7. **Non-fatal offences against the person**   214
   (Chapter 7 from Child & Ormerod: *Smith & Hogan's Essentials of
   Criminal Law* 2nd edn)

8. **Property offences**   274
   (Chapter 9 from Child & Ormerod: *Smith & Hogan's Essentials of
   Criminal Law* 2nd edn)

9. **Fraud**   333
   (Chapter 10 from Child & Ormerod: *Smith & Hogan's Essentials of
   Criminal Law* 2nd edn)

10. **General inchoate offences**   365
    (Chapter 11 from Child & Ormerod: *Smith & Hogan's Essentials of
    Criminal Law* 2nd edn)

11. **Parties to crime**   420
    (Chapter 12 from Child & Ormerod: *Smith & Hogan's Essentials of
    Criminal Law* 2nd edn)

12. **Denials of an offence**   462
(Chapter 13 from Child & Ormerod: *Smith & Hogan's Essentials of Criminal Law* 2nd edn)

13. **General defences**   506
(Chapter 14 from Child & Ormerod: *Smith & Hogan's Essentials of Criminal Law* 2nd edn)

14. **Mental Conditions, Intoxication and Mistake**   552
(Chapter 9 from Ormerod & Laird : *Smith & Hogan's Criminal Law* 15th edn)

15. **General Defences**   616
(Chapter 10 from Ormerod & Laird : *Smith & Hogan's Criminal Law* 15th edn)

16. **Voluntary Manslaughter**   685
(Chapter 13 from Ormerod & Laird : *Smith & Hogan's Criminal Law* 15th edn)

17. **Involuntary Manslaughter**   733
(Chapter 14 from Ormerod & Laird : *Smith & Hogan's Criminal Law* 15th edn)

18. **Non-fatal offences against the person**   780
(Chapter 16 from Ormerod & Laird : *Smith & Hogan's Criminal Law* 15th edn)

19. **Parties to Crime**   879
(Chapter 6 from Ormerod & Laird : *Smith & Hogan's Criminal Law* 15th edn)

20. **Making off Without Payment**   939
(Chapter 21 from Ormerod & Laird : *Smith & Hogan's Criminal Law* 15th edn)

FOREWORD

Dear De Montfort University student,

Criminal law is one of the most exciting areas of legal study, but the subject matter is vast. Nobody knows exactly how many offences exist, but they number in the thousands. This means that all courses in Criminal Law have to be selective: some offences are covered in depth; some in outline; whilst most will not feature on the syllabus. Criminal Law at De Montfort University is no different. The teaching team have given a great deal of thought to how best to introduce students to the fundamentals of criminal law, recognising that this is the first time most students have studied the subject and, for all students, it is the first time that they have studied it at degree level. Oxford University Press has compiled this book for us, which we have designed specifically for the course you are taking. It covers the entire syllabus at an appropriate level and includes additional advanced material for the topics we will address in more detail. It is tailor made to supplement the content of the lectures and to help you prepare for seminars.

Furthermore, this module coupled with this excellent textbook will enable you to accommodate and assimilate the substantive topics in order that you develop professional functional awareness through application and analysis, thereby preparing you for whichever workplace you choose.

On behalf of all of the teaching team, we hope that you enjoy studying Criminal Law and wish you every success on the course.

Professor Vanessa Bettinson
Module Leader, LLBP3015 Criminal Law

David Hodgkinson
Module Leader, LLBP1015 Criminal Law

1

Introduction

1.1   Focusing on the substantive criminal law   1
    1.1.1 What should be criminalised?   2
    1.1.2 Why do people commit crime?   4
    1.1.3 How can we prove a crime has been committed?   5
    1.1.4 What are the punishments for committing crimes?   6
    1.1.5 What is the difference between criminal and civil law?   6
    1.1.6 What is the criminal law in other jurisdictions?   7
    1.1.7 What is the process and procedure in trying a criminal case?   8
1.2   Sources of the substantive criminal law   15
    1.2.1 Statute   15
    1.2.2 Common law   16
    1.2.3 European Convention on Human Rights   17
    1.2.4 European Union   19
    1.2.5 International law   20
    1.2.6 The Law Commission and the Draft Criminal Code   21
1.3   The internal structure of offences and defences   22
1.4   The principles of the substantive criminal law   24
    1.4.1 The principle of fair warning   25
    1.4.2 The principle of fair labelling   26
    1.4.3 The principle of autonomy   27
    1.4.4 The principle of welfare   27
1.5   The subjects of the substantive criminal law   28
    1.5.1 Corporations   29
    1.5.2 Minors   31
    1.5.3 Defendants who are unfit to plead   31
1.6   Reform   33
1.7   Eye on assessment   34

1.1 Focusing on the substantive criminal law

In this book we will be exploring the criminal law of England and Wales. Many aspects of the criminal law feature in the news and debates in the media every day, which is useful and important because it reminds us about the vital role played by the criminal law in society. It makes the study of criminal law more interesting, and it can also highlight conflict and potential problems for the law. However, readers need to be aware that the focus of these debates and discussions is commonly very different from that involved in the study of substantive criminal law. The debates will often relate to sentencing, procedure, police investigation, and criminal justice matters generally. Our focus in this book is on *substantive* criminal law. It is about how offences like theft and murder are defined, not about who commits them or why (criminology), how they are investigated by the police (policing and criminal procedure), how they are prosecuted and proved in court (evidence), or how they are sentenced (sentencing). Take the following example:

> The defendant (D) kicks the victim (V) hard in the shin. D commits an offence.

Our focus involves an analysis of what D did, what circumstances she did it in, and what effect it had on V. Did D kick V while she was drunk or insane or acting in self-defence? Did V suffer serious injury or minor injury? Was V consenting (eg was it in a football match)? Questions like these lead us to identify the correct category of possible offences. Having identified the category, our task is then to explore the specific offences in detail, asking precisely what actions or omissions are criminal and comparing the offence requirements with D's behaviour. Following this, if we find the elements of an offence are satisfied, we then go on to explore possible defences.

Although our central study in this book is of the definitions of criminal offences and defences, in this introductory chapter it is important for us to set this in context. The following sections provide short descriptions of related matters that it is helpful for readers to be aware of in order to understand fully the substantive criminal rules in context, and to evaluate them effectively.

1.1.1 What should be criminalised?

When studying the substantive criminal law, it is natural to question the basis upon which certain conduct is criminalised and other conduct is not. We may ask *why* certain conduct has been made criminal (eg why is it an offence for D to kick V?);[1] we may ask why particular conduct *should* be criminal (eg why should it be an offence for D to kick V?).[2] These questions and challenges are important areas of research for those concerned with law reform and criminal law policy. If we recommend that a new offence should be created, or a present offence abolished or amended, we need to be able to explain a principled basis for our view. That basis is most often found in moral and political philosophy.[3]

Questions about the legitimate objectives for criminalisation are perhaps inevitably imprecise, resting as they do on studies of moral and political philosophy. There is no single, agreed, criterion for what makes a 'good' criminal offence. That is not to suggest that examining how and why things are criminalised is unimportant. It is extremely

---

[1] This is referred to as a 'descriptive challenge': seeking an explanation for a current state.
[2] This is referred to as a 'normative challenge': questioning the rights or wrongs of a current state.
[3] See eg Simester and Von Hirsch, *Crimes, Harms and Wrongs: On the Principles of Criminalisation* (2011); Hörnle, 'Theories of Criminalization' (2016) 10 Crim L & Phil 301.

important to study what is being criminalised because to criminalise behaviour is the most serious step a State can take: it prohibits conduct and backs that prohibition with a stigmatising label and a criminal penalty (eg fines, imprisonment, etc). Criminalisation should not, therefore be justified as a response to every form of conduct we find distasteful or anti-social, it must be reserved for only the most serious transgressions that justify the State in harming D's interests.

Traditionally, where theorists have attempted to explain and justify criminalisation, they have focused on the targeting of 'harm': conduct from D that infringes the autonomy of V (physically or otherwise), or causes serious offence.[4] Harm is a useful target because, unlike older theories based on *moral* wrongs, harm is at least relatively objective: harms can generally be observed, tested, and measured. However, although this approach is readily applicable to offences against the person such as murder, rape, or battery (eg D kicking V), it is much more difficult to present harm as the rationale for offences that can be committed before harm is caused (eg liability for attempting to commit a crime[5]) or the many regulatory offences (eg failing to have a valid road traffic licence for a vehicle). As a result, the advocates of a 'harms' or 'wrongs' approach are left with a difficult choice: maintain a narrow view of harm and fail to explain a large part of the criminal law that does not target such harm, or interpret harms and wrongs widely enough to encompass all offences (eg endangering/harming public order) but in doing so risk the concept of harm becoming so broad that it is no longer useful.[6]

In order to address the perceived problem that a theory based on harms or wrongs may too readily justify creating too many criminal offences, Duff has outlined a useful distinction between what he terms 'private wrongs' (wrongs that are not legitimate targets for criminalisation) and 'public wrongs' (which are).[7] For example, if D finishes a relationship with V in an unkind manner, we can say that D has acted wrongfully and we may even say that she has harmed V. However, D's wrong is a private wrong: answerable to V, and perhaps to friends and family, but one where the State, and thus the criminal law, has no legitimate role. In contrast, where D kicks V, it may be that the damage done to V, and society's legitimate interest in protecting others, means that D's wrong is public and deserving of criminalisation. The problem here of course, recognised by Duff, is that the distinction between a private wrong and a public wrong is politically and morally subjective, and lacks clear criteria. However, although this is a problem for those who want to establish a clear separation of legitimate and illegitimate targets of the criminal law, it may be no more than an accurate description of the political process.[8]

Theories of criminalisation provide a fascinating area for research in their own right. However, as we analyse the substantive rules of law in later chapters, such theories are rarely of direct relevance. The fact that they are not directly relevant is not to suggest

---

[4] For discussion and development of the 'harm principle', see Mill, *On Liberty* (1859); Feinberg, *Harm to Others* (1984).

[5] Criminal Attempts Act 1981.

[6] See Duff, *Answering for Crime* (2007) Ch6. For a modern defence of the harm principle, see Horder, 'Harmless Wrongdoing and the Anticipatory Perspective on Criminalisation' in Sullivan and Dennis (eds), *Seeking Security* (2012) 79; Horder, 'Bribery as a Form of Criminal Wrongdoing' (2011) 127 LQR 37.

[7] Duff, *Answering for Crime* (2007).

[8] For a more ambitious attempt to set limits on legitimate criminalisation, see Husak, *Overcriminalisation* (2008).

that they should be forgotten or ignored: drawing on theories of criminalisation to discuss why conduct has been legitimately criminalised can help in our central task (analysing the substantive criminal law) in a number of important ways. Three clear examples will suffice:

A) **When interpreting an imprecise offence/defence:** Where an offence or defence is imprecise, it is common for the courts to consider the intentions of the legislature in order to clarify and apply the rule. In the context of offences, the aim is to identify the mischief that the offence was designed to target, ensuring that it is interpreted in order to capture only that. For example, in the case of *Wilson*,[9] at his wife's (V's) request, D consensually branded his initials onto her buttocks with a hot knife. D was convicted of an offence against the person, and appealed on the basis that V's consent should have undermined liability. As we discuss in **7.8.2**, the current law regarding consent in this area is far from clear. However, the Court of Appeal allowed D's appeal and quashed his conviction, stating firmly that the criminal law had no place interfering in the private lives of the married couple when they engaged in this activity.

B) **When we are evaluating the effectiveness of an offence:** It may also be useful to consider the mischief (harms and/or wrongs) that an offence was designed to target when we are considering whether it is working well. We can then ask whether the definition of the offence has successfully targeted that mischief, and if it has, whether it has gone beyond that target to criminalise other conduct inappropriately. Indeed, the evaluation of an offence will often focus on its over-inclusivity (criminalising more than intended) or under-inclusivity (criminalising less than intended), and this analysis only makes sense once we have identified the mischief targeted.

As we will see, the potential for overly broad criminalisation in particular is a criticism that has been made of several recent statutes.[10] A useful example can be seen in the drafting of sexual offences, discussed in **Chapter 8**. In an effort to meet concerns about the ineffectiveness of some sexual offences (including claims of low conviction rates), a succession of reforms have expanded a number of the key offence definitions. However, despite the legitimate rationale for these reforms, questions now emerge about whether they have gone too far; whether the wide reach of these offences risks over-criminalisation.

C) **When discussing the potential for a new offence:** In several places in this book we discuss proposals for new criminal offences. When we do so, it is useful to consider the particular mischief that those new offences would be looking to target, and to consider whether they are adequately covered by existing law. For example, when discussing the offences against the person in **Chapter 7**, we consider the potential for specific offences relating to domestic violence and the transmission of HIV.

1.1.2 Why do people commit crime?

Exploring the reasons why people commit crimes, which types of people commit them, and whether certain groups are over-represented in criminal statistics, is a valuable

---

[9]   [1996] Crim LR 573.
[10]   See eg our discussion of the Fraud Act 2006 in **Chapter 10**, and the Serious Crime Act 2007 in **Chapter 11**.

pursuit.[11] For example, the reasons why a particular defendant assaulted or harassed a particular victim may help us to identify ways, whether legal or otherwise, to prevent such conduct in the future. It may also help us identify appropriate penalties. However, this is the focus for studies in criminology, and will not be central to the discussions in this book.

Questions about why people make bad choices are not generally relevant to the substance of the law, unless those reasons are explicitly recognised as criminal defences. D may have a good reason (a good motive if you like) for committing an offence, but unless this is recognised within the legal rules, it is irrelevant to her criminal liability.[12] When you are answering a problem question you are considering D's liability with regard to set criminal rules, you are not judging whether D is a good or a bad person.

1.1.3 How can we prove a crime has been committed?

When we consider how the criminal law is applied in practice, issues of procedure and evidence are extremely important (eg how can we prove D kicked V, or that D intended to do so?).[13] Indeed, in order to practise in the area of criminal law, the study of criminal evidence is essential. However, again, criminal evidence is not directly relevant to the identification of legal rules governing the substantive criminal law—the definition of offences and defences.

Understanding evidential issues can, however, help our understanding and evaluation of the substantive law because it sheds light on how well criminal offences operate in practice. For example, if an offence requiring proof that D *intended* a particular result is too hard to prove (evidentially), this should lead us to consider whether a new offence should be created requiring proof of something short of intention. Similarly, evidential rules and their operation are also relevant in assessing the difficulties faced in proving other offence elements. For example, criminalising conduct at a point before harm is caused (eg for attempting to harm V) would avoid the need to prove harm and allow for early intervention and harm prevention, which are both desirable. However, offences drafted in these terms will generate problems of proof (evidentially) where D's criminal behaviour at this earlier point must be considered, and may not be manifestly of a criminal kind. We discuss this further in **Chapter 11**.

Assessment matters . . .
Where the facts of a problem question state what D is thinking, it is tempting to ask how this could be proved in real life. For example, if D kicks V in a game of football you may be told in the problem that D did so intentionally. You may then question how the police and Crown Prosecution Service could ever know or prove that, in a game of football, D's kicking of V was intentional. However, this does not affect your application of the substantive criminal law. The method by which D's state of mind can be proved in court is a separate issue, and not one you need to deal with. Your task is to discuss and apply the definition of battery (the offence committed) on the facts you are given, and if you are told that D intended to kick V, then you should take this as a fact.

---

[11] Hale et al, *Criminology* (3rd edn, 2013).
[12] Although good reasons may provide mitigation affecting D's sentencing, this issue only arises *after* D has been found guilty for the relevant offence.
[13] Munday, *Evidence* (8th edn, 2015).

1.1.4 What are the punishments for committing crimes?

Where D is found guilty of a criminal offence (eg for battery when kicking V), D will be subject to a criminal sanction, most commonly a fine, a community penalty, or prison sentence. Some basic understanding of punishment and sentencing is useful when discussing the substantive criminal law, although this is not usually part of a criminal law course and is not part of our study in this book.

What may be important in the course of your study of criminal law is to note the relative gravity of offences, by reference to their maximum sentence. For example, where D intentionally kicks V without V's consent, D will have committed the relatively minor offence of battery; if V suffers some harm (eg bruising) D commits the more serious offence of assault occasioning actual bodily harm;[14] and if V suffers serious harm (eg a broken leg) D may have committed an even more serious offence of causing grievous bodily harm with intent.[15] The seriousness of these offences is graded on the basis of the maximum sentence available upon conviction. Therefore, although we are not concerned with theories of punishment, or even the precise methods employed by judges when setting a sentence in the individual case, it is important to understand some basic sentencing details in order to understand the (logically prior) role of the substantive law in setting rules at the liability stage. This will help you to decide, for example, on the appropriate offence to discuss if a defendant's conduct satisfies the requirements of multiple overlapping offences.

In practice, the substantive criminal law is concerned with one question: is D guilty or not. If the elements of an offence are satisfied then D has committed the crime, if not, D has not. There is no grey area between these two final outcomes. However, if convicted, there is much greater flexibility at the sentencing stage. D's punishment will vary depending upon the offence D has committed,[16] with different offences allowing for different maximum sentences, and the circumstances of D's offence will also be considered when setting the sentence below that maximum.[17] The Law Commission will soon be publishing a draft Bill containing a New Sentencing Code designed to bring greater clarity and consistency.[18]

1.1.5 What is the difference between criminal and civil law?

It is important to distinguish a criminal offence from any civil law tort that is similar. For example, in harassment, the criminal law offence and the tort of harassment share common definitions. This may also be relevant as certain offences are based on torts, as with false imprisonment.

Although offences and torts may share definitions and/or a common history, the civil and criminal laws are distinct systems. As with the criminal law, tort cases often centre on harms that one private party has done to another, as where D kicks V. In tort, the

---

[14] Offences Against the Person Act 1861, s47.
[15] Ibid, s18.
[16] Some offences specify a mandatory sentence, but even these have exceptions.
[17] Easton and Piper, *Sentencing and Punishment* (3rd edn, 2012).
[18] See a recent preliminary report, Law Commission, *A New Sentencing Code for England and Wales* (No 365, 2016).

injured party is seeking monetary compensation from D, and if the court is satisfied that such compensation is appropriate, it will require D to make a payment to V in proportion to the harm she has suffered.[19] V must prove her case on the balance of probabilities (the civil standard of proof). Criminal cases, in contrast, represent an action by the State (as prosecutor) against the defendant, with a successful prosecution leading to the *punishment* of D. The criminal law's focus on the wrongful conduct of D, as opposed to the compensation of V, provides an important context to our study of the substantive rules. Here, the State must prove its case against D beyond reasonable doubt (the criminal standard of proof). The criminal and civil law operate in parallel with one another, serving different priorities of justice.

1.1.6 What is the criminal law in other jurisdictions?

This book explores the substantive criminal law in England and Wales; it is not therefore directly concerned with the substantive criminal law in other jurisdictions.[20] However, this is not to say that some discussion and comparison with other jurisdictions will not aid our analysis of the law, and such comparison will arise regularly throughout this book. Where this is the case, comparison will generally be made with other common law jurisdictions such as those in the Republic of Ireland, the United States, Australia, New Zealand, and Canada. This is because with these jurisdictions employing similar systems of criminal law to our own, with a common tradition, comparisons are most easily drawn. Indeed, as the criminal law in these jurisdictions was previously administered by Britain, there are still a number of areas where offence definitions remain identical, or certainly very similar, to our own.

Our study of the substantive criminal law is aided by international comparison in two principal ways.

A) When interpreting the law: The substantive law in another jurisdiction has no bearing on the criminal law in this country. The criminal law in England and Wales, as discussed later, is established through a combination of statutes defining offences and defences, and the decisions of the courts interpreting the law and, *historically*, creating offences and defences through common law. However, the courts might find foreign law helpful when considering a problem that has arisen in that country and is now under scrutiny in the courts in England and Wales. What the foreign courts have decided does not have to be followed by the English courts, but it may be persuasive as to the best approach.[21]

B) When evaluating the law: In the years since other common law jurisdictions (eg those mentioned previously and others) have been independent from Britain, they have created and interpreted their own domestic criminal law. It is helpful to look to other countries with similar traditions of criminal law to examine how their laws are

---

[19] Deakin et al, *Markesinis and Deakin's Tort Law* (7th edn, 2012).

[20] Certain serious offences are extraterritorial in the sense that D can be convicted under English criminal law even where she has committed the criminal act in another jurisdiction.

[21] The reference to foreign case law is particularly common within smaller jurisdictions (eg the Republic of Ireland and Scotland) where the volume of cases, and therefore the body of previous case law nationally, is lower.

developing and to consider whether or not English law compares favourably. As a result, where we consider potential reform in this book, we will often consider the approaches of other common law jurisdictions.

> **Don't be confused . . .**
> When we compare the criminal law of different jurisdictions, we are not discussing international criminal law which is discussed separately later.[22] International criminal law is concerned with a distinct form of criminalisation that applies across multiple States (eg the offence of genocide) and is created through international agreement. Just as this book is focusing on the domestic criminal law of England and Wales, our comparison here is focusing on the domestic criminal law of other national jurisdictions.

1.1.7 What is the process and procedure in trying a criminal case?

Our final topic in this section relates to the administrative structure through which the substantive criminal law is interpreted and applied. For this, we are going to introduce the main actors within the criminal process and their roles (police, Crown Prosecution Service, defence, judge, and jury), and we will also introduce the court and appeals structure. The actors and the administrative structures within the criminal justice system rarely have a direct effect on the substance of criminal rules, but an awareness of both is essential in order to understand those rules in context.

1.1.7.1 The main actors within the criminal justice system

As we discuss the main actors within the criminal justice system, it is essential to remember that a criminal case is an action between the State (as prosecutor) and a private party (as defendant). The victim of the offence, where relevant, may be simply a witness for the court.[23] This is why, unlike within civil law, the victim is not on our list of main actors.

A) The police: After an offence has been committed, the role of the police is to investigate that offence in order to obtain evidence for trial. Where D kicks V, the police will arrest and interview D; try to obtain CCTV footage of the incident; locate any witnesses; record the injuries to V; and so on.

B) The Crown Prosecution Service (CPS): The CPS act as prosecutors on behalf of the State.[24] The head of the CPS, the Director of Public Prosecutions (DPP), is accountable to the Attorney General (AG) who, in turn, is directly accountable to Parliament.

Before any criminal trial commences the CPS have a duty to review the evidence gathered by the police in order to assess whether a prosecution is viable: whether there is sufficient evidence that D kicked V; whether this amounted to a particular offence; and

---

[22] See **1.2.5.**

[23] As criminal justice reform moves towards a victim-focused system, the victim is included throughout the process. However, the main action remains between the State and D.

[24] There are many other agencies with prosecution powers (eg SFO, Defra, FCA, etc) but most trials are conducted by the CPS.

whether it is in the public interest to prosecute.[25] At trial, the CPS present that evidence. In order to obtain a conviction, the CPS must demonstrate D's guilt 'beyond reasonable doubt' as to every element of the offence, the criminal standard of proof.

> **Don't be confused . . .**
> Civil law cases typically involve two private parties in opposition and are therefore referred to using both parties' names (eg *Jones v Smith*). In contrast, criminal law cases typically include only one party name (eg *R v Smith*). This is because in criminal cases the action is between the State as prosecutor (Regina: R) versus a private defendant (party name).

C) The defence: The defendant (D) is the party alleged to have committed the offence. She will be represented in court by her own legal team, where possible.[26] As the prosecution have the burden of proving D's guilt 'beyond reasonable doubt', it is the aim of the defence to raise a 'reasonable doubt' within any essential element of the prosecution's case.

Where D wishes to raise a defence (eg D kicked V in self-defence) she must satisfy what is called an evidential burden: she must provide some evidence that could lead a jury to believe the defence is satisfied. However, this evidential burden is placed on the defendant principally for reasons of efficiency. It avoids wasting the court's time by the court having to consider multiple defences that have no chance of success. This form of evidential burden should not be confused with the legal burden on the prosecution. It is for the prosecution to prove the elements of the offence beyond reasonable doubt: to prove, in our example, that D kicked V intentionally or having foreseen risk of making contact, and that V suffered some minor harm as a result. If D is able to present some evidence as to a defence, satisfying the evidential burden, it is also for the prosecution to prove the absence of that defence beyond reasonable doubt.

D) The jury: Only Crown Court trials involve a jury. The jury is made up of 12 people.[27] The role of the jury is to decide matters of fact and not matters of law. For example, if the law makes it an offence for D to kick V, it is the jury's job to decide if D did in fact kick V. If the definition of the offence requires proof that D intended to injure V, the jury must decide whether D did so intend. The judge decides on matters of law. For example, it may be that D claims she kicked V accidentally as part of a football match. The judge would rule as a matter of law whether consent by V in playing football was *capable* of providing D with a defence. The jury would then decide whether, on the facts, it was a football match, and whether V did consent.

E) The judge: The judge must adjudicate on any legal conflict between the opposing advocates relating to rules of evidence and admissibility, as well as any other matter of law. The judge is also responsible for summing up the facts and directing on the law for the jury before they retire to consider their verdict. In the magistrates' courts the magistrate must make decisions about the evidential rules, the law, *and*, because there is

---

[25] Prosecution of Offences Act 1985, s10.

[26] Defence representation is paid for privately, or through State-assisted legal aid.

[27] Jury members are randomly selected from the voting register up to the age of 75: Criminal Justice and Courts Act 2015, s68. Only those who are mentally incapable, or those with specified (serious or recent) criminal convictions, are excluded: Criminal Justice Act 2003, s321.

no jury, the facts as well. They are assisted in the first two of these by a legally qualified magistrates' clerk. Finally, in all courts, if D is found guilty of an offence, the judge is responsible for setting the appropriate sentence.[28]

Decisions of higher courts (eg the Court of Appeal and the Supreme Court) are made by panels of judges and do not include a jury. In accordance with the doctrine of precedent, the legal interpretations and decisions of these courts then bind the future interpretations of the courts below them.

1.1.7.2 The burden of proof in criminal trials

It is for the prosecution to prove D's guilt, which is known as the legal burden of proof, and they must do so beyond reasonable doubt: the criminal standard of proof. This is designed to limit the risk of innocent people being wrongly convicted.[29] It also recognises the inequality of the resources of the parties, with the State possessing vast resources for investigatory powers and personnel. The legal burden placed on the prosecution means that the defendant is presumed innocent until proven guilty. This is a long-established principle of English law,[30] also found in Article 6(2) of the European Convention on Human Rights (ECHR).

However, although the fact that the prosecution bears the legal burden of proving D's liability may be considered fundamental to the criminal law, it is not an absolute rule. In several instances, the legal burden is 'reversed' and D bears the burden of proving a particular element or defence. An example is where D claims to have been insane when kicking V, and D must prove that she was insane.[31] Reverse burdens of proof remain controversial within the law, not least for their effect on D's right to a fair trial (Art 6 ECHR). However, the use of reverse burdens in certain contexts remains common.[32]

To understand the role of reverse burdens of proof, two aspects require discussion. The first concerns the standard of proof. As highlighted previously, where the burden of proof is on the prosecution, they must prove D's liability 'beyond reasonable doubt'. However, where D bears a reverse burden, she need only prove the relevant element to the civil standard of proof: 'on the balance of probabilities'.[33]

Secondly, where reverse burdens arise, this is usually in the context of defences as opposed to offences (eg insanity[34] and diminished responsibility[35]). This is important because defences only become relevant if the prosecution have already provided evidence that D has committed the elements of the offence. Asking D to prove some element of defence once the Crown has already provided evidence of D's wrongdoing is not directly contrary to the presumption of innocence: the presumption only protects D 'until proven guilty'. In contrast, where reverse legal burdens impose an obligation on D to establish her innocence before the Crown have provided evidence of wrongdoing,

---

[28] The role of the judge is usefully summarised in *Wang* [2005] UKHL 9, [3] and [8].

[29] This is a position neatly encapsulated in the ratio attributed to William Blackstone writing in the 1760s which maintains that 'it is better that ten guilty persons escape than that one innocent suffer'.

[30] *Woolmington v DPP* [1935] AC 462.

[31] We discuss the insanity rules in **Chapters 13** and **14**.

[32] See Dennis, 'Reverse Onuses and the Presumption of Innocence' [2005] Crim LR 901; Stumer, *The Presumption of Innocence, Evidential and Human Rights Perspectives* (2010).

[33] Proving simply that it is more likely than not.

[34] See the *M'Naghten* Rules (1843) 10 Cl & Fin 200, 210.

[35] Homicide Act 1957, s2(2).

the presumption of innocence is infringed. In fact, in many cases where there appeared to be a reversed legal burden, even if this only applied to a single element within an offence, the courts have rejected it and interpreted it as an evidential burden instead to ensure compliance with Art 6 ECHR.[36] This arrangement provides some protection for D's Article 6 rights but remains problematic, particularly as the pivotal distinction between defences and offences lacks objective criteria. For example, the non-consent of V is an offence element in the context of sexual offences, but the consent of V is generally considered to be a defence in the context of other non-fatal offences against the person.[37]

The greatest effect of a reverse burden is as a matter of practice and procedure. However, it may also be directly relevant to the substantive definition of the offence. This is apparent in relation to certain mischiefs that, although deserving of criminalisation, are particularly difficult for prosecutors to prove. For example, as we will discuss in **Chapter 8**, this is true of sexual offences: although involving serious wrongs, it is difficult to prove offences that invariably take place in private, and often come down to dispute over D's and/or V's state of mind as to consent. The temptation to employ a reverse burden as to aspects of the offence (eg consent) is obvious: where we are discussing D's state of mind, surely D is in a better position to present evidence of this than the police or CPS. Indeed, within the Sexual Offences Act 2003, we already see a movement in this direction with the use of reversed rebuttable *evidential* burdens as to consent.[38] However, despite their potential practical utility, whether such reform serves the interests of justice remains a separate question.[39]

1.1.7.3 The criminal court structure and appeals process

In this section we consider the structure of the criminal appeals system.[40] It is important to understand this structure as reference to the different stages of appeal will arise regularly in our discussion of the law. It is also necessary to understand this structure when considering the doctrine of precedent. Just as legislation is binding on all courts, the doctrine of precedent dictates that interpretations of the law made by higher courts will bind (must be applied by) lower courts in future cases. Essentially, the doctrine of precedent is a common law system to ensure consistency between courts and to make future interpretations of the law more predictable. It is on this basis that when looking to identify substantive rules of law we will often do so by discussing the interpretations of the Court of Appeal (Criminal Division) and the Supreme Court (formerly the House of Lords[41]) in particular. When doing so, it is necessary, albeit not always straightforward, to distinguish legal interpretations that were required by the court to reach their decision (referred to as the *ratio decidendi* of the case, and capable of creating binding precedent)

---

[36] The courts do so using the interpretive powers within the Human Rights Act 1998, s3. See eg *Lambert* [2001] UKHL 37 relating to the possession of drugs.

[37] See **Chapters 7** and **8** respectively. It may be that consent is wrongly classified in the context of the non-fatal offences (**7.10.3**).

[38] Sexual Offences Act 2003, s75.

[39] Ashworth and Blake, 'The Presumption of Innocence in English Criminal Law' [1996] Crim LR 306.

[40] See Spencer, 'Does Our Present Criminal Appeal System Make Sense?' [2006] Crim LR 667; Law Commission, *The High Court's Jurisdiction in Relation to Criminal Proceedings* (No 324, 2010).

[41] The Supreme Court replaced the Appellate Committee of the House of Lords as the highest court in the UK in October 2009.

and interpretations that were additionally made, but not necessary to reach the decision (referred to as *obiter dicta*, creating only a persuasive and non-binding precedent).

In **Table 1.1**, we set out the role of each court within the criminal appeals system. We also highlight the potential for appeal between the courts.

Table 1.1 Criminal courts and appeals process

Magistrates' court	The magistrates' courts are the lowest criminal courts in England and Wales. They are usually made up of volunteer magistrates who are not legally qualified, and who are intended to represent the community. They rely on a legal advisor for legal guidance. In some courts there are legally qualified magistrates who sit alone (District Judges). They tend to hear the more serious cases in the magistrates' courts. The sentencing power of the magistrates' court is limited to six months' imprisonment for each offence (12 months overall), and unlimited fines.
	All 'summary only' offences (eg assault and battery) are tried in the magistrates' court. Other offences, known as triable either way offences (offences of which the seriousness can vary considerably on their facts, eg theft and criminal damage) are tried in the magistrates' court unless D elects to be tried in the Crown Court or the magistrates think the case deserves to be tried in the Crown Court. All the most serious cases (triable on indictment only) that are tried in the Crown Court also pass through the magistrates' court. In fact, over 95% of all criminal cases will be settled in the magistrates' court without appeal.
Appeal from magistrates' court	• *D may appeal her conviction to the Crown Court.* This route is available if D pleaded 'not guilty' in the magistrates' court, but was found guilty. This appeal will result in a rehearing of the case in the Crown Court.
	• *D may appeal the level of her sentence to the Crown Court.* Again, this will result in a rehearing.
	• *D and/or the Crown can appeal by 'way of case stated' to the High Court.* This appeal must contend that the magistrates made a mistake in law or acted in excess of their jurisdiction, but there can be no appeal on factual matters.
	• *D and/or the Crown can apply for judicial review to the High Court.* This application must contend that the magistrates acted beyond their power (*ultra vires*).
Crown Court	A Crown Court case will include both a professional judge (High Court Judge, Circuit Judge, or recorder) and a jury. In exceptional cases, it can be tried by judge alone—usually where the jury is discharged by the judge. As discussed earlier, the role of the judge is to decide matters of law, and the role of the jury is to decide matters of fact. The sentencing power of the Crown Court is only limited by the individually prescribed maximum sentence for each offence. In practice the judge follows the guidance from the Sentencing Council.
	We discuss very few Crown Court cases in this book. This is partly because cases at this level are not always reported, and partly because of their limited precedent value when it comes to identifying the substantive law.

Appeal from Crown Court	• In long and complex cases D and/or the Crown can make an interlocutory appeal on the judge's rulings relating to the way the trial will be conducted. The appeal is made to the Court of Appeal before the Crown Court trial commences.
	• The Crown can make an interlocutory appeal to the Court of Appeal on a point of law, if this is made before the trial judge (at Crown Court) begins summing up. This route is only available to trials on indictment, and requires leave from the trial judge or Court of Appeal. If leave to appeal is refused, or the Court of Appeal accepts but upholds the trial judge's ruling on the disputed point of law, then D is acquitted. If the appeal is successful, then the point of law will be corrected and the case will resume at the Crown Court on those amended terms. Thus, this route entails significant risks for the Crown and is rare.
	• If D is convicted at a Crown Court trial she may appeal her conviction to the Court of Appeal. The court will examine the appeal having regard to all its circumstances—'in the round'. If the Court of Appeal finds the conviction 'unsafe' it will allow the appeal, quashing the conviction and ordering a retrial in the Crown Court as appropriate.
	• D may appeal the level of her sentence to the Court of Appeal. The court has the power to quash and substitute any sentence or order as appropriate, although it may not increase its severity if D appealed. The Court of Appeal will only make such a substitution if the sentence is manifestly excessive or wrong in principle, not justified in law, or where matters were improperly considered or ignored.
	• D's conviction and or sentence can be referred to the Court of Appeal by the Criminal Cases Review Commission. If D has had an appeal rejected (or leave for appeal refused), and the CCRC believe there has been a potential miscarriage of justice (relating to conviction or sentence), it can refer it to the Court of Appeal for consideration at any time
	• The Crown may *not* appeal D's acquittal. Founded in the logic of double jeopardy (the principle that D should not face trial for the same crime twice), prosecutors cannot appeal an acquittal in the hope of convicting D. However, changes in the law relating to double jeopardy have created a narrow exception to this. If D was acquitted of one of a list of serious specified offences (eg murder or rape), and if new and compelling evidence is discovered making it more likely that D committed the offence, and if the DPP consents, the Court of Appeal may quash an acquittal and allow for new proceedings to be brought against D in the Crown Court.
	• If D is acquitted, the AG can refer a point of law to the Court of Appeal (AG's Reference cases). As stated earlier, where D has been acquitted the Crown cannot appeal against this acquittal. However, if the Crown Court's decision to acquit was based on a potentially mistaken interpretation of law, the lack of an appeal risks further damage (other courts applying similar reasoning). Therefore, this process allows the AG to refer a point of law that emerged at trial. D's acquittal is not at issue, and will remain in place irrespective of the Court of Appeal's decision. However, the mistaken point of law (if there is one) can be corrected for future cases.

(Continued)

Table 1.1 Continued

	• The AG can appeal the level of sentence to the Court of Appeal. Where D has been convicted and sentenced for certain offences identified by Parliament, the AG (on behalf of the prosecution) can refer the case to the Court of Appeal if the AG believes the sentence is 'unduly lenient'. The court is empowered to quash the previous sentence or order and replace it as appropriate, including the potential for a more severe penalty.
Court of Appeal (Criminal Division)	When the Court of Appeal sits to hear an appeal it is usually comprised of three judges presided over by a Lord Justice of Appeal (senior judge). Decisions of the Court of Appeal create precedent that binds the future interpretations of lower courts and, generally, future interpretations in the Court of Appeal as well. Occasionally, however, where a case is taken before an expanded Court of Appeal panel of five judges the court is more open to departing from its own precedents. The majority of the cases that we discuss in this book are Court of Appeal cases.
Appeal from Court of Appeal	• *D and/or the Crown may appeal to the Supreme Court.* Appeals to the Supreme Court will only be available where the disputed point of law is of 'general public importance'. Leave must be granted by the Court of Appeal or the Supreme Court. Where leave is granted, the Supreme Court may also, at its discretion, consider related issues of law that are not directly connected to the point appealed.
Supreme Court	The Supreme Court is the highest court in the UK (formerly the House of Lords), presided over by 12 Justices of the Supreme Court. Decisions of the Supreme Court create binding precedent for all lower courts, including the Court of Appeal. The Supreme Court also considers itself bound, although it may depart from its own precedent where appropriate. Supreme Court (House of Lords) cases will be discussed throughout this book. Creating the strongest judicial precedent, these decisions form a central part of our identification of the substantive law.
Privy Council	At a number of points in this book we will consider decisions of the Judicial Committee of the Privy Council. The Privy Council is based in the Supreme Court building, with roughly the same set of judges sitting in both courts. However, the Privy Council is not part of the criminal court structure for cases originating in England and Wales. Rather, the Privy Council is the court of final appeal for UK overseas territories and Crown dependencies, and for those Commonwealth countries that have retained the appeal to Her Majesty in Council or, in the case of republics, to the Judicial Committee. As the Privy Council is not directly applying the law of England and Wales, opinions of the Board have no binding effect on the courts within the structure outlined above. However, when interpreting areas of law that are identical or similar to those in this jurisdiction, bearing in mind that the judges in the Privy Council are usually also Supreme Court Justices, the Board's decisions can have a strongly persuasive effect.

1.2 Sources of the substantive criminal law

Having spent some time setting the substantive criminal law in context, and distinguishing other approaches to the study of crime, it is now possible to narrow our focus to the substantive rules themselves. The first part of this involves a discussion about the sources of the criminal law. Before we begin to interpret and apply the substantive law, we must first learn how to identify it and its basis.

Recognising the sources of the criminal law is extremely important. For example, when D kicks V causing harm, D commits a public wrong that is deserving of criminalisation. However, the formal source that criminalises D's conduct is the Offences Against the Person Act 1861.

1.2.1 Statute

Most of the substantive criminal laws in England and Wales are now set out in statutory form, the principal binding source of criminal law. There are two main benefits to this. First, as the criminal law defines and controls such an important area of interaction between State and citizen, it is appropriate that these rules should be constructed through a democratically accountable process. Secondly, statutes are more accessible to all, at least by comparison with the common law discussed later. Particularly since the development and consolidation of online resources (eg www.legislation.gov.uk), it is now possible for citizens to have access to statutory rules quickly and easily. However, a degree of caution is needed on several matters.

A) **Quantity of legislation:** Although statutes are accessible, the sheer quantity of legislation makes it impossible for the legal practitioner, let alone the public, to be fully informed.[42] Problems can also be created where, as is very common, new statutes include multiple amending provisions that make patchwork changes to other legislation.

> *Beware . . .*
> When using older sources to identify the law, or even newer ones such as legislation.gov.uk, care must be taken to ensure that you are aware of any subsequent amendments that may affect the text (even the online resources can take a long time to update).

B) **Form and detail of legislation:** Although there are formal parliamentary procedures for the creation of legislation, there are very few rules defining its form. As a result, you will find that different statutes vary greatly from one another in their detail and presentation, leading to problems at both ends of the detail spectrum. For example, the law that criminalises D as a secondary party to an offence committed by another is set out in the Accessories and Abettors Act 1861. Section 8 states, simply:

> Whoever shall aid, abet, counsel or procure the commission of any indictable offence . . . shall be liable to be tried, indicted, and punished as a principal offender.

---

[42] Chalmers and Leverick, 'Tracking the Creation of Criminal Offences' [2013] Crim LR 543.

As discussed in **Chapter 12**, although the simplicity of this provision may be superficially appealing, it quickly becomes clear that it is rather more unhelpful and misleading. With the provision leaving so many questions unanswered (eg what is it to aid, abet, counsel, or procure?), the true definition of the offence is left to the common law (see later). On the other hand, the modern trend in favour of very detailed provisions in statutes should be approached with equal caution. As we will explore in later chapters, although these statutes have been designed to pre-empt disputes and to clarify the law, some have had the opposite effect and have tended towards unnecessary complexity and impenetrability.[43]

C) Type of legislation: As long as a statute containing the offence in question is valid, then so are its provisions. In this book, we will not dwell on the types of legislation employed. However, it is worth highlighting two concerns in this area. First, criminal offences are often created in statutes that are not primarily concerned with the criminal law (eg the Insolvency Act 1986). This makes those offences more difficult to find and set in context. Secondly, and more worryingly, a great many criminal offences are created through subordinate or secondary legislation. Such legislation does not receive full parliamentary scrutiny, and therefore lacks some democratic legitimacy.[44]

1.2.2 Common law

The law in England and Wales, both civil and criminal, owes its ancient origins to societal customs and traditions. Some of these customs and traditions were formalised within codifying legislation. However, the greater part of these rules were not codified and relied on recognition and enforcement through the courts directly. Through the courts, and the system of precedent, these customs-turned-laws created a body of rules known as the 'common law'.[45] Even today, these common law rules still form the basis of the criminal law in England and Wales, as well as other 'common law jurisdictions': former British colonies that were administered using the same system. The common law system can be contrasted with the 'civil law' system that dominates most of Europe, a system that is based firmly on the creation and interpretation of legal codes (legislation that attempts to codify all areas of law) rather than law created and developed in the courts.

Importantly, despite the common law system in England and Wales, it is now firmly accepted (and has been for many years) that courts are no longer at liberty to create new offences or defences[46] or to abolish such rules.[47] This is uncontroversial. Although the development of new common law offences and defences served to create an essential body of rules, it is accepted that such rules are now more appropriately dictated by a democratically accountable Parliament. A further reason for preferring statutory law is that court-made law can be criticised as retrospective: when first recognised by the

---

[43] See eg discussion of the Serious Crime Act 2007 in **Chapter 11**. Spencer, 'The Drafting of Criminal Legislation: Need It Be So Impenetrable?' (2008) 67 CLJ 585.

[44] Criticised in Law Commission, *Criminal Liability in Regulatory Contexts* (Consultation 195, 2010) para 3.114.

[45] Holmes, *The Common Law* (2012).

[46] *Jones et al* [2006] UKHL 16.

[47] See *Goldstein and Rimmington* [2005] UKHL 63, where the House of Lords denied having power to abolish the offence of public nuisance.

court as an offence, D has had no warning as to the criminality of her action until after it has taken place and is considered by the court as a new criminal offence. Such retrospectively may allow the law to punish a certain mischief, but if that wrong was not yet recognised as a criminal wrong we cannot claim that D has *chosen* to break the law.

Although the common law no longer creates or abolishes offences or defences, it remains the source for a significant part of the current criminal law. Thus, for example, when discussing offences such as murder and manslaughter, and defences such as duress, insanity, and necessity, the relevant rules are not all defined in statute. Rather, as with many other offences and defences, we have to look to the common law and individual leading cases. This is obviously a challenge for those studying the substantive criminal law within a common law jurisdiction, but it should not be overstated. Indeed, as highlighted earlier, even when offences and defences are codified in a statute, the courts still have an important role in interpreting such legislation in practice (whether the legislation is detailed or otherwise). The difference, it is submitted, is that legislation at least allows the democratic lawmakers to choose what discretion to leave to the courts, to control the framework of the law, and to promote consistency. With the common law, all such decisions are judge made.

Assessment matters . . .

In line with the previous discussion, if you are dealing with a statutory offence/defence then your identification of the substantive rules should *always* begin with the statute. From here, you then explore case law in order to resolve any ambiguities from the statute and to see how the rules are applied in practice: the courts 'put meat on the bone'. With a common law offence/defence you need to do exactly the same thing, but this time your only source is the case law.

1.2.3 European Convention on Human Rights

The UK ratified the ECHR in 1951, allowing individual petition to the European Court of Human Rights (ECtHR) from 1966: essentially a rights-based appeal from UK courts. The Human Rights Act 1998 further incorporated the ECHR by allowing the Convention to be applied directly in domestic courts. The effect of the ECHR on substantive criminal law, as elsewhere, has been extensive.[48] However, unlike the statute and common law sources discussed earlier, the ECHR does *not* create any new criminal offences or defences. Rather, it sets out a number of 'rights' that the UK is obliged to protect in the creation and application of the law.

The role of the Human Rights Act 1998 (HRA) in particular, has been to highlight and prioritise rights jurisprudence and the ECHR at every stage of the legal process. Section 1 of the HRA formally incorporates ECHR rights into domestic law. This ensures the ECHR's influence from the earliest stages: every new piece of legislation, including criminal law matters, require a government minister to make a statement to Parliament of compatibility between the proposed legislation and the ECHR.[49] Beyond this, and very importantly, there is also an obligation on domestic courts to take account of ECHR rights when interpreting and applying *all* areas of law (not simply relying on potential

---

[48] Cooper and Colvin, *Human Rights in the Investigation and Prosecution of Crime* (2009).
[49] HRA 1998, s19.

appeal to the ECtHR in Strasbourg). Through section 3 of the HRA, domestic courts at all levels must *as far as is possible* interpret domestic legislation to give effect to ECHR rights. Under section 4, higher courts also have the power to make a 'declaration of incompatibility' where there is an inconsistency with ECHR rights and no obvious interpretive (s3-based) solution. This latter provision does not strike down or invalidate the incompatible domestic law, and has been exercised sparingly, but provides a strong incentive to maintain consistency.[50]

The main role of the ECHR with regard to the substantive criminal law, facilitated by the HRA, has been in terms of interpretation and evaluation. Below is a list of ECHR rights, and some examples of their effect on the law. The specific influence of the ECHR within each area of criminal law will be discussed throughout this book.

- Article 2: The right to life. Article 2 has affected the definition of homicide offences (murder and manslaughter),[51] abortion, euthanasia,[52] as well as leading to conflict where D kills V in self-defence.[53]

- Article 3: The prohibition of torture and inhuman and degrading treatment. Article 3 has been relevant to offences relating to parental (and school-based) application of corporal punishment,[54] as well as the treatment of criminal suspects.

- Article 4: The prohibition of slavery and forced labour. Article 4 led to the creation of a slavery offence in 2009,[55] and is particularly relevant to the discussion of human trafficking and sex workers.

- Article 5: The right to liberty and security. Article 5 has greatest effect on any defendant who has not yet been convicted (eg D's pre-trial detention, false imprisonment, and unfitness to plead), as well as D who is found not guilty by reason of insanity.[56] It might also affect the definition of offences such as false imprisonment.

- Article 6: The right to a fair trial. Article 6, including the presumption of innocence, is central to debate concerning reverse burdens of proof.[57]

- Article 7: The prohibition on criminal laws being applied retrospectively is found in Article 7. At its strongest, it applies if an offence is created and made to apply to conduct that was not criminal at the time the conduct was performed. In such a situation it would not be permissible to convict D for his conduct before the offence was created. Article 7 provides strong support for the codification of criminal law and the limitation of judicial discretion which (inevitably) is applied after the event.

- Article 8: The right to respect for private and family life. Article 8 is relevant, in particular, to offences that criminalise consensual sexual violence.[58]

---

[50] See *AG's Reference (No 4 of 2002)* [2004] UKHL 43, [28].
[51] See **Chapters 5** and **6**.
[52] See **Chapters 11** and **12**.
[53] See **Chapter 14**.
[54] See **7.3.1**.
[55] See **7.9.3**.
[56] **Chapter 13**.
[57] See, in particular, **Chapters 13** and **14**.
[58] See **7.8.2**.

- Article 9: Freedom of thought, conscience, and religion. Article 9 provides a framework for religiously aggravated offences,[59] as well as potential public order offences involving public worship.
- Article 10: Freedom of expression. Article 10 is relevant to the application of several offences and defences where D's acts are expressing protest (eg criminal damage and public order offences).
- Article 11: Freedom of assembly and association. Article 11 is most obviously relevant to public order offences as they apply to assemblies.
- Article 12: The right to family life. Article 12 has affected debates about whether married couples should be liable for an offence if they conspire (agree to commit a crime) with one another.[60]
- Article 13: The right to an effective remedy for breaches of Convention rights. Article 13 is most relevant to the civil law, but will also have an impact on what is known as restorative justice.[61]
- Article 14: The right to non-discrimination under Convention rights. Article 14, as with Article 12, is relevant to debate about whether married couples should be treated differently in certain areas of criminal law.

Articles 2 and 3 are absolute (do not allow for discretion) in the negative obligations they provide.[62] However, many of the other rights listed above are subject to important qualifications. This means that, even if there is an apparent breach of a Convention right, it can be justified by the State if it is: (a) prescribed by law; (b) necessary in the pursuit of a specified objective (eg public order, health or morals, or the freedom of others); and (c) proportionate to that objective. In view of the substantive criminal law, such qualifications are obviously essential. Substantive offences proscribe D from performing certain acts (inevitably restricting, eg, her Art 10 freedoms), as well as depriving or restricting her liberty (Art 5) where she breaks the law. Therefore, when discussing the impact of these rights on the substantive criminal law, such qualifications should always be considered.

1.2.4 European Union

Following the UK's decision to leave the European Union (EU), the future influence of the EU on UK law is uncertain. A proportion of law in the UK has been generated either directly from EU institutions[63] or indirectly through mutual recognition and cooperation. However, traditionally such provisions have not affected domestic criminal law. This is because, as the EU was originally conceived as a trade and economic union,

---

[59] See **7.9.2**.
[60] See **Chapter 11**.
[61] Restorative justice involves a novel approach to criminal processes and sentencing that focuses on the role of the victim and the community. As it is not directly relevant to the substantive criminal law, it is not considered further in this book.
[62] This is not the case where a claimant alleges a breach of a positive obligation, eg the potential right to assisted death under Art 2, *Pretty v UK* (2002) 35 EHRR 1.
[63] Secondary law from the EU takes the form of regulations, decisions, and directives. Art 288 Treaty on the Functioning of the European Union (TFEU).

criminal law was not within its competencies. As the EU has developed, however, particularly in relation to the protection of fundamental rights, its spheres of competence have expanded well beyond their original trade-based limits.

> **Don't be confused . . .**
> Although all Member States of the EU are signatories to the ECHR, the EU is not the author of the Convention; this is the separate European body, the Council of Europe. Therefore, our discussion of ECHR rights in the previous section must be distinguished from our discussion of the EU.

The expansion of EU competencies has begun to affect domestic criminal law in Member States.[64] Importantly, criminal law remains primarily an issue for individual States, with the EU gaining only limited competence. However, with the increased flow of people across borders, and the ease of technology connecting people together, there is much that can be gained from linking (or at least coordinating) criminal jurisdictions that have traditionally remained separate and insular. Coordination through the EU has therefore targeted offences that commonly involve a cross-border element (eg terrorism, human trafficking, corruption, and other organised crimes), preventing criminal groups from taking advantage of the patchwork of legal inconsistencies across Europe.[65] Such coordination has made particular strides in relation to criminal evidence and procedure,[66] and is likely to continue notwithstanding the UK exit.

Despite this expansion of EU competence, the vast majority of the substantive criminal law remains a preciously guarded area of national competence and sovereignty. Therefore, although we see an increased internationalisation of criminal offending in almost every area of the criminal law, the EU's competence remains relatively narrow and specific, with what we might call the more traditional offences (eg murder, offences against the person, etc) strictly excluded. As these more traditional offences are the subject of this book, we will largely set the influence of the EU to one side from this point forward.[67]

1.2.5 International law

International law, whether criminal or otherwise, is the product of agreements between States, and applies across those States. In this way it is fundamentally different from domestic law that is created and applied at a national level.

International law has had an effect on the substantive criminal law in England and Wales in two main ways. The first is the most direct influence, through the creation of international crimes that are applied domestically. Through Part 5 of the International Criminal Court Act 2001, a number of international offences defined in the Rome Statute[68] have been incorporated into national law. The Rome Statute focuses on a

---

[64] Criminal law emerged as a third pillar (basis for intergovernmental cooperation) within the Maastricht Treaty. Following the Lisbon Treaty, specified criminal matters come within the competence of the EU institutions. TFEU, Title V, Ch4.

[65] Art 83 TFEU.

[66] Art 82. Examples of this include measures on extradition and the European Arrest Warrant.

[67] For a wider discussion, see Baker, 'The European Union's Area of Freedom, Security and (Criminal) Justice 10 Years On' [2010] Crim LR 833; Mitsilegas, *EU Criminal Law After Lisbon* (2016).

[68] The Rome Statute 1998 is an international agreement, creating the International Criminal Court and defining core international criminal offences.

relatively small core of internationally recognised war crimes such as genocide. These offences are therefore now part of the domestic criminal law. However, they are not discussed further in this book.[69]

The second area of influence arises from softer sources of international law: conventions arising from groups such as the United Nations (UN), EU, Council of Europe, and the Organisation for Economic Co-operation and Development (OECD), where the UK agrees to create criminal offences to tackle certain agreed mischiefs.[70] In this manner, although several areas of substantive criminal law have been directly influenced or mandated by the signing of such conventions, their binding source remains the national statute (discussed earlier). Reference to such *origins* of national law, and an examination of their ambitions, can be useful when evaluating the domestic implementing offences. Such evaluation is similar to our earlier discussion of criminal wrongs: identifying the mischief which the offence is tackling in order to evaluate how effectively it has been criminalised.

1.2.6 The Law Commission and the Draft Criminal Code

As with the softer forms of international law, the work of the Law Commission and the Draft Criminal Code are not binding sources of criminal law. However, in different ways, both provide a powerful and pervasive influence affecting the reform of criminal offences and defences, as well as the interpretation of substantive rules within the courts. Both will be discussed throughout this book, and thus both require some introduction.

A) The Law Commission of England and Wales:[71] The Law Commission is a national law reform body, sponsored by the Ministry of Justice but independent from government. The Commission has been prolific, particularly in recent years, consulting on several areas of the substantive criminal law and producing reports, including draft legislation, that have directly led to several of the major reforms that will be discussed in later chapters. Where Law Commission projects have been successfully taken forward by government the Commission's papers can provide a useful background to this reform, explaining the rationale behind it and discussing examples of how it might be applied.[72] Even where the Commission's recommendations are not taken forward, these papers are also useful as summaries and evaluations of the current law, as well as providing alternative approaches that can be compared with the current position.[73] In either case, the

---

[69] See Grady, 'International Crimes in the Courts of England and Wales' [2014] Crim LR 693; Cassese and Gaeta, *Cassese's International Criminal Law* (2013).

[70] eg the Bribery Act 2010 was conceived with explicit reference to several international obligations. Law Commission, *Reforming Bribery* (Consultation 185, 2007) Appendix A.

[71] Law Commissions Act 1965. Law Commission publications can be downloaded from http://lawcommission.justice.gov.uk. Although David Ormerod is the Criminal Law Commissioner nothing in this book should be taken to represent the views of the Commission unless expressly stated to do so.

[72] See eg assisting and encouraging crime (**Chapter 11**), fraud (**Chapter 10**), and corporate manslaughter (**Chapter 6**).

[73] See eg parties to crime (**Chapter 12**), attempts and conspiracy (**Chapter 11**), intoxication (**Chapter 13**), and, most recently, insanity and automatism, hate crime, offences against the person (**Chapter 7**), kidnapping and false imprisonment (**Chapter 7**), and unfitness to plead (**1.5.3**).

accessible and authoritative nature of Law Commission material makes it a vital source for the study of criminal law.[74]

B) The Draft Criminal Code: Criminal codes have become prevalent even among common law jurisdictions. Within a code, all the major criminal offences and defences can be brought together in a single document (referred to as the 'special part' of the code), as well as general provisions such as definitions of common language (referred to as the 'general part' of the code).[75] The most recent attempt to construct a criminal code for England and Wales was published by the Law Commission in 1989,[76] following earlier proposals from an academic team in 1985.[77] The 1989 Draft Code is an exceptional piece of work, and its detailed yet succinct definitions continue to influence debate. However, very importantly, despite support from successive Lord Chief Justices, the Draft Code has never been taken forward by government and adopted into law. The approach of the Commission in most recent years, since 2009, has been focused on the reform and codification of individual areas of the law. This offers many potential benefits, but the lack of a criminal code remains regrettable.[78]

> *Beware . . .*
> The Draft Criminal Code, as with all Law Commission draft Bills, can provide a useful point of reference when evaluating the law or seeking alternatives to it. However, such material does not represent the law, and should never be presented as such: they are simply reform recommendations. Also, where a new statute is based on a prior Law Commission draft, be careful to look out for differences between the two.

1.3 The internal structure of offences and defences

Having discussed the sources of criminal offences and defences, it is useful to provide a brief introduction to the structures or forms which they might take. Strictly speaking there are very few rules that restrict how offences or defences should be framed and this is partly due to the lack of a criminal code. However, certain patterns and conventions have emerged, both within the common law and from statute, which can help to make sense of the law. These conceptual tools provide a framework for those drafting the law, for the courts applying the law, for the academic evaluating it, as well as for the student trying to do all three.

---

[74] Dyson et al, *Fifty Years of the Law Commission* (Hart, 2016); Smith, 'Criminal Law and the Law Commission 1965–2015' [2016] Crim LR 381.

[75] The language of 'general' and 'special' parts was coined by the criminal law academic Glanville Williams.

[76] Law Commission, *A Criminal Code for England and Wales*, 2 vols (No 177, 1989).

[77] Law Commission, *Codification of the Criminal Law: A Report to the Law Commission* (No 143, 1985).

[78] Dennis, 'RIP—The Criminal Code (1968–2008)' [2009] Crim LR 1. The potential benefits of a criminal code are set out in the Law Commission's Draft Code documents. See also de Búrca and Gardner, 'Codification of the Criminal Law' (1990) 10 OJLS 559.

The most important structural devises for *offences*, discussed in the following chapters, are:

- **Actus reus (guilty act):** The actus reus of an offence describes the wrongful conduct and/or consequences required for liability in proscribed circumstances. For example, when D kicks V she may have committed the crime of battery, among other potential offences. This will depend on what conduct she performed, in what circumstances (eg V must be a person), and with what consequences (ie what level of harm). The actus reus of battery describes what is prohibited: D must not make unlawful physical contact with another (V).

- **Mens rea (guilty mind):** The mens rea of an offence describes the state of mind that D must have when completing the actus reus. In battery, for example, D must either intend to make unlawful contact or at least foresee the risk that her conduct will result in unjustified contact with V.

Defences, on the other hand, do not involve guilty acts or guilty minds (quite the opposite). Thus, in this context we simply speak of the 'elements' of a defence.

- **Defence elements:** A defence will be available where its elements (its requirements) are fulfilled. For example, if D kicks V to prevent V from attacking her, she may rely on the defence of self-defence. This defence requires two central 'elements': first, that D acted with an honest belief in the need for preventative force and, secondly, that the force used (the kick) was a reasonable response based on the facts as D believed them to be.[79]

In many ways, understanding the structures of the criminal law is the most important part of our study, particularly in the context of offences. There are now well in excess of 10,000 offences known to the law of England and Wales, only a small number of which can ever be included in a book of this kind. Therefore, as well as studying the offences in their own right, our focus (particularly in the early chapters) is to develop methods of analysis that can be used to understand any offence within the law. It should be remembered, however, that these methods and conceptual tools are not essential parts of the law, they are simply methods developed to analyse it. As a result, areas of inconsistency and uncertainty have emerged within the techniques as they have been applied to different offences.

As we discuss each new offence, we will employ the structures of analysis traditionally employed in relation to that offence. This usually involves the simple separation of actus reus, mens rea, and defences introduced previously, but this will not always be the case. It is important to reflect any different forms of analysis so that when you read court judgments and other academic material that are likely to use this style, you are familiar with them. However, in order to provide you with a *consistent* structure of analysis, we will also highlight how every offence could be analysed using an approach which we will call 'element analysis'. This approach will be explored fully over the following three chapters. Based on the separation of actus reus and mens rea, element analysis further subdivides an offence into conduct, circumstances, and results. It is an approach that can be set out using simple charts, as in **Table 1.2**.

---

[79] Self-defence is discussed fully in **Chapter 14**.

Table 1.2 Offence elements chart (eg battery)

	Actus reus	**Mens rea**
Conduct element	Any physical acts or omissions required for the offence. For battery, D's act of kicking	Any mens rea required as to D's acts or omissions. For battery, that D's conduct was performed voluntarily by her
Circumstance element	Any factual circumstances required for the offence. For battery, that V is a person	Any mens rea required as to those facts or circumstances. For battery, that D knew that the thing she was kicking was a person
Result element	Any consequences of D's action/omission required for the offence. For battery, the physical contact with V	Any mens rea required as to those consequences. For battery, that D intended contact with V or foresaw a risk of that and took the risk unjustifiably

We have chosen to employ this analytical approach as our consistent tool for two main reasons. First, it allows us to explore in more detail the requirements of the offence rather than the traditional approach of analysing just actus reus and mens rea. Secondly, when we come to discuss the general inchoate offences (eg attempts and assisting and encouraging) in **Chapter 11**, as well as certain other areas,[80] the use of element analysis is essential in order to apply the law. Thus, becoming familiar with it from an early stage will be very useful.

1.4 The principles of the substantive criminal law

References to the 'principles' of criminal law, common in case law and academic debate, are drawing upon the idea that there are certain common ideals or aims underpinning the substantive rules. Led most recently by the work of Andrew Ashworth,[81] the identification and discussion of legal principles has become very important to the study of crime. Such principles are primarily employed as evaluative tools. For example, the principle of fair warning states that criminal offences should be clearly constructed and communicated in order to guide the actions of society.

The ECHR (discussed earlier) provides certain checks to the quality of the law, particularly in relation to the presumption of innocence (Art 6) and in terms of basic clarity (Art 7). However, academic discussion of the principles of criminalisation provides clearer guidance on the *ideal* qualities of the criminal law, providing points of reference that can be used to commend or criticise individual offences or defences as appropriate. As certain principles have become more widely accepted, it is clear that they also play

---

[80] eg reform proposals in relation to the intoxication rules (**Chapter 13**) and complicity (**Chapter 12**).
[81] Horder, *Ashworth's Principles of Criminal Law* (8th edn, 2016).

a role in the interpretation of the law, with certain approaches preferred by judges over others in line with underpinning principles.

The principles of criminal law have a two-pronged effect. First, they affect the substance of the law by influencing the manner of its interpretation and, secondly, they affect the reform of the law through evaluation. In the following sections we highlight a selection of the most important principles that are most closely connected to the substantive criminal law.

> **Don't be confused . . .**
> The principles of the criminal law are useful tools for evaluating the quality of an offence or defence. However, they do not affect its validity as law. As long as an offence or defence has originated from a binding source (statute or the common law), it is valid regardless of its quality in terms of legal principles and regardless of its format within element analysis or otherwise.

1.4.1 The principle of fair warning

This principle requires clear communication of the law to the public. As stated earlier, the criminal law aims to deter people from certain wrongful activities, and to punish those who *choose* to pursue wrongful ends in disregard of the law. However, to achieve either of these aims, there is an implicit assumption that the public are aware of the law in the first place: to be guided by it, or to deserve punishment for choosing to break it.

The principle of fair warning is used to discuss and evaluate how effectively offences are communicated to the public. It is a discussion that engages with several areas of debate. For example, the principle of fair warning is central to the contention that offences existing in the common law should be codified in statute, and ideally within a criminal code. In each case, public access to the law would be improved.

Fair warning is also a principle that guides *how* offences should be codified. On the one hand, offences and statutory drafting must be sufficiently detailed to allow the public to know what exactly is being criminalised, and allow them to moderate their behaviour accordingly. For example, imagine an offence drafted in simple terms such as 'it is a crime to make unlawful contact with another'. Such an offence would inform D that kicking V *may* be criminal, but without a definition of 'unlawful' the only way D could moderate her behaviour to be sure to avoid liability would be to make no contact with others at all. Hardly an ideal message! On the other hand, however, offences and statutory drafting should avoid being overly complex. For example, as we will discuss in **Chapter 8**, several sexual offences (eg voyeurism) have been defined in an extremely complex manner. The complex nature of the statutory drafting does little to provide fair warning to the legal expert trying to predict the law, let alone the public.

> **Extra detail . . .**
> For those researching this area in greater depth, some exciting work has been done by the American academic Paul Robinson. Robinson advocates the creation of multiple criminal codes, with 'rule articulation' (a code written in accessible language to tell the public what they cannot do), separated from other necessarily more complex codes that would focus on 'liability assessment' and 'grading' (codes written for those administering the law).[82]

---

[82] Robinson, 'A Functional Analysis of Criminal Law' (1994) 88 Nw UL Rev 857; Robinson, *Structure and Function in Criminal Law* (1997).

1.4.2 The principle of fair labelling

The principle of fair labelling requires accurate correlation between the name of an offence and the conduct it criminalises.[83] The rationale for this principle can be linked with that of fair warning in the previous section. The knowledge most people have of substantive crimes will not go far beyond their awareness of offence names and the implications of those names (eg kidnapping, rape, etc). Therefore, the fairness of the label dictates the fairness of the warning. However, the principle is perhaps more important when it is applied to someone after they have been convicted. This is because, as well as sentencing D as is appropriate (fines, prison, etc), the name of D's offence labels her in the eyes of the public. D is not simply sent to prison for a certain duration, she is labelled as a murderer, a thief, a robber, etc.

The role of criminal labelling is not straightforward; it has both positive and negative aspects. Labels can be very useful in terms of the clear stigma and message created: allowing the State to condemn the accused in language that the public, on whose behalf the State acts, can understand. However, labelling and stigmatisation are difficult to control and quantify, relying on changeable social constructions and attitudes. Thus, in terms of the additional punishments they provide, they cannot be objectively prescribed.

What can be controlled, however, returning us to our central focus, is that we can ensure the label given to D's offence is at least accurate, and in *this* sense fair. It is here that the principle engages most directly with the substantive law. First, it demonstrates the importance of separating different mischiefs into different offences with different labels. For example, if D1 steals V1's car, and D2 sets V2's car on fire, both Ds have caused the loss of a car. However, the mischiefs committed by D1 and D2 are different, and their conduct should be separately labelled: D1 has committed theft; D2 arson. This debate arises in later chapters, for example when we consider the creation of new offences that would relabel conduct already criminalised elsewhere (eg whether *domestic violence* should be a separate offence[84]).

The aim of fair labelling also has a direct effect on the content of offences and defences whose names are well known to the public, for example rape and robbery. This is because, as well-known labels can communicate more clearly to the public, there is often a desire that they should be maintained, even when the substantive content of the offence is changed. This is partly why, for example, there has been debate about whether the offence 'rape' should have been extended to include non-consensual anal or oral penetration.[85] The concern here is that if such labels are used inappropriately, not only is D unfairly labelled if convicted, but because D's conduct does not fit with the general understanding of the label there is a risk that a jury might acquit a defendant who fulfils the elements of the offence, and who should, therefore, be found guilty. We see this rationale, for example, behind changes in Canadian criminal law where the label of 'rape' has been removed from the sexual offences entirely.[86]

---

[83] Chalmers and Leverick, 'Fair Labelling and Criminal Law' (2008) 71 MLR 217; Williams, 'Convictions and Fair Labelling' (1983) 42 CLJ 85.

[84] See **7.10.1**.

[85] **Chapter 8**.

[86] Criminal Code of Canada, Part VIII.

1.4.3 The principle of autonomy

Where we discuss the principle of individual autonomy, we are usually referring to the autonomy of a potential offender. Again, it is a principle that can arise in various contexts. In simple terms, it can be used as a principle of minimum criminalisation. To have autonomy is to be free to act and pursue our goals unrestrained. The criminal law, by design, restricts our options by criminalising certain conduct. Indeed, in the context of criminalising failures to act, the law is limiting *all* of our options and requiring a certain course of conduct.[87] Therefore, if we see autonomy as something that should be preserved and maximised, criminal offences, particularly those involving omissions liability, that limit our autonomy should be kept to a minimum.[88]

The principle of autonomy is also the primary vehicle for the promotion of 'choice' as an essential ingredient of both moral and legal blame. The impact of this can be seen in two main areas. First, we should not criminalise conduct that D cannot avoid. The most basic implications of this would rule out the criminalisation of, for example, belonging to a certain race, breathing, or sleeping, where we have no choice at all. More interestingly, it may also affect debate on the fairness of criminalising unrealistic choices. For example, the defence of duress applies where D commits an offence to avoid threatened serious violence. However, even if we recognise that a reasonable person would have acted as D did, and therefore D's choice was in some sense a reasonably unavoidable one, duress is never allowed as a defence to murder. Thus, where D kills V whilst acting under severe duress and is convicted of murder, we may question the law's respect for her autonomy.[89]

Secondly, autonomy and choice are also central to debates about mens rea. At minimum, this can be seen in the contention that all offences should involve voluntary or intentional action: if D kicks V involuntarily, for example whilst having an epileptic seizure or when tripping over, there should be no offence. Taken more widely, we could similarly contend that every element of an actus reus should require a corresponding mens rea. For example, if D kicks V and V dies, should D only be liable for an offence related to that death if D intended or at least foresaw, in some sense chose, that level of harm? Alternatively, is it enough that D intended to kick V, and that this intentional conduct should be enough to link D with the death even if it was not foreseen? This latter debate is central to much of the discussion of mens rea in **Chapter 3**, and the distinction between what is termed subjective (choice-based) and objective (results-based) approaches to the law.

1.4.4 The principle of welfare

The principle of welfare promotes the role of the law in protecting society from harm. From a potential victim's perspective, the welfare principle is therefore in line with the

---

[87] Williams, 'Criminal Omissions—The Conventional View' (1991) 107 LQR 86; Ashworth, *Positive Obligations in Criminal Law* (2013).

[88] Husak, *Overcriminalisation* (2008).

[89] The Law Commission raises the principle of autonomy to support its recommendation that duress *should* be a defence to murder. This is discussed in **Chapter 14**.

autonomy principle discussed previously: for an individual to be autonomous and free to pursue her goals, she must be protected from others who would unfairly interfere with her, physically or otherwise. However, the protection of V requires the restriction of D. Thus, from D's perspective, the welfare principle provides a counterbalance to that of autonomy, and one that could justify a highly restrictive criminal law. For example, if D kicks V during an epileptic seizure the principle of autonomy would point towards there being no liability, D has not chosen to cause harm to V. However, D's kick has still interfered with the welfare of V. Therefore, if D is prone to such seizures, and particularly if they regularly result in injury to others, the welfare principle could be used to favour criminalisation.

The challenge for the criminal law is to find balance to promote maximum autonomy and welfare by creating the conditions, through minimum criminalisation, that allow and support people in the pursuit of legitimate social goals.[90] How effectively the law finds this balance within individual offences and defences is a something that will emerge in several later chapters. A number of these points were highlighted in our earlier discussion of autonomy, including the criminalisation of unrealistic choices (eg affecting the defence of duress), criminalising involuntary harms (affecting the requirement of voluntary movement) as well as unforeseen harms or circumstances (affecting mens rea more generally). In each case, balancing the welfare principle reminds us to consider the objective result of D's conduct as well as what D intended or foresaw. Where the result is serious harm to V, it may be that criminalisation is justified even where D has not chosen every aspect of the offence.

A final example that demonstrates the difficulty of finding balance is the defence of insanity. As discussed in **Chapters 13** and **14**, this defence means that D is not criminally liable where a disease of the mind leads her to commit an offence. However, as such defects are often more than temporary, and as D may therefore pose a continuing danger to others, a successful insanity defence will not result in simple acquittal. Rather, D is 'not guilty by reason of insanity', and a range of disposal orders, including involuntary detention in hospital, become available to the court. D is not guilty because her 'insanity' means that she did not choose to offend; but she may still have her autonomy sacrificed in the name of societal welfare.

1.5 The subjects of the substantive criminal law

As well as considering the content of the criminal law, it is also important to remember who it is aimed at: whose behaviour it seeks to regulate, and who is subject to punishment for breaking the law. The typical subject of the criminal law is a natural person. However, as we discuss briefly in the following sections, the criminal law will also apply to legal persons (ie corporations), and will not apply, or at least not in the same way, to natural persons in certain circumstances (ie minors and those unfit to plead).

---

[90] Lacey, 'Community in Legal Theory: Idea, Ideal or Ideology?' (1996) 15 Studies in Law, Politics and Society 105.

1.5.1 Corporations

Where a natural person commits an offence in the course of acting on behalf of a corporation or other legal entity, she will be liable directly for that offence.[91] However, additionally, and sometimes even in the absence of individual liability, the corporation itself, which the law treats as a legal person, may also be liable for an offence in its own right. This is referred to as corporate criminal liability.

> **Extra detail . . .**
> Beyond corporate criminal liability (targeting public limited companies (plc), private limited companies (Ltd), and limited liability partnerships (LLP)), the criminal law can also target unincorporated associations. However, in the absence of a legal personality, the rules governing such liability are often unclear.[92]

Most criminal offences with the exception of murder[93] and a few others are capable of being committed by legal as well as natural persons.[94] Indeed, in many cases, the legal *and moral* case in favour of convicting the corporation may be considerably stronger than any individual involved. An example of this would be where the negligence of a particular employee leads to harm, corporate liability may be more appropriate when that negligence is set in the context of a company that encourages risk taking and dangerous practices on a wider scale.[95]

Corporate criminal liability raises two central challenges for the law. First, in the absence of a physical entity, where do we look for the actions and mental states of the company? And secondly, where we find liability, how can we punish the company in an effective manner? In the following section, in line with the focus of this book, we focus on the first of these concerns.[96]

1.5.1.1 Vicarious criminal liability of corporations

Vicarious liability, common in the context of tortious claims for damages, allows the liability of an employee acting in the course of their duties to be attributed to the organisation they are working for. In the context of the civil law, the doctrine serves a crucial role to enable victims to be adequately compensated for their losses, with the organisation being considerably more likely than the employee to be able to bear the costs.

> **Don't be confused . . .**
> Vicarious liability does not require the organisation to have assisted, encouraged, or contributed to the actions of the employee. In this way, vicarious corporate liability should not be confused with complicity (discussed in **Chapter 12**).

[91] See generally Law Commission, *Criminal Liability in Regulatory Contexts* (Consultation 195, 2010).
[92] See discussion in *L* [2008] EWCA Crim 1970.
[93] Murder cannot be committed by a corporation because it carries a mandatory life sentence, a sentence that cannot apply to a corporate entity.
[94] The term 'person' must be interpreted in this manner, unless the contrary is specified. Interpretation Act 1978, s5 and Sch 1.
[95] Gobert, 'A Corporate Criminality: New Crimes for New Times' [1994] Crim LR 722.
[96] On the problem of effective punishment, see Jefferson, 'Corporate Criminal Liability: The Problem of Sanctions' (2001) 65 J Crim L 235.

In the context of the criminal law, where the primary aim is to punish/deter D rather than to compensate V, vicarious liability makes little sense. Where D (the organisation) has acted in a criminally blameworthy fashion then it should be targeted directly, and where it has not, the use of vicarious liability is surely unfair. However, the law does allow for the vicarious criminal liability of organisations in relation to a number of offences,[97] mainly of a regulatory nature.

1.5.1.2 Direct criminal liability of corporations

There are three primary routes to the direct criminal liability of corporations: (a) specific corporate offences; (b) the identification doctrine; and (c) liability for a failure to prevent.[98]

A) Specific corporate offences: Arguably the most efficient way to regulate corporations by criminal law is through the specific criminalisation of certain conduct. Thus, rather than attempting to reinterpret legislation drafted with natural persons in mind, corporate offences can be tailor-made: by removing mens rea requirements, by including due diligence defences, and so on. Such offences are often preferred, for example, when criminalising failure to meet certain health and safety standards. The disadvantages of such offences are that they can be perceived as purely regulatory, and thus not 'true' crimes, which can undermine the stigmatising effect of the law.

B) Identification doctrine: The identification doctrine is a mechanism created at common law to attribute criminal liability to corporations where such liability includes both actus reus and mens rea requirements. Essentially, the doctrine provides that a corporation can be liable for a crime of mens rea if that mens rea was possessed by an officer in the corporation of sufficient seniority to be considered by the court a 'controlling mind'—someone whose actions and mens rea can fairly be said to represent that of the corporation as a whole.[99] The major disadvantage of this doctrine, however, is that identifying a 'controlling officer' who had mens rea can be very difficult, particularly where the corporation is large and complex such that the 'controlling officers' are unlikely to be involved with those working at lower levels.

C) Failure to prevent: Partly as a reaction to the perceived inadequacies of the identification doctrine, modern statutes have begun to develop a form of corporate liability based around a failure to prevent. Modelled on the tort of negligence, this doctrine does not seek to blame the corporation criminally for something it has done or thought via the identification doctrine, but rather for its failure to provide adequate procedures and mechanisms to prevent the harms caused by those throughout the corporation. We can see variations of this model in place with the offences of corporate manslaughter discussed in **Chapter 6**,[100]

---

[97] *Tesco Stores Ltd v Brent LBC* [1993] 2 All ER 718.

[98] See generally Cavanagh, 'Corporate Criminal Liability: An Assessment of the Models of Fault' (2011) 75 J Crim L 414.

[99] Developed and discussed in *Bolton* [1956] 3 All ER 624; *Tesco v Nattrass* [1972] AC 153; *Re Supply of Ready Mixed Concrete (No 2)* [1995] 1 AC 456; *X Ltd* [2013] EWCA Crim 818.

[100] See **6.4.1**.

of bribery,[101] and depending upon its success, it is an approach that has the potential to be expanded across almost all criminal offences.[102]

A recent procedural development that has impacted on the criminalisation of corporations is the emergence of deferred prosecution agreements (DPAs).[103] DPAs were introduced in 2014,[104] and first used in 2015.[105] They are available to the CPS and the Serious Fraud Office (SFO), allowing these agencies to reach agreements with a corporation that defers prosecution on the proviso that the corporation agrees to a set of measures that will prevent future harms and legal violations. DPAs are controversial, and only apply to legal (as opposed to natural) persons, but can provide an efficient procedural means of regulating corporate bodies.

1.5.2 Minors

Section 50 of the Children and Young Persons Act 1933 creates a *conclusive* presumption that children under the age of 10 years cannot commit a criminal offence. Therefore, in substance, no criminal prosecution can apply to this group. This will be the case regardless of the circumstances, eg even where D (under 10) has acted intentionally and caused serious harm or death. Those under 10 years require protection and support, and this can be gained through the civil law. They do not deserve, at this young age, the punishment and stigma of criminalisation.

Once D reaches the age of 10, the criminal law will apply regardless of her lack of maturity.[106] Prior to 1998,[107] a common law doctrine (*doli incapax*) created a rebuttable presumption that those between 10 and 13 years were not capable of forming a criminal mens rea: rebutted only where the prosecution could prove that D knew that her acts were 'seriously wrong' as opposed to merely 'naughty'. The abolition of the common law doctrine, combined with the comparatively low age of criminal responsibility, has led to cogent criticism of the over-criminalisation of children within this jurisdiction.[108]

1.5.3 Defendants who are unfit to plead

In the Crown Court, D is 'unfit to plead' (or unfit to be tried) if, because of a disability, she is incapable of being tried within the normal criminal court process. The conditions for competence were set out in *M*,[109] and require D to have sufficient ability to:

(a) understand the charges;

(b) understand the plea;

---

[101] The Bribery Act 2010, s7.
[102] Law Commission, *Criminal Liability in Regulatory Contexts* (Consultation 195, 2010). See eg Criminal Finances Bill (2016), Part 3.
[103] Bisgrove and Weekes, 'Deferred Prosecution Agreements: A Practical Consideration' [2014] Crim LR 416.
[104] Crime and Courts Act 2013, Sch 17.
[105] Padfield, 'Deferred Prosecution Agreements' [2016] Crim LR 449.
[106] *T v UK* [2000] Crim LR 187: criminally punishing a 10-year-old is not contrary to Art 3 ECHR.
[107] Crime and Disorder Act 1998, s34.
[108] Keating, 'The Responsibility of Children in the Criminal Law' (2007) 19 CFLQ 183.
[109] [2003] EWCA Crim 3452. See discussion in *Marcantonio, Chitolie* [2016] EWCA Crim 14.

(c) challenge jurors;

(d) instruct legal representatives;

(e) understand the course of the trial; and

(f) give evidence (if she chooses to do so).

To establish D's unfit state, the onus of proof is on the party raising the issue: if it is raised by the defence, then they must prove D's unfitness on the balance of probabilities; if it is raised by the prosecution, then they must prove it beyond a reasonable doubt.[110] The matter is decided by a judge alone. Where D is found unfit to plead because, *at the time of trial*, one or more of the conditions in *M* is not satisfied,[111] the standard criminal process ceases. This is the case regardless of the evidence against D: even if there is overwhelming evidence that D committed the relevant offence and was competent at the time of the offence, her lack of competence at the time of trial means that a standard criminal trial would be unfair and illegitimate.

Where D is found unfit, instead of a standard criminal trial, the case will be decided through a 'trial of the facts'. This procedure is set out in sections 4 and 4A of the Criminal Procedure (Insanity) Act 1964, as amended. A trial of the facts is a trial before a jury to determine whether D committed the acts or omissions required for the offence charged. In other words, the court will explore the actus reus of the offence, but *not* the mens rea. If it is found that D did not commit the actus reus, she will be acquitted in the normal manner. However, where D is found to have committed the actus reus, although she is not liable for the full offence, a range of disposal options become open to the court. These include a hospital order, with or without a restriction order, a supervision order, or an absolute discharge.[112]

With the greater awareness of mental health issues in the criminal justice process, so the inadequacies of the current law become more apparent.[113] Chief among these has been the fact that there is no equivalent process in the magistrates' court and youth court where some of the most vulnerable defendants are tried. In the Crown Court, where the scheme outlined above applies, there are also significant difficulties. These include, for example, finding a principled and consistent separation of acts and omissions, relevant to a trial of the facts.[114] The case of *B* provides a useful example of this where, on a charge of voyeurism, the court struggled to decide whether the relevant 'act' which would have to be proved was the simple conduct of viewing of a person in a state of undress etc, or whether it also had to be shown that the viewer was motivated to do so for sexual gratification.[115] Despite the issue of motivation seeming to go beyond an analysis of acts, the Court of Appeal held that D's sexual motivation was so essential to the 'act' of

---

[110] *Podola* [1959] 3 All ER 418.

[111] Where D is competent at trial, but was suffering from a defect of reason caused by a disease of the mind when committing the criminal act, the insanity rules should be applied. See **Chapters 13** and **14**.

[112] Criminal Procedure (Insanity) Act 1964, s5.

[113] Mitchell and Howe, 'A Continued Upturn in Unfitness to Plead—More Disability in Relation to the Trial under the 1991 Act' [2007] Crim LR 530.

[114] For a useful review of this area of law, including areas of legal confusion and concern, see *Wells, Masud, Hone and Kail* [2015] EWCA Crim 2.

[115] [2012] EWCA Crim 770.

voyeurism, that it remained essential even for a trial on the facts. Similar problems have also emerged in relation to potential defences.[116]

The Law Commission has recently made recommendations for reform of the whole unfitness to plead framework;[117] including a draft Bill.[118] The Commission criticises the current law as outdated, inconsistently applied, and potentially unfair. These recommendations have been well received,[119] but whether they are taken forward by government remains to be seen.

1.6 Reform

In the penultimate section of every chapter we will have a separate discussion about legal reform. This is not to say that we will *only* discuss reform in such sections. However, where possible, we will look to separate the discussion in this way to avoid common confusions between the current law and reform recommendations. The main aim of these sections is to help you to engage critically with the current law: moving beyond an investigation of the rules themselves, to the evaluation of those rules and the consideration of alternatives. Such material is most directly relevant to essay-type questions, where you are expected to discuss and engage with your topic. However, it will also be useful for problem questions where you are asked to comment on the law as you apply it. More generally, considering the reform of offences and defences is also often the best way to gain a deeper understanding of the rules themselves.

When discussing reform proposals, it is obviously important that you understand what the proposal is attempting to do. Just as your understanding of the current law requires you to be able to identify and describe the rules, the same is true for your discussion of a reform proposal. In addition, discussion of reform requires you to engage with and to evaluate the law, and this will be a major theme of these sections. Thus, you will need to consider the law on four separate levels.

- Describe the current law: You cannot hope to discuss the reform of law that you do not understand.

- Evaluate the current law: You need to be able to identify the problems with the current law that have led to the reform proposals, evaluating the seriousness of such problems.

- Describe the reform proposal: You need to know how the reform proposal is seeking to remedy the problems identified with the current law.

- Evaluate the reform proposal: To what extent would the proposal succeed in remedying the identified problems with the current law? Would the reform create any new problems?

---

[116] *Antoine* [2000] UKHL 20.
[117] Law Commission, *Unfitness to Plead. Vol 1: Report* (No 364, 2016). See also Law Commission, *Unfitness to Plead* (Consultation 197, 2010); *Issues Paper* (2014).
[118] Law Commission, *Unfitness to Plead. Vol 2: Draft Legislation* (No 364, 2016).
[119] Loughnan, 'Between Fairness and "Dangerousness": Reforming the Law on Unfitness to Plead' [2016] Crim LR 451.

Our discussion of reform proposals will, of course, differ with each chapter. However, the tools for evaluation (both of the current law and of reform proposals) do not change, and have been introduced in this chapter. We might ask, for example, how accurately the current law or the reform proposal targets the mischiefs that it is attempting to criminalise; how similar reforms have worked out in other common law jurisdictions; whether they conform to ECHR rights, etc. In each case, we can also apply the principles of criminalisation discussed in the previous section, asking whether the current law or reform proposal fairly warns and labels, whether it respects autonomy, and whether it protects welfare.

The substantive criminal law should not be thought of as a static body of rules to be committed to memory. Rather, it is dynamic and changing, through judicial interpretation as well as through statutory reform. You should consider the evaluative tools discussed in this chapter as a toolbox, equipping you to grapple with the substantive law. The criminal law is clearest and most interesting and rewarding when you cannot only identify and apply the rules as they stand, but do so with an understanding of how those rules have developed and how they are likely to change.

1.7 Eye on assessment

The final section of every chapter will provide an 'eye on assessment'. The idea of these sections is to discuss the *application* of the current law, particularly in the context of problem questions. Having discussed the substantive rules themselves, and having discussed potential reform, this section aims to help you to structure an answer that will demonstrate that knowledge.

Without any particular offences in mind, set out below is a generic guide to structuring a *problem question* that we will return to throughout this book. Although our approach may vary from this model when discussing particular offences and defences, it remains a useful structure around which these variations can be discussed and justified.

INTRODUCTION

The introduction to a problem question should be brief. It can be useful to identify the offences and defences relevant to the question in order to show your examiner you understand, and to say how you are going to answer the question (eg chronologically, defendant by defendant, crime by crime, etc). However, be sure to get into the body of the answer as quickly as possible.

STEP 1 Identify the potential criminal event in the facts

This is unlikely to take more than a sentence, but it is essential to tell your reader where in the facts you are focusing (eg 'The first potential offence is committed when D kicks V'). If you go straight into an analysis of the law without highlighting the event in the facts then it is very difficult for a reader to follow your answer.

STEP 2 Identify the potential offence

Having identified the facts (eg D kicking V), you must now identify the offence you are going to apply. Usually, this means identifying the most serious offence that D might have committed. As an example: 'When kicking and seriously injuring V, D may have committed a grievous bodily harm offence contrary to section 18 of the Offences Against the Person Act 1861'.

STEP 3 Applying the offence to the facts

Actus reus: What does the offence require? Did D do it?

Mens rea: What does the offence require? Did D possess it?

Remember, to be liable for the offence every element of the actus reus and mens rea must be satisfied. Thus, every element should be discussed even where it is easily satisfied and little discussion is necessary. Where there is doubt, in law or in fact, highlight and discuss areas of likely dispute between prosecution and defence. Also, if the question asks you to engage critically with the law as you apply it, take particular care to include evaluation of the law.

AR and MR are satisfied	AR and/or MR are not satisfied
Continue to STEP 4.	Return to STEP 2, and look for an alternative offence. If none, then skip to STEP 5, concluding that no offence is committed.

STEP 4 Consider defences

The word 'consider' here is important, as you should not discuss every defence for every question. Rather, think whether there are any defences that *could* potentially apply. If there are, discuss those only.

STEP 5 Conclude

This is usually a single sentence either saying that it is likely that D has committed the offence, or saying that it is not likely because an offence element is not satisfied or because a defence is likely to apply. It is not often that you will be able to say categorically whether or not D has committed the offence, so it is usually best to conclude in terms of what is more 'likely'.

STEP 6 Loop

Go back up to Step 1, identifying the next potential criminal event. Continue until you have discussed all the relevant potentially criminal events.

> **CONCLUSION**
>
> It is good practice to complete your problem question answer with a brief conclusion. This is usually no more than a few sentences highlighting where you believe offences have been committed and where they have not.

 ONLINE RESOURCE CENTRE

www.oxfordtextbooks.co.uk/orc/sho/

This chapter is accompanied by a selection of online resources to help you with this topic, including:

- **Multiple-choice questions**
- **Chapter summary sheet**
- Two **sample examination questions** with answer guidance
- **Further reading**

Also available on the Online Resource Centre are:

- A selection of **videos** from the authors explaining key topics and principles
- **Legal updates**
- Useful **weblinks**

2

Actus reus

2.1   Introduction   37
2.2   Separating actus reus and mens rea   38
2.3   Actus reus elements   40
   2.3.1   The conduct element   40
   2.3.2   The circumstance element   43
   2.3.3   The result element   44
   2.3.4   Separating conduct, circumstances, and results   45
2.4   Categories of offences   46
   2.4.1   Conduct crimes   47
   2.4.2   Result crimes   47
2.5   Summary   47
2.6   Omissions liability   48
   2.6.1   Offences capable of commission by omission   49
   2.6.2   Duties to act   51
   2.6.3   Breach of duty to act   55
   2.6.4   Causation by omission   57
   2.6.5   Distinguishing acts and omissions   58
2.7   Causation   59
   2.7.1   Causation in fact   60
   2.7.2   Causation in law   61
2.8   Reform   73
   2.8.1   Omissions   73
   2.8.2   Results   75
   2.8.3   Causation   76
2.9   Eye on assessment   78

2.1 Introduction

The term 'actus reus' is loosely translated as 'guilty act', and refers to the 'external elements' of an offence. These external elements do not simply relate to the movements of D; that is, her conduct. Rather, as we will see, the actus reus of an offence includes any offence requirement that is external from the mind of D: anything that is not 'mens rea'. This will include D's acts or omissions, but also any surrounding circumstances or facts necessary for liability, for example that the stolen property belongs to another for theft. It will also include any required results of the offence, for example the causing of death in homicide offences. Additionally, it will include the necessary links between elements, for example that the results must be caused by D's conduct. So, taking the simple case of battery by kicking, the actus reus involves D's kick (conduct), of a person (circumstances), making contact with that person (result).

It should be remembered that 'actus reus' and 'mens rea' are terms of art. We separate actus reus and mens rea in our analysis because breaking down offences into their elements helps us to understand them. But we must not lose sight of the fact that no matter what methods are used to distinguish the elements of an offence, D's liability depends upon the satisfaction of *all* of them as a whole. To be liable for an offence, it must be proved beyond reasonable doubt that D satisfied *all* the requirements of *both* the actus reus and the mens rea, and D must lack a defence. This is illustrated in **Figure 2.1**.

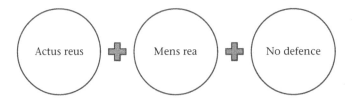

Figure 2.1 Structure of liability

The separate analysis of actus reus elements, which is the focus of this chapter, has several advantages. Most importantly, it is the physical conduct of D that identifies in time and usually in location[1] when the offence has taken place. This is why the analysis of a potential offence should always begin with actus reus, as it is only after this that we can then ask if D had the requisite mens rea *at that point*. The actus reus is also the only universal feature of all criminal offences: although offences have been created in the absence of mens rea,[2] there is no liability in the absence of actus reus, there is no 'thought crime'.[3]

2.2 Separating actus reus and mens rea

Before we explore the elements that form the actus reus, we must first learn to separate them from mens rea elements. For many offences this is relatively straightforward. Whether you are analysing a statutory or common law offence, the task is to separate any offence requirement that is external from D's state of mind (actus reus elements) from anything that is internal to D's mind, *or* concerned with such fault (mens rea elements). For example, case law tells us that the common law offence of murder is committed when D unlawfully causes the death of a person under the Queen's peace with the

---

[1] Where the offence takes place is important in relation to jurisdictional issues. Jurisdictional discussion will arise in certain chapters, but is generally not a focus of this book.
[2] See **Chapter 3** and discussion of the voluntary act requirement in particular.
[3] Duff, *Answering for Crime* (2009) Ch5.

intention to kill or the intention to cause grievous (very serious) bodily harm.[4] Here, the only part of the offence that is concerned with D's state of mind or fault is her intention to kill or cause grievous bodily harm; this is therefore the mens rea. D's actions and their results—acting to cause the unlawful death of a person—are all matters other than to do with D's state of mind or fault, and therefore represent the actus reus.

However, although these simple rules of separation are capable of consistent application, this is made more difficult when dealing with terms that appear to include both fault and external requirements.[5] Examples include 'appropriates',[6] 'cultivates',[7] 'abandons',[8] etc.[9] Where this is the case, we have two options: separate the fault and external aspects through the use of alternative terminology; or accept that actus reus elements occasionally include aspects that overlap with the fault or state of mind of D. It is contended that the former approach (separation) should always be preferred. However, this is not the consistent approach of the courts.

Below are two examples of terms that could be separated into actus reus and mens rea elements, but are popularly analysed as only one or the other.

- 'Sexual': An actus reus requirement for sexual assault,[10] as well as a number of other sexual offences,[11] is that D's conduct must be 'sexual'. Section 78 of the Sexual Offences Act 2003 states that D's conduct can be sexual (a) 'because of its nature', in the sense that a reasonable observer would describe it as sexual or (b) if its nature may be sexual and the 'circumstances' or 'purpose' of D make it sexual. Thus, although the offence element of 'sexual' is invariably referred to as an actus reus element, where it is satisfied by the 'purpose of D', this is clearly focusing on D's internal state of mind.[12]

- 'Dishonesty': One of the main elements of theft[13] and fraud[14] (and many other offences) is the requirement that D acted 'dishonestly', an element that is almost universally referred to as a mens rea requirement.[15] However, despite this, the common law definition of dishonesty set out in *Ghosh*[16] contains both external and internal elements: D acts dishonestly if her conduct would be considered dishonest by the standards of honest and reasonable people (external) and she realises that it would be considered dishonest by those standards (internal).

This kind of imperfect separation of actus reus and mens rea will arise within several of the offences discussed in later chapters. It is far from ideal, and has caused considerable

---

[4] *Cunningham* [1982] AC 566. See further *Smith and Hogan's Criminal Law* (14th edn, 2015) Ch4.
[5] Lynch, 'The Mental Element in the Actus Reus' (1982) 98 LQR 109.
[6] **Chapter 9**.
[7] *Champ* [1982] Crim LR 108 and commentary.
[8] *Hunt and Duckering* [1993] Crim LR 678.
[9] Robinson and Grall, 'Element Analysis in Defining Criminal Liability: The Model Penal Code and Beyond' (1983) 35 Stan L Rev 681.
[10] Sexual Offences Act 2003, s3.
[11] **Chapter 8**.
[12] Sullivan, 'Bad Thoughts and Bad Acts' [1990] Crim LR 559.
[13] Theft Act 1968, s1.
[14] Fraud Act 2006, s1.
[15] Discussed in **Chapter 3.6.1**.
[16] [1982] 1 WLR 409.

confusion. However, without a criminal code or some other codified source setting out the definitions of actus reus and mens rea elements,[17] such inconsistency is largely inevitable. It is also, for the most part, an inconsistency that does not damage the application of the law: D is only liable when every element of actus reus and mens rea is proved beyond reasonable doubt, whether we call them one thing or the other. Thus, the message here is to use actus reus and mens rea terminology to help with your analysis, but recognise that the law does not maintain a precise division between the two at all times.

2.3 Actus reus elements

Within the broad category of 'actus reus', it is useful further to subdivide elements into acts, circumstances, and results.[18]

- Conduct: D's physical acts or omissions required for liability.
- Circumstances: Facts surrounding D's conduct required for liability.
- Results: The effects of D's conduct required for liability.

As with the actus reus/mens rea distinction, the further separation of acts, circumstances, and results within the actus reus can be useful when setting out the detail of an offence. It is also useful to employ this terminology when singling out a particular part of the actus reus for criticism or comment. As an illustration of how this subdivision works, consider the offence of criminal damage. The actus reus requires D to have completed certain acts or omissions (conduct element) that cause damage (result element) to property belonging to another (circumstance element).

2.3.1 The conduct element

The conduct element of the actus reus is concerned with the physical movement of D's body. The conduct element, therefore, focuses only on the external movement (or, as we will see, lack of movement) of D's body. This is illustrated in **Table 2.1**.

Table 2.1 Conduct element of the actus reus

	Actus reus	Mens rea
Conduct element	D's physical acts or omissions required for liability	*
Circumstance element	*	*
Result element	*	*

---

[17] See eg definitions in the US Model Penal Code 1962, §2.02.
[18] Robinson and Grall, 'Element Analysis in Defining Criminal Liability: The Model Penal Code and Beyond' (1983) 35 Stan L Rev 681.

All criminal offences require a conduct element of some description as it is this element that locates where and usually when the offence happened. This is also the element that provides a nexus between D and the other elements required for liability. For example, we will soon ask whether the results were *caused by D's conduct element*, and whether D has a certain mens rea *at the time of the conduct element*. Therefore, when assessing potential liability within a problem question you should always begin by identifying the conduct element of the actus reus: what did D do or fail to do in breach of duty? All analysis flows from here.

The conduct required for different offences will vary considerably. For example, certain offences require quite specific acts such as penile penetration,[19] or driving.[20] However, it is also common to leave the conduct element unspecified. This is often the case when an offence is seeking to criminalise a certain harmful result no matter how it is caused by D. For example, the actus reus of murder includes *any* conduct that causes the unlawful death of a person; it does not matter if this is hitting, shooting, stabbing, pushing from a height, etc. The conduct element is still essential to D's liability, it is still the element that links D to the death, but D's method of killing is unspecified within the offence.[21]

Where a conduct element is satisfied by D's positive movements then applying the conduct element is relatively straightforward. However, certain offences are defined in such a way that liability can arise even in the absence of movement. There are three main examples.

A) Omissions liability: The major exception to any requirement of positive action is liability based on D's omission to act. Offences satisfied by omission are extremely common in the law, and in many cases largely uncontroversial.[22] For example, there will be liability where someone, whether a human or a company, fails to comply with requirements to register or file official documents such as tax returns or licences;[23] where a motorist fails to report an accident that she was involved in;[24] or where a motorist fails to provide police with a specimen of breath when lawfully required to do so.[25] These cases are easy to deal with because the statutory offence tells us what D must do, and also that if it is not done a specific crime is committed.

More controversially, outside *specific* omissions-based offences, many offences can be committed either by movement or omission. For example, the offence of murder is committed where D unlawfully shoots V (movement) with the intention to kill or cause grievous bodily harm; it is also committed where D starves her child (omission of care) with the same intention.[26] Where liability is based on an omission, three ingredients must be satisfied:

(a) *Recognised offence*: the offence charged must be recognised in law as one that is capable of being committed by omission.

---

[19] Sexual Offences Act 2003, s1.

[20] In the context of driving offences.

[21] Although the type of conduct may affect the sentence imposed, it will not affect D's substantive liability.

[22] This is a problem for those who, like Michael Moore, would prefer to represent omissions liability as a rare and mistaken option for the law: Moore, *Act and Crime* (1993) 22.

[23] See eg Companies Act 1985, s444 (Secretary of State's power to demand documents).

[24] Road Traffic Act 1988, s170(4).

[25] Ibid, s6.

[26] *Gibbins and Proctor* (1918) 13 Cr App R 134.

(b) *Duty to act*: there must be a legally recognised duty requiring D to act in a certain manner.

(c) *Breach of duty*: D's failure to act must fall below the standard expected in the performance of the duty.

More will be said about omissions liability when we continue this discussion at **2.6**.

B) Possession offences: Numerous offences are defined to criminalise the possession of certain dangerous material such as offensive weapons,[27] or offensive material such as child pornography.[28] Possession can be reconciled with the language of acts or omissions: D may have acted to gain possession, and the state of possession can be presented as D's omission to dispense of the item possessed.[29] However, it is perhaps more natural to describe 'possession' as a state of affairs where the movement, or non-movement, of D's body is not the crucial factor.[30] Thus, when discussing such offences it is perfectly acceptable to describe the conduct element as a state of possession.

C) State of affairs offences: Another category of offences that does not require positive action is referred to as 'state of affairs' or 'situational'[31] offences. Such offences should be treated with caution and can be the hallmark of tyrannical regimes that may attach criminal liability to membership of a certain political party,[32] or race or religion. However, even within England and Wales, state of affairs offences can be identified. For example, it is an offence under section 11 of the Terrorism Act 2000 to be a member, or profess to be a member, of a terrorist organisation. Other examples include offences of 'being found' in a particular situation, for example the case of *Winzar* and being found drunk in a highway contrary to section 12 of the Licensing Act 1872.

 Winzar v Chief Constable of Kent (1983) The Times, 28 March

D was taken to hospital on a stretcher, but was found to be drunk and told to leave. The police took D to their car on the highway outside the hospital. When on the highway, D was charged with being 'found drunk' in the highway.

- Divisional Court: guilty of section 12 offence.

In *Winzar*, and other similar cases,[33] it is particularly difficult to represent the conduct element of D's offence as a physical action. As with possession offences mentioned previously, we could focus on D's action, if there was any, in creating the state of affairs, or her omission in failing to remove herself from that state. Indeed, when criticising

---

[27] Prevention of Crime Act 1953, s1.
[28] Protection of Children Act 1978, s1.
[29] Moore, *Act and Crime* (1993) 20–22.
[30] Duff, *Criminal Attempts* (1996) Chs9–11; Husak, 'Does Criminal Liability Require an Act?' in Duff (ed), *Philosophy and the Criminal Law* (1998) 60.
[31] Cohen, 'The Actus Reus and Offences of Situation' (1972) 7 Is LR 186.
[32] *Scales v US*, 327 US 203 (1961) regarding communist party membership.
[33] See *Larsonneur* (1933) 24 Cr App R 74 (D was brought into the UK against her will by police, and then charged with landing in the UK illegally contrary to the Aliens Order 1920). See Lanham, '*Larsonneur* Revisited' [1976] Crim LR 276; with response from Smith [1999] Crim LR 100, and Lanham, Letter [1999] Crim LR 683.

liability in cases such as *Winzar*, reference to actions or omissions may help to highlight a significant problem with the case: the lack of voluntariness in the form of mens rea as to the conduct element.[34] However, again, it seems more natural to describe D's part in the offence without reference to bodily movement. Therefore, it is acceptable to describe the conduct element of these offences in terms of a state of affairs.

Terminology . . .

In line with the Law Commission and others, we employ the term 'conduct element' to describe the part of the offence that deals with D's physical movements or omissions. However, several statutes (as we will see) prefer the term 'act', even where that term is intended to include omissions liability. Take care with this when reading and interpreting statutes.

2.3.2 The circumstance element

Whatever D's conduct, it will be surrounded by a multitude of external circumstances: surrounding facts that are not performed by D, and not caused by D's action. Circumstances might include, for example, that V is female; V is under 18 years old; a reasonable person would be offended by D's act; V is a police officer; etc. Depending on the terms of the offence, these circumstances might be crucial to determining liability, but it should *not* be assumed that all surrounding circumstances are part of the offence. Look at the definition of the offence and identify which circumstances specified within the offence are required to be proved to exist at the time of D's potentially criminal act. This is illustrated in **Table 2.2**.

Table 2.2 Circumstance element of the actus reus

	Actus reus	Mens rea
Conduct element	D's physical acts or omissions required for liability	*
Circumstance element	Surrounding facts that must exist for liability	*
Result element	*	*

Every criminal offence will include some manner of circumstance element, used to focus in on the mischief targeted by the offence. For example, the actus reus of murder is not satisfied simply by D's conduct causing death unlawfully; D's conduct must cause the death *of a person*. Similarly, the actus reus of criminal damage is not simply conduct causing damage, but conduct causing damage *to property belonging to another*. Indeed, every offence will contain certain core circumstance elements: that D is a person, and that D is over the age of criminal responsibility (10 years old).

The examples of circumstances discussed so far are physical ones (or at least not only occurring in the mind of V or D), but this is not always the case. It is also possible for

---

[34] Smart, 'Criminal Responsibility for Failing to Do the Impossible' (1987) 103 LQR 532.

offences to require mental circumstances to exist. Rape, for example, requires D to penetrate V with his penis (conduct) without V's consent (circumstance). In this example, V's mental state is the circumstance element.

Circumstance elements will, of course, vary between offences. For example, despite the central role of the absence of consent within many sexual offences, it is irrelevant to murder. V's consent to being killed may be a circumstance of D's conduct, but it is not a circumstance element of the offence of murder and thus it has no bearing on D's liability. As we explore offences in later chapters, an important task is to identify from statute and/or common law which circumstances come within the circumstance element of each offence, and thus which circumstances are legally relevant.

> **Point to remember . . .**
> Sexual offences such as rape provide a useful example of how important circumstances can be to the targeting of a criminal wrong. Sexual penetration in the absence of consent is a serious criminal wrong; yet when the same conduct is done with legally valid consent, it is a social good.[35]

2.3.3 The result element

Just as D's conduct will take place in the context of certain circumstances, that conduct is also likely to cause a number of results. For example, when I move my fingers on the keyboard, this results in words appearing on the computer; when I throw a stone at your window, this results in damage to your window; and so on. As with the circumstance element in the previous section, however, when we refer to the result element of an offence we are not referring to every result of D's conduct. Rather, the result element of an offence is only concerned with certain results of D's conduct (and/or exceptionally the conduct of another[36]) that are required for liability, as illustrated in **Table 2.3**. For example, the result element of the actus reus of murder is 'death' (D's conduct must cause the death of V): if, in causing V's death, D's conduct also unlawfully harms a bystander and perhaps damages property, these other results are irrelevant to the charge of murder. Such results may give rise to additional criminal charges in their own right, but these will be separate from the issue of murder.

Table 2.3 Result element of the actus reus

	Actus reus	Mens rea
Conduct element	D's physical acts or omissions required for liability	*
Circumstance element	Surrounding facts that must exist for liability	*
Result element	Things caused by D's conduct required for liability	*

---

[35] The 'moral magic' performed by consent will be discussed in **Chapter 8**.
[36] This is the case, eg, in the context of vicarious liability or secondary liability. See **Chapter 12**.

Not all offences require a result element. For example, the offence of perjury applies where D lies in court when giving evidence.[37] When lying in this way, D's offence includes a conduct element (speaking) and a circumstance element (what she says is false; she is giving evidence in court), but nothing needs to result from D's conduct. Whether the court is caused to be misled, for example, is irrelevant: it is not a requirement of the offence. Other offences of this kind with no result element include the general inchoate offences of attempt, conspiracy, and assisting and encouraging.[38] D is liable for these offences as soon as she gets beyond mere preparation in trying to commit a crime (attempt), agrees with another to commit a crime (conspiracy), or assists or encourages another to commit a crime (assisting and encouraging). In each case, whether the offence tried/agreed/promoted results, or is caused, is irrelevant, D's actus reus focuses on actions and circumstances only.

Some of the most prominent offences in the criminal law, however, will require a result element. For example, murder requires D's conduct to *cause death*; offences against the person are structured around D's conduct *causing various levels of bodily harm*; criminal damage requires D's conduct to *cause damage*; and so on. Where this is the case, it is important to remember that we are not simply asking whether these results came about. Rather, the result element requires proof that the relevant results have been *caused* by D's conduct.

Therefore, whenever an offence includes a result element, this includes the requirement that the result must be causally connected to the conduct of D. There are two stages that must be satisfied to establish causation.

- **Causation in fact:** There must be a logical connection in fact. Thus, if the result would have come about in the same manner regardless of D's conduct, there is no factual causation.

- **Causation in law:** A variety of legal principles have developed to limit a finding of causation to conduct that had a substantial effect; was blameworthy; and was not superseded by subsequent events.

Causation between D's conduct and results will only be found where *both* stages of this test are satisfied. There is considerably more to say about how causation rules operate and this will be continued at **2.7**.

> *Beware . . .*
> It is common for students to think of causation as a separate issue from the actus reus. This is not correct. Causation is an essential part of the actus reus of any offence that includes a result element. It is the essential link between the conduct element and result element.

2.3.4 Separating conduct, circumstances, and results

Although the separation of conduct, circumstances, and results provides a useful structure through which to view and discuss the law, it remains controversial. The main problem is that adopting a precise and consistent separation of elements is often very difficult.[39]

---

[37] Perjury Act 1911, s1. Perjury also applies where D believes she is lying.
[38] **Chapter 11**.
[39] Buxton, 'The Working Paper on Inchoate Offences: (1) Incitement and Attempt' [1973] Crim LR 656; Buxton, 'Circumstances, Consequences and Attempted Rape' [1984] Crim LR 25; and Duff, *Criminal Attempts* (1996) 12–14.

In the absence of a criminal code or some other codified source setting out the definitions of offence elements,[40] such inconsistency is again largely inevitable. It may be, however, that a lack of consistency can be tolerated. As we discussed in relation to the problems with the actus reus/mens rea distinction, it is important to remember that D's liability requires proof of *every* element of an offence. Therefore, in practice, the criminal law will be unaffected whether we label an offence requirement as conduct, circumstance, or result; it must still be proved in the same way. However, as a device for discussing the law, it is only useful if it represents a reasonably common language: the more difference between interpretations, the less useful the technique becomes.

Below we highlight two areas where the separation of elements has proven to be particularly problematic:

A) **Expanding the conduct element:** In this book, when we refer to the conduct element we will be focusing on the physical movement of, or omission to move, D's body.[41] This is criticised by those who prefer to view action in its social context, for example that D's conduct is 'shooting'; not simply 'moving a finger'.[42] However, if we expand the definition of the conduct element beyond a focus on D's body, it is very difficult to know where to stop. For example, if D's conduct becomes 'shooting', why not 'shooting a person'? Such expansion would undermine the separation of actus reus elements.

B) **Expanding the result element:** In this book, when we refer to the result element, we will be focusing only on events *caused* by D's conduct. However, there is always a temptation to include circumstances within a discussion of the result element. For example, the academic Michael Moore would include a basic 'moral criterion' that would add further detail (eg the result of sexual assault would not simply be described as 'sexual contact', but 'sexual contact with a person').[43] Glanville Williams would also add to the result element based on what is 'customarily regarded' within elements.[44] Both approaches lack the necessary precision for maintaining the separation of actus reus elements.

> **Don't be confused . . .**
> When applying the general inchoate offences (**Chapter 11**) it is essential to use the terminology of acts, circumstances, and result. However, when discussing offences outside this you should only use it if it is useful. For example, if you wish to make a particular point about one part of an offence, then the subdivision can be helpful to identify the part of the offence you mean. However, when making more general points about the law, or summarising the requirements of an offence, it will often be easier and less cumbersome to talk of actus reus and mens rea only.

2.4 Categories of offences

The actus reus of an offence is made up of a combination of elements: the conduct element; circumstance element; and result element. However, as we have already noted,

---

[40] See eg definitions in the US Model Penal Code 1962, §2.02.
[41] In line with Robinson and Grall, 'Element Analysis in Defining Criminal Liability: The Model Penal Code and Beyond' (1983) 35 Stan L Rev 681.
[42] Duff, *Criminal Attempts* (1996) Ch9.
[43] Moore, *Act and Crime* (1993) 208.
[44] Williams, 'The Problem of Reckless Attempts' [1983] Crim LR 365, 369.

although all offences will include conduct (broadly defined) and circumstances, not all offences will include a result element. Whether an offence includes a result element or not has been used to distinguish two categories of offences.

2.4.1 Conduct crimes

Conduct crimes are so called because they do not include a result element. Examples include perjury and the general inchoate offences. The actus reus of these offences are complete as soon as D performs certain conduct in certain proscribed circumstances. As there is no result element, there is also no need to apply the rules of causation: D's conduct does not need to cause anything to satisfy the requirements of the offence.

2.4.2 Result crimes

Result crimes, unsurprisingly, are so called because they require a result element. Examples include murder and criminal damage. The actus reus of these offences is complete when D performs conduct in certain proscribed circumstances, with that conduct causing a certain proscribed result. As the result must be caused by D's conduct, the rules of causation must be applied to these cases. It is common for result crimes to specify certain circumstances and results, but to leave the conduct element unspecified. For example, the offence of murder requires the unlawful killing (result) of a person (circumstance), but it does not specify D's conduct: it must be conduct of D that has caused the result, but it does not matter what this was (eg shooting, stabbing, omitting to feed, etc) as long as the killing was unlawful.

> *Assessment matters . . .*
> All result crimes require D's conduct to have caused the result element. However, your discussion of causation does not need to be equally detailed in every case. For example, in a case where D wounds V by cutting her with a knife, the cutting and wounding happen simultaneously. As there is no space in time or proximity between conduct and result, there is little room for doubting the causal connection between the two, and so discussion of causation can be brief. In contrast, where D attacks V and V dies some time later, the gap between D's conduct and the result (death) means that a more extended discussion of causation is required.

2.5 Summary

We have provided an overview of actus reus elements, including conduct, circumstances, and results. In later chapters, a significant part of our study will be to identify the actus reus requirements of various offences, both from statute and from the common law, and to learn how they are/should be applied in practice. Understanding the elements of the actus reus in general terms will help with both.

The next two sections of this chapter revisit two areas already introduced: omissions and causation. It is important to remember the role that these play in the context of the previous discussion. However, as each of them raises a number of important issues, and has attracted significant judicial and academic attention, they require some additional examination.

2.6 Omissions liability

When looking to identify the conduct element of an offence it is always preferable to focus on D's movement as opposed to her omission to move. This is because, aside from a small number of omission-specific offences,[45] D's positive movement can *always* satisfy the conduct element of an offence, with the full offence being completed if the other elements are also satisfied. In contrast, there is reluctance from both courts and the legislature to impose liability for omissions.

A common illustration of legal reluctance in relation to omissions liability, and one that provides a useful starting point for discussion, is that *without more* there will be no liability in English law if D watches a child drown in a shallow pool, even if D could easily save the child, and even if D omits to help because she intends the child to die.[46] If the child had died as a result of D's positive action in these circumstances, D would be straightforwardly liable for murder. However, in the absence of a positive action, D's omission will not satisfy the conduct element of murder and therefore the crime will not be complete.

There are several justifications for this reluctance when it comes to omissions liability.[47] Although we might see D's failure to save the drowning child as morally blameworthy, nevertheless, with limited criminal law resources we may see the conduct of the other party who pushed the child as a more pressing target. Also, whereas a positive action makes it easy to identify the particular defendant who may be liable, D's omission to save is logically one that is shared with everyone else in the world, and so it is difficult to construct laws to isolate particular *criminal* omissions: it creates problems for fair warning, certainty, and coherence. Perhaps the most important reason for reluctance relates to respect for D's autonomy in the sense of her right to peruse person goals without undue interference from the law.[48] Let us imagine that, at any one time, D has 100,000 options when it comes to her movements (go left; right; sit; go to the shops; to work; and so on). When a criminal offence imposes liability for a positive action, D now has 99,999 options: she can act as she wishes, as long as she does not act in the proscribed manner. In contrast, when a criminal offence imposes liability for an omission to act, D has only one option: she must act in the manner required by the offence to avoid liability.[49]

Thus, although D's omission may be morally wrongful, the question of criminalisation must weigh D's wrongful omission (favouring criminalisation) against issues of practicality and respect for D's autonomy (weighing against criminalisation). This is illustrated in **Figure 2.2**.

---

[45] eg a motorist failing to provide police with a specimen of breath when properly instructed to do so, contrary to the Road Traffic Act 1988, s6.

[46] Ashworth, 'The Scope of Liability for Omissions' (1989) 105 LQR 424. Liability will only arise where D has responsibility for the child (Children and Young Persons Act 1933, s1), or a legal duty to act (discussed in the following).

[47] Williams, 'Criminal Omissions—The Conventional View' (1991) 107 LQR 86.

[48] See discussion of the principle of autonomy at **1.4.3**.

[49] There are, of course, a number of problems with this illustration. However, it serves to highlight (in general terms at least) the core of the autonomy argument.

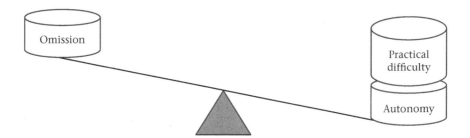

Figure 2.2 Weighing up omissions liability

In contrast to liability based on movement, D's omission alone will not generally be enough to satisfy the conduct element of an offence.[50] However, this is not to say that there is no liability for omissions, it is simply to highlight that for omissions liability to be found further ingredients are required to tip the balance. These include:

(a) D's offence must be capable of commission by omission;

(b) D must have a legally recognised duty to act; and

(c) D must have unreasonably failed to act on that duty.

This is illustrated in **Figure 2.3**.

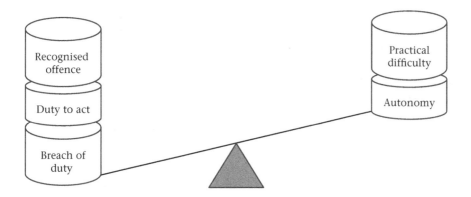

Figure 2.3 Where omissions liability is justified

For D's omission to satisfy the conduct element of an offence, each of these three requirements must be found. Following this, as long as the other offence elements are also satisfied, D will be liable for the offence.

2.6.1 Offences capable of commission by omission

In certain cases it will be clear from the statutory wording that an offence can be committed by omission. However, for the majority of offences, including all those discussed

---

[50] The only exception is the small number of omission-specific offences, eg Road Traffic Act 1988, s6.

in this book, the question of whether an offence can be committed by omission will be a matter of statutory interpretation and case law precedent.

Unfortunately, general rules have not been developed to identify whether an offence is capable of being committed by omission. For example, in the case of *Ahmad*,[51] D, who was V's landlord, omitted to undertake essential work that left V's home uninhabitable, with D intending to force V to leave. D was charged with 'doing acts calculated to interfere with [V's] peace and comfort',[52] but found not guilty on the basis that 'doing acts' could not be satisfied by omission. However, in relation to other offences, the term 'act' within a statute has not prevented liability for omissions. For example, where D remains motionless in response to sexual touching from a child, it has been held that he commits a sexual offence even where the terms of that offence require D to have acted.[53]

In the absence of general rules relating to statutory terms such as 'act', it is now clear that each offence must be assessed individually. This will be done in detail in later chapters, but a few illustrations may be useful.

- Homicide (murder and manslaughter offences): It has long been recognised that most homicide offences can be committed by omission. For example, in *Gibbins and Proctor*,[54] a man and woman were convicted of murder on the basis of their omission to feed the man's child (V). They had a duty to feed the child, they breached that duty, and they acted with the intention to cause serious harm thereby satisfying the mens rea of murder.

- Non-fatal offences against the person: Employing terms such as 'assault', 'wound', and 'battery', there has been a reluctance to find omissions liability in relation to non-fatal offences.[55] However, liability has been found. For example, in *Santana Bermudez*,[56] D misinformed a police officer that he did not have any needles, and was therefore liable when the officer (V) was pricked during the personal search. This approach, finding omissions liability in such cases, is surely correct. With reference to *Gibbins* above, for example, it would be absurd if D was liable for causing death to her child by omission, but would avoid any liability for lesser crimes if the police had intervened at a stage when V was seriously harmed but not yet dead.

- Property offences: Again, despite some doubt,[57] omissions liability has been found in relation to certain property offences. For example, in *Miller*,[58] D was convicted of arson when, having inadvertently started a fire, he did not act to try and put out the fire or call for assistance.

There appears to be a trend towards accepting omissions liability for an ever greater range of offences. However, this expansion remains controversial.[59] It is also far from

---

[51] (1986) 84 Cr App R 64.
[52] Protection from Eviction Act 1977.
[53] *Speck* [1977] 2 All ER 859. See **Chapter 8**.
[54] (1918) 13 Cr App R 134.
[55] **Chapter 7**.
[56] [2004] Crim LR 471.
[57] The Draft Criminal Code, eg, would not have allowed omissions liability for property offences.
[58] [1983] 2 AC 161.
[59] See criticism from Williams in 'Letter to the Editor' [1982] Crim LR 773.

complete; for example, there is still no liability for offences *attempted* by omission.[60] As such, when applying omissions liability within a problem question, some consideration of whether the offence is capable of commission by omission remains essential.

2.6.2 Duties to act

Having established that the offence charged is one that is capable of commission by omission, the next requirement is that D must have a legally recognised duty to act.[61] It is this duty that narrows the law's focus from *all* those who failed to act, which could be everyone in the world, to isolate those few whose omissions can be described as criminal. In this regard, duties are not simply imposed on those who are in a position to help, such as those who know about the danger and are able to provide assistance: that approach may seem appealing in order to catch D who watches the child drown for example, but it would also catch anyone who watches an aid appeal on television and chooses not to donate in the knowledge that lives could be saved. Rather, the law will only impose a duty to act in very narrow categories. These include offence-specific duties; contractual duties; familial duties; duties based on an assumption of care; and duties created through endangerment.

Unfortunately, despite the importance of these categories, the boundaries of each one are far from certain. As the common law develops, we can identify core cases, but application outside these core cases remains challenging.

> *Beware . . .*
> A 'duty to act' sounds like, and is often confused with, a 'duty of care'. A duty of care is a tort law concept essential to the tort of negligence, and identifies all those we must take care to avoid harming by our conduct. Indeed, we will discuss duties of care when we analyse the crime of gross negligence manslaughter in **Chapter 6**, a crime that borrows heavily from the tort of negligence. In contrast, duties to act identify a considerably narrower set of duties where D's criminal liability can be based on an omission. Where a duty to act is found, there will always be a duty of care; however, a duty of care will not always indicate a duty to act. Therefore, whenever D's liability is omission-based, a duty to act must be identified.

2.6.2.1 Duties to act based on the specifics of an offence

Where an offence is specifically drafted to allow for omissions liability, it is straightforward to identify the duty to act that is created. Statutory examples include section 170(4) of the Road Traffic Act 1988, which makes it an offence to fail (ie omit) to report a motor accident in which D is involved. If an accident is not reported, we can say that everyone has omitted to report it. However, the statute creates a special duty on those involved in the accident: only their omission to report is singled out as a potentially criminal omission which will satisfy the conduct element of the offence. There are also examples, albeit rare ones, in the common law. For example, the case of *Dytham* and the common law offence of misconduct in public office.[62]

---

[60] See **Chapter 11**.
[61] See Alexander, 'Criminal Liability for Omissions: An Inventory of Issues' in Shute and Simester (eds), *Criminal Law Theory* (2002) 121.
[62] See also *AG's Reference (No 3 of 2003)* [2004] 3 WLR 451.

Dytham [1979] 3 All ER 641

D, a police officer, was charged with misconduct in public office when, while on duty, he failed to intervene in an incident in which V was kicked to death by a nightclub bouncer 30 yards away. The offence of misconduct in public office creates a clear duty for public officials to act in a reasonable manner.

- Crown Court: guilty of misconduct in public office.
- Court of Appeal: conviction upheld on appeal.

Offence-specific duties of this kind are unproblematic, but they are also rather narrow: they apply only in the context of the individual offence that creates them. The other duties to act (discussed below), in contrast, can apply to provide omissions liability across multiple offences, even those that are more standardly committed by positive actions (eg murder).

2.6.2.2 Duties to act based on a contract

Where D has a contractual duty to act, such a duty is also capable of being recognised in criminal law as the basis for omissions liability. Contracts can give rise to duties between the parties where D is contracted to protect V or her property, as well as third parties such as carers and health professionals. Most commonly, as in *Pittwood*, this will involve contracts of employment.

 Pittwood (1902) 19 TLR 37

D, a railway crossing gate-keeper, opened the gate to let a cart cross the lines and then went to lunch, forgetting to close it again. As a result, a subsequent cart collided with a train, killing the train driver. D was charged with manslaughter on the basis of his omission (contractual duty to close the gate).

- Trial court: guilty of gross negligence manslaughter.

Certain contractual duties to act, particularly in relation to the caring professions, are now firmly established. However, outside these core examples, uncertainty remains. For example, how strictly will a court adhere to the terms of a contract? If a lifeguard is contracted until 5 pm, for example, is there a duty to act if she spots someone drowning at 5.05 pm as she leaves her shift?

2.6.2.3 Duties to act based on a familial relationship

Core examples where a duty to act has been found between family members include a parent's duty to care for their child (eg *Gibbins and Proctor*,[63] discussed in **2.6.1**), and between a married couple (eg *Hood*).

 Hood [2004] 1 Cr App R 431

D omitted to summon help for three weeks after his wife (V) fell and suffered broken bones. V died as a result. D was charged with manslaughter on the basis of breaching his familial duty to assist.

- Crown Court: guilty of gross negligence manslaughter.
- Court of Appeal: conviction upheld on appeal.

---

[63] (1918) 13 Cr App R 134.

Outside these core examples, however, a lack of case law has (again) led to considerable uncertainty. First, although duties have been recognised between parent and child and between a married couple, it is difficult to predict what other relationships will also give rise to similar duties. For example, if the duty is family-based, will it extend to siblings[64] or extended family? On the other hand, if the duty is based on dependence, which is arguably a more justifiable route,[65] will it extend to unmarried couples or even cohabiting friends?[66] A second layer of uncertainty relates to the boundaries of a duty within a recognised relationship. For example, will a parent still owe a duty to a fully emancipated child over the age of 18,[67] or a wife to her husband if they have been separated although perhaps not yet divorced? Again, it may be better to focus on dependence as opposed to formal relationships, but this simply leads to another question: how much dependence?[68]

2.6.2.4 Duties to act based on an assumption of care

Assumption of care duties will arise when D has voluntarily undertaken to care for V whatever the formal relationship between D and V, in circumstances where V becomes dependent upon that care.[69] A duty to act will arise where the promise of care is explicit, as in *Nicholls*.

Nicholls (1874) 13 Cox CC 75

D, V's grandmother, agreed to take care of V after the death of V's mother. V was neglected by D and died. D was charged with gross negligence manslaughter based on the duty arising from an explicit assumption of care.

- Trial court: guilty of gross negligence manslaughter.

A similar duty will also arise where the promise of care is implicit, as in *Instan*.

Instan [1893] 1 QB 450

D, V's niece, moved into V's house. V became extremely unwell with a gangrenous leg and was unable to look after herself. However, although D continued to live in the house and eat V's food, etc, she did not care for V or summon help. V died and D was charged with gross negligence manslaughter based on the duty arising from an implicit assumption of care.

- Crown Court: guilty of gross negligence manslaughter.

Although the imposition of a duty to act in these cases seems broadly just, assumption of care duties can be problematic. Most importantly, it remains unclear exactly how much, or how little, D must do before a duty will arise. Useful examples of relatively minor acts

---

[64] There is some indication of this in *Stone and Dobinson* [1977] QB 354.
[65] Fletcher, *Rethinking Criminal Law* (1978) 613.
[66] There is some indication of this in *Sinclair, Johnson and Smith* (1998) 21 August, CA.
[67] *Sheppard* (1862) Le & Ca 147 suggests not.
[68] Discussed in Ashworth, 'Manslaughter by Omission and the Rule of Law' [2015] Crim LR 563.
[69] Mead, 'Contracting into Crime: A Theory of Criminal Omissions' (1991) 11 OJLS 147.

of attempted assistance leading to the creation of a duty to act include *Ruffell*,[70] in which D briefly and unsuccessfully attempted to revive a fellow drug user after an overdose, and *Stone and Dobinson*,[71] in which D, of low intelligence, tried ineffectually to assist V before her death.

Aside from issues about when this kind of duty will arise, there is also the related problem of when it will end. It may be supposed, for example, that D could fulfil the duty by informing the authorities that she will no longer be caring for V, or perhaps if V expressly releases D from the duty.[72] However, without clarifying case law, these propositions are far from clear.

Finally, it should be highlighted that a duty to act arising from an assumption of care gives rise to an uncomfortable contrast. D who tries to help V will create a duty to continue acting that can lead to serious criminal liability if breached. Whereas D who does not try to help will not create a duty and will not therefore risk liability. The legal message, it could be said, is not to try.[73]

2.6.2.5 Duties to act based on endangerment

A duty to act will arise where D's previous conduct has created, or at least contributed to, a dangerous situation. Having created the danger, whether inadvertently or otherwise, D must act to try to prevent harm coming about.

> ### *Miller* [1983] 2 AC 161
>
> D, a squatter in V's house, went to sleep holding a lit cigarette. He awoke to find the mattress smouldering, but did nothing save move to an adjoining room. The fire caused extensive damage, and D was charged with criminal damage based on his omission to tackle the smouldering mattress or alert the authorities. The duty to do so arose from his inadvertent creation of a dangerous situation.
>
> - Crown Court: guilty of criminal damage.
> - Court of Appeal: conviction upheld on appeal.
> - House of Lords: conviction upheld on appeal.

Miller establishes a duty to act based on endangerment, arising at the point D becomes aware of the danger she has created. It is also a useful reminder that omissions liability is not restricted to cases of murder and manslaughter.[74] It should be remembered that omissions liability is not offence-specific, and may satisfy the conduct element of any offence that is capable of being committed by omission.

---

[70] [2003] EWCA Crim 122. Note, however, this conclusion is muddied by the fact that the court also stresses the close friendship between D and V.

[71] [1977] 2 All ER 341.

[72] There is some indication of this in *Smith* [1979] Crim LR 251.

[73] If this is the message, it is not indefensible. Eg when D begins to aid V, it may be that others stop helping in view of D's presence and/or that V stops asking for help. Thus, if D's assistance is then stopped, V may be worse off as a result.

[74] Murder and manslaughter are over-represented in omissions case law because the serious harm involved encourages prosecutors to find creative routes to liability.

The *Miller* principle has been extended by the more recent case of *Evans*.

 Evans [2009] EWCA Crim 650

D, V's half-sister, supplied her with heroin which she self-administered. Realising V showed symptoms of an overdose, D stayed with V but did not alert the authorities for fear of personal liability for supplying the drugs. V died and D was charged with gross negligence manslaughter on the basis of her omission to aid V. The duty arose from her contribution to the dangerous situation through drug supply.

• Crown Court: guilty of gross negligence manslaughter.

• Court of Appeal: conviction upheld on appeal.

Although *Evans* is broadly similar to *Miller*, with D's duty arising from her contribution to a dangerous situation, in *Miller* D's duty to act only arose at the point he became personally aware (subjectively) of the danger he had created. In contrast, within *Evans*, the court stated that the duty would arise when D realises *or should have realised* that the danger was created. This allows for possible omissions liability even where D did not realise the danger she had created, as long as a reasonable (objective) person would have done.[75] In *Lewin v CPS*,[76] a case that preceded *Evans*, a challenge to the CPS's decision not to prosecute D failed where D had left a heavily intoxicated friend (V) in his car in extremely hot conditions abroad leading to V's death. The court held that D did not owe a duty to V after he had parked his car. However, employing *Evans*, it could now be argued that leaving V in the car contributed to a dangerous situation that D *should have realised*, creating a duty to act and potential liability.

Assessment matters . . .
Within several cases mentioned previously, the courts have discussed more than one possible duty to act. For example, in the case of *Evans* there is discussion of potential duties based on a relationship (D was V's half-sister), assumption of care (when D begins to look after V), as well as a duty arising from endangerment. Indeed, in certain cases it is unclear on which basis the duty has been found (or whether it is found from the combination of possible duties). With this in mind, when answering a problem question, try to highlight all possible duties to act that may give rise to D's liability. Additionally, as these are common law duties, remember the list is not exhaustive: if you cannot find a recognised duty but you think liability should be found, you may wish to highlight the possibility that one of the existing duties may be extended or the, admittedly rather remote, possibility that a new duty may be recognised.

2.6.3 Breach of duty to act

After it has been established that D's offence was capable of commission by omission, and that D had a recognised duty to act, the next requirement is that D breached that

---

[75] See Williams, 'Gross Negligence Manslaughter and Duty of Care in "Drugs" Cases: *R v Evans*' [2009] Crim LR 631.

[76] [2002] EWCA 1049.

duty. This requirement is useful to focus our minds on an obvious (but easily confused) point about omissions liability: D does not satisfy the conduct element because at the relevant moment she was perfectly still (it is very likely that D will have been moving her body in one way or another); she omits in law because she fails to do what the duty to act requires of her. Thus, to test whether D has breached her duty to act, we must question what the particular duty to act required her to do.

In general terms, a duty to act obliges D to do what is *reasonable*. What is reasonable is a question for the jury. In the case of *Miller*, for example, it was required that D should attempt to put out the smouldering mattress or contact the fire brigade if this was not possible; in *Evans* to contact the emergency services; in *Dytham* to intervene in the bouncer's attack on V or at least call on other officers for backup.

Importantly, the duty to act does not require *more* than what is reasonable. For example, if Miller awoke to a roaring inferno, he would not have had a duty to charge into the fire and attempt to put it out single-handedly. In such a case, there would be a duty to act, but this would probably be satisfied by a call for help. Thus, even where harm is caused, this will not necessarily mean that D has breached her duty to act, and the question of breach must always be discussed.

Some confusion, however, should be highlighted. This is illustrated through the case of *Stone and Dobinson*.

 Stone and Dobinson [1977] 2 All ER 341

D1 (a man of low IQ) and D2 (described as 'ineffectual and inadequate') took in D1's sister (V) to live with them. V suffered from anorexia nervosa which led her to avoid food, eventually being confined to her bed. D1 and D2 made some incompetent efforts to feed and clean V, and contact a doctor, but eventually stopped. V later died in appalling conditions. D1 and D2 were charged with gross negligence manslaughter on the basis of their omission. The duty was created by a voluntary assumption of care.

- Crown Court: guilty of gross negligence manslaughter.
- Court of Appeal: conviction upheld on appeal.

This case is important because the extremely low functioning of D1 and D2 made it difficult for them to look after themselves, let alone care for V. Therefore, even after a duty to act is found on these facts, it is surely questionable what D1 and D2 were duty bound to do given their lack of capacity. If the test is whether they acted reasonably *based, subjectively, on their impaired ability to act*, then it may be that there is no clear breach. However, the little attention given to this question by the court may suggest that the test was rather: did they do what is, objectively, reasonable based on the standards of reasonable competent people? If the current law is represented by this latter test (the judgment was not clear), then there is potential for considerable injustice. Just as we should not require Miller to act beyond the capabilities of the reasonable man by putting out a house fire single-handedly, surely it is equally unfair to demand things from Stone and Dobinson that are beyond their abilities.

2.6.4 Causation by omission

If it is established that D's offence is capable of commission by omission; that D had a recognised duty to act; and that D breached that duty; then D's omission will fulfil the requirements of the conduct element. Where D's offence is a conduct crime such as a failing to report-type offence, the question then becomes whether D's omission is accompanied by the circumstances and mens rea required for the offence to be complete. However, where D's offence is a result crime, such as a homicide offence, it must also be demonstrated that a certain result came about, and that it was *caused* by the conduct element. We discuss causation in detail later. However, it is worth highlighting here the highly unusual issues that arise where D's causing conduct element is an omission.

It is arguable that an omission to act can never cause a result element. The point here is that although D's omission may allow for the result to happen, it has not materially contributed to the result any more than D's omission has contributed to every other event that takes place at that point in time.[77] This is not, however, the approach taken by the law, and it is clear that an omission can be found to have caused a result element. Although D's omission may not be the only cause, and may not even be the most significant cause, this is not definitive. Additionally, accepting the potential for omissions to cause results in certain cases does not mean that we have to conclude that D has caused (by failing to prevent) *all harms* going on in the world: the restrictive nature of duties to act will have already narrowed D's potential liability to only those events where the law requires D to act.[78]

Therefore, for D to commit a result crime by omission, the causation rules must be applied. This is not an empty requirement. The prosecution must show that it is because D had not acted in line with her duty to act that the result came about, and that if she had acted in line with her duty it would not or might not have done so. For example, if the duty in *Evans* was for D to call an ambulance as soon as it became obvious that V was suffering a drugs overdose, it must be demonstrated by the prosecution that had she done so V may not have died. If, *hypothetically*, V died immediately after self-injecting the drug, then it is highly unlikely that D could have been liable for causing death: even if she had acted in line with her duty (calling for help), V would still have died.

---

[77] Hogan, 'Omissions and the Duty Myth' in Smith (ed), *Criminal Law: Essays in Honour of JC Smith* (1987) 85. Moore, *Act and Crime* (1993) 267.

[78] Leavens, 'A Causation Approach to Criminal Omissions' (1988) 76 Cal LR 547.

Assessment matters . . .

Having established a conduct element through D's omission (relevant offence; duty to act; breach of duty), it is common for students to forget to discuss a requirement of causation. Remember, even if D has omitted in breach of her duty, unless that omission has causally contributed to the result there can be no liability for a result crime. Think about what D's duty to act required her to do and ask yourself—if D had done this might it have prevented the result? If yes, causation can be found; if not, there is no causation.

2.6.5 Distinguishing acts and omissions

In the majority of cases it will be obvious whether D has acted or omitted to act, and it will be a case of assessing her liability on that basis. However, there is a grey area between the legal understanding of act and omission that is capable of causing problems. For example, if D and V are playing tug-of-war and D lets go of the rope (causing V to fall and hurt herself), has D acted (letting go) or omitted (stopped pulling)? If a doctor turns off a life-support machine, has she acted (turning off) or omitted (stopped treatment)? And so on.[79]

This grey area between acts and omissions is capable of causing problems for the law. It is obviously crucial where the offence charged cannot be committed by omission (eg attempts). However, even where the offence (as is increasingly the case) can be committed by act or omission, it is important to remember that omissions liability is still more restrictive. For example, if D acts by movements to kill V then the conduct element of murder is satisfied immediately. However, if D kills V by omission, the conduct element requires further ingredients: a duty to act and a breach of that duty. Where there is no duty to act, D will avoid liability in the second (omissions-based) example where she would have been potentially liable in the first.

Without a rule of interpretation to guide courts in this area, it seems that the decision whether to classify D's conduct as an act or omission is one that is made on a case-by-case basis. This gives rise to inconsistency. For example, in *Fagan*[80] where D accidentally drove onto a police officer's foot and then rested the car there intentionally, D's conduct was interpreted as an action: driving on and staying on the foot rather than an omission to move off from the foot. This allowed for straightforward liability without consideration of duties to act. However, where D's behaviour is such that the courts will have a more sympathetic attitude, courts are much more likely to interpret their conduct as an omission. For example, in termination of medical care cases such as *Bland*[81] (doctor's decision to terminate care) and *Re B (A Minor)*[82] (parents' decision to terminate care), it has been held that stopping treatment will be an omission even if it involves acts such as turning off machines, and that such omissions might not breach D's duty to act where V's best interests are not served by further treatment. The issue here is not whether these cases reached the correct outcomes, but the unprincipled basis upon which those outcomes were reached.[83]

[79] Kennedy, 'Switching Off Life Support Machines: The Legal Implications' [1977] Crim LR 443.
[80] [1969] 1 QB 439. Discussed further in **Chapter 4**.
[81] *National Health Service Trust v Bland* [1993] 1 All ER 821.
[82] [1981] 1 WLR 1421.
[83] Keown, 'Restoring Moral and Intellectual Shape to the Law after *Bland*' (1997) 113 LQR 481.

Assessment matters . . .

If you are faced with conduct in a problem question that could be interpreted as an act or an omission it will usually be necessary, at least briefly, to consider both options. First, explain that the conduct element could be satisfied if we interpret D's conduct as an act. Then consider the omissions alternative, highlighting whether it is likely that D had a duty to act and breached that duty. Finally, discuss which approach you believe the court is likely to take (considering, eg, the different approaches taken by the court in relation to different cases).

2.7 Causation

When assessing liability for conduct crimes such as perjury, attempts liability, etc, there is no result element and therefore no requirement that it should be *caused* by D's conduct. In contrast, when assessing liability for a result crime such as homicide offences, criminal damage, etc, a result element must be found, and so it is also essential to demonstrate a causal link between D's conduct and that result. If D's conduct element (movement- or omission-based) did not cause the result element, there will be no liability for a result crime.

It is often quite straightforward to demonstrate that D's acts caused a particular result. For example, if D throws a stone at V's window and it breaks, there seems to be little dispute: the damage was caused by D's act. In such cases, the judge will direct the jury simply to apply their common understanding of causation. However, in real life (*and particularly in problem questions*), examples may not be this straightforward. For example, what if the window was only broken because the glass was unusually thin? What if D was not aiming for the window, but the stone was caught by a strong gust of wind? What if another stone, thrown by X, would have smashed the glass a split second later, or even made contact at the same time? In such cases, the issue of causation (whether D's conduct caused the result) is likely to be disputed between prosecution and defence. This time, although the judge will again direct the jury to apply their common understanding of causation, the judge will also guide the jury's deliberation with a number of legal principles.[84]

Assessment matters . . .

Your approach to problem questions should mirror the approach of the court. If causation is straightforwardly satisfied in your discussion of a result crime, then there is no need to discuss the full detail of the causation rules. You should highlight the presence of causation, but need not elaborate. A full discussion of the causation rules, the legal principles developed to assist with difficult cases, is only required where there are, or may be, problems identifying causation.

Legal principles have developed in the common law to assist juries where a common-sense understanding of causation does not provide a clear answer. These principles are applied via a two-stage test:

- Causation in fact: Did the result come about because of D's conduct?
- Causation in law: Was D's conduct a substantial; blameworthy; and operating cause?

---

[84] *Pagett* (1983) 76 Cr App R 279. See also *Smith and Hogan's Criminal Law* (14th edn, 2015) Ch4.

Importantly, the answer to *both* these questions must be 'yes' in order to find causation. We will discuss each in turn.

2.7.1 Causation in fact

Factual causation is always the starting point for a discussion of the causation rules, asking generally whether the result came about because of D's contributory act or her failure (omission) to prevent the result. Another way to express this is through the commonly used 'but for' test:[85] it must be proved that, *but for* D's conduct element, the result would not have come about.[86]

If D's conduct is not a factual cause, as in *White*, there can be no causation.

 White [1910] 2 KB 124

D put poison in his mother's (V's) drink intending to kill her. It was unclear on the facts whether V drank any of the poison, but she died shortly afterwards. Regardless of her potential consumption of the poison, however, medical evidence demonstrated that V died due to an unrelated heart condition.

- Crown Court: D was not guilty of murder (result crime requiring causation), but was guilty of attempted murder (conduct crime not requiring causation).
- Court of Criminal Appeal: conviction upheld on appeal.

In *White*, D had completed acts intending to cause death (conduct element of murder), and death came about (result element of murder), but liability for murder failed because of the lack of causation linking D's conduct with the result. The death would have come about in exactly the same way whether D had acted or not: he was not the factual cause. Drawing on our previous stone-throwing example, this would also rule out liability where a stone from X hits and smashes the window a split second before the stone thrown by D. Since the window is already broken and D's conduct has caused no further damage, her conduct has not in fact caused criminal damage.

The test of factual causation, therefore, will rule out liability for a result crime in cases such as *White*. However, the test remains extremely wide. This is particularly clear in two regards.

- **Accelerating the result:** As long as D's conduct caused the result to come about when it did, she is the factual cause; it is irrelevant if it would have come about later without D's involvement. For example, if V had died as a result of the poison in *White* or D's stone had hit before X's in our criminal damage example, factual causation would be established: the results may have occurred just seconds later without D's involvement, but D is still the factual cause of the result that did come about.[87] This rule holds

---

[85] Also referred to as a '*sine qua non*' cause.
[86] The only exception to this rule is where D1 and D2 act simultaneously to cause a result, where either act alone would have been sufficient (eg D1 and D2 both shoot V in the head at the same time). Here, even though we cannot say that either is a 'but for' cause of V's death, factual causation would still be found.
[87] *Dyson* [1908] 2 KB 454.

certain logic, particularly in homicide cases: as we will all die at some point, D can never do more than speed up this process.

- **More than one cause:** Again, as long as the result would not have happened in the same way but for D's conduct, it is not necessary to show that D was the only cause. This is illustrated in the case of *Benge*.

 Benge (1846) 2 Car & Kir 230

D, a railways foreman, misread a train timetable when taking up sections of track. A train arrived when the track was up and V was killed. D contended that death could have been avoided if his 'flagmen' (stationed along the track to warn unexpected trains) had placed themselves at the proper distance from the worksite, and also if the train driver had kept a proper lookout.

- Court: D was guilty of gross negligence manslaughter.

In *Benge* it may be that other actors were also 'but for' causes of V's death, and may have been independently liable for it. However, the presence of multiple causes does not undermine the fact that D was a 'but for' cause as well. Unlike the civil law, criminal liability does not seek to apportion blame or look for principal causes, it simply asks whether each defendant individually facing the prospect of liability was a factual cause. In relation to our criminal damage example, this would be the case where D, a 12-year-old, is allowed to throw the stone by her father (D2): both D (by her act) and D2 (by his omission to stop D) are factual causes of the damage.

Don't be confused . . .
The possibility of multiple causes is particularly important in relation to omissions liability. In such cases, it will often be another party who begins the course of events that will lead to the result, and so there is often at least one other obvious cause. However, this is irrelevant (even if the other cause is V herself[88]). As long as D's omission satisfies the requirements of the conduct element, it is a factual cause if D would have prevented the result by acting in line with her duty to act (the result would not have come about 'but for' her omission).

2.7.2 Causation in law

The basic test for factual causation is supplemented with a test for legal causation to avoid an overly broad catchment. For example, where D throws a stone and breaks V's window, she is the factual (but for) cause of the damage. However, we could also say that V is a factual cause if, but for V's action in annoying D, D would not have sought revenge and thrown the stone. Similarly, we could say the glass manufacturer is a 'but for' cause as, but for their creation of the glass, it would not be there to be damaged; and even D's parents might be a factual cause as, but for their decision to have children, there would be no D; and so on. The test for legal causation seeks to narrow the catchment of causation rules in terms of *fairness*: when is it fair to blame D for causing a certain result?

The role and ambition of legal causation is unproblematic. However, unlike the relative objectivism of 'but for' factual causation, any test that is formulated with reference to

---

[88] *Swindall and Osborne* (1846) 2 Car & Kir 230.

abstract notions such as 'fairness' is always likely to be controversial. And so it has proved.[89] Through common law case-by-case development, several principles of legal causation have been established. However, such is the inconsistency of their interpretation and application that several commentators have concluded that talk of established principles is misguided, with the so-called principles being used by courts to reach a *desired* conclusion in the absence of rules.[90] We discuss the principles of legal causation, insofar as the courts have declared principles of any certainty, in the following sections.

2.7.2.1 Legal cause must be 'substantial'

Probably the least controversial principle of legal causation is that D's conduct must have made a substantial contribution to the result. The term 'substantial' should not, however, imply that D must be the main cause. In fact, as long as D's role is not *de minimis* it will satisfy this requirement: D's role must be more than 'slight or trifling',[91] 'negligible',[92] 'insubstantial or insignificant'.[93]

Having been established as a factual cause of the result, it will be rare that D's conduct will not also be at least more than a *de minimis* cause. However, the fact that D's conduct is a factual cause will not automatically satisfy this requirement. For example, if D pricked V with a pin seconds before she was stabbed to death by X, it is possible to describe D's conduct as a 'but for' cause of death: where V dies of blood loss, D's conduct has caused a slight loss of blood that will have marginally speeded up the time of death. Without D's conduct V would have died only a split second later, but (as discussed previously) this does not prevent D's conduct being described as a factual cause of the death *at the time it did happen*.[94] It would be similar if D telephoned V, only for V to be startled by the ring tone and drop a vase:[95] D may not play a major role in the damage, but she remains a factual cause. In each case, we may assume that legal causation will not be found because the role played by D was negligible (*de minimis*).

2.7.2.2 Legal cause must be 'blameworthy'

As well as 'substantial', it has also been held that the result must be caused by 'blameworthy' conduct. This requirement is rarely discussed in case law and often confused by students—*so take care*.

When a result crime is created, it is usually attempting to target certain wrongful or blameworthy conduct that leads to a harmful result. For example, criminal damage criminalises D's conduct performed whilst foreseeing the risk of harming another's property (blameworthy conduct) which causes damage to that property (result). Gross negligence manslaughter criminalises D's conduct performed in a grossly negligent manner (blameworthy conduct) which causes a death (result). In each case, as with almost all result

---

[89] Hart and Honoré, *Causation in the Law* (1985).
[90] Williams, eg, describes legal causation as a 'moral reaction': Williams, *Textbook of Criminal Law* (2nd edn, 1983) 381.
[91] *Kimsey* [1996] Crim LR 35.
[92] *L* [2010] EWCA Crim 1249.
[93] *Cato* [1976] 1 All ER 260.
[94] Perkins and Boyce, *Criminal Law* (1982) 779.
[95] Based on an example from Hall, *General Principles of Criminal Law* (1960).

crimes, the wrong of the offence is established by a link not simply between conduct and result, but between blameworthy conduct and result.

Problems emerge where the link between the blameworthiness of D's conduct and the result is broken.[96] In the most problematic cases, D's conduct will be blameworthy (in line with offence requirements), D's conduct will have been the factual cause of the result, but the blameworthiness of D's conduct will have had no causal role. In this case, there will be no legal causation and D will avoid liability. This is illustrated in *Dalloway*.

 Dalloway (1847) 2 Cox CC 273

D was driving a horse and cart on a highway, whilst negligently allowing the reins to lie on the horse's back rather than keeping control of them. A small child (V) ran into the road a few yards ahead of the cart and was killed. Even if D had control of the reins, he could not have stopped in time to save V.

• Court: D was not guilty of gross negligence manslaughter.

In *Dalloway*, D was negligent in his driving and, in that sense, his conduct was blameworthy. He was also the factual cause of V's death. However, his *blameworthy conduct* was not the cause of the death: V would have died even if D was not driving negligently. The crime (gross negligence manslaughter) is seeking to criminalise deaths that are brought about because of grossly negligent behaviour; it is not intended to target deaths (as in *Dalloway*) where D's negligence has no causal effect. Thus, D was not guilty of gross negligence manslaughter.

Another example could be the offence of causing death by dangerous driving.[97] Here, again, it is possible for the requirements of 'dangerous driving' and 'causing death' to be satisfied separately but without liability. For example, whilst D is driving dangerously, V jumps from a bridge to commit suicide and lands on D's car. Liability should not arise: as with gross negligence manslaughter, it must be shown that D's dangerous driving (blameworthy act) caused the death, not simply that they both occurred. The cause must be a blameworthy cause.

Although rarely at issue, some debate has recently emerged with regard to offences such as causing death by driving without insurance or without a licence.[98] For example, in *Williams*[99] and *H*,[100] the Court of Appeal found liability for this offence even where the death caused could not have been avoided by D (was not caused by blameworthy conduct). Criticising the court, academics have pointed out that the precedent from *Dalloway* should have been applied to avoid liability.[101] The law has

---

[96] This can only arise in offences where D does not require subjective mens rea as to the result element. See **Chapter 3**.

[97] Road Traffic Act 1988, s1.

[98] Ibid, s3ZB. Discussed at **6.4.2.4**.

[99] [2010] EWCA Crim 2552.

[100] [2011] EWCA Crim 1508.

[101] Ormerod [2011] Crim LR 468; Sullivan and Simester, 'Causation Without Limits: Causing Death While Driving Without a Licence, While Disqualified, or Without Insurance' [2012] Crim LR 753.

now been clarified by the Supreme Court in *Hughes*, re-endorsing a requirement of blameworthiness.

 Hughes [2013] UKSC 56

D (driving without insurance and a full licence) was involved in a fatal collision with V. V was entirely responsible for the accident, veering onto the wrong side of the road whilst under the influence of drugs. D was charged with causing death when uninsured and without a full driving licence contrary to section 3ZB of the Road Traffic Act 1988.
- Crown Court: D did not cause death.
- Court of Appeal: appeal allowed, finding liability under section 3ZB. The offence is one of strict liability, requiring no mens rea or blameworthiness as to the causing of death.
- Supreme Court: appeal allowed, restoring the Crown Court decision. Offence requires some more than minimal fault/blameworthiness causing the result.

The approach in *Hughes* has been reaffirmed by a seven-member Supreme Court in *Taylor*,[102] a case that also involved causing death with a motor vehicle. In a unanimous judgment, the court held that D's liability required 'at least some act or omission in the control of the car which involved some element of fault, whether amounting to careless/inconsiderate driving or not, and which contributed in some more than minimal way to the death'.[103]

> **Assessment matters . . .**
> It should be remembered that for the vast majority of cases, if all offence elements are satisfied, it will be very obvious that the cause was a blameworthy cause. In such cases, you need only highlight that this requirement is satisfied. Only discuss this requirement where the result (although factually caused by D) was in some sense unavoidable, and could/would have happened if D was acting innocently.

2.7.2.3 Legal cause must be 'operative'

As well as being substantial (more than *de minimis*) and blameworthy, D's conduct must also be the operative cause of the result. The term 'operative' means that D's conduct must still be a significant cause of the result at the time it comes about; the chain of causation between conduct and result elements must not be broken. For example, where D supplies V with a dangerous drug and V self-injects causing death, D is not the legal cause of the death.[104] D is the factual cause (but for the supply of the drug V would not have died); plays a substantial role (obtaining the drug is a major step on the way to death); and her conduct is clearly a blameworthy cause (she is likely to know that the drug is dangerous); but the conduct of V breaks the chain of causation between D's conduct and the result. It is V's free and voluntary choice to self-inject the drug, and by making that choice V has taken control of the causal chain. This is illustrated in **Figure 2.4**.

---

[102] [2016] UKSC 5.
[103] At [32].
[104] *Kennedy (No 2)* [2007] UKHL 38.

Figure 2.4 Breaking the chain of causation

Breaks in the chain of causation (*novus actus interveniens*) can arise as a result of the subsequent actions of D; natural events; the actions of V; or the actions/omissions of a third party. Each will be discussed.

Lord Hoffmann stated in *Empress Car*[105] that 'it is of course the causal significance of acts of third parties . . . or natural forces that gives rise to almost all the problems about the notion of "causing" and drives judges to take refuge in metaphor [eg causal chains] or Latin [*novus actus*]'. This quotation highlights two important issues. The first is that cases of this kind arise often in the courts, and certainly more than cases questioning the 'substantial' or 'blameworthiness' of causes. The second is that judges have found these cases particularly difficult. We will see this in our discussion later, with legal principles often applied inconsistently or developed in open contradiction with one another.

Intervention from defendant

It will be very rare for D's own subsequent conduct to break the chain of causation between her initial conduct and the result. For example, where D stabs V and then shoots V within the same attack, the second act will certainly not break the chain: all of D's acts will be grouped as a single transaction causing death. The exceptional situation where a break may be found is where D's subsequent acts are part of a separate transaction. For example, D, having wounded V, visits her in hospital and accidentally infects her with smallpox from which she dies.[106] Here, D's original conduct (wounding) is effectively superseded by the primary cause of death (infection). D remains liable for a wounding offence, but that initial conduct is not the legal cause of V's death. We could focus on D's subsequent conduct (infecting) as an alternative conduct element, and this would solve our problems of causation. However, as a new conduct element we would have to find the other elements of the offence (including any mens rea) existing at this new time. In the example given, this may be problematic.

Where rare cases of this kind have arise, it is therefore important to identify the limits of a transaction (a grouping of acts within a single event). This is discussed in more detail in **Chapter 4**.

Intervention from naturally occurring events

Naturally occurring events (or 'acts of God') will only break the chain of causation if they are unforeseen by D and unforeseeable to the reasonable person. For example, if D assaults V and then leaves her on the beach at low tide, it is foreseeable that the tide will come in and that V may drown. The natural event (tide) will not break the chain of

---

[105] [1999] AC 22.
[106] See *Le Brun* (1991) 94 Cr App R 101, on quite different facts, citing *Smith and Hogan's Criminal Law*.

causation: D's original conduct (assault) is the legal cause of V's death.[107] Equally, if D attacks V (conduct) and leaves her in a coma, making V more vulnerable to potential infection, any subsequent infection (natural event) that kills V will not break the chain. D's original conduct (attack) is the legal cause of death.[108]

However, where D attacks V and then leaves her in an apparently safe environment, only for V to be killed when struck by lightning, or a falling tree, or caught in a freak earthquake, the unforeseen and unforeseeable event *will* break the causal chain.[109] Here, D remains liable for what she has caused (namely the harm from the initial attack), but cannot be liable in relation to the death. D's original conduct (attack) is not the legal cause of V's death.

Intervention from victim

As with our drugs supply example at the beginning of this section, it is clear that the acts of V can break the chain of causation between D's conduct and the result. Three main principles have emerged from judgments dealing with these cases, and they focus on: (A) the foreseeability of V's acts; (B) the voluntariness of V's acts; and (C) the unique vulnerabilities of V. We will discuss each, as well as the apparent inconsistency between them.

A) Foreseeability: As with natural events, the foreseeability of the intervention (this time the actions of V) is key to whether that intervention will break the causal chain. For example, if D jumps out and scares V who is perched on a window ledge, and V falls from the window and dies, D is the legal cause of death: V's response in fright, leading to a loss of balance, is foreseeable. However, if D jumps out and scares V who is sitting on the sofa in her living room, and V then jumps, runs up some stairs to find a window, and then jumps out, it is likely that D's conduct will not be the legal cause of death: V's response was unforeseeable and, to use the language of various cases, 'daft'. The key then, when applying this rule to problem facts, is to identify the tipping point between reactions of V that are foreseeable which do not lead to a break in the causal chain, and those that are daft that will break the chain. As *Roberts* illustrates, it is clear that courts will rarely interpret V's conduct as daft.

 Roberts (1971) 56 Cr App R 95

D, driving V home after a party, began making unwanted sexual advances towards her, threatening her, and touching her coat. V jumped out of the moving car and suffered bodily harm. D was charged with assault occasioning actual bodily harm, contrary to section 47 of the Offences Against the Person Act 1861.

- Crown Court: guilty of section 47 offence.
- Court of Appeal: conviction upheld on appeal.

D's conviction in *Roberts* demonstrates the broad interpretation that courts apply to the test of foreseeability. It is also clear that the test will vary in line with V's age, mental

---

[107] Example from *Perkins* (1946) 36 J Cr L & Cr 393.
[108] *Gowans* [2003] EWCA Crim 3935.
[109] Examples from *Perkins* and Hart and Honoré, *Causation in the Law* (1985).

capacity, and other circumstances. For example, where V is intoxicated, the court will ask if V's response was within the range of foreseeable responses for an intoxicated person.[110]

B) Voluntariness: Following D's conduct, if the result comes about because of V's free, voluntary, and informed act, the chain of causation *will* be broken. D is not the legal cause of the result. For example, if D supplies V with a hammer, and V then uses the hammer to commit criminal damage, D is not the legal cause of the damage: D is a factual 'but for' cause of the damage, but the chain of causation is broken by V's free, voluntary, and informed choice to use the hammer in this way. In contrast, where V's acts are not free, voluntary, and informed, they will not break the chain. For example, where D gives V a poisoned apple and V eats it being unaware of the poison, D will remain the legal cause of death: the chain of causation is not broken because, although V acted freely and in some sense voluntarily when eating the apple, her actions were not informed.

Problems emerge for the courts where V's acts fall between these extremes, where V's acts are *partially* free, voluntary, and informed. A useful illustration of this is *Kennedy (No 2)*.

Assessment matters . . .

Problems emerge for the courts when cases fall between extremes, but these are exactly the cases that help us the most: they indicate the borderline between acts that break the chain of causation and those that do not.

 Kennedy (No 2) [2007] UKHL 38

D supplied V with a prepared syringe of heroin. V self-injected the drug and died as a result. D was charged with manslaughter on the basis that his unlawful conduct (drug supply) caused V's death.

- Crown Court: guilty of constructive manslaughter.
- Court of Appeal: conviction upheld on appeal.
- House of Lords: quashing D's conviction on appeal—D was not guilty because he was not the legal cause of V's death.

Terminology . . .

Take care when discussing *Kennedy (No 2)*. The precedent that an informed and voluntary act by a responsible adult will break the chain of causation is *Kennedy (No 2)*—NOT *Kennedy*.[111]

In *Kennedy (No 2)* D's conduct was not the legal cause of death because V's free, voluntary, and informed choice to self-inject the drug broke the chain of causation,[112]

---

[110] *Corbett* [1996] Crim LR 594.

[111] In *Kennedy* [1999] Crim LR 65, the Court of Appeal held that D *had caused* V to take the noxious substance despite free and informed consent. *Kennedy (No 2)* arose following intervention from the Criminal Cases Review Commission.

[112] Ormerod and Fortson, 'Drug Suppliers as Manslaughterers (Again)' [2005] Crim LR 819. For an alternative view (supporting liability), see Jones, 'Causation, Homicide and the Supply of Drugs' (2006) 26 LS 139.

overruling a number of previous cases that had found liability in these circumstances.[113] *Kennedy (No 2)* demonstrates a relatively broad interpretation of what is free, voluntary, and informed: V's acts were seen as free and voluntary despite his addiction to the drug supplied. For liability to be found in these circumstances post-*Kennedy (No 2)*, it would have to be shown that D participated in the administration of the drug (if the drug is jointly administered then it is not solely the conduct of V and will not break the causal chain),[114] or to focus on D's behaviour after the self-administering to locate an alternative conduct element.[115]

C) **Vulnerabilities:** It is a long-established principle in criminal law, as in civil law, that D must 'take his victim as he finds him'. Where D punches V in such a way that would ordinarily cause no more than minor bruising, but V's 'egg-shell skull' means that V suffers much greater harm and even death, D will be the legal cause of that greater harm: V's unique vulnerability will not break the chain of causation even if unknown to D. The same principle will apply (drawing on our criminal damage example) where D's stone only smashes the window because the glass is unusually thin: D remains the legal cause of the damage. Where, as with these examples, V's vulnerabilities are physical, there is little problem. However, as we see in *Blaue*, the principle is capable of wider application.

 Blaue [1975] 3 All ER 446

D stabbed V. V required a blood transfusion to save her life, but refused on religious grounds (being a Jehovah's Witness). V died and D was charged with her manslaughter.

- Crown Court: guilty of manslaughter.
- Court of Appeal: conviction upheld on appeal—V's refusal did not break the chain of causation.

In *Blaue*, following *Holland*,[116] V's refusal of medical care was interpreted as part of her character rather than a separate, potentially intervening, event. The court held that D must take V as she is found, which meant her whole person, not just her physical person, and therefore V's refusal to have accepted a potentially life-saving blood transfusion could not be a break in the causal chain: D remained the legal cause of death. The question becomes, if V's religious convictions are part of V, what else can be similarly considered? For example, what if V simply did not like doctors, was afraid of needles, scared of catching blood-borne diseases, or even maliciously refused treatment in order to increase D's liability? The *Blaue* precedent opens the *possibility* that V's refusal in such circumstances will not break the causal chain.

---

[113] Including *Rogers* [2003] Cr App R 10; *Finlay* [2003] EWCA Crim 3868.
[114] *Burgess* [2008] EWCA Crim 516.
[115] eg an omission to assist where D has a duty to do so. See the previous omissions discussion (and *Evans* in particular).
[116] (1841) 2 Mood & R 351. In *Holland*, the state of medical safety at that date made the refusal of treatment potentially reasonable. In *Blaue*, the court clarified that reasonableness is irrelevant.

Having set out the three principles relating to foreseeability, voluntariness, and vulnerabilities, it should be highlighted that there is a certain tension between them. For example, in *Roberts* we can accept that V jumping from a car is foreseeable. But it also seems to be voluntary (breaking the causal chain as per *Kennedy (No 2)*). It may be that V's act was not *fully* voluntary in the sense that she was under threat from D, but is this any less voluntary than the consumption of drugs by an addict? Equally, in *Blaue* we could say that V's refusal of a blood transfusion was both unforeseeable (breaking the causal chain as per *Roberts*) and voluntary (breaking the causal chain as per *Kennedy (No 2)*). Perhaps the difference is that V's refusal in *Blaue* was an omission, but this is not clear. The issue here is whether the courts are using the principles to make a decision in line with the rule of law, or choosing between principles in order to justify a prior moral decision about D's culpability.[117]

A useful illustration of this concern is the courts' response to cases where V commits suicide following an attack from D.[118] On the one hand, we have a set of cases where D injures V and then V acts to exacerbate that injury and cause death. For example, in *Dear*,[119] D's conviction for murder was upheld where V intentionally aggravated his wounds that had been inflicted by D. In such cases, V's acts appear voluntary, and they are certainly unforeseeable, but may *perhaps* be justified as an extension of *Blaue*: V is acting (rather than omitting), but D's acts would have caused death anyway if untreated. However, on the other hand, the Court of Appeal has also left open the possibility of finding legal causation where D's acts would not have caused death, with death only resulting due to V's act in committing suicide.[120] Here, V's acts may be described as unforeseeable and voluntary, and do not appear to come within the *Blaue* principle either: it is hard to describe V's future actions as 'part of' V. This is not to say that liability for causing death in such cases would be unfair, where V commits suicide after prolonged abuse (physical or mental) from D there is a strong moral case that D has caused V's death. Rather, the problem is one for the rule of law: are the courts guided by legal principles, or simply by their subjective moral intuitions?

Intervention from third parties

We have already discussed the possibility of multiple causes. For example, where D, aged 12, smashes V's window and X (D's parent) allows this to happen in breach of the parental duty to control D, it may be that both D and X have caused the damage. Where this is the case, both D and X can be independently liable for criminal damage. However, there will also be cases where, following D's conduct, the result element only comes about because of the conduct of X. In such cases, the acts of X take on responsibility for what results and break the chain of causation between D and the result element.[121] For example, where D supplies X with poison, and X then poisons and kills V, D will not be the legal cause of V's death: the causal chain

---

[117] See generally Hart and Honoré, *Causation in the Law* (1985).
[118] Horder and McGowan, 'Manslaughter by Causing Another's Suicide' [2006] Crim LR 1035.
[119] [1996] Crim LR 595.
[120] *D* [2006] EWCA Crim 1139.
[121] *Latif* [1996] 2 Cr App R 92.

is broken by the acts of X. As in the previous section, the principles of (A) foreseeability and (B) voluntariness play an obvious role in the case law. However, more controversially, (C) the status of X and (D) the type of offence charged, also seems to be important considerations.

> **Don't be confused . . .**
> When discussing the potential intervention of third parties it is important to remember that we are not discussing the liability of X. Rather, we are only discussing the liability of D: if X's acts break the chain of causation, D is not liable; if they do not then D remains the cause and may be liable. The only reason you are discussing X is to ascertain the liability of D. You are not addressing X's liability, but simply whether X's conduct breaks the chain of causation between D and the result.
>
> Having discussed the liability of D, we may then go on separately to discuss the potential liability of X. The liability of one will have no bearing on the liability of the other.

A) **Foreseeability:** As with intervention of V, to break the chain of causation the acts of X must be unforeseen by D and unforeseeable to the reasonable person.

B) **Voluntariness:** To break the chain of causation, the acts of X must also be free, voluntary, and informed. For example, if D asks X to deliver a cake to V and the cake contains a secret bomb, and X does so, D is the legal cause of V's death: X has not acted in a free, voluntary, and *informed* manner. This was illustrated in the case of *Michael*.[122] D, the mother of V, sought to kill V by providing X who was V's nurse with a large dose of poison and telling her that it was medicine for V. The 'medicine' was eventually administered to V by Y, a small child living at the house. Despite the acts of both X and Y following from D, there was no break in the chain of causation: the third party acts were not free, voluntary, and informed as they did not know it was poison.

C) **Status of X:** When applying these principles, it has become clear that the courts apply different standards depending upon the status of X, the potentially intervening party. This is most obvious where X is a doctor, treating V as a result of D's previous attack. In such circumstances, negligent treatment from X that leads to greater harm will only break the chain of causation if the court considers it 'palpably wrong', and that the injuries inflicted by D are largely healed, as in *Jordan*.

 Jordan (1956) 40 Cr App R 152

> D stabbed V. At hospital, at a stage when V's wound was largely healed, X (a doctor) administered a large quantity of a drug to which V had shown he was intolerant. The treatment was described as 'palpably wrong'. D was charged with murder.
> - Crown Court: guilty of murder.
> - Court of Criminal Appeal: allowing the appeal and quashing D's conviction—X's acts broke the chain of causation such that D was not the legal cause of death.

Jordan demonstrates that the conduct of doctors *can* break the chain of causation, but its potential was narrowed considerably in two later cases of *Smith* and *Cheshire*.

---

[122] (1840) 9 C & P 356.

Smith [1959] 2 QB 35

D stabbed V in a fight between soldiers from different regiments. When carrying V to the medical reception, X dropped him twice. Y (a doctor) failed to note that the wound had pierced a lung and provided treatment later described as 'thoroughly bad'. D was charged with manslaughter.

- Crown Court: guilty of constructive manslaughter.
- Court of Criminal Appeal: upholding D's conviction—D remained a legal cause of V's death.

In *Smith*, despite poor treatment from two third parties, D remained a legal cause. The distinction here is that, unlike *Jordan*, the wounds inflicted by D were not largely healed and remained a significant and operative cause of death. As long as the injury inflicted by D is still ongoing and not 'merely part of the history' leading to injurious acts from X or Y, D will remain a legal cause.

 Cheshire [1991] 3 All ER 670

D shot V. In hospital, V was treated and the wounds ceased to be life threatening. However, following a negligently performed tracheotomy by a doctor (X), V's windpipe narrowed and he died. D was charged with murder.

- Crown Court: guilty of murder.
- Court of Appeal: upholding D's conviction—D was still a legal cause of V's death.

In *Cheshire*, unlike *Smith* (but in common with *Jordan*) V's wounds had largely healed at the point of X's negligent intervention. However, despite this, X's acts did not break the chain of causation. The court clarified that the test was not about X's mens rea, but rather whether X's act was 'so independent of [D's] acts, and in itself so potent in causing death, that [the jury] regard the contribution made by [D's] acts as insignificant'. Exactly how 'so independent' and 'so potent' should be interpreted is unclear. However, although the possibility of doctors breaking the chain of causation, as demonstrated in *Jordan*, remains open, it seems that *Cheshire* has further narrowed the already rather narrow circumstances in which it may be found.

To claim that such cases involve foreseeable and involuntary acts on the part of doctors is only possible if those principles are stretched to insignificance. Rather, the courts appear to be acting on the *understandable* basis of policy: D's acts led to V requiring care and so D should take the full consequences if things go wrong.[123] As we see in *Pagett*, it is a policy that may not be isolated to doctors.

 Pagett (1983) 76 Cr App R 279

D, to resist lawful arrest, held V in front of him as a human shield and shot at police (X). X returned fire and killed V. D was charged with the manslaughter of V.

- Crown Court: guilty of constructive manslaughter.
- Court of Appeal: upholding D's conviction—D was still a legal cause of V's death.

---

[123] Although understandable, it may be argued that attempt liability may be more appropriate: punishing D for what she was trying to do rather than maintaining the fiction that her acts achieved that end.

In *Pagett*, as with previous cases, we can understand the policy grounds on which the courts would not want to say that X's act broke the chain of causation, as this would prevent D being liable for a homicide offence. However, in order to achieve this end, the legal principles of causation are compromised. For example, in *Pagett* the court accepted that X's instinctive reaction to return fire was in some sense 'involuntary', as well as holding more generally that acts done in line with a duty to prevent crime would never break the chain of causation.

D) **Type of offence:** It has become apparent that, as well as special categories of X distorting the principles of causation, there may be a similar issue with certain types of offence.[124] We see this in *Empress Car* in relation to pollution offences.

 Empress Car Co Ltd [1999] 2 AC 22

D, a company, allowed oil to be stored on its site and failed to take precautions to prevent the fore-seeable danger that someone would release it into the river. X (an unidentified stranger) released the oil. D was charged with offences related to the pollution of the river.

- Crown Court: guilty of pollution offences.
- Court of Appeal: conviction upheld on appeal.
- House of Lords: upholding conviction—D remained a legal cause.

In *Empress Car*, despite the presumably free and voluntary act of a third party, the chain of causation was not broken. The House of Lords in *Kennedy (No 2)* has since clarified that the *Empress Car* precedent is isolated to pollution cases alone.[125] However, in allowing the exception at all, it demonstrates a further erosion of the principles of causation in this area.

Summary

It is important to remember the basic structure of the legal question: is there a break in causation between D's conduct and the results, see **Figure 2.5**.

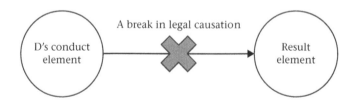

Figure 2.5 A break in legal causation

In order to answer this question, we must then consider the circumstances of the potential break. This is illustrated in **Table 2.4**.

---

124 Padfield, 'Clean Water and Muddy Causation: Is Causation a Question of Law or Fact, or Just a Way of Allocating Blame?' [1995] Crim LR 683.

125 The application of *Empress Car* is also discussed in *Day* [2014] EWCA Crim 2683, [23], suggesting that it could be applied more widely.

Table 2.4 Varieties of intervening acts

Type of intervention	Principles
Intervention from D	(1) Will only break the chain if it is part of a new transaction
Intervention from naturally occurring events	(1) Will only break the chain if it is unforeseen by D and unforeseeable by a reasonable person
Intervention from victim	(1) Will break the chain if it is unforeseen by D and unforeseeable by a reasonable person; and (2) will break the chain if it is free, voluntary, and informed; but (3) D must take the victim as he finds him
Intervention from third party	(1) Will break the chain if it is unforeseen by D and unforeseeable by a reasonable person; and (2) will break the chain if it is free, voluntary, and informed; but (3) special categories of third parties and offences will apply different rules

These principles should be applied to every case. However, it is equally important to discuss any potential conflict between principles. In some cases, with reference to academic discussion, it may be useful to identify the outcome you think the court would prefer on policy grounds, and then discuss whether the principles of causation will allow for that outcome.

2.8 Reform

With essay-type questions in mind, it is useful to pick up on three major debates that have arisen during the chapter. These include (a) the availability of omissions liability; (b) the role of results within offences; and (c) the extent of the courts' discretion when applying legal causation. We provide a brief overview of each, highlighting potential options for reform.

2.8.1 Omissions

The central debate with regard to omissions is to what extent the law should recognise a duty to act. It will be remembered from the earlier discussion that, unlike positive acts that will always satisfy the conduct element of an offence,[126] omissions will only do so if: (a) the offence is capable of commission by omission; (b) D has a recognised duty to

---

[126] The only exception being where the offence can only be committed by omission.

act; and (c) D has breached that duty. Thus, famously, if D stands and watches a small child drown in a shallow pool she will not be liable for any offence in relation to the death—even if she could easily save the child, and even if she chose not to act because she wanted the child to die. D will only be liable if she comes within a narrow legal category creating a duty to act as, for example, where she is V's parent.

Examples of this kind have led several academics to contend that liability for omissions within the current law should be expanded. There are two main examples of how this could be achieved. First, we could create a new omissions-based offence for failure to perform an 'easy rescue', of the type seen in several other jurisdictions.[127] This so-called 'bad Samaritan' offence criminalises those who fail to avert serious harm where such harm could be easily and safely prevented.[128] Secondly, building upon duties to act recognised within the current law, we could introduce a new duty to act based on 'citizenship'. Alongside duties based on familial relationships etc, a citizenship duty to act would mandate reasonable action (preventing harm) whenever D was in a position to do so for the benefit of other citizens. With D's omissions much more likely to satisfy the conduct element of an offence, the focus would then be on other offence elements to see what, if any, offence is committed. For example, if D fails to save the drowning child with the intention that it should die, her breach of a citizen's duty to act would make her liable for murder.

The case for expanding omissions liability is put most convincingly by Ashworth.[129] He terms this approach the 'social responsibility view'. For Ashworth, the current approach to omissions, which he terms the 'conventional view', falls into two main errors.

First, it assumes a moral difference between acts and omissions that is not there. In certain cases an omission may be more culpable than an act. For example, consider V1 who is caught in a house fire when D1 fails to press a button to set off a sprinkler system that would save V1; and contrast that with D2 who, seeing that V2 will die in considerable pain, and with no way to rescue her, shoots V2. Who is more culpable? Additionally, in many cases it will be difficult to determine if D has acted or omitted. For example, where D releases his grip of the tug-of-war rope, is that acting to let go or omitting to hold on?[130]

Secondly, Ashworth contends that the autonomy argument against omissions liability is misconceived. Although omissions liability restricts the options of D more than act-based liability,[131] bearing in mind that a duty will only arise in exceptional circumstances where V is in considerable danger, and bearing in mind the low expectation of D, overall autonomy is respected. Indeed, no rescue will severely restrict V's autonomy (through injury) and D will also benefit from the potential for similar assistance in the future.

---

[127] Including France and a number of US states: Ashworth and Steiner, 'Criminal Omissions and Public Duties: The French Experience' (1990) 10 LS 152.

[128] The specified level of potential harm to V and the ease of D's potential acts both vary between jurisdictions.

[129] Ashworth, *Positive Obligations in Criminal Law* (2013); Ashworth, 'The Scope of Criminal Liability for Omissions' (1989) 105 LQR 424.

[130] See **2.6.5**.

[131] See discussion of this at **2.6**.

The social responsibility view of omissions advocated by Ashworth has several benefits, including the potential for improved 'fair warning'.[132] Under the current law there are a number of duties to act, but in each case the law is very unclear as to the boundaries where these duties arise. As a result, D has to wait until after the event to find out if the court will identify a duty or not. It could be argued that a new easy-rescue offence, or a more general citizenship duty, would be fairer, clearer, and simpler.[133] The clear warning would be that omissions liability is possible whenever D unreasonably fails to act.

The arguments against such an expansion, effectively supporting the status quo, are numerous. They are also usefully summarised by Glanville Williams who in response to Ashworth, defends the conventional view.[134] Central again is the autonomy argument: whereas act-based liability stops D pursuing one course of action, omissions liability stops her pursuing *all* courses of action that are not the action required to avoid liability. Beyond this, there are also a number of other concerns. First, despite the occasional counter-example, it is contended that omissions are less culpable than actions: D is not making the world worse; she is *merely* failing to make it better. Secondly, and following from this, if the criminal law has limited resources (both in detection and punishment) it should focus on acts as the most blameworthy conduct. Thirdly, Williams contends that a citizenship duty, or specific offence of failure to rescue, would be too uncertain with no common standard of social responsibility to provide fair warning of when people may become liable for their omissions.

2.8.2 Results

One of the most interesting tensions within the criminal law is found between subjectivism (focusing on D's individual culpability) and objectivism (focusing on the harms caused by D's conduct).[135] When discussing the result elements of offences, this tension is readily apparent. On one side, results are central to liability because they usually represent the harm caused by D (objectivism); but on the other side, they are almost redundant because they are not fully controlled by D and are therefore an imperfect reflection of her culpability (subjectivism). The current law represents an *often uncomfortable* compromise between the two.

Starting with the subjectivist approach, the logic of this position is simple. Let us imagine that D1 shoots at V1 with the intention to kill. Meanwhile, D2 shoots at V2 with the intention to kill. If D1 kills V1, but D2 does not manage to kill V2 (because, eg, she is saved by doctors), the difference between D1 and D2 is simply a matter of luck. And, as luck is not a reflection of D's culpability, both D1 and D2 are equally culpable and should be punished in the same way.[136] Indeed, on this basis, *all* result crimes could be

---

[132] See **1.4.1**.
[133] Cobb, 'Compulsory Care Giving: Some Thoughts on Relational Feminism, the Ethics of Care and Omissions Liability' (2008) 39 Cam LR 11.
[134] Williams, 'Criminal Omissions—The Conventional View' (1991) 107 LQR 86.
[135] See **1.4**.
[136] Ashworth, 'Belief, Intent and Criminal Liability' in Eekelaar and Bell (eds), *Oxford Essays in Jurisprudence* (1989); Ashworth, 'Taking the Consequences' in Shute, Gardner, and Horder (eds), *Action and Value in Criminal Law* (1993); Ashworth, 'Defining Offences Without Harm' in Smith (ed), *Criminal Law: Essays in Honour of JC Smith* (1987). See also Alexander and Kessler Ferzan, *Crime and Culpability: A Theory of Criminal Law* (2009).

remodelled into 'acting with intent' conduct crimes: focusing liability on what D controls (ie her acts and her mens rea) and not being distorted by luck.[137] The subjectivist position can be seen in several areas of the law. For example, where D attempts to commit an offence with intention, but is not successful in that attempt, the same maximum sentence will generally apply to the attempt as to the principal offence attempted.[138]

An objectivist approach, in contrast, contends that *results matter*.[139] Although D1 and D2 in our example have performed the same acts, our reaction to them will be very different: we condemn D1 for her acts *and* for causing the death of V; we condemn D2 for her acts, but we are relieved that death did not result.[140] Results are therefore perceived as an additional wrong for which D is responsible. It is also contended that holding D1 responsible for the additional wrong is not punishing her on the basis of luck. As Duff makes clear, 'if I [behave in a particular way] with the intention of bringing X about . . . I have control over X's occurrence in that it depends to a significant degree on me and on what I do; X will not ensue if I do not [behave in that particular way]'.[141] The objectivist position can also be seen in several areas of the law. For example, when we discuss the non-fatal offences against the person in **Chapter 7**, it will be seen that a ladder of offences is used to label and punish D principally with reference to the seriousness of the harm inflicted upon V. An objectivist approach can also be seen in the absence, in this jurisdiction, of any general offence of reckless endangerment.[142] If D acts with the intent to cause harm she may be liable for attempt; but if she acts merely foreseeing the risk of harm, even where this is sufficient mens rea for the principal 'result-based' offence, she will not be liable for a general endangerment offence where the result does not come about.[143]

2.8.3 Causation

The causation rules dictate the required connection between the conduct and result elements of a result crime: D's conduct must cause the result in fact (but for test) *and* in law (significant, blameworthy, and operative). As we have seen earlier, the development and application of causation rules within the common law has been and remains highly problematic. In response, several alternative approaches have been advanced.

Hart and Honoré, for example, suggest an alternative based on a distinction between what they term 'normal' causal conditions such as environmental factors (not legal causes) and 'abnormal' causal conditions such as voluntary intervention (which will constitute legal causes), and may also break the chain of causation if performed by another.[144] There is much to commend this approach, but it may be that

---

[137] Although this is the logical conclusion of a subjectivist approach, few academics would support this extreme.

[138] Criminal Attempts Act 1981, s4. The only exception is attempted murder, where there is a discretionary, as opposed to mandatory, life sentence.

[139] Moore, *Placing Blame: A General Theory of the Criminal Law* (1997); Moore, *Causation and Responsibility* (2009).

[140] Duff, *Criminal Attempts* (1996) Ch4.

[141] Duff, *Answering for Crime* (2007) 63.

[142] Duff, 'Criminalising Endangerment' in Duff and Green (eds), *Defining Crimes* (2005).

[143] The English law contains several specific endangerment offences (eg speeding offences), but no general offence (akin to attempt) to catch reckless endangerment beyond these.

[144] Hart and Honoré, *Causation in the Law* (1985).

the central distinction remains too vague and subjective to perform the objectifying role intended. Another alternative can be taken from a 2002 Law Commission Criminal Team working paper on causation. The team set out its proposals in the form of a draft Bill.

(1) Subject to subsections (2) to (5), a defendant causes a result which is an element of an offence when—

    (a) he does an act which makes a substantial and operative contribution to its occurrence; or

    (b) he omits to do an act, which he is under a duty to do according to the law relating to the offence, and the failure to do the act makes a substantial and operative contribution to its occurrence.

(2) (a) The finders of fact may conclude that a defendant's act or omission did not make a substantial and operative contribution to the occurrence of a result if compared with the voluntary intervention of another person, unless:

      (i) the defendant is subject to a legal duty to guard against the very harm that the intervention or event causes; and

      (ii) the intervention was not so extraordinary as to be unforeseeable to a reasonable person in the defendant's position; and

      (iii) it would have been practicable for the defendant to have taken steps to prevent the intervention.

    (b) The intervention of another person is not voluntary unless it is:

      (i) free, deliberate and informed; and

      (ii) performed or undertaken without any physical participation from the defendant.

(3) (a) The finders of fact may conclude that a defendant's act or omission did not make a substantial and operative contribution to the occurrence of a result if compared with an unforeseeable natural event;

    (b) A natural event is not unforeseeable unless:

      (i) the defendant did not foresee it; and

      (ii) it could not have been foreseen by any reasonable person in the defendant's position.

The substance of the team's proposals is largely a reflection of the current law, and so it would do little to resolve many of the uncertainties discussed earlier. However, it may be that codification of the basic structure of causation would have advantages: creating a settled basis for the law and, equally importantly, a settled terminology. However, as the Commission has not taken these proposals forward, reform of this kind is unlikely in the near future.

Beware . . .

This is the first time, of many, that we have quoted a draft Bill from the Law Commission.[145] Remember that these do not represent the current law and you should not apply them as if they do. Rather, they are reform suggestions and should be discussed only in that context.

---

[145] Note that although David Ormerod is the Criminal Law Commissioner the views expressed in this book are not the views of the Commission unless expressly stated as such.

2.9 Eye on assessment

This section sketches a structure for analysing the actus reus of an offence when applying the law in a problem-type question. Drawing on the structure outlined at the end of **Chapter 1**, we are focusing on the first part of Step 3.

> **STEP 1 Identify the potential criminal event in the facts**
>
> This should be simply stated (eg 'The first potential criminal event arises where D kicks V'). The role of this stage is to highlight which part of the question you are answering before you begin to apply the law.

> **STEP 2 Identify the potential offence**
>
> Again, state this simply (eg 'When breaking the vase, D may be liable for criminal damage'). The role of this stage is to highlight which offence you are going to apply.

> **STEP 3 Applying the offence to the facts**
>
> Having highlighted a possible offence, Step 3 requires you to both identify the actus reus and mens rea of that offence, *and* apply them to the facts.

Step 3 will probably require most analysis within a problem question (although Steps 1 and 2 should not be forgotten). It includes the identification and application of both actus reus elements and mens rea elements. This should always begin with the actus reus: the actus reus of an offence locates it in time and space and provides a base from which to ask if D had the required mens rea *at that point*. Our analysis of actus reus requires us to answer two (deceptively) simple questions.

(1) What is the actus reus of the potential offence?

(2) Did D complete the actus reus (did she do it)?

The answer to these questions will vary between offences (question 1) and between factual scenarios (question 2). The answer to the first question will be discussed in relation to each offence covered in this book: gleaned from a combination of statutory and common law sources. However, the structure of application (question 2) is common between offences and can be usefully introduced at this point through **Table 2.5** which shows the stages of analysis.

Table 2.5 Applying the actus reus to problem facts

Actus reus	
A) Conduct element: what did D physically do?	Although there is some flexibility in stages B and C, application of the actus reus should always begin with the conduct element. This is because you need a conduct element before you can ask if the required circumstances were present when D acted or omitted, and whether D's conduct caused the result. Your analysis of the conduct element will vary between conduct and result crimes.
	Conduct crimes: conduct crimes (offences not including a result element) will usually specify a particular act or omission that D must have done. The question is therefore simple: did D do it?
	Result crimes: result crimes are a little trickier because you are usually looking for any (non-specific) conduct that caused the result. Where D performs several acts and omissions, you may have a choice of potential conduct elements. When choosing between them, always look for an action of D as opposed to an omission. This is because, if you focus on an omission, you must show the additional requirements (relevant offence; duty to act; breach of duty).
	Only focus on D's omission if: D has not acted (eg *Gibbins and Proctor*), D acted but there is an obvious problem with mens rea at that point (eg *Miller*), or D acted but there is an obvious problem with causation from that conduct (eg *Evans*). If you are forced to move on to consider omissions liability in this manner, always tell your reader the reason you are forced to do so. If there is no problem with finding liability based on D's acts, there is no need to consider her omissions as well (eg if D shoots V intentionally, then fails to get medical help and V dies—there is no need to consider D's omission to get help).
B) Circumstance element: were the required circumstances present?	All offences (conduct and result crimes) include circumstance elements (eg that D does not own the property damaged for criminal damage). Remember, when asking if these requirements are satisfied, the question is whether the circumstance is present at the time of the conduct element.
C) Result element: did D's conduct element cause the required result?	This will only be required, of course, for result crimes. This part of your analysis has two parts. First, you have to ask if the result (whatever is specified in the offence) actually happened. Secondly, you must ask if it was caused by D. Having identified the conduct element (act- or omission-based) that is most likely to have caused the result, you must now apply the causation rules (factual and legal causation) in relation to that conduct element. Thus, if D has acted but you have chosen to focus on her omission (eg because the act was involuntary), your question is whether her omission caused the result.

To illustrate this structure, take the facts of *Miller*:[146] D fell asleep with a lit cigarette, awoke to find it smouldering on the mattress, but simply left the fire to spread rather than attempt to put it out or summon help. The potential criminal event here relates to the damage to the property (Step 1) and the most likely offence is arson (Step 2). Arson is discussed in **Chapter 9**, but the actus reus essentially requires D to damage another person's property by fire.[147]

When applying this, our first task is to identify the conduct element. As D has set fire to the mattress we should begin here, with the act of dropping the cigarette. However, it is apparent that this act is not a suitable conduct element: although it causes the damage, it is done when D is asleep and is not accompanied by mens rea. Therefore, we must look for an alternative conduct element. In this case, the alternative arises when (having realised the danger) D wakes up and fails to try and prevent further damage. At this point D is most likely to have the mens rea for the offence. Focusing on this point, D's conduct element is an omission. As an omission, liability will require D's conduct to satisfy additional requirements: arson must be capable of commission by omission (*Miller* shows that it is), D must have a duty to act (D has created a dangerous situation and therefore has a duty to try to mitigate that danger), and D must have breached that duty (a reasonable person would be expected to try and put out the fire or summon help; by doing neither, D breaches his duty). D therefore satisfies the conduct element of criminal damage.

The next question is whether D's omission caused damage (result) to the property of another by fire (circumstance). It is clear from the facts that the fire does damage the property of another, so our focus turns to the causal relationship between this damage and the omission of D. Applying the causation rules, it is evident that D's omission is a factual cause of the damage: but for D's omission to take reasonable steps, the fire would not have spread and caused such extensive damage. D's omission was a blameworthy cause (he chose not to act despite foreseeing the danger), it was a substantial cause (certainly more than *de minimis*), and it was an operative cause (there were no events or other actors that could have broken the chain of causation). Therefore, the actus reus of arson is satisfied.

> *Assessment matters . . .*
> In this example, the bulk of our discussion related to the conduct element of the actus reus. This is because the facts of *Miller* present a challenge when locating a suitable conduct element, but are quite straightforward when it comes to circumstances, results, and causation. In another example, the conduct element may be straightforward and there may be more discussion of other elements. It is important in your answer not to miss out any stages in the analysis, but you need only discuss issues in detail where there is some uncertainty.

 ONLINE RESOURCE CENTRE

www.oxfordtextbooks.co.uk/orc/sho/

This chapter is accompanied by a selection of online resources to help you with this topic, including:

- **Multiple-choice questions**
- **Chapter summary sheet**

---

[146] Discussed at **2.6.2.5**.
[147] Criminal Damage Act 1971, s1.

- Two **sample examination questions** with answer guidance
- **Further reading**

Also available on the Online Resource Centre are:

- A selection of **videos** from the authors explaining key topics and principles
- **Legal updates**
- Useful **weblinks**

3

Mens rea

3.1   Introduction   **82**
    3.1.1 Identifying mens rea elements   **83**
    3.1.2 The role of mens rea elements   **85**
3.2   Mens rea in context   **86**
    3.2.1 Strict liability: actus reus with no corresponding mens rea   **88**
    3.2.2 Ulterior mens rea: mens rea with no corresponding actus reus   **89**
    3.2.3 Conclusions from mens rea in context   **90**
3.3   Voluntary act requirement   **90**
    3.3.1 The test for voluntariness   **91**
    3.3.2 The role of voluntariness   **92**
3.4   Mens rea terms   **93**
    3.4.1 Intention   **95**
    3.4.2 Knowledge   **104**
    3.4.3 Belief   **106**
    3.4.4 Recklessness   **106**
    3.4.5 Summary of mens rea terms   **112**
3.5   Objectifying 'subjective' mens rea terms   **114**
3.6   Other mens rea terms   **115**
    3.6.1 Dishonesty   **116**
    3.6.2 Negligence   **117**
3.7   Reform   **119**
    3.7.1 Codifying mens rea terms   **119**
    3.7.2 Subjective vs objective mens rea   **121**
3.8   Eye on assessment   **123**

3.1 Introduction

The Latin term 'mens rea' is loosely translated as 'guilty mind'. Where the actus reus of an offence focuses on D's conduct, the results of that conduct and the circumstances in which it takes place (external elements), mens rea focuses on what is going on in D's mind (internal elements): did she *intend* to do it, *believe* it would happen, *foresee a risk* it might happen; did she know of the circumstances, what did she believe the circumstances were; and so on. Other fault terms such as negligence are also included within this category.

As with our discussion of actus reus, it should be remembered from the outset that these terms (actus reus and mens rea) are terms of art. The ambition of the criminal law is to define *offences* which are combinations of actus reus and mens rea elements that criminalise wrongful events.[1] However, the separation of actus reus and mens rea elements is helpful when discussing and applying the criminal law, and is almost universally adopted by the courts as well as within academic writing. Mens rea is a core component of criminal law, illustrated in **Figure 3.1**.

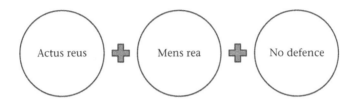

Figure 3.1 Elements of criminal liability

3.1.1 Identifying mens rea elements

If the actus reus/mens rea distinction were strictly applied, then the identification of mens rea within a statutory or common law offence would be straightforward: any requirement external to D's state of mind or fault would be an actus reus requirement, and anything internal to D's state of mind or fault would be a mens rea requirement. This remains a useful rule of thumb. For example, the common law offence of murder criminalises D who unlawfully causes the death of a person under the Queen's peace (external actus reus requirement), with the *intention* to kill or cause serious bodily harm to a person (internal mens rea requirement). However, as we have already discussed in the context of the actus reus, the precise labelling of external requirements as actus reus and internal requirements as mens rea is not always as consistent as we might hope. There are certain offence requirements that are *internal* to the mind of D and yet are traditionally referred to as part of the actus reus; as well as requirements that are *external* to the mind of D and yet are traditionally referred to as part of the mens rea.[2]

A useful terminology has developed to make sense of the distinction between internal and external mens rea.

- Subjective mens rea: The term 'subjective' is used to indicate a mens rea requirement that is looking (internally) to the mind of D. For example, criminal damage requires a mens rea of recklessness as to the causing of damage.[3] To satisfy this mens rea, the prosecution must prove that D personally foresaw a risk of causing damage. It is not enough to show that she should have done, or that a reasonable person would have done.

---

[1] See discussion at **1.1.1**.
[2] See discussion in **2.2**.
[3] Criminal Damage Act 1971, s1.

- Objective mens rea: The term 'objective' is used to indicate a requirement that is *not* looking within the mind of D; it is looking externally. For example, certain offences require proof that D was 'negligent'. Negligence is a mens rea state, but it does not focus on D's mind. Rather, to prove negligence the prosecution must show that D's conduct dropped below the standards expected of a reasonable person in her position. To have acted in this manner it is likely that D's personal state of mind is in some manner blameworthy, but this need not be demonstrated in order to prove negligence.

> **Don't be confused . . .**
> When a jury are asked to apply subjective mens rea requirements it is, of course, impossible for them to look inside D's mind. Therefore, just as a jury will look to objective factors when applying objective mens rea terms (eg what would a reasonable person have foreseen in these circumstances?), the application of subjective mens rea terms will often involve a similar process. However, important differences remain. For example, let us consider a mens rea requirement of 'foresight of damage' where the jury believe a risk of damage would have been obvious to a reasonable person.
> - **Objective test:** the fact that it was obvious to a reasonable person is definitive. D satisfies the offence requirement without needing to consider whether she actually foresaw it or not.
> - **Subjective test:** the fact that the jury think it would have been obvious to a reasonable person is evidence that may encourage the jury to think that D also foresaw it. However, if they believe D that (for whatever reason) she did not foresee it at the time, or they think that she may not have foreseen it, the offence requirement will not be satisfied.

Identifying the mens rea of an offence is not, therefore, a case of surgically separating internal from external requirements. Rather, it is a case of identifying those offence requirements that are focusing, in general terms, on D's state of mind or fault, whether these are subjective or objective requirements.[4] In more practical terms it is also about learning the vocabulary of mens rea terms that have developed in the common law (eg 'intention'; 'recklessness'; 'malice'; 'knowing'; 'belief'; etc), and looking to pick them out from the definition of an offence.

A final point to remember, when identifying and applying mens rea elements, is that your task is not a moral one. The term mens rea may imply some kind of moral evaluation in terms of *guilty* mind and the law *is* seeking to criminalise wrongful or guilty behaviour. However, the absence of moral fault should not affect how you identify and apply the law in practice: if D's behaviour satisfies the elements of an offence, then she commits that offence. Discussion of the morality of D's behaviour, if anywhere, is relevant only to a critique of the law. For example, where D kills V at V's request, and in order to relieve V from some manner of incurable illness or painful condition, her action is popularly referred to as a 'mercy killing'. For many people, the actions of D in these circumstances would not be considered wrongful or guilty. However, since she has satisfied the actus reus of murder by acting unlawfully to cause death and she does

---

[4] An alternative terminology has been to label subjective mens rea as 'mens rea', and objective mens rea as 'fault'. Unfortunately, this approach is not consistently applied by courts or academics, with 'mens rea' and 'fault' often used interchangeably to mean the same thing. Therefore, it is not employed in this chapter. Eg the Law Commission consistently employs the term 'fault element' as a simple substitute for 'mens rea'.

so with the mens rea of murder, intending to kill or cause grievous bodily harm, and she has no legal defence, she has committed the offence of murder. We may criticise the law and say that the offence should not apply in these circumstances (this is a reform discussion), but this will not affect the application of the *current* law: the elements of the offence are satisfied.[5]

> **Extra detail . . .**
> The same logic underpins the classical maxim that 'ignorance of the law is no excuse'. If D satisfies the actus reus and mens rea and has no defence she has committed the offence: it is irrelevant to her liability if she or anyone else considers what she did to be morally justifiable (as with mercy killers), and it is irrelevant whether she knew that what she was doing was a crime.

3.1.2 The role of mens rea elements

Offences are created in an attempt to criminalise wrongful behaviour. In this regard, if offences focused only on the conduct of the accused they would be rather blunt weapons. Actus reus elements can define harmful conduct and/or consequences, such as causing death, causing damage, taking another's property, etc, but such wrongs or harms alone will not necessarily justify punishing D and labelling her as a criminal. Rather, before we can properly blame D for what she has done, it is often necessary to know whether she meant to do it; knew the risk it would happen; should have known the risk; and so on. This is the role of mens rea.

Compare the following examples in which D shoots and kills V:

(a) D1 shoots V1 intending to cause death;

(b) D2 shoots at a shooting range target. V2 is (unknown to D) hiding behind the target.

In both examples, D1 and D2 have completed the actus reus of a homicide offence: their action has unlawfully caused the death of a person. However, the difference between their states of mind (D1 intending to kill; D2 knowing nothing of V2) means that our reaction to the two events is likely to be very different. D1 has killed intentionally and we therefore blame her for the death, we want her to be punished and to prevent her from acting in this manner again. D2, on the other hand, has simply shot at a target, with the death of V2 following as a terrible accident. Here, rather than blame D2 we are more likely to feel sorry for her, as someone having to live with the consequences of the accident, and we are much less likely to want to stop her doing the same thing again (ie shooting at a target). D2's conduct was not blameworthy.

The way the law distinguishes these events is through mens rea requirements. D1 has committed the offence of murder, she has unlawfully killed a person *with the intention to kill or cause serious harm*.[6] D2, in contrast, is unlikely to have committed any offence: a terrible result may have occurred (the death of V2), which is the same result caused by D1, but D2 lacks the mens rea for a homicide offence.

---

[5] See *Kingston* [1994] 3 WLR 519: liability was found despite D only committing the offence due to the wrongful actions of others.

[6] *Cunningham* [1982] AC 566.

When thinking about the role of mens rea, and the construction of offences, we should not fall into the trap of being overly simplistic. The difference between D1 who intended to kill and D2 who had no knowledge of V2 is quite straightforward; and we can appreciate the role of mens rea to catch D1 within an offence and to exclude D2. However, these examples are at the very clear ends of what is otherwise a rather murky spectrum. For example, what if, when D2 shot V2:

- D did not want to kill V, but recognised that she was virtually certain to do so, for example because she saw V standing behind the target;

- D did not want to kill V, but recognised that there was a risk she might do so, for example because of her bad aim?

- D did not know V was behind the target, but only because she failed to check the target as the gun range staff had informed her to do?

In these examples, D does not intend to kill or cause serious bodily harm to V in the conventional sense because she was not shooting in order to bring that result about.[7] However, we may still want to find liability for murder, or some other homicide offence. Thus, the mens rea of an offence must define which states of mind within the spectrum will be enough to satisfy the particular offence and which will not. To do so, the common law has developed a rich language of mens rea terms including 'intention', 'knowledge', 'belief', 'recklessness', 'negligence', 'dishonesty', and many more. Much of this chapter will be spent discussing what each of these terms means in law, allowing you to understand them when they are used within an offence and apply them to problem facts.

3.2 Mens rea in context

Although most of this chapter will be spent discussing the legal meaning of the central mens rea terms (eg 'intention'; 'recklessness'; etc), it is first important to introduce how these terms work in the context of a whole offence. The actus reus of an offence

---

[7] See discussion of intention at **3.4.1**.

can be viewed independently: we can ask whether D unlawfully caused death; damaged another's property; had non-consensual intercourse; and so on. However, this is not the case with mens rea terms. Following our discussion later, we will be able to understand what each mens rea term means, and will be able to spot them in the definition of an offence. However, on their own these terms are useless. For example, if you heard that a friend, D, had hurt one of your other friends, V, it would be natural to ask D what she was thinking. If D answered simply 'intention' or 'recklessness', this would be entirely unhelpful: even understanding the terms, they need context to provide any assistance. It makes no sense for D to intend, for example, in the abstract. However, if D were to explain that she 'intended to hurt V' or 'meant to' or realised her actions 'might hurt V', then this tells us a lot.

The same is true with the mens rea of an offence. Mens rea terms carry the same meaning across different offences: 'intention' in relation to murder means the same as 'intention' in relation to theft.[8] However, what must be intended in each case will be very different: in murder D must intend to kill or cause GBH; in theft D must intend to deprive V permanently of the property. The mens rea relates to the elements of the actus reus for the offence in question.[9] Take the offence of criminal damage set out in **Table 3.1**.[10]

Table 3.1 Criminal damage

	Actus reus	**Mens rea**
Conduct element	Any act (or omission) that causes the result	Voluntary
Circumstance element	The property damaged belongs to another	Intention or recklessness
Result element	Damage or destruction	Intention or recklessness

If we were to state the mens rea of criminal damage it would not be accurate to say that D must 'intend or be reckless': these words alone tell us nothing. Rather, we should say that D must 'intend or be reckless as to causing damage to another's property'. Or, if it was necessary to be more precise, we could state the mens rea required in relation to each element of the actus reus (as set out in **Table 3.1**).

As with criminal damage, most offences require some mens rea to correspond with each element of the actus reus. In such cases, as long as you know what the mens rea terms mean (discussed later), and as long as you know which element of the actus reus they correspond with, then you will understand the mens rea of the offence. However, there are two exceptions to this rule: two categories of offences where mens

---

[8] There are, however, unhelpful exceptions to this within certain offences: Stark, 'It's Only Words: On Meaning and Mens Rea' (2013) 72 CLJ 155.

[9] See also discussion of the correspondence principle in **Chapter 4**.

[10] Criminal Damage Act 1971, s1.

rea will not correspond with every element of the actus reus. Each requires some introduction.

3.2.1 Strict liability: actus reus with no corresponding mens rea

Certain offences are constructed to require actus reus elements with no corresponding mens rea. This can arise in two different ways, each of which will be discussed further in **Chapter 4.**

A) Strict or absolute *offences*: There are some offences in which the only mens rea required is that D's conduct must be voluntary, with no mens rea required as to any other element of the offence. Offences of this kind are usually dealing with regulatory matters and attract limited punishments to reflect the lack of mens rea. Examples include D selling defective products, or failing to observe regulatory formalities in her business.[11] Since these offences punish D for things that happen (actus reus) without regard to D's choices in bringing those things about (D's state of mind), they are criticised as lacking respect for the principle of autonomy.[12]

B) Strict liability *elements*: Much more common are offences which require mens rea as to certain actus reus elements, but not to all. Where mens rea is not required as to an element of the actus reus, it is said that liability for that element is 'strict'. Offences of this kind are generally less controversial than absolute offences where no mens rea is required as to circumstances *and* results. Nevertheless, strict liability remains problematic with regards to the principle of autonomy: liability is still possible in the absence of choice as to an essential part of what D is being blamed for.

3.2.1.1 The presumption in favour of mens rea

Although strict liability is common within many criminal offences, its controversial nature means that it will only be applied by a court if it is obvious in the drafting of the offence that it is what was intended by Parliament. Where an offence sets out a certain actus reus and is simply silent as to mens rea, there is a *presumption* that mens rea will required as to that element. As stated in the House of Lords:

> the test is not whether it is a reasonable implication that the statute rules out mens rea as a constituent part of the crime—the test is whether it is a *necessary* implication.[13]

In the case of *K*,[14] D was charged with and convicted of the (now repealed) offence of indecent assault,[15] an offence that criminalised sexual touching with victims under 16 years old. One element of the actus reus was that V must be under 16. The offence did not state that D had to 'know' or 'intend' or be 'reckless' about V's age, the statute was silent. The lower courts interpreted the element as strict: if V was under 16 it did not

---

[11] Baldwin, 'The New Punitive Regulation' (2004) 67 MLR 351. See also Law Commission, *Criminal Liability in Regulatory Contexts* (Consultation 195, 2010).
[12] See **1.4.3.**
[13] *B (A Minor) v DPP* [2000] 2 AC 428.
[14] [2002] 1 AC 462.
[15] Sexual Offences Act 1956, s14 (repealed).

matter what D's state of mind about V's age was. However, the House of Lords held that the presumption of mens rea should be applied. It was for the prosecution to prove that D lacked mens rea as to V's age, even where the terms of the offence in the statute were silent as to its requirement.

If statutory offences were carefully drafted explicitly to set out every actus reus and mens rea requirement then the presumption of mens rea would be unnecessary. Unfortunately, as we will discuss in later chapters, this has never been the case with criminal legislation where political compromise, or simple oversight, will often result in ambiguous and incomplete definitions. Therefore, a presumption of mens rea is useful to ensure such oversight does not result in overly broad legislation that criminalises D without due respect for the principle of autonomy. However, the presumption can be problematic. For example, despite the sweeping language of the House of Lords in *B* and *K*, the courts have not always been consistent in their application of the presumption.[16] Further, although it is generally accepted that the presumption will require a mens rea of at least recklessness,[17] this *rather important detail* is rarely made explicit in the case law.[18]

3.2.2 Ulterior mens rea: mens rea with no corresponding actus reus

Ulterior mens rea, which is more commonly termed 'ulterior intention', describes a mens rea requirement that does not correspond to a conduct, circumstance, or result element of the actus reus. For example, to be liable for the offence of theft, D must appropriate the property of another (actus reus) dishonestly and with the intention to permanently deprive V of that property (mens rea).[19] Here, the requirement that D must 'intend to permanently deprive V' is an ulterior mens rea requirement: D must intend something (permanent deprivation) that does not have to actually happen for the offence to be committed, something that is not part of the actus reus of the offence.

Where we see ulterior mens rea within offences, the mens rea standard that is invariably required is intention (hence the common use of the term 'ulterior intention'). However, this is not always the case. For example, section 1(2) of the Criminal Damage Act 1971 criminalises D who destroys or damages property (actus reus) intending or being reckless as to whether any property would be destroyed or damaged, *and* intending or being reckless as to whether the life of another would be thereby endangered (mens rea). The second part of this mens rea, that D must be at least reckless as to the endangerment of the life of another, constitutes ulterior mens rea: it is irrelevant whether another's life is endangered in fact as endangerment is not part of the actus reus of the offence. Thus, ulterior mens rea can include mens rea terms other than intention.[20]

---

[16] Horder, 'How Culpability Can, and Cannot, Be Denied in Under-Age Sex Crimes' [2001] Crim LR 15. See also *Brown* [2013] UKSC 43 (NI).

[17] *G* [2008] UKHL 37. This is also the level of mens rea preferred within the Law Commission's 1989 Draft Criminal Code, cl20.

[18] See eg *Tolson* (1889) 23 QBD 168, which talks ambiguously of states of mind that can make wicked acts into innocent ones.

[19] Theft Act 1968, s1.

[20] Child, 'The Structure, Coherence and Limits of Inchoate Liability: The New *Ulterior* Element' (2014) 34 LS 537.

3.2.3 Conclusions from mens rea in context

In **Chapter 2** we concluded that, when identifying the actus reus of an offence, it can be useful to identify the separate elements of which it is made up: the conduct element, the circumstance element, and for result crimes the result element. In general terms, the same approach should be taken when identifying the mens rea of an offence. Thus, in most cases the mens rea can be discussed broadly (eg the mens rea for murder is the intention to kill or cause grievous bodily harm). However, where necessary, the mens rea of an offence can also be discussed more precisely as it relates or corresponds to each element of the actus reus, as set out in **Table 3.2**.

Table 3.2 Elements of an offence

	Actus reus	**Mens rea**
Conduct element	Any physical acts or omissions required for the offence	Any mens rea required as to D's acts or omissions
Circumstance element	Any factual circumstances required to exist for the offence	Any mens rea required as to those facts or circumstances
Result element	Any consequences of D's action/omission required for the offence	Any mens rea required as to those consequences
Ulterior mens rea element	*	Any mens rea required as to something that is not part of the actus reus

3.3 Voluntary act requirement

When identifying the mens rea of an offence, we are generally looking to find which mens rea term (eg 'intention', 'recklessness', 'negligence', and so on) is required of D in relation to each element of the actus reus. For example, the offence of battery is committed by D who makes unlawful contact with V (actus reus), with a corresponding intention or recklessness as to that contact (mens rea). The same pattern is repeated when discussing potential mens rea as to circumstances, results, and ulterior mens rea.

However, mens rea as to the conduct element is different. Whether we are discussing D's movement or omission to move her body, it is not intuitive to think of D desiring to move; believing she is moving; foreseeing a risk of moving; and so on. The standard mens rea terms, defined and discussed later, are inappropriate. Rather, for the conduct element of the actus reus, it is more common to inquire as to the 'voluntariness' of D's movement or omission to move.[21] Just as *all* offences, whether conduct or result crimes,

---

[21] Some courts and academic writers refer to an 'intention' to move. However, in this context, 'intention' is being used to mean 'voluntariness'.

include a conduct element within their actus reus,[22] so in (almost) all cases must this conduct be voluntary.

> **Don't be confused . . .**
> Voluntariness is often presented as part of the actus reus of the conduct element rather than a separate corresponding mens rea requirement.[23] This is because many academics believe that the definition of action inevitably includes voluntariness, effectively merging the concepts. However, this is not the approach preferred within this book. Just as we attempt to separate internal and external offence requirements in relation to circumstances and results, the same approach can also be useful with the conduct element (for reasons of consistency if nothing else). The only difference with regard to the conduct element, as opposed to circumstances and results, is that we only ever have to apply a single mens rea term: voluntariness.

3.3.1 The test for voluntariness

This is the mens rea requirement for the conduct element of every offence. There is a great deal of philosophical and neurological debate as to the meaning of 'voluntary action'.[24] However, although this debate will influence and inform a legal definition, where possible the courts prefer to use terms in their 'natural' or 'everyday' meaning, and this is certainly easier when directing a jury. The test of voluntariness, then, is simply whether D had control over her conduct (act or omission) at the relevant time.

In a majority of cases it will be obvious that D's movement or omission to move was voluntary. This will be the case where D has considered her options before acting, as well as cases where D acts instinctively in a fight, for example. In fact it is so unlikely that D lacked control of her body that within the criminal law there is an established presumption of voluntariness. Rather than the prosecution having to prove that D's conduct was voluntary in every case, it will be *presumed* that D's conduct was voluntary unless D can produce evidence to suggest that it was not. It is only when D has discharged this evidential burden that the prosecution will then have to prove beyond reasonable doubt (the criminal standard of proof) that D's acts were in fact voluntary.[25]

A claim, by the defence, that D's conduct was involuntary can take several forms. Most obviously, this will be the case where D was unconscious or semi-conscious as, for example, where D broke an object whilst sleepwalking. However, this need not be the case. For example, if D moves her arm and stabs V because X is pushing her arm, then D's conduct will not be voluntary and she will not be liable for an offence. The same is true where D omits to move, for example, because she is physically restrained from doing so by X. Involuntariness can also result from reflex or spasm. For example, if while driving D acts on reflex because she is attacked by a 'swarm of bees' or a 'malevolent passenger',[26] her driving will not be voluntary. Similarly, if D strikes V while

---

22 See **2.3.1**.

23 See **2.3.1**. See, for support of the actus reus approach, Patient, 'Some Remarks About the Element of Voluntariness in Offences of Absolute Liability' [1968] Crim LR 23.

24 Moore, *Act and Crime* (1993), and references therein.

25 See **1.1.7.1**.

26 Examples from *Bell* [1984] 3 All ER 842.

suffering from a 'spasm' or 'convulsion',[27] again, liability will fail because D has not acted voluntarily.

The only exception to these examples of involuntariness is that D cannot claim to have acted involuntarily if the reason for her lack of control was self-induced. For example, where D voluntarily became intoxicated or where she was driving when tired and fell asleep.

> **Don't be confused . . .**
> Where D claims to have acted involuntarily, she is attempting to avoid liability by denying an element of the offence (mens rea as to the conduct element). However, because the presumption of voluntary movement places an evidential burden on D to provide some evidence of involuntariness, claims of this kind are more commonly referred to as defences: defences of automatism, intoxication, and insanity. We discuss how D can avoid liability on this basis (including issues of prior fault) in **Chapter 13**.

3.3.2 The role of voluntariness

When discussing the actus reus we explained that the conduct element represented a basic ingredient of (almost) every crime: we can only blame D for harmful results because they were caused by her act, and for circumstances because they were present when she acted. Thus, with all responsibility and liability flowing from D's conduct, the requirement that this conduct should be at least voluntary is fundamental to the law's respect for D's autonomy. Even where the offence charged is a strict liability offence where no mens rea as to circumstances and results is required, we can at least say that the basic ingredient of action was one that D must have chosen. As stated by Hart, 'unless a man has the capacity and fair opportunity to adjust his behaviour to the law, its penalties ought not to be applied to him'.[28]

Despite the vital role of voluntariness, however, there are a few absolute offences that do not seem to require any mens rea, even voluntary conduct. For example, it was an offence under the Aliens Order 1920 for D to be found in the UK when leave to land in the UK had been refused. This was the charge in *Larsonneur*.

>   **Larsonneur** (1933) 24 Cr App R 74
>
> D was ordered to depart from the UK and travelled to the Irish Free State. However, she was then arrested and brought back to the UK against her will. Having been brought back to the UK, she was then charged with the offence of being found in the UK contrary to the Aliens Order.
> - Court: guilty of the offence. The offence does not require D's presence to be voluntary.

Larsonneur is already slightly exceptional because it involves one of the few offences where D's conduct is not straightforwardly based on movement or an omission, but rather on a status (being found).[29] However, the real problem with liability in this case

---

[27] Examples from *Bratty v AG for NI* [1961] 3 All ER 523.
[28] Hart, *Punishment and Responsibility* (1968) 181.
[29] See **2.3.1**.

is not the actus reus, but rather the lack of a voluntariness requirement attached to it: D is liable for being found in the UK even though her presence is not voluntary. Despite extensive criticism of the case and the offence, however,[30] *Larsonneur* was followed by the more recent case of *Winzar v Chief Constable of Kent*,[31] and there is nothing in principle to prevent Parliament creating other offences of this kind in the future.

Despite this discussion, however, it is probably better to see exceptional offences of this kind, which do not include a voluntariness requirement, as unwelcome anomalies within the law. They should not be allowed to distort or distract our more general analysis. The requirement that D's conduct element must be performed voluntarily is all but universal within the criminal law, and certainly common between *all* of the offences discussed in the later chapters of this book.[32]

Thus, although the actus reus of the conduct element will vary in detail between different offences, the mens rea for this element will always be the same. This is illustrated in **Table 3.3**.

Table 3.3 Mens rea of the conduct element

	Actus reus	**Mens rea**
Conduct element	Any physical acts or omissions required for the offence	Voluntariness

Assessment matters . . .

As D's acts are presumed in law to be voluntary, unless D provides some evidence to rebut this presumption, the issue of voluntariness will not be discussed by the court. Likewise, when you are applying the law to problems facts, you do not need to consider the issue of voluntariness unless there is some indication that D's acts or omissions may be involuntary. If you are told, for example, that D hates V and runs over and stabs her, it would be unnecessary, and rather odd, to begin a discussion about whether D's motion to stab might have been a reflex or spasm. In contrast, if you are told, for example, that the stabbing happened whilst D was suffering from some kind of seizure, then a discussion of this kind would be important.

3.4 Mens rea terms

Although there is only a single mens rea term that applies to the conduct element (voluntariness), the standard of mens rea required for other elements will vary greatly between offences. These include, but are not limited to, 'intention', 'knowledge', 'belief', 'recklessness', 'negligence', and 'dishonesty'. The relationship between elements is set out in **Table 3.4**.

---

[30] See eg Horder, *Excusing Crime* (2004) 251.
[31] (1983) The Times, 28 March.
[32] See eg *Robinson-Pierre* [2013] EWCA Crim 2396: D's appeal allowed on the basis that liability requires voluntary conduct, even where the offence is absolute.

Table 3.4 Mens rea of the other offence elements

	Actus reus	**Mens rea**
Circumstance element	Any factual circumstances required to exist for the offence	Any mens rea required as to those facts or circumstances
Result element	Any consequences of D's action/omission required for the offence	Any mens rea required as to those consequences
Ulterior mens rea element	*	Any mens rea required as to something that is not part of the actus reus

To understand the mens rea of an offence, it is therefore necessary to identify which mens rea terms (eg intention) are used within the definition of the offence; which part of the actus reus they are referring to (eg D must intend a result); and what that mens rea term means. The first two of these tasks have already been discussed in general terms, and will be discussed in relation to various offences in later chapters. We turn to the third task now.

The criminal law has developed a rich and varied vocabulary of mens rea terms. In the sections that follow, we will set out the most important of these terms and discuss their meaning. Our aim is to clarify these terms so that when they arise in later chapters you will be able to understand them, and then to apply them in context. However, before we begin this discussion, there are three important points that should be borne in mind.

A) **Mens rea terms are usually interpreted consistently between offences:** Despite the occasional *and regrettable* exception,[33] the general rule is that each mens rea term can be defined independently of the offence in which it arises. Courts will often limit their engagement with mens rea terms to the specific case and offence before them, but because the same terms are used across numerous offences it is problematic to employ different definitions, and common definitions have developed. The idea is to identify legal definitions of mens rea terms that do not change depending upon the offence in issue.

B) **The criminal law is concerned with the legal definition of mens rea terms:** Although this sounds obvious, it is very easy to allow our common non-legal understanding of terms such as 'intention' and 'recklessness' to cloud our reading and understanding of their legal definitions. There is a consistent effort to align legal and non-legal definitions, particularly with the needs of jurors' understanding in mind. However, whereas it is acceptable for vague definitions to be used in everyday discourse, in the legal context the definitions need to be precise and consistently applied: the definitions distinguish criminal from non-criminal conduct and hence make the difference in serious offences between prison and liberty. In an effort to provide this rigidity, legal definitions depart from non-legal understandings in several areas. To understand and apply the law you must learn and apply only these legal definitions.

---

[33] Stark, 'It's Only Words: On Meaning and Mens Rea' (2013) 72 CLJ 155.

C) **Mens rea terms are (for better and for worse) defined by the common law:** Where mens rea terms are codified within a criminal code or other statute, there is an opportunity to set out a limited number of terms within a clear and defined hierarchy. We see this in the US Model Penal Code 1962, for example,[34] as well as within the 1989 Draft Criminal Code for England and Wales.[35] However, the current law in England and Wales in this area remains uncodified, with mens rea terms defined almost exclusively within the common law. There are two main consequences of this. First, the definition of mens rea terms is not fixed, but rather a matter of precedent between courts. In relation to each term, we will see that definitions have changed over time, and are not necessarily settled in their present state. Secondly, we do not have a fixed list of mens rea terms. We will discuss the most commonly used mens rea terms in this chapter, but in later chapters we will occasionally encounter other mens rea terms that have been developed by the courts.

3.4.1 Intention

Intention is the most serious standard of mens rea, demonstrating the greatest culpability and the greatest blameworthiness.[36] It can be satisfied in either of two rather different ways:

- **Direct intention:** D intends something in law if she acts with a *purpose* or *aim* towards it. So, if the actus reus requirement is a circumstance element (eg that property belongs to another), D intends it directly where she acts with the purpose or aim that it should be present. Where the actus reus requirement is a result element (eg the death of V), D acts with direct intention towards it if her purpose or aim is to bring it about by her conduct. Importantly, for direct intention, whether D thinks it is likely or not is irrelevant. The leading case defining direct intention is *Moloney.*[37]

- **Oblique intention:** D intends an actus reus requirement (whether circumstance or result) 'obliquely' where it is: (a) virtually certain to arise; (b) she recognises that it is virtually certain; and (c) the jury find that this recognition amounts to an intention. The leading case defining oblique intention is *Woollin.*[38]

Despite their differences, it is important to remember that both direct intention and oblique intention are simply alternative definitions of the same mens rea term: intention. Where an offence has a mens rea of intention, this requirement can be satisfied by *either* direct or oblique intention.

> **Don't be confused . . .**
> The mens rea for most serious offences can be satisfied by intention or recklessness. One of the few exceptions to this is murder where D must act with the intention to kill or cause serious harm (recklessness is not enough). As a result, you will notice that most of the cases defining intention tend to be

---

[34] US Model Penal Code 1962, §2.02.
[35] Law Commission, *A Criminal Code for England and Wales: Report and Draft Criminal Code Bill* (No 177, 1989) cl18.
[36] See generally Lacey, 'A Clear Concept of Intention: Elusive or Illusory?' (1993) 56 MLR 621.
[37] [1985] AC 905.
[38] [1999] AC 82.

murder cases: as only intention will suffice for this offence, it is particularly important to know where its definition starts and ends. Remember, however, that the definition of intention derived from these cases is not isolated to murder and will apply wherever the term is used.

3.4.1.1 Direct intention

Direct intention is relatively uncontroversial. In line with common understanding, the law's approach to this concept holds that D intends something if it forms part of her purpose when acting (a purely internal, subjective requirement). Such intention does not require premeditation or planning, but it must be present at the time of action. For example, D smashes V's vase in retaliation for V scratching her car. Here, D commits criminal damage with intention as to both circumstance and result elements:

- D directly intends the result element of the offence (damage) because she acts in order to cause damage;
- D directly intends the circumstance element of the offence (that the property belongs to another) because she hopes that the property belongs to V.

An alternative way of expressing direct intention, promoted by Duff,[39] is to think about success and failure. Employing this approach, we can say that D directly intends the damage because her enterprise would be a failure if the vase was not damaged. Equally, she directly intends that the vase should belong to V because, if it did not, her enterprise would be a failure.

In most cases, as with the vase example, direct intention is also synonymous with 'desire'; that is, D intends to damage the vase if she desires to damage the vase. However, this is not always true. In certain cases D may directly intend an offence element as a *means to an end* even though she does not specifically desire it. For example, if D kills her mother in order to obtain her inheritance we can say that she acts with the direct intention to cause death. D may not desire the death of her mother, she may be very sad afterwards, but the death is an essential means to her desired end: the inheritance. Using Duff's language, D directly intends to kill her mother because she will only succeed (her actions will only lead to the gaining of inheritance) if she causes death: if she does not cause death, her enterprise has failed. The same would be true, for example, where D burns down V's house in order to see her reaction. D directly intends to cause damage by fire, thereby satisfying the mens rea for arson, because even if she does not desire the fire in its own right, she intends it as a necessary means to a desired end: seeing V's reaction to the burning house. This interpretation of intention is confirmed in *Hyam v DPP*,[40] where Lord Hailsham states that intention clearly includes 'the means as well as the end'.

Very importantly, *unlike oblique intention discussed in the following section*, direct intention is not affected by a foreseen likelihood of success or failure. For example, D, a hopeless darts player, can throw a dart directly intending to hit a treble 20 even though D knows that she is very likely to fail. The same logic also applies to our earlier examples. Thus, if D throws V's vase in order to damage it, it is her direct intention to

---

[39] Duff, *Intention, Agency and Criminal Responsibility* (1990).
[40] [1975] AC 55.

cause damage even if she knows that the vase is very solid and is unlikely to be broken. Where D thinks that the vase may be hers, and not belong to V at all, she still directly intends that it belongs to another if she hopes that it belongs to V. Equally, if D tries to gain inheritance by shooting her mother, but knows that she is a bad shot or that V may be out of range, or that the gun may not fire, etc, she still directly intends to kill as a means to an end.[41]

3.4.1.2 Oblique intention

When the courts are dealing with offences that require a mens rea of intention (eg murder), the 'golden rule' for directing a jury is to avoid any elaboration on the meaning of the term unless it is truly necessary.[42] Thus, the jury are left to apply their common understanding of intention, which is likely to be broadly in line with the definition of direct intention given earlier. However, where a finding of direct intention is unlikely, it will (exceptionally[43]) be necessary to direct the jury so that they can apply a legal definition of intention that includes oblique (or indirect) intention.

> *Assessment matters . . .*
> The court's approach is the same one that you should take when discussing a requirement of intention in a problem question. Always start with direct intention. If D directly intends the offence element then there is no need to consider oblique intention. Only consider oblique intention if there is some doubt as to D's direct intent.

Oblique intention as to an offence element will arise even where it is not D's purpose or aim, and even where it is not a means to a separate purpose or aim. Oblique intention involves assessing three questions, which are similar whether intent relates to results or circumstances:

- D has obliquely intended a *result* element (eg death or GBH for murder) if that result: (a) was a virtually certain consequence of her conduct; (b) she realised that it was a virtually certain consequence of her conduct; and (c) the jury find that her realisation amounted to an intention;

- D has obliquely intended a *circumstance* element (eg V's ownership of property for theft) if: (a) the circumstance was virtually certain to be present at the time she acted; (b) she realised that it was virtually certain to be present at that time; and (c) the jury find that her realisation amounted to an intention.

The potential for oblique intention is very useful in practice. For example, let us imagine that D placed a bomb on a passenger plane, her intention being to blow up the plane and thereby to destroy certain insured items in the plane's hold. If the bomb explodes and kills the pilot and passengers, has D acted with the intention to kill? D does not have a *direct* intention to kill, as causing death is not her purpose or aim. Equally, she does not directly intend death as a means to an end. If, miraculously, the insured items were destroyed but the people on board were saved or parachuted to safety, her enterprise

---

[41] For discussion about potential differences between 'intending' and 'trying', see Horder, 'Varieties of Intention, Criminal Attempts and Endangerment' (1994) LS 335.

[42] *Moloney* [1985] AC 905, 926.

[43] *Allen* [2005] EWCA Crim 1344, [63].

would not have failed, she would still succeed in getting the insurance for the packages on board. The destruction of the insured items could be described as an intended means to an end (the end being the insurance claim), but that is not true of the deaths. However, the fact that deaths were a virtually certain consequence of her conduct, and the fact that she realised this and continued anyway, makes her state of mind look very much like an intention to kill. It is the three-part test for oblique intention that allows us to say that D intended to kill.[44]

The leading case, confirming the three-part test for oblique intention, is *Woollin*.

 Woollin [1998] 4 All ER 103

D killed his child by throwing it against a hard surface. D did not desire to kill the child. D was charged with murder, requiring a mens rea of intention to kill or cause serious bodily harm.

- Crown Court: guilty of murder—judge's direction to the jury that they could find intention if they were satisfied that D realised that his actions posed a 'substantial risk' of causing death or serious injury.
- Court of Appeal: conviction upheld on appeal—direction as to intention was acceptable.
- House of Lords: allowing D's appeal. A direction in relation to 'substantial risk' is not appropriate. Oblique intention requires the result: (a) to be virtually certain; (b) to be foreseen by D as virtually certain; and (c) for the jury to find intention.

Before we provide a little more detail on the three steps of the *Woollin* test, it is important first to understand the term 'virtual certainty'.

'Virtual certainty'

The first two parts of the three-part test use the concept of a 'virtual certainty': to be intended, the actus reus element (a) must be virtually certain to arise and (b) must be foreseen by D as a virtual certainty. The level of foresight set by this term is vitally important. It is not designed to cover cases where D foresees a future event as simply likely, very likely, or even probable: these are (as we will discuss later) states of belief or recklessness, but not intention. Rather, the standard of virtual certainty is designed to catch *only* those cases where D sees the circumstance or result as nearly inevitable. The word virtually is used largely because it is impossible to be completely certain about something that happens in the future. For example, when D puts her bomb on the plane, set to detonate in flight, she is likely to be virtually certain that deaths will result from an explosion whilst legitimately contending that without the ability to look into the future, she was not and could not be completely certain.

The high threshold set by 'virtual certainty' is essential to provide a clear definition of intention (separate from belief and recklessness). This is because as soon as we start equating intention with high levels of foresight short of a virtual certainty, it is very difficult to know where to draw the line and what language to use to do it. However, despite this importance, the common law has struggled to maintain a consistent definition. This can be illustrated in the chain of murder appeal cases in **Table 3.5**, the issue in each being whether D *intended* to kill or cause serious harm to V.

[44] Pedain, 'Intention and the Terrorist Example' [2003] Crim LR 579.

Table 3.5 History of the meaning of intention

Case reference	Case facts	Level of foresight
Hyam v DPP [1975] AC 55	D put blazing newspaper through the letterbox of her rival (X) causing a house fire. D's intention was to scare X, but in fact caused the deaths of X's children (V).	House of Lords upheld a conviction where oblique intention was defined in terms of foresight of a 'high probability'.
Moloney [1985] AC 905	D shot his stepfather V (whom he loved) in a drunken contest that involved the quick-drawing of loaded shotguns. D's gun was directed point blank at V's head.	House of Lords quashed D's conviction because it was based on an incorrect direction that D foreseeing a mere 'probability' could amount to an intention. Despite this, however, in summing up Lord Bridge talked loosely of foresight of a 'natural consequence' being sufficient.
Hancock & Shankland [1986] AC 455	D (who were striking miners) pushed a concrete block from a motorway bridge intending to scare working miners travelling below. The block hit a car and killed V.	The trial court convicted D of murder, following Lord Bridge's 'natural consequence' formulation. However, the conviction was quashed on appeal. The concern of both the Court of Appeal and the House of Lords was that foresight of a 'natural consequence' may go beyond foresight of something that is certain (or at least virtually certain). However, again, some of the language used by the Lords implied that some lower threshold may be acceptable (eg Lord Scarman's statement that 'the greater the probability of a consequence the more likely it is that the consequence was foreseen and that if that consequence was foreseen the greater the probability is that the consequence was also intended . . .').
Nedrick [1986] 1 WLR 1025	D poured paraffin through the letterbox of X's house and set it alight. A child (V) died in the house fire.	The trial court convicted D of murder, following a direction from the judge that intention could be found where D foresaw death or injury as 'highly probable'. The Court of Appeal quashed D's conviction and clarified (Lord Lane CJ) that the jury 'are not entitled to infer the necessary intention, unless they feel sure that death or serious bodily harm was a virtual certainty (barring some unforeseen intervention) as a result of the defendant's actions and that the defendant appreciated that such was the case'.

(Continued)

Table 3.5 Continued

Case reference	Case facts	Level of foresight
Woollin [1998] 4 All ER 103	D killed his child by throwing it against a hard surface. D did not desire to kill the child.	The court convicted D of murder, following a direction that intention could be found where D foresaw a 'substantial risk' of death or injury. The House of Lords allowed D's appeal, substituting a manslaughter conviction, and endorsed the standard of 'virtual certainty' set out by the Court of Appeal in Nedrick, adding it is for the jury to find whether D intended in this oblique sense.

Despite this historical inconsistency, the current law (following *Woollin*) is clear that if D's foresight of a result is less than a virtual certainty, it will not be sufficient: such foresight may amount to a belief and/or recklessness, but not to an intention.[45]

Objective part: (a) the offence element must be a virtual certainty

The first part of the test for oblique intention, it will be remembered, is that the offence element must be virtually certain in fact. This is an example of an objective mens rea requirement: it is not looking to the mind of D, but rather to the objective external world.

This first part is consistently referenced in the case law and is relatively straightforward to apply. However, it has the potential to cause problems, and we may question if it is useful within the definition. Using the plane bomber example again, let us imagine that unknown to D the hold of the plane was lined with special bomb-proof material such that the destruction of the plane was not inevitable. Where death results despite this protective material, can we still say that D obliquely intended to kill? She may have foreseen death as a virtual certainty (part (b)), but since the protective material *may* have protected those on board, we cannot say that death was virtual certain in fact (part (a)). Thus, despite the subjective part of the *Woollin* test being satisfied (part (b)), a finding of intention is undermined by an objective and external requirement (part (a)). In effect, objective facts that are not known to D (in this case the materials of the plane) are partly defining the law's view of D's state of mind.

Whilst odd, it should be noted that the first part of the *Woollin* test will rarely cause problems in practice. This is because, where part (b) is satisfied (ie D foresees a virtual certainty), this will usually be because the element is a virtual certainty in fact. However, the example in the previous paragraph at least demonstrates the potential for a problem to arise.

> **Extra detail . . .**
> Although the full three-stage test has been endorsed by later cases,[46] it will be interesting to see if it is followed by a case such as the plane bomber example (where D is virtually certain of an element, but it is not virtually certain in fact). It may be that the first part of the *Woollin* test will be removed

---

[45] The principal is usefully discussed in *Matthews and Alleyne* [2003] EWCA Crim 192.

[46] eg *Matthews and Alleyne* [2003] EWCA Crim 192.

as a requirement of oblique intention, and recognised instead as evidence relevant to the second question (evidence to help the jury decide whether D foresaw the element as a virtual certainty). If an example of this kind were to arise in a problem question, it would be useful to acknowledge this possibility.

Subjective part: (b) D must foresee the offence element as virtually certain

The requirement that D must foresee the offence element as a virtual certainty is clear and relatively uncontroversial. It should be remember that this is a subjective question that looks to the mind of D. Thus, if the jury believe that D *honestly* did not foresee or might not have foreseen the offence element as a virtual certainty, even if it was virtually certain in fact (part (a)) and even if it would have been obvious to a reasonable person, this part of the *Woollin* test will not be satisfied and the jury are not entitled to find oblique intention.[47]

Jury part: (c) the jury may find intention

The final part of the *Woollin* test is that (*only* when the first two parts are satisfied) the jury are entitled to find that D intended the offence element. It is also the most controversial. It is controversial because the fact that the jury are 'entitled' to find, or 'may' find, means that even where the first two parts of the test are satisfied, the jury are not *obliged* to find intention. Further, although this third part creates a separate and independent question from the other two, the case law does not provide criteria to guide the jury in their decision. Having found that the offence element was virtually certain and that it was foreseen as a virtual certainty by D, the jury are then left with the question 'is that intention': they may equate this with intention if they wish, or they may not.

> **Extra detail . . .**
> There has been considerable academic debate about whether satisfaction of the first two parts should oblige the jury to find intention, and thus to remove discretion from this third part.[48] This arose most recently where the court in *Woollin* described the jury as 'finding' intention rather than 'inferring' it as they had in *Nedrick*: the implication being that to 'find' intention seems to contain less discretion than to 'infer' it. However, the dominant interpretation remains that this third part is not simply a rubber stamping of the first two: satisfaction of parts (a) and (b) do not equate to intention, they merely provide the basis from which the jury may, or may not, find intention.[49]

The discretion afforded to the jury within this third part (whether or not to find intention) has both positive and negative aspects. On the positive side, allowing the jury to find that D did not intend an offence element despite it being a foreseen virtual certainty, can provide useful 'moral elbow room' within difficult cases.[50]

---

[47] In *DPP v Smith* [1961] AC 290 the House of Lords had opened the possibility for an objective definition of intention. However, post-Criminal Justice Act 1967, s8 and *Woollin*, it is clear that this objective route has been foreclosed.

[48] Norrie, 'After *Woollin*' [1999] Crim LR 532; Williams, 'Oblique Intention' (1987) 46 CLJ 417.

[49] *Matthews and Alleyne* [2003] EWCA Crim 192.

[50] Horder, 'Intention in the Criminal Law—A Rejoinder' (1995) 58 MLR 678, 688.

In the civil law case of *Gillick v West Norfolk*,[51] for example, the House of Lords ruled that it was not unlawful for a doctor (D) to prescribe the contraceptive pill to a girl under the age of 16 (X). In prescribing contraception, D's conduct fulfilled the actus reus of an offence of assisting or encouraging underage sex. However, the offence required D's encouragement to be intentional, and no intention was found.[52] Applying the first two parts of the *Woollin* test, we may conclude that there was an intention to encourage: it is virtually certain that X's boyfriend will be encouraged to have sex with X if he knows she is not going to become pregnant, and it is likely that the doctor will have foreseen this encouragement as virtually certain to follow from his prescribing X the pill. In the case itself, the House of Lords avoided this conclusion by saying that an intention to act in a patient's medical interests cannot amount to a criminal intention.[53] However, this line of reasoning is clearly unacceptable: if D (a doctor) honestly believed that it was in the best interests of a patient to die, for example, we would not say that this negated the intention to kill. Rather, a better approach may be to rely upon the third part of the *Woollin* test, accepting that the result (encouragement of X and her boyfriend) is virtually certain; accepting that D foresees it as virtually certain; but in light of D's intention to protect his patient, allow the jury to find that D did not intend to encourage such unlawful conduct. Indeed, in an analogous case of *Re A*,[54] a similar approach could have been adopted. This case involved the medical separation of conjoined twins where it was virtually certain that the operation would kill one of the twins, and the doctors (D) recognised it as such. Again, when asking if D intended to kill, it is possible that the third part of the *Woollin* test could be used to avoid this conclusion.

The main advantage of this approach, therefore, is the discretion that it allows the jury. The first two parts of the *Woollin* test cannot separate the plane bomber in the earlier example from D in *Gillick* or *Re A*: in each case the result is a virtually certain consequence of D's conduct (part (a)); and D will be aware that it is a virtual certainty consequence (part (b)). It is through the discretion in this third part that the jury may find that the plane bomber intended to kill, and that D in *Gillick* and *Re A* did not intend the relevant results.

Unfortunately, for two reasons, this same discretion (or moral elbow room) is also highly problematic. First, it is unpredictable: without criteria to guide a jury, different juries may come to different conclusions when assessing the same or similar facts. This is objectionable from a rule of law perspective since we cannot tell in advance whether conduct will be criminal, and it is also unreliable as a method of distinguishing cases such as those described previously. We may predict (or at least *hope*) that a jury will find intention in relation to the plane bomber, and no intention in relation to *Gillick* and *Re A*, but there are no guarantees of this. It is little wonder, for example, that the court and medical profession would rather rely on a defence of necessity

---

[51] [1985] 3 All ER 402.
[52] **Chapter 12**.
[53] Lord Scarman (at 19) states that the 'bona fide exercise by a doctor of his clinical judgement must be a complete negation of the guilty mind'.
[54] [2001] 2 WLR 480.

in cases such as *Re A* than they would rely on the unfettered discretion of a jury on whether to find intention.[55]

Secondly, the third part of the *Woollin* test has also been criticised for allowing the jury to, in effect, decide the law. As discussed at **1.1.7.1**, the role of the jury is meant to be isolated to issues of fact. The law as interpreted by the court tells us the elements of a crime, the law defines those elements, and it is then for the jury to decide whether or not D completed those elements in fact. However, leaving the third part of the *Woollin* test completely in the hands of the jury by not providing a legal definition to guide them, means that the jury are not only being asked to apply a legal rule, they are being asked to define it. This problem is limited, of course, because the discretion will only arise where the first two parts of the *Woollin* test are satisfied, so the jury do not have complete freedom to define any state of mind they wish as an intention, but it is still apparent.

> **Assessment matters . . .**
> When applying the *Woollin* test to problem facts, the third part presents particular difficulty. You may conclude from the facts that an offence element (eg death in murder) was a virtual certainty and that D foresaw it as such, but (like the jury) you have no criteria to apply in order to answer the third part. The best approach is to highlight this problem (as a criticism of the current law) and then to say what you think the jury are most likely to decide based on an assessment of the facts as a whole. For example, it is likely that a jury will have little sympathy for the plane bomber and are therefore likely to find an intention to kill.

3.4.1.3 Conditional intention

D conditionally intends an offence element (eg causing death) where she decides to bring it about if a certain condition arises (eg if she can buy a gun).[56] In this manner, D is committing herself to a future act with a particular mens rea, if a certain condition arises. When discussing and applying conditional intentions, two important details should be borne in mind.

First, conditional intention will only apply to mens rea as to future events.[57] D can conditionally intend something in the future (eg to kill V if the weather is clear), but D cannot conditionally intend to complete conduct that she has already done. We can ask whether it was D's purpose to kill (direct intent) or whether it was a foreseen virtual certainty (oblique intent), but talk of conditions doesn't make sense.

Secondly, we must take care to ensure that the conditions of D's intention do not undermine that intention. For example, if D intends to smash a vase, but only if she discovers that it belongs to her, then she does not (under any condition) intend to damage the property of another. Equally, we must ensure that D has a fully formed intention. For example, if D decides that she will kill V 'if she wants to tomorrow', then we might interpret this as the delaying of a decision rather than a decided conditional intention. Equally, if D says she will kill V 'if she wins the lottery twice in a row', then the extreme

---

[55] Necessity is discussed in **Chapter 14**.

[56] Williams, 'Intents in the Alternative' (1991) 50 CLJ 120; Campbell, 'Conditional Intention' (1982) 2 LS 77.

[57] This arises in the context of crimes that include an element of ulterior mens rea. See **3.2.2**.

unlikelihood of this coming about may cause us to doubt that D really does intend to go through with her plan (even if the conditions do arise).[58]

> **Point to remember . . .**
> The basic rule is that a conditional ulterior intention is still an intention. This rule is relevant to all offences that contain a requirement of mens rea as to future events, from single requirements (as with theft), to more substantial requirements (as with general inchoate offences) where D's ulterior mens rea relates to a full future offence.

3.4.2 Knowledge

The mens rea of 'knowledge' is generally seen as equivalent to 'intention' in terms of culpability. D has knowledge of an offence element if (a) she believes that it is the case and (b) she is correct in that belief.[59] This interpretation was confirmed in two cases in the House of Lords. In *Montila*:[60]

> A person cannot know something is A when in fact it is B. The proposition that a person knows that something is A is based on the premise that it is true that it is A. The fact that the property is A provides the starting point. Then there is the question whether the person knows that the property is A.

And in *Saik*:[61]

> the word 'know' should be interpreted strictly and not watered down. In this context, knowledge means true belief. . . . If D1 and D2 agree they will . . . exchange money that comes into their bureau de change, they cannot be said to be agreeing to launder money which they *know* to be from a criminal source if they merely see a risk that it might be from a criminal source.

In this manner, a mens rea of 'knowledge' includes both subjective and objective parts.

The subjective part (a) focuses on D's state of mind: she must believe that the offence element is the case. For example, D must believe that the property belongs to another in theft; or that V is a person for murder; etc. As stated in the quotation from *Saik*, belief that something 'is the case' is not satisfied by a belief that it '*may be* the case'. However, it also seems that something short of virtual certainty may be acceptable. For example, in *Hall*[62] it was accepted that D could *know* goods were stolen if she was informed by someone with first-hand experience, and in *Griffiths*,[63] it was held to be enough if D has no serious doubts. In each case, we are focusing on what D actually believed (subjective mens rea), not on what she should have believed or what a reasonable person in her position would have believed (objective mens rea).

---

[58] For a useful discussion of conditional intention, see, Alexander and Kessler Ferzan, *Crime and Culpability: A Theory of Criminal Law* (2009) 206; Alexander and Kessler, 'Mens Rea and Inchoate Crimes' (1997) 87 J Crim L & C 1138.

[59] Shute, 'Knowledge and Belief in the Criminal Law' and Sullivan, 'Knowledge, Belief and Culpability' in Shute and Simester (eds), *Criminal Law Theory* (2007) Chs8 and 9.

[60] [2004] 1 WLR 3141, [27].

[61] [2006] UKHL 18, [26].

[62] (1985) 81 Cr App R 260.

[63] (1974) 60 Cr App R 14.

The objective part (b) focuses on the objective reality: what D believes must be true in fact before we can say that she has knowledge of it. For example, if D takes property that she believes belongs to another, but in fact belongs to her, she does not *know* that the property belongs to another. This part of the legal definition is very important, and explains why the mens rea of knowledge is, *generally*,[64] only used in the context of circumstance elements. It should be remembered that D's mens rea must be identified at the time she acts.[65] As the result element of a crime relates to things *caused* by D's conduct (eg death for murder), such results will always come after D has acted, even if this is just a fraction of a second. Because of this, it is logically impossible for D to have knowledge as to a result element: at the point of acting (relevant point for mens rea) we do not know if D's belief about the future is correct or not, the objective part of the definition cannot be satisfied. In contrast, circumstance elements relate to facts that must be present at the time of D's conduct (eg that V is a person for murder). Therefore, it is possible for both parts of the 'knowledge' definition to be satisfied.

> **Don't be confused . . .**
> It is common for offences to specifically require a mens rea of knowledge as to a circumstance element. However, as knowledge is considered to be equivalent to intention, even where an offence specifies a mens rea of intention as to a circumstance element, knowledge will suffice.[66]

3.4.2.1 Wilful blindness

A state of knowledge can alternatively be found where D: (a) foresees the possibility of a certain circumstance; (b) it would be easy for D to discover the truth; (c) D deliberately avoids finding out; and (d) the circumstance is in fact present. Where this is the case, D's decision to 'shut her eyes' to the facts, or 'bury her head in the sand', is described as wilful blindness. The status of wilful blindness as sufficient to amount to knowledge was confirmed in the House of Lords in *Westminster CC v Croyalgrange Ltd*.[67]

Although there has been relatively little case law discussing the meaning of wilful blindness,[68] and not a great deal of academic scholarship,[69] it remains a useful concept. For example, let us imagine that D receives a state-of-the-art stolen television from her friend P for only a few pounds. For D to commit the offence of handling stolen goods, she must *know* or believe that the property (the television) is stolen.[70] However, even where D knows that P is a burglar, and even where she suspects that the property is stolen, she may still remain unsure as to its origins: she may lack belief. In such cases, because the route to finding out (simply asking P) is straightforward and available to her, the law translates her wilful blindness into a form of knowledge that will satisfy the offence mens rea.

There are problems with the law here, some of which are obvious from the previous example. First, in the absence of case law, there is a lack of clarity as to how the stages of

---

[64] A notable exception emerges in the context of accomplice liability, **Chapter 12**.
[65] Discussed further in **Chapter 4**.
[66] Discussed further in the context of the general inchoate offences, **Chapter 11**.
[67] (1986) 83 Cr App R 155.
[68] See, most usefully, *Roper v Taylor Garages* [1951] 2 TLR 284.
[69] Wasik and Thompson, 'Turning a Blind Eye as Constituting Mens Rea' (1981) 32 NILQ 324.
[70] Theft Act 1968, s22.

the definition should be applied. For example, it is unclear how much foresight D must have to satisfy (a); how easy it must be for her to discover the truth within (b); as well as how consciously (as opposed to absent-mindedly) D must have avoided finding out within (c). Secondly, there may be cases where wilful blindness does not appear blameworthy. For example, what if D in the previous example avoided asking her friend about the television because she had promised to trust her in the future. Imagine also a parent who does not inquire about the activities of their child because they want to encourage independence and respect privacy.

> **Assessment matters . . .**
> When applying lesser developed terms such as wilful blindness to problem questions, it is important to highlight areas of doubt. You should still apply the criteria that are available from the case law. However, where there is a lack of clarity (eg the question for (b) of how easy must it be for D to discover the truth), it is best to highlight this lack of clarity and then to predict in general terms whether, and why, you think that the court will find that D satisfied the requirement.

3.4.3 Belief

'Belief' is a mens rea term that is not as culpable as 'intention' or 'knowledge'. D has belief that a circumstance exists, or that a result will be caused, where she foresees it as highly likely. This is identical to the first subjective limb of the definition of knowledge. The difference for 'belief' is that there is no objective second limb requiring D's belief to be correct in fact. Thus, where D believes a fact and she is correct, we can say that she had knowledge or belief. However, where D believes a fact and she is not correct, we can only say that she had belief.[71] Unlike knowledge, it is possible to believe that a future event will come about, and thus belief logically can correspond to results and ulterior mens rea. However, as with knowledge, belief arises most commonly in relation to circumstance elements.

3.4.4 Recklessness

Below 'intention' and 'knowledge', and also below 'belief', 'recklessness' represents the next most culpable mens rea term. It is also one of the most important, arising in the majority of the offences discussed in this book. To satisfy a mens rea of recklessness, it must be demonstrated that D (a) foresaw a risk of the relevant element of the actus reus and (b) unreasonably continued to run that risk. This interpretation was confirmed by the House of Lords in G.[72]

Again, this general definition should be expressed and applied slightly differently depending upon the element of the actus reus at issue. For example:

- D is reckless as to a circumstance element, such as the property belonging to another for criminal damage, when she (a) foresees a risk that the circumstance is present and (b) unreasonably continues to run that risk;

---

[71] Shute, 'Knowledge and Belief in the Criminal Law' and Sullivan, 'Knowledge, Belief and Culpability' in Shute and Simester (eds), *Criminal Law Theory* (2007) Chs8 and 9.

[72] [2003] UKHL 50. The definition provided by the court is taken from the Law Commission's 1989 Draft Criminal Code, cl18.

- D is reckless as to a result element, such as property damage for criminal damage, when she (a) foresees a risk that the result will be caused by her conduct and (b) unreasonably continues to act and run that risk.

In this manner, the test includes a subjective part (a) and a minor *but necessary* objective part (b). We will discuss each in turn.

> *Beware . . .*
> We highlighted earlier the importance of understanding and applying the legal definition of mens rea terms and not being distracted by their (often different) common non-legal meanings. The term 'recklessness' is one that students often confuse in this way. In common use, the term recklessness is often used to describe a person's dangerous behaviour (eg she flailed her arms recklessly). However, where 'recklessness' is used as a mens rea term it is not concerned with D's physical behaviour. The test is simply: (a) did D foresee a risk of the offence element? And (b) did D continue unreasonably to run that risk? If the answer to both questions is 'yes', then a mens rea of recklessness is satisfied.

Subjective part: (a) D must have foreseen a risk of the offence element being satisfied

The first part of the 'recklessness' test focuses on D's state of mind: at the time of acting, D must have subjectively foreseen a risk of the relevant circumstance or result. Whether D foresaw the relevant risk or not is a simple question of fact for the jury. However, courts have provided some further guidance on exactly what the law means by the foresight of a risk.

Four useful points of clarification are set out below. These apply to any requirement of recklessness, but are more easily explained in reference to an example. We use the example of criminal damage, an offence that requires D to damage the property of another, being at least reckless as to causing such damage.[73] Let us imagine that D tries to rouse her friend by throwing small stones at her bedroom window. D does not intend to damage V's window by throwing the stones, but one of the stones causes damage.

D must foresee the risk of damage to the window: It must be remembered that this part of the 'recklessness' test is purely subjective: our focus is on D's state of mind alone. Thus, for example, if the jury believe that D did *not* foresee or might not have foreseen a risk of damaging the window with the stone then the test will not be satisfied even where the risk would have been obvious to a reasonable person in D's position. This is illustrated in *Stephenson*.

> *Stephenson* [1979] QB 695
>
> D, who suffered from schizophrenia, sheltered in a haystack and made a fire for warmth. Inevitably, the fire spread and caused damage. D was charged with criminal damage, the mens rea of which requires D to be reckless as to causing damage. Medical evidence indicated that D may not have been aware of the risk of damage as a result of his condition.
> - Crown Court: guilty of the offence. The trial judge directed the jury in terms of risks that would have been obvious to them.
> - Court of Appeal: appeal allowed against conviction. The test is purely subjective: it was a misdirection to question the obviousness of the risk; the only question is whether D foresaw a risk.

---

[73] Criminal Damage Act 1971, s1.

The size of the risk foreseen by D is irrelevant: For oblique intention, D must foresee the actus reus element (in this case damage) as virtually certain; for belief, it must be foreseen as highly likely. However, for recklessness there is no such restriction. Whether D foresees the risk as virtually certain, highly likely, likely, unlikely, etc, as long as *a* risk is foreseen, it will be sufficient. Thus, where D throws the stone at V's window foreseeing only a small chance of causing damage, it will still be enough to satisfy this part of the test. This is illustrated in *Brady*.

> ### *Brady* [2006] EWCA Crim 2413
>
> D was drunk in a nightclub. He climbed onto a railing and then fell to the dance floor beneath, causing serious injury to V. D was charged with an offence against the person that included a mens rea of recklessness as to causing harm.[74]
>
> - Crown Court: guilty of the offence against the person.
> - Court of Appeal: conviction upheld on appeal. D had appealed on the basis that the test of recklessness required D to foresee 'an obvious and significant' risk. This was rejected: foresight of any risk is sufficient.

How carefully D considers the presence of the risk is irrelevant: Before throwing the stone at V's window, D may have carefully considered the chances of causing damage. She may have selected a smaller stone and thrown it with less force. Alternatively, she may have only considered it in the fleeting moment as she began to throw the stone. However, in each case D's state of mind will be sufficient for this part of the recklessness test: some foresight of the risk is all that is required, however fleeting or superficial that is. This is a sensible rule, and it avoids the court becoming bogged down in trying to distinguish between D's degrees of thought or focus. However, the basic line between foreseeing and not foreseeing can still be problematic. In certain cases, at the very edges of subjective foresight, the courts have even been willing to accept that a risk was foreseen when it was 'suppressed', or 'driven out', or where D 'closed his mind' to it. In cases such as *Parker*, the test is satisfied on the somewhat artificial basis that the risk was foreseen by D in the back of her mind.

> ### *Parker* [1977] 1 WLR 600
>
> After a very bad day, D lost his temper when he found a public telephone out of order and proceeded to 'smash down' the receiver into the dialling box. This caused minor damage. D was charged with criminal damage, the mens rea of which requires D to be reckless as to causing damage. D claimed that, in the heat of the moment, he was not aware of this risk.
>
> - Crown Court: guilty of criminal damage.
> - Court of Appeal: conviction upheld on appeal—although D's awareness of the risk of damage was suppressed by his anger, the risk still must have entered his mind.

What D thinks about the risk is irrelevant: Having foreseen the risk of damaging V's window, D may worry and hope that no damage will be caused; she may dislike V and

---

[74] **Chapter 7**. For discussion of the implications of D's intoxication, see **Chapter 13**.

not mind the idea of the window breaking; she may not care either way. However, in each case D's state of mind will be sufficient for this part of the recklessness test: some foresight of the risk is all that is required however indifferently D may view it. This question used to arise in the context of rape and other sexual offences, before the definition of those offences changed, where D performed sexual acts and 'could not care less' whether V consented or not.[75] In such cases, it has been consistently held that D's state of mind will satisfy the test for recklessness: D may not attach any weight to the risk, but it is still foreseen.[76]

A more difficult case is where D claims that she had so little regard for her potential victims that she did not even consider the possible risks of her actions, a so-called cognitive void.[77] This is problematic because, unlike earlier examples, despite D's obvious culpability, she is claiming that she did not foresee the risk before choosing to ignore it. There is some support for the proposition that D's state of mind would still be sufficient to satisfy a mens rea of recklessness: Lord Goff in *Reid*, for example, suggested that D could be recklessly indifferent to a risk without being aware of it.[78] However, the better view, in light of *G* and other subsequent case law, is that D would not be reckless in these circumstances. The basic subjective ingredient of this mens rea term is that D must have foreseen a risk.

Objective part: (b) D must have unreasonably continued to run the risk

Having established (a) that D foresaw a risk of the circumstance or result element, it must also be demonstrated (b) that D *unreasonably* chose to run that risk. This second part of the test is objective: it does not matter whether D thought it was reasonable to run the risk, the question is whether the court think it was reasonable based on the standards of reasonable people acting in D's circumstances. For example, D may believe that it is reasonable to throw stones at her friend's window, because she wants to get her friend's attention, even though she foresees a risk of damage. The question for the court, however, is whether such conduct would be considered reasonable by others in her position. In this case, unless she has the permission of V, or she is trying to rouse V whose house is on fire, the answer is likely to be 'no': meaning that recklessness as to causing damage would be found.[79]

In many cases it will be obviously unreasonable to run the risk of causing damage or injury, and this part of the test will be easily satisfied. However, this will not always be the case. For example, a car driver may foresee a risk of someone jumping out in front of their car and being injured; when a doctor performs an operation they may foresee a chance that the patient will die; etc. However, the law does not want to discourage socially useful activities such as driving and performing operations. In such cases, D will not have a mens rea of recklessness as to causing harm: she foresees a risk (a), but it is not unreasonable to run that risk (b).

[75] The issue no longer arises in such cases because the mens rea of these offences no longer requires recklessness. See discussion in **Chapter 8**.
[76] *Satnam and Kewal Singh* (1984) 78 Cr App R 149.
[77] Ben-David, 'Cognitive Void in Relation to Attendant Circumstances as Subjective Mens Rea' [2015] New Crim LR 418.
[78] (1992) 95 Cr App R 391. Leigh, 'Recklessness after *Reid*' (1993) 56 MLR 208.
[79] Consent would also raise the possibility of a statutory defence. See discussion in **Chapter 9**.

3.4.4.1 Historical background: the rise and fall of objective recklessness

In order to understand the current definition of recklessness set out earlier, it is useful to bear in mind the common law journey that has been taken to get there.[80] This is set out in **Table 3.6**.

Table 3.6 History of the meaning of recklessness

Case reference	Case facts	Definition of 'recklessness'
Cunningham [1957] 2 QB 396	D tore a gas meter from the wall in order to steal money from it. Gas escaped into his neighbour's house and was inhaled by V. D was convicted of an offence against the person, including a mens rea of malice (which is the same as recklessness) as to the endangerment of life.[81] This was quashed on appeal.	*Subjective beginnings* The Court of Criminal Appeal quashed D's conviction because the trial judge had defined the offence term 'malicious' (meaning the same as 'reckless', see **3.4.4.1**) as synonymous with 'wicked'. The court set out a test for recklessness that is similar to the current law: D must foresee the risk. This is why the current subjective test for recklessness is often referred to as *Cunningham* recklessness.
Caldwell [1982] AC 341	D, who had been drinking heavily, started a fire in a hotel as part of an ongoing dispute. D was convicted of aggravated criminal damage, including a mens rea of recklessness as to the endangerment of life.[82] The House of Lords upheld this conviction.	*Objective recklessness* With Lords Wilberforce and Edmund-Davies dissenting, the House of Lords expanded the *Cunningham* definition of recklessness to include what is referred to as 'objective recklessness'. Under this new test, set out by Lord Diplock, D would be reckless where: (a) she foresees a risk (in line with *Cunningham*); or (b) she failed to foresee a risk that would have been obvious to the reasonable person. The second possibility here is objective because it does not look to the mind of D: it asks if the reasonable person would have foreseen the risk and allows the court to find recklessness on this basis. This is often referred to as *Caldwell* recklessness.

---

[80] Davies, 'Lawmakers, Law Lords and Legal Fault' (2004) 68 J Crim L 130; Crosby, 'Recklessness—The Continuing Search for a Definition' (2008) 72 J Crim L 313.

[81] Offences Against the Person Act 1861, s23. See **7.9.4**.

[82] Criminal Damage Act 1971, s1(2). See **Chapter 9**.

Lawrence [1982] AC 510	This case involved reckless driving, including a mens rea of recklessness as to associated dangers.	*Expanding objective recklessness* Lord Diplock reiterated his objective definition of recklessness, adding that the obvious risk must also be serious. The use of objective recklessness in this case demonstrated its general application outside criminal damage cases.
Elliott [1983] 1 WLR 939	D (a 14-year-old girl with learning difficulties) started a fire in a garden shed. The fire spread and caused damage. D was charged with criminal damage, including a mens rea of recklessness as to the damage. D claimed that she did not foresee the damage.	*Unfairness of objective recklessness* D was liable for criminal damage in this case because although she did not foresee damage (she was not subjectively reckless), the damage would have been obvious to a reasonable person. Thus, recklessness was found using the *Caldwell* test. D was liable despite not foreseeing the risk of damage, and despite her age and learning difficulties making it impossible for her to appreciate the foresight of the objective reasonable person.
G [2003] UKHL 50	D (children aged 11 and 12) set fire to some newspapers under a wheelie bin. They left the fire and it spread to surrounding buildings. They were convicted of criminal damage of the building, on the basis of their mens rea of recklessness as to the damage. They had not foreseen the chance of the fire spreading and damage being caused, although that was obvious to a reasonable person.	*Full circle: overruling* Caldwell *and back to* Cunningham The House of Lords allowed the appeal and quashed the convictions. Following extensive criticism of *Caldwell*, the House of Lords took the opportunity to overrule it and to restate the subjective recklessness test set out in *Cunningham*.
AG's Reference (No 3 of 2003) [2004] EWCA Crim 868	The case involved the offences of manslaughter and misconduct in public office. The latter including an element of recklessness.	*Expanding* Cunningham; G; *subjective recklessness* This case is useful because it confirms 'general principles' laid down in *G*: that 'recklessness' should be interpreted in a subjective manner for all offences where the term is used.

In this manner, the common law definition of recklessness has completed a full circle: from subjective to objective to subjective. Importantly, you should be clear that objective (*Caldwell*) recklessness has been overruled in *G*: it is no longer a definition of recklessness used in English law.

3.4.4.2 Maliciously and wilfully

The mens rea term 'maliciously' arises in several offences against the person.[83] The mens rea term 'wilful' also arises in a host of offences, including wilfully obstructing a police officer[84] and misconduct in public office.[85] Where such terms are applied to circumstance or result elements, it is now settled that their meaning is the same as 'recklessness'.[86] The fact that different mens rea terms are used to mean the same thing is obviously not ideal, and has the potential to cause confusion. However, aligning their meanings with recklessness in this manner at least reduces the complex variety of mens rea definitions that are present in the common law.

3.4.4.3 Intoxication as mens rea

Intoxication through drink or other drugs can cause problems for the application of recklessness in cases. The problem arises where D is charged with an offence requiring proof of recklessness as to an element, but failed to foresee the risk *due* to her intoxicated state. If we apply the definition of recklessness mentioned previously, then D is not reckless (she did not foresee a risk), and she has not committed an offence. However, the law understandably looks further than this by examining the cause of the intoxicated state.

If D was *in*voluntarily intoxicated, for example because she had her drinks laced, then she will not be liable: she did not foresee the risk and she was not at fault in bringing about that failure to see the risk.

If, however, D's lack of foresight was in some manner her own fault, brought about by her decision to become intoxicated, the situation becomes more complicated. In certain cases, the law is willing to accept that D's intoxication is equivalent to a mens rea of recklessness. Therefore, in these cases, D can be convicted of an offence that requires a mens rea of recklessness, not because she satisfies the test for recklessness set out earlier, but simply on the basis of her intoxicated state.[87] The intoxication rules will be fully discussed in **Chapter 13**.

3.4.5 Summary of mens rea terms

As we have discussed, despite their general focus on the mind of D, mens rea terms will often include objective as well as subjective parts within their definition. For example, 'oblique intention' requires that the offence element was not only subjectively foreseen as a virtual certainty, but that (objectively) it was a virtual certainty; 'knowledge' requires subjective belief in a circumstance, and also that (objectively) the belief is true; 'recklessness' requires subjective foresight of a risk, and also (objectively) a consideration of reasonableness. However, despite these objective considerations, the core of each term

---

[83] **Chapter 7.**
[84] Police Act 1996, s89.
[85] *AG's Reference (No 3 of 2003)* [2004] EWCA Crim 868.
[86] For 'maliciously' see *Cunningham* [1957] 2 QB 396. For 'wilfully' see *D* [2008] EWCA Crim 2360. In the absence of explicit authority, there remains some doubt as to whether 'malice' should be interpreted to apply the objective limb of recklessness as well as the subjective limb. However, it is contended that both should be applied.
[87] *Heard* [2007] EWCA Crim 125.

still focuses on the subjective mind of D. In each case, the prosecution must prove that D brought the relevant circumstance or result to mind in some manner before mens rea can be established.

When we discuss and apply the subjective parts of these mens rea terms, it is important to remember that they are not all about the foresight of a risk. Two forms of subjective mens rea should be distinguished.

- Where D acts in order to bring about a certain result, or a certain circumstance: This form of subjective mens rea only applies in the context of direct intention. Crucially, this form of subjective mens rea does not focus on degrees of foresight; the only question is whether the result or circumstance is D's purpose or aim.

- Where D acts foreseeing a result being caused, or the presence of a circumstance: This form of subjective mens rea requires us to assess the degree to which D foresaw the circumstance or result. Depending upon the degree of foresight, we might conclude that D is obliquely intending, has knowledge, belief, and/or recklessness.

Where D possesses the first form of subjective mens rea it is clear that she is directly intending. However, where D foresees a circumstance/result within the second form, but does not have it as her aim or purpose, we need to be able to identify the relevant mens rea across several options. The most effective way of doing this is to think about D's foresight as a spectrum between foresight of a virtual certainty at the top and lack of foresight at the bottom. At the top of the spectrum D's foresight will satisfy the test for several mens rea terms, and this will reduce as we move down the spectrum. This is set out in **Tables 3.7** (results) and **3.8** (circumstances); it can be useful to keep this in mind when applying mens rea terms, as well as discussing the differences between them.

Table 3.7 Mens rea as to the result element

D's foresight that conduct will cause a certain result	Mens rea term
Virtually certain	Intention; belief; recklessness
Very likely	Belief; recklessness
Likely	Recklessness
Possible	Recklessness
Unlikely (but still a risk)	Recklessness
Not foreseen	None

Table 3.8 Mens rea as to the circumstance element

D's foresight that circumstance will be present	Mens rea term
Virtually certain	Intention; knowledge (if true); belief; recklessness
Very likely	Knowledge (if true); belief; recklessness
Likely	Recklessness
Possible	Recklessness
Unlikely (but still a risk)	Recklessness
Not foreseen	None

Don't be confused . . .

Despite the overlap of mens rea terms, many offences list more than one mens rea term that will satisfy the offence. For example, offences will often specify a mens rea of intention or recklessness. Here, as D cannot intend without being reckless as well, it is advised that you focus on the minimum requirement (recklessness) only. It is a bit like a sign on the beach saying 'no swimming' and also 'no swimming breaststroke': they are both accurate, but the second is unnecessary because the prohibition is covered by the first.

3.5 Objectifying 'subjective' mens rea terms

It is important to understand and analyse mens rea terms in their context (ie any qualifications written into the offence). Since 2003 and the decision in *G* bringing about the demise of objective recklessness, each of the core mens rea terms ('intention', 'knowledge', 'belief', and 'recklessness') are now defined to require some degree of subjective mens rea. In each case, the mens rea term will only be satisfied if D herself possessed a certain purpose or certain foresight. However, although this positively serves the principle of autonomy,[88] it also makes the finding of mens rea more difficult: proving that D possessed a certain state of mind at the relevant time, not simply that a reasonable person in her position would have done so, can be challenging.

The greater difficulty of proving a subjective mens rea may be acceptable in view of the serious consequences of criminal prosecution, and the need for certainty that D is deserving of those consequences. However, for certain offences, where proving subjective mens rea has been particularly difficult,[89] or where Parliament simply deems

[88] See **1.4.3**.

[89] eg sexual offences or terrorism offences.

it necessary, the construction and context of mens rea terms can be adapted to reduce (or even to eliminate) their subjective parts. These offence constructions are not claiming to redefine the mens rea term more generally, and will not affect its definition when used in other offences, but they do affect the way it should be applied within that particular offence.

As the process of objectifying mens rea terms does not affect their general definitions, we will not discuss them in detail here. Rather, this will be done as they arise in relation to particular offences in later chapters. However, by way of introduction, such constructions will usually take one of two forms:

- **Objectifying the subjective part:** For certain offences you will find the subjective part of a mens rea term can alternatively be satisfied by a finding that a reasonable person in D's position would have had that mens rea. For example, harassment offences require D to know that her behaviour will cause harassment, or that she *ought to have* known that.[90] The first part of this applies the standard (subjective) use of the mens rea term 'knowledge'. However, the second alternative allows for a purely objective mens rea: the qualifying statement 'ought to have' means that, in this context, an objective test is to be applied.

- **A lack of positive belief:** An even stricter mens rea construction is to require D to have a positive and reasonable belief. For example, to commit rape D must have penetrated the vagina, anus, or mouth of V with his penis and without V's consent.[91] Mens rea as to V's non-consent is satisfied where D 'does not reasonably believe that [V] consents'. There are two aspects to this. First, there is a positive obligation on D to have held a belief in consent: if D did not believe that V consented because he did not care, for example, D will satisfy the mens rea.[92] Secondly, even where D did believe that V was consenting, that belief must be reasonably (objectively) held: unless a reasonable person in D's position would have so believed, D will satisfy the mens rea.

Point to remember . . .
The use of objective constructions is not uncommon in the law. Therefore, when identifying the mens rea of an offence, as well as looking to spot mens rea terms, it is equally important to consider their context: are they being used in the standard manner or are they adapted or objectified in some manner?

3.6 Other mens rea terms

In this section we discuss the terms 'dishonesty' and 'negligence'. Although both are described as mens rea terms, they are importantly different from the more common mens rea terms discussed previously. This is because, unlike intention and recklessness, for example, they do not correspond to separate requirements within the actus reus of an

---

[90] Protection from Harassment Act 1997.
[91] Sexual Offences Act 2003, s1.
[92] This will be the case even if a reasonable person would have believed that V was consenting.

offence. Rather, they include both external and internal requirements, and so they stand alone within an offence definition.

> **Don't be confused . . .**
>
> For the mens rea terms discussed previously (eg intention and recklessness), it has been important to identify a corresponding actus reus element. This is because it is essential to know what D must intend or foresee in order to apply the requirement to problem facts. Crucially, this is not required for dishonesty and negligence: an offence may require dishonesty and/or negligence, but these requirements stand alone, they do not correspond with other actus reus elements.

3.6.1 Dishonesty

A mens rea requirement of dishonesty appears regularly in the context of property offences (**Chapter 9**), and much of its detail can be left for consideration at this later stage. However, it is useful to provide a brief introduction.

The definition of dishonesty is now settled within the common law, set out in *Ghosh*.[93] The jury must consider two questions.

(a) Was what was done dishonest according to the ordinary standards of reasonable and honest people? If no, D is not dishonest. If yes:

(b) Did the defendant realise that reasonable and honest people regard what she did as dishonest? If yes, she is dishonest; if no, she is not.

Although it is not often necessary to set out the full test when directing a jury,[94] it is clear that both parts of the test must be satisfied for dishonesty to be found. The two parts combine both objective and subjective considerations.

A) Objective part (a): The first question is purely objective, asking the jury to assess the dishonesty of D's conduct in relation to the standards of reasonable people. The standard for dishonesty is universal, and will not vary depending upon the subject matter of the case. For example, in *Hayes*,[95] D was found to be dishonest in attempting (successfully) to manipulate lending rates between City banks, despite this practice being common within the banking industry and perceived by many as legitimate. The question is therefore not whether D perceives her conduct as dishonest, or whether it is dishonest within D's industry or sub-group, but whether it is dishonest by the general standard of all reasonable people.[96]

B) Subjective part (b): The second question is subjective, and focuses on the mind of D. When applying this test, the question is *not* whether D believed or recognised that her conduct was dishonest. Rather, the question is whether D realised that *others* would consider her conduct as dishonest. This is an important distinction. For example, if D is struggling financially and has a rather loose moral code, she may well convince herself that taking property from her workplace is not dishonest. However, it would be much

---

[93] [1982] QB 1053.
[94] *Roberts* (1985) 84 Cr App R 177.
[95] [2015] EWCA Crim 1944. See Dent [2016] Crim LR.
[96] For a discussion of the problems identifying such a universal standard, see Griew, 'Dishonesty—The Objections to *Feely and Ghosh*' [1985] Crim LR 341.

harder for her to maintain, and for a jury to believe, her claim that she did not think that reasonable honest people would consider that such taking is dishonest.[97]

3.6.2 Negligence

The test for 'negligence', even more than 'dishonesty', is not concerned with D's state of mind. Rather, negligence is used to describe a certain type of *behaviour* from D that drops below the standards that we expect from reasonable people. A requirement of negligence most commonly arises in relation to regulatory and driving offences.[98] In these cases, D is performing a lawful act (eg driving) that entails obvious risks to others. Rather than focusing on D's state of mind (eg did she foresee the risk?), a negligence requirement assumes that D must be aware of the risks and asks whether her behaviour in relation to them is reasonable.

The test for negligence in the criminal law is similarly constructed to the tort of negligence. Thus, a negligence requirement entails the following questions.

(a) What was D's duty of care?

(b) Did D breach that duty of care?

Both of these questions are objective, focusing on external standards and conduct.

A) What was D's duty of care? This question encourages us to consider who D has a duty to care for, and also, what standard of care is required. Certain statutory negligence offences will specify this within the offence, but this will not always be the case. The question of 'who' D has a duty towards, if unspecified within the offence, will be interpreted very widely in line with civil law (ie D must consider the safety of all those potentially affected by her conduct). It should be remembered that this is *not* the same as the 'duty to act' required for omissions liability, a duty to act is interpreted very narrowly.

The more difficult question is to assess the standard of care required. Here, the general rule is that D must act *reasonably* or in the manner that would be expected of the reasonable person. Where D is performing a skilled activity or holds specialised knowledge, she will be judged against the standard of a reasonable person with that knowledge. For example, negligent driving is measured against the standard of a 'competent and careful driver', and so D can be held to have driven negligently even if a reasonable non-driver could not have performed better.[99] Likewise, a surgeon must perform an operation to the standard of a reasonable surgeon, not to the standard of a reasonable layperson handed the scalpel.

Although the standard of reasonableness increases to take account of D's specialised knowledge, the same will not be true in the other direction. Therefore, when assessing the standard of the reasonable person, the jury may not take account of characteristics that may lead to D's inability to meet that standard through no fault of D. For example, it would be no defence to a charge of careless driving for D to say she was a learner driver and therefore unable at that moment to achieve the standard of the 'competent and careful driver'. Equally, if D walks into something and causes damage or injury, it will be no excuse to a negligence-based offence for D to point out that she is blind. The

---

[97] Campbell contends that this second limb is superfluous: Campbell, 'The Test for Dishonesty in *Ghosh*' (1994) 43 CLJ 349.

[98] eg the offence of driving without due care and attention: Road Traffic Act 1988, s3.

[99] *McCrone v Riding* [1938] 1 All ER 721.

strict application of the reasonable person standard in such cases has attracted criticism,[100] and there is some indication that it may be softening to allow for the age of D to be considered,[101] but the basic position remains largely unchanged.

B) **Did D breach that duty of care?** Negligence also requires D to have breached the duty of care. A breach requires the prosecution to prove that D's conduct was performed below the reasonable standard required of her. When applying this question to problem facts, some harm or injury resulting from D's conduct is an indication that D has breached their duty of care, but it is not definitive. For example, if a car (V) brakes suddenly in front of D and she crashes into it, this is an indication that she may have been driving negligently by driving too fast or being too close to V's vehicle. However, it is also possible that she was driving competently, and that the crash could not have been avoided or, at least, a reasonable driver may have had the same accident.[102]

> *Assessment matters . . .*
> When applying a negligence-based offence to problem facts, it can be easy to equate resulting harm with a breach of duty. Take care: this is not always the case. Always discuss whether D's conduct fell below, or is likely to have fallen below, the standard of the reasonable person.

3.6.2.1 Gross negligence

Gross negligence has no equivalent in the civil law and arises in the criminal law in relation to one offence only: gross negligence manslaughter.[103] To be found to have been 'grossly negligent', D must fulfil the conditions of negligence discussed earlier, and D's negligence must be sufficiently extreme to be considered by the jury as 'gross'. This definition was set out in the House of Lords in the leading case *Adomako*.[104]

> Simple lack of care such as will constitute [standard civil negligence] is not enough. For the purposes of the criminal law there are degrees of negligence, and a very high degree of negligence is required to be proved before [gross negligence] is established.

It is therefore up to the jury to consider whether D's negligence is sufficiently serious to be considered 'gross'.

> *Judge and jury . . .*
> This is another area where the law is criticised for asking the jury to decide issues of law as well as issues of fact. In this respect it is like the final part of the *Woollin* test for intention. This is because, when deciding if D's negligence is 'gross', the jury are given no definition of grossness to apply. If the jury believe that D's behaviour is really bad (if they want her to be criminalised) then they will call it gross; and if they think that it does not deserve criminalisation then they will say that it is not gross. In this manner, the jury are deciding (not applying) the boundaries of the offence.

---

[100] Simester et al, *Simester and Sullivan's Criminal Law* (6th edn, 2016) 162.
[101] *R (RSPCA) v C* [2006] EWHC 1069 (Admin). See also *obiter* statements in *Hudson* [1966] 1 QB 448.
[102] Discussed in *Simpson v Peat* [1952] 2 QB 24, 28.
[103] **Chapter 6.**
[104] [1995] 1 AC 171.

3.7 Reform

With essay-type questions in mind, it is useful to pick up on two issues in particular that have arisen within this chapter. The first is the potential benefit of codifying mens rea terms and thereby removing their core definitions from the common law. The second is to look in slightly more detail at the relative merits of subjective mens rea requirements on the one hand, and objective mens rea requirements on the other.

3.7.1 Codifying mens rea terms

Although most criminal law academics favour general codification, there is always a balancing of benefits (eg consistency and clarity) against the loss of flexibility within the common law. However, when it comes to the codification of mens rea terms, there are few if any who would oppose having statutory definitions and the chance to have avoided the continuously changing definitions that have dogged the criminal over the past 50 years. As highlighted at various points in this chapter, these changes have come in a range of forms. Some have been subtle changes, and others full redefinitions. Some have been the product of careful consideration, and some simply from an imprecise choice of words. However, in each case the general application of mens rea terms, which potentially apply to many hundreds of offences, magnifies and exacerbates problems in the law.[105]

The codification of mens rea, in a manner seen in other jurisdictions,[106] remains no more than an aspiration in England and Wales. Despite notable attempts by the Law Commission within the 1989 Draft Criminal Code,[107] and later when suggesting reforms to the offences against the person,[108] the Commission's recommendations have not been taken forward into law.[109] Probably the three main reasons in favour of codification are: (A) creating a set mens rea vocabulary; (B) creating settled core definitions; and (C) creating the clarity of definition necessary to improve the law. We will look briefly at each.

A) A settled vocabulary: One of the main advantages of the US Model Penal Code, for example, is that it reduced the amount of mens rea terminology to four key terms: intention, knowledge, recklessness, and negligence.[110] By this simple act, the host of terms that were rarely used within the law, and not well understood, were removed. The terms that remained were defined to recognise a spectrum of mens rea, but also to provide a useful core set of well understood definitions.

---

[105] For a discussion of the problems caused by a lack of codification in this area, see Law Commission, *Report on the Mental Element in Crime* (No 89, 1978).

[106] See eg Australian Model Criminal Code (1992) Div 5; US Model Penal Code 1962, §2.02; Gainer, 'The Culpability Provisions of the Model Penal Code' (1987) 19 Rut LJ 575.

[107] Law Commission's 1989 Draft Criminal Code, cl18.

[108] Law Commission, *Offences Against the Person and General Principles* (No 218, 1993) cl1.

[109] The most recent move was a 1998 Home Office Consultation Paper. See Smith, 'Offences Against the Person: The Home Office Consultation Paper' [1998] Crim LR 317. The Law Commission recently decided not to include definitions of mens rea terms in its report on offences against the person (No 361, 2015).

[110] Gainer, 'The Culpability Provisions of the Model Penal Code' (1987) 19 Rut LJ 575.

B) **A settled definition:** Codification of mens rea terms does not eliminate all discretion for the court, and there remains room for disagreement through interpretation.[111] However, a statutory definition can at least provide a core definition that will be protected from change within the common law. Thus, although we might still disagree on the exact level of foresight required for belief, for example, we would not have (as we have had with recklessness over the last 30 years) the dramatic redefinition of core terms between subjective, to objective, to subjective.[112]

Settled core definitions are important to protect against retrospective lawmaking (ie where D's state of mind fulfils the mens rea only due to its redefinition).[113] Additionally, statutory definitions protect the democratic will of Parliament, ensuring that if Parliament create offences with a certain mens rea in mind, that that mens rea term they use in drafting will continue to have the same meaning when the offence is applied. Indeed, this was one of the central criticisms of the *Caldwell*[114] objective redefinition of recklessness, as Parliament had created the Criminal Damage Act 1971 on the basis of the then subjective definition of recklessness.[115]

C) **A clear definition:** One of the main problems with common law definitions is that it is easy for precise meanings to be lost within a court's judgment, and even easier if a definition is gleaned from a combination of several judgments across multiple cases. This has been problematic, for example, in the context of oblique intention and the meaning of 'virtual certainty'.[116] Codification, in contrast, has the potential to make a definition considerably clearer, which also makes it easier to spot problems within the law and to correct them.

A useful example of improved clarity and evaluative potential can be seen in the context of oblique intention, where D obliquely intends a result element (eg unlawful killing for murder). It will be remembered that the *Woollin* definition of oblique intention requires: (a) that the result be a virtual certain consequence of D's act; (b) that D realises it is a virtually certain consequence of her act; and (c) that the jury choose to find intention. Developing this, the Law Commission defined intention within the 1989 Draft Criminal Code as:

> act[ing] in order to bring [the result] about or being aware that it would occur in the ordinary course of events.

In response to this clear statement of the (recommended) law, an interesting debate emerged that was previously hidden within the inconsistency of the common law. Even accepting that the result must be virtually certain, and that D must foresee the result as virtually certain, a question emerges as to what the *cause* of this virtual certainty must be. The most obvious answer, and that implied in the *Nedrick* and *Woollin* directions, is that

---

[111] See, on the US Model Penal Code, Simons, 'Should the Model Penal Code's Mens Rea Provisions be Amended?' (2003) 1 Ohio JCL 179.

[112] Davies, 'Lawmakers, Law Lords and Legal Fault' (2004) 68 JCL 130.

[113] Contrary to the principle of fair warning, see **1.4.1**.

[114] [1982] AC 341.

[115] McEwan and Robilliard, 'Recklessness: The House of Lords and the Criminal Law' (1981) 1 LS 267.

[116] See **3.4.1.2**.

the result must be a virtually certain consequence of D's conduct. However, this can be problematic. To go back to our plane bomber examples, what if D sets a bomb in order to destroy insured property on a plane, but thinks there is a 50 per cent chance that the bomb will malfunction and fail to explode? If the question is whether it is virtually certain that death will arise from D's *conduct* (planting the bomb), and whether it is foreseen as a virtual certainty of that *conduct*, then the answer is 'no': there is only a 50 per cent chance that the bomb will explode. However, D's purpose in acting (direct intent) is for the bomb to explode and the property to be destroyed, and if this happens then it is virtually certain (and foreseen as virtually certain) that death will result. Therefore, the Law Commission's definition of intention was adapted in their later report,[117] applying where:

(a) It is [D's] purpose to cause [the result]; or

(b) although it is not [D's] purpose to cause it, he knows that it would occur in the ordinary course of events if he were to succeed in his purpose of causing some other result.

Under the new definition, D in the previous example would satisfy an intention to kill. It is not D's purpose to kill, but she knows that death will occur in the ordinary course of events, in other words would be virtually certain, if she succeeds in her purpose (blowing up the items).

> **Assessment matters . . .**
> If an example of this kind were to arise in problem facts, it is not clear whether the courts would interpret the *Woollin* definition in line with the Law Commission's adapted approach. However, highlighting this possibility would impress examiners.

3.7.2 Subjective vs objective mens rea

As we have seen, a subjective approach to mens rea requires the prosecution to prove that D had a particular purpose or foresight at the time of acting. In contrast, an objective approach to mens rea focuses on reasonableness, asking whether a reasonable person in D's shoes would have foreseen a particular risk, and finding D culpable on that basis. As mens rea terms have developed within the common law, there has often been an apparent conflict between these two approaches. When discussing mens rea in this manner, it is important to remember that both approaches have their own advantages and disadvantages. Equally, the ideal test may well be one that incorporates elements of both.[118]

A convenient way to set out and compare the relative merits of subjective and objective approaches is to look back to our discussion of 'recklessness'.[119] It will be remembered that, following its subjective beginnings, the case of *Caldwell*[120] (and Lord Diplock in particular) redefined recklessness in an objective manner: applying where D foresaw a risk (subjective), but also where she unreasonably failed to do so (objective).

---

[117] Law Commission, *Offences Against the Person and General Principles* (No 218, 1993) cl1.

[118] Tur, 'Subjectivism and Objectivism: Towards Synthesis' in Shute, Gardner, and Horder (eds), *Action and Value in Criminal Law* (1993) 213.

[119] See **3.4.4**.

[120] [1982] AC 341.

Caldwell attracted considerable criticism because of the apparent judicial lawmaking involved, but also simply on the basis that it employed an objective approach. Sir John Smith, for example, wrote that 'the decision sets back the law concerning the mental element in criminal damage in theory to before 1861'.[121] The concern was, *and remains*, that before we are ready to convict D of a serious offence, we should be sure she has chosen to commit, or at least chosen to risk committing, that offence.[122] However, D will be reckless under *Caldwell* even where she has not made such a choice, because she has not foreseen the risk of the offence element (in this case, the risk of causing damage), it will be enough that she *should have done so*. The objection is made considerably stronger when we realise that D will be reckless under this definition even in cases where it would be impossible for her to have lived up to that reasonable standard. For example, if a blind D were to walk into and damage another's property, she will be (objectively) reckless as to that damage as long as a reasonable (sighted) person would have foreseen the risk of causing damage.[123] D is liable for a criminal offence despite not choosing to commit it; not choosing to risk it; on the basis of a reasonableness standard that was impossible for her to meet.

Criticism of *Caldwell* and the objective test led directly to it being overruled by the House of Lords in *G*,[124] with the law reverting to the old subjective test: D will only be reckless when she has foreseen the risk (in this case, of causing damage). However, the obvious problems with the purely objective test should not imply that a purely subjective one is necessarily the perfect answer. For example, what about D who damages the property of another and does not foresee the risk of damage because she could not care less about the risk to others, or because she was angry? In such cases, D may not have consciously chosen to risk the offence, but the reason for this lack of choice is in great measure D's own fault.[125] These criticisms are further strengthened by recognition that in *some* circumstances, the current law will find recklessness despite D not foreseeing the risk in the conventional sense, as for example when D is intoxicated, or when the court says D must have foreseen the risk 'in the back of her mind'.[126] If these exceptions are allowed, why not also allow recklessness where D failed to foresee a risk because of her selfishness and lack of concern for others?

Much of the current academic work in this area is not promoting complete subjectivism or complete objectivism, but rather looking for compromise approaches between them. For example, allowing recklessness to be found in cases where D has not foreseen a risk, but only if this lack of foresight was something D could be blamed for. In this manner, the blind D who causes damage will not be measured against the standard of the reasonable sighted person. However, on the other hand, D who does not care about others will not be able to rely on her callous attitude to avoid liability either.[127]

---

[121] Smith, 'Comment on *Caldwell*' [1981] Crim LR 393.

[122] For discussion of the principle of autonomy, see **1.4.3**.

[123] See *Elliott* [1983] 1 WLR 939, at **3.4.4.1**.

[124] [2003] UKHL 50.

[125] Even on the facts of *G*, the majority of the general public would support liability being found. Keating, 'Reckless Children' [2006] Crim LR 546.

[126] See **3.4.4**.

[127] See Ben-David, 'Cognitive Void in Relation to Attendant Circumstances as Subjective Mens Rea' [2015] New Crim LR 418; Lacy, 'Responsibility Without Consciousness' (2016) 36 OJLS 219; Duff, *Intention, Agency and the Criminal Law* (1990); Tadros, 'Recklessness and the Duty to Take Care' in Shute and Simester (eds), *Criminal Law Theory* (2002) 248.

3.8 Eye on assessment

This section sketches a structure for analysing the mens rea of an offence when applying the law in a problem-type question. Drawing on the structure outlined at the end of **Chapter 1**, we are focusing on the second part of Step 3.

> **STEP 1 Identify the potential criminal event in the facts**
>
> This should be simply stated (eg 'The first potential criminal event arises where D kicks V'). The role of this stage is to highlight which part of the question you are answering before you begin to apply the law.

> **STEP 2 Identify the potential offence**
>
> Again, state this simply (eg 'When breaking the vase, D may be liable for criminal damage'). The role of this stage is to highlight which offence you are going to apply.

> **STEP 3 Applying the offence to the facts**
>
> Having highlighted a possible offence, Step 3 requires you to both identify the actus reus and mens rea of that offence, *and* apply them to the facts.

Step 3 is where the bulk of your analysis will take place within a problem question (although Steps 1 and 2 should not be forgotten).

Step 3 includes the identification and application of both actus reus elements and mens rea elements. As we discussed in **Chapter 2**, this should always begin with the actus reus elements, ensuring that your analysis answers two core questions.

(1) What is the actus reus of the potential offence?

(2) Did D complete the actus reus (did she do it)?

If you conclude that D has *not* completed the actus reus of the offence, there is no need to continue to discuss mens rea elements: if there is no actus reus then there is no crime. However, if you conclude that D has completed the actus reus, or (*as is more likely in a problem question*) if you conclude that D is likely to satisfy the actus reus elements, then it is correct to move on to discuss mens rea. Again, your analysis should focus on two core questions.

(1) What is the mens rea of the potential offence?

(2) Did D have that mens rea at the point in time of her relevant conduct?

The answer to these questions will vary between offences (question 1) and between factual scenarios (question 2). The answer to the first question will be discussed in relation to each offence covered in this book: gleaned from a combination of statutory and common law sources. However, the structure of application (question 2) is common between offences and can be usefully introduced at this point. It involves the stages of analysis set out in **Table 3.9**.

Table 3.9 Applying mens rea to problem facts

Mens rea	
A) Mens rea as to the conduct element?	As we discussed earlier (*almost*) all offences require D's acts to be voluntary.[128] Thus, you must always consider whether, at the point of acting, D was in control of her movements or lack of movements.
	Although this must be considered, you do not always have to discuss it in your answer. There is a common law presumption that D's acts are voluntary. Thus, although voluntariness is a requirement for liability, and although you should always consider this (keep it in mind) when applying the law, you do not need to discuss it in your answer unless there is some indication in the facts that D's acts were not voluntary. Where this is the case, you will discuss it through the rules of automatism.[129]
B) Mens rea as to the circumstance element?	All offences (conduct and result crimes) include circumstance elements (eg that the property belongs to another for criminal damage). Examine the offence to see if these requirements must be intended; be known; believed; foreseen; or if any mens rea is required.
	If the mens rea is obviously satisfied on the case facts then do not dwell on it, simply say that it is likely to be present and move on. For example, if D stabs and kills V, it is unlikely that you need a lengthy discussion about whether D *knew* V was a person. However, if the issue is not straightforward, discuss it.
C) Mens rea as to the result element?	Only result crimes will include a result element (eg that D's acts must cause death for murder). Where such an element of the actus reus is present, examine the offence to see if it must be intended; be known; believed; foreseen; or if any mens rea is required.
	As with mens rea as to circumstances, make sure you discuss the facts of the problem to see if the required mens rea is satisfied. If it is obviously satisfied, then highlight this briefly; if it is not obviously satisfied, then discuss what is likely.
D) Ulterior mens rea?	Only certain offences will include an ulterior mens rea requirement (eg the intention to permanently deprive for theft). As above, make sure you clearly identify what mens rea term is required (intention, etc), and then apply it to the facts.

Although we have set out the table using element analysis (separating acts, circumstances, and results), this is not necessary within your answer. For example, when discussing murder, it is more common to talk generally of a mens rea of 'intention to kill or cause serious harm to a person' than it is to separate mens rea as to the unlawful killing (result) from mens rea as to the fact V is a person (circumstance). Discussing mens rea

[128] See **3.3**.
[129] **Chapter 13.**

in such general terms is perfectly acceptable (*and often more straightforward*), but you must still remember to cover every mens rea requirement within the offence: D only commits the offence if every element is satisfied. With this in mind, it can be useful to employ the language of element analysis to pinpoint certain elements for particular comment (eg if D intended to kill but did not think she was unlawfully killing a person), and it can also be useful to have it in the back of your mind as a checklist to make sure you have not left anything out.

Three final points should be noted:

- **Liability requires D to complete every element of the offence:** As with actus reus elements, if *any* element of the mens rea is or may be missing then D has not committed the offence. You may then consider if D has committed an alternative (lesser) offence.

- **Don't be afraid of the unknown:** Problem question facts are often incomplete. Particularly when applying the mens rea terms, you will often find that you are unsure if D satisfies the term or not. A common mistake students make is to pretend they are sure—stating that intention, for example, is clearly satisfied or clearly absent. In such a case, where it is not clear, this is wrong. It is much better to talk of likelihoods, particularly when predicting if a jury will find mens rea or not. Thus, unless you are very sure (eg the facts say that D intends or does not intend) then discuss whether mens rea will be proved in terms of what you think is more likely and why.

- **Intention (again):** This is a repetition from the discussion of intention, but it relates to a common mistake and so it is worth repeating. If the mens rea of an offence requires D to intend, always begin your discussion with direct intention (ie was it D's purpose or desire). Only if this is not found should you then consider oblique intention (ie was it foreseen as a virtual certainty) as a backup alternative definition.

 ONLINE RESOURCE CENTRE

www.oxfordtextbooks.co.uk/orc/sho/

This chapter is accompanied by a selection of online resources to help you with this topic, including:

- **Multiple-choice questions**
- **Chapter summary sheet**
- Two **sample examination questions** with answer guidance
- **Further reading**

Also available on the Online Resource Centre are:

- A selection of **videos** from the authors explaining key topics and principles
- **Legal updates**
- Useful **weblinks**

4

Interaction of actus reus
and mens rea

4.1 Introduction **126**
4.2 Interaction within the structure of an offence **127**
    4.2.1 Exceptions to the correspondence principle **128**
4.3 Interaction within the application of an offence **132**
    4.3.1 Actus reus and mens rea directed at different objects: transferred malice **133**
    4.3.2 Actus reus and mens rea at different times: coincidence principle **136**
4.4 Reform **141**
4.5 Eye on assessment **143**
    4.5.1 Offence content **143**
    4.5.2 Offence application **143**

4.1 Introduction

In **Chapters 2** and **3** we discussed actus reus (external requirements) and mens rea (internal/fault requirements) as largely separate concerns. However, although it is useful to discuss the law in these terms, it is important to remember that criminal liability can only be found when these two requirements are proved together in relation to the same offence. This is illustrated in **Figure 4.1**.

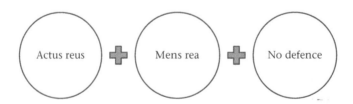

Figure 4.1 Elements of criminal liability

In this chapter, our aim is to provide some more detail about this structure, bringing together the interaction of actus reus and mens rea.

We consider the interaction of actus reus and mens rea elements in two separate contexts. First, it is important to understand how actus reus and mens rea elements relate to one another *within the structure of an offence*. We introduced this issue at the start of **Chapter 2**, but some more detail will be useful. Secondly, interaction issues also emerge when applying offence requirements to a set of problem facts. In this second context, we focus in particular on cases where actus reus and mens rea elements appear to be satisfied, but they do not take place at the same time and/or are not focused on the same target. We discuss each in turn.

4.2 Interaction within the structure of an offence

When identifying actus reus and mens rea elements within an offence, it is useful to remember how these elements interact with one another. We are looking for mens rea elements that *correspond* with elements within the actus reus.

The correspondence principle is the name given to the basic idea that each element within the actus reus of an offence should have a mens rea element that corresponds/couples with it. For example, the offence of criminal damage requires D to cause damage (actus reus) and intend or be reckless as to causing damage (mens rea).[1] From the actus reus point of view, the corresponding mens rea (intention or recklessness) provides a justification for holding D responsible for the damage: she has not only caused damage, but has (at least) chosen to risk unjustifiably doing so. Such correspondence is also essential to our understanding of mens rea. As highlighted in **Chapter 3**, it is nonsense to inquire if D intends or is reckless in the abstract; we need to know the corresponding element of the actus reus. Our question is not 'is D intending or reckless', but 'is D intending or reckless as to causing damage to property belonging to another'.[2]

When discussing an offence, it is therefore useful to think about the required correspondence of actus reus and mens rea within each offence element. For example, criminal damage is set out in **Table 4.1**.

Table 4.1 Corresponding offence elements (eg criminal damage)

	Actus reus	**Mens rea**
Conduct element	Any act (or omission) that causes the result	Voluntary
Circumstance element	The property damaged belongs to another	Intention or recklessness
Result element	Damage	Intention or recklessness

[1] Criminal Damage Act 1971, s1.
[2] See **3.2**.

As we can see, for this offence every element (conduct, circumstance, and result) includes an actus reus requirement and a corresponding mens rea requirement.

4.2.1 Exceptions to the correspondence principle

The correspondence principle does not represent an absolute rule of offence construction. Exceptions arise in two forms. First, an offence may contain actus reus elements without corresponding mens rea elements. These are called strict liability elements, arising most commonly within strict liability offences and constructive liability offences. Secondly, an offence may contain mens rea elements without corresponding actus reus elements. These elements are called ulterior mens rea elements. Both are common within the current law, but remain controversial.

4.2.1.1 Actus reus without corresponding mens rea: strict liability

We discussed strict liability[3] in **Chapter 3** to mean, simply, an absence of corresponding mens rea.[4] Where an offence contains elements of strict liability—that is, where there are actus reus elements without corresponding mens rea—that offence can be seen as contrary to the correspondence principle.

Strict liability is a label that you will find used in three main contexts. First, where an offence requires no mens rea beyond voluntary movement, it is referred to as a 'strict liability offence'. Secondly, where an offence requires mens rea for each element apart from one, this element (where no mens rea is required) is referred to as a 'strict liability element'. Thirdly, in the context of 'constructive offences', offences that include a basic offence with full actus reus and corresponding mens rea, but also include an additional actus reus element alone which is *constructed* on the basic offence to make a more serious crime.

Strict liability offences

Strict liability offences require no mens rea beyond voluntariness as to the conduct element. An example is the offence of driving when over the prescribed alcohol limit, set out in **Table 4.2**.[5]

Table 4.2 Strict liability offences (eg Road Traffic Act 1988, s5)

	Actus reus	**Mens rea**
Conduct element	Movement required to drive, attempt to drive or be in charge of vehicle	Voluntary
Circumstance element	Being in a 'motor vehicle'; being on a road or in a public place; being over the prescribed alcohol limit	None

[3] See generally Simester (ed), *Appraising Strict Liability* (2005).
[4] See **3.2.1**.
[5] Road Traffic Act 1988, s5.

Strict liability offences are controversial because they criminalise D for acting in circumstances (and sometimes causing results) without proof that D *chose* them. D need not intend them, foresee them, or even negligently miss them. For example, D would commit the driving offence in **Table 4.2** even if she did not realise that she was over the alcohol limit when driving, and even if she was not negligent as, for example, where her drink was spiked. As long as her actions satisfy the actus reus, and as long as she satisfies the basic mens rea of being voluntary in her movements, she has committed the offence.

Strict liability elements

It is common to find offences that require mens rea as to certain elements, but not to others. Where no mens rea is required to a certain element, this is commonly referred to as a strict liability element. An example is the offence of causing a child (V) to watch a sexual act, set out in **Table 4.3**.[6]

Table 4.3 Strict liability elements (eg Sexual Offences Act 2003, s12)

	Actus reus	Mens rea
Conduct element	Any act (or omission) that causes the result	Voluntary
Circumstance element	D is over 18 *and*	None
	(V is under 16	Lack of reasonable belief V is over 16
	or V is under 13)	None
Result element	Causing V to watch a third person engaging in a sexual activity *or* an image of sexual activity	Intention
Ulterior mens rea	*	Intention to gain sexual gratification

This offence provides a useful example because it includes several mens rea requirements: D's acts must be *voluntary*; she must *intend* the result element—to cause V to view sexual activity; and she must intend an ulterior mens rea requirement—to gain sexual gratification. Moreover, if V is between 13 and 16, D must also have mens rea as to this circumstance element. However, if V is under 13, the statute is clear that mens rea as to this element is strict: it is irrelevant if D intended V to be under 13; foresaw that as a risk; should have foreseen it; or had no way of knowing.

Offences of this kind where liability is strict as to one element are generally less controversial than strict liability offences, where no mens rea is required as to circumstances *and* results, but they remain problematic. After all, D is still being blamed and criminalised without choosing to cause or even risk an essential part of the actus reus.

[6] Sexual Offences Act 2003, s12.

Constructive liability offences

Constructive liability offences have an interesting and unique offence structure. At their base is a full offence that includes both actus reus and corresponding mens rea elements. At this stage there is no exception to the correspondence principle. However, in addition to this base offence, constructive crimes also include additional actus reus elements, usually in the form of result elements, that construct upon the base offence to make a more serious crime. These additional constructing elements have no corresponding mens rea, they are strict liability elements. Thus, if D satisfies the elements of the base offence, and the additional actus reus element, she becomes liable for the constructive and more serious offence.

Probably the most famous constructive crime is murder.[7] Murder is committed as a constructive offence where D intentionally causes serious harm to V (base offence), and V dies as a result (additional actus reus). This is set out in **Table 4.4**.

Table 4.4 Murder and constructive liability

	Actus reus	Mens rea
Conduct element	Any act (or omission) that causes the result	Voluntary
Circumstance element	V is a person under the Queen's peace	Knowledge
Result element	Death of V	Intention to cause death *or* intention to cause grievous bodily harm

The *minimum* mens rea required of D relates to her voluntarily and intentionally causing grievous bodily harm to a person. If D acted in line with this intention (intentionally causing grievous bodily harm) she would commit a serious offence against the person.[8] Constructing upon this base offence of intentionally causing grievous bodily harm, the offence of murder also requires an additional actus reus element: that D caused death. However, this additional actus reus element does not require any additional corresponding mens rea. In effect, the grievous bodily harm offence (actus reus and mens rea) + death (additional actus reus) = murder.

> *Beware . . .*
> Although many offences include elements of strict liability, make sure that you check the case law for a particular offence to ensure that it has been interpreted in this manner. As discussed at **3.2.1.1**, the presumption of mens rea means that several offences that appear to lack mens rea requirements have been interpreted by the courts as requiring mens rea.

---

[7] See **Chapter 5**.
[8] Offences Against the Person Act, s18.

4.2.1.2 Mens rea without corresponding actus reus: ulterior mens rea

In contrast to strict or constructive liability where an offence contains actus reus elements without corresponding mens rea, ulterior mens rea describes the opposite phenomenon; mens rea elements that lack corresponding actus reus.[9] Of course, for mens rea to make sense it must still relate to something (eg we cannot understand an intention requirement without knowing *what* D must intend). However, the object of D's mens rea, what she must intend, does not form part of the actus reus and thus does not need to come about for the crime to be completed.

For example, to be liable for the offence of theft, D must appropriate the property of another (actus reus) dishonestly and with the intention to permanently deprive V of that property (mens rea).[10] Here, the requirement that D must 'intend to permanently deprive V' is an ulterior mens rea requirement. This is illustrated in **Table 4.5**.

Table 4.5 Theft and ulterior mens rea

	Actus reus	Mens rea
Conduct element	Any act (or omission) causing the result	Voluntary
Circumstance element	What is appropriated is property	Knowledge
	What is appropriated belongs to another (ie not exclusively to D)	Knowledge
	D's appropriation is objectively dishonest	Knowledge of dishonesty
Result element	Appropriation of V's property	Intention
Ulterior mens rea element	*	**Intention to permanently deprive V of the property**

The offence requirement that D must 'intend permanently to deprive V' is an ulterior mens rea element because it lacks a corresponding actus reus element: D must *intend* permanently to deprive, but whether D actually permanently deprives V of her property is irrelevant.

Ulterior mens rea requirements are relatively common in the criminal law. Some of the advantages of ulterior mens rea include:

A) **Where corresponding actus reus would be impractical:** With offences such as theft, it is obviously impractical to include an actus reus requirement that D must 'permanently deprive' V of her property: the offence could never be complete unless the

---

[9] See Horder, 'Crimes of Ulterior Intent' in Simester and Smith (eds), *Harm and Culpability* (1996) 153.

[10] Theft Act 1968, s1.

property was destroyed, because D would always have the option of returning it and thereby negativing the actus reus. However, without the mens rea requirement of an intention to permanently deprive, the offence would be too wide, criminalising non-consensual borrowing.

B) Where we wish to intervene to prevent harm: Many offences, such as the general inchoate offences of attempt, conspiracy, and assisting and encouraging, seek to criminalise D for taking steps towards committing a future offence (trying to commit it; agreeing to commit it; assisting or encouraging another to commit it) with the intention, or in some cases recklessness, that the future offence will be completed. In these cases, we do not want to wait for the future offence to be completed before we can act to criminalise D, so such offences punish D for taking steps towards the future offence (actus reus) with ulterior mens rea as to it coming about.[11]

C) Where D has already committed a certain offence, but she does so with the intention to commit another: Where this is the case, certain offences have been drafted to criminalise D for a more serious offence that takes account of her ulterior intention. For example, section 62 of the Sexual Offences Act 2003 criminalises D who commits an offence with the (ulterior) intention to commit a sexual offence. Again, this future sexual offence does not need to come about in fact, so it is not part of the actus reus, it must simply be intended.

> **Terminology . . .**
> It is important for you to understand the terminology of strict and constructive liability, and of ulterior mens rea. However, this is simply to highlight them as exceptions to the correspondence principle. Although common within the law, you will see that offences that have been constructed in these forms are often some of the most controversial.

4.3 Interaction within the application of an offence

Having explored the different ways actus reus and mens rea elements can interact within the structure of an offence, this second part of the chapter explores their interaction when applying an offence to problem facts. With problem facts, we are looking to identify a criminal event, an event in which D completes all of the actus reus and mens rea elements of an offence.

In most cases, as long as you understand the offence requirements, and as long as the facts are clear, the application stage can be quite straightforward. Your task is to work through the offence elements: if they are all satisfied then D has committed the offence; if one or more of them is missing then she has not committed the offence.

In a minority of instances, however, additional problems relating to the interaction of actus reus and mens rea will emerge. In these cases, although D completes all the actus reus and mens rea elements, the two parts do not mesh with one another. There are two main examples of this. First is the case where D's actus reus is directed at one object (eg D hits V), but her mens rea is directed at another (eg she intended to hit X). Here, the question is whether we can we use D's mens rea directed at X as sufficient mens rea

[11] **Chapter 11.**

for an offence against V. Can we bring the elements together to create a single *whole* offence? The second set of cases is where D completes the actus reus and mens rea elements of an offence, but they do not appear to coincide with one another, they come about at different times. As highlighted in **Chapters 2** and **3**, D's mens rea must correspond with the conduct element of the actus reus. However, in a case where D has possessed that mens rea, either before or after her act, is there any way we can find liability?

4.3.1 Actus reus and mens rea at different objects: transferred malice

When D completes the actus reus of an offence (eg causing damage or injury) for which mens rea is required, that mens rea must correspond with the actus reus elements (eg D must intend to cause that damage or injury). In some cases, D's mens rea will be indiscriminate. For example, D may detonate a bomb intending to kill *anyone nearby,* or set a fire intending to *cause general damage.* Where D's mens rea is indiscriminate in this way, it is straightforward to find that D's mens rea corresponds with the actus reus and satisfies the offence. If D's bomb kills V, for example, we can say that D intended to kill V because V was within the group ('anyone nearby') that D intended to kill. Equally, if V survived and V2 was killed, we can say that D intended to kill V2 as well (V2 is within the same group).

Problems can emerge, however, where D acts with a specific target in mind. For example, D may detonate a bomb intending to kill V in particular, or start a fire intending to damage specific property. Where D succeeds in her plan, then liability is straightforward. For example, D intends to kill V in particular and does so: actus reus and mens rea elements are directed at the same target. However, where D explodes the bomb intending to kill V in particular but also kills V2, or misses V and only kills V2, then we have a problem; and if D's fire spreads in an unexpected way and damages property other than that intended, we have the same problem. In these cases, we have actus reus (death and damage), and we have mens rea (intention to cause death and damage), but the targets of the two are different: D intends to kill or damage one target, but actually kills or damages another. Is D liable for an offence?

Where D's actus reus and mens rea target different objects in this manner, liability is found through the doctrine of 'transferred malice' or, more accurately, 'transferred mens rea'. Essentially, D's targeted mens rea (eg D's intention to kill a particular person or intention to damage particular property) is *transferred* to the object that was the victim of D's actus reus (eg the actual person killed or property damaged). This was discussed in *Latimer.*

 Latimer (1886) 17 QBD 359

D swung a belt at V attempting to hit him, but only caught him slightly. Missing V, the main force of the belt hit a woman (V2), who was severely injured. D had clearly committed an offence against V. However, D was charged with a more serious offence against the person in relation to V2's injuries.[12]

- Court: guilty of offence. D's malice (mens rea) directed at V could be transferred to V2, satisfying the mens rea of the offence in relation to V2.

---

[12] Offences Against the Person Act 1861, s20. See **7.5.**

In the absence of transferred malice, D would not escape liability altogether. D would still be liable, for example, for his attempt seriously to injure V. However, attempt liability alone in these circumstances would seem odd. After all, D not only tried to cause serious injury, but he did so, albeit to an unforeseen victim. It is this intuition that D deserves liability for the full offence that has given rise to the legal fiction that is transferred malice, with the court manipulating D's mens rea towards one object into a men rea towards another. With both actus reus and mens rea now focused on the same target, using transferred malice, liability can be found. This is illustrated in **Figure 4.2**.

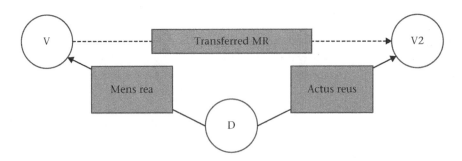

Figure 4.2 Transferred mens rea

The criminal law's rules which allow for the transfer of mens rea ensure liability by linking actus reus and mens rea elements that would otherwise lack for coincidence on a single object. This will apply for assault cases such as *Latimer*, homicide cases where D kills an unintended target,[13] as well as a host of other offences such as criminal damage where D may cause damage to an unintended target. In each case, as made clear in *Latimer*, it is not necessary for D to have foreseen harm to V2, or even for D to have been negligent in failing to foresee it. Rather, it is D's mens rea towards V that is simply transferred to bring together the elements of liability.

4.3.1.1 Limitations to the doctrine of transferred malice

There are two important limitations to the doctrine of transferred malice. First, D's mens rea can only be transferred where it relates to the same crime as her actus reus. For example, D throws a stone at V, a person, but misses and causes property damage. In this case, although D's intention to cause harm to V is hardly to her credit, an intention to hurt a person is categorically different from intention or recklessness as to property damage, and transfer of mens rea is therefore prevented.[14] The same is true where D shoots at a dog (property) in an attempt to kill it, but misses and hits its owner, V. D does not murder V because an intention to kill a dog is categorically different from an intention to kill or seriously injure a person. This is illustrated in **Figure 4.3**.

---

[13] *Mitchell* [1983] QB 741. See also *Smith and Hogan's Criminal Law* (14th edn, 2015) Ch5.
[14] *Pembliton* (1847) LR 2 CCR 119.

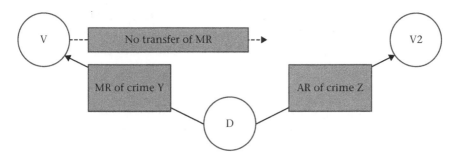

Figure 4.3 No transferred mens rea between different crimes

The second limitation to the doctrine is where liability would require a double transfer of malice. In *AG's Reference (No 3 of 1994)*,[15] D stabbed his pregnant girlfriend, V, several times with the intention required for murder. As a result of this, V gave birth prematurely to V2. V2 later died, largely as a result of the premature birth. The House of Lords rejected D's liability for the murder of V2 because such liability would require a double transfer of mens rea: from the mother, V, to her foetus, X, and then from the foetus to its changed status as a person at birth, V2.[16] This is illustrated in **Figure 4.4**.

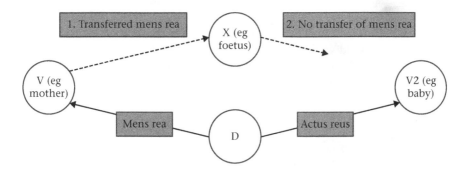

Figure 4.4 No double transfer of mens rea

Despite these two limitations, the doctrine of transferred malice remains controversial. For some, the doctrine remains too open and should be limited further. Horder has criticised the doctrine for allowing a transfer of mens rea even where the victim of the harm (V2) was unintended *and* the manner of the harm was unanticipated. For example, D shoots a gun at V1; V2, who is hiding in the bushes nearby, is startled by the noise and dies of a heart attack. Horder recommends the introduction of a 'remoteness' limitation.[17] Beyond this, others have questioned whether, given that the doctrine

---

[15] [1996] 1 Cr App R 351.

[16] D was not liable for murder. However, D was liable for manslaughter, as the offence is wide enough to be satisfied on these facts without reliance on a transfer of malice. See **Chapter 5**.

[17] Horder, 'Transferred Malice and the Remoteness of Unexpected Outcomes from Intentions' [2006] Crim LR 383. See also Eldar, 'The Limits of Transferred Malice' (2012) 32 OJLS 633.

is a legal fiction, it is necessary at all. In most cases involving transferred mens rea, it would be possible without the need for transfer to find attempt liability in relation to D's intended target, and possibly a reckless- or negligence-based offence in relation to the actual harm caused.[18]

Assessment matters . . .

Horder's article is particularly interesting here. If a case of this kind arose in problem facts (where V2 is both unintended as a victim and suffers harm in an unforeseen manner), the current law would suggest that D's mens rea towards V1 could be transferred to V2 to complete an offence. However, it may be that the court would accept Horder's approach and find a further limitation to the doctrine of transferred malice. Highlighting this possibility in your essay would be very useful.

4.3.2 Actus reus and mens rea at different times: coincidence principle

When discussing transferred malice, we highlighted the need for mens rea and actus reus to coincide, or come together, in relation to the same object (V). Beyond this, it is also essential that they should coincide at the same point in *time*—this is traditionally described as respecting the coincidence principle. For example, D forms the intention to kill her husband (V) by poisoning his food. However, when D is driving home from work someone runs in front of her car and is killed, it is V. D has not committed murder. Although D has caused V's death, which is the actus reus of murder, and she intends in general terms to kill him, she lacks the mens rea in the form of intention to kill *by this act* and *at this point in time*.

The need for temporal coincidence is the reason why our application of criminal law to problem facts should always begin with the actus reus. Once it is established that the actus reus of an offence has been completed, we can then inquire whether D possessed the mens rea for the offence *at the point in time* that she completed the conduct element of the actus reus. Whether or not she possessed the mens rea at some other point in time is irrelevant; liability demands that she must have possessed it at that particular time for liability to be established.

It is worth stressing here that we are talking about coincidence between mens rea and the *conduct element* of the actus reus (D's act or omission within the actus reus) rather than with the actus reus more generally. For example, if D laces V's food with poison with the intention to kill, and does in fact do so, she has committed murder even if she changes her mind before the poison takes effect and kills V. Indeed, she may even change her mind the split second after lacing V's food, well in advance of V ingesting the poison. As long as V's conduct is the cause of V's death, and as long as D had the required mens rea when completing that conduct, there will be coincidence and the offence will be committed.

In **Figure 4.5** the point of coincidence is represented by the vertical dotted line.

---

[18] Ashworth, 'Transferred Malice and Punishment for Unforeseen Consequences' in Glazebrook (ed), *Reshaping the Criminal Law* (1978) 77.

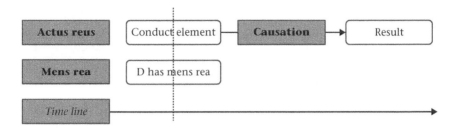

Figure 4.5 Coincidence of actus reus and mens rea

Coincidence is an absolute rule of law to which there are *no exceptions*: a lack of coincidence will mean a lack of liability. However, in rare cases where an apparent lack of coincidence is at issue, it can be very difficult to accept this conclusion. D has the mens rea for the crime at some point in time, and has completed the actus reus at some point in time, and so it can be very appealing to try to find ways around the rule. Indeed, this is what we have seen in several cases; *not* exceptions to the coincidence principle, but the courts finding often ingenious ways to identify coincidence where it looks like there is none. Such cases can be split into two categories: where actus reus seems to precede mens rea, and where mens rea seems to precede actus reus.

4.3.2.1 Actus reus and then mens rea

The first example of a potential lack of coincidence arises where D's conduct causing the result (actus reus) precedes the point in time at which D holds the required mens rea. This is illustrated in **Figure 4.6**.

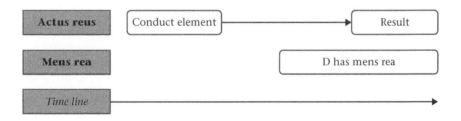

Figure 4.6 Lack of coincidence—actus reus then mens rea

Where this problem has emerged, the courts have developed two possible methods of finding coincidence.

The first, the *continuing act* approach, is exemplified in *Fagan* (see **Figure 4.7**).

 Fagan [1969] 1 QB 439

D accidentally drove his car onto a policeman's (V's) foot and, when he became aware of this, intentionally took his time moving the car in order to cause further pain. When discussing Fagan's potential liability for an offence against the person, the problem became apparent: when performing acts within the actus reus (driving onto the foot) D lacked mens rea; but when he gained mens rea (intentionally causing pain) these acts were already complete.

- Divisional Court: guilty of offence against the person. D's 'act' did not stop when driving onto the foot, but continued when on the foot. Thus, D's act did coincide with a time when he possessed the required mens rea.

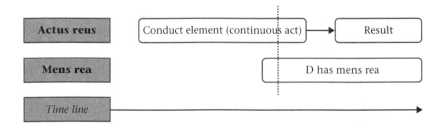

Figure 4.7 Understanding the approach in *Fagan*

By extending the conduct element, coincidence between actus reus and mens rea can be found. The courts are not creating an exception to the coincidence principle, but they are manipulating the definition of the conduct element in order to find it.

However, although the continuing act approach reaches the desired conclusion, its operation can be criticised as rather artificial. With this in mind, perhaps a better approach to the problem, as outlined in more recent case law, is to abandon a focus on D's initial acts, and to focus instead on her later omission.

The second, the *omissions approach*, is exemplified in *Miller* (see **Figure 4.8**).

  Miller [1983] 2 AC 161

D, a squatter in V's house, went to sleep holding a lit cigarette. He awoke to find he had dropped the cigarette and the mattress was smouldering, but did nothing other than move to an adjoining room. The fire caused extensive damage, and D was charged with criminal damage[19] based on his omission to tackle the smouldering mattress or alert the authorities (a duty arising from his inadvertent creation of a dangerous situation).

- Court: guilty of criminal damage.
- Court of Appeal: conviction upheld on appeal.
- House of Lords: conviction upheld on appeal.

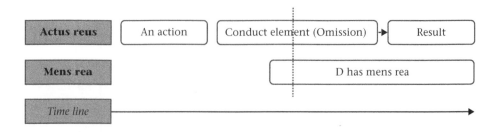

Figure 4.8 Understanding the approach in *Miller*

---

[19] Criminal Damage Act 1971, s1(1) and (3).

The fire was caused by D's positive act of dropping the cigarette. However, if the court were to focus on this act then the same coincidence problem emerges: when D acted to cause the fire he lacked mens rea as he was asleep, and when he had the mens rea (foreseeing the possibility of damage) his action was complete. Rather than trying to reinterpret and lengthen D's acts as in *Fagan*, the House of Lords instead focused on D's omission to act having become aware of the danger. As discussed in **Chapter 2**, omissions liability is only applicable where D has a duty to act. However, in this case, having created the dangerous situation and become aware of that danger, D has a clear duty to act by taking reasonable steps to prevent the harm. In failing to do so, and thereby breaching that duty, he has completed an omission that satisfies the actus reus of the offence, and has done so at a time that he possesses the requisite mens rea. Again, we have coincidence, and so we have liability.

> **Beware . . .**
> As the continuing act approach (*Fagan*) and the omissions approach (*Miller*) both provide answers to the same problem, it is tempting to think of them interchangeably. However, you should be careful not to do so. As set out previously, they are *alternatives*. It is often good to acknowledge both options, but remember that they are not the same.

4.3.2.2 Mens rea and then actus reus

The second example of a potential lack of coincidence is where D acts with the requisite mens rea for the offence, but it is her later action without mens rea that forms the actus reus of the offence. This is illustrated in **Figure 4.9**.

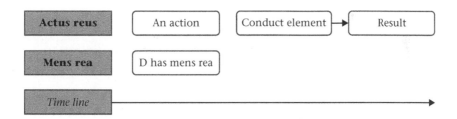

Figure 4.9 Lack of coincidence—mens rea then actus reus

Where this problem has emerged, the courts have sought to find coincidence using the *single transaction* approach. An early example of this is the Privy Council case *Thabo Meli* (see **Figure 4.10**).

 Thabo Meli [1954] 1 All ER 373

D and others hit V over the head and then, as they had planned, attempted to disguise their crime by pushing his corpse over a cliff. However, it was later discovered that V had not died from the initial blows, but rather from exposure at the bottom of the cliff. Thus, D had the mens rea for murder when striking the initial blows that did not cause death, but when completing the later act that did cause death he lacked mens rea. There was no further intention to kill because D thought V was already dead.

• Court: guilty of murder.

- Privy Council: conviction upheld on appeal. Rather than looking at each individual action separately, D's actions were better analysed as part of a general plan to cause death and to hide the body: a series of acts that could be linked within one logical transaction. Analysed in this way, since D possessed the mens rea for murder at one point during this single transaction, coincidence was found.

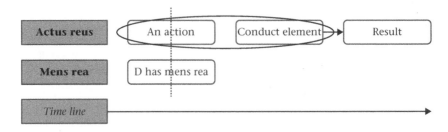

Figure 4.10 Understanding the approach in *Thabo Meli*

Within this small class of cases, where D acts with intent to kill by initial conduct but actually causes death by subsequent conduct, the transaction approach has become firmly established.

There is an appealing logic about this approach, and there is little doubt that D deserves to be found liable. However, there is also some uncertainty. Chiefly, this uncertainty relates to the basis upon which courts link D's acts within the transaction. A series of cases in **Table 4.6** set out how the courts have approached this task.

Table 4.6 Developing cases on single actus reus transactions

Case reference	Case facts	Basis for linking acts
Thabo Meli [1954] 1 All ER 373	D hit V with the intention to kill (mens rea for murder). D thought V was dead and pushed him off a cliff to make it look like an accident. D died from exposure following the fall. A single transaction links D's initial attack (with mens rea) to pushing V off the cliff (actus reus causing death).	Hitting D over the head (act 1) and pushing him off the cliff (act 2) were both part of D's single plan. Thus, they can be linked as a single transaction.
Church [1966] 1 QB 59	D fought and began to strangle V until she passed out (with mens rea for manslaughter). D thought V was dead and threw her body into a river to hide it (no mens rea as he thought she was dead). V drowned; D was convicted of manslaughter on the basis of linking his first act (with mens rea) to his second act (causing death) to find coincidence.	There was no 'plan' linking D's first act (attacking V) and second act (throwing her in the river). However, the Court of Criminal Appeal still found that they could be linked within a single transaction. It did not explain why.

Le Brun [1992] QB 61	D hit his wife (V) causing unconsciousness (with the mens rea for manslaughter). D realised that V was not dead. D dragged V home to try and cover up his offence, but dropped her accidentally and caused further head injuries from which she died. D was convicted of manslaughter on the basis of linking his first act (with mens rea) to his second act (causing death) to find coincidence.	There was no 'plan' linking D's first act (hitting V) and second act (dropping V). Also, unlike the previous cases, D did not believe V was dead. However, the Court of Appeal still found that D's acts could be linked as a single transaction on the basis that D's acts were of the same type. Thus, if D had dropped V trying to take her to a doctor, this act may not be linked with the former. However, as he was trying to conceal his crime, it could.

In light of these cases, it seems that the courts adopt a flexible approach in deciding whether D's acts can be linked within a single transaction or not. If they decide that D's acts remain of the same type, which they seem to regard in general terms as meaning they remain 'bad', then they are likely to link D's acts in order to allow for coincidence. It is only if D accidentally causes harm when later trying to help, for example, by dropping V when taking her to a hospital, that the courts are unlikely to link D's acts.

> **Extra detail . . .**
> An alternative approach to this second problem of coincidence is to focus solely on D's initial action and to establish a chain of causation from there. For example, in *Le Brun*, 'but for' D's initial attack, D would not have dragged V and she would not have died when dropped (ie D's initial action was causally connected to V's injuries). The appeal of this approach is that D's second action when dropping V (that does not coincide with mens rea) becomes irrelevant. Through the causation rules, we can say that D's first act also caused the death, and find coincidence with mens rea at this point.
>
>   This approach was discussed in *Le Brun*, but the court preferred the single transaction approach. However, were a similar case to arise in problem facts, it would be useful to highlight this as an alternative approach.[20]

4.4 Reform

In many ways, the correspondence principle remains an ideal of criminalisation: offences should consist of harmful behaviour (actus reus) that D has chosen to bring about, or risk bringing about (mens rea).[21] To the extent that this is true, the topics discussed earlier represent at least partial failures to meet that ideal:

- Through offence definitions:
  - ▷ strict and constructive liability—offences containing actus reus elements without corresponding mens rea;

[20] Arenson, '*Thabo Meli* Revisited: The Pernicious Effects of Result-Driven Decisions' (2013) 77 J Crim L 41.

[21] Horder, 'A Critique of the Correspondence Principle' [1995] Crim LR 759; Mitchell, 'In Defence of a Principle of Correspondence' [1999] Crim LR 195.

    ▷ ulterior mens rea—offences containing mens rea elements without corresponding actus reus.

- Through the application of offences:
  - ▷ transferred malice—finding liability even though D's actus reus and mens rea were targeted at different objects;
  - ▷ coincidence—finding liability even though D's actus reus and mens rea, as ordinarily understood, occurred at different times.

With this in mind, it is unsurprising that each of these areas has given rise to considerable debate, a debate that is often picked up in essay questions. Such debates have already been highlighted within our previous discussion of the law, and we do not propose to repeat them. However, when thinking about potential reform in this area, it is useful to structure your thinking, and possibly your essay, by separating two importantly distinct questions.

- Do we want liability in these circumstances at all?

This is what we might call a threshold question. If we agree that offences *should only* be committed where D demonstrates both guilty act and guilty mind, and that these should focus on the same object and occur at the same time, are we willing to tolerate any exceptions? For example, in the context of constructive liability, if D's acts cause an additional harm, for example death, should we define offences to punish D for this even if she only foresaw causing a lesser harm?[22] In the context of transferred malice, where D hits V2 when intending to hit V1, should we allow a rule that artificially transfers the mens rea from V1 to V2, or should we reject it? In this latter example, such rejection seems even more appealing when we could still charge D with an attempt offence in relation to V1, and possibly a reckless- or negligence-based offence in relation to V2.[23]

- If we do want liability in these circumstances, what is the least objectionable way to secure it?

This question is based on an acceptance that (in certain cases) constructive and strict liability, ulterior mens rea, transferred malice, or the stretching of coincidence can be acceptable. In the context of strict liability, constructive crimes, and ulterior mens rea, the debate then becomes how *widely* the practice should be available. Are such offences acceptable generally, or are they only acceptable in certain exceptional circumstances, for example to combat particularly serious harms,[24] or only where finding mens rea is particularly difficult?[25] In the context of transferred malice and coincidence, the same question arises: if these techniques can be used, where should we place the limits (eg the

---

[22] Several jurisdictions repealed offences of constructive liability. Eg the Republic of Ireland reform of the offences against the person: Non-Fatal Offences Against the Person Act 1997. The Law Commission of England and Wales has made similar recommendations for the reform of offences against the person (see **Chapter 7**).

[23] Ashworth, 'Transferred Malice and Punishment for Unforeseen Consequences' in Glazebrook (ed), *Reshaping the Criminal Law* (1978) 77.

[24] This is often a justification for punishing ulterior harmful intentions before any corresponding action is completed. See **Chapter 11**.

[25] This is often the justification for regulatory offences (especially those targeting companies) being strict. See **Chapter 3**.

additional restrictions to transferred malice suggested by Horder[26])? However, in addition to this, transferred malice and coincidence also raise issues of *method*: how are we to make sense of mens rea transfers, and how can we find coincidence when it appears to be absent? This second issue is also discussed earlier, and particularly in the context of coincidence where the common law seems to have developed multiple and alternative methods for addressing the same problem. Again, here your task is to discuss these methods and comment on which, if any, you believe is the most appropriate.

4.5 Eye on assessment

This section focuses on problem-type questions, and how the topics discussed previously should be structured into your answers. To do so we need to distinguish between those topics relating to the elements of an offence (strict, constructive liability, and ulterior mens rea), and those relating to the application of an offence (transferred malice and coincidence).

4.5.1 Offence content

The content of an offence provides you with the offence elements of actus reus and mens rea that you must apply in a problem question. Whether the offence is one that contains elements of strict liability or ulterior mens rea may therefore be useful to highlight in order to explain why it is not necessary to identify certain corresponding mens rea in the context of strict liability, or actus reus in the context of ulterior mens rea. However, unless the question specifically asks you to evaluate or discuss the law as you apply it, there is no need to enter a debate about the rights and wrongs of the offence. In most cases, you are asked to 'discuss potential liability', not to 'discuss the merits of the law'.

4.5.2 Offence application

The rules relating to coincidence of actus reus and mens rea, that is coincidence on the same object and at the same time, are essential to the application of the law. They are therefore essential considerations within all problem questions. However, although essential, it is relatively rare that a problem question, *and very rare that a real case* will involve problems in this area. The ideal approach to a problem question will therefore be to ensure coincidence, but not to waste unnecessary time discussing it unless such discussion is required.

As with **Chapters 2** and **3**, we are focusing on the third step of the problem question structure introduced in **Chapter 1**.

> **STEP 1 Identify the potential criminal event in the facts**
>
> This should be simply stated (eg 'The first potential criminal event arises where D kicks V'). The role of this stage is to highlight which part of the question you are answering before you begin to apply the law.

[26] See **4.3.1.1.**

> **STEP 2** **Identify the potential offence**
>
> Again, state this simply (eg 'When breaking the vase, D may be liable for criminal damage'). The role of this stage is to highlight which offence you are going to apply.

> **STEP 3** **Applying the offence to the facts**
>
> Having highlighted a possible offence, Step 3 requires you to both identify the actus reus and mens rea of that offence, *and* apply them to the facts.

As discussed in **Chapter 2**, your analysis within Step 3 should always begin with the actus reus elements of the offence. Identify the act/omission that D has completed, the relevant circumstances, and where necessary the unlawful results of those acts. Remember, where the actus reus does specify results, you must also show that D's acts *caused* those results.

Having examined the actus reus of the offence, you now know the point in time that D completed the relevant acts/omissions. Thus, when moving to mens rea (discussed in **Chapter 3**) you can ask more precisely whether D satisfies the mens rea at the *time* she completes the conduct element and whether it was *directed* at the relevant object.

The issues discussed in this chapter should be considered when applying mens rea elements. There are two possibilities:

- If D satisfies the mens rea at that time and directed at that object: There is no problem with coincidence. You do not need to say more on the topic: by explicitly identifying the mens rea at that relevant time and directed at that relevant object you have already demonstrated that coincidence is present.

- If D does not satisfy the mens rea at that time and directed at that object: There is a problem with coincidence. You can now highlight the problem; moving on to a full discussion of transferred malice and/or the reinterpretation of acts in order to see if coincidence can be found.

 ONLINE RESOURCE CENTRE

www.oxfordtextbooks.co.uk/orc/sho/

This chapter is accompanied by a selection of online resources to help you with this topic, including:

- **Multiple-choice questions**
- **Chapter summary sheet**
- Two **sample examination questions** with answer guidance
- **Further reading**

Also available on the Online Resource Centre are:

- A selection of **videos** from the authors explaining key topics and principles
- **Legal updates**
- Useful **weblinks**

5

Murder

5.1 Introduction   **145**

5.2 Defining murder   **146**

5.3 Actus reus of murder   **148**

    5.3.1 Acts and omissions   **148**

    5.3.2 Necessary circumstances   **148**

    5.3.3 Causing death   **150**

5.4 Mens rea of murder   **151**

    5.4.1 Other mens rea requirements   **153**

5.5 Defences to murder   **153**

    5.5.1 General defences   **153**

    5.5.2 Doctors and the treatment of terminally ill patients   **153**

    5.5.3 Partial defences   **155**

5.6 Reform   **155**

    5.6.1 Reforming the mandatory life sentence   **156**

    5.6.2 Reforming the mens rea of murder   **157**

5.7 Eye on assessment   **158**

5.1 Introduction

From this point in the book our focus narrows from the general principles and structures of criminal law, to explore particular offences and defences. We begin with a category of crimes known as homicide offences in general (offences which involve the killing of a person), and with the offence of murder in particular.

> *Terminology . . .*
> When we refer to categories of offences such as 'homicide offences', we are not referring to an offence with a distinct actus reus and mens rea. Rather, we are simply referring to a label that describes a group of offences that share certain characteristics (other categories include, eg, sexual offences; property offences; etc). It is not accurate to say D is liable for homicide. Rather, if liability is found, D is liable for a homicide offence such as murder or manslaughter.

D commits murder where she, a person,[1] unlawfully causes the death of V, also a person, with the intention to kill or cause grievous (serious) bodily harm (GBH). Murder is generally considered the most serious crime. The harm involved does not simply affect the interests of V, but undermines V's potential to experience any future 'worldly' interests of any kind. Even within the law's class of 'homicide' offences, murder is distinguished as most serious by the requirement of proof of intent: D has not simply killed V, she has done so *intending* to kill or cause GBH. It is because of its gravity as an offence that murder was until relatively recently punished with the death penalty,[2] and currently attracts a mandatory life sentence.

> **Don't be confused . . .**
> A mandatory life sentence will rarely equate to a lifetime in prison. Rather, a life sentence is made up of a tariff period (ie a minimum period in prison reflecting the circumstances of the killing), followed by a release on licence during which time D is released from prison but is monitored and may be restricted in various ways.[3] The sentence is a 'life sentence' because the licence-period restrictions continue for the life of D. The typical tariff period for a single murder in unexceptional circumstances is 15 years' imprisonment.

Despite the perceived position of murder at the apex of criminal law, it remains a problematic and controversial offence. Indeed, the Law Commission has described it as a 'rickety structure set upon shaky foundations'.[4] This is both a criticism of the offence itself, discussed in this chapter, as well as a criticism of its position and definition in the context of the other homicide offences (discussed in **Chapter 6**).

5.2 Defining murder

The Homicide Act 1957, the Coroners and Justice Act 2009 and the Corporate Manslaughter and Corporate Homicide Act 2007, have put on a statutory footing several offences and defences within the wider group of homicide offences. Crucially, however, the offence of murder remains a common law offence.

The definition of murder still quoted widely by the courts derives from a seventeenth-century book by Coke:[5]

> Murder is when a man of sound memory, and of the age of discretion, unlawfully killeth within any country of the realm any reasonable creature *in rerum natura* under the king's peace, with malice aforethought, either expressed by the party or implied by law, so as the party wounded, or hurt, etc die of that wound or hurt, etc within a year and a day after the same.

---

[1] Murder cannot be committed by a corporation or other organisation. See **Chapter 6** for the possibility of corporate manslaughter.

[2] Homicide Act 1957 marked the end of a mandatory death sentence for all convicted murderers.

[3] Criminal Justice Act 2003, Sch 21. See Padfield, 'Tariffs in Murder' [2002] Crim LR 192.

[4] Law Commission, *A New Homicide Act for England and Wales* (Consultation 177, 2005) para 1.4.

[5] 3 Inst 47. See also *Smith and Hogan's Criminal Law* (14th edn, 2015) Ch14.

Despite its continued application, the archaic and increasingly inaccurate definition contained in this quotation should not be applied straightforwardly in a modern context. Rather, although it establishes authority for the offence of murder, a contemporary translation and clarification of the offence elements is essential.

In modern language, the offence of murder requires D unlawfully to kill another person under the Queen's peace, and to do so intending to kill or cause GBH (serious bodily harm). The elements of murder are set out in **Table 5.1**.

Table 5.1 Murder

	Actus reus	**Mens rea**
Conduct element	Any conduct that causes the result	Voluntary
Circumstance element	V must be a person; under the Queen's peace; killing must be unlawful	Knowledge Knowledge Lack of belief in lawfulness
Result element	Death of V	Intention to kill or cause GBH

This represents the current definition of murder: modernising the language from Coke's definition and also recognising important changes within the law. For example, contrary to Coke, the modern definition of murder does not include a requirement for V's death to follow 'within a year and a day' of D's conduct. This requirement made some sense historically where a delay of this kind would make it almost impossible to demonstrate a causal link from V's death back to D's original conduct. However, with advances in medical science, not only has demonstrating such a causal link become easier, but the likelihood of delay before death has also increased through the use of life-support machines, etc. The rule was abolished by the Law Reform (Year and a Day Rule) Act 1996.[6] The present position is that as long as causation can be established, D may now be liable for murder regardless of the delay between her original conduct and the death of V. The only remaining restriction is that where there is considerable delay between D's conduct and V's death (over three years), or where D has already been prosecuted for a non-fatal offence relating to the same incident, the Attorney General must consent to the murder prosecution.[7]

Despite the seriousness of murder as a crime, it is important to recognise that cases caught within the definition will not always be morally straightforward. As with other offences, where D satisfies the actus reus and mens rea elements she is liable irrespective of her motive.[8] Thus, murder is committed where D kills due to hatred or spite, but it is also committed in more morally ambiguous cases such as so-called 'mercy killings'

---

[6] Yale, 'A Year and a Day in Homicide' (1989) 48 CLJ 202.
[7] Law Reform (Year and a Day Rule) Act 1996, s2.
[8] The only exception is where D's reasons/motives satisfy the elements of a criminal defence.

where D intentionally kills, often with V's consent, in order to relieve V's pain or suffering. The moral diversity of these cases is useful to keep in mind when discussing the precise requirements of the offence. It is also something that we will return to when we consider potential reforms in this area, not least the continued application of a mandatory life sentence to all murder cases.[9]

5.3 Actus reus of murder

The actus reus of murder is satisfied where D unlawfully kills another person under the Queen's peace. We discuss each element in turn.

5.3.1 Acts and omissions

As with other result crimes[10] murder does not specify particular conduct that D must perform (eg shooting, stabbing, etc), but rather proscribes the result, irrespective of what form of conduct caused that result—death. Thus, it is necessary to identify some conduct by D, but, as long as it causes the result, the type of conduct is irrelevant. D may also commit murder by omission, as in *Gibbins and Proctor*, as long as the requirements of omissions liability are satisfied.[11]

 Gibbins and Proctor (1918) 13 Cr App R 134

D1 (Gibbins) and his lover D2 (Proctor) failed to feed D1's 7-year-old child (V), resulting in V's death. D1 and D2 acted with an intention to (at least) cause serious bodily harm to V.

- Crown Court: D1 and D2 convicted for murder.
- Court of Criminal Appeal: conviction upheld on appeal. D1 liable for his omission to feed based on a familial duty owed to V; D2 based on her assumption of a duty (she was in charge of buying food).

5.3.2 Necessary circumstances

The actus reus of murder also requires proof of several circumstances that must be present for D to be liable. In most cases these will be clear, and very little discussion will be required. However, problem cases can arise.

5.3.2.1 Under the Queen's peace

Where soldiers kill alien enemies 'in the heat of war, and in actual exercise thereof',[12] the killing is not under the Queen's peace and is not, therefore, murder. This exception is important, particularly as section 9 of the Offences Against the Person Act 1861 makes any murder or manslaughter committed by a British citizen, *committed on any land outside the UK*, an offence that can be tried and punished in England. It is, however,

---

[9] See **5.6.1**.
[10] For discussion of 'result crimes', see **2.4.2**.
[11] See **2.6**.
[12] Hale, *The History of the Pleas of the Crown* (1736), vol I, 443.

a narrow exception. Where a soldier kills another, even an alien enemy in a war zone, and it is *not* done in the heat of battle, this will be considered as having been committed under the Queen's peace and D will satisfy the actus reus of murder.[13]

5.3.2.2 Unlawful killing

To say that the killing must be 'unlawful' is simply to stress that it must satisfy all actus reus and mens rea elements, and be done without lawful defence. Thus, for example, where D kills in self-defence, she is not liable for murder.[14]

> *Point to remember . . .*
> As we will see in **Chapter 14**, some defences do not apply to murder (eg duress and duress of circumstance).

5.3.2.3 V must be a person

For murder, as with other homicide offences; offences against the person; etc, the victim must be a human being. This sounds straightforward, and in the vast majority of cases it will be. However, particularly in relation to homicide offences, the status of the victim as a person will occasionally require discussion. This discussion focuses on two questions: when does life as a human being begin? And when does this status end?

A) **When does V begin to be a person:** An unborn child (foetus) is not a person within the criminal law. Thus, where D kills an unborn child she may commit an offence of child destruction or procuring a miscarriage,[15] but she cannot commit murder. In law, V only becomes a person when she is 'fully expelled from the womb' and alive.[16] Whether the umbilical cord and/or afterbirth have been expelled is irrelevant, as long as the whole of the baby's body is removed.[17] This position may be criticised in purely biological terms, the difference between a late-term foetus and a neonate is only (as Simester and Sullivan put it) a matter of location.[18] However, it is a divide that has rarely troubled the courts,[19] and the exclusion of murder from prenatal deaths is useful to allow for specific offences that can be tailored to the unique issues that arise in this area and avoid conflict with legal abortive procedures. Despite Article 2 ECHR protecting the right to life, the ECtHR has left the issue of when life begins to Member States' margin of appreciation.[20]

The focus on birth gives rise to a notable issue: prenatal harms that cause postnatal death. Where D harms a foetus that is subsequently born alive, but then dies as a result of those injuries, D has caused the death of what is a person at the time of death. Courts have long accepted that such cases satisfy the actus reus of murder,[21] although,

---

[13] Hirst, 'Murder Under the Queen's Peace' [2008] Crim LR 541; Rowe, 'The Criminal Liability of a British Soldier Merely for Participating in the Iraq War' [2010] Crim LR 752.

[14] See **5.5**.

[15] Infant Life (Preservation) Act 1929, s1 or Offences Against the Person Act 1861, s58.

[16] *Poulton* (1832) 5 C & P 329.

[17] *Reeves* (1839) 9 C & P 25.

[18] Simester et al, *Simester and Sullivan's Criminal Law: Theory and Doctrine* (6th edn, 2016) 373.

[19] The Criminal Law Revision Committee identified the last case where this was directly relevant to have been in 1874: *Handley* (1874) 13 Cox CC 79.

[20] *Vo v France* [2004] 2 FCR 577; O'Donovan, 'Taking a Neutral Stance on the Protection of the Foetus' (2006) 14 Med L Rev 115.

[21] *Senior* (1832) 1 Mood CC 346.

interestingly, this has not been applied to cases where D injures her own foetus through neglect.[22]

> **Don't be confused . . .**
>
> Where prenatal harm causes postnatal death, the actus reus of murder is satisfied. However, mens rea will often be problematic. Where D acts with the intent to seriously injure or kill the foetus, this is not the mens rea for murder (not an intent to seriously injure or kill a *person*). Additionally, where D intends to seriously injure or kill the mother, a transfer of malice to the baby is ruled out by the double transaction (from the mother to the foetus to the baby).[23] Murder, as opposed to manslaughter, will only be available in cases of this kind where D intends the foetus to be killed or seriously injured after being born alive. This will be extremely rare.

B) **When does life end for the purposes of the offence:** As a result of medical advances, the stage where life comes to an end, so there is no 'person' to kill, can also be problematic. There is no authoritative definition of death within the criminal law, but courts will often refer to medical definitions to assist them. In this regard, it is clear that death should not always be assumed where V stops breathing, or even where V's heart stops, as such occurrences can, if treated in good time, often be reversed.

However, the problem becomes acute where V's body can be kept 'alive' by medical means despite little or even no chance of recovery. In such cases, V will be considered medically dead at the point of 'brain death' (complete and irreversible non-functioning of the brain stem), and this status has been accepted by the House of Lords in *Bland*.[24] Where V's condition falls short of brain death, for example a persistent vegetative state; a profound and permanent coma; etc, V will not be considered dead and therefore remains a 'person' capable of being murdered.

5.3.3 Causing death

To complete the actus reus of murder, D's act or omission must *cause* V's death. This requires application of the general rules of factual and legal causation discussed at **2.7**. There is no need to repeat that discussion here.

One issue that should be highlighted, however, is that 'causing death' will include any 'acceleration of death'. For example, the killing of a terminally ill patient or someone who, for whatever reason, has only a short time to live, will still satisfy the actus reus of murder. As death will come to us all at some point, the act of 'causing death' must be logically synonymous with 'accelerating death'. Thus, where a doctor, family member, or anyone else intentionally ends the life of V in order to relieve pain or suffering, believing that V would not have lived long anyway, D still commits murder. This may be perceived as a problem if we believe that so-called 'mercy killing' should be permissible, but the current law offers no exception of this kind.[25]

---

[22] *Knights* (1860) 2 F & F 46. More recently, the Court of Appeal has applied this rule to dismiss an action relating to foetal alcohol syndrome: *CP (A Child) v First-Tier Tribunal* [2014] EWCA Civ 1554.

[23] See discussion of transferred malice and *AG's Reference (No 3 of 1994)* [1997] 3 All ER 936 at **4.3.1.1**.

[24] [1993] 1 AC 789.

[25] *Inglis* [2010] EWCA Crim 2637.

5.4 Mens rea of murder

Coke's definition describes the mens rea of murder as 'malice aforethought', and this term is still often used. However, malice aforethought is now simply a term of art, with its modern interpretation bearing little resemblance to the original words. For example, it is now clear that D's mens rea need not be 'malicious': that is, need not demonstrate some manner of evil character.[26] Similarly, it need not involve 'aforethought': as long as D has the mens rea at the moment of action, there is no requirement of pre-planning.[27] Rather, at the time of conduct causing death, the current law requires D to have an intention to kill or cause GBH (serious bodily harm).[28]

The meaning of the term 'intention' was discussed at **3.4.1**, and this definition applies to murder as it does to other offences requiring intention. We will not repeat the detail of that discussion here. D intends to kill or cause GBH where her conduct is carried out in order to bring about that result (direct intent); and/or where her conduct is virtually certain to cause that result, she foresees it as a virtual certainty, and the jury choose to find intention (oblique intent). At one time, the House of Lords expanded the definition of oblique intention in murder to include cases where D did not foresee a virtual certainty, but a reasonable person in D's position would have done so.[29] This created a form of objective intention. However, this is no longer good law. The current law defining intention will require *subjective* purpose or *subjective* foresight of a virtual certainty in every case.[30]

> **Don't be confused . . .**
> As we will see in later chapters, most serious offences require a mens rea of intention or recklessness as to a certain result. For such offences, the divide between intention and recklessness is unproblematic: either will suffice for liability. As murder is only satisfied by an *intention* to kill or cause GBH (recklessness is insufficient), the divide between these mens rea terms becomes very important. This is why most of the cases discussed at **3.4.1**, attempting to define intention, were murder cases.

The fact that the mens rea for murder can be satisfied by an intention to cause GBH, as an alternative to an intention to kill, is very important. D acts or omits to act with the intention to cause GBH if she intends, directly or obliquely, to cause serious bodily harm: 'grievous' being given its ordinary meaning of 'serious' or 'really serious'.[31] For example, an intention to break a major bone or severely wound V would amount to an intention to cause GBH.[32] The jury must assess what D was thinking: how much harm was D intending to cause V? Having assessed the degree of harm subjectively intended by D, the jury must then decide whether this is equivalent to the legal definition of (at least) GBH.

---

[26] eg so-called 'mercy killing' will still constitute murder.
[27] Mitchell, 'Thinking about Murder' (1992) 56 J Crim L 78.
[28] *Cunningham* [1982] AC 566; *Moloney* [1985] AC 905.
[29] *DPP v Smith* [1961] AC 290.
[30] *Woollin* [1999] AC 82, [1998] 4 All ER 103, [1998] Crim LR 890.
[31] *Bollom* [2003] EWCA Crim 2846.
[32] We discuss this further at **7.6** in relation to offences of causing GBH with intent.

Allowing liability for murder where D acts with the intention to cause merely GBH means that murder is a constructive liability offence. Where D acts with intention to kill, as in **Table 5.2**, there is uncontroversial correspondence between actus reus (causing death) and mens rea (intending to do so).

Table 5.2 Murder and intention to kill

	Actus reus	**Mens rea**
Result element	Death of V	Intention to kill

However, where D acts with intention to cause merely GBH, this does not correspond straightforwardly with the actus reus of causing death. Rather, D's mens rea corresponds with an actus reus of causing GBH, with the additional actus reus element 'causing death' constructing upon this. D is liable for murder on the basis of constructive liability.[33] This is illustrated in **Table 5.3**.

Table 5.3 Murder and intention to cause GBH

	Actus reus	**Mens rea**
Result element	Death of V	Intention to cause GBH

The possibility for constructive liability in murder, where D intends to cause merely GBH, has attracted severe criticism from academics[34] and appeal court judges[35] alike. Such criticism arises because, in these cases, D does not *choose* to kill or perhaps even to risk killing, and therefore arguably lacks the culpability to deserve liability for murder. For example, consider the case of D, a paramilitary, who shoots V in the knee as a punishment for V's disloyalty. D intends to cause GBH, but definitely does not want V to die: D wants V to be a walking deterrent to disloyal members. D is liable for a serious offence against the person.[36] However, where V, for whatever reason, whether it be lack of treatment; infection; etc, dies as a result of the shot, D's liability increases to murder and the mandatory life sentence is applied.[37] Under the current law, D satisfies the mens rea for murder even if she has no anticipation that her conduct risks killing V, as long as D intends a certain level of harm that the jury interpret as GBH. This will be discussed further in the reform section later, along

---

[33] Constructive liability is discussed at **4.2.1.1**.
[34] Mitchell, 'In Defence of the Correspondence Principle' [1999] Crim LR 195; cf Horder, 'A Critique of the Correspondence Principle in Criminal Law' [1995] Crim LR 795.
[35] *Hyam* [1975] AC 55, see the reasoning of Lord Diplock.
[36] See **7.6**.
[37] In theory, if D simply intends to prick V with a pin and V is a haemophiliac, this could lead to liability for murder (whatever D's impression, a reasonable jury are likely to see the intended pin-prick as an intention to cause serious harm to someone with this condition).

with the counter-argument that is common to constructive liability, that as soon as D intends any harm her normative position changes and she should be responsible for *all* the consequences that follow.[38]

5.4.1 Other mens rea requirements

As will be noted from **Table 5.1** setting out the offence, the mens rea of murder includes elements beyond an intention to kill or cause GBH. Most importantly, as with all other criminal offences, D can only commit murder if her act or omission causing death was performed voluntarily. Additionally, she must intend or know that what she is killing is a person under the Queen's peace.

> *Assessment matters . . .*
> In most cases, and most problem questions, it will be straightforwardly apparent that D acts voluntarily and she is aware that V is a person, and in these cases discussion of mens rea need not go beyond the required intention to kill or cause GBH. However, where there is uncertainty (eg where a spasm in D's finger causes her to pull the trigger of a gun; or where D shoots at a figure unsure if it is a person; etc) then these elements will require specific discussion.

5.5 Defences to murder

If the actus reus and mens rea elements of murder are satisfied, the next step is to explore the possibility of a defence.

5.5.1 General defences

Most of the *general* defences (so called because of their application across multiple offences) will potentially apply to murder, with the notable exception of duress and duress of circumstances. These are fully discussed later in two separate chapters. In **Chapter 13** we discuss denials of mental responsibility: D contends that he lacks responsibility for the offence due to some form of mental abnormality, whether internally or externally caused. In **Chapter 14** we discuss the general defences of self-defence and necessity: D contends that her actions were justified or should be excused because she lacked a *viable* choice not to offend. Satisfying the elements of one of these defences will lead to a complete acquittal.[39]

5.5.2 Doctors and the treatment of terminally ill patients

Over a number of years, with the increased use of powerful pain-relieving medication in hospitals, a category of cases has emerged that has put a strain on the law of murder. These cases involve the prescription of pain-relieving drugs to terminally ill patients, where doctors are aware that the patient's life expectancy will be reduced as a side effect.

---

[38] See **5.6.2**.
[39] The only exception being the insanity defence, which leads to the special verdict of 'not guilty by reason of insanity'. This is discussed in **Chapter 13**.

Such practices are very common and relatively uncontroversial in their medical context. However, to the extent that they satisfy the definition of murder, it seems that the avoidance of liability is now best explained as a form of specific defence for medical professionals.

It is important first to understand how the elements of murder will be satisfied in these cases. The doctor satisfies the actus reus of murder because her conduct in prescribing drugs accelerates the patient's death.[40] In terms of mens rea, although she does not *directly* intend to kill or cause GBH because she does not act in order to bring about that result, the shortening of life is a virtually certain consequence of her conduct and her knowledge of this is likely to amount to an *oblique* intention to kill.[41] Thus, the elements of murder are satisfied.

This problem arose in *Adams*, although the solution offered by the court did not rely on criminal defences.

 Adams [1957] Crim LR 365

D, a doctor, was charged with murder having 'eased the passing' of several patients including V with strong pain-relieving drugs.

- Crown Court: not guilty. Devlin J directed the jury that there was no special defence for doctors, but that 'he is entitled to do all that is proper and necessary to relieve pain and suffering even if measures he takes may incidentally shorten life'.

The principle applied in this case is sometimes referred to as the doctrine of double effect, which holds that intentionally causing a harmful result (eg death) can be morally defensible where it is a side effect of promoting a good end (eg pain relief). Crucial to this is Devlin J's focus on the *incidental* shortening of life, as the same act completed by another party, for example to hasten the collection of inheritance, or by a doctor where the shortening of life was the main purpose, would lead to conviction.[42] However, the direction and the principle are problematic: it is unclear whether it is actus reus (causation) or mens rea (intention) that is being displaced. It is also unclear how it is displaced: what exactly does it mean to 'incidentally shorten life'?

In line with the result of *Adams*, but moving away from the reasoning of Devlin J, we should now see this exception as a special common law defence. In *Bland*,[43] Lord Goff referred, *obiter*, to:

the established rule that a doctor may, when caring for a patient who is, for example, dying of cancer, lawfully administer painkilling drugs, despite the fact he knows that an incidental effect of that application will be to abbreviate the patient's life.

[40] As discussed at **5.3.3**, causing death includes doing an act that accelerates death.
[41] *Woollin* [1998] 4 All ER 103. We may hope that despite D's foresight the jury will choose not to 'find' intention, but this is not certain: see **3.4.1.2**. Cf *Moor* (1999, unreported) discussed in [2000] Crim LR 31 and 568.
[42] See eg *Cox* (1992) 12 BLMR 38, where the 'defence' did not apply to a doctor who prescribed non-therapeutic drugs with the principal intention of causing death. The charge was one of attempted murder.
[43] [1993] 1 AC 789.

Constructed as a defence, the rule may still lack some clarity, but it is able to provide specific protection for doctors within this category of cases. It is also able to do so without distorting the general rules of causation, or relying upon the vagaries of oblique intention.

5.5.3 Partial defences

As well as the complete defences discussed earlier (defences that, if satisfied, will lead to D's acquittal), the law of murder also includes three partial defences. If one of these partial defences is satisfied then D's liability for murder will be downgraded to voluntary manslaughter, an offence which still carries a maximum life sentence, but at the discretion of the court rather than as a mandatory sentence. These partial defences are *not* general defences, and apply *only* to the offence of murder.

The three partial defences to murder are:

- Loss of self-control: D kills while out of control owing to fear of serious violence or by seriously grave circumstances giving her a justifiable sense of being seriously wronged.[44]
- Diminished responsibility: D's recognised medical condition led to an abnormality of mind and substantially impaired her capacity, causing her to kill.[45]
- Suicide pact: D kills V in pursuance of an agreement that they will both die together.[46]

Each of the partial defences will be discussed in detail in **Chapter 6**, as their satisfaction will lead to liability for manslaughter.

> *Beware . . .*
> When considering defences to murder, students often skip straight to discussion of the partial defences. However, remember that these defences will still lead to liability for manslaughter. Therefore, you should always consider the complete defences first. Only if D lacks a complete defence would she want to consider the partial defences.

5.6 Reform

Despite sustained criticism of several aspects of the offence of murder, and despite numerous reform recommendations, the law has remained largely unchanged over the past 50 years.[47] In this section, we provide some additional discussion of the two main areas of criticism identified earlier, and sketch some of the recommendations for reform that have been offered. These relate to the maintenance of the mandatory life sentence and, secondly, the scope of the mens rea for murder. It is noted that the Justice Committee held a one-off evidence session on the law of homicide on 14 September 2016, demonstrating that reform of this area remains on the wider agenda.

---

[44] Coroners and Justice Act 2009, s54.
[45] Homicide Act 1957, s2 (as amended by the Coroners and Justice Act 2009, s52).
[46] Homicide Act 1957, s4.
[47] See generally Horder, *Homicide and the Politics of Law Reform* (2012).

5.6.1 Reforming the mandatory life sentence

In order to achieve the partial removal and subsequent abolition of the death penalty,[48] the substitution of a mandatory life sentence of imprisonment provided the necessary political compromise.[49] The death penalty could be removed, but there was, and remains, maintenance of the idea that murder as the ultimate crime should be punished with some comparable level of 'ultimate' punishment.

In the majority of cases, the mandatory life sentence does not lead to imprisonment for the rest of the offender's life. However, its terms remain uniquely draconian. Depending upon the circumstances of the murder, the minimum period of imprisonment will be set by the court at between 15 years and a whole-life term: this is known as the tariff period.[50] Importantly, and unlike standard sentences, the tariff period must be served in full before D's release is considered by a parole board. At the end of the tariff, a parole board will then decide whether D should stay in prison because she represents a continued risk to particular persons or to the public, or be released into the community. Even where D is released, this is only a release on a life-long licence: allowing administrative (not judicial) action to call D back into prison where necessary.

Despite the original utility of the mandatory life sentence as a compromise in the abolition of the death penalty, arguments against preservation of the mandatory sentence are overwhelming. Central to this is that the law of murder does not target a single specific 'ultimate' mischief, but is, rather, broad enough to catch conduct across a wide moral spectrum: from cold-blooded serial killers or sexually motivated killers, to the morally ambiguous mercy killing. This is common of most criminal offences, for example there is similar disparity between D who recklessly breaks another's pen and D who intentionally smashes another's computer, and yet both are liable for the same offence of criminal damage.[51] The difference, of course, is that a judge can reflect the moral disparity in criminal damage cases within the courts sentencing discretion from discharge to ten years' imprisonment, or potentially life imprisonment where there are aggravating factors.[52] For murder, in contrast, such discretion is removed. Over time, reflecting such criticisms, attitudes towards the mandatory life sentence have hardened academically,[53] judicially,[54] within Parliament,[55] and even among the general public.[56]

---

[48] Homicide Act 1957, s5 singled out certain types of murder that continued to attract the death penalty, before abolition through the Murder (Abolition of the Death Penalty) Act 1965.

[49] Wasik, 'Sentencing in Homicide' in Ashworth and Mitchell (eds), *Rethinking English Homicide Law* (2000) 167.

[50] Criminal Justice Act 2003, s269 and Sch 21.

[51] Criminal Damage Act 1971, s1. Discussed in **Chapter 9**.

[52] Criminal Damage Act 1971, s4.

[53] Mitchell, *Murder and Penal Policy* (1990); Mitchell, 'Identifying and Punishing the More Serious Murders' [2016] Crim LR 467.

[54] See eg *Howe* [1987] 1 All ER 771, 781.

[55] House of Lords, Select Committee on Murder and Life Imprisonment (1989) HL Paper 78, para 108-18: recommending the removal of the mandatory sentence.

[56] Law Commission, *A New Homicide Act for England and Wales?* (Consultation 177, 2005) Appendix A (Mitchell); Mitchell and Roberts, *Public Opinion and Sentencing for Murder* (2010): empirical work finding majority public support for removing the mandatory sentence.

However, despite hardening attitudes against the mandatory life sentence, the current political reality is that the sentence is unlikely to be reformed.[57] We have seen this most recently, for example, in the Law Commission's terms of reference relating to its review of murder in 2005 and 2006 where the mandatory sentence was not open for the Commission to consider.[58] In light of this reality, focus has turned to the reform of murder itself and the rules relating to it, the aim being to remove behaviour from the offence that does not warrant the mandatory sentence. Three areas are of particular interest.

- **Narrowing the definition of murder:** This possibility is discussed in the next section.
- **Reforming the partial defences:** Satisfying a partial defence allows D's liability to be mitigated from murder to manslaughter and thereby avoids the mandatory life sentence. Recent reform in relation to these defences is discussed in the next chapter.
- **Extenuating circumstances mitigation:** The idea of 'extenuating circumstances' has been introduced in other jurisdictions to allow the mandatory life sentence not to apply for certain exceptional murder cases.[59] However, despite a similar proposal (outlined by John Spencer) being advocated in this country, and even put forward as an amendment to a Bill in the House of Lords in 2009, it has not been adopted.[60] Indeed, this option seems unlikely to gain political traction, as it is perceived as an erosion of the mandatory sentence.

5.6.2 Reforming the mens rea of murder

Debates about the appropriate boundaries of murder have generally focused on mens rea elements: adapting the mens rea in order to target more effectively those seen as deserving of the label of murderer and, of course, in view of the mandatory life sentence. Two examples provide useful illustration.

A) Lord Goff: In a wide-ranging article published in 1988, Lord Goff recommends reforming the mens rea of murder in a manner that would at the same time: (a) narrow the current law by removing liability where D intends GBH, as opposed to death, and by narrowing an intention to kill to direct intention only, and also (b) widen it by allowing liability where D is 'wickedly reckless' as to death.[61] Goff would narrow the law, excluding those who intend to cause GBH, chiefly because he believes such defendants are inappropriately labelled as murderers.[62] As Goff comments, 'it seems very strange that a man should be called a murderer even though not only did he not intend to kill the victim, but he may even [in certain cases] have intended that he should not die'.[63] Conversely, Goff would find liability where D is wickedly reckless as to death, which is a concept borrowed from Scottish criminal law. This would apply where D did not

---

[57] Horder, *Homicide and the Politics of Law Reform* (2012).
[58] Law Commission, *Murder, Manslaughter and Infanticide* (No 304, 2006) para 1.1.
[59] eg in Israel and the French Penal Code, Art 345.
[60] Hansard, HL, 26 October 2009, cols 1008–9.
[61] Goff, 'The Mental Element in the Crime of Murder' (1988) 104 LQR 30.
[62] See also Wilson, 'Murder and the Structure of Homicide' in Mitchell and Ashworth (eds), *Rethinking English Homicide Law* (2000).
[63] As eg with the paramilitary punishment beating. Goff, 'The Mental Element in the Crime of Murder' (1988) 104 LQR 30, 48.

necessarily act with the purpose of killing V, but her actions demonstrated a callous or careless disregard for V's life. To understand these proposals, it is useful to also see the meticulous rebuttal of Goff's approach in the reply article of Glanville Williams.[64]

B) The Law Commission: The most recent and most comprehensive review of murder has come from the Law Commission.[65] The Commission sets out recommendations for a new ladder of homicide offences including first degree murder (punished with a mandatory life sentence); a new offence of second degree murder (punished with a discretionary life sentence); and manslaughter (punished with a discretionary life sentence).[66] The separation of first and second degree murder allows the Commission to narrow the offence of first degree murder and, thereby, the mandatory sentence.

- First degree murder: Where D kills (a) with the intention to kill, *or* (b) with the intent to cause serious injury where D was aware that her conduct involved a serious risk of causing death;

- Second degree murder: Where D kills (a) with the intention to cause serious injury; *or* (b) with the intention to cause injury or fear or risk of injury where D was aware that her conduct involved a serious risk of causing death; *or* (c) cases described in the current law as voluntary manslaughter (see **Chapter 6**);

- Manslaughter: Cases described under the current law as involuntary manslaughter (see **Chapter 6**).

Despite the merits of these recommendations, they have yet to be acted upon by the government and (at the time of writing) appear unlikely to be acted upon.

Beware . . .
When and if you discuss Law Commission (or any other) recommendations in an essay, remember that they are just that: recommendations. It is very easy to refer to such policies inaccurately as if they represent the current law. Do not fall into this trap.

5.7 Eye on assessment

The offence of murder is one of the most commonly used offences within problem scenarios. This is because, not only is the offence important and interesting in its own right, but it is also a useful vehicle through which to focus discussion on several matters. Murder is one of the few offences that is only satisfied by a mens rea of intention as opposed to recklessness; it gives rise to the most difficult issues of causation with most reported causation cases involving murder. Additionally, with the potential application of *both* partial and general defences, murder scenarios can involve a wide variety of defences.

---

[64] Williams, 'The Mens Rea of Murder: Leave It Alone' (1989) 105 LQR 387.
[65] Law Commission, *A New Homicide Act for England and Wales?* (Consultation 177, 2005); Law Commission, *Murder, Manslaughter and Infanticide* (No 304, 2006).
[66] See Ashworth, 'Principles, Pragmatism and the Law Commission's Recommendations on Homicide Law Reform' [2007] Crim LR 333.

Despite the range of potential issues, however, as with all problem questions it is important to work through the problem/offence methodically in order to discuss liability. With this in mind, we can work through the step-by-step approach outlined in previous chapters to see how this applies to a murder scenario.

> **STEP 1 Identify the potential criminal event in the facts**
>
> This is unlikely to take more than a sentence, but it is essential to tell your reader where in the facts you are focusing.

In the context of murder, or other potential homicide offences, Step 1 simply requires you to point out a death in the facts that may be connected with D. For example, 'We will first examine the potential liability of Lucy for the death of Tom'.

> **STEP 2 Identify the potential offence**
>
> Having identified the facts (eg D potentially killing V), you must now identify the offence you are going to apply. Usually, this means identifying the most serious offence that D might have committed.

Whenever there is a death in a problem question that may have been caused by D you should *always* begin with a consideration of murder, even if it is reasonably clear that an element within the offence will not be satisfied.[67] If murder is satisfied, you can then move to a discussion of defences, both full and partial. If not, depending upon which elements of murder are missing, this will lead you to the consideration of an alternative offence.

> **STEP 3 Applying the offence to the facts**
>
> Actus reus: What does the offence require? Did D do it?
>
> Mens rea: What does the offence require? Did D possess it?
>
> Remember, to be liable for the offence, every element of the actus reus and mens rea must be satisfied. Every element should be discussed, even where it is easily satisfied and little discussion is necessary. Where there is doubt, in law or in fact, highlight and discuss areas of likely dispute between prosecution and defence. Also, if the question asks you to engage critically with the law as you apply it, take particular care to include evaluation of the law.

A) Actus reus: When discussing the actus reus of murder you are looking for an act or omission that has caused V's death. This will involve the standard rules of causation and, where necessary, omissions liability discussed in **Chapter 2**. If D satisfies the actus reus of murder, continue to discuss mens rea.

If D does not satisfy every element of the actus reus she will not be liable for murder or any other homicide offence. If the question only asks you to consider liability for

---

[67] The only exception being where the problem question tells you to *only* discuss some other offence.

murder or homicide offences, then this is the end of the story: no liability. However, if the question asks you to consider D's liability more generally, having concluded that she did not cause death, your next question will be whether she has criminally contributed to the death. For example, has she assisted, encouraged, or caused another person to kill V (leading to potential liability as a secondary party: **Chapter 12**); or has she assisted or encouraged V to kill herself (leading to potential liability for assisting or encouraging suicide: **Chapter 11**)?

B) Mens rea: The mens rea of murder is only satisfied where D acts or omits to act with the intention (direct or oblique) that her conduct will cause death or GBH (serious bodily harm). It is useful to think of this as a tick-box exercise, with any one of four states of mind sufficient. This is illustrated in **Table 5.4**.

Table 5.4 Mens rea for murder

Intention . . .	to cause death . . .	or to cause GBH
Direct	1	2
Oblique	3	4

When applying the mens rea for murder to problem facts, it is useful to follow this ordering. If you find that D has acted with the direct intention to cause death (1), then there is no need to discuss the GBH rule in any detail and certainly no need to discuss the complex rules of oblique intention.[68] If it is necessary to discuss oblique intention as, for example, where D does not want to harm V at all, but recognises that her actions are extremely likely to do so, it is good practice to lead your reader to that point: tell the reader (drawing on the facts of the problem) why you think a court would be unlikely to find a direct intention. If D satisfies the mens rea for murder by one of these four means then the offence is complete; continue to discuss defences.

If D lacks mens rea then she will not be liable for murder. If the question only asks you to consider liability for murder then this is the end of the story: no liability. However, where the question is more general and asks you to consider liability for homicide offences, or all potential offences, then, assuming the actus reus was satisfied, you will now move to consider potential liability of an offence of involuntary manslaughter. These offences (discussed in **Chapter 6**) require the same actus reus as murder (an act or omission causing death), but are much less restrictive in terms of mens rea.

STEP 4 Consider defences

The word 'consider' here is important, as you should not discuss every defence for every question. Rather, think whether there are any defences that *could* potentially apply. If there are, discuss those only.

---

[68] This approach, only discussing oblique intention where necessary, is described by Lord Bridge as a 'golden rule' in *Moloney* [1985] AC 905, 926.

When discussing defences, always begin with the complete defences (**Chapters 13 and 14**) as these usually lead to a complete acquittal. Remember that the defences of duress and duress of circumstances do not apply to murder. If none of the complete defences apply, or there is some doubt over their application, also continue to discuss the partial defences (**Chapter 6**).

STEP 5 Conclude

This is usually a single sentence either saying that it is likely that D has committed the offence, or saying that it is not likely because an offence element is not satisfied or because a defence is likely to apply. It is not often that you will be able to say categorically whether or not D has committed the offence, so it is usually best to conclude in terms of what is more 'likely'.

STEP 6 Loop

Go back up to Step 1, identifying the next potential criminal event. Continue until you have discussed all the relevant potentially criminal events.

 ONLINE RESOURCE CENTRE

www.oxfordtextbooks.co.uk/orc/sho/

This chapter is accompanied by a selection of online resources to help you with this topic, including:

- **Multiple-choice questions**
- **Chapter summary sheet**
- Two **sample examination questions** with answer guidance
- **Further reading**

Also available on the Online Resource Centre are:

- A selection of **videos** from the authors explaining key topics and principles
- **Legal updates**
- Useful **weblinks**

6

Manslaughter

6.1 Introduction   **162**
6.2 Voluntary manslaughter   **164**
    6.2.1 Loss of self-control   **165**
    6.2.2 Diminished responsibility   **175**
    6.2.3 Suicide pact partial defence   **181**
6.3 Involuntary manslaughter   **182**
    6.3.1 Unlawful act manslaughter   **182**
    6.3.2 Gross negligence manslaughter   **191**
    6.3.3 Reckless manslaughter   **197**
6.4 Statutory offences of unlawful killing   **198**
    6.4.1 Corporate manslaughter   **198**
    6.4.2 Driving causing death   **201**
    6.4.3 Infanticide   **204**
    6.4.4 The killing of a foetus   **205**
6.5 Reform   **206**
    6.5.1 Reforming voluntary manslaughter   **206**
    6.5.2 Reforming involuntary manslaughter   **208**
    6.5.3 Reforming the structure of manslaughter offences   **208**
6.6 Eye on assessment   **210**
    6.6.1 Where the elements of murder are satisfied   **211**
    6.6.2 Where the elements of murder are not satisfied   **212**

6.1 Introduction

As with murder, manslaughter is a common law homicide offence: an offence with an actus reus of unlawful conduct causing the death of a person. However, the spectrum of conduct and mens rea attracting liability for manslaughter is considerably wider than that for murder, covering almost all unlawful killings that fall short of murder. The sentencing options for manslaughter are also considerably wider than those for murder: with murder, the judge must pass a 'mandatory' life sentence; with manslaughter, the judge has discretion up to a maximum of life imprisonment.[1] As the types of conduct and mens rea caught within the offence of manslaughter can differ greatly in terms

---

[1] Consistency in such sentencing discretion is managed through sentencing guidelines.

of blameworthiness, sentencing discretion allows the court to reflect those differences at the sentencing stage.

Although manslaughter is a single offence at common law, one of its complexities lies in the fact that it does not consist of a single set of offence elements. Rather, the same offence (manslaughter) can be committed in a variety of ways. Within this chapter we will explore and discuss each of these alternative forms of liability for manslaughter.

The different forms of manslaughter are separated into two distinct categories. In the first category (known as *voluntary* manslaughter), D satisfies both the actus reus and the mens rea of murder, but also fulfils the elements of a partial defence that reduces her liability to manslaughter. In the second category (known as *involuntary* manslaughter), D does not satisfy the mens rea for murder, but becomes liable for manslaughter because her conduct and mental state satisfy the elements of a lesser involuntary manslaughter offence. Thus, voluntary manslaughter involves a *partial defence* to murder, whereas involuntary manslaughter involves a separate *offence*.

Assessment matters . . .
When applying the law to a problem question, begin by considering liability for murder. Whether the elements of murder are satisfied or not will then lead to a discussion of the appropriate category of manslaughter.[2]

The structure of homicide offences is illustrated in **Figure 6.1**.

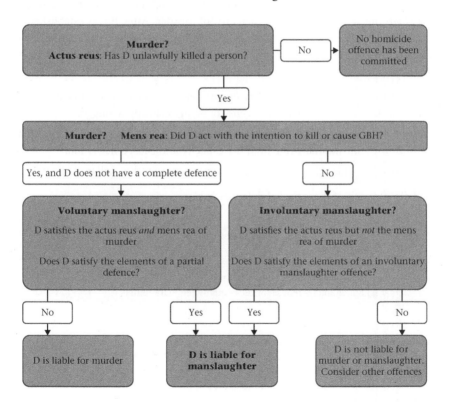

Figure 6.1 Locating homicide liability

---

[2] See **6.6**.

Although murder and manslaughter are the only homicide offences at common law, a number of statutory homicide offences have been created, particularly in recent years, to address perceived weaknesses with the common law. Some of these have employed the term manslaughter (eg corporate manslaughter[3]), whereas others have avoided it (eg causing death by dangerous driving[4]). There are also a number of offences that apply to the killing of a foetus as opposed to a legal 'person' (eg child destruction[5]). Each of these offences exists outside the common law definitions of murder and manslaughter. We will discuss these bespoke offences at **6.4**. However, we begin with a discussion of the core common law offence of manslaughter, and the categories of voluntary and involuntary manslaughter.

6.2 Voluntary manslaughter

The first category of manslaughter (voluntary manslaughter) can only arise where D satisfies *both* the actus reus and the mens rea of murder. After this is established, and assuming that D does not have a complete defence (eg self-defence[6]), it then becomes relevant to discuss the possibility for a partial defence: a defence that may reduce D's liability from murder to voluntary manslaughter. There are three partial defences:

- Loss of self-control: D kills while having lost her self-control owing to fear of *serious* violence or because of her justifiable sense of being seriously wronged.[7]

- Diminished responsibility: D's recognised medical condition led to an abnormality of mind which substantially impaired her capacity and caused her to kill.[8]

- Suicide pact: D kills V in pursuance of an agreement that they will both die together.[9]

We will discuss each of these partial defences in turn.

[3] Corporate Manslaughter and Corporate Homicide Act 2007, s1.
[4] Road Traffic Act 1988, s1 (as substituted by the Road Traffic Act 1991, s1).
[5] Infant Life (Preservation) Act 1929, s1.
[6] These defences are discussed in **Chapters 13** and **14**.
[7] Coroners and Justice Act 2009, s54.
[8] Homicide Act 1957, s2 (as amended by the Coroners and Justice Act 2009, s52).
[9] Homicide Act 1957, s4.

6.2.1 Loss of self-control

The partial defence to murder of 'loss of self-control' (LOC) is defined in sections 54 and 55 of the Coroners and Justice Act 2009.[10] The basic rationale of the partial defence is that where D kills with the intention required for murder, D's level of culpability is lower when she does so in circumstances of justified anger or acute fear, and is (in some sense) overwhelmed by a violent passion likely to have similarly affected others in her position. Paradigm examples, where the defence is intended to apply, would include cases where D kills V upon discovering V abusing D's child; or where D reacts to personal bullying or abuse by killing, in circumstances where the complete defence of self-defence does not apply.

The statutory defence represents a codification and substantial reform of the previous common law partial defence of provocation (abolished by the 2009 Act, s56).[11] Despite relative clarity within core examples, the development of the defence of provocation at common law was characterised by uncertainty and perceived unfairness. This uncertainty was often compounded by inconsistent interpretations within the appellate courts.[12] Therefore, following a number of Law Commission papers and recommendations,[13] the new partial defence of LOC was created.

Beware...

When interpreting relatively new statutes of this kind, it can be useful to read and refer back to previous cases and/or Law Commission material. However, in line with recent cautions from the Court of Appeal, such material should be used with extreme care.[14]

- Pre-2009 Act cases: The volume of cases post-2009 Act make reference to older cases almost entirely unnecessary. Such cases can be discussed when comparing the law pre- and post-2009, but should never be presented as precedent as to the interpretation of current law.

- Law Commission publications: Law Commission papers provide a very useful resource; summarising problems with the old common law and identifying a structure for reform. However, although the Commission's reform recommendations were largely accepted within the 2009 Act, a number of alterations were made.

The current LOC partial defence is defined, principally, within section 54 of the Coroners and Justice Act 2009.

(1) Where a person ('D') kills or is a party to the killing of another ('V'), D is not to be convicted of murder if—

    (a) D's acts and omissions in doing or being a party to the killing resulted from D's loss of self-control,

---

[10] Norrie, 'The Coroners and Justice Act 2009—Partial Defences to Murder (1) Loss of Control' [2010] Crim LR 275. See also *Smith and Hogan's Criminal Law* (14th edn, 2015) Ch15.

[11] For a detailed discussion of the old common law defence of provocation, see Ormerod, *Smith and Hogan's Criminal Law* (12th edn, 2008) Ch15. See also Horder, *Provocation and Responsibility* (1992).

[12] For a useful summary of these problems, see Law Commission, *Partial Defences to Murder* (Consultation 173, 2003) Part 4.

[13] Law Commission, *Partial Defences to Murder* (Consultation 173, 2003); *Partial Defences to Murder* (No 290, 2004); *A New Homicide Act for England and Wales* (Consultation 177, 2005); *Murder, Manslaughter and Infanticide* (No 304, 2006).

[14] *Gurpinar* [2015] EWCA Crim 178, [4] and [17].

(b) the loss of self-control had a qualifying trigger, and

(c) a person of D's sex and age, with a normal degree of tolerance and self-restraint and in the circumstances of D, might have reacted in the same or in a similar way to D . . .

(7) A person who, but for this section, would be liable to be convicted of murder is liable instead to be convicted of manslaughter.

In line with section 54(1), the LOC partial defence is made up of three elements, set out in **Table 6.1**. All three must be satisfied for the defence to apply.

Table 6.1 Partial defence of LOC

A) D's role in the killing must have resulted from a loss of self-control
B) D's loss of self-control must have been caused by a qualifying trigger: i) a fear of serious violence from V against D or another, *or*   ii) a thing or things done or said (or both) which constituted circumstances of an extremely grave character, *and* caused D to have a justifiable sense of being seriously wronged
C) A hypothetical person, of D's age and sex, might have reacted in the same way

Where an issue of LOC arises,[15] the legal burden is on the prosecution to prove beyond reasonable doubt that one or more of these elements is absent. If the prosecution are unable to disprove the defence, then D will be liable for manslaughter and not for murder.

> *Terminology . . .*
> Although we are again speaking of 'elements', the terms actus reus and mens rea are not applicable to defences. This is because, when discussing the elements of a defence as opposed to the elements of an offence, we are focusing on factors that makes D's conduct less blameworthy.

We will explore each element of the partial defence in turn. However, first we consider an important qualifier to the defence: D's conduct must not be motivated by a desire for revenge.

6.2.1.1 Exclusion: D must not act in a considered desire for revenge

Section 54(4) excludes the defence where D acts in a considered desire for revenge. In many cases, such a 'considered' desire will be evidence that D did not lose her self-control and so D will also lack a vital element of the defence. However, crucially, even if D satisfies the elements of the defence, it will still be excluded if this section applies. For example, D kills V following a verbal attack by V, giving D a justifiable sense of being seriously wronged. Even where D is out of control at the moment of causing death, if the

---

[15] The defence will only be put to the jury (become a live issue) where the judge is satisfied that there is sufficient evidence that a reasonable jury may find the defence elements satisfied. Coroners and Justice Act 2009, s54(6); *Gurpinar* [2015] EWCA Crim 178.

attack was 'thought about and considered' in advance, D will still be excluded from the defence.[16] This exclusion has been seen as vital to prevent the defence being used inappropriately by revenge killers.

The exclusion, however, can also cause problems. A significant criticism of the pre-2009 Act defence of provocation was that it failed to provide a partial defence to victims of abuse who killed their abusers. Particularly in the context of abused women, such defendants will not generally react on impulse, but may be driven over a period of time to kill, and choose to kill at a time when they do not endanger themselves or their children (eg when V is asleep).[17] The exclusion within the current law provides a significant hurdle for defendants of this kind trying to rely on the LOC partial defence.[18]

> **Point to remember . . .**
> It is useful to begin a discussion of the LOC defence with this exclusion because, when it applies, there is no need to move on to a discussion of the defence elements.

6.2.1.2 Element 1: D must have lost self-control

The first element of the partial defence, and perhaps its central feature, is the requirement that D's conduct (which caused V's death) must have resulted from a lack of self-control. This is a *subjective* requirement: we ask whether D herself lost self-control; it is irrelevant (for this element) whether a reasonable person in D's position would have done so or not.

There is a problem, however, in knowing exactly what the law means by 'a loss of self-control', and the term is not defined in the 2009 Act. It is clear that loss of self-control should not be interpreted too strictly by isolating it to cases where D fully lacks control over her physical bodily movement: such cases are already catered for within the complete defence of insanity, or a claim of automatism.[19] The term should be interpreted to require extreme emotion and/or a loss of rationality, but not more than this. This was accepted by the Court of Appeal in *Jewell*.[20] The court, adopting the wording of the 13th edition of *Smith and Hogan's Criminal Law*, defined loss of self-control as the 'loss of the ability to act in accordance with considered judgement or a loss of normal powers of reasoning'.[21] In this manner, a loss of self-control is not a claim that D lacked the mens rea for murder, but rather, it is an explanation why she had it.

Under the pre-2009 Act defence of provocation, there was a further requirement that D's loss of self-control had to be 'sudden and temporary'. This is no longer the case. The old requirement of a sudden and temporary loss of self-control was heavily criticised for its perceived gender bias: whilst men are more likely to react immediately to provocation, women, although similarly affected, may react later after a slow-burn period. This was discussed in *Ahluwalia*.

---

[16] See *Evans* [2012] EWCA Crim 2.

[17] Dressler, 'Battered Women Who Kill Their Sleeping Tormentors' and Horder, 'Killing the Passive Abuser: A Theoretical Defence' in Shute and Simester (eds), *Criminal Law Theory* (2002).

[18] Withey, 'Loss of Control, Loss of Opportunity?' [2011] Crim LR 263.

[19] See **Chapters 13** and **14**.

[20] [2014] EWCA Crim 414.

[21] Per Rafferty LJ at [23]. It should be noted that the Lord Chief Justice declined to endorse this approach in *Gurpinar* [2015] EWCA Crim 178, leaving the point for future consideration (at [19]).

Ahluwalia [1992] 4 All ER 889 (pre-C&JA 2009)

D killed her abusive husband (V) following years of violence. She poured petrol over V whilst he was asleep and set fire to it; V died from the burns. D admitted murder, but claimed a defence of provocation.

- Crown Court: guilty of murder.
- D appealed, questioning the trial judge's direction that D's loss of control must be sudden and temporary to qualify for the defence.
- Court of Appeal: quashed D's conviction (and ordered a retrial) on the basis that D's depression may give rise to an alternative defence of diminished responsibility (later accepted on retrial). *But* confirmed that the court was correct in finding that provocation required a 'sudden and temporary' loss of control.

The court in *Ahluwalia* allowed the defence of provocation to go to the jury on the basis that (despite the time delay between V's provocation and D's reaction) D's loss of self-control may still have been sudden and temporary. However, for a jury applying a test framed in these terms, the defence was always likely to fail.[22]

By removing the 'sudden and temporary' requirement, the potential now is that defendants such as Ahluwalia will be *more* likely to satisfy the test. However, it remains uncertain whether this will be the case. Although there is no 'sudden and temporary' condition within the current law, it is difficult to make sense of the loss of self-control requirement in the way that it has been understood (ie a 'rush of blood' or 'emotional surge'), without taking account of the time delay between provocation and reaction: a long delay implies that the trigger has not caused a loss of self-control.[23] Indeed, we see this to a certain extent in the case of *Jewell*.

 Jewell [2014] EWCA Crim 414

D killed V, a workmate, after an extended period of perceived intimidation by V. D gave evidence that he was unable to sleep in the preceding days, and was gradually 'shutting down' before he acted to kill, describing his final acts as having been done in a dream-like state. D was charged with murder.

- Crown Court: guilty of murder. LOC was not left to the jury, with the judge finding no basis for the defence.
- Court of Appeal: conviction upheld on appeal. The planning that preceded the killing undermined a claim of loss of self-control.

The approach taken in *Jewell* confirms that the requirement of loss of self-control will remain a significant hurdle for those wishing to make use of the defence, particularly in the most difficult cases such as those involving abused women, although of course the burden is on the Crown to disprove the defence. For example, if D kills her partner following domestic abuse, she may not have done so in a manic/rush of blood-type

---

[22] For a discussion of the law after *Ahluwalia*, but pre-2009, see Wells, 'Battered Women Syndrome and Defences to Homicide: Where Now?' (1994) 14 LS 266.

[23] This is recognised in the 2009 Act's Explanatory Notes, para 337 and in parliamentary debates prior to reform.

manner, but she may have felt, as a result of the abuse, that she lacked control in the sense of seeing no alternative options to protect herself. Expanding the definition of loss of self-control in this manner has an obvious appeal in the context of people who kill their abusers, and even perhaps for so-called mercy killers who are driven to kill their loved ones believing it is the only way they can assist them.[24] However, as we see in *Jewell*, it is unlikely that such an expansion will gain traction within the current law.[25]

6.2.1.3 Element 2: there must be a qualifying trigger

D's loss of self-control must have been caused by a 'qualifying trigger'. Where D loses self-control and kills in the absence of such a trigger, the LOC defence will not apply. Section 55 of the 2009 Act sets out two qualifying triggers for the defence: a fear of serious violence, and/or a sense of being seriously wronged by things said or done. Although each trigger provides a separate, alternative route into the defence, many cases will involve a combination of the two.[26]

A) Fear of serious violence from V (s55(3)): The first qualifying trigger arises where D loses self-control in fear of serious violence against herself or another identified person (eg her child). This is a *subjective* requirement: D must react to a genuine fear, and it must be a fear of *serious* violence, but this fear need not be based on a correct assessment of the facts (ie there does not need to be an actual threat) and D's fear need not be reasonable (ie a reasonable person in D's position may have realised there was no need to fear). This trigger, new to the 2009 Act, is partly designed to remove gender bias from the defence. It extends qualifying triggers from classically masculine responses to verbal or physical affronts, to include reactions to fear of serious violence. This trigger is intended to be employed, for example, in the context of abused women who kill their abusers in fear of future violence.

It is useful to consider how this trigger and the LOC *partial* defence will operate alongside the *complete* defence of self-defence, a defence discussed in **Chapter 14**. Of course, in cases where D might raise self-defence then this will be her priority: successfully pleading self-defence will result in acquittal. However, where D kills in fear of serious violence and self-defence is not available (eg because the threat to D from V was not imminent; or because the force used was unreasonably excessive; etc[27]) then the partial defence of LOC may provide a useful safety net, reducing D's liability to manslaughter.

Extra detail . . .
Whether D fears violence is a subjective question that does not rely on reasonableness. However, where that belief is unreasonable and only arises as a result of voluntary intoxication, it is unclear whether this would qualify as a trigger under the current law. Subjective requirements in self-defence, for example, apply an exception in relation to beliefs formed from voluntary intoxication,

---

[24] *Serrano* [2006] EWCA Crim 3182 (pre-C&JA 2009): a tragic case in which D's caution when killing his terminally ill wife demonstrated that he was not out of control, and thus outside the provocation defence.

[25] The current uncertainty as to the definition of 'loss of self-control' was discussed in *Gurpinar* [2015] EWCA Crim 178, but the court declined to provide further guidance.

[26] Coroners and Justice Act, s55(5); *Dawes* [2013] EWCA Crim 322, [56].

[27] See discussion of self-defence in **Chapter 14**.

not allowing such beliefs to satisfy the defence.[28] However, in line with the old common law of provocation,[29] it is contended that even intoxicated beliefs should be sufficient (should not be excluded) in the context of the LOC defence as a *partial* defence to murder.

The 'fear of serious violence' trigger has an important qualification set out in section 55(6)(a): it will not apply where D has consciously caused the conditions of her own defence. D causes the conditions of her own defence, in this context, where she has incited V to act (causing D to fear) in order to have an excuse to use violence against V. For example, where D taunts or provokes V to punch her, intending to incite V into an attack in order to kill V and rely on the partial defence. Blocking the defence in these cases is an important restriction, but will only apply where D has *consciously* manipulated the circumstances. Where D acts in a manner that is likely to provoke violence, but is not doing so consciously in order to gain an excuse to react violently, then the defence may still operate. This interpretation was confirmed in *Dawes and Ors*.

Dawes and Ors [2013] EWCA Crim 322

D discovered his estranged wife asleep with another man (V), and stabbed V with a kitchen knife, causing death. D was charged with murder and raised the defence of self-defence.

- Crown Court: guilty of murder. The jury did not accept the defence of self-defence, and the judge refused to allow the partial LOC defence to go to the jury because: (a) if D did kill in reaction to an attack from V then this only happened because D had provoked the attack; and (b) there was no evidence of a loss of self-control; D was acting in an angry but controlled manner.
- Court of Appeal: as part of a combined appeal with two other cases, Dawes's conviction was upheld. Importantly, the court clarified that the Crown Court had been wrong on point (a): although D may have provoked the attack from V, this will only undermine a LOC defence where it is done consciously in order to provide a defence for retaliatory violence. That was not the case here. However, the Crown Court was still correct not to leave LOC to the jury on the basis of point (b).

B) A sense of being seriously wronged by things said or done (s55(4)): The second qualifying trigger arises where D loses self-control as a result of a 'justifiable sense of being seriously wronged' by 'things said or done' (not necessarily by V[30]) that were of an 'extremely grave character'. This trigger requires D to identify specific actions or comments which caused the loss of self-control, with mere circumstances (eg losing money on the stock market, or a farmer losing her crops to flood) being insufficient.[31] This trigger is partly *subjective* (D must personally feel seriously wronged) and partly *objective* (the feeling of wrong must be objectively justifiable, and the circumstances must be objectively grave).

The inclusion of objective requirements within this trigger was not found in the old common law defence of provocation. It is designed to prevent the 2009 Act defence being used (or even raised[32]) in circumstances where D is provoked by trivial events

---

[28]   Ibid.
[29]   *Letenock* (1917) 12 Cr App R 221.
[30]   eg *Davies* [1975] QB 691 (pre-C&JA 2009): D killed his wife after being provoked by her lover.
[31]   *Acott* [1997] 2 Cr App R 94 (pre-C&JA 2009).
[32]   A judge will not allow the defence to go to the jury unless there is sufficient evidence upon which it might be accepted. Section 54(6).

(eg a crying baby[33] or a poorly cooked steak[34]), or by events that are only grave for D because of something objectionable about her character (eg a white supremacist provoked by a lack of deference from V, a black man[35]). In such cases, it is clear that a trivial event is not one of an 'extremely grave character', and a racist perception can never result in a '*justifiable* sense of being seriously wronged'. There is a useful discussion of this in *Dawes and Ors*, concerning the linked appeal of Barry Bowyer.

Dawes and Ors [2013] EWCA Crim 322

Bowyer (D) and V were both romantically involved with the same woman (X). D broke into V's house in order to steal items to sell. V returned home, found D, and attacked and insulted him. D retaliated, killing V. D was charged with murder.

- Crown Court: guilty of murder. The trial judge allowed the LOC defence to go to the jury, but they did not accept it.
- Court of Appeal: as part of a combined appeal with two other cases, Bowyer's conviction was upheld. The court confirmed the accuracy of the trial judge's direction on LOC, but also stated that the judge should not have left the defence to the jury at all. On the issue of the qualifying trigger, the court stated that 'it is absurd to suggest that the entirely understandable response of the deceased to finding a burglar in his home [ie attacking and insulting D] provided the appellant with the remotest beginnings of a basis for suggesting that he had a justifiable sense of being wronged, let alone seriously wronged' [66].

The introduction of objective standards within this trigger can be generally welcomed in order to exclude clear cases of this kind. And the appellate courts have been clear that trial judges should take this role seriously, evaluating the evidence rigorously before it is left to the jury.[36] However, the terms used ('extremely grave'; 'justifiable sense'; 'seriously wronged') are regrettably vague for such an important defence element. This results in considerable discretion for judges and juries when applying the law, and through this, the potential for inconsistency.[37]

Two exclusions apply to this trigger. First, as with the fear of serious violence trigger, D cannot rely on things said or done where she has incited them in order to use violence in response.[38] For example, if D encourages V to shout abuse at her so that she (D) has an excuse to react violently, the defence will not be available.

Additionally, section 55(6)(c) specifically excludes things said or done constituting 'sexual infidelity'. This exclusion was added by the government to send a clear message that killing in response to sexual infidelity should never ground a defence to murder,

---

[33] *Doughty* (1986) 83 Cr App R 319 (pre-C&JA 2009).

[34] Example from Law Commission, *Murder, Manslaughter and Infanticide* (No 304, 2006) para 1.47.

[35] The Commission, and government, were similarly keen to exclude so-called honour killings: where D kills his daughter because she has had a sexual relationship before marriage. *Mohammed* [2005] EWCA Crim 1880 (pre-2009).

[36] *Gurpinar* [2015] EWCA Crim 178, [12]–[14]. Where the LOC defence is withdrawn by a trial judge following an appropriate examination, the Court of Appeal will be reluctant to overturn that decision: *McDonald* [2016] EWCA Crim 1529.

[37] Withey, 'Loss of Control, Loss of Opportunity?' [2011] Crim LR 263, 271–274; Storey, 'Loss of Control: "Sufficient Evidence" (Again)' (2015) 79 JCL 154.

[38] Coroners and Justice Act, s55(6)(b); *Dawes* [2013] EWCA Crim 322, [56].

as it had in a number of pre-2009 Act provocation cases.[39] However, the exclusion has been highly controversial.[40] Criticism of the exclusion has focused on the principle itself: why should sexual infidelity be singled out for exclusion in cases where all other elements of the defence are satisfied, particularly as LOC is only a partial defence? More damagingly, criticism has also focused on the coherence of the exclusion: the lack of a definition of 'sexual infidelity' (eg does fidelity assume a certain status of relationship between D and V?); the potential for mixed issues (eg where D discovers her husband sexually abusing their daughter); the ambiguous drafting of things said or done that 'constituted' sexual infidelity (eg would this include V telling D that she planned to be unfaithful in the future?); and so on. These problems were discussed by the Court of Appeal in *Clinton*.

 Clinton [2012] EWCA Crim 2

D killed his wife following an argument in which she informed him that she was having an affair; that she had had sexual intercourse with a number of other men during their marriage; and she taunted him about his previous failed attempts to commit suicide. D accepted that he had completed the elements of murder, but claimed a LOC defence.

- Crown Court: guilty of murder. LOC was withdrawn from the jury because of the sexual infidelity exclusion.
- Court of Appeal: appeal allowed, and retrial ordered. Where sexual infidelity is not the sole trigger said or done (as here), it should be allowed to go to the jury alongside all other factors.

In a well-reasoned judgment, the court in *Clinton* exposed the poor drafting of the exclusion, and revealed that for coherence it could not apply in the manner that many had expected.[41] Where the sole trigger relied on by D is something said or done which amounts to sexual infidelity, then this will not apply as a qualifying trigger. However, whenever there are additional potential triggers, as will invariably be the case in complex real-world relationships, then sexual infidelity will not be excluded from those other factors when they are considered by the jury. Therefore, in most cases involving sexual infidelity, the courts are likely to focus more on the general objective standards for exclusion rather than the specific terms of section 55(6)(c).

Extra detail . . .
Although D must have been provoked or caused to fear by another party, there is no requirement that this party was V. For example, D may be taunted by X about the behaviour of V, causing D to lose control and kill V. Equally, if D loses control and attempts to kill X, but misses and kills V, D's defence may transfer to the killing of V in a manner similar to transferred malice.[42]

---

[39] Hansard, HC, 9 November 2009, col 82.

[40] Reed and Wake, 'Sexual Infidelity Killings' in Reed and Bohlander (eds), *Loss of Control and Diminished Responsibility: Domestic, Comparative and International Perspectives* (2011) 117.

[41] Morgan, 'Loss of Self-Control: Back to the Good Old Days' (2013) 77 J Crim L 119.

[42] *Gross* (1913) 23 Cox CC 445 (pre-C&JA 2009): D was provoked by her husband X, shot at him, but missed and hit V. D could use the partial defence in relation to the killing of V. Transferred malice was discussed at **4.3.1**.

6.2.1.4 Element 3: a person of normal tolerance and self-restraint might have reacted similarly

The third and final element within the LOC partial defence is that D's reaction to the qualifying trigger must have been *objectively* understandable in the sense that 'a person of D's age and sex, with a normal degree of tolerance and self-restraint, and in the circumstances of D, might have reacted in the same or in a similar way to D'.[43] This element is core to the rationale of the LOC defence: it is not simply that D has a good reason for losing self-control and killing, it is also that she was provoked, or caused to fear serious violence, to such an extent that anybody might have reacted as she did. This element is necessary to show that D's offence was, at least partially, not a reflection of an evil character. We are not saying that D acted correctly, but we can understand, and partially excuse, on the basis that, as the old adage goes, 'there but for the grace of God go I'.

Despite being at the core of the defence, the equivalent objective element under the old law of provocation caused considerable problems for the courts. This is because, when identifying the objective standard, it is necessary to decide if there is a single, fixed standard (eg that of a 'normal' human), or whether we can take account of certain characteristics of D that might affect what is a 'normal' degree of self-restraint for her (eg her age; any mental conditions; intoxication; etc: with different fixed levels required for each). On this issue, the pre-2009 Act case law diverged into two streams: one identifying the standard through a strict test of a 'normal' person of D's age and sex;[44] and the other applying a much more liberal test that allowed almost any of D's characteristics to be taken into account when identifying a 'normal' expected standard for that defendant.[45] This divergence came to an end in the case of *Holley*,[46] where a specially convened nine-member Board of the Privy Council concluded that the narrower approach (considering age and sex only) was to be preferred.[47] The academic debate surrounding this conflict provides a useful background for an evaluation of the current law.[48]

The 2009 Act does not seek to codify either of the competing positions under the old common law, but rather seeks something of a compromise position between them. In line with the old law, age and sex remain relevant considerations: the jury must consider the likely reaction of a reasonable person of D's age and sex.

> **Extra detail . . .**
> Taking account of 'age' seems sensible: it is logical that we might expect a higher degree of tolerance and self-restraint from an older person than, for example, a child. And, conversely, to hold a child

---

[43] Coroners and Justice Act, s54(1)(c).

[44] Exemplified by *Camplin* [1978] AC 705 (pre-C&JA 2009).

[45] Exemplified by *Smith (Morgan)* [2001] AC 146 (pre-C&JA 2009).

[46] *AG for Jersey v Holley* [2005] UKPC 23 (pre-C&JA 2009).

[47] Despite its status as a Privy Council decision, the Court of Appeal in *James and Karimi* [2006] EWCA Crim 14 (pre-C&JA 2009) took the radical approach of endorsing the decision in *Holley* in preference to the House of Lords case of *Smith (Morgan)*.

[48] The debate here is broadly the same as that under the pre-2009 law between *Smith (Morgan)* (liberal approach) and *Holley* (restrictive approach). See Macklem and Gardner, 'Compassion Without Respect: Nine Fallacies in *R v Smith*' [2001] Crim LR 623; cf Mitchell, Mackay, and Brookbanks, 'Pleading for Provoked Killers: In Defence of *Morgan Smith*' (2008) 124 LQR 675.

to an adult standard would seem unfair.[49] However, the inclusion of 'sex' seems to be an odd legacy from the case law, as there is no evidence that men and women have different levels of 'normal' tolerance or self-restraint.

The novelty of the current law is that, beyond age and sex, section 54(1)(c) also makes reference to 'the circumstances of D'. This implies a reversal of *Holley* and suggests that all of D's circumstances will be relevant (eg mental condition, intoxication, etc). However, opening this element to *all* of D's circumstances would take us back to the criticised position that preceded *Holley*, and was one of the major catalysts for reform of the defence. To avoid this, section 54(3) provides a vital qualification, stating that 'the circumstances of D' should be interpreted to mean:

all of D's circumstances other than those whose only relevance to D's conduct is that they bear on D's general capacity for tolerance and self-restraint.

The qualification here is quite subtle, and beyond age and sex which are always relevant, requires us to examine any potential circumstance individually to see if the jury should take it into account. Having identified a circumstance or characteristic of D that impacted on her ability to control herself (ie a potentially relevant circumstance for the current test), the court must consider whether that circumstance or characteristic was *only* relevant to D's self-control, in which case it should not be taken into account, or whether it was also relevant to some other aspect of D's defence, in which case it should be taken into account. Unfortunately, and crucially, the statute does not clarify what other aspects of D's defence must be impacted on in order for her circumstances to become relevant.

There is some clarity at the extremes. Thus, it is clear that where D's circumstances have an explicit bearing on the relevant trigger *and* D's ability to control herself then they will be taken into account. For example, if D is insulted for being mentally disabled, her status (ie her disability) may affect both the degree of the provocation and D's ability to control herself (Elements 2 and 3 of the defence).[50] Equally, at the other end of the spectrum, we know that where D's circumstances have a bearing *only* on her ability to control herself they will be excluded (Element 3 only). This was confirmed in *Asmelash* in the context of voluntary intoxication.

    Asmelash [2013] EWCA Crim 157

D and V spent the day drinking and arguing, culminating in D stabbing V twice and killing him. D was charged with murder.

- Crown Court: guilty of murder. Directing the jury as to LOC, the judge explained that they should ask whether a reasonable person sharing D's characteristics, *but not intoxicated*, might have acted in the same way.
- Court of Appeal: conviction upheld on appeal. Voluntary intoxication was only relevant to D's general capacity of self-control and was therefore rightly excluded.

[49] *Camplin* [1978] AC 705 (pre-C&JA 2009): recognising this in a case where D (a 15-year-old boy) killed V after being raped and then mocked by his rapist.
[50] Confirmed in *Asmelash* [2013] EWCA Crim 157.

However, it is the grey area between these extremes that is likely to cause problems. For example, where D has a psychiatric illness, this may not be expressly linked to the trigger (Element 2), but may still be interpreted as affecting D beyond her general capacity for self-control (Element 3) because of, for example, its effect on her ability to understand and evaluate the trigger. In view of the troubled history of this element of the defence under the old law, it is likely to be interpreted narrowly and rarely to allow more than age and sex to be considered. However, given the well-known troubled history of the old law, the ambiguity of the drafting is particularly disappointing.

> **Point to remember . . .**
> The last part of the test 'might have reacted in the same or in a similar way' should not be forgotten. Two points are important. First, it is not necessary that a normal person 'would' have reacted in a similar way, only that one 'might' have (a lower standard). Secondly, even if a normal person might have lost control and killed as D did, you must still look at the 'way' it was done. For example, if D lost control and killed V in a particularly brutal or prolonged attack, in a manner in which a normal person would never do, then she may fall outside the defence.[51]

6.2.2 Diminished responsibility

As with the LOC defence, diminished responsibility (DR) is a partial defence to murder (and only to murder[52]) that reduces D's liability from murder to 'voluntary' manslaughter, thereby avoiding the mandatory life sentence.[53] For the LOC defence, as we have seen, D claims that she should be partially excused for the killing on the basis that a 'normal' person might have reacted as she did. For DR, in contrast, D is claiming a partial excuse on the basis that she should not be held to the standard of a 'normal' person because of her medical condition.[54]

Where D's medical condition creates a defect of reason that *completely* undermines her ability to understand the nature or quality of her acts, or to know if they are wrong, then she will have a complete defence of insanity.[55] No liability is appropriate in such cases. DR is different. Where D's medical condition causes her an abnormality of mind that *substantially* impairs her abilities, she will commit an offence. However, instead of murder, D commits manslaughter.

The elements of the DR partial defence, contained in section 2 of the Homicide Act 1957, have been amended significantly by section 52 of the Coroners and Justice Act 2009. The pre-2009 DR defence was defined broadly and imprecisely to apply where D's 'abnormality of mind' substantially impaired her 'mental responsibility'. This was welcomed in certain cases, allowing for flexibility and legal equity, essentially allowing courts and juries to interpret and apply the law as they wished to find a 'fair' result. However, as discussed by the Law Commission, flexibility also resulted in 'chaotic' use of

---

[51] *Van Dongen* [2005] Crim LR 971 (pre-C&JA 2009): D's acts demonstrated abnormal savagery and fell outside the defence.

[52] *Campbell* [1997] Crim LR 495 (pre-C&JA 2009): will not apply to attempted murder.

[53] The maximum sentence for manslaughter is life imprisonment, but (unlike for murder) this sentence is not mandatory.

[54] Horder, *Excusing Crime* (2004) Ch1.

[55] *M'Naghten* (1843) 10 Cl & Fin 200, 8 Eng Rep 718. See **Chapter 14**. Although the verdict will be the 'special' one of 'Not Guilty by Reason of Insanity'.

the defence, with it being 'grossly abused' and resulting in a 'lottery' between cases.[56] In view of these problems, the Commission made recommendations for reform,[57] many of which were adopted within the 2009 Act.

The current (post-2009[58]) DR defence is set out (as amended) in section 2 of the Homicide Act 1957:[59]

(1) A person ('D') who kills or is a party to the killing of another is not to be convicted of murder if D was suffering from an abnormality of mental functioning which—

   (a) arose from a recognised medical condition,

   (b) substantially impaired D's ability to do one or more of the things mentioned in subsection (1A), and

   (c) provides an explanation for D's acts and omissions in doing or being a party to the killing.

(1A) Those things are—

   (a) to understand the nature of D's conduct;

   (b) to form a rational judgment;

   (c) to exercise self-control.

> **Don't be confused . . .**
> Both LOC and DR defences have been reformed by the 2009 Act. For LOC, as the old provocation defence (replaced by LOC) existed at common law, the new defence is located in the 2009 Act itself. In contrast, as the old DR defence was already fully codified within the Homicide Act 1957, the 2009 Act simply amended that statute. Therefore, when referring to the current DR defence, you should still refer to section 2 of the 1957 Act.

DR can be separated into four elements, set out in **Table 6.2**. All four must be satisfied, by D, for the defence to apply.

Table 6.2 Partial defence of diminished responsibility

A) D must demonstrate an abnormality of mental functioning
B) The abnormality must have arisen from a recognised medical condition

C) The abnormality must have substantially impaired D's ability to:
   i)   understand the nature of her conduct; *or*
   ii) form a rational judgement; *or*
   iii) exercise self-control

D) The abnormality must provide an explanation (or cause) of the killing

---

[56] Law Commission, *Partial Defences to Murder* (No 290, 2004) Part 5.
[57] Law Commission, *Murder, Manslaughter and Infanticide* (No 304, 2006).
[58] In force since October 2010.
[59] See generally Mackay, 'The New Diminished Responsibility Plea' [2010] Crim LR 290.

In common with the insanity defence, but in contrast to LOC, the burden of proving these elements is on the defendant and not the prosecution.[60] As we have discussed,[61] where the burden of proof is reversed in this manner, the defence only have to prove their case to the civil standard: on the balance of probabilities.[62] They must prove every element of the DR defence, and only then will D's liable be reduced from murder to 'voluntary' manslaughter. We will explore each element in turn.

6.2.2.1 Element 1: D must have had an abnormality of mental functioning

The term 'abnormality of mental functioning' is not defined in the statute and remains somewhat vague. In line with the old law, the element is designed to require a link between D's medical condition and some impact on her mind.

The language of 'mental functioning' (as opposed to 'abnormality of mind' under the pre-2009 law) demonstrates a move towards medical/psychiatric definitions that are likely to standardise the potential application of the element. For example, in *Byrne*[63] Lord Parker CJ described the pre-2009 test as 'a state of mind so different from that of ordinary human beings that the reasonable man would term it abnormal'.[64] The defence always required medical evidence to succeed, but since the 2009 Act, with the move to more medicalised elements, that has become more transparent.[65]

6.2.2.2 Element 2: the abnormality must have arisen from a recognised medical condition

The required link between D's abnormal mental functioning and a recognised medical condition is one of the most important and clearly medicalising elements of the partial defence. Therefore, although the ultimate question remains a legal one for the court, discussion of a 'recognised' medical condition will inevitably make use of medical glossaries such as the World Health Organization's *International Statistical Classification of Diseases and Related Health Problems* (ICD 10) and the American Medical Association's *Diagnostic and Statistical Manual* (SSM). Additionally, it will also be open for the court to recognise medical conditions that are not on these lists, but are supported by a reliable body of expert opinion. Both psychiatric and purely physical conditions are capable of satisfying this element, although of course purely physical conditions are less likely to satisfy the other defence elements.

> **Extra detail . . .**
> Although D must have a recognised medical condition, there is no requirement of seriousness. Thus, as long as the other defence elements are satisfied, even mild depression would be sufficient.

The rationale for linking this element of DR to medical definitions is to ensure that the legal test is not left behind by developments in medical science. However, as medical definitions are not specifically designed to assist the criminal law, problems are likely to emerge about which conditions are included and excluded by this coupling.

---

[60] Homicide Act 1957, s2(2).

[61] See **1.1.7.2**.

[62] The reverse burden for DR has been found to be compatible with the Art 6 ECHR right to a fair trial: *Lambert* [2001] 1 Cr App R 205; *Foye* [2013] EWCA Crim 475; *Wilcocks* [2016] EWCA Crim 2043.

[63] [1960] 2 QB 396 (pre-C&JA 2009).

[64] Ibid, 403.

[65] See *Bunch* [2013] EWCA Crim 2498.

A) **Included:** Popular lists of medically recognised conditions include some diagnoses which the law would not want to qualify within the DR defence (eg Hughes LJ lists references in the *Dictionary of Scientific Medicine* including 'unhappiness', 'anger', and 'paedophilia'[66]). It is now clear, however, that the fact D suffers from a condition that is 'recognised' by the medical profession is necessary but is not sufficient for it to found the defence. The condition must also be one that the courts are prepared to 'recognise' in law. This was discussed in the *Dowds* case.

 Dowds [2012] EWCA Crim 281

D killed his partner whilst heavily intoxicated, inflicting 60 stab wounds. D attempted to use the DR defence, relying on his 'acute intoxication' (extreme drunkenness) which is a medical condition recognised by the World Health Organization.

• Crown Court: guilty of murder. The judge refused to allow DR.
• Court of Appeal: conviction upheld on appeal. Although acute intoxication was a medically recognised condition, it will not qualify as such within the DR defence.

B) **Excluded:** Pre-2009, the vague terms of the DR defence meant that it could be used flexibly in the context, for example, of abused women who kill and so-called mercy killers. The current law, however, will not allow for the inclusion of such cases unless D is suffering from a recognised medical condition.[67] This is a real restriction on the scope of the defence, but should not be exaggerated. First, most defendants in such cases *will* be suffering from a recognised anxiety- or depression-related condition. Further, where there is no such condition, there are strong grounds to maintain that D's case should not come within the defence: the rationale of the defence is to provide a partial excuse for those acting as a result of their medical affliction; not as a method for courts to engage with a debate on euthanasia or other defences they might want to create (in the guise of DR) in the absence of statutory recognition of such defences by government.[68]

More troubling is the potential exclusion of developmental immaturity, particularly with young defendants: this will sometimes coincide with a recognised condition (eg autism), but will not always do so. The Law Commission recommended that developmental immaturity should be explicitly included as an alternative to a recognised medical condition.[69] This was rejected by the government as unnecessary. Government stressed the general overlap with recognised conditions. Despite this, the omission is unfortunate, and may lead to unfairness.

6.2.2.3 Element 3: the abnormality must have substantially impaired D's mental ability to . . .

Although the defence is still called 'diminished responsibility', the pre-2009 requirement of a 'substantially impaired mental responsibility' has been replaced with an element that

---

[66] *Dowds* [2012] EWCA Crim 281.
[67] Kennefick, 'Introducing a New Diminished Responsibility Defence for England and Wales' (2011) 74 MLR 750; evidence of 'Dignity in Dying' to the Joint Committee on Human Rights, 8th Report, 2008–9, para 1.150.
[68] A point made in Horder, *Ashworth's Principles of Criminal Law* (8th edn, 2016) 277–278.
[69] Law Commission, *Murder, Manslaughter and Infanticide* (No 304, 2006) paras 5.125–5.137.

makes no reference to 'responsibility' at all. Rather, D's 'substantial' impairment must be shown to relate to one of three rather more precise abilities (each capable of medical assessment). Whether D's abnormality has substantially impaired her in a relevant way remains a question for the jury. However, such is the medicalisation of the current law that if there is uncontested expert opinion on this matter (demonstrating a relevant impairment) the judge should withdraw murder from the jury unless the prosecution has made clear on what evidence a jury could convict of murder in the face of the expert opinion.[70]

Terminology . . .

The term 'substantial' is not defined in the 2009 Act, but may be crucial to the application of DR. It is clear that substantial impairment should not be interpreted to require a total destruction of capacity and blame, as this ground is already covered by the complete defence of insanity. After the courts had, over many years, adopted different interpretations of the term the Supreme Court has recently provided a concluded view. Some cases had adopted an interpretation that substantial meant only 'more than trivial';[71] whereas in other cases the word substantial had been given a narrower meaning, requiring proof of something much more significant.[72] The Supreme Court's conclusion is that the merely 'more than trivial' approach is not correct. Juries should not generally require an explanation of the word substantial since it is an ordinary English word. If they do, 'the judge should explain that whilst the impairment must indeed pass the merely trivial before it need be considered, it is not the law that *any* impairment beyond the trivial will suffice'.[73] It is surprising that the court felt it necessary to adopt a stricter test when the burden is one borne by the defendant.

. . . understand the nature of D's conduct

This first possibility carries an obvious echo of the insanity defence: which also refers to an inability to understand the nature of one's own conduct.[74] However, unlike insanity, where there must be a complete inability, DR is satisfied by a substantial impairment. An example, adapted from the Law Commission, is a child with a mental illness who obsessively plays violent video games and then kills in the belief that the victim will regenerate as they do in her games.[75] Here, D may understand the physical dynamics of her action, but she does not understand its impact on V.

. . . form a rational judgement

The second possibility is where D's abnormality substantially impairs her ability to form a rational judgement. As the Law Commission highlights,[76] this is the most likely route within DR for an abused person who kills their abuser, or for a so-called mercy killer: in each case the pressure of the circumstances may substantially impair D's ability to make rational choices.[77]

---

[70] *Golds* [2016] UKSC 55, cf *Brennan* [2014] EWCA Crim 2387; commentary by Fortson [2015] Crim LR 291.

[71] See *Ramchurn* [2010] EWCA Crim 194.

[72] *Golds* [2014] EWCA Crim 748. Rogers, 'The Amended Diminished Responsibility Plea' (2015) 74 CLJ 201.

[73] *Golds*, [43].

[74] **Chapter 14**.

[75] Law Commission, *Murder, Manslaughter and Infanticide* (No 304, 2006) para 5.21.

[76] Ibid, para 5.121.

[77] The issue is really about whether D was able rationally to make a choice rather than whether the choice made was a rational one.

. . . exercise control

The final possibility within this element, where D's ability to exercise control is substantially impaired, has the potential to be interpreted very widely. The availability of this option makes it possible to restrict the LOC defence to cases where a person of 'normal' self-restraint might have reacted similarly. Where D is incapable of living up to the standard of 'normal' self-restraint, her defence (if she satisfies all the elements) should be DR.

6.2.2.4 Element 4: the abnormality must provide an explanation (or cause) of the killing

The final element of the DR partial defence requires a causal link between D's abnormality and the killing. Although section 2(1)(c) only states that the abnormality must provide an 'explanation' for the killing, section 2(1B) clarifies that an 'explanation' will be found 'if it causes, or is a significant contributory factor in causing, D to carry out the conduct'. In this manner, the DR defence does not partially excuse D simply because of her abnormality of mental functioning and/or her recognised medical condition. It is rather because these elements combine to have affected her conduct and caused her to kill.

Demonstrating a causal link of this kind is far from straightforward. Causation in criminal law, as we discussed in **Chapter 2**, usually focuses on the external causal effect of D's conduct on a particular result, and this can be very difficult to prove. However, causation in the context of DR requires something even more challenging: assessment of the causal effect of an abnormality *within* the mind of D upon her choice of conduct. Even with the help of medical experts, this is far from an exact science.[78] It is for the defendant to prove.

Another difficulty when applying this element is the chance, which is not uncommon, of multiple causes/motivations (eg D kills as a result of her abnormality and her anger at losing her job). When applying the law to such facts, it is clear that D's abnormality can be a substantial cause without being the sole cause, satisfying this element of the defence. However, it will be necessary for D to demonstrate, on the balance of probabilities, that her condition was not merely incidental. There is a useful discussion of this in the case of *Dietschmann*.[79]

Dietschmann [2003] 1 AC 1209 (pre-C&JA 2009)

D became heavily intoxicated and killed V. D was also suffering from a mental abnormality, a form of depression following the death of his aunt to whom he was very close. D raised the DR defence.

- Crown Court: guilty of murder.
- Court of Appeal: conviction upheld on appeal.
- House of Lords: appeal allowed (D liable for voluntary manslaughter only). It was clarified that although D's killing may have been partly caused by circumstances other than D's abnormality (in this case, voluntary intoxication) it is still open to a jury to find DR as long as D's abnormality remained a substantial aspect. Ignoring the other circumstance, the DR elements were nevertheless satisfied.

---

[78] Miles, 'A Dog's Breakfast of Homicide Reform' [2009] 6 Arch News 6.
[79] Confirmed in *Dowds* [2012] EWCA Crim 281.

Where, as in *Dietschmann*, one of the causes of D's killing is intoxication, three situations should be carefully separated when applying the defence.

(a) First, as confirmed in *Dowds* (discussed earlier), acute intoxication is not a *legally* recognised condition for the purposes of DR, and so intoxication alone cannot provide a basis for the DR defence.

(b) Secondly, where D is intoxicated and has a separate recognised condition (as in *Dietschmann*), the jury should ask whether D's recognised condition caused the killing and, as far as possible, exclude the intoxication from their consideration.

(c) Thirdly, where D has a recognised condition that caused the intoxication (eg drug or alcohol dependency), the jury may take account of *both* the condition and the intoxication related to that condition when considering causation.[80]

6.2.3 Suicide pact partial defence

The third partial defence to murder arises where D kills V pursuant to an agreement that they will die together (a suicide pact). Section 4 of the Homicide Act 1957 states:

(1) It shall be manslaughter, and shall not be murder, for a person acting in pursuance of a suicide pact between him and another to kill the other or be a party to the other . . . being killed by a third person . . .

(2) For the purposes of this section 'suicide pact' means a common agreement between two or more persons having for its object the death of all of them, whether or not each is to take his own life, but nothing done by a person who enters into a suicide pact shall be treated as done by him in pursuance of the pact unless it is done while he has the settled intention of dying in pursuance of the pact.

There are two main elements to this partial defence, set out in **Table 6.3**. Both must be satisfied for D's liability to be reduced from murder to voluntary manslaughter.

Table 6.3 Partial defence of suicide pact

A) D must have agreed with V that they will die together
B) D must intend, at the point of killing V, to die herself in line with the agreement

As with the DR defence, the burden of proof is on D to establish the elements of the defence on the balance of probabilities.[81]

Assessment matters . . .
When applying the law to apparent suicides, take care to identify the correct offences. Where D kills V, then you are right to apply homicide offences and, where relevant, the partial defence of suicide

---

[80] The pre-2009 Act approach is likely to be followed here: *Stewart* [2009] EWCA Crim 593.

[81] Homicide Act 1957, s4(2). This is compatible with D's right to a fair trial under Art 6 ECHR: *AG's Reference (No 1 of 2004)* [2004] 1 WLR 2111.

pacts. However, where D assists or encourages V to kill herself, D will not have committed a homicide offence (she has not caused death). Rather, you should apply the offence of assisting or encouraging suicide.[82] The act of suicide or attempted suicide is not an offence.

6.3 Involuntary manslaughter

Involuntary manslaughter has nothing to do with 'involuntariness'. Rather, the label 'involuntary' is used to differentiate this second form of manslaughter liability from the first (voluntary manslaughter) discussed previously. Crucially, whereas voluntary manslaughter arises where D commits murder and then relies on a partial *defence*, involuntary manslaughter arises where D does not satisfy the mens rea of murder, so does not commit murder, but does commit a lesser manslaughter *offence*.[83] As with all homicide offences, involuntary manslaughter offences require the same actus reus as murder (the unlawful killing of a person). However, the mens rea requirements of involuntary manslaughter offences do not require the same mens rea as murder (an intention to kill or cause GBH).

Three main involuntary manslaughter offences will be discussed in this section. All exist at common law.

- Unlawful act manslaughter: D commits a criminal act in dangerous circumstances, and this causes the death of V.

- Gross negligence manslaughter: D causes V's death through criminal negligence.

- Reckless manslaughter: D causes V's death, being reckless as to causing death or GBH.

> **Don't be confused . . .**
> A fourth involuntary manslaughter offence is that of corporate manslaughter. However, as this offence requires a different actus reus from other manslaughter offences, it will be discussed separately at **6.4.1**.

The main point of contention within involuntary manslaughter offences has been breadth of the forms of mens rea capable of giving rise to liability. Although courts have a wide sentencing discretion, from absolute discharge to life imprisonment, it remains questionable whether all of the conduct currently captured within these offences deserves the label manslaughter. Indeed, the Law Commission has cautioned against this category becoming a 'residual, amorphous, "catch-all" homicide offence'.[84]

6.3.1 Unlawful act manslaughter

Unlawful act manslaughter (UAM) is also (interchangeably) referred to as 'unlawful and dangerous act manslaughter' or 'constructive manslaughter'. In each case, it refers to an

---

[82] Discussed in **Chapter 11**.
[83] See flowchart in **Figure 6.1**.
[84] Law Commission, *Murder, Manslaughter and Infanticide* (No 304, 2006) para 2.9.

involuntary manslaughter offence in which, by her acts, D commits a criminal offence (the base offence), the base offence carries an objective risk of harm to V, and V dies as a result. The current state of the law is presented in **Table 6.4**.

Table 6.4 Unlawful act manslaughter

	Actus reus	Mens rea
Conduct element	Any acts causing the results	Voluntary
Circumstance element	Any circumstances required for the base offence A sober and reasonable person in D's position would recognise a risk of some harm to V	As required for the base offence None
Result element	Any results required for the base offence Death of V	As required for the base offence None

The elements of UAM can be alternatively, and more simply, presented as the combination of three core requirements (illustrated in **Figure 6.2**). The presentation and analysis of UAM in this three-part structure (as opposed to a more traditional discussion of actus reus and mens rea) is the most common approach taken by courts and academics.

Figure 6.2 Unlawful act manslaughter

From the outset, the potential breadth of UAM should be highlighted. At one end of the spectrum, where D's conduct is most blameworthy, UAM will apply to cases just short of liability for murder. For example, where D kills V foreseeing that her act is likely to kill or cause GBH, but not foreseeing it as a virtual certainty,[85] UAM will most likely be applied.[86] In contrast, at the other end of the spectrum, UAM can also be satisfied by conduct which is significantly less blameworthy. For example, where D commits a relatively minor offence without foreseeing significant risks to V, but V is killed as a matter of 'bad luck', UAM is also likely to apply. The most common example of the latter

---

[85] Where D foresees causing death or GBH as a virtual certainty, it is possible that she satisfies the mens rea for murder. See **5.4**.

[86] D is alternatively liable for reckless manslaughter. See **6.3.3**.

(less blameworthy) scenario involves the so-called 'one punch killer' who commits UAM when she hits V (commits a battery), V falls, hits her head, and dies.[87]

As both **Table 6.4** and **Figure 6.2** make clear, liability for UAM does not require D to have any mens rea as to the dangerousness of her action, or as to the resulting death. UAM is a constructive liability offence; with dangerousness and the death of V constructing upon the base offence to create liability for UAM.[88] We will discuss each of these three elements in turn.

6.3.1.1 The unlawful act (base offence)

We must first identify the charge that D would have faced if no one died. We call this the base offence. Historically, this base offence was interpreted very widely to include all criminal offences, and even civil wrongs.[89] However, under the current law, it is clear that only criminal offences will be sufficient.[90]

The most common base offences within UAM are offences against the person (eg D physically attacks and kills V without the mens rea for murder, but with the mens rea for an offence against the person).[91] However, other criminal offences will also qualify. For example, UAM convictions have been based upon criminal damage (eg *Farnon & Ellis*:[92] where a homeless man was killed following a basement fire); and burglary (eg *Watson*:[93] where an elderly homeowner had a heart attack during a burglary). There are two important restrictions on the types of base offence that will satisfy this element.

A) The base offence must be one requiring subjective mens rea: In the case of *Andrews v DPP*,[94] at trial, a charge of UAM was constructed upon a negligence-based dangerous driving offence (D having killed a pedestrian whilst overtaking another car). However, on appeal to the House of Lords, it was stated that the base offence for UAM requires an intrinsically criminal offence, not satisfied by 'a lawful act with a degree of negligence that the legislature makes criminal'. The original meaning of this dictum is ambiguous and troublesome. However, it has been interpreted to mean that offences satisfied by a mens rea of negligence (eg dangerous driving),[95] or those requiring no mens rea at all (ie strict liability offences),[96] will not qualify as potential base offences for UAM. Thus, where D acts negligently to cause death, the appropriate course will be to consider liability for gross negligence manslaughter (discussed in the following section).

B) The base offence must have been completed by an act rather than an omission: Until this issue is revisited in the courts (when we anticipate it will be reversed) it is

---

[87] *Mallett* [1972] Crim LR 260. Mitchell, 'More Thoughts About Unlawful and Dangerous Act Manslaughter and the One Punch Killer' [2009] Crim LR 502.

[88] Constructive crimes are introduced at **4.2.1.1**.

[89] eg *Fenton* (1830) 1 Lew CC 179: involving civil trespass; Buxton, 'By Any Unlawful Act' (1966) 82 LQR 174.

[90] *Kennedy (No 2)* [2007] UKHL 38.

[91] For discussion of the non-fatal offences against the person, see **Chapter 7**.

[92] [2015] EWCA Crim 351.

[93] [1989] Crim LR 730.

[94] [1937] AC 576.

[95] *Lamb* [1967] 2 QB 981.

[96] There is no direct authority on this point, but it is generally accepted and must surely follow from the exclusion of negligence-based offences. See the commentary to *Andrews* [2003] Crim LR 477.

currently the case that the base offence within UAM must have been completed by an action as opposed to an omission.[97] In *Lowe*,[98] the Court of Appeal held that D was not guilty of UAM where his base offence was one of *omitting* to care for his child (an offence under the Children and Young Persons Act 1933, s1(1)). Liability in this case could have been rejected because D's base offence was satisfied by negligence (see point A). However, the court instead focused on the lack of a physical act by D.

With respect, the use of the act/omission distinction in this context lacks any coherent basis: if the criminal law beyond UAM places harm caused by omission in breach of duty alongside harm caused by action, why should it be different in this context?[99] Indeed, as we have discussed,[100] the distinction between acts and omissions is often difficult to define, and so the use of the distinction here simply adds unnecessary complexity to the law.

Assessment matters . . .

Most omissions cases can be dealt with under the alternative involuntary manslaughter offence of gross negligence manslaughter, where liability can be found for omissions. However, criticism of the act/omission rule has been included above because, if applying UAM to omissions within a problem question, it would be sensible to highlight the criticism of the rule and the potential that it may not survive future appellate decisions.

Having identified a potential qualifying base offence (a criminal offence, requiring subjective mens rea, and which is committed by D's acts), it remains essential that every element of that base offence is satisfied by D, and that she does not have a valid defence to that offence. Although this sounds self-evident (ie an 'unlawful act' is only *unlawful* if all criminal elements are completed), it is easily neglected, even by the highest courts.[101] The requirement is illustrated in *Lamb*.[102]

 Lamb [1967] 2 QB 981

D pointed a loaded revolver at V as a joke. Neither D nor V understood how a revolver worked, and so when D pulled the trigger neither realised that the barrel of the gun would revolve and the bullet would be fired. It did, and V was killed.

- Crown Court: guilty of unlawful act manslaughter.
- Court of Criminal Appeal: appeal allowed. The base offence (assault or battery) was not complete because D lacked mens rea, he did not intend or foresee a risk of harm to V or a risk of causing V to apprehend harm.

When identifying the relevant base offence upon which to construct UAM liability, it should be remembered that the general doctrines of criminal law will still apply to this

---

97 Dennis, 'Manslaughter by Omission' (1980) 33 CLP 255.
98 [1973] QB 702.
99 Ashworth, 'Editorial' [1976] Crim LR 529.
100 See **2.6.5**.
101 *DPP v Newbury* [1977] AC 500: where the House of Lords fail to specify the offence at the base of the UAM conviction.
102 See also *Arobieke* [1988] Crim LR 314: D caused V's death, but not through a completed base offence; there was no liability for UAM.

offence. This includes rules that can be used to create liability, such as the intoxication rules discussed in **Chapter 13**, as well as the rules relating to defences discussed (principally) in **Chapter 14**:

Creating liability: where D commits the actus reus of a base offence (eg hits V), but lacks mens rea due to voluntary intoxication, D remains liable for basic intent offences because the intoxication rules serve to replace the absent mens rea. With all elements of the base offence now satisfied, D may be liable for UAM.[103]

Defences: where D commits a base offence, but satisfies the elements of a complete defence, then there is no crime upon which to construct UAM liability.[104] As many UAM cases involve base offences against the person, the most common defences to consider are self-defence and consent.[105] In *Slingsby*, for example, there was no battery, and therefore no UAM, where V *consented* to acts of sexual touching, even though those acts resulted in an unexpected injury and infection from which V died.[106] However, care should always be taken to question whether a potential defence is satisfied. For example, in the case of *A*, D threw V into a river as part of a post-exam celebration, and V drowned. D claimed that V was consenting, but the Crown established that V was not consenting on the facts and D was liable for UAM.[107]

6.3.1.2 The base offence must be dangerous to V

The second element of dangerousness is important, but easily misunderstood. It is not simply a requirement that D's actions are dangerous in fact: as they have caused death, such a requirement would be self-evident and unnecessary. Rather, it is the requirement that a sober and reasonable person in D's position would have foreseen that her acts carried a risk of harm to V at the time D acted. It should be noted that this is an objective requirement. Thus, although the base offence will require some manner of subjective mens rea, the dangerousness element does not.

The full test of the dangerousness of D's conduct is usefully set out by Edmund Davies J in *Church*:[108]

> the unlawful act must be such that all sober and reasonable people would inevitably recognise that it must subject the other person to, at least, the risk of some harm resulting therefrom, albeit not serious harm.

It is important to understand and apply this test of recognition carefully. In particular, four core questions should be borne in mind.

A) **Recognising danger to whom?** The *Church* definition states that D's conduct must be dangerous to the 'other person' and, importantly, this other person should be interpreted as V. Despite some inconsistent authorities,[109] it is now clear that the first element of UAM (the base offence) does not need to be directed or targeted at V. For example, in

---

[103] *Lipman* [1970] 1 QB 152.
[104] *Scarlett* (1994) 98 Cr App R 290.
[105] See **7.3.2–7.3.3** and **7.8.2–7.8.3**.
[106] *Slingsby* [1995] Crim LR 570.
[107] *A* (2005) 69 J Crim L 394.
[108] [1996] 1 QB 59, 70.
[109] *Dalby* [1982] 1 All ER 916.

Watson,[110] D's base offence of burglary was not directed at the elderly homeowner (V), but nevertheless D was liable for UAM when V died from a stress-induced heart attack. In contrast, the second element (dangerousness) will only be satisfied if danger to V is foreseeable. For example, let's imagine that the frail householder in *Watson* died from a heart attack having watched television news footage of a violent crime perpetrated by D. In such a case, D should not be liable for UAM in relation to V unless, at the time of D's acts, there was a foreseeable risk of harm to V, and not just a risk to the more immediate victim of her violent attack. There is support for this approach in *Carey*.[111]

B) **What type of recognition?** The requirement is that a sober and reasonable person would have recognised/foreseen danger to V, *not* whether D herself foresaw it. The test is objective, it is a strict liability element,[112] and not a question of D's personal perception or mens rea. Taking *Watson* as our example again, the test for danger-ousness was satisfied in this case because a reasonable person would have foreseen the risk of causing a heart attack when restraining an elderly person and stealing from them. It is irrelevant whether D personally foresaw the risk of danger, and even whether D was capable of foreseeing the risk (eg due to low IQ).[113]

The only exception, where we take account of D's subjective mind, is where D has 'special knowledge' of risks to V that may not be obviously apparent to a reasonable person. For example, if the victim in *Watson* had been apparently young and healthy then the risk of harm from a non-violent burglary may not have been foreseeable to the sober and reasonable individual. However, if D had known (special knowledge) that the apparently healthy victim had a fragile heart condition, then this could be taken into account within the test, and would likely make danger foreseeable in the *Church* sense.

Although a risk of harm will often be foreseeable (it usually is where death has resulted!), this will not always be the case. This is illustrated in *Dawson*.[114]

Dawson (1985) 81 Cr App R 150

D and others attempted to rob a petrol station using an imitation gun. V, who died of a heart attack, was not elderly, was in apparent good health, and protected behind bullet-proof glass. D was charged with UAM.

- Crown Court: guilty of UAM. Jury directed to consider the risk of danger from the perspective of a reasonable person knowing what they (the jury) knew (including that V was, in fact, suffering from a heart condition).
- Court of Appeal: appeal allowed. Direction was wrong to include facts that were known to the jury, but would not have been apparent to a reasonable person in D's shoes at the time of the attempted robbery.

---

[110] [1989] Crim LR 730.
[111] [2006] EWCA Crim 17: an affray (involving danger/harm to others) was not foreseeably dan-gerous to V.
[112] See **4.2.1.1**.
[113] *Farnon & Ellis* [2015] EWCA Crim 351; commentary at (2015) 79 JCL 234.
[114] See also *Carey* [2006] EWCA Crim 17: death of an apparently healthy young woman when flee-ing from an affray. No foreseeable risk of danger to V: no UAM.

In cases of this kind, D has clearly completed a relevant base offence (attempted robbery); and caused death. However, as harm to V was not objectively foreseeable, this element was not satisfied and there could be no liability for UAM.

C) **What degree of recognition?** The *Church* test speaks of '*all* sober and reasonable people . . . *inevitably*' recognising a risk to V. From this, it is clear that the potential for risk/danger should not be interpreted too widely to include a mere possibility of harm (where harm is possible, but unlikely). The risk must be one that a reasonable person *would* have foreseen rather than *may* have foreseen.

D) **Recognition of what?** We have so far spoken loosely of foresight of a risk of harm or danger. However, precisely what must be foreseen is crucial. Starting again with the quotation from *Church*, we are told that D must foresee 'the risk of some harm . . . albeit not serious harm'. *Church* is therefore important authority that the foreseeable risk of harm need not be a risk of serious harm, and certainly need not be a risk of life-threatening harm. For example, if D hits V, where a reasonable person would foresee the risk of some minor bruising only, this element would be satisfied.

> **Extra detail . . .**
> Although danger of some harm to V must be objectively foreseeable, this danger does not need to be the sole or principal cause of her death. For example, in *JM and SM*,[115] V (a doorman) died after a fight with D. The fight carried an objectively foreseeable risk of harm: standard risks from fighting. However, V did not die as a result of this danger, he died due to a heart attack resulting from a rush of blood during the fight combined with an undiagnosed heart condition. D was liable for UAM.

Although there is no requirement for a foreseeable risk of *serious* harm from D's base crime, a foreseeable risk of a legally recognised harm is essential. In this regard, a foreseeable risk of unlawful physical contact with V (potentially causing various levels of bodily injury) will obviously qualify. Equally, it is clear from the case law that a base crime can be foreseeably dangerous even if no physical contact with V is anticipated, where, for example, bodily harm is still likely (eg from heart attack).[116] Although there is no UAM case to settle this point, it is likely that a foreseeable risk of psychiatric harms would also be sufficient: psychiatric harms (recognised psychiatric conditions) have been accepted as bodily harms in the context of the offences against the person, so there is no reason why they would be excluded here.[117] However, a foreseeable risk of psychological or emotional harms short of psychiatric injury (eg fear or distress) will not be sufficient.[118]

> **Extra detail . . .**
> Proving that sober and reasonable people would inevitably foresee a risk of D's acts causing a psychiatric disorder will always be extremely difficult. In practice, when courts are looking for potential dangerousness, we will almost always be talking about objective foresight of a risk of unlawful contact,

---

[115] [2012] EWCA Crim 2293. See, more recently, *Tarasov (Valodia)*, Court of Appeal, 22 November 2016.

[116] *Watson* [1989] Crim LR 730.

[117] *Ireland and Burstow* [1998] AC 147. See **7.4.1**.

[118] *Dhaliwal* [2006] EWCA Crim 1139, [32]: no UAM liability in case involving psychological abuse causing distress (short of a recognised psychiatric disorder) and ultimately suicide.

or shock/distress causing physical injury (eg heart attack). Further, even in extreme cases where a risk of psychiatric injury is objectively foreseeable (eg potentially following prolonged domestic abuse), other elements of UAM (eg *causing* death) remain major hurdles.

6.3.1.3 The base offence must cause the death of V

The third and final element of UAM is the requirement that D's base offence, as well as foreseeably endangering V, should *cause* V's death. As with the requirement of dangerousness, this is a strict liability element: D's base offence must cause death, but there is no requirement for D to have intended; known; foreseen; or had any mens rea at all as to this result. In this way, UAM is a 'constructive crime': constructing liability by the accumulation of the two strict liability elements upon the base offence. This was at issue in *AG's Reference (No 3 of 1994)*.

 AG's Reference (No 3 of 1994) [1998] AC 245

D stabbed his girlfriend (M), with the intention required for murder and knowing that she was pregnant. Although M survived, the attack later caused her to enter premature labour. The baby (V) was born, but only survived for four months in intensive care before it died. D was charged with the murder of V.

- Crown Court: no liability for murder or UAM. As D was acquitted, the AG appealed the point of law.
- Court of Appeal: D should have been liable for murder using transferred malice—transferring D's intent to kill M to V.
- House of Lords: D should not have been liable for murder as there can be no double transfer of malice.[119] However, D should have been liable for UAM.

Extra detail . . .
Liability for murder was not possible in *AG's Reference (No 3 of 1994)* because of the difficulty of demonstrating mens rea as to the death of V. However, UAM should have been found because no such mens rea is required: D need only complete a base offence (the assault of M); for that offence to be objectively dangerous to V (clearly satisfied); and for that base offence to cause the death V (when the baby dies it is a person, it is not still in the womb).

The causation element of UAM simply requires us to apply the standard causation rules discussed at **2.7**. D's act must be the cause of death in fact (the 'but for' cause); and the cause of death in law (proximate; substantial; and operating). In cases such as *AG's Reference (No 3 of 1994)*, where there is a significant gap between D's acts and the death of V, then a causal link can be more difficult to prove. However, as long as it is proven, as it was in this case, liability will still be found.[120]

Within the general rules of causation, there are three areas of particular interest for UAM.

---

[119] See **4.3.1.1**.
[120] *AG's Reference (No 3 of 1994)* [1998] AC 245: Lord Hope stated that UAM would be committed even if the death was 'many hours, days or even months' after the base offence.

A) **Fright and flight:** V flees from the scene of a crime (base offence) committed by D, and dies when in flight. This can result, for example, from a heart attack brought on from the exertion; by tripping and hitting her head; by running in front of a car; etc. D's likely lack of mens rea as to death or serious injury in these cases will undermine liability of offences such as murder, and should direct you towards the strict elements of UAM. When applying UAM, however, there are two main barriers to liability. First, where D appears healthy and there are no obvious physical hazards, it may be difficult to demonstrate an objectively foreseeable risk of harm in flight.[121] Secondly, it must be shown that V's conduct in taking flight has not broken the chain of causation between D's base offence and V's death: V's response must not be 'wholly disproportionate' or 'daft'. In *Lewis*,[122] for example, liability for UAM was found where V was killed running into a road to escape an ongoing assault from D. V's own conduct in this case clearly contributed to death being caused, but did not break the causal chain from D's assault because it was foreseeable and not 'daft'. In contrast, if V had managed to escape the immediate danger of the assault, and had clear safe options for further flight, her choice to nevertheless run into a busy road may well have passed beyond the foreseeable into the daft, and thus broken the causal chain.

B) **Drug supply:** V voluntarily takes prohibited drugs supplied by D (base offence), and dies from their effects. Following several years of confusion, the case of *Kennedy (No 2)* has now clarified that there can be no liability for UAM in these cases.

> *Kennedy (No 2)* [2007] UKHL 38
>
> D supplied V with a prepared syringe of heroin. V self-injected the drug and died as a result. D was charged with UAM on the basis that his unlawful conduct (drug supply) caused V's death.
> - Crown Court: guilty of UAM.
> - Court of Appeal: conviction upheld on appeal.
> - House of Lords: quashing D's conviction on appeal—D was not guilty because he was not the legal cause of V's death.

In such cases, V's free and voluntary act in self-administering the drug will break the chain of causation between D's base offence (supply) and V's death. It is also debatable whether the act of drug supply alone can give rise to an objectively foreseeable risk of bodily harm.[123] Therefore, to find liability for UAM in these cases it will be necessary to show that D administered the drug directly to V: this base offence[124] is foreseeably dangerous, and does not require the voluntary acts of V to cause death.

C) **Suicide:** V is distressed by D's base offence (eg physical abuse) to such an extent that she commits suicide. Two categories of cases should be distinguished. The first is where D's base offence causes physical injury to V, and V either fails to treat or exacerbates that injury in some manner to cause death. In these cases, causation (and thus

---

121 *Carey* [2006] EWCA Crim 17.
122 [2010] EWCA Crim 151. See also *Tarasov (Valodia)*, Court of Appeal, 22 November 2016: V's choice to jump out of a window (causing death) did not break the causal chain despite a gap of over one hour from D's original attack.
123 Wilson, 'Dealing with Drug Induced Homicide' in Clarkson and Cunningham (eds), *Criminal Liability for Non-Aggressive Deaths* (2008).
124 Offences Against the Person Act 1861, s23.

liability for UAM) has been found on the basis that D's original offence remains a substantial and operating cause of death; V has no duty to limit the harm caused by D; and D must take her victim as she found her.[125] The second category is where D's base offence causes psychiatric harm or where D's injuries are healed at the point of suicide. In these cases, it will be much more difficult to demonstrate that V's suicide was not a free and voluntary act that breaks the chain of causation. However, the possibility of causation in these circumstances, particularly where a history of abuse can be shown to have undermined the voluntariness of V's choice, has been left open within the case law.[126]

6.3.2 Gross negligence manslaughter

Generally, liability for serious offences will be imposed only where D has taken the *choice* to harm or *chosen* to risk harm: punishing D for the harms caused, but also for her blameworthy *choice* in bringing them about. This approach respects the principle of autonomy: someone should only be blamed for advertent wrongdoing.[127] This general approach has meant that there are not many serious offences in English law based on negligence, other than those in a regulatory context.[128] However, gross negligence manslaughter (GNM) stands as an extreme exception, punishable with a maximum of life imprisonment.

GNM provides an offence designed to catch cases where, despite the lack of a conscious choice to risk harms, D's conduct is seriously negligent (unreasonably careless or inattentive), and where that negligence causes death. For example, if D tests her new gun in a busy park and causes death, failing to foresee any potential harm to others because she does not care about and therefore does not consider the safety of others, she is likely to be liable for GNM. Such liability has been recognised for many years.[129]

Despite its long-term recognition, however, GNM has developed inconsistently at common law. For example, during the 1970s and particularly the 1980s, GNM and reckless manslaughter became confused by the use of the *Caldwell*[130] test to define recklessness.[131] However, the current law can be stated with some confidence, having been clarified in the leading case of *Adomako* in the House of Lords.

 Adomako [1994] 3 All ER 79

D (an anaesthetist) failed to notice that a tube supplying oxygen to his patient (V) had become detached. As a result, V died. D was charged with GNM on the basis that his conduct fell dramatically below the standards expected of a reasonable anaesthetist.

• Crown Court: convicted of GNM—negligent test applied without reference to objective recklessness.

---

[125] *Blaue* (1975) 61 Cr App R 271: refusal of medical treatment on religious grounds. *Dear* [1996] Crim LR 595: reopening of wounds caused by D. There is some tension here with the foreseeability principle in causation (see **2.7.2**).

[126] *D* [2006] EWCA Crim 1139; Horder and McGowan, 'Manslaughter by Causing Another's Suicide' [2006] Crim LR 1035.

[127] See **1.4.3**.

[128] See **3.6.2**.

[129] *Finney* (1874) 12 Cox CC 625; *Bateman* (1925) 94 LJKB 791.

[130] See **3.4.4**.

[131] *Stone and Dobinson* [1977] QB 354; *Seymour* [1983] 1 AC 624; *Kong Cheuk Kwan* (1986) 82 Cr App R 18.

- Court of Appeal: conviction upheld on appeal.
- House of Lords: appeal dismissed—correct test requires a duty of care between D and V; a breach of that duty; that D's conduct caused death; and that D's conduct was 'gross' in its negligence. The court clarified that objective recklessness is not part of the test.

The elements of GNM can be set out to separate actus reus and mens rea, as in **Table 6.5**.

Table 6.5 Gross negligence manslaughter

	Actus reus	**Mens rea**
Conduct element	Any conduct causing the results	Voluntary
Circumstance element	There must be a duty of care between D and V D's breach of duty must be 'grossly negligent': must pose a serious and obvious risk of death	Knowledge of facts establishing a duty None
Result element	D must breach her duty of care Death of V	None None

Setting out GNM in this manner highlights the lack of mens rea required as to circumstance or result elements. However, partly because of this lack of mens rea, and partly because of its links with the civil law concept of negligence, GNM is more commonly presented and applied (as in *Adomako*) as the four core elements in **Figure 6.3**.

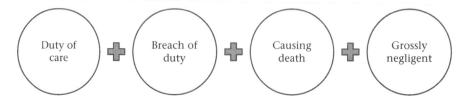

Figure 6.3 Gross negligence manslaughter

We will discuss each of these elements in turn.

6.3.2.1 Duty of care

The first element of GNM requires the prosecution to prove that, at the time of acting to cause death, D owed V a duty of care. Core examples of duties of care include doctors to patients;[132] transport carriers to passengers;[133] employers to employees;[134] etc. However,

---

[132] *Adomako* [1994] 3 All ER 79.
[133] *Barker* [2003] 2 Cr App R 110.
[134] *Dean* [2002] EWCA Crim 2410.

duties will be recognised far beyond these examples. With the definition of a 'duty of care' taken largely from the civil law, it has been interpreted broadly to apply wherever D's conduct caries a foreseeable risk to those around her.[135]

The criminal law is not, however, bound to follow the civil definition of 'duty of care'. As illustrated in *Wacker*, the criminal law has taken a more expansive approach to recognising duties.

> **Wacker** [2003] QB 1203
>
> D was engaged in smuggling 60 illegal immigrants into the UK. D shut the air vent to the container carrying the immigrants, and 58 of them suffocated as a result. D was charged with GNM.
>
> • Crown Court: convicted of GNM.
> • Court of Appeal: conviction upheld on appeal. Although the joint criminal venture between D and the victims would undermine any duty of care in civil law, this was not the case in criminal law.

The ability of the criminal law to recognise duties of care outside those recognised in civil law is important because it allows criminal courts (as in *Wacker*) to avoid complex civil rules/exclusions that do not serve the interests of the criminal law. The aims of the two bodies of law are different: civil law is structured around private compensation between individuals and the consent of both parties to a risky activity or crime may, therefore, undermine a civil claim; whereas the criminal law is structured more generally around the prevention and punishment of wrongs, the blame is coming from the State, rather than in the form of compensation to another non-innocent party.[136]

> **Judge and jury**
> Whether a relationship is capable of giving rise to a duty of care is a legal question for the judge. The jury will be directed that a duty exists if they find certain facts to be present and (where there is dispute on facts) to not find a duty if they find other facts to be present.[137]

Unlike UAM, GNM can be committed by act or *omission*. Where D's positive acts cause death (eg negligent mistreatment by a doctor), then it is only necessary to demonstrate a duty of care as discussed. However, where D's omissions cause death (eg negligent lack of treatment by a doctor), then the standard rules of omissions liability will also apply.[138] This means that as well as a duty of *care*, the court must also identify a duty from the much narrower categories of duties to *act*. We have already discussed the limited duties to act recognised in law: contractual; relationship-based; where D assumes a duty by caring for V; where D has created or contributed to a dangerous situation.[139] Although *both* a duty to act and a duty of care will be required for omission-based

---

[135] *Evans* [2009] EWCA Crim 650; Herring and Palser, 'The Duty of Care in Gross Negligence Manslaughter' [2007] Crim LR 24.

[136] See also *Willoughby* [2005] Crim LR 389: death of V when helping D to commit arson, leading to UAM liability.

[137] *Evans* [2009] EWCA Crim 650, [45].

[138] See **2.6**.

[139] See **2.6.2**.

GNM, the duties within the narrower category of duties to act will always also satisfy a duty of care. Thus, in practice, it is only necessary to identify a duty to act, which will then double as a duty of care as well.[140]

A leading case in relation to omission-based GNM is *Evans*.

 Evans [2009] EWCA Crim 650

D, V's half-sister, supplied her with heroin which she self-administered. Seeing symptoms of an over-dose, D stayed with V but did not alert the authorities for fear of personal liability for supplying the drugs. V died and D was charged with GNM on the basis of her omission to aid V (duty arising from her creation of a dangerous situation when supplying the drugs).

- Crown Court: guilty of GNM.
- Court of Appeal: conviction upheld on appeal.

Evans is an important case for two main reasons.[141] First, it demonstrates a novel way in which GNM can be used to find liability in a drug supply and overdose case. As we discussed earlier, UAM cannot operate in these cases as V's voluntary self-injection will break the chain of causation. However, by focusing on D's negligent omission *after* the self-injection, there is the potential for a causal link between this 'conduct' and V's death. This is illustrated by **Figure 6.4**, with the cross representing V's self-injection (the break in the causal chain).

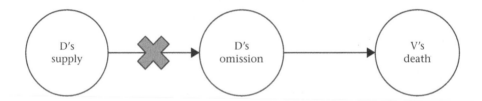

Figure 6.4 Breaking the chain of causation

Evans is also important because it demonstrates the willingness of the courts to expand the definition of a duty to act in certain cases. *Evans* had a duty as per the *Miller*[142] principle: D has a duty to make reasonable efforts to avoid a danger that she has created and then becomes aware of. In *Evans*, in order to find liability it was held that D need not have *created* the danger as long as she *contributed* to its creation: D did not cause the danger in *Evans* because V's self-injection breaks the causal chain. Equally, the court made clear that D need not become subjectively aware of the danger to which she contributed, as long as a reasonable person would have done so. Both represent significant expansions of the offence, and to this form of duty to act.

---

[140] For critical discussion, see Ashworth, 'Manslaughter by Omission and the Rule of Law' [2015] Crim LR 563.

[141] Williams, 'Gross Negligence Manslaughter and Duty of Care in "Drugs" Cases: *R v Evans*' [2009] Crim LR 631.

[142] [1983] 2 AC 161.

> **Point to remember . . .**
> The approach to a duty to act in *Evans* makes it much easier to find liability where D supplies V with a drug, V self-administers, and V dies. However, remember that the duty to act still requires a reasonable person in D's position to have foreseen life-threatening harm. This may be possible where D is present to observe V's overdose or reaction, but is very unlikely where D simply supplies the drug and leaves.

6.3.2.2 Breach of duty of care

The second element of GNM is the requirement that D breaches her duty of care, and duty to act in the context of omission-based GNM. Again, this requirement mirrors negligence in the civil law, and similar principles apply. The question is whether D's conduct has fallen below that expected of a reasonable person in her position. For action-based GNM, we ask whether a reasonable person would have refrained from the acts carried out by D and/or whether a reasonable person would have acted differently. For omission-based GNM, we ask whether a reasonable person in D's position would have acted. As with the civil law, where D purports to exercise a certain skill, the standard against which D's conduct is measured is the reasonable person with that skill. Thus, D's conduct in *Adomako* was measured against the standard of a reasonable anaesthetist, not simply a reasonable person.

> **Don't be confused . . .**
> The consent of V to D's conduct is not relevant to the issue of breach; although it may be relevant to the final element of 'grossness' discussed later. For example, the victims in *Wacker* discussed in the previous section consented to the obviously dangerous venture of attempting to be smuggled in a lorry container. Their consent did not undermine the fact that D's conduct, including the shutting of the vent which led to their deaths, was a breach of his duty to them.

6.3.2.3 Causing death

After it is established that D owed V a duty of care (including a duty to act in omission cases), and that D breached that duty, it must be proved that D's breach caused V's death. For example, where a doctor, D, breaches a duty of care to her patient with negligent treatment, and V dies, it must still be shown that V would not have died in the same way if she had been treated reasonably. The causation element here simply requires us to apply the standard causation rules discussed at **2.7**: D's conduct must be a cause of death in fact (a 'but for' cause); and a cause of death in law (proximate; substantial; and operating).

Even where D's conduct is omission-based, causation must still be found. For omission-based GNM, the question of causation requires us to ask what a reasonable person in D's position would have done, and whether that action would have prevented V dying in the manner she did. For example, D was liable for GNM in *Evans* because she failed to act reasonably to try to save V's life, watching V die of an overdose over the course of hours without calling medical help. However, if we take exactly the same facts as *Evans*, but this time we imagine that V died almost instantly, such that even if D had called for help this could not have effected V's death, then there would have been no causation and no liability.

6.3.2.4 Grossly negligent

The final element of GNM requires D's negligence to be sufficiently 'gross' (ie sufficiently bad) to be deserving of criminal as opposed to simply civil liability. This is a question for the jury. Lord Mackay sets out the question in *Adomako* as follows:

> having regard to the risk of death involved, [was] the conduct of the defendant . . . so bad in all the circumstances as to amount to a criminal act or omission?

Lord Mackay's question, as stated, needs qualification. After all, D's negligent conduct may satisfy a negligence-based criminal offence such as careless or dangerous driving, and yet still not be sufficiently gross for such a serious offence as GNM. Therefore, the grossness element is not simply about distinguishing non-criminal conduct; instead, it asks the jury if D's behaviour warrants liability for manslaughter.

The term 'gross' is rather ambiguous as an offence element, and so it is useful to consider what factors a jury should take into account when applying it to the facts of a case. The first factor is that a reasonable person in D's position must have been able to foresee a risk that D's conduct might cause death. Objective foresight of anything less than death (eg injury, or even serious injury) is insufficient. This requirement was implied within *Adomako*, and later confirmed within *Gurphal Singh*[143] and *Misra*.[144] Crucially, however, the grossness element does not require *subjective* foresight: GNM does not require subjective mens rea.[145] Subjective foresight of causing death will be powerful evidence as to the grossness of D's negligence, but unlike objective foresight, it is not a necessary component.

Although objective foresight of causing death is a necessary factor within the grossness test, it is not automatically sufficient. Rather, the second factor requires the jury to look at all the surrounding circumstances in order to make their assessment; for example, what were D's motives; was she acting maliciously; how did she explain her conduct; and so on. The discretion given to the jury here can be useful to ensure only those deserving, all things considered, of GNM liability are brought within the offence. However, the absence of clear criteria makes it difficult to predict the outcome of cases, and has given rise to powerful criticism about the potential for inconsistency[146] with different juries applying the test differently, and about the role of the jury more generally.[147]

The latter criticism, about the role of the jury, focuses on whether the grossness element is asking the jury to establish facts, which is the correct role of the jury, or whether it is asking them to establish matters of law, which is the correct role of the *judge*.[148] When applying elements of a crime, the jury should be given the legal definition of that element by the judge and then be asked to decide whether, on the facts as they

---

[143] [1999] Crim LR 582.

[144] [2004] EWCA Crim 2375.

[145] *S* [2015] EWCA Crim 558; *Misra* [2004] EWCA Crim 2375.

[146] Such inconsistency can also be reflected in decisions to prosecute. Quick, 'Prosecuting "Gross" Medical Negligence: Manslaughter, Discretion and the Crown Prosecution Service' (2006) 33 JLS 421.

[147] The Court of Appeal has recently encouraged trial judges to provide more detail to juries about what factors to consider when deciding the question of grossness: *Sellu* [2016] EWCA Crim 1716.

[148] See **1.1.7.1**.

believe them to be, that element is satisfied. With regard to the grossness element, it can appear as if this division of expertise has broken down: the jury are told to find the grossness element as having been satisfied if they find the facts to be criminal in nature, and to find the facts criminal if they find them gross. This test is circular and, in effect, it is asking the jury to define the offence (the law) as they apply it. However, despite the apparent circularity, the test has survived challenges on human rights grounds and remains valid.[149]

6.3.3 Reckless manslaughter

Reckless manslaughter is the last of the three common law involuntary manslaughter offences. D will come within this offence where she causes V's death by act or omission and is at least reckless as to causing death or GBH. The elements are set out in **Table 6.6**.

Table 6.6 Reckless manslaughter

	Actus reus	Mens rea
Conduct element	Any act or omission causing the result	Voluntary
Circumstance element	V is a person	Knowledge
Result element	Death of V	Recklessness as to death or GBH

The offence of reckless manslaughter is rarely prosecuted, and so there are few appeal cases discussing its interpretation.[150] It is rarely prosecuted because cases coming within this offence will almost always alternatively satisfy the elements of either UAM or GNM and, as these two offences do not require subjective mens rea as to death or serious harm, they will usually be easier to prosecute. The only cases where D commits reckless manslaughter *and not* UAM or GNM, arise where D kills by omission (thus no UAM), and where D's omission does not pose an objectively foreseeable risk of death (thus no GNM).

Mitchell and Mackay have found that reckless manslaughter is occasionally charged where the facts of a case involve culpability just short of murder, where it is clear that D foresaw a high risk of causing death or GBH, but it would be difficult to demonstrate that it was foreseen as a virtual certainty (ie difficult to prove the intention required for murder).[151]

---

[149] See Lord Justice Judge's attempt to explain the test in a non-circular way in *Misra* [2004] EWCA Crim 2375, [62]–[63].

[150] One of the few exceptions is *Lidar* [2000] 4 Arch News 3.

[151] Mitchell and Mackay, 'Investigating Manslaughter: An Empirical Study of 127 Cases' (2011) 31 OJLS 165.

This makes sense, both in relation to the law in practice and as an approach to problem questions. If it is clear that D foresaw death or GBH as highly likely, then a jury may find foresight equivalent to virtual certainty and thus find liability for murder, but will at the very least find a foresight that will satisfy the requirements of reckless manslaughter.

6.4 Statutory offences of unlawful killing

This chapter has focused on the traditional manslaughter conviction: voluntary manslaughter resulting from a partial defence to murder, and involuntary manslaughter resulting from a common law manslaughter offence. However, the criminal law also recognises a number of other offences of unlawful killing, some of which employ the label manslaughter. These offences are discussed briefly in this section, and their differences from the traditional forms will be highlighted.

6.4.1 Corporate manslaughter

Under standard rules of corporate liability,[152] it has been possible for a corporation to commit homicide offences: most commonly GNM. However, with the Corporate Manslaughter and Corporate Homicide Act 2007 (CMA 2007),[153] a new route to corporate liability has been created and GNM for companies has been abolished.[154] The offence is commonly presented as a form of involuntary manslaughter alongside the traditional common law offences of UAM, GNM, and reckless manslaughter. However, we have separated it in our discussion because unlike the traditional involuntary manslaughter offences, corporate manslaughter does not require the standard actus reus of murder to have been committed (the killing of a person, by a person), but can be satisfied where a variety of acts or omissions within the corporation, potentially from many different individuals, combine to cause death.

The CMA 2007 is based indirectly on preceding Law Commission recommendations.[155] The Commission and others were critical of the way the common law had failed to find GNM in relation to companies. This was because, particularly with respect to large and complex companies, it would often be impossible to identify a 'controlling mind' (ie very senior figure) within the company who was individually[156] responsible in GNM for V's death. In the absence of such a figure, even if a general culture of negligence was found within large parts of the corporation, and these were found to have caused V's death, the common law identification doctrine could not link liability to the corporation.[157] As we discuss later, the CMA 2007 seeks to address these problems

---

[152] See **1.5.1**.
[153] Ormerod and Taylor, 'The Corporate Manslaughter and Corporate Homicide Act 2007' [2008] Crim LR 589.
[154] CMA 2007, s20.
[155] Law Commission, *Involuntary Manslaughter* (No 237, 1996).
[156] The old law would not allow the acts of employees to be aggregated together and viewed as the acts of the corporation: *AG's Reference (No 2 of 1999)* [2000] QB 796.
[157] Wells, 'Corporate Manslaughter: Why Does Reform Matter?' (2006) 123 SALJ 646.

within the new offence. However, it is noteworthy that the few successful prosecutions under the offence have also (so far) focused on smaller corporations.[158]

> **Extra detail . . .**
> Directors and other individuals within a corporation cannot be charged with the corporate manslaughter offence, and cannot be a secondary party to a corporate manslaughter offence. However, they can still be individually liable under one of the standard common law involuntary manslaughter offences, or for health and safety offences.[159]

The corporate manslaughter offence is set out in section 1(1) of the CMA 2007. Where D (a corporation) is found liable under this section, it will face an unlimited fine,[160] potentially combined with a remedial order and/or a publicity order.[161]

(1) An organisation to which this section applies is guilty of an offence if the way in which its activities are managed or organised—

(a) causes a person's death, and

(b) amounts to a gross breach of a relevant duty of care owed by the organisation to the deceased.

The structure of this offence is similar to GNM, and its analysis and application should be approached in a similar manner. The elements are set out in **Figure 6.5**.

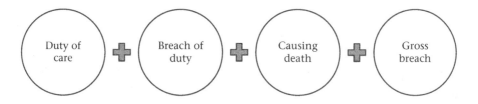

Figure 6.5 Corporate manslaughter

Before discussing these elements, it is necessary first to identify which organisations are capable of committing the offence. This is set out in section 1(2) to include most corporations, police forces, partnerships, trade unions, or employers' associations, as well as various government departments.

6.4.1.1 Duty of care

D (the relevant organisation) must owe a duty of care to V (the person killed). As with GNM, the duty requirement will be interpreted in line with established civil law duties. As set out in section 2 of the CMA 2007, the most relevant duties will be to employees;

---

[158] *Cotswold Geological Holdings Ltd* [2011] EWCA Crim 1337; Dobson, 'Shifting Sands: Multiple Counts in Prosecutions for Corporate Manslaughter' [2012] Crim LR 200.

[159] Antrobus, 'The Criminal Liability of Directors for Health and Safety Breaches and Manslaughter' [2013] Crim LR 309.

[160] CMA 2007, s1(6).

[161] Ibid, ss9–10.

visitors on premises; customers; etc. As with GNM, it is for the judge to decide as a matter of law what is capable of giving rise to a duty of care.[162]

The scope of this element and, therefore, the offence, is severely limited by a number of exceptions where a duty of care will not be found. For example, section 3 excludes public policy decisions. This will exclude a number of cases, including where government departments make potentially negligent decisions to remove funding from projects and people die as a result (eg the funding of certain medical drugs). Section 4 excludes military activities; section 5 excludes certain police activities; section 6 excludes certain activities of the emergency services; and section 7 has a similar role for child protection and probation services. In each case, these provisions are unnecessarily complex in their construction, and are likely to lead to appeals.

6.4.1.2 Breach of duty of care

This element requires D (the relevant organisation) to have breached its duty to V by failing to perform in a reasonable manner, to the standard of a relevant reasonable organisation. Importantly, and in contrast to the old identification doctrine approach discussed earlier, this breach does not need to be identified in the conduct of a single representative of the organisation, but can be found through an aggregation of the organisation's activities as a whole.

The crucial restricting qualification to this is that a 'substantial element' of the breach must be traceable to 'the way in which [D's] activities are managed or organised by its senior management'.[163] This is not as restrictive as the identification doctrine: 'senior management' is interpreted more broadly than those who would have qualified as controlling minds;[164] 'senior management' allows aggregation across those in that class; and their impact only needs to be 'substantial' as opposed to sole or even dominant. However, any restrictions of this kind relating to senior figures will inevitably make the prosecution of larger and more complex organisations more difficult.

6.4.1.3 Causing death

As with GNM, the standard rules of causation will apply.[165]

6.4.1.4 Gross breach of duty

Finally, it must be established that D's (the relevant organisation's) breach of duty was 'gross'. As with GNM, this is a question for the jury. However, unlike with GNM, the CMA 2007 provides significant guidance for the jury in their assessment. Section 1(4)(b) states that:

> a breach of a duty of care by an organisation is a 'gross' breach if the conduct alleged to amount to a breach of that duty falls far below what can reasonably be expected of the organisation in the circumstances.

---

[162] Ibid, s2(5).
[163] Ibid, s1(3).
[164] Ibid, s14(c) defines 'senior management' as those having significant roles in managing significant activities or parts of the organisation.
[165] See **2.7**.

Section 8 then goes on to provide factors for the jury to consider, including the seriousness of D's failure and how foreseeable it was that a risk of death would be created. Additional factors listed in section 8 also include an assessment of the culture towards risk within the organisation, as well as any breaches of health and safety law.[166]

6.4.2 Driving causing death

There are many statutory offences involving causing death by driving. Where D kills V with her car, there is nothing to stop her being charged with murder or manslaughter at common law, provided the relevant elements of the offence can be proved (ie including mens rea). However, for reasons of fair labelling, and in order to tailor offences to secure convictions for road-based homicides, a series of bespoke offences have been created.[167]

6.4.2.1 Causing death by dangerous driving

Section 1 of the Road Traffic Act 1988 (RTA 1988)[168] makes it an offence to cause death by driving a 'mechanically propelled vehicle dangerously on a road or other public place'.[169] The elements are set out in **Table 6.7**.

Table 6.7 RTA 1988, s1

	Actus reus	Mens rea
Conduct element	Causing the result by driving	Voluntary
Circumstance element	D's driving of a vehicle in public is dangerous	None
Result element	Death of V	None

As the table demonstrates, causing death by dangerous driving is a negligence-based offence. All that is required is that D's driving caused V's death, employing the standard rules of causation,[170] and that D's driving, at the relevant time, was objectively dangerous.

D's driving will qualify as 'dangerous' where 'the way he drives falls far below what would be expected of a competent and careful driver, *and* it would be obvious to a competent driver that driving in that way would be dangerous' (ie would risk injury or serious property damage).[171] This also includes cases where the mechanical state of the car

---

[166] Wright, 'Criminal Liability of Directors and Senior Managers for Deaths at Work' [2007] Crim LR 949.

[167] Cunningham, 'The Reality of Vehicular Homicides: Convictions for Murder, Manslaughter and Causing Death by Dangerous Driving' [2001] Crim LR 679.

[168] As amended by the Road Traffic Act 1991.

[169] The Legal Aid, Sentencing and Punishment of Offenders Act 2012, s143 has inserted a new offence in the RTA 1988, s1A of causing GBH by dangerous driving. Applying similar terms to s1, this offence applies where D causes serious harm which falls short of death.

[170] See **2.7**.

[171] RTA 1988, s2A (emphasis added).

makes driving dangerous, and this would have been obvious to a reasonable driver.[172] As with other negligence-based offences, D's knowledge of the factors making her driving dangerous are irrelevant to her liability if they would have been obvious to a reasonable person.[173] The only exception is one working against D: where she has special knowledge of potential danger beyond that of a reasonable driver, as for example where she is a mechanic and recognises signs of danger, her driving may be found to be dangerous on that basis.

6.4.2.2 Causing death by careless driving

Section 2B of the RTA 1988 makes it an offence to cause death by driving a 'mechanically propelled vehicle on a road or other public place without due care and attention, or without reasonable consideration for other persons using the road or place'.[174] The elements are set out in **Table 6.8**.

Table 6.8 RTA 1988, s2B

	Actus reus	**Mens rea**
Conduct element	Causing the result by driving	Voluntary
Circumstance element	D's driving of a vehicle in public is without due care and attention, Or without reasonable consideration for others	None
Result element	Death of V	None

Filling the perceived gap below the section 1 offence, here D's driving does not need to carry an obvious objective risk of causing harm to the person or property. Rather, it is enough that D was driving in a careless manner,[175] and that she caused death.

6.4.2.3 Causing death by careless driving when under the influence of drink or drugs

Section 3A of the RTA 1988 makes it an offence to cause death by driving a 'mechanically propelled vehicle on a road or other public place without due care and attention, or without reasonable consideration for other persons using the road or place, and he is, at the time when he is driving, unfit to drive through drink or drugs, *or* he has consumed so much alcohol that the proportion of it in his breath, blood or urine at that time exceeds the prescribed limit, *or* he is . . . required to provide a specimen . . . but without reasonable excuse fails to provide it, *or* he is required by a constable to give his permission for a laboratory test of a specimen of blood taken from him . . . but without reasonable excuse fails to do so'. The elements are set out in **Table 6.9**.

---

[172] Ibid, s2A(2) and (3); *Strong* [1995] Crim LR 428.
[173] *Roberts and George* [1997] Crim LR 209.
[174] Created by the Road Safety Act 2006, s30.
[175] Defined at RTA 1988, s3ZA.

Table 6.9 RTA 1988, s3A

	Actus reus	Mens rea
Conduct element	Causing the result by driving	Voluntary
Circumstance element	D's driving of a vehicle in public is without due care and attention, *or* without reasonable consideration for others	None
	And	
	D is unfit to drive through drink or drugs; or	None
	she exceeds the alcohol limit; or	
	she fails to provide a specimen; or	
	she does not give permission for a specimen to be tested	
Result element	Death of V	None

This offence constructs upon the section 2B offence, leading to more serious liability where one of the aggravating factors is present.

6.4.2.4 Causing death while driving unlawfully

Section 3ZB of the RTA 1988[176] makes it an offence to cause death whilst driving without a valid driving licence, or whilst uninsured. The elements are set out in **Table 6.10**.

Table 6.10 RTA 1988, s3ZB

	Actus reus	Mens rea
Conduct element	Causing the result by driving	Voluntary
Circumstance element	D is driving a vehicle in public; and	None
	D has no licence; or	
	D is uninsured	
Result element	Death of V	None

Alongside this offence, and with the same construction, section 3ZC of the RTA 1988 includes an offence of causing death whilst disqualified from driving.[177]

These offences have been controversial because, read literally, they appear to criminalise D for causing death even where she is not a blameworthy cause: her driving is

---

[176] Created by the Road Safety Act 2006, s21.
[177] As amended by the Criminal Justice and Courts Act 2015, s29.

competent. Indeed, this is how section 3ZB was originally applied.[178] However, following academic criticism,[179] the Supreme Court has now confirmed that D's driving must have caused death through some fault on her part.[180] This confirms the general principle of causation that all causes must be blameworthy.[181]

6.4.3 Infanticide

The infanticide rules apply to cases in which D (a mother) kills V (her child) within the first year of its life where, at the time of killing, D's mind was disturbed due to the birth or due to her lactation as a result of the birth.[182] These rules are specifically designed to distinguish killings of this type from traditional homicide offences. To this end, infanticide can operate *either* as an offence in its own right, *or* as a partial defence to murder or manslaughter. The law is set out in section 1 of the Infanticide Act 1938.[183]

6.4.3.1 The offence of infanticide

Section 1(1) of the 1938 Act makes it an offence:

> Where a woman by any wilful act or omission causes the death of her child being a child under the age of twelve months, but at the time of the act or omission the balance of her mind was disturbed by reason of her not having fully recovered from the effect of giving birth to the child or by reason of the effect of lactation consequent upon the birth of the child, then . . . she shall be guilty of . . . infanticide, and may for such offence be dealt with and punished as if she had been guilty of the offence of manslaughter of the child.

The elements of infanticide are set out in **Table 6.11**.

Table 6.11 Infanticide

	Actus reus	Mens rea
Conduct element	Act or omission causing the result	Voluntary
Circumstance element	D is the mother of V; and V is under 12 months old; and D's mind was disturbed by the effects of giving birth, or her lactation from giving birth	None
Result element	Death of V	None

---

[178] *Williams* [2010] EWCA Crim 2552.

[179] See Ormerod [2011] Crim LR 473, and Sullivan and Simester, 'Causation Without Limits: Causing Death Whilst Driving Without a Licence, While Disqualified, or Without Insurance' [2012] Crim LR 754.

[180] *Hughes* [2013] UKSC 56; *Taylor* [2016] UKSC 5.

[181] See **2.7.2.2**.

[182] Mackay, 'The Consequences of Killing Very Young Children' [1993] Crim LR 21; Wilczynski and Morris, 'Parents Who Kill Their Children' [1993] Crim LR 31; Brennan, 'Beyond the Medical Model: A Rationale for Infanticide Legislation' (2007) 58 NILQ 505.

[183] As amended by the Coroners and Justice Act 2009, s57.

Where D satisfies these elements, she will be liable for infanticide regardless of whether she satisfies the elements of any other homicide offence (the *offence* of infanticide is free-standing and independent of other offences).[184] The offence will often be charged where D kills V when suffering from postnatal depression, and sentences are usually relatively low.[185] It should be noted that the rather artificial link to the physical birth of the child or D's lactation has been criticised, but it seems that the courts will interpret these requirements broadly to allow appropriate cases to come within the offence.[186]

6.4.3.2 The partial defence of infanticide

Section 1(2) of the 1938 Act states that:

> Where upon the trial of a woman for the murder of her child, being a child under the age of twelve months, the jury are of opinion that she by any wilful act or omission caused its death, but that at the time of the act or omission the balance of her mind was disturbed by reason of her not having fully recovered from the effect of giving birth to the child or by reason of the effect of lactation consequent upon the birth of the child, then the jury may, notwithstanding that the circumstances were such that but for the provisions of this Act they might have returned a verdict of murder, return in lieu thereof a verdict of infanticide.

The effect of this section is that even where D is charged with, and satisfies, the elements of murder or manslaughter, if the court finds the elements of infanticide to be satisfied as well, they should find liability for infanticide only. D has an evidential burden to raise the defence, and it is then for the prosecution (if they so choose) to disprove the elements beyond a reasonable doubt.

> *Point to remember . . .*
> The infanticide rules only apply to biological mothers within the first year of birth. Outside this (eg fathers who kill), D will be potentially liable for the traditional homicide offences, and will have to rely on defences such as diminished responsibility.

6.4.4 The killing of a foetus

The unlawful killing of a foetus does not represent a homicide offence because a foetus is not a person in law until it is fully independent of its mother, by being fully expelled from the womb.[187] The abortion of a foetus within 24 weeks of conception in certain conditions, or after this point in more exceptional conditions, has been a legal practice for some time.[188] However, outside this regulated procedure, the killing of a foetus is likely to constitute an offence under one of two headings.

A) Section 1 of the Infant Life (Preservation) Act 1929: This section creates the offence of 'child destruction': the intentional killing of a foetus capable of being born

---

[184] *Gore* [2008] Crim LR 388: clarifying that infanticide does not require mens rea as to death.
[185] The maximum sentence is life imprisonment, but most cases result in community orders.
[186] *Kai-Whitewind* [2006] Crim LR 348.
[187] See **5.3.2.3**.
[188] Abortion Act 1967, s1.

alive. A foetus is capable of being born alive where it would be capable of independent breathing, from around 26 weeks.[189] The offence is punishable with a maximum of life imprisonment.

B) Section 58 of the Offences Against the Person Act 1861: This section creates the offence of attempting to procure a miscarriage: where D (whether the mother of V or any other person) intentionally attempts to cause a miscarriage at any stage by means of ingestion of a noxious thing (eg poisons) or other means.[190] The offence may be committed even where the 'mother' is not in fact pregnant, where D (any person other than the 'mother') acts with the intent to cause a miscarriage.

> **Point to remember . . .**
> As discussed earlier, although the killing of a foetus will not amount to a homicide offence, liability for a homicide offence may be possible where the foetus is injured by D when in the womb and dies later after birth.[191] As long as the foetus is born alive before it dies, it becomes a 'person' within the meaning of the law.

6.5 Reform

In this section we will highlight a number of ongoing debates in relation to manslaughter and the potential for further reform. We begin with debates focused on the core defences leading to voluntary manslaughter and offences leading to involuntary manslaughter, we then consider the overall structure of manslaughter within the law.

6.5.1 Reforming voluntary manslaughter

Despite the extensive reform of loss of control and diminished responsibility within the Coroners and Justice Act 2009, considerable debate remains about the role and construction of these partial defences. To some extent this is inevitable, particularly where academics and/or courts identify categories of defendant that should, morally, fall outside the scope of murder and the mandatory life sentence, and where the partial defences seem to be the only method of achieving this end.[192]

Beginning with the partial defence of loss of control, it is useful to look back (see **Table 6.12**) on three controversial points identified in relation to the pre-2009 law and see whether they remain a concern for the current law.

---

[189] *Rance v Mid-Downs Health Authority* [1991] 1 QB 587; Foster, 'Forty Years On' (2007) 157 NLJ 1517.
[190] *Ahmed* [2010] EWCA Crim 1949.
[191] See **6.3.1.2**, discussing *AG's Reference (No 3 of 1994)* [1998] AC 245.
[192] Such inevitability, while we retain the mandatory life sentence for murder, is recognised by the Law Commission in *Partial Defences to Murder* (No 290, 2004) para 2.68.

Table 6.12 Evaluating the current partial defence of LOC

What types of conduct can qualify as provocation (or, under the current law, as 'triggers')?	The 2009 Act defines 'qualifying triggers' in a way that both narrows and expands the previous law. It narrows the trigger based on provocative acts or omissions to only those creating a 'justifiable sense' of D being 'seriously wronged'. It expands the law by introducing a new fear of serious violence trigger. These general categories, although rather vague, have been generally welcomed.[193] However, the specific exclusion of sexual infidelity has not been successful.[194]
What characteristics of D can be taken into account when deciding if her reaction should qualify for the defence?	This question was problematic under the old law, but the 2009 Act seems to resolve it in a compromise between the two options debated within the old law. However, the slightly ambiguous reference in the statute to 'in the circumstances of D' may have the unfortunate consequence of reopening this debate.[195] Indeed, some believe that it should be reopened in order to allow the offence to have a wider application.[196]
Is the defence gender-biased in its operation?	Significant efforts have been made to make the defence more gender-neutral, including the new fear of serious violence trigger and the removal of the 'sudden and temporary' requirement for D's loss of control. However, the government's choice to retain the requirement that D should have lost control in fact (contrary to the Law Commission's recommendations) maintains a significant hurdle for female defendants who are much less likely to react through a loss of control (particularly in the context of abused women).[197]

The current LOC defence is a significant improvement on the previous common law, and has been further strengthened by a series of useful early Court of Appeal judgments. However, uncertainties remain.[198]

For diminished responsibility, it is useful to start with the general scope and aim of the defence. This is because the medicalisation of the elements of DR will almost inevitably restrict its use as a flexible (undefined) tool of legal equity: a tool for avoiding murder and the mandatory life sentence in 'deserving' cases. In this regard, we may think the law should have remained broadly defined, thereby allowing flexibility to deal more sensitively with women who kill their abusers; and even so-called mercy killers. On the other hand, we may think the law should be strictly defined, that Parliament should be

---

[193] See **6.2.1.3**.

[194] For a useful discussion of specific and general exclusions, see Crofts and Loughnan, 'Provocation, NSW Style: Reform of the Defence of Provocation in NSW' [2014] Crim LR 109.

[195] See **6.2.1.4**.

[196] Mitchell, Mackay, and Brookbanks, 'Pleading for Provoked Killers: In Defence of *Morgan Smith*' (2008) 124 LQR 675.

[197] See **6.2.1.2**.

[198] Parsons, 'The Loss of Control Defence—Fit for Purpose? (2015) 79 JCL 94.

responsible for creating defences for these classes of defendants where necessary. One's view of the new defence, and the appropriateness of future reform, will chiefly depend upon which side of this debate is preferred.

Accepting that the current law has adopted a relatively precise definition of DR, there is also room to question that detail. Two areas stand out. First, there remains a concern that developmentally immature defendants without an associated learning disability will fall outside the defence. The Law Commission's recommendations extended the defence to the developmentally immature and it is concerning that they have been omitted from the final reform.[199] Secondly, having established the first three limbs of the defence (abnormality of mental functioning; caused by a recognised condition; substantially impairing D's ability to control or understand her actions), it is arguable that the further requirement of a causal link between D's abnormality and the killing is both medically incapable of being proved and morally unnecessary.[200]

6.5.2 Reforming involuntary manslaughter

The common law offences of UAM and GNM are some of the most controversial in the criminal law. In both cases, the offences label and punish D for manslaughter without requiring her to have foreseen the possibility that her acts will cause death: they both include elements of strict liability.[201]

For UAM, this led the Law Commission at one time to recommend abolition of the offence without replacement.[202] However, more recently, the Commission has made recommendations that reduce the constructive nature of the offence by requiring *some* mens rea as to death or injury, but leaving its basic structure largely intact.[203] For those opposed to constructive liability, this remains inadequate.[204]

Similar criticisms can be made of GNM. Indeed, as GNM does not require D to have committed a base offence with necessary mens rea, it is capable of criminalising D for manslaughter where she has not chosen to commit, or risk committing, any offence at all. Rather, it will be enough that her behaviour is classified by a jury as falling grossly below the level expected. The Law Commission has consistently recommended the maintenance of GNM, although it would like it to be codified in legislation, and to make D's ability (capacity) to appreciate the risk of death as an express element.[205]

6.5.3 Reforming the structure of manslaughter offences

The Law Commission has recommended a restructuring of murder and manslaughter into three tiers (a ladder) of offences.[206] This was introduced in the context of murder in the previous chapter, where we acknowledged the unlikelihood of this structure being

---

[199] See **6.2.2.2**.
[200] Mackay, 'The New Diminished Responsibility Plea' [2010] Crim LR 299.
[201] See generally Clarkson and Cunningham (eds), *Criminal Liability for Non-Aggressive Death* (2008).
[202] Law Commission, *Involuntary Manslaughter* (Consultation 135, 1994).
[203] Law Commission, *Murder, Manslaughter and Infanticide* (No 304, 2006) para 2.163.
[204] Keating, 'The Restoration of a Serious Crime' [1996] Crim LR 535.
[205] Law Commission, *Murder, Manslaughter and Infanticide* (No 304, 2006) para 3.60.
[206] Law Commission, *Murder, Manslaughter and Infanticide* (No 304, 2006); Ashworth, 'Principles, Pragmatism and the Law Commission's Recommendations on Homicide Law Reform' [2007] Crim LR 333.

adopted into legislation.[207] However, the recommendations provide a useful insight into how that law might be rationalised. The structure recommended by the Commission is as follows:

> . . . first degree murder should encompass:

(1) intentional killings, and

(2) killings with the intent to cause serious injury where the killer was aware that his or her conduct involved a serious risk of causing death.[208]

> **Extra detail . . .**
> First degree murder is expanded beyond intentional killing to include a killing with the intention to cause serious harm (as with the current law). However, the requirement that D must foresee a serious risk of death would, if enacted, reduce the scope of the offence as where D stabs V in the leg causing GBH, but V dies following an unforeseen medical complication. The mandatory life sentence would apply to first degree murder.

> . . . second degree murder should encompass:

(1) killings intended to cause serious injury; or

(2) killings intended to cause injury or fear or risk of injury where the killer was aware that his or her conduct involved a serious risk of causing death; or

(3) killings intended to kill or to cause serious injury where the killer was aware that his or her conduct involved a serious risk of causing death but successfully pleads provocation, diminished responsibility or that he or she killed pursuant to a suicide pact.[209]

> **Extra detail . . .**
> The proposed offence of second degree murder would carry a maximum (non-mandatory) life sentence. This offence would encompass certain cases currently dealt with as murder (1), but also the more serious cases currently dealt with as manslaughter (2 and 3).

> . . . manslaughter should encompass:

(1) killing another person through gross negligence ('gross negligence manslaughter'); or

(2) killing another person:

    (a) through the commission of a criminal act intended by the defendant to cause injury, or

    (b) through the commission of a criminal act that the defendant was aware involved a serious risk of causing some injury ('criminal act manslaughter').[210]

> **Extra detail . . .**
> The least culpable form of homicide would retain the label of manslaughter, with a maximum (non-mandatory) life sentence. This would cover reformed versions of the current involuntary manslaughter offences.

---

[207] See **5.6.2**.
[208] Law Commission, *Murder, Manslaughter and Infanticide* (No 304, 2006) para 9.5.
[209] Ibid, para 9.6.
[210] Ibid, para 9.9.

6.6 Eye on assessment

In this section we discuss the potential application of manslaughter within a problem question. The same structure of analysis should be employed as we have discussed in previous chapters.

> **STEP 1 Identify the potential criminal event in the facts**
>
> This is unlikely to take more than a sentence, but it is essential to tell your reader where in the facts you are focusing. For homicide offences, this involves pointing out where a person has died (eg 'The first potential criminal event arises where Mary shoots at Vicky and Vicky dies').

> **STEP 2 Identify the potential offence**
>
> Having identified the facts (eg D potentially killing V), you must now identify the offence you are going to apply. Usually, this means identifying the most serious offence that D might have committed.

When applying Step 2, it is useful to keep in mind the flowchart with which we began the chapter, repeated in **Figure 6.6**.

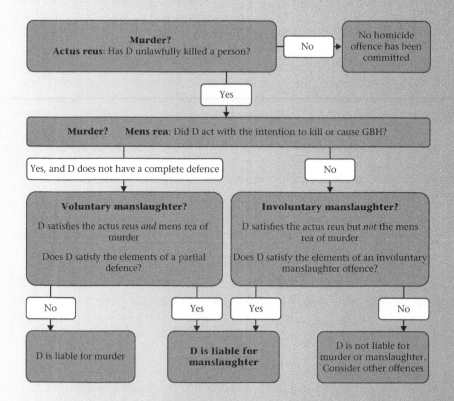

Figure 6.6 Locating homicide liability

In line with the flowchart, unless the question isolates a specific offence for discussion (eg 'Discuss Mary's potential liability for unlawful act manslaughter'),[211] you should begin with the most serious potential offence: murder.

> **STEP 3 Applying the offence to the facts**
>
> Actus reus: What does the offence require? Did D do it?
> Mens rea: What does the offence require? Did D possess it?

6.6.1 Where the elements of murder are satisfied

Where the elements of murder are satisfied, you should move on to discuss potential defences.

> **STEP 4 Consider defences**
>
> The word 'consider' here is important, as you should not discuss every defence for every question. Rather, think whether there are any defences that *could* potentially apply. If there are, discuss those only.

When discussing defences, always begin with the complete defences (**Chapters 13** and **14**) as these usually lead to a complete acquittal. Remember that the defence of duress does not apply to murder. If none of the complete defences apply, or there is some doubt over their application, continue to discuss the partial defences to murder.

When discussing the partial defences, it is usually appropriate to discuss loss of control first and then go on to consider diminished responsibility (this reflects the preference of most defendants, partly because LOC does not entail a reversal of the burden of proof). As both of these defences are statute-based, your discussion should be structured around the elements of the defences as stated in the statute. Cases that post-date the statute are most useful to identify how the courts apply the defence elements in practice. Cases pre-dating the statute may also be useful as an indication of how the statute is likely to be applied, particularly where the statute appears to be the codification of rules taken from an old case, but remember that such cases are not binding precedent and should not be presented as such.

When applying the partial defences, take care to acknowledge areas of uncertainty. Particularly in relation to diminished responsibility, many of the questions for the jury are likely to be led by expert medical evidence. If you are not told medical details about D within the problem facts (eg that she is suffering from clinical depression, etc), then you should highlight this omission of essential information. You can still apply the law on the facts that you are given, and you can still predict *likely* outcomes based on those facts, but your answer should be expressly qualified (eg 'on the facts available it seems likely that . . . ').

---

[211] Where a specific offence is isolated by the question, the elements of this offence (and potential defences to it) are all that should be discussed.

> ### STEP 5 Conclude
>
> This is usually a single sentence either saying that it is likely that D has committed the offence or saying that it is not likely, either because an offence element is not satisfied or because a defence is likely to apply. It is not often that you will be able to say categorically whether or not D has committed the offence, so it is usually best to conclude in terms of what is more 'likely'.

> ### STEP 6 Loop
>
> Go back up to Step 1, identifying the next potential criminal event. Continue until you have discussed all the relevant potentially criminal events.

6.6.2 Where the elements of murder are not satisfied

Where the actus reus of murder is not satisfied, then you need to look for other potential offences beyond homicide. Where the actus reus of murder is satisfied, but the mens rea is lacking, you should apply the involuntary manslaughter offences.

> *Beware...*
> Remember that the three common law involuntary manslaughter offences are separate and should not be confused. Apply them to the facts one at a time.

When selecting which offence to apply first, the following distinction is useful.

A) D lacks mens rea for murder, but she clearly foresaw the risk of death or GBH: Where D's mens rea is just short of that required for murder, it is logical to step down to the offence of reckless manslaughter. This is because reckless manslaughter shares a similar structure to murder, with the only difference being that D need not intend to cause death or GBH (recklessness being sufficient). Thus, there is no need to demonstrate a base offence (required for UAM), or duty of care and grossly negligent conduct (required for GNM). Rather, you can simply refer back to your discussion of several elements of murder (particularly the actus reus), and then apply the recklessness-based test for mens rea to demonstrate liability.

B) D lacks mens rea for murder, and it is unclear if she foresaw a risk of death or GBH: In many cases, the simple step down to an obviously satisfied offence of reckless manslaughter will not be possible. In these cases, reflecting the approach generally taken in the courts, it is good practice to apply UAM first, and then to apply GNM where UAM is not satisfied. In certain cases you can skip over UAM very briefly (eg where D's conduct is an omission, or there is clearly no base offence).

Where you do not find liability for any offence, then move to Step 5. Where you find a likelihood of liability, move to Step 4.

> ### STEP 4 Consider defences
>
> The word 'consider' here is important, as you should not discuss every defence for every question. Rather, think whether there are any defences that *could* potentially apply. If there are, discuss those only. Remember that the partial defences cannot apply here—they can only potentially apply where D commits murder.

STEP 5 Conclude

This is usually a single sentence either saying that it is likely that D has committed the offence, or saying that it is not likely, either because an offence element is not satisfied, or because a defence is likely to apply. It is not often that you will be able to say categorically whether or not D has committed the offence, so it is usually best to conclude in terms of what is more 'likely'.

STEP 6 Loop

Go back up to Step 1, identifying the next potential criminal event. Continue until you have discussed all the relevant potentially criminal events.

 ONLINE RESOURCE CENTRE

www.oxfordtextbooks.co.uk/orc/sho/

This chapter is accompanied by a selection of online resources to help you with this topic, including:

- **Multiple-choice questions**
- **Chapter summary sheet**
- Two **sample examination questions** with answer guidance
- **Further reading**

Also available on the Online Resource Centre are:

- A selection of **videos** from the authors explaining key topics and principles
- **Legal updates**
- Useful **weblinks**

7

Non-fatal offences against the person

7.1   Introduction   **215**

7.2   Assault and battery   **216**

    7.2.1 Assault   **217**

    7.2.2 Battery   **220**

    7.2.3 Hostility as an element of assault or battery?   **222**

    7.2.4 The relationship between assault and battery   **222**

7.3   Defences to assault and battery   **223**

    7.3.1 Lawful chastisement of children   **223**

    7.3.2 Consent to assault and battery   **223**

    7.3.3 Belief in consent to assault and battery   **229**

7.4   OAPA 1861, s47: assault occasioning actual bodily harm   **230**

    7.4.1 Actus reus of s47   **231**

    7.4.2 Mens rea of s47   **232**

7.5   OAPA 1861, s20: wounding, or inflicting grievous bodily harm   **233**

    7.5.1 Actus reus of s20   **233**

    7.5.2 Mens rea of s20   **234**

    7.5.3 Coexistence of s20 and s47   **235**

7.6   OAPA 1861, s18: wounding, or causing grievous bodily harm with intent   **235**

    7.6.1 Actus reus of s18   **236**

    7.6.2 Mens rea of s18   **236**

7.7   Sections 47, 20, and 18: alternative verdicts   **238**

7.8   Defences to sections 47, 20, and 18   **238**

    7.8.1 Defences to the base offence for s47   **238**

    7.8.2 Consent to the more serious offences against the person   **240**

    7.8.3 Belief in consent to the more serious offences against the person   **246**

7.9   Conduct-focused offences against the person   **246**

    7.9.1 Harassment and stalking   **246**

    7.9.2 Racially or religiously aggravating elements   **255**

    7.9.3 Torture and slavery   **259**

    7.9.4 Administering poison   **260**

7.10 Reform   **264**

    7.10.1 Modernisation and re-codification   **265**

    7.10.2 Constructive liability   **268**

    7.10.3 Consent   **269**

7.11 Eye on assessment   **270**

7.1 Introduction

One of the central values upon which the criminal law is constructed is that of bodily autonomy: the right not to be physically interfered with against your will.[1] We have already discussed the role of this value in the context of murder (**Chapter 5**) and manslaughter (**Chapter 6**), where D's conduct results in the ultimate loss of V's bodily autonomy through death. However, the criminal law's protection of bodily autonomy extends to conduct well short of that causing death. Grouped within the 'non-fatal offences against the person', a variety of offences have been designed to criminalise behaviour that ranges from the infliction of serious (non-fatal) injuries, through to the potential targeting of any non-consensual contact.

Although the detailed content of these offences can vary considerably, it is possible to identify patterns in the law to aid understanding. It is useful, for example, to separate the various non-fatal offences into two separate categories, result-focused and conduct-focused.

The offences in the result-focused category are defined largely by reference to the *degree* of harm suffered by V. These offences can be presented as an imperfect 'ladder', with the most serious at the top and the least serious at the bottom.

(a) Wounding with intent to cause grievous bodily harm (GBH), or causing GBH with intent.

(b) Maliciously wounding or inflicting GBH.

(c) Assault occasioning actual bodily harm (ABH).

(d) Assault and battery.

We discuss this category of offences first, and in most detail, beginning at the bottom of the ladder and working up.

The second category of non-fatal offences is 'conduct-focused'. Although offences in this category are still concerned with D causing harm to V, they are equally concerned with the *manner* in which that harm is inflicted. This can be illustrated, for example, with harassment and poisoning offences. In each case, the conduct targeted could alternatively be charged within the first category of offences, focusing on the degree of harm suffered by V. However, to do so would be to ignore the special circumstances of D's offending. By

---

[1] Respect for bodily autonomy is enshrined in Art 8 ECHR (respect for private life). For more serious infringements the protection lies in Art 3 (freedom from torture, inhuman and degrading treatment), Art 5 (freedom from unlawful deprivation of liberty), and Art 2 (right to life). See **1.1.1** and **1.4** for a more general discussion of the values protected by the criminal law. See also Wilson, *Central Issues in Criminal Theory* (2002) Ch1.

employing the more specific offences of harassment and poisoning, offences which can be defined and labelled to highlight the particularly harmful methods D has employed, and the law can send a clear message to both the individual offender as well as society more generally.

As will become clear, unlike the result-focused category of non-fatal offences, the conduct-focused category does not attempt to target a particular spectrum of resulting harms. Rather, offences in this conduct category have been developed in an ad hoc manner, arising to fill gaps found within the result category as well as reflecting social and political priorities. It is within this conduct category that we might also locate the sexual offences, a series of offences that are defined independently to reflect the uniquely serious manner of their commission. However, owing to the importance and complexity of these offences, they will be discussed separately in **Chapter 8.**

Terminology . . .

Only a natural 'person' can be a victim of an offence against the person. The meaning of 'person' has already been discussed in relation to murder and manslaughter, and these rules apply equally to the non-fatal offences (eg an unborn foetus or someone who is legally dead cannot be the victim of an offence in this chapter).

Although we use the language of 'victim' in relation to the person offended against, the implications of this label can appear inappropriate in the context of certain non-fatal offences. For example, as we will discuss later, it is possible for D to commit a non-fatal offence even when the 'victim' has consented to, and even gained pleasure from, D's actions. Think about this when evaluating the offences. If the label 'victim' seems inappropriate, does this mean you think the law is in need of reform? If not, who is the law protecting?

The Law Commission has recently published a report discussing the current law on the offences against the person, and making recommendations for fundamental reform. We make reference to the report throughout this chapter; but it repays reading in full.[2]

7.2 Assault and battery

Within the result category of non-fatal offences, and at the bottom of our imaginary ladder of harms, are the offences of assault and battery. Many of the offences in this category are defined in the Offences Against the Person Act (OAPA) 1861. However, the offences of assault and battery are not defined in statute. The power to charge assault and battery now derives from section 39 of the Criminal Justice Act 1988,[3] but they are *defined* in the common law. This has given rise to a technical dispute as to whether these offences should be *referred to* as statutory or common law offences, but for our purposes, little turns on this dispute.[4]

---

[2] Law Commission, *Reform of Offences against the Person* (No 361, 2015). Gibson, 'Getting Their "Act" Together? Implementing Statutory Reform of Offences Against the Person' [2016] Crim LR 597.

[3] 'Common assault and battery shall be summary offences and a person guilty of either of them shall be liable to a fine . . ., to imprisonment for a term not exceeding six months, or to both.'

[4] Assault and battery are also torts. As a result, the definition of these offences has been partly derived from civil law cases, and some of these cases are discussed later.

7.2.1 Assault

An assault involves any conduct by D that, intentionally or recklessly, causes V to *apprehend* imminent unlawful personal violence. In contrast, a battery (discussed in the following section) is any conduct by which D, intentionally or recklessly, *inflicts* unlawful personal violence upon V. The elements of assault are set out in **Table 7.1**.

Table 7.1 Assault

	Actus reus	**Mens rea**
Conduct element	Any conduct causing the result	Voluntary
Circumstance element	V is a person	Knowledge
Result element	V apprehends an imminent threat of unlawful force	Intention or recklessness

7.2.1.1 Actus reus of assault

In contrast to the everyday/non-legal meaning of 'assault', the legal definition does *not* require D to make any physical contact with V. Such contact is only required for the distinct offence of 'battery'. The actus reus of assault is satisfied as soon as D causes V to apprehend or believe that V is about to suffer some personal violence.

The actus reus of assault is therefore less concerned with the conduct of D, and rather more concerned with the impact of that conduct on V. The test is not whether D's conduct was likely to cause another to apprehend unlawful violence, but whether it had this impact in fact. For example, if D motions to strike V (ie performs conduct that would usually cause V the relevant apprehension), but V does not so apprehend, perhaps because she is asleep or she knows D is bluffing, the actus reus will not be satisfied.

Having clarified this central point, however, several questions must be considered in relation to V's required apprehension of unlawful personal violence.

A) **What do we mean by 'unlawful personal violence'?** The language of 'unlawful personal violence' is now well established.[5] As with battery, 'unlawful personal violence' includes any non-consensual contact; V need not believe that the 'violence' would be serious or cause injury. Care should also be taken, however, not to interpret this requirement too widely. It is not sufficient, for example, that D causes V to fear in a general sense, and indeed the term 'fear' should be avoided. D may cause V fear when showing her a scary film, for example, but this will not ordinarily cause V to apprehend the imminent application of force, and will not satisfy the actus reus. If V is made to apprehend immediate unlawful violence it does not matter whether she was in 'fear' or not; V may be stronger than D and have no fear whatsoever about D's imminent attack, but the actus reus of assault will be satisfied.

---

[5] *Ireland* [1998] AC 147. See also *Smith and Hogan's Criminal Law* (14th edn, 2015) Ch5.

B) How imminent must V believe the violence will be? V must be caused to apprehend immediate or imminent unlawful personal violence. Threats of violence at some non-imminent point in the future (eg 'I will beat you up next month'), however serious, will not constitute an assault. The distinction between imminent violence, which does satisfy the actus reus, and non-imminent violence, which does not, is therefore central to liability. The courts have applied a part subjective and part objective approach.

- Subjective: in order to establish the nature of the threat from D, the law focuses on the facts as V is caused to believe them to be.

If D points an unloaded or imitation gun at V, causing V to believe that she is about to be shot, then D has completed the actus reus of assault. In reality, under any definition of 'imminence', there is no imminent threat of V being shot by a gun that cannot be fired. However, based on the facts that V is caused to believe, a finding of imminence is possible.[6]

- Objective: although the facts are established from what V is caused to believe, the question of whether this belief amounts to an apprehension of *imminent* violence remains an objective one for the court.

If V is caused to believe she will be shot in one hour, whether this is imminent will be a question for the court. The tendency of the court has been to interpret the requirement of imminence very broadly, allowing for liability even where V knows that the threat will involve some delay.[7] This approach has been adopted consistently by the courts,[8] as illustrated by the case of *Constanza*.

 Constanza [1997] Crim LR 576

D harassed V over a period of 20 months, sending threatening letters, writing on her front door, and taking items from her washing. V suffered clinical depression as a result. D was charged with assault causing actual bodily harm, which as we will see is an offence that requires an assault to have been committed.[9] D claimed that the letters could not have caused V to anticipate an *immediate* threat.

- Crown Court: guilty of assault, and thus assault occasioning actual bodily harm.
- Court of Appeal: conviction upheld on appeal. The court found assault on the basis that V was caused to apprehend violence 'at some point not excluding the immediate future'.

Assessment matters . . .
When applying cases such as *Constanza* to problem facts, a very wide definition of 'imminence' should be employed. However, take care not to fall into the trap which the courts arguably have, by confusing an imminent anticipation of violence at some point in the future (not enough to satisfy

[6] *Logdon v DPP* [1976] Crim LR 121, DC.
[7] See Virgo, 'Offences Against the Person—Do-It-Yourself Law Reform' (1997) 56 CLJ 251.
[8] *Logdon v DPP* [1976] Crim LR 121: D showed V a pistol in a drawer, saying he would keep her hostage; *Smith v Chief Superintendent of Woking Police Station* (1983) 76 Cr App R 234: D seen looking through a window at V; *Ireland* [1998] AC 147: D made phone calls to V.
[9] Discussed at **7.4**.

the actus reus) with an anticipation of imminent violence (which will satisfy the actus reus). It is not disputed that the cases discussed earlier displayed the former, but it is debatable whether they should have been held to include the latter.

C) Can the result be caused indirectly? Most assaults will involve a threatened battery, as where D threatens to punch V in the face. However, although D must cause V to apprehend imminent unlawful violence it is not necessary that such apprehension should involve violence *from D*. Thus, where D threatens V with a dog,[10] or even attack from another person, D's conduct will satisfy the actus reus.

D) Can the conduct element be satisfied by words alone, or by omission? Words alone are capable of causing V to apprehend unlawful imminent violence, and so it is clear they are capable of fulfilling the conduct element of assault, whether communicated orally or in any written form.[11] It is also *likely* that assault can be committed by omission, although this has not yet been clarified at common law.

Assault by omission could arise where D inadvertently causes V to apprehend imminent violence, and then omits to correct the situation. For example, D checks the sights on her gun when V walks into the room, and then intentionally omits to withdraw the threat by lowering the gun. D does not commit assault by her act (when aiming the gun) as she does not possess mens rea at this point; she commits assault when omitting to lower the gun, in breach of a duty to act,[12] with the required mens rea. This example could be analysed as assault by omission *or* assault by continuing act.[13]

E) Can the threat be implied or conditional? Implied or conditional threats are most likely in the context of a verbal assault as, for example, where D says to V 'if the coin-toss lands on heads then I will hit you'. As before, provided D's threat causes V to apprehend imminent violence, the actus reus of assault will be satisfied.[14] The only exception to this is where the communicated condition undermines *any chance* of the threat being carried out. For example, D shouts at V 'I would hit you if you weren't already ugly'. D's conduct may be threatening, but her statement makes clear that there will be no imminent attack, and therefore there is no assault.[15]

7.2.1.2 Mens rea of assault

The mens rea for assault requires D to intend *or* be reckless as to causing the result: D must intend or foresee the possibility that her act will cause V to apprehend imminent unlawful violence. This was established in *Venna*.[16]

---

[10] *Dume* (1986), The Times, 16 October.

[11] As in *Constanza*.

[12] D has a duty to act to remedy her inadvertent creation of a dangerous situation: *Miller* [1983] AC 161. See **2.6**.

[13] For discussion of these alternative approaches, see **4.3.2.1**.

[14] See Williams, 'Assault and Words' [1957] Crim LR 219.

[15] See *Tuberville v Savage* (1669) 1 Mood Rep 3. D's potential assault (putting hand on sword) was undermined by the accompanying statement: 'if it were not assize time I would not take such language'.

[16] [1976] QB 421. This case involved a battery that caused actual bodily harm, but it remains good authority for the mens rea of both assault and battery.

D must also possess appropriate mens rea as to the other offence elements. As with all offences, D must have performed the relevant conduct voluntarily.[17] D must have also been aware that her victim, V, was a person.

> **Assessment matters . . .**
> Although D's mens rea as to the result of causing V to apprehend imminent violence should always be discussed in a problem answer, this is not true of the other mens rea requirements. It will usually be self-evident that D acted voluntarily and is aware that V is a person, and so these requirements need only be explicitly discussed if there is some room for doubt. This applies equally to the other offences discussed later.

7.2.2 Battery

A battery is any conduct by which D, intentionally or recklessly, inflicts unlawful personal violence upon V.[18] The elements of battery are set out in **Table 7.2**.

Table 7.2 Battery

	Actus reus	**Mens rea**
Conduct element	Any conduct causing the result	Voluntary
Circumstance element	V is a person	Knowledge
Result element	Unlawful physical contact with V	Intention or recklessness

7.2.2.1 Actus reus of battery

The actus reus of battery consists of the infliction of unlawful personal violence. The term 'violence' in this context will encompass *any* unlawful contact with another. As Blackstone explained:

> The law cannot draw the line between different degrees of violence, and therefore prohibits the first and lowest stage of it; every man's person being sacred, and no other having a right to meddle with it, in even the slightest manner.[19]

A broad approach to the actus reus of battery has been maintained by the courts, further evidenced in the legal answers to the questions below.

A) **Does battery require physical contact?** Unlike assault, where D can cause V to apprehend violence through any means, including words, battery will *always* require physical contact with V. This is a fundamental difference between the two offences.

---

[17] See **3.3**.
[18] *Rolfe* (1952) 36 Cr App R 4.
[19] *Commentaries*, iii, 120, cited in *Collins v Wilcock* [1984] 3 All ER 374, 378.

However, although some force must be applied, in line with the broad approach highlighted above, it will be satisfied even if V is unaware of the touching, as where V is asleep, and will include touching V's clothes, as illustrated in *Thomas*.

 Thomas (1985) 81 Cr App R 331

D (a school caretaker) touched the hem of a 12-year-old pupil's skirt. He was charged with the (now repealed) sexual offence of indecent assault which, like battery, required a touching.

- Court: guilty of indecent assault.
- Court of Appeal: appeal allowed on the basis that the touching was not indecent. However, it was confirmed that there was a touching: 'There could be no dispute that if you touch a person's clothes while he is wearing them that is equivalent to touching him.'[20]

Despite this wide interpretation, the requirement of contact can be problematic. For example, where D causes bodily harm in the form of psychiatric injury, this may be inflicted without any physical impact on V's body. In such a case, because there is no physical force, there will be no battery.[21]

B) **Can the result be caused indirectly?** Many cases will involve *direct* contact between D and V, as where D hits V with her fist or with a weapon. However, battery will also be found where contact is caused *indirectly*, as where D hits V by throwing things at V or spitting at V, or where D's contact with a third party impacts on V (eg D punches X, causing her to drop V, her baby[22]). Several cases confirm this point. In *DPP v K*,[23] for example, D committed battery when he poured acid into a toilet hand-dryer, causing the next user to be sprayed; in *Martin*[24] it was agreed that battery could be found where D digs a pit for V to fall into, or causes injury through the placing of an obstruction. Other cases involve battery where D sets his dog[25] or other animal[26] on V.

C) **Can the conduct element be satisfied by an omission?** Battery will invariably involve an act, and it has been generally assumed that acts are required for liability.[27] However, as with assault (**7.2.1.1**), it is likely that the courts will find battery can be committed by omission. Support for this can be found in *Santana-Bermudez*.

 Santana-Bermudez v DPP [2004] Crim LR 471

D assured V, who was a policewoman, that he was not carrying any 'sharps' (hypodermic needles) before she searched him. He was, and V was injured. D was charged with battery occasioning actual bodily harm,[28] an offence where battery must be demonstrated.

---

[20] At 334.
[21] Ormerod and Gunn, 'In Defence of *Ireland*' [1996] 3 Web JCLI.
[22] *Haystead v Chief Constable of Derbyshire* (2000) 164 JP 396. Liability could *alternatively* be found through transferred malice.
[23] [1990] 1 All ER 331, overruled on *other* grounds by *Spratt* [1991] 2 All ER 210.
[24] (1881) 8 QBD 54.
[25] *Murgatroyd v Chief Constable of West Yorkshire* [2000] All ER 1742.
[26] eg where D causes a horse to bolt: *Gibbon v Pepper* (1695) 2 Salk 637 (*obiter*).
[27] *Innes v Wylie* (1844) 1 Car & Kir 257.
[28] See **7.4.**

- Magistrates' court: guilty of battery occasioning actual bodily harm.
- Crown Court: not guilty—no actus reus.
- High Court: no retrial was ordered, but the court confirmed that D's omission was capable of giving rise to a battery.

Omissions liability, it should be remembered, requires D to have omitted in breach of a duty to act.[29] In *Santana-Bermudez*, this is established by D's creation of a dangerous situation: having sharp objects in his pocket and assuring V that he did not.[30]

7.2.2.2 Mens rea of battery

The mens rea of battery requires intention or recklessness as to causing the result: the application of unlawful force to the body of V. This was established in *Venna*.[31] D must also perform her conduct voluntarily, and know that V is a 'person'.

7.2.3 Hostility as an element of assault or battery?

It is generally accepted that hostility is *not* an element of assault or battery. Lord Lane CJ has described battery as:

> an intentional touching of another person without the consent of that person and without lawful excuse. It need not necessarily be hostile, or rude, or aggressive, as some of the cases seem to indicate.[32]

Some doubt has been raised by the House of Lords in *Brown*,[33] where the majority indicated that hostility *is* required. However, the definition of 'hostility' applied in *Brown* means that it is likely to have little impact. The facts of *Brown* involved sadomasochistic acts that were consented to for the mutual satisfaction of those involved, and such acts could not, in plain English, be described as hostile. In order to find hostility in this case, the House of Lords effectively emptied the word of its meaning: saying the acts were hostile because they were unlawful.[34] Under this approach, hostility does not seem like an offence element at all, but rather a description of events that have been found to be criminal on other grounds.

7.2.4 The relationship between assault and battery

Assault and battery are two separate offences. However, this was not always the case, and they are still often referred to interchangeably, inconsistently, and/or cumulatively in cases, academic discussion and statute. The main reason for this continued problem is that, without an acceptable verb to correspond with the noun of 'battery', the term 'assaulted' is used to describe D who commits both assault and/or battery. Take care not to be confused by this when reading cases and commentary: 'D assaulted V' can mean D committed assault, battery, or both.

---

[29] See **2.6**.
[30] *Miller* [1983] AC 161.
[31] [1976] QB 421.
[32] *Faulkner v Talbot* [1981] 3 All ER 468, 471.
[33] [1994] AC 212.
[34] Per Lord Jauncey.

7.3 Defences to assault and battery

Where D has satisfied the offence elements of assault or battery, she will nevertheless avoid liability if she has a specific defence of 'lawful chastisement', 'consent', or 'belief in consent'. These will be discussed in the following sections.

> *Assessment matters . . .*
> When considering defences, it is usually good practice to begin with specific defences. However, if these do not apply, remember that D can also avoid liability if she satisfies one of the general defences that apply across a greater part of the criminal law. See **Chapter 13**, where we discuss denials of offending, and **Chapter 14**, where we discuss the general defences.

7.3.1 Lawful chastisement of children

A lawful chastisement or 'corporal punishment' defence has traditionally applied at common law to allow parents and teachers to use physical force to discipline children.[35] However, the definition of this defence at common law was uncertain, and the subject of challenges in the ECtHR.[36]

The defence is now codified within section 58 of the Children Act 2004, and considerably restricted in scope. The defence will: (a) only apply for parents; (b) only apply to assault and battery (ie none of the more serious offences against the person); and (c) only apply where the force used was reasonable and proportionate in the circumstances, involving no cruelty.

Under section 549(4) of the Education Act 1996, a member of school staff now has no defence to any offence against the person committed on a pupil by way of punishment. This includes assault or battery. However, the Act does make clear that reasonable force can be used to restrain violent pupils (s550A), those who are endangering themselves and/or property (s548(5)), or where the teacher needs to search for a weapon (s550AA).

7.3.2 Consent to assault and battery

The defence of consent is vitally important in relation to non-fatal offences against the person.[37] Where D makes *consensual* contact with V (eg shaking V's hand), or causes V to apprehend *consensual* contact (eg motioning towards shaking V's hand), we would not want to find liability for assault or battery. Indeed, such examples are so obviously outside that intended to be criminalised that there are strong grounds for contending that 'non-consent' should be classified as an offence element, meaning that such conduct

---

[35] Keating, 'Protecting or Punishing Children: Physical Punishment, Human Rights and English Law Reform' (2006) 26 LS 394; Barton, 'Hitting Your Children: Common Assault or Common Sense?' (2008) 38 Fam L 65.

[36] *A v UK* [1998] TLR 578; Phillips, 'The Case for Corporal Punishment in the UK—Beaten into Submission in Europe' (1994) 43 ICLQ 153.

[37] There is a vast literature on this subject. See Law Commission, *Consent and Offences against the Person* (Consultation 134, 1994), on which see Ormerod, 'Consent and Offences Against the Person: LCCP No 134' (1994) 57 MLR 928; and Law Commission, *Consent in Criminal Law* (Consultation 139, 1995), on which see Ormerod and Gunn, 'Consent—A Second Bash' [1996] Crim LR 694. See also Reed et al (eds), *Consent: Domestic and Comparative Perspectives* (2017).

would not require a consent defence at all. And there is some uncertainty here at common law, with examples of contradictory classifications found in the courts and surrounding commentaries. We discuss this in the 'reform' section later (**7.10.3**). In what follows, for the sake of consistency, and in line with a slight predominance in the case law,[38] we analyse consent as a defence.

The structure of the defence of consent, as it applies to assault or battery, is set out in **Table 7.3**.

Table 7.3 Defence of consent

A) V's consent must be expressed or implied to D in a legally recognised manner
B) V's consent must be effective: V must have the capacity, freedom, and information required to make a choice

As we go on to discuss the more serious offences against the person from **7.4**, a third element to the consent defence emerges: the context of V's consensual harm must come within a legally accepted category (eg surgery).[39] However, in the context of assault and battery, due to the low levels of harm involved, no such additional limitations apply. Even where we perceive D's conduct as socially unacceptable, such as where D and V engage in a consensual fight, V's effective consent will undermine charges of simple assault or battery.

7.3.2.1 Element 1: expressed and/or implied consent

The most straightforward cases involving consent entail V expressly consenting to contact with D (eg when V motions to shake D's hand). However, particularly in the context of assault or battery, implied consent is very common.

Implied consent most commonly applies to touching which, although not explicitly consented to, is part of everyday life.[40] For example, where one is jostled in a busy street or when entering a crowded train; or even where one is embraced, within reason, as the clock strikes for New Year. The logic behind implied consent is that, by voluntarily moving in society, we agree to be exposed to the foreseeable contact that social life entails. There are, of course, limits to implied consent. For example, as demonstrated in *Wood v DPP*, contact must be genuinely within the realms of everyday activity.

 Wood v DPP [2008] EWHC 1056 (Admin)

D was restrained by V, a police officer, as he left a public house. Importantly, V was not in the process of arresting D, but merely restraining him in order to establish his identity. D resisted, and was charged with assaulting the police officer.

• Magistrates' court: D is guilty of assault.

---

[38] This was the approach preferred by the bare majority in *Brown* [1994] AC 212.
[39] See **7.8.2.1**.
[40] *Collins v Wilcock* [1984] 3 All ER 374.

- Crown Court: conviction upheld.
- High Court: appeal allowed, and D acquitted. V is not entitled to restrain D in this manner unless carrying out a lawful arrest (no implied consent). Thus, as V was assaulting D, D's resistance was lawful.

Implied consent should also not be equated with foreseeability, clarified in *H v CPS*.[41] *H* involved a teacher at a special-needs school (V) who was assaulted by a student (D). V was well aware of the risk of assault within the school, but the court rejected the submission that her awareness amounted to an implied consent for D's attack.

7.3.2.2 Element 2: effective consent

For consent to be valid in law, it must be effective. For example, if V is unaware of exactly what D is planning to do, or is mentally unable to understand, then it is highly questionable whether V's apparent acquiescence should absolve D of liability. The principal questions are the following:

- What *mental capacity* is required for V to be capable of effective consent?
- What degree of *knowledge* is required for V to be capable of effective consent?
- Can *fraud* by D undermine the effectiveness of consent?
- Can *duress* or pressure from D or another undermine the effectiveness of consent?

These questions will be considered in turn.

> *Extra detail . . .*
> In the context of implied consent to touching expected in everyday social movement (eg light contact between people on a busy train), uniquely, 'effectiveness' is assumed and becomes irrelevant. This assumption is clearly artificial, particularly where V is unable to understand the implied consent she is providing through age or mental deficiency, for example. However, despite the artificiality, bearing in mind the type of conduct involved, it is unlikely to lead to substantial problems.

Capacity

V may lack the capacity[42] to consent for a variety of reasons, including mental disorder or learning difficulties, infancy, or more temporary conditions such as intoxication. In each case, the issue of capacity should be considered.

In the interests of simplicity, it is tempting for the courts to equate a certain status with a general lack of capacity, and this has been the dominant approach historically. However, as cases such as *Burrell v Harmer* demonstrate, this approach is not appropriate.

> **Burrell v Harmer** [1967] Crim LR 169
>
> D was charged with battery causing actual bodily harm, an offence which required proof of a battery, after tattooing the arms of boys aged 12 and 13. D's defence was that the boys had consented, having actively instigated the tattooing.

---

[41] [2010] All ER 56.
[42] See Law Commission, *Consent in Criminal Law* (Consultation 139, 1995) Part 5; Law Commission, *Mental Capacity* (No 231, 1995).

> • Crown Court: guilty of the offence. The boys, as minors, were not capable of understanding the nature of the act of tattooing (ie they lacked capacity) and therefore there was no effective consent.

With the court taking little time to explain and discuss exactly what knowledge the boys lacked, this case demonstrates the rather superficial approach too often taken to the assessment of capacity.

A more nuanced approach to capacity has been set out in the Mental Capacity Act 2005, and whilst the criminal courts are not bound by it in the context of offences against the person, it has had a considerable impact on judicial reasoning.[43] The Act states that 'a person lacks capacity in relation to a matter if at the material time he is unable to make a decision for himself in relation to the matter because of a temporary or permanent impairment of, or a disturbance in the functioning of, the mind or brain'. The Act further cautions that a lack of capacity should not be inferred from '(a) a person's age or appearance, or (b) a condition of his, or an aspect of his behaviour, which might lead others to make unjustified assumptions about his capacity'.

The question of capacity must be individual and decision-specific. Capacity can change for each individual over time, and different decisions require different levels of capacity to engage with (ie V may lack capacity for complex decisions, but not for more simple ones). The resulting test is more difficult for the courts to apply, but respects the autonomy of the individuals involved.

> *Assessment matters . . .*
> Where problem facts state that V suffers from a certain mental condition, is a minor, or is intoxicated, it is tempting to assume that she lacks capacity to consent. This should certainly be discussed, but the best answers will also consider the possibility that she might have sufficient capacity despite her status. A conclusion should then be provided with an opinion of what is most likely based on the facts that have been provided.

Informed consent

Although V may have *capacity* to consent to particular conduct, she must also, logically, be aware of what that conduct entails before she can exercise her capacity and make a decision. Although logical, the amount of information V requires for effective consent it less obvious. Adopting a commonsense approach, the courts generally equate the level of knowledge required with the degree of harm to which V is consenting: the greater the harm, the more knowledge required for effective consent. It should therefore be of little surprise that most of the cases discussed here involve more serious offences than simple assault or battery. However, as the same general rules apply to assault and battery (just with a lighter touch), it is still useful to have the discussion at this stage.

Informed consent to non-fatal offences was considered in the important case of *Konzani*.

    Konzani [2005] EWCA Crim 706

> D engaged in consensual unprotected sexual intercourse with three complainants. As a result of this, each contracted HIV, a condition that D was aware he had but of which he had not informed the complainants.

---

[43] See *Re S and another (Protected Persons)* [2010] 1 WLR 1082, [53].

- Crown Court: guilty of maliciously inflicting GBH.[44]
- Court of Appeal: conviction upheld on appeal. The victims had consented to sexual intercourse, but, because of the lack of information made known to them, they had not consented to the risk of contracting HIV.

The court explained the role of informed consent in the following terms:

> If an individual who knows that he is suffering from the HIV virus conceals this stark fact from his sexual partner, the principle of her personal autonomy is not enhanced if he is exculpated when he recklessly transmits the HIV virus to her through consensual sexual intercourse. On any view, the concealment of this fact from her almost inevitably means that she is deceived. Her consent is not properly informed, and she cannot give an informed consent to something of which she is ignorant. . . . Silence [from D] in these circumstances is incongruous with honesty, or with a genuine belief that there is an informed consent. Accordingly, in such circumstances the issue either of informed consent or honest belief in it will only rarely arise: in reality, in most cases, the contention would be wholly artificial.[45]

Most important within this decision is the court's clear distinction between being informed as to the nature of the sexual intercourse (to which there *was* effective consent), and being informed as to the risk of HIV infection (to which there was *no* effective consent). This distinction is critical because if it is not made, then there is either consent to both and thus no liability at all, or there is no consent to either and thus D has also committed rape.[46]

Konzani encourages us to consider D's central activity (in this case, sexual intercourse) as *potentially* distinct from associated risks of harm (in this case, infection); and encourages us to consider V's consent separately as to each. Where D has consented to the central activity, and your analysis moves to the separate associated risks, three categories of case should be distinguished.

A) No knowledge or deception: Where D has no special knowledge of the associated risks (eg D does not know she is infected), then V's effective consent to the central activity includes consent as to the associated risks. D is not deceiving V, and V is fully informed of what D knows. Even where V is harmed, no liability will result.[47]

B) Knowledge but no deception: Where D has special knowledge of the associated risks (eg D knows she is infected), and she informs V of that fact, then V's effective consent to the central activity includes consent as to the associated risks. Even where V is harmed, no liability will result.

C) Knowledge and deception (as in *Konzani*): Where D has special knowledge of the associated risks (eg D knows she is infected) but does not inform V of that knowledge, then V's effective consent to the central activity will not include effective consent as to the associated risks. Where those risks manifest in harm, liability may be found.

---

[44] See **7.5**.

[45] At [23] per Judge LJ.

[46] For critical commentary, see Weait, 'Knowledge, Autonomy and Consent: *R v Konzani*' [2006] Crim LR 763; Munro, 'On Responsible Relationships and Irresponsible Sex' (2007) 19 CFLQ 112.

[47] D may alternatively rely on a belief in consent defence, see **7.3.3**.

Don't be confused . . .
Konzani involved risks associated with sexual intercourse, but the rule will apply in other contexts as well. For example, a doctor (D) injects V with a therapeutic drug, knowing, but not informing V, that the needles being used have often been found to be contaminated. V's consent to the injection includes consent to various associated risks. However, D's special knowledge means that V's effective consent to the injection may not include effective consent to the risks of contamination that were not disclosed, should they arise.

Consent procured by fraud

Fraud has the potential to undermine V's apparent consent in two main areas: fraud as to the identity of D; and fraud as to the nature of the act consented to.[48] Unfortunately, the current law has become complex and confused.

A) **Fraud as to the identity of D:** The basic rule is easy to apply. If D gains V's consent to being touched by impersonating X, V's consent to that touching (battery) is not legally effective. V's consent is given to X in relation to X's acts, not the impersonating D.

Problems emerge where D is not impersonating another person but, rather, D is lying about certain characteristics or qualifications. In these cases, it is much less clear if D is being fraudulent about her *identity*. The courts have generally interpreted 'identity' narrowly in such cases, as seen in *Richardson*.

  Richardson [1998] 2 Cr App R 200

D was suspended from practising dentistry, but continued to treat patients. D was charged with assault occasioning actual bodily harm in relation to her treatment of patients during this time. The patients were clear that they would not have consented to treatment if they had known that D was suspended.

- Crown Court: guilty of assault occasioning actual bodily harm. Fraud as to identity (presenting as a licensed dentist) undermined the patients' apparent consent.
- Court of Appeal: appeal allowed. No fraud as to identity: D did not lie about who she was, but rather simply about the holding of a licence.

In cases such as *Richardson*, it is arguable that D's lack of qualifications was more important to V's consent than whether D claimed to be someone else. However, the law has maintained a narrow test of 'identity' focusing only on the latter.

B) **Fraud as to the nature of D's conduct:** Fraud as to the nature of D's conduct is capable of undermining otherwise effective consent as, for example, where D tells V that it is customary to greet someone by punching them in the face. However, where V is not deceived as to the core nature of the act, but simply as to a collateral issue, this will not generally undermine consent. The courts have consistently interpreted the 'nature' of conduct very narrowly. For example, in *Mobilio*,[49] where V consented to D inserting an instrument into her vagina for diagnostic purposes, but D was secretly acting only for his sexual gratification, the court held that consent was effective: the fraud was not as to the *nature* of the act.

---

[48] See Law Commission, *Consent in Criminal Law* (Consultation 139, 1995) Part 6.
[49] [1991] 1 VR 339. Ormerod, 'A Victim's Mistaken Consent in Rape' (1992) 56 J Crim L 407.

This issue has also arisen in relation to consensual sexual intercourse where D does not inform her sexual partner of a known sexually transmitted infection. This was considered in *Dica*,[50] where D infected two sexual partners with HIV. As with the more recent case of *Konzani* (discussed earlier in relation to informed consent), the Court of Appeal in *Dica* made the crucial distinction between: (a) consent as to sexual intercourse, which was both informed and non-fraudulent, and (b) consent as to the risk of infection, which was uninformed and gained through fraud.[51] Although V was not misled as to the *nature* of the sexual act, and thus D had not committed rape, V was misled as to the *nature* of the associated risk of infection (the risk of bodily harm). D was guilty of inflicting GBH.

Consent procured through duress

V's apparent consent will not be effective if it is gained by threats (duress). For example, if D submits to a light beating only amounting to a battery in order to avoid a greater one, the threat of the greater beating is likely to undermine her consent. Similar results have emerged even where D's threats were non-criminal (eg submit to this beating or be dismissed from employment[52] or I will bring a prosecution[53]). Indeed, duress may even be implied from a relationship, such as that between a teacher and pupil.[54]

Despite these examples, however, the exact test for duress in this context remains unclear. It must be demonstrated that V's apparent consent was *caused* by D's threat as opposed to other factors, and so it is important to balance the gravity of the threat against the act consented to. However, it remains unclear whether this balancing is a purely objective procedure (asking if a person of reasonable steadfastness would have submitted to the violence), or whether it includes a subjective dimension (eg where D knew V was particularly vulnerable through mental abnormality or alcoholism, etc).

> **Assessment matters . . .**
> In order to assess whether consent is effective, it is necessary to consider each of the topics discussed in this section: capacity, level of knowledge, fraud, and duress. However, applying these to problem facts is not a tick-box exercise. Therefore, again, you should fully explore and discuss where it is relevant on the facts (eg D is a minor or is tricked in some way), but this may not be necessary if there is no such indication.

7.3.3 Belief in consent to assault and battery

D may also avoid liability if she *believed* that V provided valid consent. Thus, even if V was not consenting, and so the consent defence does not apply, D will avoid liability if she genuinely believed that consent was present. As seen in *Jones*, this will be the case even where D's belief is unreasonable.

---

[50] [2004] EWCA Crim 1103.

[51] The court in *Dica* disapplied the earlier case of *Clarence* (1888) 22 QBD 23, where the court had held that V's consent to sexual intercourse amounted to an implied consent to the risk of infection.

[52] *McCoy* 1953 (2) SA 4.

[53] *State v Volschenk* 1968 (2) PH H283, here the threat did *not* undermine consent.

[54] *Nichol* (1807) Russ & Ry 130.

Jones [1987] Crim LR 123

The defendant schoolboys threw V into the air with the intention of catching him as part of a joke. However, they missed and V suffered severe injuries. They sought to rely on the consent of V.

- Crown Court: guilty of an offence causing GBH. The judge did not allow the defence of consent to be put to the jury.
- Court of Appeal: appeal allowed. Consent should have been left to the jury. Consent could have been a valid defence if V had consented *or* if D genuinely (even if unreasonably) believed that V consented.

This defence is rarely pursued in court. D must raise enough evidence that she genuinely believed that V provided valid consent (ie express or implied, and effective).

7.4 OAPA 1861, s47: assault occasioning actual bodily harm

Section 47 is satisfied where D commits an assault or battery that causes V to suffer actual bodily harm (ABH).

47. Whosoever shall be convicted on indictment of any assault occasioning actual bodily harm shall be liable to imprisonment for not more than five years.

The elements of the section 47 offence are set out in **Table 7.4**.

Table 7.4 OAPA 1861, s47

	Actus reus	**Mens rea**
Conduct element	Any conduct causing the results	Voluntary
Circumstance element	V is a person	Knowledge
Result elements	V apprehends a threat of imminent physical contact, or, physical contact is applied	Intention or recklessness
	And	
	V suffers ABH	None

An alternative illustration of section 47 is provided in **Figure 7.1**.

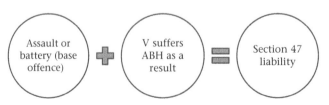

Figure 7.1 OAPA 1861, s47

7.4.1 Actus reus of s47

The actus reus of the section 47 offence requires D to commit the actus reus of assault or battery, with the additional result that V suffers ABH.

7.4.1.1 Assault or battery

The term 'assault' in section 47 should be read as 'assault or battery'. The actus reus elements of these base offences have been discussed earlier. Most cases will involve a battery that occasions ABH. However, a base offence of assault is also possible as, for example, where D causes V to apprehend imminent violence (assault) and V hurts herself when attempting to escape (ABH).[55]

7.4.1.2 Occasioning

Having demonstrated an assault or battery, the prosecution must prove that this assault or battery *occasioned* ABH. 'Occasioning', in this context, has been interpreted to mean nothing more than 'causing'.[56] Thus, D's conduct must have caused: (a) the result element of the assault or battery; and (b) ABH.

7.4.1.3 Actual bodily harm

'Actual bodily harm' is not defined in the OAPA, and so the courts have attempted to interpret it in line with the term's common meaning, influenced also by the maximum five-year sentence.[57] Distinct from mere battery, it is clear that ABH will not be found where V's injury is merely 'transient and trifling'.[58] However, ABH has been described in expansive terms to include 'any hurt or injury that is calculated to interfere with the health or comfort' of V.[59] Examples of ABH include:

- scratches, grazes, and abrasions;
- bruising and swelling;
- temporary loss of consciousness;[60]
- cutting a substantial amount of hair;[61]
- psychiatric injury; etc.[62]

The potential for ABH in the form of psychiatric injury should be applied with care. As *Ireland* (below) makes clear, psychiatric injury will amount to ABH where it manifests as an identified or recognised psychiatric condition (eg clinical depression). However, simple psychological harms, such as fear or anxiety, will never amount to ABH.

 Ireland and Burstow [1998] AC 147

These cases were combined in the House of Lords. Ireland was charged with a section 47 offence having made a series of silent telephone calls which caused V1 to suffer psychiatric harm. Burstow

---

[55] *Roberts* (1972) 56 Cr App R 95.
[56] Ibid. This interpretation is challenged in Gardner, 'Rationality and the Rule of Law in Offences Against the Person' (1994) 53 CLJ 502, 509.
[57] *DPP v Smith* [1961] AC 290 at 334 describes the term as requiring 'no explanation'.
[58] *T v DPP* [2003] Crim LR 622.
[59] *Miller* [1954] 2 QB 282.
[60] *T v DPP* [2003] Crim LR 622.
[61] *DPP v Smith* [2006] EWHC 94 (Admin).
[62] CPS Charging Standards: www.cps.gov.uk/legal/l_to_o/offences_against_the_person.

was charged with an offence of causing GBH, having harassed V2, including making silent calls, and causing her to suffer severe depression.

- Crown Court: both found guilty of the offences charged.
- Court of Appeal: both convictions upheld on appeal.
- House of Lords: appeals dismissed. Psychiatric injury is capable of amounting to actual and/or grievous bodily harm.

7.4.2 Mens rea of s47

The only mens rea requirements for section 47 are those relating to the base offence of assault (intention or recklessness as to causing V to apprehend imminent violence) or battery (intention or recklessness as to making contact with V). There is no additional mens rea required in relation to the result of ABH.

The lack of mens rea required as to causing ABH was established in *Roberts*.

Roberts (1971) 56 Cr App R 95

D made unwanted sexual advances towards V when driving her in his car. D tried to take off V's coat (a battery), and this led to V jumping out of the moving car and sustaining grazes and concussion (ABH). D was charged with a section 47 offence. D claimed that he did not foresee the risk that V would jump out of the car, and that he should therefore avoid liability.

- Crown Court: guilty of section 47 offence.
- Court of Appeal: conviction upheld on appeal. Liability does not require D to foresee the chance that his acts will cause ABH.

The rule in *Roberts* was later thrown into doubt following a remarkable series of cases.[63] However, it has now been confirmed by the House of Lords in *Savage* and *Parmenter*.[64]

Savage and **Parmenter** [1992] 1 AC 699

Cases combined in the House of Lords. Savage involved D who intended to throw the contents of her beer glass over V1, but slipped and threw the glass as well causing a wound. Parmenter involved D who handled a baby (V2) in such a way that caused serious injury. In both cases, the defendants claimed that they did not intend or foresee a risk of causing harm.

- Crown Court: both found guilty of offences involving GBH.
- Court of Appeal: appeals allowed—there was a lack of mens rea for the GBH offences. In *Savage*, liability for GBH was replaced with liability for a section 47 offence. In *Parmenter*, section 47 was not applied, the court found that mens rea was required as to causing ABH.
- House of Lords: *Parmenter* appeal allowed. *Savage* appeal dismissed. Both liable for a section 47 offence: this offence requires no mens rea as to the causing of ABH.

Section 47 is, therefore, an example of a constructive liability offence.[65]

---

[63] *Spratt* [1991] 2 All ER 220 (without reference to *Roberts*) held that recklessness was required as to the ABH. However, on the same day, *Savage* [1991] 2 All ER 210 (without reference to *Roberts*) held that no mens rea was required. Later, confronted with this conflict (but, again, without reference to *Roberts*), *Parmenter* [1992] 1 AC 699 preferred *Spratt*.

[64] Reversing *Parmenter* and overruling *Spratt* on this point.

[65] On constructive liability see **4.2.1.1**; in the context of offences against the person see **7.10.2**.

7.5 OAPA 1861, s20: wounding, or inflicting grievous bodily harm

Section 20 criminalises malicious wounding *and/or* inflicting GBH, with at least foresight of some bodily harm.

20. Whosoever shall unlawfully and maliciously wound or inflict any grievous bodily harm upon any other person, either with or without any weapon or instrument shall be guilty of [an offence triable either way] and being convicted thereof shall be liable to imprisonment for five years.

The elements of the section 20 offence are set out in **Table 7.5**.

Table 7.5 OAPA 1861, s20

	Actus reus	**Mens rea**
Conduct element	Any conduct causing the results	Voluntary
Circumstance element	V is a person	Knowledge
Result element	V is wounded	Recklessness as to some bodily injury
	Or	
	V suffers GBH	Recklessness as to some bodily injury

7.5.1 Actus reus of s20

The two ways of completing the actus reus of section 20 are through wounding and/or inflicting GBH.

7.5.1.1 Wounding

In order to constitute a wound, V's skin must be broken by, for example, stabbing.[66] The standard case will involve V's outer skin, but wounding will also be found where D breaks internal membranes that are similar to the outer skin as, for example, where D punches V and splits the inside of her cheek or lip.[67] There are limits, however. First, the whole skin (every layer) must be broken. For example, a scratch that breaks the 'surface of the skin' but not every layer will not amount to a wound.[68] Secondly, wounding cannot be *purely* internal. In *Wood*,[69] for example, despite causing V's broken collarbone, as the skin remained intact, there was no wound.

Doubt remains as to whether wounding can be caused by omission, and a case of this kind would be rare. However, it is likely that omissions liability is possible. For example, D omits to put sharp knives in a safe place having foreseen the possibility

---

[66] *Moriarty v Brooks* (1834) 6 C & P 684.
[67] *Waltham* (1849) 3 Cox CC 442.
[68] *Morris* [2005] EWCA Crim 609.
[69] (1830) 1 Mood CC 278.

that V—a young child—might injure herself with them. Breaching a duty to remove the danger created, D is likely to commit the section 20 offence by omission if injury results.

7.5.1.2 Inflicting grievous bodily harm

In the absence of a statutory definition, GBH has been defined by the House of Lords to mean 'serious bodily harm'.[70] Thus, V's injuries must be more serious than ABH, which requires only 'bodily harm'. However, it is clear that GBH does not require injury to be permanent or life-threatening,[71] with even brief unconsciousness being potentially sufficient.[72] Classic examples include broken bones and disfigurement. It is also clear that *serious* psychiatric injuries may amount to GBH, as discussed previously in *Ireland*.[73] However, as with ABH, such injury must amount to a recognised psychiatric condition; simple fear or distress is insufficient.

> *Extra detail . . .*
> As with section 47, when deciding on the degree of harm caused, the court will consider the totality of V's injuries. Thus, it is not necessary to demonstrate that V suffered ABH or GBH as a result of a single act (eg punch), provided that the harm was sustained from one attack or relevant period.[74]

Unlike the section 18 offence (discussed below) which requires D to 'cause' GBH, section 20 uses the term 'inflict'. This has given rise to some disagreement about whether the two words require different tests. For example, it has been contended that 'inflict' implies that D must cause injury through an assault or battery, as with section 47.[75] However, it is now settled law that 'inflict' should be interpreted in exactly the same way as 'cause'. D's conduct must be shown to have caused the harm to V applying the standard rules of causation, and there is *no* extra requirement of assault or battery.

> *Assessment matters . . .*
> There are two distinct ways to bring about the actus reus of section 20: by wounding or by inflicting GBH. It should be remembered that although these will often overlap (eg D stabs V in the stomach), this will not always be the case. Where D breaks one of V's bones, for example, but does not break the skin, this is GBH and not a wound.[76] Conversely, a minor wound (eg injection from a needle) will amount to a wound but not GBH. With this in mind, when applying section 20 to problem facts, it is good practice to identify which (if not both) are caused by D.

7.5.2 Mens rea of s20

Whether the allegation is of wounding, causing GBH, or both, section 20 specifies a mens rea that D must be acting 'maliciously'. This has been interpreted to mean 'intentionally

---

[70] *Smith* [1961] AC 290.
[71] *Bollom* [2004] 2 Cr App R 50.
[72] *Hicks* [2007] EWCA Crim 1500.
[73] See **7.4.1.3**.
[74] *Brown* [2005] EWCA Crim 359: case involving abuse over several days.
[75] *Wilson* [1984] AC 242, clarifying that assault and battery are *not* required for s20 liability.
[76] *Wood* (1830) 1 Mood CC 278 (broken collarbone).

or recklessly'.[77] However, although intent or foresight of a risk is required, section 20 does *not* require D to intend or foresee the full extent of the harms caused (ie wounding or GBH). Rather, liability merely requires D to intend or foresee that *some* bodily harm might be caused, not necessarily amounting to a wounding or GBH. As Diplock LJ explained in *Mowatt*:[78]

> the word 'maliciously' does import upon the part of the person who unlawfully inflicts the wound or other grievous bodily harm an awareness that his act may have the consequence of causing some physical harm to some other person. . . . It is quite unnecessary that the accused should have foreseen that his unlawful act might cause physical harm of the gravity described in [s20], ie, a wound or serious physical injury. It is enough that he should have foreseen that some physical harm to some person, albeit of a minor character, might result.

It should be remembered, however, that intent or foresight of some harm is still necessary for liability. For example, D will not commit a section 20 offence if her intention is simply to frighten V, where D does not foresee the possibility of V suffering injury as a result.

7.5.3 Coexistence of s20 and s47

As the section 47 and section 20 offences are punishable with the same maximum of five years' imprisonment, it is arguable that their coexistence is unnecessary.[79] However, as section 20 will *usually* involve greater harms,[80] and also includes a higher requirement of mens rea, section 20 is regarded in practice as the more serious offence. In this manner, conviction for section 20 will usually result in a higher sentence than for section 47.

As we have highlighted earlier, one of the aims of this first category of non-fatal offences is the creation of a ladder that provides appropriate offences and sentences in relation to different levels of harm. The lack of clarity in the current distinction between section 47 and section 20, and its reliance on prosecutors and the courts to create that distinction in practice, reflects poorly on the current law. This has been highlighted by the Law Commission,[81] and we discuss it later in the context of potential reforms.[82]

7.6 OAPA 1861, s18: wounding, or causing grievous bodily harm with intent

Section 18 criminalises malicious wounding *and/or* the causing of GBH, with intention to cause GBH or resist apprehension etc.

---

[77] *Savage* and *Parmenter* [1991] 4 All ER 698, 721. Although the term 'recklessness' is used, it remains unclear whether D must satisfy *both* limbs of the test, or whether foresight of a risk (ie the first limb) is all that is required.

[78] [1968] 1 QB 421, 426. Reiterated in *C* [2007] EWCA Crim 1068.

[79] Gardner, 'Rationality and the Rule of Law in Offences Against the Person' (1994) 53 CLJ 520.

[80] This will not always be the case. See reform discussion at **7.10.1.1**.

[81] Law Commission, *Reform of Offences against the Person* (No 361, 2015).

[82] See **7.10.1.1**.

18. Whosoever shall unlawfully and maliciously by any means whatsoever wound or cause any griev-ous bodily harm to any person with intent to do some grievous bodily harm to any person or with intent to resist or prevent the lawful apprehension or detainer of any person, shall be guilty of [an offence triable only on indictment], and being convicted thereof shall be liable to imprisonment for life.

The elements of the section 18 offence are set out in **Table 7.6**.

Table 7.6   OAPA 1861, s18

	Actus reus	**Mens rea**
Conduct element	Any conduct causing the results	Voluntary
Circumstance element	V is a person	Knowledge
Result element	V is wounded Or V suffers GBH	Intention to cause GBH *or* intention to resist apprehension etc and being reckless as to bodily harm Intention to cause GBH *or* intention to resist apprehension etc and being reckless as to bodily harm

7.6.1 Actus reus of s18

The actus reus of the section 18 offence is identical to that of section 20: D's conduct must have caused V to suffer either a wound and/or GBH.[83] There is no need to demonstrate that the elements of assault or battery were also present.

7.6.2 Mens rea of s18

The mens rea of section 18 is the same regardless of whether D has wounded V or caused GBH. The standard case of section 18 will involve D causing GBH to V with malice and an intention to cause GBH. However, section 18 is committed where *any* of the following arises:

- wounding with malice and intent to cause GBH;
- wounding with malice and intent to resist lawful apprehension;
- wounding with malice and intent to prevent lawful apprehension;
- wounding with malice and intent to resist lawful detainer;
- wounding with malice and intent to prevent lawful detainer;
- GBH with malice and intent to resist lawful apprehension;

---

[83] The only difference is that, technically, s18 does not require the harm to be caused to another.

- GBH with malice and intent to prevent lawful apprehension;
- GBH with malice and intent to resist lawful detainer; and
- GBH with malice and intent to prevent lawful detainer.

Amongst these variations, two important details should not be missed:

First, unlike other offences against the person, the mens rea of section 18 is only satisfied by an *intention* (recklessness is not sufficient). Therefore, the meaning of 'intention' as distinct from recklessness becomes crucial. As discussed in relation to murder, D intends when she either (a) acts in order to bring about the result, or (b) acts with foresight that the result is a virtually certain consequence of her action, the result is in fact a virtually certain result, and the jury choose to find that she intended it.

Secondly, as held in *Taylor*, an intention to wound is *not* sufficient mens rea for section 18.

 Taylor [2009] EWCA Crim 544

D stabbed V in the back during an altercation. There was no evidence that D intended to cause GBH.

- Crown Court: guilty of a section 18 offence. The court defined the mens rea of section 18 as an intent to wound or to cause GBH.
- Court of Appeal: appeal allowed, and liability for section 20 substituted. Section 18 requires intention to cause GBH (not simply to wound), and there was insufficient evidence of such intention in this case.

7.6.2.1 Malice

'Malice' has already been discussed in relation to section 20. It requires, broadly, for D to intend or foresee the possibility of causing V bodily harm. For the section 18 offence, the role played by the malice requirement is therefore very different between (A) cases where D intends GBH, and (B) cases where D does not intend to cause GBH but does, for example, intend to resist lawful apprehension.

A) **Where D intends to cause GBH:** In this, the most common construction of the section 18 offence, the word 'maliciously' adds nothing at all. D's intention to cause GBH incorporates the less serious malice requirement, and so it need not be discussed separately.[84]

B) **Where D does not intend GBH, but does intend to resist lawful apprehension, etc:** Here, the 'maliciously' requirement becomes central to liability. This is because D's mens rea does not otherwise make reference to harms at all. The 'maliciously' requirement means that D must foresee at least some bodily harm, and although there is no direct authority, probably also requires the foresight of GBH.[85] Thus, where D intends to prevent apprehension, etc, 'maliciously' should be interpreted to require her to *also* foresee the possibility of GBH before section 18 liability is established.

---

[84] *Brown* [2005] EWCA Crim 359, [17].
[85] This is assumed in *Morrison* (1989) 89 Cr App R 17.

7.7 Sections 47, 20, and 18: alternative verdicts

Consistent with the 'laddering' of these offences, it has been held that a charge relating to a more serious offence against the person will include the less serious offences as alternatives. Thus, if D is charged under section 18, GBH with intent, a jury may alternatively find liability under section 20 or section 47 if they believe that the essential elements of liability for section 18 are unproven.[86] In this manner, analysis of liability will generally focus on the most serious potential offence before working down the ladder if necessary.

Despite the utility of this approach, research has suggested it also led to unfortunate consequences. Particularly, because of the availability of the lesser alternatives, it seems that many juries shied away from reaching guilty verdicts for the most serious section 18 offence, even where the elements of this offence appear to be satisfied.[87] Such research demonstrates a flaw to the laddering of offences.

7.8 Defences to sections 47, 20, and 18

Where D satisfies the elements of section 47, 20, or 18, she will nevertheless avoid liability if she has a specific defence of 'consent' or 'belief in consent'. Additionally, D may also avoid liability by relying on one of the general defences discussed in **Chapter 13** (denials of offending) and **Chapter 14** (general defences). Our focus in this section will be the specific defences.

It should be noted that although the defences of 'consent' and 'belief in consent' are available in relation to sections 47, 20, and 18, these defences are *not* constructed in the same way as they were in relation to assault and battery discussed previously. To apply to the more serious offences, V's consent, or D's belief in consent, will require additional elements before being legally effective.

7.8.1 Defences to the base offence for s47

The defences to assault and battery discussed earlier (including lawful chastisement, consent, and belief in consent) will not ordinarily prevent liability for a section 47, 20, or 18 offence. However, the unique construction of section 47, requiring a base offence of assault or battery that causes ABH, opens the possibility that one of these defences might apply to undermine liability for the base offence. With the base offence removed, the construction of section 47 liability would then become impossible (assault or battery + ABH = s47). Thus, in effect, a defence to simple assault or battery could act as a defence to section 47 liability.

Where D has caused the level of harm necessary for a section 47 offence, the courts have been reluctant to allow a defence to simple assault or battery (the base offence) to undermine liability. Therefore, a line of authority has developed in relation to these cases that can prevent D from raising a defence to the base offence, depending upon

---

[86] *Mandair* (1994) 99 Cr App R 250.

[87] Genders, 'Reform of the Offences Against the Person Act: Lessons from the Law in Action' [1999] Crim LR 689.

her foresight of causing ABH. Where D is prevented from raising a defence to the base offence, she will be restricted to those defences that are available for the more serious offences (discussed later). Although the courts have struggled for consistency, their general approach can be summarised as follows.

A) D causes ABH, she intended or foresaw the possibility of causing ABH:

> *Example . . .*
> D and V agree to practise shadow boxing, intending no contact or only very light contact. D knows that she lacks really tight control of her punches and foresees she might hit V causing ABH. D does so.

V may have given effective consent to assault or battery, but D's foresight that she might cause ABH means that such consent will *not* prevent section 47 liability. Rather, D will only avoid liability if she satisfies the elements of the more restrictive consent defences discussed later. This is confirmed in *Donovan*.[88]

B) D causes ABH, she did not intend or foresee the ABH:

> *Example . . .*
> D and V play a game trying to push each other over. V falls and accidentally hits her head causing ABH.

As D does not foresee the chance of causing ABH or greater, V's effective consent to assault or battery *will* prevent section 47 liability. V has consented to the assault or battery, and there is no reason (no further fault from D) that justifies not legally recognising that consent. This is confirmed in *Meachen*.[89]

C) D causes ABH. She did not intend or foresee the ABH, although she *should* have foreseen it:

> *Example . . .*
> D and V play a game trying to push each other over. V falls and accidentally hits her head causing ABH. V hit her head on an obvious rock that was directly behind her.

This final example is the most problematic. There are conflicting cases, but following *Boyea*,[90] it is likely that V's effective consent to assault or battery will *not* prevent her potential section 47 liability. As with D's recklessness in (A), D's negligence as to causing ABH will undermine her defence. D will only avoid liability if the elements of the more restrictive consent defences discussed later are satisfied.

> *Don't be confused . . .*
> Section 47 cases where V consented to assault or battery, but did not consent to ABH, are rare. However, the approach of the courts, focusing on D's foresight of ABH, is interesting. It should be remembered that D need not foresee the chance of causing ABH to be liable for a section 47 offence, as it is a constructive liability offence. However, such foresight becomes a primary concern here, when deciding if defences to simple assault or battery can be used to undermine liability.

---

[88] [1934] 2 KB 498.
[89] [2006] EWCA Crim 2414.
[90] (1992) 156 JP 505.

7.8.2 Consent to the more serious offences against the person

Consent can be a valid defence to offences under section 47, 20, or 18. However, in addition to the defence elements required for consent as to assault or battery, consent to the more serious offences will only be available where D's conduct comes within what the courts are prepared to accept is an excepted category. For example, D cannot avoid liability for GBH if she demonstrates that V asked to be shot. However, a doctor can avoid such liability by showing that V consented to a surgical operation that was duly performed. The elements of the defence are set out in **Table 7.7**.

Table 7.7 Defence of consent to serious offences against the person

A) V's consent must be expressed or implied to D in a legally recognised manner
B) V's consent must be effective: V must have the capacity, freedom, and information to make a choice
C) The conduct and harms consented to must come within a legally recognised category

We have discussed the first two elements of the defence in the context of assault and battery earlier,[91] and the same rules apply here. Therefore, our focus will be on the additional element, identifying the categories of conduct (where D commits a s47, 20, or 18 offence) that can be validly consented to.

The third element of the defence was established in what remains the leading case, *Brown*.

 Brown [1994] AC 212

D and others were involved in sadomasochistic homosexual groupings. Within the group, the men filmed various acts causing both ABH and wounding for their mutual sexual pleasure. They were charged with offences under sections 47 and 20.

- Crown Court: guilty of section 47 and 20 offences.
- Court of Appeal: convictions upheld on appeal.
- House of Lords: appeal dismissed. The court set out the additional requirement for consent in relation to sections 47, 20, and 18. They then concluded that sadomasochism did not qualify within one of the special categories.

The recognised categories, or accepted activities, where V's consent will be legally effective, have not been designed in accordance with particular legal principles or with regard to any legal or medical notions of acceptable harm.[92] Rather, as Lord Woolf rather

---

[91] See **7.3.2**.

[92] See Tolmie, 'Consent to Harmful Assaults: The Case for Moving Away from Category Based Decision Making' [2012] Crim LR 656; Kell, 'Social Disutility and Consent' (1994) 14 OJLS 121; Giles, 'Consensual Harm and the Public Interest' (1994) 57 MLR 101.

candidly admitted in *Barnes*,[93] they have evolved as a matter of 'public policy'. This policy-based approach allows the courts flexibility to reach what they consider to be socially desirable results. However, in their attempts to do so, the list of accepted activities has developed inconsistently and, as many would now accept, incoherently. The categories that have so far been acknowledged by the courts include:

- surgery;
- body modification;
- religious flagellation;
- sports;
- horseplay; and
- sexual pleasure.

We discuss each in turn.

7.8.2.1 Surgery

Surgery is a straightforward example where V can provide valid consent to what might otherwise constitute a serious offence against the person.[94] This includes both essential and non-essential (cosmetic) treatment.[95]

7.8.2.2 Body modification

There are several common forms of body modification—involving bodily harm—that may be validly consented to (eg hair cutting, piercing, tattooing, etc).[96] There are, however, borderline cases. This can be illustrated in the comparison of *Wilson* and *Brown*.

> **Wilson** [1996] Crim LR 573
>
> At his wife's (V's) request, D consensually branded his initials onto her bottom with a hot knife. D was charged with a section 47 offence.
> - Crown Court: guilty of section 47 offence.
> - Court of Appeal: appeal allowed. D's conduct was akin to tattooing and other body modification, and V's consent was therefore valid.

The outcome of *Wilson* was decided by the Court of Appeal in a manner that gave short shrift to the prosecution, making clear that this was not a place for criminal liability. This would suggest that *Wilson* was a clear case on its facts where V's consent was valid. However, although some of the acts in *Brown* could equally have been treated as analogous to acceptable forms of body modification (eg genital piercing), the court in *Brown* found consent to be invalid.

---

93 [2005] Crim LR 381.

94 Law Commission, *Consent in Criminal Law* (Consultation 139, 1995) Part 8; Skegg, 'Medical Procedures and the Crime of Battery' [1974] Crim LR 693 and (1973) 36 MLR 370.

95 *Corbett v Corbett* [1971] P 83: sex-change operation.

96 Law Commission, *Consent in Criminal Law* (Consultation 139, 1995) Part 9; Elliott, 'Body Dismorphic Disorder, Radical Surgery and the Limits of Consent' (2009) 17 Med L Rev 149.

Body modification is also common in a religious context (eg circumcision of Jewish and Muslim males).[97] Religious body modification gains some protection from Article 9 ECHR which respects religious freedom. However, certain foreign cultural practices have not been accepted within this exception, for example cheek incision.[98] Such distinctions appear incoherent.

7.8.2.3 Religious flagellation

Although rarely practised, religious flagellation (beating or whipping as part of a religious ritual) is also likely to constitute an exception where V may validly consent to bodily harm.[99] This was recognised by Lord Mustill in *Brown*.

7.8.2.4 Sports

Various sports provide a clear social utility despite the high risk of bodily injury involved, for example rugby, roller derby, etc.[100] However, although the law seeks to allow valid consent in these cases, it must take care not to exempt acts of violence carried out under the guise of sport. A number of principles have developed.

First, we must question whether the 'sport' is recognised by the law (ie sports that can be played legally). What is included here remains, to some extent, an accident of history, and is not based on degrees or risks of harm. For example, sports like boxing allowing participants to intentionally inflict GBH, and the courts recognise this as lawful.[101] However, certain activities that might once have been considered sports, such as duelling, are no longer recognised as lawful. Where injury results from an unrecognised sport, then the sporting exception will not apply and D may be liable.

Secondly, having established that the sport is recognised, we examine the rules of the sport. The law will generally accept that no offence arises for conduct within the rules of a sport, played consensually. For example, if D tackles V in a game of rugby, injuring V, but not committing a foul, D will not be liable for an offence. These risks are implicitly consented to when V joins the game. One qualification here, however, is that the criminal law is not *mandated* to accede to any rule changes instituted by sporting bodies. For example, if the Football Association decided that footballers could hit each other with bats, this would not automatically mean that consent to such hitting would be legally recognised.

Thirdly, we must consider injuries that result *outside* the rules of a recognised game. In this regard, human imperfection dictates that for sport to be played at all, consent must

---

[97] Gilbert, 'Time to Reconsider the Lawfulness of Ritual Male Circumcision' [2007] EHRLR 279; Vickers, 'Circumcision—The Unkindest Cut of All?' (2000) 150 NLJ 1694. See also Regional Court judgment in Cologne, Germany (June 2012) where male circumcision was held unlawful (Docket No Az 151 Ns 169/11, Landgericht Köln). Female circumcision and associated conduct is criminal (Female Genital Mutilation Act 2003, as amended by the Serious Crime Act 2015).

[98] *Adesanya* (1974) The Times, 16 July; Poulter, 'Foreign Customs and the English Criminal Law' (1975) 24 ICLQ 136.

[99] Law Commission, *Consent in Criminal Law* (Consultation 139, 1995) paras 10.2–10.7.

[100] Law Commission, *Consent in Criminal Law* (Consultation 139, 1995), Part 12; Cutcheon, 'Sports, Violence and the Criminal Law' (1994) 45 NILQ 267; Livings, 'A Different Ball Game' (2007) 71 J Crim L 534.

[101] Gunn and Ormerod, 'The Legality of Boxing' (1995) 15 LS 181; Anderson, *The Legality of Boxing: A Punch Drunk Love?* (2007).

be recognised in relation to certain forms of inadvertent or reckless behaviour, such as a late tackle in football or a bouncer in cricket.[102] The task, then, is to distinguish what we might call *legitimate* foul play (conduct that breaches the rules, but is still impliedly and validly consented to), from *illegitimate* foul play (conduct that breaches the rules to such an extent that it is not validly consented to). This was discussed in *Barnes*.[103]

 Barnes [2005] 1 WLR 910

D was playing in an amateur football match. D mistimed a sliding tackle against V, and caused serious injury. D was charged with a section 20 offence.

- Crown Court: guilty of section 20 offence.
- Court of Appeal: appeal allowed. D's conduct can be outside the rules of the game (within a margin of appreciation) and still be validly consented to.

When asking if the risk is impliedly consented to by those involved, even though it is outside the rules of the game, the Court of Appeal set out a number of factors that should be considered: the type of sport, the level at which it is being played, the nature of the act, the degree of force, the extent of the risk of injury, and D's state of mind.[104] With sporting sanctions and/or civil remedies often readily available, criminal prosecutions are rare and usually reserved for only the gravest conduct.

The test in *Barnes* may be usefully imagined as a target board, as set out in **Figure 7.2**.

According to *Barnes*:
- Inner circle (rules of the game): V provides valid implied consent to any non-intentional injury occurring within the rules of the game.
- Middle circle (just outside the rules of the game): V provides valid implied consent to any non-intentional injury occurring just outside the rules of the game, but within a margin of appreciation.
- Outer circle (outside the margin of appreciation): V's implied consent to the risk of harm does not include conduct that breaks the rules of the game and is outside the margin of appreciation.

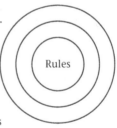

Figure 7.2 Consent and sport

Picking up on the last of the factors highlighted in *Barnes*, D's state of mind requires some special attention. This is because, with the exception of boxing and certain martial arts, playing sport should not involve D *intentionally* causing V bodily harm. Thus, although in sports such as hockey or cricket V's implicit consent will extend to the risk

---

[102] *Moore* (1898) 14 TLR 229.
[103] Anderson, 'No Licence for Thuggery: Violence, Sport and the Criminal Law' [2008] Crim LR 751.
[104] Supported by the Law Commission, *Consent and Offences against the Person* (Consultation 134, 1994). See Gardiner, 'Should More Matches End in Court?' (2005) 155 NLJ 998.

of D causing bodily harm, V has not consented to D *intentionally* causing such injury. Where D does cause injury with intent, there is, therefore, no consent.[105]

7.8.2.5 Horseplay

Focusing predominantly on children, the horseplay exception goes beyond sport to recognise consent in relation to general undisciplined play. Although such conduct carries a risk of injury, it is felt that as long as *genuinely* non-consenting individuals remain protected by law,[106] V's consent should be recognised even to the risk of GBH. Not recognising this exception would criminalise thousands of acts in playgrounds across the country and also, perhaps, deny a valuable part of growing up.[107]

The horseplay exception has been interpreted widely. For example, 'robust games' in *Aitken*[108] saw celebrating RAF officers setting fire to one another's fire-resistant clothing, eventually leading to V suffering severe burns. It was held that if V consented, such consent could be recognised within the exception.

7.8.2.6 Sexual pleasure?

Where V's consent derives from a context of sexual pleasure, as opposed to the pleasure of sport or other non-sexual play, the courts have struggled to maintain a clear or coherent approach.

Risk of sexually transmitted infection

It is now clear from *Dica*[109] that V may validly consent to the *risk* of even potentially lethal infection in the context of a sexual encounter, such as unprotected sex with a person with HIV. For such consent to be valid, V must be fully informed of the risk.[110] This will not, of course, include consent where either party is *intending* that the infection should be spread.

Unlike many recognised exceptions (discussed earlier), consent to the risk of infection is not socially desirable. However, it was found in *Dica* that not recognising this exception would involve an 'impracticality of enforcement', as well as invading a part of life that remains 'pre-eminently private'.

Harm and sexual pleasure: sadomasochism

Sadomasochism (giving and receiving targeted pain for sexual pleasure) is always likely to be problematic for the law in this area.[111] An analogy could be drawn with the risk of sexual infection, allowing consent in recognition of the impracticality of enforcement and the privacy of sexual relationships. However, unlike the risk of sexual infection and most sport, and horseplay, D is not simply *risking* bodily harm. Rather, the intentional infliction of bodily harm is essential to what both D and V are consenting to. This should not automatically disqualify V's consent as invalid. Within the recognised categories, D

---

[105] *Bradshaw* (1878) Cox CC 83.
[106] *A* [2005] All ER 38: V was clearly not consenting.
[107] *Jones* (1986) 83 Cr App R 375.
[108] [1992] 1 WLR 1006.
[109] [2004] EWCA Crim 1103.
[110] *Konzani* [2005] EWCA Crim 706.
[111] Law Commission, *Consent in Criminal Law* (Consultation 139, 1995) Part 10; Bamforth, 'Sadomasochism and Consent' [1994] Crim LR 661; Leigh, 'Sado-Masochism, Consent and the Reform of the Criminal Law' (1976) 39 MLR 130.

intends to inflict bodily harm in the context of body modification, religious flagellations, and sports such as boxing and martial arts. However, it has emboldened the courts to look more deeply into the perceived social utility of the practice. In doing so, the law has become confused, inconsistent, and indefensible.

The following cases provide an overview of the current legal position:

- *Brown*:[112] the leading case in this area, involving sadomasochistic homosexual encounters between a group of men resulting in prosecutions under sections 47 and 20. A majority in the House of Lords (3:2) upheld the convictions, reasoning that despite the consent of those involved, the actions were not 'sexual' but 'violent'; reflecting a cult of violence that endangered and corrupted those involved.

- *Donovan*:[113] this early case reflects many of the same public policy concerns that led to the decision in *Brown*. In this case, D beat a consenting 17-year-old girl with a cane for purposes of sexual gratification. D was convicted of both indecent assault and common assault. As D was charged with common assault and not GBH it is even more astounding that a conviction resulted: as discussed earlier, valid consent for these cases should not require D's conduct to come within the recognised categories. Although such a result is unlikely to be repeated, the policy aims discussed in this case (referred to in *Brown*) remain relevant to the current law.

- *Wilson*:[114] here, D's conviction under section 47, following the consensual branding of his wife's bottom, was overturned on appeal. The Court of Appeal considered the activity to be akin to tattooing, and made clear that they did not believe that this is an area in which the criminal law should interfere: 'consensual activity between husband and wife, in the privacy of the matrimonial home, is not, in our judgment, normally a proper matter for criminal investigation, let alone criminal prosecution'.

Recognising the apparent conflict between *Brown* and *Wilson* in particular, subsequent cases have attempted to find a sensible distinction. Unfortunately, however, courts have tended to do so by focusing on the degree or nature of the harms involved.[115] This is unfortunate because, as both cases involved ABH, it is hard to identify the measurement by which the harms in *Brown* can be characterised as worse. This is particularly evident when we consider that it was only in *Wilson* that hospital treatment was required.

Despite a number of appeal cases, it therefore remains unclear whether sexual gratification constitutes a recognised category through which V may provide valid consent to bodily harm in excess of simple assault or battery. This may be possible where the activity can be likened to other accepted practices such as tattooing, and more controversially, these appeal cases may also suggest that it is more acceptable in the context of heterosexual married couples. However, the courts' willingness to label certain practices as 'violent' as opposed to 'sexual', or to conclude that they involve a different 'degree' or 'nature' of harm, makes the law in this area unpredictable.

---

[112] [1994] AC 212.
[113] [1934] 2 KB 498.
[114] [1996] Crim LR 573.
[115] *Laskey v UK* (1997) 24 EHRR 39: claiming the injuries were not 'comparable in seriousness'; *Emmett* (1999) The Times, 15 October: V's consent to ABH was invalid because D's conduct went 'beyond that which was established in *Wilson*'.

7.8.3 Belief in consent to the more serious offences against the person

D has a defence if she believed that V provided valid consent. For a belief defence in this context, D's belief in V's consent must have been consistent with the legal requirements of being informed, effective, and within a recognised category. Thus, even if V was not consenting in fact, D will avoid liability if she genuinely believed that consent was present.[116] This defence is rarely pursued in court.

7.9 Conduct-focused offences against the person

The first category of non-fatal offences was primarily concerned with the *degree* of harm caused by D: creating a ladder of offences in order to label and punish the degree of harm caused most appropriately. However, in this section we move to discuss a new category of offences. These offences, although still concerned with degrees of harm, are no longer attempting to form part of the ladder explored in the result category. Rather, this group of offences is conduct-focused: created independently in order to recognise certain specifically harmful circumstances or motives, in order to fill perceived gaps in the law, and/or to reflect political and social priorities.

There are many offences that fall within this category. In the following sections we explore a sample of these, including harassment and stalking, racially or religiously aggravating elements, torture and slavery, and administering poison.

7.9.1 Harassment and stalking

The criminalisation of harassment and stalking has for many years been, and remains, a challenge for the criminal law.[117] This is because, unlike standard offences against the person, harassing conduct can take almost any form, including apparent acts of kindness such as the repeated sending of flowers. Also, whereas other offences will focus on a single attack from D, the harms associated with harassment are usually cumulative: perhaps minor in their own right, but severely debilitating in combination. With this in mind, despite the broadening of the OAPA offences to include purely verbal assaults and psychiatric injuries,[118] specific offences have been required to combat the full range of potentially harassing behaviour.[119] These are provided within the Protection from Harassment Act 1997 (PHA).

7.9.1.1 PHA 1997, s2: offence of harassment

Section 2 makes it an offence to cause harassment: to pursue a course of conduct in breach of section 1(1) or 1(1A)[120] (see **Table 7.8**).

> (1) A person must not pursue a course of conduct—
>
>> (a) which amounts to harassment of another, and

[116] *Jones* [1987] Crim LR 123.
[117] Babcock, 'The Psychology of Stalking' in Infield and Platford (eds), *The Law of Harassment and Stalking* (2000); Addison and Lawson-Cruttenden, *Harassment Law and Practice* (1998); Finch, 'Stalking the Perfect Stalking Law: An Evaluation of the Efficacy of the Protection from Harassment Act 1997' [2002] Crim LR 702.
[118] *Ireland* [1998] AC 147.
[119] See Home Office, *Stalking the Solutions* (1996).
[120] Section 1A was added by the Serious Organised Crime and Police Act 2005, s125.

(b) which he knows or ought to know amounts to harassment of the other.

(1A) A person must not pursue a course of conduct—

(a) which involves harassment of two or more persons, and

(b) which he knows or ought to know involves harassment of those persons, and

(c) by which he intends to persuade any person (whether or not one of those mentioned above)—

(i)   not to do something that he is entitled or required to do, or

(ii) to do something that he is not under any obligation to do.

Table 7.8 PHA 1997, s2

	Actus reus	Mens rea
Conduct element	Any course of conduct that causes the result	Voluntary
Circumstance element	V is a person	Knowledge
Result element	(s1(1)) Harassment of V Or (s1A) Harassment of V and others	Know *or* ought to have known Know *or* ought to have known
Ulterior mens rea element	*	(s1A) Intention to persuade V not to do something she is entitled to do, *or* to do something she is not obliged to do

Actus reus of s2

The actus reus of section 2 proscribes a course of conduct that results in V, or V and others, being harassed. The terms 'harassment' and 'course of conduct' are crucial.

A) **Harassment** is not fully defined in the PHA and leaves considerable discretion to the court to interpret the term as it is commonly understood.[121] We are told in section 7(2) that harassment includes 'the causing of alarm or distress'. However, as we are only told that harassment *includes* causing alarm or distress, it is possible that harassment can also be found without proof of either.[122] Equally, alarm and distress can be caused without harassment. This point was recently clarified in *O'Neill*: 'many actions that cause alarm or distress will not amount to harassment; hence, the requirement, well established in authority... that the conduct must also be oppressive'.[123]

---

[121] *Thomas v News Group Newspapers Ltd* [2001] EWCA Civ 1233.
[122] *DPP v Ramsdale* (2001) The Independent, 19 March.
[123] [2016] EWCA Crim 92.

We must also take care to understand D's conduct in the context of the facts of a particular case. In *Curtis*,[124] for example, D undoubtedly caused alarm and distress to V through a number of minor assaults and other dangerous behaviour. However, although D's actions were 'oppressive, unreasonable and unacceptable', the Court of Appeal quashed his conviction for harassment, finding that the relevant six incidents spread out over a nine-month relationship between D and V, involving violence on both sides, did not amount to harassment.

> **Assessment matters . . .**
> The lack of a clear definition should encourage you to discuss the law when applying it to prob-lem facts. Look for the causing of alarm or distress, and oppression, but remember that this is not conclusive.

B) A course of conduct must be shown to have *caused* the harassment. The main point here is the need for persistence from D, with a course of conduct requiring at least two separate incidents. The focus here is on D's conduct, and as established in *James v CPS*, even an active role by V will not necessarily undermine liability.

> **James v CPS** [2009] EWHC 2925 (Admin)
>
> V, the manager of a social services team, had a duty to return the calls of D (a receiver of care) despite D's persistent abuse on such calls.
> - Magistrates' court: guilty of section 2 offence.
> - Crown Court: conviction upheld on appeal.
> - High Court: conviction upheld on appeal. V's self-exposure to the harassment was irrelevant.

When identifying the incidents within D's course of conduct, it is important to distinguish between cases involving a single victim, and cases involving multiple victims. The rules are set out in section 7:

> (3) A 'course of conduct' must involve—
>
>   (a) in the case of conduct in relation to a single person (see section 1(1)), conduct on at least two occasions in relation to that person, or
>
>   (b) in the case of conduct in relation to two or more persons (see section 1(1A)), conduct on at least one occasion in relation to each of those persons.

In standard cases involving a single V under section 7(3)(a), a course of conduct will require D to repeat certain conduct on at least two occasions to that V. Although relatively simple to state, the test can cause problems, particularly where it is difficult to identify or divide incidents. For example, in *Kelly v DPP*,[125] D made three calls to V's mobile between 2.57 am and 3.02 am, leaving abusive voicemail messages on each occasion. Listening to these messages later, and without pause between messages, V was caused severe distress. *Is this more than one incident?*[126] Similarly, in an effort to find

---

[124] [2010] EWCA Crim 123.
[125] [2003] Crim LR 43, DC.
[126] See also *DPP v Hardy* [2008] All ER (D) 315: 95 phone calls within a 90-minute period held to constitute a course of conduct rather than a single incident.

multiple incidents, the courts have also been willing, whether rightly or wrongly, to accept indirect acts or harassment. For example, in *DPP v Williams*[127] D put his hand through a bathroom window startling X who was in the room showering, and causing V (X's flatmate who was later *told* of the incident) to also be fearful. Later, D looked into a bedroom window, this time frightening V directly. The court held that, as V was caused distress by both incidents, the offence was made out even though the first was indirect.[128]

In cases involving multiple victims, a course of conduct will require only a single harassing act in relation to at least two victims. In this manner, V's multiple acts of harassment are not excused from liability simply because they are not aimed at the same V. This provision is particularly useful in the context of protesters who harass those connected with animal breeding and testing.[129] Where D's course of conduct is based on section 7(3)(b), however, it must be remembered that the additional element of ulterior mens rea will be required.[130]

Alongside evidence of multiple acts, in order to establish a 'course of conduct' in either guise, it must also be demonstrated that those acts were in some way connected. In many cases, such as repeated telephone calls within a short period of time, this will be relatively easy to establish. However, what if the acts are separated by a considerable period of time, say, two birthday cards, or are of a very different nature? This was discussed in *Lau v DPP*.

 Lau v DPP [2000] Crim LR 580

The first incident involved D slapping V (his then girlfriend) on the face. The second, four months later, involved D threatening V's new partner with a brick. D was charged with a section 2 offence.

- Magistrates' court: guilty of section 2 offence.
- Crown Court: appeal allowed. Although a course of conduct can be found despite a lengthy gap, even up to a year, the incidents must have a logical connection. An example given was of racial harassment outside a synagogue on the Day of Atonement. In this case, however, there was insufficient evidence of that connection or nexus.

It is clear from *Lau* that each case will turn on its facts. The question for the court is a general one: are the incidents logically connected as a single course of conduct? To fulfil the actus reus of section 2, the answer must be 'yes'.

Mens rea of s2

Applying the mens rea for section 2 again requires a distinction to be made between cases where D harasses a single V on multiple occasions (s1(1)), and cases where D harasses multiple Vs (s1(1A)). This is because it is only in the latter that there is an additional ulterior mens rea requirement.

A) Mens rea required for *both* s1 and s1A: At the time of acting, D must have known, or ought to have known, that her course of conduct would result in harassment.

---

[127] *DPP v Williams* (DC, 27 July 1998, Rose LJ and Bell J).
[128] Section 7(3A) provides the additional possibility that where D aids and abets an act of harassment that is carried out by another, the law will also treat the act as having been completed by D.
[129] Home Office, *Animal Welfare: Human Rights—Protecting People from Animal Rights Extremists* (2004).
[130] Section 7(3A) provides the additional possibility that, where D aids and abets an act of harassment that is carried out by another, the law will also treat that act as having been completed by D.

In this manner, the mens rea of section 2 can be satisfied both subjectively by D's actual knowledge or objectively by the fact that a reasonable person would have known. The objective approach is illustrated in *Colohan*.[131]

 Colohan [2001] EWCA Crim 1251

D, who suffered from schizophrenia, sent a number of letters to his local MP (V). The letters were threatening in places and caused V substantial distress. D was charged with a section 2 offence.

- Crown Court: guilty of section 2 offence.
- Court of Appeal: conviction upheld on appeal. Although D may not have known that his letters would cause alarm or distress, a reasonable person not suffering such an illness would have done. Therefore, mens rea is satisfied.

Within this objective standard, D's lack of appreciation or inability to appreciate the effects of her conduct will not be taken into account. However, any additional information that D possesses will. This is important where D is aware of particular circumstances that make her otherwise innocuous conduct more likely to be harassing (eg D knows that V has consistently rejected her advances, and yet continues to send gifts).

B) Mens rea required _only_ where D harasses multiple Vs (s1(1A)): D must intend her course of conduct to persuade the Vs to refrain from something they are entitled to do, or to do something they are not (eg for an animal breeder to stop trading with a biological research lab). In the more common section 2 case, where D harasses a single victim (s1(1)), this additional intention is not required.

Defences for s2

With such a broadly defined offence it is important to consider any defences that D might raise to avoid liability.[132] A specific defence is provided by section 1(3), highlighting three cases where no course of conduct will be found:

(3) Subsection (1) or (1A) does not apply to a course of conduct if the person who pursued it shows—

     (a) that it was pursued for the purpose of preventing or detecting crime,

     (b) that it was pursued under any enactment or rule of law or to comply with any condition or requirement imposed by any person under any enactment, or

     (c) that in the particular circumstances the pursuit of the course of conduct was reasonable.

A) Defence 1(3)(a): This defence seems tolerably clear. Although the defence is predominantly intended to protect the police and other law enforcement agencies, it can also be used by others, such as investigative journalists, and even members of the public. However, particularly where the defence is raised by people who are not acting as officials, the court will closely scrutinise whether such conduct was required.[133]

---

131   [2001] EWCA Crim 1251.
132   Discussed in *Hayes v Willoughby* [2013] UKSC 17.
133   *Howlett v Holding* (2006) The Times, 8 February: D conducted a campaign against V, a local councillor, by flying banners from his aircraft referring to her in abusive terms.

B) **Defence 1(3)(b):** This defence is also relatively uncontroversial, protecting free speech and expression, for example, through public demonstrations.[134]

C) **Defence 1(3)(c):** This defence is more problematic, and more difficult to define.[135] The defence requires D to prove (on the balance of probabilities) that her harassing course of conduct was *reasonable* for her to pursue in the circumstances. For the court, particularly in protest-related cases, this will mean difficult policy decisions regarding the reasonableness of protest that causes others alarm or distress.[136]

Alongside these specific defences, the general defences must also be considered. We discuss these in **Chapters 13** and **14**.

7.9.1.2 PHA 1997, s4: causing fear of violence

Section 4 criminalises D's course of conduct that not only causes harassment to a particular V, but *also* leads to a fear that violence will be used against V (see **Table 7.9**):

(1) A person whose course of conduct causes another to fear, on at least two occasions, that violence will be used against him is guilty of an offence if he knows or ought to know that his course of conduct will cause the other so to fear on each of those occasions.

(2) For the purposes of this section, the person whose course of conduct is in question ought to know that it will cause another to fear that violence will be used against him on any occasion if a reasonable person in possession of the same information would think the course of conduct would cause the other so to fear on that occasion.

Table 7.9 PHA 1997, s4

	Actus reus	Mens rea
Conduct element	Any course of conduct that causes the result	Voluntary
Circumstance element	V is a person	Knowledge
Result element	Harassment of V And V fears violence will be used against her	Know or ought to have known Know or ought to have known

Actus reus of s4

Section 4 shares many of the same actus reus elements as section 2, with the addition that D must cause V to fear that violence will be used against her. Section 4 is the more

---

[134] *Huntingdon Life Sciences v Curtin* (1997) The Times, 11 December.
[135] *Baron v DPP* (13 June 2000).
[136] *Debnath* [2006] 2 Cr App R 25.

serious offence and carries the higher maximum sentence: five years' imprisonment on indictment, as opposed to six months for a summary conviction under section 2.

The requirement that D causes V to fear that violence will be used against her is therefore central to the more serious section 4 offence. In many ways, this is a similar requirement to the actus reus of assault (see **7.2.1.1**), although, importantly, section 4 does not require V to anticipate *imminent* violence. Although 'violence' is not defined in the PHA, it is clear that V must anticipate that she personally will come to harm, and it is not sufficient if V anticipates violence to another.[137] The only qualification to this is where D's threats to another cause V, indirectly, to fear for her own safety.[138]

The requirement of 'harassment' (defined earlier) is not explicit in the text of section 4. However, a series of decisions have made clear that harassment *is* an essential result element within the offence.[139] This means that harassment must be considered.[140] However, as causing a fear of violence will also *generally* cause alarm or distress (harassment), the requirement of harassment will be easily satisfied in most cases.

Finally, and also in common with section 2, it must be demonstrated that both of these result elements were caused by D's 'course of conduct' (defined earlier). An isolated event, no matter how serious, will not be sufficient. Rather, a course of conduct requires the causing of harassment and the fear of violence on at least two occasions. It should be noted that, unlike the section 2 offence, a course of conduct under section 4 will only be satisfied where it is focused on a single V. Thus, multiple acts directed at different Vs (caught within s2 through s1(1A)), will not be sufficient for section 4.

Mens rea of s4

As with the section 2 offence, D is not required to intend or even to foresee a possibility that her course of conduct will cause harassment and a fear of violence. Rather, it is sufficient mens rea if a reasonable person, imbued with any special knowledge D has, would have known that the course of conduct would cause those results.

Defences for s4

As with section 2, there are a set of specific defences set out within the PHA that apply to section 4:

(3) It is a defence for a person charged with an offence under this section to show that—

    (a) his course of conduct was pursued for the purpose of preventing or detecting crime,

    (b) his course of conduct was pursued under any enactment or rule of law or to comply with any condition or requirement imposed by any person under any enactment, or

    (c) the pursuit of his course of conduct was reasonable for the protection of himself or another or for the protection of his or another's property.

---

[137] *Henley* [2000] Crim LR 582: D harassed V and his family, including threats to kill. The trial judge wrongly failed to direct the jury that V must fear violence to himself and that foreseeing violence to others *only* is insufficient for s4.

[138] Ibid. See also *Caurti v DPP* [2002] Crim LR 131 and commentaries.

[139] eg *Curtis* [2010] EWCA Crim 123.

[140] *Widdows* [2011] EWCA Crim 1500: D's conviction for s4 quashed because the trial judge failed to make clear in summing up that harassment was required. However, see *Haque* [2011] EWCA Crim 1871: D's conviction was safe despite a similar failure.

The defences in section 4(3)(a) and (b) largely mirror those already discussed in relation to section 2: where D is attempting to prevent/detect crime, and where D is acting in accordance with a rule of law. However, the third specific defence in section 4(3)(c) contains an important difference. Although the corresponding defence to section 2 allows *any* reasonable excuse to act as a defence, in relation to section 4, D's reasonable conduct will only be a defence where it is directed at protecting herself or another, or for the protection of property. This represents a significant narrowing of the defence in light of the more harmful conduct that D has completed to come within section 4.

Alongside these specific defences, the general defences must also be considered. We discuss these in **Chapters 13** and **14**.

7.9.1.3 Stalking offences

Although the harassment offences in sections 2 and 4 of the PHA have been employed to tackle stalking, following an Independent Parliamentary Inquiry into Stalking Law Reform,[141] specific stalking offences have been created.[142] The report concluded that since sections 2 and 4 had been interpreted so widely by the courts to include, for example, neighbourhood disputes, they were no longer fit for purpose in relation to stalking. The stalking-specific offences are therefore designed to build upon sections 2 and 4, to expose the full extent of the harm associated with stalking as opposed to simple harassment. The maximum sentences, however, remain the same as the more basic section 2 and 4 offences.

The stalking offences are set out in sections 2A and 4A of the PHA. These offences do not replace sections 2 and 4. Rather, where D commits an offence under section 2 or 4, and D's course of conduct includes conduct 'associated with stalking', D may now be alternatively liable under sections 2A and 4A. Conduct associated with stalking is left undefined in the PHA, but section 2A(3) does provide a number of illustrative examples intended to aid interpretation:

(3) The following are examples of acts or omissions which, in particular circumstances, are ones associated with stalking—

(a) following a person,

(b) contacting, or attempting to contact, a person by any means,

(c) publishing any statement or other material—

(i)   relating or purporting to relate to a person, or

(ii) purporting to originate from a person,

(d) monitoring the use by a person of the internet, email or any other form of electronic communication,

(e) loitering in any place (whether public or private),

(f) interfering with any property in the possession of a person,

(g) watching or spying on a person.

---

[141] Justice Unions' Parliamentary Group, 'Independent Parliamentary Inquiry into Stalking Law Reform: Main Findings and Recommendations', February 2012.

[142] In force from November 2012. Gowland, 'Protection from Harassment Act 1997: The "New" Stalking Offences' (2013) 77 J Crim L 387.

Interestingly, the PHA does not specify any corresponding mens rea element in relation to this requirement. Thus, as long as D's course of conduct includes acts or omissions that are associated with stalking, there is no requirement for D to have realised that this was the case.

The structure of the new section 2A offence is set out in **Figure 7.3**.

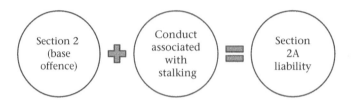

Figure 7.3 PHA 1997, s2A

The structure of the new s4A offence is set out in **Figure 7.4**.

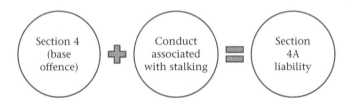

Figure 7.4 PHA 1997, s4A

Owing to a late parliamentary amendment, the section 4A offence (but *not* the s2A offence) can *also* be committed through an alternative construction. Within this alternative, the requirement that V must fear violence has been broadened considerably. This is set out in section 4A(1)(b):

(b) either—

   (i) causes another ('B') to fear, on at least two occasions, that violence will be used against B, or

   (ii) causes B serious alarm or distress which has a substantial adverse effect on B's usual day-to-day activities.

This extension was felt necessary because using section 4 as the base offence was believed to be overly restrictive: it would not have allowed for a stalking conviction under section 4A where V did not anticipate physical attack but was nevertheless caused substantial distress.

The statute does not provide a definition of what constitutes 'serious alarm or distress' or a 'substantial adverse effect on B's usual day-to-day activities'. This will be left to the courts, with the potential to be interpreted very widely indeed. As for mens rea, as with a charge based on V fearing violence, it is clear that D's mens rea as to section 4A(1)(b) (ii) is also satisfied by knowledge that such results will be caused, or by the fact that a reasonable person, imbued with any special knowledge D may have, would have known.[143]

---

[143] PHA, s4A(3).

This alternative structure for section 4A is set out in **Figure 7.5**.

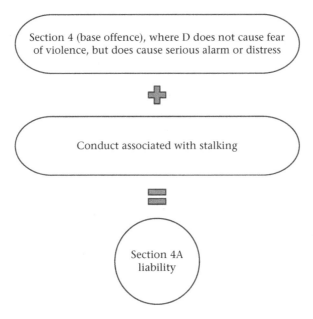

Figure 7.5 Alternative route to PHA 1997, s4A

Defences for s2A and s4A

As we have already observed, the section 2A and 4A offences are very similar to the section 2 and 4 offences discussed previously, the major difference being that the new stalking offences also require D's course of conduct to include conduct associated with stalking. Consistent with this, the specific defences discussed earlier in relation to the section 2 and 4 offences are also capable of negating liability for the section 2A and 4A offences. Thus, for section 2A (as with s2), if D acts with one of the intentions listed in section 1(3) then this will negate her liability for the course of conduct. Equally, for section 4A (as with s4), if D acts with one of the intentions listed in section 4(3)[144] she will also avoid liability.

Alongside these specific defences, the general defences must also be considered. We discuss these in **Chapters 13** and **14**.

7.9.2 Racially or religiously aggravating elements

Where D's violence has been motivated by hatred towards a particular racial or religious group, it has always been open to the court to reflect this aggravating factor at the sentencing stage.[145] And this remains the case.[146] However, first the Crime and Disorder Act

---

[144] This time the defences that are also explicitly repeated in s4A(4).

[145] Walters, 'Conceptualizing "Hostility" for Hate Crime Law: Minding "the Minutiae" When Interpreting Section 28(1)(a) of the Crime and Disorder Act 1998' (2014) 34 OJLS 47; Burney, 'Using the Law of Racially Aggravated Offences' [2003] Crim LR 28.

[146] Owusu-Bempah and Walters, 'Racially Aggravated Offences: When Does Section 145 of the Criminal Justice Act 2003 Apply?' [2016] Crim LR 116.

1998 (in relation to race) and then the Anti-Terrorism, Crime and Security Act 2001 (amending the Crime and Disorder Act in relation to religion) have adapted these aggravating factors and made them elements of a new species of offences. Although somewhat controversial,[147] these offences are now a fully established part of the law. Indeed, the Law Commission has recommended expanding the categories to include aggravation based on disability, sexual orientation, and transgender.[148]

D commits one of these 'aggravated offences' when she perpetrates one of the offences discussed earlier (assault and battery; s47 OAPA; s20 OAPA; or harassment or stalking[149]), *and* she satisfies one of the additional racially or religiously aggravating elements. Thus, for example, what would be a conviction for assault or harassment becomes a conviction for racially aggravated assault or religiously aggravated harassment. In each case involving offences against the person, the aggravated version of the relevant base offence has a maximum sentence that is increased by between one and two years.

The offences are stated in sections 29[150] and 32[151] of the Crime and Disorder Act 1998. However, it is section 28 that sets out the requirements for racial or religious aggravation:

(1) An offence is racially or religiously aggravated for the purposes of sections 29 to 32 below if—

 (a) at the time of committing the offence, or immediately before or after doing so, the offender demonstrates towards the victim of the offence hostility based on the victim's membership (or presumed membership) of a racial or religious group; or

 (b) the offence is motivated (wholly or partly) by hostility towards members of a racial or religious group based on their membership of that group.

Section 28 thereby creates two separate forms of aggravating element: actus reus-based (s28(1)(a)), and mens rea-based (s28(1)(b)). D's base offence need only satisfy *one* of these to become an aggravated offence.

7.9.2.1 Aggravated through actus reus

The first species of aggravating element is where, *regardless of D's mens rea*, her actions at the time of committing the base offence (eg assault) objectively demonstrate hostility towards a racial or religious group. In this manner, even where D's base offence is not motivated by racial or religious hostility as, for example, where D is angry after V took her parking space, if D acts so as to display such hostility in the course of her offence then she is caught by the aggravated form of liability. The question in each case will be whether D's demonstration of hostility is linked to her base offence. This was discussed in *Babbs*.

---

[147] For a useful discussion of religiously aggravated offences, and potential dangers to freedom of expression, see Iganski, Sweiry, and Culpeper, 'A Question of Faith? Prosecuting Religiously Aggravated Offences in England and Wales' [2016] Crim LR 334.

[148] Law Commission, *Hate Crime: Should the Current Offences be Extended?* (No 348, 2014). Bakalis, 'Legislating Against Hatred: The Law Commission's Report on Hate Crime' [2015] Crim LR 192.

[149] There is no need for aggravation for s18 which carries the maximum life sentence.

[150] In relation to assault and battery, s47 and s20 OAPA.

[151] In relation to harassment and stalking.

Babbs [2007] EWCA Crim 2737

D racially abused V in a takeaway restaurant, and a scuffle broke out. Some minutes later, after D had received his food, he then headbutted V. D was charged with racially aggravated assault relating to the headbutt.

• Crown Court: guilty of aggravated assault.

• Court of Appeal: conviction upheld on appeal. Despite the delay between the racial abuse and the assault, there was sufficient proximity for the prosecution to stand.[152]

This form of aggravating element is very broad in its reach, attaching increased liability where a base offence is simply accompanied by, rather than inspired by, hostile comment or action. This was intended by its drafters, who feared that proving racial or religious hatred as a sole motive would be too difficult for prosecutors. However, it has also drawn criticism, particularly when other forms of hate will have no such effect, for example where D assaults V whilst calling him a 'fat bastard'.[153] As the statute matures it will be interesting to see if it has the effect of deterring people from racist language or whether (as has been feared) it may harden the racist attitudes of those convicted.[154]

The structure of the offence is set out in **Figure 7.6**.

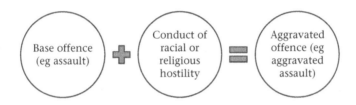

Figure 7.6 Aggravated liability (AR)

7.9.2.2 Aggravated through mens rea

The second species of aggravating element is based on D's mens rea. Set out in section 28(1)(b), D is liable for the more serious offence if her commission of the base offence (eg assault) was *motivated* by racial or religious hostility. This second aggravating element is much narrower and less controversial than that in section 28(1)(a).

Although D must be motivated by racial or religious hostility to come within this form of aggravation, as in *Kendall v DPP*, such hostility need not be her sole motivation.

Kendall v DPP [2008] EWHC 1848 (Admin)

D attached posters in public places with photos of illegal immigrants who had recently been found guilty of murder, with the heading 'Illegal Immigrant Murder Scum'. The posters also advertised the British National Party. D was charged with a public order offence, including racial aggravation under section 28(1)(b).

---

[152] Note, however, *Parry v DPP* [2004] EWHC 3112 (Admin), where a 20-minute delay was held to be too long.

[153] Noted by Maurice Kay J.

[154] Burney and Rose, 'Racially Aggravated Offences: How is the Law Working?' (2002) HORS 244.

- Magistrates' court: guilty of aggravated offence.
- High Court: conviction upheld on appeal. As long as D was partially motivated by racial hostility, it does not matter that he may have had other motives as well.

Racial or religious hostility must, however, form *part* of D's motivation. In *DPP v Howard*[155] D was charged using section 28(1)(b) after chanting 'I'd rather be a Paki than a cop' at his neighbours who were white police officers. Despite D's abusive language, it was held that he could not be liable using section 28(1)(b) because there was no evidence to demonstrate that D's words were *motivated* by hostility towards people from Pakistan, and rather more to suggest that his sole motivation was the personal dislike of his neighbours.[156]

The structure of the aggravated offence is set out in **Figure 7.7**.

Figure 7.7 Aggravated liability (MR)

7.9.2.3 Defining terms

The terms 'race' and 'religion' are core to both species of aggravating element. However, neither is defined with any detail within the Crime and Disorder Act.[157]

A) 'Race' and racial group have been interpreted by the courts in an extremely broad and non-technical manner. It will include nationality (including citizenship), ethnic origin and colour.[158] Race will also include non-inclusive expressions, so D will have demonstrated racial hostility if she refers to V as 'foreign' or 'non-white'.[159]

B) 'Religious group' is defined in the Act simply as a group of persons linked by reference to religious belief or lack thereof. As with the interpretation of 'race', and that employed in relation to Article 9 ECHR, it is likely that 'religion' will be interpreted widely. Non-inclusive terms such as 'unbeliever' will also qualify as religious hostility.[160]

In cases of racial and religious hostility the accuracy of D's assumptions about V's racial or religious status is irrelevant. So, for example, where D calls V a 'Paki' when V is from India, the element of the offence is still satisfied.[161] Equally, racial and religious

---

[155] [2008] EWHC 608 (Admin).
[156] Moses LJ cautioned: 'Prosecutors should be careful not to deploy [s28(1)(b)] where offensive words have been used, but in themselves have not in any way been the motivation for the particular offence with which a defendant is charged. It diminishes the gravity of this offence to use it in circumstances where it is unnecessary to do so and where plainly it cannot be proved', [12].
[157] Partial definitions are provided: Crime and Disorder Act 1998, s28(4) and (5).
[158] This can create problems for the court, eg *White* [2001] Crim LR 576.
[159] *Rogers* [2007] UKHL 8.
[160] *DPP v M* [2004] EWHC 1453 (Admin).
[161] *Rogers* [2007] UKHL 8.

hostility can be evident even where D and V are of the same racial or religious group. And, finally, it has been held that such hostility does not require V to be aware of D's actions, or even be present at the time.[162]

7.9.2.4 Defences to the aggravated offences

There are no *specific* defences that apply solely to these aggravated offences. However, as each of these offences will include a base offence (eg assault), any specific defences that apply to those base offences (discussed earlier) will also undermine liability for the aggravated offence. The general defences should also be considered, discussed in **Chapters 13** and **14**.

7.9.3 Torture and slavery

Conduct constituting torture and/or slavery is criminalised through various offences. Where D causes bodily harm, for example, we could employ one of the non-fatal offences from the first category discussed earlier. Equally, where V is not harmed beyond subjection to non-consensual captivity, we have the offence of false imprisonment.[163] However, specific offences of torture and slavery have been created. This is because, as with other overlapping offences, specific offences enable defendants to be labelled more appropriately, to provide a clear social message that such conduct represents a serious wrong, as well as demonstrating compatibility with ECHR rights.

7.9.3.1 Torture

A specific torture offence was created by section 134 of the Criminal Justice Act 1988, carrying a maximum sentence of life imprisonment (see **Table 7.10**). The offence is designed in accordance with Article 3 ECHR.

> 134. A public official or person acting in an official capacity, whatever his nationality, commits the offence of torture if in the United Kingdom or elsewhere he intentionally inflicts severe pain or suffering on another in the performance or purported performance of his official duties.

Table 7.10 Criminal Justice Act 1988, s134

	Actus reus	**Mens rea**
Conduct element	Any conduct causing the result	Voluntary
Circumstance element	V is a person	Knowledge
	D is acting, or purporting to act, in an official capacity	Intention
Result element	V suffers severe pain or suffering	Intention

---

[162] *Dykes v DPP* [2008] EWHC 2775 (Admin).
[163] *Pearson-Gaballonie* [2007] EWCA Crim 3504.

7.9.3.2 Slavery

Replacing a previous offence,[164] slavery is currently criminalised by section 1 of the Modern Slavery Act 2015 (MSA 2015), carrying a maximum sentence of life imprisonment (see **Table 7.11**). The offence is designed in accordance with Article 4 ECHR.

(1) A person commits an offence if—

   (a) the person holds another person in slavery or servitude and the circumstances are such that the person knows or ought to know that the other person is held in slavery or servitude, or

   (b) the person requires another person to perform forced or compulsory labour and the circumstances are such that the person knows or ought to know that the other person is being required to perform forced or compulsory labour.

Table 7.11 Modern Slavery Act 2015, s1

	Actus reus	**Mens rea**
Conduct element	Any conduct causing the result	Voluntary
Circumstance element	V is a person	Knowledge
Result element	V is held in slavery or servitude Or V performs forced or compulsory labour (in line with Art 4 ECHR)	Knew *or* ought to have known Knew *or* ought to have known

Section 2 of the MSA 2015 sets out a complementary offence relating to human trafficking.

Just as importantly, section 45 of the MSA 2015 creates specific defences for the *victims* of slavery and/or trafficking who are compelled to commit an offence. This defence, loosely based on the common law defence of duress (**14.3**), is designed to encourage victims of slavery and/or trafficking to come forward to the police in order to undermine larger criminal organisations.[165]

7.9.3.3 Defences to torture and slavery

There are no *specific* defences for those who commit either of these offences. The general defences should be considered, particularly if D lacks capacity, but they are unlikely to apply. We discuss the general defences in **Chapters 13** and **14**.

7.9.4 Administering poison

Sections 23 and 24 of the OAPA 1861 create two specific poisoning offences. In addition to more specific labelling, these offences are designed to close a potential gap in the

---

[164] Coroners and Justice Act 2009, s71.

[165] Laird, 'Evaluating the Relationship Between Section 45 of the Modern Slavery Act 2015 and the Defence of Duress: An Opportunity Missed?' [2016] Crim LR 395.

law: as poisoning is often non-violent, D's conduct may, for example, lack the assault or battery essential to section 47 of the OAPA.[166]

7.9.4.1 OAPA 1861, s23: administering poison so as to endanger life or cause GBH

Section 23 represents the more serious poisoning offence, punishable with a maximum of ten years' imprisonment (see **Table 7.12**):

> 23. Whosoever shall unlawfully and maliciously administer to or cause to be administered to or taken by any other person any poison or other destructive or noxious thing, so as thereby to endanger the life of such person, or so as thereby to inflict upon such person any grievous bodily harm, shall be guilty of [an offence] and being convicted thereof shall be liable . . . to [imprisonment] for any term not exceeding ten years . . .

Table 7.12 OAPA 1861, s23

	Actus reus	Mens rea
Conduct element	Any conduct causing the result	Voluntary
Circumstance element	V is a person	Knowledge
Result element	V takes or is administered a noxious thing V's life is endangered or V suffers GBH	Reckless None beyond recklessness as to some minor harm

Actus reus of s23

Two areas within the actus reus of section 23 require clarification: the alternative methods of poisoning; and the definition of a noxious thing.

   A) **Method of poisoning:** Section 23 criminalises D where she acts in one of three possible ways.[167] It should be remembered, however, that nothing substantively turns on which method is employed; they all result in liability for section 23.

(a) *D administers the noxious thing to V directly*: this is the most straightforward method, including cases where D injects V with a noxious thing, sprays it into her face, etc.[168]

(b) *D causes an innocent third party to administer the noxious thing to V*: this will cover cases where, for example, D asks X to inject V with the noxious thing (X believing that the syringe contains non-harmful medicine).

(c) *D causes V to take the noxious thing herself*: this final method has caused problems for the courts in terms of causation. The question is under what circumstances D

---

[166] *Hanson* (1849) 2 Car & Kir 912.
[167] For a useful overview, see *Kennedy (No 2)* [2007] UKHL 38.
[168] *Gillard* (1988) 87 Cr App R 189: spraying into V's face.

can be said to have *caused* V to take the noxious thing. The answer requires us to examine whether V's conduct was both voluntary and informed:

(i) if V is *not* aware that the thing she is taking is noxious as, for example, where she believes she is drinking tea, then, despite V's voluntariness, the law will treat D as having *caused* the taking.[169] Thus, (c) will be satisfied;

(ii) if V *is* aware that the thing is noxious, and makes a free and informed decision to take it, this will break the chain of causation from D and point (c) will not be satisfied. This point was finally settled by the House of Lords in *Kennedy (No 2)*.[170] In this case, D was charged with unlawful act manslaughter (based on s23 poisoning), having handed a syringe containing heroin to V who self-injected causing death. D was not liable under section 23, and therefore not liable for manslaughter, because he had not *caused* V to take the heroin.

B) **Noxious thing:** When defining a noxious thing, some distinction should be drawn between substances that are noxious per se, such as arsenic and other materials that will commonly lead to death, and those that are potentially noxious when administered in certain circumstances, such as when taken in large quantities.

(a) Where a substance is noxious per se, this requirement will be satisfied irrespective of whether D has administered a sufficient quantity to risk harm to V (eg not enough arsenic in the tea), and irrespective of whether V may have some resistance that makes the substance less harmful (eg having built up a resistance from regular use).[171]

(b) *Potentially* noxious substances have been interpreted widely. The court in *Marcus*,[172] for example, stated that '"noxious" mean[s] something different in quality from and of less importance than poison or other destructive things', going on to quote the *Shorter Oxford Dictionary* definition that includes the terms 'injurious, hurtful, harmful, unwholesome'. The court also made it clear that, although a substance may be harmless in small quantities, it will be held as noxious if it is administered in sufficient quantities to endanger life or cause GBH, or to injure, aggrieve, or annoy in the context of section 24.

With this expansive definition in mind, where the substance administered has caused V's life to be endangered or GBH (or injury, grievance, or annoyance in the context of s24), it is difficult to see how the court could not also conclude that it was noxious.

Mens rea of s23

Mens rea for the result element consists of two requirements, both arising from the term 'maliciously'. First, D must intend or be reckless as to the method used. D must foresee a risk that her actions will cause the administration/taking of the noxious thing. Secondly, as before, maliciously has been interpreted to require D to foresee some risk

---

[169] *Harley* (1830) 4 C & P 369; *Dale* (1852) 6 Cox CC 14.
[170] [2007] UKHL 38. See **2.7.2.3**.
[171] *Kennedy (No 2)* [2007] UKHL 38: heroin was considered noxious despite the tolerance built up through addiction.
[172] [1981] 1 WLR 774.

of bodily harm.[173] However, no fault is required as to V's suffering of life endangerment or GBH.[174]

The mens rea here contrasts with the section 24 offence, where D must act with 'intent to' bring about the harms suffered by V. This is extraordinary: a less culpable state of mind being required for the more serious offence (s23) than the less serious (s24).

7.9.4.2 OAPA 1861, s24: administering poison intending to injure, aggrieve, or annoy

Section 24 represents the less serious poisoning offence, punishable with a maximum of five years' imprisonment (see **Table 7.13**).

> 24. Whosoever shall unlawfully and maliciously administer to or cause to be administered to or taken by any other person any poison or other destructive or noxious thing, with intent to injure, aggrieve, or annoy such person, shall be guilty of a misdemeanor, and being . . . convicted thereof shall be liable to be kept in penal servitude . . .

Table 7.13 OAPA 1861, s24

	Actus reus	**Mens rea**
Conduct element	Any conduct causing the result	Voluntary
Circumstance element	V is a person	Knowledge
Result element	V takes or is administered a noxious thing	Reckless
Ulterior mens rea element	*	Intention to injure, aggrieve, or annoy

Actus reus of s24
D must expose V to a noxious thing. This has already been discussed in relation to section 23. However, unlike section 23, there is no requirement that this exposure should lead to life endangerment or GBH, or indeed to any harm at all.[175]

Mens rea of s24
Alongside mens rea elements already discussed in relation to section 23, section 24 also requires ulterior intention to 'injure, aggrieve, or annoy'. It will be remembered that *ulterior* intention is mens rea that does not correspond to an element in the actus reus—thus D must intend it, but whether it is caused in fact is irrelevant to her liability. In this

---

[173] *Cunningham* [1957] 2 QB 396: D damaged a gas meter, causing gas to seep into the neighbouring houses and endangering life.
[174] *Cato* [1976] 1 WLR 110.
[175] Ashworth, 'Defining Criminal Offences without Harm' in Smith (ed), *Criminal Law Essays in Honour of JC Smith* (1987) 13.

manner, D's *motives* become central. For example, if a paedophile administers drugs to a child in order to facilitate sexual offences, then she has intent to injure and satisfies the ulterior mens rea. However, if a parent administers a drug to their child in order to keep them awake to see fireworks or to stay up for the other parent to return from work then, although we may question D's conduct, the ulterior mens rea will not be satisfied.[176]

7.9.4.3 Defences to s23 and s24

As with several of the offences against the person, there will be a specific defence where V provided valid consent, or D believed that V provided valid consent. As the issue of consent here relates to substances that have the potential to cause bodily harm, the precedent from *Brown* must be applied. Thus, to be legally valid, V's consent must be *both* effective[177] and come within one of the recognised exception categories.[178] It is difficult to envisage how many of the recognised categories could apply in the context of poisoning.[179] However, it is certainly possible in relation to medicine, so there will be no poisoning offence where a doctor consensually administers an anaesthetic for surgery, even where V reacts to the anaesthetic and suffers serious harm. The general defences should also be considered. We discuss these in **Chapters 13** and **14**.

7.10 Reform

With much of the law in this area still governed by the OAPA of *1861*, it is perhaps unsurprising that there have been several calls for reform going beyond piecemeal amendments.[180] The Law Commission, for example, has described the law as 'defective on grounds both of effectiveness and of justice'.[181]

The following discussion aims to provide a brief overview of some of the most pressing areas of potential reform. These include:

- the case for modernisation and re-codification;
- the controversial status of constructive liability; and
- the meaning and role of consent.

Assessment matters . . .
Try to think about these topics as they could relate to essay-type questions. Think about which positions/ideas you agree with and, more importantly, why you think they are the more convincing. It is this second part in particular that your examiners want you to discuss.

---

[176] Examples from *Hill* (1986) 83 Cr App R 386. For a borderline case see *Weatherall* [1968] Crim LR 115: D put a sleeping tablet in V's drink to enable him to search her handbag for proof of adultery. Held: there was insufficient evidence of intent to injure, aggrieve, or annoy.

[177] See **7.3.2.2**.

[178] See **7.8.2**.

[179] It has even been suggested that poisoning can *never* come within one of these exceptions (*Cato* [1976] 1 WLR 110).

[180] Genders, 'Reform of the Offences Against the Person Act: Lessons from the Law in Action' [1999] Crim LR 689.

[181] Law Commission, *Legislating the Criminal Code: Offences against the Person and General Principles* (Consultation 122, 1992).

7.10.1 Modernisation and re-codification

With regard to modernisation and re-codification, it is useful to separate our discussion of the first category of non-fatal offences (result-focused) and the second category (conduct-focused).

7.10.1.1 Result-focused offences (ladder of harms)

Several attempts at re-codification and rationalisation have been made in this area, including within both the 1985 and 1989 Draft Criminal Codes.[182] The most recent attempt has come from the Law Commission, in its 2015 report *Reform of Offences against the Person*.[183]

Building from the structured hierarchy (ladder) of offences outlined by the Home Office in 1998,[184] the Commission's recommendations can be summarised as follows.

(1) **Intentionally causing serious injury:** A person is guilty of an offence if she intentionally causes serious injury to another, punishable with up to life imprisonment.

(2) **Recklessly causing serious injury:** A person is guilty of an offence if she recklessly causes serious injury to another, punishable with up to seven years' imprisonment.

(3) **Intentionally or recklessly causing injury:** A person is guilty of an offence if she intentionally or recklessly causes injury to another, punishable with up to five years' imprisonment.

(4) **Aggravated assault:** A person is guilty of an offence if—

    (a) she intentionally or recklessly applies force to or causes an impact on the body of another, or

    (b) she intentionally or recklessly causes the other to believe that any such force or impact is imminent,

and injury is caused. Punishable with up to 12 months' imprisonment, triable only in the magistrates' court.

(5) **Physical assault:** A person is guilty of an offence if she intentionally or recklessly applies force to or causes an impact on the body of another, punishable with up to six months' imprisonment, triable only in the magistrates' court.

(6) **Threatened assault:** A person is guilty of an offence if she intentionally or recklessly causes the other to believe that any such force or impact is imminent, punishable with up to six months' imprisonment, triable only in the magistrates' court.

---

[182] Law Commission, *Codification of the Criminal Law: A Report to the Law Commission* (No 143, 1985); Law Commission, *A Criminal Code for England and Wales* (2 vols) (No 177, 1989). See also Law Commission, *Legislating the Criminal Code: Offences against the Person and General Principles* (Consultation 122, 1992); Law Commission, *Offences against the Person and General Principles* (No 218, 1993).

[183] No 361, 2015. See Padfield, 'Reform of Offences Against the Person' [2015] Crim LR 175; Gibson, 'Getting Their "Act" Together? Implementing Statutory Reform of Offences Against the Person' [2016] Crim LR 597; Demetriou, 'Not Giving Up the Fight: A Review of the Law Commission's Scoping Report on Non-Fatal Offences Against the Person' (2016) 80 J Crim L 188.

[184] *Consultation Paper on Violence* (1998). Smith, 'Offences Against the Person: The Home Office Consultation Paper' [1998] Crim LR 317.

Although the Law Commission recommendations are based upon the Home Office scheme from 1998, two important differences should be highlighted. First, 'aggravated assault', triable in the magistrates' court only, is a newly conceived offence: looking to bridge the gap between the reckless causing of injury (3) and the equivalents of assault and battery (5 and 6), and aiming more accurately to label D's conduct and to move many cases involving low-level violence out of the Crown Courts.[185] Secondly, whereas the 1998 draft Bill would have merged assault and battery into a single offence, the Commission prefers the clarity of two separate offences (5 and 6).[186]

Several benefits within the proposed scheme can help to remind us of problems in the current law, as well as the relatively easy manner in which many could be resolved.

A) Clear/modern language: Unlike the current law where the courts are required to interpret and translate terms such as 'maliciously', 'inflict', and 'grievous', the language proposed in this scheme is simple and comprehensible. This provides clarity not only for the court but also for the public whose behaviour is intended to be guided by the law.[187] The Commission's recommendations also explicitly cater for the inclusion of mental as well as physical injury.[188]

B) Clear hierarchy/ladder in punishments: It is a common criticism of the OAPA that offences under sections 47 and 20 have the same maximum sentence despite section 20 involving a more serious actus reus (GBH as opposed to ABH) and a more serious mens rea (recklessness as to some harm as opposed to simple assault or battery). The recommended scheme, from the most serious offence (1) to the least serious offences (5 and 6), creates a clear sentence divide between each step on the ladder. The new aggravated assault offence (4), discussed earlier, is also intended to fill a gap within this hierarchy.

C) Clear hierarchy/ladder in harms: The current law attempts to create a ladder of harms, with different offences applicable depending on the level of harm caused. However, as we highlighted, this breaks down to some extent in relation to wounding: even the prick of a small needle may count as a wound and therefore classify D's conduct alongside GBH. This was more understandable in 1861, where any wound may have risked infection and death, but it is clearly out of step with the medical realities of the modern world. The proposed scheme deals with this by talking only of 'serious injury', 'injury', and application or anticipation of 'force'.

D) Use of constructive liability: The proposed scheme, unlike the current law, employs very few constructive liability offences: offences where parts of D's actus reus do not require any corresponding mens rea. One of the few constructive liability offences within the scheme is the new offence of aggravated assault. The controversial status of constructive liability is discussed in more detail later.

E) Problems with section 47: As we have discussed, there is a problem with the current law, that in order to commit an offence under section 47, D must be shown to have committed an assault or battery. This seems strange: if D *has caused* bodily harm,

---

[185] Law Commission, *Reform of Offences against the Person* (No 361, 2015) paras 5.30–5.68.
[186] Ibid, paras 5.3–5.29.
[187] It has been argued that reform should go even further in this regard, specifying types of harm, such as disables, disfigures, or dismembers in order to provide a clearer message and label. Horder, 'Rethinking Non-Fatal Offences Against the Person' (1994) 14 OJLS 335.
[188] Law Commission, *Reform of Offences against the Person* (No 361, 2015) paras 4.117–4.126.

why condition liability on demonstrating physical contact or a fear of such contact? The equivalent offence within the Commission's scheme (3) does not contain such a requirement.

7.10.1.2 Conduct-focused offences

In relation to conduct-focused offences against the person, debate has centred on areas where new specific offences against the person could/should be created.

One prominent example relates to the potential for a specific offence of 'domestic violence'. The idea is that a new offence could better label the distinctive wrongs involved in domestic abuse (its systematic nature, the destruction of trust, etc),[189] as well as provide a clearer social message highlighting the issue, as well as informing the public and police attitudes. However, finding a balance between the inclusion of the various species of domestic abuse on the one hand, whilst keeping the offence sufficiently focused on the distinctive wrong on the other, would be very difficult. After some useful discussion in its 2015 report, the Law Commission decided not to recommend new offences of domestic violence.[190] It is also likely that many of the perceived problems with the current law here can be addressed through the offence of coercive control, set out in section 76 of the Serious Crime Act 2015.[191]

Another possibility, and one that has attracted considerable debate, is the potential for a specific offence targeting the reckless sexual transmission of HIV.[192] This is partly driven by perceived problems within the current law, and partly by a seeming reluctance on the part of prosecutors to charge standard non-fatal offences in such cases.[193] However, as debate in this area focuses more on HIV alone, as opposed to simply all transmission of infections, then we must question the basis upon which the focus is justified, as well as the potential stigmatising effects that an offence of this kind may produce. The Commission discusses the potential for a new offence in this area at length in its 2015 report, concluding that the case for a specific offence has not yet been made.[194]

Assessment matters . . .
When writing about the potential for a new offence, it is a useful exercise to try and draft the actus reus and mens rea to consider what it might look like. In doing so, think about what form of behaviour you are trying to criminalise and why.

---

[189] Tadros, 'The Distinctiveness of Domestic Abuse: A Freedom Based Account' in Duff and Green (eds), *Defining Crimes* (2005) 119.

[190] Law Commission, *Reform of Offences against the Person* (No 361, 2015) paras 5.111–5.118.

[191] Bettinson, 'Criminalising Coercive Control in Domestic Violence Cases' [2016] Crim LR 165.

[192] Ormerod, 'Criminalizing HIV Transmission—Still No Effective Solutions' (2001) 30 CLWR 135; Bennett, 'Should We Criminalise HIV Transmission' in Erin and Ost (eds), *The Criminal Justice System and Health Care* (2007) 225; Weait, *Intimacy and Responsibility: The Criminalisation of HIV Transmission* (2007); Matthiesson, 'Should the Law Deal with Reckless HIV Infection as a Criminal Offence or as a Matter of Public Health?' (2010) 21 KLJ 123 (responding to *Weait*); Cherkassky, 'Being Informed: The Complexities of Knowledge, Deception and Consent when Transmitting HIV' (2010) 74 J Crim L 242.

[193] *Dica* [2004] EWCA Crim 1103; Weait, 'Criminal Law and the Transmission of HIV: *R v Dica*' (2005) 68 MLR 121; Spencer, 'Retrial for Reckless Infection' (2004) 154 NLJ 762.

[194] Law Commission, *Reform of Offences against the Person* (No 361, 2015) Part 6.

7.10.2 Constructive liability

Constructive liability describes an offence where D must cause a particular result, but there is no requirement for corresponding mens rea. For example, section 47 requires D's acts to cause an assault or battery, and to cause V bodily harm (all actus reus). However, in terms of mens rea, D need only have fault in relation to the assault or battery. It may be that D did not intend the bodily harm element, she may not have foreseen it as a possibility, and it may not even have been foreseeable to a reasonable person—but her mens rea as to this element is irrelevant. Rather, the simple fact that she caused ABH is *constructed* upon her liability for assault or battery and makes her liable for the more serious section 47 offence. We see a similar construction in a number of the offences against the person (discussed earlier), in unlawful act manslaughter (**6.3.1**), as well as in murder (**5.4** and **5.6.2**). An extreme version of constructive liability can be seen with strict liability offences: D does not require mens rea as to any elements of the actus reus beyond the voluntariness of her acts/omissions.[195]

Constructive liability is controversial for a number of reasons, principally relating to D's lack of choice. As we discussed in **Chapter 1**, justifications for criminal law are often tied to the notion of autonomy: people should be free to act as they wish as long as they do not choose to break the law. The problem with constructive liability is that it ignores the issue of choice. Thus, for example, if D assaults V and causes bodily harm, she will be liable under section 47 whether or not she chose to cause or risk that bodily harm. Not only does this conflict with the criminal law's general disposition towards subjectivism (requiring choice), but it also increases the role of luck. For example, D1 and D2 both intentionally push V1 and V2, each foreseeing no more harm than involved in simple contact. In the case of V1 this is all that results: D1 is liable for a minor battery offence. However, V2 falls and sustains an injury: D2 is now liable for a section 47 offence. Or worse, V2 dies: D2 is now liable for unlawful act manslaughter. The liability of D1 and D2 is very different, and yet their intentions and *choices* (ie their culpability) were the same. *Is this just?*[196]

For some, of course, the answer is 'yes'. Although D2 may not have chosen to cause bodily injury or to kill, as in the example above, that is what her actions have caused. Although we may not wish to criminalise accidents, by choosing to commit the battery on V (the push), D has chosen to break the criminal law and there is a persuasive argument that D has therefore changed her normative position: she has chosen to break the law and so must accept *all* of the consequences of her actions, even unforeseen/unforeseeable ones.[197]

Whether or not we accept this argument in support of constructive liability offences will play a central role in future re-codification of the offences against the person. Currently it seems that the dominant view is that constructive liability should be avoided: this is illustrated in the reform recommendations from the Law Commission, and can also be illustrated in other jurisdictions such as the Irish Non-Fatal Offences Against the Person Act 1997.[198] However, the debate remains open.

---

[195] Simester, *Appraising Strict Liability* (2005).

[196] Ashworth, 'The Problem of Luck' in Shute, Gardner, and Horder (eds), *Action and Value in Criminal Law* (1993) 107.

[197] Simons, 'Strict Liability in the Grading of Offences: Forfeiture, Change of Normative Position, or Moral Luck?' (2012) 32 OJLS 445; Ashworth, 'A Change of Normative Position: Determining the Contours of Culpability in Criminal Law' [2008] New Crim LR 232.

[198] This Irish statute replaces and/or codifies common law assault, as well as most of the OAPA offences formally applying in the Republic of Ireland. See Charleton, McDermott, and Bolger, *Criminal Law* (1999) paras 9.77–9.185.

7.10.3 Consent

V's consent, or D's belief in consent, will undermine liability for most of the non-fatal offences. However, it is also an area that has caused the court significant problems. By way of summary, the central problems identified include the following.

A) **Consent as a defence, or non-consent as an offence element:** In our earlier discussion, we have treated V's consent as a *defence*. However, the OAPA leaves open the possibility that non-consent could be analysed as an offence element, and this alternative has been preferred by several courts and commentators.[199] Indeed, in the leading case of *Brown*, only a bare majority of the Lords preferred to analyse consent as a defence.[200]

It would be highly desirable for this point to be clarified. It is contended that analysis of non-consent as an *offence* element represents the better view, particularly in relation to the minor offences of assault and battery.[201] The cumulative role of offence elements is to set out a specific harmful and/or wrongful event that the criminal law wishes to prevent and punish. D may be able to rely on a defence to excuse or justify her conduct, or to excuse her from liability, but the criminal event is still regrettable. In relation to V's non-consent, we believe that this requirement is an essential part to the *wrong* within the offences against the person. If V provides valid consent (eg in the context of contact sports), D is not committing a wrong that relies on a defence to justify or excuse it. Equally, when we come into consensual contact with others in our daily life, we are not committing wrongs that require justification. Rather, we believe that such conduct is only wrongful in the absence of consent and, thus, V's non-consent must form part of the offence elements rather than a defence.[202]

The two options for interpretation . . .

• *Offence*: requires (a) non-consent in fact and (b) a lack of belief in consent.

• *Defence*: satisfied by (a) consent in fact or (b) belief in consent.

On either interpretation, D's liability will always require that V does not consent and that D does not believe that consent is present.

B) **Effective consent:** Considerable work has been done to understand and define consent in relation to sexual offences.[203] However, in the context of the offences in this chapter, the meaning of consent remains elusive, ill-defined, and too often susceptible to overly broad rules. The Law Commission does not deal with the meaning of consent within its 2015 report, but there is scope for the Commission to examine this again in the future.

C) **Degree of harm that can be legally consented to:** This problem arises where V is of full capacity, is informed, and has not been misled as to the anticipated harm: at what stage (if at all) should the law nevertheless say that V's consent is invalid?[204] This discussion raises difficult moral questions, and taken to its natural conclusion, will also lead to consideration of euthanasia. Whatever moral view is preferred, the approach of the

---

[199] eg Lord Woolf stated in relation to assault that 'it is a requirement of the offence that the conduct itself should be unlawful': *Barnes* [2005] EWCA Crim 3246, [16].

[200] Although Lord Jauncey, Lord Lowry, and Lord Templeman analysed consent as a defence, Lord Mustill and Lord Slynn considered non-consent as part of the offence. See Shute, 'Something Old, Something New, Something Borrowed: Three Aspects of the Project' [1996] Crim LR 684.

[201] This approach is reflected in the latest Law Commission Recommendations. Law Commission, *Reform of Offences against the Person* (No 361, 2015) paras 5.3–5.29.

[202] Williams, 'Consent and Public Policy' [1962] Crim LR 74.

[203] **Chapter 8**.

[204] Feinberg, *The Moral Limits of the Criminal Law, Vol 1: Harm to Others* (1984).

current law is clearly unacceptable—particularly when we begin to explore the recognised exception categories where valid consent is recognised, such as sports, horseplay, and sexual gratification. Particularly in relation to the latter example, people need to know the law in order to guide and model their behaviour. The fact that the current law (in cases like *Brown*) fails to provide that guidance demonstrates a clear need for reform.

7.11 Eye on assessment

In this section we discuss the potential application of the offences against the person within a problem question. The same structure of analysis should be employed, as we have discussed in previous chapters.

> ### STEP 1 Identify the potential criminal event in the facts
>
> This is unlikely to take more than a sentence, but it is essential to tell your reader which facts of the case you are focusing on. For offences against the person, this involves pointing out where a person has been hurt (eg 'The first potential criminal event arises where Mary kicks Vicky').

> ### STEP 2 Identify the potential offence
>
> Having identified the facts (eg D potentially injuring V), you must now identify the offence you are going to apply.

When applying Step 2, it should be remembered that the main non-fatal offences can be viewed as a ladder, with the least serious offences (assault and battery) at the bottom, and the most serious (s18 GBH) at the top. When *learning* these offences it is helpful to start at the bottom of this ladder and work up, and this approach has been adopted in this chapter. However, when *applying* these offences to a problem scenario, the opposite approach should be taken.

If we apply these offences to a problem in the same order we learnt them (bottom up), then we end up with rather peculiar results:

> *Example ...*
> Take the example of D who breaks V's arm by hitting her with a bat. Here, it is likely that D will have committed assault if V saw her coming, as V is likely to have apprehended non-consensual imminent violence; D will also have committed battery, as she intentionally comes into non-consensual contact with V; D will also have committed a section 47 offence, as D's assault and battery have caused harm; D will also have committed a section 20 offence, as D has caused GBH and intends to cause harm; and D will also have committed a section 18 offence, as GBH is intentionally caused.

In this manner, D satisfies the elements of each of the offences. However, as she does so through a single act (hitting V with a bat), it is inappropriate to find liability for more than one offence. Therefore, much like Russian dolls, more serious offences subsume less serious ones committed by the same action: leaving D in our example liable for a section 18 offence only. The problem with starting our discussion at the bottom of the offence ladder, therefore, is that having discussed the elements of several offences, the only one that is relevant is the last. (*A particularly serious problem if you run out of time and miss it off!*)

With this in mind, when applying the offences against the person to a problem scenario, it is advised that you should begin by exploring the most serious *potential* offence first. The word potential here is important. Just as it is bad practice to discuss less serious offences when a more serious one has been committed, it is also important not to spend a long time discussing more serious offences if V has only suffered minor harm. Our recommended approach is set out in the simple flowchart at **Figure 7.8**.

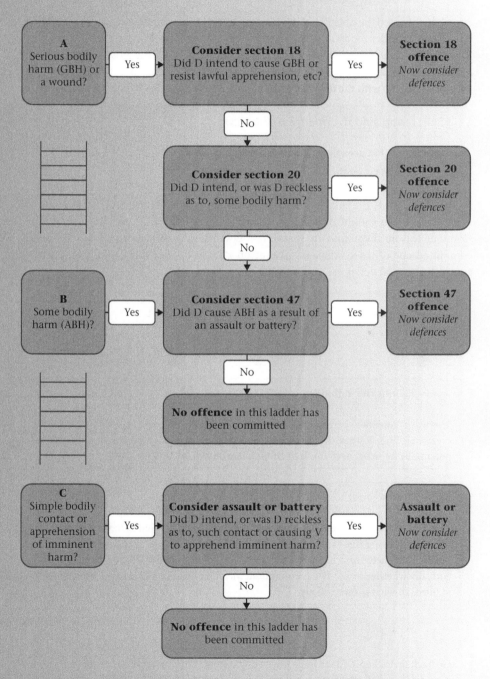

Figure 7.8 Problem question flowchart for offences against the person

Having highlighted the potential criminal event (Step 1), you should assess the level of harm caused to V in order to identify the relevant entry point to the flowchart in **Figure 7.8** (A, B, or C). Having identified the relevant entry point, this tells you the most serious potential offence that D may have committed (Step 2) (eg s18 in relation to GBH, s47 for bodily harm, etc). In line with the flowchart, the next step is to assess D's liability for that offence.

STEP 3 Applying the offence to the facts

Actus reus: What does the offence require? Did D do it?

Mens rea: What does the offence require? Did D possess it?

If D does not satisfy the elements of the most serious potential offence (eg lacks mens rea for s18), then you should go on to consider the next possible offence down the ladder. Continue this until you find an offence that D satisfies, or you conclude that D has not committed one of these offences. Where you find an offence that D satisfies, move to consider potential defences (both specific and general defences).

AR and MR are satisfied	AR and/or MR are not satisfied
Continue to STEP 4.	Return to STEP 2, and look for an alternative offence. If none, then skip to STEP 5, concluding that no offence is committed.

STEP 4 Consider defences

The word 'consider' here is important, as you should not discuss every defence for every question. Rather, think whether there are any defences (eg consent) that *could* potentially be relevant to the facts. If there are any, discuss those only.

STEP 5 Conclude

This is usually a single sentence either saying that it is likely that D has committed the offence, or saying that it is not likely either because an offence element is not satisfied or because a defence is likely to apply. It is not often that you will be able to say categorically whether or not D has committed the offence, so it is usually best to conclude in terms of what is more 'likely'.

STEP 6 Loop

Go back up to Step 1, identifying the next potential criminal event. Continue until you have discussed all the relevant potentially criminal events.

ONLINE RESOURCE CENTRE

www.oxfordtextbooks.co.uk/orc/sho/

This chapter is accompanied by a selection of online resources to help you with this topic, including:

- **Multiple-choice questions**
- **Chapter summary sheet**
- Two **sample examination questions** with answer guidance
- **Further reading**

Also available on the Online Resource Centre are:

- A selection of **videos** from the authors explaining key topics and principles
- **Legal updates**
- Useful **weblinks**

9

Property offences

9.1   Introduction   **328**

9.2   Theft   **328**

    9.2.1 Appropriation   **329**

    9.2.2 Property   **335**

    9.2.3 Belonging to another   **339**

    9.2.4 Intention permanently to deprive   **343**

    9.2.5 Dishonesty   **346**

9.3   Robbery   **350**

    9.3.1 Theft   **351**

    9.3.2 Force or the threat of force   **351**

    9.3.3 Link between theft and force   **353**

9.4   Burglary   **353**

    9.4.1 TA 1968, s9(1)(a): burglary by trespassing with intent   **354**

    9.4.2 TA 1968, s9(1)(b): burglary by offences committed following trespassory entry   **357**

    9.4.3 Aggravated burglary   **359**

9.5   Handling stolen goods   **360**

    9.5.1 Actus reus of s22   **361**

    9.5.2 Mens rea of s22   **364**

9.6   Blackmail   **365**

    9.6.1 Actus reus of s21   **366**

    9.6.2 Mens rea of s21   **368**

9.7   Criminal damage   **370**

    9.7.1 Actus reus of s1(1)   **370**

    9.7.2 Mens rea of s1(1)   **373**

    9.7.3 Defences to criminal damage   **373**

    9.7.4 Arson   **376**

    9.7.5 Aggravated criminal damage   **376**

9.8   Reform   **379**

    9.8.1 Defining theft   **379**

9.9   Eye on assessment   **381**

9.1 Introduction

Having discussed offences against the person, fatal (**Chapters 5** and **6**), non-fatal (**Chapter 7**), and sexual (**Chapter 8**), this chapter and **Chapter 10** move to consider offences against property. Offences within this category are many and varied, criminalising conduct such as the taking of another's property (eg theft, robbery, etc), possessing stolen or criminal property (eg handling stolen goods, money laundering, etc), as well as damaging another's property (eg criminal damage, arson, etc). Beyond such crimes, there are also a number of specific technical offences designed to protect particular property rights, such as those relating to intellectual and/or digital property, vehicle misuse, and so on. Through such offences, the criminal law provides protection for the full range of civil law property rights, supporting the system of rules governing civil ownership in its function.[1]

Within the wide range of property crimes, this chapter will focus on a selection of core offences.

- Theft: D dishonestly appropriates V's property.
- Robbery: D uses force to steal V's property.
- Burglary: D trespasses onto V's property, committing (or intending to commit) one of a number of offences.
- Handling stolen goods: D deals in specified ways with V's property, which has been stolen.
- Blackmail: D threatens V in order to gain her property.
- Criminal damage: D damages V's property.

Each of these offences are defined by statute, and often in considerable detail. In the following sections we discuss each in turn.

In **Chapter 10**, still focusing on property crimes, we analyse the fraud offences. We discuss these separately in light of the major revisions brought by the Fraud Act 2006. The fraud offences are also distinct from most other property offences because they are conduct crimes, focusing on D's inchoate criminal intentions: criminalising D for acting with the intention to interfere with V's property rights, rather than for actually doing so.[2]

9.2 Theft

Theft is defined in section 1(1) of the Theft Act 1968 (TA 1968), with further detail provided over sections 2–6. The maximum penalty on indictment is seven years' imprisonment.[3]

> (1) A person is guilty of theft if he dishonestly appropriates property belonging to another with the intention of permanently depriving the other of it . . .

---

[1] Ormerod and Williams, *Smith's Law of Theft* (9th edn, 2007) and *Smith and Hogan's Criminal Law* (14th edn, 2015), Ch19.
[2] We set out the meaning of inchoate liability at **4.2.1.2**.
[3] Theft Act 1968, s7.

The elements of theft are set out in **Table 9.1**.

Table 9.1 Theft

	Actus reus	Mens rea
Conduct element	Any conduct causing the result	Voluntary
Circumstance element	What is appropriated is property It belongs to another D's appropriation is dishonest	Knowledge Knowledge Knowledge
Result element	D appropriates V's property	Intention
Ulterior mens rea element	*	Intention permanently to deprive V of her property

Theft is more straightforwardly presented as five core offence elements, as in **Table 9.2**. Although consistent with **Table 9.1** (which separates actus reus and mens rea), the focus on five core elements in **Table 9.2** is generally preferred: mirroring the statutory sections of the TA 1968, and reflecting the most common approach of the courts.

Table 9.2 Theft

A) Appropriation (s3)
B) Of property (s4)
C) Belonging to another (s5)
D) With the intention of permanently depriving V of it (s6) and
E) Dishonesty (s2)

We discuss each of these offence elements in turn. Liability requires the prosecution to prove that D satisfied *every* element, and for these elements to have coincided (ie occurred at the same time).

9.2.1 Appropriation

Appropriation is defined in section 3 of the TA 1968. Section 3(1) states that:

Any assumption by a person of the rights of an owner amounts to an appropriation, and this includes, where he has come by the property (innocently or not) without stealing it, any later assumption of a right to it by keeping or dealing with it as owner.

Despite the relative clarity of section 3(1), the meaning of 'appropriation' has generated considerable dispute in the appellate courts, including four cases in the House of Lords. In resolving these disputes, the courts have generally preferred to interpret the term broadly. Three central points of debate have arisen: whether D must appropriate all of the rights of the owner; whether consensual appropriation will satisfy this element; and whether D appropriates where V has given the property as a valid gift in civil law.

9.2.1.1 Assuming the rights of an owner

Section 3(1) is clear that assuming the rights of an owner will amount to an appropriation. The most obvious cases will be where D takes V's property and treats it as her own. However, what if D only assumes certain ownership rights, but not others? For example, what if D sells V's property (assuming rights of legal ownership), but does not physically interfere with it (does not assume rights of possession or control)? Where cases of this kind emerge, it forces us to recognise ownership rights as a bundle of rights and not a singular concept. The case of *Morris* confirms that the assumption of any one property right will be sufficient to find an appropriation.

 Morris [1984] AC 320

D switched labels on supermarket goods in order to purchase the more expensive goods at the (false) lower price. He proceeded to the checkout and paid the lower price. D was then charged with theft.

- Crown Court: guilty of theft.
- Court of Appeal: conviction upheld on appeal.
- House of Lords: appeal dismissed. When swapping the labels, D assumed 'a' right of the owner (the right to price the goods) and this was sufficient (at that point) to amount to an appropriation.

It has been cogently argued that *Morris* represents an incorrect interpretation of the TA 1968 and that appropriation should only be found where D assumes all of the rights of an owner.[4] However, the approach in *Morris* has been confirmed subsequently by the House of Lords in *Gomez*[5] and so, for better or worse, this is the approach that should be applied.

Finding appropriation based on the assumption of a single property right can be complex; where a single taking, over a period of time, can amount to several separate appropriations. For example, D takes an item from V with the intention of borrowing it and returning it later, appropriating at the point she takes/assumes physical possession and control. Later, D decides to keep the item, appropriating further rights of legal ownership.[6]

---

[4] For discussion of this and support for the decision, see Melissaris, 'The Concept of Appropriation and the Offence of Theft' (2007) 70 MLR 581.

[5] [1993] AC 442.

[6] Indeed, this second appropriation (where D decides to keep the property) is explicitly catered for in the latter part of s3(1): 'this includes, where he has come by the property (innocently or not) without stealing it, any later assumption of a right to it by keeping or dealing with it as owner'.

> **Assessment matters . . .**
> The potential for multiple acts of appropriation makes it crucial to identify which act of appropriation is most likely to lead to liability for theft (ie which act also coincides with the other elements of the offence). We discuss this further in 'Eye on assessment' at **9.9**.

Following *Morris*, it is clear that D can appropriate certain property rights by omission, or through the mental 'act' of deciding to treat V's property as her own.

Where D discovers that she has taken possession of V's property accidentally, D will *not* be assumed to have appropriated that property if she has not treated it as her own or made a decision to keep it.[7] For example, where property is picked up by D's child, and only discovered when the child takes it home. However, if D does decide to keep the property, this and any other assumption of rights will be sufficient to constitute the appropriation element of the actus reus.

A final point should be clarified regarding 'continuing acts' of appropriation.[8] In most cases of theft, the act of appropriation is best analysed as a single and instantaneous event: for example, D steals V's bag when she grabs it from V and runs away; she does not continue to steal it when using it several days or weeks later. However, if we follow the logic of *Morris*, we could say that appropriation starts and finishes the moment that D touches the bag, concluding before D even begins to run away. This issue can be important where there is uncertainty as to territorial jurisdiction: for example, where D takes V's car whilst abroad and imports it to England, can we say that theft occurred in England? It will also be important in the context of other offences such as robbery, where violence must be shown to accompany the act of theft. The shorter the duration of the theft, the less likely that robbery can be found.[9] In such cases, courts have sensibly interpreted appropriation as existing beyond an instant, to include the time where D is still 'on the job', probably including D's running away but not her use of the property on following occasions.[10]

9.2.1.2 Appropriation with consent

Paradigm cases of theft will involve a non-consensual appropriation; D taking V's property without her knowledge or against her wishes. In line with this, a requirement of 'adverse' appropriation has often been assumed by the courts, such as in *Morris*.[11] However, the wording of the TA 1968 does not expressly limit the offence to these cases, stating generally that 'any assumption' of rights will constitute an appropriation. In light of this drafting, other cases such as *Lawrence* have held that the consent or non-consent of V is irrelevant.[12] The question, and the inconsistent approach of previous cases, was eventually addressed by the House of Lords in *Gomez*.

---

[7] *Broom v Crowther* (1984) 148 JP 592.
[8] For a general discussion of continuing acts, see **4.3.2.1**. See also, Williams, 'Appropriation: A Single or Continuous Act?' [1978] Crim LR 69.
[9] See **9.3**.
[10] *Atakpu* [1994] QB 69: no appropriation in England where cars were stolen in Frankfurt or Brussels and brought to England days later.
[11] [1984] AC 320. Lord Roskill (*obiter*) 'appropriation involves not an act expressly or impliedly authorised by the owner but an act by way of adverse interference with or usurpation of those rights'.
[12] *Lawrence* [1972] AC 626: D, a taxi driver, took extra money from V for a fare. V did not speak much English and 'allowed' the extra money to be taken from his wallet. The House of Lords held that there was an appropriation: it did not matter that V consented to the taking.

Gomez [1993] AC 442

D was the assistant manager of an electrical goods shop. He convinced his manager to allow a customer to buy items using cheques that D knew were stolen and therefore worthless. The manager consented to the 'sale'. D was charged with theft.

- Crown Court: guilty of theft.
- Court of Appeal: appeal allowed. Following *Morris*, the consent of V undermines the element of appropriation.
- House of Lords: appeal allowed, reaffirming D's liability and following *Lawrence*. With Lord Lowry dissenting, the Lords confirmed that, where D tricks V, appropriation will be found whenever there is an assumption of ownership rights by D, regardless of V's consent.

The decision in *Gomez* sparked considerable academic debate,[13] not least because the irrelevance of V's consent created a substantial overlap with offences of obtaining by deception which were then in force[14] (the overlap is now with fraud offences in force today).[15] Indeed, the prosecution of *Gomez* for an offence of obtaining property by deception (what would today be fraud by false representation) would have been straightforward.[16] However, for reasons unknown, the prosecutors chose to charge theft and so the question of consent in relation to theft had to be resolved. *Gomez* (again, for better or worse) confirms that as long as D assumes a right of ownership over V's property, there will be an appropriation and V's consent or non-consent is irrelevant.

9.2.1.3 Appropriation with full civil title

Gomez confirmed that D could, by deception, appropriate V's property regardless of V's consent. However, as D's appropriation was still achieved through deception when D lied about the cheques, the question remained open as to whether D's assumption of rights would still be an appropriation where V consents and there is no deception. The court in *Gomez* indicated that appropriation would be found even in the absence of deception, both through the examples they employed,[17] as well as other cases they overruled, but this did not form part of the ratio of the case.

The decision that appropriation could be found despite a lack of deception was confirmed in the case of *Hinks*. *Hinks* provides that, where D assumes ownership rights from V, this may be an appropriation even where the property is consensually transferred from V with full title (where the transfer is valid and not voidable in civil law[18]). Thus, D may be liable for theft of property in criminal law, but be entitled to keep that same property in civil law.

---

[13] Heaton, 'Deceiving Without Thieving' [2001] Crim LR 712; Davies, 'Consent After the House of Lords: Taking and Leading Astray the Law of Theft' (1993) 13 LS 308; Cooper and Allen, 'Appropriation after *Gomez*' (1993) 57 J Crim L 186.

[14] TA 1968, s15. Repealed by the Fraud Act 2006.

[15] Fraud Act 2006. See **Chapter 10**.

[16] We discuss the overlap between theft and fraud offences further at **10.8.3**.

[17] eg of a person switching labels in a supermarket, where the court said there would be appropriation at the moment D touches the labels. At that point there is no full deception offence.

[18] Transfers become voidable if there is a 'vitiating factor'. These include duress, misrepresentation, undue influence, and so on.

Hinks [2000] 4 All ER 833

D befriended V who was a man described by the court as naive, trusting, and of limited intelligence. Over a six-month period she took V to his building society almost every day and was given £300 (the maximum withdrawal), eventually totalling over £60,000. At the point of arrest, D had taken almost all of V's money as well as his television. D was charged with theft.

- Crown Court: guilty of theft.
- Court of Appeal: conviction upheld on appeal.
- House of Lords: appeal dismissed, with Lord Hutton and Lord Hobhouse dissenting. Although the transfer of the money may not have amounted to a civil wrong, this does not preclude it being an appropriation and a theft.

Extra detail . . .

It may have been arguable that the facts of *Hinks* involved a voidable contract. In other words, it could have been argued that V was mentally incapable of making a valid gift or that there must have been some undue influence from D. If the gift was voidable then D's conviction for theft (following *Gomez*) would have been uncontroversial. However, importantly, the accepted facts at the House of Lords were such that the gift was valid in civil law.

In order to appreciate the full implications of *Hinks*, it is useful to highlight the two main arguments raised and rejected by the appeal courts.

A) **Distinguishing *Hinks* and *Gomez*:** The first line of argument was that *Hinks* should be distinguished from *Gomez* because *Hinks* involved a full and valid transfer of property in civil law. Indeed, even following *Gomez*, in *Mazo*,[19] it was accepted by the Court of Appeal to be 'common ground that the receiver of a valid gift *inter vivos* could not be the subject of a conviction for theft'.[20] This argument was supported by the apparent absurdity of D being potentially liable for theft and yet, as a matter of civil law, remaining the owner of the property stolen.[21] However, this argument was rejected in *Hinks*, and *Mazo* was overruled. The court found the law clearly stated in *Gomez*. On the issue of inconsistency between civil and criminal law, Lord Steyn, with the majority, stated that:

The purposes of the civil law and the criminal law are somewhat different. In theory the two systems should be in perfect harmony. In a practical world there will sometimes be some disharmony between the two systems. In any event, it would be wrong to assume on priori grounds that the criminal law rather than the civil law is defective.

The House of Lords therefore recognised the inconsistency, but rejected it as a reason for finding no appropriation. This is particularly interesting if we consider the rationale of property offences to be for the protection of the civil system of ownership rights. Following the decision in *Hinks*, theft is not being used to protect ownership rights;

---

[19] [1996] Crim LR 435.
[20] In *Mazo*, this led to the acquittal of D on similar facts to *Hinks*.
[21] Beatson and Simester, 'Stealing One's Own Property' (1999) 115 LQR 372.

quite the opposite, it is punishing D for gaining valid ownership.[22] Theft is now targeting dishonesty or exploitation more generally. Whether this is the correct role for the offence of theft remains an open debate.[23]

B) **Challenging *Gomez*:** The second line of argument in *Hinks* was that the definition of appropriation had become too easy to satisfy following *Gomez*, rendering that element of negligible significance within the offence. The idea here is that the mischief of theft is not targeted by the consensual touching of another's property, and so other offence elements are having to do the work of narrowing liability that used to be done (at least in greater part) by appropriation.[24] The main 'other' element to bear the brunt of this narrowing has been 'dishonesty' (discussed later) and, the argument goes, the current definition of dishonesty is not suitable on its own for this task. However, the court reasoned that any fundamental change of this kind (reconsidering *Gomez*) could lead to the offence becoming unacceptably narrow. It is clear that the court wanted to find liability in cases such as *Hinks* and so, taking some comfort from one alternative academic opinion,[25] they dismissed this line of argument as well.

> **Point to remember . . .**
> *Gomez* and *Hinks* led to considerable debate about the appropriate role and construction of theft, and some of these points will be discussed further in the 'reform' section at **9.8**. However, by avoiding technical distinctions based on the civil law, the requirement of appropriation is usually straightforward to apply: we ask simply, did D assume any right of ownership over V's property? For example, if D goes to a supermarket to steal an item, she will have appropriated (and committed theft) at the first moment she comes into contact with the item. The fact that D is permitted by the shop to touch the item at this point (ie has the shop's consent) is irrelevant.

9.2.1.4 The bona fide purchaser exception

Section 3(2) of the TA 1968 creates an exception where no appropriation will be found. This arises where D purchases property in good faith (bona fide), believing that she is gaining full civil title, it then transpires that full title has not been transferred (eg because the goods were stolen), but D continues to treat the item as her own. In such a case, D appears to have assumed the rights of the owner and thus come within the definition of appropriation, however, this section prevents that from being the result in law.

It should be remembered that this exception only applies to property acquired by D for value, so it does not apply to gifts. Further, even though D is excused from theft by section 3(2), she remains potentially liable for handling stolen property[26] and/or fraud if she presents herself as the owner, for example to sell the property to another.[27]

---

[22] For an alternative view, that *Hinks* provides indirect protection for property rights, see Shute, 'Appropriation and the Law of Theft' [2002] Crim LR 445.
[23] Bogg and Stanton-Ife, 'Protecting the Vulnerable: Legality, Harm and Theft' (2003) 23 LS 402. We discuss this in the reform section at **9.8**.
[24] Smith, 'Theft or Sharp Practice: Who Cares Now?' (2001) 60 CLJ 21.
[25] Gardner, 'Appropriation in Theft: The Last Word' (1993) 109 LQR 194.
[26] See **9.5**.
[27] *Wheeler* (1990) 92 Cr App R 279.

9.2.2 Property

For theft to be committed, what D appropriated must be legally recognised as 'property'. Unlike the definition of appropriation, the definition of property is generally not controversial. However, care must be taken to understand exactly what is included. Section 4 of the TA 1968 provides a general definition of property (founded on civil law concepts), and then lists specific exclusions relating to land, things growing wild, and wild creatures.

> (1) 'Property' includes money and all other property, real or personal, including things in action and other intangible property.

Before moving to consider the specific exceptions to this definition, its key terms require some unpacking.

A) **Real property** is a reference to land. Thus, subject to the specific exclusions discussed later, D can be liable for the theft of certain land rights.

B) **Personal property** is a reference to all property that is not land and that includes property that is illegal or prohibited. For example, D commits theft where she appropriates drugs from V, even where they are illegally possessed by V.[28]

C) **Things in action** is a reference to a category of intangible property where D has the right to sue another for a particular sum. This is most commonly associated with bank accounts. Although we commonly refer to having 'money in the bank', this is, of course, not accurate: there is no specific pile of money in a bank belonging to us.[29] Rather, depositing money to a bank creates a form of intangible property, our right to sue the bank for that specific sum. This property right is a 'thing in action'. Therefore, where D dishonestly causes the bank to transfer funds from V's account, D does not steal any physical money belonging to V, she steals a thing in action (ie she steals part of V's right to sue the bank for a sum of money).[30] The same is true where D has transferred money from V's overdraft.[31] The only exception in such cases is where D has transferred funds from V's account that V had no right to sue for (ie where V had no thing in action). This can arise where D has transferred funds in excess of V's overdraft, or where D takes from her own account in excess of her overdraft.[32]

D) **Other intangible property** allows the definition of intangible property to extend beyond the most common things in action. An example can be seen in *AG of Hong Kong v Chan Nai-Keung*,[33] in which D, a director of company A and company B, sold export quotas from one company to the other at a gross undervalue. Although the export quotas did not represent a thing in action, they were held to constitute other intangible property and were therefore subject to theft.

---

[28] *Smith* [2011] EWCA Crim 66.
[29] Discussed in *Davenport* [1954] 1 All ER 602.
[30] *Chan Man-sin v AG for Hong Kong* [1988] 1 All ER 1.
[31] *Kohn* [1997] 2 Cr App R 445.
[32] *Hilton* (1979) 69 Cr App R 395; Griew, 'Stealing and Obtaining Bank Credits' [1986] Crim LR 356.
[33] [1987] 1 WLR 1339, exploring identical provisions in the law of Hong Kong.

An interesting problem of categorisation has emerged in relation to the stealing of cheques.[34] A cheque which is given by V for consideration creates a thing in action as it creates the right to sue V's bank for the specified sum. So if V is tricked, for example, into writing a cheque in D's favour, that creates a right for D to sue V's bank. However, D has not taken V's right to sue, unlike electronic bank transfers discussed earlier. Instead, the thing in action which D has gained is not property which has ever belonged to V and cannot be the subject of theft.[35] What D gains is her own brand new right to sue V's bank. We could wait for a theft to arise when D presents the cheque and thereby causes a bank transfer so that V's bank account—a thing in action—is diminished. The problem is that D does not commit theft until she presents the cheque and causes the transfer, not allowing earlier intervention. Alternatively, we could focus on the cheque as a piece of paper (tangible property) and say that D stole that from the outset. However, as D does not intend to keep the paper, in fact she intends to present it to the bank, she does not satisfy a different offence element (intention to permanently deprive) in relation to the paper: so this cannot ground our case for theft either.[36] Our final option to find liability in theft[37] is to say the cheque is a 'valuable security', a piece of property that creates or guarantees certain financial rights.[38] This approach has been accepted in Australia by the Supreme Court of Victoria[39] and, although not yet accepted in this jurisdiction, may well (and should) be followed in the future.

> **Extra detail . . .**
> The decline in the use of cheques generally has made this problem less acute. However, the same issues can arise in relation to the stealing of paper tickets.

9.2.2.1 Exceptions

Section 4 highlights a number of specific exceptions to the definition of property.

Land

The first specific exception relates to land (s4(2)). Where D takes V's land without severing it, she may have appropriated property within the civil law, but this will not constitute property for the purposes of theft.[40] For example, D moves her garden fence a few inches into V's garden.

Only certain specified land rights will amount to property within the offence of theft. First, section 4(2)(a) allows for theft of land by a trustee of property.

> (a) when he is a trustee or personal representative, or is authorised by power of attorney, or as liquidator of a company, or otherwise, to sell or dispose of land belonging to another, and he appropriates the land or anything forming part of it by dealing with it in breach of the confidence reposed in him

---

[34] Smith, 'Obtaining Cheques by Deception or Theft' [1997] Crim LR 396.
[35] *Preddy* [1996] AC 815.
[36] *Graham* [1997] 1 Cr App R 302.
[37] D may commit fraud if she dishonestly induces V to write the cheque for her, see **Chapter 10**.
[38] *Arnold* [1997] 4 All ER 1.
[39] *Parsons* [1998] 2 VR 478.
[40] It was felt that civil remedies would be more appropriate to deal with cases of this kind.

Therefore, where D is the trustee of property and disposes of that property dishonestly for her own advantage, she may commit theft.

Secondly, section 4(2)(b) allows for theft of land by D who severs part of that land, as long as D does not possess rights of ownership.[41]

> (b) when he is not in possession of the land and appropriates anything forming part of the land by severing it or causing it to be severed, or after it has been severed

The moving fence example was not theft because D was not severing (not removing) the part of V's land that she appropriated. Where there is such severance, however, these items will constitute property for the purposes of theft. For example, D takes some of V's topsoil, her plants, her garden shed, etc.

Thirdly, section 4(2)(c) allows for theft of land by a tenant who appropriates a fixture or structure from the land.

> (c) when, being in possession of the land under a tenancy, he appropriates the whole or part of any fixture or structure let to be used with the land.

Unlike D with no rights to the land, a tenant will not commit theft where she removes minor fixtures (eg topsoil).[42] However, where she appropriates a fixture (eg bath, sink, etc) or a structure (eg garden shed, greenhouse, etc), these items will constitute property for theft. In such cases, simple appropriation is all that is required, there is no additional requirement for severance.

Wild mushrooms and flowers

The second exception, where property in civil law will not amount to property for the purposes of the TA 1968, relates to wild mushrooms and flowers (s4(3)). This is defined liberally to include all fungi, and any plant or tree.

> (3) A person who picks mushrooms growing wild on any land, or who picks flowers, fruit or foliage from a plant growing wild on any land, does not (although not in possession of the land) steal what he picks, unless he does it for reward or for sale or other commercial purpose.

As with land, this exception from the definition of property is also not absolute. Although D may pick 'flowers, fruit or foliage', she may not take or dig up the whole plant, as this will amount to property. The exception also only applies to things growing wild, and so cultivated flowers or fungus are not included. Finally, the exception will only apply to those picking for non-commercial reasons.[43] Thus, where D picks berries in order to make jam for sale, she is picking property and may commit theft. However, where she is picking for her own use only, the berries are not property within the offence. How D makes use of the items picked is a useful indication of her intentions at the time of picking, but remember that it is her intention at this point (regardless of what happens later) that is crucial to liability. For example, if D picks berries to make jam for herself then she does not commit theft, even if she *later* decides to sell the jam.

---

[41] This includes, eg, the children of a tenant.
[42] Although she has appropriated the property of another (the landlord) in civil law.
[43] Welstead, 'Season of Mists and Mellow Fruitfulness' (1995) 145 NLJ 1499.

Wild creatures

The final specified exception relates to wild creatures (s4(4)).

> (4) Wild creatures, tamed or untamed, shall be regarded as property; but a person cannot steal a wild creature not tamed nor ordinarily kept in captivity, or the carcase of any such creature, unless either it has been reduced into possession by or on behalf of another person and possession of it has not since been lost or abandoned, or another person is in course of reducing it into possession.

Although wild creatures will generally not constitute property for the purposes of theft, the provision makes clear that this will not be the case with (a) non-wild creatures, or (b) wild creatures that have been killed or trapped, which become the property of the person who killed or trapped them. For example, if D kills and removes a wild animal from V's property, such as a pheasant, whilst D may be guilty of a poaching offence,[44] she will not be guilty of theft. To keep a creature in 'captivity', thus making it property, requires more than the regular feeding of a wild creature, even if the eventual aim is to trap and/or kill the creature.[45]

Other common law exceptions

Alongside the specific statutory exceptions within section 4, the common law has also developed to exempt other areas from the definition of property in theft. These include the following.

A) Electricity: Electricity is not property for the purposes of theft[46] but there is a separate offence within section 13 of the TA 1968 of wasting or diverting another's electricity.

B) Confidential information: Information does not amount to property within section 4.[47] In *Oxford v Moss*,[48] a university student who unlawfully acquired an examination paper, read and returned it, could not be liable for theft. There may be alternative offences under the Computer Misuse Act 1990, where the information is taken from a computer, and the Law Commission once provisionally proposed a new offence of misuse of trade secrets.[49] However, there is no theft in these cases.

C) Services: A service (eg a manicure, taxi journey, theatre performance, etc) is not property within section 4, and so failure to pay for a service is not theft. Such conduct is likely to be an offence of obtaining services dishonestly under section 11 of the Fraud Act 2006.

D) Bodies: Traditionally, human bodies and/or parts of bodies have not been classed as property within section 4.[50] However, this view is changing in a number of areas. For example, it has been held that bodily products which are intended to be held or

---

[44] Night Poaching Act 1828; Game Act 1831.
[45] *Cresswell v DPP* [2006] EWHC 3379 (Admin): involving the feeding of wild badgers.
[46] *Low v Blease* [1975] Crim LR 513.
[47] Christie, 'Should the Law of Theft Extend to Information?' (2005) 69 J Crim L 349; Davies, 'Protection of Intellectual Property—A Myth?' (2004) 68 J Crim L 398.
[48] (1978) 68 Cr App R 183.
[49] Law Commission, *Misuses of Trade Secrets* (Consultation 150, 1997).
[50] *Sharpe* (1857) D & B 160.

285

controlled can amount to property (eg urine samples,[51] sperm deposits,[52] etc). Thus, stealing blood from a blood bank, for example, is likely to constitute theft.

9.2.3 Belonging to another

The offence of theft is not designed simply to prevent D dishonestly assuming property rights (ie appropriating property), but more broadly to protect the ownership rights of others. Therefore, it is always essential to demonstrate that the property appropriated belonged to another at the point of appropriation. The general rule is set out in section 5(1) of the TA 1968.

> (1) Property shall be regarded as belonging to any person having possession or control of it, or having in it any proprietary right or interest (not being an equitable interest arising only from an agreement to transfer or grant an interest).

We will shortly comment on the individual terms used. However, before this, it should be highlighted that 'belonging to another' does not necessarily mean that V possessed exclusive ownership of the property appropriated. Having introduced the idea of multiple different ownership rights (**9.2.1.1**), it is important to recognise that D still appropriates V's property where V only possesses one of these rights. For example, V lends a book to X, X gives the book to Z to hold, and D snatches the book from Z and makes off with it. Here, D appropriates property belonging to V (proprietary ownership), X (possession), and Z (control). Even if only one of these could be proved, D's charge for theft of property belonging to another would be satisfied. What matters is that someone has *some* proprietary right or interest other than D.

9.2.3.1 Possession or control

V has possession or control of property where she intends to control or possess it, and maintains some degree of control over it in fact. For example, the owners of a vending machine will possess the coins inside the machine even if they do not know the quantity; and a landowner will possess the contents of their buildings even if they are not aware of every item.[53] The question in each case, turning on civil law concepts, is whether V demonstrates a sufficient claim of possession. This is illustrated in *Rostron*.

 Rostron [2003] All ER 269

D and others trespassed onto a golf course at night, with diving apparatus, and took lost golf balls from a lake which was part of the course driving range. D was charged with theft of the balls.

- Crown Court: guilty of theft.
- Court of Appeal: conviction upheld on appeal. The jury were entitled to find that the balls belonged to the golf course. Although the course owners did not intend to collect the balls themselves, they still maintained possession and control over them.

---

[51] *Welsh* [1974] RTR 550.
[52] *Yearworth v North Bristol NHS Trust* [2009] EWCA Civ 37.
[53] *Woodman* [1974] QB 754.

An interesting problem emerges where D is the owner of the property and she takes it from another who has possession or control. Does D commit theft of her own property? The requirement of dishonesty (discussed later) makes theft in these circumstances very unlikely. However, where there is dishonesty, the basic rule is that if V holds a proprietary interest in D's property, then D's taking of the property may amount to theft. This is illustrated in *Turner (No 2)*.

Turner (No 2) [1971] 2 All ER 441

D had his car repaired by V at a garage. On collecting his car, D used a spare set of keys to take his car without paying the bill. D was charged with theft of the car.

- Crown Court: guilty of theft.
- Court of Appeal: conviction upheld on appeal. The garage was in possession and control of the car and so, although D was the legal owner, he was still taking property that belonged to another (the garage).

The reasoning in *Turner (No 2)* was expressed too widely, indicating that appropriation in all such circumstances would amount to the taking of property belonging to another. This cannot be right. For example, if V snatches D's bag in the street and D takes it back, even though V takes brief control of the bag, D's re-taking is not taking property belonging to another: D has every right to take it back. This was recognised in *Meredith*, where D's dishonest appropriation of his car from a police compound was not theft.[54] *Turner (No 2)* does provide a useful illustration, however, of theft in circumstances where D does not have the right to demand his car be returned in civil law (until he pays the bill).

9.2.3.2 Proprietary interest

Proprietary interests are determined in reference to civil law rules of ownership. In most cases the ownership of property will be clear, as with the owner of the book in our opening example. However, the civil law rules are not always straightforward, as illustrated in *Marshall*.[55]

Marshall [1998] 2 Cr App R 282

D obtained part-used tickets from Underground users and resold them. London Underground Ltd (V) claimed ownership of the part-used tickets, making D's reselling an appropriation of their property. D was charged with theft.

- Crown Court: guilty of theft.
- Court of Appeal: conviction upheld on appeal. The question was whether a clause on the back of the ticket stating V's continued ownership of the ticket was sufficiently clear to buyers. If yes, then it remained V's property in civil law, but if not, then V had no interest. The court found that the clause was sufficiently clear.

As with *Marshall*, decisions in this area will often turn on the subtle rules of civil ownership. For example, property may be found to belong to the Crown if it comes within

---

[54] [1973] Crim LR 253.
[55] Smith, 'Stealing Tickets' [1998] Crim LR 723.

the rules of 'treasure',[56] property may belong (in equity) to beneficiaries of a trust,[57] property ownership may pass on contract despite V never receiving the goods,[58] and so on. Although identifying the proprietary interest may involve close scrutiny of civil rules, once such an interest is identified, it will always satisfy this element of theft. This will be the case even where D also has a proprietary interest in the property, as where one business partner takes all of the value out of a corporate partnership.[59]

9.2.3.3 Specific examples within s5

Alongside the general definition of 'belonging to another' in section 5(1), the rest of the section goes on to clarify certain potentially problematic examples.

A) Section 5(2): This subsection clarifies that where D, a trustee, dishonestly appropriates from that trust, she takes property of another. This is true where the trust has individual beneficiaries (overlapping with s5(1)), as well as purpose trusts (eg charitable trusts) where others have the ability to enforce the trust.[60]

> **Point to remember . . .**
> There is an obvious overlap with section 5(1) and (2) where the agreement between D and V creates a trust, or V retains equitable proprietary rights. In such a case, either provision may be used.[61]

B) Section 5(3): This subsection deals with property given to D for a particular purpose as, for example, where V provides D (her cleaner) with money to buy cleaning products. In such cases, even though the property is passed to D, if she deals with it in an improper manner, for example keeping it for herself, this will constitute taking the property of another.

In order to come within section 5(3), D must be under a legal, as opposed to a merely moral, duty to deal with the property in a particular way. This is a question of law for the judge.[62] In the context of money, the question is often whether D was expected to use specific money for a specific purpose (s5(3) applies), or whether the money was a general payment to D in exchange for future conduct that may be paid for from other funds (s5(3) does not apply). For example, where a travel agent receives deposits for a trip, there is an expectation that the agent will organise and pay for the trip, but no expectation that they will do so with the particular money provided. Thus, even where the company dishonestly fails to provide the trip or a refund there is no theft, although there is a breach of a civil/contractual obligation.[63] On the other side of this fine line are cases where D receives money in sponsorship, on the understanding that it will be

---

[56] *Waverley Borough Council v Fletcher* [1995] 4 All ER 756: using a metal detector, D found a gold brooch on the council's land.
[57] *Clowes (No 2)* [1994] 2 All ER 316; Davies, 'After *R v Clowes No 2*' (1997) 61 J Crim L 99.
[58] *Rose v Matt* [1951] 1 KB 810.
[59] *Bonner* [1970] 1 WLR 838.
[60] *Dyke and Munro* [2002] Crim LR 153. In the context of charitable trusts, the AG has the right of enforcement.
[61] *Hallam* [1995] Crim LR 323.
[62] *Clowes (No 2)* [1994] 2 All ER 316.
[63] *Hall* [1972] All ER 1009.

passed to the relevant charity. These cases are now likely to fall within section 5(3): those sponsoring are not paying D, but expect her to pass that money to the charity.[64]

C) Section 5(4): This subsection applies where D receives property by mistake and is under an obligation to return it or its value. A good example is where D receives an overpayment of wages. In such cases, where D appropriates the property and refuses to make restoration, she takes the property of another. This is illustrated in *Gresham*.[65]

 Gresham [2003] EWCA Crim 2070

D's mother died and yet D, who had power of attorney, did not inform her pension provider (V) who continued to make payments for ten years. D used this money as his own. D was charged with theft.

- Crown Court: guilty of theft.
- Court of Appeal: conviction upheld on appeal.[66] D had a duty under section 5(4) to return the money to V, and so his use of it amounted to the taking of another's property.

Where V mistakenly transfers property to D, this will *also* often result in V retaining some equitable proprietary ownership. In such cases, section 5(4) *and* (1) will apply.[67]

D) Section 5(5): This subsection clarifies that a legal person (a corporation) can own property. Therefore, for example, if directors of a company dishonestly appropriate company property, they are taking the property of another (the company).[68]

9.2.3.4 Abandonment by V

Where property owned by V is abandoned, it becomes ownerless, and therefore cannot be the subject of theft. It should be emphasised, however, that such abandonment is very rare: V must leave the property and be indifferent as to *any* future appropriation. For example, where V throws property into the bin, intending it to be collected and disposed of by authorised collectors, it is not abandoned; and D's taking of the property, where D is not an authorised collector, can amount to theft.[69] This is why in *Rostron* (discussed earlier), the golf course had not abandoned lost golf balls even though they had no intention of collecting the balls themselves. Other useful examples of *non*-abandonment include V who loses jewellery and gives up the search; and V who leaves property for a specific charity to collect.

9.2.3.5 The *Hinks* problem

The case of *Hinks*, discussed at **9.2.1.3**, provides an interesting problem in relation to this element: that the property must belong to another. It will be remembered that *Hinks* involved money being given to D by V, who was a vulnerable adult. These payments

---

[64] *Wain* [1995] 2 Cr App R 660.
[65] See also *AG's Reference (No 1 of 1983)* [1985] QB 182: theft of overpaid wages.
[66] Two of the 12 counts were overturned for lack of appropriation, but these are not relevant to the current discussion.
[67] *Shadrokh-Cigari* [1988] Crim LR 465; MacCormack, 'Mistaken Payments and Proprietary Claims' [1996] Conv 86.
[68] *A v Snaresbrook Crown Court* (2001) 165 JPN 495.
[69] *Williams v Phillips* (1957) 121 JP 163.

were dishonestly received, but nevertheless, crucially, represented valid gifts in civil law. Thus, at the moment the property was passed to D, D gained exclusive ownership rights. The question arises whether, at the moment of appropriation, the property belonged to D or to V? If it belonged to D then there is no appropriation of another's property—no coincidence in time—and, therefore, no theft.

In *Hinks*, this point was given little consideration and the property was assumed to belong to V at the moment of transfer. This is a useful indication that, when appropriation and the passing of property ownership are simultaneous, the courts will take a permissive approach to potential problems of coincidence. However, facts could arise that test such indulgence. For example, what if V in *Hinks* had sent the money to D by post, with D only appropriating it when later picking up her mail inside her house. In such a case, if the money is a valid gift, then when it sits in D's house it is entirely her property: thus, her appropriation of it could not, surely, be theft.

9.2.4 Intention permanently to deprive

The next major element of theft is the requirement that when appropriating the property of another, D did so with an intention permanently to deprive V of it. Section 1(2) of the TA 1968 explicitly clarifies that theft need not be for D's benefit, so this element includes an intention to give V's property to another. However, V must be deprived of her property, and, D must intend that deprivation to be permanent.

The requirement of an intention permanently to deprive is an ulterior mens rea element.[70] There is no corresponding actus reus element: whether D permanently deprives V in fact is irrelevant. Indeed, D's conduct after the appropriation, whether she returns the property and/or how she deals with it, is only relevant insofar as it provides evidence of D's intention at the moment of appropriation. For example, if D takes V's watch intending to keep it, but later discovers the sentimental value of the watch to V and returns it, she still commits theft: all the elements of the offence coincided at the moment of appropriation. Conversely, where D takes the watch intending to return it, but later loses it or changes her mind, there is no theft at the moment the watch is taken.[71]

> **Beware . . .**
> It is very easy to slip up in your discussion of this element by focusing on whether D has permanently deprived V or not. Remember, *all* discussion of this element should be focused on D's intentions at the point of appropriation only.

9.2.4.1 TA 1968, s6(1): extensions

Section 6(1) of the TA 1968 sets out a broad, and not entirely clear,[72] definition of what it means to intend to permanently deprive.

> (1) A person appropriating property belonging to another without meaning the other permanently to lose the thing itself is nevertheless to be regarded as having the intention of permanently

---

[70] See **4.2.1.2.**
[71] In such a case, prosecution for theft would rely on finding a second appropriation when D decides to keep the watch.
[72] Spencer, 'The Metamorphosis of Section 6 of the Theft Act' [1977] Crim LR 653.

depriving the other of it if his intention is to treat the thing as his own to dispose of regardless of the other's rights; and a borrowing or lending of it may amount to so treating it if, but only if, the borrowing or lending is for a period and in circumstances making it equivalent to an outright taking or disposal.

Several areas of uncertainty have arisen in the application of this section, and it is useful to trace how the courts have responded to them.

A) **Intention to ransom or sell property back to V:** Where D appropriates V's property with the intention of selling it back, or ransoming it to V, it is arguable that D does not intend *permanently* to deprive V of it. However, not surprisingly, the courts have consistently held this to come within section 6(1): D intends to treat the property as her own, and this is equivalent to the intention of an outright taking.[73] The same principle applies, for example, where D steals a ticket from a theatre, intending to return the ticket only when granted entry to the theatre (ie only when the theatre provides consideration).

B) **Intention to replace with identical property:** A problem emerges where D takes property intending to replace it with an identical equivalent. This can arise with any property. For example, where D takes a celebrity's sunglasses and replaces them with an identical pair, liability for theft is largely uncontroversial. However, it is most troublesome in the context of money. For example, where D takes money from a till at work, intending to replace it the following day with equivalent money, albeit not exactly the same notes or coins taken. All such cases will satisfy section 6(1), as clarified in *Velumyl*.

 Velumyl [1989] Crim LR 299

D, an employee, took money from the company safe, intending to return it after the weekend. D was charged with theft.

- Crown Court: guilty of theft.
- Court of Appeal: conviction upheld on appeal. D did not intend to return the exact notes or coins taken, so he must have intended to permanently deprive his employers of them.

It should be noted that although liability was found in *Velumyl*, many cases of this kind will fail for lack of dishonesty (discussed later).

C) **Intention to remove value from the property:** If D's intention is to take property and return it to V with *all* of its value removed, then there is, straightforwardly, an intention permanently to deprive. For example, D returns an animal after killing it; a car after setting it on fire; a sports season ticket at the end of the season; etc. Such conduct may be described, within section 6(1), as borrowing equivalent to an outright taking or disposal.[74] However, as illustrated in *Lloyd*, difficult questions of degree emerge where D intends only to take *some* of the value from V's property.

---

[73] *Raphael* [2008] EWCA Crim 1014: D stole V's car and then offered to sell it back.
[74] *DPP v J* [2002] EWHC 291 (Admin): intention to return headphones after breaking them.

Lloyd [1985] 3 WLR 30

D, who worked as a cinema projectionist, appropriated films with the intention of making illegal copies to sell elsewhere, but to return the originals. D was charged with theft.

- Crown Court: guilty of theft.
- Court of Appeal: appeal allowed. D's intention was merely to remove some of the value from the films, and was not sufficient to be equivalent to an outright taking.

Each case will turn on its facts. Where, for example, D intends to return the sporting season ticket halfway through the season, or the car when damaged but not destroyed, the question for the court will be one of degree: did D's intended conduct amount to an intention to remove sufficient value to be equivalent to an outright taking?

D) **Intention to abandon the property:** There will be clear cases where an intention to abandon V's property will amount to an intention to dispose of it, as where D intends to throw V's pin into a haystack. However, where D's intended abandonment may allow V to regain her property, the question is again one of degree. This is illustrated in the case of *Mitchell*.

 Mitchell [2008] EWCA Crim 850

D and three others forcibly took V's car, having crashed their own, whilst attempting to escape from the police. The car, largely undamaged, was later abandoned on the road with its hazard lights on. D was charged with robbery, which requires D to have committed theft.

- Crown Court: guilty of robbery.
- Court of Appeal: appeal allowed. The circumstances of the intended abandonment made it likely that the car would be returned to V and thus did not indicate an intention to permanently deprive.

The question in each case will focus on the manner by which D *intended* to abandon the property at the moment of appropriation.

E) **Conditional intentions:** This final problem case emerges where D appropriates property with a conditional intention to permanently deprive V of it. Examples include intention to keep V's jewellery only if the stones are genuine; to keep V's season ticket only if the team keep winning; etc. Despite doubt created by early case law,[75] it is now clear that D's conditional intention will constitute a valid intention. This was confirmed in *AG's References (Nos 1 and 2 of 1979)*.

 AG's References (Nos 1 and 2 of 1979) [1980] QB 180

Combined cases involving Ds who were arrested whilst trying to break into buildings. Both were charged with burglary, requiring an intention to steal.

- Crown Court: not guilty of burglary, a conditional intention to steal (if there was anything worth taking) is insufficient.

---

[75] *Easom* [1971] 2 QB 315; *Husseyn* (1977) 67 Cr App R 131.

> - Court of Appeal: the Crown Court was wrong: both Ds had an intention to steal, even if they had no specific property in mind. The court explicitly extended its judgment to standard theft cases.

The older case of *Easom* provides useful facts to explain how the current law should be applied. In that case, D picked up a woman's handbag and looked through it for valuables, but then replaced it having taken nothing. Pre-*AG's References (Nos 1 and 2 of 1979)*, D's conviction for theft of the handbag and its contents was quashed because of D's conditional intention. Following *AG's References*, there remains no theft of the bag: D never intended (even conditionally) permanently to deprive V of the bag. There will, however, be theft of the bag's contents: although D decided not to keep the contents because of their lack of value, he still appropriated them with the conditional intention of keeping them had they been valuable. If the bag had been empty, there would be no property for D to intend conditionally permanently to deprive, and therefore no theft. There would, however, be liability for attempted theft.[76]

9.2.4.2 TA 1968, s6(2): intention to risk the property

Although most borderline issues within section 6 have been left to the common law, one area has been clarified by section 6(2) of the TA 1968.

> (2) Without prejudice to the generality of subsection (1) above, where a person, having possession or control (lawfully or not) of property belonging to another, parts with the property under a condition as to its return which he may not be able to perform, this (if done for purposes of his own and without the other's authority) amounts to treating the property as his own to dispose of regardless of the other's rights.

This subsection makes clear that where D intends to part with V's property and cannot be sure of its return, her intention amounts to an intention permanently to deprive. For example, where D intends to risk V's money by gambling with it, or pawning it in circumstances where she is not positive of its return, her intention amounts to an intention permanently to deprive even if she hopes to be successful and give the property back.[77]

9.2.5 Dishonesty

The final element of theft is the requirement of dishonesty. D must appropriate property belonging to another, with the intention permanently to deprive, and that appropriation must be dishonest. With many of the other elements of theft being interpreted widely by the courts, and potentially applying to apparently innocent conduct, the role of dishonesty is crucial in narrowing the offence to its target mischief only.[78]

Unfortunately, despite its importance, dishonesty is not defined in the TA 1968. Rather, section 2 provides three situations when D is *not* dishonest. These will always be the starting point for a discussion of dishonesty: if the case comes within one of the examples then the discussion stops there—there is no dishonesty and therefore there is no theft.

---

[76] **Chapter 13.**
[77] *Fernandes* [1996] 1 Cr App R 175.
[78] Griew, 'Dishonesty: The Objections to *Feely* and *Ghosh*' [1985] Crim LR 341.

9.2.5.1 Statutory examples of no dishonesty

The first situation applies to cases where D believed she had a legal right to the property she appropriated (s2(1)).

> (a) if he appropriates the property in the belief that he has in law the right to deprive the other of it, on behalf of himself or of a third person;

D's belief need not be reasonable,[79] and it does not have to be based on an accurate understanding of the law.[80] As long as D *honestly* believed she had a legal (and not merely moral) right to the property, she will not be dishonest. Most commonly, this will arise where D takes V's property believing that it is hers as, for example, where D takes the wrong umbrella when leaving a restaurant.

The second example applies where D believed that V would have consented to the appropriation (s2(1)).

> (b) if he appropriates the property in the belief that he would have the other's consent if the other knew of the appropriation and the circumstances of it;

Again, D's belief need not be accurate or reasonable. As long as D honestly believed at the time of appropriation that V would have consented, then her conduct is not dishonest. Circumstances of this type are common as, for example, with family or friends using each other's property in the belief that the other would consent.

The final example applies where D appropriates property believing that the owner is undiscoverable (s2(1)).

> (c) (except where the property came to him as trustee or personal representative) if he appropriates the property in the belief that the person to whom the property belongs cannot be discovered by taking reasonable steps.

This example is intended to deal with those who discover seemingly abandoned property. D is not dishonest if she appropriates that property, as long as she honestly believes that the owner could not be found using reasonable steps. D's belief does not have to be reasonable.

D comes within this example even if she believes that the owner is potentially discoverable in certain circumstances. For example, D may believe she could find the owner of a watch if she spent weeks searching and paid for television adverts, but this is clearly more than would be reasonably expected. The value of the property will thereby affect what constitutes reasonable steps in each case.[81]

As the subsection makes clear, this example does not apply to trustees and trust property. In such a case, D must rely on one of the other examples, or the general common law definition of dishonesty.

---

[79] *Terry* [2001] EWCA Crim 2979.
[80] *Bernhard* [1938] 2 KB 264.
[81] *Sylvester* (1985) CO/559/84: D unsuccessfully raised s2(1)(c) in relation to a car he was stripping for parts.

> **Point to remember . . .**
> Section 2(2) clarifies that D may be dishonest even where she pays for the property. This is necessary to criminalise situations such as D taking her neighbour's barbeque on a hot day, but leaving some money to compensate. However, the subsection only provides that D 'may' be dishonest in such cases; thus, the common law definition must be applied.

9.2.5.2 Common law definition of dishonesty

In the absence of a statutory definition of what *is* dishonest, the test has been left to the common law. The question of dishonesty is one of fact for the jury: the jury must find what D did and what she was thinking, and whether that was dishonest.[82] The leading case, providing the test for dishonesty, is *Ghosh*.

 Ghosh [1982] QB 1053

D, who was working as a surgeon, claimed fees for carrying out certain operations where this was not appropriate. D was charged with obtaining property by deception (since repealed as an offence under the TA 1968, s15), an offence where D must act dishonestly.

- Crown Court: guilty of section 15 offence.
- Court of Appeal: conviction upheld on appeal. D acts dishonestly where (a) D's conduct is dishonest according to the standards of reasonable and honest people; and (b) D realised (at that point) that the conduct would be seen as dishonest according to those standards.

In many cases, it will not be necessary for the jury to be directed by reference to the *Ghosh* test.[83] For example, D accepts that the conduct would be dishonest but denies the conduct;[84] or D accepts that she performed apparently dishonest conduct but claims to have done so absent-mindedly (ie so the question is whether we believe her).[85] However, where dishonesty is at issue, both parts of the *Ghosh* test must be applied.

Step 1: Is D's conduct dishonest according to the standards of reasonable and honest people? The first step of the test is objective. The jury must consider what D has done and apply the objective standards of reasonable people in deciding whether that conduct is dishonest, not their own standards of dishonesty, and not D's. Such standards may change over time, and leaving this question to the jury allows the legal standard to change with society. The question will not always be obvious. For example, in *Gohill v DPP*,[86] although magistrates found D's behaviour not to be dishonest (D allowed customers to borrow tools from a hire shop for short periods without payment, and sometimes for a personal tip), this was reversed on appeal.

It may be difficult for a jury to identify a universal standard for dishonesty across all reasonable and honest people, but it is clear that this is what they are required to do. The

---

[82] *Feely* [1973] QB 530.
[83] *Roberts* (1985) 84 Cr App R 177.
[84] *Cobb* [2005] EWCA Crim 1549: D denied taking money from a till.
[85] *Atkinson* [2004] Crim LR 226.
[86] [2007] EWHC 239 (Admin).

test in *Ghosh* will not vary this standard between different groups or occupations, however specialised or unique. This was confirmed in *Hayes*.[87]

 Hayes [2015] EWCA Crim 1944

D, a banker, manipulated banking investment rates (LIBOR rates) in order to benefit his company. D admitted his conduct, but later claimed that it was not dishonest because it was widely condoned and even encouraged within the industry at that time. D was charged with conspiracy to defraud, an offence requiring dishonesty.

- Crown Court: guilty of conspiracy to defraud. Different standards within specific industries are not relevant to the objective standard of dishonesty applied from *Ghosh*.
- Court of Appeal: conviction upheld on appeal. Confirming the judgment of the lower court, Sir Brian Leveson P, commented (at [30]) that 'honesty is determined by objective standards of honest and reasonable people; persons are not free to set their own standards'.

It is therefore clear that the standard of dishonesty applied within the first limb of the *Ghosh* test is single and universal.

Step 2: Does D realise that her conduct would be considered dishonest by the standards of honest and reasonable people? As well as being dishonest by the standards of honest and reasonable people, D must *also* realise that her conduct would be so considered to satisfy the full test. The construction of this second step is important. It is a subjective question, asking what D believes, but the question relates back to an objective standard: we do not ask D if she considers her behaviour dishonest by her own standards of honesty; we ask if she knew that others would consider her conduct dishonest by the objective standard of reasonable and honest people. Thus, an animal rights protester might believe it is not dishonest to take equipment from an animal testing lab by her own standards (believing it is justified to disrupt the industry), but she is likely to concede that her conduct would be perceived as dishonest by the standards of the community.

Two common examples may be useful. The first example involves D who does not pay for public transport because, having recently arrived in the country, she does not know payment is required. D's conduct in this case is likely to be seen as dishonest by the standards of reasonable people, satisfying the first step of the *Ghosh* test, but D is likely to avoid liability on the second step. As D did not realise that payment was expected, she is unlikely at that time to have appreciated that others would consider her conduct dishonest. The second example is that of Robin Hood, and this example is useful to demonstrate some of the uncertainty of the test. On the first step, it is not certain that every jury would consider robbing from the rich to give to the poor to be dishonest, although it is likely that most would. On the second step, we have a similar problem: a perceptive folk hero might realise that most people would think her dishonest but carry on regardless, but a more self-obsessed folk hero might believe (however unreasonably) that she is acting in a way that reasonable and honest people would not think dishonest. This is important because only the more perceptive folk hero would satisfy the second step in *Ghosh*.

---

[87] Dent and Kervick, '*Ghosh*: A Change in Direction?' [2016] Crim LR 553.

9.3 Robbery

Robbery is defined in section 8(1) of the TA 1968. The maximum sentence on indictment is life imprisonment.[88]

(1) A person is guilty of robbery if he steals, and immediately before or at the time of doing so, and in order to do so, he uses force on any person or puts or seeks to put any person in fear of being then and there subjected to force.

The elements of robbery are set out in **Table 9.3**.

Table 9.3 Robbery

	Actus reus	Mens rea
Conduct element	Any conduct causing the results	Voluntary
Circumstance element	What is appropriated is property	Knowledge
	What is appropriated does not belong to D	Knowledge
	D's appropriation is dishonest	Knowledge
Result element	D appropriates V's property	Intention
	(D uses unlawful force against another, or causes another to apprehend immediate unlawful force)	Intention or recklessness
Ulterior mens rea element	*	Intention permanently to deprive V of her property
		Intention that force or threat of force will facilitate the theft
		(Where D does *not* use or cause another to apprehend unlawful force, she may still be liable if seeking to make another so apprehend)

---

[88] TA 1968, s8(2).

The elements of robbery may be more simply illustrated in line with **Figure 9.1**.

Figure 9.1 Robbery

9.3.1 Theft

D must commit theft as an essential part of the offence of robbery.[89] If D does not commit theft due to the absence of any of the elements of theft (discussed at **9.2**) then D does not commit robbery. Of course, where there is no theft but D has used unlawful force, she may still be liable for an offence against the person,[90] or for an offence of assault with intent to rob,[91] but not robbery.

9.3.2 Force or the threat of force

The requirement of 'force' can be satisfied in any one of three ways: actual infliction of force; causing an apprehension of force; and/or seeking to cause the apprehension of force. We discuss each in turn.

> *Beware . . .*
> The requirement of force or threat of force shares several similarities with the offences of assault and battery discussed at **7.2**. However, as we will see, these similarities are not complete, and so the requirement of force within robbery should not be equated with assault and battery.

9.3.2.1 Force

Most straightforward cases of robbery will involve D using force against V in the course of theft. Such force must be bodily and not simply against V's property. It must be more than negligible, but need not be serious.[92] For example, minor bodily contact when picking V's pocket will not satisfy this element,[93] but any pushing or shoving of V is likely to do so.[94] This is illustrated in *P v DPP*.

---

[89] *Guy* (1990) 93 Cr App R 108.
[90] **Chapter 7**.
[91] TA 1968, s8(2).
[92] It has been argued that different levels of force should lead to different levels of liability: Ashworth, 'Robbery Reassessed' [2002] Crim LR 851.
[93] *Monaghan and Monaghan* [2000] 1 Cr App R 6: pickpocketing and 'jostling' charged as theft.
[94] *Dawson* (1976) 64 Cr App R 170: theft and a 'nudge' charged as robbery.

P v DPP [2012] EWHC 1657 (Admin)

D snatched a lit cigarette from V's hand. No contact was made with V. D was charged with robbery.

- Youth Court: guilty of robbery.
- High Court: appeal allowed, and conviction for theft substituted. D's snatching of the cigarette did not amount to sufficient 'force' to satisfy robbery.

D's appeal was allowed in *P v DPP* because of a lack of sufficient force, not because of the lack of direct bodily contact. It has been recognised for some time that although force against another's body is required, such force may be indirect. For example, where D wrenches a shopping basket or a handbag from V's grip, causing force to be inflicted despite the lack of direct physical contact, robbery may be found.[95]

9.3.2.2 Fear of force

Section 8 describes putting V in 'fear' of being subjected to force. However, the term 'fear' is problematic to the extent that it suggests something beyond the apprehension of force. It would not be desirable, for example, for D's liability to depend on the robustness or bravery of V. Therefore, courts have interpreted 'fear' in line with the apprehension that force will be used.[96]

V must be caused to apprehend that force will be used 'then and there'. Thus, there was no robbery in *Khan*[97] where V handed money to D fearing that if he did not do so D would be in trouble with a third party (X), and that D may return and use force against V. The apprehension here was of future not present force. Where D threatens force in the future in order to gain V's property, the appropriate charge is blackmail.[98]

9.3.2.3 Seeking fear of force

D can alternatively satisfy this element of robbery if she 'seeks' to put V in fear of force. Even where D does not use force against V, or cause V to apprehend the use of force (both actus reus), D may still be liable if she acts with the intention to cause V to so apprehend (ulterior mens rea).[99] For example, robbery will be committed if D uses a fake gun to threaten V and take property, even if V realises the gun is fake.

Point to remember . . .
Where D causes another to apprehend force, or seeks to do so, the person threatened must be aware of it. For example, where D threatens V directly, or where D threatens V's family member X whilst X is present, robbery may be committed. However, where D threatens V with an attack upon one of her family, and that family member is not present and not aware of the threat, robbery is not committed.[100]

---

[95] *Clouden* [1987] Crim LR 56; *Symons* [2009] EWCA Crim 83.
[96] *R v DPP* [2007] EWHC 739 (Admin): robbery despite evidence from V that he was not afraid.
[97] [2001] EWCA Crim 923.
[98] See **9.6**.
[99] *Tennant* [1976] Crim LR 133.
[100] *Taylor* [1996] 10 Arch News 2.

9.3.3 Link between theft and force

To amount to robbery, as opposed to separate offences of theft and an offence against the person, the two major parts of the offence must be linked. This does not mean that force must necessarily be aimed at the owner of the property stolen. For example, there will be robbery where D overpowers a security guard of shop A to prevent her seeing and reporting D's thefts from shop B. However, there must be temporal *and* intentional links.

A) Temporal link: Section 8 states that the force must be 'immediately before' or 'at the time of' the theft. This means that there is no robbery where there is a large time gap between the two. However, a common-sense application of the law, as in *Hale*, allows some minor gaps in time, even where the force comes after the act of appropriation.

 Hale (1978) 68 Cr App R 415

D1 and D2 broke into V's house. Whilst D1 stole V's jewellery, D2 tied V up. D1 and D2 were charged with robbery.

- Crown Court: guilty of robbery.
- Court of Appeal: convictions upheld on appeal. Even if the appropriation by D1 might have occurred fractionally before the force used by D2, the act of theft could be interpreted as a continuing act. The elements of robbery therefore coincided in time.

Just as the courts have interpreted the 'act' of theft broadly to find that the elements coincide in time, the same has been true of the element of 'force', particularly in threat of force cases. For example, there will be robbery where D threatens V on day one and then takes property from V on day two, knowing that the threat is still operating on V (ie when approached on day two, V may fear immediate force if she refuses because of the earlier threat).[101]

B) Intentional link: D must use the force 'in order to' steal. Therefore, accidental infliction of force during a theft is not robbery. Indeed, where D assaults V with no intention to steal, but then takes the opportunity to take V's property, there is no robbery. There may be a theft and an assault in such a case but there is no intentional link between them.[102]

9.4 Burglary

The offence of burglary is set out in section 9 of the TA 1968. The maximum sentence on indictment is ten years' imprisonment, or 14 years where the burglary takes place in a dwelling.[103]

(1) A person is guilty of burglary if—

    (a) he enters any building or part of a building as a trespasser and with intent to commit any such offence as is mentioned in subsection (2) below; or

---

[101] *Donaghy and Marshall* [1981] Crim LR 644.
[102] *James* [1997] Crim LR 598.
[103] TA 1968, s9(3).

(b) having entered any building or part of a building as a trespasser he steals or attempts to steal anything in the building or that part of it or inflicts or attempts to inflict on any person therein any grievous bodily harm.

(2) The offences referred to in subsection (1)(a) above are offences of stealing anything in the building or part of a building in question, of inflicting on any person therein any grievous bodily harm therein, and of doing unlawful damage to the building or anything therein.

As is clear from the statute, the offence of burglary is more complex than its common (mis)understanding as simply breaking and entering to commit theft. In fact, the offence is best understood by splitting it into two separate offences, both leading to conviction for burglary. The first offence is set out in section 9(1)(a); the second in section 9(1)(b).

9.4.1 TA 1968, s9(1)(a): burglary by trespassing with intent

Section 9(1)(a) creates a form of inchoate offence: targeting D who trespasses with *intent* to commit theft, cause GBH, or commit criminal damage. D is liable at the point of entry provided she has the requisite intent. Whether she goes on to commit the intended offence is irrelevant to her liability under this subsection. As with other inchoate offences,[104] the rationale for this offence is to facilitate early intervention by the police, imposing liability *before* the harms associated with theft, GBH, or criminal damage have come about. The offence is set out in **Table 9.4**.

Table 9.4 Burglary: TA 1968, s9(1)(a)

	Actus reus	**Mens rea**
Conduct element	Any conduct causing the results	Voluntary
Circumstance element	D is a trespasser	Intention or recklessness
Result element	Entry into a building or part of a building	Intention
Ulterior mens rea element	*	Intent to commit theft; cause GBH; or commit criminal damage

9.4.1.1 Actus reus of s9(1)(a) burglary

The actus reus of section 9(1)(a) burglary is deceptively simple: entry to a building, or part of a building, as a trespasser. However, within this, areas of complication have arisen.

---

[104] **Chapter 11.**

A) **Entry:** D 'enters' a building, or part of a building, if any part of her person crosses the threshold. In the case of *Collins*,[105] discussed in the following section, Edmund Davies LJ said that entry must be 'effective and substantial'. However, such terms are not useful, as they erroneously suggest that D must have fully entered or that her entry must be such that she could commit the intended offence. As illustrated in *Ryan*, following *Brown*,[106] such a degree of entry is not required.

 Ryan [1996] Crim LR 320

D attempted to break into V's house but became wedged in the kitchen window with his arm and head inside the building. D was charged with section 9(1)(a) burglary.

- Crown Court: guilty of burglary.
- Court of Appeal: conviction upheld on appeal. Although most of D's body was not inside the building and, although he was not in a position to commit the intended offence, the jury were still entitled to find a valid entry.

Under the (pre-1968) common law, entry could also be found indirectly as where D uses an instrument such as a long hook rather than her body to enter the building. It is uncertain whether such conduct could constitute entry under the current law, and there is no authority directly on this point. In such cases, where D uses the instrument to commit the intended offence (eg theft), it is better to charge that intended offence rather than burglary, or an attempt of the intended offence where it is not carried out.[107]

B) **Building or part of a building:** The word 'building' is given its ordinary meaning by the courts.[108] However, a judge must still advise the jury whether the structure entered by D is capable of being found to be a building. This is not always straightforward. A standard house is clearly a building whether occupied or not, as are work buildings; outhouses; sheds; and so on. The term has been interpreted broadly to include part-built or damaged structures, as well as semi-permanent containers.[109] Section 9(4) also extends the term to include 'inhabited' vehicles or vessels whether occupied or not, which includes caravans, houseboats, and so on. However, where the vehicle or vessel is not inhabited, or the structure is insufficiently permanent (eg a tent), a court may find that there is no building and therefore no burglary.[110]

Don't be confused . . .
The orthodox interpretation of a 'building' includes the entire structure. Where D breaks into Flat 1 in order to gain access to Flat 2 to commit theft, D commits section 9(1)(a) burglary at the point of entry to the building that houses the two flats (we do not have to wait until she enters Flat 2).[111]

---

[105] [1973] QB 100.

[106] [1985] Crim LR 212: there was entry where D stood outside a shop, but was reaching through a window.

[107] **Chapter 11**.

[108] *Brutus v Cozens* [1973] AC 854. Laird, 'Conceptualising the Interpretation of "Dwelling" in Section 9 of the Theft Act 1968' [2013] Crim LR 656.

[109] *B & S v Leathley* [1979] Crim LR 314: a freezer container disconnected from its chassis could be a building.

[110] *Norfolk Constabulary v Seekings and Gould* [1986] Crim LR 167: a freezer container that was still connected to its chassis was a (non-inhabited) vehicle and not a building.

[111] *Headley v Webb* [1901] 2 Ch 126: two semi-detached houses can constitute a single building.

Reference to 'part of a building' is included to deal with cases where D has permission to enter the building (eg the shop) but not into certain areas (eg behind the counter).[112] Where such areas constitute 'part of a building', D may be liable under section 9(1)(a) for entering them as a trespasser with the required mens rea. As with the definition of 'building', there are core examples such as separate rooms within a house or hotel; behind a shop counter; etc, but there will also be uncertainty as with a roped-off area within a shop.[113]

C) **As a trespasser:** Where D enters a building without permission of the owner or possessor, or the owner or possessor's family, or some other legal authorisation,[114] she enters as a trespasser. Trespass is a tortious concept, but its definition in the criminal law need not be identical to that in tort.[115] Whether D is a trespasser will usually be clear, but two cases should be highlighted. First, where V mistakenly permits D to enter, D enters as a trespasser.[116] For example, V thinks D is the plumber. Secondly, where D enters in excess of her permission, she is also trespassing. This is illustrated in *Jones and Smith*.

 Jones and Smith [1976] 3 All ER 54

D and another entered his father's house, at night, with the intention to steal. D had a general permission to enter, but not for the purposes of stealing. D was charged with burglary.

- Crown Court: guilty of burglary.
- Court of Appeal: conviction upheld on appeal. D entered the building in excess of the general permission given by his father, thus as a trespasser.

The logical conclusion to this second rule is that D commits burglary whenever she enters a shop with intent to steal: she is a trespasser because her permission to enter does not extend to entry for the purposes of theft.[117] This seems correct on the law. However, prosecutors have been, and are likely to remain, reluctant to prosecute shoplifting as burglary unless D enters a specifically restricted area within a shop.[118]

Extra detail . . .
Interesting problems emerge where D enters with permission but the permission is then withdrawn. Where D fails to leave in a reasonable time, she becomes a trespasser. However, as she has not 'entered' as a trespasser, we would still need some kind of crossing (eg into a new area of the building) as a trespasser in order to potentially catch D within burglary.

9.4.1.2 Mens rea of s9(1)(a) burglary

There are two major elements within the mens rea of section 9(1)(a) burglary. First, D must be at least reckless as to the facts that make her a trespasser. Secondly, D must intend to commit one of the offences listed in section 9(2).

---

[112] *Walkington* [1979] 2 All ER 716: D trespassed behind a shop counter.
[113] Discussed in *Walkington*. Where the barrier is clear, it is likely to create a separate part of the building.
[114] eg police entering property pursuant to a warrant.
[115] *Collins* [1973] QB 100.
[116] Ibid. Discussed at **9.4.1.2**.
[117] Smith, 'Shoplifting and the Theft Acts' [1981] Crim LR 586.
[118] *Walkington* [1979] 2 All ER 716.

A) **Intent/reckless as to trespass:** In most cases D will be well aware when she enters a building as a trespasser. However, particularly in relation to mistaken consent cases, and cases of entry in excess of permission, mens rea may be harder to demonstrate. Take the case of *Collins*.

 Collins [1973] QB 100

D, naked apart from his socks, climbed a ladder up to V's window. D's intention was to have sex with V. Seeing the silhouette of D in her window, V mistook D for her boyfriend, invited him in, and they engaged in sexual intercourse. V turned on the light and discovered her mistake. D was charged with burglary (at this time burglary included entry as a trespasser with 'intent to rape').

• Crown Court: guilty of burglary.

• Court of Appeal: appeal allowed. Although V's mistake meant that D entered without true permission, the jury were not directed to ask the separate mens rea question: was D at least reckless as to V's mistake (ie did he at least foresee a risk of the mistake and continue unreasonably to run such a risk)?

Although *Collins* avoided liability due to (possible) lack of mens rea, this will not always be the case. For example, in *Jones and Smith* (discussed in the previous section), the fact that the youths waited to enter D's father's house at night provided evidence that they realised that they were entering in excess of their permission.

B) **Intent to steal, cause GBH, or commit criminal damage:** This element is an example of ulterior mens rea: D must intend to commit one of these offences at the time of entry, but whether she goes on to carry it out is irrelevant.[119] This element is pivotal to the mischief targeted by section 9(1)(a). Without this intention, D merely commits the civil wrong of trespass; with the intention, D commits burglary, a serious criminal offence. As a form of ulterior intention, it is clear that a conditional intention is sufficient, as where D intends to steal if she finds anything worth stealing.[120] However, nothing short of intention as to every element of the future offence will suffice.[121]

Assessment matters . . .
What if D intends to take an item from the building and damage it elsewhere (does D intend to commit criminal damage 'therein'?), or to take a person from the building and cause GBH elsewhere (does D intend to cause GBH 'therein'?). These questions have not arisen in the case law, but provide an interesting problem. As with all legal unknowns, if arising in a problem question, you should highlight the lack of authority and say what you think the likely outcome would be, based on the rationale of the offence and the general approach of the courts.[122]

9.4.2 TA 1968, s9(1)(b): burglary by offences committed following trespassory entry

Section 9(1)(b) burglary will often overlap with section 9(1)(a), but is quite different. Section 9(1)(b) applies where D enters a building or a part of a building as a trespasser and then commits theft, attempted theft, causes GBH, or attempts to cause GBH. Where

---

[119] See **4.2.1.2.**
[120] *AG's References (Nos 1 and 2 of 1979)* [1979] 3 All ER 143.
[121] *A v DPP* [2003] All ER 393: recklessness is not sufficient.
[122] White, 'Lurkers, Draggers and Kidnappers' (1986) 150 JP 37.

D enters with the intent to commit one of these offences, and then does so, she commits burglary under *both* sections 9(1)(a) and 9(1)(b). However, where she enters with intent to commit one of the listed offences, but does not commit or attempt to commit it, there is a section 9(1)(a) burglary only. Where she enters without the intent to commit one of the listed offences, but then does commit such an offence after having entered, there is a section 9(1)(b) burglary only.

To come within section 9(1)(b), D must complete the offence of theft, attempted theft, a GBH offence, or an attempted GBH offence. The elements of these offences are discussed elsewhere in this book.[123] In addition to this base offence, the other elements of section 9(1)(b) are set out in **Table 9.5**.

Table 9.5 Burglary: TA 1968, s9(1)(b)

	Actus reus	Mens rea
Conduct element	Any conduct causing the results	Voluntary
Circumstance element	D is a trespasser	Recklessness
Result element	Entry into a building or part of a building	Intent

Section 9(1)(b) burglary may be more simply illustrated, as in **Figure 9.2**.

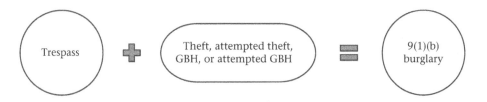

Figure 9.2 Burglary: TA 1968, s9(1)(b)

Beware . . .
The listed offences in relation to sections 9(1)(a) and 9(1)(b) are different. Importantly, criminal damage is a listed offence under section 9(1)(a) but not under section 9(1)(b). So, where D trespasses without the intention to commit criminal damage, but commits criminal damage whilst inside the building, she does not commit burglary. She will, of course, be liable for criminal damage.

9.4.2.1 Actus reus of s9(1)(b) burglary

D must enter a building or a part of a building as a trespasser. These elements were discussed above in the context of section 9(1)(a).

When inside the building, D must then complete the actus reus of theft, a GBH offence, or attempt either. We discussed the elements of theft at **9.2**; GBH offences at **7.5–7.6**; and we discuss criminal attempts at **Chapter 11**.

---

[123] Theft (**9.2**); GBH (**7.5–7.6**); Attempt (**Chapter 11**).

9.4.2.2 Mens rea of s9(1)(b) burglary

D must be at least reckless as to the facts that make her entry a trespass. We discussed this previously in relation to the case of *Collins*.

When committing one of the listed offences within the building, D must act with the mens rea required for that offence. For example, if committing theft, D must intend to permanently deprive V of her property, and do so dishonestly. We discuss the elements of theft at **9.2**; GBH offences at **7.5–7.6**; and criminal attempts at **Chapter 11**.

> *Extra detail . . .*
>
> As section 9(1)(b) does not specify a particular GBH 'offence', it was held in *Jenkins*[124] that as long as D caused GBH there was no need to demonstrate any mens rea. However, this interpretation has been heavily criticised and is unlikely to be followed by future courts. For example, D trespasses into V's house, thinking V is away. V hears someone in the house and suffers a shock-induced heart attack. D has committed the trespass, but surely not burglary.

9.4.3 Aggravated burglary

A burglary becomes aggravated burglary under section 10 of the TA 1968 if it is committed with the use of a listed weapon. The maximum sentence for aggravated burglary on indictment is life imprisonment.[125]

(1) A person is guilty of aggravated burglary if he commits any burglary and at the time has with him any firearm or imitation firearm, any weapon of offence, or any explosive; and for this purpose—

   (a) 'firearm' includes an airgun or air pistol, and 'imitation firearm' means anything which has the appearance of being a firearm, whether capable of being discharged or not; and

   (b) 'weapon of offence' means any article made or adapted for use for causing injury to or incapacitating a person, or intended by the person having it with him for such use; and

   (c) 'explosive' means any article manufactured for the purpose of producing a practical effect by explosion, or intended by the person having it with him for that purpose.

The structure of the offence is illustrated in **Figure 9.3**.

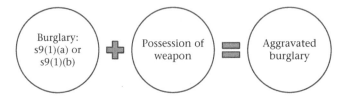

Figure 9.3 Aggravated burglary

We have already discussed the elements of burglary, and much of the possession requirement is self-explanatory from the text of section 10. However, three points should be stressed.

First, it will not always be clear if what D possesses is a 'weapon' within the meaning of section 10. Section 10(1)(b) is particularly ambiguous, but has been interpreted broadly. For example, even an otherwise innocent item such as a screwdriver will become a weapon within this section if D is carrying it to use as a weapon.[126] Note that section

---

[124] [1983] 1 All ER 1000.
[125] TA 1968, s10(2).
[126] *Kelly* [1993] Crim LR 763.

10(1)(b) also extends to 'incapacitation'. Thus, carrying sleeping pills to drug the owner of the building, or socks to tie her up, etc, will all be caught by the offence.

Secondly, the requirement that D must have the weapon 'at the time' of committing the burglary means that it is important to identify whether D is committing burglary under section 9(1)(a) or 9(1)(b). D commits section 9(1)(a) burglary at the point of entry to the building with the requisite intention. Thus, for aggravated section 9(1)(a) burglary, D must have the weapon at this point.[127] D commits section 9(1)(b) burglary at the point she commits theft, a GBH offence, or attempts either. Thus, for aggravated section 9(1)(b) burglary, D must have the weapon at this point.[128]

Thirdly, the requirement of possession ('has with him') simply means that D must be in control of the weapon and must be aware of it.[129] It is irrelevant whether D intends to use the weapon in the course of the burglary. For example, in *Stones*,[130] D's conviction was upheld where he was carrying a kitchen knife, even though he claimed to have the knife for defensive purposes only.

9.5 Handling stolen goods

The offence of handling stolen goods is set out in section 22 of the TA 1968. The maximum sentence on indictment is 14 years' imprisonment.[131]

(1) A person handles stolen goods if (otherwise than in the course of the stealing) knowing or believing them to be stolen goods he dishonestly receives the goods, or dishonestly undertakes or assists in their retention, removal, disposal or realisation by or for the benefit of another person, or if he arranges to do so.

The elements of the offence are illustrated in **Table 9.6**.

Table 9.6 Handling stolen goods

	Actus reus	**Mens rea**
Conduct element	Any conduct causing the result	Voluntary
Circumstance element	The goods are stolen	Knowledge or belief
	D's conduct is dishonest	Knowledge
Result element	D receives the goods,	Intention
	Or undertakes or assists in their retention, removal, disposal, or realisation by or for the benefit of another person, or arranges to do so	Intention

---

[127] *Wiggins* [2012] EWCA Crim 885.
[128] *Chevannes* [2009] EWCA Crim 2725.
[129] *Russell* (1985) 81 Cr App R 315.
[130] [1989] 1 WLR 156.
[131] The high maximum of 14 years (theft carries a maximum of seven years) is set to discourage trade in stolen goods and thereby discourage future thefts: *Shelton* (1993) 15 Cr App R 415.

9.5.1 Actus reus of s22

Handling stolen goods is an extremely wide-ranging offence, extending well beyond the paradigm where D takes physical possession of V's recently stolen goods from the thief (P). Core questions within the actus reus relate to the meaning of 'goods'; the meaning of 'stolen'; and the meaning of 'handling'.

9.5.1.1 Goods

The definition of 'goods' for the purpose of this offence is set out in section 34(2)(b) of the TA 1968.

> (b) 'goods', except in so far as the context otherwise requires, includes money and every other description of property except land, and includes things severed from the land by stealing.

This section explicitly links the definition of 'goods' to that of 'property', defined within section 4 and discussed earlier.[132] Therefore, (almost) everything that qualifies as property under section 4 will also be 'goods' for the purposes of section 22. Although there has been some doubt whether things in action (eg bank account credit) can constitute goods for the purpose of this offence, it is now clear that they can.[133] The only exception to the equivalence between property and goods is in relation to land: certain non-severed fixtures are capable of constituting property, whereas they will not be goods for the purpose of this offence unless severed.

9.5.1.2 Stolen

In order for the handling offence to apply, it must be demonstrated that the property was in fact 'stolen'.[134] This is set out in section 24 of the TA 1968.

> (4) For purposes of the provisions of this Act relating to goods which have been stolen . . . goods obtained in England or Wales or elsewhere either by blackmail or . . . by fraud . . . shall be regarded as stolen; and 'steal', 'theft' and 'thief' shall be construed accordingly.

The types of property that are classed as stolen goods for the purposes of this offence extend beyond those that are acquired by theft. Goods can be stolen through theft,[135] robbery,[136] burglary,[137] blackmail,[138] or fraud.[139] D need not personally have committed the relevant offence (leading to the 'stolen' status), but it must be demonstrated that someone did. This is discussed in *Defazio v DPP*.

 Defazio v DPP [2007] EWHC 3529 (Admin)

V's missing credit card was found in D's house. D was charged with handling stolen goods.

---

[132] See **9.2.2.**
[133] *AG's Reference (No 4 of 1979)* [1981] 1 All ER 1193.
[134] If the goods are not stolen, but D believes they are, she may be liable for an attempted handling offence (*Haughton v Smith* [1975] AC 476), see **Chapter 11.**
[135] See **9.2.**
[136] See **9.3.**
[137] See **9.4.**
[138] See **9.6.**
[139] **Chapter 10.**

- Magistrates' court: guilty of handling stolen goods.
- High Court: appeal allowed. The fact that the card was found does not mean that it was stolen: D had claimed that he found the card on the street and merely forgot to hand it in.

Where goods are found and there is some doubt as to their status, the fact that D has been told by another that they are stolen is not sufficient to demonstrate that they are stolen in fact.[140] However, other material evidence, such as D witnessing the goods being stolen; buying them in extremely suspicious circumstances; and/or for an unrealistically low price, may be sufficient.[141]

The types of property that can be classed as stolen under this section also extend beyond the property that was originally acquired through theft, robbery, etc. This is set out in section 24(2) of the TA 1968.

(2) For purposes of those provisions references to stolen goods shall include, in addition to the goods originally stolen and parts of them (whether in their original state or not),—

(a) any other goods which directly or indirectly represent or have at any time represented the stolen goods in the hands of the thief as being the proceeds of any disposal or realisation of the whole or part of the goods stolen or of goods so representing the stolen goods; and

(b) any other goods which directly or indirectly represent or have at any time represented the stolen goods in the hands of a handler of the stolen goods or any part of them as being the proceeds of any disposal or realisation of the whole or part of the stolen goods handled by him or of goods so representing them.

This means that, in certain cases, it will be necessary to trace the stolen goods, or their proceeds. The operation of this subsection is best illustrated by way of an example. Let us imagine that P steals an iPhone and then sells it to X for £100, and X then sells the phone to D. In line with section 24(2)(a), despite gaining the phone third-hand, D may still be liable for handling stolen goods if she has the requisite mens rea. This will be the case even if X did not commit the offence of handling because her conduct in relation to the phone was not accompanied by mens rea. In line with section 24(2)(b), it is also possible to trace the proceeds of stolen goods. Thus, where P sells the phone she stole to X for £100, the money P receives from X (the proceeds of the stolen goods) becomes stolen property in its own right. This will also be the case for D if she goes on to sell or exchange the goods bought from X. However, D's money received by X (who did *not* commit a handling offence in relation to the original goods) does not constitute stolen goods: the money received by X is not money 'in the hands of a handler of stolen goods'.

Section 24(3) sets out when goods cease to be stolen, and thus cannot form the basis of the offence when handled.

(3) But no goods shall be regarded as having continued to be stolen goods after they have been restored to the person from whom they were stolen or to other lawful possession or custody, or after that person and any other person claiming through him have otherwise ceased as regards those goods to have any right to restitution in respect of the theft.

---

[140] This is evidence of D's belief only: *Marshall* [1977] Crim LR 106.
[141] *Korniak* (1983) 76 Cr App R 145: D buying jewellery from a stranger for a very low price.

The result of this section is that where the police (or owner) regain lawful possession, the goods cease to be stolen. In such a case, where D retakes control of the goods, she is guilty of theft rather than handling stolen goods. Interesting questions emerge about what constitutes being 'restored' to an owner or custody, as in *AG's Reference (No 1 of 1974)*.

 AG's Reference (No 1 of 1974) [1974] 2 All ER 899

A police officer immobilised D's car while D was absent from it and kept watch for D's return, correctly suspecting the car contained stolen goods. D returned, and was questioned by the officer. In view of his unsatisfactory responses, D was arrested and the car searched. D was charged with handling stolen goods.

- Crown Court: not guilty of handling stolen goods. When immobilising the car, the police officer effectively took control of (restored) the goods. Thus, when D came to the car, the goods were no longer stolen.
- Court of Appeal: whether the officer had restored the goods was a question of fact for the jury, taking account of the officer's intentions. Thus, the judge at first instance was wrong not to allow this issue to be decided by the jury.

9.5.1.3 Handling

The section 22 offence specifies a number of ways (as many as 18) through which the stolen goods may be handled.

> (1) A person handles stolen goods if . . . he . . . receives the goods, or . . . undertakes or assists in their retention, removal, disposal or realisation by or for the benefit of another person, or if he arranges to do so.

Several of these terms require explanation.

A) **Receives or arranges to receive:** This is the only form of handling that does not have to be 'by or for the benefit of another person'. Thus, where D is not acting for another, this is the only potential route to liability. D receives goods where she gains possession or control from another.[142] This will typically involve physical possession, but is wide enough to include joint control, as where the goods are held by X, but X is acting as an agent of D.[143] Acts of arranging to receive will also be included as where D agrees to receive the goods from X.[144] However, the simple fact that the goods are found on D's premises will not be sufficient; it must be shown that they are there by D's invitation or agreement: receiving requires D's active participation.[145]

B) **Retention, removal, disposal, realisation:** Alongside receiving, these terms represent the other form of handling. 'Retention' requires D to act in a manner that

---

[142] 'From another' is important. Where D simply finds stolen goods, she does not receive them: *Haider* (1985) unreported.
[143] *Miller* (1854) 6 Cox CC 353; *Smith* (1855) Dears CC 494.
[144] *King* [1938] 2 All ER 662.
[145] *Cavendish* [1961] 2 All ER 856.

will make it more likely that stolen goods are kept (eg storing them for X).[146] Simple use of the goods is not sufficient.[147] 'Removal' requires D to assist with moving the goods from one location to another even if D never gains possession or control.[148] 'Disposal' requires D to destroy or sell/exchange the stolen goods.[149] 'Realisation' requires D to exchange the goods for money or other property, and as such, overlaps with disposal.[150]

C) Arranging or assisting: Just as 'receiving' extends to arranging to receive, the same is true of the other forms of handling defined above. For example, D arranges to dispose when she agrees with another to sell the stolen goods. However, beyond that which is applicable to receiving, D may also handle stolen goods under these other headings through acts of assisting or encouraging the retention, removal, disposal, or realisation of the goods. For example, lying to the police to allow the goods to be retained by X.[151] To assist, it must be shown that D actively encouraged or helped X; simply benefiting from another's handling is not sufficient.[152] When combined, these qualifications even allow for handling where D arranges to assist X to retain, remove, dispose, or realise.

D) For the benefit of another: Apart from in cases of receiving or arranging to receive (as in point A above), it must be shown that D has acted (handled) for the benefit of another. This requirement keeps the offence within limits, avoiding every theft also being an incident of handling. With this in mind, the requirement has been interpreted narrowly in *Bloxham* to apply only where D is acting on behalf of another.

 Bloxham [1983] 1 AC 109

D purchased a car from P, unaware that it was stolen. D later came to suspect that the car was stolen and sold it to X. D was charged with handling stolen goods.

- Crown Court: guilty of handling stolen goods.
- Court of Appeal: conviction upheld on appeal.
- House of Lords: appeal allowed. D clearly disposed of the stolen goods, but did not do so for the benefit of another. Although the buyer of the car (X) may have benefited, it was not sold by D for X's benefit.

9.5.2 Mens rea of s22

There are two main mens rea elements: knowledge or belief that the goods are stolen, and dishonesty.

---

[146] *Pitchley* (1972) 57 Cr App R 30.
[147] *Sanders* (1982) 75 Cr App R 84: D used a stolen heater and battery charger in his father's garage.
[148] *Gleed* (1916) 12 Cr App R 32.
[149] *Watson* [1916] 2 KB 385.
[150] *Bloxham* [1983] 1 AC 109.
[151] *Kanwar* (1982) 75 Cr App R 87.
[152] *Coleman* [1986] Crim LR 56: D's knowledge that his wife was using stolen money to pay their joint solicitor's fees did not, of itself, amount to assisting.

9.5.2.1 Knowledge or belief that the goods are stolen

D must know or believe that the goods are stolen. These are subjective mens rea terms and, as such, it will not be sufficient to show that a reasonable person would have believed or known.[153] It must be proved that D believed or knew.[154]

It is clear that suspicion or recklessness that the goods are stolen will never be sufficient.[155] Interestingly, it has also been held that wilful blindness will not be sufficient either.[156] Thus, where D is suspicious but actively avoids looking deeper in order to remain ignorant, although this may amount to a form of knowledge in other contexts,[157] this will not be the case for the purposes of handling stolen goods.

9.5.2.2 Dishonesty

The requirement of dishonesty requires us to apply the *Ghosh* test discussed previously.[158] It must be demonstrated that (a) D's acts of handling were dishonest by the standards of honest and reasonable people; and (b) D realised that her actions would be so regarded. In most cases where D handles stolen goods knowing or believing that they are stolen, it will not be difficult to demonstrate dishonesty. The exception may be where D handles the goods with an intention to return them to the owner or the police.[159]

> **Extra detail . . .**
> Similar and overlapping offences of money laundering are used in tandem with the offence of handling stolen goods. The main offences of money laundering are found in the Proceeds of Crime Act 2002. We do not discuss these offences further in this book.[160]

9.6 Blackmail

The offence of blackmail is defined in section 21 of the TA 1968. The maximum sentence on indictment is 14 years' imprisonment.[161]

> (1) A person is guilty of blackmail if, with a view to gain for himself or another or with intent to cause loss to another, he makes any unwarranted demand with menaces; and for this purpose a demand with menaces is unwarranted unless the person making it does so in the belief—
>
> (a) that he has reasonable grounds for making the demand; and
>
> (b) that the use of the menaces is a proper means of reinforcing the demand.

The elements of blackmail are set out in **Table 9.7**.

---

[153] See **3.4.2–3.4.3**. Griew, 'States of Mind, Presumptions and Inferences' in P Smith (ed), *Criminal Law: Essays in Honour of JC Smith* (1987) 63.
[154] *Atwal v Massey* [1971] 3 All ER 881.
[155] *Forsyth* [1997] Crim LR 581.
[156] *Griffiths* (1974) 60 Cr App R 14.
[157] See **3.4.2.1**.
[158] See **9.2.5**.
[159] *Matthews* [1950] 1 All ER 137.
[160] See *Smith and Hogan's Criminal Law* (14th edn, 2015) Ch27.
[161] TA 1968, s21(3).

Table 9.7 Blackmail

	Actus reus	Mens rea
Conduct element	D makes demands	Voluntary
Circumstance element	D uses menaces	Knowledge
Result element	None	None
Ulterior mens rea element	*	D intends to make a gain or cause a loss to another D does not believe that she has reasonable grounds to make the demands, *or*, D does not believe that the use of menaces is a proper means of reinforcing the demand

There is no single rationale for the offence of blackmail. It can be seen as needed to protect V from threats of unpleasant consequences; her privacy from invasive demands;[162] and her property which is the subject of the demand.[163] Blackmail also has an interesting structure: criminalising harmful conduct (ie the demand with menace), but also a significant ulterior element (ie D must intend to make a gain or cause a loss, but this need never come about, the offence requires no actual results at all).

9.6.1 Actus reus of s21

The actus reus of blackmail is formed of two principal elements: the making of a demand, and the use of menaces.

> **Don't be confused . . .**
> Although the 'unwarranted' nature of D's demand may appear to be an actus reus element, and is often described by courts in these terms, it is better understood as part of D's mens rea. This is because the question of whether D's demands are unwarranted depends solely upon her intentions and beliefs (ie her state of mind).

9.6.1.1 Demands

It must be proved that D made a demand in relation to another's property. This can be express or implied, as where D points a gun and asks if V might like to hand over her wallet; and it can be by any means of communication: orally, written, gesture, via an intermediary, etc.[164] Also, although the word 'demand' might imply some form of

---

[162] Alldridge, 'Attempted Murder of the Soul: Blackmail, Privacy and Secrets' (1993) 13 OJLS 368.
[163] Lamond, 'Coercion, Threats and the Puzzle of Blackmail' in Simester and Smith (eds), *Harm and Culpability* (1996) Ch10.
[164] *Treacy v DPP* [1971] AC 537.

harsh words, it is clear that the manner of the request, however polite, will still constitute a demand. In *Robinson*,[165] for example, 'Sir, I am now only making an appeal to your benevolence' was capable of being a demand. The requirement of a demand is satisfied as soon as it is made, regardless of whether V is aware of it, such as in cases where a letter is lost in the post, where V is deaf, etc.[166]

The lack of a demand as to property will be fatal to the offence. Where D catches V committing a crime (or doing anything she would rather keep secret), and V asks D if she will accept some property in exchange for her silence, there is no demand from D and therefore no blackmail. Equally, even where there is a demand from D, but that demand does not relate to property, such as where D demands sexual acts from V, again there is no blackmail.[167]

9.6.1.2 Menaces

A menace has been defined as 'any action detrimental to or unpleasant to the person addressed'.[168] Therefore, beyond threats of violence to persons or property, any threat of an unpleasant character (eg to reveal compromising information) can amount to a menace. The only restriction, preventing the offence applying in trivial circumstances, is that the menace must be 'of such a nature and extent that the mind of an ordinary person of normal stability and courage might be influenced or made apprehensive so as to accede unwillingly to the demand'.[169] This is a relatively low threshold (note the use of 'might'), but it is an objective one. Three situations should be distinguished.

A) V does not accede, but a reasonable person would: The use of an objective standard means that D's threats constitute a menace even if V is not intimidated in fact because, for example, she is particularly brave.[170]

B) V accedes, but a reasonable person would not: Again, the objective standard means that V's reaction is largely irrelevant and the question is whether a reasonable person *might* have acceded. Thus, in this context, there will be no menace, and therefore no blackmail.[171]

C) V accedes due to known vulnerabilities, but a reasonable person would not: As with point B, the result here is likely to be no menace. However, there is an exception. This arises where D has personal knowledge of V's vulnerability, such as V's infirmity, youth, timidity, etc, and so D realises that her threat will be particularly menacing to V. In this case, a menace will be found.[172]

As long as D's threats meet the objective standard required, it is irrelevant whether the menace is directed at V or another, whether the menace is carried out, or even whether it is possible for D to carry it out. This is illustrated in *Lambert*.

---

[165] (1796) 2 East PC 1110.
[166] *Treacy v DPP* [1971] AC 537: the demand was made when the letter was posted.
[167] Although D may be committing a sexual offence: **Chapter 8**.
[168] *Thorne v Motor Trade Association* [1937] AC 797, 817.
[169] *Clear* [1968] 1 All ER 74, 80.
[170] *Moran* [1952] 1 All ER 803.
[171] *Harry* [1974] Crim LR 32: V felt threatened by a note from a student charity event offering shopkeepers immunity from 'inconvenience' for payment: not sufficiently menacing.
[172] *Garwood* [1987] 1 All ER 1032: where D must have been aware of V's extreme timidity.

Lambert [2009] EWCA Crim 2860

D phoned his grandmother pretending to have been kidnapped, and asking her to send money to have him freed. D was charged with blackmail.

- Crown Court: guilty of blackmail.
- Court of Appeal: conviction upheld on appeal. D communicated a menace to V. The fact that D was also the victim of that menace, and that the whole scenario was untrue, did not matter.

9.6.2 Mens rea of s21

There are two core mens rea elements: D's demands must be unwarranted, and they must be made with the intention to make a gain or cause a loss. Both of these requirements are ulterior as they do not correspond to elements within the actus reus.[173]

> **Point to remember . . .**
> Unlike the property offences discussed earlier, blackmail does not require an element of dishonesty.

9.6.2.1 Unwarranted demands

Not all demands with menaces will constitute blackmail. For example, D demands payment of a debt from V and threatens civil legal action. Demands will only come within blackmail if they are unwarranted. In order to apply this element, we do not look to the content of the threat or the demands, although these will be useful evidence, but, rather, we look to the state of mind of D. It must be demonstrated by the Crown that (A) D did not believe that she had reasonable grounds to make the demands *or* (B) that D did not believe that the use of menaces was a proper means of reinforcing the demand.[174] Lack of either belief will suffice.

> **Extra detail . . .**
> The unwarranted requirement attempts to mitigate what some describe as the 'blackmail paradox'. The paradox is evident because D is legally entitled to make certain demands of V (eg ask V for money). D is also legally entitled to do certain things that are unpleasant for V (eg expose V's immoral activities). However, where D threatens the latter in exchange for the former, her conduct becomes criminal.[175]

A) Lack of belief in reasonable grounds for the demand: Even where D believes that it is proper to use menaces, she must also believe that she has reasonable grounds for her demands. The question is not whether she thinks her demands are correct, but whether she believes that others would agree they are reasonable.

B) Lack of belief in the propriety of menaces: More common is the case where D believes that her demands are reasonable, but lacks belief in the propriety of her menaces.

---

[173] See **4.2.1.2**.
[174] *Ashiq* [2015] EWCA Crim 1617: discussing unwarranted demands, and the Crown's legal burden.
[175] Lindgren, 'Unraveling the Paradox of Blackmail' (1984) 84 Col L Rev 670.

For example, in *Kewell*,[176] although D believed in the reasonableness of demanding the return of a debt, it was easy for the prosecution to show that D did not honestly believe that threatening to reveal embarrassing photos of V was a proper means of enforcing that debt. It has been argued that whenever D realises that her threat will involve committing a criminal offence, such as threats of unlawful violence, this will automatically undermine any claim of belief in propriety.[177] However, although this is undoubtedly very strong evidence that D did not believe that her threats were proper, it is unlikely to be conclusive in every case.

> **Extra detail . . .**
> Structuring this element in terms of mens rea can lead to two interesting results. First, even where (objectively) D's demands and use of menaces are entirely reasonable, if D lacks belief as to either she will still satisfy this element. Conversely, even where (objectively) D's demands and use of menaces are entirely unreasonable, unless the Crown can disprove D's claim that she honestly believed that both were proper, she will not satisfy this element.

9.6.2.2 A view to a gain or a loss

Although D need not make a gain or cause a loss in fact,[178] it is necessary that she made the demands with this intention. Gain and loss are defined in section 34(2)(a) of the TA 1968, refining the offence to focus on property only.[179]

> (a) 'gain' and 'loss' are to be construed as extending only to gain or loss in money or other property, but as extending to any such gain or loss whether temporary or permanent; and—
>
> (i) 'gain' includes a gain by keeping what one has, as well as a gain by getting what one has not; and
>
> (ii) 'loss' includes a loss by not getting what one might get, as well as a loss by parting with what one has;

An intention to make a gain *or* cause a loss is sufficient. For example, this element will be satisfied where D intends to cause a loss to V even though D makes no gain by, for example, demanding that V destroys an item of property. The same is also true where D intends to make a gain but not to cause a loss by, for example, demanding to be promoted, but intending to do a good job. It has been argued that where D demands something to which she is legally entitled, such as the payment of a debt, she cannot be intending to make a gain or cause a loss.[180] However, the court in *Lawrence and Pomroy*,[181] without specific discussion, seem to have assumed that such demands will still satisfy this element.

---

[176] [2000] 2 Cr App R 38.

[177] *Harvey, Ulyett and Plummer* (1981) 72 Cr App R 139.

[178] *Dooley* [2005] EWCA Crim 3093, see commentary [2006] Crim LR 544.

[179] As stated earlier, a demand of a sexual nature or other non-property demand will not come within the offence.

[180] Hogan, 'Blackmail' [1966] Crim LR 474.

[181] (1971) 57 Cr App R 64.

9.7 Criminal damage

In this section we discuss offences of criminal damage, arson, and aggravated criminal damage.[182] The basic offence of criminal damage is contained in section 1(1) of the Criminal Damage Act 1971.[183] The maximum sentence on indictment is ten years' imprisonment.[184]

(1) A person who without lawful excuse destroys or damages any property belonging to another intending to destroy or damage any such property or being reckless as to whether any such property would be destroyed or damaged shall be guilty of an offence.

The elements of criminal damage are set out in **Table 9.8**.

Table 9.8 Criminal damage

	Actus reus	**Mens rea**
Conduct element	Any conduct causing the result	Voluntary
Circumstance element	What is damaged is property	Intention or recklessness
	The property belongs to another	Intention or recklessness
Result element	Damage or destruction	Intention or recklessness

Following the enactment of the TA 1968 just three years earlier, the Criminal Damage Act 1971 attempts to create a coherent scheme of liability where D damages as opposed to appropriates another's property.

9.7.1 Actus reus of s1(1)

D commits the actus reus of criminal damage where she: (i) damages; (ii) property; (iii) belonging to another. Each requires discussion.

9.7.1.1 Damage

Damage is not defined in the statute, and is intended to carry its ordinary meaning.[185] Short of destruction, damage requires rendering property unusable and/or involves a

---

[182] There are also various offences of threatening criminal damage (Criminal Damage Act 1971, s2), possession of anything with intent to commit criminal damage (Criminal Damage Act 1971, s3), as well as more specific offences relating to dangerous materials such as explosives. These offences will not be discussed in this book. See further *Smith and Hogan's Criminal Law* (14th edn, 2015) Ch29.

[183] Following Law Commission recommendations: *Offences of Damage to Property* (No 29, 1970).

[184] Criminal Damage Act 1971, s4(2).

[185] *Roe v Kingerlee* [1986] Crim LR 735.

physical interference that reduces the value of property or costs money to repair. The benefit of this open-textured approach has been necessary flexibility, allowing similar acts to be considered as damage in one context but not another. For example, we may want to say that spitting in food is damage, but spitting on the pavement is not. However, the courts have struggled to maintain coherence.

A) Undermining usability: In *Drake v DPP*,[186] it was held that wheel clamping did not amount to damage because, although it prevents use of the vehicle, the physical integrity of the vehicle is not affected. Contrast *Fiak*,[187] where D stuffed blankets from his prison cell in the toilet and flushed repeatedly to cause a small flood. The fact that the blankets and the cell were rendered temporarily unusable led the courts to find that damage was caused.

B) Reduction in value: Equating damage with actions that reduce value seems apt in examples such as the scratching of a car: the car remains usable but there is clearly some damage.[188] However, this approach has been criticised[189] and has largely fallen out of favour.

C) Cost of repair: Recent cases have tended to focus on the cost of repair as opposed to any reduced value of the property. However, again, courts have struggled for coherence. In *A (A Juvenile)*,[190] there was no damage where D spat on a policeman's raincoat because the spittle could be easily removed with a damp cloth. Contrast *Samuels v Stubbs*,[191] where D jumped on a policeman's hat, and whilst the hat could be restored to its original state with little difficulty, the court still found that damage was caused. A useful case, demonstrating the problems for the court, is *Hardman v Chief Constable of Avon and Somerset Constabulary*.

 Hardman v Chief Constable of Avon and Somerset Constabulary [1986] Crim LR 330

D painted silhouettes on the pavement using water-soluble paints. The paint would have washed away in a few days, but the council paid for a jet wash to remove it. The issue was whether the painting constituted damage.

• Crown Court: taking account of the cost of removal, the painting constituted criminal damage.

This case seems correct in that the paint did cost the council money to remove. However, it opens several unanswered questions. For example, would it still have been damage if the council had left the paint to be removed by the rain? What about other mess that we leave for the council (or rain) to clear up?[192] What about graffiti that people appreciate, and D anticipates will be appreciated?[193]

---

[186] [1994] RTR 411. Note, this may now constitute a separate offence.
[187] [2005] EWCA Crim 2381.
[188] *Foster* (1852) 6 Cox CC 25.
[189] Smith, *Property Offences* (1994) para 27.16.
[190] [1978] Crim LR 689.
[191] [1972] 4 SASR 200.
[192] Alldridge, 'Incontinent Dogs and the Law' (1990) 140 NLJ 1067.
[193] Edwards, 'Banksy's Graffiti: A Not So Simple Case' (2009) 73 J Crim L 345.

9.7.1.2 Property

Property is defined by section 10(1) of the Criminal Damage Act 1971.

> (1) In this Act 'property' means property of a tangible nature, whether real or personal, including money and—
>
> > (a) including wild creatures which have been tamed or are ordinarily kept in captivity, and any other wild creatures or their carcasses if, but only if, they have been reduced into possession which has not been lost or abandoned or are in the course of being reduced into possession; but
> >
> > (b) not including mushrooms growing wild on any land or flowers, fruit or foliage of a plant growing wild on any land.
>
> For the purposes of this subsection 'mushroom' includes any fungus and 'plant' includes any shrub or tree.

This definition, particularly subsections (a) and (b), is broadly consistent with the definition of property in the TA 1968.[194] However, there are three important differences.

- Land cannot generally be the subject of theft. However, the same logic does not apply to criminal damage. For example, D may not be able to steal her neighbour's garden, but can certainly damage it. Land is property in this context.
- Intangible property, such as bank account credit, copyright, etc, is property for theft, but will not constitute property for criminal damage. Criminal damage is isolated to physical damage to tangible property only.
- Wild plants/fungi can be property for theft if picked with a commercial intention, but this will not be the case for criminal damage. Plants/fungi growing wild will not be property for the purposes of criminal damage.

9.7.1.3 Belonging to another

It is not an offence under section 1(1) for D to damage her own property. There are exceptional situations where the law creates separate offences to prevent even an owner from damaging their property, as with offences dealing with cruelty to animals. Belonging to another is defined in section 10(2)–(4) of the Criminal Damage Act 1971.

> (2) Property shall be treated for the purposes of this Act as belonging to any person—
>
> > (a) having the custody or control of it;
> >
> > (b) having in it any proprietary right or interest (not being an equitable interest arising only from an agreement to transfer or grant an interest); or
> >
> > (c) having a charge on it.

[194] See **9.2.2**.

(3) Where property is subject to a trust, the persons to whom it belongs shall be so treated as including any person having a right to enforce the trust.

(4) Property of a corporation sole shall be so treated as belonging to the corporation notwithstanding a vacancy in the corporation.

As with 'belonging to another' in the context of theft, discussed earlier,[195] it is not fatal to conviction if D had some proprietary interest in the property, as long as another person also had some proprietary interest. Thus, this element will be satisfied where D damages property that she co-owns with another, or in which another has even a minor proprietary interest as, for example, where the property is loaned to V.[196]

9.7.2 Mens rea of s1(1)

There are two principal elements to the mens rea. First, it must be shown that D intended, or was at least reckless, as to causing damage to the property. Secondly, D must also have intended/known or been reckless as to the fact that the property belonged to another. This second element of the mens rea should not be forgotten, as illustrated in *Smith*.

Smith [1974] QB 354

At the end of D's tenancy, he removed a length of wiring that he had installed, causing £130 worth of damage. Under civil law, following its installation, the wiring belonged to D's landlord. However, D was unaware of this, believing that it belonged to him. D was charged with criminal damage.

- Crown Court: guilty of criminal damage.
- Court of Appeal: appeal allowed. D did not know, and did not foresee a risk, that the wiring did not belong to him. D lacked an essential element of the mens rea.

The mens rea terms 'intention' and 'recklessness' were discussed in **Chapter 3**. It will be remembered that much of the debate and flux relating to the definition of recklessness has focused on criminal damage cases, including the leading case of *G*.[197]

9.7.3 Defences to criminal damage

In addition to the general defences such as duress, necessity, etc,[198] section 5 of the Criminal Damage Act 1971 also provides two specific defences: belief in consent; and protection of property.

(2) A person charged with an offence to which this section applies, shall, . . . be treated for those purposes as having a lawful excuse—

(a) if at the time of the act or acts alleged to constitute the offence he believed that the person or persons whom he believed to be entitled to consent to the destruction of or damage to

---

[195] See **9.2.3**.
[196] This does not extend to insurers of goods, as they hold no proprietary interest: *Denton* [1982] 1 All ER 65.
[197] [2004] AC 1034.
[198] **Chapters 13** and **14**.

the property in question had so consented, or would have so consented to it if he or they had known of the destruction or damage and its circumstances; or

(b) if he destroyed or damaged . . . in order to protect property belonging to himself or another or a right or interest in property which was or which he believed to be vested in himself or another, and at the time of the act or acts alleged to constitute the offence he believed—

   (i) that the property, right or interest was in immediate need of protection; and

   (ii) that the means of protection adopted . . . were . . . reasonable having regard to all the circumstances.

(3) For the purposes of this section it is immaterial whether a belief is justified or not if it is honestly held.

(4) For the purposes of subsection (2) above a right or interest in property includes any right or privilege in or over land, whether created by grant, licence or otherwise.

9.7.3.1 Belief in consent defence

Section 5(2)(a) provides a belief in consent defence. As confirmed by section 5(3), the test is simply whether D honestly believed that the owner did or would have consented to her causing damage, even if that belief was not reasonable. In *Denton*,[199] for example, there was no criminal damage where D honestly believed that the owner of a mill had encouraged him to burn it down, even though the reason for that belief was based on insurance fraud. Although, note that belief (however honest) that God is the owner, and would have consented, will not be sufficient.[200]

It should be remembered that even where the owner would not have consented and/or the person consenting does not have the authority to do so, and even where this would have been clear to a reasonable person, D may still satisfy the defence if she *honestly* believes that both requirements are satisfied. One of the more controversial mistake cases is *Jaggard v Dickinson*.[201] In this case, D had permission from X to treat X's house as her own. However, when arriving heavily intoxicated at what she mistakenly believed was X's house, D broke a window in V's house in order to gain entry. Her defence to criminal damage under section 5(2)(a) was accepted. Although rather shocking, the problem with this case may be the court's treatment of her intoxicated state (concluding that it made no difference) rather than the defence itself. We discuss this further in **Chapter 13**.

9.7.3.2 Belief in protection of property defence

Section 5(2)(b) creates a defence for belief in the protection of property, as where D damages a fence in order to protect/enforce her right of way, or shoots a dog to protect cattle, etc.[202] There are three main elements to this defence: belief that D or another has a vested interest in the property protected; belief that that property is in immediate need

---

[199] [1982] 1 All ER 65.
[200] *Blake v DPP* [1993] Crim LR 586.
[201] [1980] 3 All ER 716. See criticism in *Magee v CPS* [2014] EWHC 4089 (Admin).
[202] The 'threat' protected from need not be a criminal act: *Jones* [2005] QB 259.

of protection; and belief that the means of protection (ie the damage caused) is reasonable. D must have belief as to all three.

A) **Belief in vested interest:** D must believe that she or another has a vested interest in property that she is acting to protect by damaging other property.[203] She must also believe that her action is necessary 'in order to' protect that property. This sounds like a subjective requirement (did D honestly believe?), but following *Hunt*, has been given a mixed subjective/objective meaning.

 Hunt (1977) 66 Cr App R 105

D, who was assisting his wife as a warden at a set of retirement flats, set fire to some bedding in order to draw attention to the defective fire alarms. D claimed a section 5(2)(b) defence, saying that he was acting to protect the properties from future risks. D was charged with arson which requires proof of criminal damage.

- Crown Court: guilty of arson.
- Court of Appeal: conviction upheld on appeal. Whether D's acts were capable of protecting the property (were 'in order to') is an objective question. Here, D's acts provided no protection.

It is counter-intuitive to interpret a requirement of 'belief' in an objective way. However, *Hunt* has been confirmed in further judgments.[204] What is necessary, therefore, is to ask what D believes (subjectively), and then to ask if this belief in protection has any reasonable (objective) basis.

Extra detail . . .
It is open to future courts to interpret this element subjectively, which would be preferable. Defendants in cases like *Hunt* should not be able to claim the defence owing to the apparent lack of 'immediate' need; there is no need to read in an objective limb here.

B) **Belief in immediate need:** This element has been interpreted to be part subjective and part objective. First, the court must ascertain the subjective beliefs that D held at the time: how soon did she believe, reasonably or not, that the property would be in danger? Secondly, the court must decide (objectively) whether D's belief amounted to a belief of an 'immediate' need. Whether D would classify it as immediate is irrelevant.[205]

C) **Belief in reasonableness of methods:** This is a subjective requirement: we ask whether D believed her methods were reasonable, not whether others would so regard them. Even where D cuts down large parts of her neighbour's trees in order to protect her right to light, if she honestly believes that this is a reasonable method, and the jury believe she is or may be telling the truth, then the defence will be available.[206]

---

[203] *Cresswell v DPP* [2006] EWHC 3379 (Admin).
[204] *Hill and Hall* (1988) 89 Cr App R 74: D could not use the defence when damaging an air-force base in order to protect surrounding properties from being targeted by enemy forces.
[205] *Jones* [2005] QB 259.
[206] *DPP v Unsworth* [2010] EWHC 3037 (Admin).

9.7.4 Arson

Arson is preserved as a separate offence from simple criminal damage by section 1(3) of the Criminal Damage Act 1971. The maximum penalty on indictment is life imprisonment.[207]

> (3) An offence committed under this section by destroying or damaging property by fire shall be charged as arson.

The structure of arson is illustrated simply in **Figure 9.4**.

Figure 9.4 Arson

All elements of the criminal damage offence must be satisfied. Additionally, it must be demonstrated that D caused the damage by fire, and that her intention or recklessness was to cause the damage by fire. Thus, where D causes damage other that by fire, such as smoke damage, or intentionally causes damage to property that results unexpectedly in fire, there will be no liability for arson, although D may still be liable for criminal damage.[208]

9.7.4.1 Defences to arson

D may rely on the general defences such as duress, necessity, etc.[209] D may also rely on the specific defences under section 5 discussed earlier.[210]

9.7.5 Aggravated criminal damage

Aggravated criminal damage and aggravated arson are also separate offences under section 1(2) of the Criminal Damage Act 1971. The maximum sentence on indictment is life imprisonment.[211]

> (2) A person who without lawful excuse destroys or damages any property, whether belonging to himself or another—
>
> > (a) intending to destroy or damage any property or being reckless as to whether any property would be destroyed or damaged; and
> >
> > (b) intending by the destruction or damage to endanger the life of another or being reckless as to whether the life of another would be thereby endangered;<p>shall be guilty of an offence.

---

[207] Criminal Damage Act 1971, s4(1).
[208] *Drayton* [2006] Crim LR 243.
[209] **Chapters 13** and **14**.
[210] See **9.7.3**.
[211] Criminal Damage Act 1971, s4(1).

The structure of aggravated criminal damage/arson is illustrated simply in **Figure 9.5**.

Figure 9.5 Aggravated criminal damage

Aggravated criminal damage can be constructed upon either criminal damage or arson, even where the damage is to D's own property. The aggravating element is that D must intend or be reckless as to the endangerment of life by the damage she intended to cause, or was reckless about causing.

9.7.5.1 Actus reus of aggravated criminal damage

The actus reus of aggravated criminal damage, for the most part, simply mirrors that of criminal damage or arson. However, crucially, the actus reus of this offence may also be satisfied where damage is caused to D's own property. Even where D burns down her own house, for example, or takes a hammer to her own car, she will complete the actus reus.[212]

Although, as we discuss later, D must intend or be reckless as to the endangerment of life, there is no need for endangerment of life in fact. This is not part of the actus reus. In *Parker*,[213] for example, D was liable for aggravated criminal damage where he started a fire in his semi-detached house and foresaw a risk to the lives of his neighbours. This was the case even though his neighbours were unharmed, and even though they were not even in their house at the time such that the fire could not have actually endangered them.

9.7.5.2 Mens rea of aggravated criminal damage

The mens rea of aggravated criminal damage requires D to satisfy all the mens rea requirements of the base offence of criminal damage or arson discussed previously. *Additionally*, it must also be proved that D acted with the intention or was reckless as to the possibility of another person's life being endangered.[214]

D must intend or foresee endangerment arising from the damage of property that she intended or was reckless that she might cause (this is the nexus to the property offence),

---

[212] *Merrick* [1996] 1 Cr App R 130: D, with the owner's permission, exposed a cable reckless as to endangerment. There are also several cases of attempted suicide reckless as to endangerment, eg where D burns down her own house, eg, *Brewis* [2004] EWCA Crim 1919.

[213] [1993] Crim LR 856.

[214] Foresight of self-endangerment is not sufficient. *Thakar* [2010] EWCA Crim 2136: D set fire to his car when depressed following divorce.

and so foresight of endangerment from D's acts alone is not sufficient: it has to be *by* the damage. This was discussed in *Steer*.

 Steer [1988] AC 111

D shot a rifle at the windows of V's house, against whom he had a grudge, breaking the windows (criminal damage) and foreseeing the endangerment of V. D was charged with aggravated criminal damage.

- Crown Court: guilty of aggravated criminal damage.
- Court of Appeal: appeal allowed. D was reckless as to the endangerment of V from his acts (ie shooting the rifle), he was not reckless as to the endangerment of V 'by the destruction or damage of property' (ie from the broken glass from the window). Aggravated criminal damage is only satisfied by the latter.
- House of Lords: appeal dismissed, confirming the reasoning of the Court of Appeal.

The result of this case is that D will be liable for aggravated criminal damage where she foresees the endangerment of life *by* the damage she intended (eg demolishing a building that might fall on someone, breaking a gas pipe that might poison someone, etc[215]); but not where the damage is simply incidental (eg throwing a bat that might hit someone, and may also damage property). This may seem a fine and perhaps unnecessary distinction, but the House of Lords recognised that to hold otherwise would lead to undesirable results. Lord Bridge in *Steer* provided the following example:

> If A and B both discharge firearms in a public place, being reckless as to whether life would be endangered, it would be absurd that A, who incidentally causes some trifling damage to property, should be guilty of an offence punishable with life imprisonment, but that B, who causes no damage, should be guilty of no offence.

The point being made here is that our criminal law does not recognise a general offence of endangerment which would apply to reckless acts where no harm is caused,[216] and aggravated criminal damage should not be manipulated/misapplied into filling that role.

Extra detail . . .
Criminal damage under section 1(1) can alternatively be aggravated if it is accompanied by racial or religious hatred.[217] The mechanism for such aggravation is discussed at **7.9.2** in relation to offences against the person, but applies in the same way for racially or religiously aggravated criminal damage.[218]

9.7.5.3 Defences to aggravated criminal damage

D may rely on the general defences such as duress, necessity, etc.[219] However, the specific defences under section 2 do not apply to aggravated criminal damage: belief in the

---

[215] *Cunningham* [1957] 2 QB 396: breaking a gas pipe.
[216] Duff, 'Criminalising Endangerment' in Duff and Green (eds), *Defining Crimes* (2005) Ch3.
[217] Crime and Disorder Act 1998, s30.
[218] *DPP v M* [2005] Crim LR 392.
[219] **Chapters 13** and **14**.

owner's permission and/or protection of property will not excuse causing damage that might endanger a person's life.

9.8 Reform

There are numerous areas of confusion and seeming incoherence in relation to property offences, and many of the academic articles referred to in this chapter are calling for some manner of reform. In this section we focus on just one of these debates: how to define the offence of theft, although we use it to highlight questions that are common among many of the property offences.

When considering reform of property offences it is important to remember that, despite some quite powerful criticism in certain specific areas and despite a flurry of appeals cases between the 1970s and 1990s in particular, the law has been relatively settled during the last 15 years. This is not to say that reform is no longer desirable, but that stability should caution against reform that is likely to result in renewed uncertainty.

9.8.1 Defining theft

The discussion here is whether the elements of theft, as currently interpreted, are fairly and coherently targeting their intended mischief. There are two parts to this debate.

The first part of the debate is to identify the mischief of theft: what is the offence designed to target? The most obvious answer to this, and the one we began the chapter with, is that theft is designed to protect property rights. Thus, the mischief of theft is any violation of those rights. However, this is not sufficient. Where V lends D her car, for example, D gains possession and so interferes with V's property rights, but there is nothing wrongful here, and certainly nothing deserving of criminalisation. Thus, there must be something more, beyond simple interference with property rights, that justifies the use of criminal law.

At one time, this additional wrong or harm may have been identified in D's 'manifestly criminal' appropriation: theft being a *non-consensual* interference with property rights.[220] However, following *Gomez*,[221] an appropriation can be found even where V consents. Without this additional 'wrong' within the actus reus of the offence, much of the work necessary to isolate theft to those deserving of criminalisation is instead done within the mens rea, and particularly the requirement of dishonesty. Some believe that this has led to the offence becoming unacceptably broad in its application, potentially applying to minor acts of preparation that outwardly suggest little wrongdoing, such as touching an item in the supermarket with the requisite mens rea.[222]

Perhaps the most controversial point of this debate, however, relates to cases where theft has been found even though there has been no breach of civil law and no property rights have been infringed. The clearest example of this is *Hinks*,[223] where D dishonestly

---

[220] The term manifest criminality was coined by Fletcher, *Rethinking Criminal Law* (1978) 82. It means that D's external conduct is obviously wrongful.

[221] [1993] AC 442.

[222] For a good summary of the debate, see Shute, 'Appropriation and the Law of Theft' [2002] Crim LR 445.

[223] [2000] 4 All ER 833.

took advantage of a vulnerable person although the gifts from V were valid in civil law. Cases like *Hinks* are central to our identification and understanding of the mischief of theft, suggesting that the offence is targeting dishonest appropriation more generally, and not, as had generally been assumed, being structured by civil property rules. Academics have responded to *Hinks* in three main ways. For some, the inconsistency with civil law is unproblematic, and the criminal law of theft should go beyond the wrongs of civil law to protect against dishonest appropriation more generally.[224] However, a majority of commentators have seen the developing split from civil law as problematic. Within this group, many have criticised *Hinks* as a wrong turn losing sight of the specific mischief (anchored by civil law breaches) that theft should be targeting.[225] Also within this group, there has developed an interesting line of analysis that sees the split as problematic but places the fault for that split with unduly narrow interpretations of the civil law.[226]

A final, but vital part of this first debate relates to the overlap between the expanding mischief of theft and fraud offences. We discuss fraud in **Chapter 10** and will return to this debate there. Basically, the argument is that theft and fraud are designed to protect property rights in different ways, targeting and separately labelling different wrongs: theft should target non-consensual appropriation, whereas fraud should target deceptive consensual appropriation. On this view, the expansion of theft in *Gomez* and *Hinks* has broken down the distinction, potentially leading to inappropriate convictions and labelling.[227] The argument against this, from Gardner in particular, has been that overlapping offences are useful to ensure all criminally deserving cases are covered, particularly in relation to protection of the vulnerable where it may be difficult to demonstrate deception.[228] Although this argument is well put, following the reform of fraud offences within the Fraud Act 2006, where proof of deception is no longer required, it is debatable whether this justification for overlap still holds.

Point to remember . . .

Debate about the identification of the rationale of an offence is also central to academic discussion of several other property offences discussed in this chapter. This is particularly true where the offence contains a requirement of harm or endangerment of a person, leading us to consider whether the gravamen of the offence is the protection of property or the person.[229]

The second part of the debate, having discussed what the offence is attempting to achieve, is to analyse the appropriateness of its elements. If we agree that the offence of theft should be protecting against the dishonest appropriation of all property rights, or dishonest appropriation more generally, then it may be contended that the current rules are

---

[224] Bogg and Stanton-Ife, 'Theft as Exploitation' (2003) 23 LS 402.
[225] Simester and Sullivan, 'The Nature and Rationale of Property Offences' in Duff and Green (eds), *Defining Crimes* (2005).
[226] Green, 'Theft and Conversion—Tangibly Different' (2012) 128 LQR 564: discussing the interpretation of 'property' within the two regimes.
[227] Shute and Horder, 'Thieving and Deceiving: What is the Difference?' (1993) 56 MLR 548; Melissaris, 'The Concept of Appropriation and the Offence of Theft' (2007) 70 MLR 597; Green, *Thirteen Ways to Steal a Bicycle* (2012).
[228] Gardner, 'Appropriation in Theft: The Last Word?' (1993) 109 LQR 194.
[229] eg robbery. Ashworth, 'Robbery Reassessed' [2002] Crim LR 851.

too narrowly drawn. Glanville Williams, for example, makes the case that even where D's intention is to deprive V temporarily (ie not permanently) of her property, this may still have a similarly detrimental effect on V's rights, and be deserving of criminalisation.[230] Lacey, Wells, and Quick go even further to suggest that the elements of theft could be expanded to protect other rights, such as environmental and welfare rights.[231] Where the mischief of theft is identified broadly in terms of dishonest appropriation, even this level of broadening may seem appropriate.

A related discussion, if the wrong of dishonesty lies at the heart of theft and many other property offences, is whether the current definition of dishonesty is sufficient to distinguish between those deserving and not deserving of liability. When discussing the definition of dishonesty and the *Ghosh* test mentioned earlier,[232] we highlighted several problems with relying on the jury to identify common standards of honesty without legislative guidance. In the most thorough critique of the current approach, Edward Griew highlights several problems including the lack of consistency, the lack of objectivity, a tendency towards longer and more complex trials, etc.[233] However, despite these problems, it is interesting to note the even greater emphasis on dishonesty within the Fraud Act 2006, implying that perhaps the current definition of dishonesty (although flawed) lacks a more acceptable alternative.

Finally, a further discussion relating to the construction of theft and other property offences contends that there should be some distinction between amounts or types of property appropriated. In this regard, it is interesting to note that whilst offences against the person (**Chapters 5–7**) are standardly constructed to take account of the *degree* of harm suffered by V, and only exceptionally in terms of the *method* of that infliction, property offences tend to be the opposite. And this is despite research showing that the public does see a moral difference between different degrees of theft, such as the values of the property taken and/or types of property.[234] Rearranging property offences to reflect degrees of harm would represent a fundamental shift from current practice.

9.9 Eye on assessment

In this section we consider the potential application of property offences within a problem question, using the same structure of analysis discussed in previous chapters.

> **STEP 1 Identify the potential criminal event in the facts**
>
> This should be simply stated (eg 'The first potential criminal event arises where D takes the iPhone'). The role of this stage is to highlight which part of the question you are answering before you begin to apply the law.

[230] Williams, 'Temporary Appropriation Should Be Theft' [1981] Crim LR 129.
[231] Lacey, Wells, and Quick, *Reconstructing Criminal Law* (4th edn, 2010) 399.
[232] See **9.2.5**.
[233] Griew, 'Dishonesty: The Objections to *Feely* and *Ghosh*' [1985] Crim LR 341.
[234] Green and Kugler, 'Community Perceptions of Theft Seriousness' (2010) 7 J Em LS 511.

For most criminal offences, this stage is quite straightforward. However, particularly in relation to property offences, you need to take extra care. This is because, as well as obvious potential criminal events (eg D snatches V's wallet, D smashes V's vase, etc), many of the offences discussed can arise from what might appear to be quite innocent conduct when accompanied by mens rea. For example, any touching of another's property could be theft, any trespass could be section 9(1)(a) burglary, and so on. Take care not to miss potential crimes; read the question facts carefully.[235]

In addition, when dealing with a potential theft, it should be remembered that a single taking might include more than one act of appropriation. For example, where D takes physical control of the property (appropriation by control) and then later decides to keep it (appropriation of ownership rights). Although there may be only one crime in these cases, you are given a choice of conduct elements: a choice of where to identify the potentially criminal event. You should focus on the one that is most likely to find liability. Thus, in our example, if the first act of taking control was not accompanied with an intention to keep the item, then this appropriation will not be theft because D did not, at this point, have an intention permanently to deprive. You should therefore highlight the second act of appropriation (D's decision to keep the item) as the one that is most likely to lead to liability, and therefore focus your discussion of the offence on that moment.

> **STEP 2 Identify the potential offence**
>
> Again, state this simply (eg 'When taking V's iPhone, D may be liable for theft'). The role of this stage is to highlight which offence you are going to apply.

Identifying the relevant offence can also be quite challenging in relation to property offences, partly because of the overlap between offences and partly because of the common use of aggravating elements. Where more than one offence could apply to the same potentially criminal event, our advice in previous chapters has been to apply the most serious potential offence first. This advice also holds true for property offences. However, a distinction should be made between entirely separate and more serious offences (eg the difference between theft and aggravated burglary), and more serious offences that include the lesser offence with the addition of an aggravating element (eg the difference between criminal damage and racially aggravated criminal damage). Where you are dealing with a choice between offences in the first category, it always makes sense to apply the more serious offence first. However, where you are dealing with aggravating elements, it is often clearer to apply the base offence first and then to consider whether the aggravating factor applies to satisfy the more serious offence.

In relation to the property offences discussed in this chapter, this approach is illustrated in **Table 9.9**.

---

[235] Also, as always, be guided by the question as well as the facts (eg if the question asks you to consider theft only, then these potential criminal events are the only relevant ones to highlight).

Table 9.9 Identifying and applying property offences

Starting offence	Offence following aggravation
Where D appropriates property—first consider liability for **theft**	If D satisfies the elements of theft, go on to consider the following potential aggravations: • Does D use force—robbery • Is D trespassing—s9(1)(b) burglary • Where there is s9(1)(b) burglary, does D use a weapon—aggravated burglary
Where D trespasses into another's building or part of a building—first consider liability for **s9(1)(a) burglary**	If D satisfies the elements of s9(1)(a) burglary, go on to consider the following potential aggravations: • Does D use a weapon—aggravated burglary
Where D has trespassed into another's building or part of building, and then harms someone or attempts to harm someone or attempts to steal—first consider liability for **s9(1)(b) burglary**	If D satisfies the elements of s9(1)(b) burglary, go on to consider the following potential aggravations: • Does D use a weapon—aggravated burglary
Where D comes into possession of stolen property, or the proceeds of stolen property—consider liability for **handling stolen goods**	*
Where D threatens V, making demands in relation to property—consider liability for **blackmail**	*
Where D damages another's property—first consider liability for **s1(1) criminal damage**	If D satisfies the elements of s1(1) criminal damage, go on to consider the following potential aggravations: • Is there any racial or religious hatred—racial or religiously aggravated criminal damage • Is the damage caused by fire—arson • Is D at least reckless as to the endangerment of others' lives—aggravated criminal damage
Where D damages her own property—first consider liability for **s1(2) aggravated criminal damage**	If D satisfies the elements of s1(2) aggravated criminal damage, go on to consider the following potential aggravations: • Is the damage caused by fire—aggravated arson

When applying the law to problem facts, you therefore need to choose between the 'starting offences' in the left-hand column, applying the most serious potential offence. If the elements of that offence are satisfied, you should go on to consider whether that offence can be upgraded by one of the aggravating elements detailed in the right-hand column.

When discussing aggravating elements, it is common for courts and commentators to describe the process as 'constructing' upon the base offence. This is accurate, but you should take care not to confuse it with 'constructive liability', which is a specific label given to offences that include a constructive strict liability element.[236] The offences discussed in this chapter are not constructive crimes in this more specific sense. To avoid confusion and mislabelling, it may be best to avoid language like 'construction' in the context of property offences entirely.

STEP 3 Applying the offence to the facts

Having identified the relevant offence make sure you discuss each of the required elements.

Actus reus: What does the offence require? Did D do it?

Mens rea: What does the offence require? Did D possess it?

AR and MR are satisfied	AR and/or MR are not satisfied
Continue to STEP 4.	Return to STEP 2, and look for an alternative offence. If none, then skip to STEP 5, concluding that no offence is committed.

STEP 4 Consider defences

The word 'consider' here is important as you should not discuss every defence for every question. Rather, think whether there are any defences (eg duress) that *could* potentially apply. If there are, discuss those only.

When considering and discussing potential defences, remember to consider any specific defences (ie those statutory defences that only apply to certain offences) as well as the general defences (discussed in **Chapters 13** and **14**).

STEP 5 Conclude

This is usually a single sentence either saying that it is likely that D has committed the offence, or saying that it is not likely either because an offence element is not satisfied or because a defence is likely to apply. It is not often that you will be able to say categorically whether or not D has committed the offence, particularly when applying concepts such as dishonesty, so it is usually best to conclude in terms of what is more 'likely'.

---

[236] See **4.2.1.1**.

STEP 6 Loop

Go back up to Step 1, identifying the next potential criminal event. Continue until you have discussed all the relevant potentially criminal events.

 ONLINE RESOURCE CENTRE

www.oxfordtextbooks.co.uk/orc/sho/

This chapter is accompanied by a selection of online resources to help you with this topic, including:

- **Multiple-choice questions**
- **Chapter summary sheet**
- Two **sample examination questions** with answer guidance
- **Further reading**

Also available on the Online Resource Centre are:

- A selection of **videos** from the authors explaining key topics and principles
- **Legal updates**
- Useful **weblinks**

10

Fraud

10.1 Introduction   **386**

10.2 FA 2006, s2: fraud by false representation   **388**

  10.2.1 Actus reus of s2   **389**

  10.2.2 Mens rea of s2   **392**

10.3 FA 2006, s3: fraud by failure to disclose information   **395**

  10.3.1 Actus reus of s3   **396**

  10.3.2 Mens rea of s3   **397**

10.4 FA 2006, s4: fraud by abuse of position   **397**

  10.4.1 Actus reus of s4   **398**

  10.4.2 Mens rea of s4   **400**

10.5 FA 2006, s11: obtaining services dishonestly   **401**

  10.5.1 Actus reus of s11   **402**

  10.5.2 Mens rea of s11   **403**

10.6 Fraud preparation offences   **403**

  10.6.1 FA 2006, s6: possession of articles for use in frauds   **403**

  10.6.2 FA 2006, s7: making or supplying articles for use in frauds   **405**

10.7 Related fraud and deception offences   **406**

  10.7.1 Conspiracy to defraud   **406**

  10.7.2 TA 1978, s3: making off without payment   **409**

10.8 Reform   **412**

  10.8.1 The drafting of the FA 2006   **412**

  10.8.2 Fraud and the irrelevance of results   **412**

  10.8.3 Distinguishing theft and fraud   **413**

10.9 Eye on assessment   **414**

10.1 Introduction

Fraud offences are designed to criminalise D's dishonest conduct—her lies, her with-holding of information, and/or her abuse of position—where she intends V to lose or risk losing property and/or to gain property herself. This has been contrasted with theft where, put simply, D dishonestly appropriates the property of another. However, the extent to which these offences operate to target *distinct* mischief is a matter of contention, particularly since theft has been held to include consensual appropriation.[1]

Fraud is an offence under section 1 of the Fraud Act 2006 (FA 2006).[2] Prior to the FA 2006, conduct that we would now charge as fraud was criminalised through a variety of deception offences within the Theft Act 1968 (TA 1968), which have now been repealed.[3] Those deception offences were heavily and consistently criticised, both for their unnecessary complexity as well as their overly restrictive application.[4] For example, under the pre-2006 law, the prosecution had to demonstrate a 'representation' from D; that her representation *caused* V to form a false belief; that that false belief *caused* V to act in a specified manner, such as transferring property; and that V's behaviour thereby benefited D or another. Demonstrating each causal link within this chain was very difficult for prosecutors, and, more importantly, it was argued that D's behaviour may have been equally blameworthy even when certain elements were missing (eg where D failed to deceive V, but still gained the advantage[5]).

The FA 2006, based upon Law Commission recommendations,[6] recast this area of the law. Moving away from the previous result-based offences, the new fraud offence focuses on D's dishonest conduct and intentions, looking to punish those intentions whether her acts of deception are successful or not. The new offence is a conduct crime, committed regardless of whether any consequences were caused or not by D's conduct. In this manner, the new fraud offence represents a move away from the property harms discussed in **Chapter 9** (eg theft, criminal damage, etc), and shares many more characteristics with the inchoate offences discussed in **Chapter 11**.

The offence of fraud is set out in section 1 of the FA 2006. The maximum sentence on indictment is ten years' imprisonment (three years more than theft).[7]

(1) A person is guilty of fraud if he is in breach of any of the sections listed in subsection (2) (which provide for different ways of committing the offence).

(2) The sections are—

(a) section 2 (fraud by false representation),

(b) section 3 (fraud by failing to disclose information), and

(c) section 4 (fraud by abuse of position).

As made clear in section 1(1), although fraud can be committed via three different routes, it represents a single offence. However, in order to analyse the offence, it is useful to look at each of these different routes separately.

---

[1] We pick up on this debate further in the reform section (**10.8.3**).

[2] The FA 2006 came into force from 15 January 2007.

[3] Other deception offences were also contained in the Theft Acts 1978 and 1996.

[4] For an overview of this criticism, see Law Commission, *Fraud and Deception* (Consultation 155, 1999).

[5] *Edwards* [1978] Crim LR 49.

[6] Law Commission, *Fraud* (No 276, 2002). See also Home Office, *Fraud Law Reform* (Consultation, 2004).

[7] FA 2006, s1(3)(b).

After discussing the central fraud offence, we will also go on to discuss the related offences of obtaining services dishonestly (FA 2006, s11) and possession of articles for use in frauds (FA 2006, s6). We will also provide a brief overview of other related fraud and deception offences.

10.2 FA 2006, s2: fraud by false representation

Fraud by false representation is defined in section 2 of the FA 2006. The requirements of this route to fraud are exceptionally wide, and in practice section 2 is likely to be the most often prosecuted.[8]

(1) A person is in breach of this section if he—

    (a) dishonestly makes a false representation, and

    (b) intends, by making the representation—

        (i)   to make a gain for himself or another, or

        (ii) to cause loss to another or to expose another to a risk of loss.

The elements of section 2 are illustrated in **Table 10.1**.

Table 10.1 FA 2006, s2

	Actus reus	**Mens rea**
Conduct element	Making a representation	Voluntary
Circumstance element	D's representation is false D's representation is dishonest	Knowledge or foresight of a possibility Knowledge
Result element	None	None
Ulterior mens rea element	*	Intention, by the making of the representation, to make a gain or cause a loss to another or expose another to a risk of loss

There is, under section 2, fraud where D makes a false representation dishonestly, with the intention thereby to make a gain or cause a loss, or risk of loss, to another. Whether V is actually deceived by D's representation, and/or whether V loses or D gains, is irrelevant (ie no results need to be demonstrated).

---

[8] Ormerod, 'The Fraud Act 2006—Criminalising Lying' [2007] Crim LR 193.

10.2.1 Actus reus of s2

The actus reus of section 2 requires D to have made a representation, and for that representation to be false.

10.2.1.1 Making a representation

It must be shown that D made a representation. Therefore, where D dishonestly takes advantage of a false representation made by another, for example X, where X is not acting as an agent of D,[9] then unless D also makes some representation as to its truth, she will not commit the offence. Three important aspects of a 'representation' require comment: the subject of the representation; the recipient; and the method.

A) The subject of the representation: Paradigm cases will involve false representations as to facts. For example, D assures V that the painting she is selling is genuine; that the car is not stolen; that she has sufficient funds to pay for the meal; and so on. However, section 2 is not limited to representations as to facts.

(3) 'Representation' means any representation as to fact or law, including a representation as to the state of mind of—

(a) the person making the representation, or

(b) any other person.

D makes a representation as to law where she informs someone about a legal detail, such as a contractual matter; and as to a state of mind where she states her intentions or beliefs or those of another (eg her intention to pay for goods on delivery).

Difficulty has arisen in relation to statements of opinion. For example, D exaggerates the quality of sale goods; tells V that her roof would benefit from retiling; etc. Under the pre-2006 law, cases of this kind were decided inconsistently, with certain cases falling short of a representation,[10] whilst others were caught.[11] It is submitted that, under the current law, matters of opinion should always be treated as representations of D's belief as to facts. The focus then shifts, in such cases, to whether that opinion was honestly held.

B) The recipient of the representation: Representations will usually be made to a person (V). Where this is the case, there is a question whether V must be aware of the representation for it to be complete. For example, what if V does not hear D's spoken comments, because, unknown to D, she is deaf; or V does not see D's email because it is blocked by V's email filters? There is no case yet directly on this point, but it is likely that the courts will interpret 'representation' broadly to be satisfied even where V remains oblivious. This is supported by a similarly broad interpretation given to 'communication' in other areas of the law,[12] a term which is arguably more likely than 'representation' to require acknowledgement from V.

---

[9] We discuss the use of agents in point C 'The method of the representation'.

[10] *Bryan* (1957) Dears & B 265: saying watch components were as good as Elkington's (a famous brand) was a mere exaggeration.

[11] *Smith v Land and House Property Corporation* (1884) 28 Ch D 7: saying a tenant was 'most desirable' where there was a consistent history of non-payment of rent.

[12] *Collins* [2006] UKHL 40: discussing the offence of grossly offensive communications.

> **Point to remember ...**
> Although V does not need to be aware of the representation, this does not mean that D will commit the offence when she makes intentionally private representations (eg notes something inaccurate in her diary). Other elements of the offence, such as the required intention to thereby make a gain or cause a loss, mean that the offence will only catch representations that are aimed at influencing others (ie D must intend to make a representation to another or a machine).

Although D's representations will usually be aimed at a person, this need not be the case. Under the pre-2006 law, it was held that 'deception' entailed the deception of a person, and so liability in cases where D deceived a machine, such as a banking system, became highly problematic.[13] Under the current law, this is addressed by section 2(5).

> (5) For the purposes of this section a representation may be regarded as made if it (or anything implying it) is submitted in any form to any system or device designed to receive, convey or respond to communications (with or without human intervention).

Despite rather complex drafting, this subsection clearly allows for fraud by false representation where there is no intended human recipient. Indeed, if anything, it may be too broadly drafted. Read literally, it may even apply where D drafts a misrepresenting email and saves (submits) it to her computer (any system).

C) **The method of the representation:** As we intimated earlier, section 2 can apply regardless of how D chooses to communicate with V, whether orally; in writing; by gestures; etc. D may even make a representation indirectly via an agent. This is illustrated in *Idrees v DPP*.

> **Idrees v DPP** [2011] EWHC 624 (Admin)
>
> Having failed his driving theory test on multiple occasions, D arranged for another person (P) to impersonate him, and pass the test on his behalf. D was charged with fraud by false representation, the false representation being P's impersonation whilst acting as D's agent.
>
> • Magistrates' court: guilty of fraud.
> • High Court: appeal dismissed. D was making a false representation (via P), and was doing so with the intention to make a gain (pass the test).

As well as catching different methods of physical communication, section 6(2) also clarifies that both express and implied representations will be caught. Thus, just as D makes a false representation when she tells a shop assistant falsely that she has authority to use a credit card, the same is also true where D simply presents the card for payment, thereby implying that she has authority to do so.[14] The case of *Barnard*, although pre-FA 2006, provides a memorable illustration.

---

[13] *Holmes* [2004] EWHC 2020 (Admin).
[14] For a similar interpretation pre-2006, see *Lambie* [1982] AC 449.

Barnard (1837) 7 C & P 784 (pre-FA 2006)

D entered an Oxford cobblers and requested boots and straps. D was wearing a cap and gown (of the type then worn by Oxford University students), and requested the associated discount. D was not a student of the university and was charged with a deception offence.

- Crown Court: guilty. D clearly deceived through an express note which claimed that he was a student. However, Bolland B went on to say that even if D did not present the note, his dress provided an implied deception sufficient for liability.

Despite section 2 being wide enough to encompass different methods of representation, one area of uncertainty has emerged. Given that section 3 of the FA 2006 specifically criminalises fraud by omission, does section 2 also cover implied representations by omission?

It is contended that for section 2, two scenarios involving omissions can, and should, be distinguished. In the first scenario, D makes a true representation to V, the facts then change, but D omits to inform V of this change. In these circumstances, it is possible that D's representation will be interpreted as a continuing act to include her failure to inform V after the facts change, and thus it is possible that section 2 will apply. Pre-FA 2006, such implied representations were found whether D was responsible for the change of facts, or simply became aware of them.[15] This is illustrated in *DPP v Ray*.

 DPP v Ray [1974] AC 370 (pre-FA 2006)

D and others ordered and consumed a meal at a Chinese restaurant. They did so intending to pay. However, at the end of the meal they changed their minds. They continued to sit in the restaurant until the waiter left the room, and then ran out. D was charged with a deception offence relating to his debt to the restaurant.

- Crown Court: guilty of the deception offence.
- High Court: appeal allowed—D's omission was not a deception.
- House of Lords: (3:2) appeal allowed. D's representations to be a paying customer continued from his ordering and eating the food (positive acts) and included his continuing to sit in the restaurant after he had decided not to pay (omission). Thus, there was coincidence of deception and mens rea.

In cases such as *Ray*, recognition of an implied continuing representation is essential to liability and, post-FA 2006, the potential for implied representations of this kind has been confirmed in *Government of the United Arab Emirates v Allen*.[16] However, in this case, the Divisional Court cautioned that implied continuing representations would only be found where it was 'reasonable' to read such a representation into the conduct of another. Stressing the fact-specific nature of this inquiry, the court rejected that a representation was made where D failed to inform her bank that she was no longer able to honour a security cheque deposited when she received a loan.

In the second scenario, D becomes aware that V is mistaken about a certain fact, but fails to correct her mistaken belief. For example, V says 'it will be great to buy a car which

---

[15] *Rai* [2000] 1 Cr App R 242: D failed to inform the council his mother had died, and allowed them to install the disability aids to which he was no longer entitled.
[16] [2012] EWHC 1712 (Admin).

has only had one owner', where D, who is selling the car, knows the car has had many more owners. In such cases it could be argued that, despite no express false representation, D's silence could amount to an implied representation that V's beliefs are correct. However, it is contended that this route to liability should be avoided. In line with CPS charging guidelines,[17] the criminal law should take care not to undermine the civil rules of *caveat emptor* (buyer beware), and maintain a difference between active representations and a simple failure to report faults. In the most serious cases of this kind there will generally be a legal duty upon D to disclose the omitted information, and in such cases section 3 of the FA 2006, and not section 2, provides the appropriate route to fraud liability.

10.2.1.2 The representation must be false

Section 2(2) defines what is meant by a 'false' representation.

> (2) A representation is false if—
>> (a) it is untrue or misleading, and
>> (b) the person making it knows that it is, or might be, untrue or misleading.

The first part of this provision, section 2(2)(a), extends the meaning of 'false' beyond core cases of outright untruth to include representations that are misleading. A representation may be misleading, and thus come within this part of the actus reus, even if it is literally true. For example, if V asks D, a car dealer, if there has been any reported problem with a particular model in the last year, and D answers honestly that there have not, this may still be misleading if D omits to mention the several hundred reported problems every other year. Equally, where D displays a fake painting among genuine classics, although she may not state that the fake is genuine, her choice of display may still be misleading.[18]

Where D believes that her statement is false, but it is in fact true, there will be no fraud. This was the case in *Deller* (pre-FA 2006),[19] where D agreed to sell his car 'free of encumbrances' in the belief that he had mortgaged the car (ie it was encumbered). However, as the proposed mortgage was unsuccessful, his statement turned out to be true. In such cases, the appropriate charge is attempted fraud.[20]

10.2.2 Mens rea of s2

The mens rea of section 2 is made up of three core elements: D must at least foresee a risk that her representation is false; she must act dishonestly; and she must intend to make a gain, cause a loss, or cause a risk of loss to another. Each element must coincide with (ie must be present at the point in time of) D's act of false representation.

10.2.2.1 Knowledge that the statement is, or might be, false

This element is satisfied where D *either* knows her representation is false or misleading, *or* foresees that it might be (s2(2)(b)). In either case, subjective mens rea is required: simple negligence (ie a reasonable person would have foreseen) will not be sufficient. This has

---

[17] www.cps.gov.uk/legal/d_to_g/fraud_act/.
[18] *Hill v Gray* (1816) 1 Stark 434.
[19] (1952) 36 Cr App R 184.
[20] **Chapter 11**.

been confirmed in *Augunas*,[21] and will include cases where D *deliberately* closes her eyes to a risk or deliberately avoids confirming facts when she has at least foreseen a risk of falsity.

Including the foresight of a risk makes this element of mens rea very wide indeed. For example, it will be satisfied where an art dealer, D, advertises a painting for sale as an original, being aware of the risk, which seems unavoidable in the art world, that it might be a fake. As a result, the requirement of 'dishonesty' is once again crucial for avoiding liability in such cases.

10.2.2.2 Dishonesty

The FA 2006 does not provide a definition of dishonesty, and there is also no equivalent to section 2 of the TA 1968, which provides examples of conduct not to be deemed dishonest.[22] Therefore, in the absence of any statutory guidance, the term is left exclusively to the common law definition and the *Ghosh* test.[23]

The *Ghosh* test for dishonesty is discussed in detail at **9.2.5.2**. To apply the *Ghosh* test, the jury are required to answer two questions. If the answer to both is 'yes', then the element is satisfied.

- Question 1: Is D's false representation dishonest according to the standards of reasonable and honest people?
- Question 2: Does D realise that her false representation would be considered dishonest by the standards of honest and reasonable people?

At **9.2.5.2** we discuss several criticisms of the *Ghosh* test, not least the unpredictability of asking a jury to identify a common standard of honesty. The same criticisms apply equally here.

An important question has emerged within the academic literature: is lying always dishonest?[24] If the answer were 'yes', then the section 2 offence would be rendered hopelessly wide. When television adverts, for example, imply that the spraying of a deodorant will make the wearer sexually irresistible, or that an energy drink can make you play sport like a professional, such representations are clearly false, but it is unlikely that they would be considered dishonest by a reasonable person. Ironically in such cases, the more dramatic the lie, and thus the less plausible, the less likely it is to be found dishonest. However, there is a clear grey area, for example occupations such as market trading and used car dealerships where trade patter and exaggeration is common.[25] Such cases will be left to the case-by-case application of the *Ghosh* test, with the likely outcomes far from clear.

10.2.2.3 Intention to make a gain or cause a loss (or risk of loss)

Section 2 does not require D to make a gain, or to cause or risk a loss to another in fact. However, D must act with the ulterior intention to achieve at least one of these ends. For example, where D starts a false rumour about a competitor's business, this element

---

[21] [2013] EWCA Crim 2046.
[22] D thinks she has a legal right; D thinks V would consent; D thinks V is untraceable by reasonable steps.
[23] [1982] QB 1053.
[24] Ormerod, 'Criminalising Lying' [2007] Crim LR 193.
[25] It should be remembered that the standard for 'honesty' is universal, and not industry-specific. The fact that a certain lie is common within an industry is no excuse for dishonesty: *Hayes* [2015] EWCA Crim 1944.

of the offence will be satisfied as long as D at least intends to risk causing a loss to that competitor, even if she does not intend to gain anything.

The definitions of 'gain' and 'loss' are set out in section 5 of the FA 2006.

(2) 'Gain' and 'loss'—

  (a) extend only to gain or loss in money or other property;

  (b) include any such gain or loss whether temporary or permanent;

  and 'property' means any property whether real or personal (including things in action and other intangible property).

(3) 'Gain' includes a gain by keeping what one has, as well as a gain by getting what one does not have.

(4) 'Loss' includes a loss by not getting what one might get, as well as a loss by parting with what one has.

As made clear in section 5(2)(a), D's intentions must relate to property, so an intention to gain something other than property, for example sexual favours, will not be sufficient. However, the definition of property here is very wide, including all tangible and intangible property, and without the exclusions that exist under the TA 1968.[26]

The final point to remember is one that is easily overlooked: D's intention must be causal. D must intend to *cause* the gain or loss by her conduct. This is illustrated in *Gilbert*.

***Gilbert* [2012] EWCA Crim 2392**

D and others set up a bank account in order to facilitate their company's activities—developing and selling real estate. In doing so, they made false representations about their financial position. D was charged with fraud by false representation.

- Crown Court: guilty of fraud.
- Court of Appeal: appeal allowed. Although a false representation was made, the court failed to direct the jury clearly that D must intend to make a gain *from* that representation.

Importantly, the court in *Gilbert* did not rule out the possibility that D intended her false representation to cause a gain in allowing her to finance the company, thereby allowing her to make a profit. However, D's conviction in the Crown Court was unsafe because the need to demonstrate this intention-based causal link was not clarified for the jury.

Point to remember …
The requirement for D to intend her conduct to 'cause' a gain or a loss provides a further (potential) tool for limiting liability. Consider the problem examples of extreme advertising, market traders, and used car salesmen discussed earlier. In such cases, where the trader makes an extreme puff

---

[26] eg land and wild creatures. These (and other examples) are not property in the context of theft because they are excluded by the TA 1968, s4. However, they are property in the context of fraud.

(eg 'these sunglasses are the same as those worn by David Beckham'), it may be contended that she does not intend this representation to 'cause' V to buy the goods. Rather, perhaps, such comments are intended simply as friendly trade banter or humour.[27]

10.3 FA 2006, s3: fraud by failure to disclose information

The second route to liability for fraud under section 1 of the FA 2006 is fraud by failure to disclose information. Fraud by failure to disclose is set out in section 3 of the FA 2006.

3. A person is in breach of this section if he—

  (a) dishonestly fails to disclose to another person information which he is under a legal duty to disclose, and

  (b) intends, by failing to disclose the information—

    (i) to make a gain for himself or another, or

    (ii) to cause loss to another or to expose another to a risk of loss.

The elements of section 3 are illustrated in **Table 10.2**.

Table 10.2 FA 2006, s3

	Actus reus	Mens rea
Conduct element	Failing to disclose information	Voluntary
Circumstance element	D has a legal duty to disclose the information D's failure to disclose is dishonest	None Knowledge
Result element	None	None
Ulterior mens rea element	*	Intention, by failing to disclose, to make a gain or cause a loss to another or expose another to a risk of loss

As with section 2, section 3 is a conduct crime. D must dishonestly fail to disclose information where there is a legal duty to do so, D must intend thereby to make a gain or cause a loss or risk of loss to another, but no such gain or loss needs to be demonstrated in fact.

---

[27] Ormerod and Gardner discussed this point in [2007] Crim LR 660.

10.3.1 Actus reus of s3

The actus reus of section 3 requires a failure to disclose information where D has a legal duty to do so.

10.3.1.1 Identifying a legal duty to disclose information

The question whether a legal duty exists is one of law for the judge. There is no definition of 'legal duty' in the statute. However, quoting from the original Law Commission report,[28] the FA 2006 explanatory notes make clear that 'legal duty' should be interpreted in line with the civil law.

> 7.28 . . . Such a duty may derive from statute (such as the provisions governing company prospectuses), from the fact that the transaction in question is one of the utmost good faith (such as a contract of insurance), from the express or implied terms of a contract, from the custom of a particular trade or market, or from the existence of a fiduciary relationship between the parties (such as that of agent and principal).

> 7.29 For this purpose there is a legal duty to disclose information not only if the defendant's failure to disclose it gives the victim a cause of action for damages, but also if the law gives the victim a right to set aside any change in his or her legal position to which he or she may consent as a result of the non-disclosure. For example, a person in a fiduciary position has a duty to disclose material information when entering into a contract with his or her beneficiary, in the sense that a failure to make such disclosure will entitle the beneficiary to rescind the contract and to reclaim any property transferred under it.[29]

The second paragraph of this guidance is particularly informative, making it clear that a legal duty to disclose will arise whenever D's failure to disclose information would render a contract, or relevant part of a contract, voidable. Clear examples will include a failure to disclose medical conditions when taking out life insurance; failure to disclose a criminal record when applying for a job; failure, as in *Mashta*, to reveal a change of financial position when in receipt of State benefits; and so on.[30]

Mashta [2010] EWCA Crim 2595

D continued to receive asylum support on grounds of destitution whilst in gainful employment. Among other charges, D was charged with fraud by failing to disclose his employment.

- Crown Court: guilty of fraud.
- Court of Appeal: appeal on sentence allowed, reducing D's sentence from 15 to eight months' imprisonment.

Although the Law Commission had recommended that the 'legal duty to disclose' should also include 'moral duties', this extension was rejected by the Home Office.[31] This makes

---

[28] Law Commission, *Fraud* (No 276, 2002) paras 7.28–7.29.
[29] FA 2006 Explanatory Notes, s3.
[30] Salter, 'It's Criminal Not to Disclose' (2007) 37 Fam L 432: discussing divorce proceedings where D fails to disclose the true extent of her assets. See also *Razoq* [2012] EWCA Crim 674: D (a doctor) failed to disclose disciplinary hearings and suspension from hospital to other locum (ad hoc medical work) agencies.
[31] Home Office, *Fraud Law Reform* (Consultation, 2004) paras 18–25.

the court's job easier: narrowing their search for a duty to legal concepts only. However, the court will still have to grapple with complex areas of civil law in order to decide whether or not a particular duty arises on the facts.

> **Assessment matters ...**
> In most cases D's failure to disclose could also be presented as a false representation (a representation that there is nothing to disclose), and so could be prosecuted under section 2. In clear cases of a failure to disclose, section 3 is likely to be preferred because it provides the most accurate label for D's conduct. However, where the presence of a duty is more difficult to identify, it is likely that section 2 will generally be preferred. We discuss this further in 'Eye on assessment' at **10.9**.

10.3.1.2 When does D fail to disclose

In many cases, D's failure to disclose will be obvious on the facts. For example, D has a duty in *Mashta* to disclose any gainful employment whilst receiving benefits; D does not disclose, so D has 'failed' to do so. However, it is important to remember that a failure to disclose is satisfied not only where D discloses nothing at all, but also where D fails to disclose *sufficient* information in a manner that renders relevant parts of a contract voidable. Thus, even partial disclosure may still satisfy the actus reus of this offence. Again, this question will involve the judge in a detailed analysis of the relevant civil law obligation.

10.3.2 Mens rea of s3

The mens rea of section 3 requires D to have acted dishonestly, and to have intended by her failure to disclose to make a gain or to cause a loss or risk of loss to another. These two core elements have been discussed above in relation to section 2 (**10.2.2**), and should be interpreted in exactly the same way for section 3.

It should be noted that whilst the section 2 offence required mens rea of knowledge or awareness of a risk that D's representation was false, section 3 does not contain any equivalent requirement in relation to the duty to disclose. Therefore, D may be liable under section 3 even if she did not know or even foresee a possibility that she was under a legal obligation to disclose information. However, although this seems unacceptably broad, the possibility for unfairness is limited by the requirement of dishonesty and the *Ghosh* test. This is because where D is unaware of a legal duty to disclose, her failure to do so is much less likely to be considered dishonest by the standards of reasonable and honest people, and even where it was, she is unlikely to realise that it would be so considered.

10.4 FA 2006, s4: fraud by abuse of position

The final route to liability for fraud under section 1 of the FA 2006 is fraud by abuse of position. Fraud by abuse of position is set out in section 4 of the FA 2006.

(1) A person is in breach of this section if he—

    (a) occupies a position in which he is expected to safeguard, or not to act against, the financial interests of another person,

(b) dishonestly abuses that position, and

(c) intends, by means of the abuse of that position—

    (i)   to make a gain for himself or another, or

    (ii) to cause loss to another or to expose another to a risk of loss.

The elements of section 4 are illustrated in **Table 10.3**.

Table 10.3 FA 2006, s4

	Actus reus	**Mens rea**
Conduct element	Acts or omissions	Voluntary
Circumstance element	D occupies a position in which she is expected to safeguard the financial interests of another	None
	D abuses that position	None
	D's abuse of position is dishonest	Knowledge
Result element	None	None
Ulterior mens rea element	*	Intention, by abuse of position, to make a gain or cause a loss to another or expose another to a risk of loss

As with sections 2 and 3, section 4 is a conduct crime. D must dishonestly abuse a position in which she is expected to safeguard the financial interests of another, D must intend thereby to make a gain or cause a loss or risk of loss to another, but no such gain or loss needs to be demonstrated in fact.

10.4.1 Actus reus of s4

The actus reus of section 4 requires D, by act or omission,[32] to abuse a position in which she is expected to safeguard the financial interests of another.

10.4.1.1 Identifying the relevant positions

The first element of the actus reus requires D to occupy a position in which she is expected to safeguard the financial interests of another. Unfortunately, again, this core element is not defined in the statute.

The most obvious interpretation of the required 'position' is where D owes a 'fiduciary duty' to another (ie a civil law duty to act within the interests of another). Indeed, most of the examples provided by the Law Commission and government have involved such

---

[32] FA 2006, s4(2).

duties. For example, employees using insider knowledge to make secret profits; those taking advantage of vulnerable people whose finances they have agreed to administer; and so on. *Marshall* provides a useful illustration.

 Marshall [2009] EWCA Crim 2076

D was a manager of a residential care home for people with extreme learning difficulties, and in that position had control over a particular resident's (V's) finances. Over a period of time, D withdrew over £7,000 from the resident's account and used it for her own benefit. D was charged with fraud by abuse of position.

• Crown Court: guilty of fraud.
• Court of Appeal: appeal on sentence (12 months) dismissed.

Beyond cases of this kind, however, the government has made it clear in the FA 2006 Explanatory Notes that the offence will not be limited to abuse of a fiduciary duty.

The necessary relationship will be present between trustee and beneficiary, director and company, professional person and client, agent and principal, employee and employer, or between partners. It may arise otherwise, for example within a family, or in the context of voluntary work, or in any context where the parties are not at arm's length. In nearly all cases where it arises, it will be recognised by the civil law as importing fiduciary duties, and any relationship that is so recognised will suffice. We see no reason, however, why the existence of such duties should be essential. This does not of course mean that it would be entirely a matter for the fact-finders whether the necessary relationship exists. The question whether the particular facts alleged can properly be described as giving rise to that relationship will be an issue capable of being ruled upon by the judge and, if the case goes to the jury, of being the subject of directions.[33]

The guidance maintains that the question of relevant position is one for the judge, but by breaking away from the civil law concept of fiduciary duty, the task for the judge when identifying a relevant position is very difficult. Potentially, whenever D is in a position of trust, or expresses some form of loyalty to another, they may satisfy this element.[34] This question was explored in *Valujevs*.

 Valujevs [2014] EWCA Crim 2888

D and others were gangmasters (they controlled a group of casual agricultural workers, supplying accommodation and travel). In order to secure personal gain, D made unwarranted deductions from workers' pay, grossly inflated rents, and withheld work in order to force workers into debt. D was charged with fraud by abuse of position, along with specific unlicensed gangmaster offences.

• Crown Court: guilty of gangmaster offences; but no case to answer in relation to fraud. Although D treated the victims very poorly, he was not 'expected to safeguard' their 'financial interests', and so did not come within section 4.
• Court of Appeal: allowing appeal. D's conduct is capable of coming within section 4.

---

[33] FA 2006 Explanatory Notes, s4. Quoting from Law Commission, *Fraud* (No 276, 2002) para 7.38.
[34] Collins, 'Fraud by Abuse of Position: Theorising Section 4 of the Fraud Act 2006' [2011] Crim LR 513.

The Court of Appeal clarified a number of key points in the judgment. First, it was confirmed that the duty to safeguard the financial interests of another is an objective question for the court. In other words, we are not talking about legitimate expectations from D's or V's perspective, but from the perspective of the reasonable person. This is sensible, not allowing D to avoid a duty unfairly and not allowing V to artificially impose one. Secondly, the court clarified that although such a duty arose in this case, this was because D had collected the pay of his workers and was therefore responsible for delivering it to them. Crucially, the duty did not arise simply because D was charging inflated rents or paying poor wages, and such conduct alone will not be sufficient.[35]

10.4.1.2 When does D abuse this position

Once it is established to the satisfaction of the judge that the position D occupies qualifies in law as a relevant one, it is then a question of fact for the jury whether she abused this position. Where D owes a fiduciary duty to V, establishing abuse will involve directing the jury on potentially complex civil law rules relating to breach of duty. And beyond this, as the offence extends beyond formal relationships of this kind, the term 'abuse' has had to remain flexible. As a result, the term is undefined, justified in the Explanatory Notes as a conscious choice to maintain flexibility.[36] Unfortunately, what is gained in flexibility from not defining such a crucial term is almost certainly lost in lack of certainty and consistency when the offence is applied by the courts. This is illustrated in *Pennock and Pennock*.

 Pennock and Pennock [2014] EWCA Crim 598

A husband and wife (D1 and D2) opened a joint bank account with an uncle (V) aged 90. £100,000 of V's money was subsequently transferred into the account and later used to buy a house to be owned by D1 and D2's daughter (X). V later claimed to have no knowledge of the account, the transfer, or the use of the money. D1 and D2 were charged with fraud under section 4 as to (a) the money transfer, and (b) transferring the title of the property to X.

- Crown Court: guilty of fraud.

- Court of Appeal: appeal allowed. The evidence and detail of abuse was not sufficiently clear on the facts, the judge at first instance having failed to direct the jury that D1 and D2 were free to make use of funds from a joint account (where this was free of restrictions) and that the transfer of property title did not undermine V's equitable interest because X was not a bona fide purchaser. Although the court made clear that the facts could have resulted in liability under section 4, the lack of clear direction from the trial judge as to the civil law involved rendered the convictions unsafe.

10.4.2 Mens rea of s4

The mens rea of section 4 requires D to have acted dishonestly, and to have intended *by* her abuse of position to make a gain or to cause a loss or risk of loss to another.

---

[35] Collins, 'Fraud by Abuse of Position and Unlicensed Gangmasters' (2016) 79 MLR 354.
[36] FA 2006 Explanatory Notes, s4.

These two core elements have been discussed previously in relation to section 2 (**10.2.2**), and should be interpreted in exactly the same way for section 4.

In line with section 3, the additional circumstance elements for the section 4 offence are strict liability elements. Thus, although D must occupy a position in which she is expected to safeguard the financial interests of another, and although D must abuse that position, D does not require any specific mens rea as to either of these actus reus elements. D may therefore come within the offence even where she is unaware that she holds such a position.[37] However, as with section 3, although this seems unacceptably broad, the possibility for unfairness is limited by the requirement of dishonesty and the *Ghosh* test. This is because where D is unaware that she occupies a relevant position, her potential abuse of it is much less likely to be considered dishonest by the standards of reasonable and honest people, and even where it was, she may not realise that it would be so considered.

> **Point to remember …**
> We discussed in **Chapter 9** the central role of 'dishonesty' within most of the property offences, and highlighted criticism of its inability to perform this role effectively. Within the core fraud offences the same, and arguably even greater, reliance is apparent.

10.5 FA 2006, s11: obtaining services dishonestly

Obtaining services dishonestly is set out at section 11 of the FA 2006.[38] The maximum penalty on indictment is five years' imprisonment.[39]

(1) A person is guilty of an offence under this section if he obtains services for himself or another—

    (a) by a dishonest act, and

    (b) in breach of subsection (2).

(2) A person obtains services in breach of this subsection if—

    (a) they are made available on the basis that payment has been, is being or will be made for or in respect of them,

    (b) he obtains them without any payment having been made for or in respect of them or without payment having been made in full, and

    (c) when he obtains them, he knows—

        (i) that they are being made available on the basis described in paragraph (a), or

        (ii) that they might be,

    but intends that payment will not be made, or will not be made in full.

The elements of section 11 are set out in **Table 10.4**.

---

[37] The term 'abuse' implies some form of conscious or intentional wrongdoing. However, there is nothing in the statute to make such mens rea a requirement.

[38] Replacing the old offence 'obtaining services by deception' (TA 1978, s1). Withey, 'The Fraud Act 2006—Some Early Observations and Comparisons with the Former Law' (2007) 71 J Crim L 220.

[39] FA 2006, s11(3).

Table 10.4　FA 2006, s11

	Actus reus	**Mens rea**
Conduct element	Acts causing the result	Voluntary
Circumstance element	D's obtaining of services is dishonest	Knowledge
	Payment is required for the services	Knowledge or foresight of a chance
	No (or insufficient) payment is provided	Intention
Result element	Services are obtained for D or another	Intention

Unlike the offence of fraud discussed earlier, section 11 creates a result crime: D's dishonest acts must *cause* services to be obtained in circumstances where payment is knowingly withheld.

10.5.1　Actus reus of s11

The actus reus of section 11 requires D to have acquired services for which payment is required, but to have failed to pay for these services in full. Paradigm examples will include cases where D uses an illegal device (decoder) to watch satellite TV without paying; where D takes goods on hire without intending to pay for them; where D gains entry to a sporting or music event by climbing over a fence; and so on. Indeed, where the service requires payment, the offence will even cover D who opens a bank account using false details, or continues to use her account having had her authority to do so removed.[40]

Two points should be emphasised. First, unlike fraud, section 11 is a result crime: causation is crucial. Thus, where D obtains services, for example, gaining entry to a sporting event, with the intention of paying, but decides after the event that she will not do so, she does not commit a section 11 offence. This is because, at the time she acts to *cause* the services to be obtained, she is not yet dishonest; and when she is later dishonest, she has already obtained the services. The correct charge in these circumstances, discussed later, would be making off without payment.[41]

Secondly, it must be shown that D acquired a 'service'. This is not defined in the statute, but is clearly considerably wider than 'property'. The only restriction is that the service must be one for which payment is required. Thus, where D acts dishonestly to gain a gratuitous service D does not commit a section 11 offence: as, for example, where D lies about his age to obtain a free car wash for the elderly.

---

[40] *Sofroniou* [2003] EWCA Crim 3681.

[41] See **10.7**. Where D has obtained the services and continues to represent that she is willing to pay, there will be an alternative charge under the FA 2006, s2.

10.5.2 Mens rea of s11

To satisfy the mens rea of section 11, D must know that payment for the service is or might be required; must intend to obtain the service without paying; and must act dishonestly. The first two of these requirements are relatively straightforward, but should be carefully applied. For example, where D lies about her religion or postcode in order to access a selective fee-charging school, she will not commit a section 11 offence if she intends to pay the fees: she acts dishonestly to obtain a service, but she does not intend to avoid payment.[42] The final element of dishonesty requires us to apply the standard *Ghosh* test. This is discussed earlier in the context of section 2 (**10.2.2.2**), and the same approach applies here.

10.6 Fraud preparation offences

Sections 6 and 7 of the FA 2006 criminalise acts in preparation for fraud. Section 6 proscribes possession of articles for fraud; and section 7 proscribes the making or supplying of articles for use in frauds. In both cases, the law is trying to facilitate early intervention by the police, targeting D before she has caused or attempted to cause harm.

Extra detail …

It should be remembered that, under the current law, the principal fraud offence is also drafted in an inchoate or pre-emptive fashion, criminalising D where she falsely represents, fails to disclose, or abuses her position with the intent to make a gain or cause a loss, but not requiring that gain or loss (the substantive harm) to be caused. The offences under sections 6 and 7 provide even earlier criminalisation.

10.6.1 FA 2006, s6: possession of articles for use in frauds

The maximum penalty for section 6 on indictment is five years' imprisonment.[43]

(1) A person is guilty of an offence if he has in his possession or under his control any article for use in the course of or in connection with any fraud.

The elements of section 6 are set out in **Table 10.5**.

Table 10.5 FA 2006, s6

	Actus reus	**Mens rea**
Conduct element	Possessing or controlling an article	Voluntary (ie known) possession
Circumstance element	None	None

(Continued)

---

[42] Monaghan, 'Fraudsters? Putting Parents in the Dock' (2010) 174 CL&JW 581 and 'School Application Forms and the Criminal Law' [2015] Crim LR 270.

[43] FA 2006, s6(2).

Table 10.5 Continued

	Actus reus	Mens rea
Result element	None	None
Ulterior mens rea element	*	Intention to use the article in connection with fraud

As **Table 10.5** illustrates, section 6 creates an extremely broad offence, criminalising the possession or control of any article with intention to use it in connection with fraud. It is irrelevant for this offence whether any future fraud is completed or not.

10.6.1.1 Actus reus of s6

The two core elements of the actus reus are that D (A) has possession or control of (B) an article.

   A) **Possession or control:** Straightforward cases will involve physical possession of an article on D's person. This will include, for example, where D is found with fake bank notes; with a decoding machine facilitating the illegal viewing of paid satellite television; etc.[44] It will also include, as in *Nimley*, items that might be otherwise innocent, such as an iPhone.

 Nimley [2010] EWCA Crim 2752

D was caught videoing cinema films on his iPhone. D had already successfully recorded and uploaded three previous films to the internet for free consumption. D was charged with offences including possession of articles (the iPhone) for use in fraud.

- Crown Court: guilty of section 6 offence.
- Court of Appeal: appeal against sentence allowed, removing the custodial element of the sentence and replacing it with community service.

Possession or control are not, however, limited to examples of physical possession. For example, where D has relevant articles stored in her house, in her office, or in other premises, these too will be in her possession or control. In this manner, we are in possession or control of many thousands of articles at any one time.[45]

   B) **Articles:** As noted earlier, relevant articles found in D's possession may be otherwise innocent as long as D intends to use them in connection with fraud. Thus, the iPhone in *Nimley* constituted a relevant article just as much as an item, such as a decoding machine, where the sole function is to facilitate fraud. Everyday articles such as pens and paper will therefore constitute relevant articles as long as D possesses them with the

---

[44] *Kazi* [2010] EWCA Crim 2752: possession of paper that was to be used to make fake banknotes; *Ciorba* [2009] EWCA Crim 1800: possession of a memory stick used to download data from ATM machines.
[45] *Montague* [2013] EWCA Crim 1781.

required mens rea. Section 8(1) of the FA 2006 also expressly includes 'any program or data held in electronic form' as articles. Thus, where D possesses certain software or a document held in electronic form, and intends to use it in connection with fraud, she commits a section 6 offence.

> *Extra detail ...*
> We wait to see how widely these terms will be interpreted by the courts. For example, does D have possession of all the information on the internet simply by her ability to access it?

10.6.1.2 Mens rea of s6

The two core mens rea elements are D's (A) knowledge of possession or control, and (B) intention to use the article in connection with fraud.

A) **Knowledge of possession:** It is not clear from the statute whether D must have knowledge, or indeed any mens rea, as to the fact of possession. However, in line with other possession offences, particularly drug offences, it is contended that such a requirement should be found by the courts. In most cases, the fact that D must intend to use the article in connection with fraud will require in effect that D has knowledge of possession; but not always. For example, where D plans to use a piece of software without realising that the software is already installed on her computer. In such cases, it is contended that D should avoid liability under section 6.

B) **Intention to use the article in connection with fraud:** This is a common law supplement to wording of the statute, narrowing the offence to more acceptable limits. However, the intention requirement remains broadly constructed. For example, the phrase 'in connection' clearly allows for cases where D does not plan to use the article as a tool for the fraud, but simply in some related role as, for example, to help cover her tracks; or gain access to the necessary tools; etc. It is also unclear how widely 'fraud' should be interpreted: the term clearly covers an intention to commit an offence under section 1, and most likely sections 9 and 11, but beyond this it remains uncertain. One useful clarification in *Sakalauskas*[46] is that D's intention must relate to *future* acts of fraud, as opposed to past acts.

10.6.2 FA 2006, s7: making or supplying articles for use in frauds

The maximum penalty for section 7 on indictment is ten years' imprisonment.[47]

> (1) A person is guilty of an offence if he makes, adapts, supplies or offers to supply any article—
>
> > (a) knowing that it is designed or adapted for use in the course of or in connection with fraud, or
> >
> > (b) intending it to be used to commit, or assist in the commission of, fraud.

The elements of section 7 are set out in **Table 10.6**.

---

[46] [2013] EWCA Crim 2278.
[47] FA 2006, s7(2).

Table 10.6 FA 2006, s7

	Actus reus	Mens rea
Conduct element	Making, adapting, supplying, or offering to supply an article	Voluntary
Circumstance element	None	None
Result element	None	None
Ulterior mens rea element	*	Knowing the article is designed or adapted for use in connection with fraud Or Intending the article to be used to commit or assist the commission of fraud

Section 7 creates an offence capable of numerous constructions (eg making; adapting; supplying; offering; with knowledge; with intent; etc). As such, it should be applied carefully, ensuring that the correct construction is identified in relation to the particular factual event. However, at its core, the offence is designed to criminalise D who is either preparing articles for the commission of fraud herself, or doing so to assist another.

10.7 Related fraud and deception offences

There are a number of fraud-related offences within the criminal law, including false accounting;[48] making false statements as company directors;[49] suppression of documents;[50] and the common law offence of cheating the public revenue.[51] However, in this section we provide only a brief account of two such offences: conspiracy to defraud and making off without payment.

10.7.1 Conspiracy to defraud

Conspiracy to defraud is a common law offence that criminalises D who agrees with another (D2) on a dishonest course of conduct that risks prejudice to another's property rights.[52] This is a spectacularly wide offence, with the potential to criminalise an

---

[48] TA 1968, s17.
[49] Ibid, s19.
[50] Ibid, s20.
[51] Ormerod, 'Cheating the Public Revenue' [1998] Crim LR 627.
[52] Defined in *Scott v Metropolitan Police Commissioner* [1975] AC 919.

agreement to complete conduct that may not be a crime or even a civil wrong if simply undertaken by an individual. Beyond this, the exact boundaries of the offence are far from certain. As a result, unsurprisingly, it has attracted considerable criticism.[53] The Law Commission recommended abolition of conspiracy to defraud within its recommendations for the FA 2006.[54] However, concerned about possible lacunae within the new statute, and bearing in mind the popularity of the offence with prosecutors, the government favoured retention.[55] There are currently no signs that the offence will be abolished.

The elements of conspiracy to defraud are set out in **Table 10.7**. The maximum sentence is ten years' imprisonment.

Table 10.7 Conspiracy to defraud

	Actus reus	**Mens rea**
Conduct element	Agreement with another	Voluntary
Circumstance element	Agreement involves a risk to V's property interests or deception in a public duty D's agreement is dishonest	Knowledge Knowledge
Result element	None	None
Ulterior mens rea element	*	Intention that the course of conduct is completed

10.7.1.1 Actus reus of conspiracy to defraud

The core elements of the actus reus of conspiracy to defraud are (A) an agreement between two or more (B) on a course of conduct that risks the property interests of another or deception in a public duty. This is a conduct-based inchoate offence: the agreement must involve a risk to property interests or deception, but it is irrelevant whether the parties go through with their agreement and whether any property interests are imperilled.

A) Agreement between two or more: As with other conspiracy offences (**Chapter 11**), conspiracy to defraud requires an agreement (a meeting of minds) between two or more people. However, the agreement need not involve one of the defendants doing the defrauding themselves. For example, in *Hollinshead*[56] the House

---

[53] Jarvis, '*Evans* and Conspiracy to Defraud: A Postscript' [2015] Crim LR 704; ATH Smith, 'Conspiracy to Defraud' [1988] Crim LR 508; JC Smith, 'Conspiracy to Defraud: Some Comments on the Law Commission's Report' [1995] Crim LR 209.

[54] Law Commission, *Fraud* (No 276, 2002) Draft Bill, cl9.

[55] See commentary in Ormerod and Williams, *Smith's Law of Theft* (2007) paras 5.65 et seq.

[56] [1985] AC 975.

of Lords found a conspiracy to defraud where D1 and D2 agreed to produce devices designed to corrupt electricity meters, making them undercount the electricity used, even though the defrauding would be done by unidentified third parties—the customers using the device.

B) Risks the property interests of another or deception of someone's public duty: Agreements to a course of conduct that would amount to an offence under the Theft Acts and/or the FA 2006 would clearly satisfy the requirement of risking another's property interests. Conspiracy to defraud has also been used to criminalise agreements that if carried out would not amount to an offence. For example, agreements relating to the 'temporary' deprivation of another's property (short of theft);[57] to shifting land boundary fences; to inducing another to take a financial risk they would not otherwise have taken;[58] and so on. However, the case of *Evans*[59] has clarified that something unlawful is required under this route: either that the object of the agreement was unlawful, or if the object was lawful, that the means of achieving that object were unlawful.[60]

Alongside agreements that risk property interests, it has long been accepted that the deception of V to act against her public duty will also satisfy this element of the offence. Examples include D deceiving a public official to supply export licences,[61] supply information,[62] employ unqualified staff,[63] and so on. Certain cases suggest that this construction will also apply outside public officials. to those deceived into acting against any contractual duties.[64]

10.7.1.2 Mens rea of conspiracy to defraud

The mens rea of conspiracy to defraud requires: (A) knowledge of the risks involved in the agreement; (B) intention that the course of conduct will be carried out; and (C) dishonesty. As with all conspiracy offences, at least two of the parties to the agreement must *both* satisfy the mens rea (ie there must be a meeting of minds).

A) Knowledge of the risks: D must recognise the risks posed to the property interests of another, or the possible deception of V acting in a public duty.[65] D's motives, in this regard, are irrelevant. Thus, in *Wai Yu-tsang*[66] the Privy Council found that D had conspired to defraud the bank he worked for by failing to reveal financial information even though he was acting, he claimed, to protect the bank's interests.

B) Intention that the course of conduct will be completed: If the parties agree on a course of conduct, but do not intend that it will be carried out, then no offence is committed. For example, D agrees, but plans to 'whistle-blow' and prevent the course of conduct happening.

---

[57] *Scott v Metropolitan Police Commissioner* [1975] AC 919: temporary deprivation of cinema tapes.
[58] *Allsop* (1976) 64 Cr App R 29.
[59] [2014] 1 WLR 2817. Upheld by Fulford LJ when the SFO sought to reopen the prosecution: [2014] EWHC 3803 (QB).
[60] Jarvis, 'Conspiracy to Defraud: A Siren to Lure Unwary Prosecutors' [2014] Crim LR 738.
[61] *Board of Trade v Owen* [1957] AC 602.
[62] *DPP v Withers* [1975] AC 842.
[63] *Bassey* (1931) 21 Cr App R 160.
[64] *Welham* [1961] AC 103.
[65] *Cooke* [1986] AC 909.
[66] [1992] 1 AC 269.

C) **Dishonesty:** The *Ghosh* test applies here, as discussed previously at **10.2.2.2.** The potential for other elements of the offence to catch ostensibly innocent conduct makes the role of dishonesty centrally important.

10.7.2 TA 1978, s3: making off without payment

Making off without payment is an offence contrary to section 3 of the TA 1978. The maximum penalty on indictment is two years' imprisonment.[67]

(1) Subject to subsection (3) below, a person who, knowing that payment on the spot for any goods supplied or service done is required or expected from him, dishonestly makes off without having paid as required or expected and with intent to avoid payment of the amount due shall be guilty of an offence.

(2) For purposes of this section 'payment on the spot' includes payment at the time of collecting goods on which work has been done or in respect of which service has been provided.

(3) Subsection (1) above shall not apply where the supply of the goods or the doing of the service is contrary to law, or where the service done is such that payment is not legally enforceable . . .

The elements of section 3 are set out in **Table 10.8.**

Table 10.8 TA 1978, s3

	Actus reus	**Mens rea**
Conduct element	Making off	Voluntary
Circumstance element	On the spot payment is required Payment is not supplied in full D's making off is dishonest	Knowledge Intention Knowledge
Result element	None	None
Ulterior mens rea element	*	Intention to avoid payment

Making off without payment was intended to provide a simple offence to target cases where D tries to avoid payment for goods or services by taking flight. For example, running out of a restaurant without paying the bill, jumping out of a taxi without paying the fare, etc. Importantly, there is no need to demonstrate any deception, and no need to show that D has successfully avoided payment. The offence simply requires D to have dishonestly made off without paying for goods or services that she knows require payment, and doing so with the intention to avoid payment.[68]

---

[67] TA 1978, s4.
[68] *Vincent* [2001] 1 WLR 1172.

10.7.2.1 Actus reus of s3

The actus reus of section 3 requires D to: (A) make off; (B) without payment; where (C) on-the-spot payment is required.

A) Making off: Making off simply requires D to have physically moved from the location in which payment is required. This will be the case whether D leaves surreptitiously, as where D climbs out of a restaurant's bathroom window, or whether she leaves to the 'sound of trumpets'.[69] However, D must have fully left the relevant location. For example, if D is stopped before leaving the restaurant where payment is required she will not have committed the section 3 offence, although there may be liability in attempt.[70]

One point remains unresolved in the literature—does D 'make off' if V gives her permission to leave?[71] It was held in *Hammond*[72] that, however obtained, the existence of permission was incompatible with the notion of 'making off', and it is contended that this approach is correct. Where D acts honestly in gaining permission, then V has allowed her to leave and liability would seem inappropriate; where D is dishonest we may feel that liability is deserved, but again V has allowed her to leave, and section 3 is not appropriate. In this second case, liability can be found under fraud by false representation.[73]

B) Without payment: This element simply requires that D has not paid for the goods or services, or has not paid in full.

C) On-the-spot payment is required: There are two parts to this requirement. First, for payment to be 'required or expected', it must be that goods or services have been supplied.[74] This will include D taking goods that are supplied via self-service display in a supermarket, or fuel at a self-service forecourt.[75] However, where goods have not yet been supplied there will be no offence under section 3[76] as, for example, where D tries unsuccessfully to trick V out of goods and then runs away. Equally, where goods or services are supplied, but they are of a sufficiently low quality or provided in breach of contract, such that D is not legally obliged to pay for them, there will again be no liability under this section.[77] Section 3(3) also makes it clear that there will be no offence under this section where D makes off without paying for illegal goods or services, for example from a brothel, or having been supplied with illegal drugs.

The second part of this element is that the payment for goods or services must be required or expected 'on-the-spot'. This was the focus of the court in *Vincent*.

---

[69] *Brooks and Brooks* (1982) 76 Cr App R 66.
[70] *McDavitt* [1981] Crim LR 843.
[71] Spencer, Letter, 'Making Off Without Payment' [1983] Crim LR 573.
[72] [1982] Crim LR 611.
[73] See **10.2** if the making off related to property.
[74] 'Goods' are defined by the TA 1968, s34 (made applicable to the TA 1978 by s5(2)). 'Services' are not defined in statute.
[75] For an alternative view, see, Smith 'Shoplifting and the Theft Acts' [1981] Crim LR 586.
[76] The charge here, if any, would be for fraud or attempted theft.
[77] *Troughton v Metropolitan Police* [1987] Crim LR 138: taxi driver in breach of contract so payment was not required.

Vincent [2001] EWCA Crim 295

D did not settle his bill in full when leaving two different hotels. On each occasion, he dishonestly assured the owners (V) that he was about to come into some money and would pay them later, and on each occasion V allowed him to leave on this basis. D was charged with making off without payment.

- Crown Court: guilty of section 3 offence. Even though V consented to D leaving, D's dishonest obtaining of that consent meant that he still 'made off' for the purposes of section 3.
- Court of Appeal: appeal allowed. Where V consents to D leaving without payment, even where this is procured by dishonesty, D is not 'making off' for the purpose of section 3.

In *Vincent*, V's consent to later payment meant that payment was no longer required or expected on the spot (ie at that time, in that hotel). Therefore, D's leaving that spot could not amount to making off without payment. Where D acts in this manner, dishonestly avoiding immediate payment with the intention to make a gain or cause a loss, the appropriate charge would be fraud by false representation (**10.2**).

10.7.2.2 Mens rea of s3

The mens rea of section 3 requires D to have (A) known that on-the-spot payment was required; (B) intended to avoid payment; and (C) acted dishonestly.

A) Knowledge that on-the-spot payment is required: It will often be clear to D that payment for goods or services is required of her on-the-spot. However, the element will be lacking where, for example, D leaves thinking that another party is going to pay, or believing that payment is only required at some later stage.[78]

B) Intention to avoid payment: The text of section 3 requires D to intend to avoid payment, but is unclear whether this means an intention to *permanently* avoid payment or whether intention to avoid payment temporarily will suffice. This was clarified in *Allen*.

Allen [1985] AC 1029

D left a hotel without settling his bill. His intention was to pay the bill later when he could afford to do so. D was charged with making off without payment.

- Crown Court: guilty of section 3 offence. The trial judge directed the jury that D need only intend to default from payment at that time.
- Court of Appeal: appeal allowed. D must intend to make permanent default.
- House of Lords: appeal dismissed, endorsing the Court of Appeal's reasoning.

It is now clear that D will not come within section 3 unless she makes off with the intention to permanently avoid payment.

C) Dishonesty: The *Ghosh* test applies here, as discussed earlier at **10.2.2.2**. It is important to remember that we are looking for dishonesty at the point D makes off.

---

[78] *Brooks and Brooks* (1982) 76 Cr App R 66.

10.8 Reform

Despite the relatively recent reform of fraud offences in the FA 2006, the government has kept the exercise of these offences under review and further legislative change remains possible.[79] In this section, we discuss three areas of debate: the drafting of the FA 2006; the move to conduct crimes; and the disappearing distinction between theft and fraud.

10.8.1 The drafting of the FA 2006

There has been a trend in modern statutes to define offences in an unhelpfully complex manner.[80] We were critical of this in relation to the Sexual Offences Act 2003 (**8.9**), and we discuss similar criticisms in relation to inchoate offences of assisting and encouraging and the Serious Crime Act 2007 (**Chapter 11**). In comparison to these other statutes, the FA 2006 is remarkably straightforward, defining the three core routes to fraud liability over just five brief sections. It should also be recognised that in the early years of the statute, despite extensive use in the lower courts, there have been very few appeal cases, demonstrating its general success. The question emerges, however, whether this apparent simplicity and success has come at any cost? Two points should be highlighted.

First, in order to remove complex details from the statute, a number of key terms have been left undefined. We saw this earlier, for example, with terms such as 'dishonesty',[81] 'service',[82] 'position',[83] 'abuse',[84] and so on. With terms of this kind, where ordinary meanings are not self-evident, the choice not to provide a statutory definition creates uncertainty in the law.[85] In this manner, complexity is not avoided but is rather hidden within the case law.

Secondly, by removing complex requirements of deception and causation present in the pre-2006 Act offences, the current law has defined the core fraud offences in an inchoate manner, criminalising D's dishonest conduct which is *intended* to interfere with property rights as opposed to criminalising successful interferences. Attempting to simplify the law by broadening offence definitions has also been a common practice in recent years (eg sexual offences; inchoate liability; terrorism offences; etc). The disadvantage of this is the potential for over—or inappropriate—criminalisation. We discuss this further in the following sections.

10.8.2 Fraud and the irrelevance of results

Although the fraud offences are undoubtedly simpler than their equivalents were prior to the FA 2006, the move from deception-based result crimes to dishonesty-based

[79] Sarker, 'Fighting Fraud—A Missed Opportunity' (2007) 28 Comp Law 243.
[80] Spencer, 'The Drafting of Criminal Legislation: Need It Be So Impenetrable?' (2008) 67 CLJ 585.
[81] This term is central to most property offences.
[82] Central to the offence of making off without payment (**10.7.2**) and obtaining services dishonestly (**10.5**).
[83] Required for fraud by abuse of position (**10.4**).
[84] Ibid.
[85] Including potential for challenge under Art 7 ECHR.

conduct crimes has considerably widened the range of conduct caught.[86] Unlike the old deception offences, and unlike other property offences discussed in **Chapter 9**, the actus reus of fraud does not require D to gain property or cause a loss of property to another. For example, for section 2 of the FA 2006, D commits fraud as soon as she makes a false representation with the required mens rea.

The irrelevance of results has broadened liability in two important ways. First, the offence will be committed earlier when the false representation is made rather than when property is transferred. Although this change will affect all cases, it will have a particular impact on cases in which D fails to deceive V and no property is passed. Under the old law, D either commits an attempt offence or no offence at all. Under the FA 2006, D has completed the full offence of fraud.

Secondly, at the other end of the scale, the irrelevance of results also expands the offence to capture later acts. Under the pre-2006 law, it had to be demonstrated that D's deception caused property to be transferred. Thus, D could not be liable for deceptive conduct that came after the transfer of property. This caused problems in cases, for example, where D fills her car with petrol intending to pay, but then changes her mind and deceives the station attendant (V) to avoid payment. The ownership of the petrol passes to D at the moment it mingles with other petrol in her car. Therefore, by the time D deceives V there are no property rights to be passed.[87] This has traditionally been dealt with through the offence of making off without payment, and this continues to apply. However, D's conduct will now *also* be fraud by false representation: D dishonestly makes a false representation after filling her tank when she deceives V (this might be as simple as continuing to act as a paying customer), and does so to make a gain (which includes keeping what one has[88]).

Recognising the expansion of liability under the FA 2006, two questions should be considered. First, is the expansion of liability justified: are these cases criminal mischief that we want to label as fraud? Secondly, are the central terms of the new expanded offence, particularly 'dishonesty', fit for the purpose of identifying and targeting only the conduct deserving of criminalisation?

10.8.3 Distinguishing theft and fraud

Having discussed the definition of the fraud offences, it is useful to briefly return to the debate about overlap between theft and fraud. As we highlighted at the end of the last chapter (**9.8.1**), there is a concern that the offences of fraud and theft overlap to an unacceptable degree.[89] The argument here is that where theft should target D who takes V's property without consent, fraud should target those who deceive V into parting with their property voluntarily. However, as we have seen, the current law does not reflect this neat division. Rather, following *Gomez* and *Hinks*, as long as D acts dishonestly, theft can now extend to cases in which V consents to the appropriation of her property.[90] And, alongside this, fraud now requires no transfer of property at all.

---

[86] See **2.4.1**.

[87] *Collis-Smith* [1971] Crim LR 716.

[88] FA 2006, s5(3).

[89] Shute and Horder, 'Thieving and Deceiving: What is the Difference?' (1993) 56 MLR 548; Melissaris, 'The Concept of Appropriation and the Offence of Theft' (2007) 70 MLR 581.

[90] See discussion at **9.1**.

The question emerging from this is whether the current law is well served maintaining these two separate offences? If the mischief of both offences is now simply focused on dishonest conduct, would a single dishonesty offence provide a more coherent way forward?[91]

10.9 Eye on assessment

In this section we consider the potential application of fraud offences within a problem question, using the same structure of analysis discussed in previous chapters.

> **STEP 1 Identify the potential criminal event in the facts**
>
> This should be simply stated (eg 'The first potential criminal event arises where D makes a false benefit claim'). The role of this stage is to highlight which part of the question you are answering before you begin to apply the law.

When identifying a potential criminal event, it is important to remember that the main fraud offence is a conduct crime: the relevant point of potential liability is where D makes the representation (s2), fails to disclose (s3), or abuses her position (s4), not at the point if and when property rights are affected. Of course, where D possesses articles for use in fraud (s6) or makes or supplies such articles (s7), the potential event may be even earlier.

> **STEP 2 Identify the potential offence**
>
> Again, state this simply (eg 'When claiming false benefits, D may be liable for fraud by false representation'). The role of this stage is to highlight which offence you are going to apply.

Identifying the appropriate offence in this area is not easy, and you need to take time to consider your options. Chiefly, this is because many of the offences overlap with one another, and so you will usually have more than one available route to liability. One issue arising here is that it can be possible, and tempting, to answer a whole problem with reference to only one route to fraud (eg s2). Although accurate, you need to consider that assessments are about demonstrating knowledge, as well as the fair labelling of D, and so it is useful to acknowledge and discuss potential liability under different routes. The one caveat here, as always, is that if the problem question specifies a certain route (eg 'Discuss Dave's potential liability for fraud by failure to disclose') then you should *only* do what the question asks of you.

Table 10.9 sets out the offences we have discussed in this chapter (with the addition of theft), ordered in terms of when they might arise within a problem scenario. On the right, we indicate why you might discuss this offence as opposed to other overlapping options.

---

[91] This possibility is discussed (and rejected) by the Law Commission, *Fraud* (No 276, 2002) paras 5.20–5.57.

Table 10.9 Identifying and applying fraud offences

Possession of articles for use in frauds	• This offence is useful to criminalise acts where D is in possession of something with the required intent before he has done any more towards a full fraud offence. • These offences are useful to consider where, for whatever reason, D does not go on to commit the fraud or theft.
Making or supplying articles for use in frauds	• This offence is useful where D makes or supplies articles for fraud with the required intent. • Again, these offences are useful to consider where, for whatever reason, D does not go on to commit the fraud or theft.
Conspiracy to defraud	• This offence is useful where D agrees with another person to commit fraud, with the required intent. • Again, these offences are useful to consider where for whatever reason D does not go on to commit the fraud or theft.
Fraud by false representation	• This offence applies at the point D makes a false representation. • This offence is extremely wide, covering most of the conduct targeted by the two offences below. If in doubt, this is probably the one to focus on.
Fraud by failure to disclose	• This offence applies at the point D fails (omits) to disclose information where she has a legal duty to do so. • Where there is an omission and a clear legal duty, such as a failure to disclose a criminal record when applying for a job, you should try to apply this offence in preference to fraud by false representation.
Fraud by abuse of position	• This offence applies at the point D abuses her position with a view to making a gain or causing a loss. • Again, although these cases will usually involve a false representation, it is useful to apply this offence in preference to s2 where the facts are clear (eg a carer taking money from her vulnerable patients).
Theft	• Theft applies later than the offences discussed above, occurring only when property has been appropriated by D. • Remember that theft requires potentially problematic elements that fraud does not: appropriation; intention to permanently deprive. • Where you could apply theft or fraud, you should consider which offence provides the most accurate label for what D has done, but also that fraud is the more serious offence and so should usually be applied in preference.

(Continued)

Table 10.9 Continued

Obtaining services dishonestly	• Like theft, this offence only applies where results are caused: the obtaining of a service.
	• Remember that theft does not apply to services. Thus, where services are obtained, you should either apply this offence or one of the fraud offences.
Making off without payment	• This offence comes last in our timeline, applying where D has received the goods and then makes off.
	• This offence is useful where D's dishonesty does not arise until after the goods have been transferred to D. In such a case, theft will not apply due to a lack of coincidence in time of actus reus and mens rea. However, at the time of making off D will be dishonest and so will come within this offence.

Where, as is likely, you identify more than one possible offence, it is good practice to focus your analysis on the most appropriate, but also to (briefly) acknowledge the other possible routes.

STEP 3 Applying the offence to the facts

Having identified the relevant offence, make sure you discuss each of the required elements.

Actus reus: What does the offence require? Did D do it?

Mens rea: What does the offence require? Did D possess it?

AR and MR are satisfied	AR and/or MR are not satisfied
Continue to STEP 4.	Return to STEP 2, and look for an alternative offence. If none, then skip to STEP 5, concluding that no offence is committed.

STEP 4 Consider defences

The word 'consider' here is important, as you should not discuss every defence for every question. Rather, think whether there are any defences (eg duress) that *could* potentially apply. If there are, discuss those only.

STEP 5 Conclude

This is usually a single sentence either saying that it is likely that D has committed the offence, or saying that it is not likely either because an offence element is not satisfied or because a defence is likely to apply. It is not often that you will be able to say categorically whether or not D has committed the offence, particularly when applying concepts such as dishonesty, so it is usually best to conclude in terms of what is more 'likely'.

STEP 6 Loop

Go back up to Step 1, identifying the next potential criminal event. Continue until you have discussed all the relevant potentially criminal events.

 ONLINE RESOURCE CENTRE

www.oxfordtextbooks.co.uk/orc/sho/

This chapter is accompanied by a selection of online resources to help you with this topic, including:

- **Multiple-choice questions**
- **Chapter summary sheet**
- Two **sample examination questions** with answer guidance
- **Further reading**

Also available on the Online Resource Centre are:

- A selection of **videos** from the authors explaining key topics and principles
- **Legal updates**
- Useful **weblinks**

11

General inchoate offences

11.1 Introduction   418

11.2 Criminal attempts   420

    11.2.1 Actus reus of attempts   422

    11.2.2 Mens rea of attempts   429

    11.2.3 Defences to criminal attempts   436

11.3 Conspiracy   436

    11.3.1 Actus reus of conspiracy   438

    11.3.2 Mens rea of conspiracy   444

    11.3.3 Defences to conspiracy   449

    11.3.4 Common law conspiracies   450

11.4 Assisting or encouraging   450

    11.4.1 Actus reus of assisting or encouraging   451

    11.4.2 Mens rea of s44: intentionally encouraging or assisting an offence   453

    11.4.3 Mens rea of s45: encouraging or assisting an offence believing it will be committed   456

    11.4.4 Mens rea of s46: encouraging or assisting offences believing one or more will be committed   459

    11.4.5 Defences to assisting or encouraging   462

11.5 Double inchoate liability   463

11.6 Substantive offences in an inchoate form   464

    11.6.1 Assisting or encouraging suicide   465

11.7 Reform   465

    11.7.1 The actus reus of attempts   466

    11.7.2 The mens rea of attempts and conspiracy   467

    11.7.3 The future of assisting and encouraging   468

    11.7.4 The inconsistency of law reform   468

11.8 Eye on assessment   469

11.1 Introduction

'Inchoate' is a term used to describe offences that are, in some sense, not complete.[1] Standard (non-inchoate) principal offences are designed to target 'mischief' based on D's

---

[1] See **4.2.1.2.**

mens rea and, crucially, her manifestation of some harmful conduct. Inchoate offences, in contrast, will generally *not require* D to have caused significant harm to a person or property, but will target D who has made some progress towards a harmful end, foreseeing/intending harm to come about. D's conduct may be inchoate ('just begun'; 'undeveloped'), but because of her potentially harmful ambitions, it is also deserving of criminalisation.

The general inchoate offences are not defined in relation to any single protected interest, but apply across multiple principal offences.

- Attempt: D is criminalised for trying to commit a principal offence;
- Conspiracy: D is criminalised for agreeing with another to commit a principal offence; and
- Assisting or encouraging: D is criminalised for doing acts capable of assisting or encouraging another (P) to commit a principal offence.

> *Terminology . . .*
> The following will be used throughout this chapter and **Chapter 12**:
> - principal offence—this refers to the offence (eg murder, theft, etc) that D is attempting/conspiring/ assisting or encouraging. This is also commonly referred to as the 'substantive offence', the 'full offence', or the 'future offence';
> - principal offender—where D is assisting or encouraging another to commit a principal offence, the party assisted or encouraged is referred to as the principal offender (P).

In order to understand and apply the general inchoate offences, it is crucial to understand their relationship with principal offences. Two rules stand out as particularly important. First, inchoate offences only operate in combination with a principal offence. For example, D could not be liable for 'attempt', she could only be liable for 'attempted murder' or 'attempted theft' or 'attempted rape', etc. Therefore, when identifying potential liability for one of the general inchoate offences, it is essential to also identify the related principal offence. Secondly, although D's inchoate liability must relate to a principal offence, it is irrelevant (in terms of her inchoate liability) whether that principal offence attempted/ conspired/assisted or encouraged ever comes about.[2] D's liability arises as soon as she satisfies the elements of the inchoate offence.

It is universally accepted that the criminal law should include some form of general inchoate liability.[3] For example, if D shoots at V with an intention to kill, the criminal law would rightly be criticised if it did not consider D's conduct worthy of criminalisation just because, as a matter of luck,[4] D missed her target. The challenge with these offences is setting the point at which D's conduct justifies criminal intervention. We discuss this later in the context of potential reform,[5] but it is useful to keep in mind throughout. As

---

[2] Where D completes the principal offence, however, it would usually be more appropriate in terms of fair labelling to charge that offence (or complicity in a principal offence committed by P, discussed in **Chapter 12**).

[3] Cornford, 'Preventative Criminalisation' [2015] New Crim LR 1.

[4] On the role of 'luck', see Ashworth, 'Criminal Attempts and the Role of Resulting Harm' (1988) 19 Rutgers LR 725.

[5] See **11.7**.

we move into a discussion of the different inchoate offences, you should note that there is a necessary and obvious balancing of legal priorities, and you should consider which of these priorities you believe intuitively is most important in order to start thinking about your evaluation of the current law. We can present this balancing as the relationship between fairness to D and the protection of society.

A) Fairness to D: At the point D commits one of the inchoate offences, the principal offence attempted/conspired/assisted or encouraged has not yet come about and may never come about. Thus, in order to identify sufficient blameworthiness which renders it fair to criminalise D, we are not looking for the same mischief as the principal offence, but rather some kind of equivalent in terms of moral blameworthiness. In search of such equivalence, we are likely to favour mens rea requirements that only criminalise D where she has fully committed to the principal offence, with intention as to its commission. We are also likely to favour restrictive actus reus requirements, only intervening at the moment when D has unequivocally demonstrated dangerous conduct, or conduct very close to the point of committing the principal offence. We want to criminalise D who would have gone on to commit the principal offence, not D who might have changed her mind if left alone.

B) Protection of society: If we follow the 'fairness to D' approach to its natural extremes, we end up with a narrow set of inchoate offences that only target conduct very close to the commission of the principal offence. The problem with this, in many cases, is that it will be dangerous to draw the offence so narrowly. It would mean that investigators would have to wait for D to have progressed a long way on her criminal enterprise to committing the principal offence before she could be arrested for an inchoate offence. Particularly with the rise of intelligence-led policing, where we might have very good evidence of D's future intentions and planning well before the attack, there are obvious benefits to an intervention at the earliest, and therefore safest, opportunity.

The balancing of these and other[6] considerations is central to the set of offences discussed in this chapter. It is a balancing that shifts over time due to political preferences, changes in policing, and public attitudes. It is useful to consider your own views on this issue now, and to keep this in mind when considering the individual offences and cases that follow.

11.2 Criminal attempts

The offence of attempt criminalises D for doing more than merely preparatory acts towards the commission of an offence she is trying to commit.[7] Attempt is generally charged where D has failed to commit the principal offence, although this need not be the case.[8] And where D has failed to commit the principal offence, the reason for this failure is also irrelevant to her liability.[9] D may have failed for a variety of reasons; including

---

[6] We discuss the principles of criminalisation at **1.4**.

[7] See generally Law Commission, *Conspiracy and Attempts* (Consultation 183, 2007) Parts 12–16; *Conspiracy and Attempts* (No 318, 2009) Part 8; Duff, *Criminal Attempts* (1996); Yaffe, *Attempts* (2010).

[8] If D succeeds in committing the principal offence, she remains liable for the earlier attempt, but it would be inappropriate to charge both: *Webley v Buxton* [1977] QB 481.

[9] Although it may be relevant at sentencing.

367

where D changes her mind before completing the principal offence or is stopped from doing so, as well as where D has done everything she thought necessary but fails, for example because her shot misses her target (V) or V is saved by medical intervention.

Exactly when D's 'trying to commit' a principal offence becomes a criminal attempt is defined in section 1(1) of the Criminal Attempts Act 1981 (CAA 1981). The maximum sentence for attempt mirrors that of the principal offence which is being attempted.[10]

(1) If, with intent to commit an offence to which this section applies, a person does an act which is more than merely preparatory to the commission of the offence, he is guilty of attempting to commit the offence.

The elements of criminal attempt are set out in **Tables 11.1a** and **11.1b**.

Table 11.1a Criminal attempts

	Actus reus	**Mens rea**
Conduct element	Any action	Voluntary
Circumstance element	D's action goes beyond mere preparation towards the commission of a principal offence (on the facts as she believes them to be)	None
Result element	None	None
Ulterior mens rea element	*	*Set out in Table 11.1b*

Table 11.1b Ulterior mens rea element for criminal attempts

Principal offence	**D's ulterior mens rea as to the principal offence**
Conduct element	D must intend to complete the conduct required for the principal offence
Circumstance element	*Possible attempts*: D's required mens rea will mirror that required for the circumstances of the principal offence attempted, but only to a minimum of recklessness Or *Impossible attempts*: D must intend/know the circumstances required for the principal offence
Result element	D must intend to cause the results required (if any) for the principal offence

[10] CAA 1981, s4(1).

As **Tables 11.1a** and **11.1b** demonstrate, a major part of the offence of attempt is forward-looking: examining D's ulterior mens rea as to the principal offence she is trying to commit.

11.2.1 Actus reus of attempts

The actus reus of attempt requires D's conduct to have gone beyond mere preparation towards completing a principal offence. Although this sounds relatively simple, several questions must be carefully considered.

11.2.1.1 Can D attempt by omission?

The wording of section 1(1) ('a person does an act') suggests that a criminal attempt cannot be committed by omission.[11] There is also an absence of case law to contradict this. However, it is contended that section 1 can and should be interpreted to allow for this possibility where D is under a legal duty to act. For example, where D starves her child (V) with the intention of killing V, and does so, it is clear that she may be liable for murder.[12] Where V is discovered prior to death and given life-saving treatment, it would surely be appropriate to charge D with attempted murder.[13]

> *Assessment matters . . .*
> If faced with an attempt by omission in a problem question, it should be highlighted that liability may not be available within the terms of the CAA 1981. However, if there is a duty to act, as there would be in our example above, you should also acknowledge that a court may choose to interpret the CAA 1981 to allow for omissions liability.

11.2.1.2 Which principal offences can be attempted?

Our starting point is that all principal offences may be subject to an attempt. However, from this starting point, there are a number of exceptions where attempts liability will *not* apply.

A) **Summary only offences**: Attempts liability will only apply to indictable and either way offences, excluding summary only offences (ie, those triable only in the magistrates' court).[14] Notable examples of summary only offences include assault and battery.[15]

B) **Conspiracy and secondary liability**: To avoid criminalising events too far removed from the principal offence, there can be no liability for D who attempts to

---

[11] Palmer, 'Attempt by Act or Omission: Causation and the Problem of the Hypothetical Nurse' (1999) 63 J Crim L 158.

[12] *Gibbins and Proctor* (1918) 13 Cr App R 134.

[13] The Law Commission has recommended amending the CAA 1981 to make it clear that omissions liability should be possible: Law Commission, *Conspiracy and Attempts* (No 318, 2009) paras 8.142–8.151.

[14] See **1.1.7.3**.

[15] The Law Commission has recommended that attempts should not be extended to include summary only offences: Law Commission, *Conspiracy and Attempts* (No 318, 2009) paras 8.154–8.161.

conspire or attempts to aid and abet another.[16] We discuss this further in the double inchoate liability section later.[17]

C) Other exceptional cases: There are a few examples where attempt liability would be impossible, or at least unlikely, to arise. For example, it is impossible to attempt to commit an involuntary manslaughter offence. This is because attempt requires D to intend the result element of the principal offence (ie in this case, death), and if D intends this element she has committed attempted murder.

11.2.1.3 When are D's acts more than merely preparatory?

The crux of the actus reus of attempt is that D's acts must go 'beyond mere preparation' towards the commission of a relevant principal offence. The term is not defined in the CAA 1981 and should be given its natural meaning.[18] However, it is useful to understand the intentions of those drafting the law, before considering how it has been applied in the courts.

The intended role of 'more than merely preparatory'

Before the CAA 1981, the actus reus of the old common law offence of attempt was simply that D needed to have 'attempted'. Without further guidance on what conduct constituted such an attempt, the law was open to interpretations across a wide spectrum of behaviour. At either end of this spectrum were what have been termed the last act test and the series of acts test. The current law seeks a middle ground.

A) Last act test: The last act test would only allow for attempt liability where D has completed all acts that she believes are necessary to commit the principal offence.[19] Thus, where D sets out to shoot and kill V, D would only attempt after having pulled the trigger. Allowing D every opportunity to change her mind and desist, this approach would only criminalise D where she has passed the point of no return, when she has 'crossed the Rubicon and burnt h[er] boats'.[20] The downside of this approach, of course, is that it may not provide adequate protection for society: where the police can intervene prior to D's 'last act' we would surely want them to do so, and yet we could not always rely on an alternative offence to charge them with.

B) Series of acts test: The series of acts test, formulated by Stephen, would find attempts liability where D's act forms 'part of a series of acts which would constitute [the] commission [of a principal offence] if it were not interrupted'.[21] In our attempted murder by shooting example, this would allow for liability well before the firing of the gun, potentially back to the buying of the gun, planning the killing, etc. This approach allows for early criminalisation and thus early intervention by the police to protect society,

---

16 CAA 1981, s1(4). On the exclusion of attempting to aid and abet, see Bohlander, 'The Conflict Between the Serious Crime Act 2007 and Section 1(4)(b) Criminal Attempts Act 1981—A Missed Repeal?' [2010] Crim LR 483; Child, 'The Differences Between Attempted Complicity and Inchoate Assisting and Encouraging—A Reply to Professor Bohlander' [2010] Crim LR 924.

17 See **11.5**.

18 *Jones* [1990] 3 All ER 886.

19 Applied in the early case of *Eagleton* (1855) 6 Cox CC 559.

20 *Stonehouse* [1978] AC 55. Reference to the 'Rubicon' is to the river at the edge of the Roman Empire: when the Rubicon was crossed with armed men, war was declared.

21 *Digest of Criminal Law* (5th edn, 1894) Art 50.

not least V! However, as recognised by Lord Lane CJ in *Gullefer*,[22] the disadvantage of this is that D's actions at these very early stages may not yet be sufficiently proximate to the principal offence to be deserving of liability. As D's conduct may also be objectively innocent (eg legally buying a gun), there is also a problem with potential over-reliance on confession evidence and the associated risks of encouraging police malpractice.[23]

C) The CAA 1981 test: Within this spectrum of proximity to the principal offence, the CAA 1981 formulation—'more than merely preparatory'—tries to forge a midway path.[24] The idea is that, although strictly speaking all acts prior to the last act are done in preparation, there are certain acts leading to a principal offence that are sufficiently proximate as to go beyond 'mere' preparation, and are deserving of attempts liability.[25] Although somewhat vague, the test is necessarily general in its terms because it has to be adaptable to a great number of offences, including all serious ones, across the criminal law. The ideal of this approach is illustrated in *Jones*.[26]

 Jones (1990) 91 Cr App R 351

D got into the back seat of a car with V, and pointed a sawn-off shotgun at him. Following a struggle, V escaped unharmed. D was charged with attempted murder.

- Crown Court: guilty of attempted murder.
- Court of Appeal: conviction upheld on appeal. Even though D was at least three steps away from completing the principal offence (he still had to remove the safety catch, put his finger on the trigger, and pull it), his acts were still capable of being 'more than merely preparatory'.

Applying 'more than merely preparatory' in practice

The aims of the CAA 1981 formulation are relatively clear. The problem, however, is that because the test is applied in practice across multiple offences and across an infinite variety of factual circumstances, there is potential for it to be applied in unwanted and inconsistent ways.[27] In relation to 'complete attempts,' where D has completed the last acts she believes are necessary to commit the principal offence, then there is no problem as D clearly satisfies the actus reus requirement of going beyond mere preparation.[28] However, problems do emerge in the context of 'incomplete attempts,' where D still has a number of acts to complete before she commits the offence. Three areas of concern are apparent within the literature: (A) the test is being applied too narrowly; (B) the test is being applied inconsistently *between* offences; and (C) the test is being applied inconsistently *within* offences.

---

[22] [1990] 3 All ER 882.
[23] Horder, *Ashworth's Principles of Criminal Law* (8th edn, 2016) 479.
[24] See, leading to this formulation, Law Commission, *Attempt, and Impossibility in Relation to Attempt, Conspiracy and Incitement* (No 102, 1980) paras 2.19–2.52.
[25] *Tosti* [1997] Crim LR 746: the court held that D's acts were 'preparatory, but not merely so'.
[26] Discussed in Smith, 'Proximity in Attempt: Lord Lane's Midway Course' [1991] Crim LR 576.
[27] Law Commission, *Conspiracy and Attempts* (Consultation 183, 2007) Parts 1, 12–14.
[28] The only exception to this can arise where D is a secondary party to a principal offence.

A) **Applied too narrowly:** The first area of concern is that the 'more than merely pre-paratory' test is being interpreted too narrowly, inadequately weighing the need to pro-tect society from harms and failing to identify the desired midway course. This was the view of the Law Commission in its most recent consultation,[30] although it subsequently chose not to recommend reform of the current formulation. **Table 11.2** provides an overview of cases that can be used to illustrate this criticism.

Table 11.2 Is the actus reus of attempt applied too narrowly?

Case	Facts	Outcome on appeal
Gullefer [1990] 3 All ER 882	D tried to stop a dog race, in which the dog he bet on was losing, by jumping onto the track. He hoped the race would be declared a 'no race' and he would be able to reclaim his bet. D was charged and convicted of attempting to steal the money.	Appeal allowed. D's acts were not beyond mere preparation: he would still have had to go to the bookmakers, demand his money, etc.
Campbell [1991] Crim LR 268	D was arrested a yard away from the door of a Post Office that he intended to rob. He was carrying an imitation firearm, a threatening note, and he confessed to the planned robbery. D was charged and convicted of attempted robbery.	Appeal allowed. D's acts were not beyond mere preparation: he had not yet entered the Post Office or made any demands of the cashier.
Geddes [1996] Crim LR 894	D was found in the boys' toilet of a school with various kidnapping paraphernalia. D was charged and convicted of attempted false imprisonment.	Appeal allowed. D's acts were not beyond mere preparation: D was lying in wait but he had not confronted a potential victim.
K [2009] EWCA Crim 1931	D approached a 6-year-old boy playing near his work and asked him if he wanted to watch pornography on the laptop in his office. D was charged and convicted of attempting to cause a child to watch a sexual act (Sexual Offences Act 2003, s12).	Appeal allowed. D's acts were not beyond mere preparation: D had not yet led the child to the laptop (if indeed it was there).

---

[29] CAA 1981, s4(3). Discussed in *Wang* [2005] UKHL 9.
[30] Law Commission, *Conspiracy and Attempts* (Consultation 183, 2007).

B) Inconsistent between offences: The second area of concern is that the test is being applied inconsistently, and that despite the restrictive approach exemplified in the cases in **Table 11.2**, certain categories of offence have attracted a considerably broader approach.[31] An example of this is the offence of attempted rape. Although the actus reus of rape is only completed when D achieves penile penetration of V's vagina, anus, or mouth, convictions for attempted rape have been secured on the basis of conduct well short of this. In most such cases, D will be found to have attempted rape at the stage of physical confrontation with V. This is illustrated in the case of *Dagnall*.[32]

 Dagnall [2003] EWCA Crim 2441

D grabbed V with the intention of raping her and forced her against a fence. Fortunately, a passing police car saw D and intervened. There was no evidence that D had begun to remove V's clothes, let alone attempted the act of penetration. D was charged with attempted rape.

- Crown Court: guilty of attempted rape.
- Court of Appeal: conviction upheld on appeal.

C) Inconsistent within offences: The third area of concern is that the test is being applied inconsistently within individual offence groups, and even within individual offences. For example, in the case of *K*, summarised earlier (**Table 11.2**), it was held that discussing watching pornography with a child was not beyond mere preparation towards the offence of causing a child to watch a sexual act. However, in a case which was appealed in the same year, *R*,[33] it was held that there could be attempt liability where D sent a text message to a prostitute asking her if she knew of any 12-year-olds available for sex.[34] Similarly, although the court held in *Geddes* (also summarised in **Table 11.2**) that D was not beyond mere preparation to kidnapping when he was found in a school toilet, a quite different approach was taken in *Tosti* just a year later.

 Tosti [1997] Crim LR 746

D was found examining the lock of a barn. D's car was also found nearby, containing metal-cutting equipment. D was charged with attempted burglary.

- Crown Court: guilty of attempted burglary.
- Court of Appeal: conviction upheld on appeal.

For those who believe that the approach in *Geddes* was applied too narrowly, then the decision in *Tosti* is to be welcomed. However, bearing in mind that in *Tosti* the defendant was simply examining the lock, and would have had to have gone back to his car to collect the cutting equipment, etc, the two decisions are difficult to reconcile.

---

[31] For useful discussion of this, see Clarkson, 'Attempt: The Conduct Requirement' (2009) 29 OJLS 25.

[32] See also *AG's Reference (No 1 of 1992)* (1992) 96 Cr App R 298; *Paitnaik* [2000] 3 Arch News 2; *MH* [2004] WLR 137; *Bryan* [2015] EWCA Crim 433.

[33] [2009] 1 WLR 713.

[34] An attempt to arrange a sexual offence with a child (Sexual Offences Act 2003, s14).

11.2.1.4 What if the crime D is attempting is impossible for her to commit?

This question arises where D tries to commit a principal offence, *but unknown to her*,
the commission of that offence would be impossible. An offence may be impossible
for a variety of reasons. However, there are two broad categories that should be distinguished: legal impossibility and factual impossibility.

Legal impossibility

D's attempt is *legally* impossible where she tries to commit a principal offence which,
contrary to her belief, is not actually an offence known to the law. For example, if D
wrongly believes that adultery is illegal, and then tries to seduce one of her husband's
friends, we could describe her actions as an impossible attempt: she has gone beyond
mere preparation towards the commission of what she believes is a principal offence.
She has also revealed a criminal character; a willingness to break the law. However, as
adultery is not a crime known to English law, and because the actus reus of attempt
requires D to have attempted to commit 'an offence', there can be no liability in these
circumstances. This was confirmed in *Taaffe*.[35]

Factual impossibility

D's attempt is factually impossible where she tries to commit a principal offence which
does exist in English law, but the circumstances surrounding her attempt mean it could
not come about. This includes cases of physical impossibility where, for example, D tries
to kill V who is already dead, or tries to steal from an empty safe, etc; as well as cases of
inadequate means, such as where D tries to kill V by putting pins in a voodoo doll, or
tries to shoot V with an unloaded gun, etc. In these cases, D has not only demonstrated
a general willingness to break the law, but has gone beyond mere preparation—on the
facts as she believed them to be—towards committing a valid principal offence. In recognition of this culpability, the current law will find attempts liability. This is confirmed
in section 1(2) of the CAA 1981.

> (2) A person may be guilty of attempting to commit an offence to which this section applies even
> though the facts are such that the commission of the offence is impossible.

This subsection does not contradict the requirement for D's acts to have been more than
merely preparatory towards the commission of an offence. Rather, it provides an alternative route to satisfy this element. Let us take the example where D tries to shoot V with
a gun that is, unknown to her, not loaded. Applying the actus reus of attempted murder,
we first ask whether D's acts in pulling the trigger have gone beyond mere preparation
towards killing V in reality? The answer here may be 'no': D cannot cause an unloaded gun

---

[35] [1983] 2 All ER 625: D attempted to import foreign currency, believing (incorrectly) that this was
a crime. No liability for attempt.

to fire, and so, in reality, the intended shooting still requires D to go and buy bullets etc (ie it is insufficiently proximate). However, where the answer to this first question is 'no', section 1(2) allows us to ask a second question: have D's acts gone beyond mere preparation *on the facts as she believed them to be*? Where the answer to this second question is 'yes', as it would be in our example, D will have satisfied the actus reus of the attempt. Where the answer to both questions is 'no', of course, there will be no attempts liability.

In many cases, the application of this rule appears uncontroversial. In our unloaded gun case, for example, D has shown herself willing to complete all the acts she believes are necessary to kill another person, demonstrating her culpability, and the mere fact of failure on this occasion does not prevent her future dangerousness. However, isolated from D's intentions/beliefs, impossible attempts will often involve seemingly innocent conduct, such as clicking the trigger of an *unloaded* gun, putting sugar in tea *believing it is poison*, handling goods *believing them to be stolen*, and so on. Because such cases can seem so innocuous, despite the terms of section 1(2) of the CAA 1981, the courts initially wavered when applying the test. We see this in *Anderton v Ryan*.

 Anderton v Ryan [1985] UKHL 5

D admitted to police that she was in possession of a stolen video recorder. However, the police could not trace the origin of the recorder in order to prove that it was stolen. D was charged with attempting to handle stolen goods.[36]

- Magistrates' court: not guilty of attempting to handle stolen goods—ruled out by impossibility.
- Divisional Court: appeal allowed. The case was sent back with an instruction to convict—an impossible attempt is still an attempt.
- House of Lords: appeal against conviction allowed (Lord Edmund-Davies dissenting)—the majority held that section 1(2) only extended attempts liability to certain cases of factual impossibility and this was not one of them.

Anderton v Ryan created an odd precedent, contrary to the wording of section 1(2). And, indeed, just a year later, in *Shivpuri*, it was overruled. *Shivpuri* confirmed, in line with the statutes, that factual impossibility would never undermine attempts liability.[37]

 Shivpuri [1987] AC 1

D was arrested by customs officials with a suitcase which he 'confessed' contained prohibited drugs. However, analysis of the contents showed that it actually contained simple vegetable matter (ie not prohibited drugs). D was charged with attempting to be knowingly concerned in dealing with a prohibited drug.[38]

- Crown Court: guilty of attempting the drugs offence.
- Court of Appeal: conviction upheld on appeal.
- House of Lords: appeal dismissed—*Anderton v Ryan* overruled.

---

[36] The offence of handling stolen goods is discussed at **9.5**.
[37] The court was heavily influenced by Williams, 'The Lords and Impossible Attempts' (1986) 45 CLJ 33.
[38] Customs and Excise Management Act 1979, s170(1)(b).

Post-*Shivpuri*, the legal position on impossible attempts is clear. Even where D's acts do not go beyond mere preparation in fact, they may still satisfy the actus reus of attempts if they go beyond mere preparation on the facts *as D believed them to be*.

11.2.2 Mens rea of attempts

As with the other inchoate offences, and as illustrated in **Tables 11.1a** and **11.1b**, the major part of D's mens rea relates to her completion of the future principal offence. This is an ulterior mens rea: mens rea as to a principal offence (eg murder, theft, handling stolen goods, etc) that need never be completed in fact. Such mens rea is vital to D's liability, representing the gravamen of inchoate liability. Without such mens rea, D has simply completed acts that may appear entirely innocent, particularly in the context of impossible attempts. With proof of her mens rea, however, D's acts are revealed as culpable acts in pursuit of a principal offence and deserving of criminalisation. For example, D puts sugar in V's tea believing that that sugar is poison and intending to kill.

It is on this basis that section 1(1) of the CAA 1981 explicitly requires D to act 'with intent to commit an offence'. In the Law Commission's work preceding the CAA 1981, it was believed that D would only be correctly held liable for an attempt where she was fully committed (ie where she *intended*) to go on to commit every element of the actus reus of the principal offence attempted.[39] This approach was adopted within the statute. However, as we will discuss in the following section, applying the requirement that D intends the principal offence has not always been straightforward.

11.2.2.1 Intending the principal offence

The requirement that D acts with the intention to commit the actus reus of the principal offence, subject to the discussion later, applies regardless of the mens rea requirements of that principal offence. This is illustrated in the case of *Whybrow*.

Whybrow (1951) 35 Cr App R 141

D wired up a soap dish in his bathroom in order to give his wife an electric shock. D was charged with attempted murder.

- Crown Court: guilty of attempted murder. The trial judge directed the jury that the mens rea for attempted murder is the same as for murder: intention to kill or cause GBH.
- Court of Criminal Appeal: appeal dismissed. The direction was wrong to include 'intention to cause GBH', but the misdirection did not render the verdict unsafe. The mens rea for attempted murder requires D to intend to kill.

As clarified in *Whybrow*, although the mens rea of murder allows for an intention to kill *or to cause GBH*, the mens rea for attempted murder requires D to intend to complete the actus reus of the principal offence. Thus, as the actus reus for murder requires D

---

[39] Law Commission, *Attempt, and Impossibility in Relation to Attempt, Conspiracy and Incitement* (No 102, 1980).

to kill V (ie GBH is not sufficient), only an intention to kill will satisfy the mens rea of attempted murder.

The same rule applies in relation to principal offences that require a mens rea of less than intention. For example, attempted criminal damage requires an intention to cause damage despite the principal offence requiring only recklessness as to damage;[40] attempted ABH requires an intention to cause ABH despite the principal offence requiring no mens rea as to this harm at all;[41] and so on.[42] Regardless of the mens rea of the principal offence, attempts liability requires D to act with the intention to complete the actus reus elements of the principal offence.

The mens rea term 'intention' here carries the same meaning as it does at common law: including both direct (purposive) and oblique (defined in *Woollin*) intention.[43] As with all ulterior mens rea, an intention to commit the principal offence also includes a conditional intention to do so. A conditional intention, as we have discussed,[44] arises where D decides to do something (ie in this case, to commit a principal offence) *only if* a certain condition arises or, alternatively, *unless* certain conditions arise. This was discussed in *AG's References (Nos 1 and 2 of 1979)*.

AG's References (Nos 1 and 2 of 1979) [1980] QB 180

Combined cases in which D (in each case) was arrested in the process of trying to steal non-specified items (ie anything worth stealing) from another's premises. In the first case, D had entered the building and was searching for items of value (charged with s9(1)(a) burglary[45]); in the second, D was arrested when trying to enter the building (charged with attempted s9(1)(a) burglary).

• Crown Court: not guilty in either case—D did not have an intention to steal specific items but merely a conditional intention to steal items if there were any worth taking.

• Court of Appeal: Crown Court was wrong. D could have been convicted in either case. A conditional intention to steal is still an intention to steal.

The clarification of the law in *AG's References (Nos 1 and 2 of 1979)* seems entirely sensible: just as D intends to steal if she has specific items in mind, so she intends to steal if she has a conditional intention to steal unspecified items.

Confusion pre-*AG's References (Nos 1 and 2 of 1979)*, concerning how such cases should be charged, provides a useful reminder that care must be taken to identify exactly what D is intending. For example, in *Easom*,[46] D rummaged through a woman's handbag in a theatre and then, finding nothing worth taking, put it back. The bag was connected to a policewoman's wrist by a thread. The Court of Appeal correctly held that D did not commit theft or attempted theft because he was not intending to steal (ie to permanently deprive D) of the bag or those specified contents. Rather, D was attempting to steal items of value

---

[40] *Millard and Vernon* [1987] Crim LR 393. See **9.7**.

[41] See **7.4**.

[42] Horder, 'Varieties of Intention, Criminal Attempts and Endangerment' (1994) 14 LS 335.

[43] Confirmed in *Pearman* (1984) 80 Cr App R 259; *Walker* (1989) 90 Cr App R 226. For discussion of 'intention', see **3.4.1**.

[44] See **3.4.1.3**.

[45] See **9.4.1**.

[46] [1971] 2 QB 315; followed in *Husseyn* (1977) 67 Cr App R 131.

that he did not find; these were the items he intended to permanently deprive from V. If the indictment had reflected this by stating 'attempting to steal contents of the handbag' then he could and should have been found liable of a standard impossible attempt.[47]

> **Don't be confused . . .**
> Try to remember, simply, that a conditional intention as to future acts is still an intention. Indeed, all future intention can be described as conditional to some degree, whether D makes this explicit or not. Taking the example of attempted theft, if we asked any would-be thief if she intends to steal if she discovers she is being watched by the police; if she wins the lottery and becomes a millionaire; etc, the answer is likely to be 'no'—her intention to steal is conditional on these facts not arising. In this way, just because D is explicit about certain conditions in a case will not undermine her intention.

11.2.2.2 Expanding what it means to intend the principal offence

So far, so good: D must act with the intention, including conditional intention, to commit the actus reus of the future principal offence. However, unfortunately, the application of this approach in practice has revealed an apparent unfairness, and the courts have reacted to this by reinterpreting the statute.

This apparent unfairness arose in the context of attempted rape, and the case of *Khan*.

 Khan [1990] 2 All ER 783

D and others tried to have sex with V (a 16-year-old girl) who was not consenting. Each of the defendants was reckless as to her non-consent. The defendants who had achieved penetration were straightforwardly guilty of rape. However, D did not achieve penetration and was charged with attempted rape.

- Crown Court: guilty of rape—the mens rea for attempted rape is the same as for the principal offence of rape.
- Court of Appeal: *the judgment of the Court of Appeal is discussed below.*

Applying section 1(1) of the CAA 1981 literally, the judgment of the Crown Court in *Khan* appears to be wrong. If attempt liability requires D to intend *every* element of the actus reus of the principal offence, then the mens rea for attempted rape is not the same as the mens rea for rape. The principal offence of rape is satisfied by an intention to cause penile penetration of V's vagina, anus, or mouth, but it requires a lesser mens rea as to the circumstance requirement of V's non-consent (ie recklessness when *Khan* was decided; a lack of reasonable belief in consent under the current law[48]). Following a literal interpretation of the CAA 1981, therefore, the charge of attempted rape should have required a mens rea of intention as to every element of the actus reus, including intention or knowledge as to this circumstance element.[49]

The problem with this conclusion in relation to *Khan*, is that it would have undermined his liability for attempted rape: D was *reckless* as to V's non-consent; he did not *intend* or

---

[47] Campbell, 'Conditional Intention' (1982) 2 LS 77.
[48] See **8.2.**
[49] As discussed at **3.4.2**, in the context of circumstance elements, knowledge and intention are applied as equivalent states of mind.

know that she was not consenting. However, what D did in trying to have non-consensual intercourse with V, being reckless as to her non-consent, was so similar to those defendants who were liable for rape that a lack of liability for attempted rape would appear unaccept-able.[50] The Court of Appeal chose to avoid this problem by reinterpreting and expanding what it means to intend to commit the principal offence.

 Khan [1990] 2 All ER 783

- Court of Appeal: conviction upheld on appeal. Attempts liability requires D to *intend* the physical parts of the principal offence (ie in this case, the act of penetration), but need not include an intention as to attendant circumstances (ie in this case, V's lack of consent). Thus, in relation to such attendant circumstances, it is sufficient for D to have the same mens rea as required for the principal offence (ie in this case, recklessness).

For the Court of Appeal in *Khan*, 'with intent to commit an offence' should be interpreted as requiring an intention to commit the physical parts of the principal offence—that is, any conduct and result elements—but allows for mens rea less than intention as to any circumstance elements. On this basis, the court was able to find D liable for attempted rape. Following this case, the Law Commission has not only endorsed the approach in *Khan*, but has recommended the CAA 1981 be amended to make this approach clearer.[51]

Following *Khan*, the mens rea of attempt is satisfied where D *intends* the conduct and result elements of the principal offence attempted, but may be satisfied by a *lesser mens rea* as to circumstances. Applied to an offence of attempted criminal damage, for example, this would require D to intend the result element of causing damage, even though the principal offence would be satisfied by recklessness. However, it would allow for recklessness as to the circumstance element (ie that the property damaged belongs to another), mirroring the mens rea of the principal offence as to this element.

Khan represents the current law. We discuss this approach and others in the reform section later in the chapter.[52] However, even at this stage, it is useful to have an idea of some of the problems with the *Khan* approach in practice. Four criticisms should be noted.

A) **Difficulty in separating offence elements:** The approach taken in *Khan* had been mooted by the Law Commission when it was making its recommendations which led to the CAA 1981. However, the approach was rejected at that time, chiefly because of the difficulty of separating principal offences into conduct, circumstance, and result elements.[53] In order to apply the *Khan* approach, such separation is essential: although mens rea as to the circumstance element can mirror that required for the principal offence, mens rea as to the conduct and result elements are fixed at intention.

---

[50] Williams, 'The Problem of Reckless Attempts' [1983] Crim LR 365.
[51] Law Commission, *Conspiracy and Attempts* (No 318, 2009) paras 8.87–8.141.
[52] See **11.6**.
[53] Law Commission, *Attempt, and Impossibility in Relation to Attempt, Conspiracy and Incitement* (No 102, 1980) paras 2.11–2.13. Buxton, 'The Working Paper on Inchoate Offences' [1973] Crim LR 656; Buxton, 'Circumstances, Consequences and Attempted Rape' [1984] Crim LR 25.

B) Lack of clarity regarding mens rea for the circumstance element: Where the principal offence requires subjective mens rea as to the circumstance element (eg intention, recklessness etc) then it is clear from *Khan* that the mens rea for attempt should mirror this standard. However, it remains unclear whether the courts will allow a similar mirroring if the circumstance element of the principal offence allowed for negligence or strict liability. For example, in a case similar to *Khan* today (ie post-Sexual Offences Act 2003) would D have to be reckless as to V's non-consent, or would it be sufficient to mirror the principal offence mens rea (ie a lack of reasonable belief in consent)? The answer to this is uncertain. However, it is likely that courts would follow the Law Commission's interpretation that there should be a minimum mens rea of recklessness, even where the circumstance element of the principal offence would require less.[54]

C) What if the principal offence includes an ulterior mens rea element? *Khan* helps us to identify the mens rea for an attempt in relation to the conduct, circumstance, and result elements of an offence, but does not tell us what mens rea will be required as to an ulterior mens rea element within a principal offence. This issue arose in *AG's Reference (No 3 of 1992)*.

 AG's Reference (No 3 of 1992) (1993) 98 Cr App R 383

D (and others) threw petrol bombs towards a car containing V, reckless as to the endangerment of V. The throws missed. D was charged with attempted aggravated arson.[55]

- Crown Court: not guilty of attempted aggravated arson. Although the principal offence allowed for liability where D is merely reckless as to the endangerment of life (ulterior mens rea requirement), an attempt requires D to intend to endanger life.
- Court of Appeal: Crown Court was wrong. D should have been found guilty. Following *Khan*, it is sufficient for D's mens rea in attempt to reflect the mens rea required for the principal offence.

This case is highly problematic. Although the Court of Appeal claimed to be following *Khan*, the element of the principal offence they were dealing with (recklessness as to the endangerment of life) is poorly characterised as a circumstance element. However, if we see it as anything other than a circumstance element (eg as a result element) then *AG's Reference (No 3 of 1992)* represents a further extension of the *Khan* precedent (ie allowing less than intention) outside circumstances. The general confusion surrounding what this case represents makes it unlikely to be followed. It is contended that where

---

[54] Law Commission, *Conspiracy and Attempts* (No 318, 2009) para 8.133.
[55] See **9.7.5.**

a principal offence includes an ulterior mens rea element, this should be *intended* for attempts liability.[56]

D) What if the offence D is attempting is impossible? The Law Commission's rejection of a *Khan*-like approach prior to the CAA 1981 was also based on a concern about the potential for inappropriate criminalisation, where D's attempt was impossible *and* D was reckless as to circumstances.[57] For example, D intentionally breaks a vase that belongs to her, although at the time of causing the damage she was not sure if it was hers or not. Liability for attempted criminal damage in this case seems unjustified: D did not risk another's property (impossible attempt), and she did not intend to do so (reckless as to ownership).[58] Interestingly, it is this final area of concern that has led to the latest twist in the case law.

11.2.2.3 Re-narrowing what it means to intend the principal offence?

As feared, a case came before the courts that combined an impossible attempt with potential recklessness as to circumstances: *Pace*.

Pace [2014] EWCA Crim 186

Undercover police officers sold scrap metal at a scrap metal yard to D and another, intimating that the metal was stolen. D purchased the metal regardless. As the metal was not in fact stolen, D was charged with attempting to convert criminal property.[59]

- Crown Court: guilty of attempting to convert criminal property. The fact that the attempt was impossible, because the metal was not criminal property, does not bar liability; and following *Khan* it is sufficient that D had a mens rea of suspicion as to the circumstance element of the principal offence (ie suspicion rather than intention that the property was stolen).

- Court of Appeal: appeal allowed. Attempts liability requires D to intend every element of the actus reus of the principal offence, including any circumstance elements.

The Court of Appeal in *Pace* explicitly rejected the reasoning that led to the judgment in *Khan*, drawing on a number of the criticisms of *Khan* listed earlier. However, crucially, *Pace* could not overrule *Khan*, with both decided by the Court of Appeal. Instead, the court in *Pace* seek to distinguish and limit *Khan* on the dual basis that: (a) *Khan* was not intended to create a general rule for attempts; and (b) *Khan* did not involve an impossible attempt.[60] We are left with a rather unfortunate patchwork of both *Khan* and *Pace*.

11.2.2.4 Intending the principal offence under the current law

The current law, following *Khan* and *Pace*, is at something of a crossroads (see **Table 11.3**). Despite the efforts to distinguish the two cases in *Pace*, it is difficult to avoid the conclusion that the two approaches are irreconcilable, representing different

[56] Child, 'The Structure, Coherence and Limits of Inchoate Liability: The New Ulterior Element' (2014) 34 LS 537.

[57] Law Commission, *Attempt, and Impossibility in Relation to Attempt, Conspiracy and Incitement* (No 102, 1980) paras 2.99–2.100.

[58] Williams, 'The Government's Proposals on Criminal Attempts—III' (1981) 131 NLJ 128.

[59] Contrary to the Proceeds of Crime Act 2002, s327(1).

[60] *Pace* [2014] EWCA Crim 186, [52].

interpretations of the 'mischief' of attempt liability. We must therefore wait for an appeal to the Supreme Court, or for the very unlikely eventuality of legislative reform, to decide between them. In this regard, there is growing academic opinion encouraging the court in either direction.[61]

In the meantime, for the lower courts (*and for answers to problem questions*), we may see the mens rea of attempts diverging between impossible and possible attempts: impossible attempt cases applying *Pace* and requiring intention as to every element of the principal offence attempted, and attempts that are possible applying *Khan* and requiring intention as to conduct and results, but allowing mens rea as to circumstances to mirror that required for the principal offence. To illustrate this distinction, we can use the example of attempted criminal damage. Remember that the principal offence of criminal damage has a mens rea of recklessness, both as to circumstances (ownership of the property) and results (damage to the property).[62]

Table 11.3 Applying *Khan* and *Pace*

Facts	Which case to apply?
D intentionally tries to damage property, being reckless as to whether it belongs to her. The property belongs to V.	Possible attempt = apply *Khan* D is liable for attempted criminal damage because she intended the conduct and result, and her mens rea as to the circumstance mirrored that of the principal offence.
D intentionally tries to damage property, being reckless as to whether it belongs to her. The property does belong to her.	Impossible attempt = apply *Pace*. D is not liable for attempted criminal damage because she does not intend or know every element of the principal offence.
D intentionally tries to damage property that she knows belongs to V.	D is liable for attempted criminal damage (whether the attempt is possible or not) because she intends every element of the principal offence.
D is reckless as to causing damage to property that she knows belongs to V.	D is not liable for attempted criminal damage (whether the attempt is possible or not) because she does not intend the result element of the principal offence.

Distinguishing the mens rea of possible and impossible attempts in this way is no more than a temporary position until one approach (*Khan* or *Pace*) is chosen definitively over the other. Not only does the distinction make the law overly complex, but it is also unprincipled,

---

[61] In support of the approach in *Pace*, see Child and Hunt, '*Pace and Rogers* and the Mens Rea of Criminal Attempt: *Khan* on the Scrapheap?' (2014) 78 J Crim L 220; Mirfield, 'Intention and Criminal Attempts' [2015] Crim LR 142; Simester, 'The Mens Rea of Criminal Attempts' (2015) 131 LQR 169. In support of the approach in *Khan*, see Dyson, 'Scrapping *Khan*' [2014] Crim LR 445; Stark, 'The Mens Rea of a Criminal Attempt' [2014] Arch Rev 7.

[62] See **9.7**.

as the reasoning in the two cases clash; not being isolated to possible or impossible attempts. It will also be very difficult to apply in practice, since it will not always be clear whether an attempt is possible or impossible.[63]

11.2.3 Defences to criminal attempts

The general defences discussed in **Chapters 13** and **14** apply to criminal attempts in the same way that they apply to other offences. Beyond this, there are no specific defences.

Certain jurisdictions have recognised a defence of withdrawal, where D has gone beyond mere preparation with the required mens rea (ie she has committed an attempt) but then voluntarily desists from carrying it out. However, withdrawal has never been incorporated into English law.[64]

11.3 Conspiracy

Conspiracy is defined in section 1 of the Criminal Law Act 1977 (CLA 1977).[65] It is an offence for two or more defendants (D1 and D2) to agree to commit a future principal offence. As with attempts, D's liability for conspiracy is tied to the principal offence: D is not guilty of conspiracy *simpliciter*, but of conspiracy to murder, conspiracy to commit theft, conspiracy to rape, and so on. And, again, D's liability for conspiracy is not affected by the principal offence being later committed or not: D is liable as soon as the agreement is formed with the required mens rea.

> **Extra detail . . .**
> It is common to see prosecutions for conspiracy even where D has completed the principal offence agreed upon. There is nothing to bar this approach, and it can be advantageous for prosecutors in relation to the rules of evidence.[66] However, this is not good practice in terms of fair labelling; has been consistently criticised by the courts;[67] and has led to problems in practice.[68]

Alongside statutory conspiracy under the CLA 1977, there also remains a small subset of common law conspiracies. A legacy from the old law of conspiracy pre-CLA 1977, these conspiracies can apply even where D1 and D2 have agreed to do something that may not be a principal offence in its own right. The common law conspiracies which are still recognised within the law are conspiracy to defraud[69] and conspiracy to corrupt public morals or to outrage public decency. These common law conspiracy offences are highly controversial and the Law Commission has repeatedly recommended their abolition.[70] Each will be discussed briefly, after we have explored the central statutory offence.

---

[63] Child and Hunt, '*Pace and Rogers* and the Mens Rea of Criminal Attempt: *Khan* on the Scrapheap?' (2014) 78 J Crim L 220.

[64] First rejected in *Taylor* (1859) 1 F & F 511. See also Wasik, 'Abandoning Criminal Intent' [1980] Crim LR 785; Stuart, 'The Actus Reus in Attempts' [1970] Crim LR 505, 519–521.

[65] As amended by the CAA 1981, s5.

[66] Klein, 'Conspiracy—The Prosecutor's Darling' (1957) 24 Brook LR 1.

[67] We see such criticism as far back as *Boulton* (1871) 12 Cox CC 87.

[68] Jarvis and Bisgrove, 'The Use and Abuse of Conspiracy' [2014] Crim LR 261.

[69] Already discussed at **10.7.1**.

[70] eg Law Commission, *Fraud* (No 276, 2002).

The rationale for criminalising conspiracy, as with attempts, is based around the dual logic of (a) allowing for early police intervention to prevent future criminal harms, whilst (b) targeting conduct and mens rea that demonstrates a sufficient mischief to be deserving of liability, even though the full principal offence is not committed. This mischief in the context of conspiracy, however, is quite unique. Rather than requiring a certain degree of proximity to the principal offence, as with attempts, conspiracy focuses on the agreement between defendants to commit the principal offence. Agreement is crucial here because it provides powerful evidence of a committed intention to carry out the principal offence,[71] as well as introducing the increased danger posed by coordinated group offences, for example gang violence, organised property offences, etc. There is also a psychological aspect to an agreed intention, as opposed to an individual intention, which makes D more likely to go through with what she has agreed with another.

The maximum sentence for statutory conspiracy mirrors that of the principal offence which D1 and D2 have conspired to commit.[72] For example, conspiracy to murder carries life, conspiracy to steal is seven years, etc.

(1) . . . if a person agrees with any other person or persons that a course of conduct shall be pursued which, if the agreement is carried out in accordance with their intentions, either—

    (a) will necessarily amount to or involve the commission of any offence or offences by one or more of the parties to the agreement, or

    (b) would do so but for the existence of facts which render the commission of the offence or any of the offences impossible,

he is guilty of conspiracy to commit the offence or offences in question.

The elements of conspiracy are set out in **Tables 11.4a** and **11.4b**.

Table 11.4a Statutory conspiracy

	Actus reus	Mens rea
Conduct element	Any action that causes the agreement	Voluntary
Circumstance element	The agreement involves a course of conduct that will necessarily amount to the commission of an offence (on the facts as D1 and D2 believe them to be)	None
Result element	D1 forms an agreement with D2 to pursue a course of conduct	Intention of D1 and D2
Ulterior mens rea element	*	Set out in *Table 11.4b*

---

[71] Law Commission, *Conspiracy and Attempts* (Consultation 183, 2008) Part 2.
[72] CLA 1977, s3.

Table 11.4b Ulterior mens rea element for statutory conspiracy

Principal offence	D1 and D2's ulterior mens rea as to the principal offence
Conduct element	D1 and D2 must intend that the conduct required for the principal offence will be completed by at least one of them
Circumstance element	D1 and D2 must intend/know the circumstances required for the principal offence
Result element	D1 and D2 must intend that the results required (if any) for the principal offence will be completed by at least one of them

As with attempts, the focus of the mischief involved in conspiracy relates primarily to D's ulterior mens rea, to her commitment to the principal offence. However, unlike attempts, conspiracy requires us to identify actus reus and mens rea elements in at least two separate defendants. It requires a meeting of minds. This is not to say that both defendants must be found and convicted for liability to arise (eg D2 might have fled or died). But the court must be satisfied that both parties committed the offence before liability for any one D can be established.

11.3.1 Actus reus of conspiracy

The actus reus of conspiracy requires an agreement between D1 and D2 to pursue a course of conduct that will necessarily amount to the commission of a principal offence. These requirements are not defined in any detail within the CLA 1977, but have been the subject of several appellate cases.

11.3.1.1 Agreement to a course of conduct

At its core, the actus reus of conspiracy consists of an agreement between D1 and D2. This does not require the formalities of a contractual agreement valid in civil law, but a *decision* to pursue the criminal course of conduct must have been made.[73] This is illustrated in *Walker*.

 Walker [1962] Crim LR 458

D1 discussed with D2 and D3 the proposition that they should steal a payroll, but D1 later withdrew from the negotiation. D1 was later charged with conspiracy to rob.[74]

- Crown Court: guilty of conspiracy to rob.
- Court of Criminal Appeal: appeal allowed. There was no evidence of a decision, of an agreement being reached.

---

[73] Orchard, 'Agreement in Criminal Conspiracy' [1974] Crim LR 297.
[74] Robbery is discussed at **9.3**.

Negotiation, encouragement, assistance, or even actively pursuing a common goal,[75] all fall short of an agreement and cannot amount to conspiracy. However, once an agreement is found, there is no need to go beyond this to show that D has begun any further preparation towards committing the principal offence: the agreement is sufficient.[76] Such agreements may be oral, written, or by any other means. In charging D1 with conspiracy, it is obviously desirable to have identified D2 and to have direct evidence (eg observation) of their agreement. However, it should be remembered that neither of these is essential, as long as there is sufficient evidence to show that an agreement was reached between D1 and another.[77]

Care should be taken when identifying the relevant agreement, especially where the agreement involves multiple principal offences and/or multiple defendants. In the context of multiple principal offences, such as an agreement to rob *and* to murder V, it is usually appropriate to treat them as two separate conspiracies, even though they are contained within a single agreement.[78] Where there are multiple defendants, the situation may be more complex. It is not essential for every defendant within a conspiracy to have agreed with every other defendant, or even to have made contact with them. We see this, as in **Table 11.5**, in so-called wheel and chain conspiracies.

Table 11.5 Identifying wheel and chain conspiracies

Wheel conspiracies	Wheel conspiracies take place where there is a core individual or group who make agreements with a series of others. Like spokes on a bicycle wheel, these 'others' do not have contact with one another directly, but they are all joined within a single agreement (conspiracy) by the central figure. This may arise, for example, where D plans a bank robbery and contacts several others in order to play their parts, such as get-away drivers, lookouts, etc.
Chain conspiracies	Chain conspiracies take place where D1 agrees with D2, who agrees with D3, who agrees with D4, and so on. Again, although there is no direct communication between defendants beyond those either side of them in the chain, they are all signing up to a single common venture. This may arise, for example, where individuals contact others in order to organise a riot.

The examples in **Table 11.5** involve single conspiracies between multiple defendants where, although not all of the defendants are in communication with one another, they have all agreed to a course of conduct with *at least* one other, and they are all aware of the common nature of the enterprise and share the common intention to commit that offence. In such cases, the agreement between all the defendants can be charged as

---

[75] eg where both D1 and D2 are trying to kill V.
[76] *Hussain, Bhatti and Bhatti* [2002] Crim LR 407.
[77] *Mehta* [2012] EWCA Crim 2824: conspiracy with persons unknown to defraud the NatWest bank, where there was CCTV evidence of others being involved. See also Smith, 'Proving Conspiracy' [1996] Crim LR 386; Smith, 'More on Proving Conspiracy' [1997] Crim LR 333.
[78] *Taylor* [2002] Crim LR 205.

a single conspiracy. However, where there are parallel but separate agreements, those separate agreements should be charged as separate conspiracies. This is discussed in *Shillam*.[79]

 Shillam [2013] EWCA Crim 160

There was evidence of a central figure (D2) who supplied illegal drugs and cutting equipment to several others including D1 (the appellant), D3, and D4. Each was charged with a single conspiracy to supply cocaine.

- Crown Court: guilty of conspiracy to supply cocaine.
- Court of Appeal: appeal allowed. D1, D3, and D4 were not parties to a single grand conspiracy to supply cocaine across the network of dealers. Rather, they were each party to separate conspiracies with D2 in relation to their own supply of cocaine and equipment. Conviction for a conspiracy that spanned all defendants was therefore unsafe.

The same point is made within a useful example from *Griffiths*.[80]

I employ an accountant to make out my tax return. He and his clerk are both present when I am asked to sign the return. I notice an item in my expenses of £100 and say: 'I don't remember incurring this expense'. The clerk says: 'Well, actually I put it in. You didn't incur it, but I didn't think you would object to a few pounds being saved.' The accountant indicates his agreement to this attitude. After some hesitation I agree to let it stand. On those bare facts I cannot be charged with 50 others in a conspiracy to defraud the Exchequer of £100,000 on the basis that this accountant and his clerk have persuaded 500 other clients to make false returns, some being false in one way, some in another, or even all in the same way. I have not knowingly attached myself to a general agreement to defraud.

In this hypothetical scenario, as in *Shillam*, there is evidence of several separate conspiracies. Multiple defendants can only be grouped within a single conspiracy where they are all agreeing to a *common* course of action (as in **Table 11.5**).

Excluded agreements: parties to the agreement

Certain classes of agreement cannot give rise to conspiracy liability. For example, although a company can be party to a conspiracy,[81] there can be no conspiracy between a company and the sole controlling director of that company. This is because where the director (D) acts as the sole controlling mind of the company, any conspiracy between the two would involve D effectively conspiring with herself.[82] Section 2(2) of the CLA 1977 also makes three further specific exclusions.

A) **Spouses or civil partners:** Originating from the common law idea of a married couple as a single person, and currently justified on the basis of preserving the stability of marriage, there is no conspiracy where spouses or civil partners agree to commit a principal offence. Of course, where there are other co-conspirators in addition to the spouses, any agreement with these others will qualify as a relevant agreement.[83] The

---

[79] Jarvis and Bisgrove, 'The Use and Abuse of Conspiracy' [2014] Crim LR 261.
[80] [1966] 1 QB 589.
[81] *ICR Haulage Co Ltd* [1944] KB 551.
[82] *McDonnell* [1966] 1 QB 233.
[83] *Chrastny* [1991] 1 WLR 1381.

387

exclusion is also limited to marriage or civil partnership, and does not extend to cohabitation akin to marriage.[84] Despite Law Commission recommendations to abolish this exclusion entirely, it remains effective.[85]

B) Persons under the age of criminal responsibility: Where D1 agrees with a child under the age of 10, there can be no meeting of criminal minds because an infant is not legally capable of forming a criminal intent.[86]

C) The intended victim of the principal offence: There is no conspiracy where D1 agrees with D2 to commit an offence where D2 is the intended victim, and the offence involved is one designed to protect D2. For example, there is no conspiracy where D1 and D2 agree to kidnap D2, or to cause GBH to D2.[87]

Excluded agreements: principal offences

Agreements may also be excluded if they relate to certain principal offences. Care should be taken here, as the exclusions do not mirror those in relation to attempts discussed earlier. Importantly, it is possible for D to conspire to commit a summary only offence (although it is not possible to attempt summary only offences).[88] This was thought necessary, in the context of conspiracy, to guard against the planning of multiple summary only offences on a widespread scale.[89] It is also possible to conspire to commit other inchoate offences.[90]

The only major exclusion, in the context of conspiracy, is that D cannot conspire to commit an offence as a secondary party. We discuss complicity in **Chapter 12**. For example, where D1 and D2 agree to send a letter to P to encourage her to kill V, and P goes on to kill V, D1 and D2 may be liable for conspiring to commit the inchoate offence of assisting or encouraging murder (discussed later), but they will not be liable for conspiracy to commit murder as secondary parties.[91]

11.3.1.2 Necessarily amount to or involve the commission of a crime

Having established that D1 and D2 have agreed to a course of conduct, it must then be demonstrated that that course of conduct would necessarily amount to or involve the commission of the principal offence by one of the parties.

> **Point to remember . . .**
> The last part of this is simple, but easily forgotten. Where D1 and D2 agree that someone outside the agreement will commit an offence, there is no conspiracy. There is only a conspiracy where it is agreed that (at least) one of those party to the conspiracy will commit the future principal offence.

The most troublesome part of this requirement is to understand what it means for an agreement to *necessarily* amount to or involve the commission of an offence. Three

---

[84] *Suski* [2016] EWCA Crim 24. Foreign marriage will only qualify if valid in English law: *Bala* [2016] EWCA Crim 560.

[85] Law Commission, *Conspiracy and Attempts* (No 318, 2009) para 5.16.

[86] Discussed by the Law Commission, ibid, para 5.45.

[87] Ibid, para 5.35.

[88] Although consent of the DPP is required: CLA 1977, s4(1).

[89] *Blamires Transport Services Ltd* [1964] 1 QB 278: involving a conspiracy over two years to contravene certain (summary only) Road Traffic Act provisions on multiple occasions.

[90] Discussed at **11.5**.

[91] *Kenning* [2008] EWCA Crim 1534.

issues in particular have arisen: (a) where D1 and D2's agreement is vague and imprecise; (b) where the agreement is conditional; and (c) where the agreement is impossible to carry out. In each of these cases, there are grounds to argue that D1 and D2's agreement will not *necessarily* amount to or involve the commission of a principal offence. However, a blanket exclusion of this kind would not be in the interests of justice, and so the provision has been interpreted to allow for liability.

What if the agreement is imprecise?

The rule here is relatively simple, but must be applied with care. To be sure that D1 and D2 have agreed to commit a principal offence, there must be sufficient detail within that agreement to be sure that they (a) have agreed to do something criminal, so an agreement to 'get revenge on James' would not be sufficient, and (b) to identify the offence they have agreed to commit, so an agreement to 'break the law' would be equally insufficient. On the latter, it should be remembered that conspiracy requires a principal offence to attach to (eg conspiracy to murder) and so, unless we can identify that principal offence, there can be no liability for conspiracy. The agreement must, therefore, cover every element of the principal offence, including any results. For example, an agreement to put poison in V's tea is not a conspiracy to murder unless the agreement is to kill V with that poison: causing death is an essential element of murder and so, for conspiracy to murder, it must be part of the agreement.

Providing it is proved that D1 and D2 agreed that all of the elements of a particular offence will be completed, there is no requirement for the agreement to have settled the details of that offence. For example, where D1 and D2 agree to kill V, there may be a conspiracy to murder even though they have not decided when, how or where the killing will be undertaken. Indeed, as long as they have decided that the principal offence will be carried out by one of the parties to the agreement, they need not have decided which one of them will do it. All that is required is agreement to complete the elements of the principal offence.[92]

What if the agreement is conditional?

Alongside the issue of conditional mens rea, discussed later, conspiracies may also involve explicitly conditional agreements.[93] For example, D1 and D2 agree to rob a bank *if the coast is clear*. The agreement here is conditional on an external factor and, therefore, it could be argued that the agreement is not one that will *necessarily* amount to or involve the commission of robbery (ie if the coast is not clear, there will be no robbery). Where there is an agreement between multiple actors to commit a future principal offence, conditions of this kind are likely.

The basic rule here is that, as long as the condition does not fully undermine the potential for the principal offence being completed, then a conditional agreement will still satisfy the actus reus of conspiracy. For example, if D1 and D2 agree to smash a vase *only* if they discover that the vase belongs to them, or to have sexual intercourse with V *only* if V consents, then there can be no conspiracy to commit criminal damage or rape: in each case, the agreement is only to act if an essential element of the principal offence is absent. On the other hand, where the condition does not eliminate

---

[92] Ormerod, 'Making Sense of Mens Rea in Statutory Conspiracies' (2006) 59 CLP 185.
[93] See Law Commission, *Conspiracy and Attempts* (Consultation 183, 2007) paras 5.18–5.26.

the potential for the principal offence (ie specifies a condition under which, or in the absence of which, it *will* be committed) then this element of the actus reus of conspiracy will be satisfied. This is illustrated in *O'Hadhmaill*.

 O'Hadhmaill [1996] Crim LR 509

D, who was a member of the IRA, was found in possession of explosives and planned targets. D was charged with conspiracy to cause explosions. D claimed that there was no conspiracy, because the plan was not to use the explosives unless the ceasefire, which was then in operation, came to an end.

- Crown Court: guilty of conspiracy to cause explosions.
- Court of Appeal: conviction upheld on appeal—a conditional agreement to commit an offence is sufficient for liability.

In *O'Hadhmaill*, although the agreement might not have led to the use of explosives if the ceasefire held, there remained a conditional agreement to use the explosives if the ceasefire ended. This was sufficient. Even if the condition that leads to the principal offence being committed is unlikely, as long as there is a genuine agreement that, if that condition came about, it would be committed, then there is a conspiracy.[94]

When applying the law it is vital to distinguish conditional agreements, which can form valid conspiracies, from ongoing negotiations, which can't. Conditional agreement requires D1 and D2 to have made a firm commitment (agreement) that they *will* (not might) commit a future principal offence on certain conditions. For example, where D1 and D2, who work in a bureau de change, agree to 'transfer money if it is not criminal property' then there can be no conspiracy to launder: there is no agreed position on what they will do if the money is criminal property. However, if they agree to 'transfer the money even if they discover it to be criminal property' then there will be a conspiracy to launder: they have decided that if a certain condition comes about (that the property is criminal) they *will* commit the principal offence.[95]

Another area of potential confusion relates to so-called peripheral conditional agreements. The case of *Reed*[96] provides a useful hypothetical example.

D1 and D2 agree to drive from London to Edinburgh in a time which can be achieved without exceeding the speed limits but only if the traffic which they encounter is exceptionally light.

The question here is whether, alongside the central agreement to meet in Edinburgh at the set time, there is a conditional agreement and potential conspiracy to exceed speed limits if necessary. The court in *Reed* commented that this would not be a conspiracy, because the agreement to speed under certain conditions is incidental to the central agreement. However, it can be argued that this reasoning is faulty, and if accepted will only encourage uncertainty and incoherence. For example, if D1 and D2 agreed to rob a bank and to kill security guards if necessary, it would be inconceivable for a court to hold

[94] *Jackson* [1985] Crim LR 444: conspiracy to pervert the course of justice where D1 and D2 agreed to shoot V in the leg if V was found guilty of a separate crime, the idea being to encourage judicial lenience at sentencing.

[95] Campbell, 'Conditional Intention' (1982) 2 LS 77.

[96] [1982] Crim LR 819.

the conditional agreement to kill as peripheral and therefore irrelevant.[97] So what does it mean for an agreement to be peripheral?

Assessment matters . . .

If you encounter similar facts in a problem question to the hypothetical scenario in *Reed*, or any other conditional agreement where the principal offence is both conditional and incidental, you should discuss the approach suggested (*obiter*) in *Reed*. You should then decide what you think is more likely for the court to do (ie follow the guidance in *Reed* or apply the rule on conditional agreements strictly).

What if the agreement is impossible?

Just as D may attempt the impossible as, for example, where D tries to kill V unaware she is already dead, so D1 and D2 may conspire to commit an impossible offence. For example, agreeing to kill V, being unaware that she is already dead. As with attempts,[98] although D may conspire to commit a *factually* impossible offence of this kind, there can be no liability for *legally* impossible agreements. For example, agreeing to commit adultery, wrongly believing it is a crime, will not give rise to liability.

This approach is codified in section 1(1)(b) of the CLA 1977:[99]

(1) . . . if a person agrees with any other person or persons that a course of conduct shall be pursued which, if the agreement is carried out in accordance with their intentions, either—

    (a) will necessarily amount to or involve the commission of any offence or offences by one or more of the parties to the agreement, or

    (b) would do so but for the existence of facts which render the commission of the offence or any of the offences impossible,

he is guilty of conspiracy to commit the offence or offences in question.

The actus reus requirement that the agreement must necessarily amount to or involve the commission of a principal offence can therefore be satisfied in two ways: either on the objective facts of the case (s1(1)(a): possible conspiracies) or on the facts as D wrongly believed them to be (s1(1)(b): impossible conspiracies).

11.3.2 Mens rea of conspiracy

In comparison to the other general inchoate offences, the mens rea for conspiracy is relatively straightforward, and does not require us to identify the separate elements of the principal offence in order to apply it.[100] In relation to her own immediate actions, the sole requirement is that D must intend to form the agreement.[101] It is irrelevant

---

[97] Indeed, this was a paradigm example of conditional intention used by the Supreme Court in *Jogee* [2016] UKSC 8, [92]–[94].

[98] See **11.2.1.4**.

[99] As amended by the CAA 1981, s5. The old law (pre-amendment by the CAA 1981) had barred liability for conspiracy where the principal offence was impossible: *DPP v Nock* [1978] AC 979.

[100] Ormerod, 'Making Sense of Mens Rea in Statutory Conspiracies' (2006) 59 CLP 185.

[101] *Prior* [2004] Crim LR 849.

whether D realises that what she is agreeing to is a principal offence; ignorance of the law is no excuse.[102] In relation to the future principal offence, D must intend or know that, in accordance with their agreement, *every* element of that offence will be completed, whether by D or one of her co-conspirators. D and at least one other party to the agreement must have acted with this mens rea.

As with attempts, the aspect of mens rea that has caused the courts the most problems has been the ulterior mens rea requirements relating to the future principal offence. Four main issues should be highlighted.

11.3.2.1 At least two defendants must intend the principal offence

It is clear in section 1(1) of the CLA 1977 that D and *at least one other party to the agreement* must have intended for it to be carried out 'in accordance with their intentions'. Care must be taken when applying this in practice, and it should be remembered that we are looking at the parties' intentions at the point they form the agreement. A useful case to illustrate this is *Yip Chiu-Cheung*.

 Yip Chiu-Cheung [1995] 1 AC 111

D1 arranged with D2 to traffic illegal drugs between Hong Kong and Australia. Unknown to D1, D2 was an undercover police officer: D2 intended to carry out the plan, but only in order to identify both suppliers and recipients of the drugs, so both could be arrested. However, D2 later missed his flight and the plan failed. D1 was charged with conspiracy to traffic dangerous drugs.

- Hong Kong Court: guilty of conspiracy to traffic dangerous drugs.
- Hong Kong Court of Appeal: conviction upheld on appeal.
- Privy Council: appeal dismissed. Although D2's aim was to arrest D1 at a later stage, at the time of agreeing with D1, he was intending that the principal offence (drug trafficking) would happen. D2's motive for his intention is irrelevant.

This case is discussed at length by the Law Commission.[103] D1 is liable for conspiracy to traffic dangerous drugs because he made an agreement to do so with D2, satisfying the actus reus of conspiracy, and *at the time of that agreement* both D1 and D2 intended that the principal offence would be carried out, thereby satisfying the mens rea of conspiracy. D2's motives are irrelevant. Equally, the fact that D2 later changed his mind after missing his flight is also irrelevant, what matters is the state of mind of both parties at the time of the agreement.

If we vary the facts of *Yip Chiu-Cheung*, the reason for caution is clear. Let's say that the undercover officer, D2, made the original agreement with the intention of intervening *before* the principal offence took place. On these amended facts there would be no conspiracy. The actus reus of the conspiracy may have been completed by the agreement, but the mens rea is absent as they did not *both* intend that the principal offence be completed. If D1 and D2 were the only parties to the potential conspiracy, a lack of mens rea from D2 would mean that neither party commits the offence: even though D1 intended the principal offence, and even though D1 believed that D2 also intended the offence,

---

[102] *Broad* [1997] Crim LR 666.
[103] *Conspiracy and Attempts* (Consultation 183, 2007) paras 8.11–8.26.

if D2 did not intend in fact then there is no common intention. Of course, if there was another party to the agreement who did intend the principal offence (D3), then there could still be a conspiracy between D1 and D3, but not D2.[104]

> **Don't be confused . . .**
> Although this example involves undercover police officers, the same rules apply where anyone agrees with another to commit a principal offence, without the intention that it should be completed.

11.3.2.2 A conditional intention is still an intention

Earlier (**11.3.1.2**) we discussed conditional agreements as part of the actus reus of conspiracy. In line with this, where an agreement is conditional, D is likely to have a conditional intention: an intention to commit the principal offence *only* if certain conditions are present/absent. For example, where D1 and D2 agree to rob a bank as long as the coast is clear, we have both a conditional agreement and, if D1 and D2's intentions are in line with that agreement, a conditional intention. Even where the agreement between D1 and D2 is unconditional (eg simply agreeing to rob the bank), it is still possible for either or both to have a conditional intention, as where D1 agrees but only intends to go ahead with the plan if she can get a gun. Indeed, as the House of Lords recognised in *Saik*, 'In the nature of things, every agreement to do something in the future is hedged about with conditions, implicit if not explicit.'[105]

In line with the approach taken to conditional agreements, the core point here is that a conditional intention to commit a principal offence still amounts to a valid intention to commit it, and will satisfy the mens rea of conspiracy. What we are looking for is a decision from D, at the point of agreement, that if a certain condition arises/is absent then she will commit the principal offence. D is pre-empting a future choice (eg whether to rob the bank) by deciding in advance that if the condition is satisfied she will act with the required intention.

11.3.2.3 The parties must intend *every* element of the principal offence

The wording of the statute—'in accordance with their intentions'—carries the clear implication that D1 and D2 must intend every part of the principal offence will be carried out. This was also the stated policy at the time the 1977 Act was created.[106]

However, as we just saw, the court in *Khan* reinterpreted the CAA 1981 to be satisfied by something less than intention as to every element of the principal offence,[107] and the wording of the CLA 1977 could be interpreted similarly. The facts of *Khan* itself provide a useful example. *Khan*, it will be remembered, involved a number of defendants raping V, and D trying to do so. Each one was reckless as to V's non-consent, the circumstance element of the principal offence of rape. On these facts, as we discussed, the Court of Appeal held that even though D did not intend or know that V was not consenting, he could still be liable for attempted rape on the basis of his intention to complete the

---

104 *McPhillips* (1990) 6 BNIL: D not liable for conspiracy (although others were) when he intended to intervene to prevent the principal offence taking place.

105 [2006] UKHL 18, [5].

106 Law Commission, *Report on Conspiracy and Criminal Law Reform* (No 76, 1976) paras 1.41–1.43.

107 See **11.2.2.2**.

physical elements of rape (penile penetration of V's vagina), combined with a mens rea as to the circumstance element (V's non-consent) which satisfied that required by the principal offence. Adjusting these facts, what would happen if the parties had agreed their plan in advance? If conspiracy requires intention or knowledge as to *every* element of the principal offence, then there would be no conspiracy to rape: the parties lack intention or knowledge as to the circumstance of V's non-consent. However, if the *Khan* approach were applied to conspiracy, liability for conspiracy to rape could be found.

The difference between attempts and conspiracy, however, is that beyond the general requirement of intention, section 1(2) of the CLA 1977 addresses mens rea as to circumstances specifically:

> (2) Where liability for any offence may be incurred without knowledge on the part of the person committing it of any particular fact or circumstance necessary for the commission of the offence, a person shall nevertheless not be guilty of conspiracy to commit that offence by virtue of subsection (1) above unless he and at least one other party to the agreement intend or know that that fact or circumstance shall or will exist at the time when the conduct constituting the offence is to take place.

Under this subsection, a *Khan*-like approach to conspiracy is ruled out: where the principal offence requires a mens rea as to circumstances of anything less than intention or knowledge, D1 and D2 must still intend or know that circumstance for conspiracy liability.

Despite the language of section 1(2), however, in a series of conspiracy cases post-*Khan*, the potential for conspiracy liability where D did not intend or know the circumstance element of the principal offence began to gain traction.[108] For example, in *Sakavickas*[109] D was convicted of conspiracy to assist another to retain the benefit of criminal conduct following involvement with a tobacco-importing operation.[110] D claimed that he lacked intention or knowledge that the tobacco had been imported without duty being paid (the circumstance element of the principal offence) but this was held not to be necessary by the Court of Appeal, following *Khan*, as long as he had the mens rea required by the principal offence. This line of cases finally came to a head in *Saik*.

 Saik [2006] UKHL 18

D operated a bureau de change with a turnover of around £1,000 a week. However, from 2001 this increased dramatically to over £8 million in a year. Surveillance of D also witnessed him meeting his alleged co-conspirators in parked cars, rather than in the office, to exchange large sums of money. D was charged with conspiracy to launder the proceeds of crime.[111] D intended the physical elements of the principal offence, and had a mens rea of 'suspicion' as to the criminal origins of the money (the circumstance element of the principal offence). Suspicion was sufficient mens rea for the principal offence.

---

[108] Ormerod, 'Making Sense of Mens Rea in Statutory Conspiracies' (2006) 59 CLP 185.
[109] [2004] EWCA Crim 2686.
[110] Contrary to the Criminal Justice Act 1988, s93A.
[111] Contrary to the Criminal Justice Act 1998, s93C(2); and now an offence under the Proceeds of Crime Act 2002, s327.

- Crown Court: guilty of conspiracy to launder the proceeds of crime.
- Court of Appeal: conviction upheld on appeal. Mens rea as to circumstances can mirror those required by the principal offence.
- House of Lords (Baroness Hale dissenting): appeal allowed, quashing D's conviction. The mens rea of conspiracy requires D to intend or know every element of the principal offence and this is confirmed (in relation to circumstances) in section 1(2).

The House of Lords in *Saik* have brought much needed clarity to the law of conspiracy. To be liable, D and at least one other conspirator must intend every element of the principal offence. In this manner, unlike with attempts, it is not necessary to separate the principal offence into its elements in order to identify the mens rea required by D: whether act, circumstance or result, all elements must be intended.[112]

Extra detail . . .

Baroness Hale dissented in *Saik* claiming that liability could be found using conditional intention: as D intended to convert the money regardless of its origin, this could be described as a conditional intention to launder the money *if* it was criminal. However, the majority rejected this logic. The problem here is that D did not make a decision to act in the future with intention or knowledge as to the criminal origin of the money, he decided to act in the absence of such knowledge. Therefore, D did not intend or know the circumstance, even conditionally. He was reckless.[113]

11.3.2.4 A problem case: *Anderson*

In *Anderson*, the House of Lords created a great deal of uncertainty for the mens rea of conspiracy from which the current law is still recovering. The case has not been overruled. However, its conclusions have been consistently overlooked and/or ignored to the extent that it should no longer be applied.

  Anderson [1986] AC 27

D was part of a group planning to effect the escape of one of them from prison. D was paid to supply diamond wire capable of cutting through metal bars. D was charged with conspiracy to effect the escape of a prisoner. D claimed that he only wanted to be paid and did not intend the principal offence to be completed. In fact, he did not believe that it would be successful.

- Crown Court: guilty of conspiracy to effect the escape of a prisoner.
- Court of Appeal: conviction upheld on appeal.
- House of Lords: appeal dismissed. Lord Bridge, with whom the other Lords concurred, stated that conspiracy requires an agreement to commit a principal offence and an intention for D to play his part. However, it does not require an additional intention that the principal offence will be committed.

Anderson suggests that an intention to commit the principal offence is not required for conspiracy, but that D must intend to play a role towards that principal offence. Both of these conclusions are highly problematic.

---

[112] See discussion in the recent case of *Thomas* [2014] EWCA Crim 1958.
[113] Law Commission, *Conspiracy and Attempts* (Consultation 183, 2007) Part 5.

A) **D need not intend the principal offence:** If the parties to an agreement do not need to intend to commit the principal offence then we have the prospect of a conspiracy to commit an offence where no party actually wants it to come about; this is absurd. The approach has not been applied in subsequent cases.[114] For example, in *Ashton*,[115] the Court of Appeal found that there would be no conspiracy to murder where D did not intend the murder to take place: D had agreed the plan to kill V, but did not intend that it should come about.

B) **D must intend to play an active role in the principal offence:** The idea that D must intend to play an active role in the principal offence is equally problematic; it would mean having to prove, in every case, the details of D's role beyond simple agreement. This could lead to problems where D orders others (eg those in a gang) to commit an offence but does not plan to play any active role herself. Again, subsequent decisions have reinterpreted the words of Lord Bridge to, effectively, dismiss this requirement. In *Siracusa*,[116] for example, the Court of Appeal attempted to empty the requirement of any real meaning, holding that it would be satisfied where D does not actively intend to take steps to prevent the offence taking place.

The approach in *Anderson* is not likely to be followed and, we suggest, should not be followed in future cases. D1 and at least one other conspirator must intend the principal offence be committed in order for them to be liable for conspiracy. Beyond their agreement, as long as it is intended that one of them will commit the principal offence, there is no need to show that all parties will play an active role.[117]

> *Assessment matters . . .*
> If you encounter facts similar to *Anderson* in a problem question, then the case should be discussed—remember that it is a House of Lords judgment and it has not been overruled. However, it is important that your discussion should acknowledge the criticisms of *Anderson* and the approach of subsequent cases, concluding that it is unlikely to be applied.

11.3.3 Defences to conspiracy

The general defences discussed in **Chapters 13** and **14** apply to conspiracies in the same way that they apply to other offences. Beyond this, there are no specific defences.[118] As with attempts, a defence of withdrawal has been mooted (ie a defence where D conspires but then acts in order to cancel her agreement) but this has not found favour.[119]

As conspiracy is a multi-party offence, it is possible for situations to arise where D1 alone has a defence such as duress, insanity etc. Where this is the case, D1 will not be liable. However, the same is not necessarily true for D2, even where she has only agreed with D1. D2's liability will depend upon whether D1's defence undermines her ability to form an

---

[114] *McPhillips* (1990) 6 BNIL; *Edwards* [1991] Crim LR 45; *Harvey* [1999] Crim LR 70; etc.

[115] [1992] Crim LR 667.

[116] (1989) 90 Cr App R 340.

[117] This corresponds to the Law Commission's analysis of the current law: Law Commission, *Conspiracy and Attempts* (Consultation 183, 2007) paras 4.22–4.41.

[118] The Law Commission has recommended a defence of 'acting reasonably': *Conspiracy and Attempts* (No 318, 2009) Part 6.

[119] *Thomson* (1965) 50 Cr App R 1: confirming that there is no such defence; *McPhillips* (1990) 6 BNIL: providing some support for such a defence.

agreement and to share an intention to commit the principal offence. For example, where D1's defence is insanity, and it is accepted that she was not able to appreciate the nature or quality of her conduct, then it is clear that there could not have been any agreement and neither party will have committed conspiracy. However, where D1's defence is duress, for example, whereby D1 was threatened by a third party to conspire with D2, it is still possible for D1 to have agreed and to have shared the required intention. Thus, although D1 may be acquitted, D2 remains liable for conspiracy.[120]

11.3.4 Common law conspiracies

Alongside the statutory offence of conspiracy, two examples of common law conspiracy remain active. Preserved by section 5 of the CLA 1977, these offences can apply even where the object of the parties' agreement is not in itself an offence.

- Conspiracy to defraud: An agreement between two or more to dishonestly deprive or interfere with the property rights of another, or to deceive a public official into acting contrary to duty.
- Conspiracy to corrupt public morals or to outrage public decency: An agreement between two or more to act in a highly offensive way.

Conspiracy to defraud remains a frequently used offence and is discussed at **10.7.1**. Conspiracy to corrupt public morals or to outrage public decency is also retained, but lacks clear definition in statute or in case law. Rather, in the rare cases where it is applied, the reasoning tends to focus on extreme moral distaste for the subject of the agreement.[121] Examples include *Shaw v DPP*,[122] where D was liable for conspiracy to corrupt public morals when publishing a 'Ladies' Directory' detailing the names, addresses and sexual activities available from various prostitutes; and *Knuller*,[123] where, despite the legalisation of homosexual acts, D was convicted of conspiracy to corrupt public morals when publishing adverts facilitating homosexual encounters. The continued existence of this offence is further complicated by debate as to whether corrupting public morals and outraging public decency is itself a principal offence capable of being the subject of conspiracy under the CLA 1977.

> **Extra detail . . .**
> Although factual impossibility does not undermine liability for statutory conspiracy, it will undermine liability for a common law conspiracy.[124]

11.4 Assisting or encouraging

Offences of assisting or encouraging[125] are contained within Part 2 of the Serious Crime Act 2007 (SCA 2007). As with the other inchoate offences, D is not liable for assisting

---

[120] *Matusevich* (1977) 51 ALJR 657.
[121] This may be unlikely to survive an Art 7 ECHR challenge for lack of certainty.
[122] [1962] AC 220.
[123] [1973] AC 435.
[124] *DPP v Nock* [1978] AC 979.
[125] Fortson, *Blackstone's Guide to the Serious Crime Act 2007* (2008) Ch6; Ormerod and Fortson, 'Serious Crime Act 2007: Part 2 Offences' [2009] Crim LR 389.

or encouraging *simpliciter*, but rather for conduct capable of assisting or encouraging a principal offence, for example assisting murder; encouraging theft; etc. In such cases, D is not trying to commit the offence herself (as in attempts) or necessarily agreeing that it should be committed (as in conspiracy) but she is, nevertheless, criminally blameworthy for her conduct in support of the potential principal offender.[126] D is liable as soon as, with the required mens rea, she carries out the conduct capable of assisting or encouraging.

The SCA 2007 offences replace the old common law of incitement, where D encouraged P to commit a principal offence with the intention that it should be completed. The SCA 2007 offences cover this conduct, but also reach considerably further than the old offence, and considerably further than the Law Commission recommendations that led to the reform.[127] In this regard, although Law Commission material can be useful in understanding the offences, care must be taken to identify points of departure between the Commission's report and the final form of the statute.

Three separate offences are created within Part 2 of the SCA 2007. The maximum penalty for each mirrors that of the principal offence for which D has completed acts capable of assisting or encouraging.[128]

- Section 44: Intentionally encouraging or assisting an offence.
- Section 45: Encouraging or assisting an offence believing it will be committed.
- Section 46: Encouraging or assisting offences believing one or more will be committed.

As the actus reus of each offence is the same, we will deal with this collectively. We will then explore the different mens rea requirements of each offence in turn. The offences have been rightly criticised for being overly complex in their formulation and have yet to be usefully clarified in the courts; it is therefore essential to work methodically through the offence elements as presented in the statute.

11.4.1 Actus reus of assisting or encouraging

Offences under sections 44, 45, and 46 require the following actus reus. Sections 44(1)(a) and 45(a):

. . . an act capable of encouraging or assisting the commission of an offence.

Section 46(1)(a):

. . . an act capable of encouraging or assisting the commission of one or more of a number of offences.

As with attempts and conspiracy, as soon as D completes this actus reus with the required mens rea, D is liable for assisting or encouraging the offence: it is irrelevant whether P (the person assisted or encouraged) goes on to commit the principal offence.[129]

---

[126] For a discussion of the rationale of these offences, see Law Commission, *Inchoate Liability for Assisting and Encouraging Crime* (No 300, 2006) Part 4.

[127] Law Commission, *Inchoate Liability for Assisting and Encouraging Crime* (No 300, 2006).

[128] SCA 2007, s58.

[129] Ibid, s49(1).

Point to remember . . .
Although irrelevant for the inchoate charge, where P goes on to commit the principal offence D may be liable as an accomplice. We discuss this in **Chapter 12**.

Several aspects of the actus reus are clarified at other points in the statute. Section 65(2)(b) clarifies that D may assist or encourage by act *or omission*. For example, D, a disgruntled security guard, assists by omitting to turn on an alarm system in order to assist a robbery.[130] Section 65(2)(a) clarifies that assisting or encouraging an offence includes taking steps to reduce the chance of criminal proceedings being brought against P. For example, D acts as a lookout or intimidates potential witnesses of P's offence. Section 67 clarifies that the actus reus may be a 'course of conduct' as well as a one-off act. For example, D sends P a series of weapons components over a period of time.

However, despite these useful points of clarification, the central terms 'encouraging' and 'assisting' are not fully defined.

A) Encouraging: Encouraging is intended to mean the same as 'inciting' under the pre-SCA 2007 law.[131] This includes positive acts of instigation, persuasion, or emboldening, as well as negative acts such as threats.[132] Conduct capable of encouraging can include that which is express or implied,[133] and can be targeted at a particular person or addressed to the world at large.[134] Examples under the old law, demonstrating the breadth of the term, include D responding to an advert which invited readers to buy indecent pictures of children, thereby encouraging P to distribute such photos;[135] and where D subscribed to a website showing indecent pictures of children, thereby encouraging the owner of the website to continue their publication.[136]

B) Assisting: The SCA 2007 extends the old common law of incitement to include assisting as well as encouraging. This will be useful where D provides P with a tool or with advice, etc, to help with, but not necessarily encourage, the principal offence.[137] As with encouragement, there is no need for D's assistance to be substantial: any act capable of providing any assistance will suffice.

Perhaps the most important qualification of the actus reus is that D does not need to assist or encourage P in fact: D must simply perform acts *capable* of assisting or encouraging P. For example, where D encourages P to kill V, it does not matter whether this convinces P; whether it has no effect on P at all; or even if P is never aware of it; as long as D's acts were capable of encouraging P to kill then the actus reus is satisfied.[138] In the

---

[130] For omissions liability, D must have a duty to act. See **2.6.2**.
[131] Law Commission, *Inchoate Liability for Assisting and Encouraging Crime* (No 300, 2006) paras 5.32–5.45.
[132] SCA 2007, s65(1).
[133] *Jones* [2010] EWCA Crim 925: implied encouragement to grow cannabis where D gave coded advice on 'growing tomatoes'.
[134] *Parr-Moore* [2003] 1 Cr App R 425: advertising the sale of speed trap blockers, inciting speeding offences.
[135] *Goldman* [2001] Crim LR 894.
[136] *O'Shea* [2004] Crim LR 948.
[137] Law Commission, *Inchoate Liability for Assisting and Encouraging Crime* (No 300, 2006) paras 5.46–5.51; Sullivan, 'Inchoate Liability for Assisting and Encouraging' [2005] Crim LR 1047
[138] Law Commission, *Inchoate Liability for Assisting and Encouraging Crime* (No 300, 2006) paras 5.27–5.31.

latter case, the Law Commission uses the example of D who places a ladder outside V's house to assist P committing burglary. Even if P fails to discover the ladder, and knows nothing of D's efforts, D's acts are still capable of assisting P to burgle, and so the actus reus of the SCA offence is complete.

> *Extra detail . . .*
> Despite extending the offence to cover 'assisting', the SCA 2007 has left a gap where D 'procures' an offence (causes it to happen) without assisting or encouraging. For example, D spikes P's drink intending for P to commit an offence of driving over the prescribed alcohol limit. Where P goes on to commit the offence then D will be liable as a secondary party (discussed in **Chapter 12**). However, where P does not (eg because she realises what has happened), it will be difficult to show that D has performed conduct capable of assisting or encouraging the offence.[139]

11.4.2 Mens rea of s44: intentionally encouraging or assisting an offence

As with attempts and conspiracy, the gravamen of assisting or encouraging lies in the mens rea.[140] Unfortunately, the unnecessarily complex drafting of the SCA 2007 expresses this requirement across two sections. Section 44:

(1) A person commits an offence if . . .

    (a) he intends to encourage or assist its commission . . .

Section 47:

(1) Sections 44, 45 and 46 are to be read in accordance with this section.

(2) If it is alleged under section 44(1)(b) that a person (D) intended to encourage or assist the commission of an offence, it is sufficient to prove that he intended to encourage or assist the doing of an act which would amount to the commission of that offence . . .

(5) In proving for the purposes of this section whether an act is one which, if done, would amount to the commission of an offence—

    (a) if the offence is one requiring proof of fault, it must be proved that—

        (i)   D believed that, were the act to be done, it would be done with that fault;

        (ii) D was reckless as to whether or not it would be done with that fault; or

        (iii) D's state of mind was such that, were he to do it, it would be done with that fault; and

    (b) if the offence is one requiring proof of particular circumstances or consequences (or both), it must be proved that—

        (i)   D believed that, were the act to be done, it would be done in those circumstances or with those consequences; or

---

[139] Child, 'The Differences Between Attempted Complicity and Inchoate Assisting and Encouraging—A Reply to Professor Bohlander' [2010] Crim LR 924, 929. D would be liable for a poisoning offence.

[140] Child, 'Exploring the Mens Rea Requirements of the Serious Crime Act 2007 Assisting and Encouraging Offences' (2012) 76 J Crim L 220; Ormerod and Fortson, 'Serious Crime Act 2007: Part 2 Offences' [2009] Crim LR 389.

(ii)   D was reckless as to whether or not it would be done in those circumstances or with those consequences.

The elements of the section 44 offence are illustrated in **Tables 11.6a** and **11.6b**.

Table 11.6a SCA 2007, s44: assisting or encouraging

	Actus reus	**Mens rea**
Conduct element	Any action or omission	Voluntary
Circumstance element	D's conduct is capable of assisting or encouraging P to commit an offence	Intention to assist or encourage the conduct element of P's offence
Result element	None	None
Ulterior mens rea element	*	Set out in **Table 11.6b**

Table 11.6b Ulterior mens rea element for s44 assisting or encouraging

	D's ulterior mens rea as to P's principal offence
Conduct element	D must intend that P will complete the conduct element of the principal offence
Circumstance element	D must intend, believe, or be reckless as to the circumstance element of P's principal offence
Result element	D must intend, believe, or be reckless as to whether P will cause the results (if any) required by the principal offence
P's mens rea	D must intend, believe, or be reckless as to whether P will act with the mens rea required by the principal offence Or D must have the mens rea for the principal offence herself

Terminology . . .
The SCA 2007 uses the term 'fault' to mean the same as 'mens rea'; and the term 'consequences' to mean the same as 'results'.

When considering the mens rea for these offences, it is useful to separate what is required by D in relation to her own conduct, and what is required by D in relation to the future conduct and mind of P.

11.4.2.1 D's mens rea as to her own conduct

Section 44(1)(b) states that D must intend that her conduct will assist or encourage P's principal offence. This implies that D must intent to assist or encourage every element of P's offence. However, as sections 47(1) and 47(2) clarify, this is not the case. Rather, 'it is sufficient to prove that [she] intended to encourage or assist the *doing of an act* which would amount to the commission of a crime'.[141]

Therefore, D will satisfy this part of the mens rea if she intends to assist or encourage P, even minimally, to complete the conduct element of the future principal offence. For example, where D is charged with assisting murder in having provided P with a gun, it is sufficient to prove that D intended her conduct to assist P to shoot that gun (the conduct element of P's offence). There is no additional need within this element to show that D intended to assist P to shoot a person (circumstance), or cause death (result).

11.4.2.2 D's mens rea as to P's principal offence

As well as D's intentions as to the impact of her own conduct, D must also have a certain ulterior mens rea as to the future principal offence of P. Unlike conspiracy, and to a lesser extent attempts, D need not intend that every element of the principal offence should be completed.

Section 44 is silent on this part of D's mens rea, and so we look to section 47. To identify the required mens rea, and to apply it to case facts, it is necessary to separate the elements of P's principal offence.

A) D's mens rea as to the conduct element of P's principal offence: There is no mention of D's mens rea as to the conduct element of P's offence within the statute. However, as D must intend to assist or encourage this conduct element (**11.4.2.1**), it is logical that D must also *intend* that P will complete it.[142] Taking our assisting murder example, D must not only intend to assist P to shoot the gun (own conduct), she must also intend that P will shoot the gun in fact (P's conduct).

B) D's mens rea as to the circumstances of P's principal offence: This is provided by section 47(5)(b): requiring a minimum of *recklessness*. In our example, therefore, D must intend for P to shoot the gun and be at least reckless as to whether P shoots a person (the circumstance element of murder).

C) D's mens rea as to the result element of P's principal offence: This is also provided by section 47(5)(b): requiring a minimum of *recklessness*. In our example, D must intend for P to shoot the gun and be at least reckless as to whether P shoots a person (circumstance) and causes their death (the result element of murder).

D) D's mens rea as to P's mens rea when completing the principal offence: This is provided by section 47(5)(a): requiring a minimum of *recklessness*. In our example, D

---

[141] Emphasis added.

[142] For an alternative possibility, see Child, 'Exploring the Mens Rea Requirements of the Serious Crime Act 2007 Assisting and Encouraging Offences' (2012) 76 J Crim L 220. Although Child now accepts that this alternative should not be preferred. See useful rebuttal in Fortson, 'Inchoate Liability and Part 2 Offences under the Serious Crime Act 2007' in Reed and Bohlander (eds), *Participation in Crime* (2013) 173.

must intend for P to shoot the gun, be at least reckless as to whether P shoots a person (circumstance) and causes their death (result), and be at least reckless as to whether P will do so with the intention of causing death or GBH (the mens rea of murder).

Where, in an exceptional case, D lacks recklessness as to P's mens rea, D may still be liable if she possesses the mens rea for the principal offence herself. This clause (s47(5)(a)(iii)) will rarely arise, but is designed to address a potential loophole. For example, knowing that V is asleep, D provides P with a gun and encourages her to shoot V, telling P that V is already dead. Could D could be charged with assisting and encouraging murder? D clearly possesses mens rea as to her own conduct, as she intends to encourage P to shoot the gun. D also satisfies ulterior mens rea requirements as to the conduct, circumstances, and results of P's principal offence, as she intends P to shoot and kill what she knows to be a living person. However, D is not reckless as to P's mens rea; D knows that P thinks V is dead and therefore D lacks recklessness as to P acting with the mens rea for murder. In such a case, D will be liable because, although she knows that P lacks the mens rea for murder, D acts with that mens rea herself.[143]

> **Beware . . .**
> As with attempts, we must separate the elements of the principal offence in order to identify D's required mens rea in relation to each. However, in this case, our main focus is not separating the circumstance element. Rather, the most important element to separate for special treatment is the conduct element, as there is a common requirement of recklessness as to the other elements. Unfortunately, in many ways, separating the conduct element can be more troublesome than separating the circumstance element.

11.4.3 Mens rea of s45: encouraging or assisting an offence believing it will be committed

Moving beyond intentional assisting or encouraging, this offence expands liability to cases of belief.[144] The mens rea requirements for this offence are spread across sections 45 and 47.

Section 45:

> A person commits an offence if . . .
>
> (b) he believes—
>
>   (i) that the offence will be committed; and
>
>   (ii) that his act will encourage or assist its commission.

---

[143] This will also apply to encouraging rape where, eg, D encourages P to have sex with V knowing that V will not consent. Even if D assures P that V is consenting, and even if P has reasonable grounds to believe that V is consenting and so would lack mens rea when completing the principal offence, D remains liable for encouraging rape because D has the mens rea for rape him/herself.

[144] Child, 'Exploring the Mens Rea Requirements of the Serious Crime Act 2007 Assisting and Encouraging Offences' (2012) 76 J Crim L 220; Ormerod and Fortson, 'Serious Crime Act 2007: Part 2 Offences' [2009] Crim LR 389.

Section 47:

(1) Sections 44, 45 and 46 are to be read in accordance with this section . . .

(3) If it is alleged under section 45(b) that a person (D) believed that an offence would be committed and that his act would encourage or assist its commission, it is sufficient to prove that he believed—

    (a) that an act would be done which would amount to the commission of that offence; and

    (b) that his act would encourage or assist the doing of that act . . .

(5) [Extracted at **11.4.2**]

The elements of the section 45 offence are illustrated in **Tables 11.7a and 11.7b**.

Table 11.7a SCA 2007, s45: assisting or encouraging

	Actus reus	**Mens rea**
Conduct element	Any action or omission	Voluntary
Circumstance element	D's conduct is capable of assisting or encouraging P to commit an offence	Belief that it will assist or encourage the conduct element of P's offence
Result element	None	None
Ulterior mens rea element	*	Set out in *Table 11.7b*

Table 11.7b Ulterior mens rea element for s45 assisting or encouraging

	D's ulterior mens rea as to P's principal offence
Conduct element	D must believe that P will complete the conduct element of the principal offence
Circumstance element	D must believe or be reckless as to the circumstance element of P's principal offence
Result element	D must believe or be reckless as to whether P will cause the results (if any) required by the principal offence
P's mens rea	D must believe, or be reckless as to whether P will act with the mens rea required by the principal offence Or D must have the mens rea for the principal offence herself

11.4.3.1 D's mens rea as to her own conduct

Section 45(b)(ii) states that D must believe that her act will assist or encourage P's principal offence. Again, although this appears to apply to the whole of that offence, it must be read in accordance with sections 47(1) and 47(3). Section 47(3)(b) clarifies that, as with the section 44 offence, D's mens rea need only apply to the conduct element of P's offence.[145]

Therefore, this part of D's mens rea merely requires her to believe that her conduct will assist or encourage the conduct element of P's principal offence. Using our assisting murder example, this might apply where D sells P a gun simply in order to make a profit. In this case, D may not intend to assist P to fire the gun, indeed she may actively not want her to, and so D will not come within the section 44 offence. However, if she believes that she is assisting P to fire the gun, she will satisfy this part of section 45.

11.4.3.2 D's mens rea as to P's principal offence

Section 45(b)(i) states that D must believe that the principal offence will be completed, implying that D must have belief as to each element of that future offence. However, as section 47(3)(a) subsequently clarifies, this only applies to P's conduct element. Thus, again, it is necessary to separate out the elements of P's principal offence in order to identify the mens rea required of D in relation to each.

A) D's mens rea as to the conduct element of P's principal offence: This is provided by a combination of sections 45(b)(i) and 47(3)(a): requiring a minimum of *belief.* Using our gun-selling example, D not only has to believe that her conduct will assist P to shoot the gun (D's mens rea as to her own conduct), but must also believe that P will shoot the gun in fact (D's mens rea as to the conduct of P).

B) D's mens rea as to the circumstances of P's principal offence: This is provided by section 47(5)(b): requiring a minimum of *recklessness.* In our example, D must believe that P will shoot the gun and be at least reckless as to whether P shoots a person (the circumstance element of murder).

C) D's mens rea as to the result element of P's principal offence: This is also provided by section 47(5)(b): requiring a minimum of *recklessness.* In our example, D must believe that P will shoot the gun, and be at least reckless as to whether P shoots a person (circumstance) and causes their death (the result element of murder).

D) D's mens rea as to P's mens rea when completing the principal offence: This is provided by section 47(5)(a): requiring a minimum of *recklessness.* In our example, D must believe that P will shoot the gun, be at least reckless as to whether P shoots a person (circumstance) and causes their death (result), and be at least reckless as to whether P will do so with the intention of causing death or GBH (the mens rea of murder). Again, as with section 44 above, D may alternatively satisfy this element if she has the mens rea for the principal offence herself.

> **Point to remember . . .**
> Much of the mens rea between the section 44 and 45 offences are the same. The only difference (intention/belief) relates to the conduct element of the principal offence.

---

[145] The misleading use of the term 'offence' in the SCA 2007 is discussed in Fortson, 'Inchoate Liability and Part 2 Offences under the Serious Crime Act 2007' in Reed and Bohlander (eds), *Participation in Crime* (2013) 173.

11.4.4 Mens rea of s46: encouraging or assisting offences believing one or more will be committed

Section 46 applies where D does acts capable of assisting or encouraging P to commit a number of principal offences but is unsure which offence P will choose.[146] The mens rea is set out over sections 46 and 47.

Section 46:

(1) A person commits an offence if . . .

    (b) he believes—

        (i)   that one or more of those offences will be committed (but has no belief as to which); and

        (ii) that his act will encourage or assist the commission of one or more of them.

Section 47:

(1) Sections 44, 45 and 46 are to be read in accordance with this section . . .

(2) If it is alleged under section 46(1)(b) that a person (D) believed that one or more of a number of offences would be committed and that his act would encourage or assist the commission of one or more of them, it is sufficient to prove that he believed—

    (a) that one or more of a number of acts would be done which would amount to the commission of one or more of those offences; and

    (b) that his act would encourage or assist the doing of one or more of those acts.

(5) [Extracted at **11.4.2**]

The elements of the section 46 offence are illustrated in **Tables 11.8a** and **11.8b**.

Table 11.8a SCA 2007, s46: assisting or encouraging

	Actus reus	**Mens rea**
Conduct element	Any action or omission	Voluntary
Circumstance element	D's conduct is capable of assisting or encouraging P to commit one or more of a number of offences	Belief that it will assist or encourage the conduct element of one or more of P's offences (but with no belief as to which)
Result element	None	None
Ulterior mens rea element	*	Set out in **Table 11.8b**

---

[146] Child, 'Exploring the Mens Rea Requirements of the Serious Crime Act 2007 Assisting and Encouraging Offences' (2012) 76 J Crim L 220; Ormerod and Fortson, 'Serious Crime Act 2007: Part 2 Offences' [2009] Crim LR 389.

Table 11.8b Ulterior mens rea element for s46 assisting or encouraging

	D's ulterior mens rea as to P's principal offence
Conduct element	D must believe that P will complete one or more conduct elements of one or more principal offences
Circumstance element	D must believe or be reckless as to the circumstance elements of P's principal offences
Result element	D must believe or be reckless as to whether P will cause the results (if any) required by the principal offences
P's mens rea	D must believe, or be reckless as to whether P will act with the mens rea required by the principal offences Or D must have the mens rea for the principal offences herself

In order to explain the mens rea of this offence, it is useful to employ an example. As before, let us imagine that D sells V a gun, motivated purely by profit from the sale. D believes that P will use the gun to attack V. However, D is unsure whether P will use the gun to threaten and rob V,[147] or whether P will use the gun to shoot and kill V. In such a case, D may be charged under section 46 with assisting robbery and murder.

11.4.4.1 D's mens rea as to her own conduct

Section 46(b)(ii) states that D must believe that her act will assist or encourage P to commit one or more principal offences. Read in accordance with sections 47(1) and 47(4)(b), this requires D to believe that her conduct will assist or encourage (at least) the conduct element of those possible offences. In our example, D must believe that she has assisted both offences of robbery and murder.

11.4.4.2 D's mens rea as to P's principal offence

Section 46(b)(i) states that D must believe that one or more of P's principal offences will be completed, implying that D must have belief as to each element of those offences. However, as section 47(4)(a) subsequently clarifies, this only applies to P's conduct elements. Thus, again, it is necessary to separate the elements of P's principal offences in order to identify the mens rea required of D in relation to each.

A) D's mens rea as to the conduct elements of P's principal offences: This is provided by a combination of sections 46(b)(i) and 47(4)(a): requiring a minimum of *belief*. In our example, D must believe that P will *either* use the gun to threaten with *or* to shoot. D does not intend either (so s44 would be inappropriate), does not believe that P will commit one act over the other (so s45 would be inappropriate), she believes that P *will* commit one of the acts but is unsure which.

---

[147] Theft Act 1968, s8. See **9.3**.

B) D's mens rea as to the circumstances of P's principal offences: This is provided by section 47(5)(b): requiring a minimum of *recklessness*. In our example, D must believe that P will shoot or threaten with the gun, and be at least reckless as to whether P shoots or threatens a person (the circumstance element of murder and robbery).

C) D's mens rea as to the result element of P's principal offences: This is also provided by section 47(5)(b): requiring a minimum of *recklessness*. In our example, D must believe that P will shoot or threaten with the gun, be at least reckless as to whether P shoots or threatens a person (circumstance), and at least reckless as to whether D will cause death or gain V's property (the result elements of murder and robbery).

D) D's mens rea as to P's mens rea when completing the principal offences: This is provided by section 47(5)(a): requiring a minimum of *recklessness*. In our example, D must believe that P will shoot or threaten with the gun, be at least reckless as to whether P shoots or threatens a person (circumstance), be at least reckless as to whether D will cause death or gain V's property (result), and be at least reckless as to whether P will do so with the mens rea required for murder or robbery. Again, D may alternatively satisfy this element if she has the mens rea for the principal offence herself.

11.4.4.3 Applying s46: the Court of Appeal's guidance in *Sadique*

There is, arguably, a need for an offence like section 46 to cater for assisting and encouraging where D believes an offence will be committed but is unsure which offence it will be. However, as the previous section sets out, the structure of this offence is highly complex. The offence was discussed in *Sadique*.

Sadique [2011] EWCA Crim 2872

D supplied cutting agents including benzocaine and hydrochloric acid to assist the production and supply of illegal drugs. D was charged with a section 46 offence of assisting the supply of Class A or Class B drugs.

- Crown Court: appeal against charges in preparatory hearing, contending that section 46 is incompatible with Article 7 ECHR.
- Court of Appeal: appeal dismissed.

In confirming that the section 46 offence is sufficiently clear to be compatible with Article 7 ECHR, the Court of Appeal set out their interpretation of the provision. However, their analysis was problematic in two main areas.

A) Confusing ss45 and 46: The court held that section 46 requires D to believe that each of the possible offences, assisted or encouraged, *will* be committed by P. Thus, in *Sadique*, D must believe that his acts will assist the supply of Class A drugs and Class B drugs, and an indictment should ideally separate these offences into individual counts. The problem with this, as highlighted by several academics,[148] is that although it makes the sentencing exercise clearer, it undermines the purpose of section 46. Although section 45 requires D to believe that an individual offence will come about, section 46 is

---

[148] eg Virgo, 'Encouraging or Assisting More Than One Offence' [2012] Arch Rev 6.

designed to deal with cases where D only believes that one of a number of offences will be committed (but does not know/believe which). This interpretation (consistent with our discussion at **11.4.4.1–11.4.4.2**) was later accepted by the Court of Appeal following a further appeal in 2013.[149]

B) Mens rea as to circumstances, results and mens rea of the principal offence: Seeking to clarify the requirements of the offence, the court set out the mens rea in simple terms.[150] However, they do so inaccurately, suggesting that D must believe that P will complete *all* elements of the principal offence. As we set out earlier, the statute in fact requires a minimum of recklessness as to P's circumstances, results and mens rea. The court's confusion on this point is a useful illustration of over-reliance on the Law Commission report which had recommended a minimum of belief, a recommendation that was not accepted within the SCA 2007.[151]

Despite these problems with *Sadique*, much of the blame must be placed with the unnecessary complexity of the legislation. Without significant amendment, further confusions of this kind are inevitable.

11.4.5 Defences to assisting or encouraging

As well as the general defences (discussed in **Chapters 13** and **14**), the SCA 2007 creates two specific defences: acting reasonably and protection of the victim.[152]

> *Point to remember . . .*
> These defences only apply to offences under sections 44–46 of the SCA 2007. They do not apply to attempts or conspiracy, or any other offences.

Section 50 of the SCA 2007 creates a specific defence of 'acting reasonably'. This applies where circumstances exist, or D reasonably believes they exist, and these circumstances make it reasonable to act as D did.

This defence is essential in order to narrow liability to acceptable limits. The Law Commission provides the following example: D is driving at 70mph in the outside lane of a motorway but moves in when she sees P's car approaching from behind at greater speed. In this case, without the defence of acting reasonably, the Law Commission recognises that because of the astonishing breadth of the offences created, D may be liable for assisting P's speeding offence: D's act is capable of assisting by clearing the way; D believes that she will assist P to continue speeding; D believes that P will continue speeding; and D is at least reckless as to whether P will be over the speed limit, etc. The example is fanciful, of course, since it is unlikely that the SCA would be used to charge a driver in the circumstances. However, it does demonstrate the importance of

---

[149] *Sadique* [2013] EWCA Crim 1150. Commentary by Fortson [2014] Crim LR 61.
[150] *Sadique* [2011] EWCA Crim 2872, [87].
[151] For a more generous interpretation of the case, see Fortson, 'Inchoate Liability and Part 2 Offences under the Serious Crime Act 2007' in Reed and Bohlander (eds), *Participation in Crime* (2013) 173.
[152] Law Commission, *Inchoate Liability for Assisting and Encouraging Crime* (No 300, 2006) Part 6.

the defence of acting reasonably. It is unclear whether the defence will generate diffi-culties in the real world as where D claims that her acts capable of assisting terrorism were reasonable given her beliefs, or her supply of a weapon was reasonable given the previous attacks P had suffered.

Although such examples are used to illustrate the role of the defence, they may also be employed to criticise the overbroad scope of the original offences. As we discussed from the start of **Chapter 1**, the purpose of a criminal offence is to define and punish a criminal mischief. The fact that the assisting and encouraging offences apply to conduct such as moving motorway lanes, as in the example above, shows that these offences are not satisfying that task and are effectively switching the bur-den: requiring D, through the specific defence, to demonstrate the reasonableness of her own conduct to avoid liability. The criminal law would be much simpler for the prosecution if all acts were presumed criminal unless D could justify their reasonableness![153]

Less controversially, section 51 provides a specific defence where D assists or encour-ages an offence for which she is the intended victim. For example, if D (12 years old) encourages her boyfriend (16 years old) to have sex with her, *she* has a defence to a charge of encouraging rape of a child under 13.

11.5 Double inchoate liability

So-called double (or infinite) inchoate liability arises where D's inchoate offence is targeted at a principal offence which is itself inchoate.[154] For example, where D pro-vides P with access to her house so that P can plan a robbery with a third party, D may be liable for assisting a conspiracy to commit robbery. Although, as in our example, liability of this kind may be justified, it must also be recognised that D's conduct is extremely remote from the potential future harm, being at least two steps removed. Concern that such remoteness will lead to inappropriate criminalisation is limited in two ways.

First, not all combinations of inchoate offences are possible. The potential combina-tions, illustrated in **Table 11.9**, have been expanded dramatically by the SCA 2007. They have developed in the absence of a clear principle. For example, the Law Commission has rejected the potential for an offence of attempt to conspire as an overextension of the law, yet conceded that such conduct will almost always amount to encouraging a conspiracy, which is an offence.[155] The table should be read by looking to the left-hand column first.

---

[153] Newman, 'Statutory Defences of Reasonableness' in Reed and Bohlander (eds), *General Defences in Criminal Law* (2014) 145.
[154] Law Commission, *Conspiracy and Attempts* (No 318, 2009) Part 3.
[155] Ibid, para 3.22.

Table 11.9 Double inchoate liability

	Attempt	Conspiracy	SCA 2007, s44	SCA 2007, s45	SCA 2007, s46
Attempt	No offence	No offence CAA 1981, s1(4)(a)	D may attempt a s44 offence	D may attempt a s45 offence	D may attempt a s46 offence
Conspiracy	D1 and D2 may conspire to attempt	D1 and D2 may conspire to conspire	D1 and D2 may conspire to commit a s44 offence	D1 and D2 may conspire to commit a s45 offence	D1 and D2 may conspire to commit a s46 offence
SCA 2007, s44	D may assist or encourage an attempt	D may assist or encourage a conspiracy	D may assist or encourage a s44 offence	D may assist or encourage a s45 offence	D may assist or encourage a s46 offence
SCA 2007, s45	No offence SCA 2007, s49(4)–(5)	No offence SCA 2007, s49(4)–(5)	No offence SCA 2007, s49(4)–(5)	No offence SCA 2007, s49(4)–(5)	No offence SCA 2007, s49(4)–(5)
SCA 2007, s46	No offence SCA 2007, s49(4)–(5)	No offence SCA 2007, s49(4)–(5)	No offence SCA 2007, s49(4)–(5)	No offence SCA 2007, s49(4)–(5)	No offence SCA 2007, s49(4)–(5)

The second way in which double inchoate liability could be limited is through requiring D to intend the future offence. For example, where D assists a conspiracy to commit robbery, she must intend that the robbery is completed. To ensure that this second limitation is applied, courts must require that for D to commit an inchoate offence, she must intend any ulterior mens rea requirement within that principal offence. As noted previously when discussing *AG's Reference (No 3 of 1992)*,[156] however, this has not always been the case with attempts, and appears contrary to the wording of the SCA 2007 in relation to the assisting and encouraging offences. Therefore, despite some comments to the contrary, it seems that this second limitation is largely absent from the current law.[157]

11.6 Substantive offences in an inchoate form

We have discussed several offences in this book that could be described as inchoate, and there are a considerable number of such offences within the criminal law. These include, for example, the new fraud offences where D acts with the dishonest intention of making

---

[156] (1993) 98 Cr App R 383. See **11.2.2.2**.

[157] Child, 'The Structure, Coherence and Limits of Inchoate Liability: The New Ulterior Element' (2014) 34 LS 537.

a gain or causing a loss, but need not do so in fact to be liable;[158] several of the new sexual offences such as specific offences of inciting sexual activity and grooming, where no sexual contact is required;[159] several possession offences such as D's possession of illegal drugs or weapons, although not itself harmful, but posing an obvious future risk of their use; endangerment offences such as driving over the speed limit, with excess alcohol; as well as D acting in criminal violation of health and safety legislation. In each case, it should be remembered that we are criminalising D for causing the *potential* for future harms.

11.6.1 Assisting or encouraging suicide

The offence of assisting or encouraging suicide, under section 2 of the Suicide Act 1960,[160] is included here by way of contrast to the assisting or encouraging offences discussed previously (see **Table 11.10**). The general inchoate offences in the SCA 2007 do not apply to suicide, simply because suicide is not a criminal offence. However, section 2 of the Suicide Act makes special provision for the criminalisation of acts which assist or encourage it. The most controversial aspect of this offence relates to the likelihood of prosecution being brought where, for example, D assists P's travel to a jurisdiction in which euthanasia is legal.[161]

Table 11.10 Assisting or encouraging suicide

	Actus reus	Mens rea
Conduct element	Any action	Voluntary
Circumstance element	D's conduct is capable of assisting or encouraging P to commit suicide (on the facts as D believes them to be)	Intention to assist or encourage suicide
Result element	None	None

It should be noted that the offence contains no result element, so it is irrelevant whether P is in fact assisted or encouraged, or whether P commits suicide. There is also no ulterior mens rea requiring D to intend that P will, as a result, commit suicide, so a suicide website owner whose posts intend to assist P, but does not necessarily desire that P will commit suicide, will be caught by the offence. The offence, and the prosecution guidance accompanying it, remain controversial.[162]

11.7 Reform

The general inchoate offences criminalise conduct at the very fringes of the criminal law, and so it should be no surprise that there has been, and remains, considerable debate

[158] **Chapter 9.**
[159] **Chapter 8.**
[160] Amended by the Coroners and Justice Act 2009, s59.
[161] O'Sullivan, 'Mens Rea, Motive and Assisted Suicide: Does the DPP's Policy Go Too Far?' (2014) 34 LS 96.
[162] See the latest challenge in R (Kenward and others) v DPP [2015] EWHC 3508 (Admin), in which the court provides a valuable summary of current debates.

about their appropriate construction. Much of this debate relates to the overarching clash between those who would like to facilitate earlier intervention, in order to minimise the risk of future harms, and those who are concerned about the over-expansion of criminalisation to remote conduct, such that may be insufficient to demonstrate appropriate blameworthiness. In this section, we do not attempt to discuss these debates in full. Rather, we provide a brief summary combined with references to academic material that should be explored in order to get a fuller picture.

11.7.1 The actus reus of attempts

Debate surrounding the actus reus of attempts is probably the most straightforward to understand, but may also be the most intractable. Defensible academic arguments can be made for a wide variety of approaches, from very early to very late criminal intervention.

A) Early intervention with attempts: If we believe that the 'mischief' targeted by criminal attempts is D's mental commitment to completing the principal offence, rather than any physical signs of that commitment, then we can justify very early intervention by the criminal law as soon as we have sufficient evidence of that commitment.[163] However, for many, the term 'attempt' is problematic here, requiring D to do more than form an intention. It was on this basis that the Law Commission proposed the creation of a new offence of 'criminal preparation' in 2007.[164] This proposal was problematic and was ultimately rejected following consultation.[165] However, for those who favour early intervention through a general offence, the case for a preparation offence may still be appealing.[166]

B) Refining the current midway course: Most academics, and most other jurisdictions, favour something of a midway option between first and last act attempts. In this regard, it may be that an alternative form of words (eg 'substantial step' or 'unequivocal act') should be preferred to the current formulation.[167] Alternatively, or in addition, several academics recommend the use of statutory examples, as used in the US Model Penal Code[168] to supplement the statute. These could, for example, make it clear that lying in wait, as in *Geddes*,[169] should satisfy the actus reus.[170] However, this approach has been resisted in this country, partly because of the difficulty in agreeing suitable examples, and partly because statutory examples have not been part of the drafting history in England and Wales.[171]

C) Narrowing the actus reus to later acts: It may also be argued that attempts liability should be narrowed from the current formulation to apply only to the most blameworthy cases. For example, a subtle narrowing has been recommended by Duff, who conceptualises attempts as 'attacks' on protected interests, and so would only find an attempt where D's conduct could be described as an attack.[172] More radical, Alexander, Kessler Ferzan,

---

[163] Robinson, 'The Modern General Part: Three Illusions' in Shute and Simester (eds), *Criminal Law Theory* (2003) 92–93.
[164] Law Commission, *Conspiracy and Attempts* (Consultation 183, 2007) Part 16.
[165] Law Commission, *Conspiracy and Attempts* (No 318, 2009) Part 8.
[166] Rogers, 'The Codification of Attempts and the Case for "Preparation"' [2008] Crim LR 937.
[167] There is a very useful discussion of this in Law Commission (No 102, 1980) Part 2D.
[168] Model Penal Code, §5.01(2).
[169] See **11.2.1.3**.
[170] Duff, *Criminal Attempts* (1996) 57.
[171] Law Commission, *Conspiracy and Attempts* (No 318, 2009) para 8.74.
[172] *Criminal Attempts* (1996) Ch13.

and Morse have recommended that attempts should be narrowed to cases in which D has unleashed a risk, an approach that comes close to the 'last act' test discussed earlier.[173]

11.7.2 The mens rea of attempts and conspiracy

Although the current mens rea requirements for attempts and conspiracy differ, it is generally accepted that overlap between the offences means that a consistent approach would be preferable. It was partly on this basis that the court in *Pace* rejected *Khan*, and chose to adopt a position for the mens rea of impossible attempts in line with conspiracy.[174] However, a preference for consistency does not tell us what that consistent approach should be. Some of the main options for reform include the following:

A) **Intention approach:** This approach requires D to intend every element of the future principal offence. This approach was preferred and adopted within the CAA 1981 and the CLA 1977. Its benefits include its simplicity, as well as its narrowing of inchoate liability to cases where D is fully committed to completing the principal offence. However, as discussed in *Khan*, it may be too narrow: preventing liability for (eg) attempted rape, where D intends the physical parts of the offence but is reckless as to the circumstance of V's non-consent. An alternative may be to offer a standard mens rea requirement of belief, or even recklessness, as to every element.[175]

B) **Khan approach:** This approach allows D's mens rea as to circumstances to mirror that of the principal offence. This approach has been recommended, with clarification, by the Law Commission for both attempts and conspiracy.[176] Problems with this approach have been highlighted earlier.[177] To these we may also add that this approach seems to be conceptually confused: requiring less than intention as to circumstances, but not telling us why circumstances as elements of an offence warrant special treatment (beyond the desired result in the individual case).[178]

C) **Conditional intention approach:** This approach stretches a traditional understanding of conditional intention to find intention where D intends to act in the knowledge that her action may be criminal.[179] This has the advantage of focusing on intention, but also allowing for liability in *Khan*-like cases. However, it is problematic, labelling what is essentially recklessness as conditional intention, and struggling to explain why recklessness as to results (as opposed to circumstances) should be treated differently.[180]

D) **Missing element approach:** Stannard has recommended an approach in which D need only intend elements of the principal offence that are not completed despite his trying (eg in *Khan*, as V is not consenting, the only missing element is the sexual

---

[173] *Crime and Culpability: A Theory of Criminal Law* (2009).
[174] See **11.2.2.2–11.2.2.3**.
[175] Belief is preferred in Child and Hunt, 'Mens Rea and the General Inchoate Offences: Another New Culpability Framework' (2012) 63 NILQ 247.
[176] Law Commission, *Conspiracy and Attempts* (No 318, 2009).
[177] See **11.2.2.2**.
[178] Child and Hunt, 'Mens Rea and the General Inchoate Offences: Another New Culpability Framework' (2012) 63 NILQ 247.
[179] Williams, 'Intents in the Alternative' (1991) 50 CLJ 120.
[180] Duff, *Criminal Attempts* (1996) 15–16.

penetration; so D must intend the latter, but need not intend the former).[181] This approach was preferred in *AG's Reference (No 1 of 1992)*.[182] However, this case may be too broad. For example, D borrows V's tools to do a job that risks damaging them; however, in his confusion, he uses his own tools and causes damage. D would be liable for attempted criminal damage: intending the missing element (ownership) and reckless as to the non-missing element (damage).[183]

E) **Mirroring approach:** The Irish Law Commission has recommended that mens rea should mirror that required for the principal offence as to every element (with the exception of murder).[184] This has the advantage of simplicity but is highly problematic. For example, if D asks a drunken P for a lift home, D may be liable for the strict liability offence of encouraging P to drive with excess alcohol, even if D was not aware that P was intoxicated.[185]

11.7.3 The future of assisting and encouraging

Whatever the merits of the Law Commission's recommendations on assisting and encouraging,[186] the final scheme of offences created within the SCA 2007 is not fit for purpose. Spread over multiple complex sections, the current law lacks clarity and has already caused problems for the appellate courts.[187] Additionally, although its complex drafting initially discouraged its extensive use, the breadth of the offences as drafted (both in terms of actus reus and mens rea) provide for the possibility of inappropriate criminalisation—with only the uncertain defence of 'acting reasonably' to restrain it.[188]

The Justice Committee of the House of Commons engaged a review of these offences with a view to post-legislative scrutiny, a process that could end in reform or even repeal of the offences.[189] This has already revealed a consistent dissatisfaction with the law amongst those consulted. However, the Committee concluded that a full review should be delayed to see if the current law can be clarified by future court judgments.

It should be noted that changes elsewhere in the law may result in more charges being brought within the SCA 2007 assisting or encouraging provisions. Most obviously, complicity liability (cases where D assists or encourages an offence which is then committed) has been dramatically narrowed to require intentional assistance, and intention as to elements of P's offence. We discuss these changes in **Chapter 12**. Defendants who may have previously been charged with complicity offences, but who do not meet the new mens rea requirements, are likely to be charged with SCA 2007 offences.

11.7.4 The inconsistency of law reform

To help provide a critique of the current state of the law, it is useful to observe the inconsistent approach taken to the reform of the general inchoate offences. As we have

---

[181] Stannard, 'Making Up for the Missing Element—A Sideways Look at Attempts' (1987) 7 LS 194.
[182] (1992) 96 Cr App R 298.
[183] Duff, *Criminal Attempts* (1996) 14–15.
[184] Irish Law Reform Commission, *Report on Inchoate Offences* (No 99, 2010).
[185] Child and Hunt, 'Mens Rea and the General Inchoate Offences: Another New Culpability Framework' (2012) 63 NILQ 247.
[186] Law Commission, *Inchoate Liability for Assisting and Encouraging Crime* (No 300, 2006).
[187] See **11.4.4.3**.
[188] Ormerod and Fortson, 'Serious Crime Act 2007: Part 2 Offences' [2009] Crim LR 389.
[189] House of Commons, *Post-Legislative Scrutiny of Part 2 of the Serious Crime Act 2007* (2013).

415

highlighted at various points in this chapter, the codification of attempts (CAA 1981) and conspiracy (CLA 1977) resulted from a fundamental review of inchoate offences by the Law Commission at that time. Between 2006 and 2009, we saw a similar review by the Law Commission and recommendations for a consistent change of direction—particularly through the broadening of mens rea.[190] However, this time, these recommendations were not consistently taken forward into legislation. Rather, the only offences to be reformed on the basis of the later review were those of assisting or encouraging, those in least need of reform and for which reform has proved least satisfactory.

As a result, the current general inchoate offences are imbalanced. Despite the overlap between the offences (eg it is hard to think of an agreement to commit an offence that does not also involve one party encouraging the other), the approach codified within the SCA 2007 is fundamentally different from the current law of attempts and conspiracy. And as the courts seek to bridge this gap, both sides risk further confusion and incoherence. In **Chapter 12**, we discuss a similar inconsistency caused by the reform of inchoate assisting and encouraging, and the lack of complementary statutory reform of secondary liability, (again) despite Law Commission recommendations. Finally, a similar criticism can be made in relation to the creation of specific inchoate offences, such as those relating to sexual offences and terrorism, which again do not seem to have been created with a view to consistent coexistence with the general inchoate offences.[191]

11.8 Eye on assessment

As with previous chapters, this section provides advice for applying the offences discussed in practice. Although the elements of the general inchoate offences are very different from the offences discussed in previous chapters, the basic structure to follow within a problem question remains the same.

STEP 1 Identify the potential criminal event in the facts

This should be simply stated (eg 'The first potential criminal event arises where D tries to shoot V'). The role of this stage is to highlight which part of the question you are answering before you begin to apply the law.

STEP 2 Identify the potential offence

Again, state this simply (eg 'When shooting at V, D may be liable for attempted murder'). A useful way to identify the principal offence attempted/conspired/assisted or encouraged is to think about what offence D (or D2) would have committed if her plan had been successful. The role of this stage is to highlight which offence you are going to apply.

When answering a question on the general inchoate offences, it is easy to become overwhelmed by the detail. Steps 1 and 2 should be useful reminders to start simply.

---

[190] No 300, 2006; Consultation 183, 2007; No 318, 2009.
[191] Child and Hunt, 'Risk, Pre-Emption, and the Limits of the Criminal Law' in Doolin, Child, Raine, and Beech (eds), *Whose Criminal Justice? State or Community?* (2011) 51.

While looking for a potential offence, keep the basic descriptions of the offences in your mind: for example, has D tried to commit an offence (attempt); has D agreed with another to commit an offence (conspiracy); has D assisted or encouraged another to commit an offence (assisting and encouraging)?

Remember that these offences overlap, and so a single action may amount to more than one of the general offences. In this case, highlight the overlap to your reader and then proceed with your analysis of the offence you think is most appropriate: either because it more accurately describes what D has done, or because you think there is more chance of finding liability for that offence. Again, tell your reader *why* you have made the choice.

> **STEP 3 Applying the offence to the facts**
>
> Having identified the relevant offence, make sure you discuss each of the required elements.
>
> Actus reus: What does the offence require? Did D do it?
>
> Mens rea: What does the offence require? Did D possess it?

This is the most challenging part of problem questions in relation to the general inchoate offences because there are several stages of analysis that you need to lead your reader through. The most important advice here is to be clear; to separate each part of your discussion; and to be methodical. With reference to our detailed discussion of the offences earlier, the checklist approach in **Tables 11.11, 11.12,** and **11.13** can provide a useful guide to structuring your answer.

Table 11.11 Applying attempts

Attempts
D decides to cut down a tree, unsure whether it belongs to her or her neighbour V. The tree belongs to V, who stops D just before the first chop of her axe. If she was successful, she would have committed the principal offence of criminal damage.
When D tries to cut down the tree, she may have committed attempted criminal damage: • Actus reus: Has D's act gone beyond mere preparation towards damaging or destroying V's tree (the actus reus of criminal damage), either in reality or on the facts as D believes them to be?   • Mens rea: D's attempt is not impossible (ie if D continued as planned, she would have committed criminal damage); therefore we need to apply the mens rea of attempts as set out in *Khan*. Does D *intend* the conduct she has performed? Does D *intend* the conduct element of the principal offence of criminal damage (ie the chopping)? Does D *intend* the result element of the criminal damage (ie causing damage)? Does D have the same mens rea as criminal damage requires (ie *recklessness*) as to the circumstance element (ie that the tree belongs to another)?

Table 11.12 Applying statutory conspiracy

> **Conspiracy**
>
> D1 and D2 agree to smash the window of V's car. If their plan had been carried out, the principal offence of criminal damage would have been committed.
>
> ---
>
> When D1 and D2 make their plan, they may be liable for conspiracy to commit criminal damage:
>
> - Actus reus: Has D (whichever D you are considering) formed an agreement with another that will necessarily amount to or involve the commission of criminal damage by one of them, either in reality or on the facts as they believe them to be?
>
> - Mens rea: Do D1 and D2 intend to form the agreement? Do D1 and D2 *intend* that every element required for criminal damage will be completed by a party to the agreement?

Table 11.13 Applying assisting or encouraging

> **Assisting or encouraging**
>
> D sells a can of spray paint to P in her shop. D is concerned that P might use it for graffiti. If P did use it she would commit the offence of criminal damage.
>
> ---
>
> When D sells the spray paint to P, she may commit an offence of assisting criminal damage. As she does not intend the principal offence to come about, and has only one principal offence in mind, the most likely charge would be section 45 of the SCA 2007:
>
> - Actus reus: Has D done an act which is capable of assisting P to commit criminal damage?
>
> - Mens rea: Does D *believe* that her act will assist P to complete the conduct required for criminal damage (ie assist spraying the paint)? Does D *believe* that P will complete the conduct element of criminal damage (ie spraying the paint)? Is D at least *reckless* as to whether P will complete the other elements of the principal offence: the results (ie causing damage), circumstances (ie that the damaged property belongs to another), the mens rea (ie that P will be at least reckless as to causing damage to another's property)?

Remember that with the exception of conspiracy and impossible attempts, you will need to split the principal offence into conduct, circumstances, and results in order to identify and apply the mens rea required of D in relation to each. You will find this division relatively straightforward for certain offences, as with the criminal damage examples in **Tables 11.11, 11.12**, and **11.13**. Where you struggle to find a clear separation, try and do the best you can, but highlight to your reader that the separation is not clear, and reflect on this as a criticism of the changes to the law in this area that makes such separation essential.

AR and MR are satisfied	AR and/or MR are not satisfied
Continue to STEP 4.	Return to STEP 2, and look for an alternative offence. If none, then skip to STEP 5, concluding that no offence is committed.

STEP 4 Consider defences

The word 'consider' here is important, as you should not discuss every defence for every question. Rather, think whether there are any defences (eg duress) that *could* potentially apply. If there are, discuss those only.

As well as the general defences, remember that there are also a number of specific defences (as discussed earlier). Remember that where a specific defence applies to a certain offence, it only applies in this context and should *never* be applied to a different offence.

STEP 5 Conclude

This is usually a single sentence either saying that it is likely that D has committed the offence, or saying that it is not likely either because an offence element is not satisfied, or because a defence is likely to apply. It is not often that you will be able to say categorically whether or not D has committed the offence, so it is usually best to conclude in terms of what is more 'likely'.

STEP 6 Loop

Go back up to Step 1, identifying the next potential criminal event. Continue until you have discussed all the relevant potentially criminal events.

 ONLINE RESOURCE CENTRE

www.oxfordtextbooks.co.uk/orc/sho/

This chapter is accompanied by a selection of online resources to help you with this topic, including:

- **Multiple-choice questions**
- **Chapter summary sheet**
- Two **sample examination questions** with answer guidance
- **Further reading**

Also available on the Online Resource Centre are:

- A selection of **videos** from the authors explaining key topics and principles
- **Legal updates**
- Useful **weblinks**

12

Parties to crime

12.1 Introduction **473**

12.2 Principal or accomplice? **476**

    12.2.1 D as a principal offender **476**

    12.2.2 D as a co-principal **476**

    12.2.3 D as a principal via innocent agency **478**

    12.2.4 D as an accomplice **479**

    12.2.5 Uncertainty whether D is a principal or an accomplice **479**

12.3 Complicity by aiding, abetting, counselling, or procuring **481**

    12.3.1 Actus reus of aiding, abetting, counselling, or procuring **482**

    12.3.2 Mens rea of aiding, abetting, counselling, or procuring **489**

12.4 Complicity by joint enterprise? **503**

    12.4.1 Challenges following the abolition of joint enterprise **505**

12.5 The relationship between complicity and inchoate liability **506**

12.6 Defences **507**

    12.6.1 Withdrawal **507**

    12.6.2 The victim rule **508**

    12.6.3 Acting reasonably? **509**

12.7 Reform **509**

    12.7.1 Abolishing complicity **510**

    12.7.2 Law Commission 2007 recommendations **511**

12.8 Eye on assessment **512**

12.1 Introduction

Crimes are rarely committed by a single defendant acting in perfect isolation. Where P robs a bank, for example, she may have enlisted X as a getaway driver, Y as a lookout, Z to assist gathering the loot, and so on. Even before the robbery begins, these parties and others may also have encouraged P or helped her to make plans. In **Chapter 11** we discussed the potential for inchoate liability in these circumstances. Under those inchoate offences, provided they have the required mens rea, X, Y, and Z and any others involved will be liable for assisting or encouraging robbery or conspiracy to rob at the first moment of assisting, encouraging, or agreeing with

P. Those offences apply whether or not the principal offence (the robbery) ever comes about.

Moving beyond inchoate liability, accomplice liability (or complicity as it is also called) arises where P goes on to complete the principal offence. In these circumstances, the other parties are no longer simply liable for their inchoate roles,[1] but may now be additionally liable as accomplices, as parties to the crime. There is no need to prove that X, Y, and Z have done anything more than they had to trigger inchoate liability, but their liability as accomplices reflects the additional blameworthiness that is derived from the completion and associated harms of the principal offence. In this way, their accessorial liability is triggered by, or derives from, the completion of P's principal offence. Where X, Y, and Z are liable as accomplices, they are labelled and punished in the same way as P. In the example given, each will be charged with 'robbery', and if convicted, sentenced as a 'robber'.

> **Extra detail . . .**
> P may also be assisted after the principal offence (eg to hide the money or to disrupt the police investigation). There are a number of offences to deal with such acts,[2] but they will not be discussed in this chapter. Rather, our focus is on the actions of the parties before P's crime is completed or during its continuance.

Complicity, like the general inchoate offences, creates a form of general liability, applying across the criminal law unless expressly[3] or impliedly[4] excluded. Therefore, just as D may commit an offence as a principal offender, where D helps another to commit the offence D may be liable for that same offence as an accomplice. Complicity is largely a common law doctrine, but its basic structure is codified within section 8 of the Accessories and Abettors Act 1861.[5]

> 8. Whosoever shall aid, abet, counsel, or procure the commission of any indictable offence, whether the same be an offence at common law or by virtue of any Act passed or to be passed, shall be liable to be tried, indicted, and punished as a principal offender.

Where D acts as an accomplice, she does not commit the offence as a principal, but her assistance or encouragement of P's offence ('aiding, abetting, counselling, or procuring'), and her mens rea, connect her to P's crime. Where P commits murder, for example, her accomplice D will also be labelled as a murderer, and will be subject to the same mandatory life sentence. Where P commits rape, his accomplice, D, will be labelled and punished as a rapist, even if D is a woman and therefore unable to commit rape as a principal

---

[1] Although each will in theory remain liable for the inchoate offences committed, they would be unlikely to be charged.

[2] Examples include impeding the apprehension or prosecution of offenders (Criminal Law Act 1967, s4); compounding an offence (Criminal Law Act 1967, s5); and the common law offence of refusal to aid a constable.

[3] eg the Corporate Manslaughter and Corporate Homicide Act 2007 expressly excludes complicity of individuals.

[4] *Farr* [1982] Crim LR 745, and commentary.

[5] The Magistrates' Courts Act 1980, s44 creates an equivalent provision for summary offences.

because rape requires penile penetration.[6] Indeed, where D acts as an accomplice, her liability will derive directly from whatever offence is committed by P.

Despite the important role played by complicity, and perhaps partly because of it, the rules governing liability have not developed consistently within the common law. Rather, as the Law Commission has observed, the law has 'developed haphazardly and is permeated with uncertainty'.[7] There are two main reasons for the unsatisfactory state of this development.

- **Inevitable complexity:** Complicity, like the general inchoate offences, is particularly complex and challenging because it requires discussion of D's actus reus; D's mens rea as to her own conduct; and D's mens rea as to a future principal offence being committed by P. However, beyond inchoate liability, complicity also involves the *commission* of that principal offence by P. Therefore, complicity includes an additional requirement: D's mens rea as to P's principal offence must be sufficiently similar (factually) to that principal offence to ground D's increased liability. Maintaining a consistent and coherent approach to each of these separate requirements, especially within the common law, is exceptionally difficult.

- **Problem of policy:** The doctrinal rationale of complicity, as we discuss in the reform section later in the chapter,[8] remains uncertain, and so provides little structure for how complicity should be interpreted by the courts. However, at its simplest, there is a strong intuitive sense in which P's completion of the principal offence assisted or encouraged by D increases D's blameworthiness from a position where P does not commit the offence and D's liability is therefore inchoate. In other words, results matter. In addition to this, the political will to tackle gang violence and other forms of coordinated law breaking, even where the individual roles of each member are unclear, creates a powerful incentive towards expansive interpretations of the law to facilitate findings of liability.[9]

As a result of these, and other, reasons, the law of complicity has continued to provide a considerable challenge for the courts. Indeed, as recently as 2016 in the combined cases of *Jogee and Ruddock* (hereafter *Jogee*),[10] the Supreme Court has fundamentally changed the mental element of the offence, stating that the previous 30 years of jurisprudence had been the result of a 'wrong turn'. As the dust begins to settle on this and other appellate court cases, this chapter aims to provide a route to understanding and applying the current law of complicity. The challenge, as it is for courts, academics, and students alike, is to find sufficient coherence within the law to be able to discuss and apply it logically, whilst also to acknowledge an inevitable lack of certainty as to much of the law in practice.

---

[6] *Ram and Ram* (1893) 17 Cox CC 609. For the exceptional cases where a woman can commit rape as a principal, see **8.2**.

[7] Law Commission, *Participating in Crime* (No 305, 2007).

[8] See **12.7**.

[9] See eg the House of Lords case of *Powell and English* [1999] AC 1 where Lord Hutton makes repeated reference to 'practical concerns' outweighing 'strict logic'.

[10] [2016] UKSC 8, [2106] UKPC 7.

12.2 Principal or accomplice?

Where a criminal event involves multiple actors, the division between principal offenders (those committing the offence) and accomplices (those assisting, encouraging, or procuring the offence) is not always obvious. However, as the rules governing the liability of principals and accessories are different, identifying the role of D may be crucial.

The courts have struggled to maintain a clear separation of principal and accomplice, perhaps best illustrated in the Supreme Court's judgment in *Gnango*.

 Gnango [2011] UKSC 59

D and P (who was unidentified, but referred to in court as 'Bandana Man') got into a gunfight with each other following a chance meeting in a London estate. Both shot at the other with the intention to kill or to cause GBH. One of P's shots missed D and hit and killed V, an innocent pedestrian passing by. D was charged with murder through the doctrine of complicity.

- Crown Court: D guilty of murder on the basis that D and P were jointly concerned with an affray, and D foresaw the chance of murder being committed within this venture.
- Court of Appeal: appeal allowed, quashing D's conviction. There was no common purpose between D and P, and thus no way of connecting P's crime with D.
- Supreme Court: appeal allowed, restoring liability (Lord Kerr dissenting). D was liable because he assisted or encouraged P to shoot (Lords Phillips, Judge, and Wilson); or because he was a principal offender (Lord Clark); or because he was a joint principal with P (Lords Brown, Clark, and Dyson).

We discuss this case at several points later. However, for present purposes it is sufficient to highlight that despite a general agreement that liability should have been found, the case leaves open four distinct bases for that liability, all of which are revealed to be questionable and imprecise.[11] In search of clarity, we emphasise the following principles for identifying D's role within an offence.

12.2.1 D as a principal offender

D is a principal offender if she completes the actus reus and mens rea elements of the principal offence. This is the standard form of liability assumed in our discussion of the substantive offences in previous chapters.

12.2.2 D as a co-principal

Where there is more than one actor involved in an offence, this does not necessarily mean that there is a single principal offender and that the other parties are accessories. Rather, where D and another (or others) each complete the actus reus and mens rea of an offence, they commit the offence as co-principals. For example, where D1 and D2 attack V with the intention to kill or cause GBH, and V dies as a result of this

---

[11] See Lord Kerr's dissent. See also Buxton, 'Being an Accessory to One's Own Murder' [2012] Crim LR 275; Virgo, 'Joint Enterprise Liability is Dead: Long Live Accessorial Liability' [2012] Crim LR 850; Sullivan, 'Accessories and Principals after *Gnango*' in Reed and Bohlander (eds), *Participating in Crime* (2013).

combined attack, both D1 and D2 will be liable for murder as principal offenders.[12] D1 and D2 have both caused the result (death) in fact and in law, even though there were multiple causes.[13]

This contrasts with the situation where D does not commit the actus reus of the offence with P, but she does assist or encourage it. For example, where D hires P as a contract killer to murder V. In this scenario, it may be thought by a layperson that D has caused V's death, but this is not the result in law. Rather, because P has taken the free and informed choice to kill V after D's assistance or encouragement, P's free and voluntary act breaks the chain of causation between D and the killing.[14] Legally, D has not caused P's voluntary acts or their results; P is their sole author. As stated in *Kennedy (No 2)*:

> Principals cause, accomplices encourage (or otherwise influence) or help. If the instigator were regarded as causing the result he would be a principal, and the conceptual division between principals … and accessories would vanish. Indeed, it was because the instigator was not regarded as causing the crime that the notion of accessories had to be developed. This is the irrefragable argument for recognising the *novus actus* principle as one of the bases of our criminal law. The final act is done by the perpetrator, and his guilt pushes the accessories, conceptually speaking, into the background. Accessorial liability is, in the traditional theory, 'derivative' from that of the perpetrator.[15]

Despite the foundational importance of the distinction between principals and accessories, because both parties (if found guilty) will be labelled and punished in the same way, it is one that is often confused.

In *Gnango*,[16] for example, outlined previously, D does not shoot V himself, and P's shots are not caused by D, they are free and voluntary acts.[17] In short, D does not commit the actus reus of murder. However, in the Supreme Court, Lords Brown,[18] Clarke,[19] and Dyson[20] each express support for the view that D could be liable as a principal offender; and in the latter's case, this was even after recognising a break in the chain of causation.[21] If these dicta were accepted it would represent a significant change to the law, collapsing the distinction between principals and accessories set out in *Kennedy (No 2)*, and rewriting the rules of causation.[22] It cannot be correct. It is an understandable, but regrettable, confusion of distinct concepts.[23]

---

[12] *Macklin and Murphy's Case* (1838) 2 Lew CC 225.

[13] See **2.7.1**.

[14] *Kennedy (No 2)* [2007] UKHL 38.

[15] [2007] UKHL 38, [17], quoting Williams, '*Finis* for *Novus Actus?*' (1989) 48 CLJ 391.

[16] [2011] UKSC 59.

[17] Unlike in *Pagett* (1983) 76 Cr App R 279, where return fire from police was held not to break the causal chain, P's shots were not involuntary self-defence. See **2.7.2.3**.

[18] At [71].

[19] At [81].

[20] At [105].

[21] At [106].

[22] Sullivan, 'Accessories and Principals after *Gnango*' in Reed and Bohlander (eds), *Participating in Crime* (2013).

[23] Buxton, 'Being an Accessory to One's Own Murder' [2012] Crim LR 275.

12.2.3 D as a principal via innocent agency

Although the free and voluntary acts of a third party will break the chain of causation, this is not the case where the actions of that party are uninformed. Where D uses a party (X) as a tool to commit an offence, and that party is unaware of the circumstances that would make her acts criminal, D may still be liable as a *principal* offender via the doctrine of innocent agency.[24] For example, D gives X a letter bomb to deliver to V, X does so, and V is killed. In this scenario, if D had informed X that the letter contained a bomb then X's act of delivery becomes a free and voluntary act that breaks the chain of causation between D's acts and the death of V (X becomes the principal to the murder; D the accessory). In contrast, if X is unaware of the letter's contents, then her delivery to V is not an informed act and D remains the cause of V's death (D becomes the principal to the murder; X the innocent agent).

The doctrine of innocent agency is illustrated in *Michael*.[25]

Michael (1840) 9 C & P 356

D, intending to kill her baby (V), gave the nurse caring for the child (Y) a bottle of 'medicine' which she asked Y to administer. The bottle actually contained laudanum, a drug that would kill V if administered at the dose instructed by D. In the event, Y did not administer the drug but left it on the mantelpiece. Whilst Y was absent, her 5-year-old son (X) took the drug and administered it to V, causing death. X had no understanding of the drug or its danger. D was charged with murder.

- Assizes: guilty of murder. The actions of Y and X were uninformed (ie they were innocent agents) and so D's act remained the cause of V's death.

A third party will qualify as an innocent agent if she acts without essential knowledge (as with X and Y in *Michael*); where she is under the age of criminal responsibility (as X was in *Michael*); or where she is legally insane. In each case the third party becomes, in effect, a tool of D as opposed to an autonomous agent.

The doctrine of innocent agency works well with the types of offence for which the principal does not require a particular attribute to commit the offence, as for example with murder. However, for certain offences, it seems inappropriate to characterise D as a principal offender when acting through an innocent agent. For example, where D tells X to have sex with his wife (V) knowing that V will not consent, and X does so (V not making her lack of consent apparent to X because of D's threats), can we say that D rapes V as a principal offender?[26] The doctrine of innocent agency would suggest that this is possible, with X's uninformed acts not breaking the chain of causation. However, section 1 of the Sexual Offences Act 2003 defines rape in terms of D penetrating V's vagina with 'his penis', an act D has not performed. Similar problems arise in the context of bigamy: if D knows Y is married, but induces X (unaware of Y's marital status) to marry Y, it is problematic to say that D has 'married during the lifetime of his wife' (the actus reus of bigamy). In each case, the courts have preferred to describe D as 'procuring' the offence

---

[24] Williams, 'Innocent Agency and Causation' (1992) 3 Crim L Forum 289.
[25] See also *Stringer and Banks* [1991] Crim LR 639: fraud via an innocent agent.
[26] This example is based on the facts of *Cogan and Leak* [1976] QB 217, where there was some support for an innocent agency approach.

as an accomplice. This affords liability, and avoids the linguistic problems described in relation to rape and bigamy above, but it also begs an obvious question: how can D be an accomplice to X when X has not committed an offence? We return to this in our discussion of 'procuring' later.

> **Extra detail . . .**
> The Law Commission has recommended that the doctrine of innocent agency should be codified and reformed to include all cases where D acts through an innocent person. Thus, for the Commission, D should be liable for rape and bigamy as a principal offender in the examples given despite the linguistic problems applying offence definitions. This would resolve the current need to resort to procuring. However, this recommendation does not represent the current law.[27]

12.2.4 D as an accomplice

D is an accomplice to a principal offence where, rather than completing the actus reus of the offence herself, she aids, abets, counsels, or procures P to commit the offence, and P does so. In modern language, this requires D to have assisted or encouraged P, *or* to have caused P's offence to come about.[28] Each will be discussed in detail later.

> **Terminology . . .**
> Several terms are used interchangeably in the literature.
> • Complicity: the doctrine of complicity is also commonly referred to as accomplice liability; accessorial liability; and secondary liability.
> • Accomplices: accomplices are also commonly referred to as accessories and secondary parties.
> • Principals: principal offenders are sometimes referred to as perpetrators.

D's liability for the principal offence is derivative of, or parasitic on, P's conduct. This does not mean that P must be convicted of the principal offence before D can be liable, or even that P must be identified. D's liability derives from proof of the principal offence, not from P's conviction for it. Thus, D's liability depends on proof that her acts were relevant to a principal offence that has been committed by another party: D's liability *does* derive from P's criminal conduct.[29] This is crucial where, for example, P is unidentified (eg *Gnango*) or even deceased.

12.2.5 Uncertainty whether D is a principal or an accomplice

Even when the greatest care is taken to distinguish between principals and accessories, there are two circumstances where uncertainty can emerge. One is legal, and the other is factual.

A) Legal: Legal problems separating principal offenders and accomplices can emerge, as we have highlighted, in the context of innocent agency.[30] Although the doctrine of

---

[27] Law Commission, *Participating in Crime* (No 305, 2007) paras 4.8–4.27. See Taylor, 'Procuring, Causation, Innocent Agency and the Law Commission' [2008] Crim LR 32.
[28] *Ferguson v Weaving* [1951] KB 814.
[29] *Thornton v Mitchell* [1940] 1 All ER 339: no principal offence, and therefore no accessory liability.
[30] See **12.2.3**.

innocent agency operates logically in relation to most offences, its application to certain offences such as rape and bigamy is strained. As a result, despite D acting through an innocent agent (ie acting as a principal), the courts are more likely to characterise D's conduct as procuring (ie acting as an accomplice).

B) Factual: Factual problems separating principal offenders and accomplices can emerge in cases where D's role in the principal offence is unclear. For example, it might be common ground that both D1 and D2 were present at the time V was attacked and killed, but it may be disputed whether both attacked V, or whether only one of the parties attacked V, and disputed between them as to which. Where this is the case, there are two possible outcomes.

First, if it can be proved that D *either* killed V as a principal offender *or* was an accomplice to the killing of V by another because D must have, at least, assisted or encouraged the offence, then D may be convicted of the principal offence without the prosecution having to prove which role she played. *Giannetto* provides a useful illustration.

 Giannetto [1997] 1 Cr App R 1

D threatened to kill his wife (V) and hired another party (Y) to kill her. V was killed, but it could not be proved who killed her. D was charged with murder on the basis that he *either* killed V himself as a principal *or* she was killed by someone on his behalf (ie he was an accomplice).

- Crown Court: guilty of murder.
- Court of Appeal: conviction upheld on appeal. D may be liable in these circumstances even where the jury are not unanimous on what role he played, as long as they were sure that he was either a principal or an accessory.

Despite uncertainty as to D's role, because conviction as principal or accessory leads to the same result in the shape of liability for the principal offence, it has been held that this rule does not breach D's right to a fair trial under Article 6 ECHR.[31] This is often referred to as the 'forensic advantage of complicity', and provides a crucial route to liability in a number of cases.[32] For example, in the context of gang violence and other group offences it may be impossible to prove which member committed the actus reus of the principal offence, namely which member struck the fatal blow, but it is clear that each member was sufficiently involved.[33] It is also useful for domestic situations involving mistreatment of children: a parent's duty to prevent harm to their child may be enough to implicate them as an accomplice to abuse carried out by the other parent, avoiding the need to identify which parent is the principal offender.[34]

The second possibility of factual confusion arises where evidence places D at the scene of the crime, but it *cannot* be proven that D either committed the offence as a principal

---

[31] *Mercer* [2001] All ER 187.
[32] Law Commission, *Participating in Crime* (No 305, 2007) paras 2.5–2.6 and 3.3–3.4.
[33] *Bristow* [2013] EWCA Crim 1540: D convicted of manslaughter where there was uncertainty which of the group (jointly committing burglary) killed V in their escape. Commentary by Ormerod [2014] Crim LR 457.
[34] Glazebrook, 'Insufficient Child Protection' [2003] Crim LR 541.

or acted as an accessory. In other words, although D may have committed the principal offence, or may have acted as an accomplice, she may also be an innocent party; the evidence is inconclusive. In such a case, D must be acquitted. Where this is the case for both/all parties involved, even though we know one of them must have committed the offence, both/all must be acquitted: simply, guilt cannot be proved *beyond reasonable doubt*.[35]

12.3 Complicity by aiding, abetting, counselling, or procuring

Where D aids, abets, counsels, or procures P to commit a principal offence, and P does so, D is labelled and punished *as if* she committed the principal offence herself. As we have said, D's liability goes beyond inchoate liability (discussed in **Chapter 11**) because the principal offence has been committed. Equally, D does not commit the principal offence as a principal offender because P's choice to commit the offence breaks the chain of causation between D's acts and that offence. D is an accomplice, a secondary party.

Although the precise elements for liability (as an accomplice) remain uncertain within the common law, **Tables 12.1a, 12.1b,** and **12.1c** provide an overview of the likely requirements.

Table 12.1a Complicity by aiding, abetting, counselling, or procuring

	Actus reus	Mens rea
Conduct element	Any acts or omissions causing the result	Voluntary
Circumstance element	Aiding, abetting, or counselling: D's conduct is capable of assisting or encouraging P to commit the principal offence	Knowledge
	Or	
	Procuring: D's conduct is capable of causing P's principal offence	Knowledge
Result element	Aiding, abetting, or counselling: D's conduct assists or encourages P to commit the principal offence	Intention
	Or	
	Procuring: D's conduct causes P's principal offence	None

---

[35] *Abbott* [1955] 2 QB 497; *Banfield* [2013] EWCA Crim 1394; Williams, 'Which of You Did It?' (1989) 52 MLR 179.

Table 12.1b Ulterior mens rea element for complicity

	D's ulterior mens rea as to P's principal offence
Conduct element	D must intend that P will complete the conduct element of the principal offence
Circumstance element	D must intend or know the circumstance element of P's principal offence
Result element	D must intend or know that P will cause the results (if any) required by the principal offence, unless the principal offence is one of constructive liability
P's mens rea	D must intend that P will act with the mens rea required by the principal offence

Table 12.1c P's principal offence

P's principal offence	P's principal offence must be completed in the absence of a supervening event

Unlike the general inchoate offences, as P's offence is completed, we do not analyse D's actus reus and mens rea in the abstract. Rather, cases begin by identifying the crime that P has committed, and then discuss D's actus reus and mens rea *in relation to* that principal offence.

12.3.1 Actus reus of aiding, abetting, counselling, or procuring

As illustrated in **Tables 12.1a, 12.1b,** and **12.1c**, D's actus reus requires us to distinguish between aiding, abetting, or counselling on the one hand, and procuring on the other. It should be reiterated that D's conduct only needs to satisfy one of these terms to complete the actus reus.[36]

In *AG's Reference (No 1 of 1975)*,[37] Lord Widgery CJ stated that the terms 'aid', 'abet', 'counsel', and 'procure' should be given their 'ordinary meaning'. However, this is somewhat misleading, particularly in the context of counselling which should not be interpreted in line with common parlance,[38] and abetting and procuring which are not terms in common use. Rather, we need to identify legal definitions.

---

[36] *Ferguson v Weaving* [1951] KB 814.
[37] [1975] 2 All ER 684, 686.
[38] We are not talking about D providing P with emotional support or therapy.

12.3.1.1 Aiding, abetting, or counselling

Aiding, abetting, and counselling have been interpreted in modern times[39] to mean no more than assisting or encouraging. This will include, for example, D providing P with tools, with information, acting as a lookout, positively emboldening P, threatening P to commit the principal offence, and so on.

A) **Aiding**: 'Aiding' should be read as 'assisting'. D may assist at the time P commits the principal offence (eg acting as a lookout, driving the getaway car, etc), or in advance of the offence (eg providing tools, weapons, etc).[40] D may satisfy this requirement even where the assistance is unwanted by P, or even unknown to P as where D, without P's knowledge, restrains a policeman who would have intervened to stop P's offence.[41]

B) **Abetting**: 'Abetting' should be read as 'encouraging'. As we saw in the context of inchoate liability,[42] D can encourage positively by emboldening or instigating; or negatively by threatening.

An important line of case law has developed in relation to encouraging by 'mere presence' at the scene of P's offence. This is not the same as omissions liability (discussed later) because D must have *actively* gone to the scene, simply finding yourself unwittingly at the scene of a crime is not sufficient.[43] Even accepting this qualification that D must have been active in her presence, however, it may still be doubted whether the effect of mere presence should be recognised as capable of encouraging. Nevertheless, it has been consistently held that mere presence is *capable* of constituting an act of encouragement. This is illustrated in *Clarkson*.[44]

> *Clarkson* [1971] 3 All ER 344
>
> D1 and D2 entered a room in their barracks in which a woman was being raped by other soldiers. There was no evidence that they provided any assistance or encouragement beyond their choice to enter and remain present. They were charged with rape as accomplices.
>
> • Court-Martial: guilty of rape.
> • Court-Martial Appeal Court: appeal allowed. Voluntary presence is *capable* of satisfying the actus reus of complicity. However, there was insufficient proof as to mens rea: the prosecution did not prove that D1 and D2 intended to assist or encourage rape by their presence.

Clarkson provides useful clarification on the actus reus of complicity, as well as a reminder to be mindful of mens rea requirements (discussed later). Although voluntary presence is capable of constituting an act of encouragement, such encouragement should not be assumed, and must still be demonstrated on the particular facts. For example, in

---

[39] Historically, these terms have been interpreted in different ways.

[40] *Nedrick-Smith* [2006] EWHC 3015 (Admin): D was an accessory when driving P to the scene of the crime.

[41] Discussed in *Fury* [2006] EWCA Crim 1258.

[42] See **11.4.1**.

[43] eg *Kousar* [2009] EWCA Crim 139: D was not liable for possession of counterfeit goods simply because her husband was found storing them in the loft of their matrimonial home.

[44] Confirmed in *Jogee* [2016] UKSC 8, [11].

Coney,[45] D's presence at an illegal prize-fight was clearly capable of encouraging those taking part because such fights would not happen without an audience, but his conviction was quashed because the jury were incorrectly directed that such presence was *conclusive* of encouragement.[46] In fact, where encouragement is found, D has often done more than being *merely* present. For example, in *Wilcox v Jeffery*,[47] where D was complicit in P's offence of playing an illegal jazz concert,[48] D was present at the concert, but had also arranged the concert and transported P from the airport.

> **Point to remember . . .**
> Issues relating to mere presence are only necessary where there is no evidence of D's conduct at the scene, or there is evidence of inactivity. Where there is evidence of D encouraging P at the scene (eg clapping at the concert in *Wilcox*), then it will be much easier to find liability.

C) **Counselling:** 'Counselling' should also be read as 'encouraging'. At one time counselling and abetting were distinguished on the timing of D's encouragement with abetting occurring at the time of the offence and counselling in advance, but this distinction no longer operates.[49]

Can D assist or encourage by omission?

As with inchoate assisting and encouraging, D may also become complicit in P's offence by omission. This arises in two circumstances, both of which are usually analysed as providing P with tacit encouragement.

The first, and most straightforward, case applies where P's omission arises as a breach of a recognised duty to act. We highlighted such duties in our general discussion of omissions liability (ie familial duties; contractual duties; assumed duties; duties arising from the creation of a dangerous situation; and so on).[50] This will include, for example, D who does nothing whilst his wife drowns their child,[51] or a disgruntled security guard who omits to turn on an alarm system.

Controversially, complicity also recognises a second category of omission-based encouragement.[52] It applies where D has a *power or right to control* the actions of P, but deliberately refrains from doing so. The rule is illustrated in *Du Cros v Lambourne*.

 Du Cros v Lambourne [1907] 1 KB 40

D was charged with driving a motor vehicle at a dangerous speed. However, it could not be proved whether he was driving or was a passenger.

- Petty Sessions: guilty of driving at a dangerous speed. Conviction in the alternative that he was either driving, or was (as owner of the car) assenting to P's speeding by failing to intervene.

---

[45]   (1882) 8 QBD 534.
[46]   *Allen* [1965] 1 QB 130: D's presence at an affray did not constitute encouragement, even though he held a secret intention to help P if needed.
[47]   [1951] 1 All ER 464.
[48]   Paid employment was not allowed on the terms of P's permission to visit the UK.
[49]   Discussed in *NCB v Gamble* [1959] 1 QB 11.
[50]   See **2.6.2**.
[51]   *Russell* [1933] VLR 59.
[52]   This second category does *not* apply to inchoate assisting or encouraging offences.

- Quarter Sessions: conviction upheld on appeal.
- King's Bench: appeal dismissed.

More recent cases, confirming the rule, include *Tuck v Robson*, where D (a pub licensee) allowed customers to drink after hours;[53] *Webster*, where D allowed an intoxicated P to drive his car;[54] *Gaunt*, where D (a manager) failed to prevent P (his employee) racially harassing another employee;[55] and *Martin*, where D (supervising a learner driver) allowed P to drive dangerously, resulting in the deaths of P and a passenger.[56] It should be remembered that liability under this rule, although potentially extensive, is restrained by the requirements of mens rea (discussed later), particularly post-*Jogee*.

Extra detail . . .
The Law Commission recommended abolishing omissions liability where D is not in breach of a duty to act, contending that the current law demands too much of D to act as a 'good Samaritan'. The Commission used the example of D who fails to prevent an assault happening on his front lawn when woken by it in the middle of the night.[57]

Must D cause P's offence?

Having established that D's conduct is *capable* of assisting or encouraging P's principal offence, the next question is whether it must do so in fact. We have already highlighted that a strict causation between D's conduct and P's offence could never be required: where P acts voluntarily she breaks the chain of causation, and therefore there is no causal link from D's conduct; where P does not act voluntarily (ie she is an innocent agent), then D is a principal rather than an accomplice.[58] It will also be remembered that no causal link is necessary for inchoate assisting or encouraging.[59] However, as D's liability in complicity derives from P's completion of a crime, it might be thought that some causal role is essential to justify that derivation.[60] As stated in *Stringer*:[61]

It is well established that D's conduct need not cause P to commit the offence in the sense that 'but for' D's conduct P would not have committed the offence. . . . But it is also established by the [common law] that D's conduct must have some relevance to the commission of the principal offence; there must, as it has been said, be some connecting link. The moral justification for holding D responsible for the crime is that he has involved himself in the commission of the crime by assistance or encouragement, and that presupposes some form of connection between his conduct and the crime.

---

[53] [1970] 1 WLR 741.
[54] [2006] EWCA Crim 415: P crashed the car causing death. D was liable as an accomplice for causing death by dangerous driving.
[55] [2003] EWCA Crim 3925.
[56] [2010] EWCA Crim 1450.
[57] Law Commission, *Participating in Crime* (No 305, 2007) paras 3.39–3.41.
[58] See **12.2**.
[59] See **11.4.1**.
[60] Some have argued that this causal connection is/should be the basis for complicity liability. See **12.6**.
[61] [2011] EWCA Crim 1396, per Toulson LJ at [48].

It is on this rather vague basis that the current law of complicity requires *some* causal effect from D's conduct, but does not require full causation of the kind discussed in **Chapter 2**. So what does this mean in practice? To answer this question, it is useful to distinguish assistance from encouragement.

A) **D assists P (eg provides tools, acts as a lookout, etc):** It must be demonstrated that D's assistance contributed to P's offence in some way. For example, where D provides P with a gun to kill V, but P ignores the gun and kills V with a knife, there is no assistance: D's acts were capable of assisting P, but provided no assistance in fact. Thus, although D satisfies the actus reus for inchoate liability by her acts capable of assisting or encouraging,[62] D does not assist P for the purposes of complicity.

> *Assessment matters . . .*
> Where P rejects D's assistance (as in our example), the offer of help may nevertheless encourage P to commit the principal offence. With this in mind, even where D's acts look like potential assistance, remember to consider whether they also (or alternatively) encourage P (ie abet or counsel). In the absence of actual assistance or encouragement, you should remember that D may still be liable under the SCA 2007 if her acts were 'capable' of assisting or encouraging.

Once it is established that D has provided some assistance, the actus reus of complicity will be satisfied. There is no need to show that D's assistance was substantial. For example, D acts as a lookout but no one appears to disturb the crime being committed by P; D supplies weapons that P could have acquired elsewhere; D drives P to the scene but gets lost and is late: in each case D's assistance is minimal, but will still satisfy the actus reus for complicity in P's offence. This element is usefully discussed in *Bryce*.

> *Bryce* [2004] EWCA Crim 1231
>
> D drove P to a place to enable P to kill V. D foresaw that P would kill V. P did kill V, but a full 12 hours after D's involvement, and only following discussion with another party. D was charged with murder as P's accomplice.
> - Crown Court: guilty of murder.
> - Court of Appeal: conviction upheld on appeal. Despite the time delay between D's acts and the killing, and despite other contributory facts, D's acts continued to provide some assistance to the murder.

B) **D encourages P (eg emboldens, threatens, etc):** To establish a connection between D's encouragement and P's offence, it must be proved that D's encouragement was communicated to P.[63] In other words, P must know that D is encouraging her. For example, if D, present as a spectator in a football stadium, shouts for one player (P) to punch another player (V), and P does so, D will only be complicit in P's offence if P hears the shout. If P does not hear, D remains liable for inchoate

---

[62] See **11.4.1**.
[63] *Calhaem* [1985] 1 QB 808.

encouragement (ie her act is *capable* of encouraging P), but will not satisfy the actus reus of complicity.[64]

However, once it is demonstrated that P was aware of D's encouragement, even where that encouragement had little effect on P, D will satisfy the actus reus of complicity. The trial judge in *Giannetto*, discussed earlier,[65] provided a useful and often repeated example.

> If . . . [D] knew that somebody else intended to kill his wife and he just did nothing at all, then he is not guilty because he has not participated . . . Supposing somebody came up to [D] and said, 'I am going to kill your wife', if he played any part, either in encouragement, as little as patting him on the back, nodding, saying, 'Oh goody', that would be sufficient to involve him in the murder, to make him guilty, because he is encouraging the murder.

As this example illustrates, D's encouragement will be sufficient even where P has already decided to commit the principal offence. It is assumed that D's encouragement, although not changing D's settled plan, still emboldens or fortifies her intention. This assumption is only rebutted if there is evidence that P gained no encouragement from D. For example, where D encourages P to punch V, but before doing so P tells D to 'mind your own business'.[66]

12.3.1.2 Procuring

In the alternative to aiding, abetting, or counselling, the actus reus of complicity can be satisfied where D 'procures' P's offence. To procure is to 'produce by endeavour'. Procuring will apply even where D has not assisted or encouraged P, as long as D has played a causal role in the principal offence coming about. The leading case is *AG's Reference (No 1 of 1975)*.

> **AG's Reference (No 1 of 1975)** [1975] 2 All ER 684
>
> D surreptitiously laced P's drink with alcohol knowing that P would be driving home. P was unaware of this. P later committed an offence of driving with excess alcohol[67] as the principal offender and D was charged as an accomplice.
>
> - Crown Court: not guilty of driving offence, because P was unaware of D's role.
> - Court of Appeal: on a reference from the AG, D should have been liable. D procured P's offence.

In line with this case, it is clear that D can procure an offence where P is unaware of D's actions, and even though D is not encouraging or assisting P's acts (ie in this case, P's driving). It is enough that D caused the necessary circumstances of the offence to be present (ie in this case, for P to be over the proscribed alcohol limit), and thus caused P to commit the offence.

---

[64] Example taken from the Law Commission, and discussed in *Stringer* [2011] EWCA Crim 1396, [49].
[65] See **12.2.4**.
[66] Law Commission, *Participating in Crime* (No 305, 2007) para B.62.
[67] Contrary to the Road Traffic Act 1972, s6(1), now replaced by the Road Traffic Act 1988, s5.

Subject to the problem cases discussed in the following section, procuring requires D to have caused P's offence. Thus, liability for procuring will be undermined by any break in the causal chain. In *AG's Reference (No 1 of 1975)*, P chose only to drink soft drinks and then to drive. Those acts do not break the chain of causation between D's acts and the offence because they are not informed acts (ie P is unaware of the alcohol lacing his drink). If P was aware of the alcohol and chose to continue, his acts would break the chain, and D would only be liable as an accomplice if it could be shown that his acts also assisted or encouraged P. In *Beatty v Gillbanks*,[68] for example, the Salvation Army knew that a proposed meeting would provoke a violent reaction from a hostile organisation known as the 'Skeleton Army'. Although this proved to be correct, the Salvation Army could not be said to have procured the violence. This is because the free, voluntary, and informed choice of Skeleton Army members broke any potential causal chain. Provocation is not causation.

> **Extra detail . . .**
> Although D may assist or encourage by omission, it is very unlikely that D could procure an offence (produce by endeavour) without positive movement.

Problem cases and procuring

Difficulties can arise in certain cases involving procuring. Ideally, procuring cases can be logically distinguished from other cases in the following way.

- D assists or encourages P who knowingly commits a principal offence: This is *not* a procuring case because D has not caused P to commit the principal offence. This is a standard case of complicity by D assisting or encouraging P.

- D causes the unknowing P to complete the actus reus of an offence that also requires mens rea: This is not a procuring case because P commits no crime. D will be liable as the principal offender via the doctrine of innocent agency.

- D causes the unknowing P to commit a strict liability offence: This *is* a procuring case. P does commit the principal offence, and D has caused her to do so.

Unfortunately, within the innocent agency category in the second bullet point, certain cases have been decided under the heading of procuring. Thus, as well as standard cases of procuring in the last bullet point, a further category must be added.

- D causes the unknowing P to complete the actus reus of an offence that also requires mens rea, but the offence cannot be committed by an innocent agent: As highlighted earlier,[69] there are a number of offences that cannot be committed via an innocent agent (eg rape and bigamy). Therefore, for these cases, even though innocent agency might appear the correct approach (D causes P's actus reus but P does not commit an offence because she lacks mens rea), the courts are more likely to describe D's liability as complicity by procuring. This is an unfortunate description. P has not committed an offence and so it cannot be said that D's liability derives from another's crime. This is not to say that D should be acquitted—D has caused P to commit the actus reus of

---

[68] (1882) 9 QBD 308.
[69] See **12.2.3–12.2.4**.

that crime, and D has mens rea—it is simply that the approach used to find liability (ie procuring) seems inappropriate.

The case of *Cogan and Leak* provides a useful illustration.

 Cogan and Leak [1976] QB 217

D told his wife (V) to have sexual intercourse with his friend (P). V was scared of D and so, although she did not consent, she did not resist P. P was unaware that V was not consenting. P was charged with rape, with D as his accomplice.

- Crown Court: guilty of rape (both D and P).
- Court of Appeal: P's appeal allowed—there was a misdirection relating to the mens rea required of P for rape.[70] D's conviction upheld—although P was innocent, D nevertheless procured the offence of rape.

Cogan and Leak is a useful case because the Court of Appeal discusses the possibility of finding liability on the basis of innocent agency, but eventually prefers the procuring approach. Similar reasoning was adopted in *Millward*.[71] In this case D instructed an employee (P) to drive a tractor and trailer knowing that the hitch mechanism connecting them was defective. The hitch broke in transit and the detached trailer killed the driver of an oncoming car (V). P did *not* commit an offence of causing death by reckless driving[72] because he lacked mens rea. However, D *was* convicted of procuring that offence.

Point to remember . . .
Although these cases allow for complicity by procuring even though P does not commit a principal offence, it is essential that P completes the actus reus of the offence and that D has caused P to do so. We see this in *Cogan and Leak*, and in *Millward*, where D instructs or permits conduct from P knowing (but not telling P) that such conduct satisfied the actus reus of an offence. Where the actus reus of the offence is not completed by P, whatever D's role, there can be no complicity.[73]

12.3.2 Mens rea of aiding, abetting, counselling, or procuring

The mens rea for complicity has not been consistently identified or applied by the courts for many year. Indeed, the Law Commission's 2007 report highlighted four different (and inconsistent) approaches active at that time.[74] The current law is governed by the recent case of *Jogee*, in which the Supreme Court has fundamentally changed the previous law, and (to some extent) clarified the current law moving forward.

---

[70] See **8.2**.
[71] [1994] Crim LR 527.
[72] Since replaced by the offence of causing death by dangerous driving, discussed at **6.4.2.1**.
[73] *Loukes* [1996] 1 Cr App R 444: D was not an accomplice to causing death by careless driving because P (the driver) was not careless and therefore did not satisfy the actus reus of the offence.
[74] Law Commission, *Participating in Crime* (No 305, 2007) para 1.16.

Jogee and Ruddock [2016] UKSC 8, [2016] UKPC 7

Combined cases on appeal. In *Jogee*, D and P went to V's house and began a violent confrontation. P took a knife from the kitchen and killed V. D intended P to confront V with violence, and foresaw the possibility of serious harm being caused, but did not intend serious harm to be caused. In *Ruddock*, D and P combined in the robbery of V's car. V was tied up, and P killed V. D foresaw that P might act with intention to cause serious harm, but did not intend him to. Jogee and Ruddock were both charged with murder, as accessories.

- Crown Court (and court of first instance in Jamaica): guilty of murder as accessories.
- Court of Appeal (and Court of Appeal of Jamaica): convictions upheld on appeal.
- Supreme Court (and Privy Council): unanimous in allowing the appeal, and ordering retrials of both defendants. Complicity liability requires D to intend to assist or encourage P to commit the principal offence with the required mens rea, foresight is no longer sufficient for liability; it is merely evidence of intent.

The full implications of *Jogee* have already attracted considerable academic attention,[75] and are likely to require further clarification in the courts. However, as we discuss below, despite areas of continued uncertainty, the judgment is generally to be welcomed. As a unanimous judgment it avoids the inconsistencies highlighted earlier in the context of *Gnango*, and in its substance it has made positive steps towards narrowing the law to a more acceptable target.

When discussing D's mens rea, and unpacking the judgment in *Jogee*, it is useful to separate: (a) D's mens rea as to her own conduct, illustrated previously in **Table 12.1a**; and (b) D's mens rea as to the future conduct and state of mind of P, illustrated previously in **Table 12.1b**. We discuss each in turn.

> *Point to remember . . .*
> Separating our discussion of D's mens rea in this way was also recommended in relation to inchoate assisting and encouraging.[76] However, the important difference here is that we assess D's mens rea with regard to a principal offence which has been committed by P. We do not ask generally whether D had mens rea as to P committing an offence but, rather, whether D had mens rea as to P committing the offence completed. As you will see later, this difference can be important where P's offence varies from D's expectation.

12.3.2.1 D's mens rea as to her own conduct

This part of D's mens rea contains two requirements. First, as with all criminal liability, D's conduct (ie D's assisting, encouraging, or procuring) must be performed voluntarily. For example, there will be no liability where D inadvertently drops a tool which P

---

[75] Ormerod and Laird, '*Jogee*—Not the End of a Legal Saga but the Start of a New One?' [2016] Crim LR 543; Buxton, '*Jogee*: Upheaval in Secondary Liability for Murder' [2016] Crim LR 324; Dyson, 'Shorn-Off Complicity' (2016) 75 CLJ 196 (comment); Stark, 'The Demise of "Parasitic Accessorial Liability": Substantive Judicial Law Reform, not Common Law Housekeeping' (2016) 75 CLJ 550; Simester, 'Accessory Liability and Common Unlawful Purposes' (2017) 133 LQR 73.

[76] See **11.4.2–11.4.4**.

then uses to commit a crime, and/or where D omits because she is tied up and unable to move.[77]

Secondly, D must intend that her conduct will assist or encourage P to commit the principal offence, or in the context of procuring, that her conduct will cause the principal offence.[78] Importantly, this is not to say that D must intend that P will commit the principal offence (we discuss D's mens rea as to P's offence later). Of course, where D intends to assist, encourage, or cause an offence she will usually also intend that that offence should be committed, but this is not necessarily the case. For example, if D sells P a gun knowing that P could use it to kill V, D may be motivated purely by payment for the gun and may hope that P does not commit the offence, but she is still 'intentionally assisting' P to commit murder. This was discussed in *National Coal Board v Gamble*, and explicitly endorsed throughout *Jogee*.

 National Coal Board v Gamble [1959] 1 QB 11

D supplied coal to P. At the weigh-station, before P was able to leave with the coal, P's lorry was overladen to the extent that taking the lorry on the road became an offence.[79] Nevertheless D allowed P to leave with the overladen lorry. D was charged as an accomplice to P's offence.

• Court: guilty of overladen offence.

• Divisional Court: conviction upheld on appeal by case stated. Although D may have been indifferent as to P's offence, he must have obliquely intended to assist (knowing that his action, supplying the coal and allowing P to leave, was virtually certain to assist). Slade J dissented, stating that D should only be found to have intended to aid where this is his direct intention (ie oblique intent was insufficient).

Following *Gamble*, another useful example of obliquely intending to assist or encourage is supplied by *Gnango* where the gunfight between D and P resulted in V being shot.[80] In *Gnango* it was clearly not D's direct intention that P would shoot at him with the intention to kill, D would have actively not wanted this, but such encouragement was a foreseen virtual certainty from D's conduct (ie D obliquely intended it).[81] In summary, then, this element will be satisfied where D directly intends to assist, encourage, or procure P's offence because it is D's desire or purpose, *or* where it is D's oblique intention because although she may not desire it, D recognises that assistance or encouragement is the virtually certain consequence of her conduct.

Alongside useful clarification that an 'intention' to assist or encourage can be satisfied by both direct and oblique intention, it is interesting to note that the Supreme Court in *Jogee* also emphasise the potential role of conditional intention.[82] For example, for the court, D may conditionally intend to encourage P to commit murder where D intentionally encourages P to commit a bank robbery and to murder guards if necessary.

---

[77] *Bryce* [2004] EWCA Crim 1231, [41]–[42].

[78] Duff, 'Can I Help You? Accessorial Liability and the Intention to Assist' (1990) 10 LS 165.

[79] Motor Vehicles (Construction and Use) Regulations 1955, regs 68 and 104.

[80] See **12.1**.

[81] See also *Lynch v DPP for Northern Ireland* [1975] AC 653, 678: knowingly driving P to murder V is sufficient even where D would prefer the murder not to happen.

[82] At [92]–[95].

However, the court's approach here seems faulty. Conditional intention is a concept employed to understand intention as to *future* conduct; a decision to act in the future if certain conditions obtain (see **3.4.1.3**). Yet here, we are discussing intention to assist or encourage P through completed conduct. Thus, rather than describing D's intention as condition, which may lead to confusion, it is more accurate to describe D's intention as simply specific in its content: to encourage P to perform specified conduct in certain circumstances only.

The requirement that D must intend to assist, encourage, or procure P's offence is a settled element of D's liability, but problem cases have emerged. For example, it has been argued that where D supplies P with an article for use within a principal offence, D may be excused accessorial liability if the supply was required under civil law, for example where P demands the return of a gun which was lent to D.[83] However, although liability in these circumstances can appear harsh,[84] it is unlikely that such an exclusion exists.[85] As long as D intends directly or obliquely to assist, encourage, or procure P's crime, she will satisfy this element.

Don't be confused . . .

In most cases, D's intention to assist, encourage, or procure P's offence can be discussed and applied in general terms. However, this is not always required. The following represents the minimum mens rea to satisfy this element.

- Assisting or encouraging: following *Jogee*, it now seems apparent that D must intend to assist or encourage the whole principal offence (with the exception of constructive crimes, discussed later).[86] This contrasts with the law pre-*Jogee*, and that applicable to inchoate assisting or encouraging, where D need only intend to assist or encourage the conduct part of the principal offence.[87]

- Procuring: D must intend to cause the principal offence, but she need not intend to cause every element. For example, in *AG's Reference (No 1 of 1975)*,[88] where D laced P's drink with alcohol, it was enough that D intended to cause the circumstance element (alcohol level) to come about, there was no additional requirement to intend to cause D's conduct (driving).

12.3.2.2 D's mens rea as to P's principal offence

This element of D's mens rea is the most complex. Unlike inchoate assisting or encouraging where we assess D's mens rea as to a *potential* principal offence in the abstract, complicity requires us to examine D's mens rea in relation to a principal offence that has come about. Therefore, as well as exploring D's state of mind at the time of the assistance or encouragement, we must also assess whether that mens rea will be sufficient in cases in which P's actual offence is less serious than D anticipated; more serious; or simply

---

[83] Discussed in *National Coal Board v Gamble* [1959] 1 QB 11, 20.

[84] Williams, 'Obedience to Law as a Crime' (1990) 53 MLR 445.

[85] Not least because withholding property in these circumstances would not be a breach of civil law: *K v National Westminster Bank* [2006] EWCA Civ 1039. Discussed in *Bryce* [2004] EWCA Crim 1231, [63].

[86] At [88]–[99].

[87] For pre-*Jogee* complicity, see discussion in *Bryce* [2004] EWCA Crim 1231; for inchoate, see **11.4.2**.

[88] See **12.3.1.2**.

very different. We discuss each of these separately. However, we begin with the case in which P completes the principal offence in line with D's expectations.

A) P commits the principal offence as D expected: The general rule, taken from *Johnson v Youden*,[89] is that at the time of assisting, encouraging, or procuring D must 'know the essential matters' that constitute P's principal offence. This implies that D must have knowledge of what P will go on to do. However, despite consistent endorsement of the quotation from *Johnson*, it has been interpreted to mean something quite different. Rather than a requirement of knowledge, or even belief, courts began to interpret 'knowledge' in this context as being satisfied by mere 'foresight' of a risk (see **Table 12.2**).

Table 12.2 Foresight and complicity

Case reference	Case facts	Outcome
Chan Wing-Siu [1985] AC 168	D (and two others) went to V's house with knives to rob him. V was stabbed and killed, and his wife wounded. D foresaw, but did not intend, that one of his co-accused might act with intention to kill.	The Privy Council decided that in cases of this kind (described as Joint Criminal Ventures), D may be liable as an accomplice on the basis of foresight.
Powell and English [1999] AC 1	In *Powell*, D, X, and P went to the house of a drug dealer (V) to buy drugs. At the door, one of them shot V dead. In *English*, D and P attacked a police sergeant, V, with wooden posts. P produced a knife which D had not foreseen that P might carry and fatally stabbed V.	Following a line of authority from *Chan Wing-Siu*, including *Slack* [1989] QB 775, *Wakely* [1990] Crim LR 119, and *Hyde* [1991] 1 QB 134, the House of Lords endorsed the view that foresight sufficed for mens rea.
ABCD [2010] EWCA Crim 1622	C organised an attack on V in his home, carried out by A, B, and D. Unable to prove which of the defendants inflicted the fatal blows, they were each charged with murder as a principal or an accomplice.	Court of Appeal clarified that D must foresee every element of the principal offence, including the principal's required mens rea.

This line of authority has been explicitly overruled in *Jogee*, and is no longer good law.[90] Characterising *Chan Wing-Siu* as a 'wrong turn',[91] *Jogee* returns the law on this point to its position 30 years earlier, requiring D intentionally to assist, encourage, or procure, and to know that P will complete the elements of the principal offence.

Unfortunately, in contrast to the clarity of the Supreme Court's rejection of the previous case law, detail of the court's preferred construction is lacking. The court is clear that D must *intend* P to act with whatever mens rea is required for the principal offence,[92]

---

[89] [1950] 1 KB 544, 546.
[90] At [61]–[99].
[91] At [82].
[92] At [90].

but largely silent on D's required mens rea as to potential circumstance and/or result elements of P's offence. The court restates *Johnson* that D must have 'knowledge' as to the essential elements of P's offence,[93] but it is not clear what is meant by knowledge in this context. And within this vacuum, three competing theories have emerged. We prefer the first alternative, which is reflected in **Tables 12.1a, 12.1b**, and **12.1c**.

(1) D must intend or know the essential elements of P's offence: This approach would require D intentionally to assist, encourage, or procure P's offence, *and* intend that that offence should come about. This interpretation is most in line with the aims of *Jogee* to depart from the previous foresight-based approach, in line with the approach to P's mens rea, accords best with reference to a knowledge requirement,[94] and is supported by several commentators.[95] However, this approach does not sit well with all of the examples given in the case. For example, the court state (at [90]) that D who supplies weapons to P with 'no further interest' in their use may still be liable as an accomplice where the weapons are used to commit an offence. D in this example does not intend any element of the future offence and so either this approach is wrong, the example is wrong, or (more drastically) the court are implying a new definition of intention.[96]

(2) D must believe the essential elements of P's offence: This is something of a compromise approach, requiring D to foresee the elements of P's future offence as more likely than not (narrowing from mere foresight), but falling short of requiring intention. This approach was previously supported by the Law Commission and other commentators,[97] and still retains support.[98] However, the belief standard does not conform to the text in *Jogee*, and remains an unlikely possibility.

(3) D requires no mens rea as to P's offence, beyond intention as to mens rea: A literal reading of *Jogee* would suggest that D does not require any specific mens rea beyond a requirement (discussed previously) to intend to assist or encourage the principal offence, and an intention that P should act with the required mens rea. This approach relies on courts focusing on the requirement of intention to assist or encourage the *whole* of P's offence, and potentially supporting this with a new authorisation requirement, such that D must also endorse P's principal offence in some way. Indeed, if this approach were preferred, the authorisation requirement would be essential to narrow liability from the pre-*Jogee* position (as the Supreme Court clearly intended). However, this approach would be very novel, and vague, and so it would require considerable judicial clarification moving forward if it is to be preferred.

---

[93] At [9] and [16].

[94] It is logically impossible to 'know' the future, and so knowledge as to future events is often best translated into an intention.

[95] Ormerod and Laird, '*Jogee*—Not the End of a Legal Saga but the Start of a New One?' [2016] Crim LR 543; Buxton, '*Jogee*: Upheaval in Secondary Liability for Murder' [2016] Crim LR 324; Horder, *Ashworth's Principles of Criminal Law* (2016) 446–453.

[96] Discussed in Ormerod and Laird, '*Jogee*—Not the End of a Legal Saga but the Start of a New One?' [2016] Crim LR 543.

[97] Law Commission, *Participating in Crime* (No 305, 2007) para 3.122; Ormerod and Wilson, 'Simply Harsh to Fairly Simple: Joint Enterprise Reform' [2015] Crim LR 3.

[98] Dyson, 'Shorn-Off Complicity' (2016) 75 CLJ 196 (comment).

Subject to the preceding discussion, it is therefore contended that *Jogee* has narrowed D's mens rea as to P's principal offence, requiring D to intend to assist or encourage the principal offence and to intend that P will complete the offence in fact. However, before we move on, two further points require brief clarification.

First, what if D intends to assist or encourage P to commit an offence, intends an offence to come about, but is unsure which of a number of offences P will commit, or is unsure of the details of the offence? The answer, confirmed in *Jogee*,[99] is that D may be complicit if P commits an offence among those D intends. In *Bainbridge*,[100] for example, D was liable as an accessory to bank robbery even though, when supplying cutting equipment to P, he was unaware which premises would be targeted and when. The Court of Criminal Appeal clarified that although D did not know the details of the specific offence committed by P, his conviction remained safe because he knew when supplying the equipment that P might use the equipment for breaking and entering. Similar reasoning is also evident in *DPP for NI v Maxwell*.

 DPP for NI v Maxwell [1978] 1 WLR 1350

D was a member of the proscribed organisation UVF in Northern Ireland and he assisted P by driving him to a pub. D knew that P intended to attack the pub, but was unsure whether this would involve planting explosives, murder, or robbery. In the event, P damaged the pub using pipe bombs. D was charged as an accessory to the explosives offence.[101]

- NI Crown Court: guilty of explosives offence.
- NI Court of Appeal: conviction upheld on appeal.
- House of Lords: appeal dismissed. D does not need to know the details of P's offence, as long as he knows the essential matters.

Maxwell is a particularly useful case. It provides House of Lords endorsement for the principle in *Bainbridge* that D need not know the details of P's offence. Additionally, although narrowed by *Jogee* to require intention, it confirms that D may be liable even where she is unsure which of a number of offences P will commit. Of course, where P commits an offence that was not intended, for example in this scenario rape, then D would not be an accomplice to that offence.

Secondly, what if D intends P to commit a strict liability offence, must D still intend every element of that offence? This question did not arise in *Jogee*, but is likely to follow the previous case law. Although P in this case requires no mens rea, complicity liability nevertheless requires D to intend each element of the principal offence.[102] In *Callow v Tillstone*,[103] a butcher (P) committed a strict liability offence by selling tainted meat. P was liable despite genuinely believing that the meat was fit for sale, a belief based on D's negligent veterinary examination. D was not liable as an accomplice because he was not reckless as to the tainted status of the meat (the law would

---

[99] At [14]–[16].
[100] [1960] 1 QB 129.
[101] Explosive Substances Act 1883, s3(1)(a).
[102] The only exception relates to constructive offences, discussed later.
[103] (1900) 83 LT 411.

now require intention). The important point here is that although not every element of P's offence requires P to have mens rea, D must intend all the essential elements for complicity liability.

B) P commits a less serious principal offence than D intended: This situation arises where D assists, encourages, or procures P to commit an offence such as intentional GBH, but P commits a less serious offence such as battery. Regardless of P's conduct, D is likely to be liable for the inchoate offence of assisting or encouraging the more serious offence.[104] D is also likely to be complicit in the offence committed by P. For the latter, it would have to be shown that D either intended P to commit the less serious offence or, as with our example, that the less serious offence is a lesser included offence within the one intended.[105] However, there are certain cases in which D may be liable as an accomplice to the more serious offence intended, even though this offence is not completed by P. It is useful to separate our analysis into the three reasons why P may not have committed the more serious offence D intended.

P lacks actus reus: This was the case in our example, where P commits battery rather than GBH. Here, D's liability is limited by P's actus reus and will not go beyond it. D may therefore be an accessory to battery, but not to intentional GBH. This is a logical outcome, and one that remains faithful to the idea of complicity as derivative from P's offence. However, it can appear rather generous to D, particularly where P causes harm as a result of D's assistance or encouragement, but does not complete the actus reus of an offence. This was the issue in *Thornton v Mitchell*.[106]

Thornton v Mitchell [1940] 1 All ER 339

A bus conductor (D) negligently signalled for a bus driver (P) to reverse. Two pedestrians were knocked down by the bus, one of whom (V) was killed. P was charged with careless driving, D as an accomplice.[107]

- Court: P not guilty, as his driving was not careless. D was found guilty, and appealed.
- High Court: appeal by case stated allowed. Where P does not commit the actus reus of an offence, there can be no accomplice liability.

P's commission of the actus reus may therefore limit D's accomplice liability, and where no actus reus is performed by P, it may undermine it altogether. In such cases, however, remember that inchoate liability may still be available.

P lacks mens rea: Mirroring cases of incomplete actus reus, a lack of mens rea from P is also likely to minimise or even extinguish her liability; with D's derivative liability following suit. However, there is an important exception. This applies where, although P

---

[104] See **11.4**.

[105] A 'lesser included' offence is one where all of its elements are included within the more serious offence; with the more serious offence also requiring further elements. Thus, eg, where D intends P to commit intentional GBH by hitting V with a bat, then D must have also intended P to make unlawful physical contact with V (ie battery) as part of that greater offence.

[106] See also *Loukes* [1996] Crim LR 341: lack of actus reus element undermining D's accomplice liability for dangerous driving.

[107] The relevant offence under the current law is causing death by careless driving (see **6.4.2.2**).

lacks mens rea for the principal offence and although D may know that P will lack mens rea, D will nevertheless be guilty as an accomplice to that offence if she herself acted with the mens rea required for it. Lord Mackay approved the following example in the House of Lords:[108]

> [D] hands a gun to [P] informing him that it is loaded with blank ammunition only and telling him to go and scare [V] by discharging it. The ammunition is in fact live, as [D] knows, and [V] is killed. [P] is convicted only of manslaughter, as he might be on those facts. It would seem absurd that [D] should thereby escape conviction for murder.

In this example, P has not committed murder, and D did not intend that P would do so because D knew that P lacked mens rea. However, although P's lack of mens rea negates his murder liability, it would seem unfair if it also undermined D's liability for murder as an accomplice: P did not intend to kill or cause GBH (the mens rea of murder), but D certainly did. This is the crux of the exception.[109] Indeed, it is an exception that is closely mirrored in the context of inchoate assisting and encouraging as well.[110]

Where P lacks mens rea for any crime, it is possible for D to be liable as an accomplice even though P has not committed an offence. Such cases will usually more appropriately be treated within innocent agency: where P lacks any mens rea, she becomes a tool of D's offence, and her conduct does not break the causal chain.[111] However, as we have discussed, there are linguistic problems with innocent agency in the context of offences such as rape and bigamy, and so the doctrine of complicity has been preferred. *Cogan and Leak*, discussed earlier,[112] provides a useful example: D made his wife V submit to sex with P, where P was unaware that V was not consenting. In this case, P was not liable for rape or any other offence because he lacked mens rea. However, D qualifies within the exception and was liable as an accomplice to rape[113] because D acted with the mens rea for rape: D knew that V was not consenting.[114]

Alternatively, as in Lord Mackay's example, P may have mens rea for a lesser offence, with D complicit in a more serious one. These examples are more troublesome than those in which P has *no* mens rea, because P's knowledge of the lesser crime is enough to undermine her potential status as an innocent agent. Commentators have characterised P's conduct as a form of semi-innocent agency,[115] but this terminology raises more questions than it answers. Rather, as we did previously, the better approach is to apply the exception, and to ask if D had mens rea for the more serious principal offence.

---

[108] *Burke* [1987] AC 417, 457.
[109] Taylor, 'Complicity, Legal Scholarship and the Law of Unintended Consequences' (2009) 29 LS 1. See critique of the exception in Kadish, 'Complicity, Cause and Blame' in *Essays in Criminal Law* (1987) 180.
[110] See **11.4.2.2**.
[111] See **12.2.3**.
[112] See **12.3.1.2**.
[113] See also *Millward* [1994] Crim LR 527: D instructed P to drive a vehicle he knew was unfit for the road. P did so, and an accident led to the death of V. D was complicit in causing death by reckless driving, but P committed no offence.
[114] The minimum mens rea for rape at this time was recklessness as to non-consent. The current law has a minimum of a lack of reasonable belief in consent. See **8.2**.
[115] Williams, *Textbook of Criminal Law* (1978) 373.

Where she does, as with the murder in Lord Mackay's example, she should be liable as an accomplice to that more serious offence, even though P is only guilty of the minor one. This approach was rejected in *Richards*[116] but, following judicial criticism of that case in *Burke*,[117] it is contended that the exception should (and would) be applied in these circumstances today.

> **Don't be confused . . .**
> Standard cases involve an assessment of D's intention as to P's mens rea. Only when this breaks down, because P lacks mens rea, do we go on to explore the possible exception. The exception finds complicity liability where D has the mens rea required for the principal offence (ie the mens rea P lacks).

P has a defence: The last possibility, where D is complicit to a more serious offence than P has committed, arises where P has a defence. In this case, as P has committed the intended principal offence assisted, encouraged, or procured by D, our starting point is that they are both liable for that offence. If P has a successful defence, P's liability will be reduced or removed. If D does not satisfy the defence, she will remain complicit in the principal offence, even if P has been acquitted.

This rule applies both to partial and complete defences. For the partial defences to murder, the potential for D to be liable for murder despite P's satisfaction of a partial defence has been codified.[118] For the other defences, the rule exists at common law. *Bourne* provides an example in the context of duress.[119]

 Bourne (1952) 36 Cr App R 125

D compelled his wife (P) to have sex with a dog. D was charged as an accomplice to P's offence of buggery. P was not charged because she would have had a defence of duress.

- Court of Assizes: guilty of buggery.
- Court of Criminal Appeal: conviction upheld on appeal. The fact that P had a defence, and so was not liable for the principal offence, does not undermine D's liability as an accomplice.

This rule has the same effect as the last one discussed (where P lacks mens rea) but it applies very differently. In the present case, the standard complicity rules are applied, with the only difference being that P's liability (but not D's) is reduced by a defence.

C) **P commits a more serious offence than D intended:** At the other extreme from the cases just discussed, P may act in a way which goes beyond that intended by D. For example, D assists P to commit a simple battery, but P intentionally causes GBH.

Most cases of this kind can be resolved relatively simply. Since D must intend the essential elements of P's offence, D's liability cannot exceed that which was intended. In our example, as P causing GBH is likely to have included a battery in the form of some unlawful contact between P and V, D will be complicit in that battery (which D

---

[116] [1974] QB 776.
[117] [1987] AC 417, 457. Cf Kadish, 'Complicity, Cause and Blame' (1985) 73 Cal L Rev 323, 329.
[118] Diminished responsibility, Homicide Act 1957, s2(4); loss of control, Coroners and Justice Act 2009, s54(8).
[119] **Chapter 14.**

intended), but only P will be liable for the more serious GBH offence since that was intended by D.

There is an exception, however, and this applies where P commits a constructive liability offence—an offence, such as unlawful act manslaughter, where an unforeseen result increases P's liability from the base offence intended to a more serious offence.[120] Where P commits an offence of this kind, because P is not required to foresee the result element for liability (in manslaughter that is the death of V), it has been consistently held that D can also be liable as an accomplice where she does not intend or foresee the result either. For example, D encourages P to punch V, with both expecting the punch to result in no more than minor bruising amounting to only a battery. However, when P punches V and commits the base offence of battery, V unexpectedly falls backwards and hits her head on the hard floor, dying as a result. P is now liable for unlawful act manslaughter despite not foreseeing the death.[121] D is liable for unlawful act manslaughter as an accomplice; as with P, despite her lack of intention or foresight that P might cause death.

> **Don't be confused . . .**
> You may have noticed an inconsistency—where P commits a strict liability offence that does not require her to have mens rea, it has been held that D must nevertheless intend P to complete the actus reus of that offence to be liable as an accomplice; however, where P does not require mens rea as to the result element of a constructive liability offence, we are told that D may be liable as an accomplice even where she too lacks mens rea as to that result. The best explanation for this inconsistency, as explained by the Law Commission,[122] is that (unlike complicity in strict liability offences) complicity in a constructive crime still requires D to intend P to commit the base offence. Thus, her intention as to the base offence means that D is not an innocent party, and she (like P) should accept even the unforeseen consequences of her actions.

The application of this rule in manslaughter cases is exemplified in *Bristow*.[123]

> **Bristow** [2013] EWCA Crim 1540
>
> D and others undertook a planned robbery of an off-road vehicle repair yard. The owner of the yard (V) attempted to prevent the robbery and was killed, run over by one or more of the vehicles used for the robbery. It was unclear who was driving the vehicle that hit V. D and the others were charged with unlawful act manslaughter (as principal or accessory).
>
> - Crown Court: guilty of unlawful act manslaughter.
> - Court of Appeal: conviction upheld on appeal. D either (a) completed the dangerous and unlawful act (burglary) and caused death (ie acted as a principal), or (b) he assisted others to commit burglary and they caused V's death. D was liable under (a) or (b) even if he did not foresee the chance of death being caused.

Extending the mens rea of constructive liability crimes into complicity liability has been criticised for being too harsh on D. This has been particularly true for accomplices to

---

[120] See **4.2.1.1**.
[121] See **6.3.1**.
[122] Law Commission, *Participating in Crime* (No 305, 2007) para B.97.
[123] [2014] Crim LR 457 and commentary.

murder, another example of a constructive liability offence.[124] However, the rule remains valid. In *Jogee*,[125] for example, the Supreme Court makes clear that if D intended to assist or encourage P to cause serious harm to V and P kills V, even though D does not intend P to kill, D is still rightly convicted of murder. And if D intends to assist or encourage less serious harm and P kills V, even though D does not intend P to kill, D is still rightly convicted of manslaughter.[126] In this manner, although complicity liability has been narrowed in *Jogee* to require intention, application to constructive crimes still casts the net (perhaps inappropriately) wide.

D) **P commits an offence which is different from that D intended:** As we have discussed, D's foresight or lack of foresight about the details of P's offence will not affect her liability as long as she intends the essential elements. For example, if D provides P with a gun to murder V on Tuesday, but P kills V on Wednesday, D remains liable for murder as P's accomplice. However, there are occasions where P's crime is so fundamentally different from that assisted, encouraged, or procured by D that complicity liability would be inappropriate: D should only derive liability from P's crime where that crime is sufficiently similar to the one D intended. Where P's crime is fundamentally different, D remains inchoately liable for her acts of assistance or encouragement, but is not complicit in P's offence. The leading case, establishing this rule, was *English*.[127]

English [1999] AC 1

D and P attacked a police sergeant, V, with wooden posts. P produced a knife which D had not foreseen that P might carry and fatally stabbed V. D was charged with murder as an accomplice.

- Crown Court: guilty of murder.
- Court of Appeal: conviction upheld on appeal.
- House of Lords: appeal allowed. Even though D was reckless as to P causing GBH with intent (ie sufficient mens rea for complicity in murder at this time), P's conduct (stabbing with a knife) was fundamentally different from that anticipated by D (hitting with posts). Thus, D is not an accomplice to P's offence.

The continued relevance of the fundamental difference rule, however, and particularly the focus on P's weapon, has been cast into doubt by the Supreme Court in *Jogee*.[128] The Supreme Court touch only briefly on this rule as it was not relevant to the case before them, but they clearly suggest that having narrowed complicity liability to intentional assistors and encouragers, there should be less need for the fundamental difference rule to be applied in future cases.

---

[124] Mitchell and Roberts have researched public attitudes to liability in these circumstances, finding an unease at the harshness of liability, *Public Survey of the Mandatory Life Sentence for Murder* (2010).
[125] [2016] UKSC 8.
[126] At [96] and [101]–[107]. On this basis, the defendant in *Jogee* was convicted of manslaughter following retrial.
[127] The appeal of *English* was combined with *Powell and Daniels*.
[128] [2016] UKSC 8.

… there will normally be no occasion to consider the concept of 'fundamental departure' as derived from *English*. What matters is whether [D] encouraged or assisted the crime … The tendency which has developed … to focus on what [D] knew of what weapon [P] was carrying can and should give way to an examination of whether [D] intended to assist in the crime charged. If that crime is murder, then the question is whether he intended to assist the intentional infliction of grievous bodily harm at least … Very often he may intend to assist in violence using whatever weapon may come to hand. In other cases he may think that [P] has an iron bar whereas he turns out to have a knife, but the difference may not at all affect his intention to assist, if necessary, in the causing of grievous bodily harm at least. Knowledge or ignorance that weapons generally, or a particular weapon, is carried by [P] will be evidence going to what the intention of [D] was, and may be irresistible evidence one way or the other, but it is evidence and no more.[129]

Despite this statement from the Supreme Court, it is likely that the fundamental difference rule will continue to have some role within complicity liability. For the court in *Jogee*, the limited occasions when the rule continues to operate should be remodelled and renamed as 'supervening events'.[130] Below we highlight two scenarios where we believe this rule may retain some significance (the assumption being that outside this the rule has no role).

> **Judge and jury . . .**
> Whether P's conduct was fundamentally different (whether a supervening event occurred) from D's intention is a question of fact for the jury.[131]

The first and clearest example of a potential supervening event, arises where D intentionally assists or encourages an attack on a certain specified target, and P *intentionally* attacks a different target. For example, D encourages P to kill X, but P intentionally kills V; D assists P to damage X's car, but P intentionally damages V's car; and so on. In these circumstances, P's intentional change of target will probably constitute a supervening event, and D will not be liable as an accomplice to P's offence.[132] This is illustrated in *Saunders and Archer*.

> **Saunders and Archer** (1573) 2 Plowd 473
>
> P planned to kill his wife, X. D advised P, and on this advice P gave X a poisoned apple. X ate some of the apple, but gave the rest to their child, V, who ate it and died. P saw what happened and did not intervene.
>
> • Court: P is guilty of murder, his intention to kill X being moved to V via the doctrine of transferred malice.[133] X is an innocent agent. D is also not guilty of murder as an accomplice.

Although dicta in *Saunders and Archer* suggest that D will never be liable as an accomplice where P kills the wrong victim, this does not represent the current law. Rather, in line with the *outcome* of this case, D is likely to escape liability because P was aware of

---

[129] At [98].
[130] At [97].
[131] *Greatrex* [1999] 1 Cr App R 126.
[132] Recognised in *Powell* [1999] AC 1, and *Reardon* [1999] Crim LR 392.
[133] We discuss transferred malice at **4.3.1**.

the change of victim, had the power to intervene, and did not do so. In such a case the change of target was known to P, was controllable, and therefore not fully unintentional.

Three qualifications should be noted. First, there will be no fundamental difference/supervening event where P's change of target is unintentional.[134] Where P attempts to kill X, but accidentally kills V, P commits murder because her mens rea—her intention to kill X—is transferred to V. Just as the doctrine of transferred malice operates to secure P's liability, the same is true for D: her mens rea (ie intention of P killing X) is also transferred to V. Secondly, there will also be no fundamental difference/supervening event if the change is insubstantial. For example, in *Dunning and Graham*,[135] following a grievance between D and V, P offered to set fire to V's house. D accepted, and supplied V's address. In the event, P changed his mind and set fire to V's car instead. Although this was a clear change of target, the court found that it was not a substantial change from the plan envisaged by D, and so he remained complicit. Thirdly, there is unlikely to be a fundamental difference/supervening event where P carries out the principal offence as planned *and* goes on to commit an additional offence of the same type. For example, D provides P with a jemmy to assist burglary, and P burgles multiple properties; or D supplies a knife for P to kill someone, and P kills two people with it; and so on.[136] In these cases, D is likely to be complicit in the intended offence and the additional offence.

The second *potential* basis for establishing fundamental difference/supervening event arises where P acts in a considerably more dangerous way than that intended by D. Despite the court in *Jogee* emphasising that we should move away from focusing on knowledge of a weapon, it is still contended that P's conduct, whether related to the use of a weapon or not, must remain broadly in line with D's intentions for D to be fairly held as an accomplice.[137] For example, if D intends P to use a knife to cut off one of V's fingers, but P uses it to cut V's throat, we may question whether D's potential liability for manslaughter can be fairly derived from P's conduct. *AG's Reference (No 3 of 2004)* provides a useful illustration.

 AG's Reference (No 3 of 2004) [2005] EWCA Crim 1882

D recruited P and another to intimidate V by discharging a firearm near (but not at) him. P intentionally shot and killed V. D was charged with murder as P's accomplice.

- Crown Court: not guilty of murder.
- Court of Appeal: judge was correct to rule as he had to find no liability, as P's act (shooting at V) was fundamentally different from the act intended by D (shooting near V).

Along with clear examples of this kind, however, are cases that have presented more challenging facts. In *Gamble*,[138] for example, D intended that an attack on V would result

---

[134] Lanham, 'Accomplices and Transferred Malice' (1980) 96 LQR 110.

[135] Unreported, December 1985.

[136] *Reardon* [1999] Crim LR 392: D was complicit in two murders committed with his knife, despite only foreseeing one of them.

[137] *Mendez* [2010] EWCA Crim 516, [42]–[47]. The Court of Appeal in *Johnson* [2016] EWCA Crim 1613 relied on the fact that applicants were aware of the weapons possessed by principal offenders as a basis for rejecting the applicants' arguments for appeals out of time under *Jogee*.

[138] [1989] NI 268.

in GBH by kneecapping (ie shooting V in the knee joints). In the event, P killed V by cutting his throat and shooting him in the chest. As a result of this, despite D intending that P should cause GBH, the fundamental difference in P's acts meant that D was not liable for murder.

> Although the rule remains well entrenched that an intention to inflict grievous bodily harm qualifies as the mens rea of murder, it is not in my opinion necessary to apply it in such a way as to fix an accessory with liability for a consequence which he did not intend and which stems from an act which he did not have within his contemplation. I do not think that the state of the law compels me to reach such a conclusion, and it would not in my judgment accord with the public sense of what is just and fitting.[139]

We provide two examples here, but it is clear post-*Jogee* that this area will require further clarification from the courts before we can provide an outline with any confidence. It is also likely that the rule will arise in the future as a useful (flexible) tool for dealing with unexpected facts. The South African case of *Robinson* provides a useful example.[140] D, P, and V agreed that P would kill V, allowing D to claim V's life insurance and to avoid V's upcoming fraud prosecution. At the last moment V withdrew consent to being killed, but P killed V regardless. Applying an equivalent to the fundamental difference rule, the South African court found that D was not complicit in the murder because the withdrawal of consent made P's act of killing very different from that agreed to and intended by D. Whether the same approach would be adopted in this jurisdiction is not certain.

> **Point to remember . . .**
> The key to the fundamental difference/supervening event rule is not simply looking for extreme factual differences. Rather, we are looking for factual differences that break the nexus of responsibility between D and the principal offence. For example, a long time delay might appear a significant difference, but is unlikely to undermine D's liability.[141] It should also be remembered that the more specific D's intention as to P's offence (eg specific victim, etc), the more likely a finding of fundamental difference. For example, if D encourages P to kill others in general, and P goes on to kill, there is very little basis upon which D can claim that P's offence was fundamentally different from her intention.

12.4 Complicity by joint enterprise?

Alongside standard cases of complicity by assisting, encouraging, or procuring,[142] a parallel concept of complicity by joint enterprise (also known as parasitic accessory liability) was developed in the common law.[143] Crucially, as we discuss below, the concept of joint enterprise liability (as a separate route to complicity) has now been explicitly removed by the Supreme Court in *Jogee*.[144] Cases will now be prosecuted within the standard terms

---

139 Per Carswell J at 284.
140 1968 (1) SA 666.
141 *Bryce* [2004] EWCA Crim 1231.
142 Codified within the Accessories and Abettors Act 1861.
143 Krebs, 'Joint Criminal Enterprise' (2010) 73 MLR 578.
144 [2016] UKSC 8, [76]–[78].

of complicity liability discussed in previous section or not at all, and the continued use of the language of 'joint enterprise' should be avoided.

> *Terminology* . . .
> Joint enterprise is also commonly and interchangeably referred to as joint criminal enterprise, joint venture, and/or joint criminal venture.

In essence, joint enterprise has been used to describe a coordination of behaviour between D and P towards a common criminal end. It was classically described as follows: where D and P engaged together with a common purpose to commit Crime A and in the course of that P committed Crime B, then D would also be liable for Crime B if D had foreseen as a possibility that P might commit it with mens rea and the manner in which P did do was not fundamentally different from what D had foreseen might happen. For example, D and P take part in a fight with a rival gang, and P kills one of its members (V). D is not a co-principal with P in the murder of V because D does not commit the actus reus of the principal offence of murder. It may well also be that D did not provide any obvious assistance or encouragement to the acts of P in killing, and so the standard route to accomplice liability becomes difficult to establish: D has not assisted or encouraged murder directly. However, through her coordinated conduct, the doctrine of joint enterprise provided the basis for accomplice liability, and this route has been supported by several commentators.[145]

The problem with joint enterprise was that as soon as one begins to explore the actus reus and mens rea in any detail, it begins to merge back into standard complicity by assisting, encouraging, or procuring. Take our gang murder example, it is difficult to see how D can coordinate behaviour with P in any meaningful way without either committing the offence with her as a co-principal, or by assisting, encouraging, or procuring her. Where D does none of these, where her conduct is simply being proximate to P, complicity liability should not be found.[146]

The decision in *Jogee* to treat so-called joint enterprise cases within the standard rules of complicity is to confirm a previous line of Court of Appeal cases,[147] and legal commentary.[148] As Toulson LJ stated in *Stringer*:[149]

> Joint enterprise is not a legal term of art. In *R v Mendez* [2011] QB 876, the court favoured the view that joint enterprise as a basis of secondary liability involves the application of ordinary principles; it is not an independent source of liability. Participation in a joint criminal adventure involves mutual encouragement and assistance.

In line with this view, our earlier discussion of complicity by assisting, encouraging, and procuring has included several cases where courts have used the language of joint

---

[145] eg Law Commission, *Participating in Crime* (No 305, 2007); Simester, Spencer, Sullivan, and Virgo, *Simester and Sullivan's Criminal Law: Theory and Doctrine* (5th edn, 2013) 244–249.

[146] We would not want to criminalise as accomplices all those within a certain distance of a criminal offence!

[147] *ABCD* [2010] EWCA Crim 1622; *Mendez* [2011] QB 876; *Stringer* [2011] EWCA Crim 1396; *Gnango* [2011] UKSC 59.

[148] Wilson and Ormerod, 'Simply Harsh to Fairly Simple: Joint Enterprise Reform' [2015] Crim LR 3.

[149] [2011] EWCA Crim 1396, [57].

enterprise. The term 'joint enterprise' in these cases does not distinguish them as a separate form of complicity liability.

12.4.1 Challenges following the abolition of joint enterprise

For many, the doctrine of joint enterprise will not be missed. It created further layers of complexity within an already overly-complex area of law, and it has become (as the Supreme Court acknowledge), 'understood (erroneously) by some to be a form of guilt by association or of guilt by simple presence without more'.[150] However, advocates of the doctrine remain, and it is useful briefly to survey some of their reasons in order to understand the potential challenges for complicity in the coming years. Three main areas require comment.

A) **Expanding liability in coordinated encounters:** The first argument in favour of joint enterprise is policy-based, claiming that although standard complicity may be narrowed (or even abolished[151]) a wide view of joint enterprise should be maintained to allow the law to tackle coordinated (often gang-related) criminality. In *English*, Lord Hutton describes this as 'not based solely on logic' but justified by 'public policy' and 'practical concerns' in relation to group criminality.[152] This was the basis of the Law Commission's 2007 report, in which joint enterprise would have been retained with a recklessness mens rea standard.[153]

B) **Cases where D coordinates conduct with P, but does not obviously assist or encourage her:** Where D intentionally coordinates her conduct with P towards a common criminal end, it is difficult to imagine a scenario in which D does not thereby provide some manner of intentional assistance or encouragement. However, such cases are possible.[154] It is arguable that *Gnango* represents just such a case, where D and P coordinated their conduct, but D does not intentionally assist or encourage P to commit murder.[155] The facts of *Gnango*, it will be remembered, involved a shoot-out between D and P, where P shot and killed a passerby (V). In Lord Kerr's powerful dissenting judgment, the point is made that D's intentional conduct within the gunfight did not include an intention to assist or encourage P to return fire so D was not intending to assist or encourage P's offence as required for the principal offence, the murder of V. It is a convincing point: D's plan was to shoot P and thereby *stop* him shooting back, not to encourage it. Hence D lacked an essential element of mens rea, and liability could not have been found applying the normal rules of complicity discussed above.[156] However, this approach was not accepted, and a majority within the Supreme Court found that D *did* intend (at least obliquely) to encourage P to shoot back thereby finding D liable as an accessory to his

---

[150] *Jogee* [2016] UKSC 8.
[151] Sullivan, 'Doing Without Complicity' [2012] JCCL 199.
[152] *English* [1999] AC 1.
[153] Law Commission, *Participating in Crime* (No 305, 2007).
[154] An exception might be where P testifies that, although D's acts were capable of assisting or encouraging, she was not assisted or encouraged in fact. Law Commission, *Participating in Crime* (No 305, 2007) paras 3.42–3.45.
[155] Discussed at **12.1**.
[156] See **12.3.2.1**.

own attempted murder by P. The approach of the court here is not the most intuitive, but it is likely to be adopted by future courts where similar problem facts emerge.

C) Cases where D assists or encourages an offence, and anticipates P committing a second collateral offence in the course of the first: Cases of this kind emerge, for example, where D and P rob a bank and, whilst doing so, P kills a security guard. When analysing D's potential accomplice liability as to the second, collateral, offence, the language of joint enterprise became common.[157] *Powell* provides a useful example.[158]

Powell and Daniels [1999] AC 1

D, X, and P went to the house of a drug dealer (V) to buy drugs (the primary offence). At the door, one of them shot V dead (the collateral offence). D was charged with murder either as a principal offender or as an accessory.

- Crown Court: guilty of murder.
- Court of Appeal: conviction upheld on appeal.
- House of Lords: appeal dismissed.

Powell was liable as an accomplice to the collateral offence (murder) in this case despite providing no obvious assistance or encouragement as to that crime, ostensibly on the basis that her coordinated conduct with P (ie joint venture) as to the primary offence was sufficient. Thus, if we still want liability in such cases post-*Jogee*, we need to examine how they can be dealt with within standard rules of complicity.

The most likely course will be to ask whether D's assistance or encouragement of the primary offence provided some tacit assistance or encouragement as to the collateral. This approach was adopted in *Stringer*,[159] for example, and supported in *Jogee*, where the court also noted the important role of conditional intention in such cases: although D may not want P to commit the collateral offence come what may, she may have expressly or tacitly agreed with P that the collateral offence should be committed if certain circumstances arise.[160]

12.5 The relationship between complicity and inchoate liability

Just as D may be complicit in substantive offences such as rape or murder, for example, D may also be complicit in an inchoate offence such as conspiracy to rape, or assisting murder. This arises where D assists, encourages, or procures (or forms a joint enterprise to commit) the inchoate offence, and P goes on to commit that inchoate offence.[161]

---

[157] Simester, 'The Mental Element in Complicity' (2006) 122 LQR 578, 598–600.
[158] *Powell* was combined with *English* on appeal.
[159] [2011] EWCA Crim 1396.
[160] [2016] UKSC 8, [92]–[99].
[161] Smith, 'Secondary Participation and Inchoate Offences' in Tapper (ed), *Crime, Proof and Punishment* (1981) 21.

However, it is *no* offence inchoately to conspire, or to assist or encourage P to act as an accomplice.[162] There is also *no* offence of attempted complicity.[163]

12.6 Defences

The rules about denial of criminal responsibility and the general defences apply to complicity as they do across other criminal offences. These will be discussed in **Chapters 13** and **14** respectively. Here we discuss two established specific defences,[164] and one that has not yet been recognised by the courts. These are defences to complicity offences only, and will not necessarily relieve D of inchoate liability.[165]

12.6.1 Withdrawal

Where D assists or encourages P to commit a principal offence (with mens rea) she is immediately liable for an inchoate offence regardless of P's future conduct.[166] D cannot negate such inchoate liability even if she later 'withdraws' by removing or renouncing her assistance or encouragement.[167] However, if D successfully withdraws in the time between her conduct and P committing the principal offence, D will be able to limit her liability to the inchoate charge and avoid complicity liability. The ability to withdraw and prevent complicity liability in this way provides a useful incentive for D to negate or at least mitigate the effects of her criminal conduct.

What is required of D to withdraw effectively is not entirely clear within the law, and will vary between case facts, but rules have developed to help us to apply the defence. A useful starting point is that mere repentance, without any action, is not sufficient.

 Rook [1993] 2 All ER 955

D and another were recruited by X to kill his wife (V). D further recruited P. On the day of the murder, D was unexpectedly absent but P went ahead with the plan and murdered V. D was charged with murder as P's accomplice.

- Crown Court: guilty of murder.

- Court of Appeal: conviction upheld on appeal. D's absence was not sufficient to withdraw from P's offence.

---

[162] *Kenning* [2008] EWCA Crim 1534.

[163] Criminal Attempts Act 1981, s1(4)(b). For discussion, see Bohlander, 'The Conflict Between the Serious Crime Act and s4(1)(b) of the Criminal Attempts Act 1981' [2010] Crim LR 483 and Child, 'The Differences Between Attempted Complicity and Inchoate Assisting and Encouraging: A Reply to Professor Bohlander' [2010] Crim LR 924.

[164] Law Commission, *Participating in Crime* (No 305, 2007) Part 5.

[165] See **11.4.5**.

[166] See **11.4**.

[167] Reed, 'Repentance and Forgiveness: Withdrawal From Participation Liability and the Proportionality Test' in Reed and Bohlander (eds), *Participation in Crime* (2013); Smith, 'Withdrawal and Complicity' [2001] Crim LR 769.

The court in *Rook* does not specify what D should have done to withdraw successfully, but does state a minimum that he must have served 'unequivocal notice' of his withdrawal to P.[168] The focus of the defence is not on the withdrawal of D as an individual, but the withdrawal of D's assistance or encouragement, and this will always require action.

The most important detail to remember, discussed in *O'Flaherty*,[169] is that the courts will balance the weight of D's assistance or encouragement against the action taken to withdraw. Thus, the more substantial D's involvement in P's offence,[170] and the closer to P's commission of the offence that D attempts to withdraw,[171] the more the courts will require. Where D's assistance or encouragement is relatively minimal, for example where D has simply expressed the view that P's plan is a good one, it may be sufficient for D to withdraw by retracting these comments to P or removing the assistance. Where D's conduct is more substantial, she will have to do more. This does not necessarily mean that she must try and prevent P's crime taking place by going to the police, for example,[172] although this will obviously be useful evidence of withdrawal.

In certain cases D may accept liability as an accomplice for a primary offence, but claim to have withdrawn before a collateral offence was committed. This can occur where D joins an attack on V intending P to kill V, the attack ends with V still alive, D leaves, and then P returns to kill V.[173] D's argument, on these facts, would be that the second attack was not collateral to the first, but was a separate event. This is a different claim to standard cases of withdrawal, but can result in the same outcome, extracting D from continued potential liability.

12.6.2 The victim rule

Where an offence is designed for the protection of a specific class of victim,[174] someone within that class is not complicit where they assist, encourage, or procure the offence to be committed *against themselves*. This mirrors similar defences discussed in the context of inchoate assisting or encouraging and conspiracy.[175] Often referred to as the '*Tyrrell* defence', it originated in this case.

> **Tyrrell** [1894] 1 QB 710
>
> D (a girl at some point when aged between 13–16 years) encouraged P to have sexual intercourse with her. D was charged under section 5 of the Criminal Amendment Act 1885 (now the Sexual Offences Act 2003, s9) as P's accessory.
>
> • Central Criminal Court: guilty of the sexual offence.
>
> • Crown Case Reserved: appeal allowed. The statute was passed for the protection of young girls, not to criminalise them.

[168] Following *Becerra* (1975) 62 Cr App R 212.
[169] [2004] EWCA Crim 526.
[170] *Gallant* [2008] EWCA Crim 111: comparing withdrawal of instigators within gang violence compared to peripheral members.
[171] *Becerra* (1975) 62 Cr App R 212: failure to withdraw at a very late stage.
[172] *Otway* [2011] EWCA Crim 3.
[173] *Mitchell* [1999] Crim LR 496; *Robinson* [2000] 5 Arch News 2 (restricting the approach in *Mitchell*); *O'Flaherty* [2004] EWCA Crim 526.
[174] Williams, 'Victims and Other Exempt Parties in Crime' (1990) 10 LS 245.
[175] See **11.3.1.1** and **11.4.5**.

How far the victim rule extends, and exactly which offences it applies to, has not been settled. Indeed, modern statutes such as the Sexual Offences Act 2003 can be criticised for not taking full account of the rule.[176] However, it remains an important defence, and one that the Law Commission has recommended be codified in statute.

Two exceptions to the rule should be noted. First, the defence will only apply to offences designed to protect a specific sub-group of the population, not the population as a whole. Thus, for example, the defence will not apply to D who encourages P to kill her, as the offence of murder is designed to protect all people.[177] Secondly, the defence will not apply to D within the protected class if she assists or encourages P to commit the offence against *another* person within that class (eg D would have been liable in *Tyrell* had she encouraged P to have sexual intercourse with another girl aged 13).

12.6.3 Acting reasonably?

The courts have not recognised a defence of acting reasonably within the current law, although the Law Commission has recommended a defence of acting to prevent crime or limit harm.[178] Such a defence has, however, been accepted in the context of inchoate assisting or encouraging.[179] It would be open to the courts to recognise a defence of this kind where, for example, D encourages P to damage V's car in order to convince P not to attack V herself. In the absence of this as a specific defence, D would have to rely on the uncertain general defence of necessity.[180]

12.7 Reform

Any student studying the law of complicity will be struck by its complexity and, in several areas, its incoherence. The number of appellate court cases in recent years provides further demonstration of the uncertainties within the current law; and the judgments themselves seem to have done little to stem the flow. Even following *Jogee*,[181] parliamentary reform and clarification is long overdue.[182]

When seeking legal coherence, however, it is important to understand the base principles underlying liability (ie what is the 'wrong' complicity seeks to criminalise?). And it is here that we locate the source of the current law's confusion. There are at least two competing rationales for complicity, neither of which is entirely satisfactory. These are the causal theory and the derivative theory.

A) The causal theory: The causal theory holds that D is complicit in P's offence because she has materially contributed to its commission. There is support for this theory within the current law. For example, unlike inchoate assisting and encouraging

---

[176] Bohlander, 'The Sexual Offences Act 2003—The *Tyrrell* Principle—Criminalising the Victim' [2005] Crim LR 701.
[177] *Gnango* [2011] UKSC 59.
[178] Law Commission, *Participating in Crime* (No 305, 2007) paras 5.10–5.23.
[179] Serious Crime Act 2007, s50.
[180] **Chapter 14**.
[181] [2016] UKSC 8.
[182] cf Wilson and Ormerod [2015] Crim LR 3.

where D is merely required to perform acts 'capable' of assisting or encouraging, complicity will *not* be found where there is evidence that (despite conduct capable of encouraging or assisting P) D has not assisted or encouraged in fact.[183] Indeed, in *Mendez*, Toulson LJ stated that 'at its most basic level secondary liability is founded on the principle of causation'.[184] There is also support for a version of this theory from Gardner, who highlights the benefits of a causal theory in terms of respect for D's autonomy: D is liable for what she has done, not simply for her association with the actions of another.[185]

The obvious (and potentially fatal) problem with this theory, however, is that most complicity cases do not require D to have caused P's offence. Where D has caused P's offence, D has either procured P's offence or committed it as a principal via the doctrine of innocent agency.[186] For most complicity cases involving assistance or encouragement, P's free, voluntary, and informed choice to commit the principal offence will break any chain of causation between D's conduct and that offence.[187] In view of this, causal theories are forced into the murky realms of 'substantial contribution' rather than full causation. This is problematic: it does not provide clarity on what the offence should require of D, and if less than causation, as must be the case, it is arguable that it undermines the benefits of the theory highlighted earlier.

B) The derivative theory: The derivative theory holds that D's liability is a product of P's liability; D assuming co-responsibility with P because of her association with P's conduct. Again, advocates of the derivative theory can find support within the current law's treatment of D (ie labelling and punishing her in the same way as P), as well as the fact that D's liability hangs on P's completion of the principal offence.

However, the derivative theory is also problematic. In contrast to the causal theory, the derivative theory can be criticised for being too harsh to D and not respecting the principal of autonomy: D seems to be punished for P's choices rather than her own. And, in other areas, it may also be too generous to D. Where P commits a less serious offence than that intended by D, the current law (in certain cases) still allows D to be held liable for the more serious offence intended.[188] But surely, if we fully respect a derivative theory, it should not be possible to criminalise D for anything in excess of P's offence.

The current doctrinal uncertainty makes useful reform almost impossible. As Wilson comments, 'the range of problems left uncatered for by this fudging of the theoretical basis to accessorial liability spreads across the whole field of doctrine'.[189]

12.7.1 Abolishing complicity

In view of the doctrinal uncertainty discussed in the previous section, for some commentators the abolition of complicity liability becomes an attractive proposition.

---

[183] See **12.3.1.1**.
[184] [2010] EWCA Crim 516, [18].
[185] Gardner, 'Complicity and Causality' (2007) 1 Crim L & Phil 127, 136.
[186] See **12.2**.
[187] *Kennedy (No 2)* [2007] UKHL 38.
[188] **12.3.2.2**.
[189] Wilson, *Central Issues in Criminal Theory* (2002) 221.

This would not result in a complete lack of liability for D, as the inchoate offences of assisting or encouraging and conspiracy would cover almost all cases.[190] Indeed, it is an approach that once found favour with the Law Commission.[191]

However, the most recent Law Commission recommendations rejected this approach for two main reasons.[192] First, it was contended that cases where P goes on to commit the principal offence assisted or encouraged are different (ie more serious) than cases where P does not, such that only inchoate liability in both cases would fail to mark the distinction in culpability. Secondly, it was highlighted that abolition of complicity would undermine the forensic advantage of, in appropriate cases, being able to charge D as a principal *or* an accessory where D's exact role is uncertain. On both of these grounds, we agree that the Commission was right to rethink its original proposal. Interestingly, a variation on the abolition proposal has been mooted by Sullivan in a manner which seeks to address some of these concerns.[193]

12.7.2 Law Commission 2007 recommendations

We have made reference to the latest Law Commission recommendations[194] at several points during this chapter, and it is contended by some commentators that they represent the best route available to reform of this area. However, despite codification of inchoate assisting or encouraging within the Serious Crime Act 2007 (intended to work in tandem with the Commission's complicity recommendations), the Commission's complicity report remains unimplemented, and particularly post-*Jogee*, is unlikely to be taken forward by government. The Commission recommended the following scheme for complicity.

- Clause 1: Complicity liability where D assists or encourages P to commit an offence that P goes on to commit, intending to assist or encourage, and intending that P should complete at least the conduct element of that offence.

- Clause 2: Complicity liability where D forms a joint enterprise with P to commit an offence that P goes on to commit, intending to assist or encourage, and at least reckless as to P completing that offence. Note the lower 'recklessness' standard required for this offence.

- Clause 3: A new offence of 'causing a no-fault offence' where D causes (ie not just assists or encourages) P to commit a strict liability offence. This new offence provides a coherent response to cases where D causes P's offence, but P is not an innocent agent because the conduct she is caused to complete is an offence despite her lack of mens rea.

---

[190] The only exception might be cases of procuring. Child, 'The Differences Between Attempted Complicity and Inchoate Assisting and Encouraging: A Reply to Professor Bohlander' [2010] Crim LR 924.

[191] Law Commission, *Assisting and Encouraging Crime* (Consultation 131, 1993).

[192] Law Commission, *Participating in Crime* (No 305, 2007) paras 1.38–1.40.

[193] Sullivan, 'Doing Without Complicity' [2012] JCCL 199.

[194] Law Commission, *Participating in Crime* (No 305, 2007).

Academic responses to the Commission's recommendations have been mixed.[195] In 2015, the Justice Committee of the House of Commons recommended that the Law Commission start a further project on joint enterprise, not adopting its 2007 report. However, at time of writing, post-*Jogee*, this seems unlikely.

12.8 Eye on assessment

Answering problem questions on complicity is challenging, but the structure is no different to any other essay of this kind. The focus should be on clarity, leading your reader through your analysis, and keeping your discussion as simple as possible— there is no need to add to the complexity! The starting point is to identify a criminal offence from P, and then to work backwards to D's potential liability for complicity in that offence.

> **STEP 1 Identify the potential criminal event in the facts**
>
> This should be simply stated (eg 'The first potential criminal event arises where P murders V, having been encouraged to do so by D'). The role of this stage is to highlight which part of the question you are answering before you begin to apply the law.

> **STEP 2 Identify the potential principal offence**
>
> Again, state this simply (eg 'When P kills V, following D's encouragement, D may be liable for murder as P's accomplice'). The role of this stage is to highlight which offence you are going to apply.

> **STEP 3 Applying the offence to the facts**
>
> Having identified the relevant principal offence, make sure you discuss each of the required elements.
>
> Begin with the principal offence committed by P: Are we sure we have a complete offence that D may be an accomplice to? Having established P's offence, we can now explore D's potential accomplice liability:
>
> Actus reus: What does the offence require? Did D do it?
>
> Mens rea: What does the offence require? Did D possess it?

In order to apply Steps 2 and 3, you need to do two things. First, you need to lead your reader through the most likely route to liability (ie principal offender; co-principal;

---

[195] Wilson welcomes the proposals in 'A Rational Scheme of Liability for Participating in Crime' [2008] Crim LR 3, but they are criticised in Sullivan, 'Participating in Crime' [2008] Crim LR 19 and Taylor, 'Procuring, Causation, Innocent Agency and the Law Commission' [2008] Crim LR 32. Horder (Criminal Law Commissioner at the time of the Complicity Report) responds to Sullivan's criticism in Ch6 of *Homicide and the Politics of Law Reform* (2012).

459

complicity by assisting or encouraging; by procuring; etc) and, secondly, you need to apply the elements of that offence.

In **Figure 12.1** we set out a flowchart to help you to make sense of the different routes to complicity liability. Within each stage represented in the figure, you will need to take account of the detailed commentary set out in the chapter (ie this is a rough guide, not a substitution for engagement with the case law).

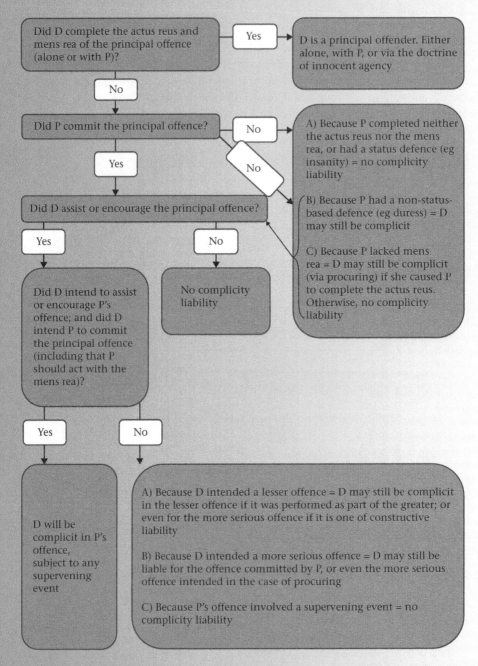

Figure 12.1 Guide to multi-party offending

AR and MR are satisfied	AR and/or MR are not satisfied
Continue to STEP 4.	Return to STEP 2, and look for an alternative offence. If none, then skip to STEP 5, concluding that no offence is committed.

STEP 4 Consider defences

The word 'consider' here is important, as you should not discuss every defence for every question. Rather, think whether there are any defences (eg duress) that *could* potentially apply. This includes the specific defences of withdrawal and the victim rule. If there are any potential defences, discuss those only.

STEP 5 Conclude

This is usually a single sentence either saying that it is likely that D has committed the offence as an accomplice, or saying that it is not likely either because an offence element is not satisfied or because a defence is likely to apply. It is not often that you will be able to say categorically whether or not D has committed the offence, so it is usually best to conclude in terms of what is more 'likely'.

STEP 6 Loop

Go back up to Step 1, identifying the next potential criminal event. Continue until you have discussed all the relevant potentially criminal events.

 ONLINE RESOURCE CENTRE

www.oxfordtextbooks.co.uk/orc/sho/

This chapter is accompanied by a selection of online resources to help you with this topic, including:

- **Multiple-choice questions**
- **Chapter summary sheet**
- Two **sample examination questions** with answer guidance
- **Further reading**

Also available on the Online Resource Centre are:

- A selection of **videos** from the authors explaining key topics and principles
- **Legal updates**
- Useful **weblinks**

13

Denials of an offence

13.1 Introduction   **515**

    13.1.1 Denials, defences, or constructors of liability?   **517**

13.2 Intoxication   **517**

    13.2.1 When is D's intoxication relevant to liability?   **518**

    13.2.2 Element 1: D's intoxication must be voluntary   **521**

    13.2.3 Element 2: D's offence must be one of basic intent   **522**

    13.2.4 Element 3: D must have taken a dangerous drug   **528**

    13.2.5 Element 4: D must have lacked mens rea *because* of intoxication   **529**

    13.2.6 Intoxication and defences   **530**

13.3 Sane automatism   **531**

    13.3.1 Automatism as a denial of offending   **532**

    13.3.2 Prior-fault automatism as a method of inculpation   **535**

    13.3.3 Automatism and defences   **539**

13.4 Insanity as a denial of mens rea   **539**

    13.4.1 The special verdict of 'not guilty by reason of insanity'   **542**

    13.4.2 Elements of legal insanity   **542**

    13.4.3 Insanity and defences   **549**

13.5 Combining intoxication, automatism, and insanity   **550**

13.6 Reform   **550**

    13.6.1 Intoxication   **551**

    13.6.2 Sane automatism   **552**

    13.6.3 Insanity   **552**

13.7 Eye on assessment   **554**

13.1 Introduction

In **Chapters 13** and **14** we shift focus from the discussion of substantive offences (ie issues of inculpation), to denials of liability (ie issues of exculpation). We have already discussed a number of specific defences in relation to particular crimes (eg withdrawal for complicity, belief in an owner's consent for criminal damage, etc). The rules discussed in these two chapters are different because, if they apply, they provide a complete[1] defence for (almost[2]) any criminal offence.

The classification of criminal law defences is controversial, not least because the term 'defence' is often employed non-specifically to describe all manner of arguments raised by a defendant.[3] In this book, between **Chapters 13** and **14**, we distinguish two sets of rules which continue to be commonly referred to as defences. This chapter focuses on the rules regulating D's denial of an offence, a denial of one or more actus reus or mens rea elements. **Chapter 14**, in contrast, focuses on defences properly so called. These rules apply where D *has* committed the actus reus and mens rea of the offence charged, but seeks to rely on an independent set of rules (ie a defence) to escape liability.

We begin with denials of an offence. Where D has not completed every element of the offence charged, strictly speaking, she does not need a defence: she has not committed the offence. We might talk loosely of a 'defence' where D states an alibi (eg that she was somewhere else when the bank was robbed), or where D denies specific offence elements (eg that she did not foresee a risk of causing criminal damage), but such statements are not appealing to independent rules beyond the terms of the offences themselves. However, there are three sets of rules that, whilst falling within this category, require specific examination.

- Intoxication: D explains her lack of mens rea (including, in extreme cases, her lack of voluntary movement) on the basis of intoxication. For example, D stabs her sleeping friend, drunkenly mistaking her friend for a theatrical dummy.[4] D, in this example, lacks subjective mens rea for any offence against the person.

- Sane automatism: D explains her lack of voluntary movement (and associated lack of mens rea) on the basis that she was rendered totally incapacitated by some *external* circumstances affecting her. For example, D drives dangerously when attacked by a swarm of bees, or punches V whilst suffering concussion following a blow to the head.[5] D, in these examples, lacks an essential element for all offences.

- Insanity (as a denial of offending): D explains her lack of mens rea (including, in extreme cases, her lack of voluntary movement) on the basis of what the law labels insanity.[6] This includes all medical conditions which cause some bodily malfunctioning, which prevent D understanding the nature or quality of her acts, or not to know they are wrong. For example, D kills V under the insane delusion that she is breaking a jar.[7]

These three sets of rules require separate discussion from other denials of offending for three main reasons. First, unlike most denials (eg simple alibis), D cannot raise issues

---

[1] Unlike the 'partial' defences to murder discussed at **6.2**, the rules discussed in **Chapters 13** and **14** lead to an acquittal.

[2] The only exception is the defence of duress (**Chapter 14**) which does not apply to murder and a small number of related offences.

[3] Williams, 'Offences and Defences' (1982) 2 LS 233.

[4] Example from Lord Denning in *AG for Northern Ireland v Gallagher* [1963] AC 349, 381.

[5] Examples from Lord Goddard CJ in *Hill v Baxter* [1958] 2 WLR 76, 82–83.

[6] The insanity rules can apply *both* as a denial of offending, and as a defence where D has committed the offence. This chapter discusses the former only, **Chapter 14** discusses the latter.

[7] Example from Stephen, *A Digest of the Criminal Law* (8th edn, 1947) 6.

463

of intoxication, automatism, and/or insanity without bringing some evidence that the relevant condition or circumstances applied to her at the time of the alleged offence.[8] This is because, although there is a general burden on the prosecution to prove D's liability, there are legal presumptions that our movements are voluntary, that we are sane, etc.[9] Secondly, where D successfully pleads insanity this will not result in an unqualified acquittal, but rather in the special verdict of 'not guilty by reason of insanity'. Thirdly, and most importantly, these rules are special because in certain circumstances they can provide alternative routes to liability where D lacks mens rea for the offence charged. In other words, if D uses evidence of her intoxication to explain the absence of mens rea or actus reus, the evidence might then be capable of being used by the prosecution to justify her conviction despite the missing offence element(s). The evidence is used as a method of *inculpation*.

13.1.1 Denials, defences, or constructors of liability?

Where the rules in this chapter apply to inculpate D for an offence, there is a potentially confusing inconsistency in the terminology used by courts and within academic writing. This is because many commentators still prefer to discuss denials of liability as 'defences'. You are likely to come across two methods of presentation.

- D satisfies the elements of the offence because, although she lacks mens rea, the relevant rules provide that her prior fault substitutes for that mens rea.
- D satisfies the elements of the offence because the relevant rules prevent D denying liability (ie prevent her using a defence).

We prefer the first method of analysis because we believe it provides a more accurate description of D's liability. Where D lacks mens rea through intoxication, for example, it seems odd to say that she satisfies the elements of the offence because she is not allowed to raise the defence of intoxication—not being allowed to raise the issue of intoxication does not mean that D somehow acted with mens rea. Rather, if we are finding D liable, it must be because D's prior fault in becoming intoxicated is substituting for her lack of mens rea.[10] We return to this discussion at several points in the chapter in relation to prior-fault intoxication, prior-fault automatism, and prior-fault insanity.

13.2 Intoxication

There is an obvious and well-documented link between intoxication, particularly alcoholic intoxication, and crime.[11] Intoxicants can lower inhibitions, warp moral and practical judgments, encourage unpredictable behaviour, and so on. In short, D's conduct

---

[8] The nature of this burden differs between the rules, discussed later.

[9] The use of reverse burdens in these areas is another reason why the terminology of 'defences' has been common.

[10] Simester, 'Intoxication is Never a Defence' [2009] Crim LR 3; Child and Reed, 'Automatism is Never a Defence' (2014) 65 NILQ 167; Child, 'Prior Fault: Blocking Defences or Constructing Crimes' in Reed and Bohlander (eds), *General Defences* (2014).

[11] Dingwall, *Alcohol and Crime* (2005).

when intoxicated may not be a reflection of her character when sober.[12] This is not, however, and never has been, a defence to criminal offences. D's claim that 'it was the drink' may provide some moral mitigation, and may become relevant at sentencing, but it is not an answer to a criminal charge. If it were, there would be a lot more space in prisons!

13.2.1 When is D's intoxication relevant to liability?

The intoxication rules *only* become relevant where, as a result of intoxication, D lacks the prescribed mens rea for the crime charged. This is illustrated in *Kingston* where, although intoxicated against his will, this intoxication was irrelevant to D's liability.

 Kingston [1994] 3 All ER 353

P was hired to take compromising photos of D to use for blackmail. P invited V (a 15-year-old boy) to his flat, gave him alcohol and drugs, and left him asleep. He then drugged D's coffee, and encouraged D to indecently assault V as he slept. D did so. D was charged with indecent assault.[13]

- Crown Court: guilty of indecent assault.
- Court of Appeal: appeal allowed. No liability: D only committed the offence as a result of P surreptitiously drugging him and thus lowering his inhibitions.
- House of Lords: appeal allowed, and D's conviction reinstated. A drunken intention is still an intention.

In *Kingston*, mens rea was proved irrespective of intoxication, so there was no need (or scope) to rely on special rules of intoxication (discussed later). Despite the disinhibiting effect of the drugs in this case, D was still able, and did in fact, form an intention to assault V, and so D satisfied all elements of the offence charged. D acted with the mens rea required for the offence. There is no defence of intoxication where D has committed an offence; a drunken intent is still an intent; an intoxicated mens rea is still a mens rea.[14] This is illustrated in **Figure 13.1**.

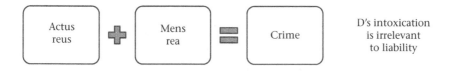

Figure 13.1 An intoxicated mens rea is still a mens rea

---

[12] This chapter only discusses the intoxication of D. The intoxication of a victim may affect D's liability (eg where it affects V's consent in sexual offences) but this is a separate issue, discussed elsewhere.

[13] D's conduct would now be charged under the Sexual Offences Act 2003.

[14] Horder has recommended an alternative approach for cases like *Kingston* based on temporary insanity: Horder, 'Sobering Up? The Law Commission on Criminal Intoxication' (1995) 58 MLR 534.

D's intoxication only becomes relevant to liability if it means that, as a result of her intoxication, an offence element does not exist. In standard intoxication cases, this is likely to be an absence of mens rea. For example, D claims that she was so drunk she did not intend to make contact with V, or damage V's property. In more extreme cases, it may also involve an absence of voluntary movement. For example, D becomes so intoxicated that she loses consciousness.[15] In all cases of this kind, special legal prior-fault intoxication rules must be applied.

> **Don't be confused . . .**
> In this book we have analysed a lack of voluntariness in movement as a lack of mens rea (mens rea as to the conduct element of a crime). However, as we explained at **3.3**, it is common to analyse 'voluntary movement' as a single actus reus element. Thus, where D uses intoxication to explain a lack of voluntary movement, some courts and commentators will describe this as explaining a lack of actus reus. The difference between the two descriptions does not affect the application of the prior-fault intoxication rules, but should be noted to avoid confusion.

Before the rules apply, D must lack mens rea as a result of intoxication. However, there is no need to demonstrate further that D was rendered 'incapable' of forming mens rea.[16] For example, if D mistakenly kills V thinking that V is a theatrical dummy due to her intoxication, D may be 'capable' of forming an intention to kill, but her intoxication still provides an explanation for her lack of mens rea in relation to V, and the prior-fault intoxication rules will still apply.

The prior-fault intoxication rules apply therefore when D is claiming that she did not have the mens rea for the offence charged because she was intoxicated by drink or drugs at the time of the offence. Once engaged, our starting point, as set out in **Figure 13.2**, is that D has not committed an offence.

Figure 13.2 Lacking mens rea due to intoxication

A lack of liability in these cases, however, is not always appropriate, and in many cases it will be possible to use D's intoxication to construct liability. Accepting that D lacked mens rea when completing the actus reus of the relevant offence (a time we will call T2), the prior-fault intoxication rules look back to D's conduct in becoming intoxicated (a time we will call T1). The question is whether D's conduct at T1 is sufficiently blameworthy that we can use D's 'prior fault' at T1 to replace or substitute for the missing offence elements at T2?[17] **Table 13.1** sets out the elements of the prior-fault intoxication rules in

---

[15] *Lipman* [1970] 1 QB 152: D took LSD (a hallucinogenic drug). Believing that he was fighting snakes at the centre of the earth, D killed V.

[16] There has been some inconsistency on this point. See *Beard* [1920] AC 479, 501–502; *Kingston* [1994] 3 All ER 353; cf *Sheehan and Moore* [1975] 2 All ER 960.

[17] Simester, 'Intoxication is Never a Defence' [2009] Crim LR 3.

a logical order that is worth following. If the conditions in these rules apply, D will be guilty of a criminal offence even though she lacked mens rea at T2.

Table 13.1 Prior-fault intoxication rules

A) D's intoxication at T1 must have been voluntary;
B) D's offence at T2 must have been one of 'basic intent', as opposed to one of 'specific intent';
C) D's intoxicant at T1 must have been 'dangerous' in the sense that it is commonly known to lead to unpredictability or aggression; and
D) D must lack mens rea at T2 *because* of that intoxication

Where these elements are satisfied, D's lack of mens rea at T2 will be substituted for by the prior-fault intoxication rules, and D will be liable as if the missing elements were satisfied.[18] This is illustrated in **Figure 13.3**.

Figure 13.3 Intoxication replacing a lack of mens rea

Extra detail . . .
Unless D claims to have lacked voluntariness, there should be no burden on D to prove she lacked mens rea through intoxication.[19] However, intoxication is usually raised by D to explain a lack of mens rea that would otherwise be difficult for a jury to believe (eg 'I thought my sleeping friend was a theatrical dummy'). In certain cases, the courts have begun to require specific evidence of intoxication from D before she is allowed to raise the issue.[20] This reflects policy concerns about allowing D to claim a lack of mens rea on the basis of intoxication too easily, and may also reflect the language of defences commonly used when discussing the prior-fault intoxication rules. However, it is submitted that no specific evidence should be required: it is for the prosecution to prove mens rea, and the law should avoid any rules requiring D to prove her innocence.

We discuss each element of the prior-fault intoxication rules in turn.

---

[18] The alternative way of expressing this, using the language of defences, is to say that if the elements of the prior-fault intoxication rules are satisfied D will *not* be able to raise intoxication as a defence. See **13.1.1**.
[19] We discuss the presumption of voluntary movement in the context of automatism later.
[20] *McKnight* (2000) The Times, 5 May; *P* [2004] EWCA Crim 1043.

13.2.2 Element 1: D's intoxication must be voluntary

D's voluntariness in becoming so intoxicated at T1 that she lacks mens rea for the crime at T2 is fundamental to establishing any kind of blameworthiness. The law is looking for some kind of equivalence between D's conduct in becoming intoxicated at T1 and her lack of mens rea at T2. Only if D became intoxicated voluntarily can we say that she *chose* to run the associated risks.[21]

13.2.2.1 Involuntary intoxication

Where D's intoxication was involuntary,[22] it would not be fair for the courts to say she has chosen to run the risks associated with intoxication, and it would be inappropriate to blame her for subsequent conduct caused by that intoxication. Where D is not responsible for her intoxicated state (ie involuntary intoxication at T1), and where that involuntary intoxication caused her to lack the relevant mens rea at the time of the offence (T2), there is no liability for any offence. However, two points should be considered carefully.

First, as discussed earlier, remember that the prior-fault intoxication rules do not apply unless offence elements are missing. The leading case is *Kingston* (discussed earlier), where D was drugged by a third party, and then sexually assaulted a minor. Understandably, the House of Lords in *Kingston* had some sympathy for D: he was aware of and claimed to be in control of his paedophilic tendencies when sober, only losing control as a result of the drugs involuntarily administered by P. Where such involuntary intoxication leads to a lack of mens rea at T2, there is no blameworthy conduct at T1 or T2, and D will not be liable for an offence. D was liable in *Kingston* because his conduct at T2 *was* accompanied by mens rea. Thus, although there was no prior fault at T1, D was liable at T2 without the need for such substitution.

Secondly, involuntariness has been narrowly defined. D's intoxication is clearly involuntary in cases like *Kingston* where D's drinks are surreptitiously laced with alcohol or other intoxicating drugs,[23] and the same may be true where D is forced to take drugs under duress. However, as illustrated in *Allen*, where D knows that she is consuming a dangerous intoxicant (eg alcohol), this does not qualify as involuntary simply because she is unaware of its quantity or possible effects.

 Allen (1988) The Times, 10 June

D committed the actus reus of buggery and indecent assault.[24] He lacked mens rea (he claimed he was not acting voluntarily) because he had consumed a large amount of wine supplied by a friend. D claimed this was involuntary intoxication because he did not realise the strength of the wine. D was charged with the sexual offences.[25]

- Crown Court: guilty of the sexual offences.
- Court of Appeal: convictions upheld on appeal. D's intoxication was voluntary.

---

[21] Note the important role of 'choice'. See our discussion of the principle of autonomy at **1.4.3**.
[22] Law Commission, *Intoxication and Criminal Liability* (No 314, 2009) Part 4.
[23] *Ross v HM Advocate* 1991 SLT 564: D's drink was involuntarily laced with various drugs including LSD, under the influence of which D injured several people. His conviction for offences against the person was quashed on appeal.
[24] Commentary at [1988] Crim LR 698.
[25] For such acts performed today D would be charged under the Sexual Offences Act 2003.

A more difficult case arises where D voluntarily consumes an intoxicant, but a further intoxicant is added without her knowledge (eg X gives D a double shot of alcohol rather than the single requested, or X laces D's alcoholic drink with another intoxicating drug). In cases of this kind, the question for the court is likely to be whether the *involuntary* proportion of D's intoxication overrides the voluntary, such to make it trivial.[26]

As illustrated in **Figure 13.4**, where D's intoxication is involuntary, and she is intoxicated to the extent that she lacks mens rea, then there is no liability. This is because there is no prior fault in her becoming intoxicated at T1 which can provide the culpability for conduct at T2.

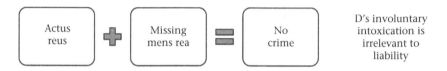

Figure 13.4 Involuntary intoxication

13.2.2.2 Voluntary intoxication

In order to satisfy this first element of the prior-fault intoxication rules, we are looking for voluntary conduct from D at T1 that causes her to become intoxicated. Standard examples include the voluntary consumption of alcohol, or the taking of illegal drugs.

13.2.3 Element 2: D's offence must be one of basic intent

Having established that D was voluntarily intoxicated at T1, we now focus on the potential offence of which D committed the actus reus (but lacked mens rea) at T2. If the crime D is charged with is one classified by the law as a 'specific intent' offence, then D is not guilty of that crime regardless of her intoxication.[27] However, if the crime D is charged with at T2 is one classified by the law as a 'basic intent' offence, then D may be liable for that offence on the basis of her prior fault in voluntarily intoxicating herself at T1.

The crucial two-part classification between basic and specific intent offences has been developed at common law.

> **Terminology . . .**
> The terms 'basic intent' and 'specific intent' are misleading, as they do not describe types of intention. Rather, they are simply labels that have been used to distinguish two classifications of offences. We discuss the basis of this distinction later, but suffice to say, it has nothing to do with different types of intention.[28]

---

[26] Law Commission, *Intoxication and Criminal Liability* (No 314, 2009) paras 3.126–3.127.

[27] Unless D had voluntarily intoxicated herself in order to commit the offence—'Dutch courage', discussed later in this section.

[28] For discussion of the origin of these terms, as well as a more general critique, see Gough, 'Intoxication and Criminal Liability: The Law Commission's Proposed Reforms' (1996) 112 LQR 335, 342.

A) **Basic intent offences:** Where D is charged with a basic intent offence, the prior fault in D's voluntary intoxication at T1 *may be* sufficient to replace her lack of mens rea at T2, subject to the other elements within the prior-fault intoxication rules. Malicious wounding or inflicting GBH[29] is an example of a basic intent offence. Thus, where D wounds V or causes GBH, but lacks mens rea (and even, potentially, lacks voluntariness in her movement) because of her voluntary intoxication, she will still be liable for the offence.[30] This is illustrated in **Figure 13.5**.

Figure 13.5 Basic intent offences

B) **Specific intent offences:** Where D is charged with a specific intent offence, D's prior fault in voluntary intoxication at T1 will *not* be sufficient to replace her lack of mens rea at T2. Wounding or causing GBH with intent[31] is an example of a specific intent offence. Thus, where D wounds V or causes GBH, but lacks mens rea (and even, potentially, lacks voluntariness in her movement) because of her voluntary intoxication, she will not be liable for this offence.[32] This is illustrated in **Figure 13.6**.

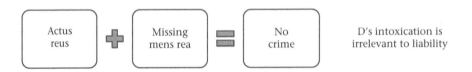

Figure 13.6 Specific intent offences

The logic of separating basic and specific intent offences is that D's voluntary intoxication at T1 is only sufficiently wrongful to replace a lack of mens rea for certain offences and not others. However, there are two major problems with this.

---

[29] Offences Against the Person Act 1861, s20.
[30] *Aitken* [1992] 1 WLR 1006.
[31] Offences Against the Person Act 1861, s18.
[32] *Davies* [1991] Crim LR 469.

The first problem is that, although D voluntarily becoming intoxicated at T1 is not obviously equivalent to *any* potential subjective mens rea missing at T2, the prior-fault intoxication rules are not limited to substituting for objective mens rea only. Equivalence with subjective mens rea is assumed within the current law in the context of basic intent offences,[33] but it is difficult to justify logically.[34] Even if we accept that voluntarily taking a dangerous drug means that D *chose* to risk committing a harmful act, that choice is necessarily non-specific. In contrast, subjective mens rea requires D to intend or be reckless as to specific elements of an offence before she is liable for it. In the context of criminal damage, for example, foresight of possible danger is not sufficient for liability; D must be reckless as to the specific risk of causing damage, and to the specific fact of ownership as to the property damaged. The criticism, therefore, is that when the prior-fault intoxication rules are used to replace a lack of subjective mens rea (including voluntariness in movement at T2), we are finding liability on the basis of an objective (negligence-based) standard at T1.[35]

The second problem is that the common law has struggled to create a clear set of rules to distinguish basic intent and specific intent offences. It should be acknowledged that in the absence of a justified equivalence between intoxication and a certain level of mens rea, a principled test of this kind is almost impossible, but the law requires one in order to function.

13.2.3.1 Distinguishing between basic and specific intent offences

The leading case discussing the separation of basic and specific intent offences is *Majewski*.[36]

DPP v Majewski [1977] AC 443

Intoxicated by a range of dangerous drugs, including alcohol, D was involved in a bar brawl where he assaulted several people. D also assaulted a number of police officers during the course of his arrest. D was charged with assault occasioning ABH, and assaulting a police officer.[37] D claimed that he lacked mens rea due to intoxication.

- Crown Court: guilty of assault offences.

- Court of Appeal: appeal dismissed.

- House of Lords: appeal dismissed. These were basic intent offences, and so D's voluntary intoxication can be used as a substitute for the mens rea he lacked at the time of his conduct.

Although *Majewski* is clear in its categorisation of assault as a basic intent offence, the Lords did not provide a unified test to apply to other offences. To the extent that a test

---

[33] *Majewski* [1977] AC 443.

[34] Horder, 'Sobering Up? The Law Commission on Criminal Intoxication' (1995) 58 MLR 534.

[35] Robinson, 'Causing the Conditions of One's Own Defence: A Study in the Limits of Theory in Criminal Law Doctrine' (1985) 71 Vir LR 1, 14–17; Husak, 'Intoxication and Culpability' (2012) 6 Crim L & Phil 363, 366–368; Williams, 'Voluntary Intoxication—A Lost Cause?' (2013) 129 LQR 264, 266–271.

[36] Law Commission, *Intoxication and Criminal Liability* (No 314, 2009) paras 2.2–2.74; Horder, 'The Classification of Crimes and the General Part' in Duff and Green (eds), *Defining Crimes* (2005).

[37] Offences Against the Person Act 1861, s47; Police Act 1996, s89.

is discernible,[38] the Lords seem to treat offences that can be satisfied by recklessness as ones of basic intent, and those requiring intention as specific intent. It is noted by Lord Edmund-Davies that this distinction 'illogical though . . . it may be' has an advantage of 'compromise' where offences are laddered on the basis of mens rea.[39] For example, where D, in her voluntarily intoxicated state lacks mens rea but causes GBH, she is not liable for a section 18 offence (specific intent), but is liable for a section 20 offence (basic intent);[40] where she lacks mens rea but causes death she is not liable for murder (specific intent), but is liable for manslaughter (basic intent); and so on.

Though rather imprecise, where the Lords attempted to be more specific, they ran into problems. For example, Lord Simon in *Majewski* discussed a test based on intention as to consequences: where D must intend the consequence element of the offence, it is a specific intent offence.[41] But this cannot be right. Murder, for example, the paradigm specific intent offence, can be committed without an intention to kill (ie where D intends to cause GBH).

An alternative specific method of distinction, but equally flawed, was considered in *Heard*.

Heard [2007] EWCA Crim 125

Whilst drunk, D exposed his penis and rubbed it on a police officer's leg. D claimed to lack mens rea due to intoxication (ie a lack of *intentional* touching). D was charged with sexual assault.[42]

- Crown Court: guilty of sexual assault, holding that sexual assault is a basic intent offence.
- Court of Appeal: conviction upheld on appeal.

Extra detail . . .

Heard should not have been a difficult case. The fact that D did not remember his actions the following day is not a basis for claiming that he did not intend to touch V when intoxicated. There was no need to discuss the classification of sexual assault as a basic or specific intent offence because his appeal to the intoxication rules should have fallen at the first hurdle: an intoxicated mens rea is still a mens rea.

Although *Heard* should not have been a difficult case, the court took the opportunity to provide an alternative test for identifying basic and specific intent offences.

crimes of specific intent are those where the offence requires proof of purpose or consequence, which are not confined to, but amongst which are included, those where the purpose goes beyond the actus reus (sometimes referred to as cases of 'ulterior intent').

In this passage, Hughes LJ accepts Lord Simon's test in *Majewski* focusing on intention as to results (despite the problems outlined earlier), and also builds upon it with reference to

---

[38] In line with *Beard* [1920] AC 479.
[39] [1977] AC 443, 495.
[40] Offences Against the Person Act 1861.
[41] [1977] AC 443, 478–479.
[42] Sexual Offences Act 2003, s3.

ulterior mens rea.[43] For Hughes LJ, any offence which requires ulterior mens rea, even an ulterior mens rea of recklessness (eg criminal damage being reckless as to the endangerment of life[44]), will be one of specific intent.

The test provided in *Heard*, however, is even more problematic than Lord Simon's in *Majewski*. As with Lord Simon's test, Hughes LJ's test is under-inclusive. It is unable to explain why murder is a specific intent offence despite lacking a requirement of intention at to results and/or ulterior mens rea. But beyond this, and of more importance, the Hughes LJ test also seems to abandon any potential for theoretical underpinning. Although problematic, *Majewski* at least makes a broad implicit claim of moral equivalence, between (a) voluntary intoxication at T1 which is of such a degree as to cause D to fail to see risks etc and (b) recklessness at T2, which can be used to explain large parts of the case law. However, in classifying sexual assault as a basic intent offence, despite a mens rea of *intentional* touching, and by classifying recklessness-based offences like aggravated criminal damage as specific intent offences, *Heard* runs counter to the intention/recklessness distinction.

Without guidance beyond these two equally unattractive alternatives, the current law remains in a state of uncertainty. The reaction of several other common law jurisdictions has been to reject the *Majewski* distinction between specific and basic intent.[45] However, we have not yet taken that step in England and Wales.[46] Rather, in the absence of a clear test, the law has developed by categorising offences as they emerge in case law. There is a pattern, with most intention-based offences being classified as specific intent, but this is not systematic.

- **Basic intent:** Manslaughter,[47] malicious wounding or causing GBH (s20),[48] assault occasioning ABH (s47),[49] assault and battery,[50] rape,[51] sexual assault,[52] criminal damage (where only recklessness is alleged),[53] etc.

- **Specific intent:** Murder,[54] wounding or causing GBH with intent (s18),[55] theft,[56] robbery,[57] section 9(1)(a) burglary,[58] attempt to commit a specific intent offence,[59] complicity,[60] etc.

---

[43] Mens rea going beyond the actus reus of the offence: see **4.2.1.2**.
[44] Criminal Damage Act 1971, s1(2). See **9.7.5**.
[45] eg Canada in *Daviault* (1994) 118 DLR (4th) 469; Australia in *O'Connor* (1980) 146 CLR 64; New Zealand in *Kamipeli* [1975] 2 NZLR 610; South Africa in *Chretien* 1981 (1) SA 1097.
[46] See the discussion of reform at **13.6**.
[47] *Beard* [1920] AC 479.
[48] *Aitken* [1992] 1 WLR 1006.
[49] *Bolton v Crawley* [1972] Crim LR 222.
[50] *Majewski* [1977] AC 443.
[51] *Grout* [2011] EWCA Crim 299.
[52] *Heard* [2007] EWCA Crim 125.
[53] *Caldwell* [1981] 1 All ER 961.
[54] *Beard* [1920] AC 479.
[55] *Davies* [1991] Crim LR 469.
[56] *Majewski* [1977] AC 443.
[57] Ibid.
[58] *Hutchins* [1988] Crim LR 379.
[59] *Clarkson* [1971] 3 All ER 344.
[60] Ibid, although note some doubt in *Lynch* [1975] AC 653.

13.2.3.2 Dutch courage

Where an intoxicated D lacks mens rea for a specific intent offence, this is usually the end of the matter: D's intoxication cannot replace her lack of mens rea, so there is no liability for that offence.[61] However, there is one possible exception to this rule. This relates to (so-called) 'Dutch courage' cases, where D becomes intoxicated at T1 *in order to* commit the specific intent offence at T2. In such cases, D's blameworthy conduct is not merely her choice to become voluntarily intoxicated, but her choice to do so in order (ie with intention) to commit the offence. This was discussed in *AG for Northern Ireland v Gallagher*.

AG for Northern Ireland v Gallagher [1963] AC 349

D decided to kill his wife. D drank most of a bottle of whisky and then did so. D claimed that, due to his intoxication, he lacked mens rea for murder as a specific intent offence. D was charged with murder.

- Crown Court: guilty of murder.
- Northern Ireland Court of Appeal: appeal allowed. The court found that D had been wrongly convicted on the basis of his mens rea at T1, rather than focusing on T2.
- House of Lords: appeal allowed, restoring D's conviction. Contrary to the Court of Appeal, the House of Lords held that the trial court had correctly focused on D's mens rea at T2. Thus, this was simply a case where intoxicated mens rea is still mens rea.

D's conviction in this case did not require an examination of 'Dutch courage' because, despite D's intoxication, it was found that D intended to kill at the time (T2) of killing his wife. However, Lord Denning went on to say that even if the Court of Appeal's interpretation was correct (ie that D only had mens rea when becoming intoxicated at T1), it would still be correct in law to find liability, even for a specific intent offence.

> I think the law on this point should take a clear stand. If a man, whilst sane and sober, forms an intention to kill and makes preparation for it . . . and then gets himself drunk so as to give himself Dutch courage to do the killing, and whilst drunk carries out his intention, he cannot rely on this self-induced drunkenness as a defence to a charge of murder, nor even as reducing it to manslaughter . . . The wickedness of his mind before he got drunk is enough to condemn him, coupled with the act which he intended to do and did do. A psychopath who goes out intending to kill, knowing it is wrong, and does kill, cannot escape the consequences by making himself drunk before doing it.

The logic of this statement is compelling. Where D becomes intoxicated *in order to* kill whilst in that state, it seems correct that D should be liable for murder even if she lacked mens rea at the moment she caused V's death (due to her intoxication). In line with the views of Lord Denning, this can be presented as an exception to the rule that intoxication cannot replace a lack of mens rea for specific intent offences.

An alternative way of analysing these (rather unlikely) facts, is that D's conduct in becoming intoxicated is the conduct element of her offence. Under this analysis, D's

---

[61] See **Figure 13.6**. D may be liable for an alternative basic intent offence.

conduct in becoming intoxicated is akin to the shooting of a bullet or the release of a stampeding herd of cattle towards V. In each case, D is in control of the release (ie becoming intoxicated; pulling the trigger; releasing the cattle) and then loses control of the weapon before it makes contact with V (ie her involuntary body; the bullet; the cattle). Analysed in these terms, there is no issue of coincidence, as D has the mens rea for murder whilst completing the conduct element (becoming intoxicated). And there is nothing to break the chain of causation. Thus, whether we recognise an exception to the prior-fault intoxication rules or we rely on standard rules of liability, D is guilty of murder.[62]

13.2.4 Element 3: D must have taken a dangerous drug

Having satisfied the first two elements of the prior-fault intoxication rules, we can say that D has made a choice at T1 (through *voluntary* intoxication) that has led to the potential commission of a relevant offence at T2 (a *basic* intent offence). However, to say that V has voluntarily taken an intoxicating substance at T1 is not yet to say that V has acted in a blameworthy manner. Rather, before we can claim any potential equivalence between D's fault at T1 and her missing mens rea at T2, we need to look at the detail of her choice. Was D's choice at T1 a blameworthy choice; did D voluntarily take a *dangerous* drug?[63]

A drug is legally classified as 'dangerous', in this context, where it is commonly known in society, or personally known to D, to cause unpredictability and/or aggression. Alcohol is a clear example where such effects are commonly known, and as established in *Lipman*,[64] other drugs such as LSD will come within the same category. Voluntary intoxication with a dangerous drug provides the blameworthy choice necessary at T1 to construct liability at T2.

Where the intoxicant consumed by D at T1 is *not* commonly known to have effects of this kind, and it is not known to D personally (eg from previous use), D's prior fault in her voluntary consumption of that drug will *not* be a sufficient substitute for the mens rea of the basic intent offence at T2. This was recognised in *Bailey*,[65] where D (a diabetic) failed to take sufficient food after insulin and committed a series of serious attacks whilst in an intoxicated state.

> It is common knowledge that those who take alcohol to excess or certain sorts of drugs may become aggressive or do dangerous or unpredictable things, they may be able to foresee the risks of causing harm to others but nevertheless persist in their conduct. But the same cannot be said without more of a man who fails to take food after an insulin injection.[66]

The same reasoning was later applied in *Hardie*.

---

[62] Child, 'Prior Fault: Blocking Defences or Constructing Crimes' in Reed and Bohlander (eds), *General Defences* (2014).

[63] See discussion in Loughnan and Wake, 'Of Blurred Boundaries and Prior Fault: Insanity, Automatism and Intoxication' in Reed and Bohlander (eds), *General Defences in Criminal Law* (2014) 113, Part 4.

[64] [1970] 1 QB 152.

[65] [1983] 1 WLR 760.

[66] Griffiths LJ at 764–765.

Hardie [1985] 1 WLR 64

D took five valium tablets (a sedative drug) to calm himself after being told to leave the house by his partner. D returned, intoxicated by the tablets, and set fire to a wardrobe in the house. D was charged with arson with intention or recklessness as to the endangerment of life.

- Crown Court: guilty of arson. D's lack of mens rea (due to intoxication) was replaced by his voluntary intoxication.
- Court of Appeal: appeal allowed. Valium was not a dangerous drug, and D had no reason to believe it would lead to the actions it caused.

Where the intoxicant is non-dangerous in the sense that it is not commonly known to be dangerous and not personally known to be dangerous by D, even where it results in potentially criminal harms, there will be no liability. This is illustrated in **Figure 13.7**.

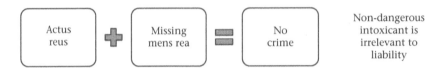

Figure 13.7 Intoxication with a non-dangerous intoxicant

It is only where D has *voluntarily* taken a *dangerous* intoxicant that we have a blameworthy choice at T1.

13.2.5 Element 4: D must have lacked mens rea *because* of intoxication

Having established that D was voluntarily intoxicated by a dangerous drug at T1, and that she lacked mens rea for the basic intent offence at T2, the final stage of the prior-fault intoxication rules looks for a nexus to connect the two. In short, D's prior fault by voluntary intoxication at T1 will only be sufficient substitute for her lack of mens rea at T2, creating liability, if her intoxication was the reason she lacked that mens rea. For example, D becomes voluntarily intoxicated with a dangerous drug at T1, and later trips on a hidden tripwire and smashes V's vase in the fall at T2 (basic intent offence of criminal damage). In this case, it would be inappropriate to use D's voluntary dangerous intoxication to substitute for a lack of mens rea in criminal damage. Even if D was sober, she would have done the same thing (ie her blameworthiness at T1 has not affected her conduct at T2).

This point was at issue in *Richardson and Irwin*.

 Richardson and Irwin [1999] 1 Cr App R 392

D and others (university students) picked up V whilst heavily intoxicated and dropped him over a balcony. D fell 10–12 feet, and was injured. D claimed that he did not foresee the potential for injury, because of his intoxication. D was charged with maliciously inflicting GBH (basic intent offence).[67]

- Crown Court: guilty of section 20 offence.

---

[67] Offences Against the Person Act 1861, s20.

> • Court of Appeal: appeal allowed. D was convicted because a *reasonable* sober person would have foreseen the risk of injury (satisfying the mens rea of s20). However, the correct question was whether *D* would have foreseen the risk of injury if sober.

In some cases, as with *Richardson and Irwin*, it may be difficult to predict what D (as opposed to a reasonable person) would have foreseen if sober. This is a question for the jury.

13.2.6 Intoxication and defences

Just as D's voluntary intoxication can create liability where she lacks mens rea, it can also affect her use of various defences. This does not mean that defences become entirely unavailable: an intoxicated person may still have good reason to act in self-defence, for example. Problems arise, however, where D makes a mistake due to intoxication. For instance, where D assaults V with the intoxicated belief that she is acting in self-defence, where in fact no defensive force was necessary.

The general rule is that D may not use a defence where, in order to satisfy the elements of that defence, she is forced to rely on an intoxicated mistake. The defence of self-defence,[68] for example, typically applies where D believes that force is required to protect herself or property, and where the amount of force used is objectively reasonable. If sober, D's belief in the necessity for force does not need to be correct, or even reasonable, as long as it is honestly held.[69] However, as stated in *Hatton*, D's belief will be disregarded if it is based on an intoxicated mistake.[70]

 Hatton [2005] EWCA Crim 2951

Heavily intoxicated, having drunk more than 20 pints of beer, D killed V with several blows of a sledgehammer. D raised self-defence on the grounds that he thought V (who had told D that he was an SAS officer) had attacked him with a stick that he thought was a samurai sword. D was charged with murder.

• Crown Court: guilty of murder. The court did not allow D to rely on his intoxicated mistake as a basis for self-defence.

• Court of Appeal: conviction upheld on appeal. The lower court was correct not to allow D to rely on his intoxicated mistake.

The decision in *Hatton*, and the policy it follows, have been subject to criticism.[71] It seems strange, for example, that although other unreasonable beliefs can ground self-defence, an intoxicated mistake is singled out for special treatment. However, it is a public policy decision (reflecting a general concern about intoxicated offenders) that has been endorsed by subsequent legislation,[72] as well as by the Law Commission.[73]

---

[68] **Chapter 14.**
[69] *Gladstone Williams* [1987] 3 All ER 411.
[70] Following *O'Connor* [1991] Crim LR 135, and *O'Grady* [1987] QB 995.
[71] Dingwall, 'Intoxicated Mistakes About the Need for Self-Defence' (2007) 70 MLR 127; Spencer, 'Drunken Defence' (2006) 65 CLJ 267.
[72] Criminal Justice and Immigration Act 2008, s76(5).
[73] Law Commission, *Intoxication and Criminal Liability* (No 314, 2009) para 3.53.

The only exception to this rule has arisen in the context of criminal damage, where D raises the specific statutory defence that she believed the owner was consenting or would have consented to the damage.[74] As shown in *Jaggard v Dickinson*, here at least D *is* able to rely on her intoxicated mistake.[75]

 Jaggard v Dickinson [1981] QB 527

D was told by X, a friend, to use his house as her own. Returning home drunk, D mistakenly tried to enter an identical house on the same street, and when her way was blocked by the owner she gained access by breaking windows. D was charged with criminal damage, and raised the defence that she believed (at the time) that the house belonged to X, and he would have consented to the damage if he had known the circumstances.

- Crown Court: guilty of criminal damage. D may not rely on an intoxicated mistake.
- Divisional Court: appeal allowed. D may use the defence, even if her belief is based on an intoxicated mistake.

This decision is anomalous, and cannot be reconciled with the general rule discussed previously. As a result, although not yet fully reversed, the precedent in *Jaggard v Dickinson* has been limited by subsequent cases. In *Maghee*,[76] for example, D attempted to rely on the rule from *Jaggard* to appeal a conviction for failing to stop after an accident:[77] D claimed his intoxicated state meant he did not realise there had been a collision. The Divisional Court dismissed Maghee's appeal, questioning the continued validity of *Jaggard*, and ruling that D could not rely on his intoxicated mistake.

Assessment matters . . .
If something similar to *Jaggard v Dickinson* were to arise in problem facts, it is important to remember that this case remains authoritative. However, it would be correct to stress the criticism of this case as anomalous and, following *Maghee*, that it is unlikely to be applied outside criminal damage.

13.3 Sane automatism

The 'defence' of sane automatism,[78] as it is commonly referred to, is structured in broadly the same way as the intoxication rules.[79] Where D raises sane automatism, she is making the claim that some external factor affected her body at T1 and caused her to lack voluntariness at T2. For example, 'I drove dangerously, but only because I had just been struck by a flying object'; 'I omitted to feed my child because I was knocked unconscious'; 'I struck out at the paramedic causing injury because I was suffering the effects of having taken insulin and not having eaten'. As we discussed at **3.3**, all criminal offences require

---

[74] Criminal Damage Act 1971, s5(2).
[75] Williams, 'Two Nocturnal Blunders' (1990) 140 NLJ 1564.
[76] [2014] EWHC 4089 (Admin).
[77] Road Traffic Act 1988, s170(4).
[78] Law Commission, *Insanity and Automatism* (Discussion Paper, 2013).
[79] Child and Reed, 'Automatism is Never a Defence' (2014) 65 NILQ 167.

voluntary conduct (actions or omission). Thus, D's claim of involuntariness at T2 is a claim that she did not commit an offence, resulting in an unqualified acquittal.

The automatism rules, however, are not simply a shorthand for expressing a lack of voluntary conduct. This is because, even where D successfully denies offending in this way, it is possible for D to be held liable on the basis of her prior fault in becoming an automaton. As with intoxication, we are again dealing with a two-part set of rules: providing a shorthand for D's claim to lack voluntariness, and providing a possible tool of inculpation for the prosecution.

Despite similarities with the intoxication rules, there are three major differences that should be highlighted from the outset. First, the automatism rules will not apply where D's state of automatism is caused by a dangerous drug (as defined within the intoxication rules). Here, only the prior-fault intoxication rules will apply.[80] Secondly, automatism will *only* apply where D loses voluntary control of her conduct. If something external causes D to lack mens rea, but not to lack voluntariness, then the automatism rules will not apply. Thus, automatism arises in far fewer cases than the prior-fault intoxication rules, which apply whenever D's intoxication causes *any* lack of mens rea. Thirdly, as automatism lacks the commonly understood link to violence associated with intoxication, the potential of prior fault and inculpation is considerably more limited.

13.3.1 Automatism as a denial of offending

Before we discuss the potential for prior-fault inculpation, it is necessary first to understand how and when a claim of automatism will be successful in denying an offence. Automatism, in this context, is a shorthand for the claim that D *totally* lacked voluntary control of her conduct at the time of her potential offence, and should therefore be acquitted. Where D acts voluntarily, even if her conduct has been influenced by external factors, automatism will not be found.[81] Just as 'an intoxicated mens rea is still mens rea', so irrational or erratic voluntariness is still voluntariness.[82]

> **Extra detail . . .**
> Although there is a general burden on the prosecution to prove that D completed the elements of the offence charged, there is a legal presumption that a person's movements are voluntary. This creates an evidential burden for D, if she wants to raise automatism, to provide some evidence of involuntariness. After she satisfies this evidential burden, it is then for the prosecution to prove to the criminal standard that her acts were voluntary.[83]

The clearest cases of sane automatism will involve D being rendered fully unconscious at T1, as with our dangerous driving example earlier. Where D is fully unconscious, it is clear that she lacks any voluntary control of her body, and so any harm her body causes cannot be the product of voluntary movement.

However, sane automatism is not limited to states of unconsciousness. Indeed, there are several clear examples of conscious automatic behaviour. For example, where X

---

[80] Mackay, 'Intoxication as a Factor in Automatism' [1982] Crim LR 146.
[81] *AG's Reference (No 4 of 2000)* [2001] Crim LR 578: accidental, but not automatic, conduct.
[82] *Coley* [2013] EWCA Crim 223, [22].
[83] Jones, 'Insanity, Automatism and the Burden of Proof on the Accused' (1995) 111 LQR 475.

overpowers D and physically manipulates her body to complete certain movements (eg to plunge a knife into V); where D's body spasms uncontrollably (eg causing her to strike V); where D reacts to a sudden noise (eg causing her to drop another's property); where D thrashes her arms in response to an attack by a swarm of bees (eg causing her to drive dangerously);[84] and so on. In each of these cases, even though D is conscious, she is not in control of her actions. As Lord Denning describes in *Bratty*:

> No act is punishable if it is done involuntarily: and an involuntary act in this context—some people nowadays prefer to speak of it as 'automatism'—means an act which is done by the muscles without any control by the mind, such as a spasm, a reflex action or a convulsion.[85]

Having accepted that conscious behaviour can satisfy automatism, however, the challenge is then to identify the line between automatism on the one hand, and non-automatic conduct brought about by external factors on the other hand. If the former is found, an essential element of liability will be undermined.

Automatism, particularly where it arises in driving offences, has been defined very narrowly. This is illustrated in *Broome v Perkins*.

 Broome v Perkins [1987] Crim LR 271

A diabetic (D) failed to take sufficient food after an injection of insulin, and slipped into a hypoglycaemic episode.[86] Whilst in this trance-like state, he drove erratically and collided with another car. D was charged with driving without due care and attention.[87]

- Magistrates' court: not guilty of driving offence due to automatism.
- Divisional Court: appeal (by way of case stated) allowed. The fact that D was able to coordinate his movements to drive, even though severely impeded, meant that he could not have been in a fully automatic state.

This extremely narrow definition of automatism was later confirmed in *AG's Reference (No 2 of 1992)*,[88] where a lorry driver was charged with causing death by reckless driving having suffered a condition known as 'driving without awareness' as a result of long hours on the road. Following D's acquittal on grounds of automatism, the Court of Appeal held that automatism should not have been left to the jury, and that only a 'total destruction of voluntary control' would suffice.

It was once believed that these decisions reflected policy considerations unique to driving offences (ie a reaction to the commonality of people driving when tired or otherwise

---

[84] Example from *Hill and Baxter* [1958] 1 QB 277, 286.

[85] [1963] AC 386, 409.

[86] Diabetes can lead to involuntariness in two main ways: (a) *hypo*glycaemia—this results from taking insulin (an external cause) and then failing to eat sufficiently; (b) *hyper*glycaemia—this results from failing to take insulin (and so the diabetes acts as an internal cause). As we discuss later, the distinction between these two is vital. This is because although hypoglycaemia causing involuntariness will be treated as a standard form of sane automatism (now under discussion), hyperglycaemia causing involuntariness (because of its internal cause) will be dealt with under the insanity rules.

[87] Road Traffic Act 1988, s3.

[88] [1994] Crim LR 692.

impaired).[89] This view was supported, to some extent, by non-driving cases such as *Charlson*,[90] where a broader view of automatism seems to have been employed: D's cerebral tumour caused him to act as an 'automaton without any *real knowledge* of what he was doing'.[91] However, a number of more recent cases have reasserted the narrow view of automatism for both driving[92] and non-driving cases.[93] In *Coley*,[94] a non-driving case in which doctors agreed that D would not have been conscious of his movements, the Court of Appeal has asserted a particularly restrictive approach:

> [D] was plainly not unconscious, in the sense of comatose. But automatism does not require that, and if it did it would be even more exceptional than it undoubtedly is. On the other hand, his mind may well, if the doctors were right, have been affected by delusions or hallucinations and in that sense his detachment from reality might be described by some as an absence of conscious action. Such condition, however, clearly falls short of involuntary, as distinct from irrational, action. . . . [T]he defendant would, despite their hypothesis of psychotic episode, have been capable of complex organised behaviour. It is plain that a person acting under a delusion may act in such a way, and clearly this defendant did. . . . The doctor said 'He is conscious in a way but it is conscious in the belief that he is a character [in a computer game]. He does not have an awareness of what he is doing.' That is a description of irrational behaviour, with a deluded or disordered mind, but it is not a description of wholly involuntary action.

If automatism is interpreted in line with this statement, it will rarely (if ever) apply outside the context of unconsciousness or physical manipulation.

Coley makes the law easier to apply (ie it creates a clear line between sane automatism and voluntariness), but raises serious questions of fairness. When discussing the voluntariness requirement at **3.3**, we explain the importance of a conscious link between D and the harmful or wrongful events attributed to her; an essential ingredient in the law's respect for individual autonomy. In the circumstances discussed in *Coley*, where D's brain is guiding movement, but that guide is not conscious or rational, it is questionable whether there is a sufficient nexus through which to blame D in criminal law for any harm caused. The current narrow view of sane automatism has therefore attracted considerable academic criticism.[95]

In view of this narrow approach, it will be little surprise that claims of *moral* involuntariness have been consistently rejected as a basis for automatism. We may feel some moral sympathy for D who commits an offence because of an 'irresistible impulse', 'hysterical amnesia', 'hysterical fugue', or where she is unaware of a legal restriction. But D is not treated as acting in an automatic manner in a legal sense.[96] Where D steals alcohol because of an irresistible craving for drink, she still commits theft;[97] where D is provoked

---

[89] Simester et al, *Simester and Sullivan's Criminal Law: Theory and Doctrine* (6th edn, 2016) 119.
[90] [1955] 1 All ER 859.
[91] Emphasis added.
[92] *C* [2007] EWCA Crim 1862.
[93] Law Commission, *Insanity and Automatism* (Discussion Paper, 2013) paras 5.24–5.31.
[94] [2013] EWCA Crim 223, [23].
[95] Horder, 'Pleading Involuntary Lack of Capacity' (1993) 52 CLJ 298; Sullivan, 'Making Excuses' in Simester and Smith (eds), *Harm and Culpability* (1996) 131.
[96] *Isitt* [1978] Crim LR 159.
[97] *Dodd* (1974) 7 SASR 151; Tolmie, 'Alcoholism and Criminal Liability' (2001) 64 MLR 688.

481

to attack V, this is still an assault. These circumstances will be considered as relevant mitigation at sentencing, but they do not affect the liability stage.[98]

To summarise, where D's conduct is fully involuntary at T2 due to an external factor at T1, as long as the intoxication rules do not apply and there is an absence of other prior fault, she will not be guilty of an offence at T2. This is illustrated in **Figure 13.8**.

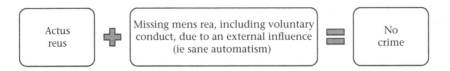

Figure 13.8 Automatism as a denial of offending

> *Terminology . . .*
> It is worth noting again that many commentators prefer to describe 'voluntary conduct' as an actus reus element, such that automatism amounts to a denial of actus reus and mens rea. In this book, we prefer to separate conduct (actus reus) from the issue of voluntariness (mens rea), and so automatism does not involve a denial of actus reus. The difference does not affect how the law is applied, but should be noted to avoid confusion when reading other sources.

Where D's conduct is affected by external stimuli but her movements remain voluntary, there is no automatism. As discussed previously, the narrow interpretation of automatism makes this scenario increasingly likely. This is illustrated in **Figure 13.9**.

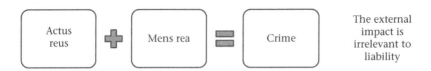

Figure 13.9 External impact not causing automatism

13.3.2 Prior-fault automatism as a method of inculpation

In many cases involving automatism there is no issue of prior fault. Therefore, automatism, if demonstrated, acts only as a denial of the offence, leading to acquittal. However, where D's automatism at T2 has arisen from her blameworthy conduct at T1 (her prior fault), missing offence elements at T2 can be substituted for by this fault. This requires us to examine the rules of prior-fault automatism. Three sets of facts must be distinguished.

- D is a sane automaton (ie suffers a total loss of control at the time of T2 owing to some external factor at T1) and the cause of the automatism is some involuntary external factor (a swarm of bees, someone knocking D unconscious by a blow to the head, etc). No liability.

[98] The only exceptions to this are extreme cases which engage defences such as duress (discussed in **Chapter 14**) or loss of control as a partial defence to murder (discussed in **Chapter 6**).

- D is a sane automaton at T2 when committing the actus reus of an offence. Her state of automatism has been caused by her prior fault at T1. However, her potential offence is one of specific intent, as defined in relation to the prior-fault intoxication rules earlier. No liability.

- D is a sane automaton at T2 when committing the actus reus of an offence. Her state of automatism has been caused by her prior fault at T1. Her potential offence is one of basic intent, as defined in relation to the prior-fault intoxication rules earlier, and so her prior fault is used to substitute for the missing offence elements. In this context, the automatism rules do not work as a defence, but as a method of inculpation.[99] Liability will be found.

Table 13.2 sets out the elements of the prior-fault automatism rules.

Table 13.2 Prior-fault automatism rules

A) D committed the actus reus of an offence at T2, but did so in a state of automatism;
B) D's automatism resulted from D's prior fault at T1; and
C) D's automatism must have caused the lack of offence elements for a basic intent offence

We discuss each element further in the following sections.

> **Don't be confused . . .**
> As with the prior-fault intoxication rules, the inculpatory work of the automatism rules is most commonly described by courts and commentators as a defence (see **13.1.1**). For example, in *Coley*,[100] Hughes LJ states that 'the defence of automatism is not available to a defendant who has induced an acute state of involuntary behaviour by his own fault'. We avoid this terminology because it is misleading: saying that D cannot raise the issue of automatism does not make her conduct voluntary or mean that she had mens rea. Rather, as we describe the same phenomenon, the automatism rules are replacing a lack of voluntariness and other mens rea with (what the law considers) equivalent prior fault. The rules are not denying a defence, they are constructing a crime.[101]

13.3.2.1 Element 1: D was in a state of automatism at T2

We discussed this requirement at **13.3.1**. It is important to remember that for the prior-fault automatism rules to apply, D must be in a state of automatism when completing the actus reus of the offence at T2. The narrow conception of automatism within the current law also therefore narrows the potential for prior-fault inculpation.

---

[99] Child and Reed, 'Automatism is Never a Defence' (2014) 65 NILQ 167.
[100] [2013] EWCA Crim 244, [24].
[101] Child and Reed, 'Automatism is Never a Defence' (2014) 65 NILQ 167.

13.3.2.2 Element 2: D acted with prior fault at T1

For the prior-fault intoxication rules, the issue of prior fault at T1 (ie when becoming intoxicated) was relatively straightforward to establish because of the commonly understood link between intoxication and certain crimes. Thus, where D voluntarily becomes intoxicated with a dangerous drug (one commonly known to create states of unpredictability), we may attribute prior fault. For automatism, in contrast, there is no equivalent common understanding (and no link in fact) between a lack of voluntariness and the causing of criminal harms.[102] Therefore, more must be required at T1 to establish sufficient prior fault that might later substitute for missing offence elements.[103]

The law in this area, however, is unfortunately vague and inconsistent. On the one hand, cases such as *Bailey*[104] suggest that D will only have sufficient prior fault where she has *subjectively* foreseen at T1 the potential for involuntariness at T2. This would be the case, for example, where D decides to drive foreseeing the chance of an (insulin-induced) hypoglycaemic episode, and foreseeing the chance that this might lead to unconsciousness whilst at the wheel. This approach is endorsed by the Law Commission,[105] and seems to be the most appropriate if D's fault is going to be used to construct liability at T2.[106] On the other hand, cases such as *Quick*[107] state that D will have sufficient fault if she *objectively* should have foreseen such risks. Thus, where D is negligent in the management of her diabetes before driving (eg fails to eat sufficiently after a dose of insulin), then this negligence will constitute sufficient prior fault even where she does not subjectively foresee the risk of hypoglycaemia herself. The Australian case of *Ryan*[108] provides a further example of the objective approach. In this case, D pointed a loaded shotgun at V (whom he had robbed) with one hand, whilst attempting to tie him up with the other. V moved, startled D, and D (according to his account) involuntarily pulled the trigger as a reflex. On Windeyer J's view, D remained liable because of the obvious danger created by his actions at T1, even if D did not subjectively foresee the risk of the involuntary reflex which followed.

> **Assessment matters . . .**
> Where there is inconsistent case law of this kind, you need to take particular care when applying it to problem facts. Do not just choose certain cases and ignore others. Rather, where D subjectively foresees a risk of involuntariness in dangerous circumstances then you can be sure that this is sufficient prior fault. Where D does not foresee the risk, but was potentially negligent in not doing so, you should highlight cases such as *Quick* and *Ryan* that suggest that this too might be sufficient, but also, ideally, note the academic criticism.

---

[102] *Bailey* [1983] 2 All ER 503, 764–765. For academic discussion of this, see Horder, 'Sobering Up? The Law Commission on Criminal Intoxication' (1995) 58 MLR 534, 544–555.

[103] Law Commission, *Insanity and Automatism* (Discussion Paper, 2013) Ch6.

[104] [1983] 2 All ER 503.

[105] Law Commission, *Insanity and Automatism* (Discussion Paper, 2013) paras 6.12–6.28.

[106] Rumbold and Wasik, 'Diabetic Drivers, Hypoglycaemic Unawareness and Automatism' [2011] Crim LR 863.

[107] [1973] QB 910.

[108] (1967) 40 ALJR 488; Elliott, 'Responsibility for Involuntary Acts: *Ryan v The Queen*' (1968) 41 ALJ 497.

13.3.2.3 Element 3: D's prior fault caused automatism at T2 for a basic intent offence

Having established prior fault from D at T1 (when losing voluntary control), our next question is to consider whether the law is prepared to treat that prior fault as sufficient to replace or substitute for the missing elements of the offence at T2 (when D commits the potential offence). Clearly, D's prior fault at T1 must be capable of replacing a lack of voluntary conduct at T2: as all cases of automatism include a lack of voluntariness, the ability to substitute for this missing element is essential for automatism to perform any inculpatory role at all. This has been consistently confirmed in all the case law involving prior fault and automatism.[109]

But what about other mens rea elements beyond voluntary conduct? Where D is effectively or in fact unconscious, she is unlikely to possess any mens rea as to any aspect of the harm she causes at T2. If the automatism rules are *only* able to substitute prior fault at T1 for a lack of voluntary conduct at T2, then they could only produce liability in the context of strict/absolute liability offences (ie offences that require no mens rea beyond voluntariness). But we know from the case law that prior fault is used as a substitute for liability for offences beyond this, most commonly for driving offences that often require mens rea as to the dangerous circumstances of D's driving.

Perhaps the most obvious question, in view of the prior-fault intoxication rules, is whether prior-fault automatism also makes a distinction between basic and specific intent offences (ie that D's prior fault can replace a lack of mens rea for a basic intent offence but not for a specific intent offence).[110] The early case law on prior fault and automatism did not recognise a basic/specific intent distinction; implying a very broad potential for the substitution of missing mens rea elements.[111] However, this position was later clarified, to some extent, in *Bailey*:[112] a case involving the specific intent offence of wounding or causing GBH with intent.[113] The court highlighted that *Quick* should not be interpreted to allow prior-fault automatism to substitute for missing mens rea elements in crimes of specific intent. Unfortunately, following this useful clarification, the court then went further to cast doubt on its ability to substitute for similar elements in crimes of basic intent as well.

> In our judgment, self-induced automatism, other than that due to intoxication from alcohol or drugs, may provide a defence to crimes of basic intent. The question in each case will be whether the prosecution have proved the necessary element of recklessness. In cases of assault, if the accused knows that his actions or inaction are likely to make him aggressive, unpredictable or uncontrolled with the result that he may cause some injury to others and he persists in the action or takes no remedial action when he knows it is required, it will be open to the jury to find that he was reckless.[114]

---

[109] Although, as we noted at **13.3.2** ('Don't be confused . . . '), the phenomenon will generally be described as the denial of a defence.

[110] See discussion at **13.2.3** in the context of intoxication.

[111] *Quick* [1972] QB 910: 'A self-induced incapacity will not excuse . . . nor will one which could have been reasonably foreseen as a result of either doing, or omitting to do something, as, for example, taking alcohol against medical advice after using certain prescribed drugs, or failing to have regular meals while taking insulin' (at 922). Criticised in Mackay, 'Intoxication as a Factor in Automatism' [1982] Crim LR 146.

[112] [1983] 2 All ER 503.

[113] Offences Against the Person Act 1861, s18.

[114] *Bailey* [1983] 1 WLR 760, 765 (Griffiths LJ).

In view of this confused position, it is likely (and hoped) that the courts will take a lead from the Law Commission Discussion Paper on automatism and insanity.[115] For the Commission, despite reservations as to the specific/basic intent distinction, there is a useful recognition that prior fault for automatism should be consistent with prior fault for intoxication. Thus, contrary to *Bailey*, D's conduct in voluntarily rendering herself an automaton should be capable of serving as a sufficient substitute fault for a lack of mens rea of basic intent offences. D's conduct in voluntarily rendering herself automaton should *not* be capable of serving as a sufficient substitute fault for a lack of mens rea of specific intent offences.[116] This is illustrated in **Figure 13.10**.

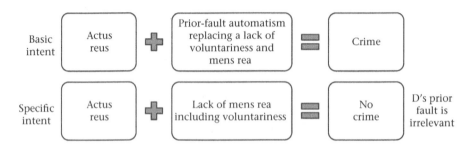

Figure 13.10 Prior-fault automatism

13.3.3 Automatism and defences

In cases where D successfully raises automatism in the absence of prior fault, she has not committed an offence, and so there is no need to consider potential defences. However, where she does so in circumstances of prior fault, and the offence is one of basic intent, she will be liable even though she was an automaton unless there is some other defence available to her.

In such cases, we do not focus on D's behaviour at T2: D's involuntariness is incompatible with the elements of criminal defences (discussed in **Chapter 14**). Instead, our focus is on D's behaviour at T1, asking whether she rendered herself incapable of voluntary action in circumstances that give rise to a defence (eg where D was threatened, was under duress, to drive even though she foresaw the chance of losing consciousness). In such circumstances, D's defence will undermine any finding of prior fault, and thereby undermine any construction of liability at T2.

13.4 Insanity as a denial of mens rea

The final category of denial of offences discussed in this chapter relates to the rules of insanity.[117] This will arise where D claims not to have fulfilled all the elements of the

---

[115] Law Commission, *Insanity and Automatism* (Discussion Paper, 2013).
[116] This is the necessary implication from the flowchart at p 95, and para 6.77.
[117] Law Commission, *Insanity and Automatism* (Discussion Paper, 2013).

offence because of some malfunctioning of her body—an *internal* factor (eg where D's insane delusions prevent her from appreciating that the thing she is stabbing is a person). This analysis of the insanity rules should be distinguished from two other related discussions elsewhere in this book,

- **Unfitness to plead:** This arises where D is mentally and/or physically unfit to stand trial, and was discussed at **1.5.3**. In contrast, the rules of insanity discussed in this chapter relate to insanity at the time of the potential offence in circumstances where D is now able to stand trial.
- **Insanity as a defence:** This arises where D *has* completed the actus reus and mens rea of an offence, and raises insanity as a way to avoid liability. This is discussed in **Chapter 14**. In contrast, the rules of insanity discussed in this chapter relate to a claim that D's insanity meant that she did not complete an offence.

> **Don't be confused . . .**
> Insanity as a defence, and insanity as a denial of offending, are often discussed together. This is because the same rules will apply to the application of insanity in either context. We separate them here (between **Chapters 13** and **14**), not to suggest that different rules apply, but to reflect the different role played by the insanity rules in the two different contexts.

As with intoxication and automatism, where D raises insanity to deny the mens rea it is not useful, although entirely commonplace, to refer to this as a defence. In this context, D raises insanity to explain her lack of mens rea (potentially, but not necessarily, including a lack of voluntariness), attempting to avoid liability for any offence.[118]

> **Extra detail . . .**
> We have seen earlier that one of the reasons the language of defences is employed has been because of the use of reverse burdens, and insanity is no different. Just as the law presumes that D is sober and in control of her conduct, so the law also presumes that D is sane. Indeed, the presumption of sanity is much stronger. Presumptions of sobriety and voluntariness only create evidential burdens on D, whereas the presumption of sanity creates a legal burden such that D must (on the balance of probabilities) prove that she was insane at the time of the offence.[119] This is extremely controversial, and the Law Commission has considered a reverse evidential burden for insanity instead.[120] Where D is claiming not to have committed the offence, it is one thing to require evidence to rebut a presumption of common behaviour, but quite another to ask D to prove her innocence![121] But this is what the current law requires.

Where insanity arises as a denial of mens rea, and D succeeds in proving that to the civil standard, the verdict will be one of 'not guilty by reason of insanity'. Where the insanity rules are satisfied, even where this involves a denial of offence elements, and even where

---

[118] It was held in *DPP v Harper* [1998] RTR 200 that the insanity rules do not apply to strict liability offences, the court reasoning that insanity amounted to a denial of mens rea and strict liability offences do not require mens rea. However, commentators agree that this decision must be wrong. First, insanity can also involve a denial of voluntary movement, which is required for strict liability offences and, secondly, because (as we discuss in **Chapter 14**) insanity can act as a defence as well as a simple denial of offending.

[119] *M'Naghten* (1843) 10 Cl & Fin 200, 210, confirmed in *Bratty* [1963] AC 386.

[120] Law Commission, *Insanity and Automatism* (Discussion Paper, 2013) para 4.163.

[121] Jones, 'Insanity, Automatism, and the Burden of Proof on the Accused' (1995) 111 LQR 475.

there is no prior fault at issue, D will be denied an unqualified acquittal. Rather, the verdict of 'not guilty by reason of insanity' is a technical acquittal which still allows the court to impose a range of compulsory orders (eg hospitalisation, supervision).[122] We discuss this further at **13.4.1**. The inculpatory status of the special verdict is acknowledged by the fact that D (uniquely) can appeal if found not guilty on this basis.[123]

The special verdict, and the disposal options which follow, mark the insanity rules out from other denials of offending which may result in an unqualified acquittal. This is not to say that D who lacks mens rea due to insanity is blameworthy; she has not committed the offence, and is rightly acquitted. However, the rationale of the insanity rules is that where D lacks mens rea as a result of insanity, as opposed to an external influence, then D's condition is more likely to reoccur and so the special verdict is required to ensure that the public are protected.[124] How effectively the current insanity rules achieve this rationale can be criticised, and is discussed later. But at this point it is important to highlight the unique status of the insanity rules as far as defendants are concerned. Faced with the uncertain outcome of the special verdict, as well as the stigma of the insanity label, defendants will generally attempt to deny liability without engaging the insanity rules. Indeed, where they are engaged, many will prefer to plead guilty.

Judge and jury . . .

Owing to its inculpatory effects, defendants will rarely try to raise insanity directly. Rather, it is the judge's role to identify whether D's denial of offence elements amounts to a denial based on insanity.[125] Where this is the case, the judge will then inform D, who will choose whether to proceed with a claim of insanity or to change her plea to guilty.

The leading case on insanity is *Sullivan*.

 Sullivan [1984] 1 AC 156

Whilst visiting an 80-year-old friend (V), D had an epileptic seizure during which he kicked V in the head and caused GBH. D was charged with GBH offences.[126]

- Crown Court: guilty of ABH offence.[127] D attempted to rely on automatism, but the court ruled that his condition amounted to insanity. On this basis, to avoid the insanity rules, D pleaded guilty to ABH.
- Court of Appeal: conviction upheld on appeal.
- House of Lords: appeal dismissed.

Sullivan is unfortunately a typical application of a set of rules which, as we will see, are not fit for purpose. A seemingly blameless man would rather plead guilty than be treated under a set of rules designed to acknowledge and protect those not deserving of blame. We offer a critique of these rules in the following sections.

---

[122] See **13.4.1**.
[123] Criminal Appeals Act 1968, s12.
[124] *Sullivan* [1984] AC 156, 172.
[125] *Roach* [2001] EWCA Crim 2698.
[126] Offences Against the Person Act 1861, s18 and s20. See **7.5** and **7.6**.
[127] Offences Against the Person Act 1861, s47. See **7.4**.

13.4.1 The special verdict of 'not guilty by reason of insanity'

Where D satisfies the insanity rules (**13.4.2**) she will be acquitted, but the verdict will be 'not guilty by reason of insanity'.[128] The judge will then choose from a range of disposal orders appropriate to D's case.

> **Terminology . . .**
> Although disposal orders can be compulsory, this is not a matter of sentencing. D has been acquitted, and so the terminology of 'disposal' is important.

Before 1991, those found not guilty by reason of insanity (as well as those unfit to plead) had to be ordered to be detained indefinitely in a hospital. Fortunately, with the exception of cases involving murder,[129] this is no longer the case. Disposal is now governed by section 5 of the Criminal Procedure (Insanity and Unfitness to Plead) Act 1991.[130] Under this Act, the judge is provided with three disposal options:

(a) a hospital order (with or without a restriction order);

(b) a supervision order; and

(c) an order for an absolute discharge.

Although the insanity plea remains underused in the courts, there is evidence that the rationalisation of disposal orders has begun to correct this.[131]

A second reason for underuse, which has not been addressed in legislation, is the enduring label 'insanity'. Insanity can be a stigmatising term for those with severe mental conditions but, as will be clear from *Sullivan* (and expanded later), the insanity rules apply well beyond those within this group. When so much progress has been made regarding public attitudes to mental illness more generally, it is staggering that the criminal law retains a label of this kind. The Law Commission has considered whether the special verdict should be amended, holding D 'not criminally responsible by reason of a recognised medical condition'.[132] The sooner the law is amended in these terms, the better.

13.4.2 Elements of legal insanity

The rationale of the insanity rules, as a denial of mens rea, is essentially forward- looking: D has not committed an offence, and this must be acknowledged with an acquittal, but D has revealed herself as someone who could pose a danger to the public in the future and so may warrant compulsory treatment and/or supervision. Despite some unease about the compulsory treatment of those who have not committed an offence, most commentators accept the public need for a set of rules of this kind.[133] For example,

---

[128] Trial of Lunatics Act 1883, s2.

[129] In this case, a fixed hospital order is mandated: Criminal Procedure Act 1991, s5(3).

[130] As amended by the Domestic Violence, Crime and Victims Act 2004.

[131] Mackay and Kearns, 'The Continued Under Use of Unfitness to Plead and the Insanity Defence' [1994] Crim LR 546; Mackay, Mitchell, and Howe, 'Yet More Facts About the Insanity Defence' [2006] Crim LR 399.

[132] Law Commission, *Insanity and Automatism* (Discussion Paper, 2013) para 10.15.

[133] For a contrary view, see Slobogin, 'An End to Insanity: Recasting the Role of Mental Illness in Criminal Cases' (2000) 86 Vir LR 1199.

489

in *Bratty*,[134] D removed a girl's stockings and strangled her with them, in circumstances where (according to medical evidence) his psychomotor epilepsy could have prevented him understanding his actions. Were this to have been the case, D might have been acquitted, but it is surely right that the courts are empowered to put compulsory measures in place to protect others in the future.

The devil, of course, is in the detail; whilst compulsory treatment may be acceptable under certain conditions, those conditions involve the complex weighing of legal and medical priorities, and will inevitably shift alongside medical advancement. However, the criminal law has not created a dynamic set of rules capable of balancing these priorities and shifting in line with medical progress. Rather, the insanity rules remain products of the common law, and remain principally based on a set of Law Lord opinions from 1843.

The current law of insanity was set out in relation to *M'Naghten*. This case involved insanity as a defence (ie D had committed an offence), but the same rules apply where D uses insanity to deny offending.

 M'Naghten (1843) 10 Cl & Fin 200

D attempted to murder Sir Robert Peel, who was then Home Secretary, and killed Edward Drummond (Peel's secretary) by mistake. D was charged with murder.

• Crown Court: not guilty of murder by reason of insanity. D was suffering from morbid delusions about the Conservative Party.

M'Naghten's acquittal provoked controversy, and was debated in the legislative chamber of the House of Lords, where the Law Lords were asked questions on the insanity rules.[135] It was the answers given to those questions, and not the case itself, which provide the basis for the modern law on insanity. The '*M'Naghten* Rules', as they have come to be known, were given binding authority by their endorsement in *Sullivan*.[136]

The *M'Naghten* Rules, crucially, are not based on a medical definition of insanity. Rather, they provide a set of legal rules to determine if D will be caught within a legal definition of insanity, and directed towards the special verdict. These rules are set out in **Table 13.3**.

Table 13.3 The *M'Naghten* Rules

A) D must suffer from a disease of the mind;
B) This must have caused a defect of reason; and
C) This must have caused a lack of responsibility, *either* because D did not know the nature or quality of her act, *or* she did not know it was wrong

We explore each in turn.

---

[134] [1963] AC 386.

[135] (1843) 4 St Tr NS 847.

[136] [1984] 1 AC 156.

13.4.2.1 Element 1: disease of the mind

The first requirement, that D must have been suffering from a disease of the mind, sounds very much like a medical question. However, although medical experts will be required to provide evidence,[137] the definition they are asked to apply ('a disease of the mind') is a legal one. This is illustrated in *Kemp*.

 Kemp [1957] 1 QB 399

D made a motiveless and irrational attack upon his wife with a hammer, causing GBH. D was suffering from arteriosclerosis, a condition which caused a congestion of blood in his brain and caused him to lapse into unconsciousness at the time of the attack. D was charged with a GBH offence.

- Court of Assizes: not guilty by reason of insanity. The fact that D's condition was physical rather than mental does not prevent the insanity rules applying.

Later confirmed in *Sullivan, Kemp* provides important clarification that D may be suffering from a disease of the mind (in legal terms) even where there is no degeneration of brain cells. As Devlin J stated:

> In my judgment the condition of the brain is irrelevant and so is the question of whether the condition of the mind is curable or incurable, transitory or permanent. There is no warranty for introducing those considerations into the definition in the *M'Naghten* Rules. Temporary insanity is sufficient to satisfy them. It does not matter whether it is incurable and permanent or not.[138]

Moving away from a medical understanding of mental illness, the legal definition of 'disease of the mind' is rather more concerned with marking the distinction between insanity (leading to the special verdict) and sane automatism or simple lack of mens rea (leading to an acquittal in the absence of prior fault). In doing so, the law focuses on a sole criterion: does D's involuntariness (and/or lack of other mens rea) stem from an internal bodily condition or from an external factor. Where D's condition is internally caused, whatever its medical classification, it will be deemed a disease of the mind for the purposes of the insanity rules.

Although most insanity cases will involve medically recognised mental illnesses (eg schizophrenia being the most common[139]), the central role of the internal/external test has led to a number of unfortunate, and largely indefensible, classifications. Perhaps the most striking of these has arisen in relation to diabetes, where a diabetic coma, and associated involuntariness, can be brought on *internally* by a lack of treatment with insulin (hyperglycaemia), or *externally* by treatment with insulin followed by an insufficient intake of food (hypoglycaemia). The origins of these conditions and their impact upon D are almost identical, but they sit either side of the internal/external divide.[140] This was discussed in *Quick*.

---

[137] Criminal Procedure (Insanity and Unfitness to Plead) Act 1991, s1. This section prevents a jury returning a verdict of not guilty by reason of insanity except on the evidence of two or more registered medical practitioners, of whom at least one must be approved as having special expertise in the field of mental disorder.

[138] At 407.

[139] Mackay, Mitchell, and Howe, 'Yet More Facts About the Insanity Defence' [2006] Crim LR 399.

[140] Rumbold, 'Diabetes and Criminal Responsibility' (2010) 174 CL&JW 21.

Quick [1973] QB 910

D, a nurse in a mental hospital, attacked a paraplegic patient causing ABH. D called evidence that he was diabetic and, at the time of the attack, was suffering from hypoglycaemia caused by a lack of food after insulin. D was told that this would amount to a claim of insanity, and so he changed his plea to guilty.

- Crown Court: guilty of assault occasioning ABH.[141]
- Court of Appeal: appeal allowed. D's hypoglycaemia was externally caused, and so he should have been allowed to raise automatism rather than insanity.

Quick can be contrasted with *Hennessy*,[142] where D also raised automatism on the basis of a diabetic coma. However, in this case D's coma was induced by a lack of insulin. The ruling, therefore, was that automatism was unavailable because D's condition was internally caused: D could rely on the insanity rules, or (as he did) change his plea to guilty.

Beyond diabetes, a number of other conditions have also been (morally inappropriately) caught within the insanity rules. Individuals treated in criminal law as insane include epileptics,[143] pre-menstrual syndrome suffers,[144] sleepwalkers,[145] and so on. These examples are problematic for the simple reason that the term 'insanity' is so obviously inappropriate both medically as well as to the ordinary citizen. But they can also be problematic for a test which seeks a neat, or at least consistent, divide between internal and external causes. In the context of sleepwalking, for example, which has attracted particular attention,[146] it is not always obvious that the cause is purely internal. For example, D's sleepwalking may arise from the external influence of hypnosis or, more trivially, it may be triggered from disturbed sleep or from eating certain foods before sleeping.[147]

Another example of uncertain classification arises in so-called psychological blow cases, where D tries to explain an internal loss of faculties on the basis of a psychologically traumatic event. D's aim here is to characterise the psychological trauma as an external cause, leading to an unqualified acquittal under the automatism rules, and avoiding insanity. One of the first cases where this line of argument was attempted was the Canadian case of *Rabey*.[148] D, a student who became infatuated with a girl (V), discovered that she was not interested in him, and reacted by hitting her on the head with a rock that he had taken from the geology laboratory. D was initially acquitted on the basis of automatism, the court accepting that the psychological blow of rejection had caused him to experience a dissociative state. However, not surprisingly, the prosecution's appeal was later accepted, with the Canadian Supreme Court clarifying that 'the common stresses and disappointments of life which are the common lot of all mankind

---

141 Offences Against the Person Act 1861, s47.
142 (1989) 89 Cr App R 10.
143 *Sullivan* [1984] AC 156; Mackay and Reuber, 'Epilepsy and the Defence of Insanity—Time for a Change' [2007] Crim LR 782.
144 *Smith* [1982] Crim LR 531; Edwards, 'Mad, Bad or Pre-Menstrual' (1988) 138 NLJ 456.
145 *Burgess* [1991] 2 All ER 769; Mackay, 'The Sleepwalker is Not Insane' (1992) 55 MLR 714.
146 Wilson et al, 'Violence, Sleepwalking and the Criminal Law' [2005] Crim LR 601 and 614; Mackay and Mitchell, 'Sleepwalking, Automatism and Insanity' [2006] Crim LR 901.
147 Law Commission, *Insanity and Automatism* (Discussion Paper, 2013) para 1.44.
148 (1977) 37 CCC 461.

do not constitute an external cause'.[149] The dissociative state it seems, if accepted, should have constituted evidence of insanity. A more difficult case is *T*.

 T [1990] Crim LR 256

A young woman (D) took part in a violent robbery with two others. She was charged with robbery. It emerged that D had been raped at some point prior to the robbery taking place, and the issue of automatism was raised by the defence: that D was acting in a dissociative state (akin to sleepwalking) as a result of the rape.

- Crown Court: guilty of robbery. Crucially, the court found that the case gave rise to the potential for automatism rather than insanity, and thus accepted the psychological blow as an external cause. However, the jury did not accept that D's conduct was fully involuntary.

This case is useful for two main reasons. First, it demonstrates that psychological blows stemming from extreme circumstances can ground a claim of automatism rather than insanity. But, secondly, it also provides a reminder of how narrowly the law has interpreted involuntariness in the context of automatism, making this route very difficult in practice.[150]

Finally, not only can the current internal/external test be criticised for leading to inappropriate labelling and uncertainty, but its practical application is also out of line with its rationale of public protection. The fact that D's condition is internally caused does not necessarily make her more likely to be dangerous in the future. This is clear, for example, if we compare D1 who suffers an *internal* congestion of blood to the brain that can be treated to prevent reoccurrence, with D2 who suffers an *external* blow to the head that causes permanent brain injury. It is also clear when we compare states of hyper- and hypoglycaemia, conditions sharply distinguished in law, yet conditions which affect D in largely identical ways.

These criticisms of the law are well acknowledged. Indeed, research has shown the Crown Courts will often ignore the detail of the rules where they lead to clear unfairness, and have been willing to apply a more common-sense approach (eg allowing automatism to run in sleepwalking cases).[151]

Assessment matters . . .
Where problem facts involve D causing harm whilst sleepwalking, for example, it is important to follow the established authorities: D's state is internally caused, and thus gives rise to the insanity rules. Acknowledging that the law 'in practice' will often see courts allowing automatism to be run will be an impressive addition to your answer, but should be a secondary point.

13.4.2.2 Element 2: causing a defect of reason

Having established that D's denial of offending is based on an internal cause (a disease of the mind), ruling out the potential application of intoxication and/or sane automatism,

---

[149] (1980) 54 CCC at 7.
[150] Horder, 'Pleading Involuntary Lack of Capacity' (1993) 53 CLJ 298, 313–315.
[151] *Lowe* (2005, unreported) and *Pooley* (2007, unreported); Mackay and Mitchell, 'Sleepwalking, Automatism and Insanity' [2006] Crim LR 901.

our next question is whether D was thereby caused to have a defect of reason. This stage is important. If D's defect of mind caused her to behave absent-mindedly, so she had the ability to reason but did not do so, or simply contributed to an attitude where she chose not think about the dangerous nature of her conduct, then the insanity rules will not apply. The leading case here is *Clarke*.

 Clarke [1972] 1 All ER 219

D took articles from a supermarket without paying for them. Evidence was raised that she did so absent-mindedly, partly as a result of mild depression. D was charged with theft. When told that her denial amounted to a plea of insanity, D changed her plea to guilty.

- Crown Court: guilty of theft.
- Court of Appeal: appeal allowed. D's condition did not prevent her being able to reason, and so the insanity rules were not satisfied. D was simply denying mens rea.

Clarke was attempting to claim a simple lack of mens rea, which would have resulted in an unqualified acquittal. However, in relying on her depression to explain this lack of mens rea, the insanity rules were applied.

Extra detail . . .
Where (as in *Clarke*) D is denying mens rea, her defence representatives will want to avoid the insanity rules. This is because insanity would direct D to the uncertain outcome of the special verdict and, if insanity does not apply, D will be acquitted on the simple basis of lack of mens rea. In contrast, where D accepts that she completed the offence elements and raises insanity as a defence (discussed in **Chapter 14**), her default position if the insanity rules do not apply will be liability. Therefore, D is much more likely to want the insanity rules to apply. Remember the insanity rules can operate as both a denial of mens rea or as a defence; context is everything.

13.4.2.3 Element 3: causing a lack of responsibility

The final stage of the insanity rules requires D's defect of mind to have caused D to lack responsibility for the harms caused, *either* because she did not understand the nature or quality of what she was doing (a denial of mens rea) *or* because she did not know it was wrong (a defence). Our focus in this chapter is the former, but both will be discussed.

The insanity rules will not apply in situations other than these two alternatives. Thus, for example, where D commits an offence as a result of an 'irresistible impulse', if she understands what she is doing and that it is wrong, she will not satisfy the insanity rules. This was considered in *Kopsch*,[152] where D admitted killing his uncle's wife, but evidence was raised that he was acting under the uncontrollable direction of his sub-conscious mind. The court held that such evidence provided no basis for a denial of criminal responsibility. An irresistible impulse will only be relevant to the insanity rules where it causes D to lack understanding of her actions, or not to know they are wrong.[153]

---

[152] (1925) 19 Cr App R 50.
[153] *AG for South Australia v Brown* [1960] AC 432.

D does not know the nature or quality of her act

In modern language, this is a claim that D 'did not know what he was doing'.[154] It is a reference to the physical nature of D's conduct, and will not include lesser states of inadvertence (eg to the moral or legal quality of the conduct).[155] It will clearly apply where D is unconscious, but will also include cases where D is acting under a delusion. Often-repeated examples include where D kills V under the insane delusion that she is breaking a jar[156] or cuts V's throat believing it is a loaf of bread.[157] However, cases outside clear examples of this kind will be more testing. For example, in the case of B,[158] a paranoid schizophrenic defendant had sex with his wife, without her consent, believing that he had sexual-healing powers. D was rightly convicted of rape on the facts, but interestingly for present purposes, the Court of Appeal also considered what would have happened if D's condition had led him to believe that V was consenting. The court said that nothing would change. But surely this would be an example of D not knowing the nature or quality of his act, consensual intercourse being categorically different from non-consensual intercourse.

In cases where D does not know the nature or quality of her act, the rejection of the insanity rules will generally lead to D's unqualified acquittal: not understanding the nature or quality of one's act is to deny mens rea. With the public's protection in mind, it will be interesting to see if a case with the amended facts of B postulated by the court would end, as the Court of Appeal suggest, outside these rules.[159]

D does not know that her act is wrong

Even where D *does* understand the nature and quality of her conduct, the insanity rules will still apply if her defect of reason caused her not to know that what she was doing was wrong. This limb of the insanity rules will usually arise where D has committed an offence (both actus reus and mens rea), and raises insanity as a defence. Insanity as a defence, as opposed to a denial of offending, will be discussed further in **Chapter 14**. However, it is useful to provide an overview here.

Crucially, and controversially, D will only satisfy this limb of the insanity rules where she is caused not to know the *legal* wrongfulness of her acts. Where her condition causes her to believe her actions are morally right, but she still understands that they are criminal, she will not come within the insanity rules. This was established in *Windle*.

 Windle [1952] 2 QB 826

D's wife was mentally ill, and often spoke to him of suicide. D, described as 'weak willed', became obsessed with this idea. Having discussed it repeatedly with his workmates, one suggested that D should give her a dozen aspirin. D gave his wife 100 aspirin tablets, which she took, and died.

---

154 *Sullivan* [1983] 2 All ER 673, 678.
155 *Codere* (1916) 12 Cr App R 219; Mackay, 'Some Observations on the Second Limb of the M'Naghten Rules' [2009] Crim LR 80.
156 Stephen, *A Digest of the Criminal Law* (8th edn, 1947) 6.
157 Kenny, *Outlines of Criminal Law* (2007) 76.
158 [2013] EWCA Crim 3.
159 Child and Sullivan, 'When Does the Insanity Defence Apply? Some Recent Cases' [2014] Crim LR 787.

Reporting her death, D told the police 'I suppose they will hang me for this'. D was charged with murder.

- Crown Court: guilty of murder. The defence of insanity was withdrawn from the jury because, although there was medical evidence of a defect of mind, it was agreed that D knew that what he did was legally wrong.
- Court of Criminal Appeal: conviction upheld on appeal.

The position in *Windle* has been confirmed in *Johnson*,[160] and so its narrow interpretation continues to apply.

Criticism of *Windle*, however, has been telling. Bearing in mind that the special verdict still allows for compulsory treatment and therefore restraint, it is difficult to see why a defendant such as Windle should be denied a defence which would recognise his lack of meaningful choice in offending. Other common law jurisdictions, notably Australia,[161] have refused to follow *Windle* in their application of the insanity rules. Indeed, even within this jurisdiction, it seems that the lower courts will often apply the wrongfulness limb without distinction between D's legal and moral awareness.[162]

Assessment matters . . .

As with other areas, the potential inconsistency here between appellate court authority and the 'law in practice' in lower courts needs to be handled with care. When applying to problem facts, always begin by applying the binding authority, which in this context is *Windle*. However, where D is unable to appreciate the moral wrongfulness of her acts, but knows that they are against the law, it is good practice to mention that although *Windle* suggests that the insanity rules will not apply, Mackay et al have found that they are often applied in practice.

13.4.3 Insanity and defences

Where insanity is raised as a denial of offending (ie to explain D's lack of mens rea), D will not require a defence. D has not committed an offence.

The only exception to this, potentially, could arise were the courts to recognise a rule of prior fault for insanity in line with intoxication and automatism. Thus, if D's prior fault resulted in a state of insanity and criminal conduct, D would be liable for the full offence rather than not guilty by reason of insanity. In such a case, with D now facing liability, defences would come back into play. D could claim a defence to undermine her prior fault at T1 and thus undermine liability (eg duress, where D is threatened to not take her medication).

Where D commits an offence and raises insanity as a defence (discussed in **Chapter 14**), a potential clash with other defences may arise. This is because if D also satisfies the elements of an alternative complete defence, she will naturally prefer that option, leading to an unqualified acquittal, rather than insanity, leading to the special verdict. We explore this potential for multiple applicable defences in **14.2.2**. However, importantly, where insanity is raised as a denial of offending, this issue does not arise.

---

[160] [2007] EWCA Crim 1978.
[161] *Stapleton* (1952) 86 CLR 358.
[162] Mackay and Kearns, 'More Fact(s) About the Insanity Defence' [1999] Crim LR 714, 722; Mackay, Mitchell, and Howe, 'Yet More Facts About the Insanity Defence' [2006] Crim LR 399.

13.5 Combining intoxication, automatism, and insanity

The three denials of offending discussed in this chapter are mutually exclusive in their application, and will in most cases lead to different outcomes. Identifying which set of rules, if any, should apply is therefore crucial. If D's lack of mens rea stems from an internal factor then *only* the insanity rules should be applied; where it stems from voluntary consumption of a dangerous drug then *only* the prior-fault intoxication rules should be applied; where D's conduct is involuntary as a result of an external factor other than a dangerous drug then *only* the automatism rules should be applied.

Certain cases, however, will test these neat divisions. Causes can be consecutive: for example, D's voluntary intoxication may cause her to fall and hit her head, causing her to commit a criminal act whilst in a state of automatism;[163] repeat intoxication can lead to addiction and a disease of the mind;[164] and so on. Causes can also be concurrent: for example, where an external blow causes automatism by aggravating an internal condition;[165] where D is suffering from a disease of the mind and is intoxicated;[166] and so on. Cases of this kind expose the problems of relying on the internal/external distinction. Courts have tended to take a pragmatic approach, looking for the dominant cause.[167]

13.6 Reform

The rules on insanity, automatism, and intoxication have attracted sustained academic criticism, and have each been discussed by the Law Commission in terms of potential reform.[168] In this section we provide a brief overview of those reform proposals.

Before dividing our analysis between the three sets of rules, however, it is useful to highlight an underlying debate that is common between them. The major function of the rules discussed in this chapter is inculpatory in nature.[169] Where D has not completed all of the elements of an offence, our starting point must be an unqualified acquittal: D's behaviour is not proscribed by the criminal law, or at least not by the offence charged. The rules governing prior-fault automatism, the potential for what we might call 'prior-fault insanity', and the prior-fault intoxication rules, and to a more limited extend the rules covering insanity in general,[170] each operate to construct liability (or the grounds for compulsory treatment) that would not otherwise be available. The underlying debate,

---

[163] *Stripp* (1979) 69 Cr App R 318.

[164] *Beard* [1920] AC 479.

[165] *Roach* [2001] EWCA Crim 2698.

[166] *Burns* (1973) 58 Cr App R 364.

[167] For a useful discussion, criticising the 'dominant cause' approach, see Loughnan and Wake, 'Of Blurred Boundaries and Prior Fault: Insanity, Automatism and Intoxication' in Reed and Bohlander (eds), *General Defences in Criminal Law* (2014) 113.

[168] Law Commission, *Intoxication and Criminal Liability* (No 314, 2009); Law Commission, *Insanity and Automatism* (Discussion Paper, 2013).

[169] Outside this, the rules simply provide a shorthand terminology for saying that D lacks essential elements for the offence charged.

[170] The special verdict of not guilty by reason of insanity provides an acquittal, but its qualified nature (including the potential for compulsory treatment) means that it is still inculpatory in effect.

then, particularly when we are discussing the construction of liability, is the question of when and how such liability should be constructed.

The dominant language of the current law, discussing automatism, insanity, and intoxication as *defences*, only serves to disguise and confuse this underlying question.[171] If we think of these rules in terms of defences, then it is natural to think about what is required of D to excuse or justify her avoidance of liability (ie liability becomes the default). In contrast, when we accept that these rules are designed to construct liability, or in the context of insanity, at least to provide a route to orders for public protection, the question changes to consider what D has done wrong to deserve liability. The difference between these two may be subtle, but it has a real impact on our interpretation, and potential reform, of the law. For example, whilst the use of objective mental states is common among defences (discussed in **Chapter 14**), serious offences will generally require subjective mens rea, holding D liable only where she has *chosen* to commit an offence.[172] When we come to consider D's prior fault for intoxication (objectively based where the drug is a dangerous one) or automatism (case law is uncertain), our perception of the rules as defences or offence constructors is crucial.

13.6.1 Intoxication

The prior-fault intoxication rules in general, and the *Majewski* principle in particular, have been consistently criticised for their lack of a theoretical basis and their confused application in practice.[173] Where other jurisdictions have abandoned the principle, the English courts have become isolated in clinging to it. It is clear that if reform is to come, it will need to be through Parliament.

When the Law Commission first considered the prior-fault intoxication rules in 1992, it proposed that the *Majewski* principle should be abolished and replaced with an intoxication offence.[174] This would have meant that rather than D's intoxication (at T1) being used to construct liability for an offence where D lacks mens rea (at T2), D's intoxication plus harm would itself constitute a separate offence. However, following criticism on consultation,[175] the Commission changed its stance and recommended codification, with only slight amendment, of the current law.[176] This recommendation was never taken forward into legislation, being widely viewed as unnecessarily complex.

The latest Law Commission project on intoxication was completed in 2009.[177] In its report, the Commission recommended the abandonment of the *Majewski* distinction between offences of basic and specific intent. However, the Commission did not reject the basic logic underlying the current law that voluntary intoxication with a dangerous drug is equivalent, in culpability terms, to a missing mens rea of recklessness. For the Commission, the main problem with the law was that this principle was not consistently

---

[171] Simester, 'Intoxication is Never a Defence' [2009] Crim LR 3; Child and Reed, 'Automatism is Never a Defence' (2014) 65 NILQ 167; Child and Sullivan, 'When Does the Insanity Defence Apply? Some Recent Cases' [2014] Crim LR 787; Child, 'Prior Fault: Blocking Defences or Constructing Crimes' in Reed and Bohlander (eds), *General Defences* (2014).

[172] G [2003] UKHL 50.

[173] Williams, 'Voluntary Intoxication—A Lost Cause?' (2013) 129 LQR 264.

[174] Law Commission, *Intoxication and Criminal Liability* (Consultation 127, 1992).

[175] Gardner, 'The Importance of *Majewski*' (1994) 14 OJLS 279.

[176] Law Commission, *Intoxication and Criminal Liability* (No 229, 1995).

[177] Law Commission, *Intoxication and Criminal Liability* (No 314, 2009).

or specifically applied. Thus, rather than distinguishing between offences that might include various mens rea requirements, the Commission recommended that each element of each offence should be analysed separately: where the missing element of mens rea is recklessness or less, then D's intoxication can substitute for it (the Commission labelled these 'non-integral' elements), but if the element requires a higher mens rea than recklessness (eg intention, knowledge, etc) then the absence of this cannot be replaced by D's intoxication (the Commission labelled these 'integral' elements). There are a number of merits to this policy as a rationalisation of the current law. However, they have also attracted criticism,[178] and have been rejected by government.

As more commentators have accepted that the prior-fault intoxication rules are essentially inculpatory, and that the debate should be about what is required to construct liability, the prospect of an intoxication offence to replace the current prior-fault intoxication rules has regained popularity.[179] Rather than the fiction of the current law, pretending that D possessed mens rea where she did not, the advantage of an intoxication offence is that it could accurately label and punish D for what she has done: become intoxicated and caused a criminal harm. The detail of such an offence remains contested,[180] but it is contended that this approach offers the best way forward.

13.6.2 Sane automatism

The automatism rules have attracted less academic attention than intoxication, but many of the same debates and criticisms can be applied. The approach of the Law Commission, in its Discussion Paper in 2013,[181] has been an attempt to rationalise the current law in the context of other denials of offending, most notably intoxication and insanity. For example, the Commission explores the wider concept of prior fault, and looks to identify consistent approaches across the three sets of rules. Focusing on automatism specifically, the Commission also looks to resolve some of the main areas of uncertainty within the current law, discussed earlier, relating to the type of foresight required by D in the context of prior fault, as well as the degree of involuntariness required to give rise to automatism at all.[182]

As with intoxication, however, if we see the automatism rules as designed to construct liability, an alternative approach could be the creation of a prior-fault automatism offence.[183] This option is not discussed by the Commission. It will be interesting to see what approach is eventually recommended by the Commission.

13.6.3 Insanity

The most widely criticised rules discussed in this chapter relate to insanity.[184] That the law remains governed by the outlined opinions of Law Lords over 170 years ago is

[178] Child, 'Drink, Drugs and Law Reform' [2009] Crim LR 488.
[179] Simester, 'Intoxication is Never a Defence' [2009] Crim LR 3.
[180] Williams, 'Voluntary Intoxication—A Lost Cause?' (2013) 129 LQR 264; Child, 'Prior Fault: Blocking Defences or Constructing Crimes' in Reed and Bohlander (eds), *General Defences* (2014).
[181] Law Commission, *Insanity and Automatism* (Discussion Paper, 2013).
[182] Ibid, Ch5.
[183] Child and Reed, 'Automatism is Never a Defence' (2014) 65 NILQ 167.
[184] Dell, 'Wanted: An Insanity Defence That Can Be Used' [1983] Crim LR 431; Loughnan, 'Manifest Madness: Towards a New Understanding of the Insanity Defence' (2007) 70 MLR 379; Hogg, 'The Insanity Defence: An Argument for Abolition' (2015) 79 J Crim L 250.

499

nothing short of remarkable; that this should be the case despite dramatic strides in medical and public understanding of mental illness is nothing short of disgraceful.

We have already discussed a number of specific problems with the insanity rules, and there is also a useful summary of these in the Law Commission's Discussion Paper.[185] One of those we have not yet discussed, but a major pressure for reform, derives from the potential incompatibility of the current law with the ECHR.[186] There are three main areas of potential challenge.

- Articles 2 and 3: Articles 2 and 3 provide for the right to life and the prohibition of inhuman or degrading treatment. In this regard, the insanity rules have a crucial role to protect mentally disordered individuals from inappropriate prosecution, and also to protect society from potentially dangerous individuals. Where the current law fails in these roles, it is open to challenge in relation to both groups.[187]

- Article 5: Article 5 provides the right to liberty and security unless certain circumstances apply, such as where D has committed an offence or requires detention in relation to an 'unsound mind'. Where D lacks mens rea she has not committed an offence, and where the cause of this lack of mens rea is a condition such as diabetes, sleepwalking, etc, it is highly questionable whether this satisfies the Article 5 exception of an unsound mind.[188] Thus, where D, in these circumstances, is caught within the insanity rules and potentially detained against her will, this may be a breach of her Article 5 right.[189] This ground centres on the current disconnect between legal definitions of insanity and medical definitions of mental illness.

- Article 6: Article 6 provides the right to a fair trial, including the presumption of innocence. The presumption of innocence entails placing the burden upon the prosecution to prove the elements of liability. However, where D's denial of offending is based upon a disease of the mind (ie caught within the insanity rules) the current law reverses the legal burden of proof; requiring D to prove that elements of the offence were missing.[190]

In light of the various criticisms levelled at the current law, it is little surprise that it has attracted several reform proposals (almost from its inception[191]). The most recent of these is again contained in the Law Commission's 2013 Discussion Paper.[192] Some of the Commission's main proposals include the following.

- Proposal 1: Abolition of the common law rules on insanity.

- Proposal 2: Creation of a new statutory test, labelled as 'not criminally responsible by reason of recognised medical condition'.

---

[185] Law Commission, *Insanity and Automatism* (Discussion Paper, 2013) paras 1.30–1.79.

[186] Mackay and Gearty, 'On Being Insane in Jersey—The Case of *AG v Jason Prior*' [2001] Crim LR 560; Mackay, 'On Being Insane in Jersey—Part Two' [2002] Crim LR 728; Mackay, 'On Being Insane in Jersey—Part Three' [2004] Crim LR 219.

[187] Law Commission, *Insanity and Automatism* (Discussion Paper, 2013) paras 1.65–1.72.

[188] For discussion of this definition, see *Winterwerp v Netherlands* (1979) 2 EHRR 387.

[189] Although, of course, detention of this kind will require the advice of two medical experts, and would not be ordered for conditions such as diabetes.

[190] *Bratty* [1963] AC 386.

[191] As early as 1923 a committee chaired by Lord Atkin recommended a test based on 'mental disease [which] in substance deprived [D] of any power to resist': Cmd 2005.

[192] Law Commission, *Insanity and Automatism* (Discussion Paper, 2013) paras 4.158–4.168.

- Proposal 3: Creation of a three-limbed test, where D's recognised medical condition must have caused D to lack capacity: (a) rationally to form a judgment about her conduct or their circumstances; (b) to understand the wrongfulness of what she is charged with, not isolated to legal wrongfulness; or (c) to control her conduct in the relevant circumstances.
- Proposal 6: Placing an *evidential* burden on D when raising the reformed rules, but placing the legal burden on the prosecution.

As with the Commission's proposals for automatism, it is important to remember that these are only the provisional proposals of a discussion paper.

13.7 Eye on assessment

In this section we consider how denials of offending based on intoxication, automatism, and insanity should be applied to problem facts. The same basic structure is employed as discussed in previous chapters.

> ### STEP 1 Identify the potential criminal event in the facts
>
> This is unlikely to take more than a sentence, but it is essential to tell your reader where in the facts you are focusing (eg 'The first potential criminal event appears where Mary drunkenly shoots and kills Amir').

It is important to take care at this stage. Where you note from the facts that D may be intoxicated (as in our example) or may be acting involuntarily or may have a mental disorder, it is correct that this should alert you to the potential application of the rules discussed in this chapter. However, Step 1 is not the time to discuss those rules! Many students make the mistake of launching into a discussion of intoxication, automatism, or insanity at this stage but, without having told the reader why these rules need to be discussed, their analysis is likely to be confused.

Rather than discussing rules of denial at this stage, you first need to identify a potential offence (Step 2) and discuss if the elements of that offence are satisfied (Step 3).

> ### STEP 2 Identify the potential offence
>
> Having identified the facts (eg D potentially killing V), you must now identify the offence you are going to apply. Usually, this means identifying the most serious offence that D might have committed, which in this case would be murder.

> ### STEP 3 Applying the offence to the facts
>
> Actus reus: What does the offence require? Did D do it?
>
> Mens rea: What does the offence require? Did D possess it?

If you conclude that D satisfies all the actus reus and mens rea elements of the offence, then the intoxication and automatism rules have no role. This can be highlighted to your reader, for example: 'Although Mary was drunk when she killed Amir, she remains liable for murder because, despite her intoxication, she still possessed the required mens rea.'

501

As the House of Lords confirmed in *Kingston*, 'a drunken intent is still an intent'. The insanity rules as a denial of mens rea will also have no application, although insanity as a defence (discussed in **Chapter 14**) may be relevant.

It is *only* when D lacks mens rea and/or voluntary movement that the rules discussed in this chapter become truly relevant. Here, having identified the missing elements, your next question is which set of rules, if any, could apply.

(a) D lacks mens rea (potentially including a lack of voluntary conduct) because of her consumption of drugs = apply the intoxication rules;

(b) D lacks voluntary movement (potentially including other mens rea) because of an external factor other than within the intoxication rules = apply the automatism rules;

(c) D lacks mens rea (potentially including a lack of voluntary conduct) because of an internal condition = apply the insanity rules;

(d) D lacks actus reus elements, or mens rea elements for any reason other than the above = D has not completed the offence and should be acquitted.

We provide detailed analysis of how each set of rules should be applied within this chapter. Here, we include **Figures 13.11, 13.12,** and **13.13** to help with the basic structuring of this application, to be used alongside the more detailed discussion.

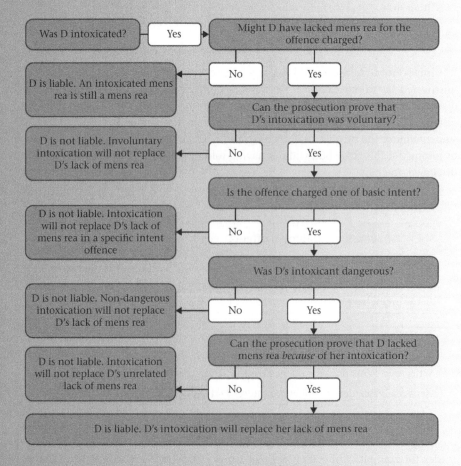

Figure 13.11 Intoxication flowchart

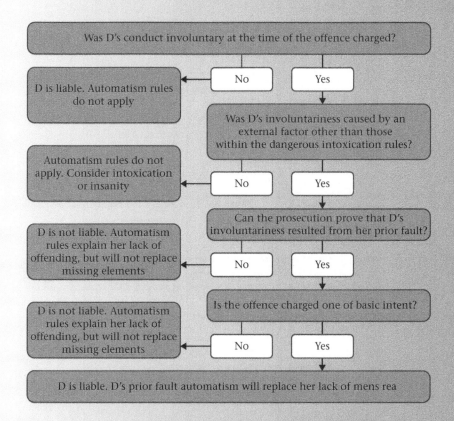

Figure 13.12 Automatism flowchart

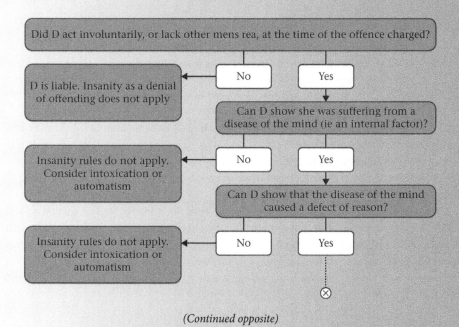

(Continued opposite)

503

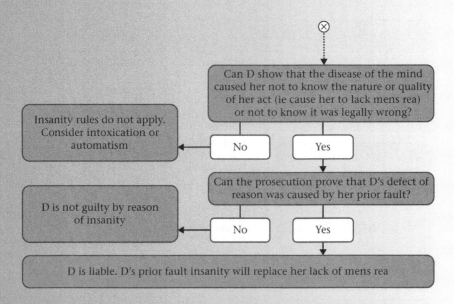

Figure 13.13 Insanity as a denial of offending flowchart (*Continued*)

AR and MR are satisfied	AR and/or MR are not satisfied
Continue to STEP 4.	Return to STEP 2, and look for an alternative offence. If none, then skip to STEP 5, concluding that no offence is committed.

STEP 4 Consider defences

The word 'consider' here is important, as you should not discuss every defence for every question. Rather, think whether there are any defences that *could* potentially apply. If you conclude there are, then discuss those only.

Where liability has been constructed on the basis of D's prior fault at T1, D may rely on a defence to undermine that fault. For example, D may rely on the defence of duress (discussed in **Chapter 14**) to deny responsibility for a failure to take medication (leading to insanity), or for taking something that causes a lack of voluntariness (leading to automatism, or intoxication).

In many cases, as we have discussed, D will have been intoxicated or mentally ill at T2, but still committed all elements of the offence. In these cases, we are not dealing with intoxication and/or insanity as a denial of mens rea because D satisfies the mens rea. However, although D's condition does not undermine liability, it may have an impact on any defences raised. For example, D will generally not be able to rely on an intoxicated mistake (**13.2.6**) when raising a defence.

STEP 5 Conclude

This is usually a single sentence either saying that it is likely that D has committed the offence, or saying that it is not likely either because an offence element is not satisfied or because a defence is likely to apply. It is not often that you will be able to say categorically whether or not D has committed the offence, so it is usually best to conclude in terms of what is more 'likely'.

STEP 6 Loop

Go back up to Step 1, identifying the next potential criminal event. Continue until you have discussed all the relevant potentially criminal events.

ONLINE RESOURCE CENTRE

www.oxfordtextbooks.co.uk/orc/sho/

This chapter is accompanied by a selection of online resources to help you with this topic, including:

- **Multiple-choice questions**
- **Chapter summary sheet**
- Two **sample examination questions** with answer guidance
- **Further reading**

Also available on the Online Resource Centre are:

- A selection of **videos** from the authors explaining key topics and principles
- **Legal updates**
- Useful **weblinks**

14

General defences

14.1 Introduction   559
    14.1.1 Excuses and justifications   561
14.2 Insanity as a defence   563
    14.2.1 The elements of insanity as a defence   564
    14.2.2 Insanity and other defences   565
14.3 Duress by threats   567
    14.3.1 Exclusions   568
    14.3.2 Element 1: X's threat and demand   572
    14.3.3 Element 2: D's response to the threat   576
14.4 Duress by circumstances   579
    14.4.1 Relationship between duress by threats and duress by circumstances   580
    14.4.2 The elements of duress by circumstances   581
14.5 Public and private defence   582
    14.5.1 Element 1: trigger—the necessity for force   585
    14.5.2 Element 2: response—a reasonable degree of force   588
14.6 Necessity   591
    14.6.1 Necessity as a defence to murder   593
14.7 Reform   595
    14.7.1 Reforming the individual defences   596
    14.7.2 Coherence between defences?   600
14.8 Eye on assessment   601

14.1 Introduction

In this chapter we discuss general complete defences. Unlike denials of offending discussed in **Chapter 13**, defences, properly so called, accept that D has committed the elements of an offence, but provide an additional set of rules that D can rely on so as to avoid liability. For example, D accepts that she intentionally pushed V to the ground thereby committing assault occasioning ABH,[1] but denies liability on the basis that she did so only to stop V attacking her child (relying on the public and private defence).[2]

---

[1] Offences Against the Person Act 1861. See **7.4**.
[2] Commonly referred to as self-defence. See **14.5**.

We have discussed a number of 'specific' defences in previous chapters—defences that only apply to a single offence or a cluster of offences, such as 'belief in owner's consent' for criminal damage.[3] In contrast, the defences discussed in this chapter, as 'general' defences, can apply, with one exception,[4] to offences throughout the criminal law. We have also previously discussed the 'partial' defences to murder—defences which have the potential to reduce liability for murder to manslaughter as, for example, where D was suffering from diminished responsibility.[5] The defences discussed in this chapter in contrast, as 'complete' defences, will result in D's acquittal.

> **Terminology . . .**
> When discussing defences, the language of actus reus (guilty act) and mens rea (guilty mind) is not appropriate. These terms are used to describe offences only. Instead, you should refer simply to the elements of defences.

Defences, and the general defences in particular, play a vital role within the criminal law as a concession to the bluntness of the criminal offence. Offence definitions attempt to isolate and identify criminal mischief, but, within the infinite variety of circumstances in the real world, it is almost impossible for these definitions to account for every eventuality. Criminal defences provide the next layers of detail; allowing the law to account for exceptional circumstances where (despite D satisfying the elements of the offence charged) liability would be inappropriate. The same analysis can be presented in more positive terms. If criminal offences have a role in guiding the behaviour of society, then relative bluntness in offence definitions is a good thing: offences can provide clear messages about conduct to be avoided, leaving defences to act as a safety net in exceptional circumstances.[6]

Defences can be problematic, however. There is considerable literature critiquing how defences are defined and applied: whether they are drawn too narrowly, failing to exculpate apparently non-blameworthy defendants; or too widely, allowing blameworthy conduct, inappropriately, to escape liability. Such criticisms are also common of criminal offences, but they may be felt particularly keenly in the context of defences as the 'safety net' or the last set of legal rules that stand between D and a criminal conviction. Indeed, it may be partly because of this that many defences lack clarity in their definitions; opening the potential for inconsistent application and criticism, but also providing flexibility to account for different factual circumstances.

In this chapter, we discuss the following defences.

- Insanity (as a defence): This arises where a medical condition caused a defect in reason, which prevented D understanding her conduct or understanding that it was wrong. For example, where D kills V under the insane delusion that she is required by law to do so.

---

[3] Criminal Damage Act 1971, s5(2)(a). See **9.7.3**.

[4] The exception is duress, which does not provide a defence to murder and certain related offences. See **14.3** and **14.4**.

[5] Homicide Act 1957, s2. See **6.2.2**.

[6] Duff, *Answering for Crime* (2007) Ch11; Wilson, 'The Structure of Criminal Defences' [2005] Crim LR 108; Wilson, 'How Criminal Defences Work' in Reed and Bohlander (eds), *General Defences in Criminal Law* (2014) 7.

- **Duress by threats:** This arises where D was threatened by someone that unless she committed the offence she is now charged with she would suffer serious injury or death, D reasonably believed that the threat would be carried out imminently, and a reasonable person in those circumstances would have reacted as D did. For example, D may plead duress when charged with robbery if she was told by X to rob a bank or else D would be killed.

- **Duress by circumstances:** This arises where D reasonably believed she faced a threat of death or serious injury, but with the threat arising from D's circumstances rather than explicitly from a person. For example, where D saw a tidal wave approaching and realised that breaking into a car to drive away was her only means of escape, D would have a defence to a charge of criminal damage to the car.

- **The public and private defence (commonly known as self-defence):** This arises where D used force against another in the genuine belief that she needed to do so to protect herself or others, or to prevent crime, and the amount of force used was reasonable in the circumstances as D believed them to be. For example, D assaults V where D believes she needs to do so in order to stop V harming her child.

- **Necessity:** This arises where D acted for the greater good, or the lesser evil. This defence, as we will see, is poorly defined and rarely applied. An example of its rare use has been to justify the separation of conjoined twins, killing one to give the other a chance of life.

These defences are not denials of actus reus or mens rea. In order to explain the moral permissibility of D's offending in circumstances of a defence, courts and commentators have occasionally referred to D's conduct as 'involuntary', or 'morally involuntary'.[7] This terminology is unhelpful. If D's conduct is involuntary then she does not commit an offence, and we apply the rules discussed in **Chapter 13**. Here, D may have been subject to an impossible choice, such that her voluntary commission of an offence is not blame-worthy, but her appeal to defences properly so called marks an acceptance that she has committed an offence.[8]

14.1.1 Excuses and justifications

Much of the theoretical writing in this area has focused on categorising types of defences in order to understand the basis upon which D is exculpated; particularly the division between excusatory and justificatory defences. The language of excuses and justifications originates from a historical question of forfeiture on acquittal: his-torically a justified killer would not have her goods forfeited, but a merely excused killer would. Forfeiture was abolished in 1828, but academic interest in the division between justifications and excuses continued, and was re-sparked by the seminal work of George Fletcher.[9]

The division between excuses and justifications can be stated quite simply, but the detail of its application and relevance to today's law is highly contested. An excusatory defence accepts that D's actions were wrongful but challenges the idea that D can be

[7] *Perka* (1984) 13 DLR (4th) 1: Canadian court discussing duress by threats.
[8] *Hasan* [2005] UKHL 22, [18].
[9] Fletcher, *Rethinking Criminal Law* (1978) Ch10.

blamed because of circumstances personal to her, whereas justifications challenge the wrongfulness of D's actions.[10] As Fletcher put it:

> A justification speaks to the rightness of the act; an excuse, to whether the actor is accountable for a concededly wrongful act.[11]

An excuse, then, tends to focus on D herself rather than her actions. For example, if D explains that she committed the offence because voices in her head compelled her to do so, we do not question whether her acts were wrongful (they clearly were), but we may question whether it is right to blame D for those acts, as through the excusatory defence of insanity. As Hart notably stated, 'unless a man has the capacity and fair opportunity or chance to adjust his behaviour to the law, its penalties ought not to be applied to him'.[12] This is the essence of an excusatory defence; whether due to a physical or mental restraint, or whether due to extreme circumstances, D did not have a *fair* opportunity to obey the law.[13] Justifications, on the other hand, focus on D's acts. For example, where D assaults V in order to stop V harming her child, D may have completed the elements of an offence, but her acts were permissible. She did the right thing.[14]

There is an appealing logic to the separation of excuses and justification, but outside core examples, it can also be problematic.[15] Take the simple example of D who assaults V in order to stop V harming D's child. Although this is a clear example of the justified defence of another, known as 'the public and private defence', D could also rely on this defence if she made a mistake, if she thought V was trying to harm her child but was wrong and V was actually no threat at all. In this case, D's actions are *justified on her beliefs*, but few would call them justified in light of the objective facts. Rather, if we accept the use of the public and private defence on these amended facts, it appears to be *excusing* D's blameworthy conduct on the basis of her mistake. Countless examples of this kind have been difficult to categorise within the excuse/justification framework, and 'bred needless confusion' in the law.[16]

Problems of categorisation have prompted two main responses. Where some commentators question why we should talk of these distinctions at all;[17] others attempt to resolve the issue by becoming ever more fine-grained in their theorising, separating subcategories of excuses and justifications.[18] This latter approach can be useful to resolve

---

[10] For criticism, see Gardner, 'Wrongs and Faults' in Simester (ed), *Appraising Strict Liability* (2005) 6–67.

[11] Fletcher, *Rethinking Criminal Law* (1978) 759.

[12] Hart, *Punishment and Responsibility* (1968) 181.

[13] See generally Horder, *Excusing Crime* (2004).

[14] It is problematic to say we 'approve' of D's acts because they still involved the commission of a criminal mischief. However, D's acts should not be condemned; they were permissible. Duff, *Answering for Crime* (2007) Ch11; Westen, 'Offences and Defences Again' (2008) 28 OJLS 563.

[15] Even within them there is a question of hierarchy, Husak, 'On the Supposed Priority of Justification to Excuse' (2005) 24 Law & Phil 557.

[16] Duff, *Answering for Crime* (2007) 263.

[17] Williams, 'The Theory of Excuses' [1982] Crim LR 732.

[18] For a particularly useful model, see Simester, 'On Justifications and Excuses' in Zedner and Roberts (eds), *Principles and Values in Criminal Law and Criminal Justice* (2012) 95.

problematic scenarios, but does so at the expense of simplicity and therefore at the expense of one of the initially appealing elements of the separation.

The current law does not rely on the explicit separation of excuses and justifications; the practical result of D's acquittal is the same for both. However, an outright rejection of these classifications, despite their critics, would be premature.[19] First, this is because the debate about these theories is useful; it forces us to question the basis upon which a defence operates. This aids our evaluation of current defences, questioning their coherence, and leads us towards potential reform options.[20] Secondly, where a separation can be made, it does appear to have certain practical consequences. For example, it seems that it is legitimate for D to use force to defend herself against an excused attacker (eg where V is attacking D under an insane delusion), but it is not legitimate for D to use force to protect herself where the attacker's conduct is justified (eg where V uses force on D in the belief that D is harming her child).[21] Further, whilst D may be an accomplice to an offence committed by P who is excused from liability, in contrast, D is absolved of liability as an accessory where P was justified in committing the offence.[22] Thirdly, and finally, the distinction seems to make a difference in what the law is trying to communicate to society. Robinson, for example, has discussed the role of defences as rule 'articulators'; that is, telling the public what they should and should not do.[23] For Robinson, whilst excuses are essential concessions to human frailty, they are not rules that the public need to know, they are not designed to adjust behaviour. Justifications, in contrast, should be communicated clearly because they tell people when it is permitted to commit certain offences for the greater good.

Assessment matters . . .
As we have said, the current law does not require an explicit identification of defences as excusatory or justificatory. Therefore, when applying a defence to problem facts, you do not need to use this terminology. However, when evaluating the law, either within a problem question or a more general essay, the terminology will be very useful.

14.2 Insanity as a defence

We have already discussed the insanity rules as a denial of offending (**13.4**), where D raises insanity to explain her lack of mens rea including in extreme cases her lack of voluntary conduct. However, uniquely, the insanity rules can *also* apply as a defence, exculpating D from liability even when she has completed the actus reus and mens rea of the offence charged. The elements of insanity as a defence are the same as those for insanity

[19] Robinson, 'Four Distinctions that Glanville Williams Did Not Make' in Baker and Horder (eds), *The Sanctity of Life and the Criminal Law* (2013).
[20] This is a common structure within academic writing. See eg Stark, 'Necessity and *Nicklinson*' [2013] Crim LR 949.
[21] Fletcher, *Rethinking Criminal Law* (1978) para 10.1.1.
[22] *Bourne* (1952) 36 Cr App R 125.
[23] Robinson, *Structure and Function in Criminal Law* (1997) Ch5.

as a denial of offending. Therefore, our discussion in this section should be read in the context of our more detailed analysis of the insanity rules in the previous chapter. Rather than repeating details from **13.4**, this section provides a brief overview of insanity as a defence, before highlighting a few areas where the difference between denial of offending and defence will affect our application of the law.

The insanity rules were set out in *M'Naghten*,[24] and confirmed in the House of Lords in its judicial capacity in *Sullivan*.[25] They are illustrated in **Table 14.1**.

Table 14.1 Insanity defence

A) D must suffer from a disease of the mind;
B) This must have caused a defect of reason; and
C) This must have caused a lack of responsibility, *either* because D did not know the nature or quality of her act, *or* she did not know it was legally wrong.

Where D satisfies these elements, even though otherwise her conduct would amount to an offence, she is entitled to a special acquittal. The burden of proof is on D on the balance of probabilities. D will be found 'not guilty by reason of insanity' (which is known as the special verdict), and the court will then choose from a range of disposal orders.[26] The special verdict ensures that D is protected from inappropriate liability through conviction, but also that the public can be protected from future danger through disposal options which include compulsory treatment and/or supervision.

Where insanity is raised as a defence, as opposed to a denial of mens rea, two main theoretical differences should be noted from our discussion at **13.4**. The first relates to the application of the elements of the insanity rules, and the second to their interaction with other defences.

14.2.1 The elements of insanity as a defence

The three elements of the insanity defence, set out in **Table 14.1**, were discussed at **13.4.2**. It should be noted here, in relation to the third element, that the either/or between 'not knowing the nature or quality of her act' and 'not knowing it was wrong' will often mark the difference between insanity as a denial of offending and insanity as a defence. Where D caused harms without an understanding of her acts as, for example, where D killed V thinking she was breaking a jar, she will not have possessed mens rea. Thus, if mens rea is required for the offence (remember that all offences require at least voluntary conduct), D's plea to the insanity rules will be a denial of offending. In contrast, where D

[24] (1843) 4 St Tr NS 847.
[25] [1984] 1 AC 156.
[26] See **13.4.1**.

has capacity to understand her acts, but her disease of the mind causes her not to know they are legally wrong, she may well possess mens rea. Indeed, understanding the legal wrongfulness of one's conduct is rarely relevant to the mens rea of an offence: ignorance of the law is no excuse.[27] Thus, an appeal to the insanity rules on this basis is likely to be an appeal to insanity as a defence.

A second point that should be noted relates to the first element of the insanity rules, which requires D to suffer from a disease of the mind and the internal/external cause distinction. Importantly, the need to show an internal cause is common to insanity as a denial of offending and insanity as a defence. However, there is likely to be an interesting switch in the priorities of the defendant. Where the plea is one amounting to a denial of offending, D will be particularly keen for the insanity rules not to be applied to her because, if the cause of her lack of capacity is external, she will receive an *unqualified* acquittal. This is why, for example, there is so much litigation around the borderline between automatism resulting in an unqualified acquittal and insanity resulting in the special verdict of not guilty by reason of insanity. In contrast, where the plea arises as a defence, the default position if the insanity rules do not apply is likely to be full criminal liability. Thus, although issues of stigma may still put off D from raising insanity, she is much more likely to do so in the hope of the special verdict.

14.2.2 Insanity and other defences

Where insanity arises as a denial of offending, it will rarely come into conflict with defences.[28] However, where insanity arises as a defence, other alternative defences may also be applicable. For example, suppose a situation where D is visiting V and has a psychotic delusion that V is possessed by the devil and is about to launch a deadly attack upon her. She makes a pre-emptive strike and is charged with assault. D will seek to raise mistaken self-defence (the public and private defence) in this case because, if successful, it would result in an unqualified acquittal. Alongside this, however, it is also clear that D's delusion will qualify for the insanity defence within the *M'Naghten* Rules. This is because D's delusion of self-defence is likely to mean that she did not know that what she was doing was wrong, and the *M'Naghten* Rules also make explicit reference to catching delusions of this kind.[29] For example, Lord Chief Justice Tindal remarked that D:

> must be considered in the same situation as to responsibility as if the facts with respect to which the delusion exists were real. For example, if under the influence of his delusion he supposes another man to be in the act of attempting to take away his life, and he kills that man, as he supposes, in self-defence, he would be exempt from punishment.[30]

---

[27] *Grant v Borg* [1982] 2 All ER 257; Ashworth, 'Ignorance of the Criminal Law, and Duties to Avoid It' (2011) 74 MLR 1.

[28] See **13.4.3**.

[29] This is sometimes referred to as a third limb of *M'Naghten*: the delusion limb: Williams, *Criminal Law: The General Part* (2nd edn, 1961) 497–507.

[30] *M'Naghten* [1843] UKHL J16, 211.

The reference to being 'exempt from punishment' in this extract is intended to mean that the insanity defence will apply. But this is very much a second best outcome for D. The insanity defence will result in acquittal, but also in the special verdict and the uncertainty of the various disposal options.

The question for the insanity rules is whether D should be allowed to rely on an alternative defence in priority to insanity, or whether the insanity rules should exclude and take preference over alternative options in order to ensure compulsory treatment and/or supervision where it is required. If D claims that her belief in the need to use force to protect herself is a belief based on her psychotic state, should D be treated as pleading self-defence, or should the fact that her claim raises insanity mean that self-defence is no longer available to her? Following the approach taken to insanity as a denial of offending, it seems right in principle and in policy that the latter option should be preferred. Whether D would favour an alternative basis for denying offending, or an alternative defence, if her satisfaction of these alternatives relies upon a defect of reason arising from a disease of the mind then the insanity rules should be applied in preference.[31] Just as D is prevented from relying on a simple denial of mens rea where that denial is based on what the law calls insanity, the same forward-looking rationale must apply equally to a choice between multiple defences: there remains a strong interest in protecting the public from future potential harm.

This issue arose in the case of *Oye*.

Oye [2013] EWCA Crim 1725

D became gripped by delusions that police officers were agents of evil spirits out to kill him, and launched a series of attacks on officers causing serious harm. D was charged with affray and maliciously inflicting GBH.[32] D raised self-defence (the public and private defence), and the judge instructed that insanity should *also* be left to the jury.

- Crown Court: guilty of affray and GBH offence. The jury rejected both defences.
- Court of Appeal: appeal allowed, substituting a special verdict of not guilty by reason of insanity.

The correct decision was reached in *Oye*, but it remains a problematic case. This is because the trial judge was in error in allowing the defences of mistaken self-defence and insanity to run in parallel. Although he was saved by the jury having rejected both defences, allowing both to run together is surely wrong in principle: if D was found not guilty on the basis of self-defence, thereby leading to an unqualified acquittal, this should be the end of the matter, and if a judge then wished to impose compulsory treatment under the separate heading of insanity this would give rise to some interesting issues under Article 5 ECHR. The Court of Appeal could have held, in line with our earlier discussion, that raising self-defence on the basis of an insane delusion amounted to raising the defence of insanity alone. However, the court achieved this same result by

---

[31] If D's appeal to self-defence does *not* rely on an insane delusion/mistake, the fact that D suffers from a disease of the mind is not relevant. The relevant conflict between defences only arises where D's claim of self-defence relies on an insane delusion/mistake.

[32] Offences Against the Person Act 1861, s20.

an alternative route. Focusing on the rules governing self-defence, the Court of Appeal held that insane delusions should be added to the list of grounds which the jury should ignore when considering whether D's use of force was reasonable (an element of the public and private defence).[33]

> **Don't be confused . . .**
> The *Oye* case is problematic, but the result (at least) is clear. Where D raises multiple defences including insanity, the insanity defence should be applied ahead of the other options. Following the approach in *Sullivan*[34] (discussing insanity as a denial of offending), it is hoped that future courts will provide clarity as to the priority of defences. Care is needed as to the application of the burden of proof.

14.3 Duress by threats

Duress, like insanity, is commonly understood as an excusatory defence.[35] D has committed an offence, but she has done so because she was threatened by X with death or serious injury if she refused. Thus, we do not agree with her conduct, the commission of the crime was not a justified act, but we can accept that she was placed in an impossible position, and so we can excuse her.

Some commentators go further and describe D's impossible position as a species of involuntariness, and it may be that D herself would protest that she 'had no choice' but to offend.[36] However, as we highlighted earlier, this kind of terminology is unhelpful in the context of defences. Where D appeals to the defence of duress, she is not claiming that she was not in control of her conduct, that would be automatism, nor is she claiming any other lack of mens rea as has been consistently recognised by the courts.[37] Rather, the defence of duress represents a concession to human frailty,[38] an acceptance that although D *did* have a choice between offending or suffering serious harm from X, her decision to offend does not reveal a dangerous character deserving of criminal punishment. We accept, essentially, that D did no more than most of us would have done in her position, and we acquit on the basis that, as the adage goes, 'there, but for the grace of God, go I'.

The defence of duress has developed at common law, and remains uncodified. As illustrated in **Table 14.2**, it consists of three main parts.[39]

---

[33] Child and Sullivan, 'When Does the Insanity Defence Apply? Some Recent Cases' [2014] Crim LR 787.

[34] [1984] AC 156.

[35] Westen and Mangiafico, 'The Criminal Defense of Duress: A Justification, Not an Excuse' (2003) 6 Buff Crim L Rev 833; Huigens, 'Duress is Not a Justification' (2004) 2 Ohio St J Crim L 303.

[36] The Canadian court in *Perka* (1984) 13 DLR (4th) 1 describe it as 'moral involuntariness'. See Wasik, 'Duress and Criminal Responsibility' [1977] Crim LR 453.

[37] *Fisher* [2004] EWCA Crim 1190; *Hasan* [2005] UKHL 22, [18].

[38] *Howe* [1987] 1 All ER 771, 779–780; *Hasan* [2005] UKHL 22, [18].

[39] Duress by threats is inconsistently presented as containing anything between two and eight elements. This inconsistency does not represent disagreement on the substance of the defence, but simply the presentation.

Table 14.2 Duress by threats

A) Exclusions: duress is not a defence to murder, attempted murder, and certain treason offences, and will not apply in circumstances of prior fault;
B) X's threat and demand: D must have reasonably believed that she or another (for whom she was responsible) was threatened with death or serious injury by X unless D committed the offence; and
C) D's response: committing a crime as D did must be something that a reasonable person in her circumstances would have done. D must show reasonable steadfastness in response to the threat, only committing the offence because her will was overborne.

It is commonly accepted that a defence of duress is needed in a criminal law system. For example, where X holds a gun to a bank manger's head and forces her to open the vault, few would want to hold D, the manager, liable as X's accomplice.[40] However, it should be highlighted from the start that there is also great concern about the limits of the defence, and scepticism about those raising it. Particularly in the context of criminal organisations and gangs, where threats and intimidation between members is common, duress can be claimed quite easily and can be very difficult for the prosecution to disprove.[41] The reaction to this has been twofold. First, as with other defences, D must provide some evidence of duress (D bears an evidential burden) before it will be considered in court, and before the prosecution are then under a legal burden to disprove it.[42] Secondly, and more controversially, scepticism about the overuse of the defence has led courts to interpret its elements increasingly narrowly. This has led to criticism in the other direction, claiming that the defence has now become overly restrictive and thus unable to apply in certain deserving circumstances.[43]

Extra detail . . .
The narrowing of duress can be witnessed across multiple cases. However, it is best illustrated by the speech of Lord Bingham in *Hasan*.[44] This speech should be carefully read in full. The minority speech of Baroness Hale, in the same case, provides useful illustration of arguments in favour of a wider interpretation.

14.3.1 Exclusions

There are two areas where duress will be excluded: in relation to certain offences; and in circumstances of prior fault.

---

[40] On accomplice liability, see **Chapter 12**.
[41] Law Commission, *Murder, Manslaughter and Infanticide* (No 304, 2006) paras 6.101–6.111.
[42] *Hasan* [2005] UKHL 22, [37]. The Law Commission has recommended reversing the legal burden of proof where duress is raised as a defence to murder (see discussion at **14.7**).
[43] For a useful discussion of this in the context of defendants suffering from domestic abuse, see Loveless, 'Domestic Violence, Coercion and Duress' [2010] Crim LR 93.
[44] [2005] UKHL 22.

14.3.1.1 Offences to which D cannot raise duress

Unlike the other general defences discussed in this chapter, which potentially apply across all criminal offences, the defence of duress (by threats and by circumstance) is not a defence to certain offences.

A) Treason: The term 'treason' refers to a bundle of offences against the state. Duress *can* be a defence to certain of these offences. In *Purdy*,[45] for example, a British prisoner of war (D) was forced to assist with German propaganda during the Second World War. In doing so, D committed a treason offence, but it was held that he could rely on duress as a defence. However, other more serious treason offences will not allow duress as a defence.[46]

B) Murder: More controversially, duress is not a defence to murder.[47] As Blackstone put it, under duress a person 'ought rather to die himself than escape by the murder of an innocent'.[48] This was recognised by a bare majority of the Privy Council in *Abbott*,[49] and later by the House of Lords in *Howe*,[50] where it was also established that duress was no defence to murder as a secondary party.[51] The harsh results of this exclusion are clearly illustrated in the case of *Wilson*.[52]

Wilson [2007] EWCA Crim 1251

D, a 13-year-old boy, assisted his father to murder his neighbour, fetching an axe and starting a fire on his father's instruction. D claimed that he only did so because of fear of his father's violence. D was charged with murder as his father's accomplice.[53]

- Crown Court: guilty of murder. The defence, being unable to rely on duress, claimed unsuccessfully that D was so swept up in fear of his father that he was not able to form mens rea.
- Court of Appeal: conviction upheld on appeal.

The Court of Appeal in *Wilson* accepted that the law could be criticised for not providing a defence of duress where a 13-year-old is forced to commit murder by a dominant and violent parent,[54] but were obliged to follow the clear precedent from *Howe*.

C) Attempted murder: It was recognised in *Gotts*[55] that if duress was no defence to murder then it would be illogical to recognise it as a defence to attempted murder.[56]

---

[45] (1946) 10 JCL 182.
[46] *Steane* [1947] KB 997, 1005.
[47] Law Commission, *Murder, Manslaughter and Infanticide* (No 304, 2006) Ch6.
[48] Blackstone, *Commentaries on the Laws of England* (1765–69) Book 4, 30.
[49] [1977] AC 755.
[50] [1987] AC 417.
[51] Walters, 'Murder Under Duress and Judicial Decision Making in the House of Lords' (1988) 18 LS 61.
[52] Ashworth, 'Commentary on *Wilson*' [2008] Crim LR 138.
[53] **Chapter 12**.
[54] At [18].
[55] [1992] 2 AC 412.
[56] Gardner, 'Duress in Attempted Murder' (1991) 107 LQR 389.

If the court had found otherwise, the results would have been bizarre: allowing D's acts to be excused, but not the results. This would have been particularly odd if V died some time after D's attack, as D would be allowed her freedom until the moment of V's death.

Unfortunately, the law remains illogical in allowing duress to apply where D commits an offence of intentionally causing GBH.[57] This is because, as the mens rea of murder includes both an intention to kill or an intention to cause GBH,[58] the same potential for problems arises here as it did in the context of attempted murder. For example, D attacks V under duress, causing V serious injury. D is not prosecuted because she has clearly acted under duress. Months later, or even longer, V dies from the injuries caused by D's original attack. D is now liable for murder, is prosecuted, and has no defence of duress.

It was confirmed by the Crown Court in *Ness* that duress remains a valid defence for conspiracy to murder, and presumably assisting or encouraging murder.[59] Unlike attempted murder, these offences will never involve the direct application of force to V as part of their actus reus. Thus, the defence can be safely recognised in this context without encountering the potential problems just discussed.

> *Point to remember . . .*
> The exclusion of duress as a defence to murder and attempted murder is one of the most controversial aspects of the defence. Echoing academic criticisms, the Law Commission has recommended that duress should be extended to cover these offences.[60] This is discussed further in the reform section at **14.7.1.2**.

14.3.1.2 Exclusion on the basis of prior fault

The general defences are designed to protect D from liability where she has been placed in a position where her offending is either excused or justified. The reference here to 'has been placed in a position' is important. Where D, either consciously or through negligence, places herself in a position where she requires a defence, the law will be much less willing to recognise that defence.[61] The defence of duress, more than any other general defence, has applied this principle progressively strictly.

Early case law allowed D some leeway where she demonstrated prior fault by voluntarily associating with X, but on reasonable grounds did not foresee the threat and demand which followed.[62] However, subsequent case law has been considerably more restrictive, illustrated in *Hasan*.

---

[57] Offences Against the Person Act 1861, s18.
[58] See **5.4**.
[59] [2011] Crim LR 645.
[60] Law Commission, *Murder, Manslaughter and Infanticide* (No 304, 2006) Ch6.
[61] Child, 'Prior Fault: Blocking Defences or Constructing Crimes' in Reed and Bohlander (eds), *General Defences* (2014) 37.
[62] *Shepherd* (1987) 86 Cr App R 47: joining a group of burglars does not mean that D should have foreseen being threatened with a gun when trying to leave; *Lewis* (1992) 96 Cr App R 412: joining a group of armed robbers does not mean that D should have foreseen being threatened not to testify against other members when in prison.

Hasan [2005] UKHL 22

D committed burglary. He did so as a result of threats from X, who was known to be violent. D acted as a minder for X's girlfriend, who was a prostitute. X also acted as a minder for his girlfriend, as well as being involved in drug dealing. D was charged with aggravated burglary.[63]

- Crown Court: guilty of aggravated burglary.
- Court of Appeal: appeal allowed, finding a defence of duress.
- House of Lords: appeal allowed, reinstating conviction. D's voluntary association with X under-mined any appeal to duress.

Hasan confirms that duress will be excluded where D voluntarily associated with X in circumstances where a reasonable person (note the objective standard) would have fore-seen a risk of future coercion. Foresight of 'coercion' need not even be specific in nature, and not even require foresight of coercion to commit a crime. As Lord Bingham states:

> The policy of the law must be to discourage association with known criminals, and it should be slow to excuse the criminal conduct of those who do so. If a person voluntarily becomes or remains asso-ciated with others engaged in criminal activity in a situation where he knows or ought reasonably to know that he may be the subject of compulsion by them or their associates, he cannot rely on the defence of duress to excuse any act which he is thereafter compelled to do by them.[64]

The breadth of this principle was criticised in a powerful minority speech from Baroness Hale, who would prefer a test based on subjective foresight,[65] and it has also attracted cogent academic criticism.[66] However, the majority approach in *Hasan* has been con-firmed in *Ali*,[67] and represents the current law.

Extra detail . . .
The quotation above from Lord Bingham includes reference to 'remains associated' as well as becom-ing associated. The potential for prior fault in these circumstances has not been well litigated, but is designed to cover cases where D joins what appears to be a non-criminal organisation, discovers that it is criminal and/or violent, but does not take an opportunity to leave. Care must be taken, however, to distinguish between cases where D has a genuine opportunity to leave (such that her choice to stay represents prior fault), and those for whom leaving the group is not a realistic or safe option (eg children brought up within a terrorist organisation) where D's decision to remain in the group might not represent prior fault.[68]

---

[63] Theft Act 1968, s10. See **9.4.3**.

[64] At [38].

[65] Hale's approach would only deny duress where D subjectively foresaw that she might be threat-ened to commit crimes.

[66] J.C. Smith, 'Comment on *Heath*' [2000] Crim LR 109. Criticising objective foresight of *any* coer-cion: 'It is one thing . . . to be aware that you are likely to be beaten up if you do not pay your debts, it is another to be aware that you may be required under threat of violence to commit other, though unspecified, crimes, if you do not.'

[67] [2008] EWCA Crim 716.

[68] This issue has arisen in the context of trafficked women: *Ajayi* [2010] EWCA Crim 471. However, a specific defence has now been created in this context: Modern Slavery Act 2015,

14.3.2 Element 1: X's threat and demand

When considering the threat and demand from X, three main questions should be considered: how serious must the threat be; who has made the threat, and who it is directed at; and how detailed must the demand be?

14.3.2.1 How serious must the threat be?

It is generally accepted that X's threat must be of death or serious personal injury,[69] as confirmed by the House of Lords in *Hasan*.[70] In this manner, the gravity of X's threat works as an important threshold for the applicability of the defence. Any threat other than that of death or serious injury, even if it is vastly more serious than the offence X is demanding of D, will not qualify. For example, X threatens D that unless she commits a minor theft of V's property, she will face the much greater theft or damage of her own property. Where D succumbs to the threat and takes V's property, even if a reasonable person in D's position would have done likewise, D will have no defence of duress.[71] Duress is not a 'balance of evils' defence. In circumstances of this kind, where D commits a minor offence in fear of greater harm that does not threaten life or serious injury, D will have to appeal to the defence of necessity, discussed later.[72]

Threats of death are straightforward, but there remains some uncertainty about what constitutes a threat of serious harm. For example, although a threat to cause non-psychiatric GBH will always be sufficient, there is uncertainty about threats to cause serious psychiatric injury (eg a threat to leave D a nervous wreck).[73] As such harm is now recognised as being capable of constituting GBH for offences against the person,[74] however, the same approach may well be followed for duress. It has also been held (*obiter*) that a threat to rape D will be sufficient to meet the gravity threshold.[75] A threat to cause ABH, however, will not be sufficient (eg where X threatens to punch D[76] unless D commits a crime).

> **Extra detail . . .**
>
> Although duress is not a balance of evils defence, there is some authority to suggest that where X demands that D commit a particularly serious offence, the gravity of the threat must be even higher (ie of life-threatening harm, or even of death only).[77] The Law Commission has taken a similar approach with its recommendations for duress as a defence to murder, saying that it should only apply where D is threatened with death or 'life-threatening injury'.[78]

s45: Laird, 'Evaluating the Relationship between Section 45 of the Modern Slavery Act 2015 and the Defence of Duress: An Opportunity Missed?' [2016] Crim LR 395.

[69] *Radford* [2004] EWCA Crim 2878.
[70] [2005] UKHL 22.
[71] *Vinh van Dao* [2012] EWCA Crim 1717 (a threat of false imprisonment); *Singh* [1973] 1 WLR 1600 (a threat of blackmail); *M'Growther* (1746) Fost 13 (a threat to property).
[72] See **14.6**.
[73] *Baker v Wilkins* [1997] Crim LR 497.
[74] *Ireland and Burstow* [1998] AC 147. See **7.4.1.3**.
[75] *Ashley* [2012] EWCA Crim 434.
[76] *Aikens* [2003] EWCA Crim 1573.
[77] *M'Growther* (1746) Fost 13; *Purdy* (1946) 10 JCL 182; *Abbott* [1976] 3 All ER 152.
[78] Law Commission, *Murder, Manslaughter and Infanticide* (No 304, 2006) para 6.76.

A problem can arise where D *believes* that she is being threatened with death or serious injury, but in fact she is not. For example, where X says she will 'do D over' unless D commits a certain crime, D may take this as a threat to her life, and therefore sufficient for duress, when in fact it is a threat to destroy D's property which is insufficient for duress. It is clear that duress is not restricted to situations where there are *in fact* threats of death or serious injury, as otherwise there would be no duress where X threatens D with an unloaded gun, but case law has been required to determine how and when the defence can be based upon D's mistaken beliefs. *Safi and others* provided useful clarification.

 Safi [2003] EWCA Crim 1809

D and others hijacked a plan in Afghanistan, eventually landing in England at Stansted. They claimed duress on the basis that they were fleeing death or serious injury from the Taliban in Afghanistan. D was charged with various offences including hijacking.[79]

- Crown Court: guilty of hijacking offences. The jury were directed that duress was only available where there was objective evidence of a threat, which on the facts there was not, and that D's beliefs in an imminent threat were insufficient.
- Court of Appeal: appeal allowed. There is no need for objective evidence of a threat, as long as D reasonably believed it existed.

Safi clarifies that duress can be founded upon a mistaken belief. Note, however, that an honest belief will not necessarily be sufficient, and D's belief must also be *reasonable*: a reasonable person in D's position would also have believed that there was a real threat of death or serious injury.[80] More recent case law has endorsed, expressly[81] or implicitly,[82] the objective approach in *Safi*, and so it is very likely that this represents the current law.

In requiring an objectively reasonable belief in the threat from X, the defence of duress is inconsistent with the public and private defence (discussed at **14.5**) where a subjectively honest belief will suffice. This may be explained on grounds that the defences apply in different circumstances, one as an excuse and the other as a justification.[83] However, the origins of the objective approach in duress were guided by the then objective approach employed for the public and private defence.[84] It is therefore at least arguable that a consistent approach favouring one alternative or the other should be preferred.[85]

Extra detail . . .
A related question has emerged asking whether the threat from X must be criminal in nature. With a threshold of death or serious injury, this question is rarely relevant to duress. However, in *Jones and others*,[86] D raised the defence of duress of circumstance against charges of criminal damage by

---

[79] Aviation Security Act 1982, s1(1).
[80] At [25].
[81] *Blake* [2004] EWCA Crim 1238, [18]; *Bronson* [2004] EWCA Crim 903, [23].
[82] *Hasan* [2005] UKHL 22.
[83] Lord Bingham expressly rejected the comparison between defences in *Hasan* [2005] UKHL 22.
[84] *Graham* [1982] 1 All ER 801.
[85] Alldridge, 'Developing the Defence of Duress' [1986] Crim LR 433; Wilson, 'The Structure of Defences' [2005] Crim LR 108, 115–116.
[86] [2004] EWCA Crim 1981. Affirmed in the House of Lords on other grounds [2006] UKHL 16.

cutting the fence at an RAF base, claiming that his actions were to prevent the UK government waging an illegal war and killing people in Iraq. The Court of Appeal avoided engaging with the question of whether the war was illegal by holding that the defence of duress could only apply to threats of death or serious injury that amounted to crimes in English and Welsh law, which the war was not. This was a convenient approach for the court, but has been cogently criticised and should be seen as isolated to its facts.[87] As we will discuss later, in the context of duress of circumstance in particular, many threats will not be criminal in nature, such as an approaching tidal wave, and the courts are unlikely to follow *Jones* in requiring them to be.

14.3.2.2 Who must the threat be from, and against whom must the threat be made?

The paradigm example of duress involves X threatening D with death or serious injury unless she commits a particular offence. Cases have emerged, however, to test this paradigm.

What if, for example, the threats do not come from another person but come from D herself in the form of suicidal thoughts? This was discussed in *Rodger and Rose*.

Rodger and Rose [1998] 1 Cr App R 143

D broke out of prison following news that the tariff period (jail time) of his life sentence had been substantially increased. It was accepted that D did this because he was depressed and suicidal, and believed that he would have committed suicide if he did not escape. D was charged with the offence of 'breaking prison'.

- Crown Court: guilty of breaking prison. Duress was not open to D because the threat was not external from himself.
- Court of Appeal: conviction upheld on appeal.

The Court of Appeal stated that to allow a defence of duress in these circumstances 'could amount to a licence to commit crime dependent on the personal characteristics and vulnerability of the offender'. The case is useful, therefore, both as a clarification that the threat must come from another person, and to help to understand duress as a defence which provides a concession to *human* frailty as opposed to *individual* frailty.

The next question asks who the threat must be aimed at: for example, what if X threatens to kill D's child unless D commits an offence? Although X's threat will invariably be aimed at D herself, the same principles are engaged where D is compelled to offend in order to protect another, and case law has progressively opened up the cases in which D can plead the defence based on her perception of threats of death or serious injury to others. In *Hurley and Murray*, an Australian court allowed duress to apply where X's threats related to D's de facto wife;[88] in *Wright*, threats against D's boyfriend sufficed;[89] in *Conway*, threats against D's car passenger were enough;[90] and so on. There is some

[87] Ormerod, Commentary [2005] Crim LR 122.
[88] [1967] VR 526.
[89] [2000] Crim LR 510.
[90] [1989] QB 290.

suggestion in *Hasan* that this class of people, other than the defendant, may be limited to 'immediate family or someone close to [D] or for whom [D] is responsible'.[91] But if this is right, it must surely be interpreted liberally. If X, a bank robber, puts a gun to a customer's (Z's) head and instructs the bank manager (D) to open the safe, D may not have any personal connection with Z, but the fact and circumstances of the threat will surely be enough to make D feel 'responsible' for Z; and it would be very harsh to deny D the defence on the basis that she was not sufficiently attached to Z. If this is correct, as dicta from other cases suggest,[92] and as the Law Commission has recommended,[93] then the class of people who the threat might be aimed at has no limits at all.

> **Extra detail . . .**
>
> It is even possible for the person threatening D and the target of that threat to be the same person. This was so in *Martin*,[94] where D's wife threatened to take her own life unless D drove whilst disqualified in order to take their son to work.[95]

14.3.2.3 Does X's demand have to specify a particular offence?

Paradigm cases will involve X demanding that D commits a particular offence, for example 'steal from the safe or else', but this will not always be the case. Sometimes it will become clear to D that she must commit a particular offence to avoid a threat, but this may not have been communicated from X: for example, 'have the money by tomorrow or else'. Where, as in our example, X does not specify a crime, it is unlikely that D will be able to rely on duress by threats although she may be able to rely on duress by circumstances.[96] This was discussed in *Cole*.

> **Cole** [1994] Crim LR 582
>
> D robbed two building societies in order to repay a debt. The money lenders had hit D with a baseball bat and threatened him and his family unless he repaid the money, although they did not specify what he should do to get it. D was charged with robbery.[97]
>
> • Crown Court: guilty of robbery.
> • Court of Appeal: conviction upheld on appeal. Duress did not apply because: (a) D's offence was not specified by the lenders; and (b) there was a lack of immediacy between the threat and D's offence.[98]

The line taken in *Cole* is very restrictive, suggesting that duress by threats will only apply where a single crime is clearly demanded. This line has been softened in *Ali*.

---

[91] [2005] UKHL 22, [21].
[92] *Shayler* [2001] 1 WLR 2206, where the Lord Chief Justice approves a statement to this effect from *Hussain*, [49].
[93] Law Commission, *Defences of General Application* (No 83, 1977) para 2.46.
[94] [1989] 1 All ER 652.
[95] The court discussed this as a duress by circumstances case, but given that there were explicit threats involved it is better analysed as one of duress by threats.
[96] See **14.4**.
[97] Theft Act 1968, s8(1). See **9.3**.
[98] We discuss this element of duress at **14.3.3.2**.

Ali [1995] Crim LR 303

D, a heroin addict, robbed a building society. D claimed that his dealer (X) had threatened him about unpaid debts, provided him with a gun, and told him to get the money from a bank or building society. D was charged with robbery.[99]

- Crown Court: guilty of robbery.
- Court of Appeal: conviction upheld on appeal. Duress did not apply because of D's prior fault in forming a relationship with X.[100] *Obiter*: the level of specificity as to the crime to be committed was sufficient for duress.

Following *Cole* and *Ali* it is clear that duress by threats requires X to have provided some indication of the type of crime that D must commit, but precise details of that crime (eg time, place, etc) are not required. Where D's defence fails on this element, the defence of duress by circumstances should be considered (see **14.4**).

14.3.3 Element 2: D's response to the threat

When analysing D's response to the threat and demand, three main questions should be considered: must the threat and demand have caused D's offence; what if D could have avoided committing the offence; and what if a reasonable person would not have acted as D did?

14.3.3.1 Must the threat and demand have caused D's offence?

The simple answer to this, unsurprisingly, is 'yes': duress only provides a defence where D's offence was compelled and therefore factually caused by X's threats and demands. If D would have done the same thing in the absence of X's threat then the defence will not apply.[101]

Problems can emerge, however, where D has several reasons for committing the offence, and only one of these constitutes a threat qualifying within the duress threshold. This was the case in *Valderrama-Vega*.

Valderrama-Vega [1985] Crim LR 220

D was involved in trafficking drugs. He claimed that he did so because of: (a) threats of serious harm from a mafia-type organisation; (b) because of financial difficulties; and (c) because of threats to expose his homosexuality. D was charged with drug trafficking offences.

- Crown Court: guilty of drug trafficking. The jury were directed that duress could only apply where D acted 'solely' due to the threats of serious injury.
- Court of Appeal: conviction upheld on appeal. However, the court clarified that the 'sole' motive test was wrong. The threats of serious injury had to be a sufficient cause, such that D would not have offended without them, but they need not be the sole cause.

---

99   Theft Act 1968, s8(1). See **9.3**.
100 We discuss this element of duress at **14.3.1.2**.
101 *DPP v Bell* [1992] Crim LR 176: in terror, D drove while over the alcohol limit. D was planning to drink drive before the threat, but as he may have been talked out of it by his passengers, it was accepted that the threat was the cause.

The approach of the court is sensible, and straightforward. Duress will only apply where the qualifying threat caused D to offend. There may have been other causes, but these are irrelevant and should be discounted.

14.3.3.2 What if D could have avoided offending?

Related to the requirement of causation, is that D must have committed the offence because she had no other option to escape before the threat would be carried out. This is often referred to as a requirement of 'imminency', because the longer the time between X's threat and D's offence, the more opportunity D is likely to have had to escape the threat without offending by, for example, going to the police.

Historically, courts were willing to interpret this requirement quite generously for D. For example, in *Abdul-Hussain*[102] the Court of Appeal allowed the appeal of D who had hijacked a plane and come to England to escape deportation and likely execution in Iraq. Although the execution was not going to happen in the 'immediate' future,[103] the threat of execution was the 'imminent' cause of D's offence, and this was sufficient. The court illustrated their approach with a useful and convincing hypothetical:

> If Anne Frank had stolen a car to escape from Amsterdam and been charged with theft, the tenets of English law would not, in our judgment, have denied her a defence of duress . . ., on the ground that she should have waited for the Gestapo's knock on the door.[104]

A similar approach was adopted in *Hudson and Taylor*.

Hudson and Taylor [1971] 2 All ER 244

D and another, aged 17 and 19, admitted committing perjury by failing to testify as to the identity of the suspect of a wounding at trial, leading to his acquittal. D claimed that she lied because she was threatened with being 'cut up' if she identified the suspect, and one of those threatening her was in the public gallery when she gave evidence. D was charged with perjury.

- Crown Court: guilty of perjury. Duress did not apply because the threat was not immediate, D was safe in the court and so the threat could not have been carried out there and then.
- Court of Appeal: appeal allowed. Although the harm threatened could not have been carried out immediately, the threat was still imminent and was the operative cause of D's offence. Duress was also not undermined by D's failure to go to the police before the trial because she believed the police could not provide adequate protection.

The test as applied in these cases simply required D to have no effective means of escape. The threatened harm may not be immediate, but as long as it is imminent and operative at the time D offends, the defence will be allowed. There is much to be said for this approach. Just because the threatened harm is not immediate, a reasonable person in D's position may still have acted as D did: there is still a need to protect D by providing a concession to human frailty.

---

[102] [1999] Crim LR 570.
[103] This is why duress was rejected at trial.
[104] Here, again, the court is focusing on the imminence of the threat rather than the immediacy of the threatened harm.

In more recent times, however, the courts have read this element narrowly. Serious doubt must now been placed on these judgments because of statements (*obiter*) in *Hasan*.[105]In this case, Lord Bingham referred to *Hudson* as having the 'unfortunate effect of weakening' the immediacy requirement, referred to as a 'cardinal feature' of duress.[106] The likelihood, therefore, is that this element will be applied more strictly in the future.[107]

14.3.3.3 What if a reasonable person would not have acted as D did?

The final element of duress applies a further objective standard; requiring that D should display a reasonable fortitude in resisting the threat and demand from X. For example, if an adult, D, is threatened with serious harm from an infant unless she commits an offence, this threat may satisfy the elements discussed previously, but it is likely that D will be expected to resist the threat. Thus, where D commits the offence in these circumstances, duress will not apply. The threat may be real, but a reasonable person would not have had their will overborne by it.[108]

The objective reasonable fortitude test has been consistently highlighted in the case law,[109] and is usefully illustrated in *Graham*.

Graham [1982] 1 All ER 801

D lived in 'a bizarre ménage a trois' with his wife (V) and homosexual partner (X). D suffered from anxiety and took Valium, making him more susceptible to bullying. X had been violent to both D and V in the past. Following a previous attack, X and D tricked V into returning home, X put a flex around V's neck and instructed D to pull. D did so in fear of X, and V died. D was charged with murder.[110] (*Note: at this time duress could be a defence to murder.*)

- Crown Court: guilty of murder.
- Court of Appeal: conviction upheld on appeal. The test for duress asks if a reasonable and sober person would have acted as D did; the fact that D's steadfastness was weakened by alcohol and valium is therefore irrelevant.

The objective nature of the test is another reflection of duress as a concession to human frailty as opposed to individual frailty. The question whether D's will was overborne is half the story; the defence is only available if a reasonable person in D's position would also have had their will overborne.

A strictly objective test of steadfastness, however, can result in unfairness. Although duress is not a concession to *individual* frailty, there are certain general characteristics, such as age, that will affect D's ability to resist threats and demands. Interestingly, in contrast to the narrowing of other elements of duress, the courts have responded to this concern by gradually liberalising the range of D's characteristics that can be taken into account when applying the reasonable steadfastness test. This is discussed in *Bowen*.

---

[105] [2005] UKHL 22.
[106] At [25]–[27].
[107] *Batchelor* [2013] EWCA Crim 2638, [15]: echoing Lord Bingham's criticism of *Hudson*, and support for stricter application of the immediacy requirement.
[108] Smith, 'Duress and Steadfastness: In Pursuit of the Unintelligible' [1999] Crim LR 363.
[109] *Howe* [1987] 1 All ER 771.
[110] **Chapter 5.**

Bowen [1996] 2 Cr App R 157

D obtained various electrical goods on credit by deception, with no way of making repayment. D claimed to be acting under duress, having been threatened to obtain the goods by two other men. Expert evidence showed that D had an IQ of 68, putting him in the bottom 2 per cent of the population, and likely to be extremely suggestible. D was charged with obtaining services by deception.[111]

- Crown Court: guilty of obtaining services by deception. Duress steadfastness test based on a reasonable person of D's age and sex.
- Court of Appeal: conviction upheld on appeal. Characteristics that affect D's ability to resist a threat and demand beyond age and sex may be relevant, but this does not include D's IQ.

The characteristics recognised in *Bowen* as potentially relevant include D's age and sex, pregnancy, serious physical disability, and recognised mental illness or psychiatric condition.[112] Where D possesses these, the test will be whether a reasonable and sober person *sharing these characteristics* might have also had their will overborne. In this way, although *Bowen* can be criticised for excluding the relevance of D's low IQ,[113] it has had a highly liberalising impact on this element of duress.

Point to remember . . .
Despite the liberalising of this element, the restrictive objectivity of other elements means that duress remains a very narrow defence. The case of *GAC* provides a useful example.[114] In this case D pleaded duress to a charge of importing drugs, having been threatened by her abusive partner (X). It was accepted that D's characteristics could be taken into account, including the fact that she was suffering from battered women syndrome. However, her defence failed on several other grounds, including the fact that the abuse she was suffering did not amount to a threat of death or serious injury.[115]

14.4 Duress by circumstances

Duress by circumstances is essentially an extension of duress by threats. It has been recognised at common law to provide a defence where there is no direct threat and/or demand from another party, but the surrounding circumstances create an equivalent overbearing of D's will. For example, if D sees a tidal wave crashing towards her on the shore, the wave does not tell her to break into a car and escape or she will be killed, but it may be very obvious that this is her choice.

Don't be confused . . .
Duress by circumstances has caused considerable confusion for the courts, mainly in terms of its place alongside other defences such as duress by threats and necessity. As a result, it has been inconsistently labelled as 'necessity' or 'necessity of circumstances', etc. Although, as we see later, this

---

[111] Now obtaining services dishonestly, Fraud Act 2006, s11. See **10.5**.
[112] Buchanan and Virgo, 'Duress and Mental Abnormality' [1999] Crim LR 517.
[113] Although D's low IQ would not make him less resistant to threats, it will make him less able to identify ways of escaping them. Thus, the threat may appear more grave.
[114] [2013] EWCA Crim 1472.
[115] Loveless, 'Domestic Violence, Coercion and Duress' [2010] Crim LR 93.

defence is similar to the necessity defence, it is better presented as a separate defence. This is because whereas necessity is hopelessly ambiguous in its application, duress by circumstances is relatively well defined. Therefore, even if we see it as a subcategory of necessity, where duress by circumstances can be applied, it provides a welcome opportunity to avoid the necessity defence.[116]

Duress by circumstances was first recognised in *Willer*.

 Willer (1986) 83 Cr App R 225

D drove his car slowly onto a pavement in order to escape from a gang of youths who were intent on doing serious injury to him and his passenger. D was charged with reckless driving, and tried to raise the defence of necessity.
- Crown Court: guilty of reckless driving. Necessity does not apply.
- Court of Appeal: appeal allowed. Necessity is irrelevant, but D does have a defence of duress.

In recognising a defence of duress, the Court of Appeal did not distinguish it as a new form of duress by circumstances. However, this was the necessary implication: the youths were not shouting 'drive on the pavement or else', the threat and demand was not specific, they were circumstantial. This was later confirmed, and to some extent clarified, in *Conway*,[117] where D drove dangerously to escape what he believed were two assailants intent on killing his passenger.[118] It was in this case that the language of duress by circumstances (or 'duress of circumstances') began to be used.

The elements of duress by circumstances are set out in **Table 14.3**.

Table 14.3 Duress by circumstances

A) Exclusions: duress is not a defence to murder, attempted murder, and certain treason offences, and will not apply in circumstances of prior fault;
B) Circumstantial threat and demand: D must have reasonably believed that the circumstances posed a threat of death or serious injury which compelled her to commit the offence; and
C) D's response: D must have shown reasonable steadfastness in response to the threat, only committing the offence because her will was overborne

14.4.1 Relationship between duress by threats and duress by circumstances

When compared to other general defences, duress by circumstances is still very new to the law. However, because of its close relationship with duress by threats, it has been

[116] Gardner, 'Necessity's Newest Invention' (1991) 11 OJLS 125.
[117] [1989] QB 290.
[118] They were in fact plain-clothes police officers, wishing to interview his passenger.

able to establish itself by mirroring most of the elements of that defence. This has led to some confusion in cases such as *Martin*,[119] where D's wife's threats to commit suicide unless he committed an offence were treated as duress by circumstances rather than the more appropriate defence of duress by threats. However, because of the similarities between the defences, both in substance and rationale, such confusions are not overly problematic.

14.4.2 The elements of duress by circumstances

Most of the elements of duress by circumstances mirror those for duress by threats, and so there is no need to repeat that discussion here. However, it is useful to highlight a few key points to illustrate how those elements apply in the context of duress by circumstances.

14.4.2.1 Exclusions

The same exclusions apply for duress by circumstances as apply to duress by threats.[120] Therefore, duress by circumstances is no defence to murder, attempted murder, and certain treason offences. Also, although there is no case on point, it is likely that duress by circumstances will be excluded where those circumstances were brought about by prior fault. Taking the example of D who breaks into a car to escape a tidal wave, she may therefore lose the defence if she is a storm chaser who has travelled to the coast to witness the devastation. This would be akin to a form of voluntary association in duress by threats.

14.4.2.2 Element 1: circumstantial threat and demand

This element represents the major difference between duress by threats and duress by circumstances. However, it also retains important similarities.[121]

A) Differences from duress by threats: Unlike duress by threats, there is no requirement to show that the threat and demand came from a person.[122] There is also no need to show that a specific crime was demanded.[123] Both of these requirements have been applied restrictively within the context of duress by threats, so duress by circumstances provides a useful alternative.

B) Similarities with duress by threats: Despite the differences, this element still retains two important and restrictive similarities. First, the threat must still be one of death or serious injury:[124] duress by circumstances retains this high threshold from duress by threats and is not a simple balance of evils defence. Where the circumstances threatening D fall below this threshold, this defence will not apply and D will have to appeal to the defence of necessity. Secondly, although the threat does not need to come from another person, it still cannot come from D.[125] Thus, the principle from *Rodger and*

---

[119] [1989] 1 All ER 652.
[120] See **14.3.1**.
[121] See **14.3.2**.
[122] See **14.3.2.2**.
[123] See **14.3.2.3**.
[124] See **14.3.2.1**.
[125] See **14.3.2.2**.

Rose applies.[126] The restrictive application of these requirements in the context of duress by circumstances is illustrated in *Quayle*.[127]

 Quayle [2005] EWCA Crim 1415

Combined cases involving possession, importation, and/or supply of cannabis for the purposes of relieving the pain of those suffering a variety of conditions. In each case, the defences of necessity and/or duress of circumstance were raised.

- Crown Court: guilty of drug offences in all but one of the cases, rejecting D's defence. One case allowed the defence to go to the jury and D was acquitted.
- Court of Appeal: convictions upheld on appeal, and the AG's Reference (concerning the acquitted D) was answered to the effect that the defence should not have been allowed to run.

Duress by circumstances was rejected in the *Quayle* appeals for two main reasons. First, the threat, in that case the additional pain resulting from not using cannabis, was not sufficient to constitute a threat of death or serious injury. Secondly, where the drug offences related to personal use, the threat was purely internal to D and was therefore disqualified by the principle in *Rodger and Rose*.

14.4.2.3 Element 2: D's response to the perceived threats

The requirements are the same here as those for duress by threats.[128] D's offending must have been caused by the threats and demands of X; D must have made reasonable efforts to avoid offending; and D must have demonstrated reasonable fortitude in resisting X's threats.

One point within this, which is particularly tricky for duress by circumstances, is identifying the beginning and end of D's compelled conduct. Unlike duress by threats, where there is another party directing what D should do and when, duress by circumstances can be rather more fluid and uncertain. For example, where an intoxicated D is compelled to drive in order to escape a tidal wave or gang of youths, how far can D drive with an operative defence of duress by circumstances? A number of cases have encountered this issue, and the general approach has been to allow the defence to operate until D is clear of the danger, such that if D continues to drive she is now committing an offence (driving over the proscribed alcohol limit) without a defence.[129]

14.5 Public and private defence

The public and private defence, which is commonly referred to as self-defence,[130] provides a complete defence to any charge where D uses force to protect her public

---

[126] [1998] 1 Cr App R 143.
[127] Watson, 'Cannabis and the Defence of Necessity' (1998) 149 NLJ 1260.
[128] See **14.3.3**.
[129] *DPP v Bell* [1992] Crim LR 176; *DPP v Jones* [1990] RTR 34; *DPP v Mullally* [2006] EWHC 3448 (Admin).
[130] The term 'self-defence' is common, but misleading. The public and private defence is not limited to the use of force to protect oneself.

or private interests.[131] Two preliminary questions are apparent: (a) what type of force can the defence justify; and (b) what are public and private interests.

As to the first, the public and private defence will only provide a defence where D's offence involved the use of force. Thus, it is most commonly applied as a defence to murder, false imprisonment, and the offences against the person more generally. For example, D relies on the public and private defence where she hits V, causing ABH, in order to prevent V stabbing her with a knife. However, the defence is not limited to offences within certain categories, and each case will be judged on its own facts to identify whether D has used force when committing the offence. For example, although dangerous driving will not always involve force, *Renouf* established that where the particular case did involve force, the public and private defence could apply.[132] This seems logical, but can lead to some rather strange results. In *Blake v DPP*,[133] for example, D was charged with criminal damage having written in felt pen on a concrete pillar outside the Houses of Parliament in protest against the Iraq war. Denying the public and private defence, the court held that D's act was 'insufficient to amount to the use of force', suggesting that D would have had more chance of using the defence if he had caused greater damage.[134]

> **Extra detail . . .**
> Although the public and private defence provides a justification for the use of force in certain circumstances, there is some uncertainty over whether it can also provide a defence to preparatory acts. For example, if D knows that V is going to try and kill her in a week's time, can D, in self-defence, purchase a gun without a licence? Or more proximately, if D is caught in a shoot-out and picks up a discarded gun for protection, can she claim self-defence for this brief moment of unlawful possession? The law would speak with a strange moral voice if it said that D was justified in these cases to use the gun to kill or injure V in defence, but has no defence to her possession of the gun. With this in mind, courts have been willing to extend the public and private defence to cover certain preparatory acts of this kind, particularly if they are proximate to or even simultaneous with the use of force.[135] To avoid confusing the limits of the public and private defence further, it is contended that such preparatory acts are more appropriately analysed using duress of circumstance.

The second preliminary question asks what we mean by public and private interests: to come within the defence, what must D be using force to achieve? The answer requires recognition that the public and private defence is actually two defences, brought together because of substantial overlap and the common rules that apply to both.

---

[131] See generally Leverick, *Killing in Self-Defence* (2006); Sangero, *Self Defence in Criminal Law* (2006).

[132] [1986] 2 All ER 449. A case of reckless driving, now abolished as an offence. Cf the dangerous driving case of *Bailey* [2013] EWCA Crim 378 where there was no force used, and the defence could not apply.

[133] [1993] Crim LR 586.

[134] The absurdity of this was noted by Brooke LJ in *Bayer v DPP* [2003] EWHC 2567 (Admin).

[135] *AG's Reference (No 2 of 1983)* [1984] QB 456 (making and storing petrol bombs to protect shop); *McAuley* [2009] EWCA Crim 2130 (carrying a knife for self-protection).

- Private defence: The private defence has developed at common law, and provides a defence where D uses force to protect herself or another from physical harm,[136] or in the protection of property.[137]
- Public defence: The public defence is provided by section 3 of the Criminal Law Act 1967, and provides a defence where D uses force to prevent a crime[138] or in effecting or assisting a lawful arrest.

There will be cases where only one of the two applies. For example, if D uses force to protect herself from V, a 9-year-old child under the age of criminal responsibility, she may be able to rely on the private defence, but the public defence will not apply because V cannot commit a crime. Equally, where D uses force to assist police making an arrest, D qualifies under the public defence, but it is quite possible that D does so despite facing no personal threat and would therefore not qualify for the private defence. However, in the majority of cases, both defences will apply simultaneously. For example, where D uses force to protect Z from attack by V, where V would commit an offence in attacking Z, D acts both to protect Z and to prevent V's crime.[139]

As a result of their common denominator—that each applies only where D uses force—and as a result of the substantial overlap between public and private interests, these defences are now best analysed as a single public and private defence. The integration of the two has been ongoing for many years within the common law, and has now been codified within section 76 of the Criminal Justice and Immigration Act 2008 (CJIA) as amended.

(1) This section applies where in proceedings for an offence—

    (a) an issue arises as to whether a person charged with the offence ('D') is entitled to rely on a defence within subsection (2), and

    (b) the question arises whether the degree of force used by D against a person ('V') was reasonable in the circumstances.

(2) The defences are—

    (a) the common law defence of self-defence; and

    (b) the defences provided by section 3(1) of the Criminal Law Act 1967 . . .

The rules in this section, which we explore later, provide a partial restatement and codification of the common law; they do not provide for reform.[140]

The two core elements of the public and private defence, usefully characterised as trigger and response, are set out in **Table 14.4.**

---

[136] *Duffy* [1967] 1 QB 63.

[137] Where D damages property to protect other property, this is governed by the Criminal Damage Act 1971, s5(2)(b) (see **9.7.3.2**). However, the public and private defence is still necessary where D uses other force to protect property (eg against the person).

[138] This only applies to the prevention of crimes in English law, as opposed to crimes in other jurisdictions or international crimes: *Jones* [2005] Crim LR 122.

[139] *Clegg* [1995] 1 All ER 334, 343.

[140] CJIA 2008, s76(9); *Keane* [2010] EWCA Crim 2514.

Table 14.4 Public and private defence

A) Trigger: D must have believed (subjective) that force was immediately required in order to protect her public or private interests; and
B) Response: the amount of force used by D must have been reasonable (objective) on the facts as D believed them to be

After D has raised the defence, the legal burden is then on the prosecution to prove beyond reasonable doubt that the elements of the defence are not satisfied.[141]

14.5.1 Element 1: trigger—the necessity for force

The trigger element within the public and private defence is essentially a threshold question: was it necessary to use *any* force against V on the facts as D believed them to exist? Questions concerning the *degree* of force used should be avoided until the second element. For example, if D sees V scratching her car and reacts by shooting V, she is likely to satisfy the first element since D may well have believed it was necessary to use *some* defensive force, but fail the second element: shooting V is an unreasonably excessive response.

The trigger element is almost entirely subjective: unlike duress,[142] we do not ask whether a reasonable person in D's position would have believed that force was necessary; we ask simply whether it was necessary on the facts as D believed them to be. Thus, this element can be satisfied even where D was wrong, and even where her mistake was unreasonable. This approach has raised concerns in relation to ECHR compatibility, particularly where D has killed V.[143] However, since being established in *Gladstone Williams*, it has been consistently applied in subsequent cases,[144] and is now codified in section 76(4)(b) of the CJIA.

 Gladstone Williams (1984) 78 Cr App R 276

V witnessed X rob a woman in the street. V caught X and held him down, knocking X to the ground on a second occasion when X attempted to get away. D witnessed the second altercation, and thought V was assaulting X. D then punched V in the face in an attempt to defend X. D was charged with assault occasioning actual bodily harm.[145]

• Crown Court: guilty of assault occasioning actual bodily harm. The judge directed that, for self-defence, D must have honestly, and on *reasonable grounds*, believed that force was necessary.

• Court of Appeal: appeal allowed. The necessity element must be based on an honest belief, but there is no requirement of reasonable grounds.

---

[141] *O'Brian* [2004] EWCA Crim 2900.
[142] See **14.3.2.1**.
[143] We discuss this in the reform section at **14.7**.
[144] *Beckford v R* [1988] AC 130 (Privy Council).
[145] Offences Against the Person Act 1861, s47. See **7.4**.

The essential question, then, is not whether D's belief in the necessity of force was reasonable, but whether it was honest. The reasonableness of D's belief will provide useful evidence in this regard, but it is not determinative.[146] This is the case whether D is defending against force to the person as in *Gladstone Williams*, property,[147] or in the context of crime prevention or criminal apprehension.[148]

The trigger element is not, however, purely subjective. Two objective considerations have been introduced.

A) **Voluntary intoxication:** D may not rely on mistakes (however honest) that have been caused by voluntary intoxication. For example, if D takes a hallucinogenic drug which causes her to mistakenly believe she is being attacked, her use of defensive force will not be considered 'necessary'. We discussed this at **13.2.5** in the context of the intoxication rules, and the case of *Hatton*.[149] It has also been confirmed, and codified, within section 76(5) of the CJIA.

B) **Mental defects:** More controversially, D may also not rely on mistakes, however honest, that have been caused by mental defect or disorder. For example, in the *Martin* case,[150] D was not able to rely on psychiatric evidence that he perceived threats to be greater than a normal person would; and in *Oye*,[151] D was not able to rely on his insane delusion that he was being attacked by evil spirits. Notably, in each case this exclusion was analysed under the second element of the defence (reasonable force) rather than the first (necessary force).[152] However, it can alternatively be analysed, as it is here, under the first element. This is because the purpose of the first element of the public and private defence is to establish the facts upon which we can question the reasonableness of D's response. Therefore, if D's insane delusion, for example, is to be excluded from the reasonableness question in the second element, little is gained by allowing it to apply within the first element. In effect, there is no difference between this exclusion and that based on voluntary intoxication.

The first element, the trigger, is therefore established from the facts as D honestly believed them to be. Whether D's belief was mistaken or unreasonable is irrelevant, unless that mistake was caused by voluntary intoxication or mental defect or disorder. Saying that the trigger element is predominantly subjective, however, does not tell us how to *assess* D's subjective belief. Although the necessity question is based on subjective belief, this does not mean that we simply ask D whether she thought force was necessary. Rather, we take the facts as she subjectively believed them, and our question is then whether we accept that *any* force was necessary. In answering this question, several sub-questions have emerged within the case law.

---

[146] *Dewar v DPP* [2010] EWHC 1050 (Admin): D's recognition that his use of force was not necessary *after* the event, does not undermine his defence (based on his beliefs at the time of the event).

[147] *Faraj* [2007] EWCA Crim 1033: D forcefully detained a gas repair man (V), believing he was a burglar.

[148] *Morris* [2013] EWCA Crim 436: D injured V with his taxi, wrongly believing that V was trying to make off without payment.

[149] [2005] EWCA Crim 2951.

[150] [2002] Crim LR 136.

[151] [2013] EWCA Crim 1725.

[152] *Oye* [2013] EWCA Crim 1725, [37]–[59].

14.5.1.1 Is it ever necessary to use force pre-emptively?

The answer here is 'yes'. Although the public and private defence will usually apply where D is responding to another's attack, this need not always be the case. In *Devlin v Armstrong*,[153] for example, the Court of Appeal in Northern Ireland held that the defence could apply where D uses force to 'ward off or prevent attack' as long as she honestly believed attack was 'imminent'.[154] The imminence requirement has been interpreted narrowly, and is seen as crucial to ensure that the defence does not extend to cover aggressive, as opposed to defensive, force. However, it also has the effect of limiting the defence in the context of abused women who kill their abusers in pre-emptive, but not imminent, circumstances.[155]

14.5.1.2 Is it ever necessary to use force where D could have retreated?

There is no duty to retreat, even where D knows that staying in a certain location is likely to result in attack from V and the need for defensive force. Over recent years, courts have treated a willingness to retreat as evidence in D's favour, suggesting that the force D then used was necessary, but force may still be necessary even where D has chosen to remain.[156] This is now confirmed, and codified, in section 76(6A) of the CJIA.

14.5.1.3 Is it ever necessary to use force where D instigated V's attack?

This question engages with prior fault. For duress, D's voluntary association where coercion was *objectively* foreseeable undermined D's defence.[157] However, this very strict rule is not applied to the public and private defence, and it is clear that D may appeal to the defence even where she instigated the violence with V (ie it does not matter 'who started it').[158] The only exception to this is where D has *consciously* manipulated V into attacking her in order to retaliate in 'apparent' defence. In these circumstances, confirmed in *Rashford*,[159] D's force will not satisfy the necessity element.

14.5.1.4 Is it ever necessary to use force against innocent/lawful force?

It is generally not permissible to use force against lawful actions. In other words, it is not necessary for D to use force against another party who is acting in lawful self-defence, or against a police officer making a lawful arrest. However, this rule is not absolute. Where D is attacked by a child under 10 or someone who is insane, the attacker may not be committing an offence, but it still may be necessary to use some defensive force.[160] Equally, the defence may apply where D has made a mistake, and we have to assess the events on the basis of D's honest beliefs as, for example, where D believes that she is defending against an unlawful attack or preventing crime, where in fact V is acting lawfully.[161]

---

[153] [1971] NI 13.
[154] At 33.
[155] McColgan, 'In Defence of Battered Women Who Kill' (1993) 13 OJLS 508.
[156] *Bird* [1985] 2 All ER 513, 516; *Duffy v DPP* [2007] EWHC 3169 (Admin).
[157] See **14.3.1.2**.
[158] *Keane* [2010] EWCA Crim 2514.
[159] [2005] EWCA Crim 3377.
[160] *Bayer v DPP* [2003] EWHC 2567 (Admin).
[161] *Gladstone Williams* (1984) 78 Cr App R 276.

> **Extra detail . . .**
>
> There was interesting use of this principle in *Re A*,[162] where Ward LJ held that the public and private defence could be employed to justify the separation of conjoined twins where separation would result in the death of one of those twins (V). Although V was an innocent party, failing to separate the twins would have inevitably resulted in both dying.

14.5.1.5 Is it ever necessary to use force where the justifying reasons are unknown to D?

With the trigger element based on D's subjective appreciation of the facts, an interesting problem emerges where D's force is in fact objectively justified but she is unaware of this. An example would be where D uses force on V, but D was not aware that V was about to launch an attack on D. D's force was, as a matter of fact, necessary, but she did not know this was the case. Where D uses force in these circumstances, it has been held in *Dadson* that she will not be able to rely on the public and private defence.[163] If D had been aware of the justifying circumstances (eg that she was about to come under attack, that V was about to commit a crime, etc) then her use of force would be necessary; but the focus of this defence on D's subjective knowledge (the facts as she believes them to be) means that it cannot apply where such circumstances are unknown.

14.5.2 Element 2: response—a reasonable degree of force

Having established the trigger (ie the facts as D believed them to be), and having established that *some* force was necessary on those facts, the second element of the public and private defence focuses on the degree of force used by D. This is a jury question.[164] Where the degree of force used was *reasonable*, or *proportionate*,[165] even if it equated to more force than was threatened by V,[166] the defence will be satisfied and D will be acquitted. Where D's degree of force was unreasonable, the defence will fail.

In order to identify 'reasonable force', the courts have adopted a middle ground between subjective and objective approaches.

- Subjective: A purely subjective approach, asking whether D believed the amount of force she used was reasonable, would be inappropriate. For example, D may honestly believe that it is reasonable to shoot V to prevent her scratching D's car, but this is not justified force.

- Objective: A purely objective approach, asking what degree of force would have been used by a reasonable person in D's circumstances, would be equally inappropriate. This is particularly true where D has made an honest mistake (eg believing that V is about to attack her). An approach to reasonable force that only takes account of the objective facts would always deny the defence in such cases: where V is not in fact threatening or involved in an offence, then no degree force is reasonable.

---

[162] [2000] 4 All ER 961.

[163] (1850) 2 Den 35. Funk, 'Justifying Justifications' (1990) 19 OJLS 630; Christopher, 'Unknowing Justification and the Logical Necessity of the *Dadson* Principle in Self-Defence' (1995) 15 OJLS 229.

[164] *AG's Reference (No 1 of 1975)* [1976] 2 All ER 937, 947.

[165] The terms 'reasonable' and 'proportionate' can be used interchangeably in this context.

[166] The public and private defence is not a balance of evils defence.

The current law combines these approaches by asking whether the degree of force D used was *objectively* reasonable based on the *subjective* facts as D believed them to be.[167] Thus, for example, where D mistakenly believes V is about to shoot her, and so responds by stabbing V, the question for the jury is whether D's force (stabbing) was objectively reasonable based on D's belief that she was about to be shot. As confirmed and codified within section 76(3)–(4) of the CJIA, this will be the case regardless of whether D's mistaken belief was reasonably or unreasonably held, as long as it was honestly held.

When applying this element, it is important to remember that we are focusing on the degree of *force* employed by D and not the degree of *harm* caused. For example, suppose V attempts to steal D's handbag in the street, and D reacts by pushing V away. It is likely, here, that D's force (the push) is both necessary and reasonable. However, what if V trips as a result of the push, hits her head on the pavement, and dies? The answer is, from the perspective of the public and private defence, that nothing has changed: our focus is on the reasonableness of the force (the push) and not the resulting harm (death). Thus, where D's force involves an obvious risk of causing death or serious harm as, for example, where D pushes V off a cliff, shoots V, etc, then this is likely to make D's force unreasonable.[168] However, just because D's reasonable use of force results in an unforeseen unreasonable degree of harm, this will not undermine D's defence.[169]

When assessing the objective reasonableness of D's degree of force, on the facts as she subjectively believed them to be, the jury must also take account of the circumstances surrounding the use of that force. Essentially, this involves a margin of appreciation for D; acknowledging that where she was in a pressured and stressful situation, she may not have been able to think entirely rationally about the level of force to be used. This rule has been expressed by the courts in various ways, including: 'it will be recognised that a person defending himself cannot weigh to a nicety the exact measure of his necessary defensive action';[170] 'one did not use jewellers' scales to measure reasonable force';[171] and so on. It has now also been confirmed, and codified, within section 76(7) of the CJIA.

Even acknowledging D's margin of appreciation, however, it should always be remembered that where the degree of force used by D is unreasonable the defence will fail. This was famously illustrated in the case of *Martin*.

 Martin [2001] EWCA Crim 2245

D lived in a remote farmhouse in Norfolk. He was woken by two people trying to burgle his premises, disturbed them, and then shot them as they tried to escape. One was killed and the other seriously injured. D was charged with murder and a serious offence against the person.[172]

- Crown Court: guilty of murder and wounding offence. The public and private defence was rejected by the jury.

---

[167] *Owino* [1996] 2 Cr App R 128; *Harvey* [2009] EWCA Crim 469.
[168] It will rarely, if ever, be reasonable to use deadly force to protect property.
[169] *Keane* [2010] EWCA Crim 2514; *Noye* [2011] EWCA Crim 650, [9] and [55].
[170] *Palmer* [1971] AC 814.
[171] *Reed v Wastie* [1972] Crim LR 221.
[172] For murder, see **Chapter 5**; for offences against the person, see **Chapter 7**.

> • Court of Appeal: appeal allowed, substituting murder for manslaughter. Public and private defence was not satisfied because of the excessive force used by D. However, new evidence provided the basis for a partial defence of diminished responsibility.

Martin is an important case for a number of reasons. First, it provides a useful example of the limits of the public and private defence: use of force by D was clearly necessary both to protect himself and his property and to prevent crime, but the force he used was excessive and so the defence failed. Secondly, it demonstrates the role that the partial defences can play where D's defensive force is excessive: in this case diminished responsibility.[173] And, thirdly, the case was also a catalyst for public, and ultimately political, concern about the operation of the defence in the context of householders who use force against unlawful intruders.

14.5.2.1 Householder cases

Following *Martin*, the public, fuelled by inaccurate media commentary, became concerned that householders were not adequately protected by the public and private defence where force is used against a trespasser. This issue became politicised, and despite the enactment of the CJIA clarifying the current law, there continued to be calls for a wider defence in these circumstances.[174] The result, contained within section 43 of the Crime and Courts Act 2013, has been the amendment of section 76 of the CJIA in the context of householders (non-trespassers[175]) who use defensive force against trespassers.

> (5A) In a householder case, the degree of force used by D is not to be regarded as having been reasonable in the circumstances as D believed them to be if it was grossly disproportionate in those circumstances.

The amendment makes clear that 'grossly disproportionate' force will never be 'reasonable', and so will always fail the second element of the defence. However, there remains some uncertainty about householders who use 'disproportionate' force which is not gross.

In line with the political aims of the amendment, it might be assumed that householders (unlike non-householders) who use disproportionate force in such cases would be treated as not having acted unreasonable. However, the recent case of *Collins* casts doubt on this interpretation, holding that disproportionate force will *not always* be reasonable.[176] For the Divisional Court, if the force in a householder case is found not to be grossly disproportionate that finding should always be followed by a second separate question as to reasonableness. The reasonableness assessment will take account of the householder's unique position (eg the court will be more

---

[173] Wake, 'Battered Women, Startled Householders and Psychological Self-Defence' (2013) 77 J Crim L 433.

[174] Skinner, 'Populist Politics and Shooting Burglars' [2005] Crim LR 275.

[175] Including guests: *Day* [2015] EWCA Crim 1646.

[176] *R (Collins) v Secretary of State for Justice* [2016] EWHC 33 (Admin): D held a burglar in a headlock, causing serious injury, before police arrived.

understanding of a failure to retreat, and perhaps her greater feelings of panic and vulnerability), but a finding of unreasonable force remains possible.

As one of the first cases discussing the householder amendment, *Collins* is an important case. However, it is also problematic, and will require further judicial clarification.[177] On a policy level, by interpreting the amendment narrowly (ie rejecting the view that householders can *always* use disproportionate force in these cases), the court seem to be out of step with Parliament's intention when passing the law. And on a more practical level, the court's decision to interpret 'proportionate force' and 'reasonable force' as separate questions within the second element of the defence is far from clear. When, for example, will force be proportionate (or at least not grossly disproportionate) and yet unreasonable? The court in *Collins* do not provide examples.

14.6 Necessity

The definition of the defence of necessity in English law remains an enigma, but it is clear that the criminal law needs such a defence. It is best understood as an imperfect safety net, a complete and general defence of last resort where no other defence is available but it is clear that liability would be inappropriate. In this way, the necessity defence represents an acceptance that within the infinite variety and complexity of human events, those crafting the criminal law will never be able to predict and account for every variation. Where unexpected facts lead to an inappropriate acquittal, this is to be regretted but tolerated. In such a case there is no broad overarching category of offences that should be applied to catch those who might otherwise avoid liability. That would be intolerable. In contrast, where unexpected facts could lead to inappropriate liability, the law rightly sacrifices principles of coherence in order to find an acquittal. The principal vehicle for this has become the defence of necessity.[178]

Extra detail . . .

Alongside necessity, other approaches have been developed to achieve the same outcome. Most notably, this has included the use of prosecutorial discretion simply to avoid bringing those who commit necessary crimes within the criminal system,[179] as well as the use of necessity in the guise of other defences or legal rules.[180] However, both of these approaches can be criticised[181] and, arguably, the defence of necessity provides a preferable route.

---

[177] Spencer, 'Using Force on Burglars' [2016] Arch Rev 6; Laird, comment [2016] Crim LR 438.

[178] Williams, 'Necessity' [1978] Crim LR 128.

[179] Following the Zeebrugge disaster, eg, no charges were brought against the corporal who ordered a man to be forcefully detached from an escape ladder (the man was frozen with fear and cold, and was blocking the escape of others): Leverick, *Killing in Self-Defence* (2006) 6–11.

[180] *Gillick* [1986] AC 112 provides a notable example, where the court applied flawed reasoning about medical judgment not being compatible with a guilty mind, in order to avoid liability where a doctor (D) prescribed the contraceptive pill to an underage girl. See **3.4.1.2**.

[181] On prosecutorial discretion, see Rogers, 'Restructuring the Exercise of Prosecutorial Discretion in England and Wales' (2006) 26 OJLS 775.

The defence of necessity has had an interesting history: its existence has often been denied by courts and commentators, but then gratefully deployed in times of legal need.[182] Where it has been recognised and applied, it seems to operate on a simple balance of evils: if D's evil (ie the offence she commits) is less serious than the evil avoided by committing it, then she is entitled to the defence; we might even say she has done the right thing.[183]

The problem lies in setting limits on the defence. If we define necessity in greater detail, then we risk sacrificing its utility as a safety net that can apply to unexpected facts. However, if the only rule defining the offence is a balance of evils test, then the defence becomes potentially impossibly wide, allowing D to raise the defence whenever she believes she has acted for good reason. The reaction of the courts has been pragmatic, to resist further definition and restriction, but to apply the defence reluctantly, and always with its potential indeterminate dangers in mind. The words of Lord Denning and Edmund Davies LJ in *Southwark London Borough v Williams* provide a useful illustration of this, discussing the potential application of necessity where a homeless person steals food or enters another's premises for shelter:

> if hunger were once allowed to be an excuse for stealing, it would open a door through which all kinds of lawlessness and disorder would pass . . . If homelessness were once admitted as a defence to trespass, no one's house would be safe. Necessity would open a door which no man could shut . . . The reason for such circumspection is clear—necessity can very easily become simply a mask for anarchy.[184]

The problem with this approach to necessity, however, is that it sends a mixed and complicated message to the public; some might even say a contradictory message. And, in this way, it can provide false hope. In recent years we have seen the defence of necessity employed on numerous occasions in an effort to justify drug offences committed to relieve severe pain,[185] and in even more extreme cases to justify assisted suicide or euthanasia.[186] Such cases, of course, were never likely to succeed. Although a case can be made for both on a balance of evils test, the courts are extremely circumspect about fundamental shifts that bring into question legislative codes and policy decisions. Despite its potential width, the necessity defence is only likely to succeed where a case arises where its precedent can be contained; only where there is a genuine belief that its unique facts have been missed or not catered for within the current law; only where it is exceptional.

Despite these problems, and despite judicial reluctance, the defence of necessity has been applied within a number of exceptional cases. It has been applied, for example, to

---

[182] Stephen went as far as to say that rules of necessity could never be laid down in advance: *A History of the Criminal Law* (1883) vol 2, 108.

[183] Where necessity is recognised, it is generally understood to operate as a justification as opposed to an excuse.

[184] [1971] 2 All ER 175, 179–181.

[185] *Quayle* [2005] EWCA Crim 1415.

[186] *R (Nicklinson) v Ministry of Justice* [2014] UKSC 38; Stark, 'Necessity and *Nicklinson*' [2013] Crim LR 949; Ost, 'Euthanasia and the Defence of Necessity' [2005] Crim LR 255.

justify detention of a person suffering from a mental disorder;[187] to justify the jettisoning of cargo from a ship to save the lives of those on board;[188] to justify the force-feeding of prisoners;[189] to justify procuring an abortion to save the mother;[190] to justify a police officer instructing cars to travel the wrong way on a one-way-street to allow ambulances access;[191] and so on.[192] The circumstances of necessity are usefully illustrated, and discussed, in *F v West Berkshire Authority*.[193]

F v West Berkshire Authority [1989] 2 All ER 545

V, a 36-year-old patient in a psychiatric hospital, formed a sexual relationship with another patient. Medical evidence found it would be 'disastrous' from a psychiatric perspective if she became pregnant, but there were problems ensuring the use of ordinary contraception. In order to allow V to continue her relationship, V's mother, acting as her next friend, applied for a court declaration that the performance of a sterilisation operation without V's consent (she was unable to consent) would be lawful.

- Court: declaration granted.
- Court of Appeal: appeal dismissed.
- House of Lords: appeal dismissed. The doctors' actions would be protected by the defence of necessity. Duress by circumstances is not available here because the 'threat' (ie pregnancy) does not meet the threshold of death or serious injury.

Interestingly, following many of these cases where it has been accepted that the courts were correct to apply a defence, legislation has followed to create a specifically tailored defence to apply in the future. In many ways, this is the ideal situation for necessity: catching the exceptional case within the imperfect safety net, alerting to the need for a defence, and then for a precise defence to be created. On a slightly grander scale, this is one way to characterise the creation of duress by circumstances.

However, there remain cases where necessity has been recognised and the creation of a specific defence has not followed. For these cases, and other exceptional cases in the future, the necessity defence remains their only imperfect option. Chief among these, because of the inapplicability of duress by threats or circumstances, is necessity as a defence to murder.

14.6.1 Necessity as a defence to murder

When considering necessity as a defence to murder, it is useful to begin with the case of *Dudley and Stephens*.

---

[187] *Bournewood Trust* [1998] 3 All ER 289.
[188] *Mouse's Case* (1608) 12 Co Rep 63.
[189] *Leigh v Gladstone* (1909) 26 TLR 139.
[190] *Bourne* [1939] 1 KB 687.
[191] *Johnson v Phillips* [1975] 3 All ER 682.
[192] The case for expanding necessity further is made in Edwards, 'Good and Harm, Excuses and Justifications, and the Moral Narratives of Necessity' in Reed and Bohlander (eds), *General Defences in Criminal Law* (2014) 75.
[193] Should now be read with the Mental Capacity Act 2005 in mind.

Dudley and Stephens (1884) 14 QBD 273

D1, D2, and V were shipwrecked, and spent 18 days drifting in an open boat. After several days without food or water, D1 and D2 decided to murder V (the cabin boy) and eat him in order to survive. They did so, and four days later they were rescued. D1 and D2 were charged with murder.

- Assizes: on instruction from the judge, the jury produced a special verdict, making findings of fact that D1 and D2 would probably have died if they had not eaten V, and that V (being very weak already) would certainly have died. The case was then adjourned to the Royal Courts of Justice.
- High Court: guilty of murder, with a sentence of death. [The prisoners were afterwards respited and their sentences commuted to six months' imprisonment without hard labour.]

The rationale for rejecting the necessity defence in *Dudley and Stephens* is disputed, but two main reasons are often highlighted from the court's judgment.[194] The first is that, at this time, necessity was not thought to provide a defence to murder. Following more recent case law, although the point is not settled, it is likely that necessity can be a defence to murder. The second reason, however, has continued to influence the application of the defence. This was the fact that D1 and D2 *chose* to kill V. This is unlike the hypothetical case of the mountain climber, D, whose partner, V, has fallen from the cliff face and is pulling D with her: D must cut the rope (allowing her partner to fall) in order to prevent them both being dragged from the cliff. In contrast, the defendants in *Dudley and Stephens* picked the cabin boy to be killed when it could have been any of their number who was selected to die. There has been some discussion of whether the drawing of lots would have led to a different result (as it was held it would have done, *obiter*, in a US case[195]) but even this was found to be unacceptable.[196]

Following this, it is notable that on the few occasions where the necessity defence has been successfully run there has been no problem of victim selection analogous to *Dudley and Stephens*. The most famous of these is the case of *Re A*.

 Re A (Children) [2000] 4 All ER 961

J and M were conjoined twins. Although they had separate vital organs, medical evidence established that the stronger twin (J) was sustaining the life of M through their common artery. If left conjoined, J's heart would fail within months and they would both die; if separated, J had the potential for a life that was worthwhile but M would die within minutes. J and M's parents refused on religious grounds to consent to an operation to separate the twins. Doctors applied for a declaration that separating the twins (killing M) would not be unlawful.

- Court: declaration granted.
- Court of Appeal: appeal dismissed.

The reasoning of the court in *Re A* is varied, but it is clear that Brooke LJ based his decision on necessity. He set out three requirements for the defence:

(a) the act is needed to avoid inevitable and irreparable evil;

194 See generally Simpson, *Cannibalism and the Common Law* (1984).
195 *US v Holmes*, 26 Fed Cas 360 (1841).
196 *Dudley and Stephens* (1884) 14 QBD 273, 285.

(b) no more should be done than is reasonably necessary for the purpose to be achieved;

(c) the evil inflicted must not be disproportionate to the evil avoided.

These requirements provide useful points of reference for the application of necessity. However, importantly, they remain vastly over-inclusive and should not be seen as criteria for the defence: they are required, but they are not sufficient. This was confirmed in the case itself, where each of the judges was obviously keen to limit the case to its particular facts. A useful illustration of the over-inclusivity of the requirements set out by Brooke LJ is also provided by Dennis:

> Suppose P, a hospital patient, urgently needs a blood transfusion to survive, but she has a very rare blood group. As it happens, Q, the patient in the next bed, has the same rare blood group, but refuses to make a donation of blood even though she could do so without risk to herself. May, D, the doctor treating P, take the blood from Q without her consent?[197]

As Dennis goes on to explain, it is arguable that if D forcefully takes blood from Q, she will satisfy the requirements set out in *Re A*. The 'rare' blood type also makes this a case, unlike *Dudley and Stephens*, where there is no problem of selection. However, if we respect the autonomy of Q, if we believe that people 'have rights to be treated as ends in themselves and not as means to the achievement of other social goals', we would surely not want the criminal law to justify such action. In short, *Re A* confirms the presence of the necessity safety net, but the problematic nature of even the barest attempt at criteria also confirms that that safety net is imperfect.[198]

Extra detail . . .
Although it has not been considered by a court, it is clear that the UK government (along with many others) believes that necessity can be a defence to murder where a hijacked passenger jet is shot down. Such action involves the intentional killing of innocent passengers, but is performed in order to limit the potential damage if the plane were to be crashed into a populated area or other target.[199]

14.7 Reform

The general defences have attracted considerable academic attention and criticism, as we have discussed, but parliamentary reform has often been piecemeal, as with the partial codification of the public and private defence, or non-existent. In this section, we first consider the potential reform of each of the defences covered in this chapter. We then widen out to discuss the current inconsistencies between defences and the importance of achieving coherence.

---

[197] Dennis, 'On Necessity as a Defence to Crime' (2009) 3 Crim L & Phil 29, 44–45.

[198] Huxtable, 'Separation of Conjoined Twins: What Next for English Law?' [2002] Crim LR 459; Rogers, 'Necessity, Private-Defence and the Killing of Mary' [2001] Crim LR 515.

[199] Hörnle, 'Hijacked Planes: May They Be Shot Down?' [2007] New Crim LR 582; Bohlander, 'In Extremis? Hijacked Airplanes, Collateral Damage and the Limits of Criminal Law' [2006] Crim LR 579. Also recognised in *R (Nicklinson) v Ministry of Justice* [2014] UKSC 38.

14.7.1 Reforming the individual defences

Each of the general defences has attracted individual comment and criticism. We consider each in turn.

14.7.1.1 Insanity as a defence

We have already considered the potential reform of the insanity rules at **13.6.3**, and we do not repeat that discussion here. However, when evaluating the insanity rules it is useful to bear in mind the distinction between insanity as a denial of offending and insanity as a defence. Indeed, in the context of our discussion of potential human rights compatibility, the difference can be crucial. For example:

- Article 6: Article 6 ECHR provides a right to fair trial including the presumption of innocence and the reverse burden of proof for insanity. This is particularly important in the context of insanity as a denial of offending: because the Crown has not established the elements of the actus reus and mens rea, then by definition the case for reversing the burden is much weaker because there is no criminal mischief. In contrast, where D has committed an offence and raises insanity as a defence, there is stronger ground for a reverse burden: D has been found to have performed the actus reus and mens rea, and therefore no longer needs to be presumed innocent. However, a reduced evidential burden may still be preferred.[200]

- Articles 2, 3, and 5: Criticisms under Articles 2, 3, and 5 will apply in largely the same way to insanity as a denial of offending and insanity as a defence. The defence of insanity, as with insanity as a denial of offending, is designed to protect the right to life, to liberty, and to protect against inhuman and degrading treatment. To the extent that the current law fails to do this, by drawing the defence too narrowly or too widely, or through its disconnect with medical knowledge about mental illness, it is rightly subject to criticism.[201]

14.7.1.2 Duress

The rules on duress by threats, and now duress by circumstances, are reasonably well established within the common law. However, as we have discussed previously, the current law has been criticised for being drawn too narrowly, excluding those deserving of an excuse.[202] Academic opposition to this narrowing has questioned the merits of criminalising people for failing to resist pressures that they are subjectively unequipped to resist, especially where those pressures may objectively have affected others in a similar way.[203] Following recent case law, it is clear that these concerns are only likely to be addressed, if at all, through legislation. However, such reform does not appear on the

---

[200] Law Commission, *Insanity and Automatism* (Discussion Paper, 2013).
[201] Ibid, paras 1.30–1.79.
[202] This stems from cases such as *Hasan* [2005] UKHL 22.
[203] Lippke, 'Chronic Temptation, Reasonable Firmness and the Criminal Law' (2014) 34 OJLS 75; Reed, 'Duress and Normative Moral Excuse' in Reed and Bohlander (eds), *General Defences in Criminal Law* (2014) 93.

current agenda. If and when this changes, the Law Commission has already provided a useful set of reform proposals.[204]

In contrast with this general lack of legislative attention, one area within the defence has attracted considerable debate: whether duress should be a defence to murder. The arguments in favour of such an extension reflect the general arguments in favour of a defence of duress to *any* crime. In simple terms, if D is threatened with death or serious harm to a degree that a reasonable person in her position would have done likewise to avoid it, D's actions are still wrong, but we can excuse the actor and sympathise with the impossible position in which she was placed. Against this, a number of arguments have been formulated to reject any extension of duress. These are most clearly stated in the reasoning of the court in *Howe*.[205] However, none of these arguments seem to hold up under analysis.

- The ordinary person of reasonable fortitude should sacrifice herself rather than take the life of an innocent.[206] *If the defence of duress were extended to cover murder, it would only apply where a jury found that a reasonable person would have yielded to the threat. If the criminal law is defining a 'reasonable' person as a hero, it is surely expecting too much.*

- One who takes the life of an innocent cannot claim to be choosing the lesser of two evils.[207] *This is not necessarily the case. For example, if D takes a single life to avoid X's threat to kill multiple people, this looks like the lesser evil. Also, the defence of duress is generally conceived as a concession to reasonable human frailty (an excuse) rather than a balance of evils defence (a justification).*

- The Law Commission had previously recommended that duress should be a defence to murder,[208] but this was not acted upon by Parliament.[209] *This proves little, as the Commission's previous recommendations were not put before Parliament to consider. We could equally claim that the failure of Parliament to overrule the House of Lords decision in* Lynch, *which suggested duress could be a defence to murder, demonstrated their approval of that approach.*

- Hard cases can be avoided though prosecutorial discretion (ie by not prosecuting).[210] *The morally innocent should not be left to the uncertain mercy of administrative discretion.*

The Law Commission has considered these arguments and others, and has recommended that the duress defence should be extended to apply to murder.[211] However, in doing so the Commission has taken the controversial step of recommending a reversed burden of proof in cases of this kind,[212] and an increased threshold so that the defence

---

[204] Law Commission, *A Criminal Code for England and Wales*, 2 vols (No 177, 1989) cll 42 and 43, and most recently *Offences against the Person and General Principles* (No 218, 1993) Part 4.
[205] [1987] 1 All ER 771.
[206] At 779–780.
[207] At 780.
[208] Law Commission, *Defences of General Application* (No 83, 1977).
[209] At 784 and 788.
[210] At 780–781 and 790–791.
[211] Law Commission, *Murder, Manslaughter and Infanticide* (No 304, 2006) Ch6.
[212] At paras 6.87–6.141.

will only apply where D is threatened with death or 'life-threatening' harm; in other words serious, non-life-threatening harm will be insufficient.[213] Whether or not the Law Commission's scheme is accepted in full, it is contended that the arguments in favour of extending the defence of duress to murder are overwhelming.[214]

14.7.1.3 The public and private defence

Unlike the other general defences, the public and private defence has attracted the recent attention of Parliament. However, as discussed earlier, the reasons for this attention have been unfortunate, being based chiefly upon public and media misunderstanding about the limits of the defence. The reaction of Parliament in partially codifying the common law within section 76 of the CJIA can be welcomed as a useful clarification, although a complete codification would have been preferable. However, the more recent amendments to this section in relation to householder cases, allowing for disproportionate force to be used in this context, demonstrates the worst features of populist unprincipled law reform.[215] This process has also distracted from two areas of potential reform that should be highlighted regarding (a) the human rights compatibility of the current law, and (b) the potential for a new defence of excessive self-defence.

Concerns have been raised about the compatibility of the current public and private defence with rights enshrined within the ECHR. In particular, this debate has focused on the potential for the defence to apply where D has killed V, and done so on the basis of an unreasonable mistaken belief that force was necessary.[216] As long as D's response in killing V was reasonable *on the facts as she believed them to be*, the defence will apply and D will be acquitted. However, what of V's Article 2 right to life?[217] As various commentators have set out,[218] although Article 2 is not an absolute right, it only permits life to be taken when it is 'absolutely necessary',[219] with the ECtHR clarifying that this requires 'good grounds' in circumstances of self-defence.[220] Arguably, D's unreasonably mistaken belief, albeit an honest one, does not constitute good grounds. It should be highlighted that neither the ECtHR[221] nor any domestic court[222] has yet found the public and private defence to be in breach of Article 2, and there are also good reasons for favouring the current subjective test over an objective alternative.[223] However, it should

---

[213] At paras 6.73–6.76.

[214] Reed, 'The Need for a New Anglo American Approach to Duress' (1996) 61 J Crim L 209. See also Arenson, 'The Paradox of Disallowing Duress as a Defence to Murder' (2014) 78 J Crim L 65.

[215] Editor, 'Defending Self-Defence' [2010] Crim LR 167.

[216] See **14.5.1**.

[217] Although debate has focused on killing and Art 2, it could equally apply where D causes lesser harm in similarly unreasonable circumstances (potentially infringing Arts 3 and/or 5).

[218] De Than and Elvin, 'Mistaken Private Defence: The Case for Reform' in Reed and Bohlander (eds), *General Defences in Criminal Law* (2014) 133; Leverick, 'Is English Self-Defence Law Incompatible with Article 2 of the ECHR?' [2002] Crim LR 347.

[219] Art 2(2) ECHR.

[220] *McCann v UK* (1996) 21 EHRR 95.

[221] *Da Silva v UK* (2016) 63 EHRR 12; *Bubbins v UK* (2005) 41 EHRR 458.

[222] *R (Bennett) v HM Coroner for Inner London* [2007] EWCA Civ 617; *Duggan* [2014] EWHC 3343 (Admin).

[223] Although mistaken, D's belief in the need for extreme force was honest and so does not reveal a blameworthy character. See the ECtHR discussion in *Da Silva v UK* (2016) 63 EHRR 12, on the death of Jean Charles de Menezes.

also be acknowledged that a case of killing under an unreasonable mistaken belief has not yet made its way to the European Court, and so the potential for a breach to be found is still very much alive.

A second area of topical debate is the potential for a new partial defence for murder where D acts with excessive force in self-defence. The public and private defence will not apply to D in these circumstances: although D's use of force may be necessary in the circumstances as she believes them to be, if they are excessive because the degree of force used is unreasonable, then the defence will fail. The potential for a new partial defence that would reduce D's liability from murder to manslaughter was considered by the House of Lords in *Clegg*.[224] However, the court concluded that a change of this kind, if it were required, would have to come from Parliament. Such reform has not been forthcoming. However, the potential for a partial defence of this kind has found consistent favour with the Law Commission and there are sound reasons for its recommendation.[225] Under the current law, someone who kills in excessive self-defence may be able to rely on one of the existing partial defences (as in *Martin*[226]), and this potential has been increased by the expansion of the loss of control defence to include a trigger based on fear of serious violence.[227] However, there will still be defendants who kill without having lost control, and who do not qualify for the partial defence of diminished responsibility, and there remains a case to be made that these defendants also warrant partial mitigation on the basis of their (semi-)defensive motivations.[228]

14.7.1.4 Necessity

At one time, the Law Commission went as far as to recommend the abolition of necessity as a defence.[229] However, as we discussed earlier, such a policy is surely ill-conceived, severely limiting the ability of the courts to deal with exceptional cases where liability is inappropriate but other defences do not apply. The recommendation was severely criticised,[230] and has been dropped. Subsequently, the Commission has recommended that necessity should remain a defence but, unlike the other defences, it should not be codified.[231] This seems to be the correct approach, allowing the necessity defence to perform its role as an imperfect safety net without the restraint of codification. Indeed, we see a similar approach in most other common law jurisdictions.[232]

---

[224] [1995] 1 All ER 334. Kaye, 'Excessive Force in Self-Defence: After *Clegg*' (1996) 61 J Crim L 448.

[225] Law Commission, *A Criminal Code for England and Wales*, 2 vols (No 177, 1989) cl59; Law Commission, *Murder, Manslaughter and Infanticide* (No 304, 2006) para 1.53.

[226] See **14.5.2**.

[227] See **6.2.1**.

[228] Stannard, 'In the Spirit of Compromise: The Irish Doctrine of Excessive Defence' in Reed and Bohlander (eds), *General Defences in Criminal Law* (2014) 171; Smith, 'Excessive Defence— A Rejection of Australian Initiative' [1972] Crim LR 524. Australian law no longer recognises a partial defence of this kind, adopting the English position in *Zecevic* (1987) 61 ALJR 375. See also, in the context of abused women who kill in excessive self-defence, Wake, 'Battered Women, Startled Householders and Psychological Self-Defence' (2013) 77 J Crim L 433.

[229] Law Commission, *Defences of General Application* (No 83, 1977).

[230] Williams, 'Necessity' [1978] Crim LR 128; Huxley, 'Proposals and Counter Proposals on the Defence of Necessity' [1978] Crim LR 141.

[231] Law Commission, *Offences against the Person and General Principles* (No 218, 1992) cl36(2).

[232] eg Canada (*Perka* (1984) 13 DLR (4th) 1); Australia (*Loughnan* [1981] VR 443); across the Oceanic countries (Forsyth, 'The Divorce and Marriage of Morality and Law' (2010) 21 Crim

14.7.2 Coherence between defences?

It is not an objection to the current general defences that they apply in various different circumstances. However, there may be a problem where the defences are inconsistent in their approach to common issues to an extent that the overall approach of the law becomes incoherent. This is undoubtedly a problem within the current law, and one in which, within denials of defences at least, the Law Commission has begun to take an interest.[233]

It is useful to provide a brief overview of some of the main areas of inconsistency within the current general defences. These inconsistencies can be explained on the basis of common law development that lacks a unifying theory of defences, and the conflict between excusatory and justificatory rationales.[234] However, although they can be explained on this basis, the law must still aim for coherence. After all, unifying theories are elusive in any area of the law.[235]

- **Subjective and objective approaches:** Probably the most striking area of inconsistency between the defences discussed in this chapter relates to their use of subjective and objective elements. For example, whereas duress requires D to have an *objectively* reasonable belief in the presence of a serious threat requiring D to offend, the public and private defence requires the equivalent belief in the necessity of force to be *subjectively* honest. If this difference was based on stated principles then it would be acceptable, but it actually originates from the defences unsuccessfully attempting to run in tandem.[236]

- **Characteristics of the defendant:** Where an objective standard is applied, there are no obvious principles underpinning the approach to which of D's characteristics can be taken into account when applying that standard. For example, for duress, it now seems that almost all of D's physical and psychiatric characteristics can be taken into account when deciding whether a reasonable person with those characteristics would have been compelled to offend.[237] In contrast, for the public and private defence, the objective degree of force test does not allow characteristics beyond age and sex to be taken into account, and explicitly excludes psychiatric characteristics.[238]

L Forum 121); and so on. One exception, where codification has been attempted, is the United States (Model Penal Code, §3.02), on which, see Alexander, 'Lesser Evils: A Closer Look at the Paradigmatic Justification' (2005) 24 Law & Phil 611; Berman, 'Lesser Evils: A Less Close Look' (2005) 24 Law & Phil 681.

[233] Law Commission, *Insanity and Automatism* (Discussion Paper, 2013).
[234] Lacy, 'Space, Time and Function: Intersecting Principles of Responsibility Across the Terrain of Criminal Justice' (2007) 1 Crim L & Phil 233.
[235] Tadros, 'The Character of Excuse' (2001) 21 OJLS 495.
[236] The court in *Graham* [1982] 1 All ER 801 equated duress with self-defence and so adopted an objective approach in line with (what was then) the accepted approach for self-defence. However, less than two years later the court in *Gladstone Williams* [1987] 3 All ER 411 opted for a subjective approach to self-defence. See also Alldridge, 'Developing the Defence of Duress' [1986] Crim LR 433.
[237] *Bowen* [1996] 2 Cr App R 157. See **14.3.3.3**.
[238] *Martin* [2001] EWCA Crim 2245. See **14.5**.

- Approaches to prior fault: The question of whether D's prior fault can undermine her appeal to a defence is equally inconsistent. For example, duress will be excluded where D voluntarily associates with others in circumstances where she *objectively* should have foreseen a risk of coercion.[239] In contrast, the public and private defence will only be similarly excluded where D has *consciously* manipulated the circumstances in order to attack V under the guise of defensive force.[240] Again, reasons for the inconsistency are not clearly articulated by the courts.[241]

An extreme response to the issue of inconsistency would be to collapse each of the general defences into a single defence, with a single set of rules and principles. A model for this approach has been set out by Clarkson.[242] However, the problem here is that a single defence becomes nothing more than a vague statement of necessity, unifying only in its inevitable preference for the lowest common denominator. Although we acknowledge that a defence of this kind (necessity) is essential as an imperfect safety net below other defences, it is surely right that other defences should exist which are capable of greater clarity and precision.

A better approach, it is contended, following the lead of the Law Commission in relation to automatism, intoxication, and insanity, is to identify common elements between the defences and make sure that the reform of any one takes account of the others, whether this means principled consistency or principled inconsistency. Wilson's work on the structure of defences provides a good example of this approach.[243]

14.8 Eye on assessment

In this section we consider the application of the general defences to problem facts. We employ the same structure as we have discussed throughout the book. However, here perhaps more than ever, it is vital to read carefully what the question, at the bottom of the problem facts, is asking you to do. In most cases, questions involving defences will be no different from any other question: they will ask you to discuss potential liability and so you will have to go through every step of the structure (which we set out later) and remember to only discuss the potential for a defence when it becomes necessary to do so, that is *only after* you have established that D is likely to have committed the actus reus with the mens rea for the offence. However, exceptionally, a question may tell you that D has committed an offence and ask you to consider potential defences only. In this case, you should skip from Step 1 (you still need to identify the criminal event) straight to Step 4 (discussion of defences).

Assuming that we are dealing with a standard question, the following structure should be applied.

---

[239] *Hasan* [2005] UKHL 22. See **14.3.1.2**.
[240] *Rashford* [2005] EWCA Crim 3377. See **14.5.1.3**.
[241] Child, 'Prior Fault: Blocking Defences or Constructing Crimes' in Reed and Bohlander (eds), *General Defences* (2014).
[242] Clarkson, 'Necessary Action: A New Defence' [2004] Crim LR 81.
[243] Wilson, 'The Structure of Defences' [2005] Crim LR 108.

STEP 1 Identify the potential criminal event in the facts

This should be simply stated (eg 'The first potential criminal event arises where D punches V'). The role of this stage is to highlight which part of the question you are answering before you begin to apply the law.

STEP 2 Identify the potential offence

Again, state this simply (eg 'When punching V, D may be liable for assault occasioning ABH'). The role of this stage is to highlight which offence you are going to apply.

STEP 3 Applying the offence to the facts

Having identified the relevant offence, make sure you discuss each of the required elements.

Actus reus: What does the offence require? Did D do it?

Mens rea: What does the offence require? Did D possess it?

AR and MR are satisfied	AR and/or MR are not satisfied
Continue to STEP 4.	Return to STEP 2, and look for an alternative offence. If none, then skip to STEP 5, concluding that no offence is committed.

STEP 4 Consider defences

The word 'consider' here is important, as you should not discuss every defence for every question. Rather, think whether there are any defences (eg duress) that *could* potentially apply. If there are, discuss those only.

Figure 14.1, on page 604, is designed to help you to identify which defence you should apply. Note that, if insanity applies, D will usually be directed to the special verdict. If insanity does not apply, you should consider duress, the public and private defence, and/or any specific defences. Remember that there is often an overlap between defences including duress and self-defence, so it may be necessary to apply more than one to the facts. Finally, if these defences do not apply, you should consider necessity as the imperfect safety net beneath. If D is liable for murder and none of the complete defences apply, you should also go on to consider the partial defences.[244]

---

[244] See **6.2.**

Remember, as we note next to Step 4, analysis of the defences is mainly a mental process. Particularly in an exam, you will not have time to lead your reader through the elements of each defence and say why each does not apply. Rather, keep **Figure 14.1** in mind to help you identify any defences that might apply (ie there are facts in the problem that suggest it might apply) and lead your reader through those defences only.

> **STEP 5 Conclude**
>
> This is usually a single sentence either saying that it is likely that D has committed the offence, or saying that it is not likely either because an offence element is not satisfied or because a defence is likely to apply. It is not often that you will be able to say categorically whether or not D has committed the offence, so it is usually best to conclude in terms of what is more 'likely'.

> **STEP 6 Loop**
>
> Go back up to Step 1, identifying the next potential criminal event. Continue until you have discussed all the relevant potentially criminal events.

 ONLINE RESOURCE CENTRE

www.oxfordtextbooks.co.uk/orc/sho/

This chapter is accompanied by a selection of online resources to help you with this topic, including:

- **Multiple-choice questions**
- **Chapter summary sheet**
- Two **sample examination questions** with answer guidance
- **Further reading**

Also available on the Online Resource Centre are:

- A selection of **videos** from the authors explaining key topics and principles
- **Legal updates**
- Useful **weblinks**

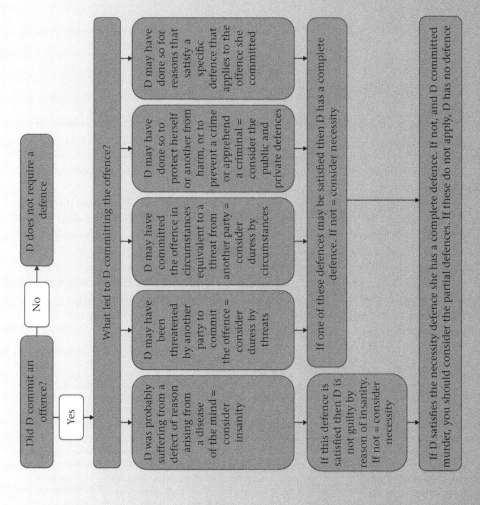

Figure 14.1 Applying the general defences

9

Mental conditions, intoxication and mistake

9.1 Introduction

In this and the next chapter the most commonly occurring 'defences' are considered. There is no accepted hierarchy of defences in English law and none is adopted in this book.[1] It should also be noted that considerable disagreement persists over the precise theoretical lines between elements which ought properly to be regarded as part of the offence and those comprising defences.[2]

In this chapter, the pleas of insanity, intoxication and mistake are examined. It would be misleading to treat all of these as 'defences' in the true sense of the word since some involve a plea which simply puts the Crown to proof of the relevant issue. The 'defences' or 'pleas' of insanity, and intoxication, are based on a denial of sufficient capacity to deserve the imposition of a criminal sanction.[3] At the core of these topics—insanity, automatism, intoxication, mistake—is the basic principle of English criminal law that the defendant should be held liable only where he is of sufficient capacity to be blameworthy for his actions.[4] As Professor Hart famously explained, a person should only be blamed if he has the 'capacity and fair opportunity to change or adjust his behaviour to the law'.[5]

---

[1] See, however, the theoretical approach in P Robinson, 'Criminal Law Defences: A Systematic Analysis' (1982) 82 Col LR 199; and for a ladder of defences see J Horder, *Excusing Crime* (2004) 103.

[2] See generally G Williams, 'Offences and Defences' (1982) 2 LS 233; K Campbell, 'Offence and Defence' in IH Dennis (ed), *Criminal Law and Criminal Justice* (1987). Tadros, *Criminal Responsibility* emphasizes the significance of the distinction. Defences, he argues, describe the conditions of criminal responsibility, but do 'not constitute essential features of D's conduct which express why he is deserving of conviction, where the defence is unavailable' (at 109). Thus, lack of consent is an element of the offence in rape.

[3] Loughnan seeks to move away from talking about defences and instead conceptualizes what are discussed in this chapter as doctrines. Her excellent account seeks to focus on the way mental condition doctrines relate to other aspects of the criminal law, rather than focusing on the moral evaluation that they might entail. See A Loughnan, *Manifest Madness: Mental Incapacity in Criminal Law* (2012). For a critique, see T Ward (2014) 77 MLR 527.

[4] Numerous theories abound as to whether criminal responsibility and defences are properly explained on the bases of D's capacity, choice or character. These philosophical arguments lie beyond the scope of this work. See, *inter alia*, Horder, *Excusing Crime* and Tadros, *Criminal Responsibility*, Ch 2.

[5] HLA Hart, *Punishment and Responsibility* (1968) 181. For discussion on the relationship of the insanity defence to questions of responsibility, see the Law Commission, *Criminal Liability: Insanity and Automatism, A Discussion Paper* (2013) (hereafter in this chapter LCDP), Appendix A. See also the supplementary material to the earlier Scoping Paper (2012) (hereafter in this chapter LCSP) available at https://consult.justice.gov.uk/law-commission/insanity-and-automatism/user_uploads/insanity_scoping_supplementary.pdf-1.

Chapter 10 deals with substantive defences in the true sense—where D has caused an actus reus with the appropriate mens rea but, despite both these elements of the offence being proved by the Crown, D is entitled to an acquittal owing to some justifying or excusing circumstance or condition. There are also special defences which apply to particular crimes (eg loss of self-control and diminished responsibility in murder). They are dealt with separately throughout the book where appropriate and their interrelationship with general defences is considered.

9.1.1 Defences and theories of justification and excuse

Historically, the common law distinguished between justification and excuse, at least in relation to homicide. Some homicides, like that done by the public hangman in carrying out the sentence of the court, were justifiable. Others, like killing by misadventure and without culpable negligence, were merely excusable. In both cases the accused who successfully raised the defence was acquitted of felony but, if the homicide was merely excusable, his goods were forfeited. In 1828, forfeiture was abolished and, ever since, there has been no difference, so far as the defendant is concerned, between the various general defences. If successfully raised, they result in a verdict of not guilty. Insanity is distinct in this respect because it results in a 'special' verdict of not guilty by reason of insanity.

There has been a revival of academic interest in a distinction between justification and excuse.[6] On one simple version of the theory, an act is justified when society does not disapprove of it or where it is permitted.[7] An act is merely excused when society disapproves of it but thinks it is nevertheless not right to punish D. The distinction is often described in simple terms: whereas the justification speaks to the rightness of the act, the excuse relates to the circumstances of the individual actor.[8] Clearly, some such distinction exists in fact. There are examples which obviously fall into one category or the other. The nine-year-old child who deliberately kills his playmate is excused but no one would say his act of killing is justified. In contrast, nearly everyone would approve of the conduct of a man who in self-defence wounds an aggressor when that is the only way he can save the lives of his family.

However, these systems of classification into justifications and excuses suffer from a number of drawbacks. First, there is no agreement on the precise hierarchy,[9] nature or definition of either classification. Duff suggests that they have 'bred needless confusion'.[10] A number of sophisticated models of justification and excuse have been developed by legal philosophers.[11]

---

[6] G Fletcher, *Rethinking Criminal Law* (1978) Ch 10; S Yeo, *Compulsion in the Criminal Law* (1990); Smith, *Justification and Excuse*; G Williams, 'The Theory of Excuses' [1982] Crim LR 732; PH Robinson (1982) 82 Col LR 199; J Gardner, 'The Gist of Excuses' (1998) Buffalo Crim LR 575; Horder, *Excusing Crime*; Tadros, *Criminal Responsibility*; Duff, *Answering for Crime*, Ch 11; A Simester, 'On Justifications and Excuses' in L Zedner and JV Roberts (eds), *Principles and Values in Criminal Law and Criminal Justice* (2012); PH Robinson, 'Four Distinctions that Glanville Williams Did Not Make: The Practical Benefit of Examining the Interrelation Among Criminal Law Doctrine' in DJ Baker and J Horder (eds), *The Sanctity of Life and the Criminal Law: The Legacy of Glanville Williams* (2013).

[7] It is problematic to suggest that the question is whether society 'approves' of the conduct. A better basis for the classification is that it is 'permitted'. See generally the account in Duff, *Answering for Crime*, Ch 11. Cf P Westen (2008) 28 OJLS 563.

[8] For criticism, see J Gardner, 'Wrongs and Faults' in Simester, *Appraising Strict Liability*, 61–67.

[9] See D Husak, 'On the Supposed Priority of Justification to Excuse' (2005) 24 L & Phil 557.

[10] *Answering for Crime*, 263.

[11] Debate continues as to whether D who relies on a justification should be seen as having done no wrong, or as having done wrong but being justified in doing it (see G Fletcher, 'The Nature of Justifications' in S Shute, S Gardner and J Horder (eds), *Action and Value in Criminal Law* (1993) 175). As for excuses, there is debate over whether D is excused because he has acted 'out of character' or because he lacked capacity (ie he has not lived up to the standards we can reasonably expect of someone in his circumstances). See generally J Gardner (1998) Buffalo Crim LR 575; V Tadros, 'The Characters of Excuses' (2001) 21 OJLS 495; and Horder, *Excusing Crime*, Ch 3.

553

Recent suggestions propose a fourfold system of classification with justifications,[12] warranted acts,[13] excuses[14] and exemptions.[15] Secondly, there is no consensus as to which classification applies to which defence—for example, many see duress as excusatory but some treat it as justificatory. Thirdly, there seems to be little agreement as to what practical difference, if any, would result from classification of a particular defence into one category or another.

Few suggest that there is any difference so far as the acquittal of the person relying on the defence is concerned,[16] but it has been argued more widely that the distinction affects third parties in that (a) it is lawful to resist an aggressor whose aggression is merely excused but not one whose aggression is justified; and (b) there may be a conviction for aiding and abetting one who is merely excused[17] but not one who is justified. Some would also argue that particular judicial decisions on excuses are not to be regarded as being of any wider significance in precedent terms.[18] As Fletcher (whose work inspired the current interest) acknowledges,[19] Anglo-American criminal law has never expressly recognized these (as he thinks) fundamental distinctions.

Applying the version of the theory as expounded by Fletcher, a citizen using force in arresting 'anyone who is in the act of committing an offence' would be justified but a person arresting 'anyone whom he has reasonable grounds for suspecting to be [but who is not in fact] committing an offence' is merely excused. But both acts are equally sanctioned by English law—the Police and Criminal Evidence Act 1984, s 24A, provides that a person other than a constable may arrest without warrant anyone who is in the act of committing an indictable offence and anyone whom he reasonably suspects to be doing so.[20] The citizen incurs no criminal liability if he arrests in these circumstances. It is true, however, that the first 'arrestee' would not be entitled to use force in self-defence (if the arrestor was using only reasonable force) whereas the second might be.[21] The law does recognize that a person's act may be excused in the criminal law, while incurring civil liability. A person who makes an unreasonable mistake of fact which, if it were true, would amount to reasonable grounds for suspecting another to be in the act of committing an offence, has a defence to a criminal prosecution for false imprisonment or assault (because he lacks mens rea) but remains liable for the corresponding torts: the act done is not the act which the 1984 Act says he *may* do. Here the terminology of justification and excuse seems appropriate. The act is 'unlawful', but the actor is excused from criminal liability.

---

[12] There are many theories of justification ranging from those based on whether the outcome of D's act was a good one; whether he acted for good reasons; etc. See Tadros, *Criminal Responsibility*, Ch 10; J Dressler, 'New Thoughts About the Concept of Justification in the Criminal Law' (1984) 32 UCLA L Rev 61; J Gardner (1998) Buffalo Crim LR 575.

[13] See Duff, *Answering for Crime*, 277 et seq. These arise where D had sufficient reason to believe he acted for a good reason.

[14] The theories of excuse are also numerous, with many accepting that there is no single definition. In short, it might be said that an excuse arises where D admits that his act was wrong, but claims not to deserve punishment because of the circumstances pertaining. See fully: Horder, *Excusing Crime*, especially Ch 6, Tadros, *Criminal Responsibility*, Ch 11; C Finkelstein, 'Excuses and Dispositions in Criminal Law' (2002) 6 Buffalo Crim LR 317. See for comparative review of approaches across Europe, J Blomsma, *Mens Rea and Defences in European Criminal Law* (2012) Chs VIII–X.

[15] Advocated by Horder, *Excusing Crime*, 103–106; Tadros, *Criminal Responsibility*, Chs 4, 10 and 11. D is exempted where his lack of capacity is a general continuing one whereas he will be excused if his lack of capacity relates to the particular incident alleged.

[16] cf Robinson (1982) 82 Col LR 199 considering special verdicts for those who are excused and also the distinctions he draws attention to in fn 6.

[17] As in *Bourne* (1952) 36 Cr App R 125 and *Cogan and Leak* [1976] QB 217, [1975] Crim LR 584. See p 223.

[18] Robinson, n 16. [19] *Rethinking Criminal Law*, n 6.

[20] Subject to the conditions in s 24A(3). See *Blackstone's Criminal Practice* (2018) D1.29.

[21] See p 396.

Any attempt to rely on the theories of justifications or excuses as the guiding principle by which to structure an analysis of defences would, in the present state of the law, be premature, and no such attempt is made in either this or the subsequent chapter.

9.1.2 Relationship between mental condition defences

Some of the pleas discussed in this chapter may overlap since they are concerned with D's denial that he was a responsible actor at the time of the commission of the offence. Their interrelationship may be usefully summarized at the outset.[22] In short, there are three categories.

(1) Situations where D suffers some malfunctioning of his body or mind owing to some disease or *internal* cause. These factors are treated in law as 'diseases of the mind' which render D liable to a special verdict of not guilty by reason of insanity. The category includes such unremarkable conditions as sleepwalking, epilepsy and diabetes. The label 'insanity' is profoundly misleading.

(2) Situations where, because of some *external* factor that has affected D's mind or body in such a way that he acts involuntarily, he is entitled to an acquittal. Examples include concussion, taking a *medically prescribed* drug or anaesthetic in accordance with instructions, and other 'external' factors. These may give rise to a defence of sane[23] automatism, but that defence is hedged with qualification and approached by the courts with considerable scepticism. A defence of sane automatism is available only where D suffers a complete loss of control over the functioning of his limbs. In addition, where the automatism is self-induced by taking alcohol or drugs, it may be a defence to crimes of specific intent (as explained later) but not generally to basic intent offences (explained later).

(3) Situations where the factors affecting D's capacity do not negate liability at all. Examples include the voluntary taking of drink or drugs (discussed at p 311), which will provide no excuse in crimes other than those of specific intent where D has become so intoxicated as to lack mens rea.

9.2 Insanity

Some form of defence *akin* to the current defence of insanity[24] is crucial to the criminal justice system.[25] It recognizes that the imposition of criminal punishment should be reserved for those who are rational and responsible beings.[26] There are two ways in which an accused

---

[22] See LCDP, Ch 6 for a thorough analysis of the relationship between insanity, automatism and intoxication.

[23] Sometimes called non-insane automatism.

[24] See generally the excellent, though now dated, discussion in RD Mackay, *Mental Condition Defences in Criminal Law* (1995). Proposals for the reform of the law are made in the Report of the Committee on Mentally Abnormal Offenders (The Butler Report, 1975) Cmnd 6244, 1975. See also the philosophical discussion in Tadros, *Criminal Responsibility*, Chs 11 and 12. For the Law Commission's review of this area and its provisional conclusions on reform, see LCDP. The present law is described in Ch 2. This paper was preceded by the LCSP in which the Commission sought evidence that the defences were causing problems in practice. See J Peay, 'Insanity and Automatism: Questions from and About the Law Commission's Scoping Paper' [2012] Crim LR 927. The supplementary materials to LCSP, Ch 2–4 (available via the **online resources**) set out the present law and problems in considerable detail.

[25] Some have suggested that the defence could be abolished and the absence of mens rea would serve as a determinant of D's liability. See n 217 and C Slobogin, 'An End to Insanity: Recasting the Role of Mental Illness in Criminal Cases' (2000) 86 Virg LR 1199. See also LCDP, Ch 2 and references therein, and the supplementary material to LCSP, Appendix A.

[26] See the valuable analysis of the relationship between the defences and responsibility in Appendix A of LCDP.

person's mental condition or illness may be relevant in a criminal trial. First, the accused may claim that he lacked mental capacity at the time of the commission of the conduct alleged to constitute the criminal offence. Secondly, the accused may be claiming that at the time of trial he lacks mental capacity to be tried. It is convenient to deal with this second category here because of its very close relationship with the defence of insanity, although technically it is a matter not of substantive criminal law but of procedure.

9.2.1 Mental illness and trial

9.2.1.1 Mental condition rendering trial impracticable

In some cases, where D is held in custody awaiting trial, his mental condition will be so serious that he is transferred to hospital. If the Secretary of State is satisfied by reports from at least two medical practitioners that D is suffering from mental disorder,[27] she may order that D be detained in a hospital, if he is suffering from mental disorder of a nature or degree which makes it appropriate for him to be detained in a hospital for medical treatment; and he is in urgent need of such treatment; and appropriate medical treatment is available for him.[28] The defendant is normally brought to trial[29] when he is well enough. The basis for this practice is:

that the issue of insanity should be determined by the jury whenever possible and the power should be exercised only when there is likely to be a scandal [ie serious concern about the propriety] if the prisoner is brought up for trial . . . [30]

Clearly, in order to maintain compatibility with Art 5(1) (deprivation of liberty only in accordance with law) and Art 6 (fair trial) of the ECHR, it is essential that this power to detain is exercised in accordance with law and sparingly.[31]

9.2.1.2 Unfitness to be tried

Introduction

It is an important principle that an accused should, wherever possible, have an opportunity to contest his guilt in a normal criminal trial.[32] Finding someone to be 'unfit' results in him being denied a full criminal trial and ought therefore to be an exceptional approach.[33]

---

[27] For definitions, see Mental Health Act 2007. The 2007 Act amends the Mental Health Act 1983, redefining 'mental disorder' as 'any disorder or disability of the mind'.

[28] Mental Health Act 1983, s 48 (as amended).

[29] See the Law Commission's description of the pathways through the criminal justice system for the mentally ill in Appendix A of supplementary material to LCSP. See also LC 364, *Unfitness to Plead* (2016) Ch 2.

[30] Report of the Royal Commission on Capital Punishment (1953) Cmd 8932. See eg *Ghanbary* [2006] EWCA Crim 2374.

[31] cf the statistics revealed by RD Mackay and D Machin, *Transfers from Prison to Hospital—The Operation of s48 of the Mental Health Act 1983* (Home Office Research Directorate, 1998) No 84. See also P Bean, *Madness and Crime* (2008) Ch 3.

[32] *R (Hasani) v Blackfriars CC* [2005] EWHC 3016 (Admin). See the Law Commission's recommendation to allow for adjournment where there is a prospect of recovery so as to enable D to have a full trial: see LC 364, para 4.97.

[33] See LC 364,*Unfitness to Plead* (2016) especially Ch 2. On fitness to plead more generally, see Mackay, *Mental Condition Defences*, Ch 5; for trends in the use of the plea see RD Mackay and G Kearns, 'An Upturn in Unfitness to Plead?' [2000] Crim LR 532; RD Mackay, B Mitchell and L Howe, 'A Continued Upturn in Unfitness to Plead—More Disability in Relation to the Trial under the 1991 Act' [2007] Crim LR 530. Research appended to the LC Report reveals that the number of unfitness cases increased and has levelled off at around 100 per year. Legal guidance for the conduct of such cases is provided by the CPS: www.cps.gov.uk/legal-guidance/mentally-disordered-offenders.

Someone who is seriously mentally ill may nevertheless be 'fit to plead to the indictment and follow the proceedings at the trial and . . . if he is, he should ordinarily be allowed to do so, because it is in principle desirable that a person charged with a criminal offence should, whenever possible, be tried, so that the question whether he committed the crime may be determined by a jury.'[34]

At any trial in the Crown Court it might be alleged by the defence or the prosecution that D is 'unfit to plead' or 'unfit to stand trial'. If D is found by the judge to be unfit, the normal trial process is not applied to him. Instead, a jury determines the narrow question whether D did the act complained of (without considering his mens rea)—this is called a trial of the facts. At that hearing D might be acquitted (having been found not to have done the act) or be found to have done the act, and thereby be subjected to a range of disposal powers which are not 'sentences' since he has not been convicted.[35]

The issue of unfitness can be raised at any time. If raised at the start of the trial on arraignment, the Crown Court follows the procedure to determine D's fitness under ss 4 and 4A of the Criminal Procedure (Insanity) Act 1964.[36] The issue may also arise where D has been found unfit, he has been hospitalized and his condition has improved so that he is brought back to court to determine whether he remains unfit.[37] If, having decided D is unfit, D appears to have recovered before the court has begun to decide the trial of the facts alleged, the court should revisit the question of whether he is fit to be tried.

What constitutes unfitness?

At the first stage—inquiring whether D is unfit—the question is whether D has sufficient understanding to be tried. Astonishingly, the law is based on a test derived from a case decided in 1836 when any concern for and understanding of mental illness and the impact that might have on the ability of an individual to participate in the trial was limited.[38] The modern-day incarnation of the test was set out in the case of *M*.[39] The trial judge directed that the defendant had to have sufficient ability in relation to *all* of the following six things: (a) to understand the charges; (b) to understand the plea; (c) to challenge jurors; (d) to instruct counsel and his solicitor; (e) to understand the course of the trial; and (f) to give evidence if he chooses. If he is able to do all these things, he has *a right* to be tried, even if he is not capable of acting in his best interests.[40] The same principle must, theoretically, be

---

[34] As expressed by witnesses before the Royal Commission on Capital Punishment, *Report* (1953) Cmd 8932, at 78. See generally LC 364, Ch 2, recommending greater availability of measures to assist defendants to participate in a full trial where possible. The judge must generally exercise this discretion to postpone where there is a reasonable chance that the prosecution case will be successfully challenged: *Webb* [1969] 2 QB 278. On the other hand, 'the case for the prosecution may appear so strong and the suggested condition of the prisoner so disabling that postponement of the trial of the issue would be wholly inexpedient': *Burles* [1970] 2 QB 191, per Parker LCJ.

[35] See LC 364, Ch 6. See *Wells et al* [2015] EWCA Crim 2, [2015] Crim LR 359; *Chinegwundoh* [2015] EWCA Crim 109.

[36] As substituted by the Criminal Procedure (Insanity and Unfitness to Plead) Act 1991 and amended by the Domestic Violence, Crime and Victims Act 2004, discussed by S White, 'The Criminal Procedure (Insanity and Unfitness to Plead) Act 1991' [1992] Crim LR 4; P Fennell, 'The Criminal Procedure (Insanity and Unfitness to Plead) Act 1991' (1992) 55 MLR 547. The 1964 Act replaced the Criminal Lunatics Act 1800. See LCCP 197, Part 2 for a history of the developments.

[37] Section 4A is mandatory and must be complied with in full in such cases: *Ferris* [2004] EWHC 1221 (Admin). See LC 364, Ch 5 and the discussion generally in *Sultan* [2014] EWCA Crim 2648. On the possibility for resumption see LC 364, Ch 9 recommending opportunities for defence and prosecution to apply for leave to resume a trial.

[38] *Pritchard* (1836) 7 C & P 303. See LC 364, Ch 3.   [39] [2003] EWCA Crim 3452.

[40] *Robertson* [1968] 3 All ER 557, [1968] 1 WLR 1767, CA. See also *R (Kenneally) v Snaresbrook Crown Court* [2002] QB 1169. For insights into how psychiatrists view these, see T Rogers et al, 'Fitness to Plead and Competence to Stand Trial' (2008) 19 J Forensic Psychiatry & Psychology 576.

applicable where the prosecution contend that D is fit to plead and he denies it; but it might be more leniently applied in such a case.

More recently the courts have sought to adopt more flexible and enlightened approaches.[41] The Law Commission Report recommends a shift in focus to whether a defendant can participate effectively given the particular allegations and likely nature of the trial, and the assistance that might be made available to him in the trial.[42] These imperatives were echoed by the Court of Appeal in *Marcantonio and Chitolie*:

In applying the *Pritchard* criteria the court is required to undertake an assessment of the defendant's capabilities *in the context of the particular proceedings*. An assessment of whether a defendant has the capacity to participate effectively in legal proceedings should require the court to have regard to what that legal process will involve and what demands it will make on the defendant. It should be addressed not in the abstract but in the context of the particular case. The degree of complexity of different legal proceedings may vary considerably. Thus the court should consider, for example, the nature and complexity of the issues arising in the particular proceedings, the likely duration of the proceedings and the number of parties. There can be no legitimate reason for depriving a defendant of the right to stand trial on the basis that he lacks capacity to participate in some theoretical proceedings when he does not lack capacity to participate in the proceedings which he faces. It is in the interests of all concerned that the criminal process should proceed in the normal way where this is possible without injustice to the defendant. Moreover, it seems to us that such an approach is essential, given the emphasis which is now placed on the necessity of considering the special measures that may assist an accused at trial. (See, for example, *Walls* [2011] EWCA Crim 443; [2011] 2 Cr App R 6 .) The effectiveness of such measures can only be assessed in the context of the particular proceedings.[43]

It was held in *Podola*[44] that a person is fit to plead where an hysterical amnesia prevents him from remembering events during the whole of the period material to the question whether he committed the crime alleged, but whose mind is otherwise completely normal. The court was prepared to concede that a deaf mute[45] is 'unfit' but declined:

to extend the meaning of the word to include persons who are mentally normal at the time of the hearing of the proceedings against them and are perfectly capable of instructing their solicitors as to what submission their counsel is to put forward with regard to the commission of the crime.[46]

But is a person suffering from hysterical amnesia capable in that sense? If the facts justify a defence of accident or alibi but D is unable to remember them, the defence cannot be raised unless there are witnesses who come forward. On the other hand, it would be unsatisfactory if, for example, there could be no trial of a motorist who had suffered concussion in an accident, alleged to have been caused by his dangerous driving, and who could not remember what he did. It would be still less satisfactory in the case of one whose failure to recall the relevant events arose from voluntary drunkenness.[47]

---

[41] See also *Walls* [2011] EWCA Crim 443 suggesting use of special measures.

[42] See LC 364, Ch 3.

[43] [2016] EWCA Crim 14, [7] per Lloyd Jones LJ. Cited with approval by Simon LJ in the subsequent case of *Ehi-Palmer* [2016] EWCA Crim 1844.

[44] [1960] 1 QB 325. The jury had found that Podola was not suffering from hysterical amnesia and the question before the Court of Criminal Appeal concerned the onus of proof of that issue; but the court held that this question could only arise if the alleged amnesia could in law bring Podola within the scope of s 2 of the Criminal Lunatics Act 1800. The court's decision on this point thus appears to be part of the *ratio decidendi* of the case.

[45] See also *Sharif* [2010] EWCA Crim 1709.

[46] [1960] 1 QB at 356. The word 'insane' was the one under consideration as that was the word used in the Criminal Lunatics Act 1800, and is not used in s 4 of the 1964 Act; but the law is unchanged. Cf CLRC, Third Report, *Criminal Procedure (Insanity)* (1963) Cmd 2149, at 7.

[47] *Broadhurst v R* [1964] AC 441 at 451, PC. Butler (by majority) recommended the retention of the *Podola* rule.

The procedure for determining unfitness

The issue of unfitness may be raised by the judge on his own initiative or at the request of the prosecution or the defence. It is usually at the request of the defence at the start of the trial. Where neither party raises the issue, the judge should do so if he has doubts about the accused's fitness.[48] The Law Commission examined in detail the problems in practice with the need for expert evidence and the difficulties in identifying the likely unfitness of the accused.[49]

The issue of whether the accused is fit used to be tried by a jury.[50] Following s 22 of the Domestic Violence, Crime and Victims Act 2004, however, the issue is now to be determined by a court without a jury. Such proceedings do not constitute 'criminal proceedings' since they cannot result in a conviction; the procedure is to ensure the protection of the defendant and the public. Accordingly, Art 6 of the ECHR does not apply.[51]

The defendant may not be found unfit to plead unless there is written or oral evidence to that effect by two or more registered medical practitioners, at least one of whom is approved by the Home Secretary as having special experience in the field of mental disorder.[52] This goes some way to ensuring that the criminal process is in step with medical practice.[53] The medical evidence is required to prove unfitness (not fitness).[54]

In *Lederman*,[55] the judge had rightly ruled that D was fit to stand trial where the medical evidence was divergent on that issue. D had attempted to commit suicide prior to his trial for causing death by dangerous driving. These suicidal intentions and mental fragility were not relevant to the *Pritchard* criteria for consideration of unfitness to plead.

When should the question of fitness to be tried be determined?

The general rule is that a defendant is presumed to be fit to be tried, and any challenge to fitness is to be determined as soon as it arises. If the accused is found by the judge to be fit and the trial proceeds, the case will be tried by a jury in the normal way.

If the defendant is found unfit, the determination of the trial of the facts occurs before a jury. The case against a person who is undoubtedly unfit to stand trial may be weak and capable of demolition by cross-examination of the prosecution witnesses by his lawyers. It would be wrong if he were to be found unfit and subjected to the disposals (including

---

[48] See LC 364, para 4.16. *MacCarthy* [1967] 1 QB 68, discussed by AR Poole, 'Standing Mute and Fitness to Plead' [1966] Crim LR 6. *Janaway* [2014] EWCA Crim 1073 demonstrates how difficult it can be to assess whether D is fit to stand trial if he refuses to cooperate. The Court of Appeal held that the trial judge's decision to continue the trial could not be criticized.

[49] See LC 364, Chs 3 and 4.

[50] Criminal Procedure (Insanity) Act 1964, s 4(5). See now *B* [2008] EWCA Crim 1997, [2009] Crim LR 608 on the position where D1 is unfit and D2 fit at the same trial. See also *MB* [2010] EWCA Crim 1684; on difficulties this creates see LCCP 197, para 7.27.

[51] *H* [2003] UKHL 1, [2003] Crim LR 817, affirming *M, K and H* [2001] EWCA Crim 2024, [2002] Crim LR 57. On ECHR concerns with the operation of the procedure, see E Baker, 'Human Rights and McNaughten and the 1991 Act' [1994] Crim LR 84; Mackay, 'On Being Insane in Jersey Part Two' [2002] Crim LR 728, 'On Being Insane in Jersey Part Three—The Case of the *Attorney General v O'Driscoll*' [2004] Crim LR 219. It is important to note, however, that the Court of Appeal has in some instances interpreted 'criminal proceedings' in a broader fashion. In *Chal* [2007] EWCA Crim 2647 the Court of Appeal held that the hearsay provisions in the Criminal Justice Act 2003 applied to proceedings under s 4A of the 1964 Act. The same approach was adopted in *Creed* [2011] EWCA Crim 144, [2011] Crim LR 644 to the bad character provisions.

[52] The 1964 Act as amended, s 4(6). See also *Borkan* [2004] EWCA Crim 1642.

[53] But see LC 364, Ch 4 on the difficulties this can generate. It recognized that other health-care professionals or support workers are better qualified to give an assessment of the accused's ability to participate in his trial. See para 4.67.

[54] See *Ghulam* [2009] EWCA Crim 2285, [2010] Crim LR 796 and commentary.

[55] [2015] EWCA Crim 1308.

559

detention) which may follow from that finding without having an opportunity to test the prosecution's case. If the judge, having regard to the nature of D's supposed disability, thinks that it is expedient and in the interests of the accused to do so, he may postpone consideration of the question of fitness to be tried until any time up to the opening of the case for the defence.[56] This gives the defence the opportunity to test the prosecution's case. If at that point the judge takes the view that the prosecution case is insufficient to justify a conviction, the jury will be directed to acquit and the question of fitness to plead will not arise. If the judge finds that there is a case to answer, that question will then be determined by the jury by whom D is being tried. The matter is regulated by statute.[57] In these exceptional cases the issue is to be determined by the same jury by which the accused is being tried.[58]

As the Court of Appeal emphasized in *Orr*,[59] s 4A is a:

mandatory statutory requirement which cannot be avoided by the court's general discretion to order proceedings otherwise however beneficial to the defendant they appear.[60]

Once it was determined that the defendant was no longer fit to fully participate, the procedure in s 4A(1) of the Criminal Procedure (Insanity) Act 1964 had to be followed.

The trial of the facts

Where D is found to be unfit, either on arraignment or at the end of the prosecution case, the trial shall not proceed, or proceed further.[61] If the matter rested there, D might again be subject to a loss of liberty on the grounds of his mental illness or condition even though he has not been proved to have committed an offence. Even if the prosecution's evidence has been heard and amounts to a case to answer, the defence may have an answer to it in the shape of evidence—for example, of alibi. Section 4A (introduced by the 1991 Act, and amended by the 2004 Act) therefore provides for a further hearing.[62] The court (ie the jury) then decides on the evidence (if any) already given and such evidence as is adduced by the prosecution or the defence. The jury determines the question whether D 'did the act or made

---

[56] See LC 364, para 4.97.

[57] Criminal Procedure (Insanity) Act 1964, as amended by the Criminal Procedure (Insanity and Unfitness to Plead) Act 1991 and the Domestic Violence, Crime and Victims Act 2004.

[58] Section 22 of the 2004 Act, amending the Criminal Procedure (Insanity) Act 1964, s 4(5) as substituted by the Criminal Procedure (Insanity and Unfitness to Plead) Act 1991, s 2.

[59] [2016] EWCA Crim 889, [2016] Crim LR 865. For comment, see A Owusu-Bempah and N Wortley, 'Unfit to Plead or Unfit to Testify?' (2016) 80 J Crim L 391.

[60] At [30] per Macur LJ.

[61] See generally LC 364, Ch 5. The judge in *O'Donnell* [1996] 1 Cr App R 286 went wrong at this point by allowing the trial to proceed, by failing to appoint someone to put the case for the defence and by not directing the trial jury that, now, the only question for them was whether D did the act. Conviction annulled and *venire de novo* ordered. See also *Norman* [2008] EWCA Crim 1810, [2009] Crim LR 346—the duty on the court is to appoint the best person to represent D. Difficulties can arise where the accused refuses to be represented. As the Law Commission notes in *Unfitness to Plead: Issues Paper* (2014) (para 2.82), questions arise as to the UK's obligations under the UN Convention on the Rights of Persons with Disabilities to respect the rights, will and preferences of disabled people.

[62] Controversy has arisen as to whether previous admissions made by D ought to be admissible in a trial of the facts. In *B* [2012] EWCA Crim 1799, the Court of Appeal held that it was difficult to see how, if D was unfit to plead, he was capable of understanding the right to caution, the caution itself and the significance of a police interview. This issue was also considered in *Swinbourne* [2013] EWCA Crim 2329, although perhaps surprisingly, the Court declined to set aside the finding of fact in that case. In *B*, the court was critical of the fact that it lacked the power to order a retrial in these circumstances and urged Parliament to address this lacuna. Such sentiments echoed those in *McKenzie* [2011] EWCA Crim 1550, [2011] Crim LR 884 where it was recognized that there is no power to order a retrial where the Court of Appeal quashes findings made under the Criminal Procedure (Insanity) Act 1964, s 4A.

the omission charged against him as the offence'.[63] The aim of such a hearing is to test the evidence rather than to hold D to account.[64] The judge should not direct the jury as to what disposal powers might then be used against D if the jury were to find that he did the act.[65]

In relation to this s 4A hearing, it was held in *Antoine*[66] that the words 'act' and 'omission' mean the actus reus of the offence and that, accordingly, D could not rely on the defence of diminished responsibility.[67] The decision creates problems by its presumption that all offences divide neatly into elements only of actus reus and mens rea that can be readily identified. On the *Antoine* approach, at a s 4A hearing, the defence can deny actus reus elements but not mens rea elements.[68] The confusion is exemplified in the judgment itself. For example, Lord Hutton, with whom all their lordships agreed, said that the jury should take into account any objective evidence of mistake, accident or self-defence and should not find that D did the act unless it is sure that the prosecution has negatived the defence. But the 'defences' of mistake and accident are simply denials of mens rea, not of the actus reus, and self-defence has a vital mental element.[69] If this *dictum* is right, it is hard to see why any other evidence, other than of a defect of reason from disease of the mind, suggesting the absence of mens rea,[70] should not be admissible, thus undermining the whole decision. Subsequently, it was held that D could not invoke the defence of provocation.[71] That defence also applied only where all the elements of murder are proved so 'the act' of murder and of manslaughter by reason of provocation seem to be identical. Presumably the same approach would be taken to the new defence of loss of control. It appears that his lordship was anticipating that the s 4A inquiry is directed not merely to the actus reus, not to the full offence of actus reus and mens rea, but to an 'unlawful act'. The difficulty lies in what constitutes 'objective' evidence. In *Wells* (at [17]), it was held to include 'the background to the incident, the antecedents of the complainants and the circumstances of the [incident] as evidenced, for example by the injuries [and any] evidence of [a] co-defendant' at [17].

It is possible to envisage some relatively straightforward cases where 'objective defences' ought to be capable of being pleaded. Difficult examples to test the precise limits of Lord Hutton's 'objective defences' might include a case in which the defence of sane automatism

---

[63] Problems arise where D has been found unfit to plead and his condition improves so that by the time of the trial of the facts he is potentially fit to stand trial. See *Omara* [2004] EWCA Crim 431. See LC 364, Ch 5.

[64] The hearing is not a trial and D cannot be convicted: *Wells* [2015] EWCA Crim 2, [9], [2015] Crim LR 359.

[65] *Moore* [2009] EWCA Crim 1672.

[66] [2001] 1 AC 340, HL, [2000] Crim LR 621, overruling *Egan* [1998] 1 Cr App R 121, [1997] Crim LR 225 which had 'held' that the words meant all the ingredients of the offence as intended by the Butler Committee (1975, Cmnd 6244, para 10.24) on whose recommendations these provisions are based. RD Mackay and G Kearns, 'The Trial of the Facts and Unfitness to Plead' [1997] Crim LR 644, however, demonstrated that this was not the meaning intended by ministers who introduced the Bill in Parliament. The same words used in the Trial of Lunatics Act 1883, s 2, refer only to the actus reus: *Felstead* [1914] AC 534, HL. An application to Strasbourg was rejected as manifestly ill-founded: *Antoine v UK* (App no 62960/00). See also Mackay [2002] Crim LR 728. For discussion see LC 364, Ch 5. The Law Commission recommends that the prosecution should have to establish all elements of the offence: para 5.85.

[67] That defence applies only when the actus reus (and, indeed, the mens rea) of murder has been established.

[68] See *Norman* [2008] EWCA Crim 1810, [2009] Crim LR 346 as a good illustration of the problems—D was charged with child abduction and suffered from Huntingdon's Disease.

[69] This passage in the 13th edition was cited with approval by the Court of Appeal in *B* [2012] EWCA Crim 770, [2013] Crim LR 90.

[70] Clearly, the finding of an act or omission may include some elements of mens rea where they are a composite element of the actus reus: *R (Young) v Central Criminal Court* [2002] 2 Cr App R 12, [2002] Crim LR 588 and commentary. See the discussion in *Wells* [2015] EWCA Crim 2, [2015] Crim LR 359.

[71] *Grant (Heather)* [2002] QB 1030, [2002] Crim LR 403.

would have been advanced at trial. Consider, for example, a case where D has been hit on the head and in a state of concussion hit and killed V, and D has by trial become so traumatized by the event that he is unfit to be tried. At the trial of the facts under s 4A, is the automatism plea a denial of mens rea and forbidden? Or is it a denial of a 'voluntary act' and expressly recognized by Lord Hutton? Or is it in some third category of 'not unlawful act'? The Court of Appeal acknowledged the problem in *M*[72] where it was accepted that the actus reus/mens rea distinction was not one that could be rigidly adhered to in every case given the diverse nature of crimes. It also poses special problems in cases of secondary liability.

The practical difficulty posed by *Antoine* arose acutely in *B*, in which D was charged with voyeurism, contrary to s 67(1) of the Sexual Offences Act 2003.[73] The Court of Appeal accepted that the requirement in s 67(1) that D did an act 'for the purpose of sexual gratification' was pre-eminently an example of a mental element. It was therefore understandable why the judge had ruled that this element ought therefore to be excluded from the jury's consideration on a trial of the facts. However, the Court of Appeal disagreed with the judge's approach. In a voyeurism case, if that element was ignored all the Crown would have to prove was that D observed V doing a private act. Simply observing someone naked or in their underwear, even if done deliberately, is not a criminal offence. Having regard to the mischief at which the offence of voyeurism was designed to address, it was held that the link between deliberate observation and the purpose of sexual gratification of the observer is central to the offence. Relying upon Lord Hutton's phraseology in *Antoine*, it is that purpose which turns the deliberate observation of another doing an intimate act in private, into an 'injurious act'. The 'relevant act charged as the offence' was held to be the deliberate observation of another doing a private act where the observer does so for the specific purpose of the observer obtaining sexual gratification. Although this decision is an important one for the analysis and application of the principles espoused in *Antoine*, it only serves to highlight the problems.

Under the present law, the broader problem lies in defining with sufficient precision the level of inquiry that is appropriate at a trial of the facts under s 4A so as to (a) avoid assessment of the accused's mental state at the time of the offence, because although he is the person best able to know that, by definition, he is now unfit to provide such evidence, or rebut allegations, and (b) prevent the hospitalization of those who would for reasons other than those of mental illness have secured a complete acquittal at a normal trial. The irony is that by seeking to protect defendants from (i) the rigours of a full trial which they would not be able to participate in effectively, and (ii) inquiry into their mental state at the time of the offence which it is supposed they are unable to defend at the trial of the facts, the system might place them in a worse position by subjecting them to a s 4A hearing.[74]

Where D has been found to be unfit and found at the s 4A hearing to have committed the actus reus, but his condition then improves and the question arises whether he is fit to be tried, the determination of his fitness and of whether he performed the actus reus must both be re-litigated. The prior determination of the actus reus being satisfied cannot be relied upon.[75]

---

[72] [2003] EWCA Crim 357, [2003] 2 Cr App R 21. See also *Wells* [2015] EWCA Crim 2. On the difficulties involved see RD Mackay and W Brookbanks, 'Protecting the Unfit to Plead' [2005] Juridical Review 173. See also the LCCP on provisional proposals to include all elements of the offence in the s 4A hearing as reformed.

[73] [2012] EWCA Crim 770, [2013] Crim LR 90. See p 820.

[74] This paragraph in the 13th edition was cited with approval by the Court of Appeal in *B* [2012] EWCA Crim 770, [2013] Crim LR 90. See LC 364, Ch 5.

[75] *Ferris* [2004] EWHC 1221 (Admin); cf *Omara*, n 63. See the Law Com Issues Paper, Ch 7.

Onus of proof

Podola's case decided, overruling earlier authorities, that where D raises the issue of fitness to plead the onus of proving that he is unfit is on him. By analogy to the rule prevailing when a defence of insanity is raised at the trial,[76] D is required to prove his case not beyond reasonable doubt but on a balance of probabilities. If the issue is raised by the prosecution and disputed by the defence then the burden is on the prosecution and the matter must be proved beyond reasonable doubt.[77] If the issue is raised by the judge and disputed by D, presumably the onus is again on the prosecution.[78]

The effect of *Podola*'s case is that a person may be convicted although a court was not satisfied that he was capable of making out a proper defence at his trial. Moreover, the reasoning of the court has been criticized on the ground, *inter alia*, that the prosecution, in bringing the charge at all, is implicitly alleging that D is fit to stand his trial; and that he, in denying that he is so fit, is merely denying that the prosecution have established all the elements in their case.

Disposal powers in relation to a person unfit to plead who 'did the act'

Until the reforms made by the 1991 Act took effect, the court was required to order that any person found unfit had to be admitted to the hospital specified by the Home Secretary where he might be detained without limitation of time, the power to discharge him being exercisable only with the Home Secretary's consent. Since the 1991 Act, a person who is found unfit but, following a s 4A hearing, not to have done the act or made the omission charged simply goes free. Where he is found to be unfit *and* to have done the act or made the omission, a wider range of disposals is now generally available, although these are frequently criticized as being inadequate.[79] Under s 24 of the 2004 Act inserting a new s 5 into the 1964 Act, in any case other than one of a fixed sentence, the court may make:[80]

(1) a hospital order (with or without a restriction order);[81]

(2) a supervision order; or

(3) an order for absolute discharge.

Magistrates' and youth courts

In magistrates' courts and youth courts[82] the procedure for dealing with defendants who may have mental illness or other difficulties preventing them participating in the trial effectively is quite different.[83] It is contained in s 37 of the Mental Health Act 1983.[84] In cases of

[76] Per Edmund Davies J at first instance, [1960] 1 QB 325 at 329; *Robertson* [1968] 1 WLR 1767, CA.

[77] *Antoine* [2001] AC 340, [2000] Crim LR 621. According to Podola's counsel, Mr FH Lawton, later Lawton LJ, it had been the normal practice in recent years for the prosecution to call the evidence.

[78] M Dean, 'Fitness to Plead' [1960] Crim LR 79 at 82.

[79] See LC 364, Ch 6 on disposals including a revised supervision order: para 6.48. The Court of Appeal in *R* [2013] EWCA Crim 591 expressed uncertainty about whether an individual who has been found unfit to be tried and has 'done the act' has been acquitted. A finding that D did the acts was not a conviction because there had been no finding that D acted with mens rea. Similarly, a finding of unfitness and that D had done the act did not amount to an acquittal. There is thus no power to make a restraining order under s 5A of the Protection from Harassment Act, 1997: *Chinegwundo* [2014] EWCA Crim 2649, [2015] EWCA Crim 109.

[80] For discussion, see A Ashworth and L Zedner, *Preventive Justice* (2014) 209–214.

[81] See *Narey v Customs and Excise* [2005] EWHC 784 (Admin).

[82] *P v Barking Youth Court* [2002] EWHC 734 (Admin), [2002] Crim LR 637.

[83] The Law Commission Consultation Paper and Issues Paper examine the many defects in the procedure in the magistrates' and youth courts. LC 364 recommends the application of a statutory procedure in the magistrates' and youth courts for defendants who are unable to participate effectively in their trial: Ch 7.

[84] See A Samuels, 'Hospital Orders without Conviction' [1995] Crim LR 220. On the need to consider the suitability of such disposal, see *IA* [2005] EWCA Crim 2077, [2006] Crim LR 79. Note that the Mental Health Act 2007, Sch 1 amended s 37, so that the s 37 powers are available if D is suffering from any disorder or disability of the mind (the limitation to cases of mental illness or severe mental impairment is removed). See LCCP 197, Ch 8.

563

alleged unfitness, *if* there exists medical evidence to justify making a hospital or guardianship order under s 37, the court has the power to make such an order in all cases. Ordinarily the court should first address whether the act alleged was done or the omission made by D. If it is not proved that D did the act or omission he will be acquitted. If the court finds that he did the act or omission it can make an order under s 37. However, if appropriate, where the court finds that D performed the act it can, instead of making an order under s 37, conduct a trial of the insanity plea.[85] At the conclusion of that trial the court's powers of disposal under s 37 remain available.

Reform

Numerous problems with the present law have been identified. It is based on an historic test and, as Toulson LJ stated in 2008, there is a 'mismatch between the legal test and the psychiatric understanding'.[86] The procedure has been cogently criticized for its focus on D's communicative ability and its failure to address the true problem—whether D is capable of providing a rational account of the incident to instruct his lawyer and of participating effectively in the trial process.[87] As the Law Commission's work has emphasized, the present test creates difficulties in practice. It fails to protect mentally ill defendants who, despite the unfitness procedure, are often tried in the normal way[88] although in some cases displaying bizarre behaviour.[89] It fails to protect enough defendants. Estimates are that 10 per cent of men on remand display signs of psychosis, but only a very small number of unfitness pleas are made each year.[90] Moreover, the test is not always well suited to cases involving those with communication or learning difficulties rather than mental illness. The s 4A hearing is also defective since it fails to provide a fair opportunity for the accused to be acquitted.

The Law Commission recommendations seek to maximize the opportunity for the defendant to continue to participate in a full trial with assistance and support.[91] An adjournment would be available if D was likely to recover sufficiently for a full trial.[92] The defendant's ability to participate effectively would be tested against a modern statutory test drafted with the modern psychological and psychiatric understanding in mind.[93] The test is based on effective participation of the accused given the context of the trial.[94] There would be the opportunity for D to plead guilty if he wished and had the capacity to do so even if he lacked the capacity for a full trial.[95] The judge would have the power to divert an unfit defendant out of the criminal justice process where it was in the interests of justice.[96]

The Law Commission recommended amendment to the trial of the facts regime to require the prosecution to prove all elements of the offence.[97] The jury would be able to return three

---

[85] *R (Singh) v Stratford MC* [2007] EWHC 1582 (Admin).

[86] *Murray* [2008] EWCA Crim 1792, [6].

[87] See also the psychiatrist's view—D Grubin, 'What Constitutes Unfitness to Plead' [1993] Crim LR 748, cf RA Duff, 'Fitness to Plead and Fair Trials' [1994] Crim LR 419.

[88] Examples include *Erskine* [2009] EWCA Crim 1425, [2010] Crim LR 48; *Moyle* [2008] EWCA Crim 3059, [2009] Crim LR 586.

[89] See *Shulman* [2010] EWCA Crim 1034; *Grant* [2008] EWCA Crim 1870.

[90] See LCCP 197, para 2.61.

[91] See LC 364, Ch 2. For comment, see A Loughnan, 'Between Fairness and "Dangerousness": Reforming the Law on Unfitness to Plead' [2016] Crim LR 451 and H Howard, 'Lack of Capacity: Reforming the Law on Unfitness to Plead' (2016) 80 J Crim L 428.

[92] LC 364, para 4.97

[93] Ch 3. Recommendations are made for more efficient use of a wider pool of relevant expertise.

[94] See para 3.136. See RD Mackay [2004] Crim LR 219. See also the Scottish Law Commission Report No 195 (2004) Ch 4 and cl 4. See LCCP 197, provisionally proposing a test of decisional competence, but awaiting a test being devised by psychiatrists. For critical comment see RD Mackay [2011] Crim LR 433.

[95] Para 3.156.   [96] Para 5.61.

[97] Para 5.85. See LCCP 197, Part 6.

possible verdicts: an acquittal, that D did the acts complained of, or that D is not g
reason of insanity.[98] The disposals available to a judge would be hospital order, sup
or absolute discharge.[99] Resumption of the full trial would be possible where D ha
ered and it was in the interests of justice subject to other safeguards where the Crown was
seeking to resume the trial. The Commission also recommends the new scheme applies to
trials in the magistrates' and youth courts.[100]

9.2.2 A plea of insanity

Whereas the plea of unfitness is concerned with the accused's mental state at the time of the
trial, insanity is concerned with the accused's mental state at the time when he is alleged to
have committed the crime.[101]

Although rarely raised in a magistrates' court, it applies in a summary trial as well as a
trial on indictment.[102] The rules governing the plea of insanity derive from the common
law, but in trials on indictment the procedure for dealing with the plea has been regulated
by statute; the unamended common law operates in magistrates' courts.[103] A successful
plea of insanity at a trial on indictment formerly resulted in a mandatory order that D be
admitted to a special hospital where he might be detained indefinitely. That was a significant
deterrent to raising the plea. Since the 1991 Act,[104] a verdict of not guilty by reason of insanity means that the judge has more discretion in the disposal and can order hospitalization,
a supervision order or an absolute discharge. Statistics suggest that this may be leading to
more frequent reliance on the defence.[105]

9.2.2.1 Operation of the insanity defence

As a preliminary point it is worth emphasizing that legal and psychiatric understandings
of 'insanity' are completely different.[106] Strangely, the fact that D suffers an extreme mental
illness recognized by psychiatrists will not necessarily be sufficient to afford a defence in
law. Conversely, the fact that D suffers an illness that no psychiatrist would normally regard
as a form of 'insanity' (eg diabetes) may qualify him for the defence.[107] It seems astonishing

---

[98] Para 5.132.   [99] Ch 6.   [100] See Ch 7.

[101] See generally Mackay, *Mental Condition Defences in Criminal Law*, Ch 2; A Loughnan, *Manifest
Madness: Mental Incapacity in Criminal Law* (2012), and for a more philosophical account see Tadros,
Criminal Responsibility, Ch 12. A comparative analysis of some European States is found in J Blosma, *Mens
Rea and Defences in European Criminal Law* (2012) 483. For the Law Commission's review of this area, see
the LCDP and the preceding LCSP, in particular, the supplementary materials available at https://consult.jus-
tice.gov.uk/law-commission/insanity-and-automatism/user_uploads/insanity_scoping_supplementary.pdf-1.
The CPS provides guidance on prosecuting people with a mental disorder: www.cps.gov.uk/legal-guidance/
mentally-disordered-offenders/.

[102] See *R (Singh) v Stratford MC* [2007] EWHC 1582 (Admin).

[103] *Horseferry Road Magistrates' Court, ex pK* [1996] 2 Cr App R 574, [1997] Crim LR 129. See T Ward,
'Magistrates, Insanity and the Common Law' [1997] Crim LR 796.

[104] As amended by the Domestic Violence, Crime and Victims Act 2004.

[105] See RD Mackay, 'Ten More Years of the Insanity Defence' [2012] Crim LR 946, noting that there has been
a gradual increase in the number of special verdicts returned but that it may now be plateauing; RD Mackay,
'Fact and Fiction About the Insanity Defence' [1990] Crim LR 247; RD Mackay and G Kearns, 'The Continued
Under use of Unfitness to Plead and the Insanity Defence' [1994] Crim LR 546; RD Mackay and G Kearns,
'More Fact(s) about the Insanity Defence' [1999] Crim LR 714; Mackay, Mitchell and Howe [2006] Crim LR 399;
A Ashworth and L Zedner, *Preventive Justice* (2014) 209–214.

[106] For an analysis of the historical interaction between the two, see A Loughnan and T Ward, 'Emergent
Authority and Expert Knowledge: Psychiatry and Criminal Responsibility in the UK' (2014) 37 Int'l J L &
Psychiatry 25.

[107] See Ch 3 of the Law Commission supplementary materials to LCSP.

565

that in the twenty-first century the law remains based not on any medical understanding of mental illness but on a distinct legal criterion of responsibility defined by the common law and set out in authoritative form in the 'M'Naghten Rules', formulated by judges as long ago as 1843.[108] Daniel M'Naghten, intending to murder Sir Robert Peel, killed Peel's secretary by mistake. His acquittal of murder[109] on the ground of insanity provoked controversy and was debated in the legislative chamber of the House of Lords, which sought the advice of the judges and submitted to them a number of questions. The answers to those questions became the famous 'Rules'. Answers to hypothetical questions, even by all the judges, are not, strictly speaking, a source of law; but in *Sullivan*[110] it was accepted by the judicial committee of the House of Lords that the Rules have provided a comprehensive definition since 1843.[111] The M'Naghten Rules are binding law.

The importance of the Rules reduced greatly on the introduction of the defence of diminished responsibility and the abolition of the death penalty. Diminished responsibility is a (partial) defence only to murder. Insanity pleas remain rare, even on charges for murder (see Ch 13). Defendants seemingly prefer to risk conviction rather than incur the stigma of a verdict of not guilty by reason of insanity. This remains true even though, since 1991, the disposal powers are not limited to automatic indefinite detention. But the stigma of the label 'insanity' remains: it is strikingly inappropriate when so much progress has been made regarding public attitudes to mental illness.

In some cases defendants will even prefer to plead guilty rather than risk a special verdict on grounds of insanity. The propriety of accepting a plea of guilty by a person who, on the evidence, is not guilty is open to question, but it has not been challenged in the Court of Appeal and the House of Lords left the matter open. It is unsatisfactory that the state of the law is such that people suffering from a mental condition feel compelled to plead guilty. One undesirable consequence is the disproportionately high number of inmates in prison with mental disorders, at least some of whom might satisfy a suitably reformed modern insanity defence.[112]

9.2.2.2 The test of insanity

Whatever the effect of the recent changes on procedure and disposal, the M'Naghten Rules remain of great importance symbolically and practically both because they provide the legal test of responsibility of the mentally abnormal and because they set a limit to the defences of automatism and, in theory, of diminished responsibility. The basic propositions of the law are to be found in the answers to Questions 2 and 3 of the M'Naghten Rules:[113]

the jurors ought to be told in all cases that every man is presumed to be sane, and to possess a sufficient degree of reason to be responsible for his crimes, until the contrary be proved to their satisfaction; and that to establish a defence on the ground of insanity, it must be clearly proved that, at the time of the committing of the act, the party accused was labouring under such a defect of reason, from disease of the mind, as not to know the nature and quality of the act he was doing, or, if he did know it, that he did not know he was doing what was wrong.

---

108 (1843) 4 St Tr NS 847. For an engaging historical analysis of the case, see A Loughnan, 'M'Naghten's Case' in P Handler, H Mares and I Williams (eds), *Landmark Cases in Criminal Law* (2017).

109 (1843) 10 Cl & Fin 200.   110 *Sullivan* [1983] 2 All ER 673 at 676.

111 In *Johnson* [2007] EWCA Crim 1978 the Court of Appeal referred enigmatically to the fact that the Rules must, given their provenance, be treated with 'some caution'.

112 See in particular Lord Bradley's report, *People with Mental Health Problems or Learning Disabilities in the Criminal Justice System* (2009).

113 10 Cl & Fin at 210, per Lord Tindal CJ. R Moran, *Knowing Right From Wrong: The Insanity Defence of Daniel McNaghten* (1981).

It will be seen that there are two lines of defence open to an accused person (often called the 'two limbs'):

(1) he must be found not guilty by reason of insanity if, because of a disease of the mind, he did not know the nature and quality of his act (effectively a denial of mens rea); or

(2) even if he did know the nature and quality of his act, he must be acquitted if, because of a disease of the mind, he did not know it was 'wrong'.

The Rules have been heavily criticized for being over-inclusive; 'disease of the mind' has been widely construed to include within the scope of insanity such commonplace illnesses as diabetes.[114] In addition, in some instances D qualifies for the defence even though he was responsible for his inability to appreciate the nature or wrongness of his actions. As Mackay has pointed out, some commentators have argued that the first limb is superfluous as anyone who did not know the nature and quality of the act must also not have known it was wrong. Others, including Glanville Williams, argued that the second limb was superfluous since anyone who did not know the nature and quality of his act must also have lacked awareness that it was wrong.[115] The Rules are also criticized for focus on the cognitive state of D (has he appreciated the nature or wrongness) rather than on whether D had the *capacity* to be held responsible or to conform with criminal regulation.[116]

Disease of the mind

The two limbs of the Rule require separate consideration but the prior question, under either limb, is whether D was suffering from 'a defect of reason from a disease of the mind'. If D was unaware of the nature and quality of his act for some reason *other than* a defect of reason from a disease of the mind (eg mistake), he will usually be entitled to a straightforward acquittal on the ground that he lacked the necessary mens rea. Moreover, in such a case the onus of proof remains on the Crown, whereas it rests on D if he tenders evidence of a defect of reason arising from disease of the mind.[117] If D was unaware that his act was 'wrong' for some reason other than from a defect of reason from a disease of the mind, this will generally not amount to a defence at all. It is a cardinal principle that neither ignorance of the law[118] nor good motive will normally afford a defence.

The question whether D has raised the defence of insanity is one of law for the judge.[119] Whether D, or indeed his medical witnesses, would call the condition on which he relies 'insanity' is immaterial. The expert witnesses may testify as to the factual nature of the condition but it is for the judge to say whether that is evidence of 'a defect of reason, from disease of the mind', because, as will become apparent, these are legal, not medical, concepts.

---

[114] See LCSP, Chs 2–4 and LCDP, Ch 2.

[115] See RD Mackay, 'Righting the Wrong? Some Observations on the Second Limb of the M'Naghten Rules' [2009] Crim LR 80.

[116] See Tadros, *Criminal Responsibility*, Ch 12; A Brudner, *Punishment and Freedom: A Liberal Theory of Penal Justice* (2009). See also LCDP, Ch 2 and the supplementary materials to the LCSP available at https://consult.justice.gov.uk/law-commission/insanity-and-automatism/user_uploads/insanity_scoping_supplementary.pdf-1.

[117] The application of the burden of proof in these cases is critically explored by T Jones, 'Insanity, Automatism and the Burden of Proof on the Accused' (1995) 111 LQR 475; A Loughnan, 'Manifest Madness' (2007) 70 MLR 379, 398. It is surprising that there has not been a direct ECtHR challenge on this basis other than in 1990 in *H v UK* (App no 15023/89) in which the Commission dismissed the application. That decision has been very heavily criticized: see Jones, ibid. See also the discussion in LCDP, Ch 8 for a full discussion of the issues and a proposal to place the ultimate burden for the reformed defence on the Crown.

[118] cf the challenge to that made by A Ashworth, 'Ignorance of the Law, and Duties to Avoid It' (2011) 74 MLR 1.

[119] See *Roach* [2001] EWCA Crim 2698.

In the leading case of *Sullivan*,[120] the defence to a charge of assault occasioning actual bodily harm was that D attacked V while recovering from a minor epileptic seizure and did not know what he was doing. The House of Lords held that the judge had rightly ruled that this raised the defence of insanity. D had then changed his plea to guilty, notwithstanding that he was thereby pleading guilty to an offence for which he was manifestly not responsible. However, his conviction was upheld.

It seems that any disease which produces a malfunctioning of the mind is a disease of the mind.[121] Commonly the insanity plea will involve mental illness (schizophrenia being the most common basis)[122] but it is not restricted to diseases of the brain. Arteriosclerosis, a tumour on the brain, epilepsy, diabetes, sleepwalking, pre-menstrual syndrome and all physical diseases, may amount in law to a disease of the mind if they produce the relevant malfunction. The lack of correlation with medical definitions of mental illness renders this aspect of the test potentially incompatible with the ECHR (see later) where it results in D's loss of liberty or loss of private life.

Although the courts have adopted a very wide definition of disease of the mind, it is not without limit, as has been illustrated. In *Coley*,[123] D had probably suffered a psychotic episode following consumption of strong cannabis. D attacked his neighbour with a hunting knife (D had dressed in combat gear and wore a balaclava). It was suggested that he might have been acting out the role of a character in a computer game. He claimed to have 'blacked out'. The trial judge refused to leave the defence of insanity to the jury and that view was endorsed by the Court of Appeal. This was a case of voluntary intoxication and not a disease of the mind amounting to insanity. Hughes LJ said:

The precise line between the law of voluntary intoxication and the law of insanity may…be difficult to identify in some borderline cases. But the present case falls comfortably on the side of the line covered by voluntary intoxication.…If the doctors were right about his state of mind, his mind was to an extent detached from reality by the direct and acute effects on it of the ingestion of cannabis. Every intoxicated person has his mind affected, and to an extent disordered, by the direct and acute effects of the ingestion of intoxicants; all intoxication operates through the brain. Not infrequently it would be perfectly legitimate to say of a very drunken man that his mind had become detached from reality by the intoxication…In order to engage the law of insanity, it is not enough that there is an effect on the mind, or, in the language of the *M'Naghten* rules, a 'defect of reason'. There must also be what the law classifies as a disease of the mind.[124]

In contrast, in *Harris*, conjoined with *Coley* on appeal, D was in the habit of binge drinking for several days at a time. Following a period of a week doing so, he took time to sober up before returning to work. After several days he then set fire to his home and was charged with aggravated arson. His defence was not one of intoxication—he was sober at the time of the fire-setting and his plea, if at all,[125] was one of insanity based on the disease of his mind caused by repeated chronic alcohol abuse. His past intoxication had produced a mental disorder—alcoholic psychosis amounting to a disease of the mind.

It is important to reiterate the distinction between pleas of insanity and pleas of sane automatism. A transitory malfunctioning of the mind is not a disease of the mind when it is

---

120 [1984] AC 156, HL.

121 *Kemp* [1957] 1 QB 399 at 406, per Devlin J, approved by Lord Denning in *Bratty*, n 133.

122 See Mackay, Mitchell and Howe [2006] Crim LR 399.

123 [2013] EWCA Crim 223, [2013] Crim LR 923. Also discussed in A Loughnan and N Wake, 'Of Blurred Boundaries and Prior Fault: Insanity, Automatism and Intoxication' in A Reed and M Bohlander (with N Wake and E Smith) (eds), *General Defences in Criminal Law—Domestic and Comparative Perspectives* (2014) 118–119 and 124.

124 At [18].   125 Not on the facts as D clearly knew what he was doing and that it was wrong.

caused by some external factor—a blow on the head causing concussion, the consumption of alcohol or drugs, or the administration of an anaesthetic. In such cases where there is a total loss of capacity sane automatism may be pleaded (discussed later in the chapter). That 'defence' imposes no burden of proof on D and, if successful, results in a complete acquittal. Insanity, on the other hand, must be proved by D (on the balance of probabilities) and results in a special verdict of not guilty by reason of insanity. In terms of process and outcome, much turns on this distinction between internal and external causes of the malfunction of the mind, yet the basis for the distinction is unsatisfactory.[126]

In determining whether D suffers from a disease of the mind, it is clear that the law considers not only D's state of mind at the time the alleged offence was committed, but how it came about.[127] Devlin J thought that the object of the inclusion of the words 'disease of the mind' was to exclude 'defects of reason caused simply by brutish stupidity without rational power'; but it seems the words exclude more than that. In *Quick*,[128] D who had caused actual bodily harm called medical evidence to show that he was a diabetic and that he was suffering from a hypoglycaemic attack at the time of the alleged offence and was unaware of what he was doing. Bridge J ruled that he had thereby raised a defence of insanity, whereupon D pleaded guilty. On appeal it was held that D's mental condition at the time of the offence was caused not by D's diabetes (an internal factor) but by his use of insulin prescribed by the doctor coupled with his failure to follow that prescription by eating after injecting insulin (an external factor). This use of the prescribed drug was an external factor and the plea of sane automatism should have been left to the jury. If D's mental condition had been caused by his diabetes the plea would have been insanity, being based on that internal factor of disease. The case illustrates the fine line between the two pleas although the consequence of pleading them successfully is markedly different.[129] The unsatisfactory nature of this distinction is further discussed in the next section.

Disease of the mind includes *physical* illnesses that manifest themselves by affecting reasoning. In *Kemp*,[130] D made an entirely motiveless and irrational attack on his wife with a hammer. He was charged with causing grievous bodily harm to her with intent. D suffered from arteriosclerosis which caused a congestion of blood in his brain, leading to a temporary lapse of consciousness during which he made the attack. It was conceded that D did not know the nature and quality of his act and that he suffered from a defect of reason but it was argued on his behalf that this arose, not from any mental disease, but from a purely physical one. It was argued that if a physical disease caused the brain cells to degenerate (as in time, it might), then it would be a disease of the mind; but until it did so, it was said, this temporary interference with the working of the brain was like a concussion or something of that sort and not a disease of the mind. Devlin J rejected this argument and held that D was suffering from a disease of the mind. He said:

The law is not concerned with the brain but with the mind, in the sense that 'mind' is ordinarily used, the mental faculties of reason, memory and understanding. If one reads for 'disease of the mind' 'disease of the brain,' it would follow that in many cases pleas of insanity would not be established because it could not be proved that the brain had been affected in any way, either by degeneration of the cells or in any other way. In my judgment the condition of the brain is irrelevant and so is the question of whether the condition of the mind is curable or incurable, transitory or permanent.

---

[126] See LCDP, Ch 6.

[127] Contrary to the *dictum* of Devlin J in *Kemp* [1957] 1 QB 399 at 407.

[128] [1973] QB 910, [1973] Crim LR 434 and commentary; cf *Hennessy*. See p 311 and *Coley* [2013] EWCA Crim 223, [2013] Crim LR 923. See also LC 314, *Intoxication and Criminal Liability* (2009) para 2.88.

[129] See *Bingham* [1991] Crim LR 433.   [130] [1957] 1 QB 399 at 407.

In the earlier case of *Charlson*,[131] where the evidence was that D was 'acting as an automaton without any real knowledge of that he was doing' as a result of a cerebral tumour, Barry J directed the jury to acquit if the defence might reasonably be true. Devlin J distinguished *Charlson* on the ground that there the doctors were agreed that D was not suffering from a mental disease.[132] As this is a question of law, the distinction seems unsound and in *Bratty*[133] Lord Denning approved *Kemp* and disagreed with *Charlson*. Lord Denning put forward his own view of a disease of the mind:

it seems to me that any mental disorder which has manifested itself in violence and is prone to recur is a disease of the mind. At any rate it is the sort of disease for which a person should be detained in hospital rather than be given an unqualified acquittal.

Quick casts some doubt on this *dictum*, and it is surely right to do so. The definition might fit a diabetic, but 'no mental hospital would admit a diabetic merely because he had a low blood sugar reaction', and it might be felt to be 'an affront to common sense' to regard such a person as insane; yet the court saw the weakness of the argument, agreeing with Devlin J that the disease might be 'curable or incurable ... transitory or permanent'; and the fact that the Home Secretary might have had a difficult problem of disposal did not affect the matter. Lord Denning's *dictum* has also been rightly criticized on the ground that it is tautologous and that a disease of the mind may manifest itself in wrongful acts other than violence, such as theft.[134]

'External' and 'internal' factors

The distinction between external causes, which may give rise to a defence of sane automatism, and internal factors which can only give rise to a defence of insanity, has been subjected to sustained and cogent criticism.[135] The supposed justification is that the internal factor will usually be a continuing condition which may cause a recurrence of the prohibited conduct, whereas the external factor—the blow on the head, the injection, the inhalation of toxic fumes,[136] etc—will usually have a transitory effect which will not recur. However, it is surely wrong to assume such a precise correlation between the source of the defect in D's 'mind' and likelihood of recurrence. The blow on the head may inflict permanent damage, which would be viewed thereafter as an internal factor giving rise to a defence of insanity. In cases of diabetes, it can hardly be suggested that there is a greater risk of recurrence from the diabetes itself causing a hyperglycaemic state (insanity) than from D forgetting to eat after taking insulin and going into a hypoglycaemic state (sane automatism). Distinguishing between external and internal causes is an unsatisfactory and deficient way of addressing the true mischief—the likelihood of danger posed by uncontrolled recurrence of the mental condition leading to a lack of capacity. The deficiency is exposed in Lord Lane's judgment in *Burgess*:

if there is a danger of recurrence that may be an added reason for categorising the condition as a disease of the mind. On the other hand, the absence of the danger of recurrence is not a reason for saying that it cannot be a disease of the mind.[137]

---

[131] [1955] 1 WLR 317.

[132] A similar argument was rejected in *Sullivan* [1983] 2 All ER 673 at 677, [1983] Crim LR 740. The nomenclature adopted by the medical profession may change but the meaning of 'disease of the mind' in the M'Naghten Rules remains unchanged.

[133] *Bratty v A-G for Northern Ireland* [1963] AC 386 at 410–412, HL.

[134] N Walker, *Crime and Insanity in England* (1963) 117.

[135] See the dissent by Dickson J in *Rabey* (1981) 114 DLR (3d) 193; RD Mackay, 'Non-Organic Automatism' [1980] Crim LR 350; Williams, TBCL, 671. See LCSP,Chs 2–4 and LCDP, Chs 2 and 6.

[136] *Oakley* (1986) 24 CCC (3d) 351 at 362, per Martin JA.   [137] [1991] WLR 1206 at 1212.

The passage serves to emphasize that the underlying bases for the courts' approach are pragmatism and policy rather than principle.

Range of conditions treated in law as 'a disease of the mind'

The reach of the M'Naghten Rules in extending to epileptics,[138] diabetics,[139] pre-menstrual syndrome sufferers,[140] sleepwalkers,[141] etc is astonishingly wide. Its application to sleepwalking has prompted interest[142] following first instance decisions taking a generous approach and allowing a defence of sane automatism to be run.[143] Even if sleepwalking is classified as insanity, a more liberal approach is evident in some cases. For example, in one case D had killed V in the course of his sleepwalking/night terror, and pleaded insanity. The CPS discontinued the case since the result of an insanity verdict would have been hospitalization for D and that was not in the public interest.[144] Pressure has also been mounting for the reclassification of epilepsy to avoid the stigma of being labelled insane.[145]

Most if not all of the reported cases involve apparently purposive conduct. In *Bratty v A-G for Northern Ireland*,[146] D took off a girl's stocking and strangled her with it. There was medical evidence that he was suffering from psychomotor epilepsy which might have prevented him from knowing the nature and quality of his act. It was held to be evidence of insanity. This seems very far removed from a convulsive movement of the body of an epilepsy sufferer. It is a complex operation which has every appearance of being controlled by the brain. Whether or not D could have prevented himself from acting in this way, he appears to be a dangerous person and, in the absence of some other form of protection for the public, a simple verdict of acquittal seems inappropriate. Sullivan's conduct, like that of Kemp, Charlson, Quick and Rabey (see later) also seems to have been apparently purposive and, though he was less obviously a danger to the public than Bratty, his case may be indistinguishable in principle. Even the examples of epilepsy referred to in recent research into insanity suggest that commonly the actions are complex purposive ones. Of course, a convulsive movement of a person in an epileptic fit may result in injury to person or property but it would seem absurd either to convict the epileptic or hold him to be insane. If insanity is available as a defence for seemingly purposive action, it is not fanciful to suggest, bearing in mind the now increased flexibility of the courts' powers of disposal, that some unscrupulous pleas of insanity will be advanced, and the courts need to be alert to that fact.

It remains deeply unsatisfactory for this crucial 'disease of the mind' element to remain so ill-defined. First, a person with a mental condition of a non-severe nature and who poses no

---

[138] *Sullivan* [1984] AC 156. RD Mackay and M Reuber, 'Epilepsy and the Defence of Insanity—Time for a Change' [2007] Crim LR 782.

[139] *Hennessy* [1989] 2 All ER 9; *Coley* [2013] EWCA Crim 223, [2013] Crim LR 923. See on diabetes and driving cases in particular, J Rumbold, 'Diabetes and Criminal Responsibility' (2010) 174 CLJW 21.

[140] *Smith* [1982] Crim LR 531 and see V John, 'Premenstrual Syndrome in the Criminal Law' [1997] Auckland Uni LR 331; SM Edwards, 'Mad, Bad or Pre-Menstrual' (1988) 138 NLJ 456.

[141] *Burgess* [1991] 2 All ER 769. I Mackay, 'The Sleepwalker is Not Insane' (1992) 55 MLR 714. Cf the Canadian Supreme Court in *Parks* (1990) 95 DLR (4th) 27.

[142] See W Wilson et al, 'Violence, Sleepwalking and the Criminal Law' [2005] Crim LR 601 and 614; RD Mackay and B Mitchell, 'Sleepwalking, Automatism and Insanity' [2006] Crim LR 901 reviewing Canadian law which adopts a more holistic approach to the question rather than relying solely on the internal/external bifurcation. See also LCDP, p 110.

[143] See *Lowe* (2005) unreported, discussed in Wilson et al, n 142, and *Pooley* (2007) unreported, discussed in Mackay and Mitchell, n 142. This has prompted CPS guidance: www.cps.gov.uk/legal-guidance/defences-sleepwalking-defence-sexual-offence-cases. See also I Ibrahim and P Fenwick, 'Sleep Related Automatism and the Law' (2008) 48 Med Sci Law 124.

[144] See http://news.bbc.co.uk/1/hi/wales/8370363.stm.

[145] See Mackay and Reuber [2007] Crim LR 782.   [146] [1963] AC 386.

real future risk to society might end up labelled and treated as insane. Secondly, a challenge to the overbroad definition of disease of the mind may arise under the ECHR. Article 5(1)(e), in guaranteeing protection against arbitrary detention, allows for the detention of those suffering from mental illness where it is necessary for the protection of the public. The European Court of Human Rights has accepted that the State's power to detain in these circumstances is limited to cases where the mental illness is one recognized by objective medical expertise, and where the medical and legal definitions of mental illness have a close correlation.[147] If a defendant were ever to be detained as a result of a special verdict of insanity when the 'disease' he was suffering from was one which medical professionals would not normally classify as insanity, there might be an incompatibility. That may be unlikely as detention is regulated by the Mental Health Act. Although medical professionals are now required to be involved in the trial of insanity,[148] it is debatable whether this ensures compatibility.[149] Medical professionals might well, in the course of providing expert evidence, be obliged to state that the disease is one that satisfies the legal test of insanity, but that is quite different from a medical professional recognizing the disease as a matter of psychiatry as one of mental illness.

Borderline cases: disease of mind (insanity) or external factor (sane automatism)?

Some of the most controversial problems on classification arise in relation to 'psychological blows'. Cases in other jurisdictions have addressed directly the question of whether a 'dissociative state' resulting from a 'psychological blow' amounts to insane or sane automatism. In the Canadian case of *Rabey*,[150] D, a student who had become infatuated by a girl, V, discovered that V did not regard him particularly highly and reacted to that news by hitting her on the head with a rock that he had taken from a geology laboratory. He was acquitted of causing bodily harm with intent on the ground of automatism. The trial judge accepted that D was in a dissociative state caused by the psychological blow of his rejection, which, it was held, was an external factor analogous to a blow to the skull where the skull is thin, causing concussion. The Ontario Court of Appeal allowed the prosecution's appeal and ordered a new trial. A further appeal to the Supreme Court of Canada was dismissed. That court approved the judgment of Martin J, who took the view that 'the ordinary stresses and disappointments of life which are the common lot of mankind do not constitute an external cause...'[151] The exceptional effect which this ordinary event had on D 'must be considered as having its source primarily in the [D's] psychological or emotional make-up'. Notwithstanding the powerful dissent by Dickson J, it is submitted that this is right and that in such a case if the evidence as to D's dissociative state is accepted at all,[152] it should

---

[147] *Winterwerp v Netherlands* [1979] 2 EHRR 387, [1994] Crim LR 84; *Luberti v Italy* (1984) 6 EHRR 440; *Reid v UK* (2003) 37 EHRR 9. See P Sutherland and C Gearty, 'Insanity and the ECHR' [1992] Crim LR 418; Baker, n 51; Emmerson, Ashworth and Macdonald, HR&CJ, paras 18.23 et seq. On the success of challenges in Jersey, see Mackay [2002] Crim LR 728. The Law Commission examines the ECHR dimension to the defence in LCSP, Ch 5.

[148] By s 1 of the 1991 Act, a jury shall not return a special verdict of not guilty by reason of insanity (NGRI) except on the written or oral evidence of two or more registered medical practitioners of whom at least one is approved by the Home Secretary as having special experience in the field of mental disorder.

[149] In addition, Mackay, Mitchell and Howe [2006] Crim LR 399 identify cases in which NGRI verdicts have been returned without medical evidence.

[150] (1977) 37 CCC (2d) 461; affd [1980] SCR 513, 54 CCC (2d) 1. See also *Parnerkar* [1974] SCR 449, 10 CCC (2d) 253 and cases discussed by Mackay [1980] Crim LR 350.

[151] (1980) 54 CCC (2d) at 7.

[152] cf the scepticism of Williams about the acceptance of the evidence of 'over enthusiastic psychiatrists' in relation to the similar case of *Parnerkar* [1974] SCR 449, 10 CCC (2d) 253; Williams, TBCL (1st edn) 612–613. See LCDP, pp 107 et seq suggesting that the concern is really whether a person of reasonable fortitude might have withstood the trauma.

be treated as evidence of insanity. Once the judge has so categorized the defence, D has the burden of proving on a balance of probabilities that he was in a dissociative state. If he and his medical witnesses are to be believed, he was not guilty, but he is a highly dangerous person.[153] Who is to say that the next ordinary stress of life will not lead him unconsciously to wield a deadly weapon? Policy clearly has a significant part to play here.

Martin J left open the question of the effect of an extraordinary event of such severity that it might reasonably be expected to cause a dissociative state in the average person. This would, it is submitted, be a case of sane automatism because D has done nothing to show that he is any more dangerous to others than anyone else; and he should be simply acquitted. It is, of course, difficult to identify what should constitute such a degree of extraordinariness. In *T*,[154] where the defendant had committed a robbery when suffering from post-traumatic stress disorder as a result of being raped, the trial judge ruled that the rape was to be treated as an external factor. It would be uncontroversial to regard the rape as an extraordinary event, but it is unclear which if any other traumatic events will suffice. Further judicial clarification of the scope of this exceptional category of sane automatism would be welcome.

In *Coley*, Hughes LJ remarked that the distinction between 'external factors inducing a condition of the mind and internal factors which can properly be described as a disease can give rise to apparently strange results at the margin'.[155] Despite the recognition that the distinction may be difficult to draw in some cases, it was ultimately confirmed that it is crucial given the different outcomes it dictates.

Defect of reason

For the insanity defence to apply, the disease of the mind must have given rise to a 'defect of reason'. It seems that D's powers of reasoning must be impaired and that D's mere failure to use powers of reasoning which he possesses does not bring him within the M'Naghten Rules. When D claimed that she had taken articles from a supermarket without paying for them because of absent-mindedness resulting from depression, it was held that even if she was suffering from a disease of the mind (which is arguable), she had not raised the defence of insanity but was simply denying that she had mens rea.[156] Tadros has suggested that this element of the defence warrants closer attention, since it could help to identify those who are morally responsible for failing to recognize either the nature and quality or wrongness of their act. This element should cause the courts to focus on whether there was a diminution of D's reasoning powers.

The nature and quality of his act: the 'first limb'

The phrase 'nature and quality of his act' refers to the physical nature and quality of the act and not to its moral or legal quality.[157] In modern terms, it means simply that D 'did not know what he was doing'.[158] It is of narrow application; illustrations given by leading writers are:

A kills B under an insane delusion that he is breaking a jar. [159]

and

the madman who cut a woman's throat under the idea that he was cutting a loaf of bread.[160]

---

[153] In fact, D's expert witness said D had no predisposition to dissociate; but the court, while bound to take account of medical evidence, may also take account of the facts of the case and apply its common sense to all the evidence.

[154] [1990] Crim LR 256. And see *Huckerby* [2004] EWCA Crim 3251.

[155] [2013] EWCA Crim 223, [2013] Crim LR 923, [20].

[156] *Clarke* [1972] 1 All ER 219. For discussion see Tadros, *Criminal Responsibility*, 333.

[157] *Codère* (1916) 12 Cr App R 21; see *Johnson* [2007] EWCA Crim 1978, [2008] Crim LR 132. For cogent criticism see Mackay [2009] Crim LR 80.

[158] *Sullivan* [1983] 2 All ER 673 at 678, [1983] Crim LR 740.   [159] Stephen, *Digest* (8th edn) 6.

[160] Kenny, *Outlines*, 76.

Of course, a person who was under a delusion such as these, apart altogether from insanity, could never be convicted of murder, simply because he had no mens rea. The important practical difference, however, is that if the delusion arose from a disease of the mind, he will be liable to be indefinitely detained in a hospital,[161] whereas if it arose from some other cause, he will go entirely free. A person whose acts are involuntary because he is unconscious does not 'know the nature and quality of his act'.[162]

Those who advocate abolition[163] of the defence of insanity suggest that the ability to plead absence of mens rea can deal with those lacking mental responsibility. The approach has been adopted in some US states, but has been criticized. The Law Commission rejected such an approach after careful examination.[164] Such an approach distorts the mens rea test to accommodate 'cases where the accused suffered from a mental disorder but could still form a mental element for specific offences'.[165] Abolishing insanity and relying on the question of mens rea also fails to accommodate the cases where D's mental illness led him to believe that he had a defence, and those for whom mens rea is present because of the mental illness.

Insanity may be pleaded in respect of an offence irrespective of whether it is an offence of mens rea. This was confirmed by the Divisional Court in *Loake v CPS*, which is discussed below.[166]

Knowledge that the act is 'wrong': the 'second limb'

This second, alternative limb is not concerned with whether the accused is able to distinguish between right and wrong in general, but whether he was able to appreciate the wrongness of the particular act he was doing at the particular time alleged to constitute a crime. It has always been clear that if D knew his act was contrary to law, he knew it was 'wrong' for this purpose. Thus, in their first answer the judges in *M'Naghten*'s case said:[167]

notwithstanding the party accused did the act complained of with a view, under the influence of insane delusion, of redressing or revenging some supposed grievance or injury, or of producing some public benefit, he is nevertheless punishable, according to the nature of the crime committed, if he knew at the time of committing such crime that he was acting contrary to law; by which expression we understand your lordships to mean the law of the land.

Even if D did not know his act was contrary to law, he was still liable if he knew that it was wrong 'according to the ordinary standard adopted by reasonable men'.[168] The fact that D thought his act was right was irrelevant if he knew that people generally considered it wrong. This again seems to be supported by the M'Naghten Rules:[169]

If the question were to be put as to the knowledge of the accused solely and exclusively with reference to the law of the land, it might tend to confound the jury, by inducing them to believe that an actual knowledge of the law of the land was essential to lead to a conviction: whereas the law is administered upon the principle that everyone must be taken conclusively to know it, without proof that he does know it. If the accused was conscious that the act was one which he ought not to do, and if that act was at the same time contrary to the law of the land, he is punishable.

Modern cases, however, suggest that the courts are concerned only with D's knowledge of legal, not moral, wrongness. In *Windle*,[170] D was unhappily married to a woman, V, who

---

[161] The disposal powers for those found not guilty by reason of insanity in cases of murder are limited.

[162] *Sullivan* [1983] 2 All ER 673 at 678, [1983] Crim LR 740, HL.

[163] eg N Morris, 'The Criminal Responsibility of the Mentally Ill' (1982) 33 Syracuse LR 477.

[164] See LCDP, Ch 2 and Appendix A.   [165] Scottish Law Commission Report, para 2.16.

[166] [2017] EWHC 2855 (Admin).   [167] (1843) 10 Cl & Fin 200 at 209.

[168] *Codère* (1916) 12 Cr App R 21 at 27.   [169] (1843) 10 Cl & Fin 200 at 210.

[170] [1952] 2 QB 826.

was always speaking of committing suicide and who, according to medical evidence at the trial, was certifiably insane. D killed V by the administration of 100 aspirins. He then gave himself up to the police, saying, 'I suppose they will hang me for this'. A medical witness for the defence said that D was suffering from a form of communicated insanity known as *folie à deux*. Rebutting medical evidence was called, but the doctors on both sides agreed that he knew he was doing an act which the law forbade. Devlin J thereupon withdrew the issue from the jury. So far the decision accords perfectly with the law as stated previously but, in the Court of Criminal Appeal, Lord Goddard CJ, in upholding the conviction, said:[171]

> Courts of law can only distinguish between that which is in accordance with the law and that which is contrary to law . . . . The law cannot embark on the question and it would be an unfortunate thing if it were left to juries to consider whether some particular act was morally right or wrong. The test must be whether it is contrary to law . . . .
>
> In the opinion of the court there is no doubt that in the M'Naghten Rules 'wrong' means contrary to law and not 'wrong' according to the opinion of one man or of a number of people on the question whether a particular act might or might not be justified.

Windle is in accordance with authority in rejecting the arguments of the defence that D should be acquitted if, knowing his act to be against the law, he also believed it to be morally right. In the Court of Appeal in *Johnson*,[172] it was confirmed that 'wrong' means only 'wrong' according to law. If D appreciates that his conduct is wrong according to law, he cannot rely on insanity. In practice it seems that juries commonly accept the defence in such cases.[173]

The High Court of Australia has refused to follow *Windle*. In *Stapleton v R*,[174] it made a detailed examination of the English law before and after *M'Naghten* and came to the conclusion that *Windle* was wrongly decided. The court's view was that if D believed his act to be right according to the ordinary standard of reasonable people, he was entitled to be acquitted even if he knew it to be legally wrong. This would extend the scope of the defence, not only beyond what was laid down in *Windle*, but beyond what the law was believed to be before that case. While such an extension of the law may be desirable, it is difficult to reconcile with the M'Naghten Rules and to justify on the authorities.[175] In *Johnson*, the court discussed *Stapleton* and rejected that approach.[176] It is not followed by the courts in England.[177] Should the defence be available where D kills a prostitute, knowing that to do so is murder, but believing that 'it is morally right to rid the streets of such women'?[178] The New Zealand Law Commission has questioned why this limb is needed or justified at all. It commented, in its 2010 report, 'it is still not clear why incapacity to reason *morally* is necessarily the right test for determining when it is not proper to hold the person responsible'.[179]

---

[171] ibid at 833, 834.

[172] [2007] EWCA Crim 1978, [2008] Crim LR 132. See RD Mackay [2009] Crim LR 79, for a valuable review.

[173] See Mackay and Kearns [1999] Crim LR 714 at 722.

[174] (1953) 86 CLR 358; see also *Weise* [1969] VR 953, especially at 960 et seq, per Barry J. See also *Chaulk* [1990] 3 SCR 1303; *Oomen* [2004] 2 SCR 507. See generally for a comparative review S Yeo, 'The Insanity Defence in the Criminal Law of the Commonwealth Nations' [2008] Sing JLS 241.

[175] *Stapleton v R* is discussed in a note by N Morris, '"Wrong" in the M'Naghten Rules' (1953) 16 MLR 435, which is criticized by J Montrose, 'The M'Naghten Rules' (1954) 17 MLR 383.

[176] Referring with approval to this para in the 11th edition.

[177] See LCSP, paras 4.67–4.74. For criticism of *Stapleton* see also the New Zealand Law Commission in *Mental Impairment Decision-Making and the Insanity Defence*, R120 (2010) para 5.6.

[178] cf *Peter Sutcliffe* (1981) 30 Apr, CCC. See A Norrie, *Crime, Reason and History* (3rd edn, 2014) 267–268; cf Tadros, *Criminal Responsibility*, 326.

[179] *Mental Impairment Decision-Making and the Insanity Defence*, R120 (2010) para 5.8 (emphasis in original).

Insane delusions and insanity

Whereas the defence of insanity is excessively broad in defining diseases of the mind, it is unsatisfactorily narrow in respect of what constitutes a sufficient awareness of wrongdoing. The judges were asked in *M'Naghten*'s case:

If a person under an insane delusion as to existing facts commits an offence in consequence thereof, is he thereby excused?

They replied:[180]

the answer must, of course, depend on the nature of the delusion: but making the same assumption as we did before, namely, that he labours under such partial delusion only, and is not in other respects insane, we think he must be considered in the same situation as to responsibility as if the facts with respect to which the delusion exists were real. For example, if under the influence of his delusion he supposes another man to be in the act of attempting to take away his life, and he kills that man, as he supposes, in self-defence, he would be exempt from punishment. If his delusion was that the deceased had inflicted a serious injury to his character and fortune, and he killed him in revenge for such supposed injury, he would be liable to punishment.

This seems to add nothing to the earlier answers. The insane delusions that the judges had in mind seem to have been factual errors of the kind which prevent a person from knowing the nature and quality of his act or knowing it is wrong. The example given seems to fall within those Rules.

Some caution is necessary with the proposition that the responsibility of the insane person 'must be considered in the same situation … as if the facts with respect to which the delusion exists were real'. It should always be remembered that there must be an actus reus, accompanied by the appropriate mens rea, for a conviction. Suppose that D strangles his wife's poodle under the insane delusion that it is her illegitimate child. If the supposed facts were real he would be guilty of murder—but that is plainly impossible as there is no actus reus.[181] In respect of the dog there is no crime because there was no mens rea (for a cruelty to animals or criminal damage offence). The Rule seems merely to emphasize that delusions which do not prevent D from having mens rea will afford no defence. As Lord Hewart CJ rather crudely put it, 'the mere fact that a man thinks he is John the Baptist does not entitle him to shoot his mother'. A case often discussed is that of a man who is under the insane delusion that he is obeying a divine command. Some US courts have held that such a belief affords a defence. Yet if the accused knows that his act is forbidden by law, it seems clear he is liable. Stephen certainly thought that this was so:

My own opinion is that if a special divine order were given to a man to commit murder, I should certainly hang him for it, unless I got a special divine order not to hang him.[182]

Irresistible impulse

It is recognized by psychiatrists that a person may know the nature and quality of an act, may even know that it is wrong and yet perform it under an impulse that is almost or quite uncontrollable. Such a person has no defence under the M'Naghten Rules. The

---

[180] (1843) 10 Cl & Fin 200 at 211.

[181] Nor, notwithstanding *Shivpuri*, p 497 should an insane delusion entail liability for an attempt.

[182] II HCL, 160 fn 1. In some jurisdictions statutory reformulations have expanded the defence to accommodate decisions. See eg *Phillip v The Queen* [2007] UKPC 31.

matter was considered in *Kopsch*:[183] D, according to his own admission, killed his uncle's wife. He said that he strangled her with his tie at her own request. (If this was an insane delusion, it would not, of course, afford a defence under the Rules stated earlier.) There was evidence that he had acted under the direction of his subconscious mind. Counsel argued that the judge should have directed the jury that a person under an impulse which he cannot control is not criminally responsible. This was described by Lord Hewart CJ as a 'fantastic theory … which if it were to become part of our criminal law, would be merely subversive'.[184]

The judges have steadily opposed acknowledging such a defence on the ground of the difficulty—or impossibility—of distinguishing between an impulse which proves irresistible because of insanity and one which is irresistible because of ordinary motives of greed, jealousy or revenge. The view has also been expressed that the harder an impulse is to resist, the greater is the need for a deterrent.[185]

English law does not recognize irresistible impulse even as a symptom from which a jury might deduce insanity within the meaning of the Rules.[186] If, however, medical evidence were tendered in a particular case that the uncontrollable impulse, to which the accused in that case had allegedly been subject, was a symptom that he did not know his act was wrong, it would be open to the jury to act on that evidence.[187] But it is not permissible for a judge to make use in one case of medical knowledge which he may have acquired from the evidence in another, in his direction to the jury.[188]

Although the M'Naghten Rules remain unaltered, a partial defence of irresistible impulse has now been admitted into the law of murder through the defence of diminished responsibility.[189]

9.2.2.3 Burden of proof

The M'Naghten Rules laid down that:

every man is presumed to be sane, and to possess a sufficient degree of reason to be responsible for his crimes, until the contrary be proved to [the jury's] satisfaction; and that to establish a defence on the ground of insanity, it must be clearly proved, etc.[190]

It seems from these words that the judges were intending to put the burden of proof squarely on the accused, and so it has always been subsequently assumed.[191] Insanity is stated to be the one exception at common law to the rule that it is the duty of the prosecution to prove the accused's guilt in all particulars.[192] He does not have to satisfy that heavy onus of proof beyond reasonable doubt which rests on the prosecution but is entitled to a verdict in his favour if he proves his case on a balance of probabilities, the standard which rests on the claimant in a civil action. If the jury think it is more likely than not that he is insane within the meaning of the Rules, then he is entitled to their verdict.

When, however, consideration is given to what has to be proved to establish insanity under the first limb of the Rules, there is an apparent conflict with the general rule requiring

---

[183] (1925) 19 Cr App R 50, CCA. See also *True* (1922) 16 Cr App R 164; *Sodeman* [1936] 2 All ER 1138, PC.

[184] (1925) 19 Cr App R 50 at 51. See LCDP, paras 4.37 et seq.

[185] As a Canadian judge, Riddell J, put it: 'If you cannot resist an impulse in any other way, we will hang a rope in front of your eyes, and perhaps that will help': *Creighton* (1909) 14 CCC 349.

[186] *A-G for State of South Australia v Brown* [1960] AC 432, [1960] 1 All ER 734, PC.

[187] ibid. See also *Sodeman* (1936) 55 CLR 192 at 203.

[188] [1960] AC 432 at 449.   [189] See Ch 13.   [190] (1843) 10 Cl & Fin 200 at 210.

[191] *Stokes* (1848) 3 Car & Kir 185; *Layton* (1849) 4 Cox CC 149; *Smith* (1910) 6 Cr App R 19; *Coelho* (1914) 10 Cr App R 210; *Bratty v A-G for Northern Ireland* [1963] AC 386.

[192] *Woolmington v DPP* [1935] AC 462, per Viscount Sankey LC at 481.

the prosecution to prove mens rea.[193] This requires proof that the accused had the required mens rea with respect to all those consequences and circumstances of his conduct which constitute the actus reus of the crime with which he is charged. But, this is a requirement to prove that the accused *did* know the nature and quality of his act—at least in cases where the mens rea of the offence is intention or knowledge. The general rule, therefore, says that the prosecution must prove these facts; the special rule relating to insanity says that the defence must disprove them![194] Williams argued[195] that the only burden on the accused is the 'evidential' one of introducing sufficient evidence to raise a reasonable doubt in the jurors' minds; and that the burden of *proof* is on the prosecution.[196] This solution appears to be the best way of resolving the inconsistency.[197]

This problem does not arise when D's defence takes the form that he did not know that his act was wrong. Here he is setting up the existence of facts which are quite outside the prosecution's case and there is no inconsistency in putting the onus on him. It is very strange that the onus of proof should be on the Crown if the defence is based on the first limb of the Rules and on D if it should be on the second. Yet the authorities[198] seem clearly to establish that the onus in the case of the second limb is on the accused. It is not possible to argue that the courts really meant the evidential burden for they have said very clearly that the burden is one of proof 'on balance of probabilities', the same standard that the claimant in a civil action must satisfy. Whatever may be the position regarding the first limb of the defence then it seems clear that, under the second, the onus is on the accused.

The anomaly is emphasized by the decision of the House of Lords in *Bratty v A-G for Northern Ireland*[199] that, where the defence is sane automatism (ie arising otherwise than through a disease of the mind), the burden of proof is on the prosecution. It is difficult to see why a person whose alleged disability arises from a disease of the mind should be convicted whereas one whose alleged disability arises from some other cause, would, in exactly the same circumstances, be acquitted.[200]

9.2.2.4 The scope of the defence

Hale[201] thought insanity was a defence only to capital charges but that opinion is no longer tenable. In *Horseferry Road Magistrates' Court, ex p K*,[202] the court accepted the misleading proposition in *Archbold*,[203] relied on by the applicant, that the defence of insanity 'is based on the absence of *mens rea*'.[204] This may be true where D asserts that he did not know the nature and quality of his act, but it is not true where he asserts that he did not know the act was wrong.[205] Awareness of 'wrongness' is not an element in mens rea. It seems that *Ex p K*

---

[193] For an explanation see *Foye* [2013] EWCA Crim 475, [2013] Crim LR 839 in which Lord Hughes stated at [35]: 'In the case of both insanity and diminished responsibility, the issue depends on the inner workings of the defendant's mind at the time of the offence. It would be a practical impossibility in many cases for the Crown to disprove (beyond reasonable doubt) an assertion that he was insane or suffering from diminished responsibility.' See also *Wilcocks* [2016] EWCA Crim 2043, [2017] Crim LR 706, Ch 13.

[194] See further Jones (1995) 111 LQR 475 for a compelling critique. [195] CLGP, 165.

[196] See LCDP, Ch 8 for full discussion. In coroners' proceedings insanity has to be disproved to the criminal standard to sustain a verdict of unlawful killing—*R (O'Connor) v HM Coroner for Avon* [2009] EWHC 854 (Admin).

[197] cf, however, *Cottle* [1958] NZLR 999 at 1019, per North J.

[198] *Sodeman v R* [1936] 2 All ER 1138; *Carr-Briant* [1943] KB 607.

[199] [1963] AC 386. [200] The Butler proposals on onus of proof appear later, see p 305.

[201] I PC, c 4, and Walker, *Crime and Insanity in England*, I, 80; S White (1984) 148 JPN 412 at 419.

[202] See n 103. [203] 1996 edn, at 17.109.

[204] In *Foye* [2013] EWCA Crim 475, [2013] Crim LR 839, Lord Hughes expressed doubt as to whether insanity is essentially a denial of mens rea. At [31]. See now *Loake v CPS* [2017] EWHC 2855 (Admin).

[205] See also *Moore v The State* [2001] UKPC 4.

misled the court in *DPP v H*[206] into holding that the defence does not apply to an offence of strict liability—in that case driving with excess alcohol.

In a welcome decision, *Loake v CPS*,[207] the Administrative Court, after a detailed examination of the law, held that the defence of insanity is not limited to denials of mens rea. L appealed against a decision of the Crown Court upholding her conviction in a magistrates' court for harassment contrary to s 2(1) of the Protection from Harassment Act 1997. L had been accused of sending a very large number of text messages to her husband, from whom she was separated. Before the magistrates and the Crown Court, she relied on the defence of insanity. However, the Crown Court ruled that the defence was not available for the offence of harassment. The prosecution argued that by creating the offence of harassment in the form that it did, and in particular by providing an objective standard in s 1(2) by specifying that the defendant 'ought to know' his conduct amounted to harassment 'if a reasonable person in possession of the same information would think the course of conduct amounted to harassment of the other', Parliament had to be taken to have excluded the defence of insanity for the s 2(1) offence. The Administrative Court held that to establish the defence of insanity, it had to be clearly proved that, when committing the act, the defendant was labouring under such a defect of reason, from disease of the mind, as not to know the nature and quality of the act he was doing, or that, if he did know it, he did not know what he was doing was wrong. The M'Naghten Rules applied to the offence of harassment under s 2(1) of the 1997 Act just as they did to all other criminal offences. Accordingly, the defence of insanity was available to a defendant charged with harassment under s 2(1).[208] As the court noted, if the sole question on which criminal liability turned was whether a reasonable person in possession of the same information as the defendant would think his course of conduct amounted to harassment, that would lead to the conclusion that D would be guilty even if he did not know the nature and quality of his act, and thus was insane under the first limb of the M'Naghten Rules. That would produce startling results. The example given was a person suffering from severe dementia who repeatedly telephoned or texted the same individual, on each occasion believing he was doing so for the first time. Such an individual would not know the nature of his act in that he would not know of the sustained nature of the calls or texts. If the prosecution were right, such a person would be guilty because, viewed objectively, his conduct amounted to harassment. Furthermore, if the prosecution were right, the court observed that the defence of insanity would not apply to any offence with an objective form of mens rea. The court held that the decisions in *DPP v H* and *Ex p K* should not be followed. Both were founded on the inaccurate proposition that the defence of insanity is based on the absence of mens rea. The court confirmed that insanity in fact rests on a broader base than the mere absence of mens rea.[209] We examine the relationship between insanity and other mental condition defences later in this chapter and its relationship with other defences such as self-defence in Ch 10.[210]

9.2.2.5 The special verdict of insanity and the right of appeal

The Trial of Lunatics Act 1883 as amended provides that if it appears to the jury that the defendant 'did the act or made the omission charged but was insane as aforesaid at the time the jury shall return a special verdict that the accused is not guilty by reason of insanity'.[211]

---

[206] [1997] 1 WLR 1406.   [207] [2017] EWHC 2855 (Admin).   [208] See [18], [61], [63].

[209] At [54]. In doing so, the court agreed with the view expressed in successive editions of this work.

[210] See p 386 and *Oye* [2013] EWCA Crim 1725, [2014] Crim LR 544 in particular.

[211] In *R* [2013] EWCA Crim 591, the Court of Appeal held that the special verdict constitutes a true acquittal, rather than something lying in between a conviction and an acquittal. This seems to have been assumed in the earlier case of *Smith* [2012] EWCA Crim 2566, [2013] Crim LR 250. Cf *Chinegwundoh* [2015] EWCA Crim 109.

In *A-G's Reference (No 3 of 1998)*,[212] it was held that the words 'act' and 'omission' mean the actus reus of the offence.[213] The prosecution do not have to prove mens rea. To require them to do so would be inconsistent with the rule that the onus is on D to prove that he did not know the nature and quality of his act.

A right of appeal to the Court of Appeal and the Supreme Court is provided by s 12 of the Criminal Appeal Act 1968, subject to the same conditions as apply in criminal appeals generally.

9.2.2.6 Function of the jury

It has been laid down for defences of both insanity and diminished responsibility that:[214]

it is for the jury and not for medical men [*sic*] of whatever eminence to determine the issue. Unless and until Parliament ordains that this question is to be determined by a panel of medical men [*sic*], it is to a jury, after a proper direction by a judge, that by the law of this country the decision is to be entrusted.

The law regarding insanity, however, is now modified by s 1 of the 1991 Act which provides that a jury shall not return a special verdict of not guilty by reason of insanity except on the written or oral evidence of two or more registered medical practitioners of whom at least one is approved by the Home Secretary as having special experience in the field of mental disorder.[215] The jury may still have to decide between conflicting medical evidence; but if the medical evidence is wholly in favour of a special verdict (or of diminished responsibility) and there is *nothing* in the facts or surrounding circumstances which could lead to a contrary conclusion, then a verdict of guilty (or guilty of murder as the case may be) will be upset.[216] If there are facts which, in the opinion of the court, justify the jury in coming to a conclusion different from that of the experts, their verdict will be upheld.

9.2.3 Proposals for reform of the insanity defence

Almost from the moment of their formulation the Rules have been subjected to vigorous criticism, primarily by doctors, but also by lawyers.[217] The Rules, being based on outdated psychiatric views, are too narrow, it is said, and exclude many persons who ought not to be held responsible. They are concerned only with defects of reason and take no account of emotional or volitional factors whereas modern medical science is unwilling to divide the mind into separate compartments and to consider the intellect apart from the emotions and the will.

There have been numerous attempts to reform the law including a 1923 review by Lord Atkin;[218] the 1953 Royal Commission on Capital Punishment;[219] and the 1978 Butler Committee review with a proposed verdict of 'not guilty on evidence of mental disorder'—'a

---

[212] [1999] 3 All ER 40, [1993] Crim LR 986.

[213] As defined in the 8th edition of this book, at p 28. See p 57.

[214] *Matheson* (1958) 42 Cr App R 145; *Bailey* (1961) 66 Cr App R 31n, [1961] Crim LR 828; *Sanders* (1991) 93 Cr App R 245, [1991] Crim LR 781—all cases concerning diminished responsibility—but the same principle surely applies to insanity.

[215] On the true input of the jury in practice, see Mackay, Mitchell and Howe [2006] Crim LR 399.

[216] See *Golds* [2016] UKSC 61, [2017] Crim LR 316 considering *Brennan* [2014] EWCA Crim 2387, [2015] Crim LR 290. See Ch 13, p 565.

[217] S Dell, 'Wanted; An Insanity Defence that Can be Used' [1983] Crim LR 431. For a reappraisal of the defence seeking to explain its operation by reference to lay conceptions of abnormality, see A Loughnan, *Manifest Madness: Mental Incapacity in Criminal Law* (2012). See Mackay [2009] Crim LR 80, and calls for a more fundamental review made by M Hathaway, 'The Moral Significance of the Insanity Defence' (2009) 73 J Crim L 310.

[218] Cmd 2005.   [219] Cmd 8932.

mental disorder verdict'. The Draft Criminal Code endorsed that approach[220] subject to including a presumption that the commission of the offence was attributable to the disorder but is rebuttable by proof beyond reasonable doubt. The Code would produce substantial improvements on the present position. It has been suggested, however, that it would still be incompatible with Art 5 of the ECHR.[221]

9.2.3.1 The Law Commission's latest proposals

In 2012 the Law Commission published a Scoping Paper on Insanity and Automatism designed to elicit some evidence of the scale of the problem the defences pose in practice. The Scoping Paper was supplemented by material exploring the statistics around the use of the defences, the comparative approaches to mental disorder defences and a summary of the previous proposals. The responses to the Scoping Paper suggested that while the academic criticisms of the offence are justified, the defences caused few problems in practice. The Commission has since produced a Discussion Paper with provisional conclusions and proposals on reform of the insanity and automatism defences.

The principal proposal is that the common law insanity defence should be abolished and replaced with a new statutory defence where someone is not criminally responsible by reason of a qualifying recognized medical condition.[222] The party seeking to raise the defence would have to adduce expert evidence that at the time of the offence D wholly lacked one of the following capacities in relation to what they are charged with having done: (a) to make a judgement rationally; (b) to understand that they are doing something wrong; or (c) to control their actions. The lack of capacity would have to be due to a qualifying recognized medical condition. Not all recognized medical conditions would qualify for the defence and it would be a matter of law, not medicine, whether the condition qualified.[223] The Commission takes the view that as a matter of policy, not all medical conditions should qualify as 'recognized medical conditions', adopting the view of Hughes LJ that 'there will inevitably be considerations of legal policy which are irrelevant to the business of medical description, classification, and statistical analysis'.[224] Acute intoxication, for example, would not qualify, nor would anti-social personality disorders. The Commission sets out in detail how the new defence would operate with the rules on intoxication.[225]

The Commission proposes that there should be an elevated evidential burden on the accused—to call evidence from two experts—but that once that burden is satisfied, then it should fall to the Crown to disprove that defence.[226] The Commission proposes to retain the requirement for evidence from two experts, but proposes that only one of them need be a medical practitioner.[227]

The new defence would be available in relation to any kind of offence and would result in a new special verdict—'not criminally responsible by reason of a recognised medical condition'. Following this verdict, both the Crown Court and the magistrates' courts would be

---

[220] For an alternative approach to reform, see the recent Scottish reform: Criminal Justice and Licensing (Scotland) Act 2010, ss 168–171. For comment see: J Chalmers, 'Section 117 of the Criminal Justice and Licensing (Scotland) Bill: A Dangerous Loophole?' [2009] SCL 1240; E Shaw, 'Psychopaths and Criminal Responsibility' (2009) 13 Edin LR 497; G Maher, 'The New Mental Disorder Defences: Some Comments' [2013] SLT 1. The new Act implements recommendations contained in the Scottish Law Commission's Report No 195, *Insanity and Diminished Responsibility* (2004).

[221] See Horder, APOCL, 163.   [222] Para 4.159.   [223] Para 4.161.

[224] See para 4.162 and *Dowds* [2012] EWCA Crim 281, [2012] 1 WLR 2576, [30].

[225] See Ch 7. For criticism, see A Loughnan and N Wake, 'Of Blurred Boundaries and Prior Fault: Insanity, Automatism and Intoxication' in A Reed and M Bohlander (with N Wake and E Smith) (eds), *General Defences in Criminal Law—Domestic and Comparative Perspectives* (2014). As the authors acknowledge, however, the Law Commission's terms of reference precluded it from reconsidering the law on intoxication.

[226] Para 4.164.   [227] Paras 4.165 and 7.53.

able to make a hospital order, a supervision order or an absolute discharge, and the Crown Court would be able to make a restriction order.[228] The Commission also recommends a new 'non-penal Youth Supervision Order' for under 18s following a special verdict.[229] Unlike the present law, under the proposals the jury verdict can be dispensed with if the accused is legally represented, no jury could reasonably reach any other verdict and the judge records the reasons for the verdict.[230]

Under the Commission's proposals, the breadth of the new recognized medical condition defence means that the defence of automatism becomes practically redundant. Physical and mental conditions can be dealt with under the new insanity defence. A new statutory defence of automatism (discussed later) would cover the situation where D had been unable to control his actions for reasons other than a recognized medical condition, for example in a reflex action case where D swerved to avoid a swarm of bees. The recognized medical condition defence and the automatism defence would be mutually exclusive. If successful, that plea would lead to an acquittal, as now. It is anticipated that very few such cases would come before the courts.[231]

The Commission also calls for a wider review of developmental immaturity as a defence. We consider that aspect of the Report in the next chapter.

9.3 Automatism

A claim by D that his consciousness was so impaired that he was acting in a state of physical involuntariness is a claim of automatism. Someone is an automaton or in a state of automatism where his conscious mind is dissociated from that part of the mind which controls action.[232] This concept—a denial of a voluntary act—has been discussed in Ch 2 in the context of the actus reus.[233]

9.3.1 Distinguishing types of automatism

The approach to automatism can be rather confusing. In reading what follows it is worth having in mind the two basic categories:

- automatism arising from an internal cause from a disease of the mind. This is a plea of insanity (insane automatism), D bears the burden of proof to show he did not know the nature and quality of his act;

- an external cause leading to total loss of control (sane automatism)—D is not guilty on any charge unless D was at fault in inducing that state of automatism.

A person who at the time he is alleged to have committed the offence was in a state of automatism (other than one induced by voluntary intoxication) cannot be guilty of it and the only question is whether he is to be found simply 'not guilty' or 'not guilty by reason of insanity'. The outcome (which is of great importance) depends on how the automatism arose. If it was caused by 'a disease of the mind', the proper verdict is not guilty by reason of insanity subject to the other elements of that defence being met. If it arose from any other cause, the

---

[228] Para 4.167.   [229] Para 4.168.   [230] Para 7.87.   [231] Para 5.123.
[232] Wilson et al [2005] Crim LR 614, 615.
[233] See the discussion in LCSP, Chs 2–4 and LCDP, Ch 5. See also the discussion in Scots law as to whether the defence is one of a denial of mens rea or actus reus (PR Ferguson, 'The Limits of the Automatism Defence' (1991) 36 J Law Soc Scotland 446; I MacDougall 'Automatism—Negation of *Mens Rea*' (1992) 37 J Law Soc Scotland 57; JM Ross, 'A Long Motor Run on a Dark Night: Reconstructing *HMA v Ritchie*' [2010] Edin LR 193).

verdict is simply not guilty. But as we have discussed earlier, whether a cause is a 'disease of the mind' is a question of law and that phrase has a wide meaning. Any 'internal factor', mental or physical, causing a malfunctioning of the mind is, in law, a disease of the mind.

So automatism caused by a cerebral tumour or arteriosclerosis, epilepsy or diabetes arises from a disease of the mind. These are all 'internal' to the accused. External factors include concussion, the administration of an anaesthetic or other drug, or hypnosis.[234] In a number of cases, acts done while sleeping have been treated as sane automatism[235] but it has now been held[236] that they are the product of a disease of the mind and thus insanity.[237]

It will be recalled that the one exception at common law to the rule that the burden of proof is on the prosecution is the defence of insanity. So if D claims that he was in a state of automatism because of an internal factor, he is raising the insanity defence and it will be for him to satisfy the jury on the balance of probabilities that this was so; but if he relies on an external factor and lays a proper foundation for the automatism defence, the onus is on the prosecution to satisfy the jury beyond reasonable doubt that it was not so.[238] If he alleges[239] that his condition was due to the administration of insulin (an external factor) inducing hypoglycaemia (too little blood sugar), he will be acquitted unless the prosecution can disprove his claim;[240] but if he alleges that it was due to diabetes (an internal factor) causing hyperglycaemia (excessive blood sugar), the onus will be on him to prove the defence on the balance of probabilities;[241] it must be supported by the evidence of two or more registered medical practitioners;[242] and, if he succeeds, he will be found not guilty by reason of insanity.[243]

A proper foundation for a defence of sane automatism (external cause) may be laid by introducing evidence from which it may reasonably be inferred that the act was involuntary. Whether such a foundation has been laid is a question of law. Lord Denning has said that D's own word will rarely be sufficient,[244] unless it is supported by medical evidence. The

---

[234] Lord Hughes in *Foye* [2013] EWCA Crim 475 observed that automatism may involve no abnormality of mind at all.

[235] *Boshears* (1961) The Times, 8 Feb; *Kemp* (1986) The Times, 3 May: D strangled his wife while experiencing a condition known as 'night terror'. Note that parasomnia caused by self-induced intoxication will not provide a defence of automatism.

[236] *Burgess* [1991] 2 QB 92, [1991] Crim LR 548, and see news reports for 21 March 2005 of a killing when sleepwalking which led to an acquittal.

[237] The Court of Appeal in *Coley* [2013] EWCA Crim 223 accepted that the distinction between external and internal factors can 'give rise to apparently strange results at the margin' but held that it was nevertheless binding upon the court.

[238] See *Roach* [2001] EWCA Crim 2698, p 292.

[239] In *De Boise* [2014] EWCA Crim 121, D sought to challenge the safety of his convictions on the basis that he was hypoglycaemic at the time he committed the relevant offences. The Court of Appeal rejected this argument on the basis that the expert instructed by D could only state that there was a possibility he was suffering from hypoglycaemia. Elias LJ affirmed that whilst the court does not look for certainty, there must be more than a mere possibility.

[240] Assuming he has not acted recklessly as to becoming automaton by failing to follow his prescription, etc.

[241] The Court of Appeal in *Coley* [2013] EWCA Crim 223 accepted that the distinction the law draws between these two scenarios is 'arguably unsatisfactory'.

[242] Criminal Procedure (Insanity and Unfitness to Plead) Act 1991, p 566.

[243] *Hennessy* [1989] 1 WLR 287, CA (this case was cited with approval by the Court of Appeal in *Coley* [2013] EWCA Crim 223); *Bingham* [1991] Crim LR 433. Cf *Pull* (1998) The Times, 20–21 Mar, discussed later. The distinction in terms of result highlights the unsatisfactorily incoherent nature of the law's categorization of automatism as sane or insane on the basis of its internal/external cause. See the cogent criticism of Wilson et al [2005] Crim LR 614.

[244] In *Dervish* [1968] Crim LR 37, *Cook v Atchison* [1968] Crim LR 266 and *Stripp* (1978) 69 Cr App R 318, CA, it was held that D's evidence that he had a 'blackout' was insufficient to raise the defence (see also *C* [2007] EWCA Crim 1862).

difficult questions that arise where there is evidence that the automatism was caused partly by a disease of the mind and partly by other factors are considered later.[245]

This basic distinction between internal and external factors has recently been subdivided further by the Law Commission.

(1) Insane automatism arising from a 'disease of the mind' (eg epilepsy). If successful, this results in a special verdict of insanity. This is a plea of insanity and is discussed in full earlier. The other elements of the defence of insanity must also be present.[246]

(2) Automatism arising from an internal malfunctioning of the body which does not constitute a disease of the mind. This should give rise to a defence of sane, not insane, automatism. An example given by the Law Commission is of D, who is driving, who experiences a sudden cramp in his leg, causing him to press the accelerator and crash the car. This is not insane automatism because there is no impairment of D's mental functioning and therefore no disease of the mind in the sense adopted in *Sullivan*[247] which could found a defence of insane automatism. This should result in a complete acquittal unless D was at fault in inducing or failing to avoid the loss of control. There do not appear to be any reported cases of such automatism.[248]

(3) Automatism arising from voluntary taking of substances (eg the accused who, having taken insulin, suffers a hypoglycaemic episode). This results in a complete acquittal unless the accused was at fault in inducing or failing to avoid the loss of control (as discussed earlier). If D was at fault, either because he foresaw the likelihood of a loss of control and unreasonably failed to avert it or because he took a drug commonly known to create loss of control, he will be liable for any offences of basic intent charged.[249]

(4) Sane automatism arising from some external physical factor other than D taking substances. A classic example is the accused being stung by a wasp while driving.[250] If successful, this leads to a not guilty verdict for any offence charged.

We have examined the plea of insanity in full earlier and that discussion is relevant to insane automatism. That leaves us to consider the approach the law takes to sane automatism and self-induced automatism.

9.3.2 Sane automatism

It should be noted that where D makes a plea of sane automatism the defence will only succeed if his loss of control was complete; an impaired consciousness is not automatism.[251] This was reiterated by the Court of Appeal in *McGhee*, a case conjoined on appeal with *Coley* in which Hughes LJ stated that there must be a 'complete destruction of voluntary control'.[252] It is not sufficient that D is disinhibited. It was accepted that it is not necessary for D to be unconscious

---

[245] See p 330.   [246] There must also be a 'disease of the mind', see *Sullivan* [1984] AC 156.

[247] [1984] AC 156.   [248] *Quick* [1973] QB 910, 922.

[249] Basic intent offences are discussed in detail at p 318. For present purposes, it can be equated with those offences for which the predominant mens rea is not intention, knowledge or dishonesty (this includes offences of recklessness, belief, negligence and strict liability).

[250] See Pearson J in *Hill v Baxter* [1958] 1 QB 277, 286; *Kay v Butterworth* (1945) 61 TLR 452, per Humphreys J. These examples are frequently used in the academic literature. See eg HLA Hart, *Punishment and Responsibility* (1968) 96.

[251] *A-G's Reference (No 2 of 1992)* [1994] QB 91. This is not always easy to establish, see *Nelson* [2004] EWCA Crim 333 (reliance on hearsay). The Draft Code would permit the defence in circumstances of impaired consciousness (cl 33).

[252] [2013] EWCA Crim 223, [2013] Crim LR 923, [22].

in the sense of being comatose. This is arguably an unduly strict approach.[253] In an indication of how strictly the courts regulate this defence, particularly in relation to diabetic drivers, the Court of Appeal has held, in an interlocutory prosecution appeal, that if D wants to advance a plea of sane automatism, he must provide evidence that:[254] he was totally unable to control his actions (driving) owing to an unforeseen hypoglycaemic attack; he could not reasonably have avoided the attack; and there were no advance warnings of its onset.[255] The narrow approach results in a further distinction from insanity: D may have some control over his actions and yet not know the nature and quality of his act or that it was wrong. He would qualify for insane automatism but not sane automatism subject to the other elements of the defences.

The plea of sane automatism can be made in relation to all offences (subject to what is said in the following section regarding self-induced automatism).

9.3.3 Self-induced sane automatism

Where D's state of automatism arises from his voluntary conduct (usually, ingesting substances), the following rules apply. The automatism plea is, of course, only available if D had a total loss of control.

(1) Where the automatism arises from D's taking a substance in bona fide compliance with his[256] medical prescription, the defence is a complete one to all crimes. For example, D has an adverse reaction to an anaesthetic and hits V. D will be acquitted on charges, whatever they may be, if he had totally lost control.

(2) Where the automatism arises *otherwise than* from D taking a substance in accordance with a medical prescription, if the crime with which D is charged is one of specific intent (discussed at p 318) the defence will result in acquittal. For example, D, a diabetic, takes insulin but ignores his prescription and takes too much, going into a coma. He punches V causing GBH. D will be acquitted on a s 18 charge.

(3) Where the automatism arises from D voluntarily taking a substance otherwise than in accordance with his medical prescription and the crime with which D is charged is one of basic intent (p 323), the automatism plea will fail if the substance ingested was one commonly known to create states of unpredictability or aggression (alcohol, alcohol combined with a drug that normally has soporific effects,[257] heroin, cannabis, cocaine, etc). Thus, D charged with reckless criminal damage will have no success with a defence based on his claim that he was 'completely out of it' and acting involuntarily when he swung his leg out and damaged V's property.

(4) Where the automatism arises from D's taking a substance otherwise than in accordance with his medical prescription and the crime with which D is charged is one of basic intent, and where the substance is not commonly known to create a state of unpredictability or aggression, the defence will result in an acquittal only if in taking the substance D was not subjectively reckless as to the effect it would have.[258] Thus, D

---

[253] See Mackay [2013] Crim LR 923.

[254] The mere possibility that D might have been experiencing a hypoglycaemic attack at the time he committed the actus reus of the offence will be insufficient, as the court confirmed in *De Boise* [2014] EWCA Crim 1121. See J Rumbold and M Wasik, 'Diabetic Drivers, Hypoglycaemic Unawareness and Automatism' [2011] Crim LR 863.

[255] *C* [2007] EWCA Crim 1862. See also *JG* [2006] EWCA Crim 1812.

[256] See the odd acceptance of the defence where D took his friend's 'pills' and mixed them with alcohol: *Buck* (2002), discussed by K Roberts (2002) 99 Law SocGaz 40.

[257] See *Coley* [2013] EWCA Crim 223, [2013] Crim LR 923.

[258] On the possible interpretations of the recklessness required, see LCDP, pp 127–131.

who is charged with reckless criminal damage after taking a soporific drug will not succeed in his plea of automatism if he was aware when taking the drug that it posed the risk for him of a state of unpredictability of aggression.

Although the defence of automatism operates to deny the actus reus of the offence, in cases of self-induced automatism the approach is founded on the same policy concerns that underpin the rules relating to the plea of intoxication which, if accepted at all, operates as a denial of mens rea—there is no voluntary conduct element. The court in *Coley*, rejecting D's plea of sane automatism, referred to *Quick* and held that automatism is not available where a defendant has induced an acute state of involuntary behaviour by his own prior fault. Hughes LJ commented:

We do not, however, think it safe to say that in every case in which automatism is indeed a possible and legitimate conclusion, it should be removed from the jury if they have a decision to make about specific intent. That may particularly be so if the jury is invited to infer intent from the action, which may be a very short-lived action; if the action might indeed have been involuntary, such inference would not be safe and the jury ought in such a case to confront the issue of involuntary automatism before it goes on to intent.[259]

This is a recognition that, having ascertained that D had a total loss of control, it is important next to identify whether the external factor was involuntary or self-induced.

9.3.3.1 Reform of automatism

The Law Commission's provisional proposals for the reform of the automatism defence are to abolish the common law defence and replace it with a statutory defence available in respect of all offences. It would be available where D had a total loss of control other than one arising from a recognized medical condition. If D's loss of capacity to control his actions is due to something he culpably did or failed to do (as provided for by the common law), then the defence of automatism should not be available. The reformed automatism defence would not lead to a special verdict. If successful, this defence would result in a simple acquittal. It would be available in a much narrower set of circumstances than the present law.

9.4 Intoxication

It will come as no surprise to read that the law in this area is heavily policy-based. There is often little by way of principle underpinning the operation of the law. The relationship between intoxication and crime, particularly violent crime and public disorder, needs no elucidation here.[260] The following discussion analyses the three key distinctions drawn by the courts in their application of the plea of intoxication.[261]

(1) Is D's intoxication voluntary or involuntary?

(2) If voluntary, is the crime charged one of specific 'intent' or 'basic' intent?

(3) If basic intent, is the drug involved one of a dangerous nature (is it one known to create states of unpredictability or aggression)?

---

[259] At [25].   [260] See generally G Dingwall, *Alcohol and Crime* (2005); LC 314, para 1.1.

[261] The focus in this chapter is exclusively on D's intoxication. V's intoxication may affect the substantive law, eg in relation to sexual offences discussed at p 764. See LC 314, *Intoxication and Criminal Liability* (2009). The report provides a useful summary of the current law in Part 2. See for critical comment on the proposals, J Child, 'Drink, Drugs and Law Reform: A Review of Law Commission Report No 314' [2009] Crim LR 488.

Before analysing these three issues, it is important to emphasize the general limits on the plea of intoxication. Intoxication is not, and never has been, a 'defence' in itself.[262] It is never a defence for D to say, however convincingly, that but for the drink he would not have behaved as he did.[263] Because alcohol and other drugs weaken the restraints and inhibitions which normally govern our conduct, a person may do things when drunk that he would never dream of doing when sober. This is echoed in the controversial judgment of the Court of Appeal in *Heard*[264] discussed in full later.

9.4.1 Intoxication as a denial of criminal responsibility

Before we examine the three key steps in detail, it is worth considering why intoxication might be relevant to criminal liability. Intoxication impairs a person's perception and judgement so that he may fail to be aware of facts, or to foresee results of his conduct, of which he would certainly have been aware, or have foreseen, if he had been sober.[265] So intoxication may be the reason why the defendant lacked the mens rea of the crime charged. When D relies on evidence of intoxication he does so for the purpose of disputing mens rea. This is its only relevance so far as liability to conviction (as opposed to sentence) is concerned.

It must always be borne in mind when considering intoxication that if D has the mens rea for the crime charged he is guilty. A drunken or drugged intent suffices for a crime of intention; a drunken or drugged awareness of a risk of the prohibited harm will suffice for a crime of recklessness. This is so even though drink or drugs impaired or negatived D's ability to judge between right and wrong or to resist temptation or provocation. It is so even though, in his drunken state, D found the impulse to act as he did irresistible. It is so if the state of intoxication was not self-induced by the accused—as where his drinks are laced. A drunken mens rea is still mens rea.

In many of the cases where intoxication is relevant, the plea, in substance, is one of mistake and the evidence of intoxication is circumstantial evidence that the mistake was made. Two examples quoted by Lord Denning[266] are: (a) where a nurse got so drunk at a christening that she put the baby on the fire in mistake for a log of wood;[267] and (b) where a drunken man thought his friend, lying in bed, was a theatrical dummy and stabbed him to death.[268] Lord Denning said there would be a defence to murder in each of these cases. These mistakes were highly unreasonable and, in the case of a sober person, it would be unlikely that a jury would believe that they might have been made. The relevance of the evidence of intoxication is simply that it makes these mistakes much more credible. Similarly where D denies that he foresaw some obvious consequence of his action, his intoxicated state makes that more plausible. A denial which would be quite incredible in the case of a sober person may be readily accepted when there is evidence that D was intoxicated.

In *Beard*, it was said that intoxication was a 'defence' only if it rendered D *incapable* of forming the mens rea.[269] This goes too far. Proof of a lack of capacity to form mens rea is

---

[262] See the review by A Simester, 'Intoxication is Never a Defence' [2009] Crim LR 3; LC 314, para 1.15.

[263] *DPP v Beard* [1920] AC 479 at 502–504. This was emphasized in emphatic terms more recently in *Dowds* [2012] EWCA Crim 281.

[264] [2007] EWCA Crim 125, [2007] Crim LR 654.

[265] For an analysis of how the modern approach to intoxication emerged at the end of the nineteenth century, see P Handler, 'Intoxication and Criminal Responsibility in England, 1819–1920' (2013) 33 OJLS 243.

[266] In *A-G for Northern Ireland v Gallagher* [1963] AC 349 at 381m.

[267] (1748) 18 *Gentleman's Magazine* 570; quoted in Kenny, *Outlines*, 29.

[268] (1951) The Times, 13 Jan.

[269] [1920] AC 479 at 501–502, HL. For further discussion, see P Handler, '*DPP v Beard*' in P Handler, H Mares and I Williams (eds), *Landmark Cases in Criminal Law* (2017).

587

of course conclusive that mens rea was not present; but it is now established that it is not necessary to go so far. It is sufficient that D lacked mens rea on that occasion even though he was capable of forming the necessary intent. Equally, an intoxicated person may be capable, notwithstanding his intoxication, of forming the intent to kill and yet not do so. The nurse at the christening was capable of forming the intent to tend the fire, so she was probably capable of forming an intention to kill. The important thing is that she did not do so—and the intoxication was highly relevant to rebut the inference which might otherwise have arisen from her conduct. When, considering the three steps to be discussed, D's mens rea may be relevant, the correct question is, taking D's intoxicated state into account, did he in fact form the necessary mens rea?[270] The onus of proof—again contrary to certain *dicta* in *Beard*[271]—is clearly on the Crown to establish that, notwithstanding the alleged intoxication, D formed the mens rea.[272]

In some modern cases, the courts have taken the unwelcome and, it is submitted, unduly restrictive approach to the question of when an intoxication plea gets off the ground. In *Soolkaland another v The State*,[273] *McKnight,*[274] and *Porceddu*,[275] the courts have suggested that D is required to provide specific evidence to show that he was intoxicated and that he lacked mens rea. This burden is not satisfied by evidence that he had consumed so much drink/drugs that he was intoxicated or by a loss of memory owing to intoxication. The courts are surely imposing too onerous a duty on D, who is not raising a defence in the true sense but rather denying the element of mens rea which it is always incumbent on the Crown to prove.

It is also necessary to emphasize that if the principles analysed in this section are to apply then D must be relying on his intoxication at the time of committing the offence as opposed to reliance on his suffering from some form of mental disorder. In *Harris*, conjoined on appeal with *Coley*,[276] the judge ruled that D's mental confusion at the time he started the fire (leading to his being charged with arson) was brought about by his previous binge drinking from which he had sobered up at the time of the act. The judge held that the rules on voluntary intoxication applied. The Court of Appeal rejected this argument, because it would represent a major expansion of the law if a mental disorder caused by D's prior fault were to be treated in the same way as drunkenness at the time of the offence.

9.4.1.1 Intoxicated mens rea

If D had the mens rea for the crime charged, it makes no difference whether his intoxication was voluntary or involuntary, nor whether the crime was one of specific or basic intent, nor whether the drug was of a dangerous or non-dangerous variety. In *Kingston*,[277] D may

---

[270] *Pordage* [1975] Crim LR 575, CA, following *dicta* in *Sheehan* [1975] 2 All ER 960, [1975] Crim LR 339 and commentary, CA, *Cole* [1993] Crim LR 300. To the same effect are *Menniss* [1973] 2 NSWLR 113 and *Kamipeli* [1975] 2 NZLR 610. But cf *Groark* [1999] Crim LR 669.

[271] [1920] AC 479 at 502.

[272] *Sheehan*, n 270. *Bowden* [1993] Crim LR 379. When evidence emerges, whatever its source, of such intoxication as might have prevented D's forming a specific intent the judge must direct the jury on it: *Bennett* [1995] Crim LR 877. Cf *McKinley* [1994] Crim LR 944, where the point was left open. The absence of a *Sheehan* direction seems to be a fertile ground of appeal: see *Golding* [2004] EWCA Crim 858. See LC 314, paras 2.27–2.33. In *White* [2017] NICA 49, Morgan LCJ held that the absence of a *Sheehan* direction in that case did not render D's conviction unsafe. His lordship did emphasize, however, that 'where the evidence does raise an issue about the effect of alcohol on the specific intention necessary for a criminal offence there is an obligation on the court, whether or not the matter is raised by counsel, to ensure that the jury is properly directed in relation to it'. At [22].

[273] [1999] 1 WLR 2011, PC.   [274] (2000) The Times, 5 May.   [275] [2004] EWCA Crim 1043.

[276] [2013] EWCA Crim 223, [2013] Crim LR 923.

[277] [1994] 3 All ER 353, [1994] Crim LR 846, HL. See J Horder, 'Pleading Involuntary Lack of Capacity' (1993) 52 CLJ 298; R Smith and L Clements, 'Involuntary Intoxication, The Threshold of Inhibition and the Instigation of Crime' (1995) 46 NILQ 210. See LC 314, para 2.75.

have given way to his paedophiliac inclinations only because E had surreptitiously laced his drink with intent that he should do so. D, however, knew what he was doing; he intended to commit a sexual assault on a 15-year-old boy. That was the mens rea of the offence. The judge had rightly directed the jury that a drugged intention is still an intention. The fact that, but for the secretly administered drug, he would not have formed the intent was a matter going only to mitigation of the penalty.[278]

9.4.2 Involuntary intoxication

Where, as a result of involuntary intoxication, D lacks the mens rea of the offence, it is submitted that he must be acquitted. This is so whether the crime charged is one of specific or basic intent. The offence has not been committed and there is absolutely no reason why the law should pretend that it has.[279] On a charge involving an offence of strict liability, the involuntary intoxication will not avail D if he claimed to lack mens rea as to that strict element since there is no mens rea for it to displace. In cases of alleged negligence, in principle, D ought only to be liable if the reasonable person would have acted in the same way had he suffered the effects of the involuntary intoxication.

In *Kingston*, Lord Mustill referred to a number of Scottish decisions to the effect that intoxication negates liability if it is 'based … on an inability to form *mens rea* as a result of some external factor which was outwith the accused's control and which he was not bound to foresee'. The *dicta* quoted all required an inability to form the intent. Inability is certainly a conclusive answer; but it is submitted that, whatever the position in Scotland, in England the ultimate question is whether D did form the mens rea and, if he did not—perhaps because he made a drunken mistake of fact—he must be acquitted, even though he was capable of forming the intent. This is the law in those cases where voluntary intoxication may be the basis of a defence to an offence of specific intent, and it ought to apply, *a fortiori*, to involuntary intoxication.

Involuntary intoxication is narrowly defined. If D knew he was drinking alcohol, he cannot claim that the resulting intoxication was involuntary merely because he underestimated the amount he was consuming[280] or the effect it would have on him. Intoxication is 'involuntary' if D was unaware that he was taking an intoxicant. So where D's lemonade is laced with vodka and he is unaware that he has consumed any alcohol, he can rely on evidence of his drunken condition.[281]

Similarly, perhaps, where D has taken drink under duress.[282] It also covers the special case where a person becomes intoxicated through taking drugs (presumably including alcohol) voluntarily in bona fide pursuance of medical treatment or prescription. This will rarely, if ever, be applicable to drink but it might apply where, for example, brandy is administered to D after an accident.

---

[278] The case prompted interesting calls for a new defence applicable where D acted out of character. See GR Sullivan, 'Involuntary Intoxication and Beyond' [1994] Crim LR 272 and 'Making Excuses' in S Shute and A Simester (eds), *Harm and Culpability* (1996) 131; Tadros (2001) 21 OJLS 495; Tadros, *Criminal Responsibility*, Ch 11; and for a more recent review see C Crosby, 'Culpability, *Kingston* and the Law Commission' (2010) 74 J Crim L 434.

[279] See LC 314, para 1.22. See also the discussion in LC 314, Part 4.

[280] *Allen* [1988] Crim LR 698; cf the definition of voluntary intoxication proposed by the Butler Committee at para 18.56 and that in the Home Office Bill (see later) cl 19(3). LC 314, Part 3 proposes a non-exhaustive list of situations amounting to involuntary intoxication.

[281] See n 277. In *Majewski*, n 288, the Lord Chancellor pointed out that the drugs taken were not medically prescribed.

[282] cf *Kingston*, n 277. But what of the much more common case where D has voluntarily taken some drink and his companions surreptitiously add more? Probably, the jury should be told to convict only if satisfied that the drink voluntarily taken *contributed* to his lack of awareness. Cf LC 314, para 3.125.

589

As intoxication is nearly always voluntary, it is probably for D to raise the issue if he wishes to contend that it is involuntary. The onus of proof will then generally be on the Crown:[283] but s 6(5) of the Public Order Act 1986, for the purposes of offences under that Act, requires D to 'show' that his intoxication was not self-induced or caused by medical treatment. As the Divisional Court stated in *DPP v Smith*, under the 1986 Act: 'a drunken defendant is treated for the purposes of the issue of awareness as if he had been sober'.[284] This was presumably intended to put the onus of proof on D; but 'show', in contrast with 'prove' which is used in other sections of the Act, might be taken to imposeno more than an evidential burden. This is more especially so given the impact of the HRA 1998, which gives force to Art 6(2) of the ECHR.[285]

9.4.3 Voluntary intoxication

9.4.3.1 Basic and specific intent crimes

D is entitled to an acquittal where his voluntary intoxication is such that he did not form the mens rea for the offence of specific intent.[286] It must be emphasized, once again, that this applies where there is a lack of mens rea, not merely a reduction of inhibition; a drunken intention is nevertheless an intention. The prosecution must prove mens rea.

In the case of a crime of basic intent, D may be convicted if he was voluntarily intoxicated at the time of committing the offence by a drug known to create unpredictability or aggression, though he did not have the mens rea required in all other circumstances for that offence and even though he was in a state of automatism at the time of doing the act; if he would have had mens rea if sober.

The problem lies in identifying a way of distinguishing between crimes of basic and specific intent. Until very recently, it appeared to be settled that the distinction was between whether the predominant mens rea element of the crime was one of intention, knowledge or dishonesty which would lead to classification as a specific intent crime, or of something less (recklessness, negligence or strict liability) in which case the crime was one of basic intent. This was a largely pragmatic, but not unprincipled, method of classification. The decision of the Court of Appeal in *Heard*[287] casts doubt on this simple and established method of classification, although technically the comments of the court on the basic/specific distinction are *obiter*.

The rule in *Majewski*

In *DPP v Majewski*,[288] the House of Lords confirmed the rule, obscurely stated in *Beard*,[289] that evidence of self-induced intoxication negativing mens rea excuses a defendant on a charge of a crime requiring a specific intent but not to a charge of any other crime. In

---

[283] *Stripp* (1978) 69 Cr App R 318 at 323; *Bailey* [1983] 2 All ER 503 at 507, [1983] Crim LR 533.

[284] [2017] EWHC 3193 (Admin), at [12] per Bean LJ.

[285] cf *Lambert* [2001] UKHL 37, [2001] Crim LR 806; *A-G's Reference (No 4 of 2002)* [2004] UKHL 40, [2005] Crim LR 200, p 23.

[286] See J Horder, 'The Classification of Crimes and the General Part' in Duff and Green, *Defining Crimes*. For extended analysis of the problems with the current law on voluntary intoxication, see R Williams, 'Voluntary Intoxication—A Lost Cause?' (2013) 129 LQR 264.

[287] [2007] EWCA Crim 125, [2007] Crim LR 654. See LC 314, paras 2.2–2.28.

[288] [1977] AC 443, [1976] Crim LR 374 and commentary; G Williams, 'Intoxication and Specific Intent' (1976) 126 NLJ 658; AD Gold, 'An Untrimmed Beard' (1976) 19 Crim LQ 34; A Dashwood, 'Logic and the Lords in *Majewski*' [1977] Crim LR 532 and 591. Discussed in LC 314, paras 2.35–2.70.

[289] [1920] AC 479. Cf P Handler, 'Intoxication and Criminal Responsibility in England, 1819–1920' (2013) 33 OJLS 243.

Majewski, D had assaulted a number of police officers when he was being restrained and arrested. He had taken a combination of drink and drugs and was very heavily intoxicated. He claimed that his self-induced intoxication had prevented him forming the mens rea, and that the evidence of the intoxication ought to be admissible to support that plea, relying on s 8 of the Criminal Justice Act 1967. He was convicted and this result was upheld by the House of Lords. He was charged with a crime of basic intent and it has long been recognized that voluntary intoxication was no defence to such a charge even if it did cause D to lack mens rea. Unfortunately, the House did not offer a unanimous basis for the distinction between crimes of specific intent and basic intent.

Rule of substantive law

On one interpretation, *Majewski* imposes a rule of substantive law that, where D relies on voluntary intoxication to a charge of a crime not requiring 'specific intent', the prosecution need not prove any intention or foresight, whatever the definition of the crime may say, nor indeed any voluntary act. D's prior fault in becoming voluntarily intoxicated supplies the mens rea. It follows that s 8 of the Criminal Justice Act 1967[290] has no application. There is, it appears, an implied qualification to every statute creating an offence and specifying a mens rea other than a specific intent. The mens rea must be proved—except, we must infer, where the accused was intoxicated through the voluntary taking of drink or drugs. It is assumed that D has the mens rea if he would have had it if sober. In *Richardson and Irwin*,[291] where DD dropped a fellow student from a balcony when drunk causing him grievous bodily harm, they were charged under s 20 of the 1861 Act. Their convictions were quashed by the Court of Appeal holding that the trial judge should have directed that the jury had to be sure that DD would have foreseen the risk of injury had they been sober.

On this first interpretation of *Majewski* it is fatal for a person charged with a crime not requiring specific intent who claims that he did not have mens rea to support his defence with evidence that he had taken drink and drugs. By so doing he dispenses the Crown from the duty, which until that moment lay upon them, of proving beyond reasonable doubt that he had mens rea. Could the Crown escape from this duty by leading evidence that D had taken drink so as to diminish his capacity to foresee the consequences of his acts? According to Lord Salmon[292] in *Majewski*, the question the House was deciding was whether the accused could rely *by way of defence* on the fact that he had voluntarily taken drink. But there are other *dicta* which suggest that D is held liable without the usual mens rea because he has taken the drink—the taking of the drink is the foundation of his liability[293]—a variety of mens rea—though not in the sense in which that term is used in this book. It is a form of 'prior fault', with D's liability for the crime based on his conduct at that time coupled with his fault in becoming intoxicated. If that is right, there is no reason why the Crown should not set out to prove it, instead of seeking to prove mens rea in the sense of intention or recklessness.

In principled terms, this first interpretation of *Majewski* is problematical. It deems the defendant's negligence or recklessness in becoming voluntarily intoxicated—his 'prior fault'—to be

---

[290] See p 131. See Simester, n 262, p 6.

[291] [1999] 1 Cr App R 192, [1999] Crim LR 494, see Simester, n 262.

[292] [1977] AC 443, [1976] Crim LR 374.

[293] 'His course of conduct in reducing himself by drugs and drink to that condition in my view supplies the evidence of *mens rea*, of guilty mind, certainly sufficient for crimes of basic intent': per Lord Elwyn-Jones LC [1976] 2 All ER 142 at 150. 'There is no juristic reason why mental incapacity (short of M'Naghten insanity) brought about by self-induced intoxication to realize what one is doing or its probable consequences should not be such a state of mind stigmatized as wrongful by the criminal law; and there is every practical reason why it should be': per Lord Simon at 153. For critical comment see LC 314, Part 2.

sufficient mens rea for the crime.[294] This is despite the fact that there is no contemporaneity between the fault in becoming intoxicated and the commission of the actus reus of the crime. And, more importantly, that prior fault is deemed to be sufficient mens rea despite the fact that the degree of fault in becoming intoxicated (foresight or awareness of becoming intoxicated) bears no correlation to the mens rea that would normally be required—foresight or awareness of a risk of a prohibited harm specified in the offence. It is, with respect, not enough to say as Hughes LJ suggests in *Heard* (discussed later) that there is 'broadly equivalent culpability'.[295]

It seems that this rule applies whatever the degree of intoxication; if D claimed that it prevented him from foreseeing or knowing what he would have foreseen or known had he been sober he is guilty of the basic intent offence. It is true that Lord Elwyn-Jones at one point[296] posed the question before the House much more narrowly. His lordship spoke of a person who 'consciously and deliberately takes alcohol and drugs not on medical prescription, but in order to escape from reality, to go "on a trip," to become hallucinated...' Such a person is readily distinguishable from the ordinary 'social drinker' who becomes intoxicated in the course of a convivial evening. The former, intending to reduce himself to a state in which he will have no control over his actions, might well be said to be in some sense reckless as to what he will do while in that state. The same cannot be said of the latter. But the general tenor of the speeches, as well as earlier and subsequent cases, is against any such distinction.[297]

Professor Duff has suggested that we can make moral sense of *Majewski* if we accept that:

recklessness can be constituted either by awareness of a relevant risk [as elsewhere in criminal law] or by unawareness that results from voluntary intoxication: recklessness must be presumed given proof of such unawareness not because it can be inferred but because it is constituted by such.[298]

A rule of evidence?

An alternative view is that *Majewski* does not create a rule of substantive law, but one of evidence. On this second interpretation, once D has been shown to be voluntarily intoxicated in a basic intent crime, the evidence of intoxication is irrelevant to the question whether D held the mens rea, but the prosecution is still obliged to prove that D had the relevant mens rea. There is some authority that a jury must be directed to decide whether D was reckless, disregarding the evidence that he was intoxicated. In *Woods*,[299] D, charged with rape under the old sexual offences law, claimed that he was so drunk that he did not realize V was not consenting. He relied on s 1(2) of the Sexual Offences (Amendment) Act 1976[300] which required the jury to have regard to the presence or absence of reasonable grounds for a belief that the woman was consenting, 'in conjunction with any other relevant matters'. He said his intoxication was a relevant matter. The court said that self-induced intoxication is not 'a legally relevant matter' but 'the subsection directs the jury to look carefully at all the other relevant evidence before making up their minds on this issue'. The evidence of intoxication is undoubtedly logically

---

[294] For a theoretical analysis of the role played by prior fault, see A Loughnan and N Wake, 'Of Blurred Boundaries and Prior Fault: Insanity, Automatism and Intoxication' in A Reed and M Bohlander (with N Wake and E Smith) (eds), *General Defences in Criminal Law—Domestic and Comparative Perspectives* (2014) and J Child, 'Prior Fault: Blocking Defences or Constructing Crimes' in the same volume.

[295] For further analysis, see R Williams, 'Voluntary Intoxication—A Lost Cause?' (2013) 129 LQR 264, 268–269.

[296] [1977] AC 443 at 471, [1976] Crim LR 374.

[297] ACE Lynch, 'The Scope of Intoxication' [1982] Crim LR 139 makes a quite different distinction between 'complete intoxication' (to which *Majewski* would apply) and 'partial intoxication' (to which it would not); but there are many degrees of intoxication and the suggested distinction seems unworkable.

[298] *Answering for Crime*, 240–241.   [299] (1981) 74 Cr App R 312, [1982] Crim LR 42.

[300] Now repealed. See now Ch 17, p 787 and the discussion of the case of *Grewal* [2010] EWCA Crim 2448.

relevant and may be the most cogent evidence. To ignore it in coming to a conclusion is to answer a hypothetical question. It is no longer, 'did he believe she was consenting?' and must become, 'would he have known she was consenting if he had not been drunk?' This is most obviously so in the case where D's intoxication has rendered him unconscious.

This second interpretation of *Majewski* as a rule of evidence also poses problems. Take *Lipman*, where D strangled V after taking LSD and believing that he was fighting off a serpent at the centre of the earth.[301] How can a judge seriously tell a jury to decide whether D *did* intend to do an unlawful and dangerous act to V—ignoring the undisputed evidence that he was unconscious at the time? Without this 'legally irrelevant' evidence, the *only* question the jury can sensibly answer is, 'would he have known that such an act was dangerous if he had not been intoxicated'? On facts like those in *Lipman*, there is only one possible answer. It is most regrettable that juries should be faced with questions which are, with all respect, nonsensical, even if their common sense will lead them to consider the only matter really in issue.

Distinguishing specific and basic intent crimes

In view of the rule in *Majewski*, the nature of 'specific intent' is a matter of great importance but a careful scrutiny of the authorities, particularly *Majewski* itself, fails to reveal any consistent principle by which specific and basic are to be distinguished.[302] A number of interpretations are possible. It is regrettable that the distinction is so obscure that the Law Commission recently felt unable confidently to state what the law was.[303]

Ulterior intent

One interpretation is that specific intent crimes are those in which there is an element of mens rea going beyond the immediate actus reus. There is, as it is often described, an 'ulterior intent'. For example, in the crime of indecent exposure it is necessary for D to have intentionally exposed his genitals with intent that someone will see them and be caused alarm or distress. There is a 'bolt on element of mens rea' (intent to cause alarm) beyond that relating to the immediate conduct of exposing his genitals. The crime would therefore on this analysis be treated as one of specific intent. This approach derives some support from *Majewski* and from the decision in *Heard*. Lord Justice Hughes suggested, *obiter*, that if an offence requires 'proof of a state of mind addressing something beyond the prohibited act itself, namely its consequences', it is one of specific intent. The court 'regard[ed] this as the best explanation of the sometimes elusive distinction between specific and basic intent in the sense used in *Majewski*'.[304] It is submitted that it is an unsatisfactory basis for distinguishing between offences. The most compelling basis for rejecting this approach is that some crimes requiring no ulterior intent—conspicuously murder—have been consistently and unequivocally treated as crimes of 'specific intent' by all levels of court including the House of Lords. If the 'ulterior intent' approach is incapable of providing the correct classification for such an obvious example as murder, it cannot be worth serious

---

301 [1970] 1 QB 152.

302 cf Gardner (1994) 14 OJLS 279 and J Horder, 'Intention in the Criminal Law—A Rejoinder' (1995) 58 MLR 678, who views the specific intent crimes as those in which the intent is integrally bound up with the nature and definition of the wrong involved. See the recommendation in LC 314. See also A Ward, 'Making Some Sense of Self-Induced Intoxication' (1986) 45 CLJ 247 and, for an historical account, A Loughnan, *Manifest Madness: Mental Incapacity in Criminal Law* (2012). Loughnan argues that the distinction between crimes of basic and specific intent has deep historical roots and is the reflection of a persistent lay understanding of the effects of alcohol. See LC 314, paras 2.29 et seq.

303 See LC 229, para 3.27. In LC 314, Part 2, it was accepted again that the law was in a confused state.

304 At [31].

consideration.305 In addition, this approach produces some very odd results. For example, an offence can be one of specific intent even if it contains no element of intent at all—provided there is an ulterior mens rea: reckless criminal damage being reckless as to whether life is endangered thereby would be a crime of specific *intention*. What of intentionally causing grievous bodily harm under s 18? On the simple form of the charge, there is no bolt on mens rea to be added. It looks then like a crime of basic intent, but every precedent confirms that it is one of specific intent.

Purposive intent

An alternative method of distinguishing between specific and basic intent is to ask whether the mens rea of the crime requires a direct or purposive intention (specific) or some other form of mens rea or strict liability (basic). This also derives some support from the speech of Lord Simon in *Majewski* who suggested that the distinguishing factor is that 'the *mens rea* in a crime of specific intent requires proof of a purposive element'. Lord Simon put it in this way:306

The best description of 'specific intent' in this sense that I know is contained in the judgment of Fauteux J in *Reg v George* (1960) 128 Can CC 289, 301—'In considering the question of mens rea, a distinction is to be made between (i) intention as applied to acts considered in relation to their purposes and (ii) intention as applied to acts apart from their purposes. A general intent attending the commission of an act is, in some cases, the only intent required to constitute the crime while, in others, there must be, in addition to that general intent, a specific intent attending the purpose for the commission of the act.'

In *Heard*, Lord Justice Hughes also endorsed the distinction between basic and specific intent found in the speech of Lord Simon in *Majewski*,307 and put it this way at [31]: 'crimes of specific intent are those where the offence requires proof of purpose or consequence, which are not confined to, but amongst which are included, those where the purpose goes beyond the *actus reus* (sometimes referred to as cases of "ulterior intent")'. It is submitted that it is also an unsatisfactory basis on which to distinguish crimes of specific and basic intent. The crime of murder, for example, has been consistently and unequivocally accepted by the Court of Appeal and House of Lords as a crime of specific intent, yet there need be no purposive element in the mens rea.308

Predominant mens rea

A third approach to distinguishing between crimes of basic and specific intent is based on whether the crime in question is one for which the predominant mens rea is (a) intention, knowledge or dishonesty (specific) or (b) some lesser mens rea of recklessness negligence or strict liability (basic). In *Majewski*, Lord Elwyn-Jones LC suggested that the test is that crimes not requiring specific intent are crimes that may be committed recklessly.309 In *Heard*, in an *obiter dictum*, the Court of Appeal rejected this simple practical approach.

The decision in *Heard*

The decision in *Heard* is a controversial one and a number of points are worth emphasizing. First, on its facts, it should never have given rise to problems. The accused had, while drunk, exposed his penis and rubbed it against the thigh of a police officer. D's plea was that he had no recollection of the incident. That is never a basis for a plea of intoxication and that should

---

305 Indeed this was one of the principal bases on which *Majewski* was criticized. See Williams, TBCL, 429.
306 At 478H.   307 At 478B–479B.   308 See LC 314, paras 2.8 et seq.
309 Lord Edmund-Davies, a party to *Majewski*, was dismayed to think that, as a result of *Caldwell*, this opinion prevailed [1982] AC 341 at 361, [1981] 1 All ER 961 at 972.

have been the end of the matter. However, D relied on his voluntary intoxication as negating his mens rea of an intention to touch for the purposes of s 3(1)(a) of the Sexual Offences Act 2003. The trial judge ruled that the intentional touching element of the offence required proof of a basic intent, and that it followed that voluntary intoxication was not a defence. Applying the predominant mens rea interpretation of *Majewski*, on a charge such as that under s 3 with the requirement of an 'intentional' touching, it was arguable at least that the crime was one of specific intent.[310] The court rejected that approach.

Secondly, we can assume that sexual offences under the 2003 Act in which the conduct is 'intended'[311] will be treated as basic intent crimes unless there is a clear ulterior purpose, as in indecent exposure, and offences in which D is acting 'for the purpose of obtaining sexual gratification'.[312] On policy grounds the court was clearly entitled to assume that Parliament had not intended to change the law, although it should be noted that under the pre-2003 law, the offence of indecent assault was not always a basic intent crime. The court could have adopted the predominant mens rea and created an exception for sex offences.

Thirdly, the court's radical reinterpretation of *Majewski* aligning specific intent with an ulterior or purposive mens rea produces difficulties, even within the scope of the s 3 offence. Someone like Lipman[313] who becomes so intoxicated that he thinks he is stroking an animal at the centre of the earth when in fact he is stroking a woman's breast will, on the court's approach, be guilty under s 3. But it is submitted that in such a case it would be difficult in any ordinary sense of the word to say that D 'intended' to touch V sexually as s 3 requires.

Fourthly, the court makes some very broad qualifications to the approach in s 3 (and other sexual offences and beyond, one assumes) in respect of accidents. Lord Justice Hughes stated that:

To flail about, stumble or barge around in an unco-ordinated manner which results in an unintended touching, objectively sexual, is not this offence. If to do so when sober is not this offence, then nor is it this offence to do so when intoxicated. It is also possible that such an action would not be judged by the jury to be objectively sexual, on the basis that it was clearly accidental, but whether that is so or not, we are satisfied that in such a case this offence is not committed. The intoxication, in such a situation, has not impacted on intention. Intention is simply not in question. What is in question is impairment of control of the limbs….'[A] drunken intent is still an intent', the corollary [is] that 'a drunken accident is still an accident'.

In respect of someone who simply trips on the dance floor and grabs at the nearest thing to steady himself this makes perfect sense. But consider someone who,[314] fooling around when heavily intoxicated, pretends to strike the bottom of a woman who is bending and who misjudges the distance and strikes her bottom. He will be acquitted on the basis that his conduct is 'accidental'.[315] It is submitted that it would be a misuse of the word 'intention' to say that he had intended to touch her sexually. He intends to move his arm and intends to come close to touching her, but not to do so. It is also misleading to say it is accidental: D is reckless about that consequence, he has seen the risk and unjustifiably gone on to take it. There is a risk that the category of 'drunken accident' endorsed by *Heard* will be misunderstood and applied in cases of what are plainly recklessness.

Finally, there are several reasons why, it is submitted, the court's *obiter dicta* rejecting the predominant mens rea interpretation of *Majewski* in favour of a purposive approach should

---

[310] R Card, *Sexual Offences: The New Law* (2004) para 1.31; P Rook and R Ward, *Sexual Offences Law and Practice* (5th edn, 2016) paras 2.81–2.82.

[311] See *Grout* [2011] EWCA Crim 299.   [312] Section 12.

[313] *Lipman* (1969) 55 Cr App R 600, CA.

[314] cf *Shimmen* (1987) 84 Cr App Rep 7, [1986] Crim LR 800, (1987) 84 Cr App Rep 7.

[315] At [23].

595

not be applied throughout the criminal law: it is more difficult to look for the 'bolt-on' element of additional mens rea in a crime in order to categorize it appropriately; the approach creates no fewer anomalies than the established interpretation of *Majewski*; and it creates confusion because specific intent might encompass crimes with no element of intent at all, such as reckless criminal damage being reckless as to whether life is endangered thereby.

9.4.3.2 The current law on basic and specific intent

Despite its obscure exposition in the House of Lords, and its unsatisfactory theoretical underpinnings, the *Majewski* approach had subsequently been knocked into pragmatic shape: the predominant mens rea approach was familiar and generally applied. Those virtues ought not to be undervalued. Despite *dicta* in *Heard*, it is submitted that any offence which may be committed recklessly ought to be held an offence of 'basic' and not 'specific' intent.

The safest approach seems to be that 'crime requiring specific intent' means a crime where evidence of voluntary intoxication negativing mens rea is a 'defence'. It may be easier to accept that the designation of crimes as requiring, or not requiring, specific intent is based on no principle but on policy. In order to know how a crime should be classified for this purpose, we can look only to the decisions of the courts. The following are crimes requiring specific intent: murder,[316] wounding or causing grievous bodily harm with intent,[317] theft,[318] robbery,[319] burglary with intent to steal,[320] handling stolen goods,[321] endeavouring to obtain money on a forged cheque,[322] causing criminal damage contrary to s 1(1) or (2) of the Criminal Damage Act 1971 where only intention to cause damage or, in the case of s 1(2), only intention to endanger life, is alleged,[323] an attempt to commit any offence requiring specific intent and possibly, post-*Jogee*, secondary participation in any offence.[324]

The following crimes do not require specific intent: manslaughter (apparently in all its forms),[325] rape,[326] sexual assault,[327] maliciously wounding or inflicting grievous bodily harm,[328] kidnapping and false imprisonment,[329] assault occasioning actual bodily harm,[330]

---

[316] *Beard*, n 289; *Gallagher* [1963] AC 349; *Sheehan* [1975] 1 WLR 739, [1975] Crim LR 339, CA.

[317] *Bratty v A-G for Northern Ireland* [1963] AC 386, per Lord Denning; *Pordage* [1975] Crim LR 575; *Davies* [1991] Crim LR 469.

[318] *Ruse v Read* [1949] 1 KB 377, [1949] 1 All ER 398 and *Majewski* per Lord Simon at 152.

[319] As a corollary of theft.

[320] *Durante* [1972] 3 All ER 962, [1972] 1 WLR 1612, [1972] Crim LR 656.   [321] ibid.

[322] *Majewski*, per Lord Salmon at 158.

[323] *Caldwell* [1981] 1 All ER 961 at 964. The Court of Appeal in *Harris* [2013] EWCA Crim 223, [2013] Crim LR 923 declined to address the issue of whether causing criminal damage being reckless to whether life would be endangered is a crime of specific intent. Hughes LJ did, however, state that there was some force in the argument that voluntary intoxication ought not to be a 'defence' to crimes involving subjective recklessness.

[324] *Clarkson* [1971] 3 All ER 344 at 347. But in *Lynch v DPP for Northern Ireland* [1975] 1 All ER 913 at 942, [1975] Crim LR 707 Lord Simon said, approving the decision of the Northern Irish Court of Criminal Appeal, that they held that the mens rea of aiding and abetting did not involve a 'specific intent'. But (a) he may have used the term in a different sense; and (b) there may be a difference depending on the nature of the alleged secondary liability—an intent to procure is different from an intent to aid; see p 198.

[325] *Beard*, *Gallagher* and *Bratty v A-G Northern Ireland* [1961] 3 All ER at 533, per Lord Denning; *Lipman* [1970] 1 QB 152.

[326] *Grewal* [2010] EWCA Crim 2448; *Grout* [2011] EWCA Crim 299, [2011] Crim LR 584. *Majewski*, per Lords Simon and Russell and *Leary v R* (1977) 74 DLR (3d) 103, SCC, discussed 55 Can Bar Rev 691. But if this is right, and it seems almost certain that it is, *Cogan and Leak* (p 223) is wrongly decided; and *Morgan* (p 332) might have been decided simply on this ground. Cf *Fotheringham* (1988) 88 Cr App R 206, [1988] Crim LR 846 and commentary.

[327] *Heard* [2007] EWCA Crim 125, [2007] Crim LR 654.

[328] *Bratty* at 533, per Lord Denning; *Majewski*, per Lords Simon and Salmon.

[329] *Hutchins* [1988] Crim LR 379. Nor child abduction: *Hunter* [2015] All ER (D) 196 (Jan).

[330] *Bolton v Crawley* [1972] Crim LR 222; *Majewski*.

assault on a constable in the execution of his duty,[331] common assault,[332] taking a convey-ance without the consent of the owner,[333] criminal damage where intention or recklessness, or only recklessness, is alleged[334] and possibly an attempt to commit an offence where reck-lessness is a sufficient element in the mens rea,[335] as in attempted rape.[336]

It will be noted that for most specific intent offences there exists a basic intent offence that can be charged in the alternative (murder and manslaughter, ss 18 and 20 of the OAPA 1861, etc). The prosecution are usually therefore able to avoid an acquittal in cases of self-induced intoxication. Two problems arise in this regard, however. First, the jury will face confusing directions on charges such as ss 18 and 20 as to what use they may make of the evidence of intoxication. Secondly, there are some specific intent offences for which there is no basic intent equivalent: theft is an obvious example.

Specific and basic: a legitimate basis of distinction?

A classification of all crimes as offences of either specific or basic intent is oversimplified. The Court of Appeal in *Heard* even hints at rejecting the two-fold classification by suggest-ing that it is not to be assumed that every offence is one of basic or specific intent.[337] It is submitted that this aspect of the Court of Appeal's decision should be taken as emphasizing that an offence is likely to have more than one element of mens rea. The question is what is the predominant mens rea.

Consider the offence under s 18 of the OAPA 1861 of unlawfully and maliciously wound-ing with intent to resist lawful apprehension. There is abundant authority to the effect that the words 'unlawfully and maliciously' when used in s 20 import only a basic intent; that is, *Cunningham* recklessness. Presumably they have the same effect in s 18. So as far as wounding goes, s 18 is an offence of basic intent. But the intent to resist lawful apprehen-sion seems a clear case of specific intent. So it seems that a drunken person who intends to resist lawful arrest but, because of his drunkenness, does not foresee the risk of wounding, might be convicted, notwithstanding his lack of *Cunningham* recklessness. If, on the other hand, because of drunkenness, he does not realize that he is resisting lawful arrest, he must be acquitted.[338]

Intoxication and *Caldwell* recklessness

Where the offence is one of *Caldwell* recklessness, assuming that any such offences still exist, the impact of *Majewski* is reduced. Where, because he was intoxicated, D gave no thought to the existence of the risk, he was reckless and is liable to conviction without the invocation of the rule in *Majewski*.[339] This was the position in *Caldwell* itself. But *Majewski* may still have a significant sphere of operation.[340] D might say that he did consider whether there was a risk and decided there was none. He was then not *Caldwell*-reckless. But, if he would have appre-ciated the existence of the risk had he been sober, he will still be liable because of *Majewski*.

---

[331] *Majewski.*   [332] *A fortiori.*

[333] *MacPherson* [1973] RTR 157; *Gannon* (1987) 87 Cr App R 254. *Diggin* (1980) 72 Cr App R 204 is not, as it first appeared: [1980] Crim LR 656, an authority on intoxicated taking: [1981] Crim LR 563; but see S White, 'Taking the Joy Out of Joyriding' [1980] Crim LR 609.

[334] See Ch 27.

[335] Commentary on *Pullen* [1991] Crim LR 457 at 458.

[336] This possibility will depend upon whether the interpretation of attempts adopted in *Pace* [2014] EWCA Crim 186 prevails. The implication of the judgment is that, on a charge of attempted rape, the Crown would have to prove that D intended that V was not consenting. For discussion, see Ch 11.

[337] At [14]. But what is this other category that now exists? And what offences might fall into it? See the Law Commission's rejection in LC 314, Part 2.

[338] *Davies* [1991] Crim LR 469.   [339] This point was overlooked in *Cullen* [1993] Crim LR 936.

[340] This is overlooked by Lord Diplock at [1981] 1 All ER 968a.

597

9.4.4 Dangerous or non-dangerous drugs in basic intent crime

In the case where D has become voluntarily intoxicated and the offence with which he is charged is one of basic intent, there remains one important issue to consider—whether the substance voluntarily ingested is 'dangerous'; that is, commonly known to create states of unpredictability or aggression.

The law in this area has developed principally in cases where D was intoxicated by alcohol. In *Lipman*,[341] it was held that the same principles apply to intoxication by other drugs but two later cases, *Bailey*[342] and *Hardie*,[343] suggest that drugs must be divided into two categories. Where it is common knowledge that a drug is liable to cause the taker to become aggressive or do dangerous or unpredictable things, that drug is to be classed alongside alcohol. Where there is no such common knowledge, as in the case of a merely soporific or sedative drug, different rules apply. There are obvious difficulties about classifying drugs in this way and it is surprising that it has not generated more case law.

In *Bailey*,[344] a diabetic failed to take sufficient food after insulin. He caused grievous bodily harm and his defence to charges under ss 18 and 20 of the OAPA was that, because of this failure, he was in a state of sane automatism. The recorder's direction to the jury that this was no defence was obviously wrong so far as s 18 was concerned for that is an offence of specific intent. The Court of Appeal held that it was also wrong for s 20 because 'self-induced automatism, other than that due to intoxication from alcohol or drugs, may provide a defence to crimes of basic intent'.[345] The court went on:

The question in each case will be whether the prosecution has proved the necessary element of recklessness. In cases of assault, if the accused knows that his actions or inaction are likely to make him aggressive, unpredictable or uncontrolled with the result that he may cause some injury to others and he persists in the action or takes no remedial action when he knows it is required, it will be open to the jury to find that he was reckless.

The automatism seems to have been treated as arising from the failure to take food, rather than from the taking of the insulin, but the court hinted at a distinction between two types of drug:

It is common knowledge that those who take alcohol to excess or certain sorts of drugs may become aggressive or do dangerous or unpredictable things....But the same cannot be said, without more, of a man who fails to take food after an insulin injection.

In *Hardie*,[346] the court developed this further. D's defence to a charge of damaging property with intent to endanger the life of another or being reckless whether another's life be endangered, was that he had taken valium, a sedative drug, to calm his nerves and that this had resulted in intoxication precluding the mens rea for the offence. The judge, following *Majewski* and *Caldwell*, directed that this could be no defence. The Court of Appeal quashed the conviction. *Majewski* was not applicable because valium:

is wholly different in kind from drugs which are liable to cause unpredictability or aggressiveness....if the effect of a drug is merely soporific or sedative the taking of it, even in some excessive quantity, cannot in the ordinary way raise a conclusive presumption against the admission of proof of intoxication for the purpose of disproving *mens rea* in ordinary crimes, such as would be the case with alcoholic intoxication or incapacity or automatism resulting from the self-administration of dangerous drugs.[347]

---

341 [1970] 1 QB 152; p 318.   342 [1983] 1 WLR 760.   343 [1985] 1 WLR 64.

344 [1983] 1 WLR 760, CA.   345 See p 315.   346 [1985] 1 WLR 64.

347 This overlooks the fact that the *Majewski* principle is stated by the House of Lords to be a rule of substantive law and that the Criminal Justice Act 1967, s 8, precludes conclusive presumptions of intention or foresight. See p 316. For further discussion, see R Williams, 'Voluntary Intoxication—A Lost Cause?' (2013) 129 LQR 264, 266–269. The distinction is also unsatisfactory in pharmacological terms: M Weller and W Somers, 'Differences in the Medical and Legal Viewpoint Illustrated by *Hardie*' (1991) 31 Med Sci Law 152.

This qualification to the normal rule for basic intent crimes applies where intoxication is self-induced otherwise than by alcohol or dangerous drugs. In these cases the test of liability is stated to be one of recklessness: 'If [D] does appreciate the risk that [failure to take food/taking the non-dangerous drug] may lead to aggressive, unpredictable and uncontrollable conduct and he nevertheless deliberately runs the risk or otherwise disregards it, this will amount to recklessness.'[348]

It is clear that the recklessness which must be proved is:

(1) subjective—an actual awareness of the risk of becoming aggressive; but

(2) 'general'—not requiring foresight of the actus reus of any particular crime, such as is required in the case of a sober person charged with an offence of *Cunningham* recklessness. D will be liable for any crime of recklessness the actus reus of which he happens to commit under the influence of the self-induced intoxication. This flows from the rule in *Majewski*.[349]

Further:

(3) being aware that one may lose consciousness may be sufficient where a failure to exercise control may result in the actus reus of a crime, as in the case of careless or dangerous driving.

D's fault in voluntarily consuming the dangerous drugs with the awareness of their likely effect provides sufficient prior fault to warrant his conviction for basic intent crimes even though at the time of the commission of the offence D lacks the mens rea for that crime.

9.4.5 Intoxication and defences

9.4.5.1 Statutory defences prescribing a belief in circumstances

The *Majewski* rule has been held inapplicable where statute expressly provides that a particular belief shall be a defence to the charge. If D held that belief, he is not guilty, even though it arose from a drunken mistake that he would not have made when sober. In *Jaggard v Dickinson*,[350] D had a friend, H, who had invited her to treat his house as if it were her own. When drunk, D went to a house which she thought was H's but which in fact belonged to R, who barred her way. D gained entry by breaking windows and damaging the curtains. Charged with criminal damage, contrary to s 1(1) of the Criminal Damage Act 1971, she relied on s 5(2) of that Act[351] which provides that a person has a lawful excuse if D believed that the person entitled to consent to the damage would have done so had he known of the circumstances. D said that she believed that H would, in the circumstances, have consented to her damaging his property. Since s 1(1) creates an offence of basic intent, D could not have relied on her drunkenness to negative her recklessness as to whether she damaged the property of another. However, it was held, she could rely on her voluntary intoxication to explain what would otherwise have been inexplicable and give colour to her evidence about the state of her belief. The court thought that this was different from using drunkenness to rebut an inference of intention or recklessness. It seems, however, to be exactly the same thing.[352]

---

[348] *Bailey* [1983] 2 All ER 503 at 507, [1983] Crim LR 533.

[349] Williams cogently argues that as a result of the current law intoxicated people can be convicted when they are inadvertent, provided they could have foreseen the risk when sober. By contrast, it is no longer permissible to convict sober people when they are inadvertent. See R Williams, 'Voluntary Intoxication—A Lost Cause?' (2013) 129 LQR 264, 270.

[350] [1981] QB 527, [1980] Crim LR 717. Cf the unsatisfactory case of *Gannon* (1987) 87 Cr App R 254, criticized by G Williams, 'Two Nocturnal Blunders' (1990) 140 NLJ 1564.

[351] See p 1077.   [352] See p 1080.

Moreover, the court thought that s 5(2) of the 1971 Act provides that it is immaterial whether a belief is justified or not if it is honestly held, and it was not open to the court to add the words 'and the honesty of the belief is not attributable only to self-induced intoxication'. Yet the courts have not hesitated to add similar words to qualify Parliament's express requirement of 'malice', that is, *Cunningham* recklessness.

The result is anomalous. Where the defendant did not intend any damage to property but was reckless about damage he may be held liable because he was drunk; but where he did intend damage to property but thought the owner would consent he is not liable, however drunk he may have been. Suppose that D, because he is drunk, believes that certain property belonging to V is his own and damages it. His belief is not a matter of defence under s 5(2)[353] but negatives recklessness as to whether property *belonging to another* be damaged.[354] If D, being drunk, destroys X's property believing that it is the property of Y who would consent to his doing so, this is a defence; but if he destroys X's property believing that it is his own, it is not. The latest Law Commission recommendation to reverse the approach in *Jaggard*,[355] is a welcome one.

In the absence of parliamentary intervention, Elias LJ in *Magee v CPS*[356] stated that the principle enunciated in *Jaggard* ought to be construed narrowly. In *Magee*, D was found guilty of failing to stop after an accident, contrary to s 170(4) of the Road Traffic Act 1988. At the time the accident occurred, D was intoxicated and as a result of her intoxicated state the magistrates found that she had a genuine belief that there had been no accident. D was nevertheless convicted. Relying upon *Jaggard*, D argued that a mistaken view of the circumstances, even if induced by drink, could constitute a defence as long as the defendant genuinely did not believe an accident had occurred. Rejecting this proposition, Elias LJ held that the continuing validity of *Jaggard* is questionable, given subsequent developments in the case law.[357] His lordship further held that the onus was on D to negate the natural inference that once the accident had occurred she would have been aware of it. It was observed that there was no reason why the common law should be construed so as to allow D to pray in aid her own state of drunkenness as the reason for the mistake, and there was every reason of policy why it should not be extended in that way. This case demonstrates that even though the Law Commission's recommendations have not been acted upon, the courts will actively work to confine the scope of *Jaggard*, which, for the reasons already given, is welcome.

9.4.5.2 Self-defence

In relation to self-defence, the law has gone quite the other way from *Jaggard*. It is now settled that when D sets up self-defence, he is to be judged on the facts as he believed them to be, whether reasonably or not.[358] However, a mistake arising from voluntary intoxication cannot be relied upon, according to *O'Grady*[359] and *Hatton*, even on a charge of murder or other crime requiring specific intent. This has now been endorsed by Parliament in s 76(5) of the Criminal Justice and Immigration Act 2008.

In *O'Grady*, this conclusion was plainly *obiter* because the appellant had been acquitted of murder and was appealing only against his conviction for manslaughter; but in *O'Connor*,[360] the court, inexplicably, treated it as binding, while quashing the conviction of murder on

---

[353] *Smith (DR)* [1974] QB 354, [1974] 1 All ER 632, [1974] Crim LR 101.   [354] ibid.

[355] LC 314, para 2.94.   [356] [2014] EWHC 4089 (Admin), [34].   [357] At [33]–[36].

[358] *Gladstone Williams* [1987] 3 All ER 411, 78 Cr App R 276, [1984] Crim LR 163, p 383.

[359] [1987] QB 995, [1987] 3 All ER 420, [1987] Crim LR 706 criticized by the Law Commission, LC 177, para 8.42, by H Milgate (1987) 46 CLJ 381 and JC Smith [1987] Crim LR 706. Relied upon in *Dowds* [2012] EWCA Crim 281, [2012] Crim LR 612 as an example of the 'general approach' that English law takes to intoxication.

[360] [1991] Crim LR 135; cf *Hatton* [2005] EWCA Crim 2951, [2006] Crim LR 353.

another ground. This was followed in *Hatton*. H who had drunk more than 20 pints of beer killed V with at least seven blows from a sledgehammer. H stated that he could not recall V's death but that he had a vague recollection that a stick fashioned in the shape of a samurai sword had been involved. H said that he believed that V had hit him with the stick and that he must have believed that V was attacking him. H wished to raise self-defence based on his own mistaken belief that he thought he was being attacked by an SAS officer (as V had earlier pretended to be) with a sword. The Court of Appeal, upholding his conviction, confirmed that the decision in *O'Grady* applied equally to cases of manslaughter and murder: a defendant seeking to rely on self-defence could not rely on a mistake induced by voluntary intoxication.[361] The case is controversial in extending the scope of *O'Grady* to murder, and in accepting unequivocally that the decisions in *O'Connor* and *O'Grady* were binding (but not, implicitly, feeling bound by *Gladstone Williams*). It is now beyond doubt by s 76(5).

As a matter of principle, this approach is flawed in a number of ways. First, it contradicts the approach taken in relation to mistakes in self-defence. If D has made a genuine but unreasonable mistake as to the need for force, he will be judged on the facts as he unreasonably believed them to be. If this is so when D is sober, logically it ought to be so when he is intoxicated since his intoxication explains the basis for the unreasonableness of his mistake. (The Law Commission rejects this argument in its report (at para 3.59).) Secondly, it is inconsistent with the application of the rules relating to specific and basic intent for offences. If D is charged with murder and pleads that he was so intoxicated that he did not form an intent, he is, if believed, entitled to an acquittal on that specific intent charge. In short, a killing in a state of voluntary intoxication is manslaughter. However, when D's intoxicated mistake to self-defence is pleaded it results in a murder conviction.

In cases of householder self-defence, Sir Brian Leveson P questioned, *obiter*, whether the same approach to intoxication should apply.[362] His lordship said this because the common law (preserved by s 76 of the 2008 Act) requires an approach which it is at least arguable is unduly restrictive for householders. There is much to be said for the proposition that those who go about in public (or anywhere outside their own homes) must take responsibility for their level of intoxication: thus by s 76(5) of the 2008 Act, a defendant cannot rely on any mistaken belief attributable to intoxication that was voluntarily induced. Why that should be so in the defendant's own home in circumstances where he is not anticipating any interaction with a trespasser is, perhaps, a more open question but that remains part of the test even in a householder case.

The law could have taken a different approach and said that D could be convicted of manslaughter by gross negligence if the jury judge his unreasonable mistake as to the need for force as a grossly negligent mistake (which a drunken mistake almost certainly is).[363] If self-defence is a defence to murder it does not necessarily follow that it needs to be a defence to manslaughter.

The Court of Appeal, in a purely policy-driven series of decisions, has created inconsistencies in an attempt to ensure that D cannot plead intoxicated self-defence: the basis for this seems to be a fear that jurors would acquit of all offences.[364] These decisions are difficult to defend. The court's attention does not appear to have been drawn to the recommendations of the Criminal Law Revision Committee, which complements those which the court

---

[361] See *Hatton* [2005] EWCA Crim 2951. Note also the Criminal Justice and Immigration Act 2008, s 76(5) which precludes D relying on a mistake in such circumstances which was attributable to him being voluntarily intoxicated. See also LC 314, paras 2.54–2.61.

[362] See *Collins* [2016] EWHC 33 (Admin), discussed in full in the next chapter.

[363] By Smith [1987] Crim LR 706. Cf the rejection arguments in LC 314, paras 3.59–3.64.

[364] See the critical comments by A Ashworth [2006] Crim LR 353; JR Spencer (2006) 65 CLJ 267; G Dingwall (2007) 70 MLR 127.

followed in *Gladstone Williams*.[365] The more logical view, it is submitted, is that a mistake arising from voluntary intoxication by alcohol or dangerous drugs ought to found a defence to crime requiring specific intent but not to one of basic intent if the prosecution prove that but for the intoxication the defendant would not have made the mistake.

9.4.5.3 Intoxication and partial defences to murder

The relevance of voluntary intoxication and alcohol dependence syndrome for the partial defences to murder (loss of control and diminished responsibility) is considered in Ch 13, p 545 and p 554.

9.4.6 Intoxication induced with the intention of committing crime

We now turn to consider the rare situation where D, intending to commit a crime, takes drink or drugs in order to give himself 'Dutch courage' and then commits the crime, having, at the time of the act, induced a state of drunkenness as to negative a 'specific intent'. The problem was raised by *A-G for Northern Ireland v Gallagher*.[366] D, having decided to kill his wife, bought a knife and a bottle of whisky. He drank much of the whisky and then killed his wife with the knife. The defence was that he was either insane or so drunk that he did not form the necessary intent at the time he did the act. The Court of Criminal Appeal in Northern Ireland reversed his conviction for murder on the ground that the judge had misdirected the jury in telling them to apply the M'Naghten Rules to D's state of mind at the time before he took the alcohol and not at the time of committing the act. The majority of the House of Lords apparently did not dissent from the view of the Court of Criminal Appeal that such a direction would be 'at variance with the specific terms of the M'Naghten Rules which definitely fix the crucial time as the time of committing the act'.[367] They differed, however, in their interpretation of the summing up and held that it did direct the jury's attention to the time of committing the act. In that case, of course, it was not necessary to decide the problem because the jury, by their verdict, had found that D had mens rea and was not insane. Lord Denning, however, seems to have taken the view that the Court of Criminal Appeal's interpretation of the summing up was correct and that the direction, so interpreted, was right in law. He said:[368]

My Lords, I think the law on this point should take a clear stand. If a man, whilst sane and sober, forms an intention to kill and makes preparation for it knowing it is a wrong thing to do, and then gets himself drunk so as to give himself Dutch courage to do the killing, and whilst drunk carries out his intention, he cannot rely on this self-induced drunkenness as a defence to a charge of murder, nor even as reducing it to manslaughter. He cannot say he got himself into such a stupid state that he was incapable of an intent to kill. So also, when he is a psychopath, he cannot by drinking rely on his self-induced defect of reason as a defence of insanity. The wickedness of his mind before he got drunk is enough to condemn him, coupled with the act which he intended to do and did do.

The difficulty about this is that an intention to do an act some time in the future is not mens rea.[369] The mens rea must generally coincide with the conduct which causes the actus reus. If D, being sober, resolves to murder his wife at midnight, drops off to sleep and, while still asleep, strangles her at midnight, it is thought that he is not guilty of murder. The case of deliberately induced drunkenness, however, is probably different. The true analogy, it is thought, is the case where a man D uses an innocent agent as an instrument with which to commit crime. It has been seen[370] that if D induces X to kill, D is guilty of murder if X is

---

365 See n 358.   366 [1963] AC 349.   367 See [1963] AC 349 at 376.
368 [1963] AC 349 at 382.   369 See p 125.   370 See p 182.

an innocent agent. Is not the position substantially the same where D induces in himself a state of irresponsibility with the intention that he shall kill while in that state?[371] Should not the responsible D be liable for the foreseen and intended acts of the irresponsible D? Regarded in this way, a conviction would not be incompatible with the wording of the M'Naghten Rules. The result, certainly, seems to be one required by policy and it is thought the courts will achieve it if the problem should be squarely raised before them.

9.4.7 Reform of intoxication

England is becoming isolated in clinging to the *Majewski* principle.[372] Its abolition elsewhere does not seem to have led, as some anticipated, to increased crime or a collapse in respect for the law.[373] The Law Commission in a Consultation Paper published in 1993 reached a provisional conclusion that *Majewski* should be abolished.[374] The radical proposal was to introduce a new offence of criminal intoxication which would reflect more appropriately, in terms of label, the responsibility of the individual who commits a crime in a state of voluntary intoxication.[375] The consultation, however, persuaded the Commission to change its mind. In LC 229 it was recommended[376] that the rule be codified with minor amendment and attempted clarification, but in a draft Bill so complex that it is impossible to commend it.[377] That has not been taken forward. The Home Office then proposed a simplified model which it intended to enact in relation to offences against the person. That too has not been taken forward.[378]

The Law Commission's latest proposals in LC 314 would have provided a statutory framework, replacing the specific/basic intent distinction. The replacement for the 'specific intent' rule is to create a statutory list of 'integral fault elements' (intention, knowledge, belief, fraud and dishonesty), and if D is charged with an offence with such an 'integral fault element' D will only be liable if the prosecution proves he had the relevant fault element despite being voluntarily intoxicated (para 3.42). The general rule for all other offences (eg those requiring recklessness) is that if D was voluntarily intoxicated he will be treated 'as having been aware at the material time of anything which D would then have been aware of but for the intoxication' (para 3.35). This effectively replaces the basic intent rule. In relation to D's mistakes induced by voluntary intoxication, D's mistaken belief should be taken into account only if D would have held the same belief if D had not been intoxicated (para 3.53). If D's intoxication is involuntary (administered without consent or under duress or under proper medical instruction or without knowledge that it was an intoxicant) or 'almost entirely involuntary', that can be considered in all cases where D is charged with a crime of subjective fault (paras 3.105–3.126). Separate complex rules are proposed in relation to secondary and inchoate liability (paras 3.85–3.104).[379] The then-government rejected the Law Commission's recommendations and stated that it would not be taking them forward.

---

[371] See the discussion in Ch 2, p 37.

[372] For extended discussion of the options for reform, see R Williams, 'Voluntary Intoxication—A Lost Cause?' (2013) 129 LQR 264. She suggests a new offence of 'committing the *actus reus* of offence X while intoxicated'. For critique see J Child, 'Prior Fault: Blocking Defences or Constructing Crimes' in A Reed and M Bohlander (with N Wake and E Smith) (eds), *General Defences in Criminal Law—Domestic and Comparative Perspectives* (2014).

[373] G Orchard, 'Surviving without *Majewski*' [1993] Crim LR 426.   [374] LCCP 127 (1993).

[375] For a defence, see G Virgo, 'Reconciling Principle and Policy' [1993] Crim LR 415; for criticism, see S Gardner, 'The Importance of *Majewski*' (1994) 14 OJLS 279.

[376] LC 229 (1995). See J Horder, 'Sobering Up' (1995) 58 MLR 534; E Paton, 'Reformulating the Intoxication Rule' [1995] Crim LR 382.

[377] See S Gough, 'Intoxication and Criminal Liability' (1996) 112 LQR 335.

[378] See JC Smith, 'Offences Against the Person: The Home Office Consultation Paper' [1998] Crim LR 317.

[379] For critical comment see J Child, 'Drink, Drugs and Law Reform' [2009] Crim LR 488.

The Code Team's report[380] to the Commission offered a simpler scheme. Other proposals for a *via media* have been made[381] but have not attracted support and are not pursued here.

The Law Commission's latest reform proposals for insanity and automatism do have one impact on intoxication. Under the Commission's proposed scheme, a defendant would be treated as pleading the new recognized medical condition defence if: he suffered from a recognized medical condition; took properly authorized medication for that condition and in accordance with the prescription (or in circumstances in which it was reasonable to take it); had no reason to believe he would suffer an adverse reaction; but suffered a total lack of a relevant capacity (see earlier).

9.5 Combined, consecutive and concurrent causes of loss of capacity

The internal and external factors which cause an individual defendant to lack capacity may operate consecutively or concurrently.[382] There is little authority on the complex questions which may arise and such as there is does not seem well thought out. From a theoretical perspective, Loughnan and Wake argue that co-morbidity poses two main issues.[383] The first relates to defendants who might have committed an offence whilst both mentally ill and intoxicated: D's mental illness might have been diagnosed prior to his committing the offence, or it may only have been stimulated by his intoxicated state. The second issue relates to defendants whose ingestion of an intoxicating substance has led them to develop some mental impairment. Their thesis is that the law currently places too much emphasis upon the cause of D's incapacity and does so in an inconsistent fashion. This part of the chapter will demonstrate that this issue poses practical problems in addition to theoretical ones. Some answers to the questions which may arise are suggested here.

9.5.1 Consecutive operation

9.5.1.1 Intoxication causes automatism

D, because he is drunk, sustains concussion and does the allegedly criminal act in a state of automatism resulting from the concussion. In *Stripp*,[384] the Court of Appeal thought, *obiter*, that D should be acquitted on the ground of automatism. That seems right—the intoxication is too remote from the act. The Law Commission concluded that the case suggests '*obiter*, the possibility that where there is a course of automatism clearly separable in time or effect from the intoxication and supported by a foundation of evidence, then a defence of automatism may be available, but when the causal factors are less easily separable it would seem that the presence of the intoxication will on policy grounds adopted in *Majewski* exclude reliance on automatism'.[385] Distinguishing the degree of separateness of the factors will not always be easy.

---

[380] LC 143 (1985) cl 26.   [381] See the 7th edition of this book, at p 230.

[382] For a discussion of the relationship between these defences see LCDP, Ch 6.

[383] A Loughnan and N Wake, 'Of Blurred Boundaries and Prior Fault: Insanity, Automatism and Intoxication' in A Reed and M Bohlander (with N Wake and E Smith) (eds), *General Defences in Criminal Law—Domestic and Comparative Perspectives* (2014).

[384] (1979) 69 Cr App R 318, 323, CA. No foundation for automatism was laid.

[385] LCCP 127, para 2.33, Report (LC 143), para 6.44.LC 314, para 2.90.

9.5.1.2 Automatism causes intoxication

D having sustained concussion, drinks a bottle of vodka under the impression that it is water and does the allegedly criminal act, not knowing what he is doing because he is intoxicated. Since the intoxication is involuntary, both causes lead to an acquittal and D must be acquitted.

9.5.1.3 Intoxication causes insanity

Beard settles that insanity caused by drink operates in the same manner as insanity arising from any other cause. If excessive drinking causes actual insanity, such as delirium tremens, then the M'Naghten Rules will be applied in exactly the same way as where insanity arises from any other causes: 'drunkenness is one thing and the diseases to which drunkenness leads are different things; and if a man by drunkenness brings on a state of disease which causes such a degree of madness, even for a time, which would have relieved him from responsibility if it had been caused in any other way, then he would not be criminally responsible.'[386]

It has already been seen[387] that there are serious difficulties in defining a 'disease of the mind' and the distinction between temporary insanity induced by drink and simple drunkenness is far from clear-cut. The distinction becomes important in the case of a person who does not know that his act is wrong because of excessive drinking. If he is suffering from temporary insanity he is entitled to a verdict of not guilty on the ground of insanity; but if he is merely drunk he should be convicted.[388]

9.5.1.4 Insanity causes intoxication or automatism

'Insanity' in the *M'Naghten* sense can strictly have no application here because it applies only in relation to a particular criminal act, whereas getting drunk or causing oneself concussion is probably not a criminal act at all and certainly not the criminal act with which we are concerned. However, D may not know the nature and quality of the act which causes the condition. The resulting intoxication is involuntary, so D should be acquitted. Insofar as automatism is caused by insanity, it is the result of an internal cause which looks as if the net result should be not guilty on the ground of insanity; but it would seem odd that, if D's insanity leads him to drink excessively, he should be acquitted absolutely whereas if it causes him to bang his head against a wall until he does not know what he is doing he should be subject to restraint. Policy may be best served by a verdict of not guilty on the ground of insanity in both cases.

9.5.1.5 Automatism causes insanity

Such cases will surely be rare, but, if one should arise, probably the answer should be as in the case where automatism and insanity are concurrent causes and for the same reason.[389]

9.5.2 Concurrent operation

9.5.2.1 Intoxication and automatism

The circumstances of non-insane automatism being pleaded where D's level of intoxication renders him an automaton are discussed earlier (p 329).

---

[386] *Davis* (1881) 14 Cox CC 563 at 564, per Stephen J approved by the House of Lords in *DPP v Beard* [1920] AC 479 at 501. For discussion, see P Handler, 'Intoxication and Criminal Responsibility in England, 1819–1920' (2013) 33 OJLS 243. See also *Coley* [2013] EWCA Crim 223, [15].

[387] See p 292.

[388] 'In a case of simple drunkenness the judge should not introduce the question whether the prisoner knew he was doing wrong—for it is a dangerous and confusing question'—per Lord Birkenhead in *DPP v Beard* [1920] AC 479 at 506. Note that in the Scottish case of *Finegan v Heywood* 2000 JC 444, (2000) The Times, 10 May, a defence of sleepwalking triggered by intoxication was treated as not being one of 'automatism'.

[389] See p 331.

9.5.2.2 Intoxication and insanity

D does not know what he is doing, partly because of a disease of the mind and partly because he is drunk. The choice is (or should be) between a verdict of not guilty on the ground of insanity and, in a crime not requiring specific intent, one of guilty. Two difficult cases cast doubt on this and illustrate the difficulty in dealing with combined causes in practice.

In *Burns*,[390] D was charged with indecent assault, a crime not requiring specific intent. He may not have been aware of what he was doing, partly because of brain damage and partly because of drink and drugs. It is unclear whether the drugs were prescribed to D.[391] The court accepted that if D did not know what he was doing, he was entitled to an absolute acquittal. If the only causes are alcohol and insanity it is difficult to see how this can be right, since neither of the concurrent causes entitled D to be absolutely acquitted. If the causes are alcohol, prescribed drugs and insanity the position is more complex. Since the crime is one of basic intent, it is arguable that the fact that D was taking non-dangerous drugs requires the prosecution to establish that D was not reckless in becoming aggressive and unpredictable.[392] Williams took the view that in such a case insanity was the correct verdict,[393] and analogy with *Beard* might suggest that this is the right verdict, but the House of Lords in *A-G for Northern Ireland v Gallagher*[394] thought otherwise, unless the alcohol caused some quite different type of disease, such as delirium tremens.[395]

9.5.2.3 Automatism and insanity

In *Roach*,[396] the Court of Appeal adopted a more pragmatic approach, focusing on which of the multiple concurrent causes of the lack of control was dominant. D was convicted of wounding with intent to cause grievous bodily harm having attacked V with a knife after a minor dispute. D claimed to have no knowledge or memory of the incident. D claimed that his voluntary intoxication by alcohol, coupled with his prescribed drugs might have had some causative effect on his latent mental illness being triggered leading to his lack of awareness. The expert evidence described a 'disease of the mind' and not surprisingly that was treated by the prosecution as the basis of a plea of insanity. Defence counsel argued that the 'disease of the mind' should lead to a defence of automatism, but the judge did not leave that defence to the jury.[397] The Court of Appeal allowed the appeal. It was accepted that automatism was sufficiently widely defined that if external factors were operative on an 'underlying condition which would not otherwise produce a state of automatism', then a defence of non-insane automatism ought to be left to the jury.[398] The court considered this to be a borderline case as identified in *Quick*, where the 'transitory effect caused by the application to the body of some external factor such as violence, drugs etc cannot fairly be said to be due to disease'. With respect, it is not clear that this is a faithful application of that principle. In *Quick*, the lack of control was due to hypoglycaemia, caused by taking insulin (an external event) on an underlying internal condition (diabetes). Is it true to say (as the Court of Appeal would) that the underlying condition in *Quick* would not otherwise have produced a state of automatism if the insulin had not been administered? Surely it would. D would have gone into a hyperglycaemic state if he had not taken the insulin. The state

---

[390] (1973) 58 Cr App R 364, [1975] Crim LR 155 and commentary.

[391] In early editions of this work, it was suggested that the combination of the causes was intoxication and insanity alone. Mackay, *Mental Condition Defences*, at 158 criticizes that narrow view of the facts.

[392] See Mackay, ibid, 159.

[393] TBCL, 681.   [394] [1963] AC 349, [1961] 3 All ER 299, p 327 (effect of drink on a psychopath).

[395] See p 554 for discussion of intoxication and the new diminished responsibility defence and *Dowds* [2012] EWCA Crim 281 in which the Court of Appeal held that acute intoxication is not a 'recognized medical condition' for the purposes of the defence.

[396] [2001] EWCA Crim 2698.   [397] At [17].   [398] At [28].

of automatism which would have resulted if the underlying condition had been left to its own devices would be hyperglycaemia, which is different from the state of automatism that resulted from the insulin—hypoglycaemia—but does that matter?

The court seems to accord precedence to the prescribed drugs rather than the internal cause and the voluntary intoxication. The lack of control seems to have been a combination of: (a) the 'psychogenic' personality (which would alone result in a special verdict); (b) prescribed drugs (which alone if taken as per the prescription would have resulted in acquittal); and (c) the voluntary intoxication (which on a specific intent charge such as this could have resulted in acquittal). It is submitted that the decision in *Roach* should be approached with considerable caution. It may be regarded as correctly decided on its facts since the judge gave confusing directions as to the relevant burdens of proof.[399]

9.6 Mistake

The rules relating to mistake are simply an application of the general principle that the prosecution must prove its case, including the mens rea or negligence which the definition of the crime requires and rebuttal of excuses raised. The so-called 'defence' is simply a denial that the prosecution has proved its case. Accordingly, only mistakes which relate to an issue which the prosecution have to prove will have any bearing on D's liability.

9.6.1 Mistakes as denials of mens rea

The 'landmark decision'[400] in *DPP v Morgan* endorsed by the House of Lords in *DPP v B*,[401] holds that D's mistake of fact will result in acquittal in all crimes of mens rea where it prevents D from possessing the relevant mens rea which the law requires for the crime with which he is charged. It is not a question of defence, but of denial of mens rea. As Lord Hailsham explains in *Morgan*:

Once one has accepted…that the prohibited act is [x], and that the guilty state of mind is an intention to commit [x], it seems to me to follow as a matter of inexorable logic that there is no room either for a defence of honest belief or mistake, or of a defence of honest and reasonable belief or mistake. Either the prosecution proves that the accused had the requisite intention, or it does not. In the former case it succeeds, and in the latter it fails.[402]

Historically, mistake had been treated as a special defence and there were many *dicta* by eminent judges that *only* reasonable mistakes would excuse.[403] Lord Lane CJ[404] and the House of Lords,[405] in the light of *Morgan*, doubted these pronouncements and the House in *B v DPP*[406] made it very clear that they are wrong.

---

[399] The Law Commission considers the effect of its proposals on insanity and automatism on intoxication and successive and concurrent causes in LCDP, pp 145–148.

[400] [1976] AC 182. It has been described by Professor Farmer as a 'curious form of landmark case'. See L Farmer, 'DPP v Morgan' in P Handler, H Mares and I Williams (eds), *Landmark Cases in Criminal Law* (2017).

[401] And subsequently by its ringing endorsement in *K* [2002] 1 AC 462 and *G* [2003] UKHL 50.

[402] Per Lord Hailsham at 214. For a powerful critique see J Horder, 'Cognition, Emotion and Criminal Culpability' (1990) 106 LQR 469.

[403] See, for historical accounts, E Keedy, 'Ignorance and Mistake in the Criminal Law' (1908) 22 Harv LR 75; Williams, CLGP, Ch 5; Hall, *General Principles*, Ch XI; G Williams, 'Homicide and the Supernatural' (1949) 65 LQR 491; C Howard, 'The Reasonableness of Mistake in the Criminal Law' (1961) 4 Univ QLJ 45.

[404] *Taaffe* [1983] 2 All ER 625, 628.

[405] *Westminster City Council v Croyalgrange Ltd* [1986] 2 All ER 353 at 399.

[406] See particularly Lord Nicholls at [2000] 1 All ER 836–839.

607

9.6.1.1 Evidence and proof

It should not be imagined that all D has to do is say 'I made a genuine mistake' to be acquitted. The reasonableness of his conduct will be important in evidential terms. Where the natural inference from D's conduct in the particular circumstances is that he intended or foresaw a particular result, the jury are very likely to convict him if he introduces no testimony that he did not in fact foresee; but the onus of proof remains throughout on the Crown and, technically, D does not bear even an evidential burden.[407] Although D's belief need not be reasonable to excuse him, as a matter of practice, the more unreasonable it is, the less likely the jury is to accept that it was genuinely held.

9.6.1.2 Mistakes in crimes of subjective mens rea

Where the law requires intention, knowledge, belief or subjective recklessness with respect to some element in the actus reus, a mistake, whether reasonable or not, which precludes that state of mind will excuse D. The fact that a genuine though unreasonable mistake will negative D's mens rea or provide an excuse stems from the courts' endorsement of subjectivism in mens rea. Obviously, if a particular crime requires D's mens rea as to the proscribed conduct, circumstance or result to be based on his subjective intentions or beliefs, and because of a mistake of fact the intentions or beliefs D holds do not relate to the proscribed conduct, circumstance or result, D cannot be liable. Thus, where D genuinely though unreasonably believes that the thing he is shooting at is a scarecrow and not a human, he will lack the mens rea for murder—an intention to kill or do grievous bodily harm *to a person in being*.

Many commentators have suggested that the wholesale application of the subjectivist principles in the context of mistake is too simplistic an approach.[408] For example, in the context of sexual offences and consent, the ease with which D can ascertain the consent of his partner and the gravity of the harm done if the sexual act is non-consensual suggest that D's mistakes as to consent should be assessed objectively. This is in fact what Parliament has required in the Sexual Offences Act 2003. Beyond sexual cases, it can be argued that where D's mistake is unreasonable, in the sense that 'holding it or acting on it in a particular situation displays an unreasonable lack of the kind of respect and concern for others that the law demands' it should not lead to acquittal.[409] However, the present law generally adopts the subjectivist stance as stated in *Morgan* and *DPP v B*. As Lord Nicholls observed in *B v DPP*, 'considered as a matter of principle, the honest belief approach must be preferable. By definition the mental element in crime is concerned with a subjective state of mind such as intent or belief.'[410]

9.6.1.3 Mistakes and crimes of negligence

Where the law requires only negligence in respect of an element of the actus reus, then only a *reasonable* mistake can afford a defence; for an unreasonable mistake, by definition, is one which a reasonable person would not make and is, therefore, a negligent one.[411] In cases

---

407 G Williams, 'The Evidential Burden' (1977) 127 NLJ 156 at 158. But there is an evidential burden on D to get a particular mistake before the jury. 'Mistake is a defence in the sense that it is raised as an issue by the accused. The Crown is rarely possessed of knowledge of the subjective factors which may have caused an accused to entertain a belief in a fallacious set of facts': *Pappajohn v R* (1980) 52 CCC (2d) 481 at 494, per Dickson J. The judge does not have to direct the jury in every case of murder: 'You must be satisfied that D did not believe V was a turkey'; but he must give such a direction if D has testified that, when he fired, he thought V was a turkey.

408 See Horder (1990) 106 LQR 469; Horder, APOCL, 237–240; R Tur, 'Subjectivism and Objectivism: Towards Synthesis' in S Shute, J Gardner and J Horder (eds), *Action and Value in Criminal Law* (1993) 213; P Alldridge, *Relocating Criminal Law* (2000) 88.

409 Duff, *Answering for Crime*, 294.

410 For criticism see J Horder, 'How Culpability Can and Cannot be Denied in Under-Age Sex Crimes' [2001] Crim LR 15, arguing that D's mistake should be relevant if it relates to his 'guiding moral reason'.

411 See Ch 4.

of gross negligence manslaughter, D's unreasonable mistake may excuse provided it is not regarded by the jury as a grossly unreasonable mistake. Parliament may, of course, specify in relation to any crime that only reasonable beliefs will excuse. An example of this is the Sexual Offences Act 2003 (see Ch 17).

9.6.1.4 Mistakes in crimes of strict liability

Where a crime is interpreted as imposing strict liability, then even a reasonable mistake as to that element of the actus reus for which liability is strict will not excuse. It is an oversimplification to say that mistakes are irrelevant in strict liability crimes since there are few such crimes in which every element of actus reus is regarded as strict.[412] Thus, in a sexual offence such as sexual assault on a child under 13 where liability as to the age of the victim is strict, D will still have to be proved to have *intentionally* touched V. Where he claims that because of a mistake he had not meant intentionally to touch a person, he will be denying mens rea, and an honest mistake will excuse. If he claims to have made a mistake about age, that is irrelevant because liability as to age is strict.

Bigamy: a special case?

On the explanation so far, the application of the principles of mistake would seem to be straightforward. However, there are skeletons lurking in the common law cupboard which suggest that in some cases D's mistake as to an element of actus reus must *always* be reasonable to provide an excuse. One particular problem relates to the cases on bigamy. In *Morgan*, the House of Lords showed no inclination to interfere with the line of authority[413] which asserted that D's mistaken belief in the death of his first spouse, or the dissolution or nullity of his first marriage, was a defence only where that mistake was reasonable. But in *B v DPP*, Lord Nicholls expressly disapproved of the requirement of reasonableness of belief in the leading bigamy case of *Tolson*.[414] It is submitted that a genuine though unreasonable belief ought now to be a sufficient excuse on a charge of bigamy.

In general terms the *Tolson* approach may be tolerable where we are concerned with so-called 'quasi-criminal', 'regulatory' or 'welfare' offences; but it should have no place in serious crimes—and, after *B v DPP*, *K* and *G* it seems less likely to do so, as discussed in Ch 5.

9.6.1.5 Identifying the relevant mistake

What the discussion on bigamy exposes is the broader problem in many crimes of identifying which elements of actus reus require a corresponding mens rea requirement. In many serious offences there will usually be a strong if not complete correspondence; that is, that elements of the actus reus will each have corresponding elements of mens rea to be proved. For example, in *Westminster City Council v Croyalgrange Ltd*,[415] Robert Goff LJ referred to 'the ordinary principle that, where it is required that an offence should have been knowingly committed, the requisite knowledge must embrace all the elements of the offence'. On orthodox subjective principles intention, knowledge, belief or recklessness is required as to all the elements of the actus reus unless that is excluded expressly or by implication; and the more serious the crime, the more reluctant should the court be to find an implied exclusion.[416]

---

[412] See SP Green, 'Six Senses of Strict Liability' in Simester, *Appraising Strict Liability*, Ch 1.

[413] *Tolson* (1889) 23 QBD 168, CCR; *King* [1964] 1 QB 285; *Gould* [1968] 2 QB 65. As the opinions in *Morgan* relating to defences have been reconsidered so too may the opinions regarding bigamy, if the matter ever arises. The House also accepted the requirement of reasonable grounds for believing the use of force to be necessary in self-defence, but see *Beckford* and *Williams*.

[414] (1889) 23 QB 168 CCR.   [415] [1986] 83 Cr App R 155, [1986] Crim LR 693.

[416] There are, admittedly, many exceptions to this principle. LCCP 195, *Criminal Liability in Regulatory Contexts* (2010) also contains discussion of the significance of this principle and of the hierarchy of mens rea, see the discussion in Ch 5.

9.6.1.6 Summary

The most logical approach to mistakes is, it is submitted: (a) to identify the relevant mistake D claims to have made; (b) identify to which element of the actus reus of the offence it relates; (c) ascertain what mens rea, if any, attaches to that element of the actus reus in dispute; (d) apply the relevant rule as stated in the previous paragraphs: if the mens rea element is subjective D is entitled to acquittal on a genuine mistake; if it is objective/negligence, D's mistake must be a reasonable one to lead to acquittal; if liability on that element of actus reus is strict, D's mistake is irrelevant.

9.6.2 Mistakes and defences

The House of Lords in *Morgan* also left untouched the traditional requirement that mistakes as to the elements of defences had to be reasonable if they were to operate to excuse the accused. *Morgan*, although a case on the mens rea for rape and for that purpose no longer good law, was a landmark case in relation to mistake generally, for which it remains an authority for offences with subjective elements. In *Beckford v R*, the Privy Council recognized this:

Looking back, *Morgan* can now be seen as a landmark decision in the development of the common law, returning the law to the path upon which it might have developed but for the inability of an accused to give evidence on his own behalf.[417]

Beckford v R is itself of great importance in that it takes the principle of *Morgan* even further than the majority of the House were, at that time, prepared to go. In *Morgan*, the plea was a simple denial of the prosecution's case relating to the elements of the offence. By charging rape, the prosecution alleged that D had intercourse with a woman who did not consent and that he either knew that she did not consent or was reckless (at that time subjective recklessness was the prescribed mens rea for rape) whether she did so. D denied that he knew or was reckless, as alleged.

   Where on the other hand D pleads a true defence, D admits the allegations made by the prosecution about actus reus and mens rea but asserts further facts which, in law, justify or excuse his action. Self-defence is an example. D admits that he intentionally killed or wounded V but asserts that he did so because V was making a deadly attack on him and this was the only way he could save his own life. It may transpire that D was mistaken. V was not in fact making a deadly attack. The courts, until the 1980s, were consistent in asserting that the defence failed if there were no reasonable grounds for his belief. The majority of the House of Lords in *Morgan* did not intend to interfere with defences. They were concerned with a mistake as to an element of the offence. *Beckford* related to a mistake as to an element of a defence. The Privy Council rejected any distinction. The Board followed *Morgan* and approved the ruling of Lord Lane CJ in *Gladstone Williams*.[418] Discussing the offence of assault, he said:

The mental element necessary to constitute guilt is the intent to apply unlawful force to the victim. We do not believe that the mental element can be substantiated by simply showing an intent to apply force and no more.[419]

If D believed, reasonably or not, in the existence of facts which would justify the force used in self-defence, he did not intend to use *unlawful* force. *Beckford* clearly applies to all

---

[417] [1987] 3 All ER 425 at 431.   [418] [1987] 3 All ER 411, 78 Cr App R 276, CA.
[419] The HRA 1998, Art 2 (right to life), was thought by some to set a more demanding standard than 'honest belief', see Ch 10. See now *Duggan* [2014] EWHC 3343 (Admin) and *Da Silva* (2016) 63 EHRR 12.

instances of private defence.[420] However, in duress, for example, the courts continue to state that D's belief in the alleged compelling facts must be based on reasonable grounds.[421] If, however, D is to be judged on the facts as he believed them to be when he sets up self-defence it is difficult to see why it is different in principle when he sets up duress. In both cases D is saying that, on the facts as he believed them to be, his act was not an offence. It is submitted that the principle of *Beckford* should be applicable to defences generally.

Since *Beckford*, *Albert v Lavin*[422] must be taken to be wrong in making a distinction in relation to assault between the definitional elements of an offence and the definitional elements of a defence. The same subjective test applies to both.

9.6.2.1 Summary

Whether the law recognizes the mistake made by D as to facts which if they existed would provide a valid defence, and whether in order to be recognized the mistake must be one of a reasonable or merely genuine nature, must be considered in the context of each defence (see the next chapter). Intoxicated mistake has been discussed previously (p 325).

The courts have adopted the subjective principle in some categories (eg self-defence),[423] but not others (eg duress).[424] Some commentators seek to distinguish the categories on the basis of whether the defence is one of a justificatory or excusatory kind, or whether the defence relates to a 'definitional element' of the offence. Since the law does not adopt such classifications, and they cannot be universally applied, it seems that these may confuse rather than illuminate matters.[425]

The correct approach to mistakes and defences is, it is submitted: (a) to identify the relevant mistake of fact the defendant claims to have made; (b) identify to which element of the defence it relates; (c) ascertain whether that element of the defence is one in which the courts have imposed an objective interpretation; (d) if the defence is one assessed objectively (eg the requirement of a reasonable belief in a threat of death or serious injury in duress) D will only be able to rely on the mistake if it is reasonable; if the element of the defence is subjective (eg the requirement that D believes in the need for force in private defence) he will be entitled to rely on the mistaken belief as to the facts even if unreasonable.

9.6.3 Irrelevant mistakes

A mistake which does not preclude mens rea (or negligence where that is in issue) is irrelevant and no defence. Suppose D believes he is smuggling a crate of Irish whiskey. In fact the crate contains Scotch whisky. Duty is, of course, chargeable on both. D believes he is importing a dutiable item and he is importing a dutiable item. The actus reus is the same whether the crate contains Irish or Scotch. He *knows*, because his belief and the facts coincide in this respect, that he is evading the duty chargeable on the goods in the crate. If D had believed the crate to contain only some non-dutiable item, for example foreign currency (even if he had mistakenly believed it was dutiable), he would have lacked the mens rea for the offence.[426]

---

[420] See Ch 10.   [421] *Hasan* [2005] UKHL 22, see Ch 10.   [422] [1982] AC 546, DC.

[423] *Williams* [1987] 3 All ER 441.   [424] *Graham* [1982] 1 All ER 801; *Hasan* [2005] UKHL 22.

[425] See TBCL, 138; Tur, 'Subjectivism and Objectivism: Towards Synthesis' in Shute, Gardner and Horder (eds), *Action and Value in Criminal Law*, 213.

[426] See commentary on *Taaffe* [1983] Crim LR 536 at 537, CA; affd [1984] AC 539. See *Forbes* [2001] UKHL 40 where D believed he was importing prohibited goods (adult pornography) and he was importing prohibited goods (child pornography). D evaded the prohibition on imports and intended to do so. See also *Matrix* [1997] 8 Arch News.

A much misunderstood case is that of *Taaffe*.[427] T imported 3.7 kilos of cannabis believing that he was importing large sums of money and that currency was subject to an import prohibition. The House of Lords upholding the decision of the Court of Appeal[428] concluded that an accused is to be judged upon the facts as he believed them to be. Taaffe held two mistaken states of mind. His mistake of fact was that he was importing currency when he was in fact importing cannabis. His mistake of law was that he thought currency was subject to a prohibition. T's belief as to the fact meant that he was not *knowingly* importing prohibited goods at all. If the jury accepted as genuine his mistaken belief as to the facts, there would be no knowing importation of prohibited goods. This is analogous to the example used earlier of D shooting the scarecrow. On that basis his mistaken belief negatived the mens rea. He could not be convicted of the substantive offence under s 170 of the Customs and Excise Management Act 1979.

T's mistaken belief as to the scope of criminal law is quite different. That belief could not, even if the jury accepted that he held it, have rendered him liable for importing the currency: there would be no criminal offence with which he could be charged either as a substantive offence under s 170 of the Customs and Excise Management Act 1979 or an attempt under s 1 of the Criminal Attempt Act 1981. The criminal law, even when inchoate forms of offending are involved, cannot extend that far: if D visits England and believes that adultery is an offence, he cannot be liable for any crime by committing adultery while here, nor for attempting to do so (see Ch 11).

The case of *Taaffe* provides for a defence only where D's belief is that he is importing goods of a particular description which, if it were true, would mean that as a matter of law he was not in fact importing goods which were subject to any prohibition. This should be contrasted with a second category of case of mistake: that in which D believes that he is importing or attempting to import prohibited goods, but in fact he is importing something not subject to a prohibition or restriction. This is illustrated by the decision in *Shivpuri* discussed at p 497. Shivpuri believed he was importing one type of prohibited goods when he was importing harmless material. The House of Lords concluded that there was no difficulty in convicting him of an attempt to import the prohibited goods. The case is, in one sense, the converse of *Taaffe*. Where D makes a mistake of fact that, if believed, would mean that he was not knowingly importing prohibited goods, he is to be acquitted: *Taaffe*. Where D makes a mistake of fact that, if believed, would mean that he was importing goods subject to a prohibition, he can be convicted of an attempt to import those goods.

9.6.4 Mistakes of law

If D makes a mistake by thinking that some form of conduct is criminal when it is not, he cannot be guilty of an offence—there is no offence with which he can be charged, as in the example of the tourist who believes adultery is a crime in England.[429] These are exceptional and unlikely ever to come to light. It does not apply where D refuses, however honestly, to accept the judgment of a court,[430] just as it would be hopeless for him to argue that he did not accept the validity of an Act of Parliament.

Suppose that X obtains goods from V by fraud and gives them to D, who knows all the facts. We have already seen that it will not avail D to say he does not know handling stolen goods is a crime. Equally, it is thought it will not avail him to say that he did not know that it is against the criminal law to obtain goods by fraud and that goods so obtained are 'stolen' for this purpose. 'Stolen' is a concept of the criminal, not the civil, law and ignorance of it is no defence.

---

[427] [1984] AC 539, HL.   [428] (1983) 77 Cr App R 82, CA.
[429] See DN Husak and A von Hirsch, 'Culpability in Mistake of Law' in Shute, Gardner and Horder (eds), *Action and Value in Criminal Law*.
[430] ibid.

On the other hand, the 'leave' granted to a visitor to remain in the UK looks like a civil law concept, but the House of Lords has held that a mistake of law is no answer to a charge of knowingly remaining without leave.[431]

9.6.4.1 Mistake of criminal law

If D mistakenly believes that conduct which is a crime in England is not criminal he will, generally, have no defence.[432] This is because *usually* knowledge that the act is forbidden by law is no part of mens rea.[433] Where, for example, D, a visitor to England believes that his conduct is lawful because it does not constitute a crime in his homeland,[434] he will have no defence if that conduct is an offence in England. The harshness of the rule is tempered somewhat by the fact that most serious criminal offences are also well recognized as moral 'wrongs'. However, it is no defence even where the crime is not one commonly known to be criminal. Thus, ignorance of any of the thousands of regulatory offences is no defence. This position is ameliorated only slightly by s 3(2) of the Statutory Instruments Act 1946 providing a defence for D charged with an offence created by Statutory Instrument to prove that, at the time of the offence, the instrument had not been published nor reasonable steps taken to bring its contents to the notice of the public or the accused.[435] By analogy, where an offence in English law involves an issue of foreign law, it is arguable that D should only be liable if it is reasonable for him to discover that law.[436] Andrew Ashworth has advanced a powerful argument against the present position. He suggests that the rule is based on shaky foundations, examines many circumstances in which the rule gives rise to unfairness and identifies government obligations to provide clearer criminal law.[437]

The arguments that every citizen should have access to a clear statement of the law is a constitutional principle supported by Art 7 of the ECHR. As Lord Bingham observed in *Rimmington*,[438] 'Article 7 sustains [the] contention that a criminal offence must be clearly defined in law, and represents the operation of "the principle of legal certainty".'[439] The principle enables each community to regulate itself:

with reference to the norms prevailing in the society in which they live. That generally entails *that the law must be adequately accessible—an individual must have an indication of the legal rules applicable in a given case—and he must be able to foresee the consequences of his actions, in particular to be able to avoid incurring the sanction of the criminal law.*[440]

---

[431] *Grant v Borg* [1982] 1 WLR 638.   [432] See 127.

[433] cf the comments of Lord Woolf in the appeal in the Privy Council in the Pitcairn case discussed later in this section: *Christian v The Queen* [2006] UKPC 47. His lordship stated that '[A]s in this case the appellants suffered no prejudice in view of their state of knowledge an argument based on abuse of process would not be established. It may be the case that the argument under this head could be freestanding and not based on abuse of process. However if this be so the need for prejudice would still be a requirement. The great majority of criminal offences require mens rea. *If you do not know and are not put on notice that the conduct with which you are charged was criminal at the time you are alleged to have committed the offence, it can be the case that you do not have the necessary criminal intent*' (emphasis added). For discussion, see D Oliver (ed), *Justice, Legality and the Rule of Law: Lessons from the Pitcairn Prosecutions* (2009) in which it is argued that the Crown lacked jurisdiction to bring the prosecutions and that they amounted to an abuse of process.

[434] See *Esop* (1836) 7 C & P 456.

[435] cf A Ashworth, 'Excusable Mistake of Law' [1974] Crim LR 652 and p 130. See for a comparison with some other European States taking a less strict approach, J Blomsa, *Mens Rea and Defences in European Criminal Law* (2012) 466.

[436] See eg the argument in relation to sex tourism where D in England might mistakenly believe that to have sex with a 15-year-old in the host country is not criminal in that country. See Alldridge, *Relocating Criminal Law*, 149, discussing the Sexual Offences (Conspiracy and Incitement) Act 1996.

[437] See p 127.   [438] [2005] UKHL 63.

[439] See eg *Brumarescu v Romania* (2001) 33 EHRR 35 at para 61 and *Kokkinakis v Greece* (1993) 17 EHRR 397 at para 52.

[440] *SW v UK; CR v UK* (1995) 21 EHRR 363 (emphasis added).

The ease with which a defendant could discover the law, and whether he might rely on a mistake as to the scope of the law where it was not readily discoverable, were in issue in the prosecution of a number of men in the Pitcairn Islands for sexual abuse of young women on the islands. In *Christian & others v The Queen (The Pitcairn Islands)*,[441] the defendants argued that the case should have been stayed as an abuse of process on the grounds, *inter alia*, that they did not know that English law applied and that they had no access on their remote Pacific island to English legal texts. Lord Woolf[442] accepted that:

it is a requirement of almost every modern system of criminal law, that persons who are intended to be bound by a criminal statute must first be given either actual or at least constructive notice of what the law requires. This is a requirement of the rule of law, which in relation to the criminal law reflects the need for legal certainty.

He had no difficulty with the principle of such an argument but found it had no application on the facts: it was clear that DD, although probably unaware of the terms of the Sexual Offences Act or even that there was legislation of that name or the sentences that could be imposed for those offences, were aware that their conduct was contrary to the criminal law. The moral wrong of rape and sexual abuse were so obvious that the claim of a lack of awareness of specific offences was irrelevant. Similarly, the Privy Council rejected the argument that the defendants could not have discovered the law had they tried[443] because the precise terms of the Sexual Offences Act had not been published on the island. This was because the fact that there were offences such as rape and possibly indecent assault was generally known because they had to be dealt with by the Pitcairn Supreme Court, requiring as they did greater punishment than was otherwise possible.

Interestingly, Lord Woolf acknowledged that:

The sheer volume of the law in England, much of which would be inapplicable…, creates real problems of access even to lawyers unless they are experts in the particular field of law in question. The criminal law can only operate…if the *onus is firmly placed on a person*, who is or ought to be on notice that conduct he is intending to embark on may contravene the criminal law, to take the action that is open to him to find out what are the provisions of that law.[444]

This places the emphasis on the duty of the citizen to ascertain the law rather than on the State to bring the law to every citizen's attention.[445]

9.6.4.2 Erroneous advice given to D

Where D has relied on erroneous advice provided by the relevant State authority he may in some circumstances be successful in an application to stay proceedings as an abuse of process.[446]

---

[441] [2006] UKPC 47. See H Power, 'Pitcairn Island' [2007] Crim LR 609.   [442] At [40].

[443] cf Lord Hope at [83] who had he not concluded that they were aware of the wrongs which were criminal at common law, would have granted a stay.

[444] At [44], emphasis added.

[445] See for discussion of some European States' approaches, J Blomsa, *Mens Rea and Defences in European Criminal Law* (2012) 473.

[446] See A Ashworth, 'Testing Fidelity to Legal Values' (2000) 63 MLR 633, 635–642 identifying the importance of Art 7 of the ECHR. One of the strongest examples is *Postermobile v LBC* (1997) 8 Dec, unreported, DC and the Editorial at [1998] Crim LR 435 (D receiving erroneous information from planning agency). See also G Williams, 'The Draft Code and Relevance of Official Statements' (1989) 9 LS 177. See for discussion of some European States' approaches, J Blomsa, *Mens Rea and Defences in European Criminal Law* (2012) 471.

9.6.5 Mistake of fact or law?

Identifying whether a mistake allegedly made by D is one of criminal law or fact is not always easy. For example, if D mistakenly believes that the person grabbing hold of him is a thug about to rob him and he resists, he has made a mistake of fact and cannot be guilty of assaulting with intent to resist arrest by what was in fact a police officer. Where, however, D is aware that the person who is grabbing him is a police officer, but mistakenly believes that the officer has no power of arrest on the facts as they exist, D has made a mistake of criminal law. But what of D who makes a mistake as to antecedent facts which, if they were as he believed them to be, would indeed preclude the officer's power of arrest?[447]

Where the mens rea involves some legal concept[448] or the absence of a claim of right then mistake may negative mens rea and be a defence.

An honest though unreasonable mistake as to the *civil* law may lead to acquittal where it prevents D from holding the mens rea of the criminal offence. For example, in *Smith (David)*,[449] D damaged property in his rented flat believing it was his own property—he made a mistake as to the ownership of the property. His conviction for criminal damage was quashed since D had no intent to damage property *belonging to another*. His mistake as to ownership prevented him having the relevant mens rea. As James LJ explained:

Applying the ordinary principles of *mens rea*, the intention and recklessness and the absence of lawful excuse required to constitute the offence have reference to property belonging to another. It follows that in our judgment no offence is committed under this section if a person destroys or causes damage to property belonging to another if he does so in the honest though mistaken belief that the property is his own, and provided that the belief is honestly held it is irrelevant to consider whether or not it is a justifiable belief.[450]

---

[447] See *Lee* [2001] Cr App R 293.   [448] See 1076.   [449] [1974] QB 354.
[450] ibid, 360.

10

General defences

This chapter deals with defences in the broader sense, not just those focused on the mental condition of the accused. In the cases in this chapter, D will usually have performed the actus reus with the appropriate mens rea, but despite both these elements of the offence being proved by the Crown, the question arises whether D is entitled to an acquittal owing to some justifying, excusing or exempting circumstance or condition. There are special or partial defences which apply to particular crimes (eg loss of self-control and diminished responsibility in murder) which are dealt with separately although where appropriate their interrelationship is considered. Some reference back to the general discussion of defences at the beginning of Ch 9 may be necessary, particularly to the introductory comments on the theoretical underpinnings of defences and the theories of justifications and excuse.

10.1 Infancy

Infants or, in more modern terminology, minors, are persons under 18 years of age.[1] Although the civil law places restrictions on certain activities (eg writing a will) the criminal law imposes no such limitations on their ability to commit crimes, for, as Kenny put it, 'a child knows right from wrong long before he knows how to make a prudent speculation or a wise will'.[2] At common law the criminal law applied different rules to minors in three categories, but under the present law only two categories remain.

10.1.1 Children under 10 years

At common law a child was entirely exempt from criminal responsibility until the day before his seventh birthday.[3] By statute, criminal responsibility now begins on the child's tenth birthday.[4] The common law rule was stated as a conclusive presumption that the child is *doli incapax*, and the statute uses the same language: 'It shall be conclusively presumed that no child under the age of ten years can be guilty of any offence.' Even though there may be the clearest evidence that the child caused an actus reus with mens rea, he cannot be convicted

---

[1] See H Keating, 'The Responsibility of Children in the Criminal Law' (2007) 19 CFLQ 183, and 'Reckless Children' [2007] Crim LR 546 and for an historical account see G Williams, 'The Criminal Responsibility of Children' [1954] Crim LR 493. Broader issues of youth justice are discussed in C Ball, 'Youth Justice: Half A Century of Responses to Youth Offending' [2004] Crim LR 167; J Fionda, *Devils and Angels: Youth, Policy and Crime* (2005); L Hoyano and C Keenan, *Child Abuse: Law and Policy* (2007).

[2] Kenny, *Outlines*, 80.

[3] A person attains a particular age at the commencement of the relevant anniversary of the date of his birth: Family Law Reform Act 1969, s 9(1).

[4] Children and Young Persons Act 1933, s 50, as amended by the Children and Young Persons Act 1963, s 16, which raised the age from eight. The Ingleby Committee had recommended that the age be raised to 12. Cmnd 1911 (1960). That is the age to be adopted in Scotland.

once it appears that he had not, at the time he did the act, attained the age of ten. This is not a mere procedural bar; no crime is committed by the child with the result that the one who instigated him to do the act is a principal and not a secondary party.[5] And where a husband and wife were charged with handling stolen goods in the form of a child's tricycle, knowing it to have been taken by their seven-year-old son, it was held that they must be acquitted on the ground that, since the child being only seven could not steal, the tricycle was not stolen.[6] Ten is a comparatively low age for the beginning of criminal responsibility, it is certainly much lower than many other European States; but, as the Ingleby Committee pointed out:[7]

In many countries the 'age of criminal responsibility' is used to signify the age at which a person becomes liable to the 'ordinary' or 'full' penalties of the law. In this sense, the age of criminal responsibility in England is difficult to state: it is certainly much higher than [ten].[8]

Numerous organizations including the UN Committee on the Rights of the Child (2002) and the European Committee on Social Rights (2005), have urged reform of English law. There is, of course, no international agreement on what the age should be.[9] As the Beijing Rules, adopted by the United Nations General Assembly in 1985 observe in their commentary on the United Nations Standard Minimum Rules for the Administration of Juvenile Justice (Beijing Rules), Art 4(1):[10]

The minimum age of criminal responsibility differs widely owing to history and culture. The modern approach would be to consider whether a child can live up to the moral and psychological components of criminal responsibility; that is, whether a child, by virtue of her or his individual discernment and understanding, can be held responsible for essentially antisocial behaviour. If the age of criminal responsibility is fixed too low or if there is no lower age limit at all, the notion of criminal responsibility would become meaningless.

10.1.2 Children aged 10 and above

At common law, there was a *rebuttable* presumption that a child aged not less than ten but under 14 years ('a young person') was *doli incapax*: incapable of committing crime. The presumption was rebutted only if the prosecution proved beyond reasonable doubt, not only that the child caused an actus reus with mens rea, but also that he knew that the particular act was not merely naughty or mischievous, but 'seriously wrong'. If there was no evidence of such knowledge, other than that implicit in the act itself, the child had no case to answer. In *C v DPP*,[11] the Divisional Court held that this ancient rule of the common law was outdated and no longer law; but the House of Lords reversed this, ruling that it was not open to the courts so to hold. That decision was followed by a series of acquittals which caused disquiet.

---

[5] See p 182.   [6] *Walters v Lunt* [1951] 2 All ER 645; and cf *Marsh v Loader* (1863) 14 CBNS 535.

[7] Cmnd 1191, at 30.

[8] The age then was eight. See n 4.

[9] See generally D Cipriani, *Children's Rights and the Minimum Age of Criminal Responsibility: A Global Perspective* (2009). The age in Scotland has now increased to 12—Criminal Justice and Licensing (Scotland) Act 2010, s 52.

[10] See further the helpful discussion in Emmerson, Ashworth and Macdonald, HR&CJ, paras 11.01–11.05 concluding that it is 'difficult to see how the [current] age of criminal responsibility is in the child's best interests'. See also J Gillen, 'Age of Criminal Responsibility: The Frontier Between Crime and Justice' [2007] Int Fam LJ 7 and A Ashworth, 'Child Defendants and the Doctrines of the Criminal Law' in J Chalmers, L Farmer and F Leverick (eds), *Essays in Criminal Law in Honour of Sir Gerald Gordon* (2010).

[11] [1996] AC 1, HL. See the 8th edition of this book for detail, at p 195.

In the Crime and Disorder Act 1998, Parliament responded by abolishing the rebuttable presumption.[12] This was intended to put children aged ten and above on an equal footing with adults, so far as liability (but not sentencing or mode of trial and procedure) is concerned. The Act is not well drafted. Section 34 of the Crime and Disorder Act 1998 provides:

> The rebuttable presumption of criminal law that a child aged 10 or over is incapable of committing an offence is abolished.

Despite cogent arguments by Professor Walker that the section[13] left it open to a child under 14 to introduce evidence that he did not know that what he did was seriously wrong, the House of Lords finally decided the defence rather than the mere presumption had been abolished. In *T*,[14] the House of Lords concluded that there was no authority for the existence of the defence separate from the presumption and that Parliament's intention was clearly to abolish the concept of *doli incapax* as having any effect in law. There is no separate defence of *doli incapax* after s 34 of the Crime and Disorder Act 1998.[15] This is a disappointing though predictable outcome. The statute is clear that it is abolishing the presumption. The House of Lords' interpretation of the parliamentary debates is strained to achieve the pragmatic result desired.[16]

In the last twenty years, the law governing the procedure for trials of child defendants has developed[17] somewhat and this may assist some children. It has been recognized explicitly that a child defendant must be able to participate effectively in proceedings.[18] One of the criteria for determining whether a child has a sufficient understanding to be tried is whether he understands the seriousness of the consequences of his actions. In some cases, the child's lack of understanding of the wrongness of his conduct will be so great that it might preclude a trial.[19] In its Discussion Paper on insanity and automatism, the Law Commission observed that it is a matter of medical fact that children are neurologically immature as compared with adults.[20] Evidence suggests that developmental delay can be relevant to the question of capacity and criminal responsibility and that it impacts upon a number of specific competencies.[21]

---

[12] Crime and Disorder Act 1998, s 34. See in particular: N Walker, 'The End of an Old Song' (1999) 149 NLJ 64; L Gelsthorpe and A Morris, 'Much Ado about Nothing—A Critical Comment on Key Provisions Relating to Children in the Crime and Disorder Act 1998' (1999) 11 CFLQ 209; J Fionda, 'New Labour, Old Hat: Youth Justice and the Crime and Disorder Act 1998' [1999] Crim LR 36; C Webb, 'Irrational Presumptions of Rationality and Comprehension' [1998] 3 Web JCLI.

[13] See Walker (1999) 149 NLJ 64.

[14] *T* [2009] UKHL 20, [2009] 1 AC 1310, HL. For critical comment see F Bennion, '*Mens Rea* and Defendants Below the Age of Discretion' [2009] Crim LR 757.

[15] T, aged 12 at the time of offending, pleaded guilty to 12 counts of causing or inciting a child under 13 to engage in sexual activity. Depending on the particular activity, this may be the sort of behaviour where a child might know that what he is doing is wrong or naughty, without seeing it as being seriously wrong resulting in his being on the sexual offender's 'register'.

[16] It has been argued that a new defence should be available for children up to the age of 14 that places emphasis on their relative lack of autonomy. See C Elliott, 'Criminal Responsibility and Children: A New Defence Required to Acknowledge the Absence of Capacity and Choice' (2011) 75 J Crim L 289.

[17] See references at n 1.   [18] *T & V v UK* (2000) 30 EHRR 121.

[19] Where there is evidence that D cannot understand, at the judge's discretion the process should switch to determining as a matter of fact whether the child performed the act alleged. There may be a sufficient delay between the act and the trial for D to have matured sufficiently to now understand the seriousness. See LCCP 197, *Unfitness to Plead* (2010); and LC 364, *Unfitness to Plead* (2016).

[20] Ch 9.

[21] P Kambam and C Thompson, 'The Development of Decision-Making Capacities in Children and Adolescents: Psychological and Neurological Perspectives and Their Implications for Juvenile Defendants' (2009) 27 Behavioral Sciences and the Law 173.

The *presumption* of *doli incapax* still poses problems in prosecutions for historic sexual abuse where the conduct alleged to have been carried out by the defendant occurred when he was between the ages of 10 and 14.[22]

10.2 Duress

10.2.1 Duress by threats and circumstances

For centuries the law has recognized a defence of duress by threats.[23] The typical case is where D is told, 'Do this [an act which would be a crime if there were no defence of duress]—or you will be killed', and, fearing for his life, D does the required act. Relatively recently, the law has recognized another form of duress—duress of circumstances. Again, D does the act alleged to constitute the crime, feeling compelled to do so out of fear, but this time no human being is demanding that he do it.[24] D does it because he reasonably believes himself to be threatened with death or serious injury and that his only reasonable way of escaping the threat is to perform the conduct element of the offence. The defences are clearly closely related. For example, D is told he will be killed unless he acts as a getaway driver for a robbery. The compulsion on D to do the act is exactly the same whether the threat comes from someone demanding that he do it, or from an aggressor, or other circumstances. His moral culpability, or lack of it, seems exactly the same.[25] The discussion of the relationship of duress, duress of circumstances and necessity is postponed until each has been examined in detail (p 378).

The law relating to duress by threats is now well developed. Duress of circumstances is still relatively new, but it has developed by analogy to duress by threats so that there is a ready-made set of principles to govern it. By a strange coincidence, all the early cases on duress of circumstances concerned road traffic offences but there is no reason why it should be limited to such offences. *Pommell*,[26] *Safi*,[27] *Shayler*[28] and a host of other cases decide that it has the same range and is governed by the same principles as duress by threats. The result is that either form of duress is a general defence, except that neither applies to some forms of treason, or to murder or attempted murder, whether the defendant is a principal or a secondary party. There are only a few differences between the two defences in application.

10.2.1.1 Duress and voluntariness

It has often been said that the duress must be such that D's act is not 'voluntary'.[29] We are not, however, concerned here with the case where a person is compelled by physical force to

---

[22] *Andrew N* [2004] EWCA Crim 1236; *H* [2010] EWCA Crim 312; *PF* [2017] EWCA Crim 983 noting that independent evidence of naughtiness beyond the mere fact of the commission of the relevant acts was required.

[23] Although somewhat dated, there is a valuable discussion of the defences in LCCP 122, *Legislating the Criminal Code: Offences Against the Person and General Principles* (1992); LCCP 218, *Legislating the Criminal Code: Offences Against the Person and General Principles* (1993); LCCP 177, *A New Homicide Act for England?* (2005) Ch 7; LC 304, *Murder Manslaughter and Infanticide* (2007) Ch 6. On the Commission's proposals, see A Ashworth, 'Principles, Pragmatism and the Law Commission Recommendations on Homicide Reform' [2007] Crim LR 333 at 340. The Law Reform Commission of Ireland has also produced a valuable analysis in its Consultation Paper, *Duress and Necessity* (2006): www.lawreform.ie; see also the review in the Victorian Law Reform Commission Report, *Defences to Homicide* (2006): www.lawreform.vic.gov.au.

[24] *Cole* [1994] Crim LR 582; *Ali* [1995] Crim LR 303.

[25] See the judicial affirmation that the defences are this closely linked: *Safi* [2003] EWCA Crim 1809, [2003] Crim LR 721; *Shayler* [2001] EWCA Crim 1977, [2001] Crim LR 986 but note p 378 later in this book.

[26] [1995] 2 Cr App R 607. The case was subsequently analysed as one of necessity rather than duress of circumstances because there is no immediate threat of death to D: see *Quayle* [2005] EWCA Crim 1415, [2006] Crim LR 148.

[27] [2003] EWCA Crim 1809, [2003] Crim LR 721.   [28] [2001] EWCA Crim 1977, [2001] Crim LR 986.

[29] See M Wasik, 'Duress and Criminal Responsibility' [1977] Crim LR 453; A Norrie, *Crime, Reason and History* (3rd edn, 2014) 218–229; ATH Smith, 'On *Actus Reus* and *Mens Rea*' in *Reshaping the Criminal Law*, 104–106.

619

go through the motions of an actus reus without any choice on his part. In such cases he will almost invariably[30] be guilty of no offence on the fundamental ground that he did no act.

If there be an actual forcing of a man, as if A by force takes the arm of B and the weapon in his hand and therewith stabs C whereof he dies, this is murder in A but B is not guilty.[31]

Nor are we concerned with the kind of involuntariness which arises from automatism where D is unable to control the movement of his body. When D pleads duress (or necessity) he admits that he was able to control his actions and chose to do the act with which he is charged, but denies responsibility for doing so.[32] He may say, 'I had no choice' but that is not strictly true.[33] The alternative to committing the crime may have been so exceedingly unattractive that no reasonable person would have chosen it; but there was a choice. It is clear that the courts recognize this because for some crimes, no matter how serious the threat D faced, he cannot rely on duress. If D is threatened with harm or even death unless he kills V, he should, according to the English courts, withstand the pressure and suffer death himself. He will not have a defence to murder if he kills: his acts were voluntary.

In Canada, the Supreme Court (holding that necessity may be an excuse, but not a justification) described the act of a person under duress as '*morally* involuntary', the 'involuntariness' being 'measured on the basis of society's expectation of appropriate and normal resistance to pressure'.[34] This seems to mean only that even a person of goodwill and reasonable fortitude might have chosen to do the 'criminal' act. Duress in English law cannot be said to be a form of involuntariness. A person who kills when acting under duress cannot rely on that plea as a defence. If he succeeded only in wounding V he could rely on duress. Surely D's act is voluntary in both cases. It would be illogical to say his act was involuntary if he only succeeded in wounding V.[35] D intends to do the act which, but for the duress, would be a crime.

It has been recognized by the Court of Appeal and the House of Lords that the defence is not a denial of mens rea, but a true defence operating despite the existence of the actus reus and mens rea of the offence.[36]

In short, duress is a defence because 'threats of immediate death or serious personal violence so great as to overbear the ordinary powers of human resistance should be accepted as a justification for acts which would otherwise be criminal'.[37]

10.2.1.2 The onus of proof

The onus of disproving duress is on the Crown.[38] If no facts from which duress might reasonably be inferred appear in the prosecution's case, then D has the 'evidential burden' of

---

[30] cf *Larsonneur*, p 43.   [31] Hale, II PC, 534.

[32] In *Southward* [2012] EWCA Crim 2779 D sought to plead duress yet at the same time deny he had committed the offence. The trial judge refused to leave duress to the jury on the basis that it would be very confusing. The Court of Appeal rightly agreed with this assessment.

[33] *Hasan* [2005] UKHL 22, per Baroness Hale at [73]. See also Duff, *Answering for Crime*, 287.

[34] *Perka* (1984) 13 DLR (4th) 1.

[35] *Howe* [1987] AC 417, HL, per Lord Hailsham LC, citing Lords Kilbrandon and Edmund-Davies in *DPP for Northern Ireland v Lynch* [1975] AC 653 at 703 and 709–710.

[36] *Fisher* [2004] EWCA Crim 1190, [2004] Crim LR 938; see also *Hasan* [2005] UKHL 22 per Lord Bingham at [18].

[37] *A-G v Whelan* [1934] IR 518, per Murnaghan J (Irish CCA). The judge probably did not have in mind any distinction between justification and excuse. If there is a material distinction, duress seems to be an excuse. Cf RA Duff, 'Rule Violations and Wrongdoing' in Shute and Simester, *Criminal Law Theory*, 63.

[38] *Hasan* [2005] UKHL 22, [37]; *Gill* [1963] 1 WLR 841, CCA; *Giaquento* [2001] EWCA Crim 2696; *Bianco* [2001] EWCA Crim 2156, endorsed in *Bloomfield* [2007] EWCA Crim 1873 and *Brandford* [2016] EWCA Crim 1794, [2017] Crim LR 554.

laying a foundation for the defence by introducing evidence of such facts.[39] There is considerable judicial scepticism regarding defences of duress and the defendant's burden to get the defence on its feet will not always be straightforward.[40] Indeed, it has been confirmed that the judge is only obliged to leave the issue to the jury if there is evidence of facts which if believed could cause a reasonable jury properly directed to accept the defence. In *Bianco*, Laws LJ stated that, 'if the case is one where no reasonable jury properly directed as to the law could fail to find the defence disproved, no legitimate purpose is served by leaving it to the jury.'[41] In *Batchelor*,[42] Elias LJ affirmed that there could be no purpose leaving a verdict to the jury that they, on considering the evidence, could not properly reach. His lordship stated that 'evidence' in this context means evidence that would, in principle, be sufficient to justify a jury concluding that the defence is established.[43] These sentiments were reaffirmed in unequivocal terms by the Court of Appeal in *Brandford*, although the court did state that the power to withdraw the defence should be exercised with caution.[44] There is a particular judicial anxiety when the defence is raised late in the trial process.

The Law Commission's recommendation in relation to the availability of the duress defence in murder is to reverse the burden, so that the accused would be obliged to prove on the balance of probabilities that the elements of the defence were made out.[45] This is a controversial approach.[46] It is a clear compromise, with the Commission being keen to see the defence of duress available to murder (which at present it is not), but prepared to reverse the burden to deter spurious and unmeritorious defences being run. The Commission acknowledges the difficulty the Crown may face in duress cases where D is often the sole source of evidence supporting the defence.[47]

10.2.1.3 The elements of the defence

Lord Bingham, in the leading modern authority from the House of Lords, *Hasan*, summarized the elements of the defence:[48]

(1) D reasonably believes there is a threat of death or serious injury;

(2) that threat must have been made to D or his immediate family or someone close to him or, someone for whom D would reasonably regard himself as responsible;

(3) D's perception of the threat and his conduct in response are to be assessed objectively—his belief that he is under such a threat must be reasonable and his decision to commit the crime in response must be reasonable;

(4) the conduct it is sought to excuse must have been directly caused by the threats D relies on;

---

[39] Radically, the Law Commission recommended reversing the burden of proof on this defence, LC 218 (1993) para 33.16. It is doubtful whether this would be compatible with the ECHR (Art 6(2)). See the doubts expressed by Lord Bingham in *Hasan* at [20]. The Law Commission has subsequently recommended that the burden be reversed should the defence become available to a charge of murder: LC 304, Ch 6.

[40] See *Hasan* at [20].   [41] [2001] EWCA Crim 2516, [15].   [42] [2013] EWCA Crim 2638.

[43] The Court of Appeal recognized in *Hammond* [2013] EWCA Crim 2709 that there is a fine line between the judge making a ruling as to the law and coming to an impermissible resolution of a case on the facts. Moses LJ stated that this problem is especially acute when duress is pleaded but that it should not deter judges from taking a robust and reasoned approach where fanciful cases of duress are raised.

[44] [2016] EWCA Crim 1794, [2017] Crim LR 554.   [45] LC 304, para 6.115.

[46] For analysis of the potential ECHR implications, see LC 304, paras 6.116 et seq.

[47] cf LCCP 177, para 7.66 where it is suggested that the days when it was easy to raise and difficult to rebut are 'long gone'!

[48] *Hasan* [2005] UKHL 22, [21]. On the decision see, *inter alia*, D Ibbetson (2005) 64 CLJ 530; R Ryan and D Ryan (2005) 56 NILQ 421.

(5) there must have been no evasive action D could reasonably take;

(6) D cannot rely on threats to which he has voluntarily laid himself open;

(7) the defence is unavailable to murder, attempted murder or treason.

(1) Threat of death or serious injury

The type of qualifying threat or danger

As a matter of policy the law places strict limits on the type of threat sufficient to trigger the defence. It is not simply a question of balancing in each case the gravity of the threat D faced against the gravity of the offence D committed in response. The threats must reach a threshold before the defence is triggered. That threshold is set at a deliberately high level. The only threat or danger which will found a defence in either type of duress is one of death or serious[49] personal injury.[50]

The House of Lords in *Hasan*, Lord Lane CJ in *Graham*[51] and Woolf LJ in *Conway*,[52] all required a threat of death or serious personal injury. This is in keeping with most modern codes in other jurisdictions.[53]

The Court of Appeal confirmed in *Brandford* that mere pressure based on the exploitation of a relationship but without a relevant threat of death or really serious harm will not be sufficient to enable D to plead duress.[54] Pressure of this nature is not entirely irrelevant, however, as the court observed that it may operate in a cumulative manner alongside a threat of death or really serious harm.

It has been held that serious psychiatric injury can be grievous bodily harm for the purposes of the OAPA 1861 and it is probable that a threat to cause such injury could amount to duress.[55] A threat to make a person a nervous wreck could be just as terrifying as a threat to cause serious physical injury. The high threshold imposed by the common law stands in contrast to the statutory offence contained in s 45 of the Modern Slavery Act 2015.[56] The statutory defence, which can only be pleaded by defendants who are victims of slavery or relevant exploitation, does not require a threat of death or really serious harm, but requires D to have been compelled to commit the criminal offence in question.[57] This compulsion must be attributable to slavery or relevant exploitation.[58]

This threshold of serious injury in duress is narrowly construed by the courts.[59] In some circumstances the high threshold can lead to harsh results. For example, in *Joseph*, a case

---

[49] In *Aikens* [2003] EWCA Crim 1573, it was doubted that a threat to punch V in the face would suffice.

[50] *Radford* [2004] EWCA Crim 2878. Cf the Criminal Damage Act 1971, s 5(2)(b).

[51] [1982] 1 WLR 294, [1982] Crim LR 365.   [52] [1989] QB 290, [1989] Crim LR 74.

[53] LC 218, para 29.1: 'the overwhelming tendency of the authorities as of modern codes, is to limit the defence to cases where death or serious injury is threatened . . . Consultation strongly supported that limitation on the defence of duress, which is imposed by clause 25(2)(a) of the Criminal Law Bill.'

[54] [2016] EWCA Crim 1794, [2017] Crim LR 554.   [55] *Baker and Wilkins* [1997] Crim LR 497.

[56] For detailed analysis, see K Laird, 'Evaluating the Relationship Between Section 45 of the Modern Slavery Act 2015 and the Defence of Duress: An Opportunity Missed?' [2016] Crim LR 395.

[57] For an interesting analysis of how the concept of compulsion is relevant to English criminal law, see S Edwards, 'Coercion and Compulsion—Re-Imagining Crimes and Defences' [2016] Crim LR 876.

[58] If D is under 18, then by virtue of s 45(4)(b) it suffices if he commits the offence as a direct consequence of being, or having been, a victim of slavery or relevant exploitation.

[59] In *Hammond* [2013] EWCA Crim 2709, D's plea of duress to the charge of breaking prison based on D's fears of being touched sexually by another inmate was rejected. The sexual advances were 'miles away' from any threat to kill or cause really serious injury; the outcome could have been different had D feared he would be raped by the other inmate. The Court of Appeal did not cite the earlier case of *A (RJ)* [2012] EWCA Crim 434, [2013] Crim LR 240 in which Lord Judge CJ observed that although duress should not be confused with pressure, the requirement that there be a threat of death or serious injury would 'no doubt' be satisfied by a threat to rape, at [63].

involving victims of human trafficking, the Court of Appeal rejected the argument that duress ought to be broadened to encompass a threat of false imprisonment.[60] As the defence in s 45 of the Modern Slavery Act 2015 does not apply retrospectively, some victims of slavery and relevant exploitation will still have to rely upon the common law defence of duress. Unless there was a threat of death or really serious harm, such individuals will be unable to plead duress successfully.[61]

What constitutes a threat of 'serious injury' for the defence has created difficulties. In *Brown*,[62] the court refused leave to appeal a conviction for possession of drugs when D, suffering from a degenerative disease, was cultivating cannabis for personal use to alleviate his pain. The court regarded the threat of 'injury' he faced as being only that additional pain he would suffer by having to rely on prescribed medication rather than the lower level of pain suffered with his condition if he used cannabis. The difference between the two levels of pain was not sufficient to constitute 'serious' injury.[63] In *Quayle*,[64] the Court of Appeal went further and rejected the pain experienced by a multiple sclerosis sufferer as sufficient to qualify as 'harm' as the defence of duress of circumstances requires.

While a threat of serious personal injury is the minimum which is acceptable to found the defence for offences to which it is available, a higher minimum may be required for crimes of great gravity. Thus, Hale required threats of death and so did the judges in *M'Growther*[65] and *Purdy*[66] but those were cases of treason. The Law Commission recommends that in a case of murder, duress will require proof that D was under a threat of death or 'life threatening injury'.[67]

The following *dictum* of Lords Wilberforce and Edmund-Davies no longer applies to killing but remains true for other acts:

the realistic view is that, the more dreadful the circumstances of the killing, the heavier the evidential burden of an accused advancing such a plea, and the stronger and more irresistible the duress needed before it could be regarded as affording any defence.[68]

Threats of blackmail, no matter how effective, are not sufficient.[69] There is no modern[70] case in which a threat of injury to property has been admitted.[71] In *M'Growther*,[72] it was held there was no defence where the Duke of Perth had threatened to burn the houses and drive off the cattle of any of his tenants who refused to follow him. But that was a case of treason and there is now clear authority that such a threat would not be enough even on some lesser charge.

If the evil D would perpetrate by submitting to the threat (eg stealing a chocolate bar) was clearly less than that which would have been inflicted had he defied it (eg burning down his house), there are cogent reasons for allowing a defence; even if the threat was not of death or even grievous bodily harm. Williams argued strongly in favour of such a principle, which

---

[60] [2017] EWCA Crim 36, [2017] Crim LR 817. The court followed what had earlier been held in *van Dao* [2012] EWCA Crim 1717 in which Gross LJ stated that 'we would in this area place the requirements of practical policy ahead of those of strict logic'. At [44]–[49]. See the commentary by Ormerod at [2013] Crim LR 234.

[61] Sch 4 to the Modern Slavery Act 2015 lists a number of offences that have been excluded from the ambit of the new defences. Therefore, depending upon the offences they are alleged to have committed, some victims of slavery and trafficking will still have to rely upon the common law even after the implementation of s 45.

[62] [2003] EWCA Crim 2637.   [63] A duress of circumstances case.

[64] [2005] EWCA Crim 1415, [2006] Crim LR 148 and commentary.   [65] (1746) Fost 13.

[66] (1946) 10 J Crim L 182.   [67] LC 304, para 6.75.   [68] *Abbott v R* [1976] 3 All ER at 152.

[69] *Singh* [1973] 1 WLR 1600.   [70] cf *Crutchley* (1831) 5 C & P 133.

[71] 'Well, the law must draw a line somewhere; and, as a result of experience and human valuation, the law draws it between threats to property and threats to the person', per Lord Simon [1975] AC 653, [1975] Crim LR 707.

[72] See n 65.

is, of course, closely analogous to that adopted in the American Model Penal Code in relation to necessity.[73] But this would in some cases still deny a defence to D even though the injury threatened was one which no ordinary person could be expected to endure; and there would be grave difficulty in balancing the two evils against one another when they are of a completely different character.[74] 'Proportionality' may be a prerequisite for necessity[75] but it seems inappropriate for duress. Duress requires a threat of death or serious injury.

From whom/what must the threat emanate

The threat must have some source extraneous to the defendant himself. In *Rodger and Rose*,[76] D who was serving a life sentence was informed that his tariff had been substantially increased. He broke out of prison and raised duress as a defence at his trial for prison-breaking. It was conceded for the purpose of the appeal that he broke out because he had become suicidal and would have committed suicide had he not done so. So there was a threat to his life, but since the threat did not come from an extraneous source, it was no defence. To allow it, said the court, 'could amount to a licence to commit crime dependent on the personal characteristics and vulnerability of the offender'. The Court of Appeal in *Quayle* relied upon this limitation to the defence to reject the defence of duress of circumstances where D cultivated cannabis for personal use to alleviate pain for his multiple sclerosis.[77]

No threat of death or GBH need exist in fact

There is no requirement for there to be a threat of death or serious injury in fact. It is sufficient that D reasonably believes that there is a threat of the relevant gravity. If the defence was only available where there was a threat in fact, D could not plead duress where threatened with an unloaded gun, nor where D escaped from prison erroneously believing it to be on fire. This would be unduly restrictive.

In *Safi and others*,[78] Afghan hijackers who had landed at Stansted airport claimed that their fear of persecution at the hands of the Taliban constituted a defence of duress of circumstances. The trial judge directed that the defence failed unless there was evidence that there was in fact, or might in fact have been, an imminent peril to the defendants or their families. S appealed on the basis that the defence should be available if he *reasonably* believed that if he had not acted in the way he had, he (and/or the family) would have been killed or seriously injured. The Court of Appeal allowed the appeal. Duress (or duress of circumstances) does not depend on there being an actual risk of death or serious injury to the accused; the defence can be made out if the accused was impelled to act as he did because, as a result of what he reasonably believed to be the situation, he had good cause to fear that otherwise death or serious injury would result.

In *Brandford*, the Court of Appeal confirmed that the threat does not have to be relayed directly to the defendant.[79] The fact that the threat was relayed to the defendant indirectly is not fatal to the defence being pleaded. The court held that the focus of the inquiry should be on immediacy, imminence and the possibility of taking evasion action. For this reason, the more indirectly the threat is relayed, then all other things being equal, the more the defendant will struggle to satisfy the elements of the defence. Therefore, although in theory a threat can be relayed indirectly, in practice it will make it very difficult for D to plead the defence successfully.

---

[73] See p 377.   [74] Law Com Working Paper No 55, paras 14–17.

[75] *Shayler* [2001] EWCA Crim 1977, [2001] Crim LR 986, see p 378.   [76] [1998] 1 Cr App R 143.

[77] [2005] EWCA Crim 415. See M Watson, 'Cannabis and the Defence of Necessity' (1998) 148 NLJ 1260. See, for a philosophical consideration of such matters, SJ Morse, 'Diminished Capacity' in S Shute, S Gardner and J Horder (eds), *Action and Value in Criminal Law* (1993) 250–263.

[78] [2003] EWCA Crim 1809, [2003] Crim LR 721.   [79] [2016] EWCA Crim 1794, [2017] Crim LR 554.

(2) Threats against whom?

Most of the cases naturally involve a threat or danger to the life or safety of D himself, but the defences are not limited to that situation. In *Hurley and Murray*,[80] the Supreme Court of Victoria held that threats to kill or seriously injure D's de facto wife amounted to duress. In *Wright*,[81] threats against D's boyfriend sufficed. In *Conway*,[82] the threat was to the passenger in D's car; and in *Martin*,[83] D's wife's threat to commit suicide if he did not drive while disqualified was held capable of founding a defence of duress of circumstances—though in fact it seems to have been one of duress by threats—'Drive or else…'.[84] So threats against the life or safety of D's family certainly suffice. In *Shayler*,[85] the Lord Chief Justice, approving a statement of Rose LJ in *Hussain*, stated that:

the evil must be directed towards the defendant or a person or persons for whom he has responsibility or, we would add, persons for whom the situation makes him responsible;…[this extends], by way of example, [to] the situation where the threat is made to set off a bomb unless the defendant performs the unlawful act. The defendant may have not have had any previous connection with those who would be injured by the bomb but the threat itself creates the defendant's responsibility for those who will be at risk if he does not give way to the threat.

Lord Bingham in *Hasan* also suggested that the threat must be 'directed against the defendant or his immediate family or someone close to him or for whom he is responsible'. So, threats to D, his family and others to whom he owes a 'duty' will qualify, but arguably this is too narrow. If a bank robber threatens to shoot a customer in the bank unless D, the clerk, hands him the keys, D surely has a defence to a charge of assisting the robbery. The concept of those for whom D is 'responsible' is ill-defined, and ought to be given a liberal construction. It is submitted that the defence is so heavily qualified by the requirement of a threat of death or serious injury and the other objective elements, that there is little need to impose restrictions on the categories of individual to whom the threat must be made.

(3) Evaluating D's response to the threat

Several difficult issues arise in determining whether by committing the crime in response to the threats D's conduct should be excused. In particular, the courts have struggled with questions of whether it is sufficient that the individual defendant regarded it as a reasonable response to the threat he believed that he faced, or whether the defence is only available if the reasonable person would have responded in the same way if faced with the threat D genuinely believed he faced.

In *Howe*, the House of Lords held that the defence fails if:

the prosecution prove that a person of reasonable firmness sharing the characteristics of the defendant would not have given way to the threats as did the defendant.

The House held that the correct direction was that stated by Lane LCJ in *Graham*:[86]

(1) Was [D], or may he have been, impelled to act as he did because, as a result of what he reasonably believed [E] had said or done, he had good cause to fear that if he did not so act [E]

---

[80] [1967] VR 526.   [81] [2000] Crim LR 510.   [82] [1989] QB 290, [1989] Crim LR 74, CA.

[83] [1989] 1 All ER 652, [1989] Crim LR 284. See also *Wright* [2000] Crim LR 510.

[84] See also *M* [2007] EWCA Crim 3228, where M sought to smuggle drugs into prison being threatened with violence by E, and hearing threats from Y in prison that if he did not get the drugs he would commit suicide.

[85] [2001] EWCA Crim 1977, [49]. This was accepted in *Hasan* [2005] UKHL 22, [2006] Crim LR 142, per Lord Bingham.

[86] [1982] 1 All ER 801 at 806, 74 Cr App R 235 at 241, [1982] Crim LR 365. Cf *Lawrence* [1980] 1 NSWLR 122.

would kill him or…cause him serious physical injury? (2) If so, have the prosecution made the jury sure that a sober person of reasonable firmness, sharing the characteristics of [D], would not have responded to whatever he reasonably believed [E] said or did by taking part in the killing?

The direction contains three objective elements:

(1) D must have *reasonably* believed in the circumstances of the threat;[87]

(2) D's belief must have amounted to *good cause* for his fear;

(3) D's response must be one which might have been expected of a *sober person of reasonable firmness*.

A fourth element is usually considered although not deriving from the *Graham* judgment:

(4) D must have had no *reasonable* opportunity to escape the threat.

In imposing this objective regime on the defence, Lord Lane in *Graham* equated duress with self-defence which, it was then generally accepted, imposed an objective test. But less than two years later in *Gladstone Williams*,[88] Lord Lane, influenced by the judgment of Lawton LJ in *Kimber*,[89] held that an unreasonable belief, if honestly held, might found self-defence. Lawton LJ appreciated and applied the general effect of *DPP v Morgan*[90] which was not cited in *Graham*. Logically, if *Morgan* applies to self-defence, it ought equally to apply to duress.[91] It is arguable, however, that the defences are distinguishable since duress is generally regarded as excusatory and self-defence as justificatory in nature.[92] The decision in *Graham* may thus have been an unfortunate accident—but subsequently it has been approved by the House of Lords in *Howe* and more recently still the House of Lords in *Hasan* certainly did not seem to be inclined to depart from it.[93]

It is submitted that, in the first two respects, the direction in *Graham* lays down too strict a rule. D should surely be judged on the basis of what he honestly believed and what he genuinely feared.[94] If his genuine fear was such that the jury conclude that no person of reasonable firmness could have been expected to resist it, he should be excused. He may have been unduly credulous or stupid, but he is no more blameworthy than a person whose

---

[87] The element of reasonableness was firmly endorsed in *Hasan* [2005] UKHL 22, [23] per Lord Bingham. See also LC 304, para 6.77. In LCCP 177, para 7.46 fn 54 the Commission suggested that in an unpublished codification project, the reasonableness test would be endorsed, reversing an earlier Law Commission Report recommendation.

[88] See p 383.

[89] [1983] 3 All ER 316, [1983] Crim LR 630 (an honest belief that V was consenting was a defence to indecent (now sexual) assault).

[90] See p 332. See JC Smith, 'The Triumph of Inexorable Logic' in *Leading Cases of the Twentieth Century* (2000).

[91] In *Martin (DP)* [2000] 2 Cr App R 42, [2000] Crim LR 615, CA (discussed in [2000] 7 Arch News 6), Mantell LJ said at 49—apparently in error—that the subjective test in self-defence had been applied to duress in *Cairns* [1999] 2 Cr App R 137 where Mantell LJ also gave the judgment. See generally on the merits of the subjective and objective approaches, P Alldridge, 'Developing the Defence of Duress' [1986] Crim LR 433.

[92] See S Yeo, *Compulsion in the Criminal Law* (1990).

[93] Lord Bingham rejected comparison with other defences in *Hasan*. Cf LCCP 177, para 7.32. It is dangerous to place too much emphasis on comparisons with other defences when seeking to interpret the scope of duress. These common law defences evolved over centuries to meet the needs of individual cases and were not the product of a coherent structured scheme as one might expect from Parliament.

[94] See W Wilson, 'The Structure of Defences' [2005] Crim LR 108, 115–116. Courts occasionally lapse into such a formula, see *Mullally v DPP* [2006] EWHC 3448 (Admin).

fear is based on reasonable grounds.[95] The Court of Appeal in *Martin (DP)*[96] held that D's characteristics—in that case a schizoid affective disorder, making him more likely to regard things said as threatening and to believe that threats would be carried out—must be taken into account. This seems to be a substantial mitigation of the objective test. It is doubtful whether that decision can stand in the light of the emphasis on the objective nature of the defence in *Hasan*.

As with mistake generally, lack of faith in the jury to detect the 'bogus defence' and the additional hardship for the prosecution probably lies at the root of the objective requirements. Also as with mistake generally, the more tenuous the grounds for his claim, the less likely is D to be believed.

The confusion and tension in this area is illustrated by the case of *Safi* (the Afghan hijack case discussed earlier). At the first trial the judge directed the jury that D's genuine belief in the threat of death was sufficient, on a retrial the second judge adopted an objective formulation. The Court of Appeal failed to clarify the position but seemed implicitly to be adopting an objective test.[97] Similarly in the case of *M*,[98] the Court of Appeal adopted an apparently subjective approach to the first question

In two subsequent cases, the Court of Appeal again endorsed the objective approach in the first limb.[99] Further clarification from the House of Lords was not forthcoming in *Hasan*, but the tenor of the speech of Lord Bingham leaves little doubt that the *objective* formulation would be preferred. That would follow the decision in *Graham* which was approved in *Howe*.

The person of reasonable steadfastness

Since duress is (according to Lord Hailsham in *Howe* and Lord Bingham in *Hasan*) a concession to human frailty[100] and some people are frailer than others, it is arguable that the standard of fortitude required should also vary,[101] and that a subjective test should apply.[102] That is not the approach adopted in English law. *Graham* is consistent with a common approach of the law in deciding that the standard is an objective one. It is for the law to lay down standards of conduct. When attacked, D may use only a reasonable degree of force in self-defence. Under the loss of self-control defence, D must display a reasonable degree of tolerance and self-restraint. Similarly, *Graham* decides that a person under duress is required to display 'the steadfastness reasonably to be expected of the ordinary citizen in his situation'.[103] The court relied particularly on the analogy with the law of provocation as

---

[95] In *DPP v Rogers* [1998] Crim LR 202, DC, Brooke LJ seems wrongly to have assumed that this is now the law, apparently anticipating a reform proposed by the Law Commission. Cf *Abdul-Hussain* [1999] Crim LR 570. If D reasonably believes there is a threat, it is immaterial that there is no threat in fact: *Cairns* [1999] 2 Cr App R 137, CA. For a criticism of the Commission's 'slavish adherence to subjectivism', see J Horder, 'Occupying the Moral High Ground' [1994] Crim LR 334 at 341 and comments by JC Smith, 'Individual Incapacities and Criminal Liability' (1998) 6 Med L Rev 138 at 155–157.

[96] [2002] 2 Cr App R 42, CA.   [97] At [25].

[98] [2003] EWCA Crim 1170. See also *Sewell* [2004] EWCA Crim 2322.

[99] *Blake* [2004] EWCA Crim 1238, [18]; *Bronson* [2004] EWCA Crim 903, [23].

[100] *Howe* [1987] 1 All ER 771 at 779–780; *Hasan* [2005] UKHL 22, [18].

[101] See KJM Smith, 'Duress and Steadfastness: In Pursuit of the Unintelligible' [1999] Crim LR 363. See also Tadros, *Criminal Responsibility*, Ch 13, on the need for defences including duress to take account of D's characteristics and RL Lippke, 'Chronic Temptation, Reasonable Firmness and the Criminal Law' (2014) 34 OJLS 75, for the argument that the law ought to make a concession for those who face chronic temptation to violate the law through no fault of their own.

[102] 'It is arguable that the standard should be purely subjective and that it is contrary to principle to require the fear to be a reasonable one': per Lord Simon [1975] 1 All ER at 931. Cf Law Com Working Paper No 55, paras 11–13 and LC 83, paras 2.27–2.28; and *Hudson* [1965] 1 All ER 721 at 724.

[103] (1982) 74 Cr App R 235 at 241.

was then in force and the decision in *Camplin*.[104] That case suggests that account should be taken of not only the gravity of the threat to D but also the sex and age of D and such of D's characteristics[105] as would affect the gravity of the threat to him. The leading case on this issue in duress is *Bowen*.[106]

In *Bowen*, it was held that for a duress plea D's age[107] and sex may be relevant, depending on the circumstances, as may pregnancy[108] and serious physical disability. These might affect the gravity of the threat and D's ability to seek evasive action. In *Bowen*,[109] the court also accepted that a 'recognized mental illness or psychiatric condition, such as post-traumatic stress disorder leading to learned helplessness'[110] would be relevant. But, D's low IQ, short of mental impairment or mental illness, is not relevant: a person of low IQ may be expected to be as courageous and able to withstand threats as anyone else. That does not necessarily answer the argument—belatedly advanced on appeal—that D's ability to seek the protection of the police might have been impaired.

Cases of 'learned helplessness' are particularly difficult.[111] In *Emery*,[112] a case of cruelty to a child, it was said, *obiter*, that it would be right to admit 'an expert account of the causes of the condition of dependent helplessness, the circumstances in which it might arise and what level of abuse would be required to produce it'. 'A woman of reasonable firmness suffering from a condition of dependent helplessness' may seem a contradiction in terms; but the point appears to be that the alleged history of violence by D's partner, said to have produced that condition, was part of the duress.[113] That explanation did not seem attractive to the court in *Bowen*.

This matter is a question for the jury and expert evidence has been held inadmissible to show that D was 'emotionally unstable' or in 'a grossly elevated neurotic state',[114] or that he is unusually pliable or vulnerable to pressure;[115] nor is evidence admissible of sexual abuse as a child, resulting in lack of firmness, not amounting to psychiatric disorder: *Hurst*,[116] where Beldam LJ said, 'we find it hard to see how the person of reasonable firmness can be invested with the characteristics of a personality which lacks reasonable firmness…'. The Court of Appeal considered this issue directly in *GAC*.[117] D unsuccessfully relied upon learned helplessness to avoid a conviction for importing Class A drugs. The Court of Appeal, dismissing D's appeal,

---

104 [1978] AC 705, [1978] 2 All ER 168, see p 543.

105 Such as the schizoid affective disorder afflicting *Martin (DP)*, n 91.

106 [1996] 2 Cr App R 157, [1996] Crim LR 577. In *Flatt* [1996] Crim LR 576, it was held that drug addiction was a self-induced condition, not a characteristic. For criticism of the approach in general for its failure to reflect psychiatric understanding, see A Buchanan and G Virgo, 'Duress and Mental Abnormality' [1999] Crim LR 517.

107 cf *Ali* [1989] Crim LR 736.

108 In *GAC* [2013] EWCA Crim 1472, Hallett LJ stated that: 'A threat of physical violence to a pregnant woman therefore might be more serious because of the risk to the unborn child' at [33].

109 [1996] 2 Cr App R 157.

110 This was held to be insufficient in *Moseley* [1999] 7 Arch News 2.

111 For extensive analysis, see J Loveless, '*R v GAC*: Battered Woman "Syndromization"' [2014] Crim LR 655.

112 (1992) 14 Cr App R (S) 394. See also J Loveless, 'Domestic Violence, Coercion and Duress' [2010] Crim LR 93 analysing how the defence is formulated in such a way as to exclude battered women. The Court of Appeal took cognizance of the criticisms made in this article without expressing a view of them in *A (RJ)* [2012] EWCA Crim 434, [2013] Crim LR 240. In this case, D's conviction was upheld. She has since alleged a violation of Art 8 of the ECHR. See *RA v UK* [2014] ECHR 1288. In 2016, the European Court of Human Rights ruled that her case was inadmissible. See *RA v UK* (App no 75321/12), 2016.

113 Arguably, in such a case D is still a person of reasonable firmness, just one with greater sensitivities.

114 *Hegarty* [1994] Crim LR 353.   115 *Horne* [1994] Crim LR 584: 'not a hero nor a coward'.

116 [1995] 1 Cr App R 82 at 90.

117 [2013] EWCA Crim 1472. For extensive analysis, see J Loveless '*R v GAC*: Battered Woman "Syndromization"' [2014] Crim LR 655.

rejected her claim that she had exhibited battered women syndrome at the time she committed the offence or that the violence against her was of sufficient severity to make out the first element of duress. Hallett LJ held that a person who has suffered domestic abuse would not be able to plead duress unless they have been 'subjected to serious physical violence so bad' that they have lost their free will.

It is no less difficult when the condition is a 'recognized mental illness'. The acceptance of such an illness as a relevant characteristic suggests that this element of the objective test has broken down and that we are moving closer to the test once proposed by the Law Commission: 'the threat is one which in all the circumstances (including any of [the defendant's] characteristics that affect its gravity) he cannot reasonably be expected to resist'.[118] Under the present law the court will be faced with drawing some fine distinctions between unusual vulnerability and recognized psychiatric conditions affecting the ability to withstand pressure.[119] This is demonstrated by *GAC*. The increasing shift towards subjectivity in this limb of the defence stands in contrast to the increased objectivity in the first limb. It highlights the incoherence of the defence as it has evolved at common law, underlining the need for a legislative response.

(4) The conduct it is sought to excuse must have been directly caused by the threats D relies on

Threats as a concurrent cause of the crime

It is said that D's will must have been 'overborne' by the threat.[120] Presumably this means only that he would not have committed the offence 'but for' the threat and that the threat was one which might cause a person of reasonable fortitude to do as he did. If the prosecution can prove that he would have done the same act even if the threat had not been made, it seems that the defence will fail.[121] But the threat need not be the only motive for D's action. In *Valderrama-Vega*,[122] D was under financial pressure and had been threatened with disclosure of his homosexual behaviour—neither matter being capable of amounting to duress—but it was wrong to direct the jury that the threats of death or serious injury also alleged to have been made must have been the sole reason for his committing the offence. If D would not have committed the offence but for the latter threats the defence was available even if he acted because of the cumulative effect of all the pressure on him. It is probably going too far to say that it is enough that the threats of death were 'the last straw' because the law will look for something more substantial than 'a straw' for an excuse; but threats of death or serious bodily harm can never be trivial, so it is probably sufficient to tell the jury that D has the defence if he would not have acted but for the threats of violence. A jury direction that the defence was available only if D acted *solely* because of the relevant threats was upheld where it was suggested that he might also have been influenced by greed but the court thought it inadvisable to use the word 'solely' in a summing up.[123]

---

[118] Draft Criminal Law Bill, cl 25, LC 218. The Commission's recommendation in relation to murder is that the jury should be permitted to take account of all the circumstances except D's capacity to withstand the duress.

[119] See *Antar* [2004] EWCA Crim 2708.

[120] cf the discussion of *Steane* [1947] KB 997, [1947] 1 All ER 813. See also GR Rubin, 'New Light on *Steane's* Case' (2003) 24 *Legal History* 143. See eg the continued use of such statements which shed little light on the defence: *Rahman* [2010] EWCA Crim 235.

[121] In *DPP v Bell (Derek)* [1992] Crim LR 176, DC, D, in terror of an aggressor, began to drive with excess alcohol. Although he admitted that, before the threat, he intended to drive, it was found as a fact (a finding with which the Divisional Court could not interfere) that he drove because of terror and so had a defence of duress of circumstances. But for the threat he might have changed his mind or been persuaded by his passengers not to drive.

[122] [1985] Crim LR 220 and commentary.   [123] *Ortiz* (1986) 83 Cr App R 173.

A nominated crime demanded?

In the paradigmatic case of duress by threats, the defendant will have been told 'perform this crime or else'. The question has arisen how specific the nomination of the crime must be for D to be able to rely on the threats.[124] In *Cole*,[125] D was convicted of robbing two building societies and pleaded duress on the basis that he had been threatened by money lenders to whom he was in debt. The Court of Appeal held that a plea of duress was not available as the money lenders had not stipulated that he commit robbery to meet their demands. This would place a very strict limitation on the defence. The Court of Appeal held, in addition, in *Cole* that there was not the degree of immediacy and directness required between the peril threatened and the offence charged. That is a better basis for the decision.

Subsequently, in *Ali*,[126] D, a heroin addict, was convicted of robbing a building society and D claimed that his supplier, X, who had a reputation for violence, had demanded repayment of the monies D owed him. Further, D claimed that X had provided D with a gun and told D to get the money by the following day from a bank or a building society. The Court of Appeal upheld his conviction but appeared to accept that a threat is capable of amounting to duress when D is charged with robbing a particular building society not specified by the person threatening him.

In a case of duress of circumstances there can be no nominated crime: D faced with an approaching tidal wave or tornado is not 'told' to 'steal that car to drive away', but he is entitled to the defence should he do so.

(5) There is no evasive action D can take

This element of the defence is more properly seen as part of a broader question which is whether the threat is still effective at the time D performs the conduct element of the offence. Historically it was recognized that:

> The only force that doth excuse, is a force upon the person, and present fear of death; and his force and fear must continue all the time the party remains with the rebels. It is incumbent on every man, who makes force his defence to show an actual force, and that he quitted the service as soon as he could.[127]

The Court of Appeal has reiterated the 'requirement that the accused must know or believe that the threat is one which will be carried out immediately or before the accused or the other person threatened, can obtain official protection'.[128] But in *Abdul-Hussain*,[129] where Iraqis hijacked an aircraft because they reasonably feared they would be killed if they were returned to Iraq, the court reinterpreted the requirement of immediacy, holding that the question was whether D's response to the 'imminent' threat was proportionate and reasonable.[130] This relaxation of the defence was controversial. In *Hasan*, Lord Bingham was at pains to reassert the primacy of the requirement of the 'immediacy of the threat' and D's inability to avoid it, which he described as the 'cardinal feature' of the

---

124 This issue was confronted directly by the Supreme Court of Canada in *Ryan* [2013] SCC 3. The court held that the defence is available only when D has been compelled to commit a specific offence under threats of death or bodily harm. See recently *Khan* [2018] EWCA Crim 78.

125 [1994] Crim LR 582. In *Hasan*, Lord Bingham approved the decision regarding the threat as lacking immediacy. See recently *Khan* [2018] EWCA Crim 78.

126 (1995) 16 Cr App R (S) 692, [1995] Crim LR 303.   127 *M'Growther* (1746) Fost 13 at 14, per Lee CJ.

128 *Hurst* [1995] 1 Cr App R 82 at 93; *Flatt* [1996] Crim LR 576.   129 [1999] Crim LR 570.

130 See *Abdul-Hussain* [1999] Crim LR 570, where the court added 'if Anne Frank had stolen a car to escape from Amsterdam and been charged with theft, the tenets of English law would not, in our judgment, have denied her a defence of duress of circumstances, on the ground that she should have waited for the Gestapo's knock on the door'.

defence.[131] His lordship was of the view that the defence would not be available if there was a delay of a day between D being threatened with being shot and his commission of the crime.[132] Surely this must depend on the circumstances, however. There may be instances where, despite the delay of a day, the defence ought to be available.

Duress where D has an opportunity to inform the police

If D is able reasonably to resort to the protection of the law, he must do so or the defence will be lost. In *Hasan*, Lord Bingham observed that it should be made clear to juries that unless D reasonably expects the threats to be carried out 'immediately or almost immediately' the defence may be lost because there may be little room for doubt that D could take evasive action. The question whether D had a reasonable opportunity to take evasive action ought *not* in Lord Bingham's view to be subsumed within the question whether D had a reasonable belief in the existence of the threat and whether a reasonable person in D's circumstances would have responded as D did.[133]

When the threat is withdrawn or becomes ineffective, D must desist from committing the crime as soon as he reasonably can. If, for example, having consumed excess alcohol, D is threatened and drives off in fear of his life, he commits a drink-driving offence only if the prosecution can prove that he continued to drive after the terror ceased.[134]

Where the threats operate, or D reasonably perceives them as operating on someone other than himself, the question whether the threat is still operative may be more difficult to determine. For example, in *Hurley*, D had ample opportunity to place himself under the protection of the police but the court held that the defence of duress might still be available because his de facto wife was held as a hostage by his oppressors. Though he himself was physically out of range, the threats against her were presently operative on his mind.

Hudson and Taylor[135] went further. Two young women, called as witnesses for the prosecution, gave false evidence because they had been threatened by a gang with serious physical injury if they told the truth, and they saw one of the gang in the public gallery of the court. The young women were charged with perjury. Duress was accepted as a defence even though they could have put themselves under the protection of the law by informing the court; and there were no threats to third parties. The court thought it immaterial that the threatened injury could not follow at once since (in its opinion) there was no opportunity for delaying tactics and they had to make up their minds whether to commit the offence while the threat was operating. The threat was no less compelling because it could not be carried out there if it could be carried out in the streets of Salford the same night. The case turns on the point that police protection could not be effective. It was recognized to extend the possible ambit of the defence widely for there would be few cases where the police can offer effective and permanent protection against such threats.[136] However, in *Hasan*, Lord Bingham regarded

---

[131] At [25]–[26].

[132] The Supreme Court of Canada in *Ryan* [2013] SCC 3 affirmed that in Canadian law it must be demonstrated that any course of action other than inflicting the injury (or committing the crime) was 'demonstrably impossible' or that there was 'no other legal way out'.

[133] At [24].

[134] *DPP v Bell (Derek)*, n 121. See the reiteration of this in *Malcolm v DPP* [2007] EWHC 363 (Admin), [2007] Crim LR 894; *Mullaley* [2006] EWHC 3448 (Admin) and in *Brown v CPS* [2007] EWHC 3274 (Admin).

[135] [1971] 2 All ER 244; followed by *Lewis* (1992) 96 Cr App R 412 at 415. Described by Ryan and Ryan (2005) 56 NILQ 421, commenting on *Hasan* as a 'historical anomaly', at 427.

[136] See comment in [1971] Crim LR 359 and (by Goodhart) in 87 LQR 299 and 121 NLJ 909 and (by Zellick) in 121 NLJ 845. In *K* (1983) 78 Cr App R 82, CA, it was held that duress might be available as a defence to contempt of court committed in the witness box by a prisoner who had been threatened with reprisals against himself and his family, by the accused, a fellow prisoner. The Law Commission originally proposed: 'The threat must be, or the defendant must believe that it is, one that will be carried out immediately, or before he (or the person under threat) can obtain official protection: Criminal Law Bill, clause 25(2)(b). This provision, by allowing the defence if the defendant believes that official protection will be ineffective, differs from previous treatments of the point'—Report, para 29.2. In LC 304, the Law Commission now recommends an objective test.

Hudson and Taylor as having had 'the unfortunate effect of weakening the requirement that execution of a threat must be reasonably believed to be imminent and immediate'.[137] Such a strict standard may be supported by the need to prevent the defence being misused and pleaded in spurious cases, but is it right that a defendant who reasonably fears he will be shot tomorrow after perjuring himself today ought not to be allowed a defence of duress? His lordship seems to be focusing the question on whether D could avoid compliance with the threat, which is in one sense practically always possible. The real question is whether D could take action which would negative the threat itself. If D genuinely, and perhaps reasonably, believes that the police or others cannot protect him from the threat, should he be denied the defence?[138] What if those under threat are held overseas beyond the protection of the British police? The Court of Appeal in *Batchelor* went even further in expressing disapproval of *Hudson and Taylor*.[139] Elias LJ, after citing Lord Bingham's reasoning in *Hasan*, stated that the Court of Appeal in *Hudson* had allowed its sympathy for the defendants to distort legal principles.[140] Even more recently, in *Brandford*,[141] one of the reasons why the Court of Appeal rejected the defendant's reliance upon duress was the fact that the relevant threats lacked the immediacy that would have precluded her from taking evasive action, such as by going to the police. As a result of this case law, it is submitted that *Hudson and Taylor* should no longer be followed. As noted earlier, however, the difficult question remains: should D be denied the threat if he genuinely, and perhaps reasonably, believes the police cannot prevent the threat being carried out?

As with the question whether the reasonable person would have withstood the pressure, similar principles apply to the rule requiring D to escape from duress if possible. His defence will fail if an ordinary person of his sex, age and other relevant characteristics would have taken an opportunity to escape. Obviously, physical disabilities, for example that he had difficulties in walking, would be taken into account.[142] Following *Graham*, however, he must presumably be taken to have been aware of opportunities of which he ought reasonably to have been aware at the time the opportunity arose.[143] A better view, it is submitted, is that if he was not in fact aware of the opportunity to escape, he should not be penalized for his stupidity or slow-wittedness. In view of recent judicial pronouncements in this area such an approach would probably be seen as too generous to the accused.

If the defence of duress is left to the jury and D seeks to explain his decision not to seek assistance from the authorities rather than commit the crime, it is not necessarily incumbent on the judge to spell out each of the risks to D if he had taken such a route.[144]

(6) D cannot rely on threats to which he has voluntarily laid himself open

A further important limitation on the defence is that the threat cannot be one that arises from D having voluntarily exposed himself to threats of violence. This has become an increasingly problematic area and the courts have sought to prevent the defence being too

---

[137] At [27]. Lord Bingham at one point suggests that the defence in *Hudson* should fail because there was no question that DD had 'no opportunity to avoid'. That is surely too strict a view. The question is whether they had a reasonable chance to avoid the threats. For examples of the strictness of *Hasan* being applied, see *N* [2007] EWCA Crim 3479 and see *Hussain* [2008] EWCA Crim 1117. and *Khan* [2018] EWCA Crim 78

[138] Consider the High Court of Australia case of *Taiapa* [2009] HCA 53 in which D was denied the opportunity to rely on the compulsion defence where, having been threatened at gun point that he, his pregnant girlfriend and his mother would be shot unless he couriered drugs, D drove to collect the drugs and did not report to the police. His asserted belief that the police would not protect him and his family was found not to give rise to the defence.

[139] [2013] EWCA Crim 2638.   [140] At [15].   [141] [2016] EWCA Crim 1794.

[142] But the fact that he was voluntarily drunk or drugged might be considered irrelevant.

[143] *Aikens*, n 49.

[144] See *Aldridge* [2006] EWCA Crim 1970 where D had been threatened that his children would be beheaded with a samurai sword if he did not participate in a robbery.

readily available to those involved in drug-related and terrorist crime, in particular where their involvement demonstrates a degree of prior culpability. The restriction is hedged in with qualifications. In *Hasan*,[145] the House of Lords expressed concern at the way in which the defence was being relied on more readily by defendants in more cases and that there was a danger that the restrictive elements of the offence were not being applied rigorously enough.[146]

Voluntary exposure to threats

D will be denied the defence if he voluntarily exposed himself to a risk of threats. An example is *Sharp*[147] where D, who was a party to a conspiracy to commit robberies, said that he wanted to withdraw when he saw his confederates equipped with guns, whereupon E threatened to blow his head off if he did not carry on with the plan. In the course of the robbery, E killed V. D's conviction for manslaughter was upheld after a jury had rejected his defence of duress. This had been the approach adopted in Northern Ireland in *Fitzpatrick* (duress no defence to a charge of robbery committed as a result of threats by the IRA because D had voluntarily joined that organization)[148] and the *dicta* of Lords Morris, Wilberforce and Simon in *Lynch*.[149] It would be different of course if D was compelled to join the violent organization by threats of death or serious bodily harm; then, in principle, he should not be deprived of the defence. Whether any lesser threat should suffice at this stage has not been decided. As Baroness Hale persuasively put the matter in *Hasan*, the question ought to be whether D by his joining exposed himself to the risk 'without reasonable excuse'.[150]

The types of organization

Most cases in this category involve D joining a criminal gang. In *Sharp*, the gang were armed robbers; in *Fitzpatrick*, a paramilitary organization. In *Lewis*,[151] the court construed this limitation on the defence strictly to be limited to associations such as 'a para-military or gangster-tyrant style of organization'. It has been applied so as to deny defendants a duress defence in wider circumstances. For example. in *Shepherd*,[152] D voluntarily joined a gang of burglars but wanted to give up after his first outing and raised the defence of duress by the gang to a charge of a later burglary, it was held that it should have been left to the jury to decide whether he was taking a risk of being subjected to such a threat of violence when he joined the gang.

In *Ali*,[153] the Court of Appeal held that if D has joined with others whom he ought to have realized might subject him to threats of violence, he is denied the defence of duress. The defence is lost irrespective of whether he has joined an existing criminal gang. D was convicted of the robbery at knife point of a vehicle owner. His plea of duress had been rejected at trial on the basis that D had voluntarily joined with the alleged duressor, BH, a co-accused in the robbery. D knew that BH carried a knife and had been warned not to associate with BH. The trial judge directed the jury that duress does not apply if:

the defendant chooses voluntarily to associate with others where he ought to foresee that he might be subjected to compulsion by threats of violence…If you choose to join very bad company, such bad company that you can foresee that you are going to be liable to threats of some kind to do things, then you cannot complain and say I was forced to do them when you had voluntarily associated with those people.

---

145 [2005] UKHL 22, [2006] Crim LR 142.   146 See especially Lord Bingham's speech at [22].
147 [1987] QB 853, [1987] Crim LR 566.   148 [1977] NI 20, CA.   149 [1975] AC 653.
150 At [78].   151 (1993) 96 Cr App R 412; *Kleijn* [2001] All ER (D) 143 (May).
152 (1987) 86 Cr App R 47.   153 [2008] EWCA Crim 716.

The judge elaborated on what was meant by 'bad company' explaining that joining bad company:

doesn't just mean people who are going about doing bad things, it means people who you should have realised could would be likely to, or may, subject you to compulsion by threats of violence.

The Court of Appeal upheld the conviction. In *Hasan*,[154] Lord Bingham had answered the certified question by saying that:

the defence of duress is excluded when as a result of the accused's voluntary association *with others engaged in criminal activity* he foresaw or ought reasonably to have foreseen the risk of being subjected to any compulsion by threats of violence.[155]

The italicized words might suggest that the defence is only lost where D joins an existing criminal gang. *Ali* rejects any such limitation.

Active membership
It is too late if D attempts to withdraw from the organization when the particular enterprise which resulted in the charge is in contemplation. No defence of duress is available. But a person who joined a paramilitary organization in his youth can hardly be held to have forfeited his right to plead duress by that organization for life. If he has done all he can to sever his connection with it before the particular incident was in contemplation, should he not be able to rely on the defence?

The risk to which D was exposing himself
In *Lewis*, D, who was serving a sentence for armed robbery, was savagely attacked in the prison yard by E, who was serving a sentence for the same robbery. D refused to testify against E because he was terrified of reprisals and was charged with contempt of court. It was held that duress ought to have been available as a defence to that charge. There was no evidence that D knew that he was exposing himself to the risk of this *sort of threat* when he participated in the armed robbery with E much earlier in time.

Initially the courts held that D would be denied the defence only where he voluntarily put himself in a position where he was aware of the risk of being subjected to pressure by way of violence *to commit offences of the type alleged* (*Baker and Ward*[156]). Subsequently a harsher view has been adopted. D will be denied the defence if he exposed himself to unlawful threats more generally: *Heath*,[157] *Harmer*.[158] Despite the cogent academic criticism of this approach,[159] the House of Lords in *Hasan* confirmed this harsh view. Lord Bingham explained that:

The defendant is, *ex hypothesi*, a person who has voluntarily surrendered his will to the domination of another. Nothing should turn on foresight of the manner in which, in the event, the dominant party chooses to exploit the defendant's subservience. There need not be foresight of coercion to commit crimes, although it is not easy to envisage circumstances in which a party might be coerced to act lawfully.[160]

---

154 [2005] UKHL 22, [39].   155 Emphasis added.   156 [1999] 2 Cr App R 355.

157 *Heath* [2000] Crim LR 109 (indebted drug user, aware that he might be subjected to threats, required to transport £300K of cannabis), distinguishing *Baker and Ward* (ibid) (inadequate direction).

158 [2001] EWCA Crim 2930, [2002] Crim LR 401.

159 As JC Smith noted in commenting on *Heath* [2000] Crim LR 109, 'it is one thing to be aware that you are likely to be beaten up if you do not pay your debts, it is another that you may be aware that you may be required under threat of violence to commit other, though unspecified crimes, if you do not'.

160 At [37]. Cf Baroness Hale's example of the battered woman compelled to perform lawful tasks of ironing, at [77].

In *Ali*,[161] the court suggested a very harsh approach whereby D could not rely on the defence if he foresaw/ought to have foreseen that he was likely to be subjected to compulsion by threats. The court drew on the approval by Lord Bingham of the trial judge's direction in *Hasan*.[162] The approach in *Ali* and in *Hasan* is to deny the defence not only on the basis of D's association with a criminal gang, but on associating with anyone he ought to have foreseen *might* put him under compulsion by threats.

D's awareness of the risk to which he is exposing himself

Hasan confirms that the duress defence is unavailable where the risk to which D exposes himself is pressure to commit any crime. A further question arises whether the defence can only be denied to D where he is proved to have been aware of that risk (subjectively), or whether it is sufficient that he ought to have been aware of that risk (objectively). As a matter of policy the House of Lords in *Hasan* suggests that the test is whether D ought to have known. Again, this restricts the availability of the defence.[163]

In *Ali*, the Court of Appeal took the objective approach, holding that duress is not available if D *ought to have foreseen* that the others might threaten him. The interpretation will operate very harshly for those involved in, *inter alia*, drug misuse. Many users of drugs will associate themselves with drug dealers and in many, if not most, cases the users ought to realize that the dealer might be likely to threaten them with violence. If the dealer does threaten the user with violence unless the user commits crimes (usually to pay the dealer), the user will be denied the defence of duress.[164] Baroness Hale's minority speech in *Hasan* adopts a more subjective approach, suggesting that the defence is denied only where D has himself foreseen a risk that he will be compelled by threats of violence to commit crime. It is submitted this is preferable approach, but it is not the law.

> The policy of the law is clearly to discourage association with known criminals, and to be slow to excuse the criminal conduct of those who do so. If a person voluntarily becomes or remains associated with others engaged in criminal activity in a situation where he knows or ought reasonably to know that he may be the subject of compulsion by them or their associates, he cannot rely on the defence to excuse any act which he is thereafter compelled to do by them. It is not necessary in this case to decide whether or to what extent that principle applies if an undercover agent penetrates a criminal gang for *bona fide* law enforcement purposes and is compelled by the gang to commit criminal acts.[165]

(7) Offences to which duress/duress of circumstances available

Duress by threats has been accepted as a defence to manslaughter,[166] criminal damage,[167] arson,[168] theft,[169] handling,[170] perjury and contempt of court,[171] perverting the course of

---

[161] [2008] EWCA Crim 716.

[162] 'Did the defendant voluntarily put himself in the position, in which he knew he was likely to be subjected to threats? You look to judge that in all the circumstances … if someone voluntarily associates with the sort of people who he knows are likely to put pressure on him, then he cannot really complain, if he finds himself under pressure. If you are sure that he did voluntarily put himself in such a position, the defence fails and he was guilty. If you are not sure and you have not been sure about all of the other questions, then you would find him not guilty.' At [14].

[163] cf Baroness Hale commenting on the attractions of the subjectivist approach advanced by the Law Commission, at [75].

[164] cf *Heath* [2000] Crim LR 109. See also *Lal* [2009] EWCA Crim 2393 and *Mullally* [2012] EWCA Crim 687.

[165] Lord Bingham at [38].   [166] *Evans and Gardiner* [1976] VR 517 and *(No 2)* 523.

[167] *Crutchley* (1831) 5 C & P 133.

[168] *Shiartos* (Lawton J, 29 Sept 1961, CCA), unreported but referred to in *Gill*, n 169.

[169] *Gill* [1963] 2 All ER 688, [1963] 1 WLR 841, CCA.   [170] *A-G v Whelan* [1934] IR 518.

[171] *K* (1983) 78 Cr App R 82, [1983] Crim LR 736, CA; *Lewis* (1992) 96 Cr App R 412.

justice,[172] offences under the Official Secrets Acts[173] and drug offences.[174] The courts have also assumed that it would apply to buggery[175] (presumably therefore also to sex offences under the 2003 Act) and conspiracy[176] to defraud. It is available to strict liability crimes,[177] but, depending on the terms of the offence, not always to status crimes.[178]

Duress of circumstances has been held to be a defence to various road traffic offences, to hijacking, contrary to s 1(1) of the Aviation Security Act 1982[179] and to unlawful possession of a firearm. It now seems safe to say that either kind of duress may be a defence to any crime,[180] except some forms of treason, murder and attempted murder.[181]

Duress and treason

Although typically it is said that treason is a crime where duress is not a defence, it is quite clear that it may be a defence to at least some forms of treason.[182] As long ago as 1419 in *Oldcastle*'s case,[183] the accused, who were charged with treason in supplying victuals (food) to Sir John Oldcastle and his fellow rebels, were acquitted on the grounds that they acted through fear of death and desisted as soon as they could. The existence of the defence was admitted, *obiter*, by Lee CJ in *M'Growther*,[184] a trial for treason committed in the 1745 rebellion and by Lord Mansfield in *Stratton*:[185]

if a man is forced to commit acts of high treason, if it appears really force, and such as human nature could not be expected to resist and the jury are of that opinion, the man is not guilty of high treason.

Much more recently, in *Purdy*,[186] Oliver J directed a jury that fear of death would be a defence to a British prisoner of war who was charged with treason in having assisted with German propaganda in the Second World War. Against this, Lord Goddard CJ said in *Steane*[187] that the defence did not apply to treason, but this remark appears to have been made *per incuriam*. Treason is an offence which may take many forms varying widely in seriousness and it would be wrong to suppose that threats, even of death, will necessarily be a defence to every act of treason. In *Oldcastle*'s case,[188] Hale emphasizes that the accuseds' act was *only* furnishing of victuals and he appears to question whether, if they had taken a more active part in the rebellion, they would have been excused. Stephen thought the defence only applied where the offender took a subordinate part.

Duress and murder

It was stated in the books from Hale onwards that duress could not be a defence to a charge of murder. As Blackstone put it, a man under duress 'ought rather to die himself than escape

---

[172] *Hudson v Taylor* [1971] 2 QB 202.   [173] *Shayler* [2001] EWCA Crim 1977, [2001] Crim LR 986.

[174] *Valderrama-Vega* [1985] Crim LR 220; *Ortiz* (1986) 83 Cr App R 173.

[175] *Bourne* (1952) 36 Cr App R 125.

[176] *Verrier* [1965] Crim LR 732. In *Abdul-Hussain* [1999] Crim LR 570, the court doubted whether duress can be a defence to conspiracy; but if it is a defence to doing the act, it must surely be a defence to agreeing to do it.

[177] *Eden DC v Braid* [1998] COD 259.

[178] See *New Forest Local Education Authority v E* [2007] EWHC 2584 (Admin), n 180.

[179] *Abdul-Hussain* [1999] Crim LR 570.

[180] Its use in relation to a charge under s 444 of the Education Act 1996, where a parent was charged with failing to secure the attendance of a child was doubted: *New Forest Local Education Authority v E* [2007] EWHC 2584 (Admin).

[181] It is not available to civil tax penalties: *Mu v Customs and Excise* [2001] VTD 17504.

[182] [1975] AC 653, [1975] 1 All ER at 920, per Lord Morris; 940, per Lord Simon; 944, per Lord Kilbrandon. In *Gotts* [1992] 2 AC 412, [1992] 2 WLR 284 at 300, Lord Lowry excepts 'most forms of treason'. This passage was cited by Lord Bingham in *Hasan*.

[183] (1419) Hale, I PC, 50, East, I PC, 70.   [184] (1746) Fost 13, 18 State Tr 391.

[185] (1779) 21 State Tr 1045.   [186] (1946) 10 J Crim L 182.

[187] [1947] KB 997 at 1005, [1947] 1 All ER 813 at 817.   [188] (1419) Hale, I PC, 50.

by the murder of an innocent'.[189] There was, however, no clear judicial authority in point and in 1969 in *Kray*[190] an inroad was made into the supposed rule when Widgery LJ said that a person charged as an accessory before the fact to murder might rely on duress. In 1975, in *Lynch v DPP for Northern Ireland*,[191] the House of Lords, by a majority of three to two, held that a person charged with aiding and abetting murder[192] could have a defence of duress. The position of the actual killer was left open and in *Abbott*[193] in 1976, again by three to two, the Privy Council distinguished *Lynch* and held that the defence was not available to the principal offender, the actual killer. This was an illogical and unsatisfactory position because it is by no means always the case that the actual killer is the most dominant or culpable member of a number of accomplices, but under the law as it then stood he alone was excluded from the defence. The distinctions involved were technical and absurd.[194] Accordingly, when the matter came before the House of Lords in *Howe*,[195] there was a strong case for either going forward and allowing the defence to all alleged parties to murder, or backward, and allowing it to none. The House chose the latter course, overruling its own decision in *Lynch*. The speeches emphasize different aspects, but the following reasons for the decision appear among them.

(1) The ordinary person of reasonable fortitude, if asked to take an innocent life, might be expected to sacrifice his own.[196] Lord Hailsham would not 'regard a law as either "just;" or "humane" which withdraws the protection of the criminal law from the innocent victim and casts the cloak of its protection on the coward and the poltroon in the name[197] of a 'concession to human frailty'.

(2) One who takes the life of an innocent person cannot claim that he is choosing the lesser of two evils.[198]

(3) The Law Commission had recommended[199] ten years previously that duress should be a defence to the alleged principal offender, but Parliament had not acted on that recommendation.[200]

(4) Hard cases could be dealt with by not prosecuting—in some cases the person under duress might be expected to be the principal witness for the prosecution[201]—or by the action of the Parole Board in ordering the early release of a person who would have had a defence if duress had been an available defence.[202]

---

[189] Blackstone, *Commentaries*, iv, 30.   [190] [1970] 1 QB 125, [1969] 3 All ER 941.

[191] [1975] AC 653, [1975] Crim LR 707.

[192] One who would have been a principal in the second degree under the law of felonies.

[193] [1977] AC 755, [1976] 3 All ER 140.

[194] *Graham* [1982] 1 All ER 801 at 804 per Lane LCJ. See also IH Dennis, 'Duress, Murder and Criminal Responsibility' (1980) 106 LQR 208.

[195] [1987] AC 417, [1987] 1 All ER 771, [1987] Crim LR 480 (sub nom *Burke*) and commentary. See also F Stark, 'R v Howe' in P Handler, H Mares and I Williams (eds), *Landmark Cases in Criminal Law* (2017); H Milgate, 'Duress and the Criminal Law: Another About Turn by the House of Lords' (1988) 47 CLJ 61; L Walters, 'Murder under Duress and Judicial Decision Making in the House of Lords' (1988) 18 LS 61; Horder, *Excusing Crime*, 133–137.

[196] *Howe* [1987] 1 All ER 771 at 779–780.   [197] Referring to the 5th edition of this book, at p 215.

[198] Lord Hailsham, *Howe* (n 195) at 780. Art 2 of the ECHR will be engaged in cases of intentional killing.

[199] Lord Bridge, ibid, at 784 and Lord Griffiths at 788.

[200] LC 83, *Report on Defences of General Application* (1977).

[201] Lord Griffiths, *Howe* (n 195) at 790.

[202] Lord Griffiths, ibid, at 791 and Lord Hailsham at 780–781. In non-murder cases the suggestion that the defence should be kept within strict limits and that no injustice will result because of the availability of sentencing discretion met with approval from Lord Bingham in *Hasan*, at [22], but cf Baroness Hale for convincing arguments against.

It is submitted that none of these reasons is at all convincing.[203]

(a) If the defence were available, it would apply only when a jury thought a person of reasonable fortitude *would* have yielded to the threat. The criminal law should not require heroism, for, as Reed argues 'it is inapt to demand heroism as a pre-requisite for exculpation'.[204] Moreover, there are circumstances in which the good citizen of reasonable fortitude not only would, but probably should, yield to the threat because—

(b) to do so might clearly be to choose the lesser of two evils, as where the threat is to kill D and all his family if he does not do, or assist in, an act which he knows will cause grievous harm but not death (though, *ex hypothesi*, it has resulted in death and so constitutes murder).

(c) Parliament's failure to act on the Law Commission recommendation proves nothing. The government has not given Parliament the opportunity to consider the matter. By parity of reason, Parliament might be taken to have approved of *Lynch*'s case, because there has been no move to overrule it.

(d) Even if he were not prosecuted, the 'duressee' would be, in law, a murderer and, if he were called as a prosecution witness, the judge would, at the time of the decision in *Howe*, have been required to tell the jury that he was an accomplice in murder on whose evidence it would be dangerous to act in the absence of corroboration. A morally innocent person should not be left at the mercy of administrative discretion on a murder charge.

There is clearly a strong argument for reversing *Howe*.[205] Lord Bingham suggested that the logic of the argument is 'irresistible'.[206] *Wilson*[207] illustrates the difficulties when duress cannot be a defence to a charge of murder, even if the person seeking to rely on that defence is a child and even if his alleged role in the murder was that of a secondary party acting out of fear of an adult perpetrator. The 13-year-old defendant was not able to plead duress, but argued instead that he had 'not known what he was doing in that his mind did not go with his actions'.[208] The Court of Appeal observed in *Wilson* that there 'might be grounds for

---

[203] This opinion was endorsed by Judge Stephen who, with Judge Cassese, was, however, dissenting in *Prosecutor v Drazen Erdemovic* (Case No IT-96–22-A) in the Appeals Chamber of the International Tribunal for the Prosecution of Persons for Serious Violations of International Humanitarian Law in the Former Yugoslavia. For an interesting discussion of whether the defence of duress ought to have been available to someone charged with war crimes for killing innocent civilians when he was threatened with death if he did not comply, see L Chiesa, 'Duress, Demanding Heroism, and Proportionality' (2008) 41 Vanderbilt J Transnt'l Crime 741.

[204] A Reed, 'Duress and Normative Moral Excuse: Comparative Standardisations and the Ambit of Affirmative Defences' in A Reed and M Bohlander (with N Wake and E Smith) (eds), *General Defences in Criminal Law* (2014) 100.

[205] On the need for reform see A Reed, 'The Need for a New Anglo American Approach to Duress' (1996) 61 J Crim L 209. See KJ Arenson, 'The Paradox of Disallowing Duress as a Defence to Murder' (2014) 78 J Crim L 65. Arenson argues that it is paradoxical that provocation operates as a partial defence to murder but duress does not.

[206] *Hasan* at [21]. It is unlikely that the Supreme Court would change the position. Cf *Dunne v DPP* [2016] IESC 24 in which the Supreme Court in Ireland declined to do so. See also *R v Ryan* (2013) 290 CCC (3d) 477, Supreme Court of Canada declining to address this issue. In *Aravena* [2015] ONCA 250, the Ontario Court of Appeal held that duress is a defence to persons charged as parties to a murder. Although the constitutionality of the murder exemption as it applies to principals was not before the court, it stated that, 'subject to any argument the Crown might advance justifying the exception as it applies to perpetrators under s. 1 of the Charter, the exception must be found unconstitutional'.

[207] [2007] EWCA Crim 1251, [2008] Crim LR 138.

[208] His police interview did not support this defence, but suggested that he acted under duress from his father—the very defence he was precluded from running.

criticising' a rule that denied a child any defence to a charge of murder on the grounds of adult or parental duress, but had no choice but to apply the law as it stood.[209]

The Law Commission in its *Murder, Manslaughter and Infanticide* Report recommended allowing the defence to the charge of murder, but controversially, recommended reversing the burden of proof.[210] The Commission[211] report addresses a range of options and concludes, rightly it is submitted, that if the jury find that D acted under duress within all the stringent requirements of the defence, he ought to be acquitted rather than guilty of manslaughter.[212]

Attempted murder and other related offences

In *Howe*, only Lord Griffiths[213] expressed a clear view that duress is not a defence to attempted murder and the House of Lords subsequently agreed with that view by a majority of three to two in *Gotts*.[214] This is logical, otherwise the effect would be that D's act would be excusable when done, and only become inexcusable if death resulted.

Logic would also require the exclusion of the defence on a charge under s 18 of the OAPA 1861 of causing grievous bodily harm with intent because here also, the offence becomes murder if death results from it. A distinction might be made between murder committed with intent to kill, where duress would not be a defence, and murder committed with intent to cause serious bodily harm, where it would. This would be reconcilable with the traditional statement of the law—a person 'ought rather to die himself than escape by the murder of an innocent'—which seems to postulate a decision to kill; but *Howe* seems too emphatic and uncompromising a decision to allow of any such refinement. *Gotts* indicates that the line is to be drawn below attempted murder, leaving the defence applicable to conspiracy to murder and assisting or encouraging murder. Indeed, in *Ness*[215] the judge ruled that duress is a defence to a charge of conspiracy to murder. Given that there exists no appellate decision directly on point, the judge chose to follow the 'closest authoritative statement' of Lord Lane in *Gotts* and endorsed the widely accepted view that duress is only excluded on a charge of murder, attempted murder and treason.

There is no point in raising the defence of duress to a murder charge; but suppose, as is frequently the case, that the evidence is such that the jury might properly acquit of murder and convict of manslaughter. If there is evidence that D may have been acting under duress[216] it is submitted that the judge should direct the jury that they must not convict of manslaughter either, unless they are sure that D was not acting under duress.

10.2.2 Duress of circumstances

10.2.2.1 The emergence of the defence

The recognition of this defence occurred, more or less by accident, in *Willer*.[217] D was charged with reckless driving after he had driven very slowly on a pavement in order to

---

[209] See commentary by A Ashworth [2008] Crim LR 138.

[210] LC 304, para 6.116. See also LCCP 177 in which the Commission took a different view. Cf O Quick and C Wells, 'Getting Tough with Defences' [2006] Crim LR 514.

[211] LCCP 177, paras 7.18–7.19.   [212] LC 304, para 6.53.   [213] *Howe* (n 195) at 780 and 790.

[214] [1992] 2 AC 412, HL. Lord Lowry, dissenting, thought it is 'the stark fact of death' which distinguishes murder from all other offences. See S Gardner, 'Duress in Attempted Murder' (1991) 107 LQR 389. The issues are discussed in LCCP 177, para 7.60.

[215] [2011] Crim LR 645 and commentary.

[216] cf *Gilmour* [2000] 2 Cr App R 407 where D was roused from his bed and, unwillingly, drove the terrorist murderers to and from the scene of the crime.

[217] (1986) 83 Cr App R 225. On the emergence of the defence more generally see S Gardner, 'Necessity's Newest Invention' (1991) 11 OJLS 125.

escape from a gang of youths who were obviously intent on doing violence to him and his passengers. The trial judge declined to leave the defence of necessity to the jury. The Court of Appeal quashed D's conviction. They said that there was no need to decide on any defence of necessity that might have existed because 'the defence of duress[218] arose but was not pursued', as it ought to have been. It should have been left to the jury to say whether D drove 'under that form of compulsion, ie, under duress'. But this was not an instance of the previously recognized defence of duress by threats—the youths were not saying, 'Drive on the pavement—or else…' There is a closer analogy with self-defence.[219] But in substance the court was simply allowing the defence of necessity which it purported to dismiss as unnecessary to the decision. It should surely make no difference whether D drove on the pavement to escape from the youths, or a herd of charging bulls, a runaway lorry or a flood, if he did so in order to escape what he reasonably believed to be a threat of death or serious bodily harm.

Subsequent cases have not dismissed *Willer* as a case decided *per incuriam*. They have treated it as rightly decided but have recognized that it is not the long-established defence of duress but an extension of it—'duress of circumstances'—the relationship of which to necessity has not been settled (see later). In *Conway*,[220] another case of reckless driving, D's passenger, Tonna, had been the target of an attack on another vehicle a few weeks earlier when another man was shot and Tonna had a narrow escape. According to D, when two young men in civilian clothes came running towards D's parked car, Tonna shouted hysterically, 'Drive off'. D drove off because he feared a deadly attack on Tonna. Being pursued by the two men in an unmarked vehicle, he drove in a manner which the jury adjudged to be reckless. The two men were police officers who wished to interview Tonna. D's conviction was quashed because the defence of duress of circumstances had not been left to the jury.

Willer and *Conway* were followed in *Martin (Colin)*.[221] D, while disqualified, drove his stepson, who had overslept, to work. He said that he did so because his wife feared that the boy would lose his job if he were late and she threatened to commit suicide if D did not drive him. The wife had suicidal tendencies and a doctor stated that it was likely that she would have carried out her threat. The defence ought to have been left to the jury. According to the Court of Appeal, the defence:

can arise from other objective dangers threatening the accused or others…the defence is available only if, from an objective standpoint, the accused can be said to be acting reasonably and proportionately in order to avoid a threat of death or serious injury….[The] jury should be directed to determine these two questions: First, was the accused, or may he have been impelled to act as he did as a result of what he reasonably believed to be the situation he had good cause to fear that otherwise death or serious physical injury would result; Second, if so, would a sober person of reasonable firmness, sharing the characteristics of the accused, have responded to that situation by acting as the accused acted?[222]

On the facts, the case seems to be strictly a case of duress by threats, where D is told, 'Commit the crime or else…' The defence, as with duress by threats, is available only so long as the 'circumstances' continue to threaten. It may have been available (though the court did not decide the point) to a driver who drove off with excess alcohol in his blood to escape assailants; but it was not necessary for him to drive the two and a half miles to his home.[223] But where it was found that D, having consumed excess alcohol, drove off in fear of his life,

---

218 The 'very different' defence of duress according to the court in *Denton* (1987) 85 Cr App R 246 at 248.
219 See p 383.   220 [1989] QB 290, [1989] Crim LR 74.
221 [1989] 1 All ER 652, [1989] Crim LR 284.   222 Per Simon Brown J at 653.
223 *DPP v Jones* [1990] RTR 34, DC. Nor to drive 72 miles when intoxicated to escape a threat, *DPP v Tomkinson* [2001] EWHC Admin 182.

he was guilty of an offence only if the prosecution could prove that he continued to drive after the terror ceased.[224] Similarly, in *Arnaot*,[225] where the court doubted there was any evidence that D was compelled by fear for her safety to drive dangerously following a road traffic incident.

In *S and L*,[226] S was charged with an offence of using unlicensed guards and sought to plead 'necessity' in that he had to deploy unlicensed guards in an emergency. The Court of Appeal referred to the trial judge's 'immaculate judgment' containing a clear and correct statement of the law of 'necessity'. For such a defence there had to be material on which a reasonable jury might conclude that:

(1) it had not been possible for S and L to obtain a licence before the threat to the premises became so acute as to compel them to deploy unlicensed guards. Although no specific threat must be identified as a matter of law, in the absence of such, it may be very difficult to identify material fit to go to a jury;[227]

(2) the deployment of the guards was directly caused by an immediate or imminent threat of death or serious injury;

(3) no other means could reasonably have been taken to avoid the risk. The judge found that the material relied on by the defence did not support the ingredients of the defence.

With respect, this sounds very much like a defence of duress of circumstances rather than one of necessity.

The Court of Appeal is clearly anxious to keep a tight degree of control over the defence of duress of circumstances (as with duress by threats).[228]

In *Quayle*,[229] the court heard a number of appeals and a related reference by the Attorney General. The issue in each case was whether the defence of necessity or 'necessity of circumstances' as it preferred to say, should be left to the jury in respect of offences of: possession, cultivation or production of cannabis where D genuinely and reasonably believed that such activities were necessary to avoid him suffering pain arising from a pre-existing medical condition or from conventional medicine to which he would otherwise resort to reduce the pain. Some of the appeals related to importation or possession with intent to supply cannabis for the purpose of alleviating pain suffered by others in similar circumstances. The defence argument was, in short, that the 'evil' of non-compliance with the Misuse of Drugs Act 1971 and the Customs and Excise Management Act 1979 was relatively minor compared with the risk of serious injury or pain to an individual defendant. It was argued that in any particular case it should be for the jury to weigh such potential ill-effects against the potential benefits to the particular defendant. This argument was supported by reference to the right to private life under Art 8 of the ECHR. The Crown argued, on policy grounds, that since Parliament had clearly and precisely regulated the medicinal use of drugs and had not provided for the use of cannabis, there were strong public policy grounds against allowing the defence of necessity. Alternatively, if the policy argument was rejected, the defence of necessity was not made out: an accused who was seeking to avoid his own pain was unable to show that there was an extraneous circumstance allegedly causing the commission of

---

[224] *DPP v Bell (Derek)*, n 121. See also *CPS v Brown* [2007] EWHC 3274 (Admin).

[225] [2008] EWCA Crim 121.   [226] [2009] EWCA Crim 85, [2009] Crim LR 723.

[227] That is a rather ambiguous but potentially wide opportunity for a defence to be run.

[228] See eg statements in *Patel* [2010] EWCA Crim 976, [47]. Imminent danger that prevents a person from acting lawfully is a necessary ingredient of the defences; *Gregory* [2011] EWCA Crim 1712 in which Lord Judge CJ stated that 'The defence of duress of circumstances is of strictly limited ambit' at [12].

[229] [2005] EWCA Crim 1415; see further the commentary at [2006] Crim LR 148.

the offence. Similarly, in the case of those who were seeking to provide the means by which others could avoid pain, they could not reasonably be said to have a responsibility towards those for whose benefit they claimed to be acting. The Attorney General submitted further that the defence of necessity did not include the avoidance of serious pain, and should not be extended (in the present context at least) to do so.

The Court of Appeal held that there was no overarching principle applicable in all cases of 'necessity' to be derived from individual authorities. 'Necessity' should be developed on a case-by-case basis. The court made more general comments about the defence including that the defence required extraneous circumstances capable of objective scrutiny by judge and jury, capable of being checked and, where appropriate, met by other evidence. Otherwise abusive defences might arise.[230] It was emphasized also that there had to be an imminent danger of physical injury; otherwise, where pain was concerned (which required a large element of subjectivity in its assessment), there would be no clear, objective basis by reference to which to test or determine the defence. Perhaps predictably, the court rejected the Art 8 argument, concluding that Parliament had sanctioned interference with the private life of the sufferer in its legislative policy.

In *Altham*,[231] the Court of Appeal dismissed an appeal in similar circumstances where the drug user who was convicted of possession sought to rely on Art 3 of the ECHR to support his defence. The Court of Appeal concluded that the condition of the appellant was made no worse by the State and that there was no Art 3 claim.

One further restriction which the Court of Appeal has sought to impose on the duress of circumstances defence is, it is submitted, unwarranted. In *Jones*,[232] involving intentional criminal damage to an air force base in an attempt to prevent the USAF and UK services continuing their bombardment of Iraq, the defendants sought to rely, *inter alia*, on defences of duress of circumstances to the charges. In particular, the defendants argued that the war on Iraq was illegal in international law and that their actions were therefore necessary to avert that crime being committed on civilians in Iraq. On an interlocutory appeal, the Court of Appeal held that the defence was not available, declaring that it is limited to a case of D being faced with a crime in national law. With respect, that cannot be right. The defence was available to *Martin* when his wife was threatening suicide (not a crime), moreover one can envisage many circumstances in which D, or those for whom he is responsible, face a threat of death or serious injury by non-criminal means (eg a rapidly engulfing forest fire leads D to steal a car to escape to safety). The House of Lords subsequently dealt with the appeal on the basis of the defence under s 3 of the Criminal Law Act 1967, and did not deal with the issues of duress of circumstances or necessity.[233]

10.3 Necessity

As with duress, we are again concerned with situations in which a person is faced with a choice between two unpleasant alternatives, one involving his committing a breach of the criminal law and the other some evil to himself or others. If the latter evil outweighs any

---

[230] At [73].

[231] [2006] EWCA Crim 7, discussed with commentary by Ashworth [2006] Crim LR 633.

[232] [2004] EWCA Crim 1981, [2005] Crim LR 122. Discussed in Norrie, *Crime, Reason and History*, 212 and S Gardner, 'Direct Action and the Defence of Necessity' [2005] Crim LR 371, although not on this point. For an analysis of the international law dimension to the case, see R Cryer, 'Aggression at the Court of Appeal' (2005) 10 J Conflict Law & Soc 209.

[233] [2006] UKHL 16, [2007] Crim LR 66.

evil involved in the breach of the letter of the law, it is arguable that the actor should have a defence of necessity. The courts have never recognized a defence in these broad terms and to what extent a defence of necessity prevails in English law is uncertain.[234] As early as 1552, Sergeant Pollard in an argument which apparently found favour with the judges of the Exchequer Chamber said that breaking the letter of laws might be justified 'where the words of them are broken to avoid greater inconveniences, or through necessity, or by compulsion…'.[235] More than 300 years later, Stephen thought the law so vague that it was open to the judges to lay down any rule they thought expedient; and that the expediency of breaking the law in some cases might be so great that a defence should be allowed—but these cases could not be defined in advance.[236]

In spite of these doubts, Glanville Williams in 1953 submitted 'with some assurance' that the defence of necessity is recognized by English law[237] and, particularly, by the criminal law,[238] arguing that the 'peculiarity of necessity as a doctrine of law is the difficulty or impossibility of formulating it with any approach to precision'.

Williams' confidence was entirely justified. Lord Goff has, on several occasions, recognized the existence of the defence and it was applied by the House of Lords in the *Bournewood Trust* case[239] to justify the detention of a person suffering from mental disorder where there was no statutory authority on point.[240] From an early period, other particular instances of necessity were recognized. It was justifiable (in the conditions of those days) to pull down a house to prevent a fire from spreading,[241] for a prisoner to leave a burning gaol contrary to the express words of a statute and for the crew of a ship or a passenger[242] to jettison the cargo in order to save the lives of the passengers. It was once held that prison officials may—indeed, must—forcibly feed prisoners if that is necessary to preserve their health and, *a fortiori*, their lives.[243] It was a defence to the offence of procuring an abortion to show that the act was done in good faith for the purpose only of preserving the life of the mother,[244] although at that time there was no provision for such a defence in any statute.[245] More recently it has been recognized that a police officer may direct other persons to disobey traffic regulations if that is reasonably necessary for the protection of life and property.[246]

---

[234] The Court of Appeal (Civ Div) has stated that there is no general defence of necessity. See *R (on the application of Nicklinson) v Ministry of Justice* [2013] EWCA Civ 961, [25]. This case examined whether necessity could be a defence to murder in the context of voluntary euthanasia and the court held that 'it is simply not appropriate for the court to fashion a defence of necessity in such a complex and controversial field; this is a matter for Parliament.' At [56].

[235] *Reniger v Forgossa* (1552) 1 Plowd 1 at 18.　　[236] II HCL, 108.　　[237] CLGP (1st edn) 216.

[238] ibid, 724 et seq.　　[239] [1998] 3 All ER 289, HL, at 297–298, 301–302.

[240] Note that the ECtHR in *HL v UK* (App no 45508/99) held that his being kept at Bournewood Hospital by doctors against the wishes of his carers under the common law of necessity amounted to a breach of Art 5(1) of the ECHR (deprivation of liberty) and of Art 5(4) (right to have lawfulness of detention reviewed by a court). Section 50 of the Mental Health Act 2007 amends the Mental Capacity Act 2005 so that it is unlawful to deprive a person of his liberty in a hospital or care home unless a standard or urgent authorization under Sch A1 to the 2005 Act is in force, or under an order of the Court of Protection. For discussion see LC 372, *Mental Capacity and Deprivation of Liberty* (2017).

[241] See now the Criminal Damage Act 1971, on which see Ch 27.

[242] *Mouse's Case* (1608) 12 Co Rep 63.

[243] *Leigh v Gladstone* (1909) 26 TLR 139 (Alverstone LCJ), not followed by Thorpe J in *Secretary of State for the Home Department v Robb* [1995] 1 All ER 677. The decision is heavily criticized—see G Zellick, 'The Forcible Feeding of Prisoners: An Examination of the Legality of Enforced Therapy' [1976] PL 153 at 159—and no longer applied in practice.

[244] *Bourne* [1939] 1 KB 687. Cf *Morgentaler* (1975) 20 CCC (2d) 449 (SCC), discussed by L Leigh, 'Necessity and the Case of Dr Morgentaler' [1978] Crim LR 151.

[245] See now Abortion Act 1967, on which see Ch 15 and *T v T* [1988] 1 All ER 613, Fam Div.

[246] *Johnson v Phillips* [1976] 1 WLR 65, [1975] Crim LR 580, DC. Cf *Wood v Richards* [1977] RTR 201, [1977] Crim LR 295, DC.

An important case law development is the emergence of duress of circumstances discussed earlier, which in many cases is treated simply as an instance of necessity. On some occasions the court has even merged the terms, as in *Quayle* where the reference is to 'necessity of circumstance'. The relationship of the defences is discussed later. Despite the explicit recognition of the defence the courts persistently adopt a restrictive approach to its application.[247] There is an underlying anxiety that the defence must be kept within strict limits to prevent defendants claiming generally that they thought their actions in breaking the law were reasonable and represented the lesser of two evils. This would be a Trojan horse for anarchy.[248] The speech of Lord Bingham in *Hasan* underlined these judicial anxieties with defences of circumstantial pressure. Norrie cogently explains why the courts have exhibited reluctance to incorporate necessity into English law in the following terms:

necessity operates to permit alternative political, ethical, economic and moral arguments to confront the formal logic of the law. Resting on a concept of moral involuntariness, it opens up the grounds upon which a defendant can say 'I could do no other'. For this reason, the law has fought shy of the defence, yet there remains at the same time a cogent reason for accepting it. It introduces broader ideas of justice, either in terms of social or environmental justice, or the requirements of a properly democratic polity. It requires the criminal law to be mindful of such ideas and the underlying social and political reasons which represent the only means of sustaining its legitimacy.[249]

10.3.1 Nature of threat

The traditional examples of necessity—escaping from the burning gaol, etc—do, like duress and duress of circumstances, involve danger to life. In relation to lesser threats, writers from Hale[250] onwards have denied that necessity can be defence to, for example, a charge of theft of food or clothing. In modern times, Lord Denning has justified that limit on the ground that 'if hunger were once allowed to be an excuse for stealing, it would open a door through which all kinds of lawlessness and disorder would pass'.[251]

In that case, a civil action, it was held that homelessness did not justify even an orderly entry into empty houses owned by the local authority: 'If homelessness were once admitted as a defence to trespass, no one's house could be safe. Necessity would open a door which no man could shut.'[252] Probably, it is now the law that if the taking or the entry was necessary to prevent death or serious injury through starvation or cold there would be a defence of duress of circumstances; but if it were merely to prevent hunger, or the discomforts of cold or homelessness, there would be no defence.

There are some cases where what was in substance a defence of necessity was allowed without identifying a threat to life or serious injury. In *Gillick's* case, one of the conditions stated of the lawfulness of the contraceptive advice or treatment given to a girl under 16 was that unless she receives it 'her physical or mental health or both are likely to suffer'.[253] In *F v West Berkshire Health Authority*,[254] it was held that it was lawful to carry out a sterilization operation on a woman who lacked the mental capacity to consent because otherwise there would be a grave risk of her becoming pregnant which would be disastrous from a psychiatric point of view.[255] Lord Goff founded his judgment on necessity. These cases would, however, involve at most a

---

247 For criticism, see S Edwards, 'Good and Harm, Excuses and Justifications, and the Moral Narratives of Necessity' in A Reed and M Bohlander (with N Wake and E Smith) (eds), *General Defences in Criminal Law* (2014).
248 cf Norrie, *Crime, Reason and History*, 207. 249 ibid, 218.
250 I PC, 54, and see Blackstone, *Commentaries*, iv, 31.
251 *Southwark London Borough v Williams* [1971] 2 All ER 175 at 179. 252 ibid.
253 Per Lord Fraser [1986] AC 112 at 174. 254 [1989] 2 All ER 545, HL.
255 See now the Mental Capacity Act 2005.

slight extension of duress of circumstances—comparable to MacNaghten J's interpretation of 'preserving the life of the mother' to include preserving her from becoming 'a physical or mental wreck' in *Bourne*,[256] a case which must now be regarded as one of duress of circumstances. Lord Goff has also said, 'That there exists a defence of necessity at common law, which may in some circumstances be invoked to justify what would otherwise be a trespass to land, is not in doubt. But the scope of the defence is by no means clear.' He found it unnecessary to decide the important question raised in that case, whether the defence could justify forcible entry (which would otherwise be a crime) into the private premises of another in the bona fide, but mistaken, belief that there exists an emergency on the premises by reason of the presence there of a person who has suffered injury and who may require urgent attention.[257] In *Pipe v DPP*,[258] Owen J ruled that magistrates had been wrong to conclude that D could not plead necessity when he drove over the speed limit in order to get a young boy with a suspected fractured leg to hospital. Despite the fact that the boy's life was not in danger, he was in severe pain and the court ruled that necessity ought to have been considered. This case, again, could be seen as being a slight extension of duress of circumstances. Indeed, Owen J cited *Conway* in his judgment.

10.3.1.1 Statutory implication or exclusion of necessity defence

In England it has been argued that there is a principle of statutory interpretation:

that it requires clear and unambiguous language before the courts will hold that a statutory provision was intended to apply to cases in which more harm will, in all probability, be caused by complying with it than by contravening it.[259]

This principle, if it exists, seems to be little noticed in modern times. In *Buckoke v Greater London Council*,[260] Lord Denning MR said, *obiter*:

A driver of a fire engine with ladders approaches the traffic lights. He sees 200 yards down the road a blazing house with a man at an upstairs window in extreme peril. The road is clear in all directions. At that moment the lights turn red. Is the driver to wait for 60 seconds or more, for the lights to turn green? If the driver waits for that time, the man's life will be lost.

Lord Denning accepted the opinion of both counsel that the driver would (at that time) commit an offence against the Road Traffic Regulations if he crossed the red light. But the threat to the fictitious man at the upstairs window seems to be no less than the threat to Willer, to the passenger in Conway's car or to Martin. Lord Denning was stating the effect of the law as he then believed it to be; but he added that the hypothetical driver 'should not be prosecuted. He should be congratulated'—so Denning would welcome the defence of duress of circumstances. As Professor Packer says:

it seems foolish to make rules (or to fail to make exceptions to rules) that discourage people from behaving as we would like them to behave. To the extent that the threat of punishment has deterrent efficacy, rules such as these would condition people confronted with dilemmas to make the wrong choice, either through action or inaction. And the actual imposition of punishment would serve no useful purpose since we assume these people are not in need of either restraint or reform.[261]

---

[256] [1939] 1 KB 687, see p 653.

[257] *Richards and Leeming* (on appeal from 81 Cr App R 125) (10 July 1986, unreported), HL. The House agreed with Lord Goff's speech (thanks to Sir Anthony Hooper for this material). By s 17(5) of PACE 'all the rules of common law under which a constable has power to enter premises without a warrant are hereby abolished'. But does this abolish a justification which (if it exists at all) is available, not only to constables, but to persons generally?

[258] [2012] EWHC 1821 (Admin).

[259] P Glazebrook, 'The Necessity Plea in English Criminal Law' (1972A) 31 CLJ 87 at 93.

[260] [1971] 1 Ch 655, [1971] 2 All ER 254 at 258. Statutory regulations now exempt the driver of the fire engine; but a contractor with a ladder on his lorry might find himself in the same position.

[261] H Packer, *The Limits of the Criminal Sanction* (1969) 114.

The terms of a statute may, in effect, 'build in' a defence of necessity or, on the other hand, positively exclude one; and in either of these situations there is no room for the application of a general, common law defence. *Quayle*[262] is a good example of the courts rejecting a possible defence on the basis of the conflict it would create with a statutory scheme in which no such defence for possession or supply of drugs was included. A defence of duress by threats or of 'necessity by circumstances' might be available where the general scheme and policy of the legislation was not in question, but the use of cannabis on an individual basis conflicted with the purposes and effect of the legislation. Norrie makes the valuable point that in cases such as *Quayle* the main problem the courts face is in not being seen to sanction a systematic policy of self-help that would undermine the law.[263]

The Court of Appeal addressed this issue again in *S (C)*.[264] D and her husband were divorced and together had a daughter. When the husband applied for contact and residence orders, D alleged that he had sexually abused the daughter but a judge found that these allegations were unfounded. D continued to believe that her daughter was being sexually abused and took her out of the jurisdiction, without the consent of either the father or the court. D was then charged with child abduction. D sought to plead necessity but the judge, referring to *Quayle*, ruled that the defence was unavailable and she pleaded guilty. Sir John Thomas P, after referring to the Child Abduction Act 1984, concluded that given the legislative policy of the Act it was impossible to see how Parliament could have intended for necessity to operate when a parent removes a child who is subject to the court's protection from England and Wales.

These cases demonstrate that if D is charged with a statutory offence and seeks to plead necessity, the judge must determine whether the defence is implicitly excluded by the terms of the legislation. This will require the judge to examine the policy objectives underpinning the legislative scheme.

10.3.1.2 Necessity and responses to non-criminal threats

As noted earlier in the case of *Jones*, the Court of Appeal sought to limit the defence to cases where D faced a criminal threat (in fact it was stipulated that the crime must be one under national law not international law). It is submitted that no such restriction applies. D may rely on the defence where he is faced with naturally occurring disasters, accidents caused by human actors or criminal threats.

10.3.1.3 Necessity and negligence?

In *DPP v Harris*,[265] McCowan LJ was inclined to think that necessity can never be a defence to what would otherwise be the offence of driving without due care because the term 'due' in the section allows for consideration of all the circumstances that would be taken into account if the general defence applied. In *Backshall*,[266] the court preferred the opinion of Curtis J who thought it contrary to common sense to allow the defence in relation to the graver offence of reckless (now dangerous) driving and not to the lesser offence of careless driving; but the court recognized that it may make no difference. A person driving as a necessity, as required, is not failing to exercise 'due' care. The reasoning of McCowan LJ might be applicable to any crime where the prosecution must prove that an act was done

---

262 [2005] EWCA Crim 1415, [2006] Crim LR 148.

263 Norrie, *Crime, Reason and History*, 209–210.

264 [2012] EWCA Crim 389, [2012] Crim LR 624, (2012) 76 J Crim L 202, applied in *Ab* [2014] EWCA Crim 1642.

265 [1995] 1 Cr App R 170, [1995] Crim LR 73, DC. Curtis J thought that if necessity (in effect, duress of circumstances) applied to reckless driving, it must apply to the lesser offence of careless driving. Cf *Symonds* [1998] Crim LR 280.

266 [1999] 1 Cr App R 35 at 41, [1999] Crim LR 662.

unreasonably: if it was necessary so to act, it could hardly be unreasonable to do so. In *Harris*, the court was concerned with a statutory regulation which prescribes the circumstances in which a fire, police or ambulance vehicle may cross a red light; and as we have seen, such a specific provision may well be taken to exclude a defence of necessity when such a vehicle crosses in other circumstances. In *Harris*, all this was *obiter* because the court found that there was no necessity for D to drive as he did.

10.3.1.4 Necessity in strict liability and situational liability offences

In *Cichon v DPP*,[267] the court held that prohibition against allowing a pit bull terrier to be unmuzzled in a public place was 'absolute' and said that it followed that Parliament had excluded any defence of necessity; but if a general defence such as self-defence or duress—or necessity—is available even in offences requiring mens rea, it should *a fortiori* be available to an offence of strict liability. If the owner had removed the dog's muzzle on the orders of an animal rights fanatic armed with a sawn-off shotgun, he would surely have had a defence of duress. So too with necessity—though the fact that the dog in *Cichon* was afflicted with kennel cough might well be held insufficient to ground any such defence.

In *Santos v CPS*,[268] the CPS conceded that the magistrates were wrong to exclude the defence of necessity on the basis that D was charged with a strict liability offence. Foskett J held that there is clear authority that establishes that the defence of necessity is available for strict liability offences, citing *Martin* and *DPP v Mullally*.[269] This echoes what was said by Lord Judge in *Gregory*.[270] Lord Judge CJ stated that while duress of circumstances/necessity is of strictly limited ambit, it is possible to envisage circumstances in which, in the context of possession of a firearm, it might arise. His lordship gave the example of a bank robber who drops his gun, which is then seized by a member of the public who runs away with it to a safe place until the police arrive. Although Lord Judge did not state emphatically that the defence would be applicable in such circumstances, he did observe that although prosecution would be unlikely that does not mean that the possible duress of circumstances/necessity defence would be bound to fail. It is submitted that despite the *obiter* nature of these observations, they have the benefit of according with common sense.

In *Hampshire County Council v E*,[271] the court held that the mother of a truanting child could not plead duress to a charge of 'being a parent of a child of compulsory school age' who was truanting.[272] The offence required no act by the mother, and thus the threats (from the child) could not affect her liability. Presumably no defence of necessity would be available to her either, which is a harsh result indeed, and seems wrong in principle.

10.3.1.5 Necessity and murder

One of the reasons given by the House of Lords in *Howe*[273] for refusing to allow a defence of duress to murder was that it had been decided in the famous case of *Dudley and Stephens*[274] that necessity was not a defence to murder. Whether that was the *ratio decidendi* of the case has been debated. One interpretation of the judgment is that the court found that no

---

[267] [1994] Crim LR 918, DC.   [268] [2013] EWHC 550 (Admin).

[269] [2006] EWHC 3448 (Admin). It was accepted in this case that duress could be a defence to a charge of drink-driving, although there was no evidence that D in fact was acting under duress.

[270] [2011] EWCA Crim 1712.   [271] [2007] EWHC 2584 (Admin).

[272] Education Act 1996, s 444.

[273] [1987] AC 417 at 429, 453, n 195, see J Donoghue (2011) 74 MLR 216, 235 et seq.

[274] (1884) 14 QBD 273. On the instructions of Huddleston B the jury found the facts in a special verdict and the judge then adjourned the assizes to the Royal Courts of Justice where the case was argued before a court of five judges (Lord Coleridge CJ, Grove and Denman JJ, Pollock and Huddleston BB).

necessity existed[275] and the House of Lords later held that the case does decide that point. The facts are well known: three men and a boy of the crew of a yacht were shipwrecked. After 18 days in an open boat, having been without food and water for several days, the two accused suggested to the third man that they should kill and eat the boy. He declined but, two days later, Dudley killed the boy who was now very weak. The three men then fed on the boy's body and, four days later, they were rescued. The accused were indicted for murder. The jury, by a special verdict, found that the men would probably have died within the four days had they not fed on the boy's body, that the boy would probably have died before them and that, at the time of the killing, there was no appreciable chance of saving life, except by killing one for the others to eat. The accused were convicted of murder, but the sentence was commuted to six months' imprisonment.

In *Dudley and Stephens*,[276] Lord Coleridge CJ examined the pronouncements of writers of authority and found nothing in them to justify[277] the extension of a defence to such a case as this. Killing by the use of force necessary to preserve one's own life in self-defence was a well-recognized, but entirely different, case from the killing of an innocent person. Moreover, 'If … Lord Hale is clear—as he is—that extreme necessity of hunger does not justify larceny, what would he have said to the doctrine that it justified murder?'[278]

Apart from authority, the court clearly thought that the law ought not to afford a defence in such a case. They thought, first, that it would be too great a departure from morality; and, secondly, that the principle would be dangerous because of the difficulty of measuring necessity and of selecting the victim. The second reason is more convincing:

Who is to be the judge of this sort of necessity? By what measure is the comparative value of lives to be measured? Is it to be strength or intellect, or what? It is plain that the principle leaves to him who is to profit by it to determine the necessity which will justify him in deliberately taking another's life to save his own.[279]

Williams finds as the 'one satisfying reason' in the judgment that it was no more necessary to kill the boy than one of the grown men and adds: 'To hinge guilt on this would indicate that lots should have been cast…'[280] If the boy had agreed to be bound by the casting of lots, he would have been consenting to die; and, arguably, consent in such a situation may be a defence. Captain Oates took his life when he left Scott and his companions; yet he was regarded not as a criminal but as a hero.[281] If the boy had not consented, the drawing of lots would be hardly more rational than trial by ordeal—yet more civilized than a free-for-all. In fact, the court disapproved, *obiter*, of a ruling in an American case, *United States v Holmes*,[282] that the drawing of lots in similar circumstances would legalize a killing. Holmes, a member of the crew of a wrecked ship, was cast adrift in an overcrowded boat. In order to prevent the boat sinking, the mate gave orders to throw the male passengers overboard and Holmes assisted in throwing over 16 men. No doubt, if his act was criminal at all, it was murder; but a grand jury refused to indict him for murder and

---

[275] Arguably this case is one of duress of circumstances as there is a threat of death or serious injury posed by the circumstances.

[276] On the case generally, see AWB Simpson, *Cannibalism and the Common Law* (1984).

[277] It has been argued that the problem with the judgment is that Lord Coleridge failed to draw a distinction between whether extreme circumstances can *justify* the taking of innocent life, and the separate question of whether such conduct, although unjustifiable, might nevertheless be *excusable*. See J Dressler, 'Reflections on *Dudley and Stephens* and Killing the Innocent: Taking the Wrong Conceptual Path' in D Baker and J Horder (eds), *The Sanctity of Life and the Criminal Law* (2013).

[278] (1884) 14 QBD at 283.   [279] ibid, 287.   [280] CLGP, 744.

[281] Should it matter that Oates killed himself?   [282] (1841) 26 Fed Cas 360.

so he was charged with manslaughter. The judge directed that the law was that passengers must be preferred to seamen; only enough seamen to navigate the boat ought to have been saved; and the passengers whom necessity requires to be cast over must be chosen by lot. As this had not been done (none of the officers or crew went down with the ship) the jury found him guilty.

Stephen thought the method of selection 'over refined'[283] and Lord Coleridge thought this 'somewhat strange ground… can hardly… be an authority satisfactory to a court in this country'.[284]

The English judges offered no alternative solution and, presumably, their view was that, in the absence of a self-sacrificing volunteer, it was the duty of all to die. This was also the view of the distinguished American judge, Cardozo J:

> Where two or more are overtaken by a common disaster, there is no right on the part of one to save the lives of some, by the killing of another. There is no rule of human jettison.[285]

The principle in *Dudley and Stephens* is distinguishable if there is no problem of selection.[286] D, a mountaineer who cuts the rope seconds before he would be dragged over a precipice by E, his falling companion, surely commits no offence. There is no question of choosing between D and E. E is going to die in a matter of seconds anyway. The question is whether he alone should die a few seconds earlier, or whether they should both die seconds later. At the inquest following the Zeebrugge ferry disaster a witness, an army corporal, gave evidence that he and numerous other passengers were trapped in the stricken ferry and in grave danger of drowning. A possible way of escape up a rope ladder was barred by a man, petrified by cold or fear, who could move neither up nor down. After fruitless attempts to persuade him to move, the corporal ordered those nearer to push him off the ladder. They did so, he fell into the water and was not seen again. The trapped passengers were then able to climb up the ladder to safety. The coroner expressed the opinion that a reasonable act of self-preservation, or the preservation of others, is 'not necessarily murder'. So far as is known, no legal proceedings against the corporal were ever contemplated. Unlike the cabin boy, but like the falling mountaineer, the man frozen on the ladder was chosen by fate as the potential victim by his immobility there. He was preventing the passengers from going where they had a right and a most urgent need to go. He was, unwittingly, imperilling their lives.[287]

Similarly, the commander of an Australian naval ship 'took the decision to save the rest of his crew by sealing four sailors in the blazing engine room, consigning them to certain death, after rescuers were beaten back by the flames'.[288] It seems likely that the decision taken by the officer is that which any prudent officer of sound judgement would have taken. If so, it is inconceivable that he would ever be charged with, much less convicted of, murder. Surely the law should recognize this. In these examples the evil avoided outweighs that caused—one dies instead of two, or instead of many—not only is there extreme duress, but the conduct is justified. Indeed, the Australian officer would probably have been in breach of his duty if he had allowed his ship and most of her crew to be lost.

---

[283] II HCL, 108.   [284] (1884) 14 QBD 273 at 285.   [285] *Selected Writings*, 390.

[286] On a more theoretical level, Dressler argues that Lord Coleridge CJ conflated justifiable with excusable conduct and that the circumstances the sailors found themselves in should have been seen as involving the latter. See n 277.

[287] See further JC Smith, *Justification and Excuse*, Ch 3. And cf self-defence against a nine-year-old or insane person.

[288] (1998) The Times, 5 May.

Re A: the conjoined twins

In the case of the conjoined twins,[289] the court held that, in the special circumstances of that case, it was lawful to kill the weaker twin, B, in order to save the life of the stronger, A. But this was not a simple choice between A and B, which the court would have been unwilling to make. The situation presented to the court was that if the operation was performed B would be killed but A would probably live—as indeed occurred—but, if the operation was not performed, both would die. Brooke LJ based his decision on necessity. The three requirements for the defence were stated to be:

(1) the act is needed to avoid inevitable and irreparable evil;

(2) no more should be done than is reasonably necessary for the purpose to be achieved; and

(3) the evil inflicted must not be disproportionate to the evil avoided.[290]

His lordship distinguished *Dudley and Stephens*. There was no problem of who was to be selected to be killed in this case. Like the man on the rope ladder in the Zeebrugge case and the falling mountaineer dragging his companion to his death, A was selected by the circumstances. Brooke LJ preferred necessity to private defence (discussed later) because here there was no 'unjust' aggression by A. But A was imperilling B's life and the private defence solution avoids the argument, valid or not, that necessity can never justify killing. Whatever its basis, the principle appears to be that it is lawful for D to kill A where, as D knows, A is doomed to imminent death but even the short continuation of his life will kill B as well. It remains important to appreciate the limited scope of this judgment. In rejecting the argument that this case is authority for the proposition that necessity is a defence to murder, the Court of Appeal has stated that, 'This case is too slender a thread on which to hang such a far-reaching development of the common law.'[291]

The most recent analysis of the issue arose in *R (on the application of Nicklinson) v Ministry of Justice*.[292] N sought to argue that voluntary euthanasia could be a defence to murder by relying upon the defence of necessity.[293] N relied upon *Re A* to demonstrate that the courts have evinced a willingness to extend the scope of the defence. Toulson LJ in the Divisional Court rejected the analogy with *Re A* and held that:

In a system governed by the rule of law, any such dispensing power requires great caution. It should not be used as a means of introducing major and controversial policy change. *In re A* was a case of highly exceptional facts, where an immediate decision was required.[294]

---

[289] *Re A (Children)* [2000] 4 All ER 961, [2001] Crim LR 400 and commentary. See also J Rogers, 'Necessity, Private-Defence and the Killing of Mary' [2001] Crim LR 515. Cf the approach of the Canadian Supreme Court in *Latimer* [2001] 1 SCR 3, denying D a defence where he killed his severely disabled daughter. The court pronounced a defence based on three criteria: (a) imminent peril; (b) no reasonable legal alternative being available; (c) D's reaction being proportionate. See S Ost, 'Euthanasia and the Defence of Necessity' in C Erin and S Ost, *The Criminal Justice System and Health Care* (2007). For criticism of Ost, see F Stark, 'Necessity and Nicklinson' [2013] Crim LR 949.

[290] *Re A (Children)*, n 289, 1051. For discussion see W Wilson, 'How Criminal Defences Work' in A Reed and M Bohlander (with N Wake and E Smith) (eds), *General Defences in Criminal Law* (2014) 21. This passage in the 13th edition was cited with approval by Lord Dyson MR in *R (on the application of Nicklinson) v Ministry of Justice* [2013] EWCA Civ 466.

[291] *Nicklinson* [2013] EWCA Civ 466, [63]. The Supreme Court also confirmed that *Re A* was an exceptional case.

[292] [2012] EWHC 2381 (Admin), [2013] EWCA Civ 466, [2014] UKSC 38.

[293] It has been argued that *Nicklinson* should not have been argued on the basis of necessity at all, but that consent would have made for a more viable argument, although one that would nevertheless have failed. See F Stark, 'Necessity and Nicklinson' [2013] Crim LR 949. Although not writing about *Nicklinson*, Professor Lewis has made the not dissimilar point that necessity is not a viable route towards the legalisation of euthanasia. See P Lewis, 'The Failure of the Defence of Necessity' in D Baker and J Horder (eds), *The Sanctity of Life and the Criminal Law* (2013).

[294] [2012] EWHC 2381 (Admin), [74].

His lordship held that the common law develops incrementally, whilst major changes involving matters of controversial social policy are for Parliament: this issue falls into the latter category.[295] This passage also demonstrates that his lordship believes that *Re A* contains an element of immediacy that the facts of the instant case lacked. The same view was taken in the Court of Appeal. In the Supreme Court Lord Neuberger observed:[296]

As Lord Dyson MR and Elias LJ explained in para 25 of their judgment in the Court of Appeal, to extend the defence of necessity to a charge of assisted suicide would be a revolutionary step, which would be wholly inconsistent with both recent judicial dicta of high authority, and the legislature's intentions. As to judicial dicta, see *R v Howe* [1987] 1 AC 417, 429B–D and 453B–F, per Lord Hailsham and Lord Mackay respectively, *Airedale NHS Trust v Bland* [1993] AC 789, 892E–893A, per Lord Mustill, and *R v Inglis* [2011] 1 WLR 1110, para 37, per Lord Judge CJ. So far as legislative intention is concerned, in 1961, Parliament decided, through section 2(1), to create a statutory offence of assisting a suicide in a provision which admitted of no exceptions, and it confirmed that decision as recently as 2009 (when section 2(1) was repealed and re-enacted in more detailed terms) following a debate in which the possibility of relaxing the law on the topic was specifically debated.

Shooting down hijacked aircraft

Following the destruction of the World Trade Center in New York by hijacked aircraft, it now appears to be recognized that it would be lawful to shoot down a plane, killing all the innocent passengers and crew if this were the only way to prevent a much greater impending disaster. This is doubted by Bohlander,[297] but without reference to the explicit statements in the Select Committee on Defence,[298] making it clear that government policy is to permit shooting down of civilian aircraft in such circumstances and that the basis for such action would be by application of a necessity principle:

In the last resort, it might be necessary to shoot down the civilian aircraft. MoD officials assured us…that they had properly examined the legal aspects of any such decision…we have satisfied our-selves with lawyers that there is a proper basis for doing this.

The MoD and Committee took the view that the test to be applied is that the act will be necessary and proportionate if:

(1) the act is needed to avoid inevitable and irreparable evil;

(2) no more should be done than is reasonably necessary for the purpose to be achieved; and

(3) the evil inflicted must not be disproportionate to the evil avoided.[299]

---

[295] The Court of Appeal agreed with this analysis. See [2013] EWCA Civ 961. The Supreme Court ([2014] UKSC 38), in a complex judgment, also refused the relief sought. For discussion see J Rogers, 'Assisted Suicide Saga—The *Nicklinson* Episode' [2014] 7 Arch Rev 7.

[296] [2014] UKSC 38, [130].

[297] '*In Extremis*? Hijacked Airplanes, Collateral Damage and the Limits of Criminal Law' [2006] Crim LR 579. See for detailed analysis Norrie, *Crime, Reason and History*, 213–214 and T Hörnle, 'Hijacked Planes: May They Be Shot Down?' (2007) 10 New Crim LR 582.

[298] Sixth Report, *Defence and Security in the UK 2001–2002*, HC 518-I, para 8.   [299] ibid, para 9.

651

10.3.1.6 A doctor's defence of necessity

Without expressly acknowledging it, the courts appear to have recognized a special defence to murder by doctors.[300] Although a doctor knows that treatment will significantly accelerate the death of his patient—that is, kill him—he is not guilty of murder if his purpose is to give what, in the circumstances as he understands them, is proper treatment to relieve pain.[301] Even if this is right, there remains the possibility, where the doctor has made a grossly negligent assessment of the circumstances, of a conviction for manslaughter.

10.3.1.7 Necessity and a duty to act

Where D owes a duty of care to E it seems that necessity may impose on him a duty to act to the detriment of—even to kill—others. The Australian naval officer referred to earlier probably had a duty to kill the four sailors. While the doctors in the conjoined twins case remained in control, they apparently had a duty to kill the weaker twin. When the 'conflict of duties'[302] is resolved, D must fulfil the prevailing duty. If A, B and C are members of a mountaineering party and A sees that B is dragging C to the deaths of both, is he not bound to cut the rope, accelerating B's death but saving the life of C, if he can do so without risk? But what about a passerby, D, who found himself in the same position as A? Presumably he would be justified in cutting the rope but probably not bound to do so.[303]

10.3.1.8 Necessity in other jurisdictions

In some other parts of the common law world a general defence of necessity is now recognized.[304]

In Australia the courts of Victoria recognized the existence of a general, if limited, defence in *Loughnan*[305] where D's defence to a charge of escaping from prison was that he feared he would otherwise be killed by other prisoners—but the defence was not made out on the facts. In *Perka*,[306] the Supreme Court of Canada held that necessity may be an 'excuse' but not a 'justification' (there seems to be no practical difference except that it perhaps made the court feel better) for an act which is 'inevitable, unavoidable and afford(s) no reasonable opportunity for an alternative course of action that does not involve a breach of the law'.

The American Model Penal Code, which has been adopted in many States of the United States, contains a general defence of necessity as follows:

Conduct which the actor believes to be necessary to avoid a harm or evil to him or to another is justifiable, provided that:

(a) the harm or evil sought to be avoided by such conduct is greater than that sought to be prevented by the law defining the offence charged . . . [307]

[300] See S Ost, 'Euthanasia and the Defence of Necessity' [2005] Crim LR 255, arguing that necessity would provide a better basis for a defence of euthanasia for doctors. For rejection of this argument, see P Lewis, 'The Failure of the Defence of Necessity' in D Baker and J Horder (eds), *The Sanctity of Life and the Criminal Law* (2013).

[301] Dr Moor's case, discussed by A Arlidge QC, 'The Trial of Dr David Moor' [2000] Crim LR 31 and a comment by JC Smith, 'A Comment on Dr Moor's Case' [2000] Crim LR 41. See also A Ashworth, 'Criminal Liability in a Medical Context: The Treatment of Good Intentions' in A Simester and ATH Smith (eds), *Harm and Culpability* (1996).

[302] See the discussion of the judgment of Wilson J in *Perka v R* (1984) 13 DLR (4th) 1 at 36 by Ward LJ in *Re A (Children)* at [2000] 4 All ER 961 at 1015–1016, by Brooke LJ at 1048–1050 and by Walker LJ at 1065–1066.

[303] On the 'duty' to assist in such cases, see Ch 2.

[304] See for a review of the position in Oceanic countries, M Forsyth, 'The Divorce or the Marriage of Morality and Law?: The Defence of Necessity in Pacific Island Countries' (2010) 21 Crim Law Forum 121.

[305] [1981] VR 443.　　[306] (1984) 13 DLR (4th) 1.

[307] §3.02. It is subject to qualifications not necessary to be noted here. See the fascinating discussions in L Alexander, 'Lesser Evils: A Closer Look at the Paradigmatic Justification' (2005) 24 L & Phil 611; M Berman, 'Lesser Evils: A Less Close Look' (2005) 24 L & Phil 681.

No such general principle exists or is likely to be developed by English courts. Edmund-Davies LJ clearly formulated the judicial attitude:

the law regards with the deepest suspicion any remedies of self-help, and permits these remedies to be resorted to only in very special circumstances. The reason for such circumspection is clear—necessity can very easily become simply a mask for anarchy.[308]

Until relatively recently, it seemed that, except in cases where necessity had already been recognized as a defence, the courts were likely to be satisfied by their power to grant an absolute discharge in hard cases.[309]

10.3.2 The relationship between duress, duress of circumstances and necessity

It seems now to be generally accepted that duress and duress of circumstances will be treated as identical by the courts as regards all elements other than the obvious one of the source of the threat.[310] This seems unobjectionable.

However, in *Shayler*,[311] it was stated that *Abdul-Hussain* 'reflects other decisions which have treated the defences of duress and necessity as being part of the same defence and the extended form of the defence [ie duress of circumstances] as being different labels for essentially the same thing'.[312] But there are strong objections to this view.

(1) It is established that duress cannot be a defence to murder or attempted murder but, following *Re A* (the case of the conjoined twins) it is now clear that necessity *may* be. This statement must be treated with due caution, however, given the Supreme Court's judgment in *Nicklinson*.[313]

(2) Imminent threats of death or grievous bodily harm are the only occasions for a defence of duress but not for necessity. It is surely a defence to a charge of battery that D was pushing a child to save him from some quite minor injury or even damage to his clothing. Suppose that in *Martin (Colin)* D's wife's threat had been not to kill herself but to leave D; and suppose further that the consequences of her doing so would have been disastrous for D and his family. Duress of circumstances is not open. Should it be a defence for D to demonstrate that the break-up of his marriage would be a social disaster beside which any effect of his driving a short distance while disqualified would pale into insignificance?

(3) Necessity is a defence only if the evil D seeks to avoid would be greater than that which he knows he is causing, whereas if D yields to torture which no ordinary person could be expected to resist, he should be excused however grave the consequences.

---

[308] *Southwark London Borough v Williams* [1971] Ch 734, [1971] 2 All ER 175 at 181.

[309] Glazebrook (1972A) 31 CLJ 87 at 118–119.

[310] See Wilson, *Central Issues*, Ch 10, pp 303 et seq; I Dennis, 'On Necessity as a Defence to Crime: Possibilities, Problems and the Limits of Justifications and Excuses' (2009) 3 Crim L & Phil 29 examining the theoretical bases for the defence. See also P Westen and J Mangiafico, 'The Criminal Defense of Duress as Justification not Excuse and Why it Matters' (2003) 6 Buffalo Crim LR 833.

[311] [2001] EWCA Crim 1977, [2001] Crim LR 986.

[312] C Clarkson, 'Necessary Action: A New Defence' [2004] Crim LR 81, made a more radical suggestion that the defences of duress, necessity, duress of circumstances and self-defence should be collapsed into one defence of 'necessary action'. This would succeed in achieving its aim of avoiding the inconsistencies of the present law, but only by adopting a lowest common denominator for the defences which seems to be simply that the jury scrutinizes D's conduct to ascertain whether he faced a crisis and responded proportionately. It would be most unlikely to be adopted by the courts since they would be concerned that it opens the floodgates for spurious claims and perverse verdicts. For criticism see AP Simester, 'On Justifications and Excuses' in L Zedner and J V Roberts, *Principles and Values in Criminal Law and Criminal Justice* (2012).

[313] [2014] UKSC 38.

(4) Recent cases allowing evidence of the vulnerability to duress of the particular defendant have nothing to do with the proportionality of evils which is said to be required for necessity but are highly relevant to whether he should be excused for giving way to threats.

(5) Necessity may create a duty to act but mere duress can hardly do so.

(6) Duress is (generally accepted to be) an excuse, and necessity a justification.[314] It is quite inappropriate to talk of a surgeon's will being 'overborne' when he decides that it is necessary to carry out a sterilization or other operation, as in the *West Berkshire* case,[315] on a person who is unable to consent. The surgeon is making a reasoned and reasonable decision. Lord Brandon thought that not only would it be lawful, but that it would be the doctor's duty to operate. There is no question of excusing 'human frailty'. All this is true, *a fortiori*, of the decision of the court when it authorizes such an operation as in *Re A* (the conjoined twins).

It is disappointing that the appellate courts have been prepared to state that 'the distinction between duress of circumstances and necessity has, correctly, been by and large ignored or blurred by the courts'.[316] More recently, the Court of Appeal in *S*, taking cognizance of the criticisms made in this section in the 13th edition, ultimately held that, 'we can leave open the question as to whether there is a distinction between necessity and duress of circumstances'.[317]

10.4 Marital coercion

The defence of marital coercion was abolished by s 177 of the Anti-social Behaviour, Crime and Policing Act 2014.[318]

10.5 Superior orders

It is not a defence for D merely to claim that the act was done by him in obedience to the orders of a superior, whether military or civil.[319] Where a security officer caused an obstruction of the highway by checking all the vehicles entering his employer's premises, it was no defence that he was obeying his employer's instructions.[320] Both the House of Lords and the Privy Council have asserted, probably *obiter*, that there is no defence of superior orders in English law.[321] Both approved the statement of the High Court of Australia[322] that 'It is

---

[314] See on this S Gardner, 'Direct Action and the Defence of Necessity' [2005] Crim LR 371.

[315] See p 369.

[316] *Shayler* (n 85) para 55; in *Hasan* [2005] UKHL 22, Lord Bingham seems to use the term necessity interchangeably with duress, eg at [22].

[317] [2012] EWCA Crim 389, [15], [2012] Crim LR 62.

[318] By virtue of s 177(3) the defence may still be pleaded in respect of an offence alleged to have been committed before the date when the provision came into force, 13 May 2014. For discussion of the defence, see the 13th edition, at p 375.

[319] See S Wallerstein, 'Why English Law Should Not Incorporate the Defence of Superior Orders' [2010] Crim LR 109 considering the influence of international law. See also P Rowe, 'The Criminal Liability of a British Soldier Merely for Participating in the Iraq War 2003' [2010] Crim LR 752 at 757.

[320] *Lewis v Dickson* [1976] RTR 431, [1976] Crim LR 442, DC.

[321] *Clegg* [1995] 1 All ER 334 at 344, [1995] Crim LR 418, HL, 407; *Yip Chiu-Cheung* [1994] 2 All ER 924 at 928, PC, p 407. The implications of *Clegg* for firearms officers and servicemen are considered in S Skinner, 'Citizens in Uniform: Public Defence, Reasonableness and Human Rights' [2000] PL 266; J Rogers, 'Justifying the Use of Firearms by Policemen and Soldiers: A Response to the Home Office's Review of the Law on the Use of Lethal Force' (1998) 18 LS 486.

[322] *A v Hayden (No 2)* (1984) 156 CLR 532 at 540.

fundamental to our legal system that the executive has no power to authorize a breach of the law and that it is no excuse for an offender to say that he acted under the authority of a superior officer.'

The fact that D was acting under orders may, nevertheless, be very relevant. It may negative mens rea by, for example, showing that D was acting under a mistake of fact or that he had a claim of right[323] to do as he did, where that is a defence; or, where the charge is one of negligence,[324] it may show that he was acting reasonably.

10.6 Public and private defence

Force causing personal injury, damage to property or even death may be justified or excused because the force was reasonably used in the defence of certain public or private interests.[325] Public and private defence is therefore a general defence to any crime of which the use of force is an element or which is alleged to have been committed by the use of force.[326] In *Riddell*, the Court of Appeal held that private defence is available as a defence to a charge of dangerous driving.[327] The court held that whilst being charged with this offence does not of itself convey that force has been used, the alleged facts relating to the driving charge may nevertheless be such that force has indeed been applied in response to threatened or actual force.[328] Private defence will therefore be available as a defence to some driving offences, dangerous driving and careless driving being the most obvious examples, but it will not be available to most other driving offences, since they necessarily do not involve the use of force.

The use of the word 'unlawfully' in a statutory definition of an offence is a reminder of the existence of the general defences but they apply whether or not the statute uses that word[329] unless expressly or impliedly excluded. It is clear that the burden of disproving claims of public or private defence rests on the prosecution.[330]

The law is to be found in a variety of sources. Defence of the person, whether oneself or another, is still regulated by the common law (a defence of private defence as it is called in this chapter) as 'clarified' in s 76 of the Criminal Justice and Immigration Act 2008; defence of property by the Criminal Damage Act 1971; and arrest and the prevention of crime by s 3 of the Criminal Law Act 1967 to be read in light of s 76.

Because of its haphazard growth, the law contains some inconsistencies and anomalies. In many cases the common law plea of private defence overlaps with the plea under s 3 of the Criminal Law Act 1967. It is important to bear in mind that s 3 is only available where D uses force *in the prevention of a crime*. Otherwise D must fall back on private defence at common law as now largely restated in s 76 of the Criminal Justice and Immigration Act 2008 (CJIA). Although the principles are very similar, technically they are different defences. One similarity that was confirmed only relatively recently is that both defences

---

[323] *James* (1837) 8 C & P 131.   [324] *Trainer* (1864) 4 F & F 105.

[325] See, *inter alia*, Norrie, *Crime, Reason and History*, Ch 10; F Leverick, *Killing in Self-Defence* (2006); B Sangero, *Self Defence in Criminal Law* (2006).

[326] *Renouf* [1986] 2 All ER 449, [1986] Crim LR 408 (reckless driving). Force was not an element of the offence of reckless driving (now abolished) but the use of force was alleged to constitute the recklessness in that case. The Court of Appeal distinguished *Renouf* in *Bailey* [2013] EWCA Crim 378.

[327] [2017] EWCA Crim 413.

[328] For criticism, see S Kyd [2017] Crim LR 637.

[329] *Renouf* (n 326); *Rothwell* [1993] Crim LR 626.

[330] The judge must give clear direction on the issue: *O'Brien* [2004] EWCA Crim 2900.

can be pleaded by D who uses force on B in order to prevent C from committing a crime. In *Hichens*, Gross LJ stated that both defences, 'are capable of extending to the use of force against an innocent third party to prevent a crime being committed by someone else'.[331] His lordship did, however, recognize that circumstances giving rise to such a defence will be rare and placed a great deal of emphasis on the requirement of immediacy. This perhaps indicates that pleas of public or private defence in circumstances such as this will only be left to the jury in exceptional cases.

Section 76 provides in part:[332]

Reasonable force for purposes of self-defence etc.

(1) This section applies where in proceedings for an offence—

    (a) an issue arises as to whether a person charged with the offence ('D') is entitled to rely on a defence within subsection (2), and

    (b) the question arises whether the degree of force used by D against a person ('V') was reasonable in the circumstances.

(2) The defences are—

    (a) the common law defence of self-defence; and

    (aa) the common law defence of defence of property; and

    (b) the defences provided by section 3(1) of the Criminal Law Act 1967 . . .

(9) This section is intended to clarify the operation of the existing defences mentioned in subsection (2).

(10) In this section—

    (a) 'legitimate purpose' means—

        (i) the purpose of self-defence under the common law,

        (ia) the purpose of defence of property under the common law; or

        (ii) the prevention of crime or effecting or assisting in the lawful arrest of persons mentioned in the provisions referred to in subsection (2)(b);

    (b) references to self-defence include acting in defence of another person; and

    (c) references to the degree of force used are to the type and amount of force used.

In a case in which D is in a dwelling and uses violence on a trespasser (a householder case), different considerations apply.

10.6.1 General principle

The defences at common law and under s 3, as now both also regulated by s 76, can be conveniently described[333] in terms of trigger and response:

- the trigger being D's belief that the circumstances as he understands them render it reasonable or necessary for him to use force;[334] and

---

[331] [2011] EWCA Crim 1626, [30], [2011] Crim LR 873.

[332] Section 76 fails to clarify the law (cf s 76(9)), seeking merely to put some common law on a statutory footing.

[333] Despite the simplicity with which private defence can be described, it is a difficult area of law and a careful direction to the jury will often be necessary. Indeed in *Hayes* [2011] EWCA Crim 2680, Moore-Bick LJ described this area of law as being 'notoriously difficult'.

[334] It is important not to lose sight of the fact that what D must have a genuine belief in is the necessity of using force. In *Yaman* [2012] EWCA Crim 1075 the judge directed the jury to evaluate whether D believed the men he attacked were burglars. It was rightly held that this was not what the jury ought to have been considering.

- the response being the use of a proportionate or reasonable amount of force to the threat that D believes he faces.[335]

The general principle is that the law allows such force to be used as is objectively reasonable in the circumstances as D genuinely believed them to be. The trigger is assessed subjectively (what did D genuinely believe);[336] the response objectively (would a reasonable person have used that much force in the circumstances as D believed them to be). For example, if D believed that he was being attacked with a deadly weapon and he used only such force as was reasonable to repel such an attack, he has a defence to any charge of an offence arising out of his use of that force. It is immaterial that he was mistaken. Indeed, it is immaterial that he was unreasonably mistaken. Section 76 of the 2008 Act confirms this established common law principle.

In terms of the force D uses in 'response' to the threat as he genuinely perceives it to be, the question, 'Was the force used reasonable in the circumstances as D supposed them to be?'[337] is a question to be answered by the jury or magistrates having regard to s 76. If D's use of force was reasonable on the threat he believed he faced, he is not liable for any harm that arises, even if the reasonable force he uses results in some greater harm which he had not foreseen. For example, D wrestles with V who is trying to steal D's wallet. V dies of a heart attack. If it was reasonable to use the amount of force to wrestle with V, D commits no offence even though it would not have been reasonable to kill V. In the important case of *Keane*[338] Hughes LJ summarized the law on these general principles set out in this paragraph. The judge need only leave private defence to the jury if there is prima facie evidence from which it could be inferred that the defence applies: *Mula*.[339]

10.6.1.1 D's belief in need for force—the trigger—is subjectively assessed

Section 76(3) of the CJIA 2008 provides:

(3) The question whether the degree of force used by D was reasonable in the circumstances is to be decided *by reference* to the circumstances as D believed them to be, and subsections (4) to (8) also apply in connection with deciding that question.[340]

By s 76(4) of the 2008 Act:

If D claims to have held a particular belief as regards the existence of any circumstances—

(a) the reasonableness or otherwise of that belief is relevant to the question whether D genuinely held it; but

---

[335] See Wilson [2005] Crim LR 108 and W Wilson, 'How Criminal Defences Work' in A Reed and M Bohlander (with N Wake and E Smith) (eds), *General Defences in Criminal Law* (2014). Wilson argues that the requirement of proportionality in private defence is, in contrast to other defences, problematic on the basis that if the defence is constituted so as to vindicate the right to personal autonomy, it is unclear why D has to do anything other than that which is necessary to vindicate that right.

[336] This element of the defence has been criticized on the basis that it focuses too much on D's subjective belief. It has been suggested that the law should require an examination of why D was mistaken. See J Rogers, 'Culpability in Self-Defence and Crime Prevention' in GR Sullivan and I Dennis, *Seeking Security: Pre-Empting the Commission of Criminal Harms* (2012).

[337] But not in relation to s 5 of the Criminal Damage Act 1971, p 1084.

[338] [2010] EWCA Crim 2514, [2011] Crim LR 393. See also *Noye* [2011] EWCA Crim 650 at [9] and [55].

[339] [2013] EWCA Crim 1293. The Court of Appeal relied upon *DPP (Jamaica) v Bailey* [1995] 1 Cr App R 257, [1995] Crim LR 313 and *Bonnick* (1978) 66 Cr App R 266, [1978] Crim LR 246.

[340] Emphasis added.

(b) if it is determined that D did genuinely hold it, D is entitled to rely on it for the purposes of subsection (3), whether or not—

(i) it was mistaken, or

(ii) (if it was mistaken) the mistake was a reasonable one to have made.

Section 76(4) makes clear that the reasonableness of the force D uses is to be assessed on the facts and circumstances as D genuinely believed them to be, even if his belief as to the circumstances was mistaken and unreasonable.[341]

The common law authority for the proposition that D is to be judged on the facts as he believed them to be is *Gladstone Williams*,[342] repeatedly applied in the Court of Appeal[343] and by the Privy Council in *Beckford v R*. Williams was charged with an assault occasioning actual bodily harm to V. D's defence was that he was preventing V from committing an assault on X. But V may have been lawfully arresting X. The jury was directed that if V was acting lawfully, D had a defence only if he believed *on reasonable grounds* that V was acting unlawfully. It was held that this was a misdirection.[344] D had a defence if he honestly held the belief that there was a need to use force against V, whether his belief was reasonable or not.[345] The court referred to the recommendation of the Criminal Law Revision Committee (CLRC) that the common law of self-defence should be replaced by a statutory defence providing:

a person may use such force as is reasonable in the circumstances as he believes them to be in the defence of himself or any other person.[346]

The court declared that this proposition represented the common law, as stated in *Morgan*[347] and *Kimber*.[348]

If D is voluntarily intoxicated he cannot rely on any mistaken belief attributable to that intoxication: s 76(5).[349]

---

[341] Subject to what is said later in relation to insane belief in the need for force. An unreasonable belief can be honestly held, but it is not a misdirection to omit this from jury directions: *Chuong* [2013] EWCA Crim 1716. On self-defence generally, see Leverick, *Killing in Self Defence*, Chs 5 and 9. On the admissibility of expert medical evidence to show why D may have been likely to perceive a threat, see *Ibrahim* [2014] EWCA Crim 121, [27] and *Press and Thompson* [2013] EWCA Crim 1849. See p 386.

[342] (1984) 78 Cr App R 276, [1984] Crim LR 163, CA. But, where D is drunk, see *O'Grady* [1987] QB 995, [1987] Crim LR 706 and *Hatton* [2005] EWCA Crim 2951, [2006] Crim LR 353, discussed at p 326. See also *Robinson* [2017] EWCA Crim 923 where D's evidence was that he panicked when he picked up a knife and stabbed V to death.

[343] *Jackson* [1985] RTR 257, [1985] Crim LR 674; *Asbury* [1986] Crim LR 258, CA; *Fisher* [1987] Crim LR 334, CA; *Beckford v R* [1988] AC 130, [1988] Crim LR 116, PC. Failure to follow this closely will render the conviction unsafe, see *Duffy v Cleveland* [2007] EWHC 3169 (Admin).

[344] It has been argued that this takes subjectivism too far for two reasons. First, that the more predisposed D is to assume unreasonably that he needs to use force, the more likely it is he will be acquitted, which puts the public at risk. Secondly, that permitting D to avoid liability altogether on the basis of an unreasonable belief could violate Art 2 and/or 3 of the ECHR. See C de Than and J Elvin, 'Mistaken Private Defence: The Case for Reform' in A Reed and M Bohlander (with N Wake and E Smith) (eds), *General Defences in Criminal Law* (2014) 135–136. Merely because the first limb of private defence is made out does not, however, mean that D will invariably be acquitted. On the ECHR point, see later.

[345] For further discussion, see Norrie, *Crime, Reason and History*, 287–291 and Horder, APOCL, 136–143.

[346] Fourteenth Report, para 72(a). The phrase 'may use' is inappropriate. The CLRC was concerned only with establishing a defence in criminal proceedings. The act should not be regarded as justified in the civil law; and, if the mistake was grossly negligent and caused death, it might be manslaughter.

[347] [1976] AC 182, [1975] Crim LR 717.

[348] [1983] 3 All ER 316, [1983] Crim LR 630, CA (D guilty of indecent assault only if he did not believe V was consenting and 'couldn't care less').

[349] See Ch 9, p 314. Cf *Goode* [2014] EWCA Crim 90, in which the Court of Appeal upheld the judge's direction to the jury that D was not entitled to rely upon a mistaken belief induced by the effects of alcohol. Section 76(5) was not cited by the Court of Appeal, it instead relied upon *Soames* [2001] EWCA Crim 2964.

10.6.1.2 Reasonableness of force—the response—is to be assessed objectively

The reasonableness of D's response and the amount of force used are to be assessed objectively on the facts as D believes them to be, by s 76(6) of the 2008 Act. Any possibility that D could have retreated is to be considered (so far as relevant) as a factor to be taken into account, rather than giving rise to a formal legal duty to retreat.[350]

The degree of force used by D is not to be regarded as having been reasonable in the circumstances as D believed them to be if it was disproportionate in those circumstances[351] (although in a householder case see the discussion below).

At common law, in *Shaw (Norman) v R*,[352] the Privy Council accepted the proposition that in determining whether D's response by using force is proportionate, D is to be judged on the circumstances *and danger* as he believed them to be. This is, it is submitted, a preferable approach. It was endorsed by the Court of Appeal in *Harvey*.[353]

D's belief that he is doing only what is reasonable may be evidence, but no more, that it *was* reasonable.[354] Lord Morris has said:[355]

If there has been an attack so that defence is reasonably necessary it will be recognized that a person defending himself cannot weigh to a nicety the exact measure of his necessary defensive action. If a jury thought that in a moment of unexpected anguish a person attacked had only done what he honestly and instinctively thought was necessary that would be most potent evidence that only reasonable defensive action had been taken. A jury will be told that the defence of self-defence, where the evidence makes its raising possible, will only fail if the prosecution show beyond doubt that what the accused did was not by way of self-defence.

This principle relates to self-defence but similar considerations apply to force used to prevent crime or to effect an arrest, etc.

10.6.1.3 Evidence of D's beliefs

There may be an issue as to what circumstances D genuinely believed to exist, especially where his claimed belief is, viewed objectively, an unreasonable one. In such a case, evidence of D's personal characteristics must, in principle, be admissible insofar as they bear upon his ability to be aware of, or to perceive, the circumstances.[356] Section 76(4)–(8) of the CJIA seeks to explain, based on the common law, what may be relevant to the question of D's beliefs. In particular, under s 76(7) in deciding whether D had a genuine belief in the need to use force:

the following considerations are to be taken into account (so far as relevant in the circumstances of the case)—

---

[350] By virtue of s 148 of the Legal Aid, Sentencing and Punishment of Offenders Act 2012, which inserts a new subs 76(6)(A).

[351] This was an issue in *Yaman* [2012] EWCA Crim 1075 in which the Court of Appeal identified a number of failings in the judge's summing up, but nevertheless upheld D's conviction. For commentary, see Ormerod [2012] Crim LR 896.

[352] [2002] 1 Cr App R 10, [2002] Crim LR 140, PC.

[353] [2009] EWCA Crim 469.

[354] *Scarlett* [1993] 4 All ER 629, [1994] Crim LR 288, appeared to have significantly modified this rule but *Owino* [1996] 2 Cr App R 128, [1995] Crim LR 743, CA and *DPP v Armstrong-Braun* [1999] Crim LR 416, DC, decide that *Scarlett* in no way qualifies the law as stated in *Gladstone Williams* (1984) 78 Cr App R 276, [1984] Crim LR 163.

[355] *Palmer v R* [1971] 1 All ER 1077 at 1078, PC, applied in *Shannon* (1980) 71 Cr App R 192, [1980] Crim LR 438 and *Whyte* [1987] 3 All ER 416.

[356] Remorse is not necessarily evidence of D's reasonableness: *Dewar v DPP* [2010] EWHC 1050 (Admin).

(a) that a person acting for a legitimate purpose may not be able to weigh to a nicety the exact measure of any necessary action; and

(b) that evidence of a person's having only done what the person honestly and instinctively thought was necessary for a legitimate purpose constitutes strong evidence that only reasonable action was taken by that person for that purpose.

By s 76(8):

Subsection (7) is not to be read as preventing other matters from being taken into account where they are relevant to deciding the question mentioned in subsection (3).

At common law, *Martin (Anthony)*[357] held that evidence of D's *physical* characteristics may be admissible. Circumstances which would not be seen as threatening by a robust young man may appear so to a frail elderly woman. However, on policy grounds, the court held that psychiatric evidence that D would have perceived the supposed circumstances as being a greater threat than would a normal person is not admissible. The court rejected an analogy with provocation[358] where such evidence would have been admissible because provocation applied only to murder and was not a complete defence. Unfortunately, the court did not consider duress, where such evidence is admissible for a defence which applies to virtually all crimes except murder and is a complete defence. In the duress case of *Martin (DP)*,[359] psychiatric evidence was admitted that D was suffering from a schizoid affective disorder which made him more likely than a 'normal' person to regard things said as threatening, and to believe that threats would be carried out.

In *Oye*, the Court of Appeal considered the extent to which the plea of private defence could be founded on insane delusions.[360] D was charged with affray and inflicting GBH on a number of police officers. There was expert evidence that D was suffering from an insane delusion at the relevant time and believed that the police officers were evil spirits. At trial there was uncontradicted psychiatric evidence that supported the insanity plea. The judge allowed private defence and insanity to be left to the jury. The jury rejected both defences and D was convicted. On appeal the court held that although there is a subjective element to the question of whether the force used was reasonable in the circumstances as D believed them to be, the standard of reasonableness makes it overwhelmingly objective. Davis LJ stated that:

An insane person cannot set the standards of reasonableness as to the degree of force used by reference to his own insanity. In truth, it makes as little sense to talk of the reasonable lunatic as it did, in the context of cases on provocation, to talk of the reasonable glue-sniffer.[361]

Support for this conclusion was derived from *Martin (Anthony)* and *Canns*,[362] in which the Court of Appeal rejected the argument that the jury ought to have been directed to consider D's delusional state in private defence. In *Oye*, Davis LJ held that the enactment of s 76 did not undermine the validity of these authorities, given that the statute merely 'clarifies' the common law defence. His lordship held that the argument advanced on behalf of D would constitute a change in the law, rather than a clarification of it.[363] The Court of Appeal

---

[357] [2001] EWCA Crim 2245, [2002] Crim LR 136. Child and Sullivan characterize this as a 'problematic authority'. See J Child and GR Sullivan, 'When Does the Insanity Defence Apply? Some Recent Cases' [2014] Crim LR 788.

[358] See p 543.   [359] [2000] 2 Cr App R 42, [2000] Crim LR 615, CA.

[360] [2013] EWCA Crim 1725, [2014] Crim LR 544, (2014) 78 J Crim L 12.   [361] At [47].

[362] [2005] EWCA Crim 2264.

[363] Since the Crown accepted the psychiatric evidence, the Court of Appeal quashed D's conviction and substituted it for one of not guilty by reason of insanity.

concluded that while D's physical condition may be taken into account in private defence, his psychiatric condition generally cannot. This outcome is unsurprising, as the argument that s 76 altered the common law in this respect was not one the Court of Appeal was ever likely to find convincing.

The decision serves to highlight the difficult interaction between private defence and insanity. As the court observed in *Oye*, ensuring that mentally ill defendants receive the treatment they require complies with policy concerns about public safety.[364] This supports the idea that once D relies on insane beliefs he should be treated as though he is pleading insanity, which ought to 'trump'[365] private defence to preclude it from being left to the jury. To permit otherwise, it is argued, undermines the rationale for the existence of the insanity plea.[366] The counter-argument is that by withdrawing private defence D is denied an opportunity to advance a defence that might lead to a full acquittal;[367] by being forced to plead insanity D is at best going to receive the special verdict. The court did not state that private defence *must* be withdrawn when D relies on insane beliefs, but rather that in considering private defence the jury should ignore those beliefs when considering the second limb of the defence. But that approach also poses problems in practice for a judge trying to direct a jury coherently: when will it be appropriate to take into consideration D's psychiatric condition short of outright legal insanity if he pleads private defence?

If D uses force and relies on insane beliefs to explain why he did so but a reasonable person in his position would have had legitimate grounds to use the amount of force D actually used, why should D be precluded from pleading private defence and the possibility of securing a complete acquittal? It is different if a reasonable person would not have used any, or such, force in the circumstances but the reason D did so is because of his insanity. It is submitted that the Court of Appeal needs to provide clarity on exactly when insanity will 'trump' private defence.

Although the courts have generally demonstrated a reluctance to permit D's psychiatric condition to be considered as relevant to the belief he held, there are some cases in which it has been admitted. For example, in *Press* D pleaded private defence to the charge of causing GBH with intent and relied on psychiatric evidence that he suffered from PTSD to substantiate his claim that he had a mistaken belief in the need to use force.[368] D was convicted and appealed. One of the issues was the extent to which expert evidence was relevant to his plea of private defence. The court distinguished *Oye* on the basis that the expert evidence did not suggest that D was acting under an insane delusion; rather, the evidence was that his PTSD could have caused D mistakenly to judge the need to use force and then exceed what was reasonable in the circumstances as he understood them to be.

---

[364] It has been argued that the policy considerations the court relies upon can apply to any unreasonable mistake made by D and not just one induced by an insane delusion, at least where D's characteristics predispose him to make unreasonable mistakes about the circumstances. See C de Than and J Elvin, 'Mistaken Private Defence: The Case for Reform' in A Reed and M Bohlander (with N Wake and E Smith) (eds), *General Defences in Criminal Law* (2014) 135.

[365] Cf R Mackay [2014] Crim LR 544.

[366] J Child and GR Sullivan, 'When Does the Insanity Defence Apply? Some Recent Cases' [2014] Crim LR 788, arguing that the same approach ought to have been adopted in *B* [2013] EWCA Crim 3, [2014] Crim LR 312.

[367] In *Oye*, the Court of Appeal observed that the order in which the jury ought to be directed to consider the defences is important, but preferred not to express a view on the matter. At [58]–[59]. As the court pointed out, s 2(1) of the Trial of Lunatics Act 1883 precludes the judge from giving a judicial direction to the jury to find D insane.

[368] [2013] EWCA Crim 1849. See also *Ibrahim* [2014] EWCA Crim 121. Jackson LJ contrasted this case with *Oye*, which was characterized as one in which D suffered from a psychiatric condition that caused him to believe in a state of affairs which did not exist, whereas in the instant case it was D's contention that his ADHD caused him to return to the fray after having initially been struck by V.

Oye and *Press* demonstrate that there is no coherence of approach as to the extent to which the personal characteristics of the defendant are relevant when pleading private defence. This issue is not confined to private defence but has also arisen in the context of duress and loss of control. There may be good reasons for this lack of coherence if each of the defences has a separate theoretical foundation. The problem is that the courts continue to make occasional comparisons between each of the defences without exploring these theoretical distinctions. They also fail to explain why an approach that has been adopted in relation to one defence is not taken in relation to another.[369]

Within private defence, the balancing of the characteristics of the relevant individuals can give rise to difficult issues. What of the relatively slight woman who uses lethal force against a physically stronger male whom she believes is about to attack her?[370] The Law Commission in its 2004 consideration of the partial defence to murder recognized the difficulty that this posed in many trials and recommended a new Judicial Studies Board Direction:

It is insufficient to weigh the weapons used on each side; sometimes there is an imbalance in size and strength. You must also consider the relationship between the defendant and [the other party]. A defendant who has experienced previous violence in a relationship may have an elevated view of the danger that they are in. They may honestly sense they are in greater danger than might appear to someone who has not lived through their experiences. All these matters should be taken into account when considering the reasonableness of the force used.[371]

10.6.1.4 Householder cases

Section 43 of the Crime and Courts Act 2013 amends s 76 by inserting the following provisions.[372]

Use of force in self-defence at place of residence

(1) Section 76 of the Criminal Justice and Immigration Act 2008 (use of reasonable force for purposes of self-defence etc) is amended as follows.

(2) Before subsection (6) (force not regarded as reasonable if it was disproportionate) insert—

'(5A) In a householder case, the degree of force used by D is not to be regarded as having been reasonable in the circumstances as D believed them to be if it was grossly disproportionate in those circumstances.'

(3) In subsection (6) at the beginning insert 'In a case other than a householder case,'.

(4) After subsection (8) insert—

'(8A) For the purposes of this section 'a householder case' is a case where—

---

[369] The Court of Appeal recognized this issue in *Oye* and declined to draw comparisons between duress and loss of control. At [43].

[370] She might now rely on s 54 of the Coroners and Justice Act 2009 if she had lost self-control. If she had not lost self-control, she must rely on the defence of self-defence.

[371] LC 290, *Partial Defences to Murder* (2004) para 4.14 (adapted from suggested formulation by Justice For Women). Cf s 76(7). See Judicial College, *Crown Court Compendium* (2017).

[372] For the background to the enactment of the provision, see S Lipscombe, *Householders and the Criminal Law of Self-Defence* (2013). Available at http://researchbriefings.parliament.uk/ResearchBriefing/Summary/SN02959. See also Norrie, *Crime, Reason and History*, 285–286 and 300; C de Than and J Elvin, 'Mistaken Private Defence: The Case for Reform' in A Reed and M Bohlander (with N Wake and E Smith) (eds), *General Defences in Criminal Law* (2014) 138–141.

   (a) the defence concerned is the common law defence of self-defence,

   (b) the force concerned is force used by D while in or partly in a building, or part of a building, that is a dwelling or is forces accommodation (or is both),

   (c) D is not a trespasser at the time the force is used, and

   (d) at that time D believed V to be in, or entering, the building or part as a trespasser.'

For a number of years, there had been calls to reform the law to provide greater legal protection for householders who use force to defend themselves in their homes.[373] These calls went unanswered until 2010, when the Coalition Government committed to 'ensuring that people have the protection they need when they defend themselves against intruders'. The government achieved this commitment through the enactment of s 43 of the Crime and Courts Act 2013 which inserts a new s 76(5A) into the 2008 Act. The policy underlying this provision is controversial. For example, Norrie has questioned whether, if a different threshold is deemed appropriate in the context of householder cases, then perhaps there are other private defence situations where a context-specific standard could be justified.[374]

Section 76(5A) provides that in a 'householder case' the degree of force used by D is not to be regarded as reasonable in the circumstances as D believed them to be if it was grossly disproportionate in those circumstances. In non-householder cases it will be recalled that if D uses merely disproportionate force, then that is not to be regarded as reasonable.

On one interpretation, the impact of this change seemed to be that in a householder case if D used grossly disproportionate force he was guilty and if not he was entitled to an acquittal. That is not the way the courts have construed the householder provision in the two leading cases, however.

In *R (on the application of Collins) v Secretary of State for Justice*, the Divisional Court rejected the argument that the statute dictates that the defendant is to be treated as having acted reasonably if the force he used was not grossly disproportionate.[375] Sir Brian Leveson P held that under s 76(5A) a householder who uses grossly disproportionate force will be guilty. Moreover, a householder can be regarded as having acted unreasonably where the degree of force used was merely disproportionate. If D has not acted grossly disproportionately the question will be whether his use of force was unreasonable. If it was, then D will be guilty.[376]

This aspect of the judgment in *Collins* has now been effectively superseded by *Ray*, in which a special Court of Appeal of five judges was convened.[377] Lord Thomas CJ, delivering the judgment of the court, endorsed the interpretation given to the legislation by Sir Brian Leveson P in *Collins*. His lordship agreed that if the degree of force used by the householder was grossly disproportionate then D will be liable. If it was not grossly disproportionate, then the question for the jury is whether that degree of force was reasonable, taking into

---

[373] See S Miller, '"Grossly Disproportionate": Home Owners' Legal Licence to Kill' (2013) 77 J Crim L 299. A number of high-profile cases acted as a catalyst for reform, in particular the case of Munir and Tokeer Hussain. For criticism of some of the earlier private members' bills that had sought to amend the law, see S Skinner, 'Populist Politics and Shooting Burglars' [2005] Crim LR 275.

[374] Norrie, *Crime, Reason and History*, 285. See also L Bleasdale-Hill, 'Householders, Self-Defence and the Right to Life' [2015] Crim LR 407.

[375] [2016] EWHC 33 (Admin), [2016] Crim LR 438.

[376] The Divisional Court's judgment generated a great deal of academic commentary. For example, see J Collins and A Ashworth, 'Householders, Self-Defence and the Right to Life' (2016) 132 LQR 377; M Dsouza, 'Understanding the "Householder Defence": Proportionality and Reasonableness in Defensive Force' (2016) 75 CLJ 192; JR Spencer, 'Using Force on Burglars' [2016] Arch Rev 6; MP Thomas, 'Defenceless Castles: The Use of Grossly Disproportionate Force by Householders in Light of *R (Collins) v Secretary of State for Justice*' (2016) 80 J Crim L 407.

[377] [2017] EWCA Crim 1391.

account all the circumstances as D believed them to be. The current state of the law is therefore as follows:

- In a householder case, D is liable if, in the circumstances as he believed them to be, the jury find he used grossly disproportionate force. He is also liable if the degree of force he used was disproportionate if and only if it was also unreasonable.

- In a non-householder case, D is liable if the amount of force used was in the jury's view unreasonable in the circumstances as he believed them to be.

In a householder case, if the jury conclude that the degree of force used by D was not grossly disproportionate, it was held that their focus should be on whether that degree of force was reasonable. In assessing the reasonableness of the degree of force used by D, the Court of Appeal held that the judge should specify the kind of circumstances that are relevant to this inquiry. Examples given by the court include the shock of coming upon an intruder, the time of day, the presence of other help, the desire to protect the home and its occupants, the vulnerability of the occupants and the conduct of the intruder.

The Court of Appeal's approach to proportionality and reasonableness

In *Keane* the Court of Appeal had treated the concepts of reasonableness and proportionality as synonymous, in a non-householder case at least. In *Ray*, the court's approach creates a more complex picture. First, the court distinguishes between reasonableness and proportionality. The use of disproportionate force which is short of being grossly disproportionate is not, on the wording of the section, necessarily the use of reasonable force. Householder cases are, on a strict matter of statutory language, focused on proportionality. Non-householder cases are focused on the reasonableness of the force used by the defendant.

When it comes to the use of force which is disproportionate, the position is now as follows:

- In a householder case, the jury are entitled to form the view, taking into account all the circumstances, that the degree of force used was either reasonable or not reasonable. Therefore, the use of disproportionate force can be reasonable, but this will not necessarily be so in every case.

- In a non-householder case the position is different, as the degree of force cannot be regarded as reasonable if it was disproportionate.

As a result of *Ray*, the difference between the two types of case is that in non-householder cases the focus is exclusively on reasonableness. The householder cases can involve a distinction between what is disproportionate and what is unreasonable. That fine distinction cuts across the earlier decision in *Keane*.

The second problem with the decision in *Ray* is that having interpreted the provision to recognize the distinction between the tests based on reasonableness alone and those tests which are based on reasonableness and proportionality, the Court of Appeal stated that juries should not be presented with 'esoteric and conceptual distinctions' between what is disproportionate on the one hand and what is unreasonable on the other.

Thirdly, this distinction is difficult when set against the historical common law position which required consideration to be given to the role of necessity and proportionality in assessing the overall reasonableness of the defendant's use of force. The Court of Appeal in *Keane* held that the enactment of s 76 of the Criminal Justice and Immigration Act 2008 did not alter the common law position. This is exactly what the Court of Appeal appears to have done in *Ray*, however.

Fourthly, there is an impact on the likely ability of a jury to apply the test. The reason why the common law required consideration to be given to the necessity and proportionality of the defendant's use of force is that, without reference to these concepts, the jury has no criteria against which to assess the reasonableness of the force used by the defendant. That the force used by the defendant must be reasonable is required by the legislation, but the legislation does not state that reasonableness ought to be divorced from the concepts that have historically been relied upon to assist juries in their assessment of whether the force used was reasonable in the circumstances. To mitigate this difficulty, the court suggests that it is important for judges to give juries 'some colour to the issue of self defence which arises'. It is unclear, however, why the court considered it preferable to rely upon fact-specific examples rather than to continue to place reliance upon concepts that have broad application, and which can apply equally to non-householder cases as they can to householder cases.

Is this what Parliament intended?

A final potential problem is that this interpretation is, arguably, not what Parliament intended. Lord Thomas CJ held that the court's 'narrow' construction of the legislation was in keeping with the aim the householder provision was intended to achieve, but as the parliamentary material cited by the court demonstrates, the government intended to amend the law to ensure it was 'on the side of people who defend themselves when confronted by an intruder in their home'. Given the court's conclusion that it is for the jury to assess whether the degree of force used was reasonable and that something less than grossly disproportionate force may be considered unreasonable, householders may be just as likely to be prosecuted now as they were before the enactment of s 76(5A). Parliament's intention has, on that view, been frustrated. Further evidence of the court's interpretation being contrary to that intended is derived from the MOJ circular that was cited by the court: 'if householders act honestly and instinctively to protect themselves or their loved ones from intruders using force that was reasonable in the circumstances as they saw them, they will not be guilty of an offence if the level of force turns out to have been disproportionate in those circumstances.' That statement of what was intended is not what *Ray* delivers. The Court of Appeal in *Ray* confirmed that the jury remain free to convict the householder on the basis that, despite the fact the degree of force he used was proportionate, it was nevertheless unreasonable in the circumstances as he believed them to be.

The fact that a five-member Court of Appeal presided over by the Lord Chief Justice was convened to consider the proper construction of s 76(5A) of the Criminal Justice and Immigration Act 2008 means that further challenge to the interpretation of the provision is now unlikely.

What is a householder case?

It is important to bear in mind that the different approach only applies in 'householder cases'. In s 76(5A), a 'householder case' is defined as one that has the following characteristics:

(1) the defence concerned is the common law of self-defence;

(2) the force concerned is force used by D while in or partly in a building, or part of a building, that is a dwelling or is forces accommodation (or is both);

(3) D is not a trespasser at the time the force is used; and

(4) at that time D believed V to be in, or entering, the building as a trespasser.

While the statute, in subsection (8F), clarifies that 'building' includes a vehicle or vessel,[378] it does not define what is meant by 'dwelling'. Historically, 'dwelling' could mean not only a person's home, but also the structures within the curtilage of a home, such as sheds, greenhouses, etc.[379] If D confronts V in his kitchen, that is clearly a householder case and the higher threshold applies. What if D confronts V attempting to steal the lawnmower from his shed? Further, what if D confronts V initially in the kitchen,

---

[378] Ensuring that inhabitants of houseboats and caravans will also be able to invoke the provision.

[379] For discussion, see K Laird, 'Conceptualising the Interpretation of "Dwelling" in Section 9 of the Theft Act 1968' [2013] Crim LR 656. For further discussion, see p 1020.

but only uses force once both are struggling in the garden? The failure explicitly to define the scope of the provision is disappointing and could lead to difficulties in practice. It is submitted that 'dwelling' in this context ought to be narrowly defined and should not extend to buildings within the curtilage of a home. This has the benefit of ensuring a relative degree of certainty whilst also fulfilling the policy objective at which the legislation is aimed. It is questionable whether confronting an intruder in one's shed is as terrifying as confronting an intruder in one's living room. In the former case, D ought to be required to take greater care to ensure that he only uses force that is proportionate in the circumstances. The minister was explicit in debates on the clause in Parliament, after all, that s 76(5A) is not intended to be a vigilantes' charter.

Subsection (8B) makes clear that if a part of a building is where D dwells and it is internally accessible to another part that is a place of work for D or another person, then it is considered part of a dwelling. This is to deal with cases such as that of the pub landlord who lives above the pub and who confronts a trespasser behind the bar. This would constitute a householder case. It would not be a householder case if the pub were not connected to the landlord's accommodation by way of an internal means of access.

It is important to note that a householder case only arises when D is not a trespasser at the time when force is used. While this ought to be uncontroversial in most cases, it could require some consideration of the civil law. Crucially, the statute does not state that D must be the homeowner; he must simply not be a trespasser.[380] This would enable a guest of the homeowner to invoke s 76(5A) for example. Whether, for example, the boyfriend of the homeowner's daughter, who surreptitiously climbed through her window, is a trespasser, poses greater difficulty.[381] Subsection (8E) makes clear that a person is a trespasser if he derives title from a trespasser or has the permission of a trespasser. The squatter's guest, therefore, is no less a trespasser because he has an invitation. Again, this limitation is in keeping with the policy objective behind the enactment of the provision.

The final point to note is that at the time force is used D must have believed V to be in or entering the dwelling, or part of it, as a trespasser. Two questions arise in relation to this element of the householder provision. First, must D's belief be reasonable or does it suffice that it is genuinely held? Secondly, can D rely upon a belief induced by voluntary intoxication? Subsection (8D) provides that the provisions in subsections (4) and (5) also apply to subsection (8A)(d). The consequence of this is twofold: it suffices for D to have had a genuine belief that V was a trespasser; and a belief induced by voluntary intoxication will not suffice. In relation to the latter, if D's mistake as to V's status as a trespasser is attributable to his voluntary consumption of alcohol, then he cannot rely upon the householder provision. This ensures there is consistency between householder cases and non-householder cases in relation to the nature of D's belief.[382] Interestingly, in *Collins*, Sir Brian Leveson P stated, *obiter*, that the common law requires an approach which it is at least arguable is unduly restrictive for householders. His lordship stated that whilst those who go about in public ought to be expected to take responsibility for their level of intoxication, whether the same ought to be expected of a defendant who is in his own home in circumstances where he is not anticipating any interaction with a trespasser is perhaps a more open question. It is submitted that there is much to be said for his lordship's characterization of the current state of the law and that this is something that merits Parliament's attention.[383]

---

[380] In *Day* [2015] EWCA Crim 1646, Laws LJ confirmed that self-defence is available not just to the property owner, but to anyone in lawful occupation of the dwelling who seeks to eject a trespasser. The court was not concerned with s 76, but the same principle applies.

[381] For discussion, see p 1008.

[382] The MOJ Circular reiterates that it suffices that D 'genuinely believed (rightly or wrongly)' that the person in respect of whom they used force is a trespasser, at para 16.

[383] [2016] EWHC 33 (Admin), [30], [2016] Crim LR 438.

10.6.1.5 The effect of the Human Rights Act 1998

There are arguments of some force[384] that the effect of Art 2 of the ECHR—the right to life—may be to invalidate the principle of *Gladstone Williams* and *Beckford* that a defendant is to be judged on the facts as he genuinely, though unreasonably, believed them to be. Article 2 provides:

(1) Everyone's right to life shall be protected by law. No one shall be deprived of his life intentionally save in the execution of a sentence of a court following his conviction of a crime for which this penalty is provided by law.

(2) Deprivation of life shall not be regarded as inflicted in contravention of this article when it results from the use of force which is no more than absolutely necessary:

   (a) in defence of any person from unlawful violence;

   (b) in order to effect a lawful arrest or to prevent the escape of a person lawfully detained;

   (c) in action lawfully taken for the purpose of quelling a riot or insurrection.

It is argued by some eminent commentators, including in particular Ashworth and Leverick, that the present English law may be incompatible with this provision since a person's right to life is not sufficiently protected if he may be killed by force used without reasonable grounds.[385]

The arguments of incompatibility highlight a number of issues. First, the Article allows for life to be taken only where 'absolutely necessary'. A defendant in England could be acquitted even though his lethal attack turns out to have been completely unnecessary. Furthermore, the European Court has underlined the restrictive nature of the exceptional circumstances in which killing is permitted.[386] In *McCann v UK* and in *Andronicou*, the Court referred to the fact that the accused must have had 'good grounds' to use force. This looks like an objective test, which is not what English law requires: *Gladstone Williams* (and s 76) requires only a genuine belief in the need to use such force. Finally, it is noted that Art 2 restricts the circumstances in which a life may be taken to the purposes of quelling riots, etc or in defence of unlawful *violence*. In English law, it is possible for a defendant to be acquitted where he uses lethal force even in response to an attack merely on property.[387]

Despite these arguments of incompatibility, it is not clear that Art 2 or the ECtHR's jurisprudence (which is typically vague) *demands* a change in the law to an objective test. The test of 'absolute necessity' applied in Strasbourg is not an inflexible one. In a recent assessment of the position, the Divisional Court in *R (Duggan) v HM Assistant Deputy Coroner*[388] recognized 'some ambiguity in the language used by the Strasbourg Court'. The court was not persuaded that an objective test of reasonableness was required to ensure that English law was compatible. The Court of Appeal subsequently agreed with this conclusion.[389]

---

[384] By A Ashworth, commenting on *Andronicou and Constantinou v Cyprus*, ECtHR, 9 Oct 1997 [1998] Crim LR 823. But see Buxton LJ, 'The Human Rights Act and the Substantive Criminal Law' [2000] Crim LR 331 at 336–337. See F Leverick, 'The Use of Force in Public or Private Defence and Article 2' [2002] Crim LR 347; JC Smith, 'The Use of Force in Public or Private Defence and Article 2' [2002] Crim LR 958; and F Leverick, 'The Use of Force in Public or Private Defence and Article 2: A Reply to Professor Sir John Smith' [2002] Crim LR 963. See also Leverick, n 325, Ch 10; Horder, APOCL, 142.

[385] See Leverick, previous note.

[386] See *Andronicou*, para 171; *Gul v Turkey* (2002) 34 EHRR 28, para 77; *McCann v UK* (1996) 21 EHRR 95. More recently, see *Ramsahai v Netherlands* (2006) 43 EHRR 39; *Huohuanainen v Finland* [2007] EHRLR 472.

[387] See the Joint Committee on Human Rights 15th Legislative Report 2007–8, para 2.35.

[388] [2014] EWHC 3343 (Admin).

[389] *R (Duggan) v North London Assistant Deputy Coroner* [2017] EWCA Civ 142.

Moreover, the ECtHR has not condemned English law when it has had the opportunity to do so. The European Court's test was reiterated in *Bubbins v UK*[390] where the Court stated that D had an 'honest belief which was perceived for good reason to be valid at the time but which was mistaken'. There was no outright condemnation of the English test. In the most recent Strasbourg authority to consider this issue, the Grand Chamber held in *Da Silva v UK*[391] that it could not be said that the test applied in the law of England and Wales is significantly different from the standard applied by the Court in *McCann*. The Court concluded that the definition of self-defence in England and Wales did not fall short of the standard required by Art 2. As Emmerson, Ashworth and Macdonald[392] point out, the truth is that there is no case yet before the Strasbourg Court in which a use of lethal force in English law has been based on a wholly irrational mistake. If such a case arose, the Court would have to face the conflict between the Strasbourg jurisprudence and English law.

The English courts' approach to the ECHR question

In the English courts, it has been accepted that the current rules of English law on the use of potentially lethal force by the police are not incompatible with the ECHR as in *R (Bennett) v HM Coroner for Inner London*[393] and *R (Duggan) v North London Assistant Deputy Coroner*.[394] In both cases the principal issue was whether a killing committed by the police as a result of an honest but mistaken act of self-defence (not amounting to a crime, but possibly involving civil liability to pay compensation, etc) could be classed by a coroner's inquest as a 'lawful homicide'.

In the High Court in *Bennett* Collins J held, having regard to the case law, that:

the European Court of Human Rights has considered what English law requires for self defence, and has not suggested that there is any incompatibility with Article 2. In truth, if any officer reasonably decides that he must use lethal force, it will inevitably be because it is absolutely necessary to do so. To kill when it is not absolutely necessary to do so is surely to act unreasonably. Thus, the reasonableness test does not in truth differ from the Article 2 test as applied in *McCann*.

The Court of Appeal upheld that decision.[395]

Subsequently, in *Ashley and others v Chief Constable of Sussex Police*,[396] the House of Lords compared self-defence when used as a defence to a criminal charge and a defence in civil proceedings. In both criminal and civil proceedings, the conduct/degree of force in self-defence must objectively be reasonable but, in judging what was reasonable, the court must in either case have regard to all the circumstances, including the fact that the action may have been taken in the heat of the moment. However, there are differences: (a) in cases of mistaken self-defence an honest but unreasonable mistake may operate as a defence only in criminal proceedings. In civil proceedings, a mistaken view of the facts provides no defence in the absence of reasonable grounds for that mistake. (b) The burden of proof is different: in criminal proceedings, the burden of negativing self-defence is on the prosecution; but in civil proceedings the burden is on the defendant to establish that he acted in reasonable self-defence.[397]

---

[390] [2005] 41 EHRR 24. See N Martin (2006) 69 MLR 242 for comment. Applied more recently in *Giuliani v Italy* (2012) 54 EHRR 10 and *Reynolds v UK* (2012) 55 EHRR 35.

[391] (2016) 63 EHRR 12.   [392] HR&CJ, para 18.33.

[393] [2006] EWHC 196 (Admin).   [394] [2017] EWCA Civ 142.

[395] [2007] EWCA Civ 617. The basis of appeal was principally that it had been a misdirection not to direct the jury to consider whether the officer's claim to have acted in self-defence was reasonable in light of the requirement in the relevant ACPO manual to reassess at all times whether it was 'absolutely necessary' to shoot.

[396] [2008] UKHL 25; see the Court of Appeal's decision: [2006] EWCA Civ 1085.

[397] Cf the decision at first instance [2005] EWHC 415 (QB).

Looking at the subject more broadly, one can argue that notwithstanding some unguarded language by the CLRC and the courts, English law does not say that D may take the life of another where there are no reasonable grounds for doing so. It says only that he is not guilty of a criminal offence, if he believes honestly though unreasonably that such ground exists. The killing is unlawful, but not criminal; D remains liable in tort. Parliament has now endorsed that principle in s 76. Where D's belief is unreasonable that will, of course, be a powerful reason for disbelieving his account and convicting him. But that is not all: the criminal law itself provides protection. If D's mistake is so unreasonable as to amount to gross negligence, D will be guilty of manslaughter.[398] That is, D will be guilty of criminal homicide if the jury think his conduct bad enough to amount to a crime—or, as is submitted later in the discussion in Ch 14, bad enough to deserve condemnation as manslaughter. The criminal law therefore does offer some protection. The fact that it is a conviction for manslaughter with a maximum life sentence cannot mean that the protection is inadequate.

Moreover, most force used in public or private defence is not intended to, and does not have, fatal results. Does the human rights argument require the *Beckford* principle to be outlawed *only* where it has fatal results? There would not seem to be any logic in that. The alternative is that it is invalidated entirely. It is submitted that this would be an undesirable and unnecessary conclusion and the English courts should not arrive at it unless compelled to do so. The present law, at least as regards protection against violence to the person, balances the need to protect life—and limb—against the ordinary rights of persons accused of crime.

In *R (Collins) v Secretary of State for Justice*, the focus of the judgment delivered by Sir Brian Leveson P was on whether the so-called 'householder provisions' were compatible with Art 2.[399] In assessing the compatibility of s 76(5A) with Art 2, the key question for the court was whether the criminal law of England and Wales effectively deters offences against the person in householder cases. His lordship held that although there may be cases when a jury consider the actions of a householder in self-defence to be more than what might be objectively described as the minimum proportionate response, this did not weaken the capacity of the criminal law to deter offences against the person in householder cases. The householder will only be able to plead self-defence if the degree of force he used was reasonable in the circumstances as he believed them to be. His lordship concluded that the criminal law provides reasonable safeguards against the commission of offences against the person in householder cases, which was sufficient to satisfy Art 2.

In addition to the right to life guaranteed in Art 2, the European Court has recognized that the rights in Arts 3 (freedom from torture and inhuman and degrading treatment) and 5 (right to liberty) are subject to an implied exception for injuries inflicted in self-defence.[400] D, who is protecting himself against an unlawful attack from V, will not infringe V's Art 5 rights by detaining him to prevent further attack.

---

[398] Cf Leverick [2002] Crim LR 347 at 361. See Leverick, *Killing in Self Defence*, Ch 10. See on the need for careful direction, *Maddocks* [2006] EWCA Crim 3112. Use of lethal force is a last resort: *Noye* [2011] EWCA Crim 650.

[399] [2016] EWHC 33 (Admin), [2016] Crim LR 438. This aspect of the court's reasoning is discussed further in S Foster and G Leigh, 'Self-Defence and the Right to Life; the Use of Lethal or Potentially Lethal Force, UK Domestic Law, the Common Law and Article 2 ECHR' [2016] EHRLR 398.

[400] *Rivas v France* [2005] Crim LR 305; *RL v France* [2005] Crim LR 306.

10.6.2 Force used in the course of preventing crime or arresting offenders

The common law on this subject was both complex and uncertain;[401] but, by s 3 of the Criminal Law Act 1967:

(1) A person may use such force as is reasonable in the circumstances in the prevention of crime, or in effecting or assisting in the lawful arrest of offenders or suspected offenders or of persons unlawfully at large.

(2) Subsection (1) above shall replace the rules of the common law on the question when force used for a purpose mentioned in the subsection is justified by that purpose.[402]

Section 3 states a rule both of civil and criminal law. When the force is 'reasonable in the circumstances' it is justified in every sense. No civil action or criminal proceeding will lie against the person using it. The section says nothing specifically about any criminal liability of the user of the force. When that is in issue the ordinary principles of mens rea should apply. The use of force may be unjustified in the civil law because it is not in fact 'reasonable in the circumstances'; but D, while liable in tort, may nevertheless be excused from criminal liability if it was 'reasonable in the circumstances *as he believed them to be*'.[403] It has been held in a civil action in Northern Ireland[404] that, for the purpose of an identical provision, the objectives of the use of force are to be determined, not by the evidence of the user of the force, but by the court, applying an objective test. D, a soldier, said that his purpose in shooting was to arrest the occupants of a vehicle whom he believed on reasonable grounds to be determined terrorists who would probably continue to commit terrorist offences if they got away; but the court held that the use of force was not reasonable to make an arrest but was justified because it was reasonable to prevent crime.[405] If this is right (and it is a persuasive opinion) in a civil action, it is also right in criminal law. The only difference is that in the criminal case D need not have reasonable grounds for his honest belief in the circumstances. The Court of Appeal confirmed in *Morris*[406] that it is a misdirection to direct the jury that D must have reasonable grounds for believing it is necessary to use force. So long as D has a genuine belief, this will suffice, even if it is a mistaken one. This case is welcome confirmation that the first limb of both private defence and the defence in s 3 embodies a subjective test.

10.6.2.1 Prevention of crime

Where D seeks to rely on the defence based on his belief that V was committing a crime, the question may well arise whether the offence was in fact occurring when D used force. In *Bowden*,[407] the issue was whether V had completed his appropriation of an article

---

401 See the 1st edition of this book, at pp 230–238.   402 See s 76 of the CJIA 2008, p 380.

403 See *Duggan*, n 394. The court held that it would be inconsistent with the statutory regime governing inquests to say that a verdict of lawful killing was available only where the coroner's jury also concluded that there would be no civil liability.

404 *Kelly v Ministry of Defence* [1989] NI 341. On whether the defence applies to British soldiers abroad, see Rowe, n 319.

405 The ECtHR (App no 17579/90) observed that the 'prevention of crime' does not appear in the justifications for taking life in Art 2 of the ECHR, but held that the shooting was justified to effect a lawful arrest. This decision is cogently criticized by JC Smith, 'The Right to Life and the Right to Kill in Law Enforcement' (1994) 144 NLJ 354.

406 [2013] EWCA Crim 436, [2013] Crim LR 995.   407 [2002] EWCA Crim 1279.

before D used violence to prevent what he understood to be a theft being perpetrated by V, but that is not a strong example. Similarly, in *Attwater*[408] D sought to rely on s 3 when he was charged with dangerous driving. He claimed that he drove in that manner (crashing with other vehicles) so that he could apprehend another driver X because X had been in an earlier incident and failed to stop. In short, D claimed to be apprehending X for his crime of failing to stop after a road traffic accident. On the facts, X's offence was probably already over.[409] In *R (DPP) v Stratford Magistrates' Court*, the Divisional Court emphasized that in order to plead the defence, there must be a link between the use of force and an imminently apprehended crime.[410] In that case, which involved protestors obstructing the passage of vehicles making their way to an exhibition centre, Simon LJ stated that there was a lack of clarity as to what crime was being committed and how force was preventing it. There was no evidence that the vehicles being obstructed were involved in anything other than lawful activity. As there was nothing to link the obstruction of the highway with an imminent or immediate crime, it was held that the defendants could not rely on the defence.

10.6.2.2 Arresting an offender

Where D seeks to rely on the defence to justify his use of force in arresting an offender, issues of civil powers of arrest may arise and the jury may well need further guidance on those powers under s 24A of PACE, namely whether on the facts as D believed them to be: (a) an offence was being committed by V (s 24A(1)(a)); or (b) D had reasonable grounds to suspect that V was committing an offence (24A(1)(b)); or (c) D reasonably suspected V to have committed the offence (s 24A(2)(b)); and (d) he reasonably believed an arrest was necessary (s 24A(3)).[411]

10.6.2.3 What is a crime for the purposes of s 3?

Section 3 operates only where D responds to prevent a 'crime'. In *Jones*,[412] the House of Lords concluded that the concept of 'crime' in this context can only have been intended to mean a crime recognized in English and Welsh law (ie not something which constitutes a crime only in international law).[413] The CLRC[414] explained the proposed s 3 in very broad terms:

the court, in considering what was reasonable force, would take into account all the circumstances, including in particular the nature and degree of force used, the seriousness of the evil to be prevented and the possibility of preventing it by other means; but there is no need to specify in the clause the criteria for deciding the question. Since the clause is framed in general terms, it is not limited to arrestable[415] or any other class of offences, though in the case of very trivial offences it would very likely be held that it would not be reasonable to use even the slightest force to prevent them.

Despite the breadth of this statement, the House of Lords' limitation in *Jones* seems warranted if the defence is to retain the degree of certainty desirable.

---

408 [2010] EWCA Crim 2399.

409 *Jackson* [1985] RTR 257. The court left open whether this was strictly speaking a matter that should have been left to the jury. The court had no doubt that a jury would have rejected the defence.

410 [2017] EWHC 1794 (Admin), [42]–[44].

411 See *Morris* [2013] EWCA Crim 436, [2013] Crim LR 995.

412 [2004] EWCA Crim 1981, [2005] Crim LR 122.

413 See Lord Bingham at [31], Lord Hoffmann at [54] and Lord Mance at [105].

414 Cmnd 2659, para 23.

415 Since the Serious Organised Crime and Police Act 2005, all offences are potentially arrestable.

10.6.2.4 When is the use of force reasonable in s 3?

The CLRC,[416] in drafting the section, described it as set out in the last paragraph: 'reasonable force, would take into account all the circumstances, including in particular the nature and degree of force used, the seriousness of the evil to be prevented and the possibility of preventing it by other means'.[417]

It cannot be reasonable to cause harm unless (a) it was *necessary* to do so in order to prevent the crime or effect the arrest and (b) the evil which would follow from failure to prevent the crime or effect the arrest is so great that a reasonable person might think himself justified in causing that harm to avert that evil. It is likely, therefore, that even killing will be justifiable to prevent unlawful killing or grievous bodily harm, or to arrest a person where there is an imminent risk of his causing death or grievous bodily harm if left at liberty. The European Court has emphasized that the use of lethal force to stop a person suspected of a non-violent offence who does not pose an immediate risk of harm to anyone is contrary to Art 2.[418] The whole question is somewhat speculative. Is it reasonable to kill or cause serious bodily harm in order to prevent rape?[419] Or robbery, when the property involved is very valuable?[420] How much force may be used to prevent the destruction of a great work of art? The most extreme cases in which the police use lethal force are because they believed D to be a terrorist suicide bomber and in which any lesser force would have been futile.

It seems that the question, 'What amount of force is reasonable in the circumstances?' is always for the jury and never a point of law for the judge.[421] If the prosecution case does not provide material to raise the issue, there is an evidential burden on the accused. If that burden is satisfied, that question for the jury is:

Are we satisfied that no reasonable person (a) with knowledge of such facts as were known to the accused[422] believed by him to exist (b) in the circumstances and time available to him for reflection (c) could be of the opinion that the prevention of the risk of harm to which others might be exposed if the suspect were allowed to escape, justified exposing the suspect to the risk of harm to him that might result from the kind of force that the accused contemplated using.[423]

At common law it was recognized that the standard of reasonableness should, as noted earlier, take account of the nature of the crisis in which the necessity to use force arises for, in circumstances of great stress, even the reasonable person cannot be expected to judge the minimum degree of force required to a nicety. This is now reflected in s 76(7) of the CJIA 2008. In holding quite considerable force to be justified to prevent an obstruction of the highway by a violent and abusive driver, Geoffrey Lane J said: 'In the circumstances one did not use jewellers' scales to measure reasonable force...'[424]

In *R (DPP) v Stratford Magistrates' Court*, the Divisional Court reiterated that citizens who apprehend a breach of the law are normally expected to call the police and not take the law into their own hands. Simon LJ emphasized that the use of force by individuals in the prevention of crime must be confined so as to avoid anarchy. His lordship stated that

---

416 Cmnd 2659, para 23.   417 Note s 76, earlier.

418 See *Nachova v Bulgaria* (2004) 39 EHRR 37.   419 See Leverick, n 325, Ch 8.

420 There are plenty of reported instances where the courts seem to have approved of the killing. See the more recent cases discussed by E Tennant (2003) 167 JP 804.

421 *Reference under s 48A of the Criminal Appeal (Northern Ireland) Act 1968 (No 1 of 1975)* [1976] 2 All ER 937 at 947, HL, per Lord Diplock.

422 Lord Diplock used the word 'reasonably' here and, in the light of his often stated opinion, it is likely that he would wish to continue to use it, were he still alive; but his remarks, in the light of *Gladstone Williams* and the cases following it, should be read as if 'reasonably' were omitted.

423 *Reference under s 48A of the Criminal Appeal (Northern Ireland) Act 1968 (No 1 of 1975)* [1976] 2 All ER 937 at 947, HL, per Lord Diplock.

424 *Reed v Wastie* [1972] Crim LR 221.

the use of force to prevent crime may be legitimate and enable D to plead the defence when individual action is necessary to prevent some imminent crime.[425]

10.6.2.5 Section 3 provides a defence only if force used

Section 3 excuses only the use of *force*. In *Blake v DPP*,[426] D, demonstrating against the Iraq war, wrote with a felt pen on a concrete pillar near the Houses of Parliament. He was charged with criminal damage and argued that his act was justified by, *inter alia*, s 3. The court held that his act was 'insufficient to amount to the use of force within the section'. This suggests that the defence might not have been ruled out on this ground (though it almost certainly would on other grounds) if D had used a hammer and chisel. It is odd that force should be excused when less serious acts might not be; but that is the effect of the section.[427]

The Court of Appeal considered this issue again in *Bailey*.[428] There was a collision between D's car and the car of a third party, C. C failed to stop and D sped after him, but struck V, who died. D sought to argue that he was using force to assist in the lawful arrest of C, who had committed the offence of failing to stop after an accident. The judge declined to leave the defence to the jury on the basis that D had not used force in attempting to stop C, indeed his evidence was that he had been a perfect gentleman throughout. Laws LJ stated: 'Giving chase in a motor car in order to ascertain the registration number of a car ahead cannot as a matter of language or good sense be regarded as a use of force.'[429] In addition, his lordship observed that D was not attempting to assist the arrest of C, rather his aim was to get his insurance details. This would also have precluded him from relying upon s 3.

In *Jones*, the House of Lords expressed doubt as to whether s 3 ought to be relied on in cases of alleged damage to property. Section 5 of the Criminal Damage Act provides the appropriate defence. The House also doubted whether s 3 was intended to apply to peaceable protest activities such as those used by the defendants in that case—cutting wire and chaining themselves to armed service vehicles.

In the most recent case to consider this issue, *R (DPP) v Stratford Magistrates' Court*,[430] Simon LJ stated that the defence applies to the direct application of force, although the force does not necessarily have to be applied directly against a person. The example given by his lordship was a defendant who attached himself to a lorry which he believed to be carrying chemical weapons. By way of contrast, it was held that the defence would not be available to those who lie down in the road in front of lorries making their way to a place where crimes are believed to be taking place or who block access by chaining themselves to gates.

10.6.3 Force used in private defence

The Criminal Law Act 1967 made no reference to the right of private defence—the right to use force in defence of oneself or another against an unjustifiable attack.[431] Insofar as that position differed in effect from s 3 of the 1967 Act, the common law was probably modified

---

[425] [2017] EWHC 1794 (Admin), [18].   [426] [1993] Crim LR 586, DC.

[427] The illogicality of this restriction was noted by Brooke LJ in *Bayer v DPP* [2003] EWHC 2567 (Admin), [2004] Crim LR 663, calling for reform of the defences. See also *Riddell*, p 407.

[428] [2013] EWCA Crim 378.

[429] At [16]. His lordship distinguished *Renouf* on the basis that D in that case had forced another car off the road and rammed it to ensure that its occupants would still be there when the police arrived. That clearly did constitute the use of force.

[430] [2017] EWHC 1794 (Admin), [50], [2018] Crim LR 157.

[431] Thus where D knows that the actual or imminent danger he faces is not from an unlawful or criminal act he cannot rely on the defence: *Bayer v DPP* [2003] EWHC 2567 (Admin). See also *Cresswell v DPP* [2006] EWHC 3379 (Admin) where the defendants could not be acting to prevent a crime when DEFRA officials were within the law to take the badgers in dispute.

by s 3. Private defence and the prevention of crime are sometimes indistinguishable. If D goes to the defence of E whom V is trying to murder, he is exercising the right of private defence but he is also seeking to prevent the commission of a crime. It would be absurd to ask D whether he was acting in defence of E or to prevent murder being committed and pre- posterous that the law should differ according to his answer. He was doing both.[432] The law cannot have two sets of criteria governing the same situation: s 3 of the Criminal Law Act is applicable. This is supported by the application of the same tests in s 76 of the 2008 Act to both the common law and s 3 defences.

The 1967 Act may be taken to have clarified the common law. Before the Criminal Law Act, the Court of Criminal Appeal equated the defence of others with the prevention of crime. In *Duffy*,[433] it was held that a woman would be justified in using reasonable force when it was necessary to do so in defence of her sister, not because they were sisters, but because 'there is a general liberty as between strangers to prevent a [crime]'. The principles applicable are the same whether the defence is put on grounds of self-defence or on grounds of prevention of crime. The degree of force permissible should not differ, for example, in the case of an employer defending his employee from the case of a brother defending his sister— or, indeed, that of a complete stranger coming to the defence of another under unlawful attack. As s 76(10)(b) of the 2008 Act makes clear, references to self-defence include acting in defence of another. The position is the same where D acts in defence of property, whether his own or that of another, which V seeks to steal, destroy or damage.

Where D is acting in defence of his own person it may be less obvious that he is also act- ing in the prevention of crime but this will usually be in fact the case. D's purpose is not the enforcement of the law but his own self-preservation; yet the degree of force which is permissible is the same.[434] An inquiry into D's motives is not practicable.[435]

As with s 3, the private law defence is limited to cases in which D responds to an unjusti- fied attack by using force. However, there is no requirement with the private law defence at common law that D is responding to a 'crime'. Therefore, where D believes that V's actions are unjustified because they are, for example, unlawful in international law, his use of force to prevent V's action may be justified.

10.6.4 Further elements of private and public defence

10.6.4.1 A duty to retreat?

There were formerly technical rules about the duty to retreat before using force, or at least fatal force. This is now simply a factor to be taken into account in deciding whether it was necessary to use force, and whether the force was reasonable.[436] The courts had developed the principle at common law (*Palmer v R*,[437] *Duffy v DPP*[438]) that it was a matter of evidence relevant to whether D was acting in self-defence but that there was no rule that a person had to retreat from threatened violence.[439] In *Jones*, the House of Lords emphasized the view that it is not for the citizen who apprehends a breach of the law to take matters into his own hands if there is an opportunity to summon official help.[440] Section 76(6)(A) now

---

[432] See *Clegg* [1995] 1 All ER 334 at 343, [1995] Crim LR 418.   [433] [1967] 1 QB 63, CCA.

[434] *Devlin v Armstrong* [1971] NI 13 at 33; *McInnes* [1971] 3 All ER 295 at 302.   [435] See p 101.

[436] *McInnes*, n 434. But cf *Whyte* [1987] 3 All ER 416 at 419, CA.

[437] [1971] AC 814, PC. This passage then appearing in the 4th edition was approved by the Court of Appeal in *Bird* [1985] 2 All ER 513 at 516, [1985] Crim LR 388. Cf Horder, APOCL, 138 arguing that this should be seen as an exception to the general principle of a duty to avoid conflict.

[438] [2007] EWHC 3169 (Admin).   [439] See *M (ZM)* [2007] EWCA Crim 376.

[440] See Lord Mance at [78]–[81]. This point was also emphasized by Simon LJ in *R (DPP) v Stratford Magistrates' Court* [2017] EWHC 1794 (Admin), [2018] Crim LR 157.

states explicitly that there is no duty to retreat. Rather, the possibility that D could have retreated is to be considered (so far as it is relevant) as a factor to be taken into account when considering whether the degree of force used by D was reasonable in the circumstances as he believed them to be. In *Ray*, discussed earlier, the Lord Chief Justice stated that if there is a threat of confrontation in the street, then the option to retreat may be important in determining whether the use of any force was reasonable. In the case of an intruder in the home, however, it was observed that the option of retreat is unlikely to arise in many cases and therefore the degree of force used, although otherwise appearing to be disproportionate, might nonetheless be assessed as reasonable.

10.6.4.2 Pre-emptive strikes

It has been accepted that a defendant need not wait for the attacker to strike the first blow before he defends himself. In *Devlin v Armstrong*,[441] following serious disturbances in Londonderry, D exhorted crowds of people who were stoning the police to build a barricade and keep the police out and fight them with petrol bombs. D claimed that she had acted in this manner because she honestly believed that the police were about to behave unlawfully in assaulting people and damaging property in the area. The Northern Ireland Court of Appeal acknowledged that a 'plea of self-defence may afford a defence [where D used force] not merely to counter an actual attack, but to ward off or prevent an attack which he honestly anticipated. In that case, however, the anticipated attack must be imminent.'[442] In *Beckford*,[443] the Privy Council also acknowledged that circumstances may justify a pre-emptive strike in self-defence. The availability of the defence in circumstances of pre-emptive strike has been narrowly construed by the courts. Where there is no evidence to support a suggestion that D has acted in pre-emptive defence, no jury direction on the issue is needed.[444]

The requirement of imminence, strictly construed, prevents the widespread reliance on the defence where battered spouses kill their abusive partners. Commonly, the physical disparity between the parties means that the woman will seize her opportunity to kill the abuser when he is not poised about to strike her, but in a position of vulnerability. This caused such individuals to rely on the partial defences of provocation and diminished responsibility.[445]

Under s 54 of the Coroners and Justice Act 2009, a defendant who kills with malice aforethought may rely on a defence of loss of control (LOSC) if he has lost his self-control and, *inter alia*, he fears serious violence from V towards himself or an identified person. The relationship between the LOSC defence and self-defence or defence of others under s 76 of the CJIA 2008 needs to be approached with caution. Self-defence is available on any charge; LOSC defence is available only on a charge of murder.[446] Self-defence results in an acquittal; LOSC in a verdict of manslaughter. With self-defence, D can only rely on a threat of (or believed threat of) *imminent* attack; with LOSC, D can rely on fear of future non-imminent attack. The defence of self-defence is available if D holds a genuine, though mistaken and

---

[441] [1971] NI 13.   [442] Per Lord MacDermott LCJ at 33.

[443] [1987] 3 All ER 425, [1988] Crim LR 116, PC.

[444] *Williams* [2005] EWCA Crim 669, cf *Carter* [2005] All ER (D) 372 (Apr); *Murphy* [2007] EWCA Crim 2810.

[445] See, generally, the discussion at p 528 and C Wells, 'Battered Woman Syndrome and Defences to Homicide: Where Now?' (1994) 14 LS 266; A McColgan, 'In Defence of Battered Women Who Kill' (1993) 13 OJLS 508; J Dressler, 'Battered Women Who Kill Their Sleeping Tormentors' in Shute and Simester, *Criminal Law Theory* arguing for a duress-type defence and J Horder, 'Killing the Passive Abuser: A Theoretical Defence' in ibid, 285.

[446] If there are multiple counts relating to different victims, care will be needed in directing the jury.

unreasonable, belief of the threat to him of *any* violence. The LOSC defence is available if D genuinely, though mistakenly and unreasonably, believes himself to be at risk of *serious* violence.[447] Violence is undefined in the LOSC defence but includes sexual violence.[448] If the degree of force used by D in killing V is, viewed objectively, excessive, that will deprive D of the defence of self-defence,[449] but will not automatically deprive D of the LOSC defence.[450]

10.6.4.3 Defence against a provoked attack

In *Browne*,[451] Lowry LCJ in Northern Ireland said, with regard to self-defence, 'The need to act must not have been created by conduct of the accused in the immediate context of the incident which was likely or intended to give rise to that need.'

Self-defence is clearly not available where D deliberately provoked the attack with the intention of killing purportedly in self-defence.[452] Where D's act was merely 'likely' to give rise to the need, the proposition, with respect, is more questionable. If D did not foresee that his actions would lead to an attack on him, it is submitted that he should not be deprived of his usual right of self-defence. Even if he did foresee the attack, he may still be entitled to act in self-defence if he did not intend it. D intervenes to stop V from ill-treating V's wife. He knows that V may react violently. V makes a deadly attack on D. Surely D's right of self-defence is unimpaired. This suggestion was cited *obiter* with approval in *Balogun*.[453]

In *Rashford*,[454] the Court of Appeal made it clear that self-defence is available to the person who started the fight, if the person whom he attacks not only defends himself but goes over to the offensive. As a matter of principle, the defence ought to be available where D has prompted V's attack, and even where D has foreseen that V was likely to respond with violence, subject to the restriction that it should not be available where D deliberately provoked the attack with the intention of killing purportedly in self-defence. Considerable care will be necessary in directing the jury in such cases. In *Rashford*, Dyson LJ approved the Scottish decision in *Burns v HM Advocate*[455] as an important decision which should be more widely known. In that case[456] it was said that the question:

depends upon whether the violence offered by the victim was so out of proportion to the accused's own actings as to give rise to the reasonable apprehension that he was in an immediate danger from which he had no other means of escape, and whether the violence which he then used was no more than was necessary to preserve his own life or protect himself from serious injury.

As the commentary in the *Criminal Law Review* points out, that test is inaccurate for English law as it suggests that the apprehension which D must have as to the threat of danger must be a reasonable one.[457]

---

447 See MOJ Circular 2010/13, para 25. Cf Leigh, p 533 n 107 who states that the test is objective.
448 MOJ CP 19/08, para 44.
449 And therefore of a complete acquittal. See *Clegg* [1995]. See also Leverick, *Self Defence* (2007) 172 et seq.
450 This analysis in the 13th edition was cited with approval by the Court of Appeal in *Dawes* [2013] EWCA Crim 322, [2013] Crim LR 770, [59].
451 [1973] NI 96 at 107, CCA, discussed 24 NILQ 527. On 'prior fault' generally, see S Yeo, *Compulsion* (1990) Ch 5.
452 Cf *Mason* (1756) Fost 132. Under the Coroners and Justice Act 2009, the loss of self-control defence is not available in such circumstances. See Ch 13, p 531.
453 [1999] 98/6762/X2.
454 [2005] EWCA Crim 3377, [2006] Crim LR 547. Considered in *Marsh v DPP* [2015] EWHC 1022 (Admin), [2015] Crim LR 713.
455 1995 SLT 1090.   456 At 1093H.
457 cf *Williams (Gladstone)* [1987] 3 All ER 411, [1984] Crim LR 163; *Beckford v R* [1988] AC 130, [1988] Crim LR 116, PC; Criminal Justice and Immigration Act 2008, s 76.

The principles were reiterated in *Harvey*[458] in relation to self-defence relied on by an initial aggressor. The court followed *Rashford*. This is subject to a principle that D cannot rely on self-defence where he has set out to engineer an attack by V which will allow him, D, to respond with greater violence under the guise of self-defence. The difficulty of course lies in how to explain that to a jury. The court in *Harvey* emphasized that the direction on self-defence for initial aggressors is not always necessary simply because there is a dispute about 'who started it'. The Court of Appeal once again returned to this in *Keane*,[459] which provides a useful review, endorsing the guidance given in *Harvey* on the application of the defence where D provokes violence from another but on whom the tables are turned. Hughes LJ said:

It seems to us that that kind of homely expression, like 'the roles being reversed', can quite well encapsulate the question which may arise if an original aggressor claims the ability to rely on self-defence. We would commend it as suitable for a great many cases, subject only to this reminder.[460]... We need to say as clearly as we may that it is not the law that if a defendant sets out to provoke another to punch him and succeeds, the defendant is then entitled to punch the other person ... The reason why it is not the law is that underlying the law of self-defence is the common-sense morality that what is not unlawful is force which is reasonably necessary ... Of course it might be different if the defendant set out to provoke a punch and the victim unexpectedly and disproportionately attacked him with a knife.

10.6.4.4 Defence against lawful force

Lord Lowry CJ of Northern Ireland stated in *Browne*:[461]

Where a police officer is acting lawfully and using only such force as is reasonable in the circumstances in the prevention of crime or in effecting the lawful arrest of offenders or suspected offenders, self-defence against him is not an available defence.

Again, it may be respectfully suggested that this proposition is too wide. If D, an innocent person, is attacked by the police who mistakenly believe him to be a gunman and the police attack is such that it would be reasonable if D were the gunman, does the law really deny D the right to resist?[462] Again, if D reasonably supposes that the police are terrorists, he surely commits no crime by resisting, even if the police are in fact acting lawfully and reasonably. In *Oraki v DPP*[463] D was convicted of obstructing an officer in the execution of his duty contrary to s 89(2) of Police Act 1996. D thought his mother was being assaulted by a police officer and intervened to prevent that from taking place. D was convicted on the basis that neither self-defence nor defence of another could be pleaded as defences to a charge of obstructing a police officer. Singh LJ stated that what was crucial was whether D genuinely believed

---

458 [2009] EWCA Crim 469.   459 [2010] EWCA Crim 2514, [2011] Crim LR 393.

460 His lordship added that: 'Lord Hope's formulation of the rule [in *Burns*] makes it clear that it is not enough to bring self-defence into issue that a defendant who started the fight is at some point during the fight for the time being getting the worst of it, merely because the victim is defending himself reasonably. In that event there has been no disproportionate act by the victim of the kind that Lord Hope is contemplating. The victim has not been turned into the aggressor. The tables have not been turned in that particular sense. The roles have not been reversed', at [18].

461 [1973] NI 96 at 107.

462 This passage in the 14th edition was cited with approval by the Divisional Court in *Oraki v DPP* [2018] EWHC 115 (Admin), [27]. *Mckoy* [2002] EWCA Crim 1628 suggests that D may resist unlawful restraint by a police officer. The judgment of Winn LJ in *Kenlin v Gardiner* [1967] 2 QB 510 is ambivalent. *Albert v Lavin* [1982] AC 546, DC (reversed by the House of Lords on another point) supports the view in the text. And see *Ansell v Swift* [1987] Crim LR 194 (Lewes Crown Court). Cf *Fennell* [1971] 1 QB 428, [1970] 3 All ER 215, [1970] Crim LR 581 and commentary; p 709. These cases must now be read in light of *Oraki*.

463 [2018] EWHC 115 (Admin).

he needed to use force to defend his mother from being assaulted. It was observed that the reasonableness of a mistaken belief on the part of a defendant is relevant to the question of whether it is a genuinely held belief but if it is a genuinely held belief, it does not matter that the belief is an unreasonable one. The Divisional Court held that the defence of self-defence or defence of another person is, as a matter of law, available in relation to the offence of obstructing a constable in the execution of his duty under s 89(2) of the Police Act 1996. It is submitted that the judgment in *Oraki* is correct as a matter of principle as it is faithful to the subjective nature of the first limb of the defences.[464] Although the judgment in *Browne* has not been overturned, it ought to be treated with considerable caution.

A person is not to be deprived of his right of self-defence because he has gone to a place where he might lawfully go, but where he knew he was likely to be attacked.

In a very limited number of cases, the attacker may not be committing a crime because, for example, he is a child under ten, insane, in a state of automatism or under a material mistake of fact. If D is unaware of the circumstances which exempt the attacker (eg the attacker's insanity), then s 3 of the Criminal Law Act will still, indirectly, afford D a defence to any criminal charge which may be brought, provided he is acting reasonably in the light of the circumstances as they appear, reasonably or not, to him; for he intends to use force in the prevention of crime, as that section allows, and therefore has no mens rea.

Where D does know of the circumstances which mean that the attack on him is not criminal, then s 3 is inapplicable, but it is submitted that the question should be decided on similar principles. A person should be allowed to use reasonable force in defending himself or another against an unjustifiable attack, even if the attacker is not criminally responsible.[465] Authority for this can now be found in the case of the conjoined twins, *Re A (Children)*.[466] The court granted a declaration that it would be lawful to carry out an operation to separate the twins to enable A to live even though the operation would inevitably kill B. B's heart and lungs were too deficient to keep her alive. She lived only because A was able to circulate sufficient oxygenated blood for both. The evidence was that if the operation was not carried out both would die. The *ratio decidendi* of the three judges differed but it is submitted that Ward LJ rightly held that this was a case of self-defence. B was, of course, completely innocent but she was killing A. He equated the case with that of a six-year-old boy shooting all and sundry in a playground. It would be lawful to kill him if that was the only way to prevent the deaths of others. There is a great difference between the boy's active conduct and the pathetic inactivity of B; but neither is committing a crime. Whatever the position regarding necessity and duress, it has always been held that private defence may be an answer to a charge of murder.

10.6.4.5 D's reliance on unknown justifying circumstances

What of D who seeks to rely on facts that existed and would justify his use of force, but of which he was unaware at the time of acting?[467] The test proposed in the CLRC's Fourteenth Report and adopted as the law in *Gladstone Williams* and s 76 is stated exclusively in terms of D's belief. Its terms do not apply where D is unaware of existing circumstances which, if he

---

[464] In the subsequent case of *Wheeldon v CPS* [2018] EWHC 249 (Admin) the Divisional Court, relying upon *Oraki*, held that in principle there was no rule that the defence of self-defence was not available to a person who assaulted a police officer who was found to be acting in the execution of their duty contrary to s 89(1).

[465] *Bayer v DPP*, n 431.   [466] [2000] 4 All ER 961, [2001] Crim LR 400, CA (Civ Div) and commentary.

[467] See TM Funk, 'Justifying Justifications' (1999) 19 OJLS 630, arguing that *Dadson* represents a 'very principled, precedented, coherent and logically compelling decision'. See also PH Robinson, 'Competing Theories of Justification: Deeds v Reasons' in Shute and Simester, *Criminal Law Theory*, 45; R Christopher, 'Unknowing Justification and the Logical Necessity of the *Dadson* Principle in Self-Defence' (1995) 15 OJLS 229; J Gardner, *Offences and Defences*, Ch 5.

knew of them, would justify his use of force. This line of reasoning accords with *Dadson*.[468] This is no accident. The Committee gave careful consideration to the matter and concluded that the *Dadson* principle was correct.[469]

Some academics take the view that where the circumstances justify his act, it is immaterial that D is not aware of them; where they can merely excuse his act, they do so only if he is aware of them.[470] Force used to make an arrest is said to be justified, not merely excused, so, it is argued, *Dadson* was a case of justification and is wrongly decided. Duress, which obviously requires awareness, is distinguishable because according to most commentators it merely excuses. But such an analysis based solely on justification and excuse is overly simplistic and does not provide a satisfactory explanation of *Dadson*. A boy who, knowing it is a wicked thing to do, deliberately kills his playmate has a defence if he was aged only nine at the time. Ten is the minimum age of criminal responsibility. He is excused, but no one would say he was 'justified' in killing his playmate because he was only nine. Is he to be liable for murder if he thought he was ten? Obviously not. He is excused by the fact, whether he knows of it or not. It is the policy of the law that a child under ten shall not be convicted of crime and the child's mistake cannot be allowed to defeat that policy.

Self-defence is, subject to s 76, still governed by the common law. Suppose that D shoots at V with intent to murder him and kills him. It turns out that D did so in the nick of time because, unknown to D, V was about to shoot D dead.[471] If D had only known he would certainly have had the defence of self-defence. Is D guilty of murder? According to orthodox justification/excuse theory, it depends on whether self-defence provides a justification or an excuse for the use of force. Glanville Williams, who at one time thought self-defence merely an excuse, later concluded that it is a justification,[472] so he thought D would have a defence. But can it really be right that a person who has fired a gun at another with intent to murder should be beyond the reach of the law? One answer is that, though not guilty of murder, he is guilty of attempted murder under the Criminal Attempts Act 1981 (since, by that Act, he is to be treated for the purpose of an attempt charge as if the facts were as he believed them to be). But how can it be said that his act was both (a) justified and (b) attempted murder? What would a jury make of a direction to that effect? The better view is that the *Dadson* principle applies and that it is generally applicable to defences unless policy (as in the case of the nine-year-old, above) otherwise requires.

10.6.4.6 Defence of property

Where D is charged with criminal damage and his defence is that he was acting in defence of his own property—as where he kills V's dog which, he claims, was attacking his sheep, the matter is regulated by the Criminal Damage Act 1971, which is considered in Ch 27.[473] Where D is charged with an offence against the person, or any other offence, and his defence is that he was defending his property, he will generally be acting in the prevention of crime and, as in defence of the person, s 3 is likely to be held to provide the criterion. Following amendment to s 76 of the CJIA, it is clear that the provisions apply to '(ia) the purpose of defence of property under the common law'.

---

468 (1850) 2 Den 35.   469 The discussion is not included in the Fourteenth Report, paras 281–287.

470 See in general GP Fletcher, *Rethinking Criminal Law* (1978); Smith, *Justification and Excuse*; ML Corrado (ed), *Justification and Excuse in the Criminal Law: A Collection of Essays* (1994); A Eser et al (eds), *Justification and Excuse: Comparative Perspectives* (1987). For monographs and essays providing sophisticated analyses of the theories, see especially R Schopp, *Justification Defences and Just Convictions* (1988) and Horder, *Excusing Crime*.

471 This paradox of the unknowing justification is analysed by R Christopher (1995) 15 OJLS 229.

472 Compare CLGP (1961) 25, (1982) 2 LS 233, 250.

473 See D Lanham, 'Defence of Property in the Criminal Law' [1966] Crim LR 368.

In *Faraj*,[474] the Court of Appeal considered the defence of protection of property where D had made a mistake in thinking that a gas repair man was a burglar and had threatened him with a knife. The court could see no reason why a householder should not be entitled to detain someone in his house whom he *genuinely* believed to be a burglar. 'The householder must honestly believe that he needs to detain the suspect and must do so in a way which is reasonable': *Gladstone Williams* applies to mistakes in relation to defence of property.

It can rarely, if ever, be reasonable to use deadly force merely for the protection of property.[475] Would it have been reasonable to kill even one of the Great Train Robbers to prevent them from getting away with their millions of pounds of loot, or to kill a man about to destroy a priceless painting (even assuming that no means short of killing could prevent the commission of the crime)? It will be recalled that Art 2 of the ECHR does not permit the use of lethal force otherwise than in preventing riot, etc, or unlawful 'violence'.

In the case of *Hussey*,[476] it was stated that it would be lawful for a person to kill one who would unlawfully dispossess him of his home. Even if this were the law at the time, it would seem difficult now to contend that such conduct would be reasonable; for legal redress would be available if the householder were wrongly evicted. Insofar as the householder was preventing crime, his conduct would be regulated by s 3 of the Criminal Law Act 1967 which replaces the rules of common law.

More recently, in *Burns*[477] the court emphasized the narrow scope of defences where D is protecting property. B was convicted of causing actual bodily harm to V, a prostitute whom B had picked up and driven to a secluded spot. Having decided not to have sex with V, and having paid her, B requested V to leave the car and when she refused, used force. The Court of Appeal upheld his conviction. B had not acted in self-defence nor in defence of anyone else; he had not been defending his property against threat or risk of damage; he was not acting for any purpose within s 3 of the Criminal Law Act 1967. The defence was one of 'self-help'. That defence was always a last resort. It was a defence which the common law would be reluctant to extend. Lord Judge CJ added:

Recognising that to be lawful the use of force must always be reasonable in the circumstances, we accept that it might be open to the owner of a vehicle, in the last resort and when all reasonably practicable alternatives have failed, forcibly to remove an individual who has entered into his vehicle without permission and refuses to leave it. However, where that individual entered the car as a passenger, in effect at the invitation of the car owner, on the basis that they mutually understood that when their dealings were completed she would be driven back in the car from whence she had come, the use of force to remove her at the appellant's unilateral whim, was unlawful.

The court also doubted, as a matter of legal theory, whether the car owner's rights could be treated as analogous to those of a landowner to remove trespassers. However, caution is required since it does not seem the point was argued in full.

10.6.4.7 To what offences is public or private defence an answer?

These defences are most naturally relied on as answers to charges of homicide, assault, false imprisonment and other offences against the person. It is not clear to what extent public or private defence may be invoked as defences to other crimes.[478]

---

474 [2007] EWCA Crim 1033. 475 See Leverick, *Killing in Self-Defence*, Ch 7.
476 (1924) 18 Cr App R 160, CCA. 477 [2010] EWCA Crim 1023.
478 Clause 44 of the Draft Code ('Use of force in public or private defence') would not justify or excuse any criminal conduct not involving the use of force (except acts immediately preparatory to the use of such force); but the Code would leave it open to the courts to develop a wider defence at common law.

In *A-G's Reference (No 2 of 1983)*,[479] D made and retained in his shop petrol bombs at a time when extensive rioting was taking place in the area. He was acquitted of an offence under s 4(1) of the Explosive Substances Act 1883 of possessing an explosive substance in such circumstances as to give rise to a reasonable suspicion that he did not have it for a law-ful object. It was a defence under the terms of the section for D to prove that he had it for a lawful object. The Court of Appeal held that there was evidence on which a jury might have decided that the use of the petrol bombs would have been reasonable force in self-defence against an apprehended attack. If so, D had the bombs for 'a lawful object' and was not guilty of the offence charged. Yet it was assumed[480] that he was committing offences of manufacturing and storing explosives contrary to the Explosives Act 1875. The court agreed with the Court of Appeal in Northern Ireland in *Fegan*[481] that possession of a firearm for the purpose of protecting the possessor may be possession of a lawful object, even though the possession was unlawful being without a licence. The judgment is strangely ambivalent.

[D] is not confined for his remedy to calling in the police or boarding up his premises. He may still arm himself for his own protection, if the exigency arises, although in so doing he may commit other offences. That he may be guilty of other offences will avoid the risk of anarchy contemplated by the reference.

To say 'He may do it—but he will commit an offence if he does' seems inconsistent. There is, however, a clear statement that acts immediately preparatory to justifiable acts of self-defence are also justified. This must surely be right. If D becomes caught up in a shoot-out between police and dangerous criminals, picks up a handgun dropped by a wounded policeman and fires in order to defend his own and police lives, it would be astonishing if he had a defence to a charge of homicide but not to possessing a firearm.[482] Possibly, then, the passage earlier refers to preparatory, but not immediately preparatory, acts. This does not resolve the ambivalence. The law must say whether a person may, or may not, do such acts; and if it says they are crimes, he may not.

The matter must now be considered in the light of the defence of duress of circum-stances.[483] A person may save himself from injury by an attacker by using force or by running away and *Willer* and *Conway*[484] are cases where this form of self-defence was an answer to a charge of reckless driving. In *Symonds*,[485] where a driver, charged under s 20 of the OAPA and with dangerous driving, raised self-defence, it was held that the same considerations applied to the driving charge as to the s 20 offence. Calling the defence to the driving charge 'duress of circumstances' may make no difference—but sometimes it may, because duress requires an objective test where the test for self-defence under s 76 is certainly subjective. As a matter of policy there is a great deal to be said for encouraging a threatened person to escape, even where that involves committing a minor offence, rather than using force against the aggressor.

A successful defendant will not care whether his defence is called 'duress of circum-stances' or 'private defence'; but whether the defence succeeds may well depend on how it is categorized, because duress of circumstance is limited to threats to the person whereas self-defence extends to defence of property; and the former is governed by an objective test

---

[479] [1984] QB 456, [1984] 1 All ER 988, [1984] Crim LR 289 and commentary.
[480] *A-G's Reference (No 2 of 1983)* [1984] 1 All ER 988 at 992–993, [1984] Crim LR 289.
[481] [1972] NI 80. Cf *Emmanuel* [1998] Crim LR 347.
[482] cf *Georgiades* (1989) 89 Cr App R 206, [1989] Crim LR 574; see also *Salih* [2007] EWCA Crim 2750; *McAuley* [2009] EWCA Crim 2130, [2010] Crim LR 336.
[483] See *Pommell*, p 344.
[484] See p 365. See DW Elliott, 'Necessity, Duress and Self-Defence' [1989] Crim LR 611.
[485] [1998] Crim LR 280.

whereas a subjective test is applied to the latter. A disqualified driver who drove his Rolls-Royce to avoid its destruction by an aggressor could not plead duress (no threat of death or serious injury). Duress would not excuse possession of the handgun even if the possessor honestly believed that life was in danger, unless his belief was based on reasonable grounds (though D's self-defence would not be impaired). For the avoidance of such anomalies, acts immediately preparatory to public or private defence are better regarded as justified or excused by those defences.

The fears of the courts regarding a general defence of necessity[486] probably militate against a recognition that public and private defence may constitute a defence to crime generally; but, where contravention of *any* law is (a) necessary to enable the right of public or private defence to be exercised, and (b) reasonable in the circumstances, it ought to be excused. It is open to the courts to move in this direction.

The availability of private defence to a charge of dangerous driving was considered by the Court of Appeal in *Riddell*.[487] It was held that although the legal elements of that offence do not inherently involve the use of force, that does not preclude the availability of the defence where, on the particular facts of the case, use of responsive force was involved in the dangerous driving alleged. The court rejected the argument that a wholly uniform approach ought to apply that would preclude private defence from being pleaded by reference to the nature of the offence charged without reference to the underlying facts. It is submitted that there is much to commend the Court of Appeal's approach, as it ensures that focus is placed on the substance of what occurred, rather than on the offence D is alleged to have committed.

In *Oraki v DPP*[488] Singh LJ doubted whether it was right as a matter of principle that private or public defence is restricted to cases involving the use of force. The example his lordship gave of such a case was someone who blocks a police car by driving his own car in front of it, and in doing so enables a third party to escape. This person would commit the offence of obstructing a police officer and Singh LJ stated that the fact force was not used should not preclude someone from pleading the defence. It is respectfully submitted that this *dictum* ought to be treated with caution, as the use of force is the hallmark of the defences discussed in this part of the chapter. Although there may appear to be an anomaly in that someone who does not use force will be unable to plead the defence, as Davis LJ stated in *Riddell*, 'self-defence ordinarily arises—putting it shortly—where a person uses force in order to meet actual or perceived force or threat of force'.[489] An individual who finds himself in the situation described by Singh LJ would be able to plead duress of circumstances, but not self-defence or defence of another.

10.6.4.8 Use of force excessive in the known circumstances

Generally, where D, being under no mistake of fact, uses force in public or private defence, he either has a complete defence or if he uses excessive force, no defence. In murder, if D used excessive force and lost his self-control he may (subject to the other elements of the defence being satisfied) be able to rely on the loss of self-control defence to reduce the offence to manslaughter. However, even in murder, if D has not lost his self-control, but has used excessive force, he will be guilty for the full offence of murder even if he genuinely (and reasonably) believed some force was necessary. This was affirmed by the House of Lords in *Clegg*.[490] D, a soldier on duty in Northern Ireland, fired four shots at a car (in fact stolen) which did not stop at the checkpoint he was guarding. The judge, sitting in a

---

486 See p 369.   487 [2017] EWCA Crim 413.

488 [2018] EWHC 115 (Admin).   489 [2017] EWCA Crim 413, [41].

490 [1995] 1 All ER 334, [1995] Crim LR 418 and commentary. See also M Kaye, 'Excessive Force in Self Defence After *Clegg*' (1996) 61 J Crim L 448.

'Diplock' court (without a jury), accepted that the first three shots had been fired in self-defence or defence of a colleague but that the fourth, which killed, was not, as the car had passed the soldiers and was already 50 feet down the road. D's conviction of murder was affirmed by the House of Lords, holding that it is established law that killing by excessive force in self-defence is murder and that if a change is to be made, it is for Parliament, not the courts, to make it. Where D has not lost control, but has used excessive force, there is no partial defence resulting in a manslaughter conviction, as with loss of control and diminished responsibility. The possibility was considered and rejected immediately after the *Clegg* decision.[491]

In *Palmer*,[492] the Privy Council explained why they saw no need for further refinement of the law in England:

> If there has been an attack so that defence is reasonably necessary it will be recognized that a person defending himself cannot weigh to a nicety the exact measure of his necessary defensive action. If a jury thought that in a moment of unexpected anguish a person attacked had only done what he honestly and instinctively thought was necessary that would be most potent evidence that only reasonable defensive action had been taken. A jury will be told that a defence of self-defence, where the evidence makes it[s] raising possible, will only fail if the prosecution show beyond doubt that what the accused did was not by way of self-defence.[493]

The CLRC was persuaded that *Howe* was right in principle and recommended its adoption in relation to private defence of person and property and the prevention of crime.[494] It is submitted that the soundness of this recommendation is not impaired by *Clegg*.[495]

10.6.5 Reform of self-defence/private defence

The Law Commission's general proposals on defences are contained in Report No 218 which provides:

> 27(1) The use of force by a person for any of the following purposes, if only such as is reasonable in the circumstances as he believes them to be, does not constitute an offence—
>
> (a) to protect himself or another from injury, assault or detention caused by a criminal act;
>
> (b) to protect himself or (with the authority of that other) another from trespass to the person;
>
> (c) to protect his property from appropriation, destruction or damage caused by a criminal act or from trespass or infringement;
>
> (d) to protect property belonging to another from appropriation, destruction or damage caused by a criminal act or (with the authority of the other) from trespass or infringement; or
>
> (e) to prevent crime or a breach of the peace.

---

[491] See the *Inter-Departmental Review of the Law on Lethal Force in Self-Defence or the Prevention of Crime* (1996) paras 83–84.

[492] [1971] AC 814.

[493] On the importance of this direction and the potential for it to be underestimated, see LC 290, Part 4, paras 4.11–4.14.

[494] Fourteenth Report, para 228. Cf PF Smith, 'Excessive Defence—A Rejection of Australian Initiative' [1972] Crim LR 524.

[495] The Law Commission in cl 59 of the Draft Code have implemented the recommendation.

(6) Where an act is lawful by reason only of a belief or suspicion which is mistaken, the defence provided by this section applies as in the case of an unlawful act, unless—

   (a) D knows or believes that the force is used against a constable or a person assisting a constable, and

   (b) the constable is acting in the execution of his duty.

10.7 Impossibility

Where the law imposes a duty to act, it has sometimes been held that it is a defence that, through no fault of his own, it was impossible for D to fulfil that duty.[496] The secretary of a limited company is not liable for failure to annex to an annual return a copy of a balance sheet laid before the company in a general meeting where there is no such balance sheet in existence: 'nobody ought to be prosecuted for that which it is impossible to do'.[497] A person is not liable for failure to leave a particular place if he is unaware of the order requiring him to do so.[498] In New Zealand, it has been held that a failure to leave the country after a revocation of a permit was not an offence if no airline would carry D because of the advanced state of her pregnancy.[499] Impossibility is a defence to a charge of failure to assist a constable to preserve the peace when called upon to do so.[500]

On the other hand, the failure of a driver to produce a test certificate is not excused by the fact that it is impossible for him to do so, the owner of the vehicle being unable or unwilling to produce it.[501]

We find here the inconsistency which is so common in relation to strict liability. It cannot be asserted, therefore, that any *general* defence of impossibility is recognized at the present time. It has to be regarded as a question of the interpretation of the particular provision, with all the uncertainty that this entails.

When impossibility might be available as a defence, it will presumably fail if the impossibility has been brought about by D's own default.[502] The defence would also seem to be confined to cases where the law imposes a duty to act and not to cases of commission where the corresponding defence, if any, is necessity.[503]

---

[496] CLGP, 746–748. See A Smart, 'Criminal Responsibility for Failing to do the Impossible' (1987) 103 LQR 532.

[497] *Stockdale v Coulson* [1974] 3 All ER 154 at 157, DC, per Melford Stevenson J.

[498] *Lim Chin Aik v R* [1963] AC 160, [1963] 1 All ER 223, PC.

[499] *Finau v Department of Labour* [1984] 2 NZLR 396.

[500] *Brown* (1841) Car & M 314, per Alderson B.

[501] *Davey v Towle* [1973] RTR 328, [1973] Crim LR 360, DC.

[502] But cf *Stockdale v Coulson*, n 497, and comment at [1974] Crim LR 375.

[503] See *Canestra* 1951 (2) SA 317 (AD) and EM Burchell and PMA Hunt, *South African Criminal Law and Procedure* (1970) 293–296.

13

Voluntary Manslaughter

At common law, all unlawful homicides which are not murder are manslaughter. The offence has a broad scope, being limited by murder at one extreme and accidental killing at the other. There are an increasing number of statutory offences of unlawful killing including, for example, causing death by dangerous driving and corporate manslaughter.[1] Some of these statutory offences preclude prosecution for manslaughter (notably corporate manslaughter) but in most cases manslaughter remains available as an alternative charge to the specific statutory offences.[2]

It is customary and useful to divide manslaughter into two main groups: 'voluntary' and 'involuntary' manslaughter. The distinction is based on D's intention at the time of the killing. Where there is no intention to kill or cause grievous bodily harm, the offence falls within the category of involuntary manslaughter. In contrast, voluntary manslaughter comprises cases where D had the intention to kill or do grievous bodily harm but some defined mitigating circumstance—loss of self-control, diminished responsibility or killing in pursuance of a suicide pact—reduces his crime to the less serious grade of criminal homicide.[3] These partial defences to murder were originally introduced to avoid the death penalty. Today they subsist unsatisfactorily in order to avoid the mandatory life sentence for murder. The partial defences to murder were radically overhauled in the Coroners and Justice Act 2009.[4]

Three partial defences to murder exist:

(1) where D kills with the mens rea for murder but at the time he had lost his self-control and one of the statutory qualifying triggers applied (governed by ss 54–56 of the Coroners and Justice Act 2009);

(2) where D kills with the mens rea for murder but he establishes on the balance of probabilities that he was suffering from diminished responsibility (under s 52 of the 2009 Act);

(3) where D kills in pursuance of a suicide pact.[5] The problem of the suicide pact is looked at in Ch 15 alongside the statutory crime of assisting or encouraging suicide.[6]

---

[1] These offences, their theoretical implications and the relationship with 'normal' manslaughter are considered in the valuable collection of essays edited by C Clarkson and S Cunningham (eds), *Criminal Liability for Non-Aggressive Death* (2008); see, in particular, A Ashworth, 'Manslaughter Generic or Nominate Offences' in that volume.

[2] See also V Tadros, 'The Limits of Manslaughter' in Clarkson and Cunningham, *Criminal Liability for Non-Aggressive Death* (2008), who argues that the special offences discriminate and fail to optimize coherence in the law; see also Tadros, *Criminal Responsibility*, 348 et seq.

[3] *A-G of Ceylon v Perera* [1953] AC 200, PC; *Lee Chun Chuen v R* [1963] AC 220; *Parker v R* [1964] AC 1369; *Smith (Clean) v R* [2002] 1 Cr App R 92; *contra*, per Viscount Simon in *Holmes v DPP* [1946] AC 588 at 598, HL.

[4] For analysis of the defences of provocation and diminished responsibility under the law before the Coroners and Justice Act 2009, see the 12th edition of this book, Ch 15.

[5] See p 619.   [6] See p 620.

13.1 Loss of self-control

13.1.1 Provocation—the old law

The common law had recognized a defence of provocation for centuries.[7] The common law defence reduced murder to manslaughter where D killed with mens rea for murder, provided at the time of the killing he had been subjected to provoking acts of such gravity that they caused him and would cause a reasonable person a sudden and temporary loss of control of a significant degree.[8] That common law rule was modified (but not codified) by s 3 of the Homicide Act 1957. The elements of that defence were that if, when D killed, he had mens rea for murder he would be guilty of manslaughter if: things said or done provoked him; and he suffered a sudden and temporary loss of self-control; and the provocation was enough to make a reasonable man do as D did (with the reasonable man sharing those of D's characteristics that would affect the gravity of the provocation but not those which affected his ability to exercise self-control).

The defence was extremely controversial.[9] Courts struggled with the application of the defence, in part because it was being used as a means of relieving the potential injustice of the mandatory life sentence for murder. There were disagreements as to the terms of the defence,[10] with numerous high-profile appeals including several to the House of Lords and Privy Council in which majority judgments added to the confusion. The core disagreement centred on whether, when addressing the question whether a reasonable person would have done as D did, the jury were to have regard to D's personal characteristics, and if so, which ones. The appellate courts failed to adopt a consistent approach, in some cases taking an objective view, but in others concluding that the jury ought to take a subjective view taking into account D's characteristics. For the appellate courts to fluctuate so often and so significantly on the interpretation of a defence in cases of such seriousness led to confusion and presented a disappointing spectacle.[11]

Even the theoretical foundation for the defence remained unclear: was the defence properly regarded as one of partial justification (D has gone beyond what would be an acceptable response to the provoking conduct, or that the deceased deserved it) or of partial excuse (D's loss of self-control was uncharacteristic, the bad character exhibited exceeds that to be expected in the circumstances)?[12] One of the most powerful influences for reform was the claim that the defence operated in a discriminatory fashion, which given its historical origins is hardly surprising.[13] Women who killed abusive partners were disadvantaged if

---

[7] For a comprehensive review of the theoretical and historical context of the defence, see J Horder, *Provocation and Responsibility* (1992). See also JM Kaye, 'Early History of Murder and Manslaughter' (1967) 83 LQR 365.

[8] *Duffy* [1949] 1 All ER 932n. On this case see S Edwards 'Justice Devlin's Legacy' [2009] Crim LR 851.

[9] There is a wealth of literature on the topic. LC 290, *Partial Defences to Murder* (2004) is a valuable starting point. The Law Commission documents leading to the new Act also include valuable discussion: see LCCP 177, *A New Homicide Act for England* (2005) and LC 304, *Murder, Manslaughter and Infanticide* (2006). Valuable articles and essays include the seminal piece by A Ashworth, 'The Doctrine of Provocation' (1976) 35 CLJ 292.

[10] See LCCP 177, para 2.78.

[11] This passage was cited with approval by Lord Judge CJ in *Clinton* [2012] EWCA Crim 2.

[12] Horder, *Provocation and Responsibility*, Chs 6–9, in particular at 130–135. See further J Dressler, 'Provocation: Partial Justification or Partial Excuse' (1988) 51 MLR 467; F McAuley, 'Anticipating the Past: The Defences of Provocation in Irish Law' (1987) 50 MLR 133; V Tadros, 'The Characters of Excuses' (2001) 21 OJLS 495. See also the discussion in LC 290, paras 3.22 et seq and the Irish Law Reform Commission, LRC Consultation Paper No 27, *Homicide: The Plea of Provocation* (2003).

[13] See Horder, *Provocation and Responsibility*.

they did not act in a state which could legally be described as one of 'sudden and temporary loss of control'.[14] In addition, until relatively recently, the cumulative effect of years of abuse was not considered. Further, the mental characteristics arising from an abusive relationship (including what some recognize as battered woman syndrome)[15] could only be taken into account if that was relevant to the gravity of the provocation (ie the sting of the words or conduct that provoked D), but not to D's ability to exercise her self-control.[16] The abused woman is unlikely as a matter of fact to kill in self-defence (as that term is understood in law). Owing to relative limited physical strength, it is uncommon for women to respond lethally when facing an attack by an abusive male partner.[17] Women charged with murder were forced to rely on diminished responsibility, which aside from requiring expert evidence and imposing a burden of proof on the accused, stigmatized them as mentally abnormal.

A further general difficulty with the defence was its relationship with the partial defence of diminished responsibility. The elements were very different, with different burdens of proof, but they overlapped in many cases.[18]

These serious problems with the provocation defence prompted reform. Law Commission papers examined numerous options for reform including whether it was even necessary or desirable to retain the defence if the mandatory sentence were to be abolished.[19] Fundamental questions included whether the purpose of the defence was to unshackle the judge from imposing the mandatory life sentence[20] or to label more distinctly those killers whose conduct might be regarded as morally different, despite their malice aforethought, owing to some mitigating feature of the killing. The unique stigmas and heightened emotions aroused by the stark fact of death generate strong views on these issues. Many other jurisdictions have faced similar difficulties where defence and reform proposals have been widely canvassed.[21]

---

[14] S Edwards, *Sex and Gender in the Legal Process* (1996) Ch 6; O'Donovan (1991) 18 J Law & Soc 219; C Wells (1994) 14 LS 266; A McColgan, 'In Defence of Battered Women who Kill' (1993) 13 OJLS 508. For a valuable summary see LCCP 173, Ch 10.

[15] See L Walker, *Battered Women Syndrome* (1st edn, 1984; 3rd edn, 2008).

[16] See C Wells, 'Provocation: The Case for Abolition' in A Ashworth and B Mitchell (eds), *Rethinking English Homicide Law* (2000).

[17] On the availability of the defence, see A McColgan (1993) 13 OJLS 508; C Wells (1994) 14 LS 266; J Dressler, 'Battered Women Who Kill Their Sleeping Tormentors' and J Horder, 'Killing the Passive Abuser: A Theoretical Defence' both in Shute and Simester, *Criminal Law Theory*.

[18] There were calls to merge the defences in something similar to that in the US Model Penal Code, § 210(3) (1)(b). See also LC 304, para 5.22. On the merits of such overlap and a potential merging of the defences, see R Mackay and B Mitchell, 'Provoking Diminished Responsibility: Two Pleas Merging into One?' [2003] Crim LR 745; J Chalmers, 'Merging Provocation and Diminished Responsibility: Some Reasons for Scepticism' [2004] Crim LR 198; J Gardner and T Macklem, 'No Provocation Without Responsibility: A Reply to Mackay and Mitchell' [2004] Crim LR 213; R Mackay and B Mitchell, 'Replacing Provocation: More on a Combined Plea' [2004] Crim LR 219. See also R Holton and S Shute, 'Self-Control in Modern Provocation Defence' (2007) 27 OJLS 49.

[19] See LC 290, Ch 2 and paras 3.35 et seq and the responses discussed to LCCP 173. Horder considers the arguments for abolition in *Provocation and Responsibility*, Ch 9.

[20] See C Wells, 'The Death Penalty for Provocation' [1978] Crim LR 662.

[21] See eg New South Wales Law Reform Commission No 83, *Partial Defences to Murder: Provocation and Infanticide* (1997); Irish Law Reform Commission, LRC Consultation Paper No 27 (2003) n 12, and LCCP 173 for a valuable summary of a number of jurisdictions. For comparative material generally, see S Yeo, *Unrestrained Killings and the Law: Provocation and Excessive Self-Defence in India, England and Australia* (1998). See also eg the Victoria Law Reform Commission, 'Law Reform Defences to Murder' [2005] Crim LR 256 and for proposals in New South Wales, T Crofts and A Loughnan, 'Provocation, NSW Style: Reform of the Defence of Provocation in NSW' [2014] Crim LR 109.

687

13.1.2 Loss of self-control—the new law

By s 56 of the Coroners and Justice Act 2009 the common law defence of provocation is abolished and replaced by a new defence of loss of control (in this chapter 'LOSC'), contained in ss 54 and 55.[22] In *Clinton*, Lord Judge CJ emphasized that the old provocation defence is irrelevant and that 'The full ambit of the defence is encompassed within these statutory provisions.'[23] The provisions derive from the Law Commission Report No 304[24] and earlier Law Commission Reports[25] and papers. Since the enacted provisions differ in important respects from the proposal put forward by the Law Commission, care is needed in relying on these documents as a source for interpretation, if they can be relied on at all.[26]

Sections 54 and 55 replace the common law defence with a related but significantly different defence labelled 'loss of control'. This is designed to be a much narrower defence than at common law and under s 3 of the 1957 Act. Section 54 provides:

(1) Where a person ('D') kills or is a party to the killing of another ('V'), D is not to be convicted of murder if—

    (a) D's acts and omissions in doing or being a party to the killing resulted from D's loss of self-control,

    (b) the loss of self-control had a qualifying trigger, and

    (c) a person of D's sex and age, with a normal degree of tolerance and self restraint and in the circumstances of D, might have reacted in the same or in a similar way to D...

(7) A person who, but for this section, would be liable to be convicted of murder is liable instead to be convicted of manslaughter.

The LOSC defence is further defined in s 55. It comprises three main elements. In short, the requirements are:[27]

(1) a loss of self-control although not one that is necessarily sudden;

(2) D's loss of control must have been attributable to one or both of two specified 'qualifying triggers':

    (a) D's fear of serious violence from V against D or another identified person, and/or

    (b) things done or said (or both) which:

---

[22] See: A Norrie, *Crime, Reason and History* (3rd edn, 2014) Ch 11; A Reed and M Bohlander (eds), *Loss of Control and Diminished Responsibility: Domestic, Comparative and International Perspectives* (2011); C Withey, 'Loss of Control, Loss of Opportunity' [2011] Crim LR 263; R Fortson and A Keene, *Current Law Statutes Annotation* (2010); J Glasson and J Knowles, *Blackstone's Guide to the Coroners and Justice Act 2009* (2010) Ch 8; S Edwards, 'Anger and Fear as Justifiable Preludes for Loss of Self-Control' (2010) 74 J Crim L 223.

[23] *Clinton* [2012] EWCA Crim 2, [2]. See also *Gurpinar* [2015] EWCA Crim 178: 'It should rarely be necessary to look at cases decided under the older law of provocation.' Per Lord Thomas CJ at [4].

[24] *Murder Manslaughter and Infanticide* (2006).

[25] LC 290, *Partial Defences to Murder* (2004). See also LCCP 173 (2003) and LCCP 177, *A New Homicide Act for England and Wales?* (2005).

[26] The Law Commission proposal had no loss of control requirement nor did it exclude reliance on sexual infidelity as a sufficient trigger, see later for discussion. Lord Judge in *Clinton* stated, at [3], that the legislation does not sufficiently follow the recommendations of the Law Commission to allow the court to discern any link between the views and recommendations of the Law Commission and the legislation as enacted. See also *Gurpinar* [2015] EWCA Crim 178.

[27] As Lord Judge CJ emphasized in *Clinton*, each of these components is integral to the defence and if one is absent, then the defence fails. His lordship stated that the components ought to be analysed sequentially and separately, at [9]. See also *Gurpinar* [2015] EWCA Crim 178 per Lord Thomas CJ.

(i) constitute circumstances of an extremely grave character, and

(ii) cause D to have a justifiable sense of being seriously wronged;

(3) A person of D's sex and age, with a normal degree of tolerance and self-restraint and in the circumstances of D, might have reacted in the same or in a similar way to D.

13.1.2.1 Commencement

Sections 54 to 56 were brought into force on 4 October 2010.[28] The LOSC defence will only apply if both D's act and V's death occurred after 4 October.[29]

13.1.2.2 The defence applies only to murder

The LOSC defence is available only to a charge of murder whether as a principal or secondary party.[30] Loss of self-control is not a defence to a charge of attempted murder or any charge other than murder. The defence should, it is submitted, have no relevance to the determination of whether D committed the acts or omissions[31] causing death when he has been found unfit to plead under s 4A of the Criminal Procedure (Insanity) Act 1964.[32]

13.1.2.3 Procedure

One of the problems with the provocation defence was that judges were compelled to leave the defence to the jury in every case in which there was some evidence of provocation even if the defence was not pleaded by D (and even if it ran counter to D's interests[33]). The LOSC defence need not be left in every case: s 54(6). Under that section the defence must be left only if 'sufficient evidence is adduced to raise an issue with respect to the defence' and this is when 'evidence is adduced on which, in the opinion of the trial judge, a jury, properly directed, could reasonably conclude that the defence might apply'. This significant change is one that the Court of Appeal was keen to assert in the early cases under the Act: *Clinton*, *Dawes*, *Gurpinar* and more recently in *Martin*. In *Clinton*, Lord Judge stated that in reaching this decision the trial judge is required to address each component of the defence, ensuring that there is sufficient evidence to establish each one.[34] Lord Judge CJ observed that this exercise:

requires a common sense judgment based on an analysis of all the evidence. To the extent that the evidence may be in dispute, the judge has to recognise that the jury may accept the evidence

---

[28] The Coroners and Justice Act 2009 (Commencement No 4, Transitional and Saving Provisions) Order 2010, SI 2010/816. For some considerable time after 4 October 2010 many homicide trials related to offences alleged to have been committed 'wholly or partly' before that date: see para 7 of Sch 22 to the Coroners and Justice Act 2009. The law of some Caribbean jurisdictions mirrors that of England prior to the enactment of the Coroners and Justice Act 2009, so the Privy Council may still have to consider provocation for some time to come.

[29] Para 7 of Sch 22 to the 2009 Act.

[30] Section 54(8): 'The fact that one party to a killing is by virtue of this section not liable to be convicted of murder does not affect the question whether the killing amounted to murder in the case of any other party to it.' This follows the position in relation to provocation: *Marks* [1998] Crim LR 676. It has been suggested that provocation (and diminished responsibility) should be available to all offences—J Horder, *Excusing Crime* (2003) 143–146.

[31] It is possible to have an omission causing death and plead LOSC. Eg D is so angered by his wife's perpetual taunts that he loses control and leaves her to die when she has fallen and is critically injured despite having a duty to assist.

[32] That was the position with provocation: *Grant* [2001] EWCA Crim 2611.

[33] eg if D was claiming that he killed V in self-defence and remained in control of his temper, if there was evidence of provocation and loss of self-control the provocation defence would be left to the jury even though that would undermine the defendant's plea of self-defence: *Bullard v R* [1957] AC 635; *Rolle v R* [1965] 3 All ER 582; *Lee Chun-Chuen v R* [1963] AC 220. Empirical work by B Mitchell ('Distinguishing Between Murder and Manslaughter in Practice' (2006) 71 J Crim L 318), reveals that 75 per cent of provocation pleas were accompanied by one or more other defence.

[34] This was reiterated in *Dawes* [2013] EWCA Crim 322, *Gurpinar* [2015] EWCA Crim 178 and *Martin* [2017] EWCA Crim 1359. This represents a change from the old law: see *Acott* [1997] 1 WLR 306, 312.

which is most favourable to the defendant, and reject that which is most favourable to the prosecution, and so tailor the ruling accordingly. That is merely another way of saying that in discharging this responsibility the judge should not reject disputed evidence which the jury might choose to believe. Guiding himself or herself in this way, the more difficult question which follows is the judgment whether the circumstances were sufficiently grave and whether the defendant had a justifiable grievance because he had been seriously wronged. These are value judgments. They are left to the jury when the judge concludes that the evidential burden has been satisfied.[35]

Lord Judge CJ further elaborated on the role of the judge in *Dawes*.[36] His lordship observed that the use of the term 'opinion' in s 54(6) does not mean there is a discretion pursuant to which different judges may reasonably form different opinions on how it ought to be exercised.[37] What the section mandates is a judgement that may be right or wrong. Lord Judge CJ sought to emphasize that, provided the evidence crosses the threshold imposed by s 54(6), the judge must leave the defence to the jury even if the defence has, for tactical reasons, decided not to plead LOSC.[38] Similarly, whether the prosecution has raised the question or not, at the end of the evidence the judge should examine it and decide whether-sufficient evidence relating to all the ingredients of the defence has been raised. The Court of Appeal emphasized in *Jewell*[39] that judges need to be cautious. There will often be no other evidence to substantiate D's claim and the judge should not reject disputed evidence that the jury may well choose to believe. It is the judge's duty to consider whether, on the whole of the evidence, the defence arises.

Sufficient evidence of each of the elements of the defence may appear in the case presented by the Crown. If not, there is an evidential burden on D.[40] If no evidence is adduced by the Crown or D that D lost his self-control, then the judge will withdraw the defence.[41] Similarly if there is no sufficient evidence of the qualifying trigger.[42] Since the burden of proof is on the Crown, evidence which might leave a reasonable jury in reasonable doubt whether or not the element is satisfied is sufficient. There must be evidence of loss of self-control and of a qualifying trigger; mere speculation will not suffice.[43] The trial judge's task is not easy and assistance from the advocates must be provided.[44] The Court of Appeal will not lightly interfere with the trial judge's decision.[45]

13.1.2.4 No considered desire for revenge

The defence cannot apply where there is 'a considered desire for revenge' (s 54(4)) even if D lost control as a result of a qualifying trigger. This is a very important qualification and in many cases will be worth considering before any other element of the defence.[46] The restriction must also be seen in combination with the requirement in s 55(6)(a): even if D has lost his self-control, if that was caused by a thing which D incited to be done or

---

[35] At [46].   [36] [2013] EWCA Crim 322, [2013] Crim LR 770.

[37] This was reiterated in *Workman* [2014] EWCA Crim 575, in which the Court of Appeal emphasized that the judge is *required* to leave the partial defence to the jury if there is sufficient evidence to raise the issue. This is not a matter of discretion.

[38] For an example of a case in which the defence was left to the jury despite not being relied upon by the defence, see *Cox* [2014] EWCA Crim 804.

[39] [2014] EWCA Crim 414. See also *Gurpinar* [2015] EWCA Crim 178 per Lord Thomas CJ.

[40] It is submitted that as in provocation mixed statements could be relied on: *Jama* [2004] EWCA Crim 960. Care will need to be taken with reliance on D's lies: *Davies* [2004] EWCA Crim 1914 (under the old law).

[41] eg *Workman* [2014] EWCA Crim 575.   [42] cf *McDonald* [2016] EWCA Crim 1529.

[43] See in relation to provocation: *Miao* [2003] EWCA Crim 3486; *Van Dongen* [2005] EWCA Crim 1728.

[44] *Gurpinar* [15] per Lord Thomas CJ.   [45] ibid.

[46] In *Davies-Jones* [2013] EWCA Crim 2809, the Court of Appeal observed that ascertaining the existence of a considered desire for revenge is a logical precursor to the consideration of loss of control.

said for the *purpose* of providing an excuse to use violence, the qualifying triggers are not available.

The courts struggled for many years to distinguish revenge killings, of a premeditated or calculated nature, from killings committed in the heat of the moment for which the partial defence is available. Under the provocation defence the requirement of the sudden loss of self-control was an (imperfect) mechanism for drawing this distinction. In *Duffy*, it was said that:[47]

circumstances which induce a desire for revenge are inconsistent with provocation, since the conscious formulation of a desire for revenge means that a person has had time to think, to reflect, and that would negative a sudden temporary loss of self-control, which is of the essence of provocation.

The Law Commission's recommendation did not include any requirement for a loss of self-control, but did propose an explicit safeguard against the defence being used for revenge killings.

With the section as enacted including a requirement for D to have lost self-control, the position is even more complex. The judge is required to identify whether there was a 'considered desire for revenge' bearing in mind that D must have lost control and satisfy a qualifying trigger. Aside from the theoretical incoherence which results from a requirement for a loss of self-control and a restriction on considered revenge killings, problems may arise in practice. An abused spouse who kills after years of torment might well have a desire for revenge and yet be out of control at the time of killing.

The judge and jury face a difficult task. The word 'considered' which suggests that there is some element of premeditation, is likely to be significant, but is unfortunately undefined.[48] Lord Judge CJ suggested in *Clinton* that 'in reality, the greater the level of deliberation, the less likely it will be that the killing followed a true loss of self-control'.[49] Whilst this may be true, it is important not to conflate what ought to be two separate inquiries. It is possible for D to have lost his self-control *and* to act out of a considered desire for revenge. If so, D cannot plead the partial defence.

It is important to note also that under the 2009 Act there is no requirement for the loss of control to be 'sudden': s 54(2). The removal of that restriction means that in some cases it will be even harder for the court to determine whether the killing is one that is motivated by a considered desire for revenge or by other emotions. For example, to take cases from the old law, there was held to be sufficient evidence to go to the jury in *Thornton*[50] where a wife had previously declared an intention to kill her brutally abusive husband, and after a fresh provocation she went to the kitchen, took and sharpened a carving knife and returned to another room where she fatally stabbed him. Is that a 'considered desire for revenge'? Similarly, under the old law, in *Pearson*,[51] although DD had armed themselves in advance with the fatal weapon and the killing was a joint enterprise, provocation was left. Is arming oneself evidence of a 'considered desire for revenge'? In *Baillie*,[52] where D, being greatly enraged, fetched a gun from an attic and drove his car to V's house (stopping for petrol on

---

[47] [1949] 1 All ER 932n.

[48] The language the Law Commission used to describe this element was adopted in the statute despite the Commission not having engaged in statutory drafting: LC 304, para 5.27. See also Horder, *Homicide and the Politics of Law Reform* (2012) 214 et seq.

[49] At [10].

[50] [1992] 1 All ER 306. The jury rejected the defence, presumably being satisfied that there was no 'sudden and temporary' loss of self-control.

[51] [1992] Crim LR 193. See on this under the old law, M Wasik, 'Cumulative Provocation and Domestic Killing' [1982] Crim LR 29.

[52] [1995] Crim LR 739.

the way) before shooting him, provocation was also left to the jury. Would this be regarded as a 'considered desire for revenge'? In *Clinton*, the Court of Appeal approved the direction of the judge that a considered desire for revenge connoted a 'deliberate and considered decision ... one that has been thought about'.[53]

If D acted in a considered desire for revenge the defence is denied whether or not the desire for revenge exists before any potential qualifying trigger—fear of serious violence or things said or done. It is enough that having been taunted, D goes away for a period of time to brood and returns to stab V. It was suggested in Parliament that the courts should look to D's dominant motive at the time of the killing. That view was rejected by ministers[54] who stated a belief that:

the expression 'considered desire for revenge' achieves the right balance in ensuring that thought-out revenge killings are excluded without automatically barring every case where revenge may be part of a complex range of motivations.

13.1.2.5 Loss of control

The requirement of a 'loss of control' lies at the heart of the loss of control defence but what that means is undefined—other than that we know it need not be a 'sudden' loss.[55] As observed in parliamentary debates, it could refer to the failure to exercise self-control or the inability to do so.[56] It is a subjective test. If D is of an unusually phlegmatic temperament and it appears that he did not lose his self-control, the fact that a reasonable person in like circumstances would have done so will not assist D in the least. It is submitted that the test may be best understood as founded on whether D has lost his ability to maintain his actions in accordance with considered judgement or whether he had lost normal powers of reasoning.[57] The threshold is a high one. As Lord Judge explained in *Dawes*: 'For the individual with normal capacity of self-restraint and tolerance, unless the circumstances are extremely grave, normal irritation, and even serious anger do not often cross the threshold into loss of control.'[58]

In deciding whether D lost his control in fact,[59] the jury are, naturally, entitled to take into account all the relevant circumstances; the nature of the conduct which constitutes the qualifying trigger, and all the relevant conditions in which it took place, the sensitivity or otherwise of D,[60] and the time, if any, which elapsed between the qualifying trigger and the act which caused death. The length of time between the qualifying trigger and the killing will be important, but unlike under the provocation defence it is not critical that the time gap is short.[61]

---

53 At [129]–[131].

54 See https://publications.parliament.uk/pa/cm200809/cmpublic/coroners/memos/ucm2802.htm.

55 The Court of Appeal observed in *McGrory* [2013] EWCA Crim 2336 that: 'It is not a requirement of the law that this legal concept be explained to the jury in any precise defined form of words...' At [30], per Maddison J. See now the *Crown Court Compendium* (2017) Ch 19, section 2.

56 See Hansard, HL, 7 July 2009, col 572.

57 This definition proposed in the 13th edition was approved in *Jewell* [2014] EWCA Crim 414. In *Gurpinar* [2015] EWCA Crim 178, this test was challenged by the Crown but the Court of Appeal found it unnecessary to resolve the issue. See the discussion on the old law in R Holton and S Shute, 'Self-Control in the Modern Provocation Defence' (2007) 27 OJLS 49.

58 At [60]. See also *Martin* [2017] EWCA Crim 1359, in which Davis LJ stated that 'a panicky or scared response to aggressive conduct of another person is not of itself necessarily indicative of the existence of an issue of loss of control'. At [47].

59 It is not sufficient that a reasonable person would have done if D did not.

60 See under s 3 *Gregson* [2006] EWCA Crim 3364 (epileptic and mentally abnormal).

61 See Hansard, HC Public Bills Committee, 3 Mar 2009, col 434.

D's failure to testify to his loss of self-control is not, it is submitted, necessarily fatal to his case. In their evaluation of the defence as a whole, the jury should, it is submitted, be directed to consider the loss of control element before examining the qualifying triggers.[62]

The requirement that there must be a loss of control is not satisfied by evidence that D acted 'instinctively', for example where a boxer punches V who had taunted him.[63] In one tragic case[64] under the old law in which D yielded to the entreaties of his incurably ill and suffering wife to put an end to her life, it was held that D had not lost his self-control. Indeed, the evidence was that he was so in control as to stop immediately when he thought, wrongly, that she had changed her mind. The case highlights the arbitrariness of a defence partially absolving those who kill in a state of anger or outrage, but not those who exercise mercy.[65]

The removal of the requirement for the loss of self-control to be sudden is a significant change from the position at common law and under the 1957 Act. Under the old law the requirement of a 'sudden and temporary loss' of control was regarded as problematic. The test had the potential to operate in a discriminatory way, rendering the defence too readily available to those who are quick to temper (more commonly men), and less accommodating of those who endure the provoking circumstances before responding with lethal force (often women who kill abusive partners).[66] The requirement was tempered by the courts in decisions such as *Thornton*[67] and *Ahluwalia*[68] to bring within the partial defence persons whose reaction to circumstances was delayed rather than instantaneous.[69]

The absence of any suddenness requirement may make it harder to establish an evidential foundation for LOSC than it had been for provocation.[70] In practical terms, it may be difficult to establish whether there was a loss of control if it was not 'sudden'.[71] In *Dawes*, Lord Judge CJ gave the following guidance on how this element of the defence ought to be understood.

Provided there was a loss of control, it does not matter whether the loss was sudden or not. A reaction to circumstances of extreme gravity may be delayed. Different individuals in different situations do not react identically, nor respond immediately. Thus, for the purposes of the new defence, the loss of control may follow from the cumulative impact of earlier events. For the purposes of this first ingredient, the response to what used to be described as 'cumulative provocation' requires consideration in the same way as it does in relation to cases in which the loss of control is said to

---

[62] This was the case under s 3: *Brown* [1972] 2 All ER 1328 at 1333.

[63] *Serrano* [2006] EWCA Crim 3182 decided under s 3.

[64] *Cocker* [1989] Crim LR 740, discussed by PR Taylor, 'Provocation and Mercy Killing' [1991] Crim LR 111.

[65] The focus of the defence on the element of anger and spontaneous loss of control as an excusing feature is critically examined by J Horder, 'Reshaping the Subjective Element in the Provocation Defence' (2005) 25 OJLS 123 who considers a defence akin to what is now s 55 of the 2009 Act.

[66] For a broader-ranging critique of the s 3 defence for its 'gendered and heterosexualist' nature and of measuring the reasonableness of killing across cultures, see H Power, 'Provocation and Culture' [2006] Crim LR 871. Other defences are also difficult to apply to these circumstances. See J Loveless, 'Domestic Violence, Coercion and Duress' [2010] Crim LR 93.

[67] [1992] 1 All ER 306, [1992] Crim LR 54. For a further appeal, see [1996] 2 Cr App R 108, [1996] Crim LR 597.

[68] [1992] 4 All ER 889, [1993] Crim LR 63. On which see D Nicolson and R Sanghvi, 'Battered Women and Provocation: The Implications of *R v Ahluwalia*' [1993] Crim LR 728.

[69] The issue has generated immense literature, see generally K O'Donovan, 'Defences for Battered Women Who Kill?' (1991) 18 J Law & Soc 219; C Wells, 'Battered Women Syndrome and Defences to Homicide: Where Now' (1994) 14 LS 266; and n 14.

[70] cf *Duffy* [1949] 1 All ER 932.

[71] The test at common law suggested that the longer the period to cool off and calm down, the more likely the killing is a revenge killing. But this assumption was not borne out by psychological/physiological evidence: see P Brett, 'The Physiology of Provocation' [1970] Crim LR 634. The requirement of suddenness was criticized for restricting the defence and excluding cases of outraged retaliation: Horder, *Excusing Crime*, 69–71 et seq.

have arisen suddenly. Given the changed description of this defence, perhaps 'cumulative impact' is the better phrase to describe this particular feature of the first requirement.

His lordship was seeking to emphasize that just because D's response to the events was delayed does not necessarily mean there was no loss of control. It will, however, remain difficult to ascertain whether D in fact reached the point at which self-control is lost.[72]

The 'loss of self control' element in s 54 raises several further issues. First, the loss of control must, presumably, still be temporary otherwise it would be a case of insanity.[73] Secondly, the burden is on the Crown to disprove the element once D has raised evidence of it. It is important to note that the judge has greater control of this LOSC defence: as has already been explained, the judge should not leave the defence to the jury unless there is sufficient evidence on which a jury, properly directed, could conclude that the defence might apply.[74] Thirdly, a further element (considered later) of the LOSC defence is that D must be judged on the basis that he possesses a 'normal degree of tolerance and self restraint' (s 54(1)(c)). It would therefore seem relevant, when considering whether at the moment that V was killed D had lost his self-control, for the jury to consider the period available to D to reflect and to cool off.[75] The cooling-off period was construed generously to D in a number of cases under the old law.[76]

By including a loss of control element, it has been argued that the government has rendered the LOSC defence incoherent.[77] The loss of control requirement was not part of the Law Commission's scheme for the proposed defence.[78] The government added it to meet concerns that there was a risk of the partial defence being used inappropriately, for example where D killed in cold blood, or the killing was gang-related, or the killing was a so-called 'honour' killing,[79] and 'where a defendant has killed while basically in full possession of his or her senses, even if he or she is frightened, other than in a situation which is complete self-defence'.[80] The Law Commission's model was based on the qualifying triggers of fear and a sense of 'justified anger'.[81] To retain these qualifying limbs but to add a loss of control element renders the scheme unnecessarily complex and lacking logic; a person who has lost control cannot easily be described as acting in a state of 'justified' anger.[82]

---

[72] In numerous reported cases the trial judge found that there was no evidence of a loss of control. See eg *Charles* [2013] EWCA Crim 1205 in which the court observed that the fact that there might have been a trigger for violence does not lead to the inference of a loss of control. In this case the trial judge observed that the deliberate nature of V's injuries was evidence that whoever had inflicted them was very much in control. In *Dawes*, D's own evidence was that he had acted out of shock rather than anger. See also *Barnsdale-Quean* [2014] EWCA Crim 1418; *Jewell* [2014] EWCA Crim 414; *Gurpinar* [2015] EWCA Crim 178.

[73] The 'temporary' nature of the loss of self-control seems irrelevant, provided only that it extended to the fatal act. D should not be deprived of a defence because he continued to be berserk for days thereafter—but sudden losses of self-control are, in practice, temporary.

[74] Section 54(6). This follows a recommendation of LC 304, para 5.11(5); and see paras 5.25–5.32.

[75] cf *Jewell* [2014] EWCA Crim 414 in which there was a 12-hour cooling-off period. The judge withdrew the defence from the jury on the basis that there was no evidence (looking not just at the delay) from which it could reasonably be concluded that the defence might apply.

[76] *Pearson* [1992] Crim LR 193; *Ibrams* (1981) 74 Cr App R 154; *Baillie* [1991] Crim LR 383. In *Mann* [2011] EWCA Crim 3292, *Baillie* was regarded as a case decided upon its own special facts.

[77] See Norrie, n 22, 322–325; S Edwards, 'Anger and Fear as Justifiable Preludes for the Loss of Self-Control' (2010) 74 J Crim L 223 discussing potential difficulties for abused spouses.

[78] The Law Commission recommended abolishing the positive requirement that D lost his self-control on the grounds that the requirement was unnecessary and undesirable and see LC 304, para 5.19.

[79] Ministry of Justice Consultation Paper 19/08, *Murder, Manslaughter and Infanticide: Proposals for Reform of the Law* (CP 19/08).

[80] ibid, para 36.   [81] What Norrie describes as 'imperfect justifications' [2009] Crim LR 278.

[82] See the powerful critique by Norrie, n 22, 312–314.

Critics have also questioned the retention of the loss of control element given the government's expressed intention to amend the law to rectify imbalances that exist in the treatment of men and women. The Law Commission recognized that women's typical reactions might make it harder for them to demonstrate a loss of self-control, and hence rejected that element in its final proposal. By retaining a requirement of loss of control, the government may have reduced the availability of the defence for abused women. It may be difficult to describe as a 'loss of control' circumstances where a person executes a plan to protect herself—as with abused women who kill their abusers while they sleep.[83]

13.1.2.6 Qualifying triggers: s 55

Under the old law, there was no restriction on the words or conduct that were capable of founding the provocation defence, provided D lost his self-control. The provocation could arise from perfectly legal acts by V or others. To take an extreme example, in *Doughty*,[84] provocation should have been left to the jury as a defence where there was evidence that the persistent crying of D's two-week-old baby had caused D to lose his self-control and kill it.

The LOSC defence under s 55 is designed to be narrower.[85] This was reiterated in *Dawes*, in which Lord Judge CJ stated that the impact of the qualifying triggers is that 'the circumstances in which the qualifying triggers will arise are much more limited than the equivalent provisions in the former provocation defence. The result is that some of the more absurd trivia which nevertheless required the judge to leave the provocation defence to the jury will no longer fall within the ambit of the qualifying triggers defined in the LOSC defence.'[86] Now, only qualifying triggers which cause the loss of self-control will be recognized. Section 55 provides:

(2) A loss of self-control had a qualifying trigger if subsection (3), (4) or (5) applies.

(3) This subsection applies if D's loss of self-control was attributable to D's fear of serious violence from V against D or another identified person.

(4) This subsection applies if D's loss of self-control was attributable to a thing or things done or said (or both) which—

(a) constituted circumstances of an extremely grave character, and

(b) caused D to have a justifiable sense of being seriously wronged.

(5) This subsection applies if D's loss of self-control was attributable to a combination of the matters mentioned in subsections (3) and (4).

Three preliminary points in relation to the qualifying triggers may be noted.[87] First, the statute requires that the loss of self-control is 'attributable to' a qualifying trigger and this

---

[83] cf B Mitchell, 'Loss of Self-Control under the Coroners and Justice Act 2009: Oh No!' in A Reed and M Bohlander (eds), *Loss of Control and Diminished Responsibility* (2011). Mitchell would prefer there to be some form of mental or emotional disturbance at the core of the defence. See B Mitchell, 'Years of Provocation, Followed by a Loss of Control' in L Zedner and JV Roberts (eds), *Principles and Values in Criminal Law and Criminal Justice* (2012).

[84] (1986) 83 Cr App R 319. See J Horder, 'The Problem of Provocative Children' [1987] Crim LR 655.

[85] For an analysis of whether they restrict the scope of the defence too much, see R Taylor, 'The Model of Tolerance and Self-Restraint' in A Reed and M Bohlander (eds), *Loss of Control and Diminished Responsibility* (2011). It has been argued that LOSC is not as restrictive as has been suggested and that it may be possible for the mercy killer to plead the partial defence. See B Livings, 'A New Partial Defence for the Mercy Killer: Revisiting Loss of Control' [2014] NILQ 187; with respect this seems unlikely.

[86] *Dawes*, [60]. Cited subsequently in *Charles* [2013] EWCA Crim 1205 and *Martin* [2017] EWCA Crim 1359.

[87] In *Clinton*, Lord Judge CJ made the additional point that, 'There is no point in pretending that the practical application of this provision will not create considerable difficulties', at [11].

raises the question whether it might be construed as requiring something less than a formal causal link. Despite the ambiguity of the word, it is submitted that the courts ought to treat this as a requirement of causation. Secondly, the presence or otherwise of a qualifying trigger is not defined or decided by D and any assertions he might make in evidence. The Court of Appeal has confirmed that the existence of a qualifying trigger requires an objective assessment by the judge at the end of the evidence[88] and, if the defence is left, by the jury considering their verdict.[89] Thirdly, what would otherwise be sufficient for a qualifying trigger is to be disregarded if D brought that state of affairs upon himself by, for example, looking for a fight by inciting something to be said or done (s 55(6)(a) or (b)), as the case may be. The restriction in s 55(6) is:

(a) D's fear of serious violence is to be disregarded to the extent that it was caused by a thing which D incited to be done or said for the purpose of providing an excuse to use violence;

(b) a sense of being seriously wronged by a thing done or said is not justifiable if D incited the thing to be done or said for the purpose of providing an excuse to use violence.

Despite some clarification in *Dawes*, the law is not as clear as it could be.[90] Under the old law, the jury were told to take into account everything both done and said according to the effect which, in their opinion, it would have on a reasonable person, even where that which was done and said was a predictable result of D's own conduct. That was the decision in *Johnson*[91] (not following *dicta* of the Privy Council in *Edwards v R*)[92] where the Court of Appeal rejected the submission 'that the mere fact that a defendant caused a reaction in others, which in turn led him to lose his self-control, should result in the issue of provocation being outside a jury's consideration'.[93]

Read literally, however, the availability of the LOSC defence is wider. LOSC would only be removed from the jury if D's *purpose* was subsequently to use violence. D will not be able to rely on LOSC where D *deliberately* induces a state of affairs that will generate a qualifying trigger—D taunts V whom he wants to kill, to do an act so that D may kill him and rely on the defence and be convicted of manslaughter only. Such a situation may seem far-fetched.[94]

In *Dawes*, Lord Judge CJ held that the impact of *Johnson* has been diminished, but not wholly extinguished by the statutory provisions contained in the 2009 Act.[95] His lordship stated that 'the mere fact that in some general way the defendant was behaving badly and looking for and provoking trouble does not of itself lead to the disapplication of the qualifying triggers based on section 55(3)(4) and (5) unless his actions were *intended* to provide him with the excuse or opportunity to use violence.'[96] The focus of the inquiry under s 55(6)(a) and (b), it is submitted, should be narrow; namely whether D's *purpose* was to provide an excuse to use violence, not whether a violent reaction was the foreseeable consequence of what D was doing. Lord Judge pointed out, however, that the judge would have to consider the additional issue of whether D did in fact 'fear' serious violence if he was out to incite it and also whether he truly had a justified sense of being seriously wronged.

---

[88] cf the exchange between the court and counsel in *McDonald* [2016] EWCA Crim 1529.

[89] *Dawes*, [61]; *Gurpinar* [2015] EWCA Crim 178.   [90] See *Dawes* [2013] EWCA Crim 322.

[91] [1980] 1 WLR 740; was preferred to the *dicta* of the Privy Council in *Edwards* [1973] AC 648.

[92] [1973] AC 648, PC.   [93] *Johnson*, 744.

[94] Analogy should be drawn with the law on self-defence where D is the initial aggressor, see *Harvey* [2009] EWCA Crim 469; *Keane* [2010] EWCA Crim 2514, on which see Ch 10.

[95] See commentary by Ashworth [2013] Crim LR 770.   [96] *Dawes*, [58].

Fear of serious violence: s 55(3)

Section 55(3) provides:

This subsection applies if D's loss of self-control was attributable to D's fear of serious violence[97] from V against D or another identified person.

And by s 55(6):

In determining whether a loss of self-control had a qualifying trigger—

  (a) D's fear of serious violence is to be disregarded to the extent that it was caused by a thing which D incited to be done or said for the purpose of providing an excuse to use violence;

This qualifying trigger is the one which renders the LOSC defence quite distinct from the defence of provocation. It flows from a Law Commission recommendation.[98] It is designed primarily to accommodate within the partial defence regime those women who kill their violent and abusive partners.[99] The sudden and temporary requirement of the common law of provocation frequently proved a stumbling block for such women. This qualifying trigger will, however, apply more widely.[100] It clearly encompasses two quite distinct sets of circumstances: (a) where D kills in order to thwart an anticipated (albeit not imminent) attack; and (b) where D overreacts to what he perceived to be an imminent threat.[101] In the first category, the defence will be particularly useful for abused spouses who kill. In that regard the reform is welcome. However, in relation to the second category, there is scope for the defence to be used in a very broad range of killings that were previously classed as murder and which attracted no defence. For example, D who stabs V in a fight in a pub might claim that he stabbed V having feared that V was going to stab him first. Even if D has used excessive force given the threat he thought he faced, and even if D has made an unreasonable mistake about the need for any force at all, he will, if the jury believe his story may be true, be convicted of manslaughter. This is a significant change in the law.

The defence is limited under this qualifying trigger to cases where D fears violence from V to himself or an identified other. That acts as a restriction, but it is unclear how narrowly it will be interpreted. What if D, who is in V's presence, hears V ordering X to commit an act of violence on D's fellow gang member who is miles away? D loses his self-control and kills V. Is this sufficient?

The relationship between the LOSC defence and self-defence or defence of others under s 76 of the Criminal Justice and Immigration Act 2008 needs to be approached

---

[97] It has been argued that despite Lord Judge CJ stating in *Dawes* that each element of the qualifying triggers requires objective evaluation, whether D feared serious violence ought to be a subjective question, ie did D himself regard this violence as 'serious'. See T Storey, 'Loss of Control: The Qualifying Triggers, Self-Induced Loss of Control and "Cumulative Impact"' (2013) 77 J Crim L 189. Such an approach has the potential to render the partial defence extremely wide.

[98] LC 304, para 5.55. Historically the common law defence of provocation *did* encompass reactions prompted by fear: LC 304, para 5.49.

[99] It has been argued that domestic violence is such a serious wrong that it would be relatively easy for women who lose control and kill their abusers to rely on the other qualifying trigger. See J Herring, 'The Serious Wrong of Domestic Abuse and the Loss of Control Defence' in A Reed and M Bohlander (eds), *Loss of Control and Diminished Responsibility* (2011).

[100] For an analysis of whether the provision will achieve this goal, see S Edwards, 'Loss of Self-Control: When His Anger is Worth More Than Her Fear' in A Reed and M Bohlander (eds), *Loss of Control and Diminished Responsibility* (2011).

[101] See MOJ CP 19/08, para 28.

with care.[102] In *Martin*,[103] the Court of Appeal emphatically rejected the suggestion that where self-defence is raised in a murder case, then that will of itself also give rise to a potential defence of loss of control. It was held that not only was such a suggestion not the law but it was wholly contrary to the designedly limited nature of the defence as confirmed by the 2009 Act. It is important to note that the defences have the following distinguishing features.

Self-defence is available on any charge; LOSC is available only on a charge of murder.[104] Self-defence results in an acquittal; LOSC in a verdict of manslaughter. With LOSC, D can rely on fear of future non-imminent attack; with self-defence he can only rely on a threat (or believed threat) of imminent attack.[105] The defence of self-defence is available if D uses force in response to a perceived threat of *any* violence (including sexual violence[106]). The LOSC defence is available if D responds to a threat of *serious* violence.[107] Violence is undefined.[108] If the degree of force used by D in killing V is, viewed objectively, excessive,[109] that will deprive D of the defence of self-defence,[110] but will not automatically deprive D of the LOSC defence. Section 54(1)(c) (see later) requires a comparison of D's behaviour with that of a person of normal self-restraint. It has therefore been argued that if D uses excessive force in self-defence and kills, since a person of normal tolerance and self-restraint would, by definition, not use excessive force, the defence ought not to be available. This view appears to be too strict. The requirement in s 54(1)(c) is to consider whether the person of normal self-restraint 'might have reacted' as D did. Even people of normal self-restraint sometimes use excessive force and kill. It is submitted that it is not appropriate to read the LOSC defence as restricted in such a way.[111]

Particular problems may arise where on the facts there is evidence that might support self-defence or LOSC. If D has used excessive force, the complete defence of self-defence will fail, but D may still be able to rely on LOSC; the excessive amount of force being explicable by reference to the 'loss of self control'. Directions to the jury will need to be approached with great care. A further problem is posed by s 54(5):

On a charge of murder, if sufficient evidence is adduced to raise an issue with respect to the defence under subsection (1), the jury must assume that the defence is satisfied unless the prosecution proves beyond reasonable doubt that it is not.

At first sight this seems to suggest that in a case where D pleads self-defence, the Crown will automatically be entitled to a manslaughter conviction in any case where D lost his

---

[102] Lord Judge CJ cited this paragraph from the 13th edition with approval in *Dawes*, [59]. In *Skilton* [2014] EWCA Crim 154, Jackson LJ observed: 'There must be a clear distinction between the defence of self-defence, on the one hand, and the partial defence of loss of control on the other hand.' At [24]. The Court of Appeal held that the trial judge was correct not to leave loss of control to the jury, as D admitted in cross-examination that he was acting out of fear and was not out of control.

[103] [2017] EWCA Crim 1359.

[104] If there are multiple counts relating to different victims, care will be needed in directing the jury.

[105] For discussion of how the two interact in the context of abused women, see N Wake, 'Battered Women, Startled Householders and Psychological Self-Defence: Anglo-Australian Perspectives' (2013) 77 J Crim L 433.

[106] MOJ CP 19/08, para 44.

[107] See MOJ Circular 2010/13, para 25. Cf L Leigh, 'Two New Partial Defences to Murder' (2010) 53 Crim L & Justice Weekly 53, who states that the test is objective.

[108] Fortson, n 22, argues that it includes psychological harm. It includes sexual harm: MOJ CP19/08, para 27.

[109] By virtue of s 43 of the Crime and Courts Act 2013, if the case is a 'householder case' then if the degree of force was grossly disproportionate or unreasonable D will be denied the defence.

[110] And therefore of a complete acquittal. See *Clegg* [1995] and Ch 10. See also Leverick, *Self Defence* (2007) Ch 6.

[111] cf the suggestion by J Miles, 'A Dog's Breakfast of Homicide Reform' [2009] 6 Arch News 8. See on this Fortson, n 22.

self-control. However, when applied properly, this provision does not create the conflict it appears to.[112] Section 54(5) requires only that sufficient evidence is adduced to raise an issue under s 54(1). Thereafter, the prosecution shoulders the legal burden of proving, to the criminal standard of proof, that the defence is not satisfied. Unless the prosecution discharges that burden, s 54(5) requires the jury to assume that the defence is satisfied.

> (6) For the purposes of subsection (5), sufficient evidence is adduced to raise an issue with respect to the defence if evidence is adduced on which, in the opinion of the trial judge, a jury, properly directed, could reasonably conclude that the defence might apply.

It is essential in cases where D pleads self-defence and LOSC that the jury deal with self-defence before LOSC. If jurors address these matters in the wrong order, a manslaughter conviction becomes compulsory. This seems to be a case in which written directions instructing jurors of the steps to verdict would be valuable.[113] Lord Judge CJ in *Dawes* confirmed this view; the appropriate approach is to leave loss of control for the jury's consideration after it has rejected self-defence.[114]

Further problems may arise if D's fear of serious violence was based on an entirely mistaken interpretation of the facts by D.[115] Under the old law the authorities suggested that where D was provoked partly as the result of a mistake of fact, he was entitled to be treated as if the facts were as he mistakenly supposed them to be. This line of reasoning accords with the approach to other defences.[116] Given that the LOSC defence based on this first qualifying trigger is similar in many respects to self-defence, and a mistaken belief in the need for self-defence will not deprive a defendant of that defence, it is submitted that the defence should be available if D has a genuine mistaken belief in facts that would amount to a qualifying trigger of a fear of serious violence.

It is unclear whether a mistake induced by voluntary intoxication precludes reliance on the defence.[117] In self-defence, on policy grounds, mistakes due to intoxication are irrelevant, notwithstanding that murder is a crime of specific intent.[118] That would suggest that the defence of LOSC was not available. However, there are several arguments that could be marshalled in favour of adopting a more generous approach in LOSC. First, the policy-driven approach in relation to self-defence and intoxicated mistakes has been heavily and cogently criticized.[119] Secondly, this is a partial defence which leads to a manslaughter conviction—it is not the case that D will leave court with a complete acquittal if he is permitted

---

[112] Maria Eagle stated that s 54(5) was to 'clarify where the burden of proof lies when a partial defence of loss of control arises in a case' and that 'the usual principles apply in relation to the burden of proof in the new partial defence'. Hansard, HC, 3 Mar 2009, col 437; see also the speech of Baroness Scotland of Asthal: Hansard, HL, 7 July 2009, col 585.

[113] See generally the *Crown Court Compendium* (2017).

[114] *Dawes*, [59].

[115] Edwards makes the important point that habituated gender thinking might impress upon what is considered sufficient to constitute both fear and serious violence. She states that women who are the victims of domestic violence can have a heightened awareness of their physical security. In cases in which D has killed in fear of an anticipated attack by V, if this is not made clear to juries then they might be inclined to think that D simply overreacted. See S Edwards, 'Loss of Self-Control: When His Anger is Worth More Than Her Fear' in A Reed and M Bohlander (eds), *Loss of Control and Diminished Responsibility* (2011).

[116] cf *Oye* [2013] EWCA Crim 1725 in which the Court of Appeal stated that it was best not to draw comparisons between loss of control and self-defence in relation to mistaken beliefs. With reference to the relationship between them, the Court of Appeal observed, *obiter*, that 'the highly complex provisions of ss.54–56 of the Coroners and Justice Act 2009 would seem to indicate no particular parliamentary intention that a corresponding approach is designed to be adopted'. At [43] per Davis LJ.

[117] See also the discussion of *Asmelash*, p 545 suggesting the Court of Appeal's reluctance to allow intoxication to be considered.

[118] *Hatton* [2006] 1 Cr App R 247, CA.   [119] See Ch 9, p 325.

to found his plea on an intoxicated mistaken view of the facts.[120] It is established that a drunken mistake may negative the mens rea of murder[121] and it is therefore consistent that such a mistake should be relevant in determining whether the killing should be reduced to manslaughter on the ground of LOSC. Thirdly, under the provocation defence an intoxicated mistake as to the facts did not preclude reliance on the defence. In *Brown*,[122] D, a soldier, wrongly, but apparently reasonably, supposed that V was a member of a gang who were attacking him and his comrade. He struck V with a sword and killed him. The judges were clearly of the opinion that this was only manslaughter. In the other cases the mistake arose from drunkenness. In *Letenock*,[123] the Court of Criminal Appeal substituted a verdict of manslaughter in the case of a soldier who had stabbed another, where the 'only element of doubt in the case is whether or not there was anything which might have caused the applicant, *in his drunken condition*, to believe that he was going to be struck'.[124] Against this is, of course, the requirement that D has by definition lost his self-control.[125]

Things said or done; circumstances of an extremely grave character, etc: s 55(4)

This form of the defence bears greatest similarity to the old law of provocation. This version of the LOSC defence is available in s 55(4) if D's loss of self-control was:

attributable to a thing or things done or said (or both) which—

(a) constituted circumstances of an extremely grave character, and

(b) caused D to have a justifiable sense of being seriously wronged.

Section 55(6) further provides that:

In determining whether a loss of self-control had a qualifying trigger—

(b) a sense of being seriously wronged by a thing done or said is not justifiable if D incited the thing to be done or said for the purpose of providing an excuse to use violence.

Under the provocation defence a wide range of situations in which D claimed that he had been provoked by things said and/or done could be left for the jury's consideration (eg the crying of a 17-day-old baby in *Doughty*[126]). This broad interpretation of the trigger for the defence meant that there was no requirement that the provoking acts or words were performed consciously, let alone with the deliberate intention to provoke.[127] The test under the LOSC defence is much stricter[128] although the statutory language is disappointingly vague.

---

[120] Although that is also true in relation to self-defence in murder because an unreasonable intoxicated mistake will lead to a conviction for manslaughter despite the courts' gloss on this in *O'Grady*. See p 326.

[121] See p 321.   [122] (1776) 1 Leach 148.   [123] (1917) 12 Cr App R 221, CCA.   [124] ibid, 224.

[125] This is one example of how the insertion of the loss of control element to the Law Commission's original proposal creates difficulties and illogicalities.

[126] (1986) 83 Cr App R 319, CA.

[127] This dilution of the concept of 'provocation' to mean merely words or conduct that *cause* the loss of control in the defendant has been heavily criticized by academics. See, in particular, T Macklem and J Gardner, 'Provocation and Pluralism' (2001) 64 MLR 815, and Tadros, *Criminal Responsibility*, 355–368. See LCCP 173, paras 4.8–4.11.

[128] The facts of *Zebedee* [2012] EWCA Crim 1428 illuminate how strict the qualifying triggers now are: D was convicted of the murder of his father. V was aged 94, suffered from senile dementia and was doubly incontinent. D claimed that he had lost his self-control after V soiled himself during the night, after which D cleaned him up, only for V to soil himself again 20 minutes later. The jury rejected his plea of loss of control. In the Court of Appeal, Spencer J observed that the jury must have concluded that whatever had triggered D's violence did not constitute circumstances of an extremely grave nature. For an analysis of some of the cases that were successful under the old law, but which would now probably fail, see T Storey, 'Raising the Bar: Loss of Control and the Qualifying Triggers' (2013) 77 J Crim L 17.

Even if a person with a normal degree of tolerance and self-restraint might have reacted in the circumstances as D did (see s 54(1)(c) and s 54(3)), this will not be enough unless those circumstances meet the thresholds as specified in s 55(4) of the 2009 Act. The Court of Appeal has confirmed that all the elements of s 55(4) require objective evaluation.[129]

Things done or said

As under the provocation defence, mere circumstances (rather than something said or done) no matter how provocative, cannot be a sufficient basis for this qualifying trigger.[130] Loss of control by a farmer on his crops being destroyed by a flood, or his flocks by foot-and-mouth, or an author on his manuscript being destroyed by lightning, cannot constitute a qualifying trigger. An 'act of God' could hardly be regarded as 'something done' within s 55(4). There is no requirement that the things said or done be said or done by the victim (subject to the other elements of the defence). This follows the old law. For example, in *Davies*, D killed his wife, V having been provoked by X, her lover.[131] Bearing in mind that there is no restriction on the source of the words or conduct which cause D to lose control, it seems odd to distinguish cases where the trigger is words by a third party (defence available) and mere circumstances (defence unavailable). If D may rely on the defence where the crops or the manuscript were destroyed by an unknown arsonist, why should it be different where no human agency was involved?

There must, as with the provocation defence, be some evidence of the qualifying trigger. In *Acott*,[132] the House of Lords held that for the defence of provocation it was not enough that D's loss of control may possibly have been the result of some unidentified words or actions by another. There must be 'some evidence of *what* was done or *what* was said to provoke the homicidal reaction'.[133] The trial judge is best placed to make this assessment.

There is no express provision in the 2009 Act to deal with the situation where D mistakenly believes that things were done or said. Several different situations may need to be distinguished. First, there is the position where D mistakenly believes that things were said or done when nothing was in fact said or done at all. In that case, it would be hard to see how the qualifying trigger is satisfied on a literal interpretation of the section. Secondly, there is the case in which words or acts occur, but D mistakes what was said or done. What of D who mishears V and thinks that V has issued a racist taunt when in fact V's words were completely innocuous? In that case, it could be argued that the defence ought to be available (subject to the other elements), even if D's mistake is an unreasonable one.[134] That raises the question of whether D can rely on this trigger for the LOSC defence if D acts on a mistaken belief induced by voluntary intoxication. Arguably, since the 'things done or said' must lead to a 'justifiable' sense of being seriously wronged, it will be appropriate to ignore intoxicated mistakes unless the mistake was one which D would have made had he been sober.

It is submitted that the defence will be available, as provocation was, if D sought to kill the person responsible for the acts or words but, by accident, missed him and killed an innocent person. The doctrine of transferred malice[135] should operate and D would be guilty of only

---

[129] See *Clinton*, [12] and *Dawes*, [61].   [130] *Acott* [1997] 2 Cr App R 94.

[131] [1975] QB 691. Cf to the same effect by Lawton J in *Twine* [1967] Crim LR 710, where D's girlfriend's conduct caused D to lose his self-control and strike and kill the man she was with.

[132] [1997] 1 All ER 706, HL, [1997] Crim LR 541. See also *Bharj* [2005] EWCA Crim 499 emphasizing that the jury would be looking at *all* the evidence.

[133] Emphasis in the original.

[134] Elvin questions whether an unreasonable belief could ever lead to a justifiable sense of being seriously wronged. See J Elvin, 'Killing in Response to "Circumstances of an Extremely Grave Character": Improving the Law on Homicide' in A Reed and M Bohlander (eds), *Loss of Control and Diminished Responsibility* (2011). Whether the two are in fact mutually exclusive is questionable.

[135] See p 122. For discussion, see M Bohlander, 'Transferred Malice and Transferred Defences' (2010) 13 New Crim LR 555.

manslaughter, as was held for provocation in *Gross*[136] where D, provoked by blows from her husband, shot at him, intending to kill him but missed and killed V.[137] If D knew it was virtually certain that she would hit V, she would have an independent mens rea with respect to V, probably sufficient to fix her with liability for murder[138] at common law; but now the acts or words of the third party would be a partial defence even for D's acts towards V.

Historically, it used to be said that there was no defence if acts or words were not done to the defendant;[139] but the 2009 Act as with the 1957 Act has no such explicit requirement.[140] D can rely on the defence if V does acts to P that might cause D to lose his self-control and, in circumstances of extreme gravity, to kill V with intent and with a justifiable sense of being seriously wronged. For example, D might find V raping his child P.[141]

There is no statutory limitation to prevent a third party description or report being sufficient to satisfy the trigger, as where D loses his temper following X's report of V's admission that V had attacked D's child. That is, of course, subject to the other elements of the defence, and in particular it must be noted that the less plausible the account relayed to D, the less likely it will cause a loss of self-control and the less likely it will give rise to a justifiable sense of being seriously wronged.

There is nothing to prevent a lawful act by V being sufficient to constitute the trigger, although the fact that the acts or words were lawful will cast doubt on whether D had a justifiable sense of being seriously wronged (see later).[142] In particular, where the act is one which is not merely permitted, but which is positively praiseworthy, it is doubtful that a jury would find that it would cause D to lose his temper and to have a justifiable sense of being seriously wronged and that such action might have been performed by a person of normal tolerance and self-restraint in D's position.

Must constitute circumstances of an 'extremely grave character'

For the purposes of this second 'qualifying trigger' (s 55(4)), the threshold is that things said and done must constitute circumstances of an 'extremely grave character'. Presumably, grave means in all the circumstances. The intention is to restrict the scope of the defence from what was the position under the defence of provocation. The Law Commission offered the following guidance:

The jury should be trusted to evaluate the relative grossness of provocation, in whatever form it comes, according to their own sense of justice in an individual case.[143]

It is disappointing that such a key term of the defence is left undefined. In *Hatter* (one of the cases conjoined with *Dawes*), it was observed that the break-up of a relationship, of itself, will not normally constitute circumstances of an extremely grave nature entitling the aggrieved party to feel a justifiable sense of being seriously wronged. Lord Judge CJ did state,

---

[136] (1913) 23 Cox CC 455 (Darling J); and see *Porritt* [1961] 1 WLR 1372. Bohlander, n 135, doubts whether this case is one concerning the transfer of defences at all. Bohlander argues that in the same way that a temporary mental disease may exempt any and all actions D committed in that state from liability, so a temporary loss of control exempts any and all actions committed under its influence. We disagree. Given that the statute mandates that the defence is only available on a charge of murder, it is difficult to see how it exempts D from all liability. If D loses his self-control and causes criminal damage to his rival's car, he cannot plead loss of control.

[137] 23 Cox CC at 456.   [138] See p 99.

[139] But see *Fisher* (1837) 8 C & P 182 (Park J, *obiter*) (D discovering V raping D's son) and *Harrington* (1866) 10 Cox CC 370 (Cockburn CJ contemplating the possibility of a defence where D found his daughter being violently assaulted by her husband).

[140] cf J Elvin, 'Killing in Response to "Circumstances of an Extremely Grave Character": Improving the Law on Homicide' in A Reed and M Bohlander (eds), *Loss of Control and Diminished Responsibility* (2011).

[141] Examples under the 1957 Act included *Pearson* [1992] Crim LR 193.

[142] *Doughty* (1986) 83 Cr App R 319.   [143] LC 304, p 85 fn 31.

however, that just as issues relating to sexual infidelity have to be examined in their overall circumstances, so the events surrounding the circumstances in the breakdown of a relationship will often but not always fall to be disqualified by s 55(6).[144]

'justifiable sense of being seriously wronged'

The defendant must have been caused by the things done or said to have a 'justifiable sense of being seriously wronged' (s 55(4)). This is much narrower than for provocation. It is intended to be an objective test.[145] It is, again, disappointing that the Act provides no further guidance on how the jury will approach this question. It was intended that it would provide an opportunity to take into consideration cumulative abuse, which will be particularly important in domestic killings by abused women. At the same time, it was intended to exclude from the scope of the defence the cases of racist or 'honour' killings. For example, it is difficult to see how the defence could be left to the jury if D, a white supremacist, killed V, a black man, because V refused to give way to D on the staircase. No reasonable jury properly directed could conclude that D had a *justifiable* sense of being seriously wronged. The defence should be withdrawn from the jury. Similarly where D, a devout Muslim, kills his daughter because she has a sexual relationship before marriage, he cannot be said to have a justifiable sense of being seriously wronged.[146]

In many cases, of course, the judge will be obliged to leave the defence to the jury for their good sense. Note that the question for them is not whether D's act in *killing* was justifiable, but whether D had a justifiable sense of being seriously wronged. Again, it is presumably a question of whether the sense of serious wrong would be felt by someone in D's circumstances. In *Bowyer*, the other conjoined appeal in *Dawes*, D was a burglar who killed the householder from whose home he was intending to steal. Given the circumstances, the Court of Appeal held that it could hardly be said that V had given D any cause to feel justifiably wronged.[147] The same was true in *Meanza*.[148] In that case D's evidence was that he felt aggrieved at being asked to turn down the television in the secure unit in which he was being detained. He also felt aggrieved by the fact his meetings and encounters with his girlfriend had to take place on a supervised basis. The Court of Appeal held, rightly it is submitted, that D could have no justifiable grievance in relation to hospital and restriction orders that were lawfully imposed, nor in relation to the restrictions imposed upon his relationship with his girlfriend.

Sexual infidelity

Historically, one of the classic examples of extreme provocation recognized by the courts for centuries was where D killed having found his spouse in the act of adultery.[149] The

---

[144] *Dawes*, [65].

[145] Some commentators (eg Liberty) suggested that the provision was insufficiently clear and that it might be construed subjectively.

[146] cf *Mohammed* [2005] EWCA Crim 1880 where in cross-examination D claimed that 'it is part of our religion' to do as he did in killing his sexually active unmarried daughter. D's perception cannot be determinative of what is justifiable.

[147] *Dawes*, [66].   [148] [2017] EWCA Crim 445.

[149] Killing, in such a case, was 'of the lowest degree of [manslaughter]; and therefore... the court directed the burning in the hand to be gently inflicted, because there could not be a greater provocation': Blackstone, *Commentaries*, iv, 192. See also the case of *Manning* (1671) T Raym 212. For a contemporary case with exactly these facts, see *Christie* [2004] EWCA Crim 1338, D was convicted of murder. As an example of how significant this factor was, see *Evans* [2009] EWCA Crim 2243 where the Court of Appeal accepted that had E been aware of the infidelity of his wife he might have been able to plead provocation. For an analysis of the way sexual infidelity-related evidence has influenced perceptions of a homicide defendant's culpability, see J Horder and K Fitz-Gibbon, 'When Sexual Infidelity Triggers Murder: Examining the Impact of Homicide Law Reform on Judicial Attitudes in Sentencing' (2015) 74 CLJ 307.

government's intention was to prevent the LOSC defence from being run in such a case and to prevent obsessively jealous men using suspected infidelity on the part of the spouse or partner as a defence for killing.[150]

Under the LOSC defence, D's loss of control that is attributed to anything said or done which constitutes sexual infidelity is to be disregarded (s 55(6)(c)). This limitation did not form part of the Law Commission's original proposals and was introduced amid much controversy in the debates in Parliament. The restriction was met with anxiety by Lord Phillips who admitted he was 'uneasy about a law which so diminishes the significance of sexual infidelity as expressly to exclude it from even the possibility of amounting to provocation'.[151]

It is important to be clear about what s 55(6) forbids:

In determining whether a loss of self-control had a qualifying trigger . . .

   (b) the fact that a thing done or said constituted sexual infidelity is to be disregarded.

The restriction on the defence is likely to present difficulties of interpretation and application. In addition, it may well fail to defeat the intended mischief. The concern is that men are able to rely on loss of self-control defences when their anger and loss of control results from sexual jealousy. As Lord Judge CJ emphasized in *Clinton*, however, D remains at liberty to tell the jury the whole story about the relevant events, including the fact and impact of sexual infidelity.[152] The jury must still consider and ultimately evaluate this evidence.

Numerous problems of interpretation arise as recognized by the Court of Appeal in *Clinton*.[153] First, there is no definition of what 'sexual infidelity' means. Clearly, there can be infidelity outside marriage, but how 'solid' a relationship must there be before sexual acts with others outside that relationship constitute infidelity?[154] Lord Judge in *Clinton* accepted that 'infidelity' connotes a continuing relationship. His lordship accepted that the consequence of this is that a killing by a spouse or partner might fall outside the defence, but a killing by a jealous stalker would not.[155]

Secondly, the term 'sexual' infidelity can be read narrowly, so as to comprise only those incidents of, and conduct directly related to, sexual activity. Lord Judge accepted that a betrayal by one partner that involved telling others about an illicit relationship was capable of falling within the prohibition.[156]

Thirdly, it seems that words might constitute sexual infidelity where, for example, D overhears his wife V saying 'I love you' to her lover, X.[157] But what of words spoken by V telling D that she loves X? Do her words 'I love someone else' constitute infidelity or are they a report of her infidelity? On a narrow view of the section, it can be argued that the words do

---

[150] See Hansard, HC Public Bills Committee, 3 Mar 2009, col 439. For consideration of the more conceptual issues, see A Reed and N Wake, 'Sexual Infidelity Killings: Contemporary Standardisations and Comparative Stereotypes' in A Reed and M Bohlander (eds), *Loss of Control and Diminished Responsibility* (2011).

[151] *The Times*, 7 Nov 2008.   [152] At [28].

[153] Apart from the specific problems that arise from the drafting of this provision, it has been argued that exclusionary clauses in general give rise to difficulties when invoked in this context. See N Wake, 'Political Rhetoric or Principled Reform of Loss of Control? Anglo-Australian Perspectives on the Exclusionary Conduct Model' (2013) 77 J Crim L 512.

[154] The debates in Parliament do not reveal what types of relationship will qualify, but the references are usually to spouses, civil partners and in some instances to 'partners'.

[155] At [18].   [156] ibid.

[157] In *Clinton*, Lord Judge CJ stated that this may, or may not, provide evidence of *sexual* infidelity. In addition, his lordship observed that it may not *constitute* sexual infidelity. Whether it does so will depend upon the relationship between the parties, the person by whom and to whom it is spoken and the circumstances. His lordship stated that situations seemingly as simple as this one 'will give rise to manifold difficulties in the context of the prohibition on sexual infidelity as a qualifying trigger'. At [25]–[27].

not constitute sexual infidelity and they are not to be disregarded under s 55(6)(c).[158] In the debates in Parliament, in response to a question whether V bragging to D that he had been having an affair with D's wife would be sexual infidelity, the government spokesman said that the defence would turn on the facts, but that:

sexual infidelity in itself cannot and should not be an acceptable reason for a defence for murder.[159]

Fourthly, read literally s 55(6)(c) only forbids regard being had to the *fact* that the thing said or done constituted sexual infidelity when determining if there is a qualifying trigger sufficient for the defence to be left to the jury. The *effect on D* of the sexual infidelity is not to be disregarded, merely the words or acts that constituted it. This is disappointing legislative drafting.

Fifthly, provided there is some other thing besides the fact of sexual infidelity said or done which amounts to extreme circumstances which D claims caused him to lose his self-control and to have a justifiable sense of being seriously wronged, the trigger will be satisfied. It may be difficult to discern whether D's loss of self-control is attributable to things done or said by his sexual partner *other than* her act of infidelity. What related aspects can be taken into account in determining if the trigger is present? The MOJ[160] makes clear that:

it is only the fact of sexual infidelity that must be disregarded. The thing said or done can still potentially amount to a 'qualifying trigger' if (ignoring the sexual infidelity) it amounts to circumstances of an extremely grave character which caused the defendant to have a justifiable sense of being seriously wronged.[161]

Examples of the sorts of activity that might trigger the defence and would not be excluded by s 55(6)(c) include D who has found his wife in bed with her lover and killed the lover, saying in defence of the killing that it was not the act of sex that triggered the loss of self-control but the fact that the lover was D's best friend. Some such claims will be plausible: D will claim the thing that caused him to lose self-control in extremely grave circumstances having a justifiable sense of being seriously wronged was not the sex but, for example, 'the fact that V threatened to take the kids', or 'the fact that she taunted me about my erectile dysfunction' or 'the fact that she smashed up my prized possession as she was leaving', etc. In debates, the government spokesman stated:

it is important to set out the position precisely and uncompromisingly—namely that sexual infidelity is not the kind of thing done that is ever *sufficient on its own* to found a successful plea of loss of control so as to reduce the verdict from murder to manslaughter.[162]

More extreme examples are easier to classify and were recognized in the debates: for example, where D comes home to find her husband, V, having sex with his young stepdaughter. In such a case, if D killed V, it would be open to D to argue that it was the fact of sexual abuse and not the sexual infidelity per se that formed the qualifying trigger. As has also been pointed out by others,[163] the combined impact of the statutory drafting and the judgment

---

[158] It was confirmed in *Clinton* that 'things said' includes admissions of sexual infidelity (even if untrue) as well as reports by others. Therefore it seems to be the case that if D is told by C that his wife, V, is having an affair, then that will be a 'thing said' for the purposes of the section.

[159] Hansard, HC, 9 Nov 2009, col 82 (Claire Ward) (emphasis added).

[160] MOJ Circular 2010/13.

[161] Para 30. This echoes statements in Parliament where the spokeswoman stated: 'If other factors come into play, the court will of course have an opportunity to consider them, but it will not be able to make the decision exclusively on the ground of sexual infidelity.' Hansard, HC, 9 Nov 2009, col 80 (Claire Ward).

[162] Hansard, HC, 9 Nov 2009, col 83 (Claire Ward) (emphasis added).

[163] N Wake, 'Loss of Control Beyond Sexual Infidelity' (2012) 76 J Crim L 193; A Clough, 'Sexual Infidelity: The Exclusion That Never Was?' (2012) 76 J Crim L 382; F Stark, 'Killing the Unfaithful' (2012) 71 CLJ 260.

in *Clinton* is to undermine the practical impact of s 55(6)(c), given that it will be a rare case where sexual infidelity stands alone as a potential qualifying trigger.[164]

Finally what is perhaps most astonishing is that the drafting means that s 55(6)(c) only forbids regard to the sexual infidelity when considering whether there is a trigger, not for the defence as a whole. As Lord Judge recognized in *Clinton*, sexual infidelity may be relevant to the third component of the defence: s 54(3) expressly excludes some of the defendant's circumstances from being considered and the fact that he has been 'sexually betrayed' is not one of them. Therefore:

sexual infidelity is not subject to a blanket exclusion when the loss of control defence is under consideration. Evidence of these matters may be deployed by the defendant and therefore the legislation proceeds on the basis that sexual infidelity is a permissible feature of the loss of control defence.[165]

Provided there is some other thing said or done which amounts to extreme circumstances which could have caused D to lose his self-control and to have a justifiable sense of being seriously wronged, the trigger will be satisfied. If the trigger is satisfied, s 54(1)(c) then requires the jury to consider whether:

(c) a person of D's sex and age, with a normal degree of tolerance and self restraint and in the circumstances of D, might have reacted in the same or in a similar way to D.

And by s 54(3):

(3) In subsection (1)(c) the reference to 'the circumstances of D' is a reference to all of D's circumstances other than those whose only relevance to D's conduct is that they bear on D's general capacity for tolerance or self-restraint.

The statute does not *at this final stage of the defence* preclude consideration of the fact of sexual infidelity. There are really two arguments. First, it can be said that what is being considered in s 54(1)(c) is not the sexual infidelity but the effects of the sexual infidelity on D. A defendant in such cases might be exceptionally vulnerable in the sense of being more easily 'wounded' by such actions.[166] In psychiatric or psychological terms, the act causing the loss of control would be the *effects* of the unfaithfulness and the betrayal rather than the 'things said or done' which constitute sexual infidelity.[167] Section 54(1)(c) does not preclude reliance on such factors provided they are 'circumstances' and that they are relevant. They clearly are, and do not solely bear only on D's general capacity for tolerance and self-restraint. Secondly, it can be argued that the terms of s 54(1)(c) do not preclude reliance on the 'circumstance' of D discovering the sexual infidelity itself. This would allow the jury to have regard to the act/words in determining whether a person of D's age and sex, etc in his 'circumstances' (ie just discovering sexual infidelity) might have reacted as he did.[168]

On one view, these interpretations of s 54(1)(c) would seem to undermine the purpose of the provision in s 55. On another view, there is no conflict because there must be some trigger other than the mere fact of sexual infidelity for the defence to get to the jury, and what

---

[164] A point echoed by Norrie, n 22, 316.   [165] At [37].

[166] See eg the acceptance that someone who was sexually abused is more likely to take offence at sexual advances than someone who was not: *Hill* [2008] EWCA Crim 76.

[167] But the government rejected an amendment that would have limited s 55(6)(c) to cases in which the motive for killing was punishment, sexual jealousy or sexual envy. Hansard, HC, 9 Nov 2009, col 84 (Claire Ward).

[168] The Court of Appeal in *Clinton* stated that this is the correct approach. Lord Judge observed that there will therefore be occasions when the jury will be both disregarding and considering the same evidence. His lordship characterized this as being 'counter intuitive', which is to put it mildly.

the government was seeking to prohibit was sexual infidelity as a sole basis for the trigger. It was acknowledged that:

If something else is relied on as the qualifying trigger, *any sexual infidelity that forms part of the background can be considered* but it cannot be the trigger. That is essentially what the legislation seeks to do—to stop the act of sexual infidelity being the trigger that enables people to say that these are extremely serious and grave circumstances.[169]

The Court of Appeal in *Clinton*, relying upon much of the analysis contained in this section in the 13th edition, was extremely critical of this component of the LOSC defence. Indeed, rather than stating that the court was interpreting the provision, Lord Judge CJ character-ized the court's role as 'mak[ing] sense of it'. Lord Judge stated that the rationale behind the inclusion of the provision is to prohibit the 'misuse' of sexual infidelity as a potential qualifying trigger for loss of control in circumstances in which it was thought to have been misused in the former defence of provocation.

His lordship stated that to compartmentalize sexual infidelity and exclude it when it was integral to the facts as a whole would be difficult, unrealistic and could lead to injustice.[170] His lordship derived support for this conclusion from statements made by the minister that the government did not believe that sexual infidelity *by itself* ought to enable D to avoid liability for murder. This implies the government accepted that if there is evidence other than the sexual infidelity, then the partial defence should be left to the jury.

Despite the criticisms that have been made of *Clinton*,[171] it is submitted that the judgment is a pragmatic one that avoids the potential injustice alluded to by Lord Phillips. *Clinton* ensures that D will not be able to plead the partial defence if the only evidence is the sexual infidelity. Trial judges will have to make a judgement as to whether the sexual infidelity pro-vides the context for the killing, in which case it may be considered, or whether it was the cause of it, in which case it is to be disregarded. As Ashworth pointed out in his commen-tary, Lord Judge's interpretation of the language utilized in s 55(6)(c) is not the only plausible one.[172] Ashworth also states, correctly it is submitted, that interpreting s 55(6)(c) so that it only precludes sexual infidelity from constituting the sole trigger conforms with statements made by the minister explaining what the government intended to achieve through the enactment of the provision. For this reason, those who argue that Lord Judge has frustrated Parliament's intention seem somewhat misguided.

Combined qualifying triggers: s 55(5)

Section 55(5) provides:

This subsection applies if D's loss of self-control was attributable to a combination of the matters mentioned in subsections (3) and (4).

It is possible for D to rely on both qualifying triggers under s 55 in combination—that he killed having lost control because he was in fear of serious violence and that he also had a justifiable sense of being seriously wronged. In *Dawes*, Lord Judge CJ observed that 'there are unlikely to be many cases where the only feature of the evidence relating to the qualifying

---

[169] Hansard, HC 9 Nov 2009, col 94 (Claire Ward) (emphasis added).

[170] So long as sexual infidelity is 'integral to and forms an integral part of the context in which to make a just evaluation of whether a qualifying trigger properly falls within the ambit of subsections 55(3) and 55(4), the prohibition in section 55(6)(c) does not operate to exclude it'. At [39].

[171] See DJ Baker and LX Zhao, 'Contributory Qualifying and Non-Qualifying Triggers in the Loss of Control Defence: A Wrong Turn on Sexual Infidelity' (2012) 76 J Crim L 254.

[172] [2012] Crim LR 539.

trigger in the context of fear of violence will arise in total isolation from things done or said within section 55(4). In most cases the qualifying trigger based on a fear of violence will almost inevitably include consideration of things said and done; in short, a combination of the features identified in section 55(3) and (4).'[173] A striking example would be where D kills V whom he found raping his daughter at knifepoint. The two limbs might also be relied on by the woman who kills her abusive partner after years of torment when she lost control fearing another violent attack by him.

Where D relies on both limbs but there is insufficient evidence of each limb in isolation though in combination the evidence would satisfy s 54(5), it is submitted that the defence ought to be available. Lord Judge's *dicta* in *Clinton* support that approach.

13.1.2.7 Degree of tolerance and self-restraint: s 54(1)(c)

In addition to the loss of control and the qualifying trigger, the third element of the defence is an important limitation on its scope in the form of an objective requirement enacted in s 54(1)(c). The requirement is that 'a person of D's sex and age, with a normal degree of tolerance and self-restraint and in the *circumstances* of D, *might* have reacted in the same or in a similar way to D'.[174] By s 54(3):

In subsection (1)(c) the reference to 'the circumstances of D' is a reference to all of D's circumstances other than those whose only relevance to D's conduct is that they bear on D's general capacity for tolerance or self-restraint.

In some respects the test is similar to the test under the 1957 Act which centred on whether a reasonable man might have done as D did. This element of the old test gave rise to confusion and numerous visits to the House of Lords.[175]

Under the old provocation defence the House of Lords and Privy Council had struggled to identify a clear position on which of the defendant's characteristics were to be considered when evaluating whether a reasonable person would have done as D did. In *Camplin*,[176] the House decided that the jury should be told that the reasonable man is a person having the power of self-control to be expected of an ordinary person of the sex and age of the accused, but in other respects sharing such of the accused's characteristics as they think would affect the gravity of the provocation to him; and that the question is not merely whether such a person would in like circumstances be provoked to lose his self-control but also whether he would react to the provocation as the accused did.[177] The distinction was central to subsequent decisions of the House of Lords: *Morhall*,[178] and Privy Council in *Luc Thiet Thuan v R*,[179] but the House shifted towards a much more subjective test in *Smith*

---

[173] *Dawes*, [56].   [174] Emphasis added.

[175] *Camplin* [1978] AC 705; *Morgan Smith* [2001] AC 146: not followed in *A-G for Jersey v Holley* [2005] 2 AC 580.

[176] [1978] AC 705.

[177] This line of reasoning accords with the argument made earlier by Ashworth in a seminal article. The proper distinction is that individual peculiarities which bear on the gravity of the provocation should be taken into account, whereas individual peculiarities bearing on the accused's level of self-control should not: (1976) 35 CLJ 292. Cf the distinction made between provocativeness and provocability made in the commentary on *Morhall* [1995] Crim LR 890. For consideration of whether the questions can be kept separate, see A Norrie, 'From Criminal Law to Legal Theory: The Mysterious Case of the Reasonable Glue Sniffer' (2002) 65 MLR 538 at 547.

[178] [1996] AC 90, HL, [1995] Crim LR 890. A unanimous decision of the House which was virtually ignored in *Smith* [2001] AC 146.

[179] [1996] 2 All ER 1033 (Lord Goff, Sir Brian Hutton and Sir Michael Hardie Boys, and Lord Steyn). Noted, [1996] Crim LR 433.

(*Morgan*).[180] Finally, in *A-G for Jersey v Holley*,[181] a specially convened nine-member Board of the Privy Council concluded that a distinction should be drawn between characteristics of the accused that were to be taken into account because they affected the gravity of the provocation, and those relating to the ability to exercise self-control which were not to be taken into account.[182] In *James and Karimi*,[183] the Court of Appeal took the radical and controversial step of endorsing the Privy Council decision in *Holley* over that of the House of Lords in *Smith*.[184]

The position under the LOSC defence

The requirement is that 'a person of D's sex and age, with a normal degree of tolerance and self-restraint and in the *circumstances* of D, *might* have reacted in the same or in a similar way to D'. It would therefore be wrong to assume that the combined effect of s 54(1)(c) and s 54(3) is to codify the decision of the majority of their lordships in *Holley*.[185] What constitutes a 'normal degree of tolerance and self-restraint' is a matter for the jury to determine according to their judgement and their collective experience of life. The reference to 'D's sex and age' is consistent with statements made in *Camplin*, and *Holley*, that the 'powers of self-control possessed by ordinary people vary according to their age and … their sex'.[186] Why sex was included at all[187] and why these are always relevant circumstances is not clear. Difficulties may arise for defendants of mental abnormality for their age since if read restrictively it is the age that is to be taken into account.[188]

However, in other respects the test is quite different.[189] First, the words that a person '*might* have reacted in the same or similar way to D' creates a test that is more generous to D than the requirement in s 3 of the 1957 Act which was that 'the provocation is enough *to make* reasonable man do as he did'. There is no express restriction that D's acts must

---

[180] [2001] AC 146 [2000] Crim LR 1004, HL. For critical comment see, *inter alia*, T Macklem and J Gardner, 'Compassion without Respect: Nine Fallacies in *R v Smith*' [2001] Crim LR 623 and 'Provocation and Pluralism' (2001) 64 MLR 815. For a defence of the case see B Mitchell, R Mackay and W Brookbanks, 'Pleading for Provoked Killers: In Defence of *Morgan Smith*' (2008) 124 LQR 675 arguing that the approach allowed for those who lacked capacity to control themselves to rely on the defence. *Rowland* [2003] EWCA Crim 3636, [41]. See Part 2 of LCCP 173, especially paras 21–22; LC 304, para 5.41.

[181] [2005] UKPC 23. For commentary see Ashworth [2005] Crim LR 966; Virgo (2005) 64 CLJ 532. See also the discussion in LC 304, paras 5.34–5.39.

[182] The minority disagreed. Lords Bingham and Hoffmann suggest that it is not rationally possible to consider the two in isolation. The majority regarded any difficulties of 'mental gymnastics' required of jurors in having regard to a defendant's 'characteristics' for one purpose of the law of provocation but not another as having been exaggerated. At [26]. Lord Carswell in dissent challenged that view, at [73].

[183] [2006] EWCA Crim 14, [2006] 1 Cr App R 29.

[184] On the precedent issue, see J Elvin, 'The Doctrine of Precedent and the Provocation Defence' (2006) 69 MLR 819.

[185] See on *Holley* the comments of Lord Lloyd, Hansard, HL, 7 July 2009, col 572, and Lord Thomas, col 579.

[186] *Holley* [2005] UKPC 23, [13].

[187] For criticism, see N Cobb and A Gausden, 'Feminism, "Typical" Women and Losing Control' in A Reed and M Bohlander (eds), *Loss of Control and Diminished Responsibility* (2011). The authors question exactly how sex is relevant to capacity and argue that its inclusion could exacerbate the stereotyping and essentialism of women.

[188] cf Norrie, who makes the cogent point that what matters is not D's age, but rather his maturity. As he points out, 'age is no more than a rough and ready way of marking maturity'. See Norrie, n 22, 319–320.

[189] Norrie argues that the old law was 'under-demanding and over-enabling', but that the new law is 'narrow, harsh, and censorious'. He states that neither the new nor the old law fully captures the morally appropriate group. See Norrie, n 22, 308–312 and 316–319. It is submitted that for the reasons given in this section, the LOSC defence is in fact in many ways more generous to defendants because *all* the circumstances other than those solely relevant to general capacity for tolerance and self-restraint may be considered.

be proportionate to the threat/trigger he faced.[190] In *Clinton*, Lord Judge CJ explained the operation of this component of the defence in the following way:

The defendant's reaction (that is what he actually did, rather than the fact that he lost his self-control) may therefore be understandable in the sense that another person in his situation and the circumstances in which he found himself, might have reacted in the same or in a similar way.[191]

Secondly it is important to note that s 54(3) clarifies s 54(1)(c) so that the reference to 'the circumstances of D' includes '*all* of D's circumstances' except those which bear on D's 'general capacity for tolerance and self-restraint' (eg a propensity to violent outbursts). The words 'in the circumstances of D' may enable a jury to adopt a more generous approach when judging D's response than might have been possible under the old law. This opens up a broader range of subjective considerations than under the *Holley* test.[192] Judges will have to be vigilant to ensure that the broad nature of the test for including D's circumstances in considering how a person of his age, etc might have reacted does not lead to evidence of tenuous relevance being admitted and distracting the jury from the central inquiry.

A third distinguishing feature from the old law is that s 54(3) only appears to exclude a circumstance on which D seeks to rely if its *sole* relevance is to diminish D's self-restraint.[193] This could open up the opportunity for D to claim, for example, that his intake of alcohol or other intoxicants was a relevant circumstance and that the intoxication did not simply diminish his self-restraint, but also had some other relevance—for example, that it caused a relevant mistake. This may amount to no more than a plea of lack of intent on grounds of intoxication, but it will make directing the jury more complex. In *Asmelash*,[194] Lord Judge CJ held that there was nothing in the statutory language to indicate that Parliament had intended for the normal rules governing voluntary intoxication not to apply.[195] D's voluntarily intoxicated state is therefore not a matter to be taken into account by the jury when considering whether D exercised ordinary self-control. It was observed that if a sober individual in D's circumstances, with normal levels of tolerance and self-restraint, might have behaved in the same way as the defendant when confronted by the relevant qualifying trigger, then D would not be deprived of the loss of control defence just because he was not sober. It was held that the trial judge was correct to direct the jury that they had to be sure that a person of D's sex and age with a normal degree of tolerance and self-restraint in the same circumstances, but unaffected by alcohol, would not have reacted in the same or a similar way.

Equally, evidence that D was suffering from chronic alcoholism is *not* (unless the taunts related to D's alcoholism) a matter to be taken into account by the jury. If D had a severe

---

[190] cf *Van Dongen* [2005] EWCA Crim 1728 where the Court of Appeal seemed to imply such despite the decision against in *Phillips v R* [2005] Crim LR 971.

[191] At [30].

[192] Indeed in *Clinton* it was held that sexual infidelity may be a circumstance. At [31].

[193] It is important not to lose sight of the fact that a circumstance is excluded only if its *sole* relevance is that it bears on D's general capacity for tolerance and self-restraint.

[194] [2013] EWCA Crim 157, [2013] Crim LR 599.

[195] The Court of Appeal was heavily influenced by the earlier case of *Dowds*, see n 237, in which Hughes LJ held that voluntary intoxication could not constitute a recognized medical condition for the purposes of diminished responsibility. Lord Judge CJ held that the two partial defences ought to adopt the same approach to intoxication because 'in a fair proportion of cases both defences are canvassed before the jury, the potential for uncertainty and confusion which would follow the necessarily very different directions on the issue of intoxication, depending on which partial defence was under consideration, does not bear contemplation'. At [24]. However, since murder is a crime of specific intent and D will often seek to argue that his intoxication meant that he did not form the necessary mens rea, the jury will already have to approach the relevance of intoxication from more than one perspective.

problem with alcohol and was taunted about his addiction, then it was held that to the extent that it constituted a qualifying trigger, D's alcohol dependency would form part of the circumstances.

Although the facts of *Asmelash* did not present this possibility, an additional situation in which D's voluntary intoxication ought to be deemed a circumstance is if it causes him to make a relevant mistake. Suppose that D was so intoxicated that he mistook V's slap on the back as an attack rather than an exuberant act of friendship and consequently kills him. Although D's intoxication might bear on his general capacity for tolerance and self-restraint, in this situation it would not be its *sole* relevance and so falls within the 'gap'[196] left by the legislation.[197]

Section 54(3) excludes circumstances 'whose only relevance to D's conduct is that they bear on D's general capacity for tolerance or self restraint'. That restriction is similar to the old law in *excluding* certain features. However, there is now no positive requirement that D's individual circumstances have to affect the gravity of the triggering conduct in order for them to be *included* in the jury's assessment of what the person of D's age and sex might have done. So, where D has a learning disability and is provoked, his disability will be relevant even if the taunts relate to something completely different. Again, there is a need to be vigilant in avoiding evidence of marginal relevance from distracting the jury.

The question that arises is which, if any, of D's mental conditions are relevant. There are now a number of cases that have considered this issue. In *McGrory*,[198] the Court of Appeal held that the judge was correct not to refer the jury to the evidence of the medical expert who testified that D's depression would have meant that he had a 'reduced ability to deal with taunting and to cope with those sorts of pressures compared to someone not suffering from depression'. Maddison J stated that this was not a relevant circumstance, as it was excluded by s 54(3). In *B*, Hughes LJ, as he then was, stated that: 's.54 of the Coroners and Justice Act 2009 . . . excludes from consideration those characteristics of the defendant which bear on his capacity for tolerance and self-restraint. Thus mental illness reducing that capacity would not be relevant to the partial defence of loss of control, but would be material if it amounted to insanity or (in the particular case of a murder charge alone) fulfilled the different criteria for the separate (also partial) defence of diminished responsibility.'[199]

The answer, it is submitted, lies in the statutory formula. The evidence of D's mental illness would be a relevant circumstance so long as it had some relevance other than it bore on his general capacity for tolerance and self-restraint. One example already mentioned is that it induced D to make a relevant mistake. In *Wilcocks*,[200] Holroyde J, as he then was, directed the jury that:

If and insofar as you conclude a personality disorder reduced his general capacity for tolerance and self-restraint, that would not be a relevant circumstance when you are considering the defence of loss of control. But it is important to emphasise that this exclusion only relates to any feature of a personality disorder which reduced his general capacity for tolerance and self-restraint. Let me give you an illustration. If you thought that [D] suffered from a personality disorder which made him unusually likely to become angry and aggressive at the slightest provocation, that would of course

---

[196] Ashworth [2013] Crim LR 599.

[197] Some commentators have expressed concern that this might lead to defendants making spurious claims with the aim of establishing that their intoxicated state had some other relevance. A Jackson and N Wortley, 'Loss of Control and the "Normal" Person: The Relevance of Self-Induced Intoxication' (2013) 77 J Crim L 292. No doubt, however, trial judges will be alive to this possibility and will scrutinize D's claim closely. Further, just because D's intoxicated state is permitted to be considered by the jury as a 'circumstance' in some situations, does not necessarily mean the partial defence will be pleaded successfully.

[198] [2013] EWCA Crim 2336.　　[199] [2013] EWCA Crim 3, [38].

[200] [2016] EWCA Crim 2043, [40].

be relevant to diminished responsibility but it could not assist him in relation to loss of control. But if you thought that a personality disorder had caused him to attempt suicide, then you would be entitled to take into account as one of his circumstances the effect on him of being taunted that he should have killed himself.

The Court of Appeal endorsed this direction and it seems to reflect the statutory intent—that provided the mental condition is relevant to some aspect other than D's *general* capacity for tolerance and self restraint, it should be considered by the jury in their deliberations on s 54(3). If, on the other hand, the mental condition's only relevance is that it bears on the defendant's general capacity for tolerance and self-restraint, then it should not be considered. For example, in *Meanza* it was conceded that D's paranoid schizophrenia and anti-social personality disorder could not be relevant circumstances within the meaning of s 54(1)(c).[201]

The leading case is now *Rejmanski*, in which the Court of Appeal accepted the analysis of the legislation that was advanced above.[202] The Court of Appeal held that the potential relevance of mental disorder to each of the elements of the LOSC defence is fact-specific: it depends on the nature of the defendant's disorder, the effect it has on the defendant and the facts of the case. In relation to the final element of the partial defence, the court held that the wording of s 54(1)(c) makes clear that:

the defendant is to be judged against the standard of a person with a normal degree, and not an abnormal degree, of tolerance and self-restraint. If, and in so far as, a personality disorder reduced the defendant's general capacity for tolerance or self-restraint, that would not be a relevant consideration. Moreover, it would not be a relevant consideration even if the personality disorder was one of the 'circumstances' of the defendant because it was relevant to the gravity of the trigger. Expert evidence about the impact of the disorder would be irrelevant and inadmissible on the issue of whether it would have reduced the capacity for tolerance and self-restraint of the hypothetical 'person of D's sex and age, with a normal degree of tolerance and self-restraint'.[203]

If the mental disorder has some relevance to D's conduct other than it bears on his general capacity for tolerance and self-restraint, it is not excluded by subs (3) and the jury will be entitled to take it into account as one of D's circumstances. The court emphasized, however, that it will be necessary to identify 'with some care' how the mental disorder is said to be relevant as one of D's circumstances. The court also emphasized that the disorder must not be relied upon to undermine the principle that D's conduct is to be judged against 'normal' standards, rather than the abnormal standard of an individual defendant. The court emphatically rejected the argument that if a disorder is relevant to the gravity of the qualifying trigger, and evidence of the disorder is admitted in relation to the gravity of the trigger, the jury would also be entitled to take it into account insofar as it bore on D's general capacity for tolerance and self-restraint. Whilst the disorder would be a relevant circumstance of the defendant, it would not be relevant to the question of the degree of tolerance and self-restraint which would be expected of the hypothetical person referred to in s 54(1)(c). Citing *Holley* and *Wilcocks*, the court accepted that a mental disorder may be a relevant circumstance where it is relevant to the gravity of the qualifying trigger. The example given by the court is a woman suffering from 'Battered Woman's Syndrome' or a personality disorder, who kills her abuser, and who may adduce evidence of her condition, on the basis that it may be relevant to both the loss of self-control and to the gravity of the provocation for her. Given that loss of control and diminished responsibility may be pleaded together as alternatives, the court emphasized that the law does not ignore a mental disorder that, through no fault of the defendant, renders him unable to exercise the degree of self-control of a 'normal' person. In a case such as this, the defendant could still plead diminished responsibility.

---

[201] [2017] EWCA Crim 445. [202] [2017] EWCA Crim 2061. [203] ibid, [25].

Rejmanski is a welcome judgment and ensures that D's reaction to the qualifying trigger is assessed against the objective standard required by the legislation. Before permitting evidence of a mental disorder to be considered by the jury, trial judges must ensure that a sufficiently cogent case has been advanced that the disorder is relevant to something other than D's general capacity for tolerance or self-restraint. As the Court of Appeal observed, in the majority of cases the disorder will be relevant to the gravity of the qualifying trigger. The court must not, however, be taken to have laid down a rule that this is the only relevance it can have. It is possible to envisage other ways in which the mental disorder may be relevant. In this regard, the judgment in *Rejmanski* confirms that the LOSC defence is more generous to defendants than provocation given that there is no positive requirement for D's circumstances to affect the gravity of the triggering conduct.

13.2 Diminished responsibility

Section 2 of the Homicide Act 1957 introduced a new defence to murder: 'diminished responsibility'.[204] The defence has been substituted with one of the same name contained in s 52 of the Coroners and Justice Act 2009.

If successful, the defence allows D to be found guilty only of manslaughter.[205] By s 2(2) of the 1957 Act the burden of proof is on D. It was held in *Foye*,[206] a case brought under the old law, that placing the burden upon D did not infringe the presumption of innocence enshrined in Art 6(2) of the ECHR. That was endorsed by the Court of Appeal in relation to the new law in *Wilcocks*.[207] Imposing a burden on D is said to be justified on the basis that: (a) diminished responsibility is an exceptional defence; (b) the defence depends upon the 'internal functioning of [D's] mental process'; (c) it would be impractical to require the Crown to disprove diminished responsibility whenever it was raised on the evidence. It has been held that, as in the case of insanity, the standard of proof required is not beyond reasonable doubt but on a balance of probabilities.[208] Diminished responsibility is not a general defence, but applies only to murder.[209] It is

---

[204] For historical and general accounts see Norrie, *Crime, Reason and History*, 248–256; RD Mackay, 'Diminished Responsibility and Mentally Disordered Killers' in Ashworth and Mitchell (eds), *Rethinking English Homicide Law* (2000); E Tennant, *The Future of the Diminished Responsibility Defence to Murder* (2001); S Dell, *Murder into Manslaughter: The Diminished Responsibility Defence in Practice* (1984).

[205] The defence derives from the law of Scotland, where it was a judicial creation, originating in the decision of Lord Deas in *HM Advocate v Dingwall* (1867) 5 Irv 466. See TB Smith, 'Diminished Responsibility' [1957] Crim LR 354 and Lord Keith, 'Some Observations on Diminished Responsibility' [1959] Jur Rev 109. The Scottish version was redefined in the Criminal Procedure (Scotland) Act 1995, s 51B, inserted by s 168 of the Criminal Justice and Licensing (Scotland) Act 2010. The defence in Scotland now results in a conviction for 'culpable homicide on grounds of diminished responsibility'. The new statutory provisions implement recommendations made by the Scottish Law Commission in Report No 195, *Insanity and Diminished Responsibility* (2004); see for comment on those recommendations (2013) 77 J Crim L 512 and [2014] Crim LR 109.

[206] [2013] EWCA Crim 475. For compelling criticism, see Ashworth [2013] Crim LR 839.

[207] [2016] EWCA Crim 2043.

[208] *Dunbar* [1958] 1 QB 1, [1957] 2 All ER 737. This rule is not affected by the HRA 1998: *Ali and Jordan* [2001] 1 All ER 1014, CA. Where the medical evidence of diminished responsibility is based on certain facts, it is for the defence to prove those facts by admissible evidence: *Ahmed Din* (1962) 46 Cr App R 269; *Bradshaw* (1985) 82 Cr App R 79, [1985] Crim LR 733 and commentary.

[209] Given that LOSC and diminished responsibility will often be pleaded together (a fact noted by Lord Judge in *Dawes* (earlier)), Mitchell argues that the differences in the burdens and standards of proof of the respective partial defences could cause considerable difficulties for juries. See B Mitchell, 'Years of Provocation, Followed by a Loss of Control' in L Zedner and JV Roberts, *Principles and Values in Criminal Law and Criminal Justice* (2012). See also Norrie, n 204, 256–257.

not available as a defence to attempted murder,[210] nor can it be raised on a finding of unfitness to plead.[211]

13.2.1 The old law

Only the briefest outline of the old law is required. Under s 2 of the 1957 Act as enacted, the defence was available on a charge of murder where D could prove that 'he was suffering from such abnormality of mind (whether arising from a condition of arrested or retarded development of mind or any inherent causes or induced by disease or injury) as substantially impaired his mental responsibility for his acts and omissions in doing or being a party to the killing'.

The elements of the defence were therefore: (a) an abnormality of mind (b) which arose from one of the specified conditions (c) which substantially impaired (d) D's mental responsibility. None of the elements was defined with any precision and arguably the courts in collusion with psychiatrists were content to avoid definition so that the defence maintained its flexibility, thereby allowing for its application in deserving cases in which the mandatory sentence for murder would otherwise apply.[212]

There had been numerous calls for reform. The Law Commission Report No 290, *Partial Defences to Murder*, concluded that[213] there was 'overwhelming support' for reform. The old law was regarded by many as 'chaotic' and it was suggested that a rational sentencing exercise would be a better response for meeting the needs of mentally ill defendants. It was noted that the defence was 'grossly abused' and whether a defendant 'finds a psychiatrist who will be prepared to testify that, for example, depression was responsible for his behaviour is "a lottery"'. There was some pressure for abolition, particularly if the mandatory sentence was removed, but the Law Commission identified several arguments[214] for retention, including the need for 'fair and just labelling'.[215]

The Commission refined its original proposal from the Partial Defences Project.[216] The proposals were taken forward by the MOJ and the new defence as enacted in 2009 is very similar to those proposals (but note the omission of a defence of developmental immaturity).

13.2.2 The new defence

Section 52 of the Coroners and Justice Act 2009 provides:[217]

(1) In section 2 of the Homicide Act 1957 (persons suffering from diminished responsibility), for subsection (1) substitute—

---

[210] *Campbell* [1997] Crim LR 495, Sedley J. See also *Farrar* [1992] 1 VR 207.

[211] *Antoine* [2001] AC 340.   [212] LC 304, para 5.107.

[213] LC 290, para 5.10 and see Scottish Law Commission, Report No 195, *Insanity and Diminished Responsibility* (2004). See also J Horder, *Homicide and the Politics of Law Reform* (2012) 226.

[214] Justifications included the need for some defence other than insanity given the 'out-dated nature of the insanity defence' and its unsatisfactory scope and operation; the stigmatization of the label 'insanity'; the need to prevent jurors being faced with only the option of murder or acquittal lest they perversely acquit; allowing the central issue of culpability to be determined by a jury and not by the judge as part of the sentencing process; the need to ensure public confidence in sentencing which is more likely on a diminished verdict than on murder; the need for a jury to evaluate the expert evidence; the need to retain the defence for abused women 'driven to kill'; and the opportunity for the defence to provide a merciful but just disposition of mercy killing cases.

[215] LC 290, para 5.18.   [216] See V Tadros, *Criminal Liability for Non-Aggressive Death* (2008).

[217] See in particular Norrie, n 204, 251–254; A Reed and M Bohlander (eds), *Loss of Control and Diminished Responsibility—Domestic, Comparative and International Perspectives* (2011); L Kennefick, 'Introducing a New Diminished Responsibility Defence for England and Wales' (2011) 74 MLR 750; R Fortson and AR Keene, *Current Law Statutes Annotation* (2010); J Glasson and J Knowles, *Blackstone's Guide to the Coroners and Justice Act 2009* (2010) Ch 8; LH Leigh, 'Two New Partial Defences to Murder' (2010) Crim L & Justice Weekly 53; R Mackay, 'The New Diminished Responsibility Plea' [2010] Crim LR 290.

'(1) A person ('D') who kills or is a party to the killing of another is not to be convicted of murder if D was suffering from an abnormality of mental functioning which—

    (a) arose from a recognised medical condition,

    (b) substantially impaired D's ability to do one or more of the things mentioned in subsection (1A), and

    (c) provides an explanation for D's acts and omissions in doing or being a party to the killing.

(1A) Those things are—

    (a) to understand the nature of D's conduct;

    (b) to form a rational judgment;

    (c) to exercise self-control.

(1B) For the purposes of subsection (1)(c), an abnormality of mental functioning provides an explanation for D's conduct if it causes, or is a significant contributory factor in causing, D to carry out that conduct.'

Section 52 was brought into force on 4 October 2010.[218] Since the provision relates exclusively to a matter of substantive law, it will apply in relation to any murder which occurred on or after that date.[219]

13.2.2.1 The elements of the defence

Section 52 makes significant changes to the defence of diminished responsibility. The main aim is to modernize and clarify the defence. In particular, the aim is to redraft the provision with the needs and practices of medical experts in mind, and to clarify what is involved in the 'substantial impairment of the defendant's mental responsibility'. Strikingly, the word 'responsibility' no longer features in the terms of the defence at all.[220] The practical effects are, it would appear, to narrow the scope of the defence and to create the opportunity for experts to have even greater influence over the outcome.[221] Because the experts have a greater opportunity to provide a more definitive opinion on more of the elements of the offence, it is unclear whether this will lead to a greater proportion of cases in which there will be accepted pleas. In 2017 Professors Mackay and Mitchell conducted a review into cases which have applied the partial defence in its current form. They compared CPS research into the new law (limited to only 90 cases) with the Law Commission's study of the old law.[222] Statistics reveal that the total number of successful diminished responsibility pleas under the old law was around 20 per year in the years immediately preceding amendment (down from around 70–85 per year in the 1980s).[223] The recent CPS study found a

---

[218] The Coroners and Justice Act 2009 (Commencement No 4, Transitional and Saving Provisions) Order 2010, SI 2010/816.

[219] Para 7 of Sch 22 to the Coroners and Justice Act 2009.

[220] There has been a divergence of views expressed on whether this is desirable. Contrast L Kennefick, 'Introducing a New Diminished Responsibility Defence for England and Wales' (2011) 74 MLR 750 with R Fortson, 'The Modern Partial Defence of Diminished Responsibility' in A Reed and M Bohlander (eds), *Loss of Control and Diminished Responsibility* (2011).

[221] Jurors remain at liberty to disregard the expert evidence left to them and find D guilty of murder. *Golds* [2016] UKSC 61 provides a vivid example of this, as the jury rejected the unanimous evidence of the three experts, two for the defence and one for the Crown, who testified that the elements of the partial defence were present. See also *Brennan* [2014] EWCA Crim 2387. For further discussion, see p 565.

[222] See R Mackay and B Mitchell, 'The New Diminished Responsibility Plea in Operation: Some Initial Findings' [2017] Crim LR 18.

[223] See LC 290; LC 304, para 5.84.

higher proportion of cases being dealt with as jury trials (43.3 per cent) than occurred in the earlier research (22.9 per cent) which indicates that more cases are being contested under the new law.[224]

The elements of the new defence are the following.

(1) An 'abnormality of mental functioning'. In itself this is not intended to be a change of substance, but rather one to adopt language preferred by psychiatrists.[225]

(2) The abnormality must arise 'from a recognised medical condition'. This is designed to be wider than the old list of bracketed causes in the original definition in s 2 of the 1957 Act. Again, it is designed to allow expert evidence to be received on a more meaningful basis.

(3) D's 'mental responsibility' must be substantially impaired. This means that his *ability* to do one or more of the things in s 2(1A), must be substantially impaired. The three things are:

(a) to understand the nature of D's conduct;

(b) to form a rational judgement;

(c) to exercise self-control.

This is a dramatic change from the old law. It is more specific and leaves less moral elbow room for the jury and is arguably harder for D to prove.

(4) The abnormality of mental functioning from a 'recognised medical condition' must be a cause or contributory cause of D's conduct in killing. There is some ambiguity as to whether the section requires a cause or merely an explanation.

Each element of the offence deserves more detailed consideration.

(1) 'an abnormality of mental functioning'

Under the old s 2 test (of 'abnormality of mind') the determination of 'abnormality' could be left entirely to the jury. In *Byrne*,[226] Lord Parker CJ stated[227] that 'abnormality' of mind:

means a state of mind so different from that of ordinary human beings that the reasonable man would term it abnormal. It appears to us to be wide enough to cover the mind's activities in all its aspects, not only the perception of physical acts and matters and the ability to form a rational judgment whether an act is right or wrong, but also the ability to exercise will-power to control physical acts in accordance with that rational judgement.

That formula was appropriate when a jury was considering a concept as loose and general as the 'mind' and asking whether D's 'mind' deviated from the norm. But the expression 'abnormality of mind' has been superseded by the test of abnormality of 'mental functioning'. That test is, even if not a formal psychiatric test, one with a psychiatric flavour. The jury cannot have a sound grasp of that concept without expert evidence.[228] Nor, therefore, can the jury understand how far D's mental functioning deviates from the norm without

---

224 R Mackay and B Mitchell, 'The New Diminished Responsibility Plea in Operation: Some Initial Findings' [2017] Crim LR 18 at 26.

225 See LC 304, para 5.114. It received support in Parliament from Baroness Murphy (Visiting Professor of Psychiatry at Queen Mary, University of London): Hansard, HL, 30 June 2009, vol 712, col 177.

226 [1960] 2 QB 396.   227 At 403.

228 This remains, however, a legal rather than a medical term. It has been argued that this fact demonstrates that the 'Law and psychiatry are based on opposing paradigms, they cannot work together'. See L Kennefick, 'Introducing a New Diminished Responsibility Defence for England and Wales' (2011) 74 MLR 750, 765. See also the discussion in Norrie, n 204, Ch 9.

expert evidence to assist them. As such, it is doubtful whether they can be left with as open a direction as in *Byrne*. Experts will express an opinion on whether there is an abnormal mental functioning. If there is uncontradicted expert evidence of the defence, the judge may withdraw murder from the jury, but should be cautious in doing so.[229] In such a case 'the judge needs to ensure that the Crown explains the basis on which it is inviting the jury to reject [the expert] evidence. He needs to ensure that the basis advanced is one which the jury can properly adopt.'[230] In *Blackman*,[231] the Lord Chief Justice emphasized that:

The fact that the prosecution calls no evidence to contradict a psychiatrist called by the defence is not in itself sufficient justification for doing so. In the light of the judgment in *Golds*, we see no reason not to follow the broad approach of this court in *R v Khan (Dawood)* [2009] EWCA Crim 1569, [2010] 1 Cr App R 4, to which reference was made in *Brennan*, which we would express as follows: it will be a rare case where a judge will exercise the power to withdraw a charge of murder from the jury when the prosecution do not accept that the evidence gives rise to the defence of diminished responsibility.[232]

The new law probably is stricter than the original s 2. Nevertheless, there is little doubt that on facts such as those in *Byrne*, the defence would still be available. Byrne strangled a young woman in a YWCA hostel and mutilated her corpse. Evidence was tendered that from an early age he had been subject to perverted violent desires; that the impulse or urge of those desires was stronger than the normal impulse or urge of sex, that he found it very difficult or, perhaps, impossible in some cases to resist putting the desire into practice and that the act of killing the girl was done under such an impulse or urge.[233] That would be an abnormality of mental functioning.

(2) 'a recognised medical condition'

The abnormality of mental functioning must arise 'from a recognised medical condition'. This new element to the test is designed to be wider than the list of sufficient causes in the original s 2 of the 1957 Act.[234] It is intended to produce clearer expert evidence from psychiatrists and psychologists and to allow sufficient flexibility for the new defence to develop in line with medical understanding and practice.[235] The immediate questions arising are: What kind(s) of medical condition? Recognized by whom?

'medical condition'

This new element of the definition will provide a clearer foundation for the defence. As the Royal College of Psychiatrists explained, it will:

encourage reference within expert evidence to diagnosis in terms of one or two of the accepted internationally classificatory systems of mental conditions (i.e. the World Health Organisation: International Classification of Diseases (ICD-10); and the American Psychiatric Association: Diagnostic and Statistical Manual of Mental Disorders (DSM-1V)) without explicitly writing those systems into the legislation.[236]

---

[229] This is examined further at p 565.   [230] Per Lord Hughes in *Golds* [2016] UKSC 61, [51].
[231] [2017] EWCA Crim 190 (CMAC).   [232] At [43].
[233] The defence of irresistible impulse, which is not within the defence of insanity, is therefore included in the law (but only of murder) by way of diminished responsibility.
[234] The Law Commission originally wanted a wider formulation: that the source of the abnormality should be an 'underlying condition' (LCCP 177, para 10.21), which would not be limited to a mental condition existing independently of the external circumstances that gave rise to the commission of an offence. It would therefore have 'include[d] cases in which the origins of the condition itself lie in adverse circumstances with which the offender has had to cope': LCCP 177, para 6.54.
[235] See the MOJ CP 19/08.   [236] LC 304, para 5.114. See MOJ CP 19/08, fn 13.

It must be noted that *any* medical condition *might* suffice subject to the restriction imposed in *Dowds*.[237] It will include physical conditions as well as psychological or psychiatric ones[238] and conditions such as diabetes or ADHD. Depressive illnesses resulting from prolonged abuse will qualify,[239] and hence the defence remains available to battered women on those terms.[240]

Acute intoxication, that is, being drunk, does not constitute a recognized medical condition.[241] Alcoholic dependency will, however, qualify as a medical condition irrespective of whether it resulted in brain damage.[242] The Court of Appeal strongly doubted in *Lindo* whether a drug-induced psychosis standing alone would be sufficient to constitute a recognized medical condition. In this case, it was submitted on behalf of L that he had entered what the expert called a 'prodromal state', which put him at risk of developing a mental illness. The court held that even if this were to be combined with the drug-induced psychosis, it would still be doubtful whether it was sufficient to trigger the operation of the partial defence. Hallett LJ stated that, 'public policy proceeds on the basis that an offender who voluntarily takes alcohol or drugs and behaves a way in which he would not have behaved when sober is not normally excused responsibility. People who take drugs run the risk of suffering side effects such as psychosis.'[243] Her ladyship held that it would be wrong to permit individuals such as L to escape full responsibility for their actions simply on the basis that they took drugs at a time when they were at risk of developing a mental illness. So, if D voluntarily consumes drink or drugs which cause him immediately to suffer some medical condition or mental illness, he will not be able to plead the partial defence. We discuss the implications of this further later.

Although this element of the defence is much broader than the equivalent element under the 1957 Act, it should not create excessive breadth in the defence overall since the other elements are all, arguably, narrower.

In discussions during the reform exercise, groups expressed concern that this element may in some circumstances be narrower than the old law because it will not apply to those who kill terminally ill relatives when the killer has 'acted rationally in response to persistent

---

[237] See p 554. In *Dowds* [2012] EWCA Crim 281, the Court of Appeal stated that just because a condition is transient or temporary does not preclude it from fulfilling this element of the partial defence. Hughes LJ suggested that concussion may be an example of such a condition, but did not resolve the matter conclusively, at [39].

[238] See the MOJ CP 19/08, para 49.

[239] The Law Commission also took the view that most cases of 'mercy' killing, in which there was evidence of an abnormality of mental functioning resulting from depression arising from long-term care, would be covered by its proposed changes. See LC 304, paras 7.34–7.37. Mackay doubts whether the Law Commission's view was correct, on the basis that there may be no recognized medical condition from which D is suffering. See R Mackay, 'The New Diminished Responsibility Plea: More than Mere Modernisation?' in A Reed and M Bohlander (eds), *Loss of Control and Diminished Responsibility*. See also M Gibson, 'Pragmatism Preserved? The Challenges of Accommodating Mercy Killers in the Reformed Diminished Responsibility Plea' (2017) 81 J Crim L 177. It has been argued that a specific provision ought to be enacted that provides a partial excusatory defence for those who kill out of compassion. See H Keating and J Bridgeman, 'Compassionate Killings: The Case for a Partial Defence' (2012) 75 MLR 697.

[240] Battered women's syndrome, having been included in 1992 in the standard British classification of mental diseases, is a relevant condition: *Hobson* [1998] 1 Cr App R 31.

[241] cf *Dowds* [2012] EWCA Crim 281.

[242] See *Kay and Joyce* [2017] EWCA Crim 647 and *Bunch* [2013] EWCA Crim 2489. Historically this was a confused area until the decision of the House of Lords in *Dietschman*. See *Tandy* [1989] 1 All ER 267. See since *Dietschman*; *Wood* [2008] EWCA Crim 1305; *Stewart* [2009] EWCA Crim 593; *Stewart (No 2)* [2010] EWCA Crim 2159.

[243] [2016] EWCA Crim 1940, [42].

requests from a seriously ill loved-one'.[244] However, it may be that some depressive illness would be likely to be diagnosed, as a 'medical condition'.[245]

'recognised'

The requirement that the medical condition is a 'recognised' one is also intended to prevent 'idiosyncratic diagnoses' being advanced as a basis for a plea of diminished responsibility.[246] However, during the debates in Committee in Parliament, the government recognized that it is important that the legislation must be sufficiently flexible to cater for emerging medical conditions. It expressed the view that it is open to the defence to call a 'recognized specialist who has had their work peer-reviewed, although it has *not quite got on the list* [ie in the psychiatric manuals DSM V or ICD-10] and that it would be for the jury to decide whether the evidence met the partial defence requirements'.[247] Care will be needed to ensure that 'quack' opinions are not received. The comment in Parliament might have been better expressed in terms of the recognized specialist being *not yet on the list*. This would reflect the desire to ensure flexibility for development.

Whether a condition in the manuals is 'recognised' is a matter of law. The Court of Appeal in *Dowds*[248] stated that it is necessary, but not always sufficient, that a condition is included in one of the diagnostic manuals. D sought to argue that voluntary acute intoxication (which is different from alcohol dependency syndrome) was a recognized medical condition for the purposes of diminished responsibility.[249] Hughes LJ observed that the general principle that voluntary intoxication is no defence 'is well-entrenched and formed the unspoken backdrop for the new statutory formula'.[250] If Parliament had sought to alter this principle, then Hughes LJ stated that it would have made its intention to do so explicit.[251] It was observed that the diagnostic manuals are extremely broad and include many conditions of questionable legal impact. His lordship gave pyromania, unhappiness, suspiciousness and marked evasiveness, paedophilia and intermittent explosive disorder as some vivid examples.

Whilst the Court of Appeal's judgment in *Dowds* is uncontroversial as it applies to voluntary intoxication, it leaves open the question as to how trial judges ought to determine whether a condition recognized by medical experts is a 'recognised medical condition' for the purposes of the law. The issue is that the term 'recognised medical condition' is extremely broad. Requiring trial judges to pick and choose which ones ought to be capable of founding the defence of diminished responsibility is inimical to the aim of reforming the

---

[244] See the evidence of 'Dignity in Dying' to Joint Committee on Human Rights, Eighth Report, 2008–09, para 1.150; evidence 44–45. Cf *Cocker* [1989] Crim LR 740 who would not fit within this defence nor LOSC. It has been argued that loss of control will provide a more viable defence for mercy killers, see B Livings, 'A New Partial Defence for the Mercy Killer: Revisiting Loss of Control' [2014] NILQ 187.

[245] See the evidence presented to the Public Bill Committee, 3 February 2009, written evidence (CJ/01); Joint Committee on Human Rights, Eighth Report, 2008–09; para 1.151. For an engaging discussion of this issue, see M Gibson, 'Pragmatism Preserved? The Challenges of Accommodating Mercy Killers in the Reformed Diminished Responsibility Plea' (2017) 81 J Crim L 177.

[246] LC 304, para 5.114.

[247] Public Bill Committee Debates, 3 Mar 2009, col 414. Emphasis added.

[248] [2012] EWCA Crim 281, [2012] Crim LR 612.

[249] For discussion of how this issue is addressed in other common law jurisdictions, see N Wake, 'Recognising Acute Intoxication as Diminished Responsibility? A Comparative Analysis?' (2012) 76 J Crim L 71. For an early analysis, see M Gibson, 'Intoxicants and Diminished Responsibility: The Impact of the Coroners and Justice Act 2009' [2011] Crim LR 909.

[250] At [35].

[251] It has been suggested that one way of avoiding the issue that arose in *Dowds* would have been for Parliament to state explicitly that intoxication is incapable of forming the basis of the partial defence, as is the case in Scotland. See N Wake, 'Diminished Responsibility and Acute Intoxication: Raising the Bar?' (2012) 76 J Crim L 197.

law to ensure it conforms with modern psychiatric practice. Hughes LJ made explicit that the question of whether the classification system addresses the legal issue in a particular case 'will inevitably [involve] considerations of legal policy which are irrelevant to the business of medical description, classification, and statistical analysis'.[252] The Court of Appeal did not, however, elucidate what D will have to prove in addition to the fact that the medical condition is accepted by the medical profession in order to satisfy this element of the defence. It seems that the list of conditions that are capable of constituting 'recognised medial conditions' will be determined on a case-by-case basis. The diagnostic manuals will be indicative and not determinative of the matter.

Developmental immaturity as a 'medical condition'?[253] The new diminished defence differs from the Law Commission's proposal principally because the new definition does not include, as a cause of impairment, 'developmental immaturity in a defendant under the age of 18', alongside abnormality of mental functioning arising from a mental condition. So, as it was put in debates:

> An adult who acts like a 10-year-old gets that taken into account, but a 10-year-old who acts like a 10-year-old does not.[254]

The government rejected this proposal on the grounds that this was unnecessary and because the concept of a 'recognised medical condition' is designed to be wide enough to cover relevant conditions affecting those under 18 (eg learning disabilities and autistic spectrum disorders).[255]

There was widespread support for the Law Commission proposal.[256] Lord Phillips is on record as regretting the omission of any reference to developmental immaturity, saying:

> The Government has not accepted this argument for two reasons. The first is that they do not believe that the absence of such a provision is causing serious problems in practice. The second is, I quote: We think there is a risk that such a provision would open up the defence too widely and catch inappropriate cases.[257]

Since there is now no defence of *doli incapax*[258] the child killer has limited defence options. Arguably, there will be cases where a young defendant might be able to bring his developmental immaturity within the rubric of a 'recognised medical condition' for the purposes of the new defence. However, whatever the cause of the developmental immaturity, whether it is nature or nurture, unless it results in an *abnormal* mental functioning, D will not be able to meet the requirement under the new s 2(1)(a). The Law Commission was concerned that experts may find it impossible to distinguish between the impact of developmental immaturity on D's functioning and the impact of a mental abnormality on that functioning process. It concluded that it was 'wholly unrealistic and unfair' to expect medical experts to assess the impact of abnormal mental functioning whilst disregarding developmental

---

252 *Dowds*, [30].

253 For further discussion, see R Fortson, 'The Modern Partial Defence of Diminished Responsibility' in A Reed and M Bohlander (eds), *Loss of Control and Diminished Responsibility* (2011), and A Ashworth *Positive Obligations in Criminal Law* (2013) 184.

254 Public Bill Committee Debates, 3 Mar 2009, col 411.

255 See CP 19/08, para 55.

256 Supported by the Crown Court judges, the Criminal Bar Association, the Youth Justice Board, the Royal College of Psychiatrists, Dr Eileen Vizard, the NSPCC and a number of lawyers in Parliament.

257 Lord Phillips' Essex University/Clifford Chance lecture on *Reforming the Law of Homicide*, delivered on 6 Nov 2008. What should matter, it is submitted, is whether there is disfunction of ability to exercise control and judgement, etc.

258 *R v T* [2009] UKHL 20, Ch 10.

immaturity.[259] The harshness of the inability to rely on developmental immaturity to found a diminished responsibility plea might be felt most keenly in some cases of joint venture murder where a young vulnerable defendant has joined with an older gang, one of whose members kills V.

It must not be forgotten that the mere fact that D suffers from a particular medical condition is only one part of the defence; all the elements need to be established by D.[260]

(3) 'a substantial impairment of mental ability'

Under the old law, the matter that had to be substantially impaired was D's *mental responsibility* for acting as he did.[261] The test of *substantial* impairment of responsibility[262] was one of moral responsibility.[263] Under the new law, the matter that now has to be shown to be substantially impaired is D's *ability to do* any of the things mentioned in the new s 2(1A).

Under the old law the most authoritative case on the meaning of 'substantially' was *Lloyd*.[264] In that case counsel for D contended that 'substantially' can mean one of two things: that the impairment was real and not illusory, or that it was of a considerable amount. That decision was seen by some to be inconsistent with that of Lord Parker CJ in the earlier case of *Simcox*.[265] In *Ramchurn*,[266] the Lord Chief Justice rejected the argument that the meaning of 'substantially' had been inconsistently applied under the 1957 Act. Lord Judge remarked that 'substantially' is an ordinary English word. The purpose of the term is to ensure that D does not escape liability for murder on account of any impairment of mental responsibility, no matter how trivial and insignificant, but also to ensure that D is not unduly burdened by having to prove that his mental responsibility was so grossly impaired as to be extinguished.

Two questions arose recently. First, did the directions approved in *Lloyd* and *Simcox* really say the same thing and, secondly, did the 2009 reformulation of the partial defence alter the meaning to be attributed to the term 'substantial'?

The correct interpretation is now governed by the Supreme Court's decision in *Golds*.[267] G appealed against his conviction for murder. He had admitted killing his partner; the only question for the jury was whether he was guilty of murder or manslaughter by reason of his diminished responsibility. Three medical experts gave evidence that the conditions for establishing diminished responsibility were satisfied. The jury rejected the defence, however, after hearing evidence that G had committed acts of domestic violence against his partner on the day of her murder. One of the issues on appeal was whether the judge had erred in refusing to direct the jury as to the meaning of the word 'substantial' in relation to the question of whether G was suffering from an abnormality of mental functioning so as to substantially impair his ability to understand the nature of what he was doing, form a rational judgement, and/or exercise self-control. The Court of Appeal held that trial judges ordinarily should not direct juries on how the word 'substantial' ought to be interpreted,

---

[259] LC 304, para 5.128.

[260] Under the old law it was held that D's ADHD was not of itself enough to satisfy the defence: *Osborne* [2010] EWCA Crim 547 where D killed V in an unprovoked attack in anger and his illness was not a cause of the conduct.

[261] *Byrne*, n 226; *Simcox* [1964] Crim LR 402; *Lloyd* [1967] 1 QB 175. But cf R Sparks, 'Diminished Responsibility in Theory and Practice' (1964) 27 MLR 9, 16–19.

[262] *Campbell* (1986) 84 Cr App R 255 at 259.

[263] A person whose impulse is irresistible bears *no* moral responsibility for his act, for he has no choice; a person whose impulse is much more difficult to resist than that of an ordinary person bears a diminished degree of moral responsibility for his act.

[264] [1967] 1 QB 175.   [265] [1964] Crim LR 402.   [266] [2010] EWCA Crim 194, [15].

[267] [2016] UKSC 61. K Laird, 'R v Golds' [2017] Crim LR 316, 318–319.

but that if the issue does arise, the jury should be directed that a more than merely trivial impairment is insufficient to establish the partial defence. G appealed to the Supreme Court. The certified questions asked, first, whether the judge is required to direct the jury on the meaning of 'substantial', and secondly, whether it is 'to be defined as "something more than merely trivial," or alternatively in a way that connotes more than this, such as "something whilst short of total impairment is nevertheless significant and appreciable"?'[268]

The Supreme Court examined the history of the defence and the cases dealing with the concept of 'substantial' under the old law. The court concluded that the word 'substantially' had historically been held, in the diminished responsibility context, to mean 'having some substance' or 'important or weighty'. It was not synonymous with 'anything more than merely trivial'. The court held that that same interpretation applies to the defence under its new formulation in the Coroners and Justice Act 2009. In the absence of any indication to the contrary, Parliament was to be taken to have adopted the established sense in which the word 'substantially' had been used. The court observed that:

(1) Ordinarily in a murder trial where diminished responsibility is in issue the judge need not direct the jury beyond the terms of the statute and should not attempt to define the meaning of 'substantially'. Experience has shown that the issue of its correct interpretation is unlikely to arise in many cases. The jury should normally be given to understand that the expression is an ordinary English word, that it imports a question of degree, and that whether in the case before it the impairment can properly be described as substantial is for it to resolve.

(2) If, however, the jury has been introduced to the question of whether *any* impairment beyond the merely trivial will suffice, or if it has been introduced to the concept of a spectrum between the greater than trivial and the total, the judge should explain that whilst the impairment must indeed pass the merely trivial before it need be considered, it is not the law that *any* impairment beyond the trivial will suffice. The judge should likewise make this clear if a risk arises that the jury might misunderstand the import of the expression; whether this risk arises or not is a judgment to be arrived at by the trial judge who is charged with overseeing the dynamics of the trial. Diminished responsibility involves an impairment of one or more of the abilities listed in the statute to an extent which the jury judges to be substantial, and which it is satisfied significantly contributed to his committing the offence. Illustrative expressions of the sense of the word may be employed so long as the jury is given clearly to understand that no single synonym is to be substituted for the statutory word... .[269]

The Supreme Court's judgment was surprising given that Lord Judge CJ seemed to have adopted the more generous interpretation of 'substantial' as recently as 2010 in *Ramchurn*. It is submitted that there are a number of problems with the judgment. First, the Supreme Court's conclusion serves to narrow the defence, which has already been narrowed by its more medicalized recasting in 2009. Gibson argues that the judgment, 'unduly compromises access to diminished responsibility'.[270] Limiting access to the partial defence could have harsh consequences. Professor Mackay gives the example of a post-natal mother who kills her 13-month-old child and who, because of the age of the child, cannot rely upon the statutory defence of infanticide. She may also be unable to rely upon diminished responsibility because the psychiatrists and/or the jury consider the degree of impairment insufficient to reach the level now required by *Golds*.[271] Secondly, it is not clear that the decision is faithful to its own premise. The Supreme Court suggests that 'substantial' is an

---

[268] [2016] UKSC 61, [43].   [269] At [43].

[270] M Gibson, 'Diminished Responsibility in *Golds* and Beyond: Insights and Implications' [2017] Crim LR 543.

[271] R Mackay, '*R v Golds*' [2017] Arch Rev 4.

ordinary English word and that the jury needs no assistance on how it ought to be interpreted, *unless* someone has suggested otherwise, in which case the jury is not simply to be told it is an ordinary English word but are to be given a further definition. If there is a technical definition that juries ought to adopt beyond the 'ordinary English one', why should every jury not hear it in all cases from the outset? Consequently, this may risk an inconsistent application of the law; some juries may receive an elaborate definition whereas others will not. Finally, the decision may generate more appeals. There is little to be lost in appealing a murder conviction in any event, but in light of the vagueness of the basic instruction to the jury—to draw the line of 'substantially impaired' according to degree—future appeals on this point are unavoidable.

Golds was subsequently applied in *Squelch*.[272] S killed his victim and was caught on CCTV. Three forensic psychiatrists agreed that S suffered from paranoid personality disorder (PPD), that he had an abnormality of mental functioning arising from that condition which had played some part in the killing. They disagreed, however, on whether it had substantially impaired S's ability to do one or more of the things listed in s 2 of the Homicide Act 1957. Two considered that it had, but the third concluded that the impairment was not substantial, only that it might be a partial cause for the incident. The judge directed the jury that:

'substantially' is an ordinary English word on which you will reach a conclusion in this case, based upon your own experience of ordinary life. It means less than total and more than trivial. Where you, the jury, draw the line is a matter for your collective judgment.

The Court of Appeal commended the judge's direction as concise and accurate. The *Crown Court Compendium* suggests that judges direct juries in the following terms: 'The abnormality of mental functioning substantially impaired D's ability to understand the nature of his conduct and/or to form a rational judgment and/or to exercise self-control. Substantially means that the impairment need not be total but must be more than merely trivial.'[273]

Under the current formulation of the law, D has to show a substantial impairment of his ability to do one or more of these:

(1) to understand the nature of his own conduct;

(2) to form a rational judgement;

(3) to exercise self-control.[274]

Whether D has these abilities is a matter of psychiatry. The question is whether there is a 'substantial impairment' of one or more of these. It is submitted that it is a psychiatric question how far D's ability deviates from the normal level of ability to do those things. Giving the medical expert a greater role to play in this regard does not take the determination of the ultimate issue away from the jury, but merely ensures that they reach a verdict that is informed by medical expertise rather than lay intuition.[275]

If (1) and (2) are construed narrowly, they will be very similar to insanity and hence may be difficult for D to satisfy. If they are akin to insanity, in many cases D might well plead that complete defence rather than the partial defence of diminished responsibility.

---

[272] [2017] EWCA Crim 204. For further discussion, see Gibson, n 270.

[273] *Crown Court Compendium* (2017) Part 1, Ch 19, section 5.

[274] See *Byrne* [1960] 2 QB 396; and *Khan* [2009] EWCA Crim 1569.

[275] See also the suggestion of LC 304, para 5.198 that it will be a question for the jury. See the most recent research by Mackay and Mitchell examining how often experts' reports deal with these matters, see n 222.

To understand the nature of D's conduct

As commentators have observed, this is similar to the first limb of the insanity plea.[276] An example of how this element might be satisfied provided by the Law Commission[277] was of a ten-year-old boy with a recognized medical condition:[278]

> who has been left to play very violent video games for hours on end for much of his life, loses his temper and kills another child when the child attempts to take a game from him. When interviewed, he shows no real understanding that, when a person is killed they cannot simply be later revived, as happens in the games he has been continually playing.

One aspect of this form of the defence is that the focus is exclusively on whether D has the ability to understand the nature of his own conduct; it does not encompass his ability to understand anyone else's. Will this accommodate D who believes that his victim is, for example, possessed? Does this apply to the person with a very distorted thinking process? Baroness Murphy raised doubts about these in Parliament,[279] and such cases may be difficult to fit within limb (1).

Substantially impaired capacity to form a rational judgement

Examples from the Law Commission included:

(1) a woman who has been diagnosed as being in a state of learned helplessness consequent upon violent abuse suffered at her husband's hands comes to believe that only burning her husband to death will rid the world of his sins;

(2) a mentally subnormal boy believes that he must follow his older brother's instructions, even when they involve taking part in a killing. He says, 'I wouldn't dream of disobeying my brother and he would never tell me to do something if it was really wrong';

(3) a depressed man who has been caring for many years for a terminally ill spouse, kills her, at her request. He says that he had found it progressively more difficult to stop her repeated requests dominating his thoughts to the exclusion of all else, so that 'I felt I would never think straight again until I had given her what she wanted.'

In addition, Lord Judge CJ in *Clinton* observed that D's discovery that his partner has been sexually unfaithful may, and often will, be said to impair his ability to form a rational judgement (and/or exercise control).[280]

The recent case of *Conroy*[281] suggests that understanding the ability to form a rational judgement should not be 'over-refined'. The Court of Appeal held that the ability to form a rational judgement connotes not only rationality of outcome, but also rationality of thought process in achieving that outcome. All of a defendant's 'relevant circumstances preceding (and perhaps preceding over a very long period) the killing as well as any relevant circumstances following the killing',[282] can be taken into account. The judge instructed the jury to ask if the thought process leading to that was irrational, and whether his ability rationally to form a judgement had been substantially impaired. On appeal, D submitted that the summing up had significantly misdirected the jury because s 2 of the 1957 Act refers to the 'ability to form a rational judgment', requiring some rationality as to the final judgment,

---

[276] See Mackay, n 217. [277] LC 304, para 5.21.

[278] To reflect the provision as enacted we must amend the example so that he has an *abnormality* of mental functioning.

[279] Hansard, HL, 30 June 2009, vol 712, col 180.

[280] At [33]. Note that the defence also requires proof of the recognized medical condition, etc.

[281] [2017] EWCA Crim 81, [37]. [282] ibid, [32].

not the 'ability rationally to form a judgment'. The Court of Appeal dismissed the appeal and stated:

As it seems to us, while of course any jury will need in the light of the available psychiatric evidence to assess a defendant's thinking processes in the context of assessing his ability to form a rational judgment, it is likely to be over-refined to divorce that consideration relating to a defendant's think-ing processes from the actual outcome. Indeed, in some cases it may actually be extremely difficult to separate out the thought processes on the one hand from the 'outcome' on the other hand. In some cases it may well be that the two may be entirely enmeshed. In our view, there is a potential danger in a direction such as this straying beyond what is actually stated in section 2 itself. The ele-ments of section 2 should so far as possible not be glossed in a summing-up to the jury.[283]

The courts seem willing to take a wide interpretation of what constitutes a substantial impairment of the ability to form a rational judgement. In *Blackman*,[284] for example, the Court Martial Appeal Court (CMAC) found that, despite B's immediate recognition and admission that his actions constituted a breach of the Geneva Convention, his ability to form a rational judgement was substantially impaired.

The ability to exercise control

This might be construed very much more widely and render the defence available in a broader range of circumstances than under (1) and (2). As Rudi Fortson points out, it might be difficult to distinguish between cases of actual impairment of D's ability to exercise self-control from cases where D chose not to control his conduct.[285] It was acknowledged in *Blackman* that the defendant's ability to exercise self-control may be sufficiently impaired even where no loss of self-control is externally discernible. In that case, despite the delib-erate nature of B's actions, the CMAC still felt that he had exhibited a substantial loss of self-control.

(4) An explanation for (or cause of) the killing

The defence is narrowed by the further requirement that the abnormality of mental func-tioning, arising from a 'recognised medical condition' substantially impairing D's ability in a relevant manner must also 'explain' his acts in killing. By s 2(1B) 'an explanation' for D's conduct is provided 'if it causes, or is a significant contributory factor in causing, D to carry out that conduct'. Several problems arise. Section 2(1B) does not say that for the defence to succeed a sufficient explanation can *only* be provided if the abnormality of mental function-ing is a 'cause'.[286] On this basis, a causal link is just one of the ways in which the killing might be explained. It has been suggested that the medical experts could agree that all the other elements of the defence are present, but then disagree about the presence of this one. Mackay argues that one way of circumventing this difficulty is for the courts to interpret this provision so that once all the other elements are established it is assumed that it is pre-sent also, unless there is evidence to the contrary.[287]

Although the wording of s 2(1B) might lend itself to the argument that the subsection provides merely one way in which the killing might be 'explained', the language of the debates was clearly envisaging a causal link, although not necessarily 'but for' causation. In

---

[283] Per Davis LJ at [37].   [284] [2017] EWCA Crim 190 (CMAC).

[285] R Fortson, 'The Modern Partial Defence of Diminished Responsibility' in A Reed and M Bohlander (eds), *Loss of Control and Diminished Responsibility* (2011). As he also points out, given that the burden of proof is on the defendant, the problem weighs most heavily on his shoulders.

[286] See further *Blackstone's Criminal Practice* (2018) B1.

[287] See R Mackay, 'The New Diminished Responsibility Plea: More than Mere Modernisation?' in A Reed and M Bohlander (eds), *Loss of Control and Diminished Responsibility*.

describing this element of the partial defence, the Supreme Court in *Golds* also used language that connoted the existence of some causal link. There may be cases where the abnormality provides an explanation sufficient to mitigate the conduct to manslaughter even if there is no causal link. In debates, the minister stated that:

We do not believe that the partial defence should succeed where random coincidence has brought together the activity of the person and the recognised medical condition.... *there must have been at least a significant contributory factor in causing the defendant to act as he did. We do not require the defence to prove that it was the only cause or the main cause or the most important factor, but there must be something that is more than a merely trivial factor.*[288]

Even if it is accepted that there must be some causal link, it is clear that the abnormality of mental functioning, etc need not be the sole cause of the killing. The Law Commission was clear that, for example, provocation might also be a relevant factor that caused D to kill. The government agreed with the Law Commission that it would be 'impracticable to require abnormality to be the sole explanation [for D's acts]' and that there must be 'some connection between the condition and the killing in order for the partial defence to be justified'.[289]

Some commentators suggest[290] that it seems that s 2(1B) is merely giving effect to the interpretation of the old s 2 in *Dietschmann*[291] and *Fenton*.[292] Under the old law, in *Dietschmann*[293] D killed the victim while D was heavily intoxicated. He was also suffering from a mental abnormality which all the medical witnesses described as an adjustment disorder arising from a 'depressed grief reaction' to the death of his aunt with whom he had a close physical and emotional relationship. In the House of Lords, Lord Hutton stressed that:[294] 'even if the defendant would not have killed if he had not taken drink, the causative effect of the drink does not necessarily prevent an abnormality of mind suffered by the defendant from substantially impairing his mental responsibility for his fatal acts'.[295] In other words, even if a factor (in that case, alcohol) other than the abnormality was the principal cause of the defendant killing V, the defence would be available. Adopting that approach to the amended section, it would not matter that the abnormality of mental functioning from a recognized medical condition was not the principal cause of the killing. The Court of Appeal in *Kay and Joyce* stated that the killing must be caused by, or significantly caused by, the recognized medical condition. Therefore, an intoxicated defendant who would have killed even if he had not been suffering an abnormality will not be entitled to the defence.

Some commentators challenge the need for any causal element. Why should D have to prove a causal link given that the abnormality of mental functioning must be proved under s 2(1A) to have substantially impaired D's ability to understand his conduct or form a rational judgement or exercise control *in relation to the acts or omissions*, that is, killing?[296]

Intoxicated defendants

The issue of the extent to which there must be a causal link between the abnormal mental functioning and the killing is most likely to arise in cases where D kills when he suffers from

---

[288] Hansard, HC, 4 Mar 2009, col 416. Emphasis added.

[289] CP 19/08, para 51; and see Hansard, HC, 3 Mar 2009, col 414 (Maria Eagle).

[290] For discussion, see R Fortson, 'The Modern Partial Defence of Diminished Responsibility' in A Reed and M Bohlander (eds), *Loss of Control and Diminished Responsibility* (2011).

[291] [2003] 1 AC 1209, HL.   [292] (1975) 61 Cr App R 261, CA; *Gittins* [1984] QB 698, CA.

[293] [2003] 1 AC 1209, [2003] Crim LR 550.

[294] Note that this case did not involve alcohol dependence syndrome.   [295] At [18].

[296] See Mackay [2010] Crim LR 299 and n 287.

an abnormality of mental functioning and at the time of the killing D had also taken alcohol or other intoxicants.

As noted, in *Dietschmann* the House of Lords accepted that if a voluntarily intoxicated defendant kills, he is entitled to rely on diminished responsibility if the elements of the defence are made out even though he was intoxicated at the time of the killing. Subsequently in *Wood*[297] the Court of Appeal applied this reasoning to a case where D was suffering from alcohol dependency syndrome. D stated that giving in to his alcohol craving was not an involuntary act, and argued that an alcoholic not suffering from severe withdrawal symptoms who chose to accept a drink after he reached his normal quota was not drinking 'involuntarily'.[298] The Court of Appeal held that in light of the decision in *Dietschmann* it was wrong to imply that unless the jury were of the opinion that every drink consumed by D was involuntary his alcohol dependency syndrome had to be disregarded. That was too strict an approach. The jury could have regard to D's alcoholism in considering the plea of diminished responsibility even if not every drink consumed that day by D was involuntary.[299]

The position under the new form of the defence was considered by the Court of Appeal in *Kay and Joyce*, in which the court confirmed that 'the law does not debar someone suffering from schizophrenia [the medical condition in this case] from relying on the partial defence of diminished responsibility where voluntary intoxication has triggered the psychotic state, but he must meet the criteria in section 2(1)'.[300] The court held that the authorities in *Dietschmann* and *Wood* apply with equal force to the amended version of diminished responsibility as they did under the former version. On the facts, there was no medical evidence available to K to show that his underlying illness was of such a degree that, independent of drug or alcohol abuse, it impaired his responsibility substantially. Therefore, once the jury rejected the defence's assertion that K was suffering from alcohol dependency syndrome, he no longer had a defence.

Applying the policy behind *Dietschmann* and *Wood*, as endorsed with reference to the amended defence in *Kay and Joyce*,[301] the position is as follows:

(1) Where D has no medical condition other than acute intoxication, he cannot rely on the defence as there is no recognized medical condition: *Dowds*.

(2) Where D suffers from a recognized medical condition other than alcohol dependency syndrome and is voluntarily intoxicated at the time of the killing,[302] the defence will succeed if: D proves that, ignoring his voluntary intoxication, he suffered an abnormality of mental functioning arising from a 'recognised medical condition' so as to substantially impair his ability in a relevant way, and that abnormality of mental functioning was a cause, or a significant contributing factor, of the conduct by which D killed. D should be entitled to the defence even if D might not have killed had he been sober, provided the abnormality of mental functioning arising from the 'recognised medical condition' nevertheless 'explains' or 'causes' his conduct in killing.

(3) Where D suffers from a recognized medical condition in the form of alcohol dependency syndrome and is intoxicated at the time of the killing, the same approach should

---

[297] [2008] EWCA Crim 1305. See also *Stewart* [2010] EWCA Crim 2159.

[298] The trial judge directed in accordance with *Tandy* [1989] 1 All ER 267 which drew distinctions between alcoholism that caused brain damage and otherwise. For critical comment see J Tolmie, 'Alcoholism and Criminal Liability' (2001) 64 MLR 688.

[299] This approach was more confirmed as being the correct one in *Williams* [2013] EWCA Crim 2749, a reference by the CCRC under the old law.

[300] [2017] EWCA Crim 647, [16].

[301] [2017] EWCA Crim. See K Laird, '*R v Kay and Joyce*' [2017] Crim LR 881.

[302] But not suffering from acute intoxication which is not a recognized medical condition.

be taken. The jury should be entitled to have regard to the alcohol dependency syndrome and D's intoxication, leaving out of account, insofar as it is possible, his voluntary intoxication. D is entitled to the defence if he proves he suffered an abnormality of mental functioning arising from a 'recognised medical condition' so as to substantially impair his ability in a relevant way, and that abnormality of mental functioning explains or was a cause of the conduct by which D killed.

(4) In categories (2) and (3), if an intoxicated defendant with a recognized medical condition would have killed even if he had not had an abnormality of mental functioning, the availability of the defence depends on whether s 2(1B) is interpreted as requiring proof of a causal link in every case. If a causal link is required, a voluntarily intoxicated defendant who would have killed even if he had not been suffering an abnormality will not be entitled to the defence. If, on the other hand, s 2(1B) is interpreted as meaning that the abnormality might explain the killing even if it did not cause it, the defence may be available. This is most likely to be relevant where the ability substantially impaired under s 2(1A) 'was D's ability to form a rational judgement rather than to exercise self-control'.[303]

The amendment to s 2 of the 1957 Act by the 2009 Act does not diminish the authority of cases such as *Byrne* and *Dix*,[304] confirming that medical evidence was a 'practical necessity' if the defence were to succeed.[305] This has been confirmed in *Bunch*[306] and more recently by the Privy Council's advice to the Queen in the Jamaican case of *Brown*.[307]

Must D's medical condition cause the killing?

As to proof of a causal link generally, in many cases the causal link between the abnormality of mental functioning and D's act of killing, or being a party to the killing, may be self-evident. It is not going to be easy to prove that an intoxicated defendant with an abnormality of mind would have killed even if he had not had an abnormality of mental functioning.[308] Some commentators have questioned whether 'from a psychiatric perspective proving even a contributory causal link can be extremely difficult, if not impossible, to do in practice'.[309] Moreover, although the Royal College of Psychiatrists did not object to the requirement, it cautioned against 'creating a situation in which experts might be called on to "demonstrate" causation on a scientific basis, rather than indicating, from an assessment of the nature of the abnormality, what its likely impact would be on thinking, emotion, volition, and so forth'.[310]

The prior fault policy

The Court of Appeal's approach to intoxication and diminished responsibility is heavily influenced by the policy against allowing D to rely on his intoxicated state when it is self-induced. It is unclear, however, how fair that policy can be when it is taken in priority to the recognition of the medical condition.

The following situations may arise:

(1) D is acutely intoxicated and that is the sole claim of a recognized medical condition—no defence: *Dowds* adopting the prior fault policy.

---

[303] See further *Blackstone's Criminal Practice* (2018) Part B1, 24.

[304] [1960] 2 QB 396 and (1982) 74 Cr App R 306 respectively.   [305] At [11].

[306] [2013] EWCA Crim 2498.   [307] [2016] UKPC 6.

[308] Even if D made an admission to that effect, how much reliance is to be placed on a confession made by someone who has an abnormality of mental functioning?

[309] J Miles, 'A Dog's Breakfast of Homicide Reform' [2009] 6 Arch News 8 and see the speech of Baroness Murphy, Hansard, HL, 30 June 2009, cols 177–180.

[310] LC 304, para 5.123.

(2) D suffers from a recognized medical condition and is intoxicated at the time of the killing—defence may be available: *Dietschmann, Kay,* etc. D's recognized medical condition is not ousted by his also being voluntarily intoxicated.

(3) D's recognized medical condition was caused by his chronic substance misuse (eg he has developed alcohol dependency syndrome) and D was intoxicated at the time of the killing—defence may be available (this is merely an example of (2), but in the context of D's sustained 'fault' in his substance abuse bringing about the recognized medical condition).

(4) An underlying recognized medical condition suffered by D is triggered by his voluntary intoxication. For example, D has schizophrenia and is aware of that fact. He takes drugs voluntarily and triggers a schizophrenic episode. In such a case the defence is available, even if D was warned that taking drugs may trigger the schizophrenia: *Kay.*

(5) D's voluntary intoxication causes a recognized medical condition (eg drug induced psychosis) where there was no pre-existing recognized medical condition—no defence: *Dowds; Lindo.*

It may seem odd that D can rely on the defence in (3) despite the fact that his sustained prior fault caused the recognized medical condition. It may also seem odd that D can rely on the defence in (4) where there is a considerable degree of prior fault in D triggering an existing recognized medical condition, but not in (5). Is the degree of prior fault in (5) that much greater than (4), or even (3)? It is submitted that these issues merit further consideration by the Court of Appeal.

13.2.2.2 The role of the expert and the jury

There is no statutory requirement of medical evidence, as there is with insanity, but surely the jury may not find that D is suffering from diminished responsibility unless there is medical evidence of a recognized medical condition and abnormality of mental functioning.[311] Indeed, in *Brennan*[312] Davis LJ stated that, 'most, if not all, of the aspects of the new provisions relate entirely to psychiatric matters. In our view it is both legitimate and helpful, given the structure of the new provisions, for an expert psychiatrist to include in his or her evidence a view on all four stages'. Under the old law, as with insanity,[313] whether the defence succeeded was a decision to be made by the jury, not the medical experts. They could reject unanimous medical evidence that D is suffering from diminished responsibility if there is nothing in the circumstances of the case to prevent them doing so.[314] The extent to which the jury remains free to do this will be considered later.

Under the old law, the 'abnormality of mind' element was a matter on which the psychiatric evidence was likely to be highly persuasive, but because the concept was a vague one, there was still an opportunity for the jury to apply its own understanding of the concept. Similarly, the crucial element of the old s 2 test involved moral rather than medical or legal evaluation: the 'substantial impairment' related not just to D's mental state, but to his 'responsibility'. In contrast, under the amended partial defence the expert may be offering opinions on: (a) whether there is an abnormality of mental functioning; (b) whether

---

[311] Medical evidence was required under the old law, indeed it was described as being a 'practical necessity' because the onus is placed on the defendant: *Byrne* [1960] 2 QB 396 at 402; *Dix* (1981) 74 Cr App R 306 at 311. The Court of Appeal in *Bunch* [2013] EWCA Crim 2498 confirmed the continued validity of *Byrne.* For further discussion, see T Storey, 'Diminished Responsibility: No Defence Without Evidence' (2014) 78 J Crim L 113.

[312] [2014] EWCA Crim 2387, [51].   [313] See p 305.

[314] eg *Salmon* [2005] EWCA Crim 70; *Eifinger* [2001] EWCA Crim 1855; cf the position if there is uncontradicted expert evidence and no other live issue: *Sanders* [1991] Crim LR 781. See generally LCCP 177, para 6.99.

729

there is a recognized medical condition; (c) whether D had a substantial impairment of ability to understand/form a rational judgement/exercise control; and (d) whether it is a cause or explanation for the killing. The Royal College of Psychiatrists expressed the view that medical experts ought not to be called upon to express an opinion on the 'ultimate issue'.[315] However, it is submitted that, in practice, it will often be difficult for an expert not to express an opinion from which it will be possible for the jury to draw a very clear inference as to the ultimate issue.

On one view, since the elements of the defence are now *all* capable of being subject to an opinion from an expert, there is much less, if anything, for the jury to consider, particularly if there was uncontradicted medical evidence for the defence. On the other hand, the courts may well continue to take the view that although the elements of the defence are now all capable of being subject to strong opinion evidence from an expert, the ultimate issue remains one for the jury. They must consider all the evidence, and the opinion of the expert is only that: an opinion. As was noted under the old law in *Walton v The Queen*:[316]

upon an issue of diminished responsibility the jury are entitled and indeed bound to consider not only the medical evidence but the evidence upon the whole facts and circumstances of the case.[317]

The Court of Appeal confronted this issue with reference to the amended partial defence in *Brennan*[318] and the Supreme Court considered it in *Golds*.

In *Brennan*, D was convicted of murder despite the fact that there was uncontradicted evidence from the experts that all the elements of the partial defence were satisfied. There was some evidence to suggest that V's murder was well planned. The defence expert, who was the only expert called, stated that such planning was not inconsistent with her finding that all the elements of the partial defence were satisfied, rather it was a facet of the mental condition from which D was suffering. Davis LJ characterized the case as one that brought to the fore two conflicting, but equally fundamental, principles. The first is that the ultimate issue on whether the partial defence is satisfied is a matter for the jury. The second is that the jury must base its verdict upon the evidence.[319] Davis LJ held that the experts can and should express a view on the ultimate issue. After reviewing the authorities analysed in this section, his lordship held that the judge ought to withdraw the murder charge from the jury if (a) the expert evidence is uncontested and (b) there is no other evidence which, looked at in the round, is at least capable of rebutting the defence.[320] In relation to this latter point, Davis LJ stated that even if there is some other evidence that might rebut the defence, there might be instances when that other evidence is too tenuous or, even if taken at its highest, is simply insufficient to permit a rational rejection of the partial defence.

In *Golds*,[321] the Supreme Court examined the reasoning in *Brennan*. The court commented, *obiter*, on the circumstances in which a judge should withdraw murder from the jury where there is uncontradicted medical evidence of diminished responsibility. The court made the preliminary observation that if a murder trial is contested, it is of considerable importance that the verdict be that of the jury. Therefore, despite the more medicalized nature of the amended partial defence, the Supreme Court affirmed in unequivocal terms that it is for the jury to determine whether all the elements are satisfied. The court also observed that the presence of a causal link between the mental abnormality and the killing and whether the impairment was substantial are elements of the partial defence that are essentially jury questions.

---

[315] Paras 5.118–5.120; and see *Khan* [2009] EWCA Crim 1569.   [316] [1978] AC 788, PC.

[317] Lord Keith (at 793F), and see *Khan* [2009] EWCA Crim 1569, noting, in particular, the observations of the court at [18].

[318] [2014] EWCA Crim 2387.   [319] At [43]–[44].   [320] At [65]–[66].

[321] [2016] UKSC 61.

Lord Hughes offered the following, valuable guidance:

Where, however, in a diminished responsibility trial the medical evidence supports the plea and is uncontradicted, the judge needs to ensure that the Crown explains the basis on which it is inviting the jury to reject that evidence. He needs to ensure that the basis advanced is one which the jury can properly adopt. If the facts of the case give rise to it, he needs to warn the jury that brutal killings may be the product of disordered minds and that planning, whilst it may be relevant to self- control, may well be consistent with disordered thinking. While he needs to make it clear to the jury that, if there is a proper basis for rejecting the expert evidence, the decision is theirs—that trial is by jury and not by expert—it will also ordinarily be wise to advise the jury against attempting to make themselves amateur psychiatrists, and that if there is undisputed expert evidence the jury will probably wish to accept it, unless there is some identified reason for not doing so. To this extent, the approach of the court in *Brennan* is to be endorsed.[322]

The point was reiterated subsequently in *Blackman*, in which the Lord Chief Justice emphasized that the judge should exercise caution before accepting the applicability of the partial defence and removing the murder charge from the jury. It was held that the fact the prosecution call no evidence to contradict a psychiatrist called by the defence is not in itself sufficient justification for the judge to take that course of action. His lordship stated that, 'it will be a rare case where a judge will exercise the power to withdraw a charge of murder from the jury when the prosecution do not accept that the evidence gives rise to the defence of diminished responsibility'.[323] These judgments demonstrate that despite the more medicalized nature of the partial defence, the crucial function of determining whether all the elements are satisfied rests firmly with the jury.

13.2.2.3 Procedural relationship with insanity

One might assume that defendants charged with murder who have killed with malice aforethought would prefer a conviction for manslaughter on the ground of diminished responsibility to an acquittal by reason of insanity, and that would explain why reliance on the M'Naghten Rules has been greatly reduced since 1957 (see Ch 9). Where D, being charged with murder, raises the defence of diminished responsibility and the Crown have evidence that he is insane within the M'Naghten Rules, they may adduce or elicit evidence tending to show that this is so. This is now settled by s 6 of the Criminal Procedure (Insanity and Unfitness to Plead) Act 1964[324]—resolving a conflict in the cases. That Act also provides for the converse situation: where D sets up insanity, the prosecution may contend that he was suffering only from diminished responsibility.[325] The roles of the prosecution and defence may be strangely reversed, according to which of them are contending that D is insane. It seems clear in principle that the Crown must establish whichever contention it puts forward is beyond reasonable doubt.[326] It must follow that D rebuts the Crown's case if he can raise a doubt. Where D relies on some other defence, such as loss of self-control, and evidence of diminished responsibility emerges, it seems that the most the judge should do is to draw the attention of D's counsel to it.[327] Diminished responsibility is an 'optional defence'. The defences of loss of self-control and diminished responsibility

---

322 At [51].   323 [2017] EWCA Crim 190 (CMAC), [43].

324 By s 52(2) of the 2009 Act, 'In section 6 of the Criminal Procedure (Insanity) Act 1964 (c. 84) (evidence by prosecution of insanity or diminished responsibility), in paragraph (b) for "mind" substitute "mental functioning".'

325 It had been so held at common law by Elwes J in *Nott* (1958) 43 Cr App R 8.

326 *Grant* [1960] Crim LR 424, per Paull J.

327 *Campbell* (1986) 84 Cr App R 255 at 259–260; *Kooken* (1981) 74 Cr App R 30.

overlap in some respects,[328] and this can lead to a complex decision regarding trial tactics since the defences carry differing burdens. Similarly, a jury will have to be directed carefully on the respective burdens.

Where the defence rely on D's abnormal state of mind of whatever kind, it is open to the prosecution to allege, and to call evidence to prove, that the abnormality amounts to insanity or diminished responsibility and it is submitted this is so even where D is alleging that he was an automaton. This view is supported by the fact that the CLRC[329] was of the view that the prosecution could call evidence in cases such as *Kemp*.[330] The prosecution may not, however, lead evidence of D's insanity where the defence have not put the abnormality of D's mind in issue,[331] even though this course is desired by the defence.

Sentencing

The sentence available to the judge is discretionary with the maximum sentence being life imprisonment. The available disposals on conviction are not something for the jury's consideration: *Edgington*.[332]

---

[328] On the merits of such overlap and a potential merging of the defences under the old law before the 2009 Act, see Mackay and Mitchell [2003] Crim LR 745; Chalmers [2004] Crim LR 198; Gardner and Macklem [2004] Crim LR 213; Mackay and Mitchell [2004] Crim LR 219.

[329] (1963) Cmnd 2149, para 41.   [330] See p 294.

[331] *Dixon* [1961] 3 All ER 460n, [1961] 1 WLR 337, per Jones J.   [332] [2013] EWCA Crim 2185.

14

Involuntary manslaughter

In the previous chapter we considered those categories of manslaughter in which the defendant has been proved to have killed with the mens rea for murder, but has a partial defence which results in a manslaughter verdict. In this chapter we consider the other forms of manslaughter—known collectively as involuntary manslaughter. This category of manslaughter includes varieties of homicide which are unlawful at common law but committed without the mens rea for murder. Given the breadth of cases that involuntary manslaughter must cover, it is not surprising that more than one form of the offence has evolved, and that the elements of each form of involuntary manslaughter are distinct, particularly as to the fault required. Equally, as the limits of the mens rea for murder are uncertain, it follows inevitably that there is a corresponding uncertainty at the boundary between murder and manslaughter. The difficulties do not end there, for there is another vague borderline between manslaughter and accidental death. Indeed, Lord Atkin said that:[1]

of all crimes manslaughter appears to afford most difficulties of definition, for it concerns homicide in so many and so varying conditions...the law...recognizes murder on the one hand based mainly, though not exclusively,[2] on an intention to kill, and manslaughter on the other hand, based mainly, though not exclusively,[3] on the absence of intent to kill, but with the presence of an element of 'unlawfulness' which is the elusive factor.

This ambiguity is unfortunate, since the offence is one of the most serious in the criminal calendar and carries a maximum life sentence. The upper and lower limits of the offence remain obscure, and there is little internal coherence between the forms of manslaughter currently recognized—other than the fact that D causes a death. Lumping together the many different types of behaviour that give rise to an unintentional unlawful killing under one label is unsatisfactory in principle, and can engender unmerited disparities in sentencing.[4] The Law Commission concluded that the offence of manslaughter was at risk of being devalued by being left as a 'residual, amorphous, "catch–all" homicide offence'.[5]

The forms of manslaughter overlap considerably. There are four broad categories of involuntary manslaughter:

(1) manslaughter by an unlawful and dangerous act;

(2) manslaughter by gross negligence;

(3) manslaughter by subjective recklessness;

(4) statutory corporate manslaughter.

The constituents of each of these categories require some degree of analysis.

---

[1] In *Andrews v DPP* [1937] AC 576 at 581, [1937] 2 All ER 552 at 554–555.

[2] See p 513.   [3] See p 521.

[4] See M Wasik, 'Form and Function in the Law of Involuntary Manslaughter' [1994] Crim LR 883.

[5] LC 304, para 2.9. To avoid drawing an arbitrary line between murder and manslaughter, the Commission recommended a middle tier of second degree murder. See Ch 12. For an argument that there ought to be aggravated murder and aggravated manslaughter to reflect different forms of killing, see C Elliot and C de Than (2009) 20 *King's College Journal* 69.

14.1 Manslaughter by an unlawful and dangerous act

The modern form of this offence has evolved from a very harsh one dating to at least the seventeenth century. The institutional writer Coke stated that an intention to commit *any* unlawful act was a sufficient mens rea for murder,[6] so that if D shot at V's hen with intent to kill it and accidentally killed V by the shot, this was murder, 'for the act was unlawful'. This savage doctrine was criticized by Holt CJ[7] and by the time Foster wrote his *Crown Law*,[8] it appears to have been modified by the proviso that to constitute murder the unlawful act which D intended to carry out had to be a felony (and not merely a misdemeanour or civil law wrong such as a tort). So, if D shot at the hen intending to steal it (a felony), the killing of V was murder even though D did not intend to kill any human. This doctrine of 'constructive murder' existed until the Homicide Act 1957. Alongside this doctrine of constructive murder, there existed a parallel doctrine of constructive manslaughter: any death caused while in the course of committing an unlawful act, other than a felony, was manslaughter. An act was unlawful for this purpose even if it was only a tort, so that the only mens rea which needed to be proved was an intention to commit the tort.

The present law is that D is guilty of unlawful act manslaughter (UAM) if he kills by an unlawful and dangerous act. The only mens rea required is an intention to do the unlawful act and any fault required to render it unlawful. It is irrelevant that D is unaware that it is unlawful or that it is dangerous.[9] It is enough that a reasonable and sober person would have been aware of the danger in the sense of a risk of some harm (not necessarily serious harm) to a person.[10] The offence is heavily and cogently criticized because of this constructive element by which D's liability for manslaughter turns on the consequence of death, which will often be unforeseen by D and indeed be regarded as a matter of 'bad luck' beyond his control.[11] The offender is labelled as a manslaughterer when he might only have foreseen, if at all, a risk of *some minor harm* being caused.[12]

It is a notoriously difficult crime to apply. A good starting point is to ask what offence D would have been charged with had no one died. That is the unlawful act on which the manslaughter may be constructed.

The crime comprises:[13]

(1) an unlawful act;

(2) intentionally performed;

(3) in circumstances rendering it dangerous;

(4) causing death.

---

6 Co 3 Inst 56. See Turner, MACL, 195 at 212 et seq for a discussion of the historical development.

7 *Keate* (1697) Comb 406 at 409.   8 *Discourses* (1762).

9 *Newbury* [1977] AC 500; *Ball* [1989] Crim LR 730; *JF* [2015] EWCA Crim 351.

10 *Watson* [1989] 2 All ER 865, [1989] Crim LR 733.

11 See RA Duff, 'Whose Luck is it Anyway?' in C Clarkson and S Cunningham (eds), *Criminal Liability for Non-Aggressive Death* (2008). See generally on liability for consequences, A Ashworth, 'Taking the Consequences' in S Shute, J Gardner and J Horder (eds), *Action and Value in Criminal Law* (1993).

12 On the issue generally, see G Williams, 'Convictions and Fair Labelling' (1983) 42 CLJ 85; B Mitchell, 'In Defence of a Principle of Correspondence' [1999] Crim LR 195; cf J Horder, 'A Critique of the Correspondence Principle in Criminal Law' [1995] Crim LR 759 and 'Questioning the Correspondence Principle: A Reply' [1999] Crim LR 206. See also the criticism in LC 304, paras 3.42 et seq.

13 Per Lord Hope, *A-G's Reference (No 3 of 1994)* [1998] AC 830. Numerous cases have relied upon this formulation of the offence, for examples see *Webster v CPS* [2014] EWHC 2516 (Admin) and *Bristow* [2013] EWCA Crim 1540.

As a simple example, consider D who throws a stone at V's greenhouse intending to break the window or being reckless as to the window being broken. V is kneeling close to the greenhouse tending his plants when the pane of glass shatters and a shard penetrates his eye and kills him. There is an unlawful act (criminal damage), the act (throwing the stone) is intentionally performed, the reasonable and sober person would consider that there was a risk of some harm (not necessarily serious harm) to V by D's actions, and V's death is caused. D is guilty of manslaughter. The offence is commonly prosecuted where D has thrown a punch at V or scuffled with V in a drunken dispute.[14] If V falls as a result of the, perhaps minor, contact and on hitting his head V dies, D will be liable for manslaughter even though he intended or was reckless as to an assault. Several elements require further examination.

14.1.1 The unlawfulness

Issues requiring elaboration are whether the unlawful act must: (a) be criminal; (b) involve a completed crime; (c) be a crime of mens rea; (d) be one dependent on proof of an act, or whether an omission will suffice; (e) be a crime involving an offence against the person.

The current state of the law is that to be sufficient for unlawful act manslaughter, the unlawful act may be any criminal offence involving an act (but not an omission), with mens rea of more than mere negligence.

14.1.1.1 A crime

At one time it was thought that even a tort which led to a death was sufficiently unlawful to trigger this offence. In *Fenton*,[15] D was liable for manslaughter when he threw stones down a mine and broke some scaffolding which caused a wagon to overturn with fatal results. D's act was a trespass and the only question was whether it caused V's death. Even in the nineteenth century the judges were sometimes troubled by the harshness of this approach. Some judges refused to apply it. For example, in *Franklin*,[16] D, walking on Brighton pier, took up 'a good sized box' from a refreshment stall and threw it into the sea where it struck a swimmer, V, and killed him. The prosecution argued that apart from any question of negligence, it was manslaughter if the commission of the tort of trespass against the stall-keeper had caused death. Field J, after consulting Mathew J who agreed, held that the case must go to the jury 'on the broad ground of negligence'. Expressing his 'great abhorrence of constructive crime', Field J asserted that 'The mere fact of a civil wrong committed by one person against another ought not to be used as an incident which is a necessary step to a criminal case.'

It is clear that under the present law D's 'act' must be a crime to found liability for manslaughter. In *Kennedy (No 2)*,[17] the House of Lords affirmed that to establish the crime of unlawful act manslaughter it must be shown: (a) that the defendant committed an unlawful act; (b) that such unlawful act *was a crime*; and (c) *that the defendant's unlawful act was a significant cause of the death of the deceased*. A good rule of thumb, as noted, is to identify the criminal charge that could be laid against D if no one had died as a result of his conduct.

In *Lamb*,[18] D pointed a loaded gun at his friend, V, in jest. He did not intend to injure or alarm V and V was not alarmed. There was therefore no assault. Because they did not understand how a revolver works, both thought there was no danger in pulling the trigger; but, when D did so, he shot V dead. D was not guilty of a criminal assault or battery because he

---

[14] For critical comment on the offence in such cases see B Mitchell, 'More Thoughts about Unlawful and Dangerous Act Manslaughter and the One Punch Killer' [2009] Crim LR 502.

[15] (1830) 1 Lew CC 179.   [16] (1883) 15 Cox CC 163.   [17] [2007] UKHL 38.

[18] [1967] 2 QB 981. The case is a controversial one. Glanville Williams wrote that 'Lamb was a fool but there is no need to punish fools to that degree. There is no need to punish Lamb at all. He had killed his friend and that was punishment enough': 'Recklessness Redefined' (1981) 40 CLJ 252 at 281.

did not foresee that V would be alarmed or injured. It was, therefore, a misdirection to tell the jury that this was 'an unlawful and dangerous act'. Sachs LJ, stated that it was not 'unlawful in the criminal sense of the word'; and, referring to *Franklin*, 'it is not in point to consider whether an act is unlawful merely from the angle of civil liabilities'. This was confirmed by *Scarlett*.[19] D, a licensee, caused death by using excessive force while lawfully expelling a trespasser from his pub. His conviction for manslaughter was quashed because the judge had directed that D was guilty if he had committed a battery (used unnecessary and unreasonable force). What the judge should have said was that it was necessary to prove that the force used was excessive in the circumstances which D believed to exist[20]—that would be more than a mere tort of battery as D would then have the mens rea of the *crime* of battery.

The House of Lords in *DPP v Newbury*[21] appeared to cast doubt on these cases. D threw a piece of paving stone from a bridge as a train approached. It killed the driver. The House of Lords failed to identify any crime rendering D's act unlawful. Throwing concrete in this way certainly looks like a criminal act, which explains why it was not argued to be lawful before the House.[22] The question for the House was whether D could properly be convicted of manslaughter if he did not foresee that his act might cause harm to another. The question is then what crime D committed *with* mens rea. As we have already outlined, UAM can be committed if D commits a crime by an intentional act provided also that a reasonable and sober person would see the risk of some harm to a person. The question is not whether D foresaw death or a risk of injury. It is whether he had mens rea for the offence that he would have been charged with if no one had died. In *Newbury*, D's act was not, on the facts, an assault or any of the usual offences against the person, all of which require mens rea. The only other likely crimes with which D could be charged were the offence of endangering passengers contrary to s 34 of the OAPA 1861 or an offence of criminal damage.[23] The House did not specify what offence was the base crime on which manslaughter was constructed.

The better view, it is submitted, is that as in *Lamb* and *Scarlett*, a criminal act must be identified and proved. *Kennedy* (*No 2*) supports this requirement.

The ambiguity of the concept of an 'unlawful' act has sometimes led the courts to gloss over the requirement for proof of a criminal offence. In *Cato*,[24] D caused V's death by injecting him with heroin with his consent. The court accepted that this was not an offence under the Misuse of Drugs Act and assumed for this purpose that it was not an offence under s 23 of the OAPA 1861[25] but said 'the unlawful act would be described as injecting the deceased with a mixture of heroin and water which at the time of the injection and for the purposes of the injection Cato had unlawfully taken into his possession'. The act was closely associated with other acts which are offences but it is submitted that neither this nor any moral condemnation attaching to that act should be enough to found liability for manslaughter. In the light of the House of Lords decision in *Kennedy* (*No 2*), such reasoning is untenable.

14.1.1.2 The 'base' crime must be proved in full

The requirement of a criminal offence prompts a further question: whether it is necessary for the prosecution to establish all of the elements of the crime that would have been

---

[19] [1993] 4 All ER 629. The case must be read in the light of *Owino* [1995] Crim LR 743, p 384. See also *Jennings* [1990] Crim LR 588.

[20] *Gladstone Williams*, p 383.   [21] [1977] AC 500, [1976] 2 All ER 365.

[22] '... no question arose whether [Newbury's] actions were or were not unlawful': *Scarlett* [1993] 4 All ER at 635, per Beldam LJ.

[23] Using an offence against property seems as objectionable a basis for convicting of manslaughter as a tort (see later). There is no doubt criminal damage will suffice as the base offence: *JF* [2015] EWCA Crim 351.

[24] [1976] 1 All ER 260.

[25] See p 715. In fact D was convicted of the s 23 offence so the remarks discussed in the text may be *obiter*.

charged had no one died—that is, the 'base' crime on which the unlawful act manslaughter charge is constructed. In principled terms the element of 'unlawfulness' should require the prosecution to prove *all* the elements (mens rea and actus reus with no defence) of the base offence. Unfortunately, this apparently obvious interpretation of 'unlawful' has not been put completely beyond doubt by the case law.

It seems clear that the prosecution must prove the full mens rea of the base offence. In *Lamb*, the trial judge had directed the jury that it is an unlawful act 'whether or not it falls within any recognized category of crime'. The Court of Appeal found this to be a misdirection because '*mens rea* is now an essential element of the offence'.[26] The courts all too often gloss over this aspect, using language that implies that a mere voluntary act by D might suffice, as, for example, in *A-G's Reference (No 3 of 1994)*,[27] where Lord Hope referred to the requirement merely that D 'did what he did intentionally'.[28]

The proof of mens rea of the base offence is a necessary but not sufficient condition of unlawful act manslaughter. Where D, on facts similar to *Lamb*, thinks that the revolver is loaded and dangerous and he only intends to cause V to be frightened, but V does not apprehend violence because he does not believe the gun to be loaded, there is no complete assault. D has the mens rea, but the actus reus is not satisfied.[29] Again, it is submitted that a conviction for unlawful act manslaughter cannot be maintained.[30] In *Lamb* itself, L's conduct did not constitute an assault *both* because he lacked the mens rea (he had no intention to frighten, nor because of his common lack of understanding of the operation of the firearm was he reckless as to causing apprehension in his victim), and there was no actus reus because his friend, believing that the whole thing was a joke, had no apprehension of immediate unlawful violence.[31] The court was categorical as to '*mens rea* being now an essential element of the offence', and also accepted that counsel had put forward the correct view that for the 'act to be unlawful it must constitute at least what he then termed a technical assault'. Support also derives from *Arobieke*.[32] D pursued V onto railway lines 'looking for him'. V was killed. There was no evidence that D had actually threatened V, so no actus reus of assault could be established. The conviction for manslaughter was quashed.[33]

In addition to proving the mens rea and actus reus of the base offence, the prosecution must disprove any defences to the base offence raised by D.[34] If the defence itself is clearly defined, there is little difficulty in applying it in the unlawful act manslaughter context. Two particular problems fall for further discussion.

14.1.1.3 Problems of consent and unlawful act manslaughter

It is a matter of policy whether the law will recognize as valid the factual consent of an individual (ie an adult of full mental capacity), which leads to conduct where harm is intended

---

[26] At 986. See also *Reid* (1975) 62 Cr App R 109 (fright by threat to use firearm was sufficient).

[27] [1998] AC 245.   [28] Per Lord Hope, at 274.

[29] It may be possible to charge a battery. There is no crime of attempted assault since it is a summary only offence. This point was not argued in *Lewis* [2010] EWCA Crim 151.

[30] If these fractions of crimes are sufficient to form the basis for a UAM charge, that may tell us something about the underlying purpose of UAM. It would be clear that the punishment is based on the 'dangerousness' of the activity rather than on the technical 'unlawfulness'.

[31] *Bruce* (1847) Cox CC 262, Erle J supports this—on the facts no assault as no apprehension by V nor intent by D.

[32] [1988] Crim LR 314.

[33] Compare *Lewis* [2010] EWCA Crim 151 where D chased V and thereby assaulted him before V was knocked down.

[34] *Jennings* [1990] Crim LR 588; *Scarlett* (1994) 98 Cr App R 290.

or foreseen: *Brown*.[35] If D pleads that V consented to the base crime, that will be accepted where D's conduct falls within an established category for which V's consent is accepted in law; for example, boxing, surgery or horseplay. Since D commits no base crime as he has V's consent, there is no unlawful act manslaughter liability.[36] Similarly, where D has not intended that a consensual assault would lead to any greater degree of harm than the mere assault or battery consented to by V, there is no base offence and can be no manslaughter conviction: *Slingsby*.[37]

In *A*,[38] D's post-exam celebrations included throwing V into a river where he drowned. D claimed that he was entitled to a defence of belief in consent to the assault, his actions being mere horseplay. If he had consent to the assault there could be no manslaughter. The Court of Appeal confirmed that if D had caused V to fall in the river by a non-accidental act and D did not have a genuine belief in V's consent to the assault, D would be liable if all sober and reasonable people realized it was dangerous in the sense discussed later.

14.1.1.4 Problems of intoxication and the unlawful act

Where the prosecution rely on an unlawful act which does not require a specific intent (eg a base crime that can be committed recklessly) and D was intoxicated at the time, it is immaterial that he lacked the mens rea of the crime in question and even that he was unconscious: *Lipman*.[39] In this memorable case D killed V by cramming a sheet into her mouth and striking her while he was on an LSD 'trip' and believed he was in the centre of the earth being attacked by serpents.[40] The unlawful act—the base crime—was the battery committed on V while D was unconscious. That battery required only the mens rea of recklessness, it was therefore a crime of basic intent, and D's self-induced intoxication provided no excuse. His prior fault satisfied that mens rea requirement.

14.1.1.5 A crime of mens rea?

It is implicit in the decision in *Church*[41] that the base crime cannot be one where the fault is merely that D performed the act negligently. That case stipulates that for UAM the crime must involve an act which all sober and reasonable people would realize entailed the risk (ie an unjustifiable risk) of harm to others.[42] This is in accordance with the well-established rule that negligence sufficient to found liability in tort is not necessarily enough for criminal guilt and that death caused in the course of committing the tort of negligence is not

---

[35] [1994] AC 212; *A-G's Reference (No 6 of 1980)* [1981] QB 715.

[36] eg *Bruce* (1847) Cox CC 262 (no assault where D spun boy round in jest and killed V), and see Lord Mustill's speech in *Brown* [1994] AC 212 at 264. In *R v Morton* (14 July 2017, Nottingham CC) D was charged with unlawful act manslaughter having caused V's death by strangulation in the course of what he argued was consensual sex. Carr J left the issue of consent to the jury on the basis that the relevant authorities do not impose a blanket prohibition on consent being relevant to D's liability in such circumstances.

[37] [1995] Crim LR 570 (D injuring V with ring in course of consensual sexual touching, V dies of infection from wound).

[38] (2005) 69 J Crim L 394.

[39] [1970] 1 QB 152. The case was heavily criticized. See commentary by I Hooker [1969] Crim LR 547; G Orchard, 'Drunkenness, Drugs and Manslaughter' [1970] Crim LR 132; P Glazebrook, 'Constructive Manslaughter and the Threshold Tort' (1970) 28 CLJ 21; R Buxton, *Annual Survey of Commonwealth Law* (1970) 128 and 134. It was not followed in Australia: *Haywood* [1971] VR 755 (Crockett J) but was affirmed by the House of Lords in *Majewski* (p 315). Cf the decision in *Heard* [2007] EWCA Crim 125.

[40] Though the jury convicted on the grounds that D was reckless or grossly negligent when, quite consciously, he took the drugs, the Court of Appeal upheld the conviction by applying the *Church* doctrine (p 577).

[41] [1996] 1 QB 59.

[42] The reference to 'an unlawful act' would be otiose if it did not mean unlawful in some other respect than negligence.

necessarily manslaughter. Not only is it insufficient that D was negligent in civil law, it is insufficient for UAM if the unlawfulness of the criminal act arises *solely* from the negligent manner in which it is performed. Death caused by such an act will not necessarily be manslaughter. This follows from the decision of the House of Lords in *Andrews v DPP*.[43] In that case Du Parcq J told the jury that if D killed V in the course of dangerous driving contrary to s 11 of the Road Traffic Act 1930, he was guilty of manslaughter. Lord Atkin (who clearly regarded dangerous driving in the 1930 Act as a crime of negligence)[44] said that, if the summing up had rested there, there would have been misdirection:

There can be no doubt that this section covers driving with such a high degree of negligence as that, if death were caused, the offender would have committed manslaughter. But the converse is not true, and it is perfectly possible that a man may drive at a speed or in a manner dangerous to the public, and cause death, and yet not be guilty of manslaughter.[45]

Lord Atkin expressly distinguished[46] between acts which are unlawful because of the negligent manner in which they are performed and acts which are unlawful for some other reason:

There is an obvious difference in the law of manslaughter between doing an unlawful act and doing a lawful act with a degree of carelessness which the legislature makes criminal.

His lordship's next sentence implies that killing in the course of unlawful acts generally *was* manslaughter:

If it were otherwise a man who killed another while driving without due care and attention would *ex necessitate* commit manslaughter.

This passage has been severely criticized[47] and it is certainly unhappily phrased: 'doing a lawful act with a degree of carelessness which the legislature makes criminal' is a contradiction in terms, for the act so done is plainly not a lawful act. But the distinction evidently intended, *viz*, between acts which are unlawful because of negligent performance and acts which are unlawful for some other reason, is at least intelligible and, in view of the established distinction between civil and criminal negligence, a necessary limitation.

The natural reading of Lord Atkin's opinion is that the distinction is between acts which are unlawful because of negligent performance and acts which are unlawful for some other reason. An alternative (strained, but more attractive) reading is that only crimes of more than mere negligence will suffice to ground an unlawful act manslaughter conviction. This is supported by the comments of Sachs LJ in *Lamb*: '*mens rea* being now an essential ingredient in manslaughter'.[48]

This issue was confronted recently at first instance. In the case of *R v Alliston*, D was charged with unlawful act manslaughter after V died as a result of his bicycle colliding with her as she was crossing the road.[49] The unlawful act relied upon by the Crown was the offence of riding a bicycle on a public road without a front brake contrary to s 91 of the Road Traffic Offenders Act 1988 in conjunction with regs 6 and 7 of the Pedal Cycles (Construction and

---

43 [1937] AC 576.

44 See Ch 32. The offence of dangerous driving was abolished by the Criminal Law Act 1977 but restored in a new form by the Road Traffic Act 1991, s 2.

45 [1937] AC 576 at 584.   46 ibid, 585.

47 Turner, MACL, 238. Referred to by Devlin as 'the only obscure speech the great Lord Atkin ever made': 'Criminal Responsibility and Punishment: Function of Judge and Jury' [1954] Crim LR 661 at 672.

48 [1967] 2 QB 981 at 988.

49 See BBC News Online, 'Cyclist detained over pedestrian death', 18 Sept 2017 at www.bbc.co.uk/news/uk-england-41306738.

Use) Regulations 1983. HHJ Joseph QC accepted the prosecution's argument that there was nothing in the authorities to the effect that something more than a strict liability or 'regulatory offence' is necessary to establish the base offence of unlawful act manslaughter. She therefore concluded that there was no prohibition in law on a prosecution for unlawful act manslaughter being based upon the offence found in s 91 of the 1988 Act.[50]

Despite the existence of authorities to the contrary, as a matter of principle, it is submitted that the offence should be read restrictively and should be based on offences that require mens rea proper.[51] Gross negligence manslaughter is more than broad enough to deal with cases in which deaths are caused in other culpable circumstances.

A further issue which then arises is whether if it is insufficient to construct a manslaughter charge on a base crime of mere negligence, it is acceptable to construct such a charge on a base crime of strict liability. The issue has not been directly addressed by the courts.[52] In the case of *Andrews*,[53] D gave V, with her consent, an injection of insulin in order to give her a 'rush'. V, who was also voluntarily intoxicated at the time, died as a result of the injection of insulin. D appealed against his conviction on the basis that the judge was wrong to rule that he would direct the jury that V's consent to the injection did not render D's act lawful. The Court of Appeal upheld the conviction, holding that ss 58(2)(b) and 67 of the Medicines Act 1968 made D's act unlawful because no consent could be pleaded to that offence. The fact that these offences are of strict liability was not challenged in the appeal.

14.1.1.6 Omissions as 'unlawful acts'

In *Lowe*,[54] the Court of Appeal held that D is not guilty of UAM simply on the ground that he has committed the offence under s 1(1) of the Children and Young Persons Act 1933 of neglecting his child so as to cause unnecessary suffering or injury to its health, and that neglect has caused death. The court disapproved *Senior*,[55] which, on similar facts, held that this was manslaughter. *Lowe* has now been overruled on its interpretation of the 1933 Act[56] but on this point *Lowe* and not *Senior* represents the law. Death had certainly been caused by unlawful and dangerous conduct, but the court distinguished between omission and commission:

if I strike a child in a manner likely to cause harm it is right that if that child dies I may be charged with manslaughter. If, however, I omit to do something with the result that it suffers injury to its health which results in its death, we think that a charge of manslaughter should not be an inevitable consequence even if the omission is deliberate.

If the omission is no more than an act of negligence then it is right that the doctrine of the unlawful and dangerous act does not apply and D is not guilty of UAM (but may be of gross negligence manslaughter); but if the omission is truly *wilful*—a deliberate omission to

---

[50] *R v Alliston*, Central Criminal Court, 17 Sept 2017.

[51] It is for this reason that *Meeking* [2012] EWCA Crim 641 ought to be treated with considerable caution. In that case the unlawful act relied upon was the offence of endangering road users, contrary to s 22A(1) of the Road Traffic Act 1988. As Ashworth points out, [2013] Crim LR 333, this is an offence of negligence and for that reason D should not have been prosecuted with UAM. As the Court of Appeal observes, D could have been charged with gross negligence manslaughter instead.

[52] For discussion, see Ormerod at [2003] Crim LR 477; M Dyson, 'The Smallest Fault in Manslaughter' [2017] 6 Arch Rev 4.

[53] [2002] EWCA Crim 3021. See the commentary by Ormerod at [2003] Crim LR 477.

[54] [1973] QB 702. See, generally, IH Dennis, 'Manslaughter by Omission' (1980) 33 CLP 255.

[55] [1899] 1 QB 283. On the difficulties of UAM in child abuse cases, see L Hoyano and C Keenan, *Child Abuse Law and Policy* (2007) 142.

[56] *Sheppard* [1981] AC 394, per Lord Edmund-Davies at 410.

summon medical aid, knowing it to be necessary—there seems to be no valid ground for the distinction.[57]

14.1.1.7 Other limitations of the category of unlawfulness

It has been questioned whether: (a) an inchoate offence might suffice for the base crime and (b) whether the base crime must be one involving an offence to the person.

As for inchoate offences, attempted offences of violence would be the most obvious scenarios in which such an issue might arise. Consider D who intends to poison V and adds what he thinks to be poison to V's tea, but he has made a mistake and is simply adding a very concentrated sweetener. V is a diabetic and dies. There is probably no completed offence under s 23 of the OAPA 1861, but there is a possible attempted poisoning.[58] The issue does not appear to have arisen in any reported case. In *Willoughby*,[59] D had poured petrol around a building which he owned and which he planned to burn down and to claim the insurance money. D claimed that he was absent from the premises when a spark ignited the petrol and his associate who was assisting in spreading the petrol was killed. The conviction for manslaughter was upheld by the court, with the conclusion that the base offence was one of causing criminal damage to property being reckless as to whether life was endangered thereby, as the jury found. It is unclear if the question was raised whether D pouring petrol was a completed act of criminal damage, or one that was merely preparatory.[60]

There are plenty of examples to suggest that the base crime need not be an offence against the person. Public order offences are capable of founding an unlawful act manslaughter charge. In *Carey*, the Court of Appeal held that there might be circumstances in which a verdict of UAM could properly be entered where the unlawful act was affray, although on the evidence that was not possible in that case.[61] On the facts the Court of Appeal quashed convictions where D1, D2 and D3 had committed an affray and D1 had hit V, a 15-year-old, apparently healthy, girl. V ran 109 metres away from DD. She died as a result of a heart condition which had not been diagnosed. The only sufficient dangerous act perpetrated on V had been the physical strike by D1. The other acts and threats used in the course of the affray were not dangerous in the relevant sense as against V. The judge should therefore have withdrawn the charge of manslaughter based on those acts. It would, it is submitted, have been easier for the Crown to argue that DD had assaulted V; that was an unlawful act, it was dangerous, and her death arose from V's foreseeable and reasonable flight and there was no break in the chain of causation since they must 'take their victim' as they find her.

Convictions have been upheld where D's unlawful act constituted criminal damage (eg *Goodfellow*)[62] and burglary (eg *Watson* (discussed later) and *Kennedy*).[63] In *JF*,[64] the arson committed in a derelict building in which homeless men were living was enough. In *Ball*[65] (discussed later), the court distinguished examples posed by D's counsel on the ground that, unlike the case before the court, they were of acts 'not directed at V' (but with respect,

---

[57] See editorial comment in [1976] Crim LR 529, where Andrew Ashworth is heavily critical.

[58] Arguably D would not be liable not because of the unlawfulness element, but because there would be no objective risk of injury from the act.

[59] [2004] EWCA Crim 3365, [2004] Crim LR 389.

[60] In such cases, a gross negligence charge might be difficult to substantiate.

[61] [2006] EWCA Crim 17, [2006] Crim LR 842 and commentary.

[62] (1986) 83 Cr App R 23.

[63] (1993) 15 Cr App R (S) 141 (burglar dropped a match used to illuminate search of house).

[64] [2015] EWCA Crim 351.

[65] The point of law certified for the House of Lords postulated 'an act [not directed against V] which is the substantial cause of the death' and the court left open the question whether D was guilty of manslaughter by gross negligence which it could scarcely have done if it was deciding that D did not cause death.

that is irrelevant). The court therefore expressed no opinion on the example of D 'storing goods known to be stolen; if unknown to him the goods contain unstable explosive which explodes killing another, is that manslaughter?' The answer must surely be no, unless the sober and reasonable observer would have known of the danger. There is something to be said in favour of imposing some limitation to the offence if it is to be retained. It does not seem appropriate that a person's guilt for homicide should depend on whether he was handling stolen goods or committing criminal damage or burglary. Cases of this sort would be better left to the next category of killing by gross negligence.[66]

14.1.1.8 No requirement that the unlawful act be 'directed at' the victim?

For a period in the 1990s the cases seemed to require that the unlawful act was directed at the victim. That was based on a statement in *Dalby*,[67] where Waller LJ said that, 'where the charge of manslaughter is based on an unlawful and dangerous act, it must be an act directed at the victim and likely to cause immediate injury however slight'. In *Goodfellow*,[68] D's argument that he was not guilty of manslaughter because his act was not directed against V was rejected. D, wanting to move from his local authority housing and seeing no prospect of exchanging it, set it on fire, attempting to make it appear that the cause was a petrol bomb. V died in the fire. The court said that in *Dalby*, Waller LJ was 'intending to say that there must be no fresh intervening cause between the act and the death'. It is true that that case could, and probably should,[69] have been decided on this ground, but it does not seem to have been the *ratio decidendi*.[70] It is also true that the act of burglary which causes the death of the obviously frail householder is not directed at him, but it is accepted in *Watson* that it may be manslaughter.[71] It now seems clear that there is no requirement that the unlawful act is directed at V.

14.1.2 Dangerousness

Until 1966, it was possible to argue that any unlawful act, other than a merely negligent act, causing death was manslaughter; but in that year in *Church* the Court of Criminal Appeal rejected such a view. Edmund-Davies J said:

For such a verdict inexorably to follow, the unlawful act must be such as all sober and reasonable people would inevitably recognize must[72] subject the other person to, at least, the risk of some harm resulting therefrom, albeit not serious harm.[73]

---

66 For a suggestion that the offence ought to be restricted to cases of 'attack' on another person, see C Clarkson, 'Context and Culpability in Involuntary Manslaughter: Principle or Instinct' in A Ashworth and B Mitchell (eds), *Rethinking English Homicide Law* (2000). The basis for this suggestion is that there is no wrong done by convicting D of a constructive crime of manslaughter because by attacking V, D has shifted his moral stance vis-à-vis V. Since the concept of 'attack' has no foundation in English law, the proposal may generate uncertainty. As Ashworth and Mitchell observe, asking whether it is enough to say that choosing to engage in violence means you make your own luck begs the question (ibid, 13). See also J Gardner, *Offences and Defences* (2007) Ch 12.

67 [1982] 1 All ER 916.

68 (1986) 83 Cr App R 23. The conviction was upheld on the grounds of both unlawful act and reckless manslaughter.

69 *Kennedy (No 1)* [1999] 1 Cr App R 54. In *Kennedy (No 2)* [2005] EWCA Crim 685, it was rightly accepted that there was no requirement that the act be 'aimed' at V.

70 See n 66.   71 [1989] Crim LR 730, CA.

72 The degree of risk entailed is not further elaborated. See R Sparks, 'The Elusive Element of Unlawfulness' (1965) 28 MLR 601.

73 [1966] 1 QB 59 at 70. Cf R Buxton, 'By Any Unlawful Act' (1966) 82 LQR 174 suggesting that the law could return to a position whereby unlawful act manslaughter is restricted to cases where D intends to cause *serious injury*.

The test of dangerousness is objective. In *Newbury*, Lord Salmon stressed that 'the test is not did the accused recognize that it was dangerous but would all sober and reasonable people recognize its danger'.

The test describes the kind of act which gives rise to liability for manslaughter, not the intention or foresight, real or assumed, of the accused. Hence, the enactment of s 8 of the Criminal Justice Act 1967[74] had no effect on the law as stated in *Church*. The question is whether the sober and reasonable person would have appreciated that the act was dangerous in the light, not only of the circumstances actually known to the accused, but also of any additional circumstances of which that hypothetical person would have been aware.[75] There is, of course, a risk that in practice the fact that a death has occurred will be treated by the jury as conclusive evidence of the fact that the activity was dangerous. Judges' directions need to caution against such simplistic reasoning.

If the victim has some peculiarity that is relevant if it would have been known to the sober and reasonable observer of the event, even if it was not known to the accused. This principle can be explained by comparing two cases. The burglary of a house in which V, a frail 87-year-old man resides, becomes a 'dangerous' act as soon as V's frailty and great age would be apparent to the reasonable observer. The unlawful act continues through the 'whole of the burglarious intrusion' so that if V dies of a heart attack caused by D's continuing in the burglary after it has become a dangerous, as well as unlawful, act, he will be guilty of manslaughter.[76] In contrast, where a petrol station attendant with a weak heart died in consequence of an attempted robbery where D was outside the station behind armour-plated glass, this was not manslaughter. The reasonable observer would not, at any point in the continuance of the robbery, have known of V's peculiar susceptibility—the act was not 'dangerous'.[77]

In the recent case of *JF*,[78] F, aged 14, and E, aged 16, were convicted of manslaughter. They had entered a derelict building and set alight a duvet on a pile of tyres before fleeing the building. They were unaware that anyone was in the building. In fact several homeless men lived in the building, and one of the men died. F had a low IQ (his understanding was comparable to a six-year-old child). At trial they were convicted of unlawful act manslaughter on the basis of the act of simple arson, which a reasonable person would have foreseen might have caused someone some harm, and which did in fact cause death. They were acquitted of the less serious charge of aggravated arson which required proof that they had been reckless as to a life being endangered. The Court of Appeal upheld the convictions. The judge had directed the jury on the objective test as follows:

It is immaterial whether or not the defendant actually knew or actually realised that the act was dangerous in the sense I have defined it for you and whether or not he intended *any* harm to result therefrom. And the sober and reasonable man is endowed with the knowledge which the defendant possessed before and at the time of starting the fire.

---

[74] See p 131.

[75] Confirmed as being the correct approach by the Court of Appeal in *Bristow* [2013] EWCA Crim 1540, [2014] Crim LR 457.

[76] *Watson* [1989] 2 All ER 865, [1989] Crim LR 733. D's conviction was quashed because causation was not established. V's death may have been caused by the arrival of the emergency services. But did this predictable event break the chain of causation? Cf commentary [1989] Crim LR 734. If V has sustained a fatal shock before D has any opportunity to observe his frailty, D's liability seems to depend on whether his acts after he had that opportunity (now 'dangerous' acts) contributed to the death.

[77] *Dawson* (1985) 81 Cr App R 150. Yet, before the Homicide Act 1957, this would have been murder (killing in the course or furtherance of a violent felony) and, according to one theory, Parliament's provision that it was not murder left it manslaughter. See the 1st edition of this book, at pp 19–20. The theory has not taken root.

[78] [2015] EWCA Crim 351.

The Court of Appeal rejected the argument that the objective test as to whether the act was a dangerous one was a test which should have been adapted to take into account the appellant's ages and, in the case of the appellant F, his mental capacity. The court held that it was for Parliament to act if there was a desire for a change in the law.

It is worth underlining three aspects of the *Church* doctrine. First, that there must be a 'likelihood' of harm. This suggests more than a mere possibility, but not perhaps that harm is more probable than not. Secondly, that the type of harm involved is only 'some' harm, not serious harm. This contrasts with the requirement in gross negligence manslaughter of a serious and obvious risk of death. Thirdly, that there is no requirement that D himself foresees any risk of harm.[79] Historically, UAM was limited to cases in which the accused had at least foreseen injury of his victim resulting from his crime.[80] The *Fourth Report of HM Commissioners on Criminal Law*[81] described the offence in terms of 'death result[ing] from any unlawful act or omission done or omitted with intent to hurt the person'.[82] The decision in *Church* may have marked a significant deviation from the historical position. Buxton, writing extrajudicially, described it as a 'staggeringly severe ruling, and one which turns its back on the major part of the 19th century development of the law'.[83] There have been many suggestions to limit the offence to cases where D has committed an unlawful act likely to cause at least serious personal injury, and to restrict it further by a requirement that D intend or be reckless as to such.[84]

14.1.2.1 'Dangerousness' in crimes committed by multiple accused

An interesting issue arose in *Carey* (discussed earlier) as to whether, in considering the 'dangerousness of an act', it is permissible to aggregate the conduct of co-accused. It is submitted that there is no difficulty in aggregating the threats of violence offered by D1, D2 and D3 where they acted together for the purposes of ascertaining whether there was a crime of a sufficiently dangerous nature to satisfy the *Church* test. If D1 is waving a machete around and D2 is shaking his fist at V, their affray comprises their combined conduct. Likewise, the dangerousness of the acts is properly assessed by looking at the combination of their conduct. Nor, it is submitted, is there a problem in aggregating the conduct of D1, D2 and D3 towards V1 and V2. Take a case where, in the course of a robbery, D1 issues serious threats against V1 and D2 issues threats to V2, and the obviously frail V2 died from a heart attack induced by the shock. It is submitted that the actions of D1 and D2 could be aggregated in determining whether the conduct was sufficiently 'dangerous' in the sense required by *Church*.[85]

---

[79] Reiterated by the Court of Appeal in *M(J)* [2012] EWCA Crim 2293, [20]. There is no requirement for D to foresee any harm let alone the type of harm V suffers.

[80] The case law bears examples, including *Sullivan* (1836) 7 C & P 641, where removing the trap-stick from a cart was sufficient to ground liability as D foresaw the risk of some harm arising.

[81] (1839); see Russell, 588.   [82] ibid, 589.   [83] See n 73.

[84] See also the Draft Scots Criminal Code, cl 38. A further attempt to narrow the offence was rejected by the Court of Appeal in *M(J)* [2012] EWCA Crim 2293. The Crown appealed against the judge's ruling that D could not be guilty unless 'the victim died as a result of the *sort of* physical harm that any reasonable and sober person would inevitably realise the unlawful act in question risked causing'. The Court of Appeal held that this placed 'a gloss on the ingredients of this offence which is not justified by the authorities and does not follow from the reasoning' (at [18]) and allowed the Crown's appeal. See Ashworth [2013] Crim LR 335.

[85] Difficulties may arise in terms of different jurors concluding that the danger emanated from one defendant rather than the other. See the discussion in *Lewis* [2010] EWCA Crim 496.

14.1.2.2 Fright, shock and harm as dangerous acts?

Psychiatric injury is now acknowledged to be actual bodily harm,[86] but it would be hard to prove that the risk of such harm would inevitably be recognized by all sober and reasonable people, especially as the law requires expert evidence to prove it. Fright and shock do not amount to 'actual bodily harm' but it does not necessarily follow that they are not 'harm' for the purposes of constructive manslaughter. In *Reid*,[87] Lawton LJ, upholding a conviction for manslaughter, said that 'the very least kind of harm is causing fright by threats'—in that case, by the use of firearms—but he was discussing the mental element of an accessory rather than the nature of the act, which is our present concern. The act was, in the opinion of the court, likely to cause death or serious injury and therefore was certainly 'dangerous'. In *Dawson*,[88] the court assumed without deciding that in the context of manslaughter 'harm' includes 'injury to the person through the operation of shock emanating from fright'. So it seems that it is not enough that the act is likely to frighten. It must be likely to cause such shock as to result in injury.[89]

Confusion was also caused by Lord Denning's *dictum* in the civil case of *Gray v Barr*,[90] which was criticized by Lord Salmon in *Newbury*.[91] Lord Denning said: 'the accused must do a dangerous act with the *intention* of frightening or harming someone or with *realisation* that it is likely to frighten or harm someone'. This is simply to require the mens rea of assault or battery. However, an act which is intended or known to be likely to frighten is not necessarily a 'dangerous' act; and whether it is dangerous is a question to be answered by an objective test. The *dictum* is correct if it is confined to the case where the unlawful act relied on is assault or battery.

In *Dhaliwal*,[92] D had struck his partner a minor blow and she had then committed suicide. This was against a history of domestic abuse amounting to psychological but not psychiatric injury by D. It was held that the infliction of mere psychological harm would not suffice to construct a manslaughter charge. The prosecution sought to rely for the relevant unlawful and dangerous act on D's conduct which caused psychological injury to V. The trial judge in his 'meticulous' judgment, and the Court of Appeal in turn, rejected this approach. It would have required an extension to the definition of grievous bodily harm. *Chan-Fook* and *Burstow* make it clear that psychiatric illness may amount to actual or indeed grievous bodily harm.[93] However, it is also clear that the Court of Appeal and House of Lords in those cases were not prepared to extend the definition of bodily harm to include emotional distress or any condition less than a 'recognisable psychiatric injury'. Attempts to dilute the definition further would exacerbate the already considerable problems of certainty in definition and proof.[94] However, in an *obiter dictum*, the Court of Appeal in *Dhaliwal*[95] left open the possibility that a manslaughter conviction might be available:

---

[86] *Chan-Fook*, p 688.   [87] (1975) 62 Cr App R 109 at 112.

[88] (1985) 81 Cr App R 150 at 155.

[89] See M Stallworthy, 'Can Death by Shock be Manslaughter?' (1986) 136 NLJ 51; A Busuttil and A McCall Smith, 'Fright, Stress and Homicide' (1990) 54 J Crim L 257.

[90] [1971] 2 QB 554 at 568, p 41. Lord Denning's emphasis.

[91] [1977] AC 500. Cf Blackstone, *Commentaries*, i, 109.   [92] [2006] EWCA Crim 1139.

[93] Expert evidence will be needed to prove the condition and that D caused it: *Morris* [1998] 1 Cr App R 386.

[94] Under the Offences Against the Person Bill (Home Office, *Reforming the Offences Against the Person Act 1861* (1998)) the definition of injury includes mental injury which encompasses any impairment of a person's mental health. See also LC 361, *Reform of Offences Against the Person* (2015) para 2.32.

[95] [2006] EWCA Crim 1139, [2006] Crim LR 923.

where a decision to commit suicide has been triggered by a physical assault which represents the culmination of a course of abusive conduct, it would be possible . . . to argue that the final assault played a significant part in causing the victim's death.[96]

14.1.3 Causing death

The principles of causation discussed in Ch 2 are applicable. The unlawful and dangerous act must cause death. Causation often gives rise to problems in UAM cases where there is frequently a factor other than D's unlawful dangerous act which plays a causal role in V's death. In the case of *Johnstone*,[97] for example, it could not be established that D's unlawful injury to V, fracturing his cheek and being abusive, had triggered the most direct cause of V's death which was a heart attack.[98]

14.1.3.1 Fright and flight cases

The question for the court is always: if there is a sufficient dangerous act, did *that* unlawful and dangerous act cause death? In some cases where D has performed a number of acts it depends which dangerous act is relied on. The tests to be applied are discussed in Ch 2. In short, the victim's conduct in trying to escape D will not break the chain of causation if it is 'reasonably foreseeable'.[99] Another variation which has developed is that V's conduct will break the chain if it is beyond a range of responses which might be regarded as reasonable, given the threat posed by D and V's circumstances.[100] In evaluating the reasonableness of the response the jury are to have regard to V's circumstances. In *Lewis*,[101] D was convicted of UAM having chased V into the road, where V was hit and killed by an oncoming car. The judge directed the jury to consider whether V running away from D was one of the responses which might have been expected from someone who found himself in V's situation. The Court of Appeal dismissed the appeal. In cases of death during flight from an unlawful act it had to be shown that there was cause and effect; that is, but for the unlawful act, flight and therefore death would not have taken place: *Williams*.[102] The court suggested that it would be appropriate to direct the jury to consider whether V's response was 'wholly disproportionate' or a 'daft response' to the nature of the threat posed by D.

14.1.3.2 Causation in drug supply cases

After a number of years in which the Court of Appeal created confusion in this area, the orthodox approach to causation was reasserted by the House of Lords in *Kennedy (No 2)*.[103] It was held that where D provides V with a syringe for immediate injection in the case of a fully informed and responsible adult V, it is 'never' appropriate to find D guilty of UAM. The criminal law generally assumes the existence of free will.[104] In its remarkably short unanimous judgment delivered by Lord Bingham, the House concluded that the Court of Appeal had been in error repeatedly in recent years in imposing liability in such cases.[105] There was

---

96 See further, J Horder and L McGowan, 'Manslaughter by Causing Another's Suicide' [2006] Crim LR 1035, arguing that in an abusive relationship case V would not be a free actor, and that general gross negligence manslaughter ought to be relied on.

97 [2007] EWCA Crim 3133.

98 See also *Warburton* [2006] EWCA Crim 627; *Fitzgerald* [2006] EWCA Crim 1655 (D, during a burglary, pushed 92-year-old V, injuring her, and she died later in hospital of pneumonia).

99 *Roberts* (1971) Cr App R 95.   100 *Williams* (1991) 95 Cr App R 1.

101 [2010] EWCA Crim 151.   102 (1991) 95 Cr App R 1.

103 *Kennedy (No 2)* [2007] UKHL 38; see generally W Wilson, 'Dealing With Drug Induced Homicide' in Clarkson and Cunningham, *Criminal Liability for Non-Aggressive Deaths*.

104 At [14].   105 [2007] UKHL 38, [2008] 1 AC 269. Cf *Keen* [2008] 1 Cr App R (S) 8.

no doubt that D committed an unlawful and criminal act by supplying the heroin to V. But that act of supplying, without more, could not harm V in any physical way, let alone cause his death. The crucial question was not whether D facilitated or contributed to administration of the noxious thing by supplying V but whether he went further and 'administered' it, that is, completed the offence under s 23 of the OAPA 1861. *Rogers*[106] was wrongly decided in concluding that where D assisted V by holding the tourniquet he had administered to V and could be liable for his death.[107]

14.1.3.3 Suicide

Homicide convictions have been upheld in a series of cases in which V has effectively committed suicide consequent upon being injured by D, but in each the decision was based on the fact that the injury inflicted by D was still an operating and substantial cause of the death, as, for example, in *Blaue*.[108] Similarly, in *Dear*,[109] the wounds inflicted by D were a continuing and substantial cause of death when V reopened them and bled to death. Similarly, in *People v Lewis*,[110] the conviction for murder was upheld where V had cut his throat to hasten his death when languishing from a gunshot wound inflicted by D, but again the decision was based on the gunshot wound being a substantial and operating cause.

Can D ever be liable for UAM where V has committed suicide and D's unlawful dangerous act is *not* at that moment of the suicide a continuing and operative cause of death? What if V jumps from a tower block fearing that D might be about to inflict an attack in physical terms? What of an abused spouse who takes her own life being in fear of D's continued psychological abuse?

If D has inflicted an injury, the question is whether that remains an operative cause of death. If V is seeking to escape the infliction (or further infliction) of injury by D the test to be applied is that from the flight cases discussed earlier: is V's act a proportionate one or a reasonably foreseeable one given the threat faced? That would cause the court to ask: can suicide ever be a reasonably foreseeable response to violence or further psychological harm? To adopt the language from *Williams* and *Lewis* discussed previously, that would mean asking: can suicide ever be within a range of reasonable responses to a threat of such harm? In *Dhaliwal*, the Court of Appeal gives *obiter* support to a suggestion that an unlawful and dangerous act (eg an assault) may be enough for a manslaughter conviction where the victim was of a 'fragile and vulnerable personality'.[111] There was no reference to any of the case law or issues in the discussion in this paragraph, and it is submitted that the Court of Appeal's *obiter dictum* ought to be treated with considerable caution.[112]

Where D's act *is* still a substantial and operative cause in the sense that the injury is persisting and V commits suicide to avoid further suffering, it is submitted that it is open to a jury to decide that V's act is a reasonably foreseeable and proportionate response (depending on the suffering) and hence not 'daft' and therefore not a break in the chain of causation.

---

[106] [2003] 1 WLR 1374.

[107] ibid, [31]. In *Burgess* [2008] EWCA Crim 516, the court considered convictions secured pre-*Kennedy (No 2)* where D had laid the tip of the needle against the vein for V. It was held that the fact that V depresses the plunger does not automatically entitle D to an acquittal. Cf the position in Scotland where *Kennedy (No 2)* was rejected: *MacAngus and Kane v HM Advocate* [2009] HCJAC 8.

[108] (1975) 61 Cr App R 271.

[109] [1996] Crim LR 595.

[110] 124 Cal 551 (1899).

[111] A Bill was introduced into Parliament to criminalize causing suicide, Hansard, HC Debates, 18 Dec 2006. It was not enacted.

[112] cf J Horder and L McGowan, 'Manslaughter by Causing Another's Suicide' [2006] Crim LR 1035.

In *W*[113] the Court of Appeal confirmed that the suicide of the victim will not necessarily break the chain of causation. In this case, V was left severely disfigured, permanently paralysed, and in a state of unbearable physical and psychological suffering as a result of injuries alleged to have been inflicted by D. V travelled home to Belgium, where euthanasia is lawful, and was euthanized by doctors in accordance with Belgian law. The Court of Appeal held that it was open to a jury to conclude that neither the acts of V in taking the decision to be euthanized nor the acts of the doctors in Belgium in carrying out his wishes broke the chain of causation. The judgment of the Court of Appeal confirms that, provided the jury concludes that the victim's act was a reasonably foreseeable response to the injuries inflicted by the defendant, there will be no break in the chain of causation between the defendant's unlawful act and the victim's death. This will remain the case even if the victim commits suicide. The defendant can therefore be guilty not only of manslaughter, but also of murder if he has the requisite mens rea.

14.2 Gross negligence manslaughter

The offence of gross negligence manslaughter has been the subject of considerable interest and controversy. It is the subject of numerous recent appeals. In the judgment in *Rose*, Sir Brian Leveson P authoritatively stated the terms of the offence as follows:

(1) The offence of gross negligence manslaughter requires breach of an existing duty of care which it is reasonably foreseeable gives rise to a serious and obvious risk of death and does, in fact, cause death in circumstances where, having regard to the risk of death, the conduct of the defendant was so bad in all the circumstances as to go beyond the requirement of compensation but to amount to a criminal act or omission.

(2) There are, therefore, five elements which the prosecution must prove in order for a person to be guilty of an offence of manslaughter by gross negligence:

(a) the defendant owed an existing duty of care to the victim;

(b) the defendant negligently breached that duty of care;

(c) it was reasonably foreseeable that the breach of that duty gave rise to a serious and obvious risk of death;

(d) the breach of that duty caused the death of the victim;

(e) the circumstances of the breach were truly exceptionally bad and so reprehensible as to justify the conclusion that it amounted to gross negligence and required criminal sanction.

(3) The question of whether there is a serious and obvious risk of death must exist at, and is to be assessed with respect to, knowledge at the time of the breach of duty.

(4) A recognisable risk of something serious is not the same as a recognisable risk of death.

(5) A mere possibility that an assessment might reveal something life-threatening is not the same as an obvious risk of death: an obvious risk is a present risk which is clear and unambiguous, not one which might become apparent on further investigation.[114]

This test is based on the decision of the House of Lords in *Adomako*.[115] In that landmark decision the House of Lords rejected the argument that gross negligence manslaughter required proof of objective recklessness as to death, as had been held in one House of

---

[113] [2018] EWCA Crim 690.
[114] [2017] EWCA Crim 1168, [77].   [115] [1994] 3 All ER 79, [1994] Crim LR 757.

Lords' case.[116] The House reasserted the approach of Lord Hewart CJ in *Bateman* that the crime turns on whether, in the opinion of the jury, the negligence of the accused went beyond a mere matter of compensation between subjects and showed such disregard for the life and safety of others as to amount to a crime against the State and conduct deserving of punishment.[117]

14.2.1 *Adomako* in the Court of Appeal

In three appeals considered together in *Prentice (Holloway and Adomako)*, the Court of Appeal sought to restrict the objective recklessness to cases of 'motor manslaughter'— causing death by driving a motor vehicle.[118] Prentice and Holloway's appeals were allowed. Adomako's appeal was dismissed by the Court of Appeal and by the House of Lords.

In *Prentice*, doctors had administered an injection which created an obvious risk of causing death and in fact did so. The jury were directed in accordance with objective recklessness that the doctors were guilty if they never gave thought to the possibility of there being any such risk. The Court of Appeal held that the question should have been whether their failure to ascertain and use the correct method of administering the drug was 'grossly negligent to the point of criminality'. In *Holloway*, D, an electrician, had given no thought to the obvious risk of death created by the way he installed the electric element of a central heating system. Applying the objective recklessness test, D would be convicted but the Court of Appeal held that that was the wrong test: the further question should have been asked, whether it was grossly negligent to have such a state of mind.

In *Adomako*, D, an anaesthetist, failed to notice that the tube supplying oxygen to a patient had become detached. According to expert evidence, any competent anaesthetist would have recognized this immediately. The judge directed the jury that a high degree of negligence was required. The Court of Appeal upheld the conviction as this was the appropriate test to apply, and the appellant appealed to the House of Lords.

14.2.2 The House of Lords' decision in *Adomako*

The House held that:[119]

(1) there is no separate offence of motor manslaughter. As Lord Atkin said in *Andrews*, 'The principle to be observed is that cases of manslaughter in driving motor cars are but instances of a general rule applicable to all charges of homicide by negligence';[120]

(2) there is no manslaughter by *objective* recklessness, in effect, though not formally, overruling *Seymour*. It would now be wrong to direct a jury on any charge of manslaughter in terms of *objective* recklessness (since the decision in *G* overruling *Caldwell*, it would be unthinkable to apply that test);[121]

---

[116] [1983] 2 AC 493. See PA Ashall, 'Manslaughter: The Impact of *Caldwell*' [1984] Crim LR 467; A Briggs, 'In Defence of Manslaughter' [1983] Crim LR 764; G Syrota, '*Mens Rea* in Gross Negligence Manslaughter' [1983] Crim LR 776.

[117] (1925) 19 Cr App R 8 at 11.

[118] See G Williams, 'Misadventures of Manslaughter' (1993) 153 NLJ 1413.

[119] See commentary at [1994] Crim LR 757 and S Gardner, 'Manslaughter by Gross Negligence' (1995) 111 LQR 22. On the safety of convictions based on recklessness, see *Morgan* [2007] EWCA Crim 3313.

[120] See generally ID Brownlee and M Seneviratne, 'Killing with Cars After *Adomako*: Time for Some Alternatives' [1995] Crim LR 389. See also *Brown* [2005] UKPC 18.

[121] For a clear review of the development of fault in manslaughter from gross negligence, through forms of recklessness and back to gross negligence, see J Stannard, 'From *Andrews* to *Seymour* and Back Again' (1996) 47 NILQ 1.

(3) there is now a single, 'simple' test of gross negligence. D must have been in breach of a duty of care under the ordinary principles of negligence; the negligence must have caused death; and it must, in the opinion of the jury, amount to *gross* negligence. The question, 'supremely a jury question', is:

having regard to the risk of death involved, [was] the conduct of the defendant . . . so bad in all the circumstances as to amount in [the jury's judgement] to a criminal act or omission?

Before examining the elements of the test in detail, it is necessary to point out that trials for gross negligence manslaughter often involve a great deal of expert evidence. Usually this evidence relates to whether D breached the duty of care he owed to V and whether the breach of duty was grossly negligent. The Court of Appeal emphasized in *Sellu* that despite the fact evidence of this nature will be crucial to the jury's assessment of whether D committed the offence, the experts cannot be permitted to undermine the role of the jury as the ultimate arbiter of guilt.[122]

14.2.3 A duty of care

The most obvious categories of duty in which liability might arise are those involving doctor and patient,[123] optometrist and patient,[124] transport carrier and passenger,[125] employer and employee,[126] parent and child,[127] landlord and tenant,[128] restaurateur and customer,[129] etc but the categories are limitless and involve duties arising in the course of hazardous activity (eg on the road,[130] smuggling illegal immigrants,[131] smuggling cocaine,[132] taking heroin,[133]

---

[122] *Sellu* [2016] EWCA Crim 1716, [142]. His lordship cited Lord Kerr's opinion for the Board in *Pora v The Queen* [2015] UKPC 9.

[123] See *Adomako* itself; *Misra* [2004] EWCA Crim 2375, [2005] Crim LR 234 and R Ferner, 'Medication Errors that Led to Manslaughter Charges' (2000) 321 BMJ 1212; RE Ferner and SE McDowell, 'Doctors Charged with Manslaughter in the Course of Medical Practice 1795–2005: A Literature Review' (2006) 99 J Royal Society of Medicine 309; O Quick, 'Prosecuting Gross Medical Negligence' (2006) 33 J Law Sco 421; M Childs, 'Medical Manslaughter and Corporate Liability' (1999) 19 LS 316. See also O Quick, 'Medical Killing: Need for a Special Offence' in Clarkson and Cunningham, *Criminal Liability for Non-Aggressive Death*, arguing that medical professionals do not deserve to be charged under the category of manslaughter based on gross negligence, but one based on recklessness. See his similar argument in 'Medical Manslaughter: The Rise and Replacement of a Contested Issue' in C Erin and S Ost (eds), *The Criminal Justice System and Health Care* (2007). See also in that volume the essay by M Brazier and N Allen 'Criminalising Medical Malpractice'. For a discussion of the issues that arise when sentencing doctors who are convicted of gross negligence manslaughter, see H Quirk, 'Sentencing White Coat Crime: The Need for Guidance in Medical Manslaughter Cases' [2013] Crim LR 871.

[124] *Rose* [2017] EWCA Crim 1168.

[125] See *Litchfield* [1998] Crim LR 507 (schooner); *Barker* [2003] 2 Cr App R (S) 22; *McGee* [2013] EWCA Crim 1012.

[126] *R v DPP, ex pJones* [2000] IRLR 373; *Dean* [2002] EWCA Crim 2410; *Clothier* [2004] EWCA Crim 2629; *Crow* [2001] EWCA Crim 2968. For an analysis of the extent to which employers owe their employees a duty of care, see S Antrobus, 'The Criminal Liability of Directors for Health and Safety Breaches and Manslaughter' [2013] Crim LR 309.

[127] *Reeves* [2012] EWCA Crim 2613.   [128] *Harrison* [2011] EWCA Crim 3139.

[129] *Zaman* [2017] EWCA Crim 1783.

[130] Including a pedestrian killing a motorcyclist by being knocked down: *Devine* [1999] 2 Cr App R (S) 409.

[131] *Wacker* [2002] EWCA Crim 1944, [2003] Crim LR 108.

[132] See news reports for 14 Aug 2010 reporting conviction of Mr Newman. N had smuggled cocaine in concentrated form in a bottle of rum. V, who had been given the bottle, was unaware of the content, drank some and died.

[133] *Ruffell* [2003] Cr App R (S) 53; *Parfeni* [2003] EWCA Crim 159 (although this must surely have been a case of unlawful act manslaughter by D injecting V with heroin in order to steal from him).

storing fireworks,[134] minding a firearm[135]), or duties arising from relationships (eg failing to seek medical assistance for a spouse or someone to whose danger D has contributed).[136]

It is impossible to catalogue all circumstances in which a duty will arise; rather, the approach is to apply the 'ordinary principles of negligence' to determine whether the defendant owed a duty to the victim. So, for example, in *Yaqoob*,[137] D was a manager of a minicab firm and he had failed to inspect the tyres of a minibus involved in a fatal accident. It was held that it was *open to the jury* to find that there was a duty to inspect and maintain beyond that required for an MOT test, council inspections and other duties imposed by regulation. Moreover, the jury did not require expert evidence to assess that duty.[138]

In cases of positive acts, it is relatively easy to identify whether there was a duty based on whether the acts created a risk of death which was obvious to the ordinary prudent individual. In cases of omission, much greater care needs to be exercised as there will be situations in which a risk of death would be obvious, but where D has no duty—as with D witnessing a blind stranger walking towards a cliff. No doubt the courts will be prepared in many cases to recognize a duty arising from a combination of circumstances.[139] In *Willoughby*,[140] for example, D had, with V, spread petrol around D's property with the intention of burning it down to claim on the insurance. V died when the petrol ignited. The Court of Appeal concluded that D's ownership per se did not give rise to a duty, but because D engaged the deceased to participate in spreading petrol, and with a view to setting fire to D's premises for D's benefit, a duty existed.

The courts have been willing to take an expansive interpretation of the scope of the duty where that appears appropriate on policy grounds. In *Evans*,[141] D was convicted of gross negligence manslaughter having supplied heroin to her half-sister V (a recovering addict). V self-administered the drug in the house with D and her mother (who was also convicted of manslaughter). D noticed that V looked as if she had overdosed, a condition D was familiar with. D, fearful of attracting the attention of the police, chose not to seek medical assistance and V died. The jury was directed that without D's involvement in the supply of heroin, there was no duty on D to act, even after she became aware of the serious adverse effect on V of the drug-taking. They were directed that if D *was* involved in supply, that fact, taken with the other undisputed facts, would and did give rise to a duty on D to act. On appeal, a five-member Court of Appeal held that having regard to the authorities on gross negligence manslaughter, it was an essential requirement of any potential basis for conviction that D was under a duty to act. The duty necessary to found gross negligence was plainly not confined to cases of a familial or professional relationship between the defendant and the deceased. For the purposes of gross negligence, a duty could arise if, *inter alia*, D had created *or contributed* to the creation of a state of affairs (V's danger) which D knew, or ought reasonably to have known, had become life-threatening. The duty on D was to act by taking reasonable steps to save the other's life by calling medical assistance. This is a controversial decision.[142]

---

[134] *Winter and Winter* [2010] EWCA Crim 1474.

[135] *S* [2015] EWCA Crim 558, [2015] Crim LR 553.

[136] *Hood* [2004] 1 Cr App R (S) 73. See also *Sogunro* [1997] 2 Cr App R (S) 89 (starving V believing her to be possessed) and see *Evans*, n 141. See also the sentencing case of *Barrass* [2011] EWCA Crim 2629 in which D pleaded guilty to the gross negligence manslaughter of his sister. It is unclear from the judgment whether the duty arose because of the familial relationship or because V was dependent upon D.

[137] [2005] EWCA Crim 2169.   [138] *Oughton* [2010] EWCA Crim 1540.

[139] As in the cases of omission, especially in *Stone and Dobinson* [1977] QB 354 in which the duty arose from the cohabitation, blood relationship and voluntary assumption of responsibility.

[140] [2005] Crim LR 383.   [141] [2009] EWCA Crim 650.

[142] There are other reported instances of drug suppliers being convicted on this basis. For an example, see *Phillips* [2013] EWCA Crim 358.

From where does the duty on D derive? A duty might be thought to arise at the time of and from the mere act of supply. That is not the law. Following the decision of the House of Lords in *Kennedy (No 2)*,[143] D cannot be convicted of unlawful act manslaughter on the basis of the act of supply to V who self-administers the drugs. D cannot be guilty of unlawful act manslaughter because if V is a free, informed, voluntary actor he breaks the chain of causation between D's unlawful act of supply and the resulting death.[144] If on such facts the prosecution was for gross negligence manslaughter, the same problem would arise: the mere act of supply will *not*, it is submitted, be sufficient to establish liability for manslaughter when V self-administers in a free, informed manner and dies. Although D might be said to owe a duty, have breached it and for there to have been a risk of death, the difficulty is that V's free, informed, voluntary act of self-administration breaks the chain of causation (as in cases of unlawful act manslaughter under *Kennedy (No 2)*).[145] Dealers who supply to their users to self-inject are not liable for manslaughter—at least provided the dealer does not stay with the user and witness the user becoming ill.

The duty arises, the court held in *Evans*, at the point in time when D realized or ought to have realized that V was suffering life-threatening illness. The duty arises at that time because D created *or contributed to* the creation of the life-threatening situation. This conclusion was reached by an extended application of the decision in *Miller*. In that case D was liable for criminal damage when, having fallen asleep with a lit cigarette, he awoke, realized his accidental conduct had created a danger but did not take reasonable steps to prevent further harm arising.[146] In this case the defendants had deliberately supplied the drugs, but V had self-injected. How, applying *Miller* in this extended form, can D be said to be under a duty of care given V's free, informed act to take the drugs? If D has not caused V's death when V self-injects (*Kennedy*), how can D have caused V to become ill when V has self-injected and therefore how can D owe a duty when V does become ill? The answer lies in the fact that the Court of Appeal used the broader expression 'created *or contributed*'.[147] A court may, it is submitted, conclude that a duty arises, applying that test, when D became aware (or ought to have become aware) of V's dangerous illness and either: (a) he was concerned in the supply to V; (b) D was in a pre-existing relationship with V (parent, carer, etc) which persists irrespective of V's self-administration (eg the husband of a woman who has self-injected and who realizes or ought to have realized that she is having breathing difficulty); (c) because D and V were engaged in a dangerous joint enterprise which went wrong;[148] or (d) where D has voluntarily assumed a duty to care for V who is in such a state[149] (eg where V becomes dependent on D's assistance as where D starts to care for V, who has overdosed

---

[143] [2008] 1 AC 269.

[144] There will be rare instances in which D is engaged in the act of injection to such an extent as to be liable for unlawful act manslaughter: *Burgess* [2008] EWCA Crim 516, p 75.

[145] In *Evans*, the Court of Appeal emphasized that 'The question in this appeal *is not whether the appellant may be guilty of manslaughter for having been concerned in the supply of the heroin which caused the deceased's death*.' Emphasis added.

[146] Although Miller was charged with criminal damage which at that time was satisfied by proof of objective recklessness, the House of Lords held that his duty only arose on his subjective realization of the danger. Gross negligence manslaughter is also a crime based on objective fault, but in *Evans* the court holds that the duty arises when D realizes or *ought* to have realized the danger.

[147] See for criticism, Glenys Williams [2009] Crim LR 631 and J Rogers [2009] 6 Arch News 6. The court's response might well be that V's free, deliberate, informed act might break the chain of causation if it was alleged that D's breach by supply per se caused V's death, but V's acts of supply do not become irrelevant when considering whether D *contributed* to the danger V now faces.

[148] See W Wilson, *Criminal Law Theory and Doctrine* (2008) 87.

[149] The court in *Evans* does not rule out this final possibility of duty in drug administration cases although it did not arise on the facts, at [36]. Arguably this is the basis for the decision in *Ruffell* [2003] 2 Cr App R (S) 53.

at a party by moving him from one room to a more secluded space, but then abandons him, leaving V worse off as he is less likely to be seen and rescued by others).

The decision has been heavily criticized but, in policy terms, it might be asked when someone has died, what is wrong with looking to the conduct of those who contributed in some way to the danger *if they also* did not take reasonable steps to alleviate the danger when aware of it? To take an example unencumbered by the policy considerations of the drug supply cases, consider an electrician, D, who leaves half-completed wiring creating a risk of death and V makes an informed choice to use the electrical equipment, aware of its hazardous status. If V is in the process of being electrocuted and D realizes that, surely D has a duty to act responsibly to avoid a life-threatening situation to which he has contributed. Why should a failure at least to seek help on realizing V has been electrocuted not be considered manslaughter if the jury determines the breach sufficiently 'gross'?[150]

The duty question in gross negligence should, according to Lord MacKay in *Adomako*, be founded on the 'ordinary principles of negligence'. However, this should not be regarded as incorporating all of the technicalities of the tort of negligence into the gross negligence offence. Thus, in *Wacker*,[151] it was held that where D had smuggled 60 illegal immigrants into the UK and 58 had died of suffocation owing to his having shut the air vent in their container, he could not displace the duty by relying on the victims' being jointly engaged with him in a criminal enterprise—that is, a plea of *ex turpi causa*.[152]

The courts are clearly anxious to retain a degree of simplicity in this element of the offence which must be put before the jury. On some occasions the criminal courts seem readily to accept the existence of a civil law duty. In the case of *Winter and Winter*,[153] for example, MW and NW were convicted of manslaughter by gross negligence having stored fireworks of an extremely hazardous nature, in breach of their licence, in a container on a farm. A large explosion occurred, killing the fire service's civilian media awareness officer (V), who had been filming the fire for training purposes. V had ignored instructions to keep back from the container. The judge ruled that MW and NW owed a duty to take proper care in the storage and handling of explosives and that that duty was owed to all persons who were on the site or in the surrounding vicinity. The Court of Appeal held that it was reasonably foreseeable that civilian employees of the fire service might come on to and close to the site of a fire in order to film or photograph a fire.[154]

Until relatively recently, confusion reigned over whether the duty issue involved a pure question of law to be determined by the judge,[155] or whether the judge was to rule on whether there was evidence capable of establishing a duty, in which case that was to be left to be determined by the jury.[156] The matter has finally been resolved in *Evans*[157] in which

---

[150] An issue might arise as to whether D discharged the duty of care despite the fact that he failed to summon assistance. The facts of *Phillips* [2013] EWCA Crim 358 are instructive. D became aware that V was suffering from the effects of an overdose, but instead of summoning help, administered adrenaline. The Court of Appeal stated that 'the "gross negligence" alleged therefore was the appellant's failure to act once he knew that [V]'s life was in danger'. D did not fail to act, however. It is important not to lose sight of the fact that the jury must be sure that there was a breach of duty, taking into consideration any steps D took to mitigate the life-threatening situation.

[151] [2003] QB 1203, [2003] Crim LR 108 and commentary. Cf Scots law, *Transco plc v HM Advocate* 2004 SLT 41.

[152] cf the statutory recognition in relation to corporate manslaughter (see later).

[153] *Winter and Winter* [2010] EWCA Crim 1474.

[154] It was held that V's failure to comply with instructions might be relevant to the issue of causation and, in civil cases, to the issue of causation, *volenti* and contributory negligence. It was not arguable in the instant case that any failure to comply with instructions had the consequence that no duty of care was owed to V.

[155] *Gurphal Singh* [1999] Crim LR 582.　　　[156] *Khan* [1998] Crim LR 830; *Sinclair* (1998) unreported.

[157] [2009] EWCA Crim 650. The court approved the commentary in *Willoughby* [2004] EWCA Crim 3365, [2005] Crim LR 389. On alternative interpretations that might have drawn from tort law, see J Herring and E Palser, 'A Duty of Care in Gross Negligence Manslaughter' [2007] Crim LR 24.

the Court of Appeal held 'that whether a duty of care exists is a matter for the jury once the judge has decided that there is evidence capable of establishing a duty'. The court stated:[158]

> In some cases, such as those arising from a doctor/patient relationship where the existence of the duty is not in dispute, the Judge may well direct the jury that a duty of care exists. Such a direction would be proper. But if, for example, the doctor were on holiday at the material time, and the deceased asked a casual question over a drink, it may very well be that the question whether a doctor/patient relationship existed, and accordingly whether a duty of care arose, would be in dispute. In any cases where the issue is in dispute, and therefore in more complex cases, and assuming that the Judge has found that it would be open to the jury to find that there was a duty of care, or a duty to act, the jury should be directed that if facts A + B and/or C or D are established, then in law a duty will arise, but if facts X or Y or Z were present, the duty would be negatived. In this sense, of course, the jury is deciding whether the duty situation has been established. In our judgment this is the way in which *Willoughby* should be understood and, understood in this way, no potential problems arising from art.6 and art.7 of the ECHR are engaged.

14.2.4 Breach of duty

The breach can be by positive act or by omission.[159]

14.2.5 Risk of death

The proposition in *Adomako* refers to a risk of *death*, a point emphasized in *Gurphal Singh*.[160] If we are to have an offence of homicide by gross negligence at all, it seems right that it should be so limited.[161] The circumstances must be such that a reasonably prudent person would have foreseen a serious risk, not merely of injury, even serious injury, but of death. The Court of Appeal confirmed this narrower interpretation in *Misra*.[162] As a matter of policy, the CPS will not prosecute on evidence of anything less. In *Yaqoob* (discussed earlier), the Court of Appeal emphasized that a direction should expressly refer to the fact that it is the risk of death and not merely serious injury that is relevant. The direction in *Singh*[163] should be followed: 'the circumstances must be such that a reasonably prudent person would have foreseen a serious and obvious risk not merely of injury, even serious injury, but of death'.

The Court of Appeal has emphasized that the question of whether there was a risk of death is an objective question—not a question about whether D himself foresaw any such risk. In *S*,[164] S, aged 15, shot his girlfriend, aged 15, when a prohibited firearm (which he was minding) went off at close range while he was showing it to her. There was no evidence that S had either known or believed the gun to be loaded. At trial, S claimed to have removed the magazine from the weapon and therefore believed that it was safe. Expert evidence was to the effect that an inexperienced 15-year-old may have reasonably believed it was safe (not being aware of the risk of a bullet still being in the chamber). The Court of Appeal rejected the argument that there could be no gross negligence when S did not know, believe or foresee the risk of death. Gross negligence manslaughter involved an objective test: whether a reasonable and prudent person of S's age and experience would have foreseen a serious risk

---

158 At [45].   159 See, on omissions, *Watts* [1998] Crim LR 833; *Litchfield* [1998] Crim LR 507.

160 *Gurphal Singh* [1999] Crim LR 582. In *Brown* [2005] UKPC 18, the suggestion was of a 'high' risk of death. *Singh* was cited in *Webster v CPS* [2014] EWHC 2516 (Admin).

161 cf the view of LH Leigh, 'Liability for Inadvertence: A Lordly Legacy?' (1995) 58 MLR 457 at 459.

162 [2004] EWCA Crim 2375, [51].   163 [1999] Crim LR 582.

164 [2015] EWCA Crim 558, [2015] Crim LR 553.

of death and, if so, whether S's conduct fell so far below the standard of care required that it was grossly negligent such that it constituted a crime. Cranston J stated that:

In answering that objective question, it was open to the jury to conclude on the evidence before it that [S's] conduct fell below the standard of care in pointing a gun and pulling the trigger when just a short distance away from [V]. The judge distinguished ordinary negligence and said that whether this was gross negligence turned on the circumstances.[165]

A recent spate of cases involving medical error has led to a further refinement of the test. The focus of the Court of Appeal's attention has been on at what point the risk of death must be assessed as being obvious and in what context. The Court of Appeal has now decided that the risk must be obvious to the reasonable professional in D's shoes, who demonstrates the same level of negligence as D. In other words, the test is not whether the reasonable professional who had not been negligent would have appreciated the existence of a serious and obvious risk of death. The risk must be assessed with reference to D's negligent standard. The difference between these two approaches can be seen in the cases in which the applicable test has been forged.

In *Rudling*,[166] V, a 12-year-old boy, had died of Addison's disease (a very rare condition) after D, his GP, had failed to attend him. Addison's disease was not something any GP could be expected to recognize, but it was argued by the prosecution that the symptoms described to her by V's mother (including vomiting, soiling and black genitals) were so alarming that D ought to have visited him and had she done so she would then have seen that V needed immediate hospital admission. Had she arranged this, V would have been diagnosed and given life-saving treatment. The trial judge nevertheless accepted a submission of no case to answer and the Court of Appeal agreed with this. The thrust of the prosecution case was that a reasonably competent GP would have said to herself 'I cannot eliminate the possibility that this child may be suffering from a rare risk to life without the child being seen urgently', which equated to a serious and obvious risk of death. But according to the Court of Appeal:

At the time of the breach of duty, there must be a risk of death, not merely serious illness; the risk must be serious; and the risk must be obvious. A GP faced with an unusual presentation which is worrying and undiagnosed may need to ensure a face to face assessment urgently in order to investigate further. That may be in order to assess whether it is something serious . . . which may or may not be so serious as to be life-threatening. A recognisable risk of something serious is not the same as a recognisable risk of death.

What does not follow is that if a reasonably competent GP requires an urgent assessment of a worrying and undiagnosed condition, it is necessarily reasonably foreseeable that there is a risk of death. Still less does it demonstrate a serious risk of death, which is not to be equated with an 'inability to eliminate a possibility'. There may be numerous remote possibilities of very rare conditions which cannot be eliminated but which do not present a serious risk of death. Further, and perhaps most importantly, a mere possibility that an assessment might reveal something life-threatening is not the same as an obvious risk of death. An obvious risk is a present risk which is clear and unambiguous, not one which might become apparent on further investigation.

These distinctions are not a matter of semantics but represent real differences in the practical assessments which fall to be made by doctors... .[167]

In the yet more recent case of *Rose*, the Court of Appeal addressed this issue more directly.[168] In *Rose*, the Court of Appeal, drawing on its earlier decision in *Rudling*, held that in assessing either the foreseeability of the risk of death or the grossness of the

---

[165] At [20].   [166] [2016] EWCA Crim 741.
[167] At [39]–[41].   [168] *Rose* [2017] EWCA Crim 1168.

conduct in question, the jury were not entitled to take into account information which would, could or should have been available to the defendant had he not breached the duty in question: the test is objective and prospective. Turning to the facts of *Rose*, D was a registered optometrist who conducted a routine eye test and examination on V. D failed to examine the internal structure of D's eyes, however, as she was required to do by statute. A few months after the eye examination, V died of acute hydrocephalus. Had D examined V's eyes in accordance with her statutory duty, she would have noticed the swelling of his optic nerve, the significance of which would have been clear. The experts agreed that a competent optometrist would have known the significance of that swelling and would immediately have referred the case on to others for urgent treatment. The judge rejected a submission of no case to answer, determining that D had failed to conduct a full examination of the internal structure of V's eyes, there was no good reason for that failure and thus she had breached her duty of care. The judge further found that the risk of death caused by the breach of duty was reasonably foreseeable. He directed the jury to consider whether that risk would have been obvious to a reasonably competent optometrist with the knowledge that the appellant would have had 'if she had not acted in breach of her duty to investigate the true position'. D appealed on the basis that the judge was incorrect to direct the jury that in evaluating whether the risk of death was reasonably foreseeable, they were entitled to consider the knowledge D would have had if she had conducted the eye examination in accordance with her statutory duty.

The Court of Appeal accepted D's submission. It was held that the objective nature of the test requires the notional exercise of putting a reasonably prudent professional in the shoes of the person whose conduct is under scrutiny and asking whether, at the moment of the breach of the duty relied on by the prosecution, that person ought reasonably to have foreseen a serious and obvious risk of death. On the facts of the case, the risk of death would only have been serious and obvious had D examined the internal structure of V's eyes. Sir Brian Leveson P concluded that there was no legitimate basis for altering what is a prospective test of foresight into one which judges with hindsight. D's conviction was therefore quashed. When directing the jury on whether it was reasonably foreseeable that D's breach of the duty gave rise to a serious and obvious risk of death, the reasonably prudent professional is to be endowed with the knowledge D had at the time of the breach of duty, not the knowledge D would or might have had if the breach had not occurred.

The court did add a caveat, however. It was held that the position might be different if V presented with symptoms which themselves either pointed to the risk of a potentially life-threatening condition or provided a flag that alerted a competent optometrist to that risk. Sir Brian Leveson P stated that was not this case, however, given that D was conducting an entirely routine examination with no material pre-existing history.

It is respectfully submitted that there are several problems with framing the test in these terms.[169] First, it seems, in policy terms, to be counterintuitive since it appears to incentivize the person who owes the duty to do less—the less D engages, the less likely the reasonably competent person in his shoes would realize there was a risk of death. The optometrist who does not bother to examine the internal structure of the eye is less likely to be liable than one who does so badly. The counter-argument to this is that the test avoids the risk of medical and other professions being charged with gross negligence manslaughter by reason of negligent omissions to carry out routine eye, blood and other tests which in fact would have revealed fatal conditions notwithstanding that the circumstances were such that it

---

[169] See further K Laird, '*R v Rose*' [2018] Crim LR 76 and K Laird, 'The Evolution of Gross Negligence Manslaughter' [2018] 1 Arch Rev 6.

was not reasonably foreseeable that failure to carry out such tests would carry a serious and obvious risk of death.[170]

Secondly, by endowing the reasonably competent professional with D's shortcomings, the Court of Appeal diminishes the objective nature of the test established in *Adomako*. The House of Lords in *Adomako* held that the standard against which D's conduct ought to be evaluated is that of a reasonably competent anaesthetist, optometrist, etc. If a reasonably competent optometrist would have performed a proper examination of the internal eye, why should D benefit from the fact that she failed to do so and therefore fell far below the standard expected of her? There is an important distinction between the facts of *Rose* and the facts of *Rudling* in this regard. In *Rose*, as D was an optometrist, any eye examination she conducted had to be in accordance with the Opticians Act 1989 and the Sight Test (Examination and Prescription) (No 2) Regulations 1989. These provisions specify that an optometrist, when conducting an eye examination, must perform an intra-ocular examination. There can be no doubt that the reasonably competent optometrist would have conducted V's eye examination in accordance with the duty imposed upon her by the applicable legislation. Had a proper intra-ocular examination been conducted, the reasonably prudent optometrist would have noticed the swelling of V's optic nerve and would have referred him for urgent medical treatment. As has already been pointed out, on the court's interpretation of the test, had D conducted an intra-ocular examination but failed to appreciate the significance of the swelling of the optic nerve, she might have been guilty. By failing to conduct an intra-ocular examination, she was able to avoid liability altogether. The facts of *Rudling* are different, however. Owing to the equivocal nature of V's symptoms, there was disagreement as to whether a reasonably competent GP would have attended V having been told of the symptoms from which he was suffering. If a reasonably competent GP might not have attended V and therefore would also have failed to appreciate the seriousness of his condition, then D should not be penalized for also failing to do so. As the House of Lords confirmed in *Adomako*, D is not to be judged against the standard of more skilled professionals but by the standard of a reasonably competent professional. In *Rose*, had the Court of Appeal agreed with the trial judge's formulation of the relevant test, this would not necessarily lead to the adverse consequences for medical and other professionals described by the Court of Appeal and set out in the previous paragraph.

A final difficulty is that the inquiry into whether the foresight of death was objectively identifiable will turn not just on the specific duty owed by D but by the critical context in which it arose. That will often be a less precise inquiry. Take a simple example of D the plumber who did not remove the front plate from a boiler to check its functioning. If the boiler subsequently explodes killing V, applying *Rose*, the question is whether the reasonable plumber in his shoes (not having taken off the front plate) would have realized there was a serious and obvious risk of death. That can only be determined by asking what the plumber was told to do when hired to examine the boiler. In a case where the plumber was called out because of a smell of gas, he may well be found liable; in a case where the call-out was to provide a routine service to the boiler, the jury may be less inclined to convict.

The problem is one which arises acutely in medical cases where the evidence of the 'context' will often be disputed and be based on what the deceased said. For example, in *Rudling*, the issue may turn on whether the mother described the boy's genitals as black (would have

---

[170] This concern was expressed by the Court of Appeal in *Rose*, but whether a doctor's failure to diagnose a condition amounts to negligence depends upon a number of factors, including the symptoms presented, the diagnostic techniques available and the dangers associated with the alternative diagnoses. See M Jones, *Medical Negligence* (2017), para 4-018.

triggered a realization in a reasonable doctor of a risk of death) or discoloured (not immediately obvious that that suggests life-threatening illness).[171]

14.2.6 'Gross' negligence

The test is objective—the question is whether the risk would have been obvious to the reasonably prudent and skilful doctor, anaesthetist, electrician, motorist, restaurateur or person on the Clapham omnibus, as the circumstances require.

14.2.6.1 Relationship with recklessness

It is, at first sight, surprising that the gross negligence test should be more favourable to the defendant than a recklessness test—even *objective* recklessness.[172] The difference is that the recklessness test did not include the requirement that the jury must be satisfied that the defendant's conduct was bad enough to be a crime. A direction based on the test in *Lawrence* terms deprived D of the chance of acquittal on that ground.[173] In *Prentice*, for example, there were many strongly mitigating factors in the doctors' conduct, which were irrelevant if the jury were concerned only with what was foreseeable, but highly relevant to question whether their behaviour was bad enough to deserve condemnation as manslaughter. Ever since *Bateman*, the courts have asserted that the test is whether the negligence goes beyond a mere matter of compensation and is bad enough to amount to a crime; but this is incomplete, if not plainly wrong. Careless driving amounts to a crime and deserves punishment but, manifestly, it does not on that ground alone amount to manslaughter, if it happens to cause death. Even dangerous driving causing death is not necessarily manslaughter. There are degrees of *criminal* negligence, and manslaughter requires a very high degree. Should not the jury be asked whether the negligence is bad enough to be condemned, not merely as a crime, but as the very grave crime of manslaughter?[174]

In *Misra*,[175] the defendants argued that gross negligence should be replaced with an offence of reckless manslaughter, relying on the fundamental rejection of objectivism in G, and the *dicta* in that case that all serious offences require proof of a blameworthy *state of mind*. The Court of Appeal concluded that such arguments had been duly considered and rejected in *Adomako*, and saw nothing in G[176] to cause them to regard *Adomako* as no longer binding.[177]

14.2.6.2 Relevance of D's state of mind

Since the test of gross negligence is purely objective, it might be thought that the state of mind of the particular accused is irrelevant to the inquiry. However, the courts have held that proof of the defendant's state of mind and in particular his foresight of the risk of harm or death is 'not a prerequisite to a conviction' whilst recognizing also that there may be

---

[171] See also *Bawa-Garba* [2016] EWCA Crim 1841.

[172] See Leigh (1995) 58 MLR 457, and A Norrie, *Crime, Reason and History* (3rd edn, 2014) 66–69.

[173] Lord Mackay in *Adomako* did accept that 'it is perfectly open to the trial judge to use the word "reckless" in its ordinary meaning as part of his exposition of the law if he deems it appropriate in the circumstances of the particular case'. See the direction in *Winter and Winter* [2010] EWCA Crim 1474.

[174] cf *Litchfield* [1998] Crim LR 507 and commentary. Whether evidence was sufficient to satisfy a jury, and whether evidence of subjective recklessness is admissible on a charge of manslaughter by gross negligence, is considered in *DPP, ex p Jones* [2000] Crim LR 858 and commentary.

[175] [2004] EWCA Crim 2375. See O Quick, 'Medicine, Mistakes and Manslaughter: A Criminal Combination?' (2010) 69 CLJ 186 discussing a statistical breakdown of such prosecutions revealing low success rates and potential racial bias in prosecutions against doctors.

[176] [2004] 1 AC 1034.   [177] See also the same conclusion in *Mark* [2004] EWCA Crim 2490.

cases in which the defendant's state of mind is 'relevant to the jury's consideration when assessing the grossness and criminality of his conduct'.[178] This approach has been endorsed on a number of occasions, and it has been recognized that it may operate in the accused's favour.[179] The Court of Appeal held in *Bannister*,[180] however, that taking into account the defendant's special skills in assessing liability in the context of s 2A(1) of the Road Traffic Act 1988 was inconsistent with the objective nature of the test.

14.2.6.3 Circularity of test

As Lord MacKay acknowledged, the test involves a degree of circularity. It may also be criticized, as was its predecessor, the '*Bateman* test', on the ground that it leaves a question of law to the jury. It has always been held that the negligence which suffices for civil liability is not necessarily enough for manslaughter, so someone has to decide whether the particular negligence is bad enough to amount to a crime, indeed this very grave crime. It is not necessary for the judge to refer to the distinction between civil and criminal liability, which might tend to confuse the jury.[181]

The jury appear to be left with the task of deciding the scope of the offence. The task is quite unlike that in, say, applying the definition of intention, which has been supplied by the judge. In such a case, the jury looks at the facts and applies the legal definition of intention as provided by the judge. In gross negligence, the jury has to determine whether on their view the conduct should be called grossly negligent, and if so that amounts to the crime. This seems objectionable in principle. In rejecting a challenge that the offence was insufficiently certain to be compatible with Art 7 of the ECHR, the Court of Appeal in *Misra* held that the jury's function in gross negligence cases is not to decide a point of law, but one of fact:

> The decision whether the conduct was criminal is described [in *Adomako*] not as 'the' test, but as 'a' test as to how far the conduct in question must depart from accepted standards to be 'characterized as criminal'. On proper analysis, therefore, the jury is not deciding whether the particular defendant ought to be convicted on some unprincipled basis. The question for the jury is not whether the defendant's negligence was gross, and whether, *additionally*, it was a crime, but whether his behaviour was grossly negligent and *consequently* criminal. This is not a question of law, but one of fact, for decision in the individual case.[182]

With respect, it is doubtful whether this meets the criticisms that the test is circular, and that it requires the jury to determine the scope of the criminal law.

14.2.6.4 Guiding the jury

The Court of Appeal has recognized the need for the jury to receive greater assistance in determining whether a particular failing is 'grossly negligent'. The issue has arisen most acutely in cases of medical negligence.

In *Sellu*,[183] an experienced colorectal surgeon was convicted of gross negligence manslaughter for a series of errors in his treatment of the deceased who had undergone elective

---

[178] *A-G's Reference (No 2 of 1999)* [2000] Crim LR 475 (Southall Rail crash case). Cf *S* [2015] EWCA Crim 558.

[179] *R v DPP, ex p Jones* [2000] IRLR 373, DC; *R (Rowley) v DPP* [2003] EWHC 693 (Admin). Whether the two are consistent on this is debatable.

[180] [2009] EWCA Crim 1571.

[181] *Becker*, No 199905228/Y5, 19 June 2000, CA. For an argument that the circularity is not pernicious, see V Tadros, 'The Limits of Manslaughter' in Clarkson and Cunningham, *Criminal Liability for Non-Aggressive Death*.

[182] At [62], emphasis in original.   [183] [2016] EWCA Crim 1716.

knee surgery. The post-operative treatment of a gastro-intestinal complication led to V's death. The prosecution alleged that three specific breaches of S's duty of care to his patient had occurred: S failed to take urgent action when an x-ray showed that an intestinal perforation was likely; S failed to visit the deceased when learning of his condition despite the potential need to perform emergency surgery; S failed to operate within eight hours of CT scan results confirming the diagnosis and the need to operate to avoid fatal peritonitis. In summing up, the jury were directed that the issue to be assessed by them was as follows: first, did S behave negligently, in that no reasonable consultant colorectal surgeon in his position would have behaved as he did. Secondly, whether any gross negligence caused or significantly contributed to the deceased's death. Furthermore, and crucially, the trial judge's description of the required level of culpability referred only to whether S's conduct fell below the standard 'in a way that was gross or severe'.

The Court of Appeal held that the trial judge's approach to gross negligence, and in particular his direction to the jury, was inadequate. Following *Adomako, Bateman, Andrews* and *Misra* the direction ought to have made clear to the jury that the required conduct must have been 'truly exceptionally bad' and such a departure from the requisite standard that it consequently amounted to it being criminal. The conviction was therefore quashed. The Court of Appeal was also critical of the judge for not giving a route to verdict although he had given written directions. It was confirmed that, in complex cases, routes to verdict are now routinely expected.

The court gave further guidance to judges on how juries should be directed on this element of the offence. To repeat the word 'gross' is insufficient. The jury need to understand that they must be sure of a failure that was not just serious or very serious but 'truly exceptionally bad'.[184] Sir Brian Leveson P accepted that when directing the jury in cases of alleged gross negligence manslaughter, no formulation of the concept of gross negligence is mandatory, but, he added:

What is mandatory is that the jury are assisted sufficiently to understand how to approach their task of identifying the line that separates even serious or very serious mistakes or lapses, from conduct which was 'truly exceptionally bad and was such a departure from that standard [of a reasonably competent doctor] that it consequently amounted to being criminal'.[185]

In the subsequent case of *Bawa-Garba*, the Court of Appeal emphasized once again that juries should be left in no doubt as to the truly exceptional degree of negligence which must be established if gross negligence is to be made out.[186] This emphasis on the high threshold for the very serious offence to be committed will have an impact on the likelihood of medical professionals being convicted (and prosecuted).

The court in *Sellu* also emphasized the importance of ensuring that the evidence elicited from the experts assists the jury in determining whether D's degree of negligence crossed the high threshold necessary for it to constitute gross negligence. Finally, the court reaffirmed that whether D's breach or omission was grossly negligent is ultimately a matter for the jury, not the experts. Trial judges must therefore take care to ensure that the jury's role is not usurped by the experts.

14.2.6.5 ECHR compatibility

The Court of Appeal in *Misra* concluded that gross negligence manslaughter was sufficiently clear and did not offend the requirement of legal certainty imposed by Art 7 or the common

---

184 At [152].
185 ibid. Langley J's direction to the jury in *Misra* [2005] 1 Cr App R 21 was cited with approval.
186 *Bawa-Garba* [2016] EWCA Crim 1841, [36].

law. The court referred to the writings of Bacon and Blackstone to support its view that Art 7 merely confirmed the common law position on the principle of legal certainty. Thus, the court felt confident that the House of Lords, when framing the offence in *Adomako*, was not 'indifferent to or unaware of the need for the criminal law in particular to be predictable and certain'.[187] The court observed that Art 7 does not require absolute certainty but that offences are defined 'with sufficient precision to enable the citizen to regulate his conduct: he must be able—if need be with appropriate advice—to foresee to a degree that is reasonable in the circumstances, the consequences which any given action may entail'.[188] On the court's view, even applying the stricter interpretation of the test in *Hashman and Harrup v UK*,[189] the offence would be likely to satisfy Art 7, since gross negligence manslaughter depends on jury evaluation of conduct by reference to its consequences, and in gross negligence manslaughter the jury must be satisfied as to the 'risk of death' and of causation.

14.2.6.6 Causation

The breach of duty which posed a serious and obvious risk of death must be the cause of the death. Principles of causation in Ch 2 apply here. The prosecution is required to prove that D's breach of duty caused or made a significant contribution to the death.[190] The issue can be a difficult one in the context of medical negligence in particular. For example, in *Sellu*, Sir Brian Leveson P stated that what was crucial in that case was that the jury were sure D's failings were grossly negligent and went on to consider the question of causation, understanding that causation would not be established if that gross negligence occurred after the time that they could be sure V would have survived.[191] Similarly, in *Bawa-Garba*, the Court of Appeal held that the judge's direction to the jury that D could only be guilty if her acts or omissions made a significant contribution to D's dying as and when he did was unassailable.[192] Expert evidence will be necessary to help the jury assess whether D's gross negligence occurred at a time when V could still have survived.

14.3 Reckless manslaughter

Gross negligence is a sufficient, but not necessarily the only, fault for manslaughter. To some extent manslaughter by advertent recklessness—conscious risk-taking—still survives.[193] Where D kills by a reckless lawful act (therefore no UAM available) which he foresees might cause serious bodily harm (no gross negligence manslaughter available as no serious and obvious risk of death), this ought to be capable of being manslaughter. Similarly, where D kills by a reckless omission (no UAM) which does not pose a risk of death (no gross negligence manslaughter), reckless manslaughter may apply if D foresaw a risk of serious injury to V. These used to be murder (*Hyam*) before the decision in *Moloney*,[194] so must still be manslaughter. Where death is so caused, the jury do not have to decide whether D's conduct is bad enough to amount to a crime. That question is appropriate only when we are concerned with degrees of negligence, there being no other way of determining the criminal degree. The jury are not

---

[187] At [34]; cf commentary on *Misra* [2005] Crim LR 234.
[188] *Sunday Times v UK* [1979] 2 EHRR 245.   [189] [2000] Crim LR 185.
[190] *Zaman* [2017] EWCA Crim 1783.   [191] [2016] EWCA Crim 1716, [127].
[192] [2016] EWCA Crim 1841, [33].
[193] For an engaging analysis see F Stark, 'Reckless Manslaughter' [2017] Crim 763 arguing that the offence does not exist but it ought to. We suggest that it already does for the reasons explained in this section.
[194] See p 91.

asked this question in non-fatal offences against the person, which may be committed reck-lessly, so it would be quite inconsistent if it applied when death is caused.

The main concern with this least controversial form of manslaughter is to distinguish 'subjective recklessness' (manslaughter) from 'oblique intention' (murder).[195] The leading case is *Lidar*,[196] in which V died when run over by D's car to which he had been hanging on when pursuing D in the course of a fight. Although the trial judge directed that D's fault element would be satisfied by proof of recklessness (ie D's personal foresight) as to mere injury, the Court of Appeal held that this was not fatal to the safety of the conviction. Subjective reckless manslaughter requires proof that D foresaw a risk that V would suffer serious injury (or death) and took the risk unjustifiably. In a sentencing appeal, the Court of Appeal recognized the existence of the offence. In *Hussain*,[197] D had killed a child, V, by driving with V trapped under the car. At trial the Crown expressly put its case on the basis that D 'knew that it was a child who was under the car rather than some other object, that he foresaw the risk of serious injury or death by continuing to drive and yet chose to take that risk and death resulted'.

14.4 Reform

The reform debate[198] was rekindled by the Law Commission and MOJ agenda for reform of homicide which, although focusing principally on the appropriate scheme of murder and partial defences, has produced a coherent regime which integrates involuntary manslaugh-ter offences.[199] The ladder structure of the Law Commission proposals allows for a clearer analysis of the relative degrees of culpability in the different forms of homicide.[200]

When considering the offences of manslaughter alongside that of murder and the pro-posed forms of murder, it is essential to bear in mind the numerous statutory offences of homicide—causing death by dangerous driving, causing death by careless driving, etc.[201]

14.4.1 Unlawful act manslaughter (UAM)

In view of the sustained principled criticism of the offence, it is no surprise that there have been calls for reform and indeed abolition. In the Law Commission's Consultation Paper No 135, *Involuntary Manslaughter*, it was observed that there was 'no prospect' of being able to devise any clear principled statement of the law based on concepts of unlawful act manslaughter.[202] In LCCP 135 the Law Commission provisionally proposed abolition

---

[195] See p 92. See also J Horder, 'The Changing Face of the Law of Homicide' in J Horder (ed), *Homicide Law in Comparative Perspective* (2007) 26–33.

[196] [2000] 4 Arch News 3.   [197] [2012] EWCA Crim 188.

[198] For a compelling review of the defects with the present law see LC 237, *Involuntary Manslaughter* (1996) Part III. See also the Law Reform Commission of Ireland Report: *Homicide* (2008).

[199] See, generally, on the common law development of the homicide offences, J Horder, 'Homicide Reform and the Changing Character of Legal Thought' in Clarkson and Cunningham, *Criminal Liability for Non-Aggressive Death*.

[200] See, *inter alia*, Tadros, 'The Limits of Manslaughter' in Clarkson and Cunningham, *Criminal Liability for Non-Aggressive Death* suggesting that there needs to be a lower category of homicide offence for the least serious cases.

[201] See Ashworth, '"Manslaughter": Generic or Nominate Offences?' in Clarkson and Cunningham, *Criminal Liability for Non-Aggressive Death*, and S Yeo, 'Manslaughter versus Special Homicide Offences: An Australian Perspective' in the same volume.

[202] Para 5.4. On earlier reform proposals including those of the CLRC, Fourteenth Report; see S Prevezer, 'Criminal Homicides Other Than Murder' [1980] Crim LR 530.

of UAM without replacement.[203] By the time of the Report two years later, its opinion had changed. The Law Commission's final recommendation was that a person is guilty of careless killing (GCK) if he has intended to cause injury, or is aware of the risk of a new offence of injury and unreasonably takes the risk where the conduct causing or intended to cause the injury constitutes an offence. Keating[204] is critical of the failure to secure correspondence between the fault (foresight of injury) and the harm caused, regarding it as 'unfortunate' for the Law Commission to include a version of unlawful act manslaughter. The Home Office subsequently questioned whether some version of the constructive manslaughter offence ought to be retained.[205] It was unconvinced by the merits of the Law Commission proposal that it was wrong in principle to convict of an offence of death where the offender was aware only of a risk of injury. The example given by the Home Office is an extreme one of a person causing a minor wound to the victim who is a haemophiliac.[206] The Home Office proposal would create liability where the accused intended some injury, in the course of the commission of a violent crime, and the death was not foreseen. As with the Law Commission proposal, there is no full correspondence between the fault (foresight of injury) and the harm (death) for which the defendant is punished. The Home Office offers no justification for basing liability on an accidental outcome rather than intention or foresight.

The Law Commission's latest recommendation is that the offence will be recast as killing another person:

(a) through the commission of a criminal act intended by the defendant to cause injury, or

(b) through the commission of a criminal act that the defendant was aware involved a serious risk of causing some injury ('criminal act manslaughter').[207]

14.4.2 Gross negligence manslaughter

In 1997, the Law Commission[208] proposed the reform, rather than abolition, of the gross negligence offence. The Law Commission's recommendations as part of the *Murder, Manslaughter and Infanticide* Report[209] are that gross negligence be recast as follows. A person is guilty of gross negligence manslaughter if:

(1) a person by his or her conduct causes the death of another;

(2) a risk that his or her conduct will cause death … would be obvious to a reasonable person in his or her position;

(3) he or she is capable of appreciating that risk at the material time;

and

(4) . . . his or her conduct falls far below what can reasonably be expected of him or her in the circumstances . . .

---

[203] See Wasik [1994] Crim LR 883.

[204] See H Keating, 'The Restoration of a Serious Crime' [1996] Crim LR 535.

[205] Consultation Paper, *Reforming the Law of Involuntary Manslaughter* (2000) para 2.11.

[206] This seemingly fanciful scenario has occurred: see *State v Frazier*, 98 SW 2d 707 (1936) (Mo).

[207] LC 304, para 2.163. In *JF* [2015] EWCA Crim 351, the Court of Appeal emphasized that it is for Parliament to change the law, not the courts.

[208] LC 237, *Legislating the Criminal Code: Involuntary Manslaughter* (1996). See also J Spencer and AM Brajeux, 'Criminal Liability for Negligence—A Lesson from Across the Channel' (2010) 59 ICLQ 1.

[209] LC 304, para 3.60.

14.4.3 Reckless manslaughter

The Law Commission recommends abolition of this category of manslaughter. It is suggested that all cases will now be adequately catered for in either: (a) the new second degree murder offence where D realizes there is a serious risk of death from his conduct and intends to cause injury, or (b) the new version of gross negligence proposed earlier. What of D who has specialist knowledge of a risk of his lawful activity which is not known to the reasonable person and who foresees a risk of injury but not death by his conduct, but who kills V? D cannot be liable for gross negligence even though D's mental state can be considered by the jury in evaluating whether his conduct is grossly negligent, as there is no objective risk of death. Nor is D guilty of second degree murder unless he sees a risk of death.

14.5 The Corporate Manslaughter and Corporate Homicide Act 2007

14.5.1 Introduction

This long-awaited Act, which extends to the whole of the UK, received Royal Assent on 26 July 2007[210] and most of the Act was brought into force on 6 April 2008. Although the Act appears to create a broad-reaching offence in terms of bodies to which it will apply and the duties of care which will trigger liability, these are severely curtailed by the technical qualifications integral to the all important duty question and by the numerous and far-reaching exclusions designed to protect public bodies. The layers of technicality serve to restrict the scope of liability far more than would at first appear, and are also likely to lead to substantial practical difficulties in prosecution.[211]

14.5.1.1 Background

Public disquiet with the lack of a specific offence for corporate killing increased with each successive failure to secure convictions for gross negligence manslaughter in any of the large-scale disasters such as the Southall, Paddington, Hatfield and Potter's Bar rail crashes, the Zeebrugge (*Herald of Free Enterprise*) and *Marchioness* shipping disasters and the Piper Alpha and King's Cross fires. With that list in mind, it seems startling that the Act was such a long time in coming. The immediate background to the Act is traceable to the Law Commission Report from 1996[212] recommending the creation of a new offence of 'corporate

---

[210] On the Act, see generally D Ormerod and R Taylor, 'The Corporate Manslaughter and Corporate Homicide Act 2007' [2008] Crim LR 589. In this part of the chapter we have drawn heavily on that article. See also A Norrie, *Crime, Reason and History* (3rd edn, 2014) 124–128, who argues that the offence takes an 'uncomfortable' hybrid 'organizational–identitarian' approach; J Gobert, 'The Corporate Manslaughter and Corporate Homicide Act 2007' (2008) 71 MLR 413; J Horder, 'The Criminal Liability of Organisations for Manslaughter and Other Serious Offences' in S Hetherington (ed), *Halsbury's Laws of England Centenary Essays* (2007); M Hsaio, 'Abandonment of the Doctrine of Attribution in Favour of Gross Negligence Test in the Corporate Manslaughter and Corporate Homicide Act 2007' (2009) 30 *Company Lawyer* 110. Other background documents are on the Home Office website.

[211] It has been argued that the 2007 Act has failed to increase accountability, see S Field and L Jones, 'Five Years On: The Impact of the Corporate Manslaughter and Corporate Homicide Act 2007: Plus ça change?' (2013) 6 ICCLR 239. For an analysis of some of the criticisms that have been made of the legislation, see P Almond, *Corporate Manslaughter and Regulatory Reform* (2013). See also C Wells, 'Corporate Criminal Liability: A Ten Year Review' [2014] Crim LR 847.

[212] LC 237, *Legislating the Criminal Code: Involuntary Manslaughter* (1996).

killing'.[213] A corporation would commit this offence if its 'management failure' were a cause of a person's death, and that failure fell far below what could reasonably be expected of the corporation in the circumstances. That proposal was, as Professor Wells noted, the start of the fundamental change in the UK to move the corporate manslaughter offence away from individual liability, bedevilled as it was by the identification doctrine discussed in Ch 8, towards liability based on 'management failure'.[214]

The Law Commission Report was followed by a Home Office Consultation Paper in which the government accepted the need for reform,[215] recognizing the need to restore public confidence that companies responsible for loss of life can properly be held accountable in law. The government stated its belief that 'the creation of a new offence of corporate killing would give useful emphasis to the seriousness of health and safety offences and would give force to the need to consider health and safety as a management issue'.[216] The government was prepared to go further than the Law Commission proposal by extending the offence to all 'undertakings' including unincorporated associations and other trades or businesses. Following a Report of the Home Affairs and Work and Pensions Committees in 2005,[217] the government produced another Bill[218] which, after much controversy in Parliament, became the present Act.

14.5.1.2 Problems with the old law

Aside from the symbolic benefits of a specifically labelled offence reflecting the particular wrongdoing involved in death caused by organizational mismanagement, three legal reasons for reform were apparent.

Identification doctrine

The identification principle was a major obstacle to securing a conviction under the common law offence of gross negligence manslaughter, particularly with a company of any size or with any complexity in its management structure. The doctrine is discussed in full in Ch 8. It required there to be an individual holding a sufficiently senior position in the company who could be identified with the company as its 'directing mind and will' and who individually fulfilled the elements of the gross negligence offence: fatality following a gross breach of a duty of care which posed a risk of death. The only successful prosecutions against corporate entities for gross negligence were in relation to small companies,[219] where there was more likely to be a single person directly and immediately responsible for

---

[213] On which see H Keating, 'The Law Commission Report on Involuntary Manslaughter: (1) The Restoration of a Serious Crime' [1998] Crim LR 535; A McColgan, 'Heralding Corporate Liability' [1994] Crim LR 547. See also S Field and N Jorg, 'Corporate Liability and Manslaughter: Should We Be Going Dutch?' [1991] Crim LR 156.

[214] C Wells, 'The Corporate Manslaughter Proposals: Pragmatism, Paradox or Peninsularity' [1996] Crim LR 545 at 553. C Wells, 'Corporate Liability: A Ten Year Review' [2014] Crim LR 847 suggests that the Act provides 'an over-complex offence [with a] definition full of ambiguities and interpretive uncertainty'.

[215] *Reforming the Law on Involuntary Manslaughter: The Government's Proposals* (2000): www.corporateaccountability.org.uk/dl/manslaughter/reform/archive/homeofficedraft2000.pdf. See J Gobert, 'Corporate Killing at Home and Abroad: Reflections on the Government Proposals' (2002) 118 LQR 72; GR Sullivan, 'Corporate Killing—Some Government Proposals' [2001] Crim LR 31. For a different proposal based on causing death in the course of a specified 'scheduled' offence (eg one contrary to the Health and Safety at Work Act), see PR Glazebrook, 'A Better Way of Convicting Businesses of Avoidable Deaths and Injuries' (2002) 61 CLJ 405; see also C Clarkson, 'Corporate Manslaughter—Yet More Government Proposals' [2005] Crim LR 677.

[216] Para 3.1.9.   [217] HC 540 I-III.   [218] Cm 6755.

[219] See eg *Kite and OLL Ltd*, Winchester Crown Court, 8 Dec 1994 (1994) The Independent, 9 Dec; *R v Jackson Transport (Ossett) Ltd*, reported in Health and Safety at Work, Nov 1996, p 4; *R v Great Western Trains Company (GWT)*, Central Criminal Court, 30 June 1999; *Roy Bowles Transport Ltd* (1999) The Times, 11 Dec.

the death and who was senior enough to be regarded as the 'directing mind and will' of the company. There were few successful prosecutions for gross negligence manslaughter against corporations. Arguably, the new law retains this disproportionate effect on smaller companies since there is now a requirement that the senior manager(s) played a substantial part in the organizational failure leading to death. The smaller the company, the more likely the 'senior managers' will have had a hand in formulating and implementing the relevant policy on safety, etc; the breach of which led to the death.

Aggregation

Many critics of the identification doctrine questioned whether it must be proved that an *individual* controlling officer (whether identifiable or not) was guilty or whether it is permissible to 'aggregate' the conduct of a number of officers, none of whom would individually be guilty, so as to constitute, in sum, the elements of the offence.[220] In the context of gross negligence manslaughter, the argument was that *a company* owes a duty of care, and if its operation falls far below the standard required it is guilty of gross negligence. A series of minor failures by officers of the company might add up to a gross breach by *the company* of its duty of care. The argument was strengthened by the fact that such aggregation is permissible in tort[221] and the concept of negligence is the same in the criminal law, the difference being one of degree—criminal negligence must be 'gross'. This argument was, however, rejected by the Court of Appeal in *A-G's Reference (No 2 of 1999)*.[222] The prosecution arose from the Southall train crash in which seven passengers died. The trial judge ruled that the gross negligence manslaughter offence requires negligence to be proved under the identification doctrine. The Court of Appeal approved that ruling, holding that unless an identified individual's conduct, characterized as gross criminal negligence, could be attributed to the company, the company was not liable for manslaughter at common law.[223]

Killing of a human by a human

It was at one time thought[224] that a corporation could not be convicted of an offence involving personal violence but, in *P&O European Ferries Ltd*,[225] Turner J held that an indictment for manslaughter would lie against the company in respect of the Zeebrugge disaster. The persuasive authority of this ruling is not impaired by the judge's subsequent decision that, on the evidence before him, the company had no case to answer. The rejected

---

[220] See RD Taylor, *Blackstone's Criminal Practice Bulletin* (Oct 2007).

[221] *WB Anderson & Sons Ltd v Rhodes (Liverpool) Ltd* [1967] 2 All ER 850, Cairns J, discussed by M Dean, 'Hedley Byrne and the Eager Business Man' (1968) 31 MLR 322.

[222] [2000] QB 796; considering *Great Western Trains Co* (1999) 3 June, CCC. It was also rejected in Scotland in *Transco v HM Advocate* 2004 SLT 41. See also *R (Bodycote) v HM Coroner for Hertfordshire* [2008] EWCA Crim 164.

[223] The court's conclusion that there can *in general* be no corporate liability in the absence of an identified human offender ignores the principle discussed earlier of corporate liability where a duty is specifically imposed on the corporation as a legal person: *Birmingham & Gloucester Railway* (1842) 3 QB 223.

[224] *Cory Bros Ltd* [1927] 1 KB 810 (Finlay J, holding that a corporation could not be indicted for manslaughter or an offence under the OAPA 1861, s 31), a ruling of which Stable J said in *ICR Haulage Ltd* [1944] KB 551, 'if the matter came before the court today, the result might well be different'.

[225] (1990) 93 Cr App R 72, [1991] Crim LR 695 and commentary. Streatfield J ruled that an indictment for manslaughter would lie in *Northern Strip Mining Construction Co Ltd* ((1965) 1 Feb, unreported, Glamorgan Assizes) but the corporation was acquitted on the merits. Maurice J's decision in a civil action, *S and Y Investments (No 2) Pty Ltd v Commercial Co of Australia Ltd* (1986) 21 App R 204 at 217, required a ruling that a company was guilty of manslaughter. A company, *OLL Ltd*, was convicted of manslaughter at Winchester Crown Court, 8 Dec 1994, following a canoeing tragedy in Lyme Bay.

argument was based on the fact that, from the time of Coke (1601), authoritative books had described manslaughter as 'the killing of a human being by *a human being*'.[226] This definition found its way into the law of some states of the USA and, via Stephen's draft Code Bill of 1880, into the New Zealand Crimes Acts of 1908 and 1961. The effect was that the New Zealand Court of Appeal decided in *Murray Wright Ltd*[227] that a corporation could not be guilty of manslaughter as a principal. Turner J did not follow that decision. Coke's purpose in using the phrase 'by a human being' was not to exclude corporations from liability—corporations were not indictable for any crime at that time—but to distinguish killings by an inanimate thing or an animal without the fault of any person. Such killings at the time of his writing had legal consequences but were not murder or manslaughter. Moreover, the requirement of an act or omission by a human being is not peculiar to manslaughter. All crimes involve acts or omissions, or the results of acts or omissions, by human beings. It is not manslaughter if a person is killed by an earthquake, or a thunderbolt, or a wild animal in the jungle.

14.5.2 The 2007 Act

14.5.2.1 The offence

Section 1 of the 2007 Act provides:

(1) An organisation to which this section applies is guilty of an offence if the way in which its activities are managed or organised—

(a) causes a person's death, and

(b) amounts to a gross breach of a relevant duty of care owed by the organisation to the deceased . . .

(3) An organisation is guilty of an offence under this section only if the way in which its activities are managed or organised by its senior management is a substantial element in the breach referred to in subsection (1).

The offence follows many of the core aspects of gross negligence manslaughter. The crucial difference is that 'rather than being contingent on the guilt of one or more individuals, liability for the new offence depends on a finding of gross negligence in the way in which the activities of the organisation are run'.[228] The statutory offence, in a reversal of the common law, is focused on the aggregate responsibility of the senior managers. The Home Office Explanatory Notes describe this as the 'management failure', but that phrase is not part of the statute.[229]

The first successful prosecution was of a small firm (eight employees) for the death of a 27-year-old geologist who was buried under earth when a 3.5m trench collapsed on him when he was unsupervised.[230] The company's sole director was directly implicated in the acts.[231]

---

[226] See eg Stephen, *Digest* (1st edn, 1877) art 218 and subsequent editions.

[227] [1970] NZLR 476.   [228] Home Office Explanatory Notes, para 14.

[229] On the ambiguities of the term 'management' in the Act, see C Wells, 'Corporate Criminal Liability: A Ten Year Review' [2014] Crim LR 847, 854: 'the CMCH Act slips between two grammatical uses of the word management. "Management" can mean either "the action or manner of managing", or the "power of managing", or it could function as a collective noun for "a governing body".'

[230] *Cotswold Geotechnical Holdings Ltd* [2011] EWCA Crim 1337, The Times, 20 July 2011. See CPS blog relating to the Cotswold Geotechnical prosecution (available at http://blog.cps.gov.uk/2011/02/tuesday-15-february-afternoon-update.html).

[231] For a list of the prosecutions, see C Wells [2014] Crim LR 847, 860.

14.5.2.2 Relationship to other homicide offences

The Act abolishes gross negligence manslaughter as far as it applies to corporations and other bodies to which the 2007 Act applies (s 20).[232] The Act also provides that individuals cannot be liable as secondary parties to an offence of corporate manslaughter (s 18(1)). Individuals within companies can, of course, still be prosecuted for gross negligence manslaughter as principal offenders subject to what has been said previously.[233] This attempt at a strict division between organizational and individual fault may pose problems. If an individual defendant is charged alongside a company in the same proceedings, the jury will be faced with two different tests of manslaughter liability.

An organization can, although this is much less likely,[234] be convicted of unlawful act manslaughter in appropriate circumstances (eg where D is the manager of a company who encourages employee X to set fire to the company premises in an insurance scam which leads to the death of V on the premises). The corporation may also be liable as an accessory to the principal individual offender in other homicide offences, such as causing death by dangerous driving.[235]

In terms of Health and Safety Act offences,[236] an offending organization can be liable under the 2007 Act and under the relevant health and safety legislation (s 19(1)).[237] Additionally, nothing in the 2007 Act precludes prosecution of an organization which has already been convicted of corporate manslaughter for a health and safety offence (s 19(2)). The relationship between the health and safety legislation and the 2007 Act offence is an interesting one.[238] The government eschewed a model of constructive manslaughter where a breach of health and safety legislation which led to death could found liability for corporate manslaughter. Liability under the Act is, instead, based on duties founded in the civil law of negligence. However, the breaches of health and safety legislation will not be irrelevant since the jury are directed that they must have regard to such breaches in establishing whether the organization has been grossly at fault (s 8).[239]

---

[232] By s 27(4) 'any liability, investigation, legal proceeding or penalty for or in respect of an offence committed wholly or partly before the commencement of that section' remains, and by s 27(5) an offence is committed wholly or partly before the commencement if 'any of the conduct or events alleged to constitute the offence occurred before that commencement'. It is clear that there is no gap left in the law: gross negligence manslaughter remains available in all other relevant circumstances. In *R v Cornish; Maidstone and Tunbridge Wells NHS Trust* [2015] EWHC 2967 (QB), Coulson J rejected the submission that any prosecution for corporate manslaughter would have to be abandoned simply because it referred to an event that occurred before the commencement of the 2007 Act. Pre-commencement events could not *found* the charges, but it was held that they could be *relevant* to the charges that were brought under the 2007 Act.

[233] The Home Office Consultation Paper in 2000 had suggested that there should be responsibility for corporate manslaughter placed on individual directors in appropriate cases but this attracted strong opposition. For an analysis of the extent to which individual corporate officers can be liable for other homicide offences, see S Antrobus, 'The Criminal Liability of Directors for Health and Safety Breaches and Manslaughter' [2013] Crim LR 309. Wells [2014] Crim LR 847 is heavily critical of this aspect of the new offence.

[234] cf the argument advanced by C Wells, *Corporations and Criminal Liability* (2001) 120.

[235] See *JF Alford* [1997] 2 Cr App R 326, [1997] Crim LR 745.

[236] Defined in s 25 to mean 'any statutory provision dealing with health and safety matters, including in particular provision contained in the Health and Safety at Work etc Act 1974, and provisions dealing with health and safety matters contained in Part 3 of the Energy Act 2013'. See on corporate liability under the 1974 Act, *Chargot Ltd (trading as Contract Services) and others* [2008] UKHL 73.

[237] The overlap is considered by Wells [2014] Crim LR 847.

[238] cf Antrobus, n 233, and P Almond, *Corporate Manslaughter and Regulatory Reform* (2013). For criticism of the way the Act impacts on this relationship, see Wells [2014] Crim LR 847.

[239] See also FB Wright, 'Criminal Liability of Directors and Senior Managers for Deaths at Work' [2007] Crim LR 949.

14.5.2.3 Which 'organizations' are caught?

Section 1(5) provides that the offence under this section is called: (a) 'corporate manslaughter', insofar as it is an offence under the law of England and Wales. This is rather misleading because it can also be committed by certain organizations other than corporations, for example an NHS Trust.[240] Section 1(2) defines the organizations to which the new offence applies, which includes, most obviously, corporations.[241] Section 1(2) also applies the offence to police forces, partnerships[242] (partnerships under the Limited Liability Partnerships Act 2000 are caught by the definition of corporation in any event), trade unions[243] and employers' associations,[244] if the organization concerned is an employer. Schedule 1 lists the government departments to which the offence applies. There are some 40 such departments.[245] These include some in which it is not difficult to imagine how corporate manslaughter liability might arise because of the functions they perform, for example Department for Transport, Department of Health, Forestry Commission. With some it may seem a little less likely, for example Revenue and Customs, CPS, National Audit Office—but since liability can arise as a result of being an employer or occupier, it is not difficult so see how they might be liable for a death.[246]

In the course of debates in the House of Lords it was emphasized how important is the extension of the offence to public bodies:

there is no reason why the death of an individual in one situation should be considered less of a death, or less deserving of justice, merely because that situation was presided over by government officials as opposed to privately employed foremen. Indeed, it is all the more of a tragedy and contravention of the natural principle of justice where the state itself acts with such gross negligence that the very lives of its own citizens are forfeit.[247]

Crown Immunity is removed by s 11. Section 11(2) provides that a Crown organization is to be treated as owing whatever duties of care it would owe if it were a corporation that was not a servant or agent of the Crown. However, as will be explained later there are a number of respects in which that liability is very heavily qualified in ss 3 to 7.

Partnerships are to be treated as owing whatever duties of care they would owe if they were a body corporate (s 14(2)).

---

[240] See *R v Cornish; Maidstone and Tunbridge Wells NHS Trust* [2015] EWHC 2967 (QB).

[241] By s 25, 'corporation' does not include a corporation sole but includes any body corporate wherever incorporated. This includes companies incorporated under companies legislation, as well as bodies incorporated under statute (as is the case with many non-departmental public bodies and other bodies in the public sector) or by Royal Charter.

[242] By s 25, 'partnership' means: '(a) a partnership within the Partnership Act 1890, or (b) a limited partnership registered under the Limited Partnerships Act 1907, or a firm or entity of a similar character formed under the law of a country or territory outside the United Kingdom.' See also *Stevenson & Sons*, p 260.

[243] By s 25, 'trade union' has the meaning given by s 1 of the Trade Union and Labour Relations (Consolidation) Act 1992.

[244] By s 25, 'employers' association' has the meaning given by s 122 of the Trade Union and Labour Relations (Consolidation) Act 1992.

[245] Provision is made in s 16 for the circumstances in which relevant functions are transferred between one government department and another or between the other bodies listed in Sch 1, and for cases in which a relevant government agency is privatized.

[246] The list of organizations to which the offence applies can be further extended by secondary legislation, eg to further types of unincorporated association, subject to the affirmative resolution procedure (s 21). The list of government departments in Sch 1 may be changed by the negative resolution procedure (eg the name of a particular department) unless the change is to alter the range of activities or functions in relation to which the s 1 offence applies, in which case the affirmative resolution procedure applies. Since the Act was passed, the list in Sch 1 has been amended on a number of occasions.

[247] Hansard, HL, text for 15 Jan 2007, col GC189 (Lord Hunt).

14.5.3 Elements of the offence

In summary there must be:

- a relevant duty owed to the victim;
- the breach of the duty by the organization must be as a result of the way the activities are managed or organized;
- a substantial element of the breach of the duty must be due to the way the senior management managed or organized activities;
- the breach of the duty must be a gross one;
- V's death was caused by the breach of the duty.

14.5.3.1 A relevant duty

The definition of a 'relevant duty of care' is provided in s 2 of the Act:

(1) A 'relevant duty of care', in relation to an organisation, means any of the following duties owed by it under the law of negligence—

    (a) a duty owed to its employees or to other persons working for the organisation or performing services for it;

    (b) a duty owed as occupier of premises;

    (c) a duty owed in connection with—

        (i) the supply by the organisation of goods or services (whether for consideration or not),

        (ii) the carrying on by the organisation of any construction or maintenance operations,

        (iii) the carrying on by the organisation of any other activity on a commercial basis, or

        (iv) the use or keeping by the organisation of any plant, vehicle or other thing;

    (d) duty owed to a person who, by reason of being a person within subsection (2), is someone for whose safety the organisation is responsible [arising where V is in custody].

(2) Subsection (1) is subject to sections 3 to 7.

The duties reflect the duties of care arising at common law. The duty is that owed in the common law of negligence[248] or, where applicable, the statutory duty which has superseded the common law duty, for example the Occupiers' Liability Act 1957. It is made clear by s 2(4) that a duty owed under the law of negligence will apply if the common law duty of negligence has been superseded by statutory provision imposing strict liability. The Explanatory Notes give the example of the Carriage by Air Act 1961. The most important thing to remember is that the criminal offence does not impose new duties; it is based on the existing duties which are present in civil law—either by statute or common law. The requirement of proving a duty will add to the complexity of the prosecution.

The most frequently arising duties are likely to be from relationships as employers and occupiers, and duties arising from these activities are also of special significance when it comes to identifying the scope of the exemptions for certain types of organization/activity.[249]

---

[248] Section 2(7) specifies, for the avoidance of doubt, that 'the law of negligence' includes, in relation to England and Wales, the Occupiers' Liability Act 1957, the Defective Premises Act 1972 and the Occupiers' Liability Act 1984.

[249] See p 609.

It is easy to see how the categories might give rise to duties of care which, if breached, could lead to fatalities. Duties as employer would, for example, include duties to provide safe places of work. Note that the duty as an employer extends beyond the scope of employees as strictly defined and includes subcontractors, and volunteer workers, etc. Duties as occupiers of premises will render organizations liable if there are, for example, faulty electrical wiring, dangerous staircases, etc. 'Premises' includes land, buildings and moveable structures (s 25); a duty owed in connection with the supply by the organization of goods might arise from provision of foodstuffs; duties arising from the provision of services (whether for consideration or not), would include most obviously rail travel and other transport; duties from the carrying on by the organization of any construction or maintenance operations[250] would include building operations.[251] Duties arising from the carrying on by the organization of any other activity on a commercial basis was a category included in case activities such as farming or mining were not regarded as involving the provision of services, etc. Duties arising from the use or keeping by the organization of any plant, vehicle or 'other thing' could be extremely wide-ranging.

The most controversial category is that relating to duties arising from detention. Lord Ramsbotham, former Chief Inspector of Prisons, was successful in the House of Lords in amending the Bill to include what is now s 2(1)(d). There was considerable government opposition and the Bill almost lapsed. The final compromise position reached was that the commencement of this element required the further approval of Parliament. The most difficult issue, and one which engaged the House of Lords, was the question whether suicides in detention would give rise to liability where the relevant agency, for example the Prison Service, could or should have prevented it.[252]

Section 2(2) lists the various forms of custody or detention[253] which will trigger a duty:

(2) A person is within this subsection if—

    (a) he is detained at a custodial institution or in a custody area at a court or police station;

    (b) he is detained at a removal centre or short-term holding facility;

    (c) he is being transported in a vehicle, or being held in any premises, in pursuance of prison escort arrangements or immigration escort arrangements;

    (d) he is living in secure accommodation in which he has been placed;

    (e) he is a detained patient.

Deaths in custody give rise to problems because of the particular status of the victim; that by definition the activities will be occurring within 'premises'; and the fact that the

---

[250] Section 2(7) further defines 'construction or maintenance operations' to mean 'operations of any of the following descriptions—(a) construction, installation, alteration, extension, improvement, repair, maintenance, decoration, cleaning, demolition or dismantling of—(i) any building or structure, (ii) anything else that forms, or is to form, part of the land, or (iii) any plant, vehicle or other thing; (b) operations that form an integral part of, or are preparatory to, or are for rendering complete, any operations within paragraph (a).'

[251] This provision overlaps significantly with the previous category of supply of goods or services. It was included to avoid any lacunae where the construction operator was not acting 'commercially'—as might be argued with some public sector bodies.

[252] Under the new division of power, prisons come under the responsibility of the Ministry of Justice.

[253] The various categories are further defined in s 2(7). Section 23 provides a power to the Secretary of State to add to those categories listed in s 2(2), to whom a 'relevant duty of care' is owed by reason of s 2(1)(d). Eg by virtue of para 15(a) of Sch 9(2) to the Immigration Act 2014, s 2(2)(b) now mandates that a person is owed a duty of care if he is detained at a short-term holding facility or in pre-departure accommodation.

organization providing the detention 'service' is one which will have to make public policy decisions as to allocation of resources, etc (and therefore in some cases the duty would be excluded under s 3).[254]

Even before s 2(1)(d) was introduced, the broad terms of s 2(1) could trigger liability for a death in custody in some circumstances. Subject to the exceptions in ss 3 to 7, there was possible liability under s 2(1)(b) if the organization's duty was as an occupier. As parliamentary debates accepted, if a brick fell off a wall because of poor maintenance and killed a prisoner that would trigger liability under the provisions already in force since the duty of care was the ordinary one owed by an occupier of premises.[255]

Duty issues under s 2

Given the potential breadth of the categories of duty and examination of the common law which might be necessary to determine whether a duty does exist, it is reassuring to see that the question whether a duty of care is owed is a question of law. It is for the judge to decide: s 2(5). Moreover, 'the judge must make any findings of fact necessary to decide that question'. This latter provision about the judge finding facts is highly unusual and should be contrasted with the common law position on gross negligence manslaughter[256] where whether a duty of care exists is a matter for the jury once the judge has decided that there is evidence capable of establishing a duty.

Section 2(6) makes it clear that the duty of care will not be excluded by *ex turpi causa* and *volenti* doctrines.[257] This is potentially very important. The scope of liability at civil law is restricted in practice by the operation of these doctrines. However, the reason that they are excluded as defences or limits on criminal liability in this context is easy enough to deduce. The victim will in many cases not be properly described as taking a truly voluntary risk since he will be compelled to do so by the organization acting as his employer, etc.

14.5.3.2 The breach must be as a result of the way the activities are managed or organized

This second element of the offence is designed to ensure that the focus is on the so-called 'management failure'. This test is not linked to a particular level of management but considers how an activity was managed within the organization as a whole. It will now be possible to combine the shortcomings of a wide number of individuals within the organization to prove a failure of management *by the organization*. The language is designed to reflect the concentration on things done consistently with the organization's culture and policies more generally. It remains to be seen how easily this can be proved.

Senior management

The Act does, however, place a significant restriction on the organizational failure test. Under s 1(3), the offence is committed by an organization only if 'the way in which its activities are managed and organised by its senior management is a substantial element in the breach referred to in subsection (1)'.[258] Who are the senior managers? By s 1(4)(c): 'senior management', in relation to an organization, means the persons who play 'significant roles' in making:

---

[254] See p 609.

[255] See Taylor, n 220. See also S Griffin, 'Accountability for Deaths Attributable to the Gross Negligent Act or Omission of a Police Force: The Impact of the Corporate Manslaughter and Corporate Homicide Act 2007' (2010) 74 J Crim L 648.

[256] *Evans* [2009] EWCA Crim 650.   [257] *Wacker* [2003] QB 1203.

[258] cf Norrie for the argument that this element of the offence demonstrates a problematic return to the identification approach. Norrie, *Crime, Reason and History*, 125.

decisions about how the whole or a substantial part of its activities are to be managed or organised, or the actual managing or organising of the whole or a substantial part of those activities.

This extends beyond the narrow category of senior individuals who would be caught at common law by the identification doctrine being the 'directing mind and will'.[259]

The senior managers' management and organization must be a 'substantial element' in the breach of duty leading to death. Two important consequences flow from this aspect of the offence. First, since the senior managers' involvement need only be a substantial element in the organization, etc, the involvement and conduct of others—'non-senior managers' who are involved in the management and organization of activities—is also relevant. Secondly, when assessing the management failure the contribution of those individuals who are not senior management can be taken into account even if their involvement is 'substantial' provided it is not so great as to render the senior managers' involvement something less than substantial. There can be more than one substantial element. No doubt the courts will say that a 'substantial' involvement is something that the jury can evaluate as an ordinary English word meaning more than trivial.

14.5.3.3 A 'gross' breach of duty?

The requirement of a gross breach of duty is clearly designed to echo the gross negligence manslaughter offence at common law. Section 2(4)(b) provides a more detailed explanation of the concept—a breach of a duty of care by an organization is a 'gross' breach if the conduct alleged to amount to a breach of that duty *falls far below* what can reasonably be expected of the organization in the circumstances. The language chosen is similar to that proposed by the Law Commission as a suitable form of words to replace gross negligence. The test retains a degree of circularity, although not to the extent of that in the common law offence of gross negligence manslaughter.

The jury's duty in relation to determining the breach of duty is provided in s 8:

(1) This section applies where—

  (a) it is established that an organisation owed a relevant duty of care to a person, and

  (b) it falls to the jury to decide whether there was a gross breach of that duty.

(2) The jury must consider whether the evidence shows that the organisation failed to comply with any health and safety legislation[260] that relates to the alleged breach, and if so—

  (a) how serious that failure was;

  (b) how much of a risk of death it posed.

(3) The jury may also—

  (a) consider the extent to which the evidence shows that there were attitudes, policies, systems or accepted practices within the organisation that were likely to have encouraged any such failure as is mentioned in subsection (2), or to have produced tolerance of it;

  (b) have regard to any health and safety guidance that relates to the alleged breach.

(4) This section does not prevent the jury from having regard to any other matters they consider relevant.

---

[259] Is the test too restrictive? Will companies seek to avoid this by nominating people in less senior positions to take responsibility for all health and safety policies?

[260] Defined in s 8(5): '"health and safety guidance" means any code, guidance, manual or similar publication that is concerned with health and safety matters and is made or issued (under a statutory provision or otherwise) by an authority responsible for the enforcement of any health and safety legislation'.

This section deals with factors to be taken into account by the jury (the offence is only triable on indictment). Note that the jury *'must'* consider these issues. Note also that the jury is obliged to consider whether the 'organization' complied, not just whether its senior management complied. This further supports the argument that the activities of non-senior managers are relevant in determining whether there has been a management failure. Section 8(3) emphasizes that the jury may have reference to general organizational and systems failures.[261] The inability to do so under the old law was a source of common complaint. How the 'attitudes, etc' are proved is problematic. There is the potential for lengthy arguments and evidence comparing practices across the particular sector or industry. Imagine a prosecution of a rail company and the potential for the company to adduce evidence of safety procedures and policies across the sector to demonstrate the quality of its own. No doubt the jury will have regard to the organization's overall objectives, published policy statements on safety, monitoring and compliance policies, attitudes to development of safety and to training and awareness, approaches to remedying previous health and safety infringements, etc.

14.5.3.4 Causing death

There must be a death of a person. Causation must be established in accordance with orthodox principles.[262] Difficulties may arise where the organization alleges that the individual employee has, with his free, voluntary, informed fatal act, broken the chain of causation.[263]

14.5.4 Excluded duties

The most important aspect of the legislation is not the scope of relevant duty and of potential liability under s 1 and s 2, but rather what the government excluded from the scope of liability under ss 3 to 7. The excluded categories of duty are considerable. The different categories and sub-categories of duty also make the interpretation of whether a duty is owed rather more complex to unravel.

14.5.4.1 Public policy

The broadest exclusion is provided in s 3(1) and deals with decisions of public policy taken by public authorities.

Any duty of care owed by a public authority in respect of a decision as to matters of public policy (including in particular the allocation of public resources or the weighing of competing public interests) is not a 'relevant duty of care'.

This excludes liability where a death is due to a public authority's decision not to allocate appropriate resources to a particular service. The section is seeking to reflect the distinction between 'operational' and 'public' policy matters in the law of tort.[264] The manner in which a public authority implements its duty in practice is justiciable in negligence, but the way it exercises its statutory discretion is not. In *X v Bedfordshire County Council*,[265] Lord Browne-Wilkinson said that, 'a common law duty of care in relation to the taking of decisions involving policy matters cannot exist'.[266] The courts have continually struggled

---

[261] This section has been influenced, as has much of this Act, by the Australian legislation and academic comment in Australia. See further B Fisse and J Braithwaite, *Corporations, Crime and Accountability* (1993).

[262] See Ch 2.

[263] See *Kennedy (No 2)* [2007] UKHL 38. However, it is arguable that the decision in *Latif* [1996] 1 WLR 104 would apply because the employee and organization are acting in concert.

[264] See *Anns v Merton Borough Council* [1978] AC 728, HL. See Horder, n 210, at 115.

[265] [1995] 2 AC 633, HL.   [266] ibid, 738.

with the dividing line and it has been recognized that the test is very difficult to apply.[267] It remains to be seen to what extent the criminal courts will be willing to engage in detailed evaluations of the common law on this issue.

As an example of the difficulty, if a relevant public authority decides not to deploy resources to buy a particular drug for patients suffering a particular illness, no duty arises. If, having made the decision to supply the drug, there is negligence in the way it is supplied/administered, etc, liability may arise. Interesting issues could arise in a trial in which the breach is of a duty owed by a private company and a public body where they have joint responsibility for managing an activity. The effect of the exemptions would be stark.

Section 3(2) provides a less extensive exclusion in relation to things done 'in the exercise of an exclusively public function':

(2) Any duty of care owed in respect of things done in the exercise of an exclusively public function is not a 'relevant duty of care' unless it falls within section 2(1)(a), (b) or (d).

(3) Any duty of care owed by a public authority in respect of inspections carried out in the exercise of a statutory function is not a 'relevant duty of care' unless it falls within section 2(1)(a) or (b).

(4) In this section—

'exclusively public function' means a function that falls within the prerogative of the Crown or is, by its nature, exercisable only with authority conferred—

(a) by the exercise of that prerogative, or

(b) by or under a statutory provision;

'statutory function' means a function conferred by or under a statutory provision.

The duty of care owed as employer or occupier or custodian under s 2(1)(a) or (b) or (d) still applies in these circumstances. This excludes only public functions involved in s 2(1)(c), notably the supply of goods or services and construction work, etc. The exemption was not supported by consultees in the government's consultation exercise.[268]

14.5.4.2 Military activities: s 4

Many of the activities performed by the armed forces[269] will be excluded by virtue of s 3(2) (above), but s 3(2) does not prevent liability arising as an employer or occupier. Section 4 goes further by providing a total exclusion for some activities. There is no relevant duty for:

operations, including peacekeeping operations and operations for dealing with terrorism, civil unrest or serious public disorder, in the course of which members of the armed forces come under attack or face the threat of attack or violent resistance.

Liability is also excluded for preparation and support of military operations of that description, or training of a hazardous nature, or training carried out in a hazardous way, which it is considered needs to be carried out, or carried out in that way, in order to improve or maintain the effectiveness of the armed forces with respect to such operations.[270]

---

[267] See *Phelps v Hillingdon LBC* [2001] 2 AC 619, HL, and also: *Gorringe v Calderdale Metropolitan Borough Council* [2004] UKHL 15; *Carty v Croydon London Borough Council* [2005] EWCA Civ 19; *Connor v Surrey County Council* [2010] EWCA Civ 286. See further, Horder, n 210.

[268] Home Office, *Summary of Responses to Corporate Manslaughter: The Government's Draft Bill for Reform*, Mar 2005, para 9.

[269] By s 12(1) 'the "armed forces" means any of the naval, military or air forces of the Crown raised under the law of the United Kingdom'.

[270] Will there be a problem in ECHR terms if the army cannot be prosecuted for killing? Arguably there will be no breach of Art 2 because an intentional killing will be prosecutable as murder on the part of the officer involved.

The armed forces will owe a duty as an employer[271] or occupier other than in those circumstances.[272]

14.5.4.3 The police: s 5

The exemptions provided for police activities are also complex.[273] Two categories exist. Sections 5(1) and 5(2) create a total exemption—that is, no relevant duty arises for some types of policing activity—where, in short, there are operations in relation to terrorism or civil unrest. More fully, there is no duty on the organization where officers or employees[274] of the public authority[275] in question are engaged in operations for dealing with terrorism, civil unrest or serious disorder, which involve them coming under attack, or facing the threat of attack or violent resistance, or those involving the carrying on of policing or law enforcement activities (s 5(2)). Nor is there a duty when the police are preparing for those types of operations or training to enable them to carry out such operations.

In other circumstances, by s 5(3) a 'relevant duty of care' is owed where the organization is acting as employer, occupier or custodian (ie s 2(1)(a), (b) or (d)). This exemption will exclude circumstances where a member of the public has been killed in the pursuit of law enforcement activities. The Explanatory Notes suggest that this includes:

decisions about and responses to emergency calls, the manner in which particular police operations are conducted, the way in which law enforcement and other coercive powers are exercised, measures taken to protect witnesses and the arrest and detention of suspects.

Professor Horder has suggested[276] that the extent of the exceptions in ss 4 and 5 is unwarranted and that the result may be to leave individuals at risk of liability when the agency is the one at fault. He suggests also that the exemption was unnecessary having regard to the need for the DPP's consent.[277] This is debatable. For Parliament to have fixed these activities as off-limits is one thing. To expect the DPP to have to make policy decisions such as the exemption of the police in a case of fatality is to subject him or her to media censure for whatever decision is made, and to diminish the level of certainty in the law.

14.5.4.4 Emergency services: s 6

In the law of tort, considerable difficulties have arisen in identifying the scope of the duty of care owed by the emergency and rescue services in the course of performing rescue activity. Section 6 puts beyond doubt that the corporate manslaughter offence does not apply

---

[271] By s 12(2), a person who is a member of the armed forces is to be treated as employed by the Ministry of Defence.

[272] There is no liability for special forces: 'Any duty of care owed by the Ministry of Defence in respect of activities carried on by members of the special forces is not a "relevant duty of care"' (s 4(3)). This is presumably necessary to allow for more extreme forms of training. By s 4(4), 'the "special forces" means those units of the armed forces the maintenance of whose capabilities is the responsibility of the Director of Special Forces or which are for the time being subject to the operational command of that Director'.

[273] See S Griffin, 'Accountability for Deaths Attributable to the Gross Negligent Act or Omission of a Police Force: The Impact of the Corporate Manslaughter and Corporate Homicide Act 2007' (2010) 74 J Crim L 648.

[274] Section 13 provides that police officers are to be treated as the employees of the police force for which they work (and are therefore owed the employer's duty of care by the force). It also ensures that police forces are treated as occupiers of premises and that other conduct is attributable to them as if they were distinctly constituted bodies.

[275] This could include other authorities such as NCA or immigration officials: s 5(4).

[276] See n 210, at 119.

[277] See www.cps.gov.uk/legal-guidance/corporate-manslaughter. In reality this consent can be granted by any prosecutor. It is not a significant safeguard.

generally to these agencies when responding to emergencies.[278] Approximate consistency with the civil law is secured by excluding liability arising from delay in response to an emergency, or the level of skill exercised in responding to the operation. The relevant emergency services protected by this exclusion are: the fire and rescue authorities and other emergency response organizations providing fire and rescue services; NHS bodies and ambulance services or blood/organ transport; the Coastguard and RNLI;[279] the armed forces (either responding to a military emergency such as a fire on a base or when assisting the civilian rescue services). By s 6(7), emergency circumstances are defined in terms of those that are life-threatening or which are causing, or threaten to cause, serious injury or illness or serious harm to the environment or buildings or other property.

The emergency services may still be liable for a death arising from their status as employer or occupier even where the death arises in the course of an emergency (s 6(5)). The exemption also does not apply to duties that do not relate to *the way in which* a body responds to an emergency, for example duties to maintain vehicles in a safe condition; these will be capable of prosecution under the offence. There is no exemption from liability for medical treatment itself, or decisions about this (other than decisions that establish the priority for treating patients). Matters relating to the organization and management of medical services will therefore be within the ambit of the offence (s 6(4)).

14.5.4.5 Child protection and probation: s 7

Section 7 limits the duty of care that a local authority or other public authority owes in respect of the exercise of its functions under Parts IV and V of the Children Act 1989. In relation to the carrying on of those duties, a relevant duty arises for the purposes of s 1 only in relation to its activities as employer, occupier and duties relating to detention (s 2(1)(a), (b), (d)). There is no relevant duty, for example, if a child was not identified as being at risk and taken into care and was subsequently fatally injured. Similarly, any duty of care that a local probation board, provider of probation services or other public authority owes in respect of the exercise by it of functions under Chapter 1 of Part 1 of the Criminal Justice and Court Services Act 2000 or the Offender Management Act 2007 is excluded. In relation to carrying out those duties, a relevant duty arises for the purposes of s 1 only in relation to its activities as employer, occupier and duties relating to detention (s 2(1)(a), (b), (d)).

14.5.5 Procedure

The offence of corporate manslaughter is triable only on indictment (s 1(6)), and a prosecution may not be instituted without the consent of the DPP (s 17(1)).[280] Proceedings against partnerships[281] for the offence are to be brought in the name of the partnership (and not in that of any of its members) (s 14(2)). Any fine imposed on a partnership is to be paid out of the funds of the partnership (s 14(3)). Further provision is made in s 15 for evidential and procedural mechanisms to apply to organizations which are not corporations. The section ensures that the relevant evidential and procedural provisions apply, in the same way as they apply to corporations, to all those government departments or other bodies listed in Sch 1, as well as to police forces and those unincorporated associations covered by the offence.

---

[278] Emergency circumstances include circumstances that are believed to be emergency circumstances: s 6(8). This deals with the circumstances in which the response is to a hoax call.

[279] Those effecting sea rescue are also exempt in a very wide exclusionary provision.

[280] cf L Jones and S Field, 'Corporate Criminal Liability for Manslaughter: The Evolving Approach of the Prosecuting Authorities and Courts in England and Wales' (2011) 32 JBL 80.

[281] Other than limited liability partnerships, which are corporate bodies and covered by the new offence as such.

14.5.5.1 Jurisdiction

Section 28 deals with extent and territorial application. The Act extends to the whole of the UK. Section 1 applies if the harm resulting in death is sustained: in the UK; or within the seaward limits of the territorial sea adjacent to the UK; on a British registered ship, British-controlled aircraft; a British-controlled hovercraft; in, on or above, or within 500 metres of, an offshore installation in UK territorial waters or a designated area of the UK's continental shelf (s 28(3)).[282]

Section 28(4) provides that:

For the purposes of subsection (3)(b) to (d) harm sustained on a ship, aircraft or hovercraft includes harm sustained by a person who—

(a) is then no longer on board the ship, aircraft or hovercraft in consequence of the wrecking of it or of some other mishap affecting it or occurring on it, and

(b) sustains the harm in consequence of that event.

Section 1 will therefore still apply if the harm resulting in death is sustained as a result of an incident involving a British vessel, but the victim is not physically on board when he suffers that harm. It will not apply if the incident involves a non-British vessel in international waters.

14.5.5.2 Penalties

An organization guilty of corporate manslaughter is liable to an unlimited fine (s 1(6)).[283] Cotswold Geotechnical Holdings Ltd was fined £385,000. This fine was upheld despite the fact that it would lead the company into liquidation.[284] It was held that in some bad cases this may be an acceptable consequence. In addition, the court has power on the application of the prosecution to impose a remedial order against an organization convicted of corporate manslaughter requiring it to take specified steps to remedy: the breach; any matter appearing to have resulted from it and to have been a cause of the death; or any health and safety deficiency in the 'organisation's policies, systems or practices' appearing to be indicated by the breach (s 9(1) and (2)). This provision is also heavily influenced by Australian experience. Any such order must be on 'such terms (whether those proposed or others) as the court considers appropriate having regard to any representations made, and any evidence adduced, in relation to that matter by the prosecution or on behalf of the organisation' (s 9(2)).

Section 9(4) provides for the form of a remedial order. It must specify a period within which the remedial steps are to be taken and may require the organization to supply evidence of compliance. Periods specified may be extended or further extended by order of the court on an application made before the end of that period or extended period. An organization which fails to comply with a remedial order commits an offence triable only

---

[282] For difficulties in international waters see the investigation into the death of a fisherman 15 miles off Cherbourg after a collision which resulted in no prosecution. See P Binning, 'Corporate Manslaughter on the High Seas' (2010) The Times, 28 Oct. Our thanks to Ms Chaynee Hodgetts for background information.

[283] The Sentencing Council has issued a definitive sentencing guideline which includes guidance on sentencing for corporate manslaughter and which is entitled *Health and safety offences, corporate manslaughter and food safety and hygiene offences: Definitive guideline* (2015). It has effect from 1 February 2016. It is available in full at www.sentencingcouncil.org.uk/publications/item/health-and-safety-offences-corporate-manslaughter-and-food-safety-and-hygiene-offences-definitive-guideline/. For discussion of sentencing issues see M Woodley, 'Bargaining Over Corporate Manslaughter—What Price a Life?' (2013) 77 J Crim L 33.

[284] [2011] EWCA Crim 1337.

on indictment and punishable with an unlimited fine (s 9(5)). There appears to be nothing to prevent the conviction of a director as an accessory to this offence.

In addition, the court has power to impose a 'publicity order' under s 10 'requiring the organisation to publicise in a specified manner' its conviction, specified particulars, the amount of any fine and the terms of any remedial order. Before imposing such an order, the court must ascertain the views of any relevant enforcement authority as it considers appropriate, and have regard to any representations made by the prosecution or the organization. The form of a remedial order must specify a period within which the publicity order must be complied with, and may require the organization to supply evidence of compliance. An organization which fails to comply with an order commits an offence triable only on indictment and punishable with an unlimited fine (s 10(4)). Section 10 was added to the Bill during its passage in the House of Lords. It is clearly predicated on the assumption (probably correct) that large organizations are more concerned about adverse publicity than a fine.

16

Non-fatal offences against the person

This chapter deals with offences against the 'person', and in relation to the offences under discussion that term means a human being; associations, whether corporate or unincorporated, cannot be victims of these offences though these bodies might be guilty of committing some of the offences either as principal or as an accessory.[1] The meaning of 'person' as a victim has been discussed almost exclusively in relation to murder but it seems clear that the same principles must apply to non-fatal offences. The common law[2] position is usefully summarized in the Draft Criminal Code which provides[3] that victim 'means a person who has been born and has an existence independent of his mother and, unless the context otherwise requires, "death" and "personal harm" mean the death of, or personal harm to, such a person'.[4]

A foetus or a child in the process of being born could not, therefore, be the victim of an assault or any other offence against the person.[5] The attack might be an offence against the expectant mother where it affected her person, as distinct from the foetus which is not part of her. Statutory offences are probably to be construed in accordance with the common law.

16.1 Assault and battery

Assault and battery were two distinct crimes at common law and their separate existence (though now as statutory offences) is confirmed by s 39 of the Criminal Justice Act 1988:

Common assault and battery shall be summary offences and a person guilty of either of them shall be liable to an unlimited fine, to imprisonment for a term not exceeding six months, or to both.

Section 39 offers a valuable simplification of the law,[6] replacing the complex provisions in the OAPA 1861.

---

[1] If a corporation may be guilty of manslaughter there is no logical reason why it should not be guilty of lesser offences against the person. See on corporate manslaughter, p 599. The 2007 Act deals only with corporate killings. In *R (on the application of Gladstone plc) v Manchester City Magistrates' Court* [2004] All ER (D) 296 (Nov), it was held that a private prosecution for assault may be brought by a registered company (the victim being the Chief Executive who was kneed in the groin at the AGM). The company's memorandum of association included power to lay an information in respect of the assault.

[2] cf *Tait*, p 617.   [3] Cl 53(1).   [4] For further reform, see p 697.

[5] In *A-G's Reference (No 3 of 1994)*, p 124, the Court of Appeal held that the foetus is part of the mother; but the House of Lords decided that it is not: [1997] 3 All ER 936, 943. 'The mother and the foetus were two distinct organisms living symbiotically, not a single organism with two aspects', per Lord Mustill.

[6] Common assault and battery were indictable offences at common law and under s 47, that element of s 47 was repealed by the 1988 Act, together with ss 42 and 43.

16.1.1 Definitions

An assault is any conduct by which D, intentionally or recklessly,[7] causes V to apprehend immediate and unlawful personal violence.[8] A battery is any conduct by which D, intentionally or recklessly, inflicts unlawful personal violence upon V.[9] But 'violence' here includes any unlawful touching[10] of another, however slight. As Blackstone explained:[11]

the law cannot draw the line between different degrees of violence, and therefore prohibits the first and lowest stage of it; every man's person being sacred, and no other having a right to meddle with it, in any the slightest manner.

This reflects the fact that the offences against the person protect the individual's personal autonomy by providing at least the opportunity for criminal punishment for the slightest unjustified infringement. This is supported by the protection offered by the ECHR, in Art 8 (respect for private life).[12] The other dimension to autonomy in this context—the purported freedom to do as you will with your body[13]—is less well respected in the current state of the law.[14]

In modern times, Lord Lane CJ described battery in expansive terms:

an intentional touching of another person without the consent of that person and without lawful excuse. It need not necessarily be hostile, or rude, or aggressive, as some of the cases seem to indicate.[15]

However, in *Brown*,[16] the majority of the House of Lords seem to have thought that hostility is an element in assault. But their lordships then interpreted 'hostile' in such a way as to deprive the word of all meaning. The case concerned sadomasochistic acts performed by a group of men on each other. All the acts were done for the mutual enjoyment of the participants, so they could not be assaults if hostility, in any ordinary meaning of the word, were required. The House of Lords suggested hostility was required but then upheld the convictions! Lord Jauncey said, 'If the appellants' activities in relation to the receivers [of the painful acts] were unlawful they were also hostile and a necessary ingredient of assault was present.' But the acts were only unlawful if they amounted to assaults. The reasoning appears to be circular. Notwithstanding the opinions of their lordships, it is submitted that the actual decision confirms the view that hostility is not an essential ingredient in the criminal offences of assault or battery. Some commentators suggest that there is value in requiring proof of hostility because otherwise an intentional touching which is nothing more than a faux pas—D's exuberant hug of a stranger at midnight on New Year's Eve—is

---

[7] *Venna* [1976] QB 421, CA (a case of battery but the same principle surely applies to assault); *Savage* [1992] 1 AC 699, 740.

[8] In *Ireland* [1998] AC 147, [1997] 4 All ER 225, 236, 239, the House of Lords applied this definition, originating in the 1st edition of this book, at p 262, adopted in *Fagan v Metropolitan Police Comr* [1969] 1 QB 439, [1968] 3 All ER 442 at 445 and approved in *Savage* [1992] AC 699, 740.

[9] *Rolfe* (1952) 36 Cr App R 4. Any amount of force will suffice, as emphasised in *Afolabi* [2017] EWHC 2960.

[10] Note that the concept of touching may achieve a greater significance since it now forms the core of a number of offences under the Sexual Offences Act 2003. In *H* [2005] Crim LR 734, it was confirmed that touching of clothes would constitute the offence under s 3 of that Act. See Ch 17.

[11] *Commentaries*, iii, 120, cited by Goff LJ in *Collins v Wilcock* [1984] 3 All ER 374 at 378.

[12] For serious infringements, protection lies in Art 3—freedom from torture, inhuman and degrading treatment—and Art 5—freedom from unlawful deprivation of liberty. Art 4 protects against slavery. See the offence in the Modern Slavery Act 2015, s 1.

[13] On which see J Gardner, *Offences and Defences* (2007) 12.

[14] See the discussion of *Brown* later in this section.

[15] *Faulkner v Talbot* [1981] 3 All ER 468 at 471, applied in *Thomas* (1985) 81 Cr App R 331 at 334; and see *Collins v Wilcock* [1984] 3 All ER 374 at 379, DC; *Wilson v Pringle* [1987] QB 237, CA (Civ Div), criticized by Wood J in *T v T* [1988] 2 WLR 189 at 200, 203 (Fam Div); *Brown* [1992] 2 WLR 441 at 446, CA.

[16] [1994] AC 212, [1993] Crim LR 583.

781

potentially criminal.[17] It is submitted that such cases are not criminal because D will have a genuine belief in consent to that level of touching on that occasion. The concept of 'hostility' is unnecessary and ambiguous; it could cause undesirable complications in an offence which, because of the volume and summary nature of prosecutions, needs to be kept simple. The Court of Appeal has potentially added further confusion by conflating the issue of V's consent with whether D evinced hostility towards V. In B, Hughes LJ stated:[18]

The element of assault frequently and usefully described as hostility is a means of conveying to the jury that some non-hostile contact is an ordinary incident of life to which we all impliedly consent.

It is respectfully submitted that hostility is not an element of the offence and that the issue of consent ought not to be confused with it.

Assault and battery form the basis of many aggravated offences—for example, assaulting a police officer, assault with intent to resist arrest, etc.[19] It should be noted that assault and battery are also torts; and many, though not all, of the principles appear to be equally applicable in both branches of the law. Consequently, some of the cases cited here are civil actions.

The CPS Charging Standards now advise charging assault and battery where there is 'no injury or injuries which are not serious'. Previous versions of the guidance advised charging assault where: the injuries sustained amount to no more than: grazes; scratches; abrasions; minor bruising; swellings; reddening of the skin; superficial cuts; or a 'black eye'[20] and there are no aggravating features. The breadth of the offences results in wide prosecutorial discretion.

16.1.2 The relationship between assault and battery

Assault and battery are separate crimes, although they were not always recognized to be such.[21] The reason for this stems from the terminological problem: there is no acceptable verb corresponding to the noun, battery. As a result, 'assaulted' is almost invariably used to mean 'committed a battery against'. Sometimes, even statutes use the term 'assault' to mean 'assault or battery' but on other occasions both words are used.[22]

Problems of substance as well as terminology flow from the offences of assault and battery being separate and these have long been ignored. In DPP v Little,[23] a charge alleging that 'D… did unlawfully assault and batter J' was held to charge two offences and so to be 'bad for duplicity'.[24] More recently, in R (on the application of Kracher) v Leicester Magistrates' Court it was observed that:

---

[17] Simester, Spencer, Stark, Sullivan and Virgo, CLT&D, 441.   [18] [2013] EWCA Crim 3.

[19] The Home Office identified over 70 such offences: Violence. Reforming the Offences Against the Person Act 1861 (1998) para 3.5. See also LCCP 217, Reform of Offences Against the Person: A Scoping Consultation Paper (2014) Ch 2.

[20] See www.cps.gov.uk/legal-guidance/offences-against-person-incorporating-charging-standard#P48_1458. See also C Clarkson, A Cretney, G Davis and J Shepherd, 'Assaults: The Relationship between Seriousness, Criminalisation and Punishment' [1994] Crim LR 4.

[21] The CLRC Fourteenth Report, para 148, treated them as a single offence which may be committed in two ways and the Draft Code, cl 75, follows the CLRC's recommendation.

[22] There is a deplorable inconsistency in the statutory terminology. Even the Criminal Justice Act 1988, having made it crystal clear in s 39 that there are two offences, goes on in s 40(3)(a) to use 'common assault' in a context in which it can only sensibly mean—and has now been held to mean—'common assault or battery': Lyndsey [1995] 3 All ER 654.

[23] [1992] 1 All ER 299, [1991] Crim LR 900, DC.

[24] ie that it makes more than one allegation in the same charge against the defendant. That is not generally permitted. Many earlier cases decided that a charge of assault and/or battery in a single information is duplicitous: Jones v Sherwood [1942] 1 KB 127, DC and Mansfield Justices, ex p Sharkey [1985] QB 613, DC. But a blind eye appears to have been turned in Notman [1994] Crim LR 518.

the offence of common assault can be committed in two ways which amount in law to different offences, namely assault by beating and an assault by putting another in fear of immediate silence [sic]. It is not possible to charge common assault in the alternative within the same charge.[25]

This has repercussions for aggravated offences which depend on proof of an assault or battery. Consider the offence under s 47 of the OAPA 1861: 'Whosoever shall be convicted of an assault occasioning actual bodily harm shall be liable to [imprisonment for five years].' If D is charged under s 47 is it necessary for the Crown to spell out whether he assaulted or battered and occasioned ABH as a result or is it enough to use the term 'assault'? In *Savage*,[26] Lord Ackner's language when discussing s 47 suggests that that offence can be satisfied by proof of an assault only but it would be incredible if D, who battered V without assaulting him (eg by hitting him on the back of the head so V did not apprehend the violence), was not guilty of an 'assault occasioning actual bodily harm'. If the word 'assault' in s 47 embraces both the offence of assault and the offence of battery it seems to follow that the usual form of indictment for that offence—'AB... assaulted JN, thereby occasioning him actual bodily harm'—is defective because it actually alleges two offences.[27]

There were further procedural problems which flowed from the failure to recognize the separateness of the offences,[28] but the Domestic Violence, Crime and Victims Act 2004 remedied these.[29]

16.1.3 Common law or statutory offences?

On a literal reading, s 39 of the 1988 Act does not create any offence. It assumes the existence of offences of common assault and battery and merely prescribes the mode of trial and penalty. Nevertheless, in *DPP v Little*,[30] it was held that common assault and battery have been statutory offences since the enactment of s 47 of the OAPA 1861. The better view is that s 47 merely prescribed the penalty for the common law offences of common assault—as statutes do for other common law offences, for example murder, manslaughter and conspiracy to defraud.[31] Those offences all continue to exist at common law. Although Laws LJ has asserted unequivocally that 'in truth, common assault by beating remains a common law offence',[32] the prosecutor is probably well advised, pending review by a

---

[25] [2013] EWHC 4627 (Admin) at [11], per Saunders J.   [26] [1991] 4 All ER 698 at 711.

[27] The same considerations apply to other aggravated assaults. The effect is that thousands of people were convicted on defective indictments since 1861—but this in no way detracts from the inescapable logic of the argument.

[28] An indictment alleging assault occasioning actual bodily harm required a separate count for s 39 assault because it was not an included offence for an alternative verdict: *Mearns* [1990] 3 All ER 989; *Disalvo* [2004] All ER (D) 316 (Jul). Arguably these were wrongly decided.

[29] Section 11 makes common assault an alternative verdict to more serious offences of assault, even if the count has not been preferred in the indictment. See *Nelson* [2013] EWCA Crim 30, [2013] Crim LR 689 for discussion although the decision is, it is submitted, in error. The court held that where a count for assault by beating is included in an indictment under the Criminal Justice Act 1988, s 40, then s 6(3A) does *not* enable a jury to return an alternative verdict of common assault on that count. The jury may return a verdict of assault on a charge of ABH. The court reasoned that if D threw a punch that missed, a verdict of 'attempted battery' may be returned on a charge of assault by beating. This overlooks the fact that attempted battery is not an offence known to law. The court's conclusion that common assault is not a permissible alternative on a charge of battery (because a battery can be inflicted on a victim who never saw the blow coming) is *per incuriam* because the case of *MPC v Wilson* [1984] AC 242, was not referred to.

[30] See n 23.

[31] See [1991] Crim LR 900; *Blackstone* (2018) B2.1. The court in *Lyndsey*, n 22, noted the criticisms that have been made of *Little* but found it unnecessary to express any opinion.

[32] *Haystead v Chief Constable of Derbyshire* (2000) 164 JP 396, [2000] Crim LR 758, DC. The defendant was in fact charged under s 39.

higher court, to follow *DPP v Little* and to charge common assault or battery as a statutory offence, contrary to s 39.

16.1.4 Actus reus of assault

The typical case of an assault as distinct from a battery is that where D, by some physical movement, causes V to apprehend that he is about to be struck. D runs towards or drives at V, or acts so as to appear to V to be on the point of striking, stabbing or shooting him. Assault was once regarded as 'attempted battery': D had embarked on an act which, if not stopped, would immediately result in an impact of some kind on V. Many 'attempted batteries' are assaults, but this is not necessarily so: D's acts may be unobserved by V, as where D approaches V from behind, or V is asleep, or insensible, or too young to appreciate what D appears likely to do. And there may be an assault where D has no intention to commit a battery but only to cause V to apprehend one.[33] The requirement is for apprehension, not fear.

16.1.4.1 Immediacy

There is a tendency to enlarge the concept of assault by taking a generous, arguably too generous, view of 'immediacy' and to include threats to V where the impending impact is remote. In more recent years this approach was precipitated by the courts' desire to provide protection for those suffering harassment at a time before the Protection from Harassment Act 1997 was in force.[34]

In *Lewis*,[35] D was uttering threats to V from another room but was convicted of maliciously inflicting grievous bodily harm and therefore impliedly of an assault.[36] In *Logdon v DPP*,[37] D committed an assault by showing V a pistol in a drawer and declaring that he would hold her hostage. In *Ireland*,[38] the House of Lords held that words alone, or even silent telephone calls, are capable of amounting to an assault; but they found it unnecessary to decide whether they did so in that case. If the caller said, 'There is bomb under your house which I am about to detonate', that would seem a clear case of assault. Lord Steyn said that the caller *may* be guilty of assault if he said, 'I will be at your door in a minute or two.' It seems to be a question of fact. Did the call in fact cause V to apprehend immediate unlawful violence? In *Constanza*,[39] V, who had for some time been harassed by D, received two letters from him eight days apart which she interpreted as clear threats. It was held that they amounted to an assault occasioning actual bodily harm. Was this two assaults or one continuing assault? It is easy to see that the letters might have caused V *immediate apprehension* of violence at some time in the future, but less easy to suppose that, as V read them, she apprehended *immediate violence*.

In *Smith v Chief Superintendent of Woking Police Station*,[40] D was convicted of assault by looking through the window of a bed-sitting room at V in her nightclothes with intent to frighten her. Kerr LJ limited his decision to a case where D 'is immediately adjacent, albeit on

---

[33] *Logdon v DPP* [1976] Crim LR 121, DC.

[34] See C Wells, 'Stalking: The Criminal Law's Response' [1997] Crim LR 463.

[35] [1970] Crim LR 647, CA.   [36] But see now *Wilson* [1984] AC 242, p 696.

[37] See earlier.

[38] See earlier. See G Virgo, 'Offences Against the Person—Do-It-Yourself Law Reform' (1997) 56 CLJ 251. J Horder, 'Reconsidering Psychic Assault' [1998] Crim LR 392, regards this dilution of the immediacy requirement as a welcome shift to an offence based on causing fear. On the merits of general threat offences, see P Alldridge, 'Threat Offences: A Case for Reform' [1994] Crim LR 176. See also LCCP 217, Ch 5.

[39] [1997] Crim LR 576. The court used ambiguous language, referring to the fact that she apprehended violence 'at some time not excluding the immediate future'. The House of Lords refused leave to appeal, but that does not imply approval of the decision.

[40] (1983) 76 Cr App R 234.

the other side of a window'. His lordship distinguished, without dissenting from, the opinion in the fourth edition of this book that 'there can be no assault if it is obvious to V that D is unable to carry out his threat, as where D shakes his fist at V who is safely locked inside his car'. There may, of course, be an assault although D has no means of carrying out the threat.[41] The question is whether D intends to cause V to believe that he can and will carry it out immediately and whether V does so believe. The question arises most obviously where D points an unloaded or imitation gun at V. If V knows the gun is unloaded or an imitation, there is no assault, for then he could not apprehend being shot.[42] If V believes it is, or may be a real, loaded gun, there is an actus reus by D, for now V suffers the apprehension which is an essential element of assault.[43]

16.1.4.2 Assault by words alone

Ireland has now settled that an assault can be committed by words alone. This seems right— as a matter of fact, words, no less than a gesture, are capable of causing an apprehension of immediate violence.[44] It follows from *Constanza* that an assault by writing, fax, email, tweet, text, etc is also possible.

Where D's actions would be an assault, but his words negate the effect of his actions, there is no offence.[45] If D's words are such that they amount to an implied threat or a conditional threat (eg 'as soon as we are alone I will hit you'), there may be an assault.[46]

It has generally been assumed that an act of some kind—even if it is only making a telephone call and remaining silent—is an essential ingredient of assault. One case[47] seems to support assault by omission but the court's actual decision was that D's conduct was a 'continuing act'. Where D inadvertently causes V to apprehend immediate violence (D is checking the sights on his gun when V walks into the room) and subsequently wilfully declines to withdraw the threat (by lowering the gun), his 'omission' might therefore constitute an assault.

16.1.4.3 Attempt to assault

There can be no conviction for attempt to commit a common assault since common assault is a summary only offence.[48] There is no reason why there should not be attempt to commit a more serious offence of which assault forms an element; as where D points an unloaded gun at V, intending to frighten him in order to resist lawful arrest, but V, knowing the gun is unloaded, is unperturbed.[49]

16.1.5 Actus reus of battery

The actus reus consists in the infliction of unlawful personal violence by D upon V. V need not be aware of the touching as, for example, where he is asleep.[50] It used to be said that every battery involves an assault; but this is plainly not so, for in battery there need be no apprehension of the impending violence. A blow from behind is a battery even though

---

[41] *Pace*, Tindal CJ in *Stephens v Myers* (1830) 4 C & P 349.
[42] *Lamb*, p 570.   [43] *Logdon v DPP*, n 33.
[44] Previously the law was unclear although many authoritative writers asserted that words could not amount to an assault. See generally G Williams, 'Assault and Words' [1957] Crim LR 219.
[45] See *Tuberville v Savage* (1669) 1 Mood Rep 3—words 'if it were not assize time I would not take such language' negatived what would otherwise be an assault of D putting his hand on a sword in V's presence.
[46] See J Horder, 'Psychic Assault' [1998] Crim LR 392.
[47] *Fagan v Metropolitan Police Comr* [1969] 1 QB 439.
[48] The point was not argued in *Lewis* [2010] EWCA Crim 151 (manslaughter where D chased V into the path of oncoming traffic).
[49] AF Noyes, 'Is Criminal Assault a Separate Substantive Crime or is it an Attempted Battery?' (1945) 33 Ky LJ 189; *State v Wilson*, 218 Ore 575, 346 P 2d 115 (1955). See also D White, 'Attempts: Initiatives in the Common Law Caribbean' [1980] Crim LR 780.
[50] See also *Thomas* (1985) 81 Cr App R 331.

V was unaware that it was coming.[51] It is generally said that D must have done some act and that it is not enough that he stood still and obstructed V's passage[52] like an inanimate object. But suppose D is sitting at the corner of a corridor with his legs stretched across it. He hears V running down the corridor and deliberately remains still with the intention that V, on turning the corner, shall fall over his legs. Why should this not be a battery? It would be if D had put out his legs with the intention of tripping up V. It would not be too difficult to conclude that D has a duty to V from the creation of the dangerous situation, applying the general principle recognized in *Miller*.[53] Further support for this proposition derives from *Santana-Bermudez*,[54] where D, an intravenous drug user, assured a police officer who was about to search him that he was carrying no 'sharps' and the officer stabbed her finger on a syringe in D's pocket. The court upheld the conviction, applying *Miller*:[55]

where someone (by act or word or a combination of the two) creates a danger and thereby exposes another to a reasonably foreseeable risk of injury which materializes, there is an evidential basis for the *actus reus* of an assault occasioning actual bodily harm. It remains necessary for the prosecution to prove an intention to assault or appropriate recklessness.[56]

By having the needles in his pocket and assuring the police officer about the contents of his pockets, D created a situation of danger. There may also be a battery where D inadvertently applies force to V and then wrongfully refuses to withdraw it. In *Fagan*,[57] where D accidentally drove his car on to a constable's foot and then intentionally left it there, the court held that there was a continuing act, not a mere omission.

There is certainly no battery where D has no control over the incident which causes the touching of V, as where D's horse unexpectedly runs away with him and into V;[58] but this might equally be explained because there is no mens rea. It might be otherwise if D foresaw, when he mounted the animal, that there was an unacceptable risk that this might happen.

16.1.5.1 Battery with or via an instrument

Most batteries are *directly* inflicted, for example by D striking V with his fist or an instrument, or by a missile thrown by him, or by spitting upon V. But this is not essential: there can be an indirect battery. Where D punched W causing her to drop her baby, V, he was guilty of battery on V. It was found as a fact that D was reckless whether he injured V.[59]

In *Martin*,[60] Stephen and Wills JJ thought there would be a battery where D digs a pit for V to fall into or where he causes V to rush into an obstruction. The Divisional Court has since recognized a battery by indirect means: in *DPP v K*,[61] D was convicted where he poured acid into a hand-drier in a toilet so that the next user sprayed himself with it.[62]

---

[51] This passage in the 13th edition of this book was cited with approval by the Court of Appeal in *Nelson* [2013] EWCA Crim 30, [2013] Crim LR 689. The Court of Appeal held that the judge was wrong to leave a verdict of common assault to the jury as an alternative to battery. See n 29.

[52] *Innes v Wylie* (1844) 1 Car & Kir 257.   [53] [1983] AC 161.

[54] [2004] Crim LR 471, [2003] EWHC 2908 (Admin).   [55] [1983] AC 161.

[56] At [10].   [57] [1969] 1 QB 439.   [58] *Gibbons v Pepper* (1695) 2 Salk 637.

[59] *Haystead v Chief Constable of Derbyshire* (2000) 164 JP 396, [2000] Crim LR 758, DC, citing the 9th edition of this work. D could, alternatively, have been held guilty of an intentional assault by reason of transferred malice: p 122.

[60] (1881) 8 QBD 54, CCR.

[61] [1990] 1 All ER 331, [1990] Crim LR 321, DC, overruled on other grounds by *Spratt* [1991] 2 All ER 210, CA.

[62] It has been argued (M Hirst, 'Assault, Battery and Indirect Violence' [1999] Crim LR 557) that these authorities are inconsistent with the decision of the House of Lords in *MPC v Wilson* ([1984] AC 242, p 696) but all that case decided was that, though the word 'inflict' does not necessarily imply an assault, an allegation of inflicting harm may do so, and assault is therefore an 'included offence'. It does not follow that no indirect injury can ever be a battery.

The courts have now interpreted 'bodily' harm to include psychiatric harm, and that may be inflicted without any impact on V's body by, for example, harassment over the phone. That certainly does not involve a battery.[63] Where, however, D has caused an impact on V, indirectly with no fully voluntary intervening act, it is submitted that D should, subject to mens rea, be guilty of battery.[64]

It is not a battery (nor an assault) for D to pull himself free from V who is detaining him, even though D uses force.[65]

It is submitted that it would undoubtedly be a battery to set a dog on another.[66] If D hit O's horse causing it to run down V, this would be battery by D.[67] No doubt the famous civil case of *Scott v Shepherd*[68] is equally applicable to the criminal law. D threw a squib (a firework) into a crowded area. First E and then F flung the squib away in order to save themselves from injury. It exploded and injured V. The acts of E and F were not 'fully voluntary' intervening acts which broke the chain of causation. This was battery by D.

If there is no violence at all, there is no battery; as where D puts harmful matter into a drink which is consumed by V.[69]

16.1.6 Mens rea of assault and battery

It is convenient to consider the mens rea of the two offences together. They are inextricably confused in some of the leading cases but need to be kept distinct if the separateness of the two offences is to be taken seriously. It was established by *Venna*[70] in 1975 that assault and battery may be committed recklessly as well as intentionally. *Venna* was a case of battery occasioning actual bodily harm but *dicta* concerning assault were relied on and it is safe to assume that the same principles apply to both offences.

The mens rea of assault is an intention to cause V to apprehend immediate and unlawful violence, or recklessness whether such apprehension be caused.[71] Technically there is an argument that D should be shown to have intended or been reckless not only as to V's apprehension, but to have intended or been reckless that V's apprehension would be of *immediate* violence. It is unlikely the courts will adopt such a sophistication.

The mens rea of battery is an intention to apply force to the body of another or recklessness whether force be so applied.

16.1.6.1 Subjective recklessness

Venna approved the test of subjective, *Cunningham*-style recklessness. Despite some attempts to apply the *Caldwell* formulation of recklessness in *DPP v K*,[72] that decision was quickly overruled by the Court of Appeal in *Spratt*[73] which was followed by that court in *Parmenter*.[74] The

---

[63] cf D Ormerod and M Gunn, 'In Defence of *Ireland*' [1996] 3 Web JCLI.

[64] The criminal law is not governed by the ancient forms of action at common law which would require directness.

[65] *Sheriff* [1969] Crim LR 260.

[66] *Murgatroyd v Chief Constable of West Yorkshire* [2000] All ER (D) 1742. But note the court's caution in *Dume* (1986) The Times, 16 Oct, CA.

[67] *Gibbon v Pepper* (1695) 2 Salk 637 (*obiter*).   [68] (1773) 2 Wm Bl 892.

[69] *Hanson* (1849) 2 Car & Kir 912; but see p 713.   [70] [1976] QB 421.

[71] cf *Savage* [1992] 1 AC 699, [1991] 4 All ER 698 at 711, HL.

[72] [1990] 1 All ER 331, [1990] Crim LR 321, DC.

[73] [1991] 2 All ER 210, [1990] Crim LR 797. In *Pinkney v DPP* [2017] EWHC 854 (Admin) despite the fact the district judge appeared to apply an objective test, D's conviction was upheld as Sir Wyn Williams reached the conclusion that on the facts D did commit an offence. With respect, the outcome of this case is surprising.

[74] [1992] 1 AC 699.

House of Lords was not asked to decide the point but *dicta*[75] assume that *Cunningham* reck-lessness is required; and with the overruling of *Caldwell* in *G*, the point is surely unarguable. The law is that D must actually foresee the risk of causing apprehension of immediate violence, or the application of it, as the case may be, and go on unjustifiably to take that risk.[76]

16.1.6.2 Is the mens rea of assault and battery interchangeable?

Is it an offence to cause the actus reus of battery with the mens rea only of assault or the actus reus of assault with the mens rea only of battery? In principle, the answer is no.[77] D waves his fist, intending to alarm (assault) V but not to strike him and not foreseeing any risk of doing so; but V who does not see D, moves, and is hit. D creeps up behind V, intend-ing to hit him over the head without attracting his attention (battery), but V unexpectedly turns round and moves to avoid the blow. Taking the distinction between assault and bat-tery seriously, in the former case D does not commit a battery but is attempting to commit an assault; and in the latter he does not commit an assault but is attempting to commit a battery; and these 'attempts' to commit summary offences are not offences. It remains to be seen how seriously the courts will take the separateness of the offences.

16.1.6.3 Assault and battery by an intoxicated person

Assault and battery are classified as offences of 'basic intent'[78] so it is no defence that D had no mens rea because of his voluntary intoxication. The reason appears to be that the offences may be committed by recklessness. If the prosecution specifically allege that D has *intentionally* assaulted or battered, it may be that they will be required to prove a 'specific intent' and intoxication will be a defence.[79] Given the demonstrable link between alcohol and offences of violence, the courts might find this approach unpalatable.

16.2 Defences to assault and battery

16.2.1 Consent

It is clear that consent is an answer to a charge of common assault or battery (though not necessarily to the offence of assault occasioning actual bodily harm[80]). It remains unclear

---

[75] 'Where the defendant neither intends nor adverts to the possibility that there will be any physical contact at all, then the offence under s 47 would not be made out. This is because there would have been *no assault*, let alone an assault occasioning actual bodily harm' ([1991] 4 All ER at 707): Lord Ackner of course means 'no bat-tery'. Other *dicta* show that he recognized that an assault in the strict sense suffices for an offence under s 47 if it occasions actual bodily harm.

[76] Despite the ease with which the test can be stated, cases with questionable outcomes still occur. Cf *Katsonis v CPS* [2011] EWHC 1860 (Admin).

[77] See also LCCP 217, Chs 3 and 5.

[78] Subject to any radical reappraisal of that concept following *Heard* [2007] EWCA Crim 125, p 319.

[79] cf *Caldwell* [1982] AC 341, [1981] 1 All ER 961 at 964.

[80] There is a vast literature on this subject. Accessible discussions include LCCP 134, *Consent and Offences against the Person* (1994), on which see D Ormerod, 'Consent and Offences Against the Person: LCCP No 134' (1994) 57 MLR 928; and LCCP 139, *Consent in Criminal Law* (1995), on which see D Ormerod and M Gunn, 'Consent—A Second Bash' [1996] Crim LR 694; S Shute, 'Something Old, Something New, Something Borrowed—Three Aspects of the Consent Project' [1996] Crim LR 684. For a multifaceted analysis, see A Reed and M Bohlander (with N Wake and E Smith) (eds), *Consent—Domestic and Comparative Perspectives* (2017). For a review of the philosophical arguments, see P Roberts, 'The Philosophical Foundations of Consent in the Criminal Law' (1997) 17 OJLS 389. On consent more generally, see D Beyleveld and R Brownsword, *Consent in the Law* (2007).

how consent negates liability for assault or battery. Is it because the *absence of consent* is an essential element in the offence, as in rape;[81] or is *consent* a defence to the charge? In *Brown*, Lord Jauncey, with whose reasoning Lord Lowry agreed, said that if it had been necessary to answer this question, which it was not, he would have held consent to be a defence. Lord Templeman also treated consent as a defence. Lord Mustill, on the other hand, regarded it as one factor negativing an actus reus; while Lord Slynn emphatically agreed with Glanville Williams that 'It is... inherent in the concept of assault and battery that the victim does not consent.'[82] The Law Commission regarded it as a defence.[83] However, Lord Woolf CJ stated that 'it is a requirement of *the offence* that the conduct itself should be unlawful'.[84]

This view—that it is an element of the offence—is, it is submitted, the better one. The importance of the question is demonstrated by the dissent of Lords Mustill and Slynn in *Brown*. The majority held that the sadomasochistic defendants were guilty of assaults occasioning actual bodily harm on, and unlawful wounding of, one another, notwithstanding the defendants' enthusiastic submission to, and the pleasure which they all derived from, the sadomasochistic 'assaults'. The question the majority asked themselves was 'Does the public interest require the invention of a new defence?' This is quite different from the question the minority were answering: 'Does the public interest require the offence to be construed to include sadomasochistic conduct?' It is not surprising that they led to different conclusions.[85]

While the distinction between offence and defence is fundamental in theory and in judicial law-making, in the practical functioning of the law in this area it is probably not very important.[86] It affects the evidential burden—if the absence of consent is an element of the offence, the prosecution must set out to prove it; if it is a defence, it is for the defendant to introduce evidence of it; but, in either case, the ultimate burden of proof is on the prosecution. In *Shabbir*,[87] S and others were acquitted by the magistrates of charges including assault. The charges arose from a prolonged violent attack in a city centre. The defendants raised the plea of consent, arguing that the Crown had the burden of proving that V had not consented to being assaulted. The magistrates found that the Crown had failed to prove that matter and acquitted. The Divisional Court held that a lack of consent could be inferred from evidence (violent attack on strangers shown on CCTV) other than the direct evidence of the victim.

Whether or not consent is properly regarded as a defence or as an element of the offences of assault and battery (and therefore as an element of the aggravated assaults discussed later), it is valuable to consider its meaning here. In recent years the courts have been forced to deal with difficult issues including defining what constitutes effective 'consent' (ie whether frauds or pressure vitiate consent) and, if such factual consent is present, whether it ought to be recognized in law. In other words, in what circumstances it is appropriate for

---

[81] *Larter* [1995] Crim LR 75, see Ch 17, p 774, n 128.

[82] G Williams, 'Consent and Public Policy' [1962] Crim LR 74, 75.

[83] For criticism see S Shute [1996] Crim LR 684.

[84] *Barnes* [2005] EWCA Crim 3246, [16], [2005] Crim LR 381.

[85] cf *Wilson*, p 682, where the court asked, 'Does public policy or the public interest demand that the appellant's activities [branding of wife's buttocks at her request] be visited by the sanctions of the criminal law?' and, unsurprisingly, answered, 'No.' By way of contrast see *BM* [2018] EWCA Crim 560, which concerned body modification such as tongue splitting by a tattooist who had no medical qualification.

[86] The Criminal Injuries Compensation Appeal Panel takes the view that the victim's consent is not determinative of whether an offence of violence has been committed: *R (E) v CICA* [2003] EWCA Civ 234.

[87] [2009] EWHC 2754 (Admin). Goldring LJ expressed astonishment and disappointment that such a 'wholly spurious' point would be taken on the facts of that case.

789

the State to apply the criminal sanction to punish conduct voluntarily engaged in by adults of full mental capacity. There are three distinct questions to address:

(1) Was there implied or express consent?

(2) Did the 'victim'[88] give effective consent to the act?

(3) Was the conduct performed in a context in which the law accepts that consent be validly given? [89]

16.2.1.1 Implied consent

Since the merest touching without consent is a battery, the exigencies of everyday life demand that there be an implied consent to that degree of contact which is necessary or customary in the ordinary course of daily life.

Generally speaking, consent is a defence to battery; and most of the physical contacts of ordinary life are not actionable because they are impliedly consented to by all who move in society and so expose themselves to the risk of bodily contact. So no one can complain of the jostling which is inevitable from his presence in, for example, a supermarket, an underground station or a busy street; nor can a person who attends a party complain if his hand is seized in friendship, or even if his back is (within reason) slapped. Although such cases are regarded as examples of implied consent, it is more common nowadays to treat them as falling within a general exception embracing the limited physical contact which is generally to be expected and accepted in the ordinary conduct of daily life.[90]

Touching a person for the purpose of engaging his attention has been held to be acceptable[91] but physical restraint is not. A police officer who catches hold of a boy, not for the purpose of arresting him but in order to detain him for questioning, is acting unlawfully.[92] So is a constable who takes hold of the arm of a woman found soliciting in order to caution her. The fact that the practice of cautioning sex workers is recognized by statute does not imply

---

[88] The term 'victim' is adopted throughout this chapter, although it is acknowledged that if V has truly consented, it is illogical to view him as such.

[89] It has been argued that English law relies too much upon category-based decision-making and that a more suitable approach is the one propounded by the New Zealand Court of Appeal in *Lee* (2006) 22 CRNZ 568. This approach requires the court to engage with the facts of the individual case in a substantive fashion rather than simply basing its decision on the generic category of behaviour to which the facts belong. See J Tolmie, 'Consent to Harmful Assaults: The Case for Moving Away from Category Based Decision Making' [2012] Crim LR 656 and W Wilson, 'Consenting to Personal Injury' in A Reed and M Bohlander (with N Wake and E Smith) (eds), *Consent—Domestic and Comparative Perspectives* (2017).

[90] *Collins v Wilcock* [1984] 3 All ER 374 at 378, per Robert Goff LJ. In *F v West Berkshire Health Authority* [1990] 2 AC 1, [1989] 2 All ER 545 at 563, HL, Lord Goff was more emphatic that the consent rationalization is 'artificial', pointing out that it is difficult to impute consent to those who through youth or mental disorder are unable to give it. See *Mepstead v DPP* [1996] Crim LR 111, DC. In *Wainwright v Home Office* [2003] UKHL 53, Goff LJ was described as having 'redefined' the concept, at [9].

[91] *Wiffin v Kincard* (1807) 2 Bos & PNR 471; *Coward v Baddeley* (1859) 4 H & N 478. *Donnelly v Jackman* [1970] 1 All ER 987, [1970] 1 WLR 562, where a police officer was held to be acting in the execution of his duty although he persisted in tapping V on the shoulder when V had made it clear that he had no intention of stopping to speak, is 'an extreme case': [1984] 3 All ER 374 at 379. See also *Walker v Commissioner of Police of the Metropolis* (2014) The Times, 16 July, CA (Civ Div) where the officer went beyond the permissible.

[92] *Kenlin v Gardiner* [1967] 2 QB 510. See *McKoy* [2002] EWCA Crim 1628. See for more recent examples *Iqbal* [2011] EWCA Crim 273; *Wood v DPP* [2008] EWHC 1056 (Admin); *Metcalf v CPS* [2015] EWHC 1091 (Admin), D may be guilty of obstructing a constable (making a lawful arrest, keeping the peace, etc) even if the officer, at some point, acts unlawfully (eg in pushing D out of the way). For discussion of whether the defences of private defence or defence of another can be pleaded in respect of these offences, see p 407.

any power to stop and detain.[93] But to 'detain' without any actual touching cannot be a battery. If the detention is effected by the threat of force, then it may be false imprisonment.[94] Article 5 of the ECHR has potential significance, but has been interpreted to protect against a 'deprivation of liberty not a minor restriction on freedom of movement'.[95]

In *H v CPS*,[96] the court rejected the submission that teachers in special needs schools must by their post 'impliedly consent' to the use of violence against them by pupils. The court accepted that the teachers were accepting a heightened risk of violence but that was not the same as saying that they implicitly consented to its infliction.

For this purpose, touching the 'person' of the victim includes the clothes he is wearing.[97] It is not necessary that V should be able to feel the impact through the clothes. In *Thomas*,[98] where D touched the bottom of V's skirt and rubbed it, the court said, *obiter*, that 'There could be no dispute that if you touch a person's clothes while he is wearing them that is equivalent to touching him.' Section 79 of the Sexual Offences Act 2003 defines touching for the purpose of that Act, as including touching with any part of the body, with anything else or *through anything*, and in *H*[99] the Court of Appeal confirmed that touching V's clothes sufficed.

In *Dica*,[100] the Court of Appeal confirmed that where V, who was unaware of D's infected state, had consented to the act of unprotected sexual intercourse she could not be said to have *impliedly* consented to the risk of infection from that intercourse.

16.2.1.2 Effective consent

The principal problems to address in this context are:

- what mental capacity V must possess to be capable of issuing effective consent;
- what degree of knowledge of the acts V must have to be capable of giving a valid consent to them;
- what effect on V's apparent consent a fraud by D will have; and
- whether duress or pressure from D or another will vitiate consent by V.

We are not at this point examining D's belief in V's consent, but it must be borne in mind that D's belief that V is consenting to an act for which V's factual consent would be recognized in law[101] is a defence whether D's belief is based on reasonable grounds or not, provided D's belief is honestly held.[102]

---

[93] *Collins v Wilcock*, n 90; see eg *McMillan v CPS* [2008] EWHC 1457 (Admin) (touching when steadying a drunk person).

[94] See p 717.

[95] See discussion in Emmerson, Ashworth, and Macdonald, HR&CJ, paras 5.02 et seq; *Guzzardi v Italy* (1981) 3 EHRR 333, para 92. See the discussion of *Austin v MPC* [2009] UKHL 12, p 718. See also *R (AP) v Secretary of State for the Home Department* [2010] UKSC 24, in which it was held that when deciding if there is a deprivation of liberty within the meaning of Art 5 of the ECHR regard should be had to the subjective factors peculiar to the particular individual.

[96] [2010] All ER (D) 56 (Apr).   [97] *Day* (1845) 1 Cox CC 207. D slashed V's clothes with a knife.

[98] (1985) 81 Cr App R 331 at 334, CA.   [99] [2005] EWCA Crim 732, [2005] Crim LR 734.

[100] [2004] EWCA Crim 1103, [2004] Crim LR 944 and commentary. The House of Lords refused leave to appeal—see House of Lords Session 2005–06, 15 Dec 2005. See for criticism of the case: M Weait, 'Criminal Law and the Transmission of HIV: R v Dica' (2005) 68 MLR 121; M Weait, 'Dica: Knowledge, Consent and the Transmission of HIV' (2004) 154 NLJ 826; cf for a positive view of the case: JR Spencer, 'Retrial for Reckless Infection' (2004) 154 NLJ 762. See also M Davies, 'R v Dica: Lessons in Practising Unsafe Sex' (2004) 68 J Crim L 498.

[101] *Konzani* [2005] EWCA Crim 706.

[102] *Morgan* [1976] AC 182, HL; p 332; *Albert v Lavin* [1981] 1 All ER 628, DC.

Capacity

Those with a mental disorder or learning difficulty may lack sufficient capacity[103] to give consent,[104] as may someone who is temporarily incapacitated by intoxication or otherwise. Youth or immaturity is clearly also a potential impediment to the giving of effective consent.[105] In *Burrell v Harmer*,[106] where D tattooed boys aged 12 and 13, causing their arms to become inflamed and painful, the boys' apparent consent was held to be no defence to a charge of assault occasioning actual bodily harm. The court took the view that the boys were unable to understand the nature of the act. But in what sense did they not understand it? The case highlights the relative superficiality of the English criminal courts' approach to such fundamental questions underlying the issue of consent.

The Mental Capacity Act 2005 provides a definition, at least for the purposes of that Act, of 'people who lack capacity'. The definition is as follows: 'a person lacks capacity in relation to a matter if at the material time he is unable to make a decision for himself in relation to the matter because of a temporary or permanent impairment of, or a disturbance in the functioning of, the mind or brain'. The section further provides that a lack of capacity cannot be established merely by reference to '(a) a person's age or appearance, or (b) a condition of his, or an aspect of his behaviour, which might lead others to make unjustified assumptions about his capacity'.

Even if the criminal courts do not adopt that definition directly in the context of offences against the person, they may be influenced in deciding whether a person lacks capacity by the 'principles' set out in s 1 of the Mental Capacity Act 2005 which include that a person: must be assumed to have capacity unless it is established to the contrary, and that a person is not to be treated as unable to make a decision merely because he makes an unwise decision.[107] The Act provides 'official recognition that capacity is not a blunt "all or nothing" condition, but is more complex, and is to be treated as being issue-specific. A person may not have sufficient capacity to be able to make complex, refined or major decisions but may still have the capacity to make simpler or less momentous ones, or to hold genuine views as to what he wants to be the outcome of more complex decisions or situations.'[108]

Informed consent

In principle, V cannot consent to some form of conduct without adequate knowledge of its nature, and the degree of knowledge required should depend on the degree of harm and risk of that harm to which V is exposing himself. In offences against the person, this issue seems to have received little attention until very recently. In sexual offences, it is implicit in the statutory formulation of the more serious non-consensual offences that V must have capacity and have 'freely agreed', and that there must have been adequate information available to V to render his consent effective.[109] The issue overlaps with the next to be discussed—that of V's apparent consent in the face of deception by D. In sexual offences, the 2003 Act provides,

---

[103] LCCP 139, Part V; LC 231, *Mental Capacity* (1995); see E Jackson, *Medical Law: Text, Cases, and Materials* (4th edn, 2016) Chs 4 and 5.

[104] See *Re MB (An Adult) (Medical Treatment)* [1997] 2 FCR 541. Medical treatment in defiance of the (mentally normal) adult patient's wishes or in the case of a child in defiance of those of a parent will infringe Art 8: *Glass v UK* (App no 61827/00) 2000.

[105] See generally *Gillick v West Norfolk and Wisbech AHA* [1986] AC 112.

[106] [1967] Crim LR 169 and commentary thereon. It is now an offence to tattoo a person under the age of 18, except tattooing by a doctor for medical reasons: Tattooing of Minors Act 1969.

[107] The Act is supplemented by a Code of Practice published in 2007. See also *C* [2009] UKHL 42, dealing with the offence in s 30 of the Sexual Offences Act 2003, discussed at p 763.

[108] See *Re S and another (Protected Persons)* [2010] 1 WLR 1082, [53] concerning powers of attorney.

[109] See Ch 17.

inter alia, that it is conclusively presumed that there is no consent where D has deceived V as to the nature or purpose of D's act.[110] In non-sexual offences against the person, it remains unclear whether V can be said to have consented without having knowledge of the *purpose* of D's conduct even if V is aware of its *nature*. The issue has arisen in relation to cases in which D has infected V with HIV[111] in the course of sexual acts.[112]

In *Konzani*,[113] the Court of Appeal confirmed that if D engages in unprotected sexual intercourse with V, and D recklessly infects V with HIV, any defence of consent D seeks to advance will not be available unless V had made an informed consent to the risk of infection.[114] As the court explained:

If an individual who knows that he is suffering from the HIV virus conceals this stark fact from his sexual partner, the principle of V's personal autonomy is not enhanced if D is exculpated when he recklessly transmits the HIV virus to V through consensual sexual intercourse. On any view, the concealment of this fact from her almost inevitably means that she is deceived. Her consent is not properly informed, and she cannot give an informed consent to something of which she is ignorant. Equally, her personal autonomy is not normally protected by allowing a defendant who knows that he is suffering from the HIV virus which he deliberately conceals, to assert an honest belief in his partner's informed consent to the risk of the transmission of the HIV virus. Silence in these circumstances not consistent with honesty, or with a genuine belief that there is an informed consent. Accordingly, in such circumstances the issue either of informed consent, or honest belief in it will only rarely arise: in reality, in most cases, the contention would be wholly artificial.[115]

Several aspects of the decision are of importance. First, to be effective, V's consent must be to the risk of HIV infection; V might well have consented to the act of sexual intercourse without consenting to the risk of HIV infection. Secondly, V cannot in law consent to intentional

---

[110] See s 76, p 775. As will be discussed later, deception is also relevant when considering the general definition of consent in s 74.

[111] See also *Golding* [2014] EWCA Crim 889, [2014] Crim LR 686 in which D pleaded guilty to transmitting genital herpes. See also LCCP 217, Ch 6.

[112] For detailed examination of the appropriate uses of the criminal law to tackle HIV transmission, see S Bronnit, 'Spreading Disease and the Criminal Law' [1994] Crim LR 21; D Ormerod and M Gunn, 'Criminal Liability for the Transmission of HIV' [1996] Web JCLI; D Ormerod, 'Criminalizing HIV Transmission—Still No Effective Solutions' (2001) 30 Common L World Rev 135; M Weait and Y Azad, 'The Criminalisation of HIV Transmission in England and Wales: Questions of Law and Policy' (2005) 10 HIV/AIDS Policy & Law Rev 1. See more generally, M Weait, *Intimacy and Responsibility: The Criminalisaiton of HIV Transmission* (2007). Cf S Matthiesson, 'Should the Law Deal with Reckless HIV Infection as a Criminal Offence or as a Matter of Public Health?' (2010) 21 KLJ 123 responding to Weait; R Bennett, 'Should We Criminalise HIV Transmission' in C Erin and S Ost (eds), *The Criminal Justice System and Health Care* (2007) 225; L Cherkassky, 'Being Informed: The Complexities of Knowledge, Deception and Consent when Transmitting HIV' (2010) 74 J Crim L 242; J Slater, 'HIV, Trust and the Criminal Law' (2011) 75 J Crim L 309; JG Francis and LP Francis, 'HIV Treatment as Prevention: Not an Argument for Continuing Criminalisation of HIV Transmission' (2013) 9 Int'l J Crim L in Context 520; the chapters in C Stanton and H Quirk (eds), *Criminalising Contagion—Legal and Ethical Challenges of Disease Transmission and the Criminal Law* (2016). The CPS has a dedicated policy for prosecuting cases involving the intentional or reckless sexual transmission of infection. See www.cps.gov.uk/legal-guidance/intentional-or-reckless-sexual-transmission-infection-policy-prosecuting-cases. The policy was reviewed after one year and was found to be 'broadly effective' (para 5.1). Note that this is not limited to HIV transmission.

[113] [2005] EWCA Crim 706; M Weait, 'Knowledge, Autonomy and Consent: R v Konzani' [2005] Crim LR 763 arguing that the case extends the criminal law too far by criminalizing *reckless* non-disclosure of HIV-positive status. See more generally M Weait, *Intimacy and Responsibility: The Criminalisation of HIV Transmission* (2007) arguing that the act of recklessly exposing a sexual partner to the risk of HIV infection without her consent should be decriminalized and treated as a public health issue.

[114] For sentencing considerations in such cases, see *P (SJ)* [2006] EWCA Crim 2599—32 months on a plea. Darryl Rowe was sentenced to life imprisonment for intentionally transmitting HIV to a number of his sexual partners. See news reports for 18 April 2018.   [115] At [23].

infection; V's consent is only effective if D is merely reckless as to transmission.[116] Thirdly, the decision appears to criminalize D who suspects that he is HIV-positive, without knowing that fact, if he then goes on to have unprotected intercourse with V without her consent as to the risk of infection.[117] This aspect of the decision has been heavily criticized for over-criminalizing.[118] Fourthly, the decision treats D's failure to disclose his HIV-positive status to V as sufficient to preclude informed consent by V. Several commentators have been critical of this aspect of the decision, arguing that V has some responsibility for taking precautions about her sexual safety, and that by assuming that by D's concealment V is not consenting, the law ignores that responsibility on V.[119] The question of whether D is liable where he has not informed V of his HIV status but, despite using a condom, he has infected V remains unresolved. D will surely argue that he was not reckless as to the risk of infection.[120]

It was accepted in *Konzani* that there may be circumstances in which V will have informed consent without express disclosure from D, as where the fact of D's HIV status becomes known in the course of medical treatment. That qualification to the general principle—that informed consent depends on D's honest disclosure—also poses problems. D will be able to plead that he did not know that V was not consenting to the risk, since he had a genuine belief that she knew of his HIV status although he had not disclosed the fact to her. In addition, D may be acquitted where V has in fact consented to the risk even if D did not know that she had consented because he was unaware of her having secured knowledge of his status from other sources. If absence of consent is an element of the actus reus, D cannot be guilty in such a case because the actus reus is not complete where V has, in fact, consented. If consent is a defence, D will have actus reus (infection) and mens rea (recklessness as to infection); but can he rely on the defence of consent based on the fact of V's awareness of his infected state of which D was ignorant at the time as it derived from other sources? Does the defence require proof that D was aware of the circumstances which would render his conduct justified? Cooper and Reed[121] suggest that this resurrects the problems posed by *Dadson* (p 34). They point to the fact that D will be relying on a justifying circumstance (V's consent) of which D was unaware at the time of the act, and that this drives 'a coach and horses' through established doctrines of informed consent.

Parliamentary clarification of the issues would be welcome, but is unlikely given the controversial nature of such legislation in terms of broader public health policies and the desire to encourage responsible sexual behaviour.[122] The Law Commission has consulted on whether future reform of the offences against the person ought to include specific offences dealing with sexually transmitted infection.[123] In the subsequent Report, the Law Commission recommended that in any new statute governing offences against the person based upon the draft Home Office Bill, the offences of causing serious injury should be capable of including the intentional or (as the case may be) reckless transmission of disease. The

---

[116] See later.

[117] Some argue that D has a 'right' not to know what his HIV status is and a right to act on that lack of knowledge: Tadros, *Criminal Responsibility*, 247.

[118] See S Ryan, 'Reckless Transmission of HIV: Knowledge and Culpability' [2006] Crim LR 981.

[119] See Weait (2005) 68 MLR at 128 and [2005] Crim LR 763. See also V Munro, 'On Responsible Relationships and Irresponsible Sex' (2007) 19 CFLQ 112.

[120] There are those who argue that consent may not be D's only way of avoiding liability in cases such as these and that there is ambiguity as to whether, in the absence of disclosure, D could avoid liability by using a condom and/or demonstrating that his viral load was very low, thereby diminishing the risk of transmission. It is argued that in these circumstances D is not being reckless and so lacks the requisite mens rea. See D Hughes, 'Condom Use, Viral Load and the Type of Sexual Activity as Defences to the Sexual Transmission of HIV' (2013) 77 J Crim L 136. See also LCCP 217, Ch 2.

[121] S Cooper and A Reed, 'Informed Consent and the Transmission of Sexual Disease: *Dadson* Revivified' (2007) 71 J Crim L 461.

[122] See J Rogers (2005) 64 CLJ 20, 22 pointing out that no government is likely to want to legislate.

[123] See LCCP 217, *Reform of Offences Against the Person: A Scoping Consultation Paper* (2014) Ch 6.

Law Commission also recommended that if the government wished to consider the possibility of excluding criminal liability for the reckless transmission of disease, or of creating special offences for such transmission, this should follow a wider review.[124]

The approach in *Konzani*, by which V's informed consent rests on D providing information as to the relevant risk, does not sit easily with the courts' approach in sexual offences, where it is unclear whether every fraud by D as to the purpose of his actions will vitiate consent.[125]

Consent procured by fraud

In offences against the person, D's fraud as to the conduct does not necessarily negative V's consent: it does so only if it deceives V as to D's identity or the nature of the act.[126] The common law approach to frauds vitiating consent remains unsatisfactorily complex and confused.

If V agrees to X touching her in a manner amounting to a mere battery, her consent is prima facie vitiated if D impersonates X and touches her. V's autonomy includes a right (generally) to choose *who* touches her. In *Richardson*,[127] D, a registered dental practitioner who was suspended from practice, carried out dentistry on patients who said they would not have consented had they known that D was suspended. D was convicted of assault occasioning actual bodily harm, the trial judge ruling that the mistake vitiated consent, being equivalent to a mistake of identity. The Court of Appeal disagreed since that would be to strain and distort the everyday meaning of 'identity'. The fraud was not as to who she was but whether she was licensed as a dentist. There is, to date, no recognition of a principle in offences against the person whereby a fraud as to an attribute (eg being medically qualified) suffices to vitiate consent. It could be argued that there are some situations in which the status or attribute of the individual is inextricably bound up with his identity for the purposes of the specific activity he is performing. Indeed, it could be that the attribute is actually *more* important than the identity. For example, would a patient visiting a general practitioner and being told that a new doctor is taking the surgery be more concerned as to the 'status' of the person or his 'identity'? The same argument might apply to the attribute of being a police officer.[128]

The courts have had even greater difficulty dealing with the effect of frauds as to the nature of the act, and in particular in distinguishing frauds that relate to issues that affect the nature of the act and frauds that relate to a collateral issue. It would be undesirable for the law to treat all frauds as vitiating consent; otherwise the most trivial lies about the conduct could give rise to liability.[129] In *Bolduc and Bird*, where D1, a doctor, by falsely pretending that D2 was a medical student, obtained V's consent to D2's presence at a necessary vaginal examination of

---

[124] See LC 361, *Reform of Offences Against the Person* (2015) Ch 6.

[125] See *Jheeta* [2007] EWCA Crim 1699, *Assange v Sweden* [2011] EWHC 2849 (Admin), *B* [2013] EWCA Crim 823; p 776. For discussion, see A Reed and E Smith, 'Caveat Amator—The Transmission of HIV and the Parameters of Consent and Bad Character Evidence' in A Reed and M Bohlander (with N Wake and E Smith) (eds), *Consent—Domestic and Comparative Perspectives* (2017) 125–130.

[126] See generally LCCP 139, Part VI.

[127] [1998] 2 Cr App R 200. *Richardson* now has to be read with *Tabassum* [2000] 2 Cr App R 328, p 673.

[128] With powers to arrest, search, etc. See *Wellard* [1978] 1 WLR 921. It could be argued that there are circumstances in which the attribute or status of the actor is so crucial as to alter the *nature* of the act performed, as perhaps in a medical context. This would require the court to adopt a much wider reading of 'nature' than the orthodox interpretation which restricts the meaning to the mechanical acts, see eg *Williams* [1923] 1 KB 340. There is some Canadian authority supporting a wider test. See *Maurantonio* (1967) 65 DLR (2d) 674; *Harms* [1944] 2 DLR 61.

[129] In appropriate cases the law lowers the threshold of what constitutes a sufficient fraud or threat, as where the victim is mentally disordered—see Sexual Offences Act 2003, ss 30–44, p 815.

V, it was held that there was no assault because the fraud was not as to the nature and quality of what was to be done.[130] Similarly, a woman was held to have consented to the nature of the act by agreeing to the introduction of an instrument into her vagina for diagnostic purposes when the operator was secretly acting only for sexual gratification.[131]

One of the leading cases in this area, and one which gave rise to considerable controversy, was *Clarence*.[132] D was charged with causing grievous bodily harm to his wife, V, when knowing that he was suffering from a sexually transmitted disease, he had unprotected sex with her and infected her. It was held that V had consented to intercourse with D and, although she would not have consented to the act of intercourse had she been aware of the disease from which D knew he was suffering, this was no assault. The court concluded that she had not been defrauded as to the *nature* of the act of intercourse (ie the physical mechanics of that act)[133] but merely as to the associated risk of disease. The flaw in this approach was in focusing on V's awareness of the nature of the act of intercourse. This was not a rape case where her understanding of the nature of sex might have been important. The court should have focused on the more important question: was V aware or was she deceived about the (risk of) harm which D was charged with causing—that of the infection. It was her awareness of the nature of *that* risk that ought to have been considered.

In the important case of *Dica*,[134] where D had infected two sexual partners with HIV, *Clarence* was regarded by the Court of Appeal as being no longer of useful application.[135] Where V, who was unaware of D's infected state, had consented to the act of unprotected sexual intercourse she could not be said to have impliedly consented to the risk of infection from that intercourse. In *Dica*, the court focused, appropriately it is submitted, on the question of whether D's fraud on V related to the infection—which represents the harm alleged—rather than the intercourse. The conclusion was that the victims had been defrauded as to the risk of infection and hence had not consented to bodily harm, but had not been defrauded as to the nature of the act of sexual intercourse and hence had not been raped.[136] The nature of intercourse is the same whether with an HIV-infected person or not. Where V has not consented to the risk of infection, D could be liable under s 20 of the OAPA 1861 if he was reckless as to whether he might infect V.[137] Subsequently, in *Konzani*[138] the court emphasized that 'there is a critical distinction between taking a risk of the various, potentially adverse and possibly problematic consequences of sexual intercourse and giving an informed consent to the risk of infection with a fatal disease'.[139] D will be liable if he fails to disclose or lies about his infection and is reckless whether he infects V.

Frauds as to the *nature* of the act (which, as *Dica* demonstrates, must be accurately categorized) are clearly sufficient to vitiate consent. Following *Tabassum*, it became unclear whether

---

130 *Bolduc and Bird* (1967) 63 DLR (2d) 82 (Sup Ct of Canada, Spence J dissenting), reversing British Columbia CA, 61 DLR (2d) 494; cf *Rosinski* (1824) 1 Mood CC 19.

131 *Mobilio* [1991] 1 VR 339. See D Ormerod, 'A Victim's Mistaken Consent in Rape' (1992) 56 J Crim L 407.

132 (1888) 22 QBD 23. For an interesting historical account of the case, see K Gleeson, 'The Problem of *Clarence*' (2005) 14 Nottingham LJ 1.

133 cf *Williams* [1923] KB 340.

134 [2004] EWCA Crim 1103, [2004] Crim LR 944 and commentary. See references in n 113.

135 The various aspects of that decision had been eroded by the courts over recent years, with *R* [1992] 1 AC 599 dispensing with the marital rape exemption, and *Ireland and Burstow* [1998] AC 147 accepting that 'infliction' need not involve an assault or direct contact.

136 The Court of Appeal allowed the appeal overturning the trial judge's ruling that the decision in *Brown* [1994] 1 AC 212 deprived V of the legal capacity to consent to such serious harm and that consent provided no defence. At his retrial Dica was convicted of inflicting grievous bodily harm contrary to s 20 and sentenced to four-and-a-half years' imprisonment. The House of Lords refused leave to appeal—see House of Lords Session 2005–06, 15 Dec 2005.

137 If D intended to infect V he would be liable under s 18 irrespective of consent.

138 [2005] EWCA Crim 706.   139 At [22].

a fraud as to the 'quality' of the act (rather than its nature) would be sufficient to vitiate consent. In that case, D had persuaded three women to allow him to examine their breasts by falsely informing them that he was medically qualified and conducting research work for a cancer charity. D's conviction for indecent assault was upheld. The court accepted that the women had been aware of the nature of the act of touching their breasts, but defrauded as to the 'quality' of the act—they believed it to be for a medical purpose—and that vitiated their consent.[140] This was recognized to have profound repercussions. Where D has sexual intercourse with V knowing (or possibly even being reckless as to whether) he is HIV-positive, D's fraud as to the infection could, on the *Tabassum* approach, be regarded as a fraud as to the 'quality' of the act. This could render V's consent to the intercourse invalid and D would be a rapist.[141]

The question of frauds as to purpose also arises. In *B*,[142] the Court of Appeal rejected the argument that D who has intercourse with V and conceals his HIV status is defrauding V as to the 'purpose' of the act of intercourse. Under the Sexual Offences Act 2003, it is conclusively presumed that V did not consent if D has defrauded V as to the nature *or purpose* of his act. The court in *B* concluded that concealment of HIV will not be a fraud as to purpose in sex cases. It is submitted that at common law, in relation to offences against the person where the requirement is of a fraud or mistake as to the *nature* of the act and not merely its purpose, the court is now extremely unlikely to adopt a contrary view.

It is important to point out that the facts of *B* were framed as involving non-disclosure rather than fraud and the Court of Appeal treated the two as quite distinct. The outcome of the case could have been different had V specifically asked D about his HIV status and he lied to her about it. The effect of the distinction that was drawn in *B*, between non-disclosure and fraud, means that there is a divergence of approach depending upon whether D is charged with a non-fatal offence against the person or a sexual offence.[143]

In terms of failure to disclose: D will not be liable for an offence against the person, if he discloses his HIV status and obtains V's consent to the risk of transmission.[144] But, in the context of sexual offences the burden is placed on the non-infected partner to ask about D's HIV status. If D says nothing and infects V, he may be guilty of inflicting GBH but not of rape.

In terms of lies: if V asks D about his HIV status and he lies, then he may be guilty of rape, and if V is infected, offences against the person. If V is not infected, then D may be guilty of rape but nothing else. At this juncture, it is worth recalling what the Court of Appeal observed in *Richardson*:[145]

There is no basis for the proposition that the rules which determine the circumstances in which consent is vitiated can be different according to whether the case is one of sexual assault or one where the assault is non-sexual.[146]

Duress

Duress may negative apparently valid consent. A threat to imprison V unless he submitted to a beating would probably invalidate V's consent to the beating. Possibly a threat to

---

[140] There is no guidance in *Tabassum* on what might constitute the 'quality' of a particular act.

[141] Under the Sexual Offences Act 2003, s 76 a fraud as to the 'nature or purpose' (not quality) of the act is conclusively presumed to vitiate consent. Whether other frauds vitiate consent requires consideration to be given to the terms of the general definition of consent in s 74. See Ch 17 for discussion.

[142] [2006] EWCA Crim 2945. For criticism see L Leigh, 'Two Cases on Consent in Rape' [2007] 5 Arch News 6.

[143] For further discussion, see K Laird, 'Rapist or Rogue? Deception, Consent and the Sexual Offences Act 2003' [2014] Crim LR 491.

[144] Unless he takes steps to avoid transmission and therefore might lack mens rea—eg where he uses a condom.

[145] [1999] QB 444.   [146] At 450.

dismiss from employment[147] or to bring a prosecution[148] would have a similar effect. It is submitted that non-criminal threats and even threats of lawful action may also be sufficient. It is unclear whether, to negative consent, the threats must be such that they would have caused a person of reasonable firmness to succumb to the violence. An alternative view would be that consent should be invalid if D knew of the particular vulnerabilities of V which caused V to succumb although they might not have caused a reasonable person to do so. If the test is whether the threat would be sufficient to overcome the will of a reasonably steadfast person, the outcome must depend to some extent on the relationship between the gravity of the threat and the act to which V is asked to submit.

Duress may be implied from the relationship between the parties—for example, where D is a teacher and V is a young pupil.[149] As in sexual offences,[150] submission is not consent. As noted, if D genuinely believes that V is consenting, even though she is in fact only submitting, D will lack mens rea.

16.2.1.3 Legal limits on the validity of consent

Having examined the circumstances in which V's apparent consent will be invalidated, we must turn to the yet more difficult question: if V has in fact given valid consent, is that consent recognized in law? Fundamental questions of morality are raised by the extent to which the State ought to use criminal sanctions to restrict an adult with full mental capacity in his consent to the infliction of harm on his person.[151] On a public policy basis, English law restricts the validity of consent by reference to the level of harm *and* the circumstances in which it is inflicted. Factual consent to mere assault or battery is valid in law. Factual consent to actual bodily harm or more serious levels of harm (wounding, serious harm, death) is not legally recognized unless the activity involved is one which the courts or Parliament have recognized to be in the public interest. Thus, as a matter of public policy, it is no defence to a charge of murder for D to say that V asked to be killed. On the other hand, V's consent to D's taking a high degree of risk of killing him is effective where it is justified by the purpose of the act, as it may be in the case of a surgical operation. Where the act has some social purpose, recognized by the law as valid, it is a question of balancing the degree of harm which will or may be caused against the value of that purpose.

Three issues require elucidation: what level of harm is caused, what level of harm is foreseen or intended and whether the activity in which the harm arises is one of the exceptional categories in which consent is recognized. Unfortunately, since this is an area in which the decisions of the appellate courts are based so heavily on public policy, it is not always easy to identify clear principles.

The level of harm

Consent to an assault or battery will always be valid consent, no matter what the circumstances (eg even if it is in a sadomasochist encounter) provided the consent is effective, as discussed earlier.

If D has caused actual bodily harm—injury of more than a merely transient or trifling nature—with intent to do so,[152] the factual consent of the victim will *not* be legally valid

---

[147] *McCoy* 1953 (2) SA 4 (AD) (threat to ground air hostess negativing her apparent consent to being caned).

[148] *State v Volschenk* 1968 (2) PH H283 (threat to prosecute held *not* to negative consent on rape charge).

[149] *Nichol* (1807) Russ & Ry 130.

[150] See p 760. See *Doyle* [2010] EWCA Crim 119, and *Ali* [2015] EWCA Crim 1279.

[151] See Williams [1962] Crim LR 74 and 154; LCCP 139, Part II, Appendix C; P Roberts (1997) 17 OJLS 389; J Feinberg, *The Moral Limits of the Criminal Law, Vol 1: Harm to Others* (1984).

[152] And probably also in cases where he does so recklessly. See the discussion of *Dica* earlier.

unless the conduct falls within one of the recognized exceptional categories discussed later. It is arguable that the law should recognize a person's consent as a valid defence to a graver level of harm than ABH. The Law Commission at one time proposed raising the level of harm to which a person is entitled to consent in general circumstances to harm falling below its proposed concept of 'serious disabling injury'.[153]

The role of intention and foresight of harms

Where D has intended or has been reckless as to the causing of actual bodily harm, liability arises even if V consents, subject to the exceptional cases later. The law has struggled with cases where D has not caused that level of harm intentionally—where he intends or is reckless as to causing only assault or battery with consent, but the conduct leads to actual bodily harm. Some *obiter dicta* suggest that D is guilty if the harm was foreseen by D (if not intended), or even if it was objectively likely to occur. The problem flowed from an overbroad statement in the *A-G's Reference (No 6 of 1980)*[154] where two youths of 18 and 17 settled an argument by a fist fight and when one sustained a bleeding nose and bruises to his face, it was held that the other was guilty of assault occasioning actual bodily harm:

> it is not in the public interest that people should try to cause or *should cause* each other actual bodily harm for no good reason. Minor struggles are another matter. So, in our judgment, it is immaterial whether the act occurs in private or in public; it is an assault if actual bodily harm *is intended and/or caused*. This means that most fights will be unlawful regardless of consent.[155]

This passage was quoted with approval by all three of the majority in the leading case of *Brown* (discussed in the following section). It is submitted, however, that it goes too far. The difficulty is the words 'or should cause' and 'and/or'. These words imply that an offence is committed if D assaults or batters V with V's consent and D does not intend to cause bodily harm, but does so in fact. The passage suggests that D will be liable even if the bodily harm was not foreseen or even foreseeable. That seems a wholly unreasonable result. Subsequent case law is difficult to reconcile with the position, and it is submitted that the *dictum* no longer represents the law.

It is submitted that the following reflects the current state of the law.

(1) D intends to cause actual bodily harm and causes that level of harm (or worse) to V with consent (or belief in V's consent). V's consent is invalid unless the harm occurs in the course of conduct within an exceptional category discussed later (pp 675 et seq). Unless it is an exceptional category case, D is liable for actual bodily harm. A good illustration is *Donovan*[156] where D caned V, with her consent, for their mutual sexual enjoyment: D would be liable under s 47.

(2) D is reckless as to causing actual bodily harm and has V's consent (or belief in V's consent) to the risk of causing that level of injury which actually occurs. It is less clear whether V's consent is invalid in all cases irrespective of whether they fall within an exceptional category. *Dicta* in *Brown* and some decisions such as *Dica* suggest that the law treats V's factual consent as invalid only in respect of intentionally inflicted harms.

(3) D intends only to make physical contact with V at the level of battery with V's consent (or a belief in V's consent), but in fact D causes actual bodily harm not intending or

---

[153] See LCCP 139. For criticisms of the proposal and its incoherence with the offences against the person, see Ormerod and Gunn [1996] Crim LR 694. Many jurisdictions adopt a much higher threshold: see LCCP 139, Appendix B. See also LCCP 217, Ch 5 in which it is noted that creating a new offence of minor injury might allow for the threshold of harm to which consent is valid to rise to the proposed new form of ABH.

[154] [1981] QB 715.   [155] *A-G's Reference (No 6 of 1980)* [1981] 2 All ER 1057 at 1059 (emphasis added).

[156] [1934] 2 KB 498.

being reckless as to that result. According to the *dictum* in *A-G's Reference* D is guilty, it being sufficient that actual bodily harm *is* caused.[157] This *dictum* has been rejected. The Court of Appeal in *Meachen*[158] concluded, correctly it is submitted, that where D intends[159] to cause the level of harm amounting to battery and has V's consent to that level of harm, if D then causes actual bodily harm or worse, without being reckless in doing so or intending to do so, he is not guilty. There is no unlawful battery as the foundational element of the actual bodily harm.[160] The facts of *Meachen* illustrate how this operates. On D's account he intentionally digitally penetrated V's anus with her consent for their mutual sexual gratification. D had no intention to cause any injury, nor did he see the risk of doing so. V suffered serious anal injury and required a colostomy. D's conviction for inflicting grievous bodily harm contrary to s 20 (and indecent assault under the Sexual Offences Act 1956) was quashed because the trial judge had erroneously ruled that V's consent could not avail D in these circumstances.

(4) The *dictum* from the *A-G's Reference* was also rejected in *Slingsby*:[161] D and V engaged in 'vigorous' sexual activity, including D inserting his hand into V's vagina and rectum. This battery was activity to which V could lawfully, and did, consent. D was wearing a signet ring which caused internal injury to V resulting in infection which led to her death. D was charged with manslaughter by an unlawful and dangerous act. Judge J ruled that it would be contrary to principle to treat as criminal, activity which would not otherwise amount to an assault merely because an injury was caused. It is respectfully submitted that this is right.

(5) The decision in *Boyea*,[162] also needs to be re-evaluated in light of the decision in *Meachen*. In *Boyea*, D's act of inserting his hand into V's vagina and twisting it caused actual bodily harm. It was held that there was an assault because the act was 'likely' to cause harm and D was guilty of an (indecent) assault even if he did not intend or foresee that harm was likely to be caused. This suggests that if, objectively, D's conduct is likely to lead to actual bodily harm there can be no defence of consent, even if D does not intend or foresee any harm over and above the battery to which he has consent. The Court of Appeal in *Meachen*, following *dicta* in *Dica*, concluded that *Boyea* is best treated as a decision in which V had not consented even to the assault/battery in the circumstances in which it was inflicted.

(6) D intends to cause actual bodily harm with V's consent (or belief in V's consent) but in fact causes only a battery. D ought not to be convicted of that offence. Consent is a valid defence to assault/battery; D has not caused actual bodily harm.[163] In *Barnes*,[164] Lord Woolf asserted that 'When no bodily harm is caused, the consent of the victim to what happened is *always* a defence to a charge.'[165] It is submitted that this is the correct approach, even though D intended a level of harm to which consent would be no defence.[166]

(7) D is reckless as to causing actual bodily harm with V's consent (or belief in V's consent) as to that risk, but in fact causes only a battery. Arguably, since D has caused only a battery and has consent to that level of harm, he ought to be acquitted.

---

[157] D has committed the actus reus of actual bodily harm. He has the mens rea for actual bodily harm (it being the same as for assault/battery).

[158] [2006] EWCA Crim 2414.

[159] The court did not have to consider the case where D is reckless as to that harm; see [43].

[160] This passage in the 11th edition was referred to in *Meachen*, at [36].

[161] [1995] Crim LR 570.   [162] (1992) 156 JP 505, [1992] Crim LR 574.

[163] cf the view in *Donovan* [1934] 2 KB 498, CCA.   [164] [2005] Crim LR 381.

[165] Para 7 (emphasis added).

[166] Arguably D may be liable for attempted actual bodily harm provided he has the requisite mens rea.

It need hardly be said if this analysis is correct, that the law is in a dreadfully confused and unsatisfactory state.

Type of activity involved

In *Brown*, a group of sadomasochistic men who had engaged in consensual beatings and genital torture which had not resulted in any participant receiving medical attention, were convicted of offences of assault occasioning actual bodily harm. The House of Lords, by a majority of three to two, upheld the convictions. In doing so, the House recognized certain categories of activity in which the law would recognize effective factual consent to injury as valid in law.[167]

Subsequently, in *Barnes*,[168] Lord Woolf candidly admitted that whether a particular activity is regarded as one to which consent may be valid is a matter of public policy. This 'renders it unnecessary to find a separate jurisprudential basis for the application of the defence in various different factual contexts in which an offence could be committed'. This will do little to satisfy those advocating the need for a clear moral foundation to the law's approach, but is not a great surprise. This policy-based approach allows the courts to maintain the incoherent list of exceptions and to add or subtract from that list based on its perception of the social utility of particular conduct and the circumstances in which it occurs. Thus, the courts may continue to allow consensual buttock branding as akin to tattooing (*Wilson*)[169] but not sadomasochistic caning on the buttocks (*Brown*; *Donovan*). It has been argued that these cases demonstrate that criminality depends too much on an arbitrary assignment of the activity in question into one category or another and that this arbitrariness is compounded by the fact that the same activity could conceivably fall within two categories, one in which consent would provide a defence and another in which it would not.[170]

This categorization, on grounds of perceived public utility, of activities to which consent may and may not be validly given can be illustrated by comparing the case of a fist fight and a boxing match, both of which are intended or likely to cause actual bodily harm or worse. Boxing under the Queensberry Rules is lawful. A boxer, trying to knock out his opponent, certainly has an intention to cause harm, possibly even serious harm, which is a sufficient mens rea for murder, but no prosecutions have been brought against fighters operating under the professional rules and in *Brown* all of their lordships accepted that boxing is lawful. According to Lord Mustill, boxing is best regarded as a special case which, 'for the time being stands outside the ordinary law of violence because society chooses to tolerate it'.[171] Where, however, two youths decide to settle an argument by a fight with fists[172] and one sustains a bleeding nose and bruises to his face, the other is guilty of assault occasioning actual bodily harm.

---

[167] On this, one of the most controversial decisions of the House of Lords in that period, see LCCP 139. D Kell, 'Social Disutility and Consent' (1994) 14 OJLS 121; M Giles, 'Consensual Harm and the Public Interest' (1994) 57 MLR 101; M Allen, 'Consent and Assault' (1994) 58 J Crim Law 183; N Bamforth, 'Sadomasochism and Consent' [1994] Crim LR 661; P Alldridge, *Relocating Criminal Law* (2000) 122 et seq. For an interesting analysis of the issues raised by the case that it is argued have been overlooked by many commentators, see J Herring, 'R v Brown' in P Handler, H Mares and I Williams (eds), *Landmark Cases in Criminal Law* (2017).

[168] [2005] Crim LR 381.   [169] [1996] 2 Cr App R 241.

[170] J Tolmie, 'Consent to Harmful Assaults: The Case for Moving Away From Category Based Decision Making' [2012] Crim LR 656.

[171] For a full discussion, see M Gunn and D Ormerod, 'The Legality of Boxing' (1995) 15 LS 181, and LCCP 139, XII. See also S Greenfield and G Osborn (eds), *Law and Sport in Contemporary Society* (2000); J Anderson, *The Legality of Boxing: A Punch Drunk Love?* (2007).

[172] A 'prize-fight' in public is unlawful at common law as a breach of the peace tending to public disorder. *Brown* [1994] AC 212, [1993] 2 All ER 75 at 79, 86, 106, 119, HL. Because the whole enterprise is unlawful, consent is not a defence even to a charge of common assault against the contestants: *Coney* (1882) 8 QBD 534.

The court in *A-G's Reference* sought to catalogue the types of activity to which V will be entitled to consent in law:

Nothing which we have said is intended to cast doubt on the accepted legality of properly conducted games and sports, lawful chastisement or correction, reasonable surgical interference, dangerous exhibitions, etc. These apparent exceptions can be justified as involving the exercise of a legal right, in the case of chastisement or correction, or as needed in the public interest, in the other cases.

Exceptional categories in which consent to (intentionally inflicted)[173] harm has been recognized by the courts or Parliament to be valid include the following.

Sports

The law has long recognized the social utility of sport in enhancing the fitness of the population.[174] A number of principles seem to have developed. First, although by playing the sport V consents to whatever the rules permit, if the rules permit an unacceptably dangerous act, the law need not recognize the validity of V's factual consent. That is a matter of public policy. However, boxing continues to be lawful despite the life-threatening injury and participants' intention to cause grievous bodily harm. Secondly, where unlike boxing and martial arts, playing within the rules of the particular sport does not *necessarily* involve D causing actual bodily harm, but D intentionally inflicts actual bodily harm or worse, V's consent is irrelevant and D commits the offence: *Bradshaw*.[175] Thirdly, and most difficult in practical terms to apply, if in playing such a sport D was reckless only as to the causing of the injury, the question will be whether V impliedly consented to the risk of that level of injury in the context in which it was inflicted.

The question of whether the conduct was within the rules of the game is not the sole determinant of liability.[176] It would be too simplistic to suggest that V's consent is only valid for that which the rules of the game permit. V may well, as a matter of fact, impliedly consent to the *risk* of injury occurring in conduct outside the rules as in a late tackle in football, or an illegitimate bouncer in cricket.[177] It is therefore necessary to look to a broader range of factors. In *Barnes*, the Court of Appeal confirmed that it is appropriate to make an objective evaluation of these circumstances. The court adopted the approach in Canadian law[178] and advocated at one time by the Law Commission.[179] Relevant circumstances include the type of sport, the level at which it was being played, the nature of the act, the degree of force used, the extent of the risk of injury and D's state of mind. Prosecution is usually reserved for sufficiently grave conduct deserving to be regarded as criminal, having regard to the fact that most organized sports have their own disciplinary procedures and to the availability of civil remedies. What is accepted in one sport might

---

[173] See earlier. Arguably the consent defence is only invalid where D has *intentionally* caused harm. See further *Dica* discussed earlier.

[174] See LCCP 139, Part XII and M Cutcheon, 'Sports, Violence and the Criminal Law' (1994) 45 NILQ 267. For an analysis that questions the objective approach to consent in sports, but denying the need for a uniform approach throughout the criminal law, see B Livings, 'A Different Ball Game' (2007) 71 J Crim L 534, disputing the arguments in C Elliott and C de Than, 'The Case for a Rational Reconstruction of Consent in Criminal Law' (2007) 70 MLR 225 who call for a unitary approach to consent throughout the criminal law. More recently, see M James, 'Consent—Revisiting the Exemption for Contact Sports' in A Reed and M Bohlander (with N Wake and E Smith) (eds), *Consent—Domestic and Comparative Perspectives* (2017).

[175] (1878) Cox CC 83.   [176] ibid.   [177] See *Moore* (1898) 14 TLR 229.

[178] See *Cicarelli* (1989) 54 CCC (3d) 121.

[179] LCCP 134. That approach was criticized by S Gardiner, 'The Law and the Sports Field' [1994] Crim LR 513, see also S Gardiner, 'Should More Matches End in Court' (2005) 155 NLJ 998 but received generally favourable responses: LCCP 139, paras 12.6–12.23. On *Barnes*, see also J Anderson, 'No Licence for Thuggery: Violence, Sport and the Criminal Law' [2008] Crim LR 751. See also B Livings [2018] Crim LR 430 on the CPS policy on prosecution in such cases.

not be covered by the implied consent in another. In highly competitive sports, conduct 'outside the rules' might be expected to occur in the heat of the moment, but even if such conduct justified not only being penalized but, for example, being sent off, it might not reach the threshold required for it to be criminal.

Horseplay

This exception is not confined to organized games. Consent by children to rough and undisciplined play may be a defence to a charge of inflicting grievous bodily harm if there is no intention to cause injury.[180] Equally, a genuine belief in consent, even an unreasonable belief, apparently negatives recklessness: *Jones*[181] where boys were injured by being tossed in the air by schoolmates. The decision recognizes that children have always indulged in rough and undisciplined play among themselves and probably always will; but the non-consenting child is rightly protected by the criminal law. The 'horseplay' exception seems to have been taken to extreme lengths in *Aitken*,[182] where the 'robust games' of Royal Air Force officers at a celebration in the mess included setting fire to one another's fire-resistant clothing. Two such incidents apparently caused no harm but on a third occasion V sustained severe burns. It was held that a ruling that it was not open to the court-martial to find that the 'activities' were lawful was wrong. If V consented to them, or if D believed, reasonably or not, that V consented to them, it was open to the trial court to find that there was no offence.

The courts have emphasized that horseplay can only be relied upon where V is consenting or D genuinely believes that to be the case. In the case of *A*,[183] D dropped V, a non-swimmer, off a bridge into a river where V drowned. V had been fighting for this not to happen and was clearly not consenting, nor was it credible that D believed he was. D's conviction for manslaughter was upheld.

Surgery

Consent to a surgical operation[184] for a purpose recognized as valid by the law is effective.[185] This includes gender reassignment surgery[186] and, presumably, cosmetic surgery and organ transplants. Where an adult of full mental capacity refuses consent to medical treatment, a failure to respect that decision will render the doctor liable for criminal offences, even in circumstances in which the treatment will be life-preserving.[187]

Body modification

Having one's hair cut is clearly lawful. Since cutting hair might amount to actual bodily harm, it is implicit that the law recognizes that consent to that activity will prevent liability: *DPP v Smith*.[188] Ritual[189] circumcision of males,[190] ear-piercing and tattooing of adults are generally assumed

---

[180] See LCCP 139.   [181] [1987] Crim LR 123, CA.

[182] [1992] 1 WLR 1006, at 1011 (C-MAC).   [183] [2005] All ER 38 (D).

[184] See LCCP 139, Part VIII.

[185] Stephen, *Digest*, art 310. See P Skegg, 'Medical Procedures and the Crime of Battery' [1974] Crim LR 693 and (1973) 36 MLR 370. It was held in *BM* [2018] EWCA Crim 560 that there is a clear difference between surgery and body modification.   [186] *Corbett v Corbett* [1971] P 83 at 99.

[187] *St George's Healthcare NHS Trust v S* [1998] 3 All ER 673. See also the discussion previously of the Mental Capacity Act 2005.   [188] [2006] EWHC 94 (Admin).

[189] ie that performed otherwise than for medical reasons. See further LCCP 139. See *Brown* [1994] 1 AC 212 and *Re J* [2000] 1 FCR 307, CA (Civ). Professor Feldman advised the Law Commission that non-therapeutic circumcision might be in breach of Art 3 of the ECHR, para 3.25; see further H Gilbert, 'Time to Reconsider the Lawfulness of Ritual Male Circumcision' [2007] EHRLR 279; PW Edge, 'Male Circumcision after the Human Rights Act' (1998) 5 J Civil Liberties 320, see also L Vickers, 'Circumcision—The Unkindest Cut of All?' (2000) 150 NLJ 1694.

[190] See the Female Genital Mutilation Act 2003. Amendments made by the Serious Crime Act 2015, ss 70–75 extend the extraterritorial effect of the offence. By s 72, a new s 3A creates an offence of failing to protect a girl from the risk of genital mutilation (punishable on indictment with up to seven years' imprisonment).

to be lawful.[191] Presumably the same is true of more exotic body-piercing of adults, although the Court of Appeal has recently held that unlicensed activities such as tongue splitting and ear removal cannot be consented to. Lord Burnett CJ stated: [192]

we can see no good reason why body modification should be placed in a special category of exemption from the general rule that the consent of an individual to injury provides no defence to the person who inflicts that injury if the violence causes actual bodily harm or more serious injury. Even were the general rule to be revisited by Parliament or the Supreme Court and a different line drawn which allows consent to act as a defence to causing actual bodily harm and wounding, body modification causes really serious harm.

In *Wilson*,[193] D's branding of his initials on his wife's buttocks, at her request, in lieu of tattooing, was held to be equally lawful. The only distinction from *Donovan*[194] appears to be that Donovan's motive in caning V was sexual gratification whereas Wilson's was to bestow on his wife an adornment which she desired. Where the purpose of the act is one which the law condemns, consent may be no answer to the charge.[195] This is now the case with ear removal and tongue splitting, despite the fact the customer may desire such extreme body modification.

Coke tells us that in 1604, 'a young strong and lustie rogue, to make himself impotent, thereby to have the more colour to begge or to be relieved without putting himself to any labour, caused his companion to strike off his left hand' and that both of them were convicted of mayhem.[196] Maiming, even with consent, was unlawful because it deprived the king of a fighting man. In early Victorian times when soldiers, as part of their training drill, had to bite cartridges, a soldier got a dentist to pull out his front teeth to avoid the drill. Stephen J thought that both were guilty of a crime.[197] Denning LJ followed these instances in discussing, *obiter*, the legality of a sterilization operation.[198] His opinion (that the operation is unlawful if done only to enable the man to have the pleasure of intercourse without the responsibility) is no longer tenable,[199] but it illustrates the continuing and changing influence of public policy.

In circumstances where the body modification is for religious reasons, reliance on Art 9 of the ECHR guaranteeing respect for religious freedom would support the validity of consent. However, the courts have been unwilling to accommodate foreign cultural practices involving children, such as incision of cheeks.[200] In view of the recognition that ritual male circumcision practised by Jews and Muslims is lawful, the law's approach appears incoherent.

Sadomasochism

Sadomasochism beyond that amounting to mere assault or battery is not an activity that can be consented to.[201] Public policy is also at the root of the decision in *Brown*. In the opinion of the majority, policy requires the conviction of men participating in consensual sadomasochistic encounters, resulting in actual bodily harm and wounding, to protect society against a cult of violence with the danger of the corruption and proselytization of young

---

[191] On consent in relation to medical treatment and body modification, see T Elliott, 'Body Dismorphic Disorder, Radical Surgery and the Limits of Consent' (2009) 17 Med L Rev 149. See also See LCCP 139, Part IX.

[192] *BM* [2018] EWCA Crim 560. See also *Oversby* (1990) unreported, cited in LCCP 139, para 9.7.

[193] [1996] Crim LR 573, CA. [194] [1934] 2 KB 498.

[195] The court was also influenced by the fact that W was married to his victim, but this must be an irrelevance. If the criminal law governing consensual injury is applied differently to homosexuals and heterosexuals (or to men and women) or on the basis of marriage, this would almost certainly involve a violation of Arts 8 and 14 of the ECHR taken together.

[196] Co 1 Inst, 127a and b. [197] *Digest* (3rd edn) 142.

[198] *Bravery v Bravery* [1954] 3 All ER 59 at 67, 68.

[199] The National Health Service (Family Planning) Amendment Act 1972 first authorized vasectomy services.

[200] *Adesanya* (1974) The Times, 16 July. See S Poulter, 'Foreign Customs and the English Criminal Law' (1975) 24 ICLQ 136. [201] See LCCP 139, Part X.

men and the potential for the infliction of serious injury: this notwithstanding that there was in fact no permanent injury, no infection and no evidence of medical attention being required.[202] The majority's reasoning that this was violence rather than sexual activity led to the conclusion that the activity should be unlawful.[203]

Public policy was invoked to justify conviction for a relatively slight degree of harm in *Donovan*.[204] D, for his sexual gratification, beat a 17-year-old girl with a cane in circumstances of indecency. He was convicted of both indecent assault and common assault. The judge failed to direct the jury that the onus of negativing consent was on the Crown, but the Court of Criminal Appeal held that, if the blows were likely or intended to cause bodily harm, this omission was immaterial because D was guilty whether V consented or not.[205]

In *Brown*, the whole House agreed that consent is a complete defence to the two offences—common and indecent assault—with which Donovan was charged. The Court of Criminal Appeal's opinion (that he could have been convicted of these offences because he was guilty of assault occasioning actual bodily harm, an offence with which he was not charged), was unacceptable in *Brown* to both Lord Lowry[206] of the majority and Lord Mustill[207] of the minority. Subsequent cases nevertheless seem to treat the *dicta* in *Donovan* as correct, but in light of the decision in *Meachen* discussed earlier, it is submitted that if D intended to inflict a battery, the consent he had to that level of harm should mean there is no criminal liability unless D intentionally or recklessly inflicted actual bodily harm.

The *dicta* in *Donovan* were distinguished in *Wilson*[208] (wife's buttock branding) on the basis that Donovan was seeking sexual gratification, whereas Wilson was not—his conduct was like that of a professional tattooist who embellishes (intimate) parts at the request of their owner. In *Laskey* (a reference on the *Brown* case), the European Court distinguished *Wilson* because the injuries were not at all 'comparable in seriousness' with those in *Brown* even though they equally amounted to assault occasioning actual bodily harm.

The decision in *Wilson* was distinguished, and *Brown* followed, in a further case of sadomasochism: *Emmett*.[209] D's conviction for recklessly occasioning actual bodily harm to V by, *inter alia*, setting fire to lighter fuel on her breasts with her consent, was upheld by the Court of Appeal. The court described the conduct as going 'beyond that which was established in *Wilson*'. But the charge was the same—assault occasioning actual bodily harm. Are the courts to start evaluating the validity of consent on the basis of some undeclared judicial barometer of the severity of harm? In *Meachen* and in *Dica*, *Emmett* appears to have been treated as a case of intentional infliction of actual bodily harm.

---

[202] The majority cited no empirical evidence to substantiate their claim that those who engage in consensual sadomasochistic cruelty are prone to have their inhibitions loosened and escalate their conduct to more harmful acts of cruelty. See J Tolmie, 'Consent to Harmful Assaults: The Case for Moving Away From Category Based Decision Making' [2012] Crim LR 656.

[203] Peter Murphy argues that the real motivation for sadomasochistic acts is sexual gratification and therefore suggests it would be more appropriate to charge D with a sexual offence in such cases. See P Murphy, 'Flogging Live Complainants and Dead Horses: We May No Longer Need to Be in Bondage to *Brown*' [2011] Crim LR 758.

[204] [1934] 2 KB 498. See L Leigh, 'Sado-Masochism, Consent and the Reform of the Criminal Law' (1976) 39 MLR 130.

[205] The conviction was quashed because the question whether the blows were likely or intended to cause bodily harm was not put to the jury.

[206] 'If the jury, properly directed, had found that consent was not disproved, they must have acquitted the appellant of the only charges brought against him' [1993] 2 All ER 75 at 97.

[207] 'There is something amiss here' [1993] 2 All ER 75 at 112.

[208] [1996] Crim LR 573.   [209] (1999) The Times, 15 Oct.

Religious flagellation

In *Brown*, Lord Mustill accepted this as a recognized, though rarely practised, exception. The protection of religious freedoms under Art 9 of the ECHR would support such a conclusion.[210]

The risk of sexually transmitted infection

The decision of the Court of Appeal in *Dica*[211] is that an adult is entitled to give valid consent to the risk of being infected with a potentially lethal sexually transmitted disease such as HIV.[212] The court distinguished between consensual acts of sexual intercourse where there might be a known risk to the health of one or other participants (consent valid) and those cases where participants were intent on spreading, or becoming infected with, disease (consent invalid). The court took the view that criminalization of consensual taking of risks would involve an 'impracticality of enforcement' and would undermine the general understanding of the community that sexual relationships were 'pre-eminently private'. Such arguments had not persuaded the House of Lords in *Brown*, albeit that case involved intentional harm. *Dica* might be seen as against the trend of post-*Brown* cases that treat consent even to a risk of harm as invalid.[213] Many will find unconvincing the distinction in *Dica* between 'sexual' and 'violent' acts, with cases such as *Emmett* and *Boyea* treated as having 'sexual overtones' but being really concerned with 'violent crime'. These cases must all be read carefully in light of *Meachen*. In *Konzani*,[214] the court confirmed that the consent will only be valid if V is informed of the risk of infection.

ECHR compatibility

The case of *Brown* was considered by the ECtHR in *Laskey v UK*,[215] with the Court unanimously holding that the prosecution, conviction and sentence did not contravene Art 8 of the ECHR.[216] It should be noted that the Court doubted whether the activities even fell within the protection of Art 8. On the assumption that they did, the Court concluded that the prosecution was necessary and proportionate to the legitimate aim of the protection of health (and possibly also the protection of morals). The Court recognized that the margin of appreciation provided national courts the scope to prescribe the level of physical harm to which the law should permit an adult to consent.

16.2.2 Lawful chastisement

It was always the common law rule that punishment was unlawful:[217]

If it be administered for the gratification of passion or rage or if it be immoderate or excessive in its nature or degree, or if it be protracted beyond the child's powers of endurance or with an instrument unfitted for the purpose and calculated to produce danger to life and limb...[218]

---

[210] See LCCP 139, paras 10.2–10.7. However, note the conviction of Syed Mustafa Zaidi, a Shia Muslim, for child cruelty after he forced two boys (13 and 15) to whip themselves during a religious ritual using a handled implement with curved blades. See news reports for 28 Aug 2008.

[211] [2004] EWCA 1103, [2004] Crim LR 944 and commentary.

[212] For discussion of the potential criminalization of other types of infectious disease, see K Laird, 'Criminalising Contagion—Questioning the Paradigm' in H Quirk and C Stanton (eds), *Criminalising Contagion: Legal and Ethical Challenges of Disease Transmission and the Criminal Law* (2016).

[213] eg *Emett* (1999) The Times, 15 Oct but note *BM* [2018] EWCA Crim 560.   [214] [2005] EWCA Crim 706.

[215] (1997) 24 EHRR 39; L Moran, 'Learning the Limits of Privacy' (1998) 61 MLR 77. See also *KA & AD v Belgium* (App no 42758/98) 2005.

[216] LCCP 139, Part III.

[217] For a valuable discussion, see H Keating, 'Protecting or Punishing Children: Physical Punishment, Human Rights and English Law Reform' (2006) 26 LS 394.

[218] *Hopley* (1860) 2 F & F 202 at 206, per Cockburn CJ. Cf *Smith* [1985] Crim LR 42, CA.

In *A v UK*,[219] the rule of the common law entitling parents to inflict moderate and reasonable physical chastisement on their children was held to offend Art 3 of the ECHR, prohibiting torture and inhuman or degrading treatment or punishment. In that case, a jury had acquitted a man who had caned his nine-year-old stepson. It was accepted that the law then needed reform but there was considerable disagreement as what form reform should take. The English courts continued to acknowledge the parental right to chastise: *H*.[220] The judge had to give detailed directions to the jury to take account of the nature, context and duration of D's behaviour, the physical and mental effect on the child, the reasons for the punishment, and so on.

16.2.2.1 The Children Act 2004

Section 58 of the Children Act 2004 now provides:

(1) In relation to any offence specified in subsection (2), battery of a child cannot be justified on the ground that it constituted reasonable punishment.

(2) The offences referred to in subsection (1) are—

    (a) an offence under section 18 or 20 of the Offences against the Person Act 1861 (wounding and causing grievous bodily harm);

    (b) an offence under section 47 of that Act (assault occasioning actual bodily harm);

    an offence under section 1 of the Children and Young Persons Act 1933 (cruelty to persons under 16).

(3) Battery of a child causing actual bodily harm to the child cannot be justified in any civil proceedings on the ground that it constituted reasonable punishment.

(4) For the purposes of subsection (3) 'actual bodily harm' has the same meaning as it has for the purposes of section 47 of the Offences against the Person Act 1861.

The effect is that reasonable and proportionate punishment amounting only to an assault or battery (that does not involve cruelty) is still protected by the defence of lawful chastisement. There is no longer a defence of lawful chastisement for punishment that involves a touching of the child and which constitutes the higher level of harm—actual bodily harm or cruelty.[221]

Given the ambiguity of the boundary between assault and actual bodily harm, neither parents nor children have gained a clear position of their rights. Reliance on Art 9 of the ECHR by parents claiming a right to inflict corporal punishment as an aspect of their religion will not preclude prosecution.[222]

---

[219] [1998] TLR 578, (1999) 27 EHRR 611. See also *Costello-Roberts v UK* (1993) 19 EHRR 112 (seven-year-old slippered at public school); *Y v UK* (1992) 17 EHRR 238 (16-year-old caned at school). See generally B Phillips, 'The Case for Corporal Punishment in the UK—Beaten into Submission in Europe' (1994) 43 ICLQ 153.

[220] [2002] 1 Cr App R 59. J Rogers, 'A Criminal Lawyer's Response to Chastisement in the European Court' [2002] Crim LR 98; for trenchant criticism of the present law, see C Barton, 'Hitting Your Children: Common Assault or Common Sense' [2008] Fam Law 65.

[221] A case may arise where, on the same facts, a charge under s 47 would be available but a prosecution for common assault would fail because of the defence.

[222] *R (on the application of Williamson) v Secretary of State for Education and Employment* [2002] EWCA Civ 1820. Confirmed in *R (Williamson) v Secretary of State for Education* [2005] UKHL 15. Baroness Hale's speech warrants close attention on these matters. See also *Seven Individuals v Sweden* (App no 8811/79) 29 DR 104, EComHR. The ECHR issues are discussed in Emmerson, Ashworth and Macdonald, HR&CJ, paras 18–19. See also the conviction of Syed Mustafa Zaidi for child cruelty after he forced two boys (13 and 15) to whip themselves during a religious ritual. See news reports for 28 Aug 2008.

The CPS reviewed a sample of cases where a child was assaulted by a parent or an adult acting *in loco parentis* after the coming into force of s 58 of the Children Act 2004. The report identified 12 cases where the reasonable chastisement defence was raised, which resulted in an acquittal or discontinuance. The report concluded that there is 'evidence to suggest that there have been cases where defendants charged with common assault have been acquitted or the case was discontinued, after running the reasonable chastisement defence. Of those cases, the file review suggests that it was possible that some defendants could have been charged differently.'[223]

16.2.2.2 Corporal punishment in schools

At common law, school teachers were in the same position as parents with regard to the conduct of the child at or on his way to or from school.[224] Now, by s 548 of the Education Act 1996, a 'member of staff' of a school has no right, by virtue of his position as such, to administer corporal punishment to a child.[225] 'Corporal punishment' does not include anything done for the purposes of averting an immediate danger of personal injury or damage to property (s 548(5)). Staff may use reasonable force to search a pupil for a prohibited item (ss 550ZA and 550ZB)[226] or to restrain pupils who are violent or disruptive (s 93 of the Education and Inspections Act 2006).

16.2.3 Necessity

As noted in Ch 10, necessity may negative what would otherwise be an assault, as where D pushes V out of the path of a vehicle which is about to run him down. The fireman, the paramedic, the surgeon and nurse may all do things to a person rendered unconscious in an accident, or by sudden illness, which would ordinarily be battery (or, in the case of the surgeon, wounding or grievous bodily harm) if done without consent; but they commit no offence if they are only doing what is necessary to save life or ensure improvement, or prevent deterioration, in health.[227]

Perhaps this is based on the presumption that V would consent if he knew of the circumstances, a principle which excuses conduct in other parts of the criminal law.[228] This is consistent with the view[229] that intervention cannot be justified if it is against V's known wishes.

So it seems that a passerby who prevents V, an adult of mental capacity, from committing suicide by dragging him from the parapet of a bridge is guilty of battery.[230]

16.2.4 Self-help

The circumstances in which a person may use reasonable force to protect himself or his property are dealt with in Ch 10. The Criminal Justice and Immigration Act 2008 regulates most such circumstances. *Burns*[231] dealt with a situation falling outside the scope of that

---

[223] *Reasonable Chastisement Research Report* (2007), http://dera.ioe.ac.uk/6886/10/chastisement.html.

[224] *Cleary v Booth* [1893] 1 QB 465; *Newport (Salop) Justices* [1929] 2 KB 416; *Mansell v Griffin* [1908] 1 KB 160.

[225] As substituted by the School Standards and Framework Act 1998.

[226] The powers in ss 550ZA and 550ZB apply only to schools in England. In Wales, members of staff may use reasonable force to search for weapons: s 550AA.

[227] *F v West Berkshire Health Authority* [1990] 2 AC 1, [1989] 2 All ER 545 at 564, 566, HL, per Lord Goff.

[228] eg the Theft Act 1968, ss 2(1)(b), 12(6), Criminal Damage Act 1971, s 5(2)(b).

[229] *F v West Berks*, n 227, at 566, per Lord Goff.

[230] cf Williams, TBCL, 616. Otherwise, perhaps, if V is in police custody: *Kirkham v Chief Constable of the Greater Manchester Police* [1990] 2 QB 283, CA.

[231] [2010] EWCA Crim 1023.

Act. B was not in danger or protecting himself, others or his property. B was convicted of causing actual bodily harm to a sex worker V. B had picked her up, agreed a price for sex and driven her to a secluded place. He then changed his mind about the sex act and asked her to get out of his car. She refused to get out until he drove her back to where they had met. He forcibly removed her, causing minor injury. The Court of Appeal, having referred to authority from the seventeenth century, dismissed B's argument that he was entitled to use force as V became a trespasser on his property when he asked her to leave and she refused. B had not acted in self-defence nor in defence of anyone else; he had not been defending his property against threat or risk of damage; he was not acting for any purpose within s 3 of the Criminal Law Act 1967. The defence was one of 'self-help'. That defence was always a last resort. It was a defence which the common law would be reluctant to extend. Lord Judge CJ added:

Recognising that to be lawful the use of force must always be reasonable in the circumstances, we accept that it might be open to the owner of a vehicle, in the last resort and when all reasonably practicable alternatives have failed, forcibly to remove an individual who has entered into his vehicle without permission and refuses to leave it. However, where that individual entered the car as a passenger, in effect at the invitation of the car owner, on the basis that they mutually understood that when their dealings were completed she would be driven back in the car from whence she had come, the use of force to remove her at the appellant's unilateral whim, was unlawful.

16.3 Assault occasioning actual bodily harm

By s 47 of the OAPA 1861, 'whosoever shall be convicted on indictment of any assault occasioning actual bodily harm shall be liable to imprisonment for not more than five years'.

16.3.1 Actus reus

16.3.1.1 Assault or battery

On its face, the section does not appear to create a separate offence but merely to provide a higher penalty for an assault at common law where actual bodily harm is occasioned, that is, caused. Consequently the offence was treated as a common law offence until the decision in *Courtie*,[232] and indeed for a period thereafter because it took some time for 'the penny to drop'. We now know that s 47 created a separate statutory offence[233] or, more accurately, two offences, assault occasioning actual bodily harm and battery occasioning actual bodily harm. Confusion on this still persists. For example, Lord Ackner in *Savage*[234] at one point describes the mens rea of the offence exclusively in terms of the battery and, at another, exclusively in terms of the assault. It is safe to assume that there are two offences and that their constituents, so far as the word 'assault' goes, are precisely the same as those of common assault and battery discussed previously. Most cases will involve battery, but not all. An assault occasioning actual bodily harm might be committed by words or gestures alone, without the need for any physical contact between the assailant and the body of the victim. D may cause V to apprehend immediate unlawful violence and V might injure himself in making reasonable escape attempts.

---

[232] [1984] AC 463, [1984] 1 All ER 740, HL, p 31.
[233] *Harrow Justices, ex p Osaseri* [1986] QB 589 DC.
[234] [1992] 1 AC 699, [1991] 4 All ER 698 at 707 and 711.

16.3.1.2 Occasioning

Once an assault or battery with appropriate mens rea is proved, it remains only to prove that it occasioned actual bodily harm. That is a question of causation[235] not requiring proof of any further mens rea or fault. This was established in *Roberts*,[236] where D in a moving car 'assaulted' V by trying to take off her coat (a battery), whereupon she jumped out and sustained injury. It was held that the only question was whether the 'assault' caused V's action—only if it was something that no reasonable person could be expected to foresee would the chain of causation be broken.[237] It is now firmly established that this is the law, after a remarkable series of cases had thrown the matter into doubt.[238] In *Savage* and *Parmenter*, the House of Lords held that the law was correctly stated in *Roberts*.[239]

The offence may be committed in circumstances of omission where D has created a dangerous situation, as in the case of *Santana-Bermudez v DPP*.[240]

16.3.1.3 Bodily harm

'Bodily harm', according to the House of Lords in *DPP v Smith*,[241] 'needs no explanation'. Since 'Grievous means no more and no less than really serious' it seems to follow that, under s 47, the harm need not be really serious. In *Miller*,[242] it was described as any hurt or injury calculated to interfere with the health or comfort of the victim. This is a very low threshold for an offence carrying a five-year maximum sentence in the Crown Court. It includes a temporary loss of consciousness.[243] It would seem sufficient that the harm was more than merely transient and trifling.[244] It can include the cutting of a substantial amount of hair.[245] In *DPP v Smith*, the court held that having regard to the dictionary definitions, in ordinary language 'harm' was not limited to 'injury' and extended to 'hurt' or 'damage'. 'Bodily', whether used as an adjective or adverb, was 'concerned with the body'. It is settled law that evidence of external bodily injury, or a break in or bruise to the surface of the skin, is not required for there to be actual bodily harm. 'Bodily' encompasses all parts of the body including the victim's organs, his nervous system and his brain. Physical pain consequent on an assault is not a necessary ingredient of the offence, otherwise there could be no conviction where V was unconscious. Bodily harm can occur whether the tissue is alive beneath the surface of the skin or dead tissue above the surface of the skin; thus, hair is an attribute and part of the human body. There is no need for the harm to be permanent: a bruise suffices. The fact that hair will regrow is irrelevant; cutting hair is bodily harm.

It has been held that actual bodily harm is not limited to physical injury. It includes psychiatric injury. This represents a significant judicial extension of the offence. Neurotic disorders are included because they affect the central nervous system of the body, but emotions

---

[235] cf the view of J Gardner, 'Rationality and the Rule of Law in Offences Against the Person' (1994) 53 CLJ 502 at 509; J Gardner, *Offences and Defences: Selected Essays in the Philosophy of Criminal Law* (2007). See also J Stanton-Ife, 'Horrific Crimes' in RA Duff et al (eds), *Boundaries of the Criminal Law* (2010).

[236] (1971) 56 Cr App R 95, [1972] Crim LR 27.

[237] cf *Williams and Davies* (1991) 95 Cr App R 1.

[238] In *Spratt* [1991] 2 All ER 210, the court, very properly overruling *DPP v K* [1990] 1 All ER 331, held that only *Cunningham*, not *Caldwell*, recklessness would suffice to establish the assault but then went on, not referring to *Roberts*, to hold there must be recklessness as to the occasioning of actual bodily harm. *Savage* [1991] 2 All ER 220, decided on the same day, applied the law as stated in *Roberts* but without reference to that case. In *Parmenter* [1991] 2 All ER 225, CA, the court, confronted with this conflict, preferred *Spratt*, again without reference to *Roberts*.

[239] [1992] 1 AC 699, reversing *Parmenter* (CA) and overruling *Spratt* on this point.

[240] [2003] Crim LR 471, discussed previously.   [241] [1961] AC 290 at 334.

[242] [1954] 2 QB 282.   [243] *T v DPP* [2003] Crim LR 622.   [244] ibid.

[245] *DPP v Smith* [2006] EWHC 94 (Admin). Presumably the same is true if D damages V's hair substantially by applying a permanent colouring.

such as fear and anxiety ('brain functions') are not. While physical injury is within the ordinary experience of a jury, psychiatric injury is not; so, if the prosecution wish to rely on it, they must call expert evidence to prove that the alleged condition amounts to psychiatric injury.[246] Even where the victim can give evidence of physical and mental symptoms of psychiatric injury, expert evidence is necessary to prove causation.[247] The Court of Appeal has declined to extend the scope of the offence: psychological injury, not amounting to an identified or recognized psychological condition, cannot amount to 'bodily harm'.[248]

The CPS Charging Standard recommends s 47 be charged for injuries which are 'serious'. In determining 'seriousness', relevant factors may include the fact that there has been significant medical intervention, or that permanent effects have resulted. Examples may include injuries requiring a number of stitches (but not superficial steri-strips) or a hospital procedure under anaesthetic. Psychological harm which involves 'more than mere emotions such as fear, distress or panic' may suffice for this offence.[249]

16.3.2 Mens rea

The only mens rea that needs to be proved is that necessary for the assault or battery.

The absence of any requirement that D intends or foresees the additional harm for which he is punished over and above an assault or battery demonstrates the lack of correspondence of actus reus and mens rea in the offence and the conflict with the general principles of subjectivism.[250] This is a very clear example of a constructive crime.

16.4 Wounding and grievous bodily harm: OAPA 1861, s 20

Section 20 of the OAPA 1861 creates two forms of offence: wounding and inflicting grievous bodily harm. By s 20:

Whosoever shall unlawfully and maliciously wound or inflict any grievous bodily harm upon any other person, either with or without any weapon or instrument shall be guilty of [an offence triable either way] and being convicted thereof shall be liable to imprisonment for five years.

The two ways of committing the offence are: (a) malicious wounding, and (b) maliciously inflicting grievous bodily harm.

The element of unlawfulness should not be overlooked and should always be drawn to the jury's attention.[251]

---

[246] *Ireland* [1998] AC 147, [1997] 4 All ER 225 at 230–233, HL, approving *Chan-Fook* [1994] 2 All ER 552, [1994] Crim LR 432. See also LCCP 217, Ch 5.

[247] *Morris* [1998] 1 Cr App R 386.   [248] *Dhaliwal* [2006] EWCA Crim 1139, [2006] 2 Cr App R 348.

[249] (2005). See www.cps.gov.uk/legal-guidance/offences-against-person-incorporating-charging-standard#P189_14382.

[250] Its constructive nature is defended on the basis that D has 'altered his normative position' towards V by choosing to assault V, and therefore must take the consequences of the further harm. See Gardner (1994) 53 CLJ 502; J Horder, 'A Critique of the Correspondence Principle in Criminal Law' [1995] Crim LR 759. Cf B Mitchell, 'In Defence of a Principle of Correspondence' [1999] Crim LR 195. See on this the important article by A Ashworth, 'A Change of Normative Position: Determining the Contours of Culpability in Criminal Law' [2008] 11 New Crim LR 232. See also I Hare, 'A Compelling Case for the Code' (1993) 56 MLR 74.

[251] *Stokes* [2003] EWCA Crim 2977. In *Horwood* [2012] EWCA Crim 253, Hooper LJ stated, 'The word there [ie unlawful] means and relates to an absence of lawful justification such as self-defence or a similar kind of defence' at [7].

16.4.1 Malicious wounding

16.4.1.1 To wound

In order to constitute a wound, the continuity of the whole skin must be broken.[252] Where a pellet fired by an air pistol hit V in the eye but caused only an internal rupturing of blood vessels and not a break in the skin, there was no wound.[253] It is not enough that the cuticle or outer skin be broken if the inner skin remains intact.[254] Where V was treated with such violence that his collarbone was broken, it was held that there was no wound if his skin was intact.[255] It was held to be a wound, however, where the lining membrane of the urethra was ruptured and bled. Evidence was given that that membrane is precisely the same in character as the membrane lining the cheek and the external and internal skin of the lip.[256] It is wrong to direct a jury that 'the surface of the skin' must be broken. On that direction a scratch would suffice which is clearly inadequate.[257]

Under a predecessor offence to s 20[258] it was held that there was no wounding where V, in warding off D's attempt to cut his throat, struck his hands against a knife held by D and cut them;[259] nor where V was knocked down by D and wounded by falling on iron trams.[260] That old offence did not contain the words 'by any means whatsoever', and it is probable that these cases would now be decided differently. Even under the earlier law, D was guilty where he struck V on the hat with a gun and the hard rim of the hat caused a wound.[261] It is unclear whether there can be a wounding by omission. It was formerly held that wounding must be the result of a battery but it is probably now sufficient that the wound be directly inflicted whether by a battery or not.[262] In *Marsh*,[263] D was convicted of wounding with intent to do grievous bodily harm after his Staffordshire terrier attacked V and D failed to call the dog off. The judge directed the jury that they could not convict D unless he had 'set his dog on' V. The Court of Appeal rejected the argument that there was no act sufficient to constitute the actus reus of wounding, which lends weight to the proposition that this is an offence that can be committed indirectly.

It is doubtful whether this specific form of injury (or indeed others in the OAPA such as choking and throwing acid) warrants a separate offence in a modern code of offences. Some suggest that the specificity of label and the distinctions between the harms and the manner in which they are inflicted reflect important moral differences.[264]

16.4.1.2 Malice

The court in *Cunningham*[265] quoted with approval the definition of recklessness in Kenny's *Outlines of Criminal Law*: 'the accused has foreseen that the particular kind of harm might be done, and yet has gone on to take the risk of it'. According to that case, this definition applies whenever a statute defines a crime using the word 'malice'.

There is no doubt that malice in this context is a subjective test—*Caldwell* has no part to play, particularly since the decision of the House of Lords in *G*. It is submitted that the

---

252 *Moriarty v Brooks* (1834) 6 C & P 684.

253 *C (A Minor) v Eisenhower* [1984] QB 331, 78 Cr App R 48, DC.

254 *M'Loughlin* (1838) 8 C & P 635.   255 *Wood* (1830) 1 Mood CC 278.

256 *Waltham* (1849) 3 Cox CC 442. Contrast *Jones* (1849) 3 Cox CC 441.

257 *Morris* [2005] EWCA Crim 609.   258 7 Will 4 & 1 Vic, c 85, s 4.

259 *Beckett* (1836) 1 Mood & R 526 (Parke B); *Day* (1845) 1 Cox CC 207. Cf *Coleman* (1920) 84 JP 112.

260 *Spooner* (1853) 6 Cox CC 392.   261 *Sheard* (1837) 2 Mood CC 13.

262 *Wilson*, p 696. Cf *Taylor* (1869) LR 1 CCR 194; *Austin* (1973) 58 Cr App R 163, CA.

263 [2012] EWCA Crim 1442.

264 See the illuminating account by Gardner (1994) 53 CLJ 502 and in J Gardner, *Offences and Defences* (2007) Ch 2.

265 [1957] 2 QB 396. The case is described more fully at p 102.

term 'malice' should be understood as meaning 'intentionally or recklessly' and 'reckless' should carry the definition used in G.[266] In *Brady*,[267] the Court of Appeal held that G does not require proof that D had foreseen 'an obvious and significant risk' in order to establish that he had acted recklessly. D was drunk when he climbed on railings at a nightclub and fell onto the dance floor below causing serious injuries to V. The court allowed the appeal, because the judge had failed to direct the jury as to recklessness in sufficiently clear and careful terms.

Although the definition of malice provided in *Cunningham* refers to D's foresight of a risk, there is no mention of the further element of the modern test of recklessness—that it is unjustifiable for D to take that risk known to him. There is no clear authority on whether malice includes that requirement under the 1861 Act. *Mowatt*[268] and *Savage*[269] involve discussion of intention or foresight, in accordance with *Cunningham*, but do not address the question whether it was justified to take the risk.[270] The court in *Brady*[271] did not specifically discuss the point, but the approach taken seemed consistent with that rule. It is submitted that the test of malice should incorporate the G definition of recklessness in its full measure: D acts with malice if he intends or foresees a risk and takes that risk unjustifiably.

D must intend or be reckless, but what is 'the particular kind of harm' that must be intended or foreseen? As a matter of general principle, the answer might be expected to be that it is necessary that D has mens rea as to all the elements of the actus reus—including the wounding or grievous bodily harm.[272] The law has developed differently. The law is that it is enough that D foresaw that *some* bodily harm, not necessarily amounting to grievous bodily harm or wounding, might occur.[273] Diplock LJ said in *Mowatt*:[274]

the word 'maliciously' does import upon the part of the person who unlawfully inflicts the wound or other grievous bodily harm an awareness that his act may have the consequence of causing some physical harm to some other person. That is what is meant by 'the particular kind of harm' in the citation from Professor Kenny.[275] It is quite unnecessary that the accused should have foreseen that his unlawful act might cause physical harm of the gravity described in [s 20], ie, a wound or serious physical injury. It is enough that he should have foreseen that some physical harm to some person, albeit of a minor character, might result.

It is sufficient to prove that D foresaw that *some* harm *might* result and took the risk unjustifiably. To tell the jury that it must be proved that D foresaw that it *would* result is too generous to the defendant.[276] It is not enough, however, whether the charge is one of wounding or inflicting grievous bodily harm[277] that D intended to frighten (unless he foresaw that the fright might result in psychiatric injury).

---

[266] See [1992] 1 AC 699. *Savage and Parmenter* [1991] 4 All ER at 721, HL, affirming *Mowatt* [1968] 1 QB 421.
[267] [2006] EWCA Crim 2413.   [268] [1968] 1 QB 421.   [269] [1992] 1 AC 699, 750.
[270] The leading speech in *Savage* describes the dissent in *Caldwell v Metropolitan Police Commissioner* [1982] AC 341, which does refer to justification, but the final conclusion was based on *Cunningham* and does not adopt the dissent in *Caldwell*.
[271] [2006] EWCA Crim 2413, [2007] Crim LR 564.   [272] cf p 120.   [273] See n 250.
[274] [1968] 1 QB 421 at 426. Reiterated post-G in *C* [2007] EWCA Crim 1068. See also *Dakou* [2002] EWCA Crim 3156, oversimplifying the issue of malice in s 18. Courts continue to make errors with this—see eg *DPP v W* [2006] EWHC 92 (Admin), where magistrates had acquitted on the basis that D had not foreseen the level of harm V suffered.
[275] *Outlines*, 211. The citation is the passage approved by the Court of Criminal Appeal in *Cunningham* [1957] 2 QB 396, [1957] 2 All ER 412; p 102.
[276] *Rushworth* (1992) 95 Cr App R 252 at 255, cited in *Pearson* [1994] Crim LR 534 which nevertheless left this point in the air. Earlier *dicta* by Lords Diplock and Ackner are ambiguous.
[277] *Flack v Hunt* (1979) 70 Cr App R 51; *Sullivan* [1981] Crim LR 46, CA.

16.4.2 Maliciously inflicting grievous bodily harm

'Grievous bodily harm' was formerly interpreted to include any harm which seriously interferes with health or comfort;[278] but, in *Smith*,[279] the House of Lords said that the words should bear their ordinary and natural meaning.[280] It is not always necessary for the jury to be told to look for 'really' serious harm,[281] and it is not clear precisely what that word means when it is included. The jury may take into consideration the totality of the injuries,[282] provided they have been inflicted in one attack or the charge accurately reflects the relevant period.[283] Although the determination of whether the injury constitutes grievous bodily harm is to be assessed objectively, and not merely on the basis of the victim's perception,[284] the characteristics of the victim may be taken into account—what is grievous bodily harm to a child might not be for an adult.[285] There is no need for the injury to be permanent or life-threatening.[286] Unconsciousness is capable of constituting grievous bodily harm.[287]

Grievous bodily harm may cover cases where there is no wounding as, for instance, the broken collarbone in *Wood*.[288] Conversely, there might be a technical 'wounding' which could not be said to amount to grievous bodily harm—as with an injection by a needle.[289] The absence of any clear definition of the term and the associated risk of inconsistent applications and a lack of predictability in verdicts is disappointing.[290]

It is settled that *serious* psychiatric injury amounts to grievous bodily harm.[291] This results in the possibility of convictions for inflicting grievous bodily harm by telephone—for example, a series of extreme obscene phone calls.[292] There is no legal difficulty with the actus reus—that is established simply by proving that D inflicted the serious psychiatric injury. Proof of mens rea in such a case may be more difficult. The Court of Appeal in *Golding* reiterated that 'the ambit of bodily harm is restricted to recognisable psychiatric illness and does not cover psychological disturbance'.[293] The anguish V suffered as a result of learning that D had infected her with the genital herpes virus was therefore incapable of constituting grievous bodily harm.

Although the level of harm is ill-defined and rests on the jury's interpretation in each individual case, it has been held in Northern Ireland not to be contrary to Art 7 for want of certainty.[294]

---

[278] *Ashman* (1858) 1 F & F 88.   [279] [1961] AC 290; n 241; followed in *Metharam* [1961] 3 All ER 200.

[280] The Court of Appeal confirmed in *Golding* [2014] EWCA Crim 889 that the assessment of harm done in an individual case is a matter for the jury, applying contemporary social standards. For criticism, see K Laird [2014] Crim LR 686.

[281] *Janjua* [1999] 1 Cr App R 91. This was reiterated more recently in *Carey* [2013] EWCA Crim 482.

[282] *Grundy* [1977] Crim LR 543; *Birmingham* [2002] EWCA Crim 2608.

[283] See *Brown* [2005] EWCA Crim 359 (abuse of V over several days).

[284] *Brown* [1998] Crim LR 484.   [285] *Bollom* [2004] 2 Cr App R 50.   [286] ibid.

[287] *Hicks* [2007] EWCA Crim 1500—the issue being raised by the jury! See also *Foster* [2009] EWCA Crim 2214, [28] discussing the levels of unconsciousness and whether the 'Glasgow coma score' might assist in determining the severity of the unconsciousness in law.

[288] See n 255. *Lashley* [2017] EWCA Crim 260 provides a vivid example, in which V was on the ground when D reversed over him with his car.

[289] Although that is often charged under s 47. See eg *Gower* [2007] EWCA Crim 1655.

[290] In *Townsend* [2013] EWCA Crim 771, D was convicted of inflicting grievous bodily harm on the basis that he had fractured V's jawbone. It subsequently transpired, however, that V's jawbone was not in fact fractured and the Crown conceded that D's conviction therefore had to be quashed.

[291] *Ireland*, p 662.   [292] *Gelder* (1994) The Times, 25 May (news item).

[293] [2014] EWCA Crim 889, [63] per Treacy LJ.   [294] See *Anderson* [2003] NICA 12.

16.4.2.1 Inflict

In a series of cases[295] from 1861 until 1983, it was held or assumed that the words 'inflict' and 'wound' both imply an 'assault'. D could be convicted of an offence under s 20 only if it was proved that he wounded or caused grievous bodily harm by committing an assault. *Clarence*[296] held that D caused V harm by infecting her with gonorrhoea, but did not *inflict* it unless there was an assault. But a second line of cases[297] simply ignored the requirement of an assault and upheld convictions where D so frightened V that V jumped through a window,[298] or accidentally injured himself by putting his hand through a glass door under a 'well-grounded apprehension of violence'.[299] In *Martin*,[300] where, shortly before the end of a performance in a theatre, D put out the lights and placed an iron bar across the doorway, he was convicted of inflicting grievous bodily harm on those injured in the panic. In 1983 the House of Lords in *Wilson*[301] resolved the matter by deciding, following the Australian case of *Salisbury*,[302] that 'inflict' does not, after all, imply an assault.[303]

Arguably, the case decided no more than that; but Lord Roskill cited the opinion of the Australian court that 'inflict' has a narrower meaning than 'cause' (as used in s 18 discussed later) and requires 'force being violently applied to the body of the victim'. In *Burstow*,[304] the House of Lords decided that 'inflict' does not bear this narrow meaning and that grievous bodily harm might be inflicted over the telephone or by other harassment, not involving the use of violence to the body or an assault. It remains necessary, as noted earlier, to prove that D foresaw that he might cause some harm, not necessarily serious psychiatric injury.

The distinction between 'cause' and 'inflict' seems then to have been substantially eliminated. The House thought that, while the words are not synonymous, there is 'no radical divergence' of meaning. Perhaps this is to be read to mean no 'material' difference.[305] If the courts were interpreting a modern statute, the use of different words in adjacent sections might compel the conclusion that different meanings were intended; but no such inference can be drawn in the 1861 Act because it was never intended, and does not purport, to be a consistent whole.[306] *Clarence* can no longer be justified on the ground that there was no assault or violent application of force or that V consented.[307] It was not overruled but it

---

[295] *Yeadon and Birch* (1861) 9 Cox CC 91; *Taylor* (1869) LR 1 CCR 194; *Clarence* (1888) 22 QBD 23; *Snewing* [1972] Crim LR 267; *Carpenter* (1979) 76 Cr App R 320n, cited [1983] 1 All ER 1004.

[296] (1888) 22 QBD 23.

[297] *Halliday* (1889) 61 LT 701; *Lewis* [1970] Crim LR 647, CA; *Mackie* [1973] Crim LR 54; *Boswell* [1973] Crim LR 307; *Cartledge v Allen* [1973] Crim LR 530, DC.

[298] *Halliday* (1889) 61 LT 701.   [299] *Cartledge v Allen* [1973] Crim LR 530.

[300] (1881) 8 QBD 54, CCR.   [301] [1984] AC 242 at 260.   [302] [1976] VR 452 at 461.

[303] The House nevertheless contrived to hold that a person charged under s 20 could be convicted on that indictment of a common assault by virtue of s 6(3) of the Criminal Law Act 1967—a much-criticized decision but approved by the House in *Savage* [1991] 4 All ER 698 at 711. See G Williams, 'Alternative Elements and Included Offences' (1984) 43 CLJ 290 and commentary at [1984] Crim LR 37.

[304] Heard and decided together with *Ireland* [1998] AC 147. Arguably the case is restricted to those cases involving the infliction of psychiatric injury. This would create an undesirable confusion in the law.

[305] Lord Hope, however, said that 'inflict' implies that the consequence of the act is something that the victim is likely to find unpleasant or harmful whereas 'cause' may embrace pleasure as well as pain. But, if that is so, the sadomasochists in *Brown* [1994] 1 AC 212, discussed earlier, could not have been held to have been guilty of *inflicting* grievous bodily harm, contrary to s 20, because everyone was having a jolly good time. This would be surprising, as they were guilty of wounding, contrary to the same subsection on the ground that consent was no defence.

[306] CS Greaves, *The Criminal Law Consolidation and Amendment Acts* (2nd edn, 1862) 3–4, cited by Lord Steyn at 234.

[307] cf p 673.

appears to have been wrongly decided.[308] Following *Dica*, it now seems clear that as a matter of practice the terms can be treated as synonymous in almost every instance.[309]

In *Brady*, discussed earlier, the Court of Appeal questioned, *obiter*, whether it may be arguable that there was no actus reus, that is, no 'deliberate non-accidental conduct on the part of the accused that inflicted grievous bodily harm'. On D's account, he had deliberately perched precariously on a low railing above a crowded dance floor having consumed considerable quantities of alcohol and drugs. D argued that the act of falling was not deliberate and must, therefore, have been accidental; and that, since the actus reus of the offence contrary to s 20 required the inflicting of grievous bodily harm, the physical act of the falling that had caused the injury was not a direct assault. With respect, that argument is difficult to follow. There is no doubt that V suffered grievous bodily harm as she was rendered paraplegic. There is also no doubt that that injury was inflicted by D. The question is whether it was inflicted by D's blameworthy conduct. If the jury were satisfied that D realized that in perching as he did there was a risk of his falling and causing some injury to a person below, and that he went on unreasonably to take that risk, it is submitted that he would have committed the s 20 offence. Although the act of perching may look innocuous viewed in isolation, that is not the actus reus of the offence: the actus reus is D's whole conduct in perching *and* the resulting harm to the victim on the dance floor. The incident of D losing his balance and falling does not represent a break in the chain of causation; it is the very incident about which D was alleged to have been reckless/malicious. His reckless conduct in perching as he did caused the loss of balance which caused the fall and the resulting injury.[310]

16.4.2.2 Coexistence of s 20 and s 47

The coexistence of s 47 with that of maliciously inflicting grievous bodily harm contrary to s 20 of the same Act, also punishable with a maximum of five years' imprisonment, makes little sense.[311] The prosecutor's task is slightly easier under s 47 since it is not necessary to prove even the foresight of some bodily harm which is necessary under s 20. Proof of an assault or battery is required under s 47, but is not necessary under s 20; and s 20 no longer requires proof of a direct application of force. Section 20 is regarded in practice as the more serious offence. In *Parmenter*,[312] the Court of Appeal said that:

although the sentences imposed in practice for the worst s 47 offences will overlap those imposed at the lower end of s 20, nobody could doubt that the two offences are seen in quite different terms, whether by defendants and their advisers contemplating pleas of guilty, or by judges passing sentence under s 47 on defendants whose pleas of guilty have been accepted by the prosecution, or by subsequent sentencers casting an eye down lists of previous convictions.

This is reflected in the CPS Charging Standard which recommends s 20 in cases of really serious harm such as: injury resulting in permanent disability or permanent, loss of sensory function or visible disfigurement; broken or displaced limbs or bones, including a fractured skull; compound fractures, broken cheek bone, jaw, ribs, etc; injuries which cause

---

308 The draft Bill in the Home Office Consultation Paper of Feb 1998 expressly excludes from the proposed offences recklessly (but not intentionally) causing anything by disease. See now *Dica* [2004] EWCA Crim 1103, p 673. See also LCCP 217, Ch 6 and LC 361 Ch 4.

309 The High Court of Australia in *Aubrey v The Queen* [2017] HCA 18 arrived at the same conclusion in respect of the equivalent legislation in New South Wales.

310 Part of the problem in the court's analysis is that the events are all categorized as either deliberate or accidental. It is unclear what is meant by this, but it stems from the unsatisfactory way in which the case was presented.

311 cf the view of Gardner (1994) 53 CLJ 502, and Ashworth, n 250.

312 [1991] 2 All ER 225 at 233.

substantial loss of blood, usually necessitating a transfusion; injuries resulting in lengthy treatment or incapacity; serious psychiatric injury.[313]

16.5 Section 18 of the Offences Against the Person Act 1861

By s 18, as amended by the Criminal Law Act 1967:

Whosoever shall unlawfully and maliciously by any means whatsoever wound or cause any grievous bodily harm to any person with intent to do some grievous bodily harm to any person or with intent to resist or prevent the lawful apprehension or detainer of any person, shall be guilty of [an offence triable only on indictment], and being convicted thereof shall be liable to [imprisonment] for life.

The elements of the actus reus have been considered previously in relation to s 20. Note that under s 18 there is, technically, no need for the harm to be caused to another.

16.5.1 Mens rea

The mens rea of the offence differs slightly depending on which form of the offence is charged.

16.5.1.1 Intention

In every case the Crown must establish an ulterior intent which may be either intent to do grievous bodily harm or intent to resist or prevent the lawful apprehension or detainer of any person. Recklessness is not enough.[314] Where the allegation is of intentionally causing grievous bodily harm, it is sufficient that D intended to cause the harm he did, irrespective of whether *he personally* would regard that level of harm as really serious. As noted earlier in the context of s 20, proving an intention to cause psychiatric injury may be very difficult.

Intention has the same meaning as in the law of murder.[315] The prosecution must prove either: (a) that D acted in order to cause grievous bodily harm, or, if it was not his purpose, (b) that he knew that grievous bodily harm was a virtually certain consequence of his act. In case (b), the jury may then find that he had the requisite intent.[316] The jury need not be directed on this oblique intention definition except in rare cases.[317]

If D intends to cause grievous bodily harm to X and, striking at X, he accidentally wounds another person, V, he may be indicted for wounding V with intent to cause grievous bodily harm to X.[318] If D intends to cause grievous bodily harm to X, and strikes the person he aims at, who is in fact V, he may be convicted of wounding V with intent to cause grievous bodily harm to V.[319] In addition, if D intends to kill X, for example by shooting him, but misses and instead causes really serious harm to V, D can be guilty of an offence contrary

---

[313] See CPS Charging Standard, www.cps.gov.uk/legal-guidance/offences-against-person-incorporating-charging-standard#P189_14382.

[314] *Re Knight's Appeal* (1968) FLR 81.

[315] *Bryson* [1985] Crim LR 669; cf *Belfon* [1976] 3 All ER 46, CA.

[316] See p 90.

[317] See *Phillips* [2004] EWCA Crim 112.

[318] *Monger* [1973] Crim LR 301, per Mocatta J holding that D could not be convicted where the indictment alleged intent to harm V. This is in accord with *Ryan* (1839) 2 Mood & R 213 and *Hewlett* (1858) 1 F & F 91 but contrary to *Hunt* (1825) 1 Mood CC 93 and *Jarvis, Langdon and Stear* (1837) 2 Mood & R 40. Cf the doctrine of transferred malice, p 122 and the comment on *Monger* in [1973] Crim LR 301.

[319] *Smith* (1855) Dears CC 559 at 560; *Stopford* (1870) 11 Cox CC 643.

to s 18 for the harm caused to V. Additionally, the Court of Appeal in *Grant*[320] accepted the proposition that an intention to kill necessarily includes an intention to cause grievous bodily harm. The argument that the two are mutually exclusive or inconsistent was rejected.

Where the indictment specifies a particular form of the offence, the intent prescribed in that form of the offence must be proved; it is not enough to prove another variety of intent described in the section.[321] So D had to be acquitted where the charge was intent to do some grievous bodily harm and the jury found that the acts were done to resist and prevent D's apprehension *and for no other purpose*.[322] But if D intends to prevent his apprehension and, in order to do so, intends to cause grievous bodily harm, he may be convicted under an indictment charging only the latter intent. It is immaterial which is the principal and which the subordinate intent.[323]

The courts continue to create difficulties with the form of the mens rea. In *Taylor*,[324] the judge had directed that the jury on a s 18 charge must be sure that the prosecution had proved that D had intended to cause grievous bodily harm or to wound. This was a misdirection to the jury.

An intent to wound is insufficient. There must be an intent to cause really serious bodily injury.[325]

There was no evidence, upon which the jury could have relied, to show that D had intended really serious injury. The conviction was quashed and was replaced with a conviction for unlawful wounding. In *Purcell*,[326] the Court of Appeal suggested that at a trial of a person charged with causing grievous bodily harm the following direction should be given to the jury on the issue of intent:

You must feel sure that the defendant intended to cause serious bodily harm to the victim. You can only decide what his intention was by considering all the relevant circumstances and in particular what he did and what he said about it.

16.5.1.2 Malice

The meaning of malice has been considered earlier in relation to s 20.

Where, under s 18, the charge is of causing grievous bodily harm with intent to do grievous bodily harm, the word 'maliciously' obviously has no part to play. Any mens rea which it might import is comprehended within the ulterior intent. Even if 'wounding' is not foreseen, it is 'malicious'. The Court of Appeal has emphasized that generally judges ought not to give a direction on malice under s 18 in these cases.[327]

Where the charge is of malicious wounding or causing grievous bodily harm with intent to resist lawful apprehension, there is no difficulty in giving meaning to 'maliciously' and it is submitted that meaning should be given to that word.[328] A mere intent to resist lawful apprehension should not found liability for a charge of wounding or causing grievous bodily

---

[320] [2014] EWCA Crim 143. The court declined to consider the issue of whether D could be guilty of two or more attempted murders for a single act by which he intended to kill only one person. For criticism, see T Storey (2014) 78 J Crim L 214.

[321] There are numerous forms of the s 18 offence other than that commonly relied upon—grievous bodily harm with intent to do grievous bodily harm—wounding with intent to do grievous bodily harm; causing grievous bodily harm with intent to do grievous bodily harm; wounding with intent to resist or prevent apprehension or detention; causing grievous bodily harm with intent to resist or prevent apprehension or detention.

[322] *Duffin and Marshall* (1818) Russ & Ry 365; cf *Boyce* (1824) 1 Mood CC 29.

[323] *Gillow* (1825) 1 Mood CC 85.

[324] [2009] EWCA Crim 544. See also *Gregory* [2009] EWCA Crim 1374.   [325] ibid, [3].

[326] (1986) 83 Cr App R 45, CA.   [327] See *Brown* [2005] EWCA Crim 359, [17].

[328] *Morrison* (1989) 89 Cr App R 17. D was seized by a WPC as she was arresting him. D dived through a window pane and the WPC was dragged with him suffering serious facial injury. D clearly *intended* to resist arrest, the Court of Appeal held he must also be subjectively (*Cunningham*) reckless as to the grievous bodily harm.

harm. It is submitted that the Court of Appeal went too far in *Mowatt*[329] in saying that 'In section 18 the word "maliciously" adds nothing.'

The indictment should spell out the alleged mens rea.[330] It is clear that there must be proof that D actually foresaw the specified result. Any doubt there may have been about this was dispelled by s 8 of the Criminal Justice Act 1967.[331] *Mowatt* was decided before the Act came into force, and certain observations in the case are therefore suspect.

If D has not admitted his malice, then it is submitted that it must be proved like every other element in the crime. The fact that the evidence appears to the judge to be overwhelming is not a good reason for not leaving it to the jury.

16.5.2 Alternative verdicts

A charge of 'causing' grievous bodily harm with intent contrary to s 18 has been held to include a charge of 'inflicting' grievous bodily harm contrary to s 20[332] which, in turn, includes a charge of assault occasioning actual bodily harm contrary to s 47.[333] The effect is that, on an indictment for the s 18 offence, the jury may find D guilty of an offence under s 20, or under s 47; and, on an indictment for the s 20 offence, of an offence under s 47. Whether to direct the jury that if they acquit of the offence charged they may convict of a lesser included offence is a matter for the discretion of the judge. Following *Coutts*,[334] if the possibility that D is guilty only of a lesser offence (s 20 or s 47) has been raised in the course of the evidence, the judge should leave the alternative offence to the jury, even in cases in which neither prosecution nor defence want the alternative offence to be left to the jury.[335] The Court of Appeal has reiterated the importance of this.[336]

In *Lahaye*,[337] the Court of Appeal's *per curiam* recommendation seems to have been that a s 20 offence ought to be included in the indictment from the outset in *any* s 18 case, and this goes beyond what was suggested by the House of Lords (Lords Mackay, Goff and Mustill) in *Mandair*,[338] namely that it may be desirable to include as an alternative where appropriate. Automatic inclusion of a s 20 count reduces the prosecution's freedom to select their indictment of choice, and increases the risk of compromise verdicts but it seems that such verdicts are already the practical reality. Beatson LJ's suggestion is, it is submitted, a sensible approach:

It is, on the authorities, the ultimate responsibility of the trial judge to leave an alternative verdict which is obviously raised by the evidence to the jury. While there is no universal rule about

---

[329] [1968] 1 QB 421. See R Buxton, 'Negligence and Constructive Crime' [1969] Crim LR 112. See also *Ward* (1872) LR 1 CCR 356.

[330] *Hodgson* [2008] EWCA Crim 895.   [331] See p 131.

[332] *Mandair* (1994) 99 Cr App R 250, [1994] Crim LR 666, HL.

[333] *Wilson* [1984] AC 242, [1984] Crim LR 36, HL.   [334] [2006] 1 WLR 2154.

[335] See *Ali* [2006] EWCA Crim 2906; cf *Foster* [2007] EWCA Crim 2869.

[336] *Foster* [2009] EWCA Crim 2214; *Green* [2009] EWCA Crim 2609; *Mathew* [2010] EWCA Crim 29; *Hodson* [2009] EWCA Crim 1590, [2010] Crim LR 249 and commentary. If s 20 is a realistically available verdict on the evidence, as an interpretation properly open to the jury, without trivializing the offending conduct, then the alternative should be left to the jury. The court emphasizes that it is particularly important that an alternative verdict was left to a jury where the offence charged required proof of a specific intent (s 18) and the alternative offence (s 20) did not. In *Caven* [2011] EWCA Crim 3239, the failure to leave the alternative offence resulted in D's conviction for an offence contrary to s 18 being quashed. In *Brown* [2014] All ER (D) 176 (Oct), D was charged with an offence of wounding with intent. Expert witnesses, however, agreed that no more than mild to moderate force would have been required to inflict the wound in question, which could easily have been sustained during a struggle, rather than as a result of a deliberate stabbing action. The jury should thus have been invited to consider the unlawful wounding option, but this was not done, so D's conviction for wounding with intent was quashed as unsafe and a conviction for the lesser offence was substituted.

[337] [2005] EWCA Crim 2847. See also *Hodson* [2010] Crim LR 248, CA; *Brown* [2014] All ER (D) 176 (Oct).

[338] [1995] AC 208.

including a section 20 count in the indictment where there is an allegation of a section 18 offence, the decision of this court in *Lahaye* states that such a count should normally be included.[339]

Research has suggested that the moral distinction between the s 18 and s 20 offences has been eroded by the availability of the alternative verdicts and the frequency with which they are returned. In one study, only 23 per cent of those indicted for s 18 were convicted of that offence, whilst 53 per cent were convicted of s 20 and only one in ten of the contested s 18 trials led to an outright acquittal.[340]

16.6 Reform

The case for reform of these offences against the person (assault, battery, s 47, s 20, s 18) is compelling.[341] The Law Commission has commented that the law is 'defective on grounds both of effectiveness and of justice'.[342] In 2014 the Commission[343] published a scoping consultation paper in which it sought to assess the strength of the case for reform and in particular whether any future reform should be based on the draft Bill from the Home Office, *Consultation Paper on Violence*[344] in 1998. That Bill proposed a structured hierarchy of offences as follows:

1.—(1) A person is guilty of an offence if he intentionally causes serious injury to another.

(2) A person is guilty of an offence if he omits to do an act which he has a duty to do at common law, the omission results in serious injury to another, and he intends the omission to have that result...

(4) A person guilty of an offence under this section is liable on conviction on indictment to imprisonment for life.

2.—(1) A person is guilty of an offence if he recklessly causes serious injury to another...

(3) A person guilty of an offence under this section is liable—

(a) on conviction on indictment, to imprisonment for a term not exceeding 7 years;

(b) on summary conviction, to imprisonment for a term not exceeding 6 months or a fine not exceeding the statutory maximum or both.

3.—(1) A person is guilty of an offence if he intentionally or recklessly causes injury to another...

(3) A person guilty of an offence under this section is liable—

(a) on conviction on indictment, to imprisonment for a term not exceeding 5 years;

(b) on summary conviction, to imprisonment for a term not exceeding 6 months or a fine not exceeding the statutory maximum or both.

4.—(1) A person is guilty of an offence if—

(a) he intentionally or recklessly applies force to or causes an impact on the body of another, or

(b) he intentionally or recklessly causes the other to believe that any such force or impact is imminent.

---

[339] *Vaughan* [2014] EWCA Crim 1456, [22].

[340] E Genders, 'Reform of the Offences Against the Person Act: Lessons from the Law in Action' [1999] Crim LR 689. See also LCCP 217, Ch 5.

[341] M Jefferson, 'Offences Against the Person: Into the 21st Century' (2012) 76 J Crim L 472; Genders [1999] Crim LR 689.

[342] LCCP 122, *Legislating the Criminal Code: Offences Against the Person and General Principles* (1992), on which see S Gardner, 'Reiterating the Criminal Code' (1992) 55 MLR 839; ATH Smith, 'Legislating the Criminal Code' [1992] Crim LR 396. See also LC 218, *Offences Against the Person and General Principles* (1993).

[343] LCCP 217.

[344] (1998) on which see JC Smith, 'Offences Against The Person: The Home Office Consultation Paper' [1998] Crim LR 317.

(2) No such offence is committed if the force or impact, not being intended or likely to cause injury, is in the circumstances such as is generally acceptable in the ordinary conduct of daily life and the defendant does not know or believe that it is in fact unacceptable to the other person.

(3) A person guilty of an offence under this section is liable on summary conviction to imprisonment for a term not exceeding 6 months or [an unlimited fine] or both.

15.—(1) In this Act 'injury' means—

(a) physical injury, or

(b) mental injury.

(2) Physical injury does not include anything caused by disease but (subject to that) it includes pain, unconsciousness and any other impairment of a person's physical condition.

(3) Mental injury does not include anything caused by disease but (subject to that) it includes any impairment of a person's mental health.

[(4) In its application to section 1 this section applies without the exceptions relating to things caused by disease.] (The Law Commission recommended removing this clause.)

In 2015, the Law Commission published a scoping report, in which it recommended that future reform should be based upon the draft Home Office Bill.[345] The consequence of this is that the main injury offences would follow the correspondence principle, in which the harm required to be intended or foreseen matches the harm done. The Commission also recommended the creation of a new offence of 'aggravated assault', that would sit between the offence of intentionally or recklessly causing harm and the basic assault offences. It would be triable only in the magistrates' court.

16.7 Racially or religiously aggravated assaults

The Crime and Disorder Act 1998 created a new category of racially aggravated crimes, and the Anti-terrorism Crime and Security Act 2001 extended these to include religiously aggravated offences.[346] There has been a growing concern at the rise in violent hate crime.[347]

It is possible for a judge when sentencing to take into account hostility on grounds of race, religion, sexual orientation, gender identity or disability.[348] Some questioned,

---

[345] LC 361. For commentary, see S Demetriou, 'Not Giving Up the Fight: A Review of the Law Commission's Scoping Report on Non-Fatal Offences Against the Person' (2016) J Crim L 188; A Jackson and T Storey, 'Reforming Offences Against the Person: In Defence of "Moderate" Constructivism' (2015) 79 J Crim L 437; V Scully, 'Reforming Offences Against the Person—Seventh Time Lucky?' [2015] 10 Arch Rev 4.

[346] See generally M Malik, 'Racist Crime: Racially Aggravated Offences in the Crime and Disorder Act 1998' (1999) 62 MLR 409; M Idriss, 'Religion and the Anti-Terrorism, Crime and Security Act 2001' [2002] Crim LR 890; A Tomkins, 'Legislating Against Terror: The Anti-terrorism, Crime and Security Act 2001' [2002] PL 205; PW Edge, 'Extending Hate Crime to Religion' (2003) 10 J Civ Lib 5; E Burney, 'Using the Law of Racially Aggravated Offences' [2003] Crim LR 28; and LCCP 213, *Hate Crime: The Case for Extending the Existing Offences* (2013) and LC 348, *Hate Crime: Should the Current Offences be Extended* (2014). For a theoretical discussion, see J Waldron, *The Harm in Hate Speech* (2012).

[347] See T Fowles and D Wilson, 'Racist and Religious Crime Data' (2004) 43 Howard J of Crim Justice 441. See also CPS, www.cps.gov.uk/news/south-east-conviction-rates-hate-crime-amongst-highest-country. In 2016/17, there were 80,393 offences recorded by the police in which one or more hate crime strands were deemed to be a motivating factor. This was an increase of 29 per cent compared with the 62,518 hate crimes recorded in 2015/16, the largest percentage increase seen since the statistical count began in 2011/12: A O'Neill, CPS Statistical Bulletin, *Hate Crime, England and Wales 2016/17* (2017).

[348] It has been held that where D pleads to a non-aggravated form of the offence and no evidence is offered on the racially aggravated form of the offence, the judge cannot then sentence on the basis that the offence was racially aggravated: *McGillivray* [2005] Crim LR 484, CA. See LC 348, paras 2.65 et seq.

therefore, whether it was necessary to create offences applicable where certain categories of base offence (including many offences of violence) are committed with racial or religious hostility.

In a clear statement the House of Lords unequivocally supported such offences. Baroness Hale opined that they properly reflect the 'qualitatively distinct order of gravity' involved when racial hostility is demonstrated.[349] In addition, establishing separate offences rather than leaving matters of racial aggravation purely for sentencing means that *the jury* must be satisfied of that distinctive stigmatizing aspect of the alleged wrongdoing.

16.7.1 The offences

Section 28(1) of the Crime and Disorder Act provides two forms which the racial and religious aggravation can take. The difference between the two is extremely important but unfortunately appears to be frequently overlooked.[350]

Offences involving a demonstration of hostility. Section 28(1)(a) applies where at the time of[351] committing the relevant offence (assault, s 47, s 20, public order offences, harassment, etc) or immediately[352] before or after doing so, the offender demonstrates towards the victim[353] of the offence racial or religious hostility based on the victim's membership of a racial or religious group. The question is whether, *objectively*, D's words or conduct demonstrate hostility based on race or religion. D's motivation is not relevant.

Offences motivated by hostility. Section 28(1)(b) applies where the relevant offence is motivated wholly or partly by hostility towards members of a racial or religious group based on their membership of that group. This is a *subjective* question. D's motivation for the use of the words or conduct is crucial in determining whether it was racially or religiously hostile.

There are numerous offences (some public order offences, harassment, criminal damage, etc) that can be aggravated in either of these ways (by demonstrations of hostility or motivated by hostility) but for the purposes of this part of this chapter, the relevant offences are contained in s 29. A person commits an offence under s 29 if he commits:

(1) an offence under s 20[354] of the OAPA 1861 (malicious wounding or grievous bodily harm); or

(2) an offence under s 47 of that Act (p 686); or

(3) a common assault;

which is 'racially aggravated' for the purposes of s 29.

---

[349] See note I Hare, 'Legislating Against Hate—The Legal Response to Bias Crimes' (1997) 17 OJLS 415 at 416–417.

[350] See *Jones v Bedford and Mid Bedfordshire Magistrates' Court* [2010] EWHC 523 (Admin). See LC 348, Ch 2.

[351] Where D uttered racist words and then attacked V several minutes later, the Court of Appeal regarded the incident as properly viewed as one in which D's racial hostility was present throughout: *Babbs* [2007] EWCA Crim 2737.

[352] This qualifies both acts before and after—a 20-minute delay after the act before D made the racist remark demonstrating hostility was too long: *Parry v DPP* [2004] EWHC 3112 (Admin).

[353] Who need not be present: *Parry v DPP* [2004] EWHC 3112 (Admin). In *Valentine* [2017] EWCA Crim 207, the Court of Appeal held that the trial judge had erred in presenting the child to the jury as the victim in his summing up, as it was the mother who had presented evidence of distress. The charge had therefore lacked accuracy.

[354] There is no need for aggravation for s 18 which carries the maximum life sentence.

Offences (1) and (2) are punishable on indictment with seven years' imprisonment (compared with five years for the basic, non-aggravated offence) and offence (3) with two years, the basic offence being triable only summarily.

16.7.2 Definitions

'Race' is widely defined to include colour, nationality (including citizenship) or ethnic or national origins.[355] The courts have taken an extremely wide and non-technical view of what constitutes a 'race' and racial group. It has been confirmed that the terms will be satisfied by non-inclusive expressions if, for example, D demonstrates hostility to V by calling him 'non-white' or 'foreign'.[356] 'Religious group' means a group of persons defined by reference to religious belief or lack of religious belief.[357] The Act gives no further guidance. Given the broad interpretation in Art 9 of the ECHR, it would seem likely that the domestic courts will interpret the offence as affording protection to a religion as widely understood.[358] By analogy with the interpretation of race, non-inclusive terms will suffice, for example 'unbeliever' or 'gentile'.[359]

Racial or religious hostility can be demonstrated by D towards someone of his own racial or religious group.[360] Note also that there is no need for D's presumption about V's race or religion to be accurate: as where D calls V a 'Paki' when V is from India. In *Rogers*,[361] the House of Lords confirmed that though D must have formed the view about V's racial group, the words used by D and which are alleged to demonstrate racial hostility need not refer expressly to that group to which V belongs. A racially aggravated assault might also be committed by one white person on another if the former were, for example, to call the latter 'nigger lover'.[362] It is submitted that this is a perfectly appropriate interpretation of the Act. There is no need for the aggravating words to be repeated, or for the intended target to hear them or be present.[363]

16.7.2.1 Assault and contemporaneous demonstration of hostility: s 28(1)(a)

The courts have made clear that the offence under s 28(1)(a) is not limited to cases in which D is motivated solely or even mainly by racial malevolence. It is designed to extend to cases which may have a racially neutral gravamen but in the course of which there is, *objectively viewed*, hostility demonstrated towards the victim based on V's race (or presumed

---

[355] 'African' does not denote an ethnic, but does denote a racial, group: *White* [2001] Crim LR 576, but see commentary on difficulties this creates. Applying the House of Lords' approach in *Rogers*, both terms are capable of being construed as demonstrations of hostility based on the victim's membership of a racial group. For further analysis see MA Walters, 'Conceptualizing "Hostility" for Hate Crime Law: Minding "the Minutiae" when Interpreting Section 28(1)(a) of the Crime and Disorder Act 1998' (2014) 34 OJLS 47.

[356] *Rogers* [2007] UKHL 8. See also *DPP v M* [2004] EWHC 1453 (Admin), [2005] Crim LR 392; *A-G's Reference (No 4 of 2004)* [2005] EWCA Crim 889; *H* [2010] EWCA Crim 1931 (question for jury whether D's repeated references to V as a 'monkey' or 'black monkey' constituted a *demonstration* of hostility based wholly or partly on race or whether it was mere vulgar abuse unconnected with hostility based on race).

[357] In *Hewlett* [2016] EWCA Crim 673, the Court of Appeal held that Romany gypsies were capable of being recognized as a racial group. D's reference to his neighbour as a 'pikey' was capable of being seen as a pejorative reference to Romany gypsies, which meant that he had committed the offence.

[358] See *Pendragon v UK* (1999) 27 EHRR CD 179.

[359] *DPP v M* [2004] EWHC 1453 (Admin), [2005] Crim LR 392.

[360] *White* [2001] Crim LR 576, CA.   [361] [2007] UKHL 8.

[362] *DPP v Pal* [2000] Crim LR 756 per Simon Brown LJ. Cf *Johnson v DPP* [2008] EWHC 509 (Admin).

[363] *Dykes v DPP* [2008] EWHC 2775 (Admin).

membership of that race).[364] So, for example, the offence applies where other bases for hostility exist—because V has, for example, taken D's car parking space, etc. In relation to s 28(1)(a), it has been held that no subjective intent needs to be proved. It is not a question of D intending to express hostility; the test is objective and the Crown merely has to show the hostile behaviour.[365] As a matter of statutory interpretation, the key term in the section is that the hostility is '*based on*' V's race. By contrast, under s 28(1)(b) the motivation behind the behaviour has to be proved—that is a requirement expressed in the section.[366]

The parliamentary debates show that this broad interpretation of s 28(1)(a) was intended, since it was felt that proving a sole racial motive for the offence would be too difficult a task for the prosecution.[367] In consequence, s 28(1)(a) is extremely broad. Lord Monson in the debates on the Bill described the section as Orwellian in that it seeks to police people's emotions.[368] At present, only insults relating to religion and race are criminalized in this way. This highlights the arbitrariness of the legislation. In terms of broader social objectives of the legislation, the section may be regarded as a success if it deters individuals from using racist language in any context. Whether this will be the effect or whether those convicted will bear such resentment at the stigma as to become hardened in their racist attitudes is debatable.[369]

16.7.2.2 Racially/religiously motivated assaults: s 28(1)(b)

The s 28(1)(b) offence is much narrower and less controversial, being focused on the defendant's state of mind and one of his *motivations* for the crime being one of racial or religious hostility, although not necessarily against the victim in person. It provides an interesting example of an offence in which the motivations rather than intentions of the defendant become crucial in substantive criminal law, and not merely as a matter of evidence.

There must be evidence of racial or religious motivation for the offence. In *DPP v Howard*,[370] D chanted 'I'd rather be a Paki than a cop' at his neighbours who were white police officers. Charges were based on s 28(1)(b). The magistrates concluded that there was insufficient evidence on which they could be satisfied that the racially aggravated public order offence had been made out. They found that the evidence showed that D's hostility was

---

[364] Per Maurice Kay J in *Woods* [2002] EWHC 85 (Admin), [11]. See also *DPP v Green* [2004] All ER (D) 70 (May); *DPP v MacFarlane* [2002] All ER (D) 78 (Mar); *DPP v M* [2004] EWHC 1453 (Admin), [2005] Crim LR 392.

[365] See *Jones v Bedford and Mid Bedfordshire Magistrates' Court* [2010] EWHC 523 (Admin), the magistrates erred in applying the reasoning from s 28(1)(b) when dealing with a case that was charged under s 28(1)(a).

[366] See *Jones v Bedford and Mid Bedfordshire Magistrates' Court* [2010] EWHC 523 (Admin). Section 28(3) provides that it is irrelevant whether in a s 28(1)(a) case D's hostility is 'also' based to any extent on another factor besides his racism. Read literally, this suggests that the section does include an examination of whether D had some racialist intent in his hostility. On that interpretation, if D's hostility was exclusively based on non-racialist grounds, he would not be within the s 28(1)(a) offence. The decision in *Jones* precludes that argument.

[367] In *Pal* [2000] Crim LR 756, the Divisional Court accepted that the racial statement 'whiteman's arse licker' was not in itself sufficient to prove hostility based on racial grounds. Simon Brown LJ stated that he did 'not regard the fact that D would not have used such a term but for V's race as a *sine qua non* of the racial hostility'. His lordship did note that the use of racially abusive insults will 'ordinarily no doubt be found sufficient'. *Pal* has since been described as turning on its own facts. In *Rogers*, Baroness Hale suggests at [15] that the case might also have been disposed of by arguing that the racial hostility was based on the caretaker's association with whites. With respect, that argument was addressed by the Divisional Court at [12] and it is not clear that that alternative approach meets the problem—the argument could still be made that the basis for hostility was the ejection and V's conduct, not his race or affinity with members of other races.

[368] HL, 12 Feb 1998, col 1266.

[369] See generally E Burney and G Rose, *Racially Aggravated Offences: How is the Law Working?* (2002) HORS 244.

[370] [2008] EWHC 608 (Admin).

motivated *only* by his intense dislike of the neighbours and not even as a result of his intense dislike of the police. There was, they concluded, insufficient evidence to establish (even in part) that the reason why those words were shouted was hostility towards Pakistani people. The Divisional Court dismissed the prosecution appeal, concluding that the magistrates were entitled to come to the conclusion they did: there was an abundance of evidence that the *sole* motivation for D's chanting was his hostility toward the officers personally. Moses LJ suggested that:

prosecutors should be careful not to deploy [s 28(1)(b)] where offensive words have been used, but in themselves have not in any way been the motivation for the particular offence with which a defendant is charged. It diminishes the gravity of this offence to use it in circumstances where it is unnecessary to do so and where plainly it cannot be proved.[371]

It is a question of fact whether the motivation is found to be exclusively for non-racist reasons. Thus, in contrast to *Howard*, in *Kendall v DPP*[372] the magistrates were entitled to find that displaying posters of black men convicted of manslaughter with the title 'Illegal Immigrant Murder Scum' was evidence of motive even though D claimed that his purpose was to drum up support for the BNP.

Reform

The Law Commission has recommended that the offences could be extended to deal with hostility towards people on grounds of disability, sexual orientation and transgender identity. Definitions of those characteristics are based on the definitions in s 146 of the Criminal Justice Act 2003. The Commission's preferred recommendation is for a wider review to assess which if any characteristics ought to be protected by aggravated offences and which if any offences should be capable of being aggravated. The Commission also recommends a new Sentencing Council guideline to deal with hate crime and that the Police National Computer records any hostility-based sentence and whether it was an aggravated offence or a matter of sentencing uplift under ss 145 and 146 of the Criminal Justice Act 2003.[373]

16.8 Aggravated assaults

Assault forms the basis for a number of more serious offences based on attacks on specified classes of people or in particular circumstances—we can call these aggravated assaults. Three introductory points should be noted about this. First, a person cannot be convicted of an aggravated assault unless he is guilty of assault. Subject to what was said earlier relating to consents and assault, if D has a defence to the charge of assault, he is not guilty of the aggravated assault.

This proposition is not always understood. For example, in *Blackburn v Bowering*,[374] D was convicted of assaulting an officer of the court in the execution of his duty.[375] His defence was that he did not believe V was a bailiff—he thought he was using reasonable

---

[371] At [12]. Cf *Johnson v DPP* [2008] EWHC 509 (Admin).

[372] [2008] EWHC 1848 (Admin).

[373] For comment see C Bakalis, 'Legislating Against Hatred: The Law Commission's Report on Hate Crime' [2015] Crim LR 192. See also recently the work of M Walters et al, *Preventing Hate Crime* (2017).

[374] [1994] 3 All ER 380, CA (Civ Div). The appeal came to the Civil Division because the offence was in the nature of a contempt of court. Referred to by Lord Nicholls in *B v DPP* [2000] 2 AC 428 at 463: 'The Crown advanced no suggestion to your Lordships that any of these recent cases was wrongly decided. This is not surprising, because the reasoning in these cases is compelling.'

[375] Contrary to the County Courts Act 1984, s 14(1)(b). See LCCP 217, paras 2.139 et seq; LC 361 Ch 5.

force against a trespasser. D's mistake was as to the legal status of the victim. The trial judge ruled correctly that liability as to that element of the offence was strict,[376] but he held that D's mistaken belief was no defence, remarking on the 'extraordinary situation' if that could have been a defence to common assault. D's conviction was quashed. If D was not guilty of assault because he lacked mens rea owing to a mistake, he could not be guilty of the aggravated form of the offence of assault on an officer of the court. Liability is strict as regards the status of the person assaulted, but there must still be an assault.[377] If the assault had been proved—for example, if D had used force which was excessive even against a trespasser—it would have been no defence that he believed (even on reasonable grounds) that V was not an officer but a thug.

Secondly, this range of aggravated offences do not form a coherent scheme, let alone a nicely structured ladder of offences. Rather they form a motley collection which has evolved over time. Many of the offences are found within the OAPA 1861. Some of these were, no doubt, intended to deal with matters causing public concern at the time, and appear rather curious today. Thus, obstructing or assaulting a clergyman in the discharge of his duties in a place of worship or burial place, or who is on his way to or from such duties, is an offence triable either way, punishable on indictment with two years' imprisonment under s 36![378] Assaulting a magistrate or other person in the exercise of his duty concerning the preservation of a vessel in distress or a wreck is an offence punishable on indictment with seven years' imprisonment under s 37. Such provisions are rarely invoked in the modern day and need not be considered further, save to note that for some, the explicit labelling and differentiation between the offences by reference to the manner and circumstances in which they were caused reflects important moral distinctions that ought to be retained and replicated in a modern criminal code.[379]

Thirdly, these aggravated offences, including those considered in this chapter, represent some of the starkest examples of constructive crimes—those which do not respect the correspondence principle—that is, D may be convicted of an offence requiring proof of actus reus elements A *and* B even though he has mens rea relating only to element A.[380]

16.8.1 Assault with intent to resist arrest

By s 38 of the OAPA 1861:

Whosoever shall assault any person with intent to resist or prevent the lawful apprehension or detainer of himself or of any other person for any offence is guilty of an offence triable either way and punishable with two years' imprisonment.

It may be assumed that the section creates two offences, assault with intent and battery with intent. For each version, D must be shown to have committed all the elements of the assault/battery *and* that he intended to resist, etc. Thus, threatening the arrester (V) with a weapon

---

[376] Following *Forbes and Webb* (1865) 10 Cox CC 362 (assaulting constable). In this regard s 14 was rightly treated as akin to s 51 of the Police Act 1964 which has now replaced by s 89 of the Police Act 1996, p 704.

[377] See p 661. This offence is an example of 'constructive crime' because the mens rea of a lesser offence, common assault, must be proved.

[378] There was one reported instance of this offence in 2001, and one in 2002: HC Written Answer, 21 Nov 2005 (Hazel Blears). The number of prosecutions is miniscule: see the Law Commission Scoping Paper, para 2.148 and Ch 5.123.

[379] See J Horder, 'Rethinking Non-Fatal Offences Against the Person' (1994) 14 OJLS 335 arguing that the offences serve valuable labelling functions and Gardner (1994) 53 CLJ 500 arguing that they are valuable in terms of clarity. See LCCP 217, Ch 3; LC 361 Ch 5.

[380] Horder [1995] Crim LR 759; cf Mitchell [1999] Crim LR 195, and see references in n 250.

to make him let go of the arrestee would be the assault, poking him with it would be battery. Dragging the arrestee from V's grasp, being reckless whether this causes V to fall to the ground, will be a reckless battery with intent to resist arrest if V does fall. D has an intention to prevent 'apprehension' when he tries to prevent the arrest taking place, and an intention to prevent the 'detainer' when he tries to bring the arrest to an end. The section applies only where the arrest is 'for any offence'; so it does not apply to an arrest in civil process or for a breach of the peace not amounting to crime. It is immaterial whether the arrest is by a police officer or a citizen; but D's claim that he did not know the arrester was a plain-clothes officer may be crucial where his defence is that he believed he was being attacked by thugs.[381]

The intent must be to resist 'lawful' arrest.[382] It is important to distinguish between D's mistakes of fact and law. If D knows of the factual circumstances which make the arrest lawful, he probably has a sufficient intent even though he believes, on the circumstances known to him, the arrest to be unlawful: for example, having read in an out-of-date law book that conspiracy is not an arrestable offence, he resists arrest for conspiracy. The law of arrest is treated as part of the criminal law for this purpose[383] and his mistake or ignorance of criminal law is no defence.[384] D's honest and, indeed, true belief that he is not, in fact, guilty of any offence is not per se a defence: the arrest may be lawful because the arrester has reasonable grounds for suspicion. But, if D makes a mistake of fact he should be judged on the circumstances as he believed them to be—in accordance with general principle. If D believes the arrester has no reasonable grounds to suspect that D is guilty, and D believes that the arrester knows he has no such grounds,—matters of fact—D should be acquitted if he resists. Whatever the true facts, D does not *intend* to resist *lawful* arrest. It may be that the principle of *Fennell*[385] leaves D liable for common assault or battery but it would be wrong in principle to convict him of the aggravated offence when mens rea with respect to the aggravating factor is not proved.

16.8.2 Assault on, resistance to, or obstruction of constables

By s 89 of the Police Act 1996:

(1) Any person who assaults a constable in the execution of his duty, or a person assisting a constable in the execution of his duty, shall be guilty of an offence and liable on summary conviction to [an unlimited] fine or to imprisonment for a term not exceeding six months or to both.

(2) Any person who resists or wilfully obstructs a constable in the execution of his duty, or a person assisting a constable in the execution of his duty, shall be guilty of an offence and liable on summary conviction to imprisonment for a term not exceeding one month or to a fine not exceeding level 3 on the standard scale, or to both.[386]

---

[381] *Brightling* [1991] Crim LR 364, CA; *Blackburn v Bowering*, p 702.

[382] *Lee* [2001] 1 Cr App R 293, CA, and see commentary at [2001] Crim LR 991. 'Whether or not an offence has actually been committed or is believed by the defendant not to have been committed is irrelevant', per Rose LJ.

[383] cf cl 25(2)(b) of the Code Team's Draft Code (LC 143), a provision not included in the Law Commission's draft (LC 177).

[384] Talfourd J put his decision on this ground in *Bentley* (1850) 4 Cox CC 406. See more recently *Hewitt v DPP* [2002] EWHC 2801 (Admin).

[385] [1971] 1 QB 428. Cf *Ball* (1989) 90 Cr App R 378, [1978] Crim LR 580. See the quashing of the conviction in *McKoy* [2002] EWCA Crim 1628.

[386] See LCCP 217, paras 2.139 and 2.145 on the volume of offending. See the Sentencing Council's revised Magistrates' Court Sentencing Guidelines (in force 24 Apr 2017) in respect of the sentencing of offenders aged 18 and older who are sentenced on or after 24 Apr 2017 in relation to s 89(2) of the Police Act 1996.

Though the section is headed 'Assaults on Constables', it contains three crimes, only one of which necessarily amounts to an assault. Resistance to a constable may occur without an assault, as where D has been arrested by V and D tears himself from V's grasp and escapes.[387] Obstruction, as explained later, includes many situations which do not amount to an assault. On the other hand, both resistance and obstruction clearly may include assaults. The nature of assault and resistance requires no further consideration but obstruction presents problems and is examined in some detail later.

Common to all three crimes is the requirement that the constable[388] is acting in the course of his duty. But the mens rea of assault and resistance, on the one hand, and obstruction on the other require separate consideration.

16.8.2.1 A constable acting in the execution of his duty

Identifying whether a police officer[389] is acting in the course of his duty is a question which can give rise to difficult problems.[390] There are numerous examples of an officer's action falling on the wrong side of the line, taking him outside his duty such that when he is assaulted this offence is not committed.[391] Police officers have no power to detain a person (in ways that go beyond levels of conduct that would be acceptable from any ordinary member of the public). If an officer does so, even briefly, without intending to exercise the power of arrest, the detention is a false arrest and amounts to false imprisonment.[392] A constable directing a motorist to leave the road to take part in a traffic census, before there was a statutory power to do so,[393] was not acting in the execution of his duty since his right at common law to regulate traffic derives only from his duty to protect life and property.[394] A constable who restrained D under the mistaken belief that D had been lawfully arrested by another officer was held not to be acting in the execution of his duty.[395]

Caution is required when interpreting the word duty. There are many things which a constable on duty may do (eg rescuing a stranded cat or helping to deliver a baby)[396] which he is probably not under any 'duty' in the strict sense to do; that is, he would commit no crime or

---

387 *Sheriff* [1969] Crim LR 260.

388 ie a person holding the *office*, not the rank of constable. A prison officer acting as such is a constable for this purpose: Prison Act 1952, s 8 see also the extended power in s 8A (but immigration detention centre officials are not constables—*Yarl's Wood Immigration v Bedfordshire Police Authority* [2008] EWHC 2207 (Admin)). It is also an offence to assault a member of other police-related agencies such as the NCA.

389 On the duties of the police, see the discussion in S Bailey, D Harris and N Taylor, *Civil Liberties, Cases and Materials* (6th edn, 2009) at Ch 4(2). See also *Metropolitan Police Comr, ex p Blackburn* [1968] 2 QB 118 CA, and *(No 3)* [1973] QB 241 CA; K Lidstone, 'A Policeman's Duty Not to Take Liberties' [1976] Crim LR 617; U Ross, 'Two Cases on Obstructing a Constable' [1977] Crim LR 187.

390 It is for the prosecution to prove: *R (Ahmad) v Bradford MC* [2008] EWHC 2934 (Admin).

391 For a recent example, see *Ahmed v CPS* (2017) 4 May, unreported, QBD (Admin), in which the injunction and power of arrest had erroneously cited repealed statutory provisions.

392 In *Walker v MPC* [2014] EWCA Civ 897, it was held that if a police officer detains a person in a way that goes beyond what would be considered acceptable conduct by a member of the public, then the police officer is committing false imprisonment unless he is exercising the power of arrest. The court granted the claimant nominal damages of £5 on the basis that since in *Bird v Jones* (1845) 7 QB 742 the law has deemed it unacceptable for an ordinary citizen to interfere with another citizen's liberty by confining him in a doorway, no matter how short the period of time might be.

393 See now the Road Traffic Act 1988, s 35 as amended.

394 *Hoffman v Thomas* [1974] 2 All ER 233, DC. In the pursuance of that duty, a constable may require a motorist to disobey a traffic regulation: *Johnson v Phillips* [1975] 3 All ER 682, DC; and remove a vehicle to the police station when the driver is arrested; *Liepins v Spearman* [1985] Crim LR 229. Cf *Saunders* [1978] Crim LR 98 (Judge Heald) and commentary.

395 *Kerr v DPP* [1995] Crim LR 394.

396 Or assisting a landlord to expel drunk and disorderly people under the Licensing Act 2003, s 143(4) (see *Semple v DPP* [2009] EWHC 3241 (Admin)).

tort or even breach of police regulations by not doing it. In *Coffin v Smith*,[397] the Divisional Court held that a constable could be in the execution of his duty for the purposes of this section even if he was doing something that he was not obliged to do.[398] Officers, who had been summoned to a club to ensure that certain people left, were assaulted. It was held that the officers were there in fulfilment of their duty to keep the peace and were plainly acting in the execution of their duty. But duty surely cannot be equated with being 'on duty'.

A constable may be acting in the execution of his duty by being present, and by intervening when a breach of the peace occurs or is imminent, but acting outside his duty if he takes it upon himself to expel a trespasser.[399] In a leading case, *Waterfield*,[400] the Court of Criminal Appeal provided welcome clarification:

> it would be difficult, and in the present case it is unnecessary, to reduce within specific limits the general terms in which the duties of police constables have been expressed. In most cases it is probably more convenient to consider what the police constable was actually doing and in particular whether such conduct was *prima facie* an unlawful interference with a person's liberty or property. If so, it is then relevant to consider whether (a) such conduct falls within the general scope of any duty imposed by statute or recognized at common law and (b) whether such conduct, albeit within the general scope of such a duty, involved an unjustifiable use of powers associated with the duty.

If the police officer's conduct falls within the general scope of the 'duty' to prevent crime and to bring offenders to justice, then it would seem to be within the protection of the statute, if it was lawful. The officer may ask questions of individuals whom he suspects to be involved in offending.[401]

If, in the course of carrying out his duty to prevent crime and to bring offenders to justice, the officer exceeds his powers, then he is no longer acting in the execution of his duty for this purpose.[402]

Where the charge against D is that he assaulted or obstructed etc a police officer, V, in the execution of his duty and the assault etc occurred in the course of V performing an arrest for a criminal offence, the fact that the offence for which the officer was effecting an arrest is subsequently not prosecuted to conviction does not mean that V was not acting in the execution of his duty.[403] However, where the constable has not arrested D and uses violence on D, D's resistance will not be an offence even if the constable would have been empowered to arrest D in the first place.[404]

Where D is arrested or detained by an officer unlawfully, for example where the officer has not used words of arrest or told D the grounds of arrest, the officer is not acting in the execution of his duty.[405] In such a case, D cannot be liable for resisting other officers in the

---

[397] (1980) 71 Cr App R 221. Cf the approval of Sedley LJ in *Porter v MPC* (1999) 20 Nov, unreported, CA (Civ).

[398] The court doubted older cases: *Prebble* (1858) 1 F & F 325 and *Roxburgh* (1871) 12 Cox CC 8. See also *Betts v Stevens* [1910] 1 KB 1 and the 4th edition of this book, at pp 361–372. *Prebble* may be distinguishable as a case where the officer was doing no more than assist a citizen in the enforcement of private rights.

[399] In *Chief Constable of Devon and Cornwall, ex p Central Electricity Generating Board* [1982] QB 458. On the police powers to prevent breach of the peace, see also P Thornton et al, *The Law of Public Order and Protest* (2010) paras 6.125 et seq.

[400] [1964] 1 QB 164 at 170.

[401] *Sekfali v DPP* [2006] EWHC 894 (Admin); cf *D v DPP* [2010] EWHC 3400 (Admin) dealing with powers of a PCSO.

[402] *Ludlow v Burgess* [1971] Crim LR 238, CA; *Pedro v Diss* (1981) 72 Cr App R 193.

[403] *Burrell v DPP* [2005] EWHC 786 (Admin).   [404] *Wood v DPP* [2008] EWHC 1056 (Admin).

[405] cf *Saliu v DPP* [2005] EWHC 2689 (Admin), D assaulted PC who had yet to arrest. See also *Sobczak v DPP* [2012] EWHC 1319 (Admin), [2013] Crim LR 516 in which the officer failed to follow s 2 of PACE by not informing D of his name, police station, the object of the search and the grounds for making it. The police officer was, however, attempting to remove B's leg from the jaws of a police dog. For that reason it was held that the police officer was acting in the exercise of his duty and D's conviction was therefore upheld.

execution of their duty when they are merely assisting the unlawful arrest.[406] A constable who is not acting in the execution of his duty because he is a trespasser begins to act in the execution of his duty as soon as circumstances justifying his presence arise—as where he reasonably apprehends a breach of the peace. He does not have to leave the premises and re-enter.[407] Even if an officer is not acting in the execution of his duty, for example where he is trespassing, the conduct of the defendant might nevertheless constitute a simple assault.[408]

Importantly, the Divisional Court in *Oraki v DPP*[409] confirmed that the defences of self-defence and defence of another person are, as a matter of law, available in relation to the offence of obstructing a constable in the execution of his duty contrary to s 89(2) of the 1996 Act.

16.8.2.2 Trivial touchings by officers

A police officer investigating crime is entitled to speak to any person from whom he thinks useful information can be obtained, even though that person declares that he is unwilling to reply,[410] but the officer has no power to detain for questioning so the use of reasonable force to escape from such detention is not an assault;[411] (it may be obstructing[412]) and the use of excessive force, while it may be a common assault (or wounding, etc) would not be an offence under s 89.

Where the question is whether something is trivial or *de minimis*, it is perhaps to be expected that assessments will differ. In *C v DPP*,[413] the officer's taking hold of a 14-year-old girl's arm to escort her home when she was reported missing by her parents was not in the exercise of his duty and hence her boyfriend was not guilty of assaulting the officer in the execution of his duty.

Officer preventing breach of peace

Probably the most important application of s 89 is in the context of the constable's duty to prevent breaches of the peace which he reasonably apprehends.[414] That power is one which must be scrutinized with the utmost care since it allows an officer (and indeed a civilian) to restrain or arrest D where D has not committed, and is perhaps not even about to commit, a crime. The House of Lords confirmed that a power to arrest or take less intrusive action arises where: (a) a breach of the peace has been committed; or (b) a breach has occurred and a further breach is threatened; or (c) the officer reasonably believes that a breach will be committed imminently. If an officer reasonably believes one of the above three circumstances pertains, he is under a duty to take such steps, whether by arrest or otherwise,[415] as he reasonably thinks are necessary.[416] Where a reasonable apprehension of an imminent breach of the peace exists, the preventive action taken must be reasonable and proportionate; and there is no power to take action short of an arrest when a breach of the peace is not so imminent as would be necessary to justify arrest.[417]

---

[406] *Cumberbatch v CPS* [2009] EWHC 3353 (Admin).   [407] *Lamb* [1990] Crim LR 58, DC.

[408] See eg *Syed v DPP* [2010] EWHC 81 (Admin).

[409] [2018] EWHC 115 (Admin). See also *Wheeldon v CPS* [2018] EWHC 249 (Admin). For further discussion, see p 402. See also E Cape [2018] Crim LR 388.

[410] Code of Practice A, code issued under the Police and Criminal Evidence Act (1984); *Weight v Long* [1986] Crim LR 746. See also *Sekfali*, p 710.

[411] *Kenlin v Gardner* [1967] 2 QB 510; *Ludlow v Burgess* [1971] Crim LR 238; *Lemsatef* [1977] 1 WLR 812. Cf *Daniel v Morrison* (1980) 70 Cr App R 142, DC.

[412] See *Sekfali*, p 710.   [413] [2003] All ER (D) 37 (Nov).

[414] *Duncan v Jones* [1936] 1 KB 218.

[415] *King v Hodges* [1974] Crim LR 424; *Blench v DPP* [2004] All ER (D) 86 (Nov). The requirement for an 'imminent' breach of the peace was interpreted very widely in *Wragg v DPP* [2005] EWHC 1389 (Admin).

[416] *Piddington v Bates* [1960] 3 All ER 660.

[417] *R (Laporte) v Chief Constable of Gloucestershire* [2007] 2 WLR 46, HL.

The most difficult cases are likely to be those in which the police seek to intervene to prevent conduct which is not objectively violent nor provocative to others but which may amount to a breach of the peace. In *Laporte*, Lord Rodger observed that:

Sometimes lawful and proper conduct by A may be liable to result in a violent reaction from B, even though it is not directed against B. If B's resort to violence can be regarded as the natural consequence of A's conduct, and there is no other way of preserving the peace, a police officer may order A to desist from his conduct, even though it is lawful. If A refuses he may be arrested for obstructing a police officer in the execution of his duty.[418]

Even where no breach of the peace is anticipated, a constable may be under some other duty to give instructions to members of the public—for example, to remove an obstruction from the highway[419]—and a deliberate refusal to obey such an instruction may amount to an obstruction of the police.

A constable who makes a lawful arrest is acting in the execution of his duty even though the arrest subsequently becomes unlawful when he fails to communicate the ground to the arrestee.[420]

16.8.2.3 Mens rea in cases of assault and resistance

The only mens rea required in the case of an allegation of assaulting a constable is the mens rea for assault or battery. In a case of resisting, the mens rea is an intention to resist. A reckless battery might be inflicted by hitting or flailing arms or legs around at arresting officers or even by biting, as where D uses his teeth to try to snatch something from the hand of the officer restraining him, being aware that he might make contact with the officer's hand in the process.[421]

There is no requirement to prove that D knew that the person he was assaulting was a police officer, still less that V was on duty. Liability in relation to the status of the arrester and whether the constable was in the execution of his duty is strict. Although the original authority for this was a ruling by a recorder in a direction to a jury in *Forbes and Webb*,[422] this has now been repeatedly accepted.[423] It is submitted that a better view[424] is that D should only be liable if he was at least reckless as to whether V was a police officer in the execution of his duty when he committed the assault.[425] Such a view avoids any difficulty arising from the fact that s 36[426] of the 1861 Act used the words 'to the knowledge of the offender', whereas no such words were used in s 38 or its successors. Nevertheless, the present English law is that laid down in *Forbes*. This is implicit in *McBride v Turnock*,[427] where D struck at O, who was not a constable, and hit V, who was. Although he had no

---

[418] At [78]. See *R (Moos) v MPC* [2012] EWCA Civ 12.

[419] It is in the course of a constable's duty to require pickets to move where they would otherwise obstruct lawful passage on the highway by others; *Kavanagh v Hiscock* [1974] QB 600, CA, applying *Broome v DPP* [1974] AC 587, HL. See also *Austin v MPC*, text accompanying n 524.

[420] *DPP v Hawkins* [1988] 3 All ER 673, [1988] Crim LR 741.

[421] *DPP v D* [2005] EWHC 967 (Admin).

[422] (1865) 10 Cox CC 362, applying s 38 of the OAPA 1861.

[423] in *Prince* (1875) LR 2 CCR 154 (six judges accepted it as correct); *Maxwell* (1909) 73 JP 176, (1909) 2 Cr App R 26; *Mark* [1961] Crim LR 173 (Judge Maxwell Turner). See also *Blackburn v Bowering*, p 702. See F Fairweather and S Levy, 'Assaults on the Police: A Case of Mistaken Identity' [1994] Crim LR 817.

[424] See the dissenting judges in *Reynhoudt* (1962) 36 ALJR 26.

[425] This was the view of the majority of the court in *Galvin (No 2)* [1961] VR 740, overruling *Galvin (No 1)* [1961] VR 733. Barry J thought actual knowledge necessary. Scholl J adhered to his view in *Galvin (No 1)* that the offence was one of strict liability. See also *McLeod* (1954) 111 CCC 106.

[426] See p 703.

[427] [1964] Crim LR 456, DC. This was also assumed to be the law in *Blackburn v Bowering*, p 702.

intention of assaulting V, the Divisional Court held that he was guilty of assaulting a constable in the execution of his duty. The mens rea for this crime being only that of a common assault/battery, D's 'malice' was transferable.[428] No better illustration could be given of the unsatisfactory nature of strict liability in this context. Following the landmark decisions of the House of Lords in *DPP v B*[429] and *R v K*,[430] it is arguable that this approach deserves reconsideration.[431]

If D is unaware (whether reasonably or not) that V is a constable and believes in the existence of circumstances of justification or excuse for his use of force, he should be acquitted:[432] he will not intend or be reckless as to an *unlawful* assault. If, however, D knows that V is a constable, it seems that a mistaken belief—even an honest and reasonable belief—that the constable is acting outside the course of his duty will not always be a defence. In *Fennell*,[433] the court assumed that a father might lawfully use reasonable force to free his son from unlawful arrest by the police; but he acted at his peril and, if the arrest proved to be lawful, he was guilty.

16.8.2.4 Wilful obstruction

The meaning of obstruction

There must be obstruction in fact. If D does an act with intent to obstruct but which fails to do so he commits no offence—and it cannot be an attempt.[434] A wide interpretation of 'obstruction' has been accepted in England.[435] It is not necessary that there should be any interference with the officer himself by physical force or threats.

Where the police tell an offender to desist from an offence, his deliberate refusal may amount to an obstruction, as where D is obstructing the highway and refuses to obey the instructions of a constable to move.[436] It is not necessary that the constable should anticipate a breach of the peace. But a constable has no power to arrest D for obstructing him, unless the obstruction was such that it actually caused, or was likely to cause, a breach of the peace.[437]

Equally, to give a warning to a person who *has* committed a crime so as to enable him to escape detection by police is enough. Thus, in *Betts v Stevens*,[438] D committed the offence by warning drivers who were exceeding the speed limit that there was a police trap ahead. *Hinchliffe v Sheldon*[439] might be thought to go further than *Betts v Stevens* in that it was only *suspected*, and not proved, that an offence was being committed; but there the warning was tantamount to a physical obstruction.[440] D, a publican's son, shouted a warning to his parents that the police were outside the public house. It was 11.17 pm and the lights were on in the bar, so presumably the police suspected that liquor was being consumed after hours. There was a delay of eight minutes before the police were admitted and no offence was detected.

---

428 See p 122.   429 [2000] 2 AC 428, see Ch 5.   430 *K* [2002] 1 AC 462, see Ch 5.

431 See also the criticism in LCCP 217, paras 5.123 et seq.

432 *Gladstone Williams* (1984) 78 Cr App R 276, p 383. *Mark*, n 423, requiring reasonable grounds for the belief, can no longer be regarded as good law.

433 [1971] 1 QB 428, [1970] Crim LR 581 and commentary, CA; and cf *Ball* (1989) 90 Cr App R 378, [1989] Crim LR 579 and commentary.

434 Because it is triable only summarily. Cf *Bennett v Bale* [1986] Crim LR 404, DC and commentary.

435 See for an historical account, J Coutts, 'Obstructing the Police' (1956) 19 MLR 411.

436 *Tynan v Balmer* [1967] 1 QB 91; *Donaldson v Police* [1968] NZLR 32.

437 *Wershof v Metropolitan Police Comr* [1978] 3 All ER 540 (May J); *Gelberg v Miller* [1961] 1 WLR 153; *Riley v DPP* [1990] Crim LR 422, DC.

438 [1910] 1 KB 1.   439 [1955] 3 All ER 406, [1955] 1 WLR 1207.

440 See Coutts (1956) 19 MLR 411.

The police had a right to enter under statute[441] whether an offence was being committed or not; an entry under this statutory right was in execution of their duty; and their *entry* was obstructed. Lord Goddard CJ defined 'obstructing' as 'Making it more difficult for the police to carry out their duties.'[442] This is far wider than was necessary for the decision.

Where defendants warn individuals who *are about to commit* offences, the courts have had difficulties. In *Green v Moore*,[443] the distinction was drawn between advising a person to *suspend* his criminal activity, so that he will not be found out by the police (warning motorists so they do not speed until past the speed trap), which is an offence; and advising him to give it up altogether (ie never speed again)—in which case he will not be found out by the police—which is not an offence.[444]

Presumably it must be proved that some named officer was obstructed;[445] it would hardly be enough that D warned E in general terms that if he did not stop committing an offence he would be found out.

Obstructing by not assisting

Lord Goddard CJ's *dictum* defining 'obstructing' as 'Making it more difficult for the police to carry out their duties'[446] goes too far. Surely a solicitor who advises his client to say nothing cannot be guilty of an offence, though he undoubtedly makes things more difficult for the police; and why should a solicitor be in a different situation from anyone else? The fact that the refusal is expressed in abusive and obscene terms should, in principle, make no difference.[447] If D's language amounts to some other offence, such as that under s 4 of the Public Order Act 1986,[448] he should be charged with that.

It has been held that refusal to answer a constable's question, though it undoubtedly makes it more difficult for the police to carry out their duties, does not amount to wilful obstruction: *Rice v Connolly*.[449] However, where there is more than a mere refusal the offence may be committed. In *Sekfali v DPP*,[450] police officers approached the defendants who had been acting suspiciously. The officers identified themselves as such whereupon the defendants all ran off. They were convicted of wilfully obstructing police officers in the execution of their duty. The Divisional Court held that the police officers were entitled in the execution of their duty to approach the men and ask questions. The court confirmed that a citizen has no legal duty to assist the police, whilst noting that most people would accept that they have a moral and social duty to do so. The court then went on:

section 89(2) makes it an offence to willfully obstruct a police officer in the execution of his duty. The appellants would have been entitled to remain silent and not answer any questions put to them. They could have refused, if they had not been arrested, to accompany the police to any particular place to which they might have been requested by the police to go. They could have said that they had no intention of answering questions and they could, no doubt, have said that as a result they were intent on going on their way and have done so without giving rise to a case which would entitle the court to conclude that in departing they were intending to impede the police officers and

---

[441] See now Licensing Act 2003, s 180(1).   [442] [1955] 3 All ER 406 at 408.

[443] [1982] QB 1044. Cf *Moore v Green* [1983] 1 All ER 663, DC. Explaining *Bastable v Little* [1907] 1 KB 59. See also *DPP v Glendinning* [2005] EWHC 2333 (Admin), holding that warning motorists of a speed trap was not necessarily sufficient to amount to the offence of obstructing a police officer in the execution of his duty unless the drivers being warned were speeding or were likely to be speeding. How fine a line is that? How will anyone know if they are likely to be?

[444] What then of the maps and apps published of all speed camera sites, or the devices which warn motorists as they approach a speed trap?

[445] *Syce v Harrison* [1981] Crim LR 110n.   [446] [1955] 3 All ER 406 at 408.

[447] See Marshall J in *Rice v Connolly* at 420.   [448] See Ch 31.

[449] [1966] 2 QB 414, DC.   [450] [2006] EWHC 894 (Admin).

obstruct the police officers in the execution of their duty. Had they responded in that way, then it would have been for the police to have decided whether to arrest them; but they ran off, as the magistrates found to avoid apprehension. That being a wilful act, taken so as to obstruct the police, was an act capable of constituting an offence contrary to section 89(2).

Telling the police a false story is also quite different from merely remaining silent and is clearly an obstruction.[451] Refusing to reveal the whereabouts of a prohibited drug is not an obstruction; but burying it to hide it from an officer searching for it might be, when the officer's task is made more difficult.[452] These difficulties would not arise if the Act had been held to be limited to physical interference; and it has been held[453] to be so limited in Scotland where 'obstruct' has been construed *ejusdem generis* with 'assault' and 'resist'.[454] D was held not guilty when he told lies to the police to conceal an offence of which he was guilty. There is much to be said in favour of the Scottish view.[455]

Lawful acts as obstruction?

It is not necessary that the act relied on as an obstruction should be unlawful independently of its operation as an obstruction of the police.[456] The conferment of powers and imposition of duties on the police may, impliedly, impose duties on others not to impede the exercise by the police of these powers and duties: the right of a constable to enter licensed premises where he believes an offence might be committed imposes an obligation on the licensee and others to let him in;[457] the right to conduct a lawful search of premises;[458] the right of a constable to require a driver in certain circumstances to provide a specimen of breath[459] implies a duty on the motorist (though he has not been arrested) to remain 'there or nearby' until the constable has had a reasonable opportunity to carry out the test.[460] If, when D is found to have consumed an excess of alcohol, it is the duty of a constable to remove D's car from the highway, there is an implied duty on D to hand over the keys of the car.[461]

Whether a duty thus to cooperate with the police is to be implied depends on whether this is a compelling inference from the nature of the police duty or right. To some extent it is a question of policy—so, the courts have held there is no duty to answer police questions but there is a duty not to give misleading answers.[462] Whether D's conduct is an act rather than an omission is only one factor in determining whether there is an obstruction. Omissions may amount to obstruction even when the omission is not an offence independently of s 89.[463] There is a separate common law offence of refusing to aid a constable who is attempting to prevent or to quell a breach of the peace and who calls for assistance.[464]

Mens rea for obstruction

Unlike 'assault' and 'resist', if D is charged with 'obstruction', it must be proved that that was 'wilful'. D must intend to behave in such a way as to make it more difficult for the police to

---

[451] *Rice v Connolly*, n 449; *Mathews v Dwan* [1949] NZLR 1037.

[452] See note on *Syce v Harrison* [1981] Crim LR 110.

[453] *Curlett v M'Kechnie* 1938 JC 176.

[454] The rearrangement of these offences by the Police Act precludes the application of the *ejusdem generis* rule; but it could have been applied when they were contained in the OAPA 1861.

[455] See Coutts (1956) 19 MLR 411.

[456] *Dibble v Ingleton* [1972] 1 QB 480. See G Williams, 'Criminal Law—The Duty Not To Obstruct Your Own Conviction' (1972) 30 CLJ 193.

[457] Licensing Act 2003, s 180.   [458] *Sykes v CPS (Manchester)* [2013] EWHC 3600 (Admin).

[459] Road Traffic Act 1988, s 7.   [460] *DPP v Carey* [1970] AC 1072 at 1097.

[461] *Stunt v Bolton* [1972] RTR 435, [1972] Crim LR 561.

[462] *Rice v Connolly*, n 449.   [463] eg *Stunt v Bolton*, n 461. Cf *Dibble v Ingleton*, n 456.

[464] *Waugh* (1976) The Times, 1 Oct 1976.

carry out their duties. His conduct need be neither hostile to, nor aimed at, the police, as some cases have suggested.[465] So, in *Lewis v Cox*[466] where D persisted in opening the door of a van in which X, who had been arrested, was about to be driven away, D's purpose was not to obstruct the police but to find out where X was being taken, but, since he must have known that he was preventing the police officer from driving off, the justices were bound to find that he intended to make it more difficult for them to carry out their duty.[467]

In *Rice v Connolly*,[468] it was said that 'wilfully' means not only 'intentionally' but also 'without lawful excuse'. This is difficult to follow. 'Wilfully' must surely refer to the state of mind of the defendant. But whether he has a lawful excuse for what he does generally depends on D's conduct and the circumstances in which he acts.[469] In that case, D would have been no more 'wilful' if he had told a false story. The difference seems to lie in the conduct which the court considers to be permissible. 'Wilfully' may of course import the absence of any *belief* on D's part of circumstances of lawful excuse. If the story told by D were in fact false, but D believed it to be true, the constable might be obstructed, but he would not be 'wilfully' obstructed.

As to mistakes about the status of the officer, in cases of obstruction, liability is not strict. In *Ostler v Elliott*,[470] it was held that D's reasonable belief that the police officers were robbers was a defence to wilful obstruction. Now, since the decision in *Gladstone Williams*,[471] it is sufficient that the mistaken belief was genuinely held even if it was unreasonable.

Note also the summary offence of obstructing without reasonable excuse an emergency worker—fire and rescue personnel, paramedics, lifeboat crew, etc—under the Emergency Workers (Obstruction) Act 2006. By s 1(3), a person is responding to emergency circumstances if the person: (a) is going anywhere for the purpose of dealing with emergency circumstances occurring there; or (b) is dealing with emergency circumstances or preparing to do so. Emergency is defined in s 1(4).[472]

16.9 Ill-treatment or neglect

Section 44 of the Mental Capacity Act 2005, which has been in force since 1 April 2007, creates the offences of ill-treatment and wilful neglect.[473] On summary conviction, D is liable to imprisonment for a term not exceeding 12 months or a fine not exceeding the statutory maximum, or both. On conviction on indictment, D may be imprisoned for a term not exceeding five years or a fine or both. As is evident, the offence can be committed if D either ill-treats P or wilfully neglects P.[474] In *Turbill*,[475] the Court of Appeal held that 'wilful' denotes a subjective state of mind, but it is not equivalent to subjective recklessness. It is respectfully submitted that 'wilful' is now generally accepted to mean intention or subjective recklessness.[476]

---

[465] *Willmott v Atack* [1977] QB 498; *Hills v Ellis* [1983] QB 680.

[466] [1985] QB 509, [1984] 3 All ER 672.   [467] cf the discussion of intention, p 90.

[468] See p 710.   [469] See comment at [1966] Crim LR 390.

[470] [1980] Crim LR 584. Note that, if he had assaulted the officers, his reasonable belief that they were not officers would not, in itself, have been a defence to a charge of assaulting them in the execution of their duty. See commentary at [1980] Crim LR 585.

[471] [1987] 78 Cr App R 276, CA, p 383.

[472] The offence can include eg making hoax calls: *McMenemy* [2009] EWCA Crim 42.

[473] See A Brammer, 'Carers and the Mental Capacity Act 2005: Angels Permitted, Devils Prosecuted?' [2014] Crim LR 589 evaluating whether the offence adds to the pre-existing legal framework.

[474] It was confirmed in *Nursing* [2012] EWCA Crim 2521 that the section creates two separate offences.

[475] [2013] EWCA Crim 1422.

[476] See the further discussion at Ch 3 and the case comment at [2014] Crim LR 388.

Section 20 of the Criminal Justice and Courts Act 2015 creates a new offence for care workers who ill-treat or wilfully neglect those in their care. By s 21, corporate or unincorporated care providers may be liable for negligence or neglect in the way their activities are organized which amounts to a gross breach of a duty of care owed to the individual receiving care.[477]

The offence in s 44 is only made out if D has care of a person who lacks, or whom D reasonably believes lacks, capacity. It is important to point out that lack of capacity is defined by reference to ss 2 and 3 of the 2005 Act. These provide a complex series of tests that purport to define the circumstances in which an individual is to be treated as if he is unable to make decisions for himself.[478] The Lord Chief Justice, in *Nursing*, held that s 44 does not create an absolute offence and that 'actions or omissions, or a combination of both, which reflect or are believed to reflect the protected autonomy of the individual needing care do not constitute wilful neglect'.[479]

16.10 Administering poison

Sections 23 and 24 of the OAPA 1861 create offences, punishable with ten and five years' imprisonment respectively, with a similar actus reus.

16.10.1 Section 23

The section (as amended) provides:

Whosoever shall unlawfully and maliciously administer to or cause to be administered to or taken by any other person any poison or other destructive or noxious thing, so as thereby to endanger the life of such person, or so as thereby to inflict upon such person any grievous bodily harm, shall be guilty of [an offence] and being convicted thereof shall be liable…to [imprisonment] for any term not exceeding ten years…

By s 25, a person charged under s 23 may be convicted of an offence under s 24.[480]

16.10.1.1 Actus reus

Administer, cause to be administered, cause to be taken

Lord Bingham described s 23 as providing three distinct offences: (a) administering a noxious thing to any other person; (b) causing a noxious thing to be administered to any other person; and (c) causing a noxious thing to be taken by any other person. His lordship explained:

Offence (1) is committed where D administers the noxious thing directly to V, as by injecting V with the noxious thing, holding a glass containing the noxious thing to V's lips, spraying V with acid or corrosive substances, or (as in *R v Gillard*[481]) spraying the noxious thing in V's face. Offence (2) is typically committed where D does not directly administer the noxious thing to V but causes

---

[477] For detailed discussion of these offences, see K Laird, 'Filling a Lacuna: The Care Worker and Care Provider Offences in the Criminal Justice and Courts Act 2015' (2016) 36 Stat LR 1.

[478] See *A* [2014] EWCA Crim 299.

[479] [2012] EWCA Crim 2521, [18].

[480] See generally LCCP 217, paras 2.189 et seq and LC 361, Ch 7.

[481] *Gillard* (1988) 87 Cr App R 189. See also *Cronin-Simpson* [2000] 1 Cr App R (S) 54, D surreptitiously pouring petrol into neighbour's house through loft pipe; *Potter* [2005] EWCA Crim 3050—splashing petrol on V and threatening to ignite (surely better charged as a threat to kill?).

an innocent third party TP to administer it to V. If D, knowing a syringe to be filled with poison instructs TP to inject V, TP believing the syringe to contain a legitimate therapeutic substance, D would commit this offence. Offence (3) covers the situation where the noxious thing is not administered to V but taken by him, provided D causes the noxious thing to be taken by V and V does not make a voluntary and informed decision to take it. If D puts a noxious thing in food which V is about to eat and V, ignorant of the presence of the noxious thing, eats it, D commits offence (3).[482]

The words 'administer' and 'take' are to be construed by the court and not left as a question of fact to the jury.[483] The words are disjunctive. 'Takes' assumes some 'ingestion' by the victim. It seems that the thing is not 'administered' until it is taken into the body.[484] To leave the poison, intending it to be taken by an unwitting victim, may be an attempt to administer it.[485] There is no requirement that the 'administration' under s 23 involves surreptitious conduct.[486]

In *Kennedy*,[487] D handed to V a syringe containing heroin with which V injected himself and, in consequence, died. At his trial he was convicted of manslaughter. The Court of Appeal said, *obiter*, that it could see no reason why D should not have been convicted of an offence under s 23. There is a very good reason, simply that D did not administer the thing to V or cause V to take it. V, a person of full age and capacity, not labouring under any mistake, administered it to himself. Such an act breaks the chain of causation. After seemingly returning to orthodoxy in *Dias*, the Court of Appeal again returned to this revolutionary approach to causation in *Rogers*,[488] and *Finlay*.[489] In *Kennedy (No 2)*,[490] the House of Lords finally laid this heresy to rest. Where D hands V a syringe with which V injects himself, there is no administering by D. Nor is it possible to say that D is jointly responsible or jointly engaged in administering the heroin.[491] In *Kennedy (No 2)*, the House of Lords also rejected the approach of the Court of Appeal in *Finlay* which had adopted the *Empress* approach to causation. Since V has voluntarily taken the decision to inject himself, his free, informed act breaks the chain of causation. It is different if D secretly puts the noxious thing into V's drink and V consumes it. V's consumption is then not a fully voluntary act—he believes he is drinking nothing but, say, coffee and has no intention to take the noxious thing. D has then 'administered' it to him or caused him to take it.[492]

Noxious

Some substances are noxious per se, as, for example, with radioactive isotope polonium-210 used to murder Russian dissident, Alexander Litvinenko. In *Marcus*,[493] a case under s 24, 'noxious' was broadly interpreted. A substance which may be harmless if taken in small quantities is noxious if administered in sufficient quantity to injure, aggrieve or annoy.[494] The meaning is taken to be coloured by the purpose which D may have in view. It is not

---

[482] *Kennedy (No 2)* [2007] UKHL 38, [9]–[10].   [483] *Gillard* (1988) 87 Cr App R 189 at 194.

[484] *Cadman* (1825) Carrington's Supplement 237. The report to the contrary in Ryan and Moody 114 is said to be inaccurate: *Harley*, n 492 per Parke J: and 6 Cox CC 16 n (c). But see *Walford* (1899) 34 L Jo 116, per Wills J.

[485] Prior to the Criminal Attempts Act, a judge could tell a jury it was an attempt, as Wightman J did in *Dale* (1852) 6 Cox CC 14.

[486] It has been prosecuted where eg D doused people with petrol and threatened to ignite it: *Potter* [2005] EWCA Crim 3050.

[487] [1999] Crim LR 65. Cf *Khan* [1998] Crim LR 830.   [488] [2003] Crim LR 555.

[489] [2003] EWCA Crim 3868.   [490] [2005] EWCA Crim 685.

[491] See Ch 2 for detailed comment. But see *Burgess* [2008] EWCA Crim 516.

[492] *Harley* (1830) 4 C & P 369; *Dale* (1852) 6 Cox CC 14. D would have been more appropriately charged with 'causing ... to be taken'.

[493] [1981] 1 WLR 774, CA.

[494] Following *Hennah* (1877) 13 Cox CC 547 and *Cramp* (1880) 5 QBD 307.Cf *Marlow* (1964) 49 Cr App R 49 (Brabin J).

necessary that the substance should be injurious to bodily health: '"noxious" mean[s] something different in quality from and of less importance than poison or other destructive things'. The court quoted the *Shorter Oxford Dictionary* meaning, 'injurious, hurtful, harmful, unwholesome', and suggested that the insertion of the celebrated snail allegedly in the ginger beer bottle in *Donoghue v Stevenson*[495] would create a noxious substance. It was held that the insertion of sedative and sleeping tablets into a bottle of milk was an attempt to commit an offence under s 24. While the tablets would cause no more than sedation or possibly sleep, they might be a danger to a person doing such normal but potentially hazardous acts as driving or crossing the street.[496]

The court 'explained' *Cato*,[497] a case under s 23, where it was said that a thing could not be noxious merely because it was harmful if taken in large quantities. That observation was not 'explicable' but wrong. The actual decision, however, that heroin is a noxious thing even where it is administered to a person with a high tolerance to whom it is unlikely to do any particular harm, is right.[498] Heroin is noxious because 'it is liable to cause injury in common use'.[499] It was no answer that V was experienced in taking heroin and had a high tolerance. Ecstasy has been held to be a noxious substance for these purposes.[500] It has been argued that HIV could be regarded as a noxious substance capable of being administered in the course of sexual activity.[501] Charges under s 20 (discussed earlier) are more likely.

Whether consenting to the administration of a noxious substance that might cause grievous bodily harm or endanger life is valid consent in law must be subject to the policy on consent adopted in *Brown*.[502] The courts have repeatedly asserted that factual consent will not necessarily provide a legal defence to a charge under s 23.[503] However, it must be the case that V can consent in some contexts to the administration of a noxious substance, even one that is potentially fatal. Otherwise, V could not consent to anaesthetic for surgery. The validity of consent will, it seems, turn on public policy factors, so that while informed adult consent in a medical context or in horseplay may be legally recognized, in other contexts it will not be. In *Dica*, it was accepted that V could validly consent to the risk of infection by HIV. The court acknowledged that in some instances a person would be willing to take that risk, for example to conceive or to respect a religious prohibition on contraception. The court held that V could not consent to an intentional infection.

Section 23 was considered by the Court of Appeal (Civil Division) in *CP (A Child) v First-tier Tribunal (Criminal Injuries Compensation)*.[504] The claimant was a child who was born with foetal alcohol syndrome after her mother drank excessively during pregnancy. CP claimed compensation from the Criminal Injuries Compensation Authority. It was argued on behalf of CP that her mother had maliciously administered a noxious thing to her contrary to s 23 of the OAPA 1861 whilst she was in the womb. In rejecting this contention, both Treacy LJ and Lord Dyson MR held that 'it is well established that a foetus is not a "person;" rather it is a sui generis organism'.[505] A foetus was not 'any other person' for the purposes of s 23, and as the harm had been inflicted on the child while she was in the womb, the child was not entitled to criminal injuries compensation.[506]

[495] [1932] AC 562.

[496] See also *T* [2006] EWCA Crim 2557, where D (46) plied V (14) with alcohol and amphetamines.

[497] [1976] 1 WLR 110; cf *Dalby* [1982] 1 WLR 425, CA.

[498] 'It is not in doubt that heroin is a noxious thing, and the contrary was not contended', per Lord Bingham in *Kennedy (No 2)* [2007] UKHL 38 [10].

[499] [1976] 1 All ER at 268. See also *MK* [2008] 2 Cr App R (S) 437 (administering methadone to child).

[500] See *Gantz* [2004] EWCA Crim 2862.

[501] See Ormerod and Gunn [1996] 1 Web JCLI; Bronnit [1994] Crim LR 21.

[502] [1994] AC 212.

[503] *Cato; McShane* (1977) 66 Cr App R 97. Cf the CLRC Fourteenth Report, para 190.

[504] [2014] EWCA Civ 1554.   [505] At [39] and [62].

[506] *A-G's Reference (No 3 of 1994)* in relation to homicide does not undermine that conclusion.

838

'Thereby'

The use of the term 'thereby' in s 23 could represent a significant restriction on the offence if it is interpreted in as narrow a fashion as that term has been understood in relation to the life-endangering offences under the Criminal Damage Act 1971. If the life endangerment arises from consequences other than the noxious substance itself, it is arguable that the offence is not committed. For example, if D laces V's coffee and V then drives to work, if V's life is endangered by the manner of his driving which was affected by the noxious substance which induced drowsiness,[507] but not by the noxious substance administered, it is arguable that life is not endangered thereby.

16.10.1.2 Mens rea

Under s 23, the only mens rea required is intention or recklessness as to the administration of a noxious thing. The use in the section of the word 'maliciously' makes this clear as held in the leading case of *Cunningham*.[508] Whereas in s 24 the offence uses the expression 'with intent to', in s 23 the expression is simply 'so as thereby to'. This suggests that in s 23 no additional mens rea is required as to the element of endangering life or inflicting grievous bodily harm. That was the interpretation adopted in *Cato*. The requirement of 'malice' was satisfied by the deliberate injection of heroin into V's body. No mens rea was required as to the danger to life or the infliction of grievous bodily harm. In *Cunningham*, the Court of Criminal Appeal thought the jury should have been told that D must have foreseen that the gas he caused to be administered to V by breaking the gas pipe might cause injury to someone. The court did not say D must have foreseen that life would be endangered. This is an extraordinary result, in that a less culpable state of mind is required for the more serious offence (s 23) than the less serious (s 24).

16.10.2 Section 24

The section as amended provides:

Whosoever shall unlawfully and maliciously administer to or cause to be administered to or taken by any other person any poison or other destructive or noxious thing, with intent to injure, aggrieve, or annoy such person, shall be guilty of [an offence], and being…convicted thereof shall be liable to [imprisonment for a term not exceeding 5 years]…

By s 25, a person charged under s 24 may not be convicted of an offence under s 23.[509]

16.10.2.1 Actus reus

The elements of administration, etc have been considered earlier in relation to s 23. Section 24 might be seen as an inchoate offence, with the focus on the conduct whereas s 23 is a result-oriented crime.[510]

It is arguable that V ought to be able to provide valid consent to the administration of a substance under s 24. However, the level of harm likely is that of injury, which seems to be on a par with the threshold at which consent is generally treated as invalid in *Brown*.[511] The public policy exceptions as in *Brown* will apply.

---

[507] cf *Steer* [1988] AC 111.

[508] [1957] 2 QB 396: D tore the gas meter from the wall of an unoccupied house to steal money from it. The gas seeped into the neighbouring houses and was inhaled by V, whose life was endangered. D's conviction under s 23 was quashed because the judge directed the jury only that 'malicious' meant 'wicked'. See now Criminal Damage Act 1971, s 1(2), see Ch 29.

[509] cf *Stokes* (1925) 19 Cr App R 71.

[510] See A Ashworth, 'Defining Criminal Offences without Harm' in *Criminal Law Essays*, 13.

[511] cf the remarks in sentencing in *Sky* [2000] 2 Cr App R (S) 260, [6].

16.10.2.2 Mens rea

This offence requires an ulterior intent: 'with intent to injure, aggrieve, or annoy such person'.

When a drug is given to V with intent to keep him awake it seems that whether this amounts to an intention to injure depends on whether D has a malevolent or a benevolent purpose. If D, a paedophile, gives the drug to V, a child, with the motive of ingratiating himself with V or rendering him susceptible to sexual offences, he has an intention to injure: *Hill*.[512] It would probably be otherwise if D's intention was to enable V to stay awake to enjoy the fireworks or greet his father on return from work. The administration of a drug to the pilot of an aircraft to keep him awake is probably not an offence. The administration of the same drug for the purpose of carrying out a prolonged interrogation may be.[513] This casts doubt on *Weatherall*.[514] D put a sleeping tablet in V's tea to enable him to search her handbag for letters proving that she was committing adultery. It was held that there was insufficient evidence of intent to injure, aggrieve or annoy: but there was surely evidence of a 'malevolent' purpose, as there would be if D gave V a sleeping tablet with intent to rape her. The test of malevolence is presumably objective. The paedophile's belief that the drugged child will enjoy and profit from the sexual experience is never going to be regarded as capable of being a 'benevolent' purpose. The question of intention comes perilously close to being one of motive, and at least on orthodox approaches to mens rea, this is irrelevant.

16.10.3 Other poisoning offences

16.10.3.1 Administering substances in relation to sexual offences

The Sexual Offences Act 2003 introduced s 61—intentional administration of a substance/causing it to be taken by V without consent with intent to stupefy/overpower to enable any person to engage in sex with V. See Ch 17.

16.10.3.2 Terrorist related poisonings

Section 38 of the Public Order Act 1986 creates what is in effect an offence of food terrorism applicable where, for example, D puts poisons or harmful objects in food products in supermarkets. Sections 113 and 114 of the Anti-terrorism, Crime and Security Act 2001 create very broad offences of using or threatening to use a noxious substance or thing to cause harm and intimidate.[515]

16.11 False imprisonment

False imprisonment, like assault and battery, is both a crime at common law and a tort.[516] The civil remedy is commonly invoked and most of the reported cases on this subject are civil actions, but it features as a count in many indictments. As will appear, there are some important distinctions between the crime and the tort.

---

[512] (1986) 83 Cr App Rep 386, HL. The offence under s 61 of the Sexual Offences Act 2003 will apply, see p 817.

[513] Examples taken from *Hill*, ibid.

[514] [1968] Crim LR 115 (Judge Broderick). See also *A-G's Reference (No 71 of 2012)* [2012] EWCA Crim 3071 where D laced his colleagues' coffee with amphetamine and reported them to a supervisor for drug taking.

[515] For discussion, see C Walker, *Blackstone's Guide to the Anti-Terrorism Legislation* (3rd edn, 2014) 215–216.

[516] See E Peel and J Goudkamp, *Winfield and Jolowicz on Tort* (19th edn, 2014) Ch 4. See also the discussion in LC 355, *Simplification of Criminal Law: Kidnapping and Related Offences* (2014).

False imprisonment is committed where D unlawfully and intentionally or recklessly restrains V's freedom of movement from a particular place without lawful justification. 'Imprisonment' is probably a wider term than, and includes, 'arrest'.[517]

16.11.1 Article 5: deprivations of liberty and arrest

Article 5 of the ECHR provides a guarantee against arbitrary deprivation of liberty, but that has been interpreted more narrowly than the concept of 'restricting movement' which lies at the heart of false imprisonment. 'Article 5 is concerned with the *deprivation* of liberty and not with mere *restrictions* on freedom of movement.'[518] The distinction is not always easy to identify since the difference is 'merely one of degrees or intensity, and not one of nature or substance'.[519] In *Gillan v MPC*,[520] the House of Lords held that a brief stop (20 mins) could not be regarded as a 'deprivation of liberty' within the meaning of Art 5; those subjected to a stop and search were merely 'detained in the sense of kept from proceeding or kept waiting'. The ECtHR disagreed, unanimously finding a violation of Art 8, that the use of coercive powers to require an individual to submit to a detailed search of his person, his clothing and his personal belongings amounted to a clear interference with the right to respect for private life: *Gillan and Quinton v UK*.[521] The Strasbourg Court expressly disagreed with the assessment of the House of Lords that the safeguards provided by the English legislation provided adequate protection against arbitrary interference.[522] In *Austin v MPC*,[523] the House of Lords concluded that the police detention of several thousand people on Oxford Street did not amount to a deprivation of liberty within the meaning of Art 5.[524] The Grand Chamber of the Strasbourg Court agreed and held that there was no violation of Art 5, basing its decision upon the exceptional facts of the case.[525] The Court reiterated that determining whether there has been a deprivation of liberty as that term is utilized in Art 5 as opposed to a mere restriction on liberty is one of degree or intensity as opposed to nature or substance. Extraordinarily, the Grand Chamber reached its conclusion without referring to the earlier judgment in *Gillan and Quinton*. Given that the applicants in *Austin* were detained for hours as opposed to the 20-minute police stop in *Gillan and Quinton*, the two cases are hard to reconcile.[526]

---

[517] *Rahman* (1985) 81 Cr App R 349 at 353, CA. *Brown* [1977] Crim LR 291, CA, and commentary thereon and articles by D Telling, 'Arrest and Detention—The Conceptual Maze' [1978] Crim LR 320 and K Lidstone, 'A Maze in Law!' [1978] Crim LR 332. Care must be taken with the articles' references to powers of arrest as these have changed significantly. See LC 355, Ch 2.

[518] *Engel v Netherlands* (1976) 1 EHRR 647, para 58; *Guzzardi v Italy* (1980) 3 EHRR 333, para 92; *Raimondo v Italy* (1994) 18 EHRR 237, para 39; *HM v Switzerland* (App no 39187/98), 26 Feb 2002. See generally Emmerson, Ashworth and Macdonald, HR&CJ, Ch 5.

[519] *Guzzardi v Italy* (1980) 3 EHRR 333, para 92; *Ashingdane v UK* (1985) 7 EHRR 528, para 41; *Engel v Netherlands* (1976) 1 EHRR 647, paras 58–59. See also *Blume v Spain* (2000) 30 EHRR 632.

[520] [2006] UKHL 12; see [2006] Crim LR 751 and commentary.

[521] (2010) 50 EHRR 45. See also *R (AP) v Secretary of State for the Home Department* [2010] UKSC 24, in which it was held that when deciding if there is a deprivation of liberty within the meaning of Art 5 of the ECHR regard should be had to the subjective factors peculiar to the particular individual.

[522] The authorization power under the Terrorism Act 2000, s 44 required only that it be expedient to make the authorization, not that it be necessary or proportionate. See Ashworth, commentary [2010] Crim LR 415. See now: the Protection of Freedoms Act 2012 dealing with the maximum length of detention without trial in terrorism cases, and stop and search under the Terrorism Act 2000. On which see E Cape, 'The Counter-Terrorism Provisions of the Protection of Freedoms Act 2012: Preventing Misuse or a Case of Smoke and Mirrors?' [2013] Crim LR 385.

[523] [2009] UKHL 5, [2009] 2 WLR 372.   [524] See Ashworth, commentary [2010] Crim LR 415.

[525] (2012) 55 EHRR 14.   [526] See Ashworth's criticisms at [2012] Crim LR 545.

16.11.2 Actus reus

16.11.2.1 'Imprisonment'

For the purposes of the offence of false imprisonment, the 'imprisonment' may consist in confining V in a prison,[527] a house,[528] even V's own house,[529] a mine[530] or a vehicle;[531] or simply in detaining V in a public street[532] or any other place.

A false imprisonment may arise for a short duration. The restraint need be only momentary, so that the offence would be complete if D tapped V on the shoulder and said, 'You are my prisoner.'[533] It is not necessary that the victim be physically detained; there may be an arrest by words alone, but only if V submits. If V is not physically detained and does not realize he is under constraint, he is not imprisoned.[534] If V agrees to go to a police station voluntarily, he has not been arrested even if the constable would have arrested him if V had refused to go.[535] If it is then made clear to V that he will not be allowed to leave until he provides a laboratory specimen, it has been suggested that, though he has never been 'arrested', he is 'under arrest'.[536] If this distinction is valid it would seem to be enough for false imprisonment that V is 'under arrest'.

It is enough that D orders V to accompany him to another place, and V goes because he feels constrained to do so. V is not imprisoned if, on hearing D use words of arrest, he runs away or makes his escape by a trick.[537] An invitation by D to V to accompany him cannot be an imprisonment if it is made clear to V that he is entitled to refuse to go. Thus, Lord Lyndhurst CB thought there was no imprisonment where D asked a policeman to take V into custody, and the policeman objected, but said that if D and V 'would be so good as to go with him', he would take the advice of his superior.[538] The distinction between a command, amounting to an imprisonment, and a request not doing so, is a difficult one.[539] Probably Alderson B went too far in *Peters v Stanway*[540] in holding that V was imprisoned if she went to the police station with a constable voluntarily but nevertheless in consequence of a charge against her.

Though some of the older authorities[541] speak of false imprisonment as a species of assault, it is quite clear that no assault need be proved.[542] In *Linsberg*,[543] the Common Sergeant held

---

[527] *Cobbett v Grey* (1849) 4 Exch 729; *R v Govenor of Brockhill Prison, ex p Evans (No 2)* [2001] 2 AC 19. On the difference between positive acts of imprisonment and omissions, see *Iqbal v Prison Officers Association* [2009] EWCA Civ 1312.

[528] *Warner v Riddiford* (1858) 4 CBNS 180.

[529] *Termes de la Ley*, approved by Warrington and Atkin LJJ (1920) 122 LT at 51 and 53. See also *Secretary of State for the Home Department v JJ* [2007] UKHL 45 considering the power to make control orders: s 1(2) of the Prevention of Terrorism Act 2005. See also *Secretary of State for the Home Department v E* [2007] UKHL 47; *Secretary of State for the Home Department v MB; Secretary of State v AF* [2007] UKHL 46.

[530] *Herd v Weardale Steel, Coal and Coke Co Ltd* [1915] AC 67.

[531] By driving at such a speed that V dare not alight: *McDaniel v State*, 15 Tex Crim 115 (1942); *Burton v Davies* [1953] QSR 26. See also *Bowell* [2003] EWCA Crim 3896, single count of false imprisonment split where D detained V in the car, and detained her again when she escaped and injured herself.

[532] Blackstone, *Commentaries*, iii, 127; *Ludlow v Burgess* [1971] Crim LR 238; *Austin v MPC*, discussed earlier.

[533] *Simpson v Hill* (1795) 1 Esp 431, per Eyre CJ; *Sandon v Jervis* (1859) EB & E 942, 'a mere touch constitutes an arrest, though the party be not actually taken', per Crowder J.

[534] *Alderson v Booth* [1969] 2 QB 216, [1969] 2 All ER 271.

[535] *Campbell v Tormey* [1969] 1 WLR 189. See Emmerson, Ashworth and Macdonald, HR&CJ, para 5.03.

[536] ibid, per Ashworth J.   [537] *Russen v Lucas* (1824) 1 C & P 153.

[538] *Cant v Parsons* (1834) 6 C & P 504.

[539] G Williams, 'Police Interrogation Privileges and Limitations under Foreign Law: England' in CR Sowle (ed), *Police Power and Individual Freedom: The Quest for Balance* (1962) at 43.

[540] (1835) 6 C & P 737, followed in *Conn v David Spencer Ltd* [1930] 1 DLR 805.

[541] Eg Hawkins, I PC, c 60, s 7; *Pocock v Moore* (1825) Ry & M 321.

[542] *Grainger v Hill* (1838) 4 Bing NC 212; *Warner v Riddiford* (1858) 4 CBNS 180.   [543] (1905) 69 JP 107.

that V, a doctor, was falsely imprisoned where D locked the door to prevent him leaving a woman in childbirth. A battery is not necessarily an imprisonment. In *Bird v Jones*,[544] V was involved in 'a struggle during which no momentary detention of his person took place'.

There is little authority on the question of how large the area of confinement may be. It is not an imprisonment wrongfully to prevent V from going in a particular direction, if he is free to go in other directions. This was decided in *Bird v Jones*,[545] where Coleridge J said: 'A prison may have its boundary large or narrow, visible and tangible, or, though real, still in the conception only;[546] it may itself be moveable or fixed: but a boundary it must have...' It would be otherwise if V could move off in other directions only by taking an unreasonable risk. It could hardly be said that a man locked in a second-floor room was not imprisoned because he could have climbed down the drainpipe. It has been suggested that it would be tortious to confine V to a large country estate or the Isle of Man;[547] but it could hardly be false imprisonment to prevent V from leaving Great Britain, still less to prevent him from entering. However, a person who has actually landed and is not allowed to leave an airport building is imprisoned.[548] Is V also imprisoned, then, if he is not allowed to leave the ship which has docked in a British port?

Merely deciding to restrain a person if he attempts to leave does not amount to imprisonment.[549] But if steps are in fact taken to prevent his leaving, as by placing a policeman at the door, he is imprisoned although he is not aware of it: *Meering v Grahame-White Aviation Co Ltd*[550] where Atkin LJ said:

It appears to me that a person could be imprisoned without his knowing it. I think a person can be imprisoned while he is asleep, while he is in a state of drunkenness, while he is unconscious, and while he is a lunatic...though the imprisonment began and ceased while he was in that state.

A contrary decision[551] was not cited and *Meering* has been heavily criticized,[552] although cited with approval by the House of Lords in *Murray v Minister of Defence*;[553] the arguments advanced against awarding damages in this situation are, however, not applicable to the crime. D's conduct may not be damaging to V if V knows nothing about it, but it is not necessarily any less blameworthy for, in most cases, the fact that V remains in ignorance must be a matter of mere chance.

Like other crimes, false imprisonment can be committed through an innocent agent.[554] So D is responsible for the actus reus if, at his direction or request, a policeman takes V into

---

[544] See later.   [545] (1845) 7 QB 742 (Denman CJ dissenting).

[546] Eg V is forbidden to move more than ten yards from the village pump.

[547] (1845) 7 QB 742. But 'Napoleon was certainly imprisoned on St Helena': *Winfield and Jolowicz on Torts* (15th edn, 1998) 71. In *Re Mwenya* [1960] 1 QB 241 a writ of *habeas corpus* was sought for V who was confined to an area of some 1,500 square miles but he was released before it became necessary to decide whether he was imprisoned for the purpose of *habeas corpus*.

[548] *Kuchenmeister v Home Office* [1958] 1 QB 496.

[549] *Bournewood Community and Mental Health NHS Trust, ex p L* [1998] 3 All ER 289 at 298, HL; but Lord Steyn, dissenting, more realistically thought (at 306): 'The suggestion that L was free to go is a fairy tale.' Note the European Court's finding of a breach of Art 5 in *HL v UK* (App no 45508/99), and see the Mental Health Act 2007, ss 4 and 5. See also the discussion of *Cheshire West and Chester Council v P* [2014] UKSC 19 that 'deprivation of liberty' in the context of the living arrangements of a mentally incapacitated person was to be given the same meaning in domestic law as in Art 5 of the ECHR.

[550] (1919) 122 LT 44, Duke LJ dissenting, where two policemen were stationed outside the door of a room to prevent V leaving. He was as effectively imprisoned as if the door had been locked. *Meering* was approved in *Murray v Ministry of Defence* [1988] 2 All ER 521 at 529, HL.

[551] *Herring v Boyle* (1834) 1 Cr M & R 377 (Court of Exchequer).

[552] G Williams in *Police Power and Individual Freedom* (1962) 45–46; C Witting, *Street on Torts* (14th edn, 2015) Ch 9.

[553] [1998] 1 WLR 692.

[554] There is no vicarious liability for false imprisonment (nor generally in criminal law for common law offences: *R (Craik) v Newcastle Magistrates' Court* [2010] EWHC 935 (Admin)).

custody,[555] or he signs the charge-sheet when the police have said they will not take the responsibility of detaining V unless he does.[556] However, if D merely gives information to a constable, which causes him to make an arrest, that is not a false imprisonment in tort by D, if D is acting in a bona fide way.[557] *A fortiori*, it should not be *criminal*, because D will also lack mens rea. But this raises the question whether D will be guilty if he deliberately supplies false information to a constable who, acting on his own authority but relying exclusively on D's information, arrests V.[558] D has surely caused the actus reus with mens rea. Note that where D is initially liable for false imprisonment, his liability ceases on the intervention of some judicial act[559] authorizing the detention or on any other event, breaking the chain of causation.[560] So, in the case of the false information leading to arrest, D may be liable for the act of the constable but not the judicial act of the magistrate.[561]

Whatever the position in the law of tort,[562] it should be immaterial in the criminal law that the imprisonment was not 'directly' caused by D; and it ought to be sufficient that D caused it with mens rea—as by digging a pit into which V falls and is trapped.[563]

Another issue in the law of tort is whether, in view of the requirement of a trespass, it is possible to falsely imprison by mere omission. In *Herd v Weardale Steel, Coal and Coke Co Ltd*,[564] V voluntarily descended into D's mine and, in breach of contract, stopped work and asked to be brought to the surface before the end of the shift. D's refusal to accede to this request was not a false imprisonment: he was under no duty to provide facilities for V to leave in breach of contract. Clearly, the result would be different if D were to take positive steps to prevent V from leaving in breach of contract,[565] as by locking him in a factory. Buckley and Hamilton LJJ[566] thought that mere omission could not have been false imprisonment, even if it occurred when the shift was over. V's only civil remedy would have been in contract; but the House of Lords expressed no opinion on this point.

In *Mee v Cruickshank*,[567] Wills J held that a prison governor was under a duty to take steps to ensure that his officers did not detain a prisoner who had been acquitted. In that case there were acts of imprisonment by the prison officers but they were not the servants of D, the governor, and it seems to have been D's omission which rendered him liable in tort. As the House of Lords accepted in *Ex p Evans*, the failure to release a prisoner on the due

---

[555] *Gosden v Elphick and Bennett* (1849) 4 Exch 445. Note also the tort of procuring an arrest, see *Martin v Watson* [1996] 1 AC 74.

[556] *Austin v Dowling* (1870) LR 5 CP 534. It is otherwise if D signs the charge-sheet as a matter of form, when the police are detaining V on their own responsibility: *Grinham v Willey* (1859) 4 H & N 496.

[557] *Gosden v Elphick and Bennett*, n 555; *Grinham v Willey*, n 556; 'We ought to take care that people are not put in peril for making complaint when a crime has been committed', per Pollock CB. Cf *O'Hara v Chief Constable of RUC* [1997] AC 286.

[558] See *Hough v Chief Constable of Staffordshire* [2001] EWCA Civ 39.

[559] *Lock v Ashton* (1848) 12 QB 871. Cf *Marrinan v Vibart* [1963] 1 QB 528, [1962] 3 All ER 380.

[560] *Harnett v Bond* [1925] AC 669. D's report caused V to be taken to an asylum; D was not liable for the imprisonment after the doctor at the asylum had examined V and decided to detain him. Cf *Pike v Waldrum* [1952] 1 Lloyd's Rep 431.

[561] See *Austin v Dowling* (1870) LR 5 C & P 534 at 540.

[562] R Clayton and H Tomlinson, *Civil Actions against the Police* (3rd edn, 2005) para 4-046. See also *Ahmed v Shafique* [2009] EWHC 618 (QB).

[563] cf *Clarence* (1888) 22 QBD 23 at 36, per Wills J.   [564] [1915] AC 67, HL.

[565] Unless, perhaps, the contract was that V should be entitled to leave only on the fulfilment of some reasonable condition: *Robinson v Balmain New Ferry Co Ltd* [1910] AC 295, PC. *Sed quaere* whether one is entitled to restrain another from leaving even if it is a breach of contract for him to do so. The contract can hardly be specifically enforceable.

[566] [1913] 3 KB at 787 and 793.   [567] (1902) 20 Cox CC 210.

date gives rise to an action in false imprisonment, even if the failure was in good faith. And it ought to make no difference that D's duty to release V arises out of a contract:

If a man gets into an express train and the doors are locked pending its arrival at its destination, he is not entitled, merely because the train has been stopped by signal, to call for the doors to be opened to let him out.[568]

But if he is kept locked in for a day at his destination this surely ought to be false imprisonment. And even if there is no remedy in tort this is no reason why the omission should not be held to be criminal. The CLRC were of the opinion that the crime of false imprisonment is, and ought to be, capable of commission by omission.[569]

16.11.2.2 Unlawful restraint

The imprisonment must be 'false'; that is, unlawful. A convicted person sentenced to imprisonment may be lawfully confined in any prison and, as against prison officers so confining him in good faith, he has no 'residual liberty'. If he is subjected to intolerable conditions he may have other remedies[570] but he cannot sue (or, it may be assumed, prosecute) the officers for false imprisonment.[571] It might, however, be false imprisonment for a fellow prisoner, or an officer acting in bad faith outside the scope of his duty, to lock him in a confined space, such as a hut, within the prison. In *Iqbal v Prison Officers Association*,[572] the failure to allow I, a serving prisoner, out of his cell on the day of unlawful strike action by prison officers, did not give rise to a claim for false imprisonment against the officers.

A parent may lawfully exercise restraint over a child, so long as he remains within the bounds of reasonable parental discipline and does not act in contravention of a court order,[573] or s 58 of the Children Act 2004. Where a girl of 14 or 15 was fostered out by her father with the consent and assistance of the local authority and he abducted her against her will and with intent to take her to her country of origin, it was for the jury to say whether they were satisfied that this was outside the bounds of legitimate parental discipline and correction.[574] A defendant charged with false imprisonment may rely on other justifications, such as the prevention of crime.[575]

The question of false imprisonment most commonly arises in connection with the exercise of powers of arrest. If such powers are exceeded, there is a false imprisonment. The principal powers are as follows.

Arrest by a constable under a valid warrant

Where a warrant is issued but the justice lacks jurisdiction to issue the warrant, the constable who arrests under the warrant is statutorily protected[576] from any 'action' if he acts in

---

[568] *Herd v Weardale Steel, Coal and Coke Co Ltd* [1915] AC 67 at 71, per Lord Haldane. See M Amos, 'A Note on Contractual Restraint of Liberty' (1928) 44 LQR 464; KF Tan, 'A Misconceived Issue in the Tort of False Imprisonment' (1981) 44 MLR 166.

[569] Fourteenth Report, paras 253, 254.

[570] See *Krgozlu v MPC* [2006] EWCA Civ 1691.

[571] *Hague v Deputy Governor of Parkhurst Prison* [1991] 3 All ER 733, HL. What if the conditions are so intolerable as to found a defence of necessity to a charge of escape (see Ch 10)? Is it false imprisonment to prevent such a prisoner from leaving the prison?

[572] [2009] EWCA Civ 1312.

[573] *Rahman* (1985) 81 Cr App R 349, CA. Cf *D* [1984] AC 778, [1984] 1 All ER 574.

[574] *Rahman*, ibid. In fact, D pleaded guilty, and his appeal was dismissed. Note s 121 of the Anti-social Behaviour, Crime and Policing Act 2014 which makes it an offence to use violence, threats or any other form of coercion for the purpose of causing another person to enter into marriage and the Forced Marriage (Civil Protection) Act 2007, which creates forced marriage protection orders.

[575] D acting to prevent theft relied on s 3 of the Criminal Law Act 1967: *Bowden* [2002] EWCA Civ 1279. See also *Morris* [2013] EWCA Crim 436, p 395; *Faraj* [2007] EWCA Crim 1033 (see Ch 10, p 405).

[576] The Constables Protection Act 1750. See *O'Connor v Isaacs* [1956] 2 QB 288.

obedience to it. As the term 'action' is inappropriate to a criminal proceeding, a constable could not rely on the Act as a defence to criminal prosecution; but he would probably have a good defence on the ground of lack of mens rea.[577] An arrest under warrant for a civil matter is unlawful if the arresting officer does not have the warrant in his possession.[578]

Arrest without warrant under PACE

The powers of police constables and others to arrest are governed by PACE. See ss 24 and 24A and the common law powers preserved under PACE.

Arrest for breach of the peace

The House of Lords held in *R (Laporte) v Chief Constable of Gloucestershire*[579] that an arrest for an anticipated breach of the peace can only be legitimate where there is a reasonable apprehension[580] of an *imminent* breach of the peace.[581] Moreover, in the absence of such an apprehension, there is no power to take preventive action falling short of arrest.

In *Austin v MPC*,[582] the House of Lords held that there was no false imprisonment when, in order to maintain order and public safety and to prevent the commission of offences, the police held several thousand people in a cordon on Oxford Street in London. Some of those people were not demonstrators. The containment of the individuals amounted to imprisonment, but it was not false imprisonment because the police were acting lawfully. The police action was found to be necessary in order to avoid an imminent breach of the peace (and the causing of serious injury) by some members of the crowd. The circumstances in which the police can detain V in order to avoid danger because of an imminent breach of the peace by X were said to be very strictly limited to extreme and exceptional circumstances. There is a breach of the peace whenever harm is actually done or is likely to be done to a person, or in his presence to his property, or a person is in fear of being so harmed through an assault, an affray, a riot or other disturbance.[583] Public alarm, excitement or disturbance is not of itself a breach of the peace, unless it arises from actual or threatened violence.

16.11.3 Mens rea

Since the great majority of the reported cases are civil actions,[584] there is little authority on the nature of the mens rea required for false imprisonment but, in *Rahman*,[585] the court stated that 'false imprisonment consists in the unlawful and intentional or reckless restraint of a victim's freedom of movement from a particular place'. This was confirmed by *Hutchins*[586] which held that the offence is one of 'basic intent' so that a belief caused by self-induced intoxication that the victim is consenting is no defence. The courts did not specify what kind of recklessness they had in mind; but a common law offence would naturally require *Cunningham* recklessness. This may be taken to be established now that it is settled

---

577 See later.   578 *De Costa Small v Kirkpatrick* (1978) 68 Cr App R 186, [1979] Crim LR 41.

579 [2007] 2 WLR 46.

580 The Court of Appeal has confirmed that on appeal it is not for the court to form its own assessment of whether a breach of the peace was imminent, rather it must evaluate the reasonableness of the apprehension of the police. See *R (Moos) v Commissioner of Police of the Metropolis* [2012] EWCA Civ 12.

581 This principle was affirmed in *R (Wright) v Commissioner of Police for the Metropolis* [2013] EWHC 2739 (QB) and *R (Hicks) v Commissioner of Police of the Metropolis* [2014] EWCA Civ 3, [2014] Crim LR 681.

582 [2009] UKHL 5, [2009] 2 WLR 372. The Grand Chamber of the Strasbourg Court dismissed the claimants' application. See (2012) 55 EHRR 14.

583 *Howell* (1981) 73 Cr App R 31 at 37. Lord Denning has said that even the lawful use of force is a breach of the peace: *Chief Constable of Devon and Cornwall, ex p Central Electricity Generating Board* [1981] 3 All ER 826 at 832; but this can hardly subject the person using such force to arrest.

584 Reckless indifference suffices for the tort: *Muuse v Secretary of State for the Home Department* [2010] EWCA Civ 453.

585 (1985) 81 Cr App R 349 at 353, CA, n 573.   586 [1988] Crim LR 379.

that assault requires *Cunningham* recklessness.[587] Assault and false imprisonment are both common law offences and are so closely related that it is inconceivable that they should be governed by different principles of mens rea.

16.11.4 Reform

The Law Commission recommends the replacement of the common law offence of false imprisonment with a statutory offence entitled 'unlawful detention' but which in other respects retains the elements of the current law.[588] The offence would be indictable only and carry a maximum life sentence.[589]

16.12 Kidnapping

Kidnapping has long been regarded as an aggravated form of false imprisonment[590] so the rules of lawful excuse are, no doubt, the same. Both are common law offences, punishable with imprisonment or fine at the discretion of the court. It is generally regarded as important to have a separate offence of kidnap to reflect the distinctive wrongdoing involved in the taking or carrying away which distinguishes kidnap from false imprisonment.[591]

In *R v D*,[592] the House of Lords gave what purported to be an authoritative account of the law of kidnapping:

First, the nature of the offence is an attack on, and infringement of, the personal liberty of an individual. Second, the offence contains four ingredients as follows: (1) the taking or carrying away of one person by another, (2) by force or by fraud, (3) without the consent of the person so taken or carried away and (4) without lawful excuse. Third, until the comparatively recent abolition by statute of the division of criminal offences into the two categories of felonies and misdemeanours (see s1 of the Criminal Law Act 1967), the offence of kidnapping was categorised by the common law as a misdemeanour only. Fourth, despite that, kidnapping was always regarded, by reason of its nature, as a grave and (to use the language of an earlier age) heinous offence. Fifth, in earlier days the offence contained a further ingredient, namely that the taking or carrying away should be from a place within the jurisdiction to another place outside it; this further ingredient has, however, long been obsolete and forms no necessary part of the offence today. Sixth, the offence was in former days described not merely as taking or carrying away a person but further or alternatively as secreting him; this element of secretion has, however, also become obsolete, so that, although it may be present in a particular case, it adds nothing to the basic ingredient of taking or carrying away.

---

[587] See p 102.   [588] See LC 355, para 4.238.

[589] See *Trifonova (Rossitza)* [2017] EWCA Crim 240.

[590] East, I PC, 429. On the history, see D Napier, 'Detention Offences at Common Law' in *Reshaping the Criminal Law*, 198. More recently, in *Vu* [2012] 2 SCR 411, the Supreme Court of Canada analysed the common law origins of the offence.

[591] See the analysis in LC 355, paras 4.66 et seq in which the Law Commission identifies the additional mischiefs in kidnap over and above those, or at least different to those, in false imprisonment, including the additional danger in which V is placed by being made to travel with D, the greater anxiety that would cause V and the enhanced wrong on D's part by demonstrating such control over V's autonomy by compelling V to remain in his continued presence. These aggravated harms and wrongs are most obvious when D uses force or threats to cause V to move with him.

[592] [1984] AC 778, [1984] Crim LR 558. Kidnapping had not previously been satisfactorily defined: see Napier, n 590. The Law Commission Draft Criminal Code, cl 81, proposed radical amendment to the offence by restricting it to cases of carrying away for ulterior purposes—to commit a serious offence.

In defining the offence in that way, Lord Brandon's attempts to consolidate earlier interpretations resulted in a considerable degree of overlap and this prompted the Law Commission to recommend a simplification of the offence in a statutory form.

Following decisions in which the Court of Appeal has struggled to identify whether the core of the offence lies in the wrong of taking and carrying away by fraud or force or the harm in terms of deprivation of liberty, the law is in a state of some confusion.[593]

In *Cort*,[594] D had on a number of occasions stopped his car at bus stops, falsely stating to women in the queue that the bus they awaited had broken down and offered them a lift. On two occasions women got into the car. One changed her mind and asked to be let out of the car and D complied; the other was taken to her destination without being assaulted by D in any way. D was convicted of two counts of kidnapping. The Court of Appeal upheld the conviction, finding that D had defrauded VV as to the nature of the act. In this case it was held that the complainants did not consent to the events; they only consented to a ride in the car, but the ride in the car was a 'different thing' from that with which D was charged. That decision is no longer to be followed in light of the decision in *Hendy-Freegard*.[595] H was convicted of two offences of kidnapping and a number of offences of dishonesty. H had 'an astonishing capacity to deceive', and managed to persuade three victims that he was an MI5 agent who had been investigating an IRA cell at their college. He persuaded them to leave the college and travel around the country, with periods of settlement, for a period of up to ten years. During that period, he financially exploited them. H's conviction for kidnapping was quashed as the Court of Appeal, rightly it is submitted, concluded that because H did not accompany the victims this meant that there was no kidnap. In the course of the judgment, the Lord Chief Justice emphasized that the prosecution had to establish that the victim was deprived of his or her liberty.

Confusion remains as to the relationship between the elements of: (a) the deprivation of liberty; (b) the absence of consent; (c) being taken or carried away; (d) the use of force or fraud; and (e) the absence of a lawful excuse. In particular, it is difficult to determine whether the force or fraud must be the means of carrying away (as Lord Brandon's speech and *Cort* suggest) or the reason for the lack of consent. A further question is whether the consent must be: (a) to the taking or carrying away; (b) the deprivation of liberty; (c) both; or (d) being taken by force or fraud.[596]

It is submitted that there must be an act of force or fraud which results in V being taken or carried away and that by that act of taking or carrying away without consent, V must be deprived of liberty without lawful excuse.

16.12.1 Deprivation of liberty

The definition offered in *D* fails to clarify whether the offence requires proof of a deprivation of liberty. Prior to *D*, commentators had expressly defined the offence in terms of a deprivation of liberty and carrying away from the place where the victim wanted to be.[597] It is difficult to see how there could be a kidnap if V was not deprived of his liberty. It is submitted that following the decision in *Hendy-Freegard*, this is now reconfirmed as a core element of the offence. Whether someone is deprived of his liberty is to be determined in the same

---

[593] For further analysis, see LCCP 200, *Simplification of the Criminal Law: Kidnapping* (2011). See also J Herring, 'What's Wrong with Kidnapping?' [2012] Crim LR 343; LC 355, para 2.10.

[594] [2003] EWCA Crim 2149, [2004] Crim LR 64.

[595] [2007] EWCA Crim 1236, CA.

[596] These criticisms were cited with approval by the Lord Chief Justice in *Kayani* [2011] EWCA Crim 2871, [2012] Crim LR 232.

[597] See the 5th edition of this book, at p 388; *Archbold* (40th edn, 1979) para 2796.

way as for the offence of false imprisonment. A deprivation of liberty is a necessary but not a sufficient basis of liability for kidnap.

It seems clear that if V has consented to the deprivation of liberty there can be no kidnapping. If V consents, for example, to being locked up (either as part of a prank or a role play in sadomasochism, etc) there is no offence of false imprisonment or of kidnap. There is consent to the deprivation of liberty.

Applying orthodox principles discussed earlier in this chapter, if D has deprived V of her liberty by deceiving her as to the nature of the act or as to his identity, there will be no valid consent. The usual difficulties will arise as to whether the fraud was as to the nature or identity. The case of *Wellard*[598] might be best interpreted as involving a fraud as to identity. In *Wellard*, D was held to have 'taken' V when by impersonating a police officer he tricked V into his car in order to submit to a 'drugs search'. That case also suggests that there is a sufficient deprivation of liberty if V does not believe that she can move. This will usually arise because of D's deception.[599]

16.12.2 Taking and carrying away

There is no doubt that this is also an important element of the offence. The requirements of carrying away and the use of force or fraud seem to be the principal factors distinguishing kidnapping from false imprisonment.[600] It seems that every kidnapping is also a false imprisonment but a detention without any taking away or force or fraud (eg D merely turns the key intentionally locking V in the room) is only the latter offence. Where D has taken or carried V away by force or fraud, he may be convicted of both offences.[601] The crime is complete when V is deprived of her liberty and carried away from the place where she wished to be.[602]

The courts have failed to define what the term 'taking or carrying away' means. Lord Brandon used the terms as alternatives, which suggests that there is some difference between them. Carried implies some movement, and as we know from *Hendy-Freegard*, D must accompany V. If 'takes' implies a different action, it could mean 'seizes', but if that means no more than a stationary capture of V by D, that would be difficult to reconcile with the requirement in *Hendy-Freegard*. It is submitted that the word 'takes' here should not be construed so as to extend the offence of kidnap to include stationary detention that would amount to no more than false imprisonment.

The courts have failed to spell out the relationship between the element of taking or carrying away and the deprivation of liberty.[603] It is submitted that the most logical interpretation of the offence may be that the act of taking or carrying away must be the *cause of* the deprivation of liberty. The decision in *Hendy-Freegard* supports this interpretation by concluding that there is no kidnap where V is taken or carried away by force or fraud (as in *Cort*) if not also deprived of her liberty. In *Cort*, for example, it would now seem to be accepted that the passengers accepting the lifts were defrauded as to being carried away, but not deprived of their liberty since they would be free to leave at any time they wished—as demonstrated by the fact that D did let one of the women out of the car immediately when

---

[598] [1978] 3 All ER 161.   [599] See LC 355, para 4.190.

[600] See also the Canadian Supreme Court's analysis of the English common law in *Vu* [2012] 2 SCR 411. It was observed that, 'it is the element of movement that differentiated kidnapping from the lesser included offence of false imprisonment and made kidnapping an aggravated form of false imprisonment. The underlying concern was that by carrying the victim away, the kidnappers would be taking him or her beyond the protection of the country's laws.' At [31].

[601] *Brown* [1985] Crim LR 398, CA (five years' imprisonment concurrent on both counts upheld).

[602] *Wellard* [1978] 1 WLR 921.   [603] See LC 355, paras 2.4 and 4.197.

she so requested. *D* could be interpreted more narrowly, to require deprivation of liberty in the course of taking or carrying away.

In *Hendy-Freegard*, Lord Phillips CJ stated that:

We cannot see that there was justification for extending the offence of kidnapping to cover the situation in which the driver of the car has no intention of detaining his passenger against her will nor of doing other than taking her to the destination to which she wishes to go, simply because in some such circumstances the driver may have an objectionable ulterior motive. The consequence of the decision in Cort would seem to be that the mini-cab driver, who obtains a fare by falsely pretending to be an authorised taxi, will be guilty of kidnapping.[604]

It is clear, following *Hendy-Freegard*, that D must accompany V at the time that V is alleged to be taken or carried away. The Crown's expansive interpretation argued for in *Hendy-Freegard* would have rendered guilty the practical joker who telephoned V and induced him to attend a hospital and remain there on the pretext that his wife had been in an accident. That would clearly go too far.[605]

Interpreting *D* in light of subsequent cases, the taking and carrying away must be by force or fraud (see the following section). It is not enough, then, that D asks V to accompany him and practises no fraud and offers no menace or threat to V, even if V is then deprived of liberty at their destination. As noted previously, it is submitted that to constitute kidnapping, the taking or carrying away must also be such as will deprive V of her liberty at that time. On a narrow interpretation of *D*, it is not sufficient that D persuades V by some fraud to accompany him to a place where he proposes to deprive her of her liberty if, during the period of her transmission to that place, D is prepared to release her at any time she requests. That would seem to follow from the decision in *Hendy-Freegard* interpreting *Cort*.[606]

In *D*, Lord Brandon states, explicitly, that the taking or carrying away must be by force or fraud *and without consent*. If a deprivation of liberty is also an essential element of the offence, and a lack of consent is an integral part of that element of the offence, the question arises: what part does consent have to play in taking and carrying away? If V is not consenting to the deprivation of her liberty, D ought to be guilty of kidnap irrespective of whether the force or fraud used to take or carry V away was sufficient to vitiate V's consent *to that act* of being carried or taken away.[607]

16.12.2.1 'Force or fraud'

The formulation in *D* creates problems. It is necessary to prove a taking or carrying away by force or fraud and absence of consent (whether that absence of consent was because of the force or fraud or not). If D's force or fraud taking V away also causes V's lack of consent, then no problem arises. If D's force or fraud that causes V to be taken or carried away is not of such gravity that it vitiates consent (eg a deception about a peripheral matter), it must be shown that V did not consent for some other reason. More problematic still is a case where

---

604 At [55]. The Lord Chief Justice referred to the criticisms of *Cort* made in the 11th edition. *Cort* was also doubted by the Court of Appeal in *Nnamdi* [2005] EWCA Crim 74.

605 The difficulty is to identify any serious offence in such cases. If D phones V and tells her falsely that D holds X hostage and that he will kill X unless V goes to a particular venue and remains there, what crime has been committed? There is no threat to X, nor to V.

606 In *Archer* [2011] EWCA Crim 2252, [2012] Crim LR 292, the Court of Appeal upheld D's conviction for kidnapping when he forced D, by threatening her with serious assault, to drive V and two others to a particular location. D did not take control of the car, it was driven by V. As Ashworth notes, this amounts to a 'carrying away' if not literally a 'taking' but nevertheless falls within the mischief at which the offence is aimed. Problematically, the Court of Appeal came to this conclusion with little citation of authority.

607 That may be an assault.

D uses force or fraud and V is not consenting for a reason unconnected to force or fraud (eg a general lack of capacity). There would, on a literal reading of *D*, be no offence unless the taking was shown to be 'by' force or fraud.

Force or fraud and consent

For the reasons discussed in the previous paragraph, it is submitted that if the force or fraud vitiates the consent to the taking or carrying away and that taking or carrying away causes V to be deprived of her liberty without consent, the offence will be committed.

Force

Clearly, where D forces V by violence or threats[608] of violence to be taken or carried away that should be sufficient to satisfy this element of the offence. It may be that lesser threats or trivial force ought to be sufficient for kidnapping. The Court of Appeal has suggested that the element of force sufficient to vitiate consent may be established by no more than submission.[609] Presumably the same is true of force sufficient to lead to taking away. The force used must be sufficient to cause V to be taken or carried away. In addition, if it is alleged that the taking or carrying away is by force, that taking or carrying away (and hence the force used to achieve it) must be sufficient to deprive V of her liberty without her consent. The relationship between deprivation of liberty and being taken away once again arises.

Fraud

What types of fraud will suffice? The answer is, it is submitted, contained within the previous analysis. The fraud used must be sufficient to cause V to be taken or carried away. Any fraud (not just those as to identity and nature) may suffice to cause V to be carried away. There is also a question of whether V is consenting to being taken and carried away. The absence of consent may arise from D's fraud or from some other basis (eg lack of capacity). It is possible to envisage a case in which D uses fraud on V to cause her to be carried away, but in which V is not actually deprived of her liberty by that act of taking away. This would seem to follow from *Hendy-Freegard*'s interpretation of *Cort*.

Adopting general principles to frauds vitiating consent, any fraud as to the identity of the actor should suffice. In this context, it is submitted that there is a stronger claim than in most circumstances for a fraud as to certain attributes of the actor and not just his correct name or identity being sufficient. Thus, as in *Wellard*,[610] the impersonation of a police officer should suffice to negative the consent of the person. Other examples might include impersonation of State officials, paramedics, etc.

In addition to frauds as to identity, it is recognized that frauds as to the *nature* of the act will vitiate consent. This is where the most significant difficulties arise, as illustrated by the cases on sexual offences discussed in Ch 17. There is also the question of whether a fraud as to the 'purpose' of the taking will suffice to vitiate consent. Consider D who falsely tells V that her husband is injured and he drives her home (because he enjoys her company). Or consider D, who tells his 17-year-old daughter that they are to travel abroad to visit an ailing relative when his true motive is for her to take part in an arranged marriage. The destination, manner of transport, etc are identical so the nature of the carrying away is not affected by the fraud. But note the decision in *Nnamdi*,[611] in which on the facts the court did not find

---

[608] The Court of Appeal accepted in *Archer*, n 606, that the reference to force in *D* extends to a threat of force and is not limited to the actual infliction of force. As noted earlier, there was little analysis of previous authorities.

[609] See *Greenhalgh* [2001] EWCA Crim 1367.   [610] [1978] 3 All ER 161.

[611] [2005] EWCA Crim 74.

it necessary to determine, on a charge of conspiracy to kidnap, whether telling V that she should meet D to join his modelling agency would be a sufficient fraud.

Force or fraud sufficient to vitiate consent to deprivation of liberty

On this literal approach to D, the elements of force or fraud represent routes through which the prosecution might establish the absence of consent to the fundamental question whether V was consenting to the deprivation of liberty arising from the taking or carrying away. It is an interpretation which resonates with Lord Brandon's emphasis in D that, 'the nature of the offence is an attack on, and infringement of, the personal liberty of an individual'.

16.12.2.2 Without lawful excuse

What amounts to a lawful excuse is left completely at large; and whether a taking by a parent amounts to kidnapping is likely to be resolved in the same way whether the court proceeds by the route of deciding (as the majority in Reid[612] would), whether there is a lawful excuse or by deciding (as Lord Bridge would) whether the offence extends to those further circumstances. If a 12-year-old child refuses to return home from a visit to his grandmother's and his father forcibly carries him off, he surely commits no offence. The majority would say, presumably, because the father has a lawful excuse and Lord Bridge, because kidnapping does not extend to those circumstances. The result is the same. The question must be whether the parent has gone beyond what is reasonable in the exercise of parental authority.

Where V is not D's child and D is not acting in pursuance of any statutory authority or power of arrest, 'lawful excuse' is likely to be narrowly confined. In Henman,[613] D was guilty of attempted kidnapping when he tried to take by force an acquaintance whom he believed to be in moral and spiritual danger from a religious sect to which she belonged. There was no lawful excuse because there was no 'necessity recognized by the law as such' for D's conduct.

16.12.2.3 Who may be kidnapped?

It was held in Reid[614] that a husband may be convicted of kidnapping his wife and in D that a father may be guilty of kidnapping his child. It was recognized that, until modern times, it may be that an indictment of a father for kidnapping his child would have failed because of the paramount stature of his position in the family; but common law principles adapt and develop in the light of radically changed social conventions and conditions. Lord Bridge held that parental kidnapping includes the case (as in D) where the parent acts in contravention of the order of a competent court, leaving open the question whether a parent might be convicted in any other circumstances; but the majority preferred to hold simply that the parent is guilty where he acts 'without lawful excuse'.[615]

In cases of fraud, the offence might be regarded as seriously deficient in protecting children. V must be deprived of her liberty without consent, and it will be possible to say that in the case of a young child[616] who lacks the understanding or intelligence to give consent, the absence of

---

[612] [1973] QB 299. [613] [1987] Crim LR 333, CA. [614] [1973] QB 299.

[615] In Kayani [2011] EWCA Crim 2871, Lord Judge CJ observed that simply because a child has been taken by a parent, it no longer necessarily follows that for policy reasons a charge of kidnapping must always be deemed inappropriate. The court invited the Law Commission to address the question whether cases in which children are removed from one parent by the other should be treated as kidnapping offences. See now LC 355, Ch 5.

[616] In the case of an older child, it is a question of fact for the jury whether (a) the child has sufficient understanding and, if so, (b) it in fact consented. Lord Brandon thought that a jury would usually find that a child under 14 lacked sufficient understanding to give consent; but this surely underestimates the capacity of the modern child. Reliance might be placed on the Mental Capacity Act 2005, discussed earlier. Cf Cooper [2009] UKHL 42 on the capacity concept in consent in sex cases (p 763).

consent is a necessary inference. However, the present definition requires there to be a carrying or taking away *by* force or fraud. In the case of a young child, D may not need to use force or fraud (unless those words are very broadly construed) to succeed in taking V away, as where a toddler is persuaded by true statements ('I'll buy you sweets') to accompany D. Arguably, such cases need not be kidnapping since they constitute false imprisonment which is equally punishable so, though it looks a little odd if a baby cannot be kidnapped,[617] no great harm is done.

16.12.2.4 Reform

The Law Commission has recommended that the common law offence be abolished and a simple statutory offence of kidnapping be created. The offence would be committed where D: (a) without lawful authority or reasonable excuse; (b) intentionally uses force or threats of force; (c) in order to take V or otherwise cause V to move with him. The offence would be indictable only and carry a maximum life sentence.[618]

16.13 Other abduction offences

16.13.1 Abduction of children

The Child Abduction Act 1984, as amended including by the Children Act 1989, creates two offences of abduction of a child under the age of 16. The offences encompass a broad spectrum of criminal behaviour, as Lord Judge CJ recognized in *Kayani*.[619]

16.13.1.1 Abduction by parents/guardians

The first offence, under s 1, arises where a child is taken or sent out[620] of the UK 'without the appropriate consent'.

Takes or sends

There is a clear lacuna since as the Divisional Court held in *Nicolaou* that the expression 'takes or send out of the United Kingdom' relates to the removal of the child from the jurisdiction, not to the position once the child has left the country. The issue is whether the appropriate consent existed at the time the child left the jurisdiction. The court rejected the submission that the phrase connotes a continuing activity. The Law Commission has recommended that the lacuna be closed and that the offence apply to detaining[621] as well as taking and sending.

---

[617] See G Williams, 'Can Babies be Kidnapped?' [1989] Crim LR 473. See the comments of Munby LJ in *Re HM* [2010] EWHC 870 (Fam) calling for law reform in this area.

[618] LC 355, para 4.231.

[619] [2011] EWCA Crim 2871, [2012] Crim LR 232. His lordship stated that: 'Child abduction, like every other offence, can take many forms. It may include the abduction of a child for a few days, or even a week or two, followed by the child's return, effectively undamaged, and, more important, although the parent from whom the separation was effected has suffered distress and anxiety in the meantime, with the loving relationship between parent and child quite unharmed. At the other extreme there are offences of forced marriage which ultimately culminate in what in reality is rape, or cases like the present, where the child is deliberately taken abroad and separated from one of its parents for many years, and the ordinary loving relationship which each should enjoy with the other is irremediably severed.' At [2]. *Kayani* [2012] 2 Cr App R (S) 38 and *SB* [2012] 2 Cr App R (S) 408 and 'a number of other decisions of this court' were considered in *RH* [2016] EWCA Crim 1754.

[620] In *R (Nicolaou) v Redbridge Magistrates' Court* [2012] EWHC 1647 (Admin). Given the fact that the purpose of the offence is the protection of children, such a narrow interpretation of s 1 is somewhat surprising. For further criticism see [2013] Crim LR 54.

[621] See LC 355, Ch 5.

Connection with the child

The offence may be committed as a principal[622] only by a person 'connected with' the child. A person 'connected with' a child is: (a) the child's parent; (b) in the case of a child whose parents were not married at the time of birth, a man in respect of whom there are reasonable grounds for believing him to be the father; (c) a guardian; (d) a special guardian;[623] (e) a person in whose favour 'a residence order'[624] is in force with respect to the child; or (f) a person having custody.

The 'appropriate consent' is the consent of *each* of the child's mother, the child's father if he has 'parental responsibility'[625] for him, any guardian, any special guardian, any person in whose favour a residence order is in force with respect to the child *and* any person having custody of him; *or* the leave of the court under the Children Act 1989,[626] or, in the case of any person having custody, the leave of the court which awarded custody.

The offence is not committed where a person in whose favour a residence order is in force takes or sends the child out of the UK for a period of less than one month or if he is a special guardian of the child and he takes or sends the child out of the UK for a period of less than three months unless, in either case, this is a breach of an order under Part II of the Children Act 1989.

The Act provides defences for which D bears an evidential burden and the prosecution the burden of proof where:

(1) D believes that he has the appropriate consent or that he would have it if the person or persons whose consent is required were aware of all the relevant circumstances; or

(2) he has taken all reasonable steps to communicate with those persons but has been unsuccessful; or

(3) the other person has unreasonably refused to consent.

The Court of Appeal held in *S(C)*[627] that necessity cannot be pleaded as a defence to a charge under s 1. The court reasoned that it would be inimical to the aims of the legislation for individuals to avoid liability by pleading such a defence. Whether this is true of other common law defences remains to be seen, but it is submitted that the court's reasoning applies with equal force to duress of circumstances. It may therefore be the case that the only defences that can be pleaded to a charge of child abduction are those that exist within the legislative scheme.

16.13.1.2 Abduction otherwise than by parents/guardians

The second offence, which arises under s 2, requires an intentional or reckless taking or detention of a child under the age of 16.[628] It is committed where a person who is:

(1) not the mother of 'the child in question';[629] or

---

[622] A person who is not 'connected with' the child may be convicted as a secondary party or conspirator: *Sherry and El Yamani* [1993] Crim LR 537.

[623] As inserted by the Adoption Act 2002.   [624] As defined in s 8(1) of the Children Act 1989.

[625] As defined in s 3 of the Children Act 1989.

[626] Note the amendments under the Adoption and Children Act 2002, s 139(1).

[627] [2012] EWCA Crim 389, [2012] Crim LR 623.

[628] D will not be guilty if he had a genuine belief that V was over the age of 16: s 2(3)(b). The court emphasized in *Heys and Murtagh* [2011] EWCA Crim 2112 that the belief need not be reasonable.

[629] This means the child actually taken: *Berry* [1996] 2 Cr App R 226, [1996] Crim LR 574 where D, the father of S1, took S2, believing she was S1. For criticism, see the commentary by JC Smith in [1996] Crim LR 386.

(2) where the parents were married at the time of the birth, his father or guardian, custodian or a person in whose favour a residence order is in force, takes or detains the
child without lawful authority or reasonable excuse:

    (a) so as to remove him from the lawful control of any person having lawful control of
him; or

    (b) so as to keep him out of the lawful control of any person entitled to lawful control
of him.

There are therefore four ways in which the offences can be committed.

'Detaining' is defined in s 3 to include causing the child to be detained or inducing the child
to remain with the accused or another person. 'Taking' is defined in s 3 so as to include causing or inducing the child to accompany the accused or any other person or causing the child
to be taken. 'Remove' does not require any 'geographical' removal—it is not the removal of
the child but removal of control of the child which is material. 'Lawful control' is not defined
in the Act and the courts have declined to define it. The concept varies according to the person said to have control—for example, parent, schoolteacher or nanny. A relevant question
is whether the child was deflected by D from doing that to which his lawful controller had
consented into some other activity. Has D substituted his authority or will for that of the lawful controller? There was evidence on which a jury could find that D had taken control where
he persuaded a 14-year-old boy on his way home from school to go to D's flat,[630] and where
he persuaded children to go with him to look for a bicycle which he said had been stolen.[631]

It is immaterial that the child consented to the lawful removal from the lawful control.[632]
In the case of X,[633] D was convicted of abducting a child, V, contrary to s 2(1)(b). D, a
woman, was a drug addict and sex worker and had befriended V aged 13. V was dressed in
a manner suggesting she was soliciting.[634] V persistently ran away from home. V was found
in the company of D in the red light district. V said in her evidence that she had no intention
of returning to her mother whether she was with D or not. On those facts, it was debatable
whether the conduct of D was any cause at all of V's absence, but the Court of Appeal held
that the issue was rightly left to the jury.[635]

The words 'so as to' are ambiguous. Two conflicting decisions added to the confusion.
In Mousir, the Court of Appeal held that the words import an element of actus reus (that
D's conduct had the objective consequence of removing the child from lawful control) but
not mens rea (that D intended to remove lawful control) but in the extradition case of Re
Owens[636] the Divisional Court, without being referred to Mousir, concluded that proof of
mens rea was required. The Divisional Court in Foster[637] favoured the conclusion in Mousir.

In Mousir, the court held that D's conduct had to bring about a sufficient degree of interference with the lawful control of the child,[638] but that the concept of control did not require an
assessment of the individual child's maturity. The conclusion that the words import such an

---

[630] Mousir [1987] Crim LR 561.

[631] Leather (1993) 98 Cr App R 179. See also Norman [2008] EWCA Crim 1810 (D unfit to plead on facts).

[632] A [2001] Cr App R 418.   [633] [2010] EWCA Crim 2367.

[634] The judge's direction on recklessness was appealed but, although unnecessary on the facts, was held not
to be in error following, as it did, Foster v DPP [2005] 1 WLR 1400 discussed later.

[635] See also R v A [2000] 2 All ER 177.

[636] [2000] 1 Cr App R 195.

[637] [2004] EWHC 2955 (Admin), [2005] Crim LR 639. Cf Wakeman [2011] EWCA Crim 1649. See also
Hunter [2015] All ER (D) 196 (Jan): the crime is one of basic intent. The judge had correctly explained that the
prosecution had to prove their allegation that the defendant had deliberately encouraged the complainant to get
into his car, following which she had been raped by his co-defendants.

[638] Where, as in that case, the charge is one of attempt, the issue is whether the acts are more than merely
preparatory to that effect.

element of actus reus seems, with respect, to be correct in principle. The natural meaning of the term 'so as to' is 'with the effect of' removing the child from lawful control. It introduces a causal element additional to the actus reus of 'taking' or 'detaining'.[639] *Owens* does not contradict this. Simon Brown LJ stated that 'the words "so as to" mean "with the intention of" rather than *merely* with the effect of'.[640] In *Re Owens*, the Divisional Court expressly held that D must 'intend' to interfere with another person's lawful control of the child.[641] The court in *Mousir* had accepted counsel's concession that the phrase did not import an element of mens rea—that D had knowledge as to the effect of his conduct being the removal of the child from lawful control. Since the offence charged in that case was one of attempt, the element of intention would be required separately under the Criminal Attempts Act 1981.

In *Foster*,[642] the court concluded that the emphasis on mens rea in *Owens* was unnecessary to reach the result in that case, suggesting that *Owens* should have been treated as a case in which D had a lawful excuse rather than one in which she lacked mens rea. The court stated that the mens rea for the s 2 offence is:

an intentional or reckless taking or detention of a child under the age of sixteen, the effect or objective consequence of which is to remove or to keep that child within the meaning of section 2(1)(a) or (b).

The Divisional Court considered the scope of the offence is *Shepherd v CPS*.[643] The appellant had been served with a Child Abduction Warning Notice informing him that a mother had not given him permission to communicate with her daughter or allow her daughter to enter or stay in his home or be in his company. The daughter, who was 14 years old at the time, went to the appellant's house and asked if she could come in to make a roll-up cigarette. The appellant allowed her in and he was charged with detaining a child without lawful authority. It was submitted on behalf of the appellant that the child had voluntarily entered his home and that he had therefore done nothing to cause her to be detained so as to be out of her mother's lawful control. The Divisional Court, in dismissing his appeal, held that the wishes of the child were irrelevant to whether the appellant had committed the offence. There was an inducement by the appellant's positive act of allowing the child to remain. Furthermore, the appellant's action in allowing the child to enter and remain in his house was sufficient to constitute the keeping of a child who was under the control of her mother.

Note that Art 8 of the ECHR—the right to respect for private life—may impose positive obligations on the State to respect family life. This may include an obligation on the State to provide safeguards against abduction.[644]

16.14 Harassment

16.14.1 Background

Prior to 1997, the criminal law struggled to provide protection for those who suffered at the hands of so-called 'stalkers'.[645] It was difficult for the law to tackle an activity which was in

---

[639] It is possible that D might remove or detain a child without lawful excuse but without causing him to be removed from lawful custody where D also removed or detained the lawful custodian.

[640] Emphasis added, at 201.   [641] [2000] 1 Cr App R 195.   [642] [2004] EWHC 2955 (Admin).

[643] [2017] EWHC 2566 (Admin).

[644] *Iglesias Gil and AIU v Spain* (App no 56673/00) 2003; *Maire v Portugal* (App no 48206/99) 2003; *D (A Child) (Abduction: Rights of Custody)* [2006] UKHL 51. See also *Ljungkvist v Sweden* [2014] ACD 173(60), DC.

[645] See R Babcock, 'The Psychology of Stalking' in P Infield and G Platford, *The Law of Harassment and Stalking* (2000); N Addison and T Lawson-Cruttenden, *Harassment Law and Practice* (1998). The offence is further amended by the Serious Organised Crime and Police Act 2005, s 125.

part an infringement of privacy,[646] in part an offence against the person, with some forms of the conduct also having a public order dimension. The use of tortious remedies to tackle behaviour which amounted to stalking was severely curtailed by the decision of the House of Lords in *Hunter v Canary Wharf*.[647] The Lords held that only those who had a right to exclusive possession of the land could sue in nuisance. Recourse was had to the criminal law and prosecutors relied on offences of public nuisance, specific offences relating to malicious communications or telecommunications where possible, or public order offences and offences against the person. These efforts to combat what was perceived as a growing social menace were assisted by the courts' acceptance that psychiatric injury was a sufficient basis for a finding of actual or grievous bodily harm[648] and by the House of Lords' acceptance that assault could be committed by words alone or even by a silent telephone call.[649] These extended interpretations were not always well received[650] but led to convictions.

Parliament nevertheless felt that a specific offence was needed and, following consultation[651] and an unseemly rush through Parliament, the Protection from Harassment Act 1997 was enacted.[652] The draftsman faced a formidable difficulty in defining 'stalking' without over-criminalizing. The conduct complained of as harassing behaviour may include acts of apparent kindness, such as repeated sending of flowers or seemingly innocuous conduct, such as walking by the victim's house. As the minister stated:

Stalkers do not stick to activities on a list. Stalkers and other weirdos [*sic*] who pursue women, [*sic*] cause racial harassment and annoy their neighbours have a wide range of activity which it is impossible to define.[653]

As Wells observes, the Act follows a pattern all too common in recent years of 'addressing a narrowly conceived social harm with a widely drawn provision, often supplementing and overlapping with existing offences'.[654] The flexibility allows for the offence to be used in respect of stalking, persistent protestors, bullying,[655] etc.

In *Smith*,[656] the Court of Appeal defined 'harassment' as follows: 'Essentially, it involves persistent conduct of a seriously oppressive nature, either physically or mentally, targeted at an individual and resulting in fear or distress.' The definition was considered more recently in *N*.[657] At trial the judge defined harassment by reference to s 7(2), but equated harassment with alarm or distress, rather than directing the jury that harassment *includes* alarm or distress. The Court of Appeal held that this was a misdirection. The danger of equating harassment with alarm or distress, according to the court, is that not all conduct, even though it may be unattractive, unreasonable and does in fact cause alarm or distress, will be

---

[646] See Alldridge, *Relocating Criminal Law*, Ch 4.

[647] [1997] 2 All ER 426. See also *Wong v Parkside Health NHS Trust* [2003] 3 All ER 932, CA.

[648] *Chan Fook* [1994] 2 All ER 552, CA; *Burstow* [1998] AC 147.

[649] *Ireland* [1998] AC 147.

[650] C Wells, 'Stalking the Criminal Law Response' [1997] Crim LR 463.

[651] See Home Office, *Stalking: The Solutions* (1996).

[652] See the analysis by E Finch, *The Criminalisation of Stalking* (2001); M Allen, 'Look Who's Stalking' [1996] Web JCLI. For a comparative review of stalking laws, see B Clarke and L Meintjes-Van der Valt (1998) 115 South African LJ 729.

[653] D MacLean, Home Office Minister, HC, 17 Dec 1996, col 827.

[654] C Wells [1997] Crim LR 463 at 464.

[655] See A Gillespie, 'Cyber-Bullying and Harassment of Teenagers: The Legal Response' [2006] JSWFL 123; N Geach, 'Regulating Harassment: Is the Law Fit for the Social Networking Age?' (2009) 73 J Crim L 241. The House of Lords in *Majrowski v Guy's and St Thomas' Hospital* [2006] UKHL 34, [2007] 1 AC 224, held that the Act applies in the workplace and that employers may be vicariously liable for failing to take appropriate preventative action to prevent employees being bullied. Note also the powers inserted by the Domestic Violence, Crime and Victims Act 2004, in respect of restraining orders in domestic violence cases.

[656] [2012] EWCA Crim 2566, [24].   [657] [2016] EWCA Crim 92.

sufficient to justify the sanction of the criminal law. The judge's direction to the jury failed to include a reference for the need to be sure that D's conduct was oppressive. The court held that the requirement of oppression serves as a yardstick that helps the law to draw a sensible line between, 'the give and take of daily life and conduct which justifies the sanctions of the criminal law'.[658] The definition provided by s 7 is clearly inclusive and not exhaustive. 'Harassment' is generally understood to involve improper oppressive and unreasonable conduct that is targeted at an individual and calculated to produce the consequences described in s 7. By s 1(3) of the Act, reasonable and/or lawful courses of conduct may be excluded.

The CPS has issued guidance on prosecuting harassment.[659] The CPS introduces the guidance by stating:

This legal guidance addresses behaviour which is repeated and unwanted by the victim and which causes the victim to have a negative reaction in terms of alarm or distress. Cases involving stalking and harassment can be difficult to prosecute, and because of their nature are likely to require sensitive handling, especially with regard to victim care. The provision of accurate and up-to-date information to the victim throughout the life of the case, together with quality support, and careful consideration of any special measures requirements are essential factors for the CPS to consider.

16.14.2 Harassment defined

1.—(1) A person must not pursue a course of conduct—

    (a) which amounts to harassment of another, and

    (b) which he knows or ought to know amounts to harassment of the other.

(1A)   A person must not pursue a course of conduct—

    (a) which involves harassment of two or more persons, and

    (b) which he knows or ought to know involves harassment of those persons, and

    (c) by which he intends to persuade any person (whether or not one of those mentioned above)—

        (i) not to do something that he is entitled or required to do, or

        (ii) to do something that he is not under any obligation to do.

2.—(1) A person who pursues a course of conduct in breach of section 1(1) or (1A) is guilty of an offence.[660]

16.14.2.1 Course of conduct

The offences under the Act are dependent on proof of a course of conduct, which is merely an element of each offence and not a crime in itself.

By s 7:

(1) A 'course of conduct' must involve—

    (a) in the case of conduct in relation to a single person (see section 1(1)), conduct on at least two occasions in relation to that person, or

    (b) in the case of conduct in relation to two or more persons (see section 1(1A)), conduct on at least one occasion in relation to each of those persons.

---

[658] At [32]. In the subsequent case of *Tan* [2017] EWCA Crim 493, D's conviction was upheld on the basis that despite the fact the judge did not use the word 'oppression', his direction nevertheless accurately conveyed to the jury the threshold that must be crossed before an offence is committed.

[659] See www.cps.gov.uk/legal-guidance/stalking-and-harassment.

[660] Section 1A was added by the Serious Organised Crime and Police Act 2005, s 125.

(3A) A person's conduct on any occasion shall be taken, if aided, abetted, counselled or procured by another—

   (a) to be conduct on that occasion of the other (as well as conduct of the person whose conduct it is); and

   (b) to be conduct in relation to which the other's knowledge and purpose, and what he ought to have known, are the same as they were in relation to what was contemplated or reasonably foreseeable at the time of the aiding, abetting, counselling or procuring.

The course of conduct is at the core of both crimes (and the tort). The provision is far from clear, with little further elaboration other than that words are sufficient (s 7(4)). One of the major problems under the Act has been in determining when two incidents are sufficiently closely associated to constitute a course of conduct. Although seeking to identify the idea of 'persistence' that lies at the heart of stalking, Parliament refrained from attempting further to define the proscribed behaviour. In debates on the Bill, Michael Howard, then Home Secretary, referred to the lack of definition, but regarded harassment as a concept 'interpreted regularly by the courts since 1986'.[661] It is extremely wide in scope and applies to protest and neighbourhood disputes[662] as well as what might more usually be regarded as stalking.

It has been accepted that D's conduct can amount to a course of conduct even where that involves some action by V. In *James v CPS*,[663] D was receiving care from a social services team in his area. D repeatedly phoned the services team to complain about his care. The team manager, V, returned D's calls as she was duty-bound to do and D was abusive to her. That pattern of behaviour was repeated. The Divisional Court held that the fact that V returned the calls was irrelevant. As Elias LJ observed:

If I am continually abusive to someone who comes within my vicinity, that may still be capable of constituting a course of conduct, even if the victim chooses to come within my vicinity. The fact that he or she chooses to do so might arguably be relevant to the question of whether there is harassment, but not to the question of whether there is a course of conduct.[664]

As the court observed in *Curtis*,[665] s 7 of the Act does not provide an exhaustive definition of harassment. There will be conduct which might alarm or distress someone without being harassing.[666]

One act or two?

Is there a 'course of conduct' when an individual engages in one continuous activity—for example, sitting outside V's house for a whole day? In *Hills*,[667] it was stressed that it is not just enough to count the incidents, nor to direct the jury in such terms.[668] In *Kelly v DPP*,[669] D, who had just been released on licence after conviction for harassing V, made three abusive and threatening telephone calls to a mobile telephone belonging to V between 2.57 am and 3.02 am. V did not answer any of the calls at the time and they were recorded on her voicemail. V subsequently listened to the messages one after the other, without pause. It was held that the closeness of time within which the calls were made was only *a* factor to be taken into account when determining whether there had been repetitious behaviour for the purposes of proving the commission of an offence of harassment. The case raises questions

---

[661] HC, 17 Dec 1996, vol 287, col 784.

[662] Inciting a dog to bark is sufficient to form part of a course of conduct: *Tafurelli v DPP* [2004] EWHC 2791 (Admin).

[663] [2009] EWHC 2925 (Admin).   [664] At [12].   [665] [2010] EWCA Crim 123.

[666] In that case repeated incidents of domestic violence.   [667] [2001] Crim LR 318.

[668] *Patel* [2005] Crim LR 649, [2004] EWCA Crim 3284.   [669] [2003] Crim LR 43, DC.

about where the courts will draw the line. Consider D who telephones V, V answers the call and immediately she identifies D and terminates the call. D calls back immediately. V sees that D's number appears on the 'caller ID' facility. Is this a course of conduct? In *Loake v CPS*, D was convicted of harassment after sending her husband, from whom she was separated, a very large number of text messages over a period of time.[670]

In *Hills*, Latham LJ stated that repetition was a significant factor in determining whether there is a course of conduct, but there is no requirement that acts be similar or repeated. Any combination of bouquets of flowers, menacing calls or letters, loitering outside the victim's home, etc will suffice. As was suggested in *Lau*,[671] the question of whether there is a course of conduct should be determined by whether there is a sufficient nexus between the two acts, taking account of all of the circumstances. The courts have acknowledged that the question is a difficult one.[672] In *DPP v Hardy*,[673] the court accepted that 95 phone calls made over a 90-minute period were capable of constituting harassment, especially since they included threats to continue that behaviour all night.[674]

One actor or two?

Section 7(3A)[675] ensures that where A performs a harassing act towards V aided by B, and subsequently A alone commits a further act of harassment towards V, the two acts may be regarded as a course of conduct. This extension of the scope of a 'course of conduct' was enacted to deal with protestors. A campaign of collective harassment by two or more people can amount to a 'course of conduct'. The knowledge and purpose of the aider, abetter, counsellor or procurer is judged at the time that the conduct was planned and not when it is carried out. The provision seeks to pre-empt a defence by A that when he counselled B to commit a second act towards V, A was unaware that his first act towards V had caused distress. Since it is enough that A ought to have known that the act would cause distress at the time that the subsequent act was commissioned, he will be liable.

The offence can be committed by D communicating with X which causes harassment to V.[676]

One victim or two?

The course of conduct under s 1(1) must relate to 'another'. In *DPP v Williams*,[677] D had put his hand through a bathroom window startling the occupant V1 who was showering. She then informed V2, her flatmate, who was scared by the event as reported to her. Two days later D peered through the bedroom window, this time frightening V2 directly. The magistrates convicted, holding that 'another' could be read as 'others'. The Divisional Court decided the case on the basis that V2 had been distressed on both occasions and therefore the offence was made out. The interpretation was rightly criticized for extending the offence considerably and for giving rise to practical problems.[678] In *Caurti v DPP*,[679] it was held that

---

670 [2017] EWHC 2855 (Admin).   671 [2000] Crim LR 580 and commentary.

672 See *Buckley* [2008] EWHC 136 (Admin) graveside altercation and spitting at V in cemetery car park.

673 [2008] All ER (D) 315 (Oct).

674 D had called an employment agency to request information about why he had been rejected for a job, so his calls had been legitimate to begin with, but they had clearly escalated into conduct that was capable of constituting harassment.

675 As inserted by the Criminal Justice and Police Act 2001.

676 *C v CPS* [2008] EWHC 148 (Admin).   677 *DPP v Williams* (DC, 27 July 1998, Rose LJ and Bell J).

678 A charge under the 1997 Act, s 1(1), might be bad for duplicity where it names two complainants when they are members of a 'close knit identifiable group': *Mills v DPP* (1998) 17 Dec, DC.

679 [2002] Crim LR 131 and commentary.

in relation to the more serious s 4 offence (causing fear of violence, see later) the course of conduct must have its impact on *one* complainant, even where it is aimed at another.

Under s 1(1A), it is clear that the harassment can be to two or more persons, provided the additional element of intention in s 1(1A)(c) can be established. The provision will prove useful in criminalizing, for example, the conduct of protestors who target people connected with animal breeding and vivisection organizations.[680] Section 1(1A) will catch threats and intimidation intended to force an individual or individuals to stop trading.

The complainant must be an individual and not a corporate body:[681] s 7(5) of the Act provides that references to a 'person' are references to 'a person who is an individual'. But a company can commit the offence.[682]

No need for temporal proximity or similarity

Is there a course of conduct where different acts are separated by a considerable period of time? For example, are two acts separated by one year, say, two birthday cards, a 'course of conduct'? In *Lau v DPP*,[683] two incidents four months apart were held to be capable of amounting to a course of conduct. The court observed that 'one can conceive of circumstances where incidents, as far apart as a year, could constitute a course of conduct'. The example given was of racial harassment outside a synagogue on the Day of Atonement. In *Baron v CPS*,[684] it was accepted that the less proximate in time and the more limited in number the incidents, the less likely that there was a course of conduct. In *Pratt v DPP*,[685] D threw water over his estranged wife and three months later chased her through the matrimonial home swearing and questioning her constantly. The magistrates found these to be a course of conduct and the Divisional Court did not find this to be an irrational decision. However, it was noted that prosecuting authorities should be cautious in bringing charges for the offence of harassment in circumstances where only a small number of incidents had occurred. The prosecution should ensure not merely that two or more incidents had occurred, but that such repetitious behaviour had caused harassment to the other person.[686] Examples of prosecution agencies overusing harassment charges persist. In *Curtis*,[687] D had in the course of a relationship with V, a fellow police officer, engaged in conduct including minor assaults on V and pulling the handbrake of a car V was driving, causing it to skid. This was charged as harassment. The court quashed the conviction. The court defined harassment as 'tormenting a person by subjecting them to constant interference or intimidation'. The conduct had to be oppressive, unreasonable and unacceptable to a degree that would sustain criminal liability. Although D's conduct had been deplorable and the incidents had been far from trivial, it could not be concluded that, in the course of a volatile relationship where there had been aggression on both sides, the six incidents over a nine-month period amounted to a course of conduct amounting to harassment within the meaning of the Act. Reference was made to *Majrowski* (see earlier)[688] where it was emphasized that:

Courts are well able to recognise the boundary between conduct which is unattractive, even unreasonable, and conduct which is oppressive and unacceptable. To cross the boundary from the

---

[680] See the Home Office document: *Animal Welfare: Human Rights—Protecting People from Animal Rights Extremists* (2004). See the Serious Organised Crime and Police Act 2005, s 145.

[681] *DPP v Dziurzynski* (2002) 166 JP 545; cf *Daiichi UK Ltd and others v Huntingdon Animal Cruelty and others* [2003] EWHC 2337 (QB): person does not include a limited company as a victim.

[682] See *Kosar v Bank of Scotland* [2011] EWHC 1050 (Admin).

[683] [2000] Crim LR, [2000] 1 FLR 799.   [684] (2000) 13 June, unreported.

[685] [2001] EWHC 483 (Admin).

[686] Note that the CPS acknowledges that the Act is 'widely drafted, and could incorporate many minor forms of behaviour'. Reference should be had to Home Office Circular 34/1997, making it clear that the Act is not intended to supplant existing powers to deal with incidents that do not reach the threshold of harassment.

[687] [2010] EWCA Crim 123.   [688] [2007] 1 AC 224 per Lord Nicholls at [30].

regrettable to the unacceptable the gravity of the misconduct must be of an order which would sustain criminal liability under section 2.

Baroness Hale observed[689] that the definition had been deliberately left wide open and it had been left to the wisdom of the courts to distinguish between the ordinary banter and badinage of life and genuinely offensive and unacceptable behaviour. It cannot be a requirement that each of the acts alleged to constitute part of the course of conduct is itself criminal.[690]

It is submitted that the events making up the 'course of conduct' under the Act require a nexus, as is implicit within the expression, which suggests a 'series' of events with some connection. The main connecting factor will be that the acts are aimed at a particular victim, but that will not of itself be sufficient, in the same way that two visits to the hospital by the same patient would not necessarily be described as a course of treatment. There must be something more connecting them—in the case of the treatment, one would expect it to be for the same ailment. The mere fact that D made two harassing calls to the same victim a year apart will not necessarily constitute a course of conduct. If the calls were made on a particular anniversary, there would be a greater nexus and the course of conduct would be more likely to be established. The question must turn on all the circumstances of the case.

When does the course of conduct begin?

In many instances, D will be involved in what might be considered to be, initially at least, neutral conduct towards V. Does his course of conduct only begin when he is aware of the distress he is causing V, or when it causes V harassment or when the reasonable person would see it as harassing? In *King v DPP*,[691] the alleged harassment was by offering the victim a plant, writing letters to her, rummaging in her rubbish, stealing her discarded underwear from refuse bags and filming her secretly. The Divisional Court held that 'repeated offers of unwelcome gifts or the repeated sending of letters could well amount to harassment, nevertheless, the *single* offer of a gift of modest value *and* the sending of one innocuous letter in the circumstances of this case cannot amount to harassment within the meaning of the 1997 Act. Nor could the letter and the gift be treated as the first stage or the first two stages of a course of conduct amounting to harassment...' The magistrates were wrong to treat these incidents as forming part of a course of conduct. The decision is difficult to square with the terms of the section. There is no limitation as to the types of conduct amounting to harassment in the statute.

A victim may be held to be aware of a course of conduct through indirect knowledge, as where V is told that D has been calling her, provided there is evidence on the basis of which the court can properly conclude that D was pursuing a course of conduct with the necessary mens rea.[692]

Mens rea as to the course of conduct

There is no requirement that the harasser intended or directed his conduct to harass V, it is sufficient that 'a reasonable person in possession of the same information would think the course of conduct amounted to harassment of another'.[693] The leading case is that of *Colohan*[694] where it was held that the test is entirely objective.[695] In that case it was held that D's schizophrenia could not be taken into consideration in evaluating whether the reasonable person would have realized that the conduct was harassing. On the facts, it was unclear whether D

---

689 ibid, [66].   690 See *R (Jones) v Bedfordshire MC* [2010] EWHC 523 (Admin), [27].

691 20 June 2000, DC.   692 *Kellett v DPP* [2001] EWHC 107 (Admin).

693 Section 1(2).   694 [2001] EWCA Crim 1251, [2001] Crim LR 845. See Ch 4.

695 Affirmed more recently by the Divisional Court in *R (Aylesbury Crown Court) v CPS* [2013] EWHC 3228 (Admin). Note that in *Loake v CPS* [2017] EWHC 2855 (Admin) the Divisional Court confirmed that insanity is available as a defence to harassment. See p 304.

was denying that he knew what he was doing in writing the allegedly harassing letters, or denying that he knew that the letters constituted a course of harassing conduct, or was claiming simply that the harassment was reasonable. Given the clear policy behind the legislation, it is not surprising that the court rejected the defence claims. The prosecution of mentally disordered individuals under this offence not only ensures the protection for victims of stalking, but also increases the chances of the offender receiving psychiatric assessment and treatment.

To be liable under s 1(1A), D must also intend to persuade the person(s) to refrain from something that they are entitled or to do something they are not; for example, for an animal breeding unit to stop trading with a vivisection lab.

In possession of the same information

Section 1(2) is unusual in requiring that the person whose course of conduct is in question *ought to know* that it amounts to harassment of another if a reasonable person 'in possession of the same information' would do so. The section is designed to endow the reasonable person with knowledge of circumstances that would render otherwise seemingly innocuous conduct harassing (eg when D knows that previous advances towards V have been rejected and continues to send gifts). In such cases D's inculpatory state of mind is taken into account. Should the reasonable person also be possessed with knowledge about D's exculpatory states of mind in order to assess whether the conduct is harassment? This is not the same as asking whether a reasonable person with the characteristics of D would regard it as harassment, particularly where the characteristic inhibits cognition of the wrongdoing. In *Colohan*, the strong policy grounds of protection on which the Act is founded justified the court's rejection of any attempt to diminish the purely objective stance. In *Pelham*,[696] D was charged under the racially aggravated form of the offence and denied that she had the mens rea on the basis that she was of low IQ and lacked an understanding of the racial nature of her comments. The court refused to allow expert evidence as to this aspect of the mens rea, in line with the general rule against expert evidence being permitted on mens rea issues.

Defences justifying the course of conduct

Section 1 provides:

(1) Subsection (1) or (1A) does not apply to a course of conduct if the person who pursued it shows—

   (a) that it was pursued for the purpose of preventing or detecting crime;

   (b) that it was pursued under any enactment or rule of law or to comply with any condition or requirement imposed by any person under any enactment, or

   (c) that in the particular circumstances the pursuit of the course of conduct was reasonable.

Paragraph (a) seems clear, although debate might arise over whether it is restricted to State officials engaged in criminal investigations or whether investigative journalists might also be able to rely on this defence.[697] It might apply to the busybody Neighbourhood Watch coordinator, although the courts have suggested that s 1(3)(a) was framed with law enforcement

---

[696] [2007] EWCA Crim 1321.

[697] Note also s 12 providing that the Secretary of State may issue certificates that render conduct of specified individuals conclusively reasonable (eg security service operatives). Note *Trimingham v Associated Newspapers Ltd* [2012] EWHC 1296 (QB), where Tugendhat J referred to *Thomas v News Group Newspapers Ltd* [2001] EWCA Civ 1233 to hold that journalism amounting to a course of conduct is reasonable under s 1(3)(c) unless, in the particular circumstances of the case, the course of conduct is so unreasonable that under Art 10 of the ECHR it is necessary proportionately to prohibit or sanction it under Art 10(2) including the protection of the rights of others.

agencies and not private individuals in mind. If a private individual relies on s 1(3)(a) he must show some rational basis for his conduct, judged on an objective basis.[698]

The Supreme Court considered what the appropriate standard ought to be in *Hayes v Willoughby*,[699] a civil case. Lord Sumption, who delivered the judgment of the majority, held that the word 'purpose' connotes a subjective state of mind.[700] Section 1(3)(a) does not, therefore, embody a wholly objective test. His lordship further stated, however, that Parliament could not have intended for there to be no limits placed on the pursuit of the course of conduct, no matter how irrational D's state of mind. It was held that the necessary control mechanism is found in the concept of rationality. His lordship distinguished rationality from reasonableness, which was characterized as an 'external, objective standard applied to the outcome of a person's thoughts or intentions'. Rationality, on the other hand:

applies a minimum objective standard to the relevant person's mental processes. It imports a requirement of good faith, a requirement that there should be some logical connection between the evidence and the ostensible reasons for the decision, and (which will usually amount to the same thing) an absence of arbitrariness, of capriciousness or of reasoning so outrageous in its defiance of logic as to be perverse.[701]

In future, therefore, before an alleged harasser can be said to have had the purpose of preventing or detecting crime, he must have sufficiently applied his mind to the matter. He must have thought rationally about the material suggesting the possibility of criminality and formed the view that the conduct said to constitute harassment was appropriate for the purpose of preventing or detecting it. Lord Sumption stated explicitly that the court should not test D's conclusions against the standard of what a reasonable person in D's circumstances would have concluded. Lord Reed dissented on the basis that Parliament did not specify that D's pursuit of the course of conduct had to be rational; the statute should not be construed as extending beyond the limits which Parliament itself made clear in its enactment; and that criminal liability should not turn on the subtle distinction between what is unreasonable and what is irrational. It is submitted that there is considerable force in Lord Reed's three points. The most pertinent one is, however, his lordship's third point. Formulating a new test of rationality adds an additional layer of uncertainty. It is submitted that not only might judges find it difficult to direct juries on how they ought to approach the test of rationality, judges themselves might have difficulty in delineating between the various states of mind now demanded by the Supreme Court's judgment when determining whether the defence ought to be left. A better approach, it is submitted, would be the one suggested by Lord Reed, namely a wholly subjective test. This would not necessarily lead to specious defences being pleaded successfully, as the jury could still conclude that D did not have as his purpose the prevention or detection of crime.

Paragraph (b) is uncontroversial. It protects the right of free speech and expression. In a civil case which was one of the first cases under the Act, Eady J commented that the Act was not intended to be used to stifle discussion of public interest on public demonstrations.[702]

---

[698] *Howlett v Holding* (2006) The Times, 8 Feb, QBD (D conducted a campaign against the V, a local councillor, by flying banners from his aircraft referring to her in derogatory and abusive terms).

[699] [2013] UKSC 17.

[700] The Supreme Court did not reach a conclusion on whether preventing or detecting crime must be the sole purpose, or whether the dominant purpose will suffice. His lordship did intimate, however, that he favoured the latter formulation. The Commercial Court in the subsequent case of *Starbev GP Ltd v Interbrew Central European Holdings* [2014] EWHC 1311 (Comm) stated that the relevant purpose is the dominant one.

[701] At [14].

[702] *Huntingdon Life Sciences v Curtin* (1997) The Times, 11 Dec, [1998] Env LR D9. See also *Bayer Crop Science Ltd* [2009] WL 4872821.

More difficult is the defence under para (c), particularly in cases where D claims that his action was part of a campaign of legitimate protest. In *Baron v DPP*,[703] the court emphasized that:

a line must be drawn between legitimate expression of disgust at the way a public agency has behaved and conduct amounting to harassment. The right to free speech requires a broad degree of tolerance in relation to communications. It is a legitimate exercise of that right to say things which are unpleasant or possibly hurtful to the recipient.

The defence under s 1(3)(c) does not involve the question whether the reasonable person regards the course of conduct as harassment, but whether it *is* reasonable harassment.[704]

It seems to arise only where it is accepted that the course of conduct is harassing. Furthermore, the question is whether the conduct was, as a whole, 'reasonable' which suggests a purely objective assessment. In some cases involving protest campaigns the courts may face difficult issues of evaluating the reasonableness of a form of protest. These may involve arguments based on rights of freedom of expression under Art 10 of the ECHR.[705]

The burden is on the defendant to prove, on the balance of probabilities,[706] that the conduct is reasonable. It has been held that pursuit of conduct in breach of an injunction will preclude a defence under s 1(3)(c).[707]

16.14.2.2 The s 2 offence

2.—(1) A person who pursues a course of conduct in breach of section 1(1) or (1A) is guilty of an offence.

(2) A person guilty of an offence under this section is liable on summary conviction to imprisonment for a term not exceeding six months, or [an unlimited] fine, or both.

The offence is based on the course of conduct and it has been held that prosecutions are not therefore time-barred if at least one of the incidents forming part of the course of conduct occurs within the six-month limitation period for the laying of informations in the magistrates' court.[708]

The s 2 offence requires two or more acts by D constituting a course of conduct. There need be only one result from their cumulative effect—the harassment of the victim. Section 7(2) provides that 'harassing a person' includes 'alarming the person or causing the person distress' and this has been treated as a non-exhaustive definition.[709] There is no requirement that any violence is threatened (or feared) for the offence under s 2. The section criminalizes conduct such as that in *Chambers and Edwards v DPP*[710] where protestors persistently but non-violently blocked the surveyor's theodolite beam, since the Divisional Court held that such conduct would amount to harassment for the purposes of the Public Order Act 1986. In many cases the section has been used successfully in respect of 'classic' stalking behaviour.[711]

---

[703] (2000) 13 June, unreported.

[704] Nothing that involves cultural or racial differences should be taken into account, unless it is relevant and supported by proper evidence: *C v CPS* [2008] EWHC 148 (Admin).

[705] See *Debnath* [2006] 2 Cr App R (S) 25, where a restraining order against D prohibiting any publication against V whether true or not was upheld.

[706] See p 23, on the appropriateness of the burden under the HRA 1998 and Art 6(2).

[707] *DPP v Mosely* (1999) The Times, 23 June.   [708] *DPP v Baker* [2004] EWHC 2782 (Admin).

[709] *DPP v Ramsdale* (2001) The Independent, 19 Mar.   [710] [1995] Crim LR 896.

[711] For critical comment on the scope of the offence, see E Finch, 'Stalking the Perfect Stalking Law: An Evaluation of the Efficacy of the Protection from Harassment Act 1997' [2002] Crim LR 702. See also J Harris, Home Office Research Study No 203, *An Evaluation of the Use and Effectiveness of the Protection from Harassment Act 1997* (2000).

865

16.14.2.3 Causing a fear of violence: s 4

Section 4 provides:

(1) A person whose course of conduct causes another to fear, on at least two occasions, that violence will be used against him is guilty of an offence if he knows or ought to know that his course of conduct will cause the other so to fear on each of those occasions.

(2) For the purposes of this section, the person whose course of conduct is in question ought to know that it will cause another to fear that violence will be used against him on any occasion if a reasonable person in possession of the same information would think the course of conduct would cause the other so to fear on that occasion.

(3) It is a defence for a person charged with an offence under this section to show that—

(a) his course of conduct was pursued for the purpose of preventing or detecting crime,

(b) his course of conduct was pursued under any enactment or rule of law or to comply with any condition or requirement imposed by any person under any enactment, or

(c) the pursuit of his course of conduct was reasonable for the protection of himself or another or for the protection of his or another's property.

Section 4 is triable either way, carrying a maximum sentence on indictment of ten[712] years' imprisonment, or a fine or both. This is a high maximum sentence for a negligence-based offence. A judge who rules that there is no case to answer on a charge under s 4 may allow the jury to consider an alternative verdict under s 2.[713]

The essential difference between this offence and that in s 2 (and the tort in s 3) is that the victim must be caused to fear on at least two occasions, that violence will be used 'against him'. The other important difference is that the only defence available to this charge is that the harasser proves that his conduct was for the purpose of preventing or detecting crime, was lawfully authorized or was reasonable for the protection of *himself or another or of property*.[714]

Section 4 has been criticized as being too narrow because of this requirement.[715] Whereas s 2 explicitly requires, *inter alia*: (a) a course of conduct (b) which must amount to harassment of another, s 4 requires that the victim is caused, by the course of conduct, to fear violence on at least two occasions. In *Curtis*, the court concluded that the s 4 offence requires proof also that the course of conduct has to amount to harassment.[716] Section 4 does not expressly require that the course of conduct which causes the victim to fear violence constitutes harassment. Section 4 contains the stricter limitation that the course of conduct has to cause fear (it being insufficient even to frighten the victim as to what might happen (*Henley*)). Arguably, s 4 represents a distinct offence focused not on harassment but on the graver wrong of creating fear of violence. However, the court's preferred interpretation is one which construes s 4 in the broader context of the Act and sits more comfortably with the fact that s 2 is an included alternative offence.[717] Interpreting s 4 so as not to require the

---

[712] See s 175 of the Policing and Crime Act 2017 (in force from 3 Apr 2017).

[713] *Livesey* [2006] EWCA Crim 3344.

[714] A failure to direct on these defences may well render a conviction unsafe—*Wilkes* [2004] EWCA Crim 3136.

[715] See Finch [2002] Crim LR 702, n 711, suggesting a new offence of intentional harassment to bridge the gap between the narrow s 4 and the wide and overused s 2.

[716] *Curtis* was followed in the subsequent case of *Widdows* [2011] EWCA Crim 1500. Although these authorities ultimately bound it as a matter of precedent, the Court of Appeal in *Haque* [2011] EWCA Crim 1871 stated that it applied them 'reluctantly'. The court took cognizance of the scepticism expressed in the comment at [2011] Crim LR 959.

[717] Furthermore, it is consistent with the approach that seems to have been taken in previous authorities holding that the victim has been put in 'fear of violence *by harassment*', such as *Patel* [2004] EWCA Crim 3284 (emphasis added).

course of conduct to constitute 'harassment' would only be of practical significance if there are circumstances in which two or more incidents with a sufficient nexus caused a fear of violence without also being harassing. That would seem unlikely.

Section 4 has no requirement of immediacy as in assault. In *Qosja*,[718] Carr J stated that:

In our judgment, a plain and natural reading of the wording of section 4A(1)(b)(i) of the Protection from Harassment Act 1997 reveals that the section is wide enough to look to incidents of violence in the future and not only to incidents giving rise to a fear of violence arising directly out of the incident in question. Nor is there any requirement for the fear to be of violence on a particular date or time in the future, or at a particular place or in a particular manner, or for there to be a specific threat of violence. There can be a fear of violence sufficient for the statute where that fear of violence is of violence on a separate and later occasion. The position can be tested simply by reference to the example of somebody saying 'I'll come back and get you'. On [counsel for D's] interpretation that would be insufficient fear to fall within the scope of the section; that is not a position that we consider to be correct.[719]

It is submitted that this interpretation of the offence is in keeping with the broad approach intended by Parliament and that it ought to apply equally to the offence in s 4(1).

Unlike s 8 of the Public Order Act 1986, no definition of violence is provided in the 1997 Act. In *Henley*,[720] H's harassment of the complainant and her family included threats to kill. He was charged under s 4. The trial judge failed properly to direct the jury, wrongly suggesting that to 'seriously frighten her' would suffice and failed to clarify that the person must *himself* fear violence, not violence towards others. It was emphasized that a direction on the mens rea under s 4(2) should be routinely given. It is 'good practice' for the judge to direct the jury to consider whether the incidents about which they were sure were so connected in type and in context as to justify the conclusion that they could amount to a course of conduct.[721]

A fear of violence may be inferred from threats and behaviour other than explicit threats of violence issued to the victim in person (eg threats to his dog), but the victim must fear that violence will be used against himself.[722] Threats to burn down the family house will suffice.[723]

16.14.2.4 Racially and religiously aggravated harassment

The Crime and Disorder Act 1998, as amended by the Anti-terrorism, Crime and Security Act 2001, provides racially and religiously aggravated offences of harassment and putting people in fear of violence.

Section 32:

(1) A person is guilty of an offence under this section if he commits—

   (a) an offence under s 2 of the Protection from Harassment Act 1997 (offence of harassment); or

   (b) an offence under s 4 of that Act (putting people in fear of violence),

which is [racially or religiously aggravated] for the purposes of this section.

An aggravated offence under s 32(1)(a) is triable either way and punishable on indictment with a maximum sentence of two years' imprisonment. An offence under s 32(1)(b) is triable

---

[718] [2016] EWCA Crim 1543.   [719] At [31].

[720] [2000] Crim LR 582. See also *Curtis* [2010] EWCA Crim 123.

[721] *Sahin* [2009] EWCA Crim 2616.

[722] *R v DPP* [2001] Crim LR 396; *Henley* [2000] Crim LR 582; *Caurti v DPP* [2002] Crim LR 131 and commentaries.

[723] *R (A) v DPP* [2005] ACD 61.

either way and carries a maximum 14 years' imprisonment on conviction on indictment. The nature of racial and religious aggravation is discussed earlier.[724]

16.14.2.5 Harassment in the home

Section 126 of the Serious Organised Crime and Police Act 2005 introduced a new offence into s 42A of the Criminal Justice and Police Act 2001. This offence is triable summarily only[725] and carries a maximum sentence of six months' imprisonment or a fine not exceeding level 4 on the standard scale, or both. 'Dwelling' has the same meaning as in s 8 of the Public Order Act (see Ch 31).[726]

Regard should also be had to s 1(3)–(3A) of the Protection from Eviction Act 1977. In short, it is an offence to do acts likely to interfere with the peace or comfort of the residential occupier or members of his household, or persistently withdraw or withhold services reasonably required for residential occupation with intent to cause the residential occupier either: (a) to give up the occupation or (b) to refrain from exercising any right or pursuing any remedy in respect of the premises.

16.14.2.6 Stalking

In February 2012 the report of the Independent Parliamentary Inquiry into Stalking Law Reform was published.[727] The report concluded that the current legislative regime was inadequate and in need of reform. Sections 111 and 112 of the Protection of Freedoms Act 2012 amend the 1997 Act with the effect that stalking is, for the first time in England and Wales, a criminal offence in its own right. These provisions have been in force since November 2012 and amend ss 2 and 4 of the 1997 Act in the following ways: s 2A(1) contains the offence of stalking; s 4A(1)(b)(i) creates the offences of 'stalking causing fear of violence'; and s 4A(1)(b)(ii) creates the offence of 'stalking causing serious alarm or distress'. As was stated earlier, conduct constituting 'stalking' as that term is commonly understood already falls within the terms of the 1997 Act.[728] What these news provisions do, therefore, is to label explicitly conduct of this nature as 'stalking', rather than harassment. Section 2A(2) provides:[729]

> (2) For the purposes of subsection (1)(b) (and section 4A(1)(a)) a person's course of conduct amounts to stalking of another person if—
>
> (a) it amounts to harassment of that person,
>
> (b) the acts or omissions involved are ones associated with stalking, and
>
> (c) the person whose course of conduct it is knows or ought to know that the course of conduct amounts to harassment of the other person.

The legislation provides some guidance as to what is meant by the requirement that D's 'acts or omissions … are ones associated with stalking'. The legislation does not, however, provide a definition of stalking. Section 2A(3) gives the following examples:

> (a) following a person,
>
> (b) contacting, or attempting to contact, a person by any means,

---

[724] Note also the Law Commission recommendations to extend the aggravated offences to protect characteristics of disability, sexual orientation and transgender identity. See text at n 373.

[725] Section 42A(4).   [726] Section 42A(7).

[727] The Justice Unions' Parliamentary Group, 'Independent Parliamentary Inquiry into Stalking Law Reform: Main Findings and Recommendations' (2012).

[728] For an analysis of whether the new provisions will deal with the phenomenon of 'cyberstalking', see N MacEwan, 'The New Stalking Offences in English Law: Will They Provide Effective Protection From Cyberstalking?' [2012] Crim LR 767.

[729] By virtue of s 2(A)(4) this is a summary only offence.

   (c)　publishing any statement or other material—

      (i)　relating or purporting to relate to a person, or

      (ii)　purporting to originate from a person,

   (d)　monitoring the use by a person of the internet, email or any other form of electronic communication,

   (e)　loitering in any place (whether public or private),

   (f)　interfering with any property in the possession of a person,

   (g)　watching or spying on a person.

D cannot be guilty unless his conduct first constitutes harassment. It is important that this element of the offence is considered separately from whether D's acts or omissions are ones associated with stalking. The list of examples provided in the legislation is not exhaustive and it is possible for an act or omission not included on the list to constitute an act or omission associated with stalking.

Section 4A(1)(b)(i) and (ii) creates the aggravated offences of 'stalking causing fear of violence' and 'stalking causing serious alarm or distress which has a substantial adverse impact on day-to-day activities'.[730] These are either way offences. Section 4A provides:

4A Stalking involving fear of violence or serious alarm or distress

  (1)　A person ('A') whose course of conduct—

    (a)　amounts to stalking, and

    (b)　either—

      (i)　causes another ('B') to fear, on at least two occasions, that violence will be used against B, or

      (ii)　causes B serious alarm or distress which has a substantial adverse effect on B's usual day-to-day activities, is guilty of an offence if A knows or ought to know that A's course of conduct will cause B so to fear on each of those occasions or (as the case may be) will cause such alarm or distress.

  (2)　For the purposes of this section A ought to know that A's course of conduct will cause B to fear that violence will be used against B on any occasion if a reasonable person in possession of the same information would think the course of conduct would cause B so to fear on that occasion.

  (3)　For the purposes of this section A ought to know that A's course of conduct will cause B serious alarm or distress which has a substantial adverse effect on B's usual day-to-day activities if a reasonable person in possession of the same information would think the course of conduct would cause B such alarm or distress.

  (4)　It is a defence for A to show that—

    (a)　A's course of conduct was pursued for the purpose of preventing or detecting crime,

    (b)　A's course of conduct was pursued under any enactment or rule of law or to comply with any condition or requirement imposed by any person under any enactment, or

    (c)　the pursuit of A's course of conduct was reasonable for the protection of A or another or for the protection of A's or another's property.

This offence is similar to the one in s 4. There are, however, a number of important differences. First, D's course of conduct must amount to stalking. Secondly, in addition to D causing

---

[730]　By virtue of s 4(A)(5)(a) a person convicted is liable on conviction on indictment to imprisonment for a term not exceeding ten years, or a fine, or both. On summary conviction, the maximum term of imprisonment is six months or a fine not exceeding the statutory maximum.

another, B, to fear on at least two occasions that violence will be used against her, D can also be guilty if he 'causes another serious alarm or distress which has a substantial adverse effect on her usual day-to-day activities'.[731] None of these terms are defined.[732] It submitted that this is a subjective question, so irrespective of whether B's 'usual day-to-day activities' are idiosyncratic, if they are substantially adversely affected then that will suffice. Section 4A(3) makes clear that D commits the offence if a reasonable person with the same information as D would think the course of conduct would have a substantial adverse impact on B's day-to-day activities. Therefore D cannot escape liability by claiming that he did not realize that his conduct would have this effect; the test is an objective one. It is also clear that the legislation imposes a threshold, as D will not be guilty unless he causes B *serious* alarm or distress that has a *substantial* adverse effect on her usual day-to-day activities. If tried on indictment, the maximum sentence for this offence is ten years' imprisonment and/or a fine.[733] If tried summarily, the maximum sentence is six months' imprisonment and/or a fine.

16.15 Offensive weapons

Legislation regulating the possession and use of firearms and offensive weapons is of major importance in the prevention of offences against the person. In earlier editions of this book[734] an account was given of the principal offences under the Firearms Act 1968 and other legislation. This is omitted from the present edition and the reader is referred to *Blackstone's Criminal Practice* (2018) Part B12 and *Archbold* (2018) Ch 24.[735] Consideration is, however, given here to an important offence of general interest, created by the Prevention of Crime Act 1953.

16.15.1 The Prevention of Crime Act 1953

The Prevention of Crime Act 1953 is, according to its long title, 'An Act to prohibit the carrying of offensive weapons in public places, without lawful authority or reasonable excuse.'
  The Act provides:

1.—(1) Any person who without lawful authority or reasonable excuse, the proof whereof shall lie on him, has with him in any public place any offensive weapon shall be guilty of an offence, and shall be liable—

  (a) on summary conviction, to imprisonment for a term not exceeding six months or a fine not exceeding [the statutory maximum], or both;

  (b) on conviction on indictment, to imprisonment for a term not exceeding four years or a fine, or both.

---

[731] Home Office Circular 018/2012 states that the offence 'is designed to recognize the serious impact that stalking may have on victims, even where an explicit fear of violence is not created by each incident of stalking behaviour'. Available at www.gov.uk/government/publications/a-change-to-the-protection-from-harassment-act-1997-introduction-of-two-new-specific-offences-of-stalking.

[732] This is recognized in the circular. The Home Office does, however, give some examples of what it considers will constitute 'substantial adverse effect': the victim changing their routes to work, work patterns or employment; the victim arranging for friends or family to pick up children from school (to avoid contact with the stalker); the victim putting in place additional security measures in their home; the victim moving home; physical or mental ill-health; the victim's deterioration in performance at work due to stress; the victim stopping/or changing the way they socialize.

[733] The maximum sentence was increased from five years by s 175(1)(b) of the Policing and Crime Act 2017.

[734] See the 6th edition, at pp 416–422.

[735] The Violent Crime Reduction Act 2006 introduced further offences in relation to imitation firearms, minding a weapon for a person, etc. The legislation has recently been further amended by Part 6 of the Policing and Crime Act 2017.

(2) Where any person is convicted of an offence under subsection (1) of this section the court may make an order for the forfeiture or disposal of any weapon in respect of which the offence was committed.

16.15.1.1 Offensive weapons

'Offensive weapon' is defined by s 1(4), as amended by the Public Order Act 1986, to mean 'any article made or adapted for use for causing injury to the person, or intended by the person having it with him for such use by him or by some other person'.

It will be noted that this definition is narrower than that of 'weapon of offence' in s 10(1)(b) of the Theft Act 1968. It does not include, as the Theft Act does, articles made, adapted or intended for *incapacitating* a person.[736]

According to the Court of Appeal in *Simpson*,[737] there are three categories of offensive weapon.

(1) Articles *made* for causing injury would include a rifle or bayonet, a revolver, a cosh, a truncheon,[738] a knuckle-duster,[739] a pair of 'sand gloves',[740] a dagger, swordstick[741] or flick knife.[742] It has been held that the fact that rice flails are *used* as weapons is sufficient evidence that they are *made* for that purpose[743] but this seems doubtful. Whether an article is 'made for' causing injury requires the jury to consider whether it is of a kind which is, generally speaking, made for such use.[744] Categorization is a matter of fact, although judicial notice has been taken of the fact that flick-knives and butterfly knives are offensive per se.[745] The judge is entitled to direct the jury that this element of the offence is established, but never to direct a conviction per se.[746]

(2) Articles *adapted* for causing injury would include razor blades inserted in a potato or a bottle broken for the purpose, a chair leg studded with nails and so on. 'Adapted' probably means altered so as to become suitable.[747] It has been held that unscrewing a pool cue so that the butt end could be used for violence might amount to adapting

---

[736] See p 1022. Ormerod and Williams, *Smith's Law of Theft*, Ch 9.

[737] [1983] 1 WLR 1494. See also *Samuels* [2016] EWCA Crim 1876.

[738] *Houghton v Chief Constable of Greater Manchester* (1986) 84 Cr App R 319.

[739] '... bludgeons, properly so-called, clubs and anything that is not in common use for any other purpose but a weapon are clearly offensive weapons within the meaning of the legislature' (the Smuggling Acts): (1784) 1 Leach 342 n (a). In *DPP v Christof* [2015] EWHC 4096 (Admin), the Divisional Court held that a leather belt which, when disassembled, was found to incorporate a detachable buckle in the form of a knuckleduster, was an offensive weapon.

[740] ie gloves into which iron powder is inserted to give weight and protect the knuckles: *R v R* (2007) 15 Nov, unreported, CA (Crim).

[741] *Butler* [1988] Crim LR 695.

[742] An offensive weapon per se because judicially noticed as such: *Simpson* [1983] 3 All ER 789, [1983] 1 WLR 1494; cf *Gibson v Wales* [1983] 1 All ER 869, [1983] Crim LR 113, DC and commentary; and *DPP v Hynde* [1998] Crim LR 72, DC (butterfly knife). In *Vasili* [2011] EWCA Crim 615, the Court of Appeal rejected the submission that an article that was both a flick-knife and a lighter was not 'made ... for causing injury to the person'. It was just as much an offensive weapon and potentially dangerous if the lighter function was not present.

[743] *Copus v DPP* [1989] Crim LR 577 and commentary. It was conceded at the trial in *Malnik* [1989] Crim LR 451 that a rice flail was an offensive weapon.

[744] *Warne* [1997] 7 Arch News 2. A petrol bomb is an offensive weapon per se: *Akhtar* [2015] EWCA Crim 176.

[745] See also the Criminal Justice Act 1988 (Offensive Weapons) Order 1988, SI 1988/2019.

[746] *Wang* [2005] UKHL 9; *Dhindsa* [2005] EWCA Crim 1198.

[747] cf *Davison v Birmingham Industrial Co-operative Society* (1920) 90 LJKB 206; *Flower Freight Co Ltd v Hammond* [1963] 1 QB 275; and *Herrmann v Metropolitan Leather Co Ltd* [1942] Ch 248, [1942] 1 All ER 294; *Maddox v Storer* [1963] 1 QB 451; *Formosa* (1990) 92 Cr App R 11, [1990] Crim LR 868, CA.

it, but this seems to be taking things too far.[748] It is not certain whether the intention of the adaptor is relevant.[749] Is an *accidentally* broken milk bottle 'adapted for use for causing injury to the person'? It is submitted that it is not and that if the article was not adapted with intent, it can only be an offensive weapon in the third category.

(3) It is very important to distinguish the third category of articles which are neither made nor adapted for causing injury, but are *carried for that purpose*. Whether D carried the article with the necessary purpose is a question of fact.[750] Articles which have been held to be carried with such intent include a cricket bat,[751] a sheath-knife,[752] a shotgun,[753] a razor,[754] a sandbag,[755] a pick-axe handle,[756] a stone[757] and a drum of pepper.[758] *Any* article is capable of being an offensive weapon; but if it is of such a nature that it is unlikely to cause injury when brought into contact with the person, then the onus of proving the necessary intent will be very heavy.

Articles adapted or intended by the carrier to injure himself

It was held by the Crown Court in *Bryan v Mott*[759] that a bottle broken for the purpose of committing suicide is 'adapted' for causing injury to the person. In *Fleming*,[760] on the other hand, the judge ruled that a large domestic carving knife carried by D to injure himself was not 'intended' for causing injury to the person: though the Act does not say 'another person', that is what it means. The view of the judge in *Fleming* is to be preferred. The question is whether the thing is 'an offensive weapon' and since 'offensive' implies an attack on *another* the injury which the adaptor or carrier must contemplate must be injury to another. The cases may, however, be distinguishable if 'adapt' does not imply any intention on the part of the adaptor. Breaking the milk bottle in fact makes it more suitable for injuring others, even if the adaptor intends injury only to himself. But such a distinction does not seem justified in principle.

Burdens of proof

In the case of articles 'made or adapted', the prosecution have to prove no more than possession in a public place.[761] D will then be convicted unless he can prove, on a balance of probability, that he had lawful authority or reasonable excuse.[762] But if the article falls into the third category the onus is on the prosecution to show that it was carried with intent to injure.[763] The prosecution must satisfy the jury that the article is either offensive per se (made or adapted) or, if it is not, that D had it with him with intent. If some of the jury think it is the one, and some the other, the case, it is submitted, is not made out.[764]

---

[748] *Sills v DPP* [2006] EWHC 3383 (Admin); the case is better seen as one of purposive carrying.

[749] *Maddox v Storer* [1963] 1 QB 451, [1962] 1 All ER 831.

[750] *Williamson* (1977) 67 Cr App R 35, [1978] Crim LR 229. See also *Dhindsa* [2005] EWCA Crim 1198 (ring with name of appellant across several fingers wrongly treated by judge as a weapon when matter should have been left to jury).

[751] *Tucker* [2016] EWCA Crim 593.   [752] *Woodward v Koessler* [1958] 3 All ER 557.

[753] *Gipson* [1956] Crim LR 281; *Hodgson* [1954] Crim LR 379.

[754] *Petrie* [1961] 1 All ER 466; *Gibson v Wales* [1983] 1 All ER 869.

[755] ibid.

[756] *Cugullere* [1961] 2 All ER 343.

[757] *Harrison v Thornton* (1966) 68 Cr App R 28, [1966] Crim LR 388, DC.

[758] 120 JP 250. Also, no doubt, a stiletto heel, which can be a very dangerous weapon: (1964) The Times, 25 Sept.

[759] (1975) 62 Cr App R 71. The point was not decided by the Divisional Court.

[760] [1989] Crim LR 71 (Judge Fricker QC).   [761] *Davis v Alexander* (1970) 54 Cr App R 398.

[762] See *L v DPP* [2003] QB 137.   [763] *Petrie* [1961] 1 All ER 466; *Leer* [1982] Crim LR 310.

[764] *Flynn* (1985) 82 Cr App R 319, [1986] Crim LR 239 and commentary.

The requisite intention

The question in *Woodward v Koessler*[765] was whether D intends to 'cause injury to the person' if he intends merely to frighten or intimidate by displaying a knife rather than by making physical contact. It is now established that he does not. If there is no intention to cause physical injury, the offence is only committed if there is an intention to cause injury by shock, a psychiatric injury—and only in very exceptional circumstances could evidence of such an intention be found.[766] Recklessness as to use will not be sufficient mens rea for the offence.[767] A conditional intention to use the article is sufficient but it must be an intention to use the article in the future. If D sets out from Berkshire intending, if the occasion arises, to use a domestic knife for causing injury in Cornwall, the knife is an offensive weapon so long as it is carried in a public place and the intention continues. Once D believes that there is no possibility of the knife being used for causing injury—because, for example, his purpose has been accomplished—it ceases to be an offensive weapon.[768] It may, therefore, be no offence to carry the knife—whether or not it had been used—from Cornwall back to Berkshire.

Offences of carrying, not using

After some hesitation, the courts have construed the Act in the light of its long title. It is aimed at the *carrying* of offensive weapons *in public places*. It is not aimed at the actual *use* of the weapon, which can invariably be adequately dealt with under some other offence. Possession of a weapon does not necessarily lead to an offence against the person, but that does not mean that possession offences are not justified.[769] It has been suggested that there are a growing number of possession-type offences which are acquiring a greater significance in the criminal law.[770] They are often easy to detect and prove and can carry substantial sentences.[771]

In *Jura*,[772] D was holding an air rifle at a shooting gallery when, on being suddenly provoked, he shot and wounded a woman. It was held that he had a reasonable excuse for *carrying* the rifle though not, of course, for using it in that way. But he had committed one offence, not two. It was as if a gamekeeper at a shooting party were suddenly to lose his temper and shoot at someone. The position is therefore that if D is lawfully in possession of the article, whether it be an offensive weapon per se or not, his decision unlawfully to use, and immediate use of it, does not amount to an offence under the Act. In *Dayle*,[773] D took a car jack from the boot of his car and threw it at V in the course of a fight. In *Ohlson v Hylton*,[774] D, a carpenter, took a hammer from his tool bag in the course of a fight and struck V. In neither case was D guilty of an offence under the Act. It seems that if D is not in possession

---

765 [1958] 3 All ER 557.

766 *Edmonds* [1963] 2 QB 142; *Rapier* (1979) 70 Cr App R 17; *Snooks* [1997] Crim LR 230. See more recently *Ali* [2012] EWCA Crim 934 in which it was conceded by the Crown that the judge's summing up was defective as it invited the jury to convict on the basis that D had used the weapon in question only to frighten.

767 See *Byrne* [2003] EWCA Crim 3253, [2004] Crim LR 582 and commentary.

768 *Allamby* [1974] 3 All ER 126, CA. Cf *Ellames* [1974] 3 All ER 130.

769 See on this D Husak, 'The Nature and Justifiability of Non-Consummate Offences' (1995) 37 Ariz LR 151.

770 See eg the offences under the Terrorism Acts and see C Walker, *Blackstone's Guide to the Anti-Terrorism Legislation* (3rd edn, 2014) Ch 6. For an interesting account of possession offences, see MD Drubber, 'The Possession Paradigm' in Duff and Green, *Defining Crimes*, 91.

771 The CPS has published its policy on prosecuting those who carry weapons: www.cps.gov.uk/legal-guidance/offensive-weapons-knives-bladed-and-pointed-articles; see also www.cps.gov.uk/legal-guidance/offences-against-person-incorporating-charging-standard.

772 [1954] 1 QB 503, CA.   773 [1973] 3 All ER 1151. See also *Sundas* [2011] EWCA Crim 985.

774 [1975] 2 All ER 490, DC. See also *Police v Smith* [1974] 2 NZLR 32 (guest in restaurant using table knife offensively); *Humphreys* [1977] Crim LR 225, CA (penknife).

873

of the article until an occasion for its use arises and he then takes it up for immediate use, he commits no offence under the Act.[775] The law was so stated in *Ohlson v Hylton*:[776]

To support a conviction under the Act the prosecution must show that the defendant was carrying or otherwise equipped with the weapon, and had the intent to use it offensively before any occasion for its actual use had arisen.[777]

This interpretation avoids the formidable difficulty which would otherwise arise where D picks up an article in the course of a fight, allegedly for self-defence. The onus of proving that this was an unreasonable step for the purposes of self-defence is on the Crown but, if it was capable of being an offence under the Act, it would be for D to prove he had a reasonable excuse.

Duration of offence

An 'occasion' has a beginning and it must also have an end.[778] If D picks up a glass to defend himself in the course of a pub brawl he does not commit an offence under the Act; but suppose, when the fight is over, he declines to put the glass down and insists on carrying it home through two miles of streets? Probably the 'occasion' has come to an end, and the question is whether D has a reasonable excuse to carry the article.

16.15.1.2 Lawful authority or reasonable excuse

It may be that the existence of lawful authority is a pure question of law, whereas whether there is a reasonable excuse is a question of fact, subject to the usual judicial control.[779]

The term 'lawful authority' presents difficulties. Before the Act, it was presumably generally lawful to be in possession of an offensive weapon in a public place—otherwise there would have been no necessity for the Act. Now it is generally unlawful. 'Lawful authority' suggests some legal exception to the general rule of the Act; yet none is provided for and the words themselves are certainly not self-explanatory. In *Bryan v Mott*, Lord Widgery CJ said[780] that 'lawful authority' refers to those 'people who from time to time carry an offensive weapon as a matter of duty—the soldier with his rifle and the police officer with his truncheon'. It seems that the 'duty' must be a public one—an employer cannot authorize his employees to carry offensive weapons simply by getting them to contract to do so.

Whether there is a reasonable excuse is said to depend on whether a reasonable person would think it excusable to carry the weapon,[781] and, in *Butler*,[782] D's argument that he had a reasonable excuse because he never considered whether the swordstick he was carrying was an article made or adapted for causing injury was left to the jury; but that may have been too generous. What did he suppose a swordstick was for, if not injuring people? A possible answer is that he thought it was made as a curio or 'collector's item'. Generally the courts have construed the provision strictly and exercised close control over magistrates and juries. It is not enough that D's intentions for use of the article were entirely lawful.[783] All of the circumstances must be considered, so, for example, it was a reasonable excuse for a male stripper to possess a truncheon as part of his uniform.[784]

---

[775] A point seemingly overlooked in *Byrne* [2004] Crim LR 582.

[776] [1975] 2 All ER 490 at 496. The requirement that the intention to use the weapon has to be formed before the occasion of its use was reaffirmed in *Veasey* [1999] Crim LR 158 and *C v DPP* [2002] Crim LR 202 and commentaries.

[777] *Powell* [1963] Crim LR 511, CCA, and *Harrison v Thornton* [1966] Crim LR 388, DC, therefore appear to be wrongly decided.

[778] cf *Giles* [1976] Crim LR 253 (Judge Jones).

[779] *Peacock* [1973] Crim LR 639; *Leer* [1982] Crim LR 310, CA.

[780] (1975) 62 Cr App R 71 at 73, DC.   [781] *Bryan v Mott*, ibid.   [782] [1988] Crim LR 695.

[783] *Bryan v Mott*, n 780.   [784] See *Frame v Kennedy* 2008 HCJAC 25 (K performed as 'Sergeant Eros').

A belief, however reasonable and honest, that an extendable baton (an offensive weapon) is an aerial or some other innocent article is not a reasonable excuse.[785] It is not necessarily a reasonable excuse that the weapon is carried only for self-defence. D must show that there was 'an imminent[786] particular threat affecting the particular circumstances in which the weapon was carried'.[787] One who is under constant threat it is said, must resort to the police. He commits an offence if he regularly goes out armed for self-defence.[788] So, there was held to be no excuse for carrying around an iron bar, though D had reasonable cause to fear and did fear that he would be violently attacked and intended to use the bar for defence only.[789] It is not reasonable for an Edinburgh taxi driver to carry two feet of rubber hose with a piece of metal inserted at one end, though he does so for defence against violent passengers whom taxi drivers sometimes encounter at night.[790] It has been held that possession of a broken milk bottle (an article adapted for causing injury) is not excused by the fact that D intended to use it to commit suicide.[791] It is an offence for security guards at clubs to carry truncheons 'as a deterrent' and as 'part of the uniform'.[792]

Unlawful possession may become lawful if circumstances change so as to give rise to a reasonable excuse. When a person is attacked he may use anything that he can lay his hands on to defend himself, so long as he uses no more force than is reasonable in the circumstances. It may, then, be reasonable to use an offensive weapon that he is unlawfully carrying. When Butler[793] was viciously attacked, his use of the swordstick to defend himself was justified, so possession of it must have become lawful, but that could not undo the possession offence already committed.[794] The narrow interpretation of reasonable excuse may qualify the important principle that a person cannot be driven off the streets and compelled not to go to a public place where he might lawfully be because he will be confronted by people intending to attack him.[795] If he decides that he cannot go to that place unless armed with an offensive weapon, it seems that he must stay away. He commits an offence if he goes armed.[796] The effectiveness of the legislation in preventing the carrying of arms would be seriously impaired if anyone who reasonably feared that he might be attacked was allowed to carry a weapon.[797]

Where D had an explanation for possession of the weapon, for example by putting it in his work trousers and forgetting 'that he was wearing those trousers' and was found in possession in public, the defence of a reasonable excuse ought still to have been left to the jury.[798] Forgetfulness alone is not a sufficiently good reason, but coupled with other factors

---

[785] *Densu* [1998] 1 Cr App R 400, [1998] Crim LR 345.

[786] But this word does not appear in the statute and should not be elevated to such: *McAuley* [2009] EWCA Crim 2130 decided under the 1988 Act, s 139.

[787] *Evans v Hughes* [1972] 3 All ER 412 at 415, DC; *Evans v Wright* [1964] Crim LR 466. The case was misapplied by the trial judge in *Archbold* [2007] EWCA Crim 2125, where D had phoned the police to report that V was attacking D's home and car and D had then gone in search of him with a knife. The trial judge's direction gave the jury no opportunity to apply a defence of reasonable excuse if D was facing imminent attack. See also *McAuley* [2009] EWCA Crim 2130 decided under the 1988 Act, s 139, emphasizing that the matter should be left to the jury.

[788] For a comparative view, see D Lanham, 'Offensive Weapons and Self-Defence' [2005] Crim LR 85.

[789] *Evans v Hughes*, n 787. See also *Bradley v Moss* [1974] Crim LR 430, DC; *Pittard v Mahoney* [1977] Crim LR 169, DC.

[790] *Grieve v MacLeod* 1967 SLT 70.

[791] *Bryan v Mott*, n 780. See also *Bown* [2003] EWCA Crim 1989, [2004] 1 Cr App R 13, decided under the 1988 Act, s 139. See also *Miller* [2007] EWCA Crim 1891, possession of butterfly knife having confiscated from girlfriend with history of self-harm.

[792] *Spanner* [1973] Crim LR 704.   [793] See n 782.

[794] Smith, *Justification and Excuse*, 117–123.   [795] *Field* [1972] Crim LR 435.

[796] *Malnik v DPP* [1989] Crim LR 451, DC.

[797] *Salih* [2007] EWCA Crim 2750. See *Deyemi* [2007] EWCA Crim 2060 and *Zahid* [2010] EWCA Crim 2158 on this approach with firearms.

[798] *Bird* [2004] EWCA Crim 964.

may be and should be left to the jury.[799] In *Jolie*, the court offered two examples of facts on which there might be a valid good reason based on forgetfulness: a parent who, having bought a kitchen knife, put it in the glove compartment of a car out of the reach of a child (reason 1), forgetting (reason 2) later to retrieve it. Similarly, in *Glidewell*,[800] a taxi driver discovered weapons left by a passenger (reason 1), and forgot to remove them because he was busy (reason 2).

The imposition of a burden of proof on D can cause great difficulty where he is charged in a second count with another offence which imposes no such burden. In *Snooks and Sergeant*,[801] DD were also charged with possessing an explosive, contrary to s 64 of the OAPA. They relied on self-defence. For s 64, the onus was on the prosecution, under the 1953 Act the onus is on DD. The jury have an impossible task.

16.15.1.3 A 'public place'

Section 1(4) of the Prevention of Crime Act 1953 provides:

'public place' includes any highway and any other premises or place to which at the material time the public have or are permitted to have access whether on payment or otherwise.

This is very similar to the interpretation which has been placed upon s 192 of the Road Traffic Act 1988 and to the definition of public place, etc in other Acts. It should always be borne in mind that the same term may bear different meanings according to the context in which it is used and that whether a place is public is a question of fact.[802]

A public place could not include land adjoining that to which the public had access even if D could have inflicted harm from such land.[803] A householder impliedly invites persons having legitimate business to walk up his garden path to the door, but this does not render the garden a 'public place'. The class of persons invited to enter is too restricted for them to constitute 'the public'.[804] On the other hand, the communal landing of a block of flats has been held to be a public place on the ground that the public had access in fact, whether or not they were permitted to have it.[805] In the absence of a notice restricting entry, there was evidence on which justices could find that the unrestricted access of the public to a local authority housing estate extended to the stairways and landings of the flats.[806] The jury are, of course, entitled to draw reasonable inferences; so that where D produced an air pistol in a private dwelling-house which he was visiting, it was open to them to infer that he brought it to or took it away from the house through the public street.[807] Possession of an article (truncheon) in a car on a public road is possession in a public place.[808]

16.15.1.4 Possession and mens rea

It must be proved that D 'has with him' the article. The prosecution must prove the minimum mental element which is necessary to constitute possession and, in addition, the 'closer contact' than mere possession which the phrase 'has with him' implies.[809] The question then is

---

[799] *Jolie* [2004] EWCA Crim 1543; *Tsap* [2008] EWCA Crim 2679; *Chahal v DPP* [2010] EWHC 439 (Admin).

[800] (1999) 163 JP 557.   [801] [1997] Crim LR 230.   [802] *Theodolou* [1963] Crim LR 573.

[803] *Roberts* [2004] 1 Cr App R 16, [2003] EWCA Crim 2753 (garden 1m wide).

[804] *Edwards and Roberts* (1978) 67 Cr App R 228, [1978] Crim LR 564 (a case under s 5 of the Public Order Act 1936).

[805] *Knox v Anderton* (1982) 76 Cr App R 156, [1983] Crim LR 114, DC, and commentary. But a public place is not synonymous with a place from which the public are not excluded: *Harriott v DPP* [2005] EWHC 965 (Admin).

[806] See also *Hanrahan* [2004] All ER (D) 144 (Nov) (rehabilitation centre to which access gained through intercom).

[807] *Mehmed* [1963] Crim LR 780.   [808] *Ellis* [2010] EWCA Crim 163.

[809] *McCalla* (1988) 87 Cr App R 372 at 378.

whether the offence is one of strict liability or whether any mens rea is required. The case law is in disarray. Some cases suggest that the prosecution must prove D knowingly 'has with him': *Cugullere*,[810] *Russell*.[811] Subsequent decisions (*Martindale*,[812] and *McCalla*[813]) have erroneously treated *Russell* as simply a decision, and therefore a wrong decision, on the meaning of possession. The prevailing view, following *McCalla*, is that the offence is one of strict liability; but the better opinion is that *Russell*, though treated as overruled, should be regarded as the binding authority.[814]

In *Jolie*,[815] D was found in possession of a knife in a car he was driving and claimed that he had forgotten it was there, although he admitted putting it there as he had used it to start the broken ignition. Kennedy LJ suggested that in the cases of *McCalla*, *Martindale* and *Buswell* it had been clear that the article had remained under D's control. His lordship suggested that the jury should be directed that they may find possession if either D was aware of the presence of the weapon or he was responsible for putting it where it was mislaid.[816]

As regards the relevant mens rea as to the offensiveness of the weapon, in *Densu*,[817] counsel abandoned an argument before the Court of Appeal that the ruling of the trial judge was wrong insofar as it suggested that the proof that D 'has with him' is satisfied on proof that D knew that he had the weapon (a baton) with him but did not know that it was a weapon. The prevailing view is that liability is strict.

16.15.1.5 Articles with blades or points

The Prevention of Crime Act is supplemented by an offence triable either way, punishable on summary conviction by six months', and, on indictment, by four years' imprisonment[818] under s 139 of the Criminal Justice Act 1988, of having with one in a public place an article 'which has a blade[819] or is sharply pointed except a folding pocket knife[820] [with a cutting edge not exceeding three inches[821]]'. The article need not be made or adapted for causing injury, nor intended by D for such use. The fact that a blade might be used for other functions than as a weapon (eg a Swiss Army knife) does not mean that it is not prima facie a bladed article within s 139.[822] Otherwise, the constituents of the offence are similar to those required by the 1953 Act. It is a defence for D to prove that he had *good reason* or lawful authority for having the article with him. In *Jolie*, the court regarded the words 'good reason' in the 1988 Act as intended to be narrower than 'reasonable excuse' in the 1953 Act.

---

[810] [1961] 2 All ER 343. Arguably the court was concerned only with the question of possession.

[811] (1984) 81 Cr App R 315.   [812] (1986) 84 Cr App R 31.   [813] See n 809.

[814] See commentary on *Wright* [1992] Crim LR 596.

[815] [2003] EWCA Crim 1543, [2003] Crim LR 730.

[816] See also *Hilton* [2009] EWHC 2867 (Admin) on the importance of distinguishing whether D knew he had something with him and whether he had a good reason for possessing it (decided under s 139).

[817] [1998] 1 Cr App R 400.

[818] Increased from two years by the Violent Crime Reduction Act 2006, s 42.

[819] This probably means a blade which has a cutting edge. A screwdriver, even if it may be properly described as having a blade, is not within the section: *Davis* [1998] Crim LR 564. However, in *Brooker v DPP* (2005) 169 JP 368, a butter knife with no cutting edge and no point was held to be a bladed article.

[820] Which means a knife which is 'readily and indeed immediately foldable at all times, simply by the folding process': *Fehmi v DPP* (1993) 96 Cr App R 235, DC, so that a pocket knife which locks into position is not 'folding': *Deegan* [1998] 2 Cr App R 121, [1998] Crim LR 562.

[821] On the difficulties on proving length where the weapon is lost, see *Banton* [2009] EWCA Crim 240.

[822] *Giles* [2003] All ER (D) 68 (Feb). A grapefruit knife qualifies: *R (on the application of Windsor and Maidenhead RIBC) v East Berkshire Justices* [2010] EWHC 3020 (Admin).

The court concluded that the words 'good reason' do not generally require a judicial gloss in directing the jury.[823]

Self-defence against an anticipated imminent attack may be a good reason.[824] In *Davis*,[825] the court thought that the section imposed 'a very significant limitation on the citizen's freedom. It should not be assumed that it has been achieved except by the use of clear words.' It is specifically provided that it is a defence for D to prove that he had the article with him for use at work,[826] religious reasons[827] or as part of national costume. It is necessary to prove that he had it with him for a specific reason *in public* on this occasion.[828]

A new s 139A was inserted by the Offensive Weapons Act 1996, creating offences of having on school premises (a) an article to which s 139 applies (punishable on indictment with four years' imprisonment[829]) and (b) an offensive weapon within the meaning of the Prevention of Crime Act 1953 (punishable on indictment with four years' imprisonment). It is a defence to both offences to prove 'good reason or lawful authority'.

Under the Legal Aid, Sentencing and Punishment of Offenders Act 2012 the offence was extended further: a person is guilty of an offence if he (a) has an article to with him or her in a public place or on school premises; (b) unlawfully and intentionally threatens another person with the article; and (c) does so in such a way that there is an immediate risk of serious physical harm to that other person.[830] In the Crown Court it carries a mandatory minimum sentence of six months. Note also that s 28 of the Criminal Justice and Courts Act 2015 introduces a minimum custodial sentence for a second (or further) conviction for possession of a knife or offensive weapon.

---

[823] See *Chahal v DPP* [2010] EWHC 439 (Admin); *Hilton* [2009] EWHC 2867 (Admin). In *Clancy* [2012] EWCA Crim 8, the Court of Appeal accepted that fear of attack would constitute a 'good reason' within the meaning of s 139(4). The court held that D's state of mind is not wholly irrelevant, but it is not determinative either. For criticism see [2012] Crim LR 549. See also *Smith v Shanks* 2014 SLT 626.

[824] *Emmanuel* [1998] Crim LR 347.

[825] [1998] Crim LR 564. Contrast the attitude of the court in *Deegan*, n 820.

[826] A question of fact for the jury: *Manning* [1998] Crim LR 198 (knife carried to do repairs to D's own car). This can include casual or part-time work: *Chahal v DPP* [2010] EWHC 439 (Admin).

[827] Which must be the dominant reason: *Wang* [2003] EWCA Crim 3228. D must show that the religion was the reason for his possession on this occasion, ie that he was to use it in some religious connection. The court acknowledged, *per curiam*, that Art 9 of the ECHR might require the State authorities to allow persons to carry bladed instruments in public in pursuit of their religious beliefs.

[828] *Giles*, n 822.

[829] Increased from two years by the Violent Crime Reduction Act 2006, s 42.

[830] Criminal Justice Act 1988, s 139AA(1) (s 139AA added by Legal Aid, Sentencing and Punishment of Offenders Act 2012, s 142(2)).

6

Parties to crime

6.1 Introduction

A person may be liable for an offence as a 'principal' or 'joint principal' where he has played a part in the commission of the actus reus of the offence.[1] To be a principal offender the person must directly and immediately perform the actus reus of an offence (in this chapter we will refer to the principal as 'P').

Plainly, the principal is not necessarily the only one who can be criminally liable for an offence. A person (in this chapter, D), might also be liable as an 'accessory', or as it is also called, a 'secondary party'. Specific common law and statutory rules govern whether a person is liable as an accessory; these rules apply to all offences, unless expressly[2] or impliedly excluded.[3] Where D is liable as an accessory, he is liable because he aided, abetted, counselled or procured (for convenience we can say 'assisted or encouraged') P who committed the principal offence.

A person, D, other than the principal, P, might also be liable for an inchoate offence—assisting or encouraging P under the Serious Crime Act 2007 (SCA 2007) or for conspiring with P that the offence would be committed. There is a crucial difference from secondary liability: D's liability for inchoate offences arises irrespective of whether P has committed the offence. We deal with inchoate liability in Ch 11.

In secondary liability we can describe D's liability as 'derivative' on the commission of the principal offence.[4] Logically, therefore, the easiest way of ascertaining D's potential liability is to assess whether the principal offence has been committed, then to consider whether D has fulfilled the requirements of aiding and abetting it. This does *not* involve asking whether D fulfilled the actus reus and mens rea of the principal offence. Instead, we ask whether D performed the relevant conduct sufficient to constitute assisting or encouraging and did so with the mens rea required for liability as an accessory.

Occasionally, statutory offences are drafted in such a way that assisting or encouraging someone to commit an offence is itself a statutory offence[5] (the statute provides: it is an

---

[1] See generally KJM Smith, *A Modern Treatise on Complicity* (1991). For an excellent discussion of the current law, see LC 305, *Participating in Crime* (2007) Part 2 and Appendix B.

[2] eg under the Corporate Manslaughter and Corporate Homicide Act 2007 there is no secondary liability for individuals.

[3] Arguably this occurs where a statute creates offences of 'using or causing or permitting to be used'. See *Carmichael & Sons (Worcester) Ltd v Cottle* [1971] RTR 11. Cf *Farr* [1982] Crim LR 745, CA, and commentary.

[4] Russell, 128; *Surujpaul v R* [1958] 3 All ER 300 at 301, PC. This is now subject to the rule in *Millward* [1994] Crim LR 527, p 223.

[5] See eg Female Genital Mutilation Act 2003. Note the Serious Crime Act 2015, ss 70–75, extending the extraterritorial effect of the offence, adding protective orders and adding an offence of failing to protect a girl from the risk of genital mutilation.

offence to 'do x' and it is an offence to assist any person 'to do x'). In those cases D can be liable for the statutory offence of assisting even if the offence D has assisted is not committed. There are numerous offences of 'being knowingly concerned in' a type of behaviour such as drug importation or supply of drugs, and the person 'knowingly concerned in' the conduct commits an offence of his own accord not merely as an accessory to someone else's.[6]

Within the scope of secondary liability there also existed at common law a controversial and much misunderstood form of liability known as joint enterprise liability. We will consider that in detail later in this chapter, but following the seminal[7] decision of the Supreme Court in *Jogee*[8] that doctrine no longer exists as a separate basis of liability.

6.1.1 Summary

Before discussing in detail the different bases of liability,[9] it is worth summarizing them to provide an overview. D may be liable in the following ways:

(1) As a principal or joint principal where he has played a part in the commission of the actus reus of the offence; or where he acts through an innocent agent.[10]

(2) As an accessory under s 8 of the Accessories and Abettors Act 1861 where D has aided, abetted, counselled or procured P in his conduct which constituted the principal crime.

(3) For the commission of a full statutory offence itself if it is one defined in terms of assisting or encouraging.

(4) Prior to the Supreme Court's judgment in *Jogee*,[11] there was an additional basis upon which D could be liable. Under the common law, D could be liable on the basis of what was known as 'joint enterprise' or 'parasitic accessory'[12] liability. This was a controversial doctrine that was held by the Supreme Court in *Jogee* to have been the result of a 'legal wrong turn' that the court concluded it was necessary to correct. The rise and fall of this doctrine is discussed later in this chapter.[13]

Despite the Supreme Court's efforts to clarify the law in *Jogee*, the current law of secondary liability remains unsatisfactorily complex, and displays many of the characteristic weaknesses of a common law doctrine that has been allowed to develop in a pragmatic and unprincipled way. Statutory reform would be welcome, although there is considerable doubt whether that should be in the form the Law Commission proposed in 2007 (Report No 305 discussed later).[14]

---

[6] See eg the Misuse of Drugs Act 1971, s 4(3)(b).

[7] The term used by Sir Brian Leveson P in *Anwar* [2016] EWCA Crim 551, [20].

[8] [2016] UKSC 8.

[9] We do not include in this summary any possible inchoate liability. See Ch 11.

[10] See p 179. See recently *Lewis and others* [2017] EWCA Crim 1734.

[11] [2016] UKSC 8. For extensive discussion, see p 214.

[12] This expression was coined by Professor Sir John Smith. See JC Smith, 'Criminal Liability of Accessories: Law and Law Reform' (1997) 113 LQR 453.

[13] At the risk of oversimplifying, D could be liable for P's crime B where D and P had set out with a common purpose to commit crime A and P had gone on to commit crime B and D foresaw as a real possibility that P might commit crime B.

[14] See R Buxton [2009] Crim LR 230; cf W Wilson, 'A Rational Scheme of Liability for Participation in Crime' [2008] Crim LR 3, suggesting the proposals generally 'succeed admirably'; cf GR Sullivan, 'Participating in Crime' [2008] Crim LR 19, suggesting the proposals on joint ventures show a 'disregard for the minimum standards of clarity and comprehensibility' and RD Taylor 'Procuring, Causation, Innocent Agency and the Law Commission' [2008] Crim LR 32, who is also critical of the complexity and incoherence of the proposals.

6.2 Bases of liability

By s 8 of the Accessories and Abettors Act 1861, as amended by the Criminal Law Act 1977:

Whosoever shall aid, abet, counsel or procure the commission of any indictable offence whether the same be an offence at common law or by virtue of any act passed or to be passed, shall be liable to be tried, indicted and punished as a principal offender.[15]

The section does not create an offence. It specifies the procedure and punishment for the aiders, abettors, counsellors and procurers, conveniently called 'accessories'.

6.2.1 Distinguishing accessories and principals

English law treats the accessory and principal in identical terms for the purposes of procedure and punishment. It has always been sufficient to prove that the defendant was either the principal[16] or accessory.[17] A person who is charged with an offence, say theft, may be convicted whether the evidence proves that he committed the theft (ie was a principal), or aided, abetted, counselled or procured it (ie was an accessory). But the charge should, wherever possible, specify whether the accused is alleged to have been the principal offender or an accessory.[18] The prosecution can nevertheless secure a conviction without specifying precisely what role they allege D played. So, in *Giannetto*, it was acceptable for the prosecution to allege that D killed his wife or that he was an accessory to her killing (by contracting a killer to do so).[19] The jury could convict on that basis. The prosecution could not be sure whether D was the principal offender or an accessory, but could establish beyond doubt that he was involved in plotting her killing.[20] The Supreme Court confirmed in *Jogee* that, 'in some cases the prosecution may not be able to prove whether a defendant was principal or accessory, but it is sufficient to be able to prove that he participated in the crime in one way or another'.[21]

Difficulties of this type are commonplace as, for example, where V is attacked by a group of individuals and killed but the medical evidence points to death resulting from a single stab wound.[22] Unless the evidence can establish that a particular member of the group must have been responsible for inflicting the fatal wound, the prosecution may have no alternative but to allege that each member was either the principal offender or an accessory. Considerable difficulty would arise in such cases if the prosecution had to choose. If there is only one fatal stab wound, the Crown cannot simply allege that each defendant was the principal. As a matter of fact, that is most unlikely to be true; only one person will have plunged the knife in. Equally, the Crown would face difficulty if they alleged that each

---

[15] Similar provisions relating to summary trial are to be found in the Magistrates' Courts Act 1980, s 44.

[16] The common law of felonies designated the actual perpetrator 'the principal in the first degree' and distinguished secondary parties into principals in the second degree—those who participated at the time when the felony was actually perpetrated—and accessories before the fact—those who participated at an earlier time. It was traditional to state that the distinction was that the principal in the second degree was *present* at the commission of the offence; but in fact he might be a considerable distance away—in a US case (*State v Hamilton and Lawrie*, 13 Nev 386 (1878)—signals from mountain top, 30–40 miles away), so long as he was assisting or available to assist, at the time. Hawkins, II PC, c 29, ss 7 and 8; Foster, *Crown Law*, 350. The abolition of felonies in the Criminal Law Act 1967 renders the distinction redundant.

[17] *Mackalley's Case* (1611) 9 Co Rep 61b; *Fitzgerald* [1992] Crim LR 660.

[18] *DPP for Northern Ireland v Maxwell* [1978] 3 All ER 1140, HL; *Taylor* [1998] Crim LR 582.

[19] [1997] 1 Cr App R 1, CA and commentary [1996] Crim LR 722 for criticism. See also *Morton* [2004] Crim LR 73.

[20] See also *Montague* [2013] EWCA Crim 1781, [2014] Crim LR 615 and commentary.

[21] *Jogee* [2016] UKSC 8, [88].

[22] cf the observations made by Davis LJ in *Lewis* [2017] EWCA Crim 1734, [46].

defendant was an accessory; unless the jury could be sure when considering the case against a particular defendant that he was not the principal, he would have to be acquitted. In view of these forensic difficulties, the pragmatic solution of being able to charge D with being either an accessory or principal is understandable. The lack of precision in such an indictment has been held not to render it incompatible with Art 6 of the ECHR on the basis of the requirement that a defendant must know 'in detail' the nature of the case against him.[23]

Although the law treats the accessory and principal in identical terms for the purposes of procedure and punishment, it is important to distinguish them for several reasons.

First, the accessory is only liable once the principal offence has been committed.[24] Secondary liability derives from the commission of the principal offence.[25] This derivative approach to secondary liability means that, with a murder for example, D may supply the weapon to P, who kills V, but it is not until that killing takes place (or is attempted) that D can be liable as an accessory. This contrasts with inchoate liability where D who supplies the weapon is liable (depending on his mens rea) as soon as he performs his act of supply, irrespective of whether P goes on to kill V or, indeed, whether P does any further act.

Secondly, in some cases, it is only an offence to do something *to another* and not to assist someone to do it to themselves (eg injecting drugs). It is essential to establish if it is alleged that D helped P to perform the conduct on himself (no liability), or whether D performed it on P (potential liability).[26]

A third reason for distinguishing principals and accessories is that, even in offences of strict liability, accessories must always be proved to have mens rea.[27]

Fourthly, in some cases offences are defined in such a way that they can be committed, as a principal offender, only by someone who is a member of a particular group or who has a particular qualification (eg the 'driver' of a vehicle or the licensee of a pub).[28]

Fifthly, in some offences vicarious liability may be imposed for the act of another who is a principal offender or does the act of a principal offender; but there is no vicarious liability for the act of an accessory.[29]

Finally, in some exceptional cases the available sentencing differs significantly between principal and accessory.[30]

6.2.2 Secondary as distinct from inchoate liability

As noted, with inchoate offences D's liability crystallizes as soon as he has assisted or encouraged P or agreed with him to commit an offence irrespective of whether that leads

---

[23] *Mercer* [2001] All ER (D) 187. Cf A Ashworth, 'A Decade of Human Rights in Criminal Justice' [2014] Crim LR 325, 327.

[24] Committing the offence includes 'attempting' to commit the offence. If P, with D's aid, has attempted to murder V, D, as well as P, can be convicted of the offence of attempted murder.

[25] See GP Fletcher, *Rethinking Criminal Law* (1978) Ch 8; KJM Smith, *A Modern Treatise on Complicity* (1991) Ch 4; D Lanham, 'Primary and Derivative Criminal Liability: An Australian Perspective' [2000] Crim LR 707; LC 300, paras 2.7 et seq. The law in application fails to remain true to this theory: Wilson describes English law as 'fudging' the theoretical basis: *Central Issues*, Ch 7. An alternative analysis sees the secondary as causally responsible for the principal's crime (see Smith, above, Ch 3; M Moore, *Causation and Responsibility An Essay in Law, Morals and Metaphysics* (2009); J Gardner, *Offences and Defences: Selected Essays in the Philosophy of Criminal Law* (2007), Ch 4). See p 180.

[26] *Kennedy (No 2)* [2008] 1 AC 269; cf *Empress Car* [1999] 2 AC 22.

[27] See p 205.   [28] See p 205.

[29] See p 192. There is no vicarious liability at common law, as confirmed in *Craik v CC of Northumbria Police* [2010] EWHC 935 (Admin).

[30] In road traffic offences, where disqualification of the principal is obligatory, disqualification of accessories is discretionary: Road Traffic Offenders Act 1988, s 34(5).

to P committing or even attempting to commit the substantive offence.[31] Under ss 44 to 46 of the SCA 2007 there is an overlap with secondary liability. Where D does an act which is capable of encouraging or assisting, for example supplying a gun to P for him to murder V, D will be liable under ss 44 to 46 (see Ch 11), subject to mens rea, irrespective of whether the anticipated offence is committed or attempted by P. The offences in ss 44 to 46 are extremely wide-reaching. If P commits the murder, D can be charged as an accessory *or* under ss 44 to 46. There will often be little advantage in charging D as an accessory.[32] The procedure and sentence will be the same for the offence under the SCA 2007 as for the anticipated substantive offence.

There is an even more complex relationship between conspiracy and secondary liability. A conspiracy is complete as soon as A and B agree to commit an offence (say, murder) with the intention[33] that the offence should be committed. There is no secondary liability for anyone unless and until the murder is committed. If B commits murder, A is liable as an accessory to murder by having agreed with B and thereby provided B with encouragement.[34] Liability as an accessory might also arise in this scenario if A assists or encourages B even without an agreement.[35] If B commits the offence, A and B can also still be charged with conspiracy to do so (see Ch 11). Finally, there is the issue of being an accessory to a conspiracy—for example, A intentionally assists D1 and D2 (eg providing D1 and D2 with facilities to meet) when they are making an agreement to murder V; A does not assist in the murder itself, but merely in setting up the agreement. If D1 commits murder as part of his conspiracy with D2, D2 is liable as an accessory (as well as for the conspiracy) because D2 has encouraged D1. Arguably, A has assisted D1 and D2 to commit the conduct element of conspiracy, but it cannot reasonably be said that A has done any act that has assisted or encouraged[36] D1 to *perpetrate the conduct element* of murder. It is submitted that A's act is not enough to render him an accessory to murder.

6.3 The principal offender

It is important to identify the principal offender.[37] Where there are several participants in a crime, the principal offender is the one whose act is the most immediate cause of the actus reus. In murder, for example, he is the person who, with mens rea, fires the gun or administers the poison which causes death; in theft, the person who, with mens rea, appropriates

[31] At common law D had no inchoate liability for assisting P to commit an offence which P did not subsequently commit or attempt to commit. The SCA 2007, ss 44–46, introduced such offences following the recommendation of the Law Commission in LC 300, *Inchoate Liability for Assisting and Encouraging Crime* (2006). See the discussion in Buxton, n 14.

[32] Section 45 requires that D should believe that P *will* commit the conduct element of the actus reus of the principal offence. In some respects this may actually be narrower than accessorial liability. Eg D, sells P a knife believing that P will use it in the kitchen, if D also believes that P *might* use it to murder his wife, D is not liable under s 45, but may be liable as an accessory if P does commit murder subject to mens rea. See Ch 11.

[33] cf *Anderson* [1986] AC 27 which is surely wrong on this.

[34] Even in the unusual case where it is not A's intention that the murder be committed. See p 453.

[35] *Rook* [1993] 2 All ER 955, [1993] Crim LR 698 and commentary. Cf Stephen, *Digest* (9th edn) art 28; Williams, CLGP, 363; *Pinkerton v United States*, 328 US 640 (1946). See, however, D Lanham, 'Complicity, Concert and Conspiracy' (1980) 4 Crim LJ 276.

[36] Arguably there is no encouragement by A in this conduct. Some light may be shed on the meaning of that concept when the courts grapple more fully with the SCA 2007 provisions.

[37] Sometimes this is overlooked, as is evident from the judge's direction in *Bristow* [2013] EWCA Crim 1540, [2014] Crim LR 457. Even if P cannot be identified, it is crucial that the jury are directed to consider first whether there was a principal offender before going on to evaluate the other possible bases of liability.

the property which is stolen; in bigamy, the person who, knowing himself to be already married, goes through a second ceremony of marriage; and so on. With offences in which there is no result or consequence to be proved, the principal offender is perhaps more accurately the person who engages in the conduct element of the actus reus. In the case of statutory offences, whether a person is a principal offender will turn on whether he satisfies the precise form of words used to describe the conduct element of the offence.[38] One of the reasons why it is important to identify the principal is because he can be guilty if liability is strict as to one of the elements of the substantive offence, but this will not be the case with the secondary party. The Supreme Court confirmed in *Jogee* that to be guilty the secondary party must have knowledge of any facts or circumstances necessary for the principal's conduct to be criminal.[39] To take an example, the principal can be guilty of making an indecent image of a child even though he may not have known that the victim was under the age of 18. This is because liability as to the age of V is strict. To be guilty of being an accomplice to this offence, however, the secondary party must have known that the victim was under the age of 18. Failure to identify accurately who is the principal and who is the secondary party risks the latter being convicted even though he may not have possessed the requisite mens rea.

It is a fundamental principle that criminal liability arises from wrongdoing for which a person is himself responsible and not for the wrongdoing of others. If, by performing acts of assistance, an accessory were taken to have brought about the commission of the offence he would for all purposes become a principal offender. If D, having persuaded P to murder V, were taken to have caused V's death, that is, killed V, he would satisfy the definition of murder as a principal. Anyone whose assistance or encouragement in fact caused another to commit a crime would then be a principal. That is not the law. Accessorial liability is based on the assumption that the accessory does not cause the actus reus.[40] The distinction between principal and accessory is fundamental and the two ought not to be elided.[41] As Lord Kerr pointed out in *Gnango*: 'To speak of joint principal offenders being involved in a joint enterprise is, at least potentially, misleading. The essential ingredient for joint principal offending is a contribution to the cause of the *actus reus*.'[42]

The House of Lords in *Kennedy (No 2)*[43] reaffirmed these fundamental principles.[44] As Lord Bingham made clear, referring to Glanville Williams' article '*Finis for Novus Actus*', the doctrine of secondary liability was developed precisely because an informed voluntary choice was ordinarily regarded as a *novus actus interveniens* breaking the chain of causation:

Principals cause, accomplices encourage (or otherwise influence) or help. If the instigator were regarded as causing the result he would be a principal, and the conceptual division between principals (or, as I prefer to call them, perpetrators) and accessories would vanish. Indeed, it was because the instigator was not regarded as causing the crime that the notion of accessories had to be developed. This is the irrefragable argument for recognising the *novus actus* principle as one of the bases of our criminal law. The final act is done by the perpetrator, and his guilt pushes the accessories, conceptually speaking, into the background. Accessorial liability is, in the traditional theory, 'derivative' from that of the perpetrator.[45]

---

[38] See eg *Corporation of London v Eurostar* [2004] EWHC 187 (Admin), where Eurostar were guilty as principals for 'landing' an Alsatian dog as prohibited under anti-rabies legislation.

[39] *Jogee* [2016] UKSC 8, [99].

[40] HLA Hart and T Honoré, *Causation in the Law* (2nd edn, 1985) 380; SH Kadish, *Blame and Punishment: Essays in the Criminal Law* (1987) 143–144.

[41] This passage in the 14th edition of this work was cited with approval by Spencer J in *R v Maughan and others* (CCC, 29 July 2016).

[42] [2011] UKSC 59, [129]. It is submitted that the reference to 'contributing to the cause of the actus reus' should be treated with caution.

[43] [2007] UKHL 38, [2008] Crim LR 223.   [44] See p 74.   [45] [2007] UKHL 38, [17].

Despite these clear statements, the courts still occasionally refer to D as a 'cause' of P's act. In *Mendez and Thompson*,[46] Toulson LJ, after a scholarly analysis of the historical position, concluded that 'at its most basic level secondary liability is founded on a principle of causation, that a defendant (D) is liable for an offence committed by a principal actor (P) if by his conduct he has caused or materially contributed to the commission of the offence (with the requisite mental element); and a person who knowingly assists or encourages another to commit an offence is taken to have contributed to its commission'.[47] If cause is read strictly, this approach seems to run contrary to the fundamental principle reiterated in *Kennedy (No 2)* and does not reflect the practical reality that D might be liable for providing assistance to someone who had already made up his mind to commit the offence. There would be no causal contribution to the offence in such a case.[48] In *Stringer*,[49] Toulson LJ acknowledged that the accessory need not 'cause' the principal to commit the offence in the sense that 'but for' the defendant's conduct, the principal would not have committed the offence. His Lordship suggests instead that the accessory's conduct has to have some relevance to the commission of the principal offence; there had to be a 'connecting link'.[50] This is far less controversial:[51]

The way that the court put it in *Mendez and Thompson* was that D's conduct must (objectively) have constituted assistance or encouragement, even if P (subjectively) did not need assistance or encouragement. Whereas the provision of assistance need not involve communication between D and P, encouragement by its nature involves some form of transmission of the encouragement by words or conduct, whether directly or via an intermediary. An un-posted letter of encouragement would not be encouragement unless P chanced to discover it and read it. Similarly, it would be unreal to regard P as acting with the assistance or encouragement of D if the only encouragement took the form of words spoken by D out of P's earshot.[52]

Writing extrajudicially, Sir Roger Toulson elaborated as follows:

It is plainly right and just that there should have to be some 'connecting link'. It would be morally repugnant to find a person guilty of murder for behaving in a way which on a fair view was unconnected with the crime...This analysis involves a concept of causation which is appropriate to the context. I do not see an alternative foundation on which secondary liability can satisfactorily be said to rest.[53]

Whilst this may seem relatively uncontroversial, the spectre of further case law on causation and secondary liabilities arises because of the disagreement between Lords Clarke and Dyson and Lord Kerr in the case of *Gnango*.[54] In that infamous case[55] D was convicted of murder. He had voluntarily engaged in an exchange of gunfire with an opponent (P) in

---

[46] [2010] EWCA Crim 516, criticized by G Virgo [2010] 5 Arch Rev 4 and D Ormerod [2011] Crim LR 151.

[47] At [18], referring to *Foster's Crown Law* (3rd edn, 1809) 369. Toulson LJ does add 'contributing to'.

[48] See, however, the argument advanced by Gardner, *Offences and Defences*, n 25.

[49] [2011] EWCA Crim 1396, [2011] Crim LR 886.   [50] At [48].

[51] Virgo contends, however, that in order to conform with existing doctrine, the connection justification would need to be extended in an artificial fashion. See G Virgo, 'Joint Enterprise Liability is Dead: Long Live Accessorial Liability' [2012] Crim LR 850.

[52] See also *Jogee* [2016] UKSC 8, [12].

[53] R Toulson, 'Complicity in Murder' in DJ Baker and J Horder (eds), *The Sanctity of Life and the Criminal Law. The Legacy of Glanville Williams* (2012) 239.

[54] [2011] UKSC 59. For criticism, see GR Sullivan, 'Accessories and Principals after *Gnango*' in A Reed and M Bohlander (eds), *Participation in Crime: Domestic and Comparative Perspectives* (2013) and R Buxton, 'Being an Accessory to One's Own Murder' [2012] Crim LR 275.

[55] [2010] EWCA Crim 1691.

885

a public place. One of P's shots, aimed at D, killed a passer-by. P was not prosecuted, but would have been guilty of murder by the law of transferred malice. D was convicted of possessing a firearm with intent to endanger life, attempted murder and, by way of joint enterprise, the murder of the passer-by. Lord Dyson felt that it was not possible to uphold D's liability on the basis that D's act of shooting was a cause of the death. If P's act of shooting at D was a free, deliberate and informed act, it broke the chain of causation between D's shooting at P and P's shooting and killing V.[56] His lordship agreed with Lord Clarke that the court could not uphold the conviction on the basis that D caused P to fire the fatal shot. But Lord Clarke took the view that the mere fact that the immediate cause of the death was a criminal and deliberate act on the part of P does not as a matter of law break the chain of causation.[57] It might have been possible to hold D liable for murder on the basis of his shot at P, but that was not left to the jury.[58] Resurrecting the debate about secondary liability and causation would be undesirable after the House of Lords had so definitively and succinctly clarified the law in *Kennedy (No 2)*.[59] It is submitted that the statement from Lord Bingham quoted earlier should be faithfully followed.[60]

6.3.1 Innocent agency

The actus reus of a crime may be directly brought about by the conduct of someone who has no mens rea, or who has some defence,[61] for example infancy or insanity. Such a person is usually described as an 'innocent agent'.[62] The principal offender in such a case is the participant whose act is the most immediate[63] cause of the innocent agent's act. Examples are plentiful. If D sends to V through the post a letter-bomb which injures V when it explodes, the postman who delivers the letter being unaware of its contents is an innocent agent. If D, intending to kill V, provides to V's daughter a poison which he says will cure V's cold, and the daughter innocently (ie without knowing the true nature of the drug) administers the poison, causing V's death, then D is guilty of murder as the principal offender and the daughter is an innocent agent.[64] If in these examples the daughter or the postman had mens rea then he or she would, of course, be a principal offender. Where D, an employee, makes a false statement to his employer's accountant, knowing that the statement will be entered in the accounts, and the innocent accountant does enter it, D is guilty, as a principal offender, of falsifying his employer's accounts.[65] Where D induces a child, aged nine, to take money from a till and give it to D, D is a principal offender as the child is exempt from criminal

---

[56] [2011] UKSC 59, [106].

[57] The only case his lordship relied upon was *Pagett* (1983) 76 Cr App R 279. In that case, however, PP were police officers acting in the execution of a duty and/or in self-defence, which is why it could be said that their acts were no longer voluntary and were caused by D in the strict sense of the term.

[58] [2011] UKSC 59, [91].   [59] [2007] UKHL 37.

[60] Lord Kerr in dissent in *Gnango* placed significant reliance upon Lord Bingham's *dicta* in *Kennedy (No 2)*. His lordship observed that even if it could be said that D's firing at P made it more likely that P would fire again, that is simply insufficient to demonstrate that D *caused* P to shoot.

[61] Other than duress: *Bourne* (1952) 36 Cr App R 125.

[62] See P Alldridge, 'The Doctrine of Innocent Agency' (1990) 2 Crim Law Forum 45; G Williams, 'Innocent Agency and Causation' (1992) 3 Crim Law Forum 289; RD Taylor, 'Complicity and Excuses' [1983] Crim LR 656.

[63] This description of relative proximity can be problematical. D1 passes poison to D2, who passes it to D3 who, unaware that it is poison, passes it to V who dies. D3 is the innocent agent. Is D2 the principal offender and D1 a secondary party? Are both D1 and D2 principal offenders? See Smith, *A Modern Treatise on Complicity*, 98. We are grateful to David Hughes for this example.

[64] *Anon* (1634) Kel 53; *Michael* (1840) 9 C & P 356.   [65] *Butt* (1884) 15 Cox CC 564.

liability. If the child is over ten and liable to conviction, then he is the principal offender if he has mens rea and D is an accessory.[66]

There are some crimes to which the doctrine of innocent agency is inapplicable because it is impossible to say that D has *personally* performed the conduct required by the definition of the actus reus.[67] Bigamy[68] is a good example. Compare it with murder. If D causes an innocent person, say the postman E, to kill V by delivering a letter which E does not know contains a bomb, it is right for the law to take the view that *D has killed V*—the actus reus of murder. In contrast take the case of bigamy, if D knows that F is married, but induces E, an innocent person who has no knowledge of F's marital status, to marry F it is impossible to say that *D has married during the lifetime of his wife*—the actus reus of bigamy. He has not done so. The innocent agency doctrine seems equally inapplicable, it is submitted, in rape and other crimes involving sexual intercourse.[69] After *Jogee*, to be an accessory, D must intend P to have mens rea. Innocent agency therefore appears to be an exception to this rule, although the issue was not discussed in *Jogee*.

6.3.2 Joint principal offenders

There may be more than one person engaged in perpetrating the conduct element of the actus reus of the principal offence. So there may be two or more principal offenders in the same crime. If D1 and D2 make an attack on V intending to kill or cause him serious injury and the combined effect of their blows is to kill him, both are guilty of murder[70] as joint principal offenders. A different type of joint responsibility is where each of two or more parties does an act which is an element of, or part of, the actus reus of the principal offence.[71]

There is, however, no joint principalship if D induces another person, P (not an innocent agent), by persuasion or otherwise, to commit the offence: that does not amount to D causing the actus reus. P's voluntary intervening act 'breaks the chain of causation'[72] so that D is not a principal offender. P is the principal offender; D may be an accessory.[73]

What if the principal offender himself is not present at the moment of the completion of the crime? This can arise in the context of innocent agency. If D1 and D2 agree to employ an innocent agent, E, both D1 and D2 are liable as principal offenders for E's acts when they are committed and it is immaterial that E was instructed by the one in the absence of the other.[74] The innocent agent's acts are considered the acts of both conspirators.[75] Where there is no innocent agent, the same considerations cannot apply. D encourages or assists P, who leaves poison to be taken by V, or sets a trap into which V falls. D is liable as a secondary party; P as the principal offender.

---

[66] *Manley* (1844) 1 Cox CC 104 In *DPP v K & B* [1997] 1 Cr App R 36, DC, it was said, *obiter*, that if D procured a child under ten to have sexual intercourse without consent, D could not be guilty of rape because there would be no actus reus. That seems wrong: see [1997] Crim LR 121, 122. See also *Mazeau* (1840) 9 C & P 676.

[67] cf *Woby v AJB and LCO* [1986] Crim LR 183, DC (boys under 18 not guilty of buying intoxicating liquor in licensed premises when they sent in an adult to buy it).

[68] Except in the case of a marriage by proxy.

[69] There are *dicta* in *Cogan and Leak* [1976] QB 217, [1975] Crim LR 584, p 223, that rape may be committed through an innocent agent but these are contrary to principle. The Law Commission propose replacing the innocent agency doctrine with a specific offence; see p 234.

[70] *Macklin and Murphy's Case* (1838) 2 Lew CC 225.

[71] *Bingley* (1821) Russ & Ry 446 (A and B each forged part of a banknote).

[72] See *Kennedy (No 2)* [2007] UKHL 38.

[73] Or under ss 44–46 of the SCA 2007 depending on his mens rea.

[74] This qualifies the idea that generally the principal is the person who is the immediate cause of the conduct element of the actus reus.

[75] *Bull and Schmidt* (1845) 1 Cox CC 281. Arguably D1 is liable as an accessory to D2 who causes E to act.

6.3.3 Joint principals or principal and accessory?

The distinction between a joint principal offender and a secondary party is sometimes a fine one. There is a view that all who act together with a common purpose are principal offenders.[76] That would mean that if D provided assistance to P by providing a gun for him to murder V and P alone fired the shot, D might be liable as a principal for murder if he shared P's purpose to kill V, even though D did not perform the actus reus of murder. This is not the law in England.[77] As noted, under s 8 of the 1861 Act generally it is immaterial whether D is alleged to have participated in the crime as principal or accessory. Either way, he is equally responsible and liable to conviction. When it is necessary to distinguish, the test would seem to be: did D by his own act (as distinct from anything done by P with D's advice or assistance) contribute to the actus reus? If he did, he is a principal or joint principal offender. The distinction may be important where the jury acquit P and convict D. If D caused the actus reus by his own act, he is a principal offender and there is no problem. But, if he did not, there is a difficulty. If P is innocent, there is no crime which D can have aided or abetted. The difficulty can be overcome (a) if P can be regarded as an innocent agent, or (b) under a somewhat uncertain principle[78] that it is an offence for D to procure the commission of P's actus reus;[79] but it is surely wrong to overcome it by a fiction, a pretence that D 'did it', if he did not.

Where the actus reus is a 'state of affairs'[80]—for example, being in the UK illegally—the test for determining who is a principal offender is: ignoring D, does the statutory description of the state of affairs fit P?

6.4 The liability of secondary parties who assist or encourage crime

To be liable as a secondary party, a person who is not the principal offender must be proved to have aided, abetted, counselled[81] or procured, though it is quite sufficient to show that he did one of these things.[82]

An accessory is liable when and where the principal offence he has aided, abetted, counselled or procured is committed. So an employer, D, who sends P to drive a lorry, which D and P know to be in a dangerous condition, from Scotland to England may be held liable in England for a death caused by P in England because of the lorry's condition.[83]

---

[76] Some jurisdictions adopt such a rule. See in Australia *Osland v R* (1998) 73 ALJR 173, HC of A. See further JC Smith, 'Joint Enterprise and Secondary Liability' (1999) 50 NILQ 153; cf A Simester, 'The Mental Element in Complicity' (2006) 122 LQR 578.

[77] See, historically, Stephen's *Digest*, arts 37 and 38. In *Gnango* [2011] UKSC 59 the approach adopted by Lords Brown and Clarke comes close to suggesting that D can be the principal even though he has not caused the actus reus of the substantive offence. With respect, this is incorrect for the reasons given above. Cf GR Sullivan, 'Accessories and Principals after *Gnango*' in A Reed and M Bohlander (eds), *Participation in Crime: Domestic and Comparative Perspectives* (2013); R Buxton, 'Being an Accessory to One's Own Murder' [2012] Crim LR 275 and G Virgo, 'Joint Enterprise is Dead: Long Live Accessorial Liability' [2012] Crim LR 850.

[78] See p 223.   [79] *Millward*, p 223.   [80] See p 42.

[81] 'Counselling' must not be taken literally. Mere incitement to commit an offence, not followed by its actual commission, is not 'counselling'—*Assistant Recorder of Kingston-upon-Hull, ex p Morgan* [1969] 2 QB 58, DC.

[82] *Ferguson v Weaving* [1951] KB 814.

[83] *Robert Millar (Contractors) Ltd* [1970] 2 QB 54. See Law Commission proposals on jurisdiction: LC 305, Ch 6.

6.4.1 Actus reus of the accessory

The actus reus and mens rea of the principal offender will be prescribed by the relevant statute or common law, so with murder it would be killing a human being with malice afore-thought, etc; with assault it will be intentionally or recklessly causing a person to apprehend immediate unlawful personal violence, etc. If D is alleged to be an accessory to any crime, his liability as an accessory comprises the actus reus of aiding, abetting, counselling or procuring, with the relevant mens rea of an accessory (intention to assist, intention for P to have mens rea, knowledge of the relevant circumstances rendering P's act criminal). The conduct sufficient to satisfy the elements of being an accessory will often contrast starkly with the requirements of the principal offence. In a case of murder, D can be convicted as an accessory as a result of *conduct* that consists of no more than acting as a lookout whereas P must be shown to have killed V, but under s 8 of the 1861 Act both D and P will be convicted as murderers, labelled as such and punished as such.

It is important to remember that there is no secondary liability for a person whose participation in the relevant events does not involve him advising or encouraging P to commit the crime, and who does not assist P in the commission of it in any way. Accepting a lift on a motorbike known to have been taken without consent does not amount to aiding and abetting the use of the vehicle without insurance.[84] It would be different if D had participated in or assisted/encouraged the taking.[85] Liability as an accessory does not extend to cases where D has not assisted or encouraged in fact, but has merely attempted or conspired to do so.[86]

Once encouragement or assistance is proved to have been given by D, the Supreme Court in *Jogee*[87] stated that the prosecution does not have to prove that it had a positive effect on either P's conduct or the outcome. The court expressed concern that such a positive effect would, in many cases, be impossible to prove. The example given by the court is where there were many supporters encouraging P. The court stated that it would be difficult to prove that the encouragement of a single one made a difference. According to the court, that does not mean that D will be guilty if he counselled P to commit the offence many years before. The Supreme Court held that it is ultimately a question of fact and degree whether D's act of assistance or encouragement was so distanced in time, place or circumstances from the conduct of P that it would be unrealistic to regard P's offence as having been encouraged or assisted by it.

It is submitted that there is a risk that these comments will be taken out of context. If it is truly the case that there is no requirement for D's act of assistance or encouragement to have had a positive effect on P, then why does it matter whether D's conduct was committed a long time ago, or has faded to the point of mere background? It is respectfully submitted that the Supreme Court in *Jogee* may have overstated its position. As was discussed earlier, secondary liability is not based upon causation, so the Supreme Court was correct not to resurrect the misleading proposition that D's act of assistance or encouragement must have caused P to commit the offence in question. As Toulson LJ confirmed in *Stringer*, however, there must be some connecting link between D's act of assistance or encouragement and P's offence. Therefore, whilst it is true that the prosecution does not have to prove that D's act of assistance or encouragement was the cause of D's conduct, there must be some connecting link between the two. In most cases, the presence of this connecting link will be self-evident. In more marginal cases, the sufficiency of the connecting link between D's act

---

[84] *D (Infant) v Parsons* [1960] 1 WLR 797.

[85] *Ross v Rivenall* [1959] 1 WLR 713. Cf the Theft Act 1968, s 12(1) and *Boldizsar v Knight* [1980] Crim LR 653, p 914.

[86] *Kenning* [2008] EWCA Crim 1534. Liability might arise under the SCA 2007, ss 44–46 or for conspiracy.

[87] [2016] UKSC 8, [12].

of assistance or encouragement and P's conduct will be a question of fact and degree, taking into consideration all the surrounding circumstances. It is disappointing that the Supreme Court in *Jogee* chose to 'fudge'[88] this issue and rely so much upon the jury to decide whether D made a sufficient contribution to be liable as an accessory to P's offence. The decision not to engage with this issue directly perhaps reveals a lack of clarity on the theoretical foundations underpinning secondary liability.

It is also necessary to bear in mind that in *Jogee* the Supreme Court abolished what had become known as the 'fundamental difference rule', which enabled D to avoid liability if the weapon P used to kill V was more dangerous than any weapon D contemplated he might use.[89] The Supreme Court did state, however, that 'it is possible for death to be caused by some overwhelming supervening act by the perpetrator which nobody in the defendant's shoes could have contemplated might happen and is of such a character as to relegate his acts to history'.[90] In such a case, the court stated that D will bear no responsibility for the death. The court's use of the concept of an 'overwhelming supervening event' has replaced the fundamental difference rule and is arguably of broader application.[91] The trial judge is not required, however, to direct the jury in such terms in every case. In *Ibrar*, for example, Hallett LJ concluded that on the facts of the case, P's use of a knife was not an 'overwhelming supervening act' that D could not have contemplated so as to require the judge to direct the jury more fully on the issue of fundamental departure.[92] The Supreme Court's reliance upon the concept suggests a degree of incoherence. The court holds that D's conduct need not have a causative impact on P's crime (causation not necessary to inculpate D), but when considering the exculpation, the court's use of the language of supervening event is that associated with a break in the chain of causation (causation is relevant to exculpation).

6.4.1.1 Aid, abet, counsel, procure
In *A-G's Reference (No 1 of 1975)* Lord Widgery CJ said:

We approach s 8 of the 1861 Act on the basis that the words should be given their ordinary meaning, if possible. We approach the section on the basis also that if four words are employed here, 'aid, abet, counsel or procure', the probability is that there is a difference between each of those four words and the other three, because, if there were no such difference, then Parliament would be wasting time in using four words where two or three would do.[93]

The four words had previously been regarded as technical terms and it is clear that they cannot be given their ordinary meaning in all respects.[94]

In the modern law, secondary participation almost invariably consists of 'assisting' or 'encouraging' the commission of the crime. In *Jogee*, the Supreme Court held that the requisite conduct element is that D has encouraged or assisted the commission of the offence by

---

88 M Dyson, 'Letter to the Editor' [2016] Crim LR 638.

89 *Powell and Daniels*; *English* [1999] 1 AC 1, 30. Historically, the doctrine also applied if the principal committed the murder in a manner not contemplated by the secondary party. The secondary party's knowledge that the principal was in possession of a weapon is now relevant to the jury's assessment of whether he possessed the requisite intent. See p 201.

90 *Jogee* [2016] UKSC 8, [97]. The Supreme Court cited *Anderson and Morris* [1966] 2 QB 110; *Wesley* [1963] 1 WLR 1200.

91 cf M Dyson, 'Shorn-Off Complicity' (2016) 75 CLJ 196.   92 [2017] EWCA Crim 1841.

93 [1975] 2 All ER 684 at 686.

94 Under the old law of felonies, 'aiding and abetting' was used to describe the activity of the principal 'in the second degree' and 'counselling and procuring' that of the accessory before the fact: *Ferguson v Weaving*, n 82, at 818–819; Stephen, *Digest* (4th edn) arts 37–39; *Bowker v Premier Drug Co Ltd* [1928] 1 KB 217 ('aid and abet' implies presence). Aid and abet was, however, sometimes used in relation to acts committed before the actual perpetration of the crime.

P.[95] As this section will discuss, the terms used in s 8 have historically been interpreted to mean subtly different things.

The only possible exception to the use of the terms 'assisting' or 'encouraging' may be the procurer who succeeds in causing the principal to commit the crime (as in the *A-G's Reference*) without doing anything which could be fairly described as encouragement or assistance. Assisting or encouraging can be by practically any means—supply of weapons, tools, information, support, keeping watch, filming an attack on a mobile phone, etc. It is generally irrelevant whether the accessory is present or absent or whether his assistance or encouragement was given before or at the time of the commission of the offence.

All four words—aid, abet, counsel, procure—may be used together to charge a person, D, who is alleged to have participated in an offence otherwise than as a principal offender.[96] As long as the evidence establishes that D's conduct satisfied one of the words, that is enough to prove his actus reus as an accessory. However, where the indictment uses only one term—for example, 'procures'—it is necessary to prove that D's conduct fits that term.

Each element of the actus reus of the accessory deserves further brief examination to consider three particular issues: (a) what forms of conduct constitute aiding, abetting, counselling or procuring; (b) whether there need be a causal link between the aiding, etc and the principal offence; and (c) whether there need be a meeting of minds or consensus between the aider, etc and the principal offender.

In short, the law is almost certainly that:

(1) 'aiding' requires actual assistance but neither consensus nor causation;[97]

(2) 'abetting' and 'counselling' imply consensus but not causation;

(3) 'procuring' implies causation but not consensus.

Aiding

It has sometimes been said[98] that 'aid and abet' is a single concept, 'aid' denoting the actus reus and 'abet', the mens rea. The natural meaning of s 8 is, however, that stated in the *A-G's Reference*. Moreover, the words aid and abet do connote different kinds of activity. The natural meaning of to 'aid' is to 'give help, support or assistance to'.[99] The courts have taken a broad view of what suffices for 'aid'. Although historically the term was commonly used to describe someone present assisting the principal at the time of the offence, there is now no such restriction.

Aiding can be satisfied by any act of assistance before or at the time of the offence.[100] Supplying a weapon or transporting P to the scene of the crime[101] are obvious examples.

Aiding does not imply any causal connection between D's act and P's. D may assist P and enable him to commit the offence more easily, earlier or with greater safety and, if so, D is surely guilty even if P would have committed the same offence if D had not intervened.[102]

---

95 [2016] UKSC 8, [8].

96 *Re Smith* (1858) 3 H & N 227; *Ferguson v Weaving* [1951] KB 814.

97 cf Stephen, *Digest* (4th edn) who argued that D who abets or counsels or commands (as well as procures) is liable and, by implication liable only, for an offence 'which is committed *in consequence* of such counselling, procuring, or commandment'.

98 *Lynch v DPP for Northern Ireland* [1975] 1 All ER 913 at 941, per Lord Simon quoting the 3rd edition of this book and Devlin J in *National Coal Board v Gamble* [1959] 1 QB 11 at 20.

99 *Oxford English Dictionary.*   100 *Coney* (1882) 8 QBD 534.

101 See eg *Nedrick-Smith* [2006] EWHC 3015 (Admin) where D3 was a party to D2 and D1 attacking V in her home. D3 drove them and stood watching as they attacked. The magistrates were entitled to find her guilty as an accessory.

102 See WR Le Fave and AW Scott, *Criminal Law* (1986) 504. See also *Luffman* [2008] EWCA Crim 1739, n 116. Cf *Mendez*, n 46.

In *Bryce*,[103] however, the court seemed to imply a causal requirement. D was convicted of murder as an accessory. In the course of a drug dealers' dispute D assisted P, who was acting on the orders of the gang leader B. D transported P and a gun to a caravan near V's home. More than 12 hours later, P, acting alone, shot V. D's ground of appeal was that the delay meant that what D did (transporting P) was too remote in time and place to the killing to constitute assistance, particularly since at that stage P had not formed the intention to kill. The Court of Appeal, after a comprehensive survey of the case law, upheld D's conviction concluding that no intervening event occurred hindering the plan, this despite the fact that in the 12-hour delay P's gun barrel was shortened and B visited P to encourage him. The court concluded that there was no 'overwhelming supervening event' sufficient to break the chain of causation, nor had D effected a withdrawal in that time. This implies a causal requirement. More explicit statements to this effect were made in *Mendez*[104] discussed earlier. In light of the explanation given in *Stringer*,[105] and the powerful statement of Lord Bingham for a unanimous House of Lords in *Kennedy (No 2)*, it is submitted that despite these *dicta*, it remains the case that there is no need for D's acts to have caused the commission of the actus reus of the principal offence. This is supported by the statements of the Supreme Court in *Jogee*.[106] Although there must be some link between D and P in the sense that D must have provided assistance or encouragement in fact, that is a far cry from establishing causation.[107]

Nor does aiding imply any consensus between D and P. If D sees P committing a crime and comes to his assistance by, for example, restraining the policeman who would have prevented P from committing the crime, D is surely guilty even though his assistance is unforeseen and unwanted by P and unknown to him. The same might apply to aid given beforehand. D, knowing that P is going to meet a blackmailer, V, slips a gun into P's pocket in the hope that he will kill V—which P does.[108]

Abetting

The natural meaning of 'abet' is 'to incite, instigate or encourage'.[109] Abetting is usually defined in terms of encouragement. There is little to distinguish abetting from counselling;[110] perhaps there is no difference except that historically 'abet' was used to refer to encouragement at the time of the offence and 'counsel' to encouragement at an earlier time.[111] It is clear that either type of activity is sufficient to found liability as an accessory.

The natural meaning of 'abet' does not imply any causal element, because the word (like counselling[112]) does not even imply that the offence has been committed.[113] As a matter of law, however, the principal offence must have been committed before anyone can be convicted as an abettor or counsellor of it.[114] But, even when the principal offence has been committed, it is true to say that D 'abetted' or 'counselled' it, in the ordinary

---

[103] [2004] EWCA Crim 1231. D would be liable for an offence under s 45 or 46 of the SCA 2007.

[104] [2010] EWCA Crim 516.   [105] See p 181.   [106] At [12].

[107] Virgo suggests that 'association' might provide the link. See G Virgo, 'Joint Enterprise is Dead: Long Live Accessorial Liability' [2012] Crim LR 850.

[108] D would on those facts be liable under s 44 of the SCA 2007. The passage in the text was quoted with approval by the Court of Appeal in *Fury* [2006] EWCA Crim 1258.

[109] *Oxford English Dictionary*.

[110] Lord Widgery's analysis of the four terms leaves considerable confusion. His lordship suggests that 'abet' and 'counsel' do imply different forms of activity.

[111] Per Lowry CJ in *DPP v Maxwell* [1978] 3 All ER 1140, 1158.

[112] See eg *Wilcox v Jeffery* [1951] 1 All ER 464; p 195; *Du Cros v Lambourne* [1907] KB 40.

[113] As a matter of ordinary language one would say that D had instigated, incited, encouraged, counselled, P even though P did not then commit the principal offence.

[114] Liability under the SCA 2007, Part 2 will arise if the anticipated offence does not occur. See p 474.

meaning of the words, even if his encouragement or counsel was ignored by P. Abetting and counselling may be treated alike on causation and, although historically there was scholarly opinion to the contrary,[115] the courts have unequivocally confirmed that there need not be any causal link between D's encouragement and P's commission of the offence in a case alleging counselling: *Luffman*.[116] The Supreme Court adopted the same approach in *Jogee*.[117]

Where the prosecution relies on counselling as the basis for D's secondary liability it must, however, establish that the commission of the offence was within the scope of the principal's authority.[118] Requiring proof of causation in abetting or counselling cases would present problems. To require that before D could be liable as an accessory his abetting/counselling must have caused P to commit the principal offence could, if causation is interpreted strictly, be to insist that, but for D's abetting/counselling, P's offence would not have been committed.[119] This would confine abetting and counselling much too narrowly. Moreover, D would then not be liable if, when he encouraged P, he knew that P had already made up his mind to commit the offence.[120] That is not to deny that D must have counselled in fact:[121] proffered advice or encouragement which has no effect on the mind of P is not counselling.[122]

As for consensus, there must be some connection between D's abetting (or counselling) and the commission of the principal offence. It is probably not necessary to prove that P was influenced in any way by D, but P must at least be aware that he has the authority, or the encouragement or the approval, of D to do the relevant acts.

For example, if the principal offender happened to be involved in a football riot in the course of which he laid about him with a weapon of some sort and killed someone who, unknown to him, was the person whom he had been counselled to kill, he would not, in our view, have been acting within the scope of his authority; he would have been acting outside it, albeit what he had done was what he had been counselled to do.[123]

It was suggested in *A-G's Reference (No 1 of 1975)* that in the case of abetting and counselling the concepts might require a meeting of minds of secondary party and principal. If counselling and abetting must be, in some degree, operative, as suggested previously, this is clearly right.[124]

---

[115] Stephen argued that if D is charged with abetting or counselling, his acts must have caused P to commit the offence. Stephen, *Digest* (4th edn) art 39. On his view, D who abets or counsels or commands (as well as procures) P is liable only for an offence by P 'which is committed *in consequence* of such counselling, procuring, or commandment'.

[116] [2008] EWCA Crim 1752. See also the explanation by Toulson LJ in *Stringer* [2011] EWCA Crim 1396 (p 181).

[117] At [12].   [118] *Calhaem* [1985] QB 808, CA.

[119] '… it does not make any difference that the person [*sc*, the person counselled] would have tried to commit suicide anyway': *A-G v Able* [1984] 1 All ER 277 at 288, per Woolf J.

[120] *Giannetto* [1997] 1 Cr App R 1, [1996] Crim LR 722. Trial judge's example: 'I am going to kill your wife'; husband: 'Oh goody.'

[121] But, it is clearly the law that an attempt to counsel does not amount to counselling. Liability for D's acts capable of encouraging P arises under ss 44–46 of the SCA 2007, and this includes attempts by D to encourage P which fail to do so.

[122] *Clarkson* [1971] 1 WLR 1402, C-MAC.

[123] *Calhaem* [1985] QB 808, CA, per Parker LJ; *Schriek* [1997] 2 NZLR 139, 149. Cf the view taken in W Wilson, *Criminal Law Doctrine* (2008).

[124] Consider the case of D, a persistent troublemaker, who comes across P and V in the middle of an argument. D urges P to punch V. Just before doing so, P tells D to 'mind your own business'. See LC 305, Appendix B, para B.63.

Counselling

To 'counsel' means to advise or solicit or encourage. The relevance of causation and consensus has been examined in the discussion of abetting in the previous section.

Procuring

'To procure means to produce by endeavour.'[125] 'You cannot procure an offence unless there is a causal link between what you do and the commission of the offence.'[126] In *A-G's Reference*, D added alcohol to P's drink without P's knowledge or consent. P drove home and thereby committed a strict liability offence of driving with a blood/alcohol concentration above the prescribed limit.[127] D was held to have procured that offence by P if it was proved that D knew that P was going to drive and that the ordinary and natural result of the added alcohol would be to bring P's blood/alcohol concentration above the prescribed limit. D had caused the actus reus (circumstance element) of the offence by putting P over the limit. This is in accordance with the natural meaning of 'procure'.[128] It is different if the driver is aware of the 'lacing'. In that situation P has, by his free, informed act of choosing to imbibe the laced drink, caused the actus reus (circumstance element) of the offence.[129] D might then be convicted as an accessory to P's offence of drink-driving on the basis that, although D has not procured its commission, he has certainly assisted its commission.[130]

What must be proved by way of a causal link in procuring? Glanville Williams cast doubt on the language of the court in *A-G's Reference*.[131] Williams relied on the facts of the famous case of *Beatty v Gillbanks*[132] to suggest that causation and procuring are not synonymous. In *Beatty*, Salvation Army members held a lawful meeting in Weston-super-Mare even though the members knew from experience that this would cause a hostile organization, 'the Skeleton Army', to attack them. The Salvation Army members clearly anticipated that the Skeleton Army would attack them and that the attack would result in damage to others, for example broken shop windows. Williams regarded it as absurd to say that the Salvationists were liable as accessories for the attack on themselves.

There are three responses to Williams' criticism: (a) Lord Widgery did not say that 'procure' means merely 'cause'. He said 'To procure means to produce by endeavour.' The Salvationists may have caused the Skeletons to make the attack (and to break the supposed windows) but these were certainly not results that they were 'endeavouring' to produce. Against this, it might be said that in *A-G's Reference*, D's awareness that he was causing the commission of the offence also fell short of proof of an endeavour to cause it; and, in *Blakely*,[133] the court thought *obiter* that D 'procured' a result if he contemplated it as a possible result of his act—which is far removed from endeavouring to produce it. (b) The Skeletons knew exactly what they were doing and in *A-G's Reference* Lord Widgery made it clear that the decision would not necessarily be the same where a driver knew that his drink was laced. The unaware driver 'in most instances… would have no means of preventing the offence from being committed', whereas the aware driver would. Lord Widgery thus contemplated that the act of the aware driver might break the chain of causation even for the purposes of secondary liability, but it is unclear whether his lordship meant that there would be no secondary liability. (c) The Supreme Court

---

[125] *A-G's Reference (No 1 of 1975)* [1975] 2 All ER 684 at 686; *Reed* [1982] Crim LR 819. See KJM Smith, 'Complicity and Causation' [1986] Crim LR 663; H Beynon, 'Causation, Omissions and Complicity' [1987] Crim LR 539.

[126] ibid, 687.   [127] Road Traffic Act 1972, s 6(1), now replaced by Road Traffic Act 1988, s 5.

[128] cf P Glazebrook, 'Attempting to Procure' [1959] Crim LR 774.

[129] See *Kennedy (No 2)* [2007] UKHL 38.   [130] LC 300, para 5.25.

[131] 'in so far as [it] purports to decide that merely causing an offence can be said to be a procuring of it, it should be regarded as too incautious a generalisation'.

[132] (1882) 9 QBD 308; TBCL, 339.   [133] See p 190.

in *Gnango*[134] accepted that D could be liable as an accessory to a crime on himself where he encouraged P in the commission of that crime. That extension, making D liable as a secondary party to crimes on himself, would seem to apply at least if the Salvationists and the Skeletons 'formed a mutual plan or agreement to have a fight'. If this approach were held to apply generally, it would mean that in the context of a street brawl, P would be liable for inflicting GBH on D and D would be liable as an accessory to his own GBH provided he were taken to have encouraged P to hit him, which would be possible even if P threw the first punch. The Supreme Court recognized that this could lead to incongruous results and advised restraint on the part of prosecuting authorities.[135] Liability is of course subject to D having the requisite mens rea.

If D procures X, an innocent agent, to commit an offence D is taken to have caused the actus reus for all purposes.[136] If D procures P, a guilty agent, to commit the offence, to be liable as an accessory D must be proved to have in fact 'produced by endeavour' the act of P; but, in law, D is not regarded as having caused the actus reus.

In *A-G's Reference (No 1 of 1975)*, D's act of procuring was done without the knowledge or consent, and perhaps against the will, of P. The impact of *Jogee* on procuring is unclear. As discussed later, D must intend P to have the mens rea for the offence. In cases such as this, D did not have that intent. Whether procuring will be treated as an exception to *Jogee* remains to be seen.

6.4.1.2 The timing of the accessory's assistance/encouragement

Assistance given by D before P even starts to commit the principal offence may be sufficient to found D's liability as an accessory if P then completes the offence. What is more important is to ascertain whether D has assisted or encouraged P before P has *concluded* the offence. Assistance given when P is no longer in the course of the commission of the offence—for example, help to enable P to escape or to reap the benefits of the commission of the offence—does not make D an accessory. Where P broke into a warehouse, stole butter and deposited it in the street 30 yards from the warehouse door, D who then came to assist in carrying it off was held not guilty of abetting P's theft.[137] Assistance given by D to a murderer, after his victim is dead or to a rapist after the act of penetration has concluded, does not render D an accessory.[138] D who, without any prearranged plan, joins P in an attack on V after V has received a fatal injury, is not guilty of homicide (though he may be guilty of an attempt) if his action in no way contributes to V's subsequent death.[139] If D1 and D2 carry out an armed robbery, and D3 drives past the bank as D1 and D2 flee from the scene of the crime with the proceeds, is D3 a party to the robbery if he allows D1 and D2 to get in the car to make good their escape?[140]

6.4.1.3 Omission as a sufficient actus reus of secondary liability?

As discussed in Ch 2, the law does not generally impose criminal liability for a failure to act. In the context of secondary liability, the question that arises is whether D's omission to

---

134 [2011] UKSC 59.

135 For criticism, see R Buxton, 'Being an Accessory to One's Own Murder' [2012] Crim LR 275, 280. For similar criticism, see GR Sullivan, 'Accessories and Principals after *Gnango*' in A Reed and M Bohlander (eds), *Participation in Crime: Domestic and Comparative Perspectives* (2013).

136 The driver whose drink, unknown to him, is 'laced' is not an innocent agent because the offence he is guilty of is a strict liability offence.

137 *King* (1817) Russ & Ry 332; see also *Kelly* (1820) Russ & Ry 421.

138 The act is a continuing one: Sexual Offences Act 2003, s 79.

139 *S v Thomo* 1969 (1) SA 385 (AD); EM Burchell and PMA Hunt, *South African Criminal Law and Procedure* (1970) 352. Some fine distinctions have begun to be drawn. In *Grundy* (1989) 89 Cr App R 333, it was held that if D struck a blow to V after P had caused grievous bodily harm, D might still be liable for assisting grievous bodily harm. In *Percival* [2003] EWCA Crim 1561, D who punched V after P had wounded V could not be liable as an aider and abettor to wounding.

140 See also *Self* [1992] Crim LR 574 and commentary.

prevent P committing the crime is sufficient to make D an accessory. Two categories of case need to be distinguished.

First, there are the established categories in which the law imposes a *duty* on an individual to act. Thus, a husband who stands by and watches his wife drown their children is guilty as an accessory to the homicide, subject to his having the requisite mens rea.[141]

Secondly, the law extends liability even wider: where D has a *power or right to control* the actions of P and he deliberately refrains from exercising that control, his inactivity *may* be a positive encouragement to P to perform an illegal act and, therefore, an aiding and abetting by D subject to D's mens rea. So, for example, if a licensee of a pub stands by and watches his customers drinking after hours, he is guilty of aiding and abetting them in doing so.[142] In *Du Cros v Lambourne*,[143] it was proved that D's car had been driven at a dangerous speed but it was not proved whether D or E was driving. It was held, nevertheless, that D could be convicted. If E was driving she was doing so in D's presence, with his consent and approval; for he was in control and could and ought to have prevented her from driving in a dangerous manner. D was equally liable whether he was a principal or an accessory.[144] The result would presumably have been different if it had been E's own car, for D would then have had no right of control, and could only have been convicted if proved to have actively encouraged E to drive at such speed.

In *Webster*,[145] the Court of Appeal approved *Du Cros v Lambourne*, holding that 'a defendant might be convicted of aiding and abetting dangerous driving if the driver drives dangerously in the owner's presence *and with the owner's consent and approval*'.[146] *Webster* emphasizes that it must be proved that D knew of those features of P's driving which rendered it dangerous and failed to take action within a reasonable time.[147] The court in *Webster* recognized the:

need to establish not only knowledge of the dangerous driving but knowledge at a time when there was an opportunity to intervene….We conclude that the prosecution had to prove that [D] knew that [P] was, by virtue of the speed the vehicle was travelling, driving dangerously at a time when there was an opportunity to intervene. It was [D's] failure to take that opportunity and, exercise his right as owner of the vehicle, which would lead to the inference that he was associating himself with the dangerous driving.

In *Baldessare*,[148] P and D unlawfully took X's car and P drove it recklessly and caused V's death. It was held that D was guilty of manslaughter as an accessory. In this case (as prosecuting counsel put it):

The common purpose to drive recklessly was…shown by the fact that both men were driving in a car which did not belong to them and the jury were entitled to infer that the driver was the agent of the passenger. It matters not whose hand was actually controlling the car at the time.

In the more recent case of *Martin*,[149] D was convicted as an accessory to P's offence of causing death by dangerous driving. P was a learner driver and D was supervising him. P lost

---

141 *Russell* [1933] VLR 59.

142 *Tuck v Robson* [1970] 1 WLR 741, DC. The principal offence is committed by the drinkers, not the licensee.

143 [1907] 1 KB 40; cf also *Rubie v Faulkner* [1940] 1 KB 571; *Harris* [1964] Crim LR 54. See D Lanham, 'Drivers, Control and Accomplices' [1982] Crim LR 419; M Wasik, 'A Learner's Careless Driving' [1982] Crim LR 411.

144 cf *Swindall and Osborne* (1846) 2 Car & Kir 230: *Salmon* (1880) 6 QBD 79; *Iremonger v Wynne* [1957] Crim LR 624; G Williams, CLGP, 137 fn 23.

145 [2006] EWCA Crim 415.

146 The court quashed the conviction in that case on the ground that the trial judge had not directed the jury that they had to consider whether there was an opportunity for Webster to intervene.

147 *Dennis v Pight* (1968) 11 FLR 458 at 463.   148 (1930) 22 Cr App R 70.

149 [2010] EWCA Crim 1450.

control of the vehicle on a bend and crashed, killing himself and a passenger.[150] Unlike *Baldessare*, there was no evidence that D had shared a common purpose with P to drive in this manner. The Court of Appeal, having considered *Webster*, tentatively proffered a direction that ought to have been given. D would be liable if: (a) P committed the offence; (b) D knew that P was driving in a manner which D knew fell far below the standard of a competent and careful driver [whether it is necessary for D to have knowledge is debatable]; (c) knowing that he had an opportunity to stop P from driving in that manner, D deliberately did not take that opportunity; and (d) by not taking that opportunity D intended to assist or encourage P to drive in this manner and D did in fact by his presence and failure to intervene encourage P to drive dangerously.[151]

Whichever category of exception (duty or control) is relied on to prove the actus reus by omission, it is not necessary that the inactive accessory be present at the commission of the offence. For example, a company and its directors may be convicted as accessories to the false making of tachograph records by the company's drivers if they knew that their inactivity was encouraging the practice on the roads miles away.[152]

6.4.1.4 Mere presence at the crime as a sufficient basis for secondary liability?

Can D's mere voluntary presence at P's commission of the principal offence, without anything more, satisfy the actus reus of secondary liability? If there is some conduct on the part of D which goes beyond 'mere' presence, then the principles already discussed will apply. The question will be whether D assisted or encouraged P by his actions or by his failure to act when under a duty/power to control. Where the case involves D's *mere* presence, several issues will commonly call for consideration including: whether D voluntarily attended the location where an offence is being or is about to be committed; the effect that D's presence has on P; and D's state of mind when present.

Mere presence at the scene of a crime is *capable* of constituting encouragement or assistance, but D is not necessarily guilty as an accessory merely because he is present and does nothing to prevent P's crime.[153] In some cases, D's presence will constitute encouragement or assistance because he is present in pursuance of an agreement that the crime be committed. In other cases, D's presence may be sufficient even though there was no prior agreement,[154] and no positive act,[155] provided that by his presence D intentionally provides assistance or encouragement to the principal.[156] In *Jogee*, the Supreme Court observed that both association and presence are likely to be very relevant evidence on the question of whether assistance or encouragement was provided. The Supreme Court did confirm,

---

[150] The conviction for being an accessory to P causing his own death by dangerous driving was quashed as there is no such offence: it is an offence to cause the death of another by driving.

[151] At [32] per Hooper LJ. A further possible element advanced by the court is not necessary (relating to D's foresight of death). See n 164 for discussion of the question whether liability might arise for D by reason of his participation in dangerous driving by P earlier in the journey, coupled with D's foresight that P might commit the offence of causing death by dangerous driving.

[152] *JF Alford Transport Ltd* [1997] 2 Cr App R 326, [1997] Crim LR 745, citing the 8th edition of this book, at p 334. See also *Gaunt* [2003] EWCA Crim 3925, where D, the manager, failed to control P (employees) in racial harassment of V (employee).

[153] *Atkinson* (1869) 11 Cox CC 330; but it is an offence to refuse to assist a constable to suppress a breach of the peace when called upon to do so: *Brown* (1841) Car & M 314. See Ch 7.

[154] *Rannath Mohan v R* [1967] 2 AC 187.

[155] *Wilcox v Jeffery* [1951] 1 All ER 464.

[156] It is insufficient to prove that D arrived even only 30 seconds after P has finished attacking V if there is no evidence of D encouraging P: *Rose* [2004] EWCA Crim 764.

however, that neither association nor presence is necessarily proof of assistance or encouragement; it depends on the facts.[157]

There are numerous examples of these principles in operation. D who stands outside a building while his friends commit a burglary inside cannot be convicted of burglary without proof that he was assisting or encouraging by, for example, acting as lookout.[158] Similarly, for D to continue to sit beside the driver of a car, P, until the end of a journey after learning that P is uninsured does not amount to abetting P's uninsured driving.[159] If D continues to share a room with a person known to be in unlawful possession of drugs, D is not an accessory unless encouragement or control is proved.[160] If prohibited drugs, found in a van belonging to a party of tourists, are the property of and under the exclusive control of one of them, the others are not guilty as accessories simply because they are present and know of the existence of the drugs.[161]

Both assistance or encouragement in fact *and* an intention to assist or encourage must be proved.[162] When these are proved, it is immaterial that D joined in the offence without any prior agreement.[163] The same principle applies in the case of omissions as in that of positive acts, and it has been held that where two drivers, without any previous arrangement between them, enter into competitive driving on the highway so as knowingly to encourage each other to drive at a dangerous speed or in a dangerous manner, the one is liable as a secondary party for a death or other criminal result caused by the other.[164]

Intention alone without encouragement or assistance in fact is insufficient. In *Allan*,[165] it was held that D who remains present at an affray, nursing a secret intention to help P if the need arises but doing nothing to evince that intention, does not thereby become an accessory. This was reiterated by the Privy Council in *Robinson*:[166]

The commission of most criminal offences, and certainly most offences of violence, could be assisted by the forbidding presence of another as back-up and support. If D's presence could properly be held to amount to communicating to P (whether expressly or by implication) that he was there to help in any way he could if the opportunity or need arose, that was perfectly capable of amounting to aiding....It is important to make clear to juries that mere approval of (ie 'assent' to, or 'concurrence' in) the offence by a bystander who gives no assistance, does not without more amount to aiding.[167]

If some positive act of assistance or encouragement is voluntarily performed by D, with knowledge of the circumstances constituting the offence, it is irrelevant that it is not done

---

[157] *Jogee* [2016] UKSC 8, [11].

[158] *S v DPP* [2003] EWHC 2717 (Admin); *L v CPS* [2013] EWHC 4127 (Admin). See also *Rose* [2004] EWCA Crim 764 where D's only actions at the scene were to discourage P from his attack on V. Cf *Ellis* [2008] EWCA Crim 886.

[159] *Smith v Baker* [1971] RTR 350.

[160] *Bland* [1988] Crim LR 41; see also *Kousar* [2009] EWCA Crim 139.

[161] *Searle* [1971] Crim LR 592 and commentary thereon; see also *Montague* [2013] EWCA Crim 1781, [2014] Crim LR 615 and commentary.

[162] *Clarkson* [1971] 1 WLR 1402; *Jones and Mirrless* (1977) 65 Cr App R 250, CA.

[163] *Rannath Mohan v R* [1967] 2 AC 187.

[164] *Turner* [1991] Crim LR 57 and commentary. (Williams, TBCL, 360, thinks otherwise, citing *Mastin* (1834) 6 C & P 396.) If one of two racing drivers is killed, the other may be convicted of causing death by dangerous driving; and it is immaterial whether his act or that of the deceased was the immediate cause of death: *Kimsey* [1996] Crim LR 35; *Lee* [2006] EWCA Crim 240. See also *Martin* [2010] EWCA Crim 1450, n 149.

[165] [1965] 1 QB 130; see also *Tansley v Painter* (1968) 112 Sol Jo 1005; *Danquah* [2004] EWCA Crim 1248 (presence alone insufficient to show that Ds formed part of the gang that robbed V when no evidence of contribution to the intimidation or threats).

[166] [2011] UKPC 3.

[167] At [14] per Sir Anthony Hughes. This passage was cited with approval by the Court of Appeal in *Robinson* [2014] EWCA Crim 2385, [15].

with the motive or purpose of encouraging the crime.[168] Nevertheless, the onus on the Crown to prove D's intent can be a heavy one where liability is based solely on D's presence at the scene.[169]

In the case of *Coney*[170] it was held that proof of D's mere voluntary presence at a prize-fight (illegal boxing match), without more, was, at the most, only prima facie and not conclusive evidence of abetting the offence of which the contestants were guilty. Presence at such an event is certainly capable of amounting to an actual encouragement. As has already been explained, this point was made by the Supreme Court in *Jogee*. If there were no spectators there would be no fight and, therefore, each spectator, by his presence, contributes to the incentive to the contestants. In the words of the Supreme Court, 'most people are bolder when supported or fortified by others than they are when they are alone'.[171] Voluntary presence at such an event is some evidence on which a jury might find that D was there with the intention of encouraging P's fight. Coney's conviction was quashed because the majority of the court thought that the judge's direction was capable of being understood to mean that voluntary presence was *conclusive* evidence of an intention to encourage. If the direction had made it clear that presence was only prima facie evidence, no doubt the conviction would have been sustained. So, in *Wilcox v Jeffrey*,[172] D was found to be an accessory by his presence at a public jazz performance by P. P was the celebrated American saxophonist Coleman Hawkins, who had been given permission to enter the UK only on condition that he would take no employment. D's presence at P's performance was a sufficient aiding and abetting of P in his contravention of the relevant immigration provisions. D's behaviour before and after P's performance supplied further evidence of D's intention to encourage P; he had met P at the airport and D afterwards reported the performance in laudatory terms in his jazz periodical. There was no finding that D applauded the performance. Had there been such a finding then the normal principles described earlier would apply—it would not have been a case of 'mere' voluntary presence but one of active encouragement by D.

Public order offences often raise particular problems in this context since the principal offence will often turn on proof of acts by a specific number of individuals, and in cases of spontaneous violence between groups, it is difficult to identify who is a principal involved in the fight, who is present actively encouraging and who is merely present without more.[173]

Note that there is no requirement that D is present when P commits the offence. As Toulson LJ observed in *Stringer*: 'for centuries secondary liability has attached to a person who aided or abetted another to commit an offence but was absent at the time of the offence….To require D to be present assisting at the time of the offence is unsupported by authority and would be wrong in principle.' It is one thing to say that D cannot be liable as an aider or abettor unless P acted with D's assistance or encouragement when he committed the offence; it is quite another to suggest that the act or words providing the assistance or encouragement must be performed or spoken at the moment of the commission of the offence. Such a limitation would exclude, for example, a person who supplied a murder weapon in advance of the crime knowing the purpose for which P wanted it. The law would be defective if an aider and abettor could escape liability by saying that there was a gap in time between his conduct and the conduct of P. This makes the Supreme Court's statement in *Jogee* about an 'overwhelming supervening event' all the more obscure.

---

168 *National Coal Board v Gamble* [1959] 1 QB 11; see p 198.
169 eg *Miah* [2004] EWCA Crim 63.   170 (1882) 8 QBD 534.   171 *Jogee* [2016] UKSC 8, [11].
172 [1951] 1 All ER 464. It is arguable that Art 11 of the ECHR may be engaged where the effect is to restrict D's right to assemble with others, see Horder, APOCL, 439.
173 See *Blackwood and others* [2002] EWCA Crim 3102 and *Ellis* [2008] EWCA Crim 886.

6.4.1.5 Problems of proving the accessory's actus reus

If all that can be proved is that the principal offence was committed either by P1 or by P2, both must be acquitted.[174] Only if it can be proved that the one who did not commit the crime as principal must have aided, abetted, counselled or procured the other to commit it can both be convicted.[175] Take the case of two nurses, P1 and P2, whose patient V is injured while in their care. The injuries might have been inflicted by P1 alone, P2 alone, by P1 with P2's as accessory or vice versa. It is for the prosecution to prove to the criminal standard that the nurse who did not inflict the injuries must have aided or abetted the infliction either by positive acts or by failure to fulfil the duty owed as a health-care worker.[176] This problem often arises in a domestic situation. It differs from most other cases only because parents owe a duty to intervene to prevent the ill-treatment of their child when a stranger would have no such duty. The case of the parent or carer of the child or vulnerable adult who dies or suffers serious injury in their household is now governed by an exceptional procedure under the Domestic Violence, Crime and Victims Acts 2004 and 2012,[177] but the general principle remains: if all that can be proved is that the offence was committed by *either* the first or second defendant, both must be acquitted. The most recent affirmation of that principle is *Banfield*.[178] S and L were convicted of the murder of V. S was his wife and L his daughter. V had disappeared but no body had ever been found. There were five postulations as to what might have explained the death: (a) S killed V and L encouraged her; (b) L killed him and S encouraged her; (c) S killed him in the absence of L; (d) L killed him in the absence of S; and (e) S and L acted together to kill him.[179] Rafferty LJ concluded:

The first four show how obvious were the tenable alternatives which could have led to [V]'s death. Once the Crown was unable to identify of which of the four options the jury could be sure, the fifth could not on the evidence provide a backstop.[180]

6.4.2 Mens rea of the accessory

The mens rea requirements of the accessory were restated in *Jogee*. They can be summarized as follows:

(1) the accessory must intend to assist or encourage the principal's conduct, or in the case of procuring, to bring the offence about;

(2) if the crime requires a particular mens rea, the accessory must intend to assist or encourage the principal to act with that mens rea.[181] Innocent agency and procuring an actus reus would appear to be exceptions to this rule;

(3) the accessory must have knowledge of any existing facts or circumstances necessary for the principal's conduct to be criminal.

We discuss each in detail here noting that this is where the decision of the Supreme Court in *Jogee* has had the greatest impact.

---

[174] *Richardson* (1785) 1 Leach 387; *Abbott* [1955] 2 QB 497.

[175] *Russell and Russell* [1987] Crim LR 494; *Lane and Lane* (1985) 82 Cr App R 5. For a valuable direction where one of two interrogating police officers has caused injury, see *Forman* [1988] Crim LR 677 (Judge Woods). See generally G Williams, 'Which of You Did It?' (1989) 52 MLR 179; EJ Griew, 'It Must Have Been One of Them' [1989] Crim LR 129. *Gibson and Gibson* (1984) 80 Cr App R 24 is misleading and should be used with care; see commentary at [1984] Crim LR 615.

[176] See for an extreme case *Pinto* [2006] EWCA Crim 749 (D aided and abetted torture of V by P believing V to be possessed).

[177] Considered at p 634. For comment see P Glazebrook, 'Insufficient Child Protection' [2003] Crim LR 541.

[178] [2013] EWCA Crim 1394, [2014] Crim LR 147.   [179] At [61].

[180] At [62]. The court cited the 13th edition of this work with approval.   [181] *Jogee* [2016] UKSC 8, [9]–[10].

6.4.2.1 Mens rea (1): an intention to aid, etc

It must be proved that D intended to do the acts which he knew to be capable of assisting or encouraging the commission of the crime. There are two elements: an intention to perform the act capable of encouraging or assisting, and an intention, or a belief, that that act will be of assistance. So, where D supplies a weapon to P, which P uses in a murder, proof of D's intention will turn on whether he meant to hand it over (as opposed to accidentally leaving it and P discovering it) and whether D intended that his supply would assist P; there is no further element that D must intend the consequences of P's conduct—that the murder be committed. As Devlin J said:[182]

If one man deliberately sells to another a gun to be used for murdering a third, he may be indifferent whether the third man lives or dies and interested only in the cash profit to be made out of the sale, but he can still be an aider and abettor.

The Supreme Court confirmed in *Jogee* that D's intention to assist or encourage P to commit the offence, and to act with whatever mental element is required of P, will often be coextensive on the facts with an intention by D that the offence be committed. The court did confirm, however, that there will be cases where D gives intentional assistance or encouragement to P, but without D having a positive intent that the particular offence be committed. The example given by the court is where, at the time that the encouragement is given, it remains uncertain what P might do.[183] It has been suggested that the law would have been clearer and better if the court had held that D must intend P to, or believe that P will, commit the crime.[184]

Intention to perform the act of assistance

This element of the mens rea is unlikely to give rise to difficulty. D must intend to perform the act that does in fact provide assistance. There is only likely to be a problem in circumstances of potential involuntariness and other rare situations.

Intention thereby to assist

There is no judicial agreement on what the requirement of an intention to assist actually means and unfortunately there was no explicit consideration of this issue in *Jogee*. It is clearly a requirement of intention,[185] but must it be proved that D acted in order to assist P (direct intent); or is it sufficient to prove only that D knew his acts would be virtually certain to assist P (oblique intent)?[186] It seems to be generally accepted that D's knowledge that his act will assist is sufficient.[187] The weight of authority certainly supports the view that it is not necessary to prove that D had as his purpose or desire to assist and if D had the (oblique) intention, it is no excuse that D's motives in performing the act of assistance were unimpeachable.[188]

---

182 [1959] 1 QB 11 at 23, applied in *JF Alford Transport Ltd* [1997] 2 Cr App R 326, 334–335.

183 *Jogee* [2016] UKSC 8, [11].

184 M Dyson, 'Letter to the Editor' [2016] Crim LR 638.

185 The offence is therefore one of specific intent for the purposes of rules on voluntary intoxication: see Ch 9: *McNamara* [2009] EWCA Crim 2530.

186 See RA Duff, 'Can I Help You? Accessorial Liability and the Intention to Assist' (1990) LS 165. See generally KJM Smith, *A Modern Treatise on Complicity* (1991) Ch 5.

187 cf IH Dennis, 'The Mental Element for Accessories' in *Essays in Honour of JC Smith* (1987); *contra* GR Sullivan, 'Intent, Purpose and Complicity' [1988] Crim LR 641; and IH Dennis, 'Intention and Complicity: A Reply' [1988] Crim LR 649; Williams [1990] Crim LR 4, 12.

188 Woolf J in *Gillick v West Norfolk and Wisbech Area Health Authority* [1984] QB 581 at 589. Woolf J's discussion of the criminal aspects of this case was adopted by Lords Scarman and Bridge in the House of Lords [1986] AC 112.

Oblique intention to assist sufficient

In *National Coal Board v Gamble*,[189] P, a lorry driver, had his employer's lorry filled with coal at a colliery belonging to the defendant Board [D1]. When the lorry was driven on to the weighbridge operated by the defendants' employee, D2, it appeared that its load greatly exceeded that permitted by the relevant regulation.[190] D2 informed P of this but P said he would take the risk, D2 gave him a weighbridge ticket and P committed the offence as principal by driving the overloaded lorry on the highway. As a matter of contract law, the property in the coal did not pass until the ticket was handed over and, therefore, P could not properly have left the colliery without the ticket from D2. It was held that the Board, D1, through its employee D2,[191] was guilty of the offence as an accessory. The decision was based on the assumption that D2 knew that he had the right to prevent the lorry leaving the colliery with the coal. Had D2 not known this, he should have been acquitted. Presumably D2 was indifferent whether P drove his overloaded lorry on the road or not—he probably thought that it was none of his business—but D2's motive was irrelevant and it was enough that his positive act of assistance had been voluntarily done (ie intentional performance of the act of assistance) with knowledge that by doing so he would be assisting P and knowledge of the circumstances constituting the offence.[192]

Despite the fact that it did not say so explicitly, the Supreme Court's judgment in *Jogee* confirms that oblique intention will suffice. The court stated that there is a difference between intention and desire and that the jury may have to be reminded of this fact. This echoes what was earlier held in *Lynch v DPP for Northern Ireland*, where D drove P to the place where he knew that P intended to murder a policeman. It was held that the fact that D does not 'want' or 'aim' to assist does not prevent him being liable as an accessory if he has an oblique intent to assist, so D's intentional driving of the car was aiding and abetting, 'even though he regretted the plan or indeed was horrified by it'.[193]

Must D intend that his conduct 'will' or 'might' assist?

There is a potential difficulty where D believes his act is capable of assisting P but does not believe that in fact it *will* assist P. An example is offered by the Law Commission[194] where D, believing that P is going to murder V, sells P rat poison. If D believes that there is only a 50 per cent chance that P will use it to murder V but D foresees the risk that P *might* murder V by some other means, it cannot be said that D believes that his act *will* assist P. The Law Commission suggest that the case law is inconclusive as to whether D is liable.[195] The judgment of the Supreme Court in *Jogee* has not necessarily clarified matters very much. The court confirmed that D must intend to assist or encourage P. The court also confirmed, however, that D need not intend for P to commit the offence in question.[196] The example of such a scenario given by the court is where, at the time that the encouragement is given, it remains uncertain what P might do. An arms supplier was the example the court gave of such a scenario. This seems to suggest that it is sufficient for D to intend that his conduct *might* assist, even though he cannot be sure that it necessarily *will* assist.

---

[189] [1959] 1 QB 11 DC, Slade J dissenting.

[190] Motor Vehicles (Construction and Use) Regulations 1955.   [191] See, however, p 199.

[192] D2 would commit an offence under s 45 of the SCA 2007.

[193] [1975] AC 653 at 678 per Lord Morris, approving the judgment of Lowry LCJ on this point. *Fretwell* (1862) Le & Ca 161 appears to be a merciful decision and unsound in principle.

[194] Taken from LC 305, Appendix B, para B.75.

[195] See the speech of Lord Simon in *Lynch* [1975] AC 653, 698h.

[196] *Jogee* [2016] UKSC 8, [10].

'Intention' even if D is legally obliged to supply to P?

If P has loaned a weapon to D, and P demands it back, when D hands it over, it is arguable that D aids in the commission of P's subsequent crime committed with that weapon as much as if D had sold or lent the article to P in the first place, but this has never been held to be aiding in law.[197] *National Coal Board v Gamble* suggests a distinction between the cases:

(1) where the seller (D) is aware before ownership has passed to the buyer (P) of P's illegal purpose the delivery amounts to abetting, but

(2) where the seller (D) learns of the illegal purpose for the first time after ownership has passed but before delivery to P the supply does not amount to abetting. The seller is merely complying with his legal duty to give P what is by then P's own property.

This seems to be an unsatisfactory distinction. If D delivers weedkiller to P, knowing that P intends to use it to murder his wife, it would be remarkable if D's guilt as an accessory to murder turned on whether the ownership passed before or after D learned of P's intention.[198] The important thing is that D knows of P's intention when he makes delivery. It should not be an answer that P has a right to possession of the thing in the civil law because the civil law should not afford a right in such a case.[199] In *Garrett v Arthur Churchill (Glass) Ltd*,[200] D, who had bought a goblet as agent of P, was held guilty of being knowingly concerned in the exportation of goods without a licence, when, on P's instructions, he delivered P's own goblet to P's agent who was to take it to the United States:

…albeit there was a legal duty in ordinary circumstances to hand over the goblet to the owners once the agency was determined, I do not think that an action would lie for breach of that duty if the handing over would constitute the offence of being knowingly concerned in its exportation.[201]

It is probably the law that the seller is liable whether or not the ownership has passed before delivery. Williams' view, however, is that the seller ought to be liable in neither case. He argues:[202]

The seller of an ordinary marketable commodity is not his buyer's keeper in criminal law unless he is specifically made so by statute. Any other rule would be too wide an extension of criminal responsibility.

A rule based on the nature of the thing as 'an ordinary marketable commodity' is not workable. Weedkiller is an ordinary marketable commodity but it may be acquired and used to commit murder. A more feasible distinction is one based on the seriousness of the offence contemplated:

The gravity of the social harm resulting from the unlawful conduct is used to determine whether mere knowledge of the intended use will be sufficient to carry the taint of illegality.[203]

---

197 [1959] 1 QB 11 at 20 per Devlin J.

198 D would be liable under ss 44–46 of the SCA 2007.

199 See G Williams, CLGP, s 124 and JC Smith, 'Civil Law Concepts in the Criminal Law' (1972) 31 CLJ 197 at 208. In *K v National Westminster Bank Plc* [2006] EWCA Civ 1039, the court noted that if the criminal law (under POCA 2002) makes it an offence for a bank to honour a customer's instructions to transfer money which it is suspected is criminal property, there can be no breach of contract for the bank to refuse to do so.

200 [1970] 1 QB 92. How far does this go? If X lends a picture to a museum, does the museum really commit an offence if, on demand, it returns the picture to X, knowing that he intends to export it without the licence required by law?

201 [1969] 2 All ER 1141 at 1145 per Parker LCJ.   202 CLGP, s 124 at 373. TBCL (1st edn) 293–294.

203 Perkins and Boyce, *Criminal Law*, 746. See also G Williams, 'Obedience to Law as a Crime' (1990) 53 MLR 445.

This could operate on the basis of some balance of the respective harms, but would have the disadvantage of being uncertain. No such distinction has been made in English law. Alternatively, a distinction could be drawn between summary and indictable offences. This would create some arbitrary results.[204] A third approach would be to restrict the scope of the liability of the seller, D, to cases in which his purpose was to assist P. There would be difficulties in establishing that mens rea in some cases.

At present, English authorities suggest a general rule of liability for sellers subject to mens rea, which after *Jogee* requires an intention to assist or encourage. This applies, *a fortiori*, in the case of lenders or those who rent out premises intended for unlawful purposes. In such cases, the owner has a continuing interest in and right to control the property.[205]

6.4.2.2 Mens rea (2): intention that P commit the crime with the requisite mens rea

In *Jogee*, the Supreme Court restated the principle that D must intend to assist P to act with the requisite mens rea for the offence. D must intend that P will have the mental element when P is performing the conduct element of the offence. As the court explained:

The second issue is likely to be whether the accessory intended to encourage or assist [P] to commit the crime, *acting with whatever mental element the offence requires of [P]*. If the crime requires a particular intent, [D] must intend (it may be conditionally) to assist [P] to act with such intent. To take a homely example, if [D] encourages [P] to take another's bicycle without permission of the owner and return it after use, but [P] takes it and keeps it, [P] will be guilty of theft but [D] of the lesser offence of unauthorised taking, since he will not have encouraged [P] to act with intent permanently to deprive. In cases of concerted physical attack there may often be no practical distinction to draw between an intention by [D] to assist [P] to act with the intention of causing grievous bodily harm at least and [D] having the intention himself that such harm be caused. In such cases it may be simpler, and will generally be perfectly safe, to direct the jury . . . that the Crown must prove that [D] intended that the victim should suffer grievous bodily harm at least. However, as a matter of law, it is enough that [D] intended to assist [P] to act with the requisite intent. That may well be the situation if the assistance or encouragement is rendered some time before the crime is committed and at a time when it is not clear what [P] may or may not decide to do. Another example might be where [D] supplies a weapon to [P], who has no lawful purpose in having it, intending to help [P] by giving him the means to commit a crime (or one of a range of crimes), but having no further interest in what he does, or indeed whether he uses it at all.[206]

The significant shift from the *Chan Wing-Siu* doctrine, which is discussed in full later, is that D *must intend* that P will intentionally commit the offence (say murder) whereas under the *Chan Wing-Siu* doctrine it was enough that D foresaw as a possibility that P might intentionally commit the offence.

This begs the question of what 'intention' means in this context. It is clear that it is not limited to purpose, as the court confirmed that:

It will therefore in some cases be important when directing juries to remind them of the difference between intention and desire.[207]

The question then remains whether intention can be inferred from foresight. In *Jogee*, the Supreme Court recognized that in the common law foresight of what might happen is evidence from which a jury can infer the presence of the requisite intention.[208] The court

---

[204] GR Sullivan [1994] Crim LR 272.

[205] eg the hotelier who lets a room to a man accompanied by a 15-year-old girl, knowing that he intends to have sex with her.

[206] *Jogee* [2016] UKSC 8, [90] (emphasis added).　　　[207] ibid, [91].　　　[208] ibid, [83].

observed that, 'foresight may be good evidence of intention but it is not synonymous with it'.[209] Inferring intention from foresight is the hallmark of oblique or indirect intention. Therefore, although foresight cannot be equated with intention as a matter of law, it is evidence the jury can take into account when they are considering whether D intended to assist or encourage P to act with whatever mens rea is necessary for him to commit the full offence. In the subsequent case of *Anwar*, Sir Brian Leveson P confirmed that, 'the jury will, of course, continue to look at the full picture or factual matrix in order to determine whether the relevant necessary intent can be inferred'.[210]

That the jury may infer intent from foresight begs the following questions: (a) in what circumstances, (b) foresight of what and (c) foresight to what degree?

One of the factors identified by the Supreme Court that may be relevant to the assessment of whether D possessed the requisite intent is whether there was a common purpose between D and P to commit the offence in question.[211] The Supreme Court confirmed, however, that liability as a secondary party does not depend on there being some form of agreement between the parties.[212] The Supreme Court also clarified that knowledge or ignorance that weapons generally, or a particular weapon, is being carried by P will be evidence going to what the intention of D was, and indeed may be irresistible evidence one way or the other, but it is evidence and no more.[213] This was confirmed by the Court of Appeal in the subsequent case of *Brown*, in which Hallett LJ stated that, 'Post-*Jogee*, knowledge of a weapon used by a principal to inflict harm is not determinative of secondary party liability. It is evidence that may inform a jury's decision as to whether a defendant who did not himself wield a weapon intended to cause harm to the victim; and if he did, the level of harm.'[214] Her ladyship therefore rejected the submission that the judge ought to have directed the jury that they could only convict D if they were sure that he knew P had a knife.

What the Supreme Court did not address, however, is whether oblique intention in the context of secondary liability has the same strict meaning it has, for example, in the law of murder. As a result of the judgment of the House of Lords in *Woollin*,[215] in a murder trial the jury are only entitled to find that D had the necessary intention if death or GBH was a *virtually certain* consequence and D appreciated that this was the case. If death or GBH was not virtually certain, then the jury are not entitled to find that D had the requisite intention. In the context of secondary liability, the Supreme Court confirmed that the jury can infer intention from foresight, but did not address the question of whether D's foresight of even the slightest possibility of P intentionally acting in the proscribed way is sufficient for the jury to be entitled to infer that he possessed the requisite intention.

To take an example of why this is not merely a theoretical problem, consider *Matthews and Alleyne*.[216] The defendants were convicted of murder after throwing the victim from a bridge and into a river, where he drowned. In light of *Woollin*, the judge directed the jury that in relation to each defendant they could only convict him of murder as a principal if, when he threw the victim from the bridge and into the river, he appreciated that death or really serious harm was a virtually certain consequence, barring some unforeseen intervention. To amend the facts, rather than being joint principals, if P was the principal and D was the accessory, how should the judge direct the jury in relation to D's liability? What is clear is that the judge should direct the jury that they can only convict D of murder as a secondary party if they are sure that he intended to assist or encourage the principal intentionally to

---

[209] ibid, [73].   [210] [2016] EWCA Crim 551, [20].   [211] *Jogee* [2016] UKSC 8, [87].
[212] ibid, [95].   [213] ibid, [98].
[214] [2017] EWCA Crim 1870, [28]. See also *Ibrar* [2017] EWCA Crim 1841.
[215] [1999] 1 AC 82. For discussion, see p 92.
[216] [2003] EWCA Crim 192. For discussion, see p 93.

kill or do GBH. If D admits being present when V was murdered by P, but denies having the requisite intent, should the judge direct the jury that they can only infer the requisite intent if D foresaw that the principal might intentionally kill or do GBH, so long as D's foresight of that was more than *de minimis*? Alternatively, should the jury be directed that they are only entitled to infer the requisite intent if D foresaw intentional GBH or killing by P as a *virtually certain* consequence of D's act of assistance or encouragement?

The issue becomes particularly striking if the Crown cannot establish the identity of the principal. As discussed earlier, this is not an uncommon scenario. Can the jury be directed that: (a) they can infer the requisite intent if the defendant they are considering foresaw that the other might intentionally kill or cause GBH so long as this foresight was more than *de minimis*; but (b) to be sure D is guilty as a principal he must have foreseen that death or GBH was a virtually certain consequence barring some unforeseen intervention. The jury would then have to be told that there are two different routes to 'finding' intention, depending upon whether the defendant whose guilt they are considering is the principal or the accessory. Given that the jury would have to be sure that a murder was committed by one of the defendants, there is potentially no avoiding directing the jury as to the applicability of two different routes. This is surely an undesirable state of affairs in directing a jury on the same word in the gravest of crimes.[217]

It is submitted that there are three significant practical issues arising as a result of this uncertainty around foresight and intention. First, it is unclear how judges are to direct juries on the law. Different judges may direct juries in different ways, which makes resolution of this issue a priority. Secondly, as a matter of principle, there is lack of clarity on whether there ought to be parity as to the level of foresight required of the principal and the accessory.[218] Resolution of this issue is made more complicated by the fact that two different questions are being asked. In relation to the principal, the issue relates to a consequence, whereas for the accessory, the issue is partly about someone else's state of mind. Thirdly, without speedy resolution by the Court of Appeal there is the danger that the debate the House of Lords sought to put an end to in *Woollin* will be replayed, which would be undesirable as the law would be thrown into a state of confusion.[219] One solution is for the jury to be directed in the following terms:

You (the jury) are entitled to conclude that the greater the likelihood or chance of X happening that you are sure that the defendant foresaw, the more weight you can place on this conclusion when you come to decide, as a matter of fact, whether the defendant intended X. So if you conclude that the defendant either did not foresee X or thought it a remote possibility only, you may conclude that he did not intend X to happen; if he foresaw that it was virtually certain to happen but carried on assisting, it may not be difficult to conclude that he intended X. How you weigh up that evidence to decide what the defendant intended is a matter for you.

It is important to bear in mind that even if D did not intend to assist or encourage P to kill or cause really serious harm, but the violence escalates and results in death, although D will not be guilty of murder he will be guilty of manslaughter. D will also be guilty of manslaughter if he participates by encouragement or assistance in any other unlawful act which all sober and reasonable people would realize carried the risk of some harm (not necessarily serious) to another and death in fact results.[220] When applied in the context of secondary

---

217 Judicial College, *Crown Court Compendium* (2017).

218 This issue is considered further at p 217.

219 For further discussion, see D Ormerod and K Laird, 'Jogee: Not the End of a Legal Saga But the Start of One?' [2016] Crim LR 539.

220 *Jogee* [2016] UKSC 8, [96].

liability, the law of manslaughter may seem particularly harsh, especially since the test of harm is an objective one.

Conditional intent

The Supreme Court confirmed in *Jogee* that D must intend to assist or encourage P to commit the offence, and to act with whatever mental element is required of P. Importantly, the Supreme Court stated that in some cases arising out of a prior joint criminal venture, it will also often be necessary to draw the jury's attention to the fact that the intention to assist, and perhaps also the intention that the crime should be committed, may be conditional.[221] The Supreme Court's discussion of conditional intent was confined to those cases in which D and P are engaged in a joint prior criminal venture, such as a burglary, during the course of which a further offence is committed. Whilst conditional intent may be particularly apposite in scenarios such as these, it can apply with equal force to cases in which there was no prior joint criminal venture.[222]

This aspect of the Supreme Court's judgment could prove controversial in three respects. First, there is the practical question of how the concept of conditional intent ought to be explained to the jury. The court gave the following example of a scenario where it might be necessary to draw to the jury's attention the fact that D's intent can be conditional:

The bank robbers who attack the bank when one or more of them is armed no doubt hope that it will not be necessary to use the guns, but it may be a perfectly proper inference that all were intending that if they met resistance the weapons should be used with the intent to do grievous bodily harm at least.

In this example, the Supreme Court seems to be suggesting that the jury will only be entitled to infer that D had the requisite intent if he foresaw that it might be *necessary* for the guns to be used in the course of the robbery. If necessity were the test, then it would impose a high threshold. In the next paragraph of the judgment, however, the Supreme Court gives an example which seems to suggest that the test is not as stringent as this:

If the jury is satisfied that there was an agreed common purpose to commit crime A, and if it is satisfied also that [D] must have foreseen that, in the course of committing crime A, [P] might well commit crime B, it may in appropriate cases be justified in drawing the conclusion that [D] had the necessary conditional intent that crime B should be committed, if the occasion arose; or in other words that it was within the scope of the plan to which [D] gave his assent and intentional support.

This paragraph could be interpreted as entitling the jury to find that D had the requisite intent if he foresaw that the further offence might be committed, not out of necessity, but merely if the opportunity arose. In the subsequent case of *Anwar* Sir Brian Leveson P offered the following formulation: 'What is now required is that [D] intended that [P] cause grievous bodily harm or kill *if the circumstances arise.*'[223] There is the danger that the misapplication of conditional intention could lead to the reintroduction of the problems the Supreme Court sought to address in *Jogee*. For example, the prosecution could invite the jury to infer that merely because D foresaw as a possibility that P might, in the course of their joint venture to burgle V's house, commit murder, that D must have conditionally intended to assist P to commit that crime. Such a formulation bears a striking resemblance to parasitic accessory liability and cannot be what the Supreme Court intended to achieve in *Jogee*.

---

[221] ibid, [92]. Conditional intention is a concept that is also discussed in Ch 11, in the context of statutory conspiracies. This section deals exclusively with the concept as it relates to accessorial liability.

[222] For discussion, see Horder, APOCL, 451–452.

[223] *Anwar* [2016] EWCA Crim 551, [22]. Emphasis added.

What must not be lost sight of is the fact that the requisite mens rea is intention. As Krebs explains, 'intent contingent upon the existence of certain facts still requires proof of full-blown intent'.[224] This point ought to be emphasized to the jury, to ensure that they do not labour under the misapprehension that by referring to conditional intention the judge is somehow sanctioning the application of a less demanding form of mens rea. In *Chan Kam Shing*, Ribeiro PJ stated that the Court of Appeal's analysis of conditional intent in *Anwar* and *Johnson* suggests that English law is 'drifting back' to a position resembling parasitic accessory liability.[225] It is submitted that to avoid this the jury ought to be directed that D will be liable if he intended to assist or encourage P to commit the offence if a particular condition was met. For example, where D and P engage in a joint criminal venture to commit robbery, during the course of which P murders the bank clerk, D will be guilty of murder if he intended to assist or encourage P to murder the bank clerk should the bank clerk attempt to raise the alarm during the course of the robbery.

Many factors will be relevant to the jury's assessment of whether D possessed the requisite intention. Of particular relevance will be the jury's assessment of the range of responses D foresaw from P in the event that the bank clerk attempted to raise the alarm during the robbery. Evidence that D, when he embarked on the robbery with P, foresaw that P might murder the bank clerk should he attempt to raise the alarm, but nevertheless continued in the joint venture,[226] would be strong evidence from which the jury could infer that D intended to assist or encourage P to commit murder should that eventuality arise. Foresight is only evidence from which the jury will be entitled to infer the requisite intention, however. Even if D foresaw that P's response to the bank clerk's attempt to raise the alarm might be to commit murder, the jury could conclude that D lacked the requisite intent because, for example, he explicitly told P that he did not want violence to be used. Again, it is crucial to ensure that the jury understands that the requisite mens rea is nothing less than intention.

Secondly, the Supreme Court's discussion of conditional intent was subject to sustained criticism by the Hong Kong Court of Final Appeal in *Chan Kam Shing*.[227] Ribeiro PJ stated that the Supreme Court relied upon the idea of conditional intent in order to deal with what his lordship characterized as 'situational uncertainties'.[228] The Court of Final Appeal took the view, however, that conditional intent is unsuited to this purpose and criticized the Supreme Court for explaining the concept solely 'in the context of joint criminal enterprise'. The court also stated that, 'The proposition that a finding of foresight is only evidence of conditional intent [was] . . . difficult to follow.'[229] Krebs agrees that the Supreme Court's analysis of conditional intent was 'somewhat opaque' but concludes that the language of joint enterprise is consistent with using the concept to determine the scope of the undertaking that was to be assisted or encouraged.[230] In *Miller v The Queen*, the High Court of Australia was also critical of the Supreme Court's reliance upon conditional intention.[231]

The final reason why the Supreme Court's discussion of conditional intention could prove controversial is of a more theoretical nature.[232] The Supreme Court's discussion of conditional intent has been found wanting by a number of commentators. For example, it has been argued

---

[224] B Krebs, 'Accessory Liability: Persisting in Error' (2017) 76 CLJ 7, 10.

[225] [2016] HKCFA 87, [92]–[93].

[226] The Court of Appeal in *Johnson* [2016] EWCA Crim 1613 made reference to the fact that the court could safely draw the conclusion that DD had the necessary conditional intent that the knife would be used with intent to kill or cause GBH should the occasion arise, on the basis that use of the knife with intent to kill or cause GBH was *within the scope of the plan* to which they gave their assent and conditional support. At [82].

[227] [2016] HKCFA 87.   [228] ibid, [72].   [229] ibid, [78].

[230] B Krebs, 'Hong Kong Court of Final Appeal: Divided by a Common Purpose' (2017) 81 J Crim L 271.

[231] [2016] HCA 30, [21] and [38].

[232] For further discussion, see DJ Baker, *Reinterpreting Criminal Complicity and Inchoate Participation Offences* (2016) Ch 2.

that particularly problematic is the fact the Supreme Court referred to D's conditional intention to assist or encourage by his *present* conduct. Simester argues that any reference to conditional intention in a scenario where D's act of assistance or encouragement is rendered some time before the crime is committed is a 'red herring'.[233] He argues that once D renders his act of assistance or encouragement, there can be no question of D having any conditional intention. This is because D's part in the commission of the crime has been fulfilled and that any conditional intention to do something requires that the thing to be done lies in the future. At the time of D's act of assistance or encouragement, he must therefore hold the crystallized, unconditional intention to assist or encourage the very crime that P ultimately commits. Simester makes the point that what lies in the future are P's actions and that as D cannot intend P's actions, nor P's mens rea, he cannot conditionally intend them either.[234] Child argues that conditional intention can never apply in these circumstances on the basis that it is irrational to apply conditional intention to present conduct and results. It is argued that, 'D's intention to aid or abet murder at t1 [time 1] cannot be conditioned by an event that happens later at t2 [time 2]. D's intention may be specific to a certain future view of the world (i.e. to encourage killing on specific terms), but once it has motivated conduct which provides that encouraging effect, it can no longer be conditional.'[235]

Despite the compelling nature of these criticisms, the Supreme Court confirmed in unequivocal terms that D's intent can be conditional. For the reasons that have already been given, it is imperative to convey to juries that conditional intent is not a less stringent form of intention and that foresight is merely evidence from which the requisite intention can be inferred.

6.4.2.3 Mens rea (3): knowledge of facts or circumstances

In addition to proof of intention to do the acts and to assist or encourage, there is a further element of the accessory's mens rea: D must 'know' of the facts or circumstances necessary for P's conduct to be criminal.[236] He need not actually know that an offence has been committed, because he may not know that the facts constitute an offence and because ignorance of the criminal law is not a defence.[237] In *Jogee*, the Supreme Court expressed this element in the following terms: 'knowledge of any existing facts necessary for [P's conduct] to be criminal'.[238]

Two questions arise:

(1) What does 'knowledge' mean in this context?

(2) As to what must D have knowledge—what are the 'facts or circumstances necessary for P's conduct to be criminal'?

Knowledge/foresight/wilful blindness

A requirement to prove D's knowledge is especially difficult to apply in the context of secondary liability. D's knowledge must relate to P's conduct and the prescribed

---

[233] AP Simester, 'Accessory Liability and Common Unlawful Purposes' (2017) 133 LQR 73.

[234] For an alternative view, see DJ Baker, 'Unlawfulness's Doctrinal and Normative Irrelevance to Complicity Liability: A Reply to Simester' (2017) 81 J Crim L 393.

[235] J Child, 'Understanding Ulterior Mens Rea: Future Conduct Intention is Conditional Intention' (2017) 76 CLJ 311.

[236] See generally KJM Smith, *A Modern Treatise on Complicity*, Ch 6 and LC 305, Appendix B.

[237] *Johnson v Youden* [1950] 1 KB 544 at 546 per Lord Goddard CJ. See also *Ackroyds Air Travel Ltd v DPP* [1950] 1 All ER 933 at 936; *Thomas v Lindop* [1950] 1 All ER 966 at 968; *Ferguson v Weaving* [1951] 1 KB 814; *Bateman v Evans* [1964] Crim LR 601; *Smith v Jenner* [1968] Crim LR 99; *Dial Contracts Ltd v Vickers* [1971] RTR 386; *D Stanton & Sons Ltd v Webber* [1973] RTR 87, [1972] Crim LR 544 and commentary thereon.

[238] *Jogee* [2016] UKSC 8, [9] and [99].

909

circumstances. The conduct may or may not be happening contemporaneously with D's act(s) of assistance or encouragement. Frequently, D's acts of assistance or encouragement will have occurred before the commission of the offence by P, and D cannot have 'knowledge' of something that has yet to occur.[239] Where the circumstances have yet to arise or materialize, D cannot know them because they are not yet in existence. The problem of proving knowledge may even arise if the principal offence *has* materialized contemporaneously with D's assistance.

In the face of practical difficulties in applying a strict test of knowledge, the concept was diluted by the courts to such an extent that this element of mens rea required of D could more accurately be expressed as a realization of a possibility of the essential elements of P's offence.[240] Knowledge in this context was the equivalent to D foreseeing (or in some cases turning a blind eye to) the likelihood of the essential matters. As a matter of substance this was more like a test of subjective recklessness. For example, the court adopted a relaxed interpretation of 'knowledge' in *Carter v Richardson*[241] where D, the supervisor of a learner driver, P, was convicted of abetting P's driving with excess alcohol. The court said, *obiter*, that it was sufficient that D knew that it was 'probable' that P was 'over the limit'—that D was, in effect, 'reckless' in the *Cunningham* sense[242] to the circumstance element of the crime that P was over the limit. In *Carter v Richardson*, P's offence comprised two main elements: a conduct element—driving—and a circumstances element—with excess alcohol. D intentionally encouraged the act of driving and was reckless as to the circumstance of the excess alcohol. That was sufficient to render him liable. There were a number of cases in which a similar formulation was adopted. For example, in *Bryce* it was held that D's foresight of the 'real or substantial risk' of P's crime was sufficient.[243]

The correctness of this approach must now be doubted in light of *Jogee*. Unfortunately, the Supreme Court did not discuss the body of case law that had developed in the years since *Johnson v Youden* that sanctioned the application of a less stringent test than knowledge. The court did, however, explicitly endorse the approach in *Johnson v Youden* and stated that the mental element in assisting or encouraging is an intention to assist or encourage the commission of the crime, which requires knowledge of any existing facts necessary for it to be criminal.[244] Although the Supreme Court did not do so explicitly, those cases in which knowledge seemed to have been equated with recklessness have been implicitly overturned and should no longer be applied. Knowledge in the context of secondary liability therefore now bears a stricter meaning than the one that had previously been sanctioned. As we discuss later, however, D does not have to intend to assist or encourage a specific offence. It will suffice for D to have intended to assist or encourage P to commit one of a range of offences which might take various forms, such as a terrorism offence or a sexual offence.

---

[239] For discussion of the philosophical nature of knowledge and its relevance to the criminal law, see S Shute, 'Knowledge and Belief in the Criminal Law' at 171 and GR Sullivan, 'Knowledge, Belief and Culpability' at 207 both in Shute and Simester, *Criminal Law Theory*. See also the essay by R Bagshaw, 'Legal Proof of Knowledge' in P Mirfield and R Smith (eds), *Essays in Honour of Colin Tapper* (2003) on evidential influences of substantive law definitions of knowledge.

[240] See LC 305, para 2.65. For a defence of the dilution of mens rea, see A Simester (2006) 122 LQR 578 at 588–592.

[241] [1974] RTR 314, discussed by G Williams (1975) 34 CLJ 182 and TBCL, 309. But in *Giogianni* (1984) 156 CLR 473 the High Court of Australia held that recklessness is not sufficient on a charge of aiding and abetting.

[242] It is quite clear that inadvertent *Caldwell/Lawrence* recklessness was never enough: *Blakely and Sutton v DPP* [1991] Crim LR 763, DC.

[243] [2004] EWCA Crim 1231, [71].   [244] [2016] UKSC 8, [9] and [16].

D must know any 'existing' facts necessary for P's conduct to be criminal

As has already been explained, D must have 'knowledge of any existing facts necessary for [P's conduct] to be criminal'.[245] As Horder points out, given that P's conduct will take place in the future, there are as of yet no 'existing facts' necessary to make P's act criminal. Therefore, what the Supreme Court must have meant is that what matters is whether D knows that, when P acts on D's assistance or encouragement, the facts making P's act criminal will exist at that later time.[246]

Knowledge in abetting an offence of strict liability

Where P's offence is one of strict liability, D must have mens rea, namely 'knowledge' of the essential elements of P's wrongdoing. The principal may, but an accessory may not, be convicted without mens rea. The reason is that secondary participation is a common law notion.[247] Application of the normal common law principles of liability requiring mens rea highlights the peculiar nature of offences of strict liability. In a strict liability offence, an accessory who has no mens rea must be acquitted even if he was negligent,[248] whereas the principal who has caused the actus reus must be convicted even if he took all proper care and was not even negligent. In *Jogee*, the Supreme Court, citing *National Coal Board v Gamble*, held that where the offence charged does not require mens rea, the only mens rea required of the secondary party is that he intended to assist or encourage P to do the prohibited act, with knowledge of any facts or circumstances necessary for it to be a prohibited act.[249]

The Supreme Court was simply recognizing the application of a longstanding principle. For example, in *Callow v Tillstone*,[250] D, a veterinary surgeon, was charged with abetting the exposure for sale of unsound meat. At the request of a butcher, P, he examined the carcass and gave P a certificate that the meat was sound. The examination had been negligently conducted and the meat was tainted. P, relying on the certificate, exposed the meat for sale and was convicted. The magistrates, holding that D's negligence had caused the exposure, convicted him of abetting. It was held that his conviction must be quashed.[251]

The principle would apply also in a case where, for example, P is charged with taking indecent images of a child under 18. If P had been assisted in his taking of the images by D, who had supplied the camera, it would have been a defence for D (even though not for P) to show that he believed the child to be over 18 or even (at least if he was unaware of the relevance of the age of 18) that he did not know what age she was.

The same principle must apply, *a fortiori*, to offences where negligence as to circumstances will found liability for the principal. Take the offence of bigamy as an example. If D encourages P to marry, both believing honestly but mistakenly and on unreasonable grounds that P's husband is dead, P may be convicted of bigamy but D cannot be convicted as an accessory. This principle applies only to D's negligence as to circumstances forming part of P's crime. Whether a secondary party may be liable for unforeseen consequences of P's crime is considered later.[252]

---

[245] ibid, [9] and [99]. See also LC 305, paras 2.51 et seq.

[246] Horder, APOCL, 448.

[247] It was never necessary for a statute creating an offence to specify that it should also be an offence to aid, etc, its commission. Cf *McCarthy* [1964] Crim LR 225.

[248] *Carter v Mace* [1949] 2 All ER 714, DC, is to the contrary, but in *Davies, Turner & Co Ltd v Brodie* [1954] 1 WLR 1364, DC, that case was said to lay down no principle of law and to be decided on its own particular facts. See J Montgomerie in 'Aiding and Abetting Statutory Offences' (1950) 66 LQR 222.

[249] *Jogee* [2016] UKSC 8, [99]. See *W(P)* [2016] EWCA Crim 745.

[250] (1900) 83 LT 411, DC.   [251] See also *Bowker v Premier Drug Co Ltd* [1928] 1 KB 217 at 227.

[252] See p 211.

Knowledge of what type of crime?

Liability for crimes of same type

If D aids, abets, counsels or procures, that is, performs acts of assistance or encouragement to P and D intends that P will commit an offence of a certain 'type' (X), neither party specifying any particular victim, time or place, D may be convicted as a secondary party to any crime *of that type* which P commits. For example, D intentionally provides P with a knife, knowing that P intends to threaten someone: if P does, D is liable.

The principle applies where, as is common, D and P have a shared common purpose to commit an offence, say burglary, but the act of P alone is the immediate cause of the commission of that offence. D is liable as an accessory for that crime provided he intentionally performed acts of assistance or encouragement (driving P to the scene) intending thereby to assist/encourage.

The principle also applies where D does not have a common purpose with P, but assists/encourages being indifferent whether P commits the crime. A leading case is *Bainbridge*.[253] D purchased some oxygen-cutting equipment which was used six weeks later for breaking into a bank at Stoke Newington. D's story was that he had bought the equipment for P, that he suspected P wanted it for something illegal—perhaps melting down stolen goods—but that he did not know that it was going to be used for any such purpose as it was in fact used. It was held that it was essential to prove that D knew the *type of crime* that was going to be committed: it was not enough that he knew that some kind of illegality was contemplated; but that, if D knew breaking and entering and stealing were intended, it was not necessary to prove that D knew the precise details, for example that the Midland Bank, Stoke Newington, was going to be broken into.[254] That would be too great a degree of specificity for the prosecution to establish and would narrow the scope of secondary liability unduly.

The principle applies equally whether D has assisted by supplying equipment or assisted or encouraged P in some other way. For example, D is liable as an accessory where he provides P with information on how to commit a crime of a particular type, although neither D nor P has any particular crime in view when the advice is given.[255] Where D opened a bank account for P, giving P a false name, D was convicted of aiding and abetting P in the fraudulent use of the particular forged cheque which P subsequently drew upon the account. D had demonstrated an intention that the account be used as a vehicle for presenting forged cheques like the one in fact presented.[256] D knew the type of crime. D is liable even though he does not share P's intent that the offence be committed as, for example, with the supplier of the gun in Devlin's example in *Gamble*. This principle might be regarded as unduly broad. Can it really be said that where D does not even know the precise crime that P will commit he 'knows the essential elements'?

In *DPP for Northern Ireland v Maxwell*,[257] the House of Lords, relying upon the principle enunciated in *Bainbridge*, held that there was no strict requirement that D knows the precise offence P will commit. D assisted P by intentionally driving him to a pub, realizing that P

---

[253] [1960] 1 QB 129, CCA. The result would be different under the LC 305 proposals because D can only be liable for those offences by P as to which D intended P commit the conduct element. If D has not intended P to commit the conduct element of burglary (as opposed to handling) he is not liable. He would be liable under the SCA 2007, s 46.

[254] cf the narrower interpretation that the Law Commission placed on it in para B85 of Appendix B of LC 305.

[255] *Baker* (1909) 28 NZLR 536. G Williams thinks the case is wrongly decided: CLGP, s 125. But is it distinguishable in principle from *Bainbridge*? Cf *McLeod and Georgia Straight Publishing Co Ltd* (1970) 75 WWR 161 (newspaper liable for incitement through article on how to cultivate marijuana).

[256] *Thambiah v R* [1966] AC 37, PC.   [257] [1978] 1 WLR 1350, HL.

intended to commit one or more of a number of offences, including: planting a bomb at the pub, shooting people at the pub or committing a robbery at the pub. In fact, P intended to plant, and did plant, a bomb there. D was liable as an accessory to that offence. Lord Scarman held that, 'an accessory who leaves it to his principal to choose is liable, provided always the choice is made from the range of offences from which the accessory contemplates the choice will be made'.[258] The principle derived from *Maxwell* was that if D gives assistance to P, knowing that P intends to commit a crime, *foreseeing* that it is one or more of crime X, or crime Y, or crime Z, but being uncertain as to which, D was liable as a secondary party to whichever of those crimes P in fact committed. He would not be liable for crime W, even if it was the same (type) as XYZ, unless it was one D contemplated that P might commit with mens rea.[259] It is not difficult to understand why the court reached the decision it did. A narrow approach to the mental element might lead to the acquittal of those who are sufficiently culpable.

The approach adopted by the House of Lords did not permit blanket liability, however. On the facts of *Maxwell*, D would have been liable for murder if P had shot and killed: murder was an offence D had foreseen that P might commit in that manner with mens rea and P carried out that crime. D would not be liable if P had committed a 'type' of offence not in D's contemplation when D performed his acts of assistance.[260] So, D would not have been liable if, on arrival at the pub, P had raped V. Nor would it be enough if D had a 'general criminal intention'. So an intention to abet another in the possession of a bag, whatever its contents may be, is insufficient to found an indictment for abetting the possession of cannabis.[261] If D had guessed that the bag contained either cannabis or some other article, proscribed or not, that should have been enough.

The Supreme Court in *Jogee* endorsed the approach in *Maxwell*, but in doing so narrowed it. The court held that the intention to assist or encourage will often be specific to a particular offence. The court recognized, however, that in other cases it may not be. In endorsing *Maxwell* the court recognized that D may intentionally assist or encourage P to commit one of a range of offences, such as an act of terrorism which might take various forms. In such cases the court held that:

[D] does not have to 'know' (or intend) in advance the specific form which the crime will take. It is enough that the offence committed by [P] is within the range of possible offences which [D] intentionally assisted or encouraged him to commit.[262]

The court held that the decision in *Maxwell* did not derogate from the principle that an intention to assist or encourage the commission of an offence requires *knowledge* by D of any facts necessary to give P's conduct or intended conduct its criminal character. As has already been explained, the principle in *Maxwell* had been interpreted to mean that it was sufficient that P committed one of a range of offences that D had in mind as possibilities. In holding that D will be guilty only if he intentionally assists or encourages P to commit one of a range of offences which D *intends* P will commit, so long as P commits an offence within that range, the Supreme Court has narrowed the approach in *Maxwell*.

[258] ibid, 1363.

[259] The prosecution may well now prefer to lay charges under s 46 of the SCA 2007. See p 489.

[260] cf Lord Scarman who, unlike Lord Hailsham who refers to the type of offence, relies on the judgment of Lowry LCJ in the Northern Ireland Court of Appeal, upholding the conviction on the basis that D 'knew' that P was going to commit one or more offences and although D did not 'know' which offence he knew that at least one would be committed and the offence P committed was one of those.

[261] *Patel* [1970] Crim LR 274 and commentary thereon. Cf *Fernandez* [1970] Crim LR 277.

[262] *Jogee* [2016] UKSC 8, [14]–[15].

913

Where are the limits to such liability? If D has supplied P with the means of committing, or information on how to commit, a crime of a particular type, is D to be held liable for *all* the crimes of that type which P may thereafter commit? What if the Midland Bank at Stoke Newington was the second, third or fourth bank which P had burgled with Bainbridge's apparatus? Glanville Williams questioned whether D should be subject to such unforeseeable and perhaps far-reaching liability.[263] If D can be liable for any one crime of *the type* contemplated even if he need not know the details of any specific crime, should D not also be liable for *others* of that type.[264] In endorsing *Maxwell*, the Supreme Court in *Jogee* must be taken to have confirmed the correctness of this approach subject to the narrowing that has already been discussed.

There are further unresolved problems in relation to this principle. None of these were considered by the Supreme Court in *Jogee*. Whether a crime is of the 'same type' as another may not always be easy to discover. If D lends a jemmy to P, contemplating that P intends to enter a house in order to steal (burglary), is D guilty of any offence if P enters a house intending to commit grievous bodily harm (which is also burglary)? Clearly, D cannot be convicted of grievous bodily harm, because that is an offence of a different type; but he is probably guilty of burglary, because burglary was the crime he had in view—though this particular variety of burglary may be abhorrent to him. If D contemplates theft and P commits robbery, D is not guilty of robbery but might be convicted of the theft which is an essential element of robbery and included in it. Is theft an offence of the same type as removing an article from a place open to the public[265] or taking a motor vehicle without authority?[266] Is robbery an offence of the same type as blackmail? What of D who provides a stolen credit card to P assuming it will be used in fraud, but P uses it to slip the latch on V's door and commit theft. Is it sufficient that these are both dishonesty offences? This is an aspect of the law desperately in need of clarification, at least from a theoretical perspective; in practice, the principle does not seem to have given rise to problems.

D not liable if P intentionally changes victim/target of crime X

If D aids, abets, counsels or procures, that is, assists or encourages, P to commit a crime of a certain 'type' (X), against a particular person, or in respect of a particular thing, D is *not* liable if P *intentionally* commits an offence of the same type against some other person, or in respect of some other thing.

As an example of the principle in operation, consider D who intentionally provides P with a knife, knowing that P intends to use the knife to threaten his ex-wife V and rape her. P deliberately rapes W, a complete stranger, instead. D had not known or intended that. D is not liable for P's act of rape.[267] In *Reardon*,[268] it was accepted[269] that if D intentionally gives assistance to P to kill an identified person, V, D is not liable if P *deliberately* kills a different person, W.

This principle is described well by Hawkins:[270]

But if a man command another to commit a felony on a particular person or thing and he do it on another; as to kill A and he kill B or to burn the house of A and he burn the house of B or to steal an ox and he steal an horse; or to steal such an horse and he steal another; or to commit a felony of one kind and he commit another of a quite different nature; as to rob J S of his plate as he is going to market, and he break open his house in the night and there steal the plate; it is said that the commander is not an accessory because the act done varies in substance from that which was commanded.

---

[263] CLGP, s 124.   [264] On the question of the withdrawal of an accessory, see p 225.

[265] Theft Act 1968, s 11. See p 903.   [266] ibid, s 12. See p 907.

[267] This is different from the case where D gives P a gun to shoot V. P shoots at V and misses killing X. P is liable for murder because his intent is transferred. D is liable as an accessory. See p 212.

[268] [1999] Crim LR 392, CA.

[269] Referring to the 8th edition of this book, at p 142.

[270] II PC, c 29, s 21. See also Foster, *Crown Law*, 369. Stephen, *Digest* (4th edn) art 43.

As the second part of that quotation makes clear, the principle applies where there is an intentional substantial variation from the proposed course of conduct, even if the victim and property are the same. Hawkins also stated:[271]

if the felony committed be the same in substance with that which was intended, and variant only in some circumstance, as in respect of the time or place, at which, or the means whereby it was effected, the abettor of the intent is altogether as much an accessory as if there had been no variance at all between it and the execution of it; as where a man advises another to kill such a one in the night, and he kills him in the day, or to kill him in the fields, and he kills him in the town, or to poison him, and he stabs or shoots him.[272]

The distinction depends on whether the variation is one 'of substance' and any such distinction must produce difficult borderline cases.

In *Dunning and Graham*, an unreported case at Preston Crown Court,[273] D had a grievance against V. P offered to set fire to V's house. D accepted the offer and gave P V's address. P went to V's house, changed his mind, and set fire to V's Mercedes instead. D did not know that V owned such a car. Nevertheless, Macpherson J held that it was open to the jury to convict D on the ground that she must have authorized or envisaged the possibility of property such as a car in the driveway being damaged by fire. If the car had been so damaged as a consequence of P's setting fire to the house, D would have been liable for arson of the car on the basis of transferred malice discussed in the following section. The actual case, however, seems to involve a deliberate variation from the plan. The result might be justified on this basis that D had authorized P to take revenge on V by damaging his property and that it did not really matter to her what the property was. Whether the variation is, or is not, one of substance, depends on the purpose of D as expressed to P.

The South African case of *S v Robinson*[274] provides a controversial illustration of the difficulties of applying this principle. It is an especially difficult case because there is no change of victim as such, but arguably a fundamental change of substance relating to the proposed offence. D1, D2 and P agreed with V that P should kill V to procure the money for which V's life was insured and to avoid V's prosecution for fraud. At the last moment, V withdrew his consent to die but P nevertheless killed him. It was not proved that D1 and D2 foresaw the possibility that P might kill V even if he withdrew his consent or that they had been reckless whether he did so kill him. It was held that the common purpose was murder with the consent of the victim and that P had acted outside that common purpose. D1 and D2, accordingly, were not guilty of murder—though they were guilty of attempted murder, since P had reached the stage of an attempt before V withdrew his consent. Holmes JA, dissenting, thought 'looking squarely at the whole train of events, the conspiracy was fulfilled in death, and there is no room for exquisite niceties of logic about the exact limits of the mandate in the conspiratorial common purpose'.

The division of judicial opinion in this case highlights the problem. What constitutes a change of 'substance' could be interpreted narrowly, being limited to changes which would alter the nature of the criminal charge that could be prosecuted. A broader view of change of 'substance' seems more desirable, but the problem then arises of how to delimit 'changes of substance'. If P knows that a condition precedent of the agreement has not been performed (whether or not forming part of the definition of the crime), he might naturally be said to be no longer engaged on the joint enterprise. If D agrees with P that P shall murder V if he finds out that V is committing adultery with D's wife and P, having discovered that V is *not*

---

271 ibid, s 20.
272 This is related to the principle in *Bainbridge* that D need not know all the details of P's offence.
273 December 1985, unreported.   274 1968 (1) SA 666.

committing adultery, nevertheless kills him, D should not be liable for murder, though, if this conditional intention is enough, he may be liable for conspiracy to murder.

D liable if P commits crime X by doctrine of transferred malice

If D intentionally aids, abets, counsels or procures P to commit a crime against a particular person V and P, endeavouring to commit that crime against V, mistakenly commits the crime against another (W), P is liable under the doctrine of transferred malice;[275] and so, therefore, is D. To take an example, if D assists P by intentionally supplying a knife intending to assist P, and P kills W mistaking W for V, D is guilty as a secondary party, and P as a principal offender, of murder. It is important to note that in this scenario P has not *deliberately* departed from the course that D assisted him with; P was attempting to commit the crime which D has assisted him with and D is as responsible for the unintended results of the acts he has assisted.

The old and famous case of *Saunders and Archer*,[276] in its result at least, is reconcilable with this principle. P intended to murder his wife. Following the advice of D, P gave her a poisoned apple to eat. She ate a little of it and gave the rest to their child. P loved the child, yet he stood by and watched it eat the poison, of which it soon died. It was held that P was guilty of murder of the child, but the judges agreed that D who, of course, was not present when the child ate the apple, was not an accessory to this murder. If P had been absent when the child ate the apple it is thought that this would have been a case of transferred malice and D would have been liable; but P's presence and failure to act made the killing of the child, in effect, a deliberate, and not an accidental, departure from the agreed plan. It was—as Kenny explained—'as if Saunders had changed his mind and on a later occasion had used such poison as Archer had named in order to murder some quite different person of whom Archer had never heard'.[277]

6.4.2.4 Summary

For liability as a secondary party:

- a criminal offence must have been committed by P (whether P is identified or not);
- D must have intentionally aided, abetted, counselled or procured P, or in other words assisted or encouraged him, to commit an offence of the type that P in fact committed;
- D must have intended to assist or encourage P's conduct, or in the case of procuring, to bring the offence about, it being sufficient that D has oblique intent;
- D must have knowledge of any existing facts or circumstances necessary for P's conduct to be criminal; and
- if the offence is one of mens rea, D must intend to assist or encourage P to act with that mens rea. Procuring and innocent agency appear to be exceptions to this rule although this has yet to be determined.

6.5 The rise and fall of 'parasitic accessory' or 'joint enterprise' liability

6.5.1 Introduction

Prior to the Supreme Court deciding that it was the consequence of a legal 'wrong turn', the problem in identifying the scope of D's liability for P's offences arose most keenly in the context of so-called 'joint enterprise' or 'parasitic accessory' liability. That doctrine gave rise to a vast number of

---

[275] Hawkins, I PC, c 29, s 22; Foster, *Crown Law*, 370; Stephen, *Digest* (4th edn) art 41, illustration (1). See also D Lanham, 'Accomplices and Transferred Malice' (1980) 96 LQR 110.

[276] (1573) 2 Plowd 473.

[277] *Outlines* at 112. See the perceptive jury questions and clear directions in *Gordon-Butt* [2004] EWCA Crim 961 on changes of victim.

appeals and to much academic debate.[278] To understand why the Supreme Court characterized the doctrine as a legal wrong turn, it is necessary to set out the basis upon which it enabled D to be liable for a crime committed by P. D was liable as a parasitic accessory where:

(1) D intentionally participated in the commission of crime 'A' with P or Ps (D's role could be either as a principal or accessory); and

(2) D shared a common purpose with P to commit crime 'A'; and

(3) P or Ps (whether identified or not) committed crime 'B' with the relevant mens rea for that crime; and

(4) P's commission of crime B was in the course or furtherance of crime 'A';

(5) D foresaw as a possibility that P or Ps might commit crime 'B' with the relevant mens rea; and

(6) P or Ps did commit it in a not fundamentally different manner from that which D foresaw; and

(7) D was at the time of the commission of crime 'B' still an active participant with P or Ps in crime 'A'.

It was said by the Supreme Court that this form of liability was developed by the Privy Council in *Chan Wing-Siu v R*,[279] as interpreted in *Hyde* and *Hui Chi-ming* and approved by the House of Lords in *Powell and Daniels, English* [280] and *Rahman*.[281] It was also endorsed in numerous Court of Appeal decisions[282] and by the Supreme Court in *Gnango*.[283]

The House of Lords in *Powell and Daniels, English*[284] confirmed that it was sufficient to found a conviction for murder for D to have realized that P *might* kill with intent to do so or with intent to cause GBH. It was not necessary that D himself held an intention to kill. The particular difficulties in application in murder stemmed from the breadth of the mens rea of that offence and the fact that it is a constructive crime—it is sufficient that P has intended GBH.

The consequences of the joint enterprise principle were especially significant in cases of murder. Once it had been proved that a murder was committed, even if the principal could not be identified, the fact that the jury could not be sure which of the members of a group delivered the fatal blow did not prevent murder convictions for all or any members of the joint enterprise who foresaw that intentional GBH might occur: *Rahman*.[285]

Parasitic accessory liability meant that D could be liable for an offence requiring proof of an intention on the part of the principal offender, P, although D was only reckless about P's likely intentional conduct.[286] Recklessness whether death be caused is a sufficient mens

---

[278] See JC Smith, 'Criminal Liability of Accessories: Law and Law Reform' (1997) 113 LQR 453; J Burchell, 'Joint Enterprise and Common Purpose' (1997) 10 SACJ 125; cf A Simester, 'The Mental Element in Complicity' (2006) 122 LQR 578, for a review see LC 305. See B Krebs, 'Joint Criminal Enterprise' (2010) 73 MLR 578; G Virgo, 'Joint Enterprise is Dead: Long Live Accessorial Liability' [2012] Crim LR 850; W Wilson and D Ormerod, 'Simply Harsh to Fairly Simple: Joint Enterprise Reform' [2015] Crim LR 3.

[279] (1985) 80 Cr App R 117. See the 7th edition of this book, at pp 143–145, for an account of the cases ending in *Chan Wing-Siu* in *Hyde* (1991) 92 Cr App R 131 and the decision in *Hui Chi-ming* (1992) 94 Cr App R 236, PC.

[280] [1999] AC 1, [1997] 4 All ER 545, HL. See also the comment by G Virgo (1998) 33 CLJ 3. See also *Neary* [2002] EWCA Crim 1736.

[281] [2008] UKHL 45.

[282] See eg *Smith* [2008] EWCA Crim 1342; *ABCD* [2010] EWCA Crim 1622; *Mendez* [2010] EWCA Crim 516; *Lewis* [2010] EWCA Crim 496; *Badza* [2010] EWCA Crim 1363; *Montague* [2013] EWCA Crim 1781; *Bristow* [2013] EWCA Crim 1540; *Ali* [2014] EWCA Crim 2169.

[283] [2011] UKSC 59.   [284] [1999] 1 AC 1.   [285] [2008] UKHL 45.

[286] For extensive analysis of why parasitic accessory liability was controversial, see W Wilson and D Ormerod, 'Simply Harsh to Fairly Simple: Joint Enterprise Reform' [2015] Crim LR 3; B Crewe, A Liebling, N Padfield and G Virgo, 'Joint Enterprise: The Implications of an Unfair and Unclear Law' [2015] Crim LR 252; M Dyson, 'Might Alone Does Not Make Right: Justifying Secondary Liability' [2015] Crim LR 967.

917

rea for manslaughter but not for murder; yet in a joint enterprise case D could be convicted if D was reckless as to whether P might intentionally perpetrate the conduct element of the actus reus of murder. In *Powell and Daniels, English*, Lord Steyn rejected the argument that joint enterprise imposed a form of constructive liability for murder. His lordship held that if this were the case it would be contrary to principle and would be a defect of the criminal law. It was accepted that the liability of the secondary party is 'undoubtedly' predicated upon a lesser form of mens rea, but his lordship went on to state that it was unrealistic to say that joint enterprise *as such* imposed constructive criminal liability. What D must have foreseen was P's *intentional* act: recklessness *whether the conduct element of the offence of murder be committed* is a different and more culpable state of mind than recklessness *whether death be caused*—a point which was regarded as persuasive by Lord Steyn.[287]

An example will illustrate how this form of secondary liability applied. Where D intentionally performed acts of assistance or encouragement to P, intending for P to have the mens rea for the offence in question: he gave P a gun to assist in his robbery, for example. D is liable as an accessory to the robbery even though P was the one who completed the offence. That is orthodox accessorial liability as we have discussed it so far in this chapter. But, if in the course of the robbery P shot and murdered V, D was *also* liable as an accessory for murder which he did *not* intend or assist or encourage P to commit, provided: (a) D intentionally encouraged or assisted P to commit robbery; (b) D foresaw that in the course of[288] committing robbery, P might perform the conduct element of murder in the prescribed circumstances making that an offence; (c) D foresaw that P might do so with the mens rea of murder; and (d) the manner of P committing the murder was not fundamentally different from what D foresaw might occur.

Consider a second example. D, the accessory, intentionally assisted or encouraged P to commit theft by shoplifting from a major electrical retailer, contemplating that in the course of committing that offence P 'might well' do an act with intent to cause grievous bodily harm if challenged by the security staff. If P did an act of the kind D foresaw/contemplated and punched V in order to make off with the goods he was stealing, P was guilty of robbery. D was guilty as accessory to both the theft and to the robbery.

These principles applied: whether D was present with P or not;[289] irrespective of whether D caused any conduct by P; irrespective of whether D agreed with P that P might do so; and irrespective of whether D shared a common intent with P to commit crime B (eg murder).[290]

6.5.1.1 The judgment in *Jogee*

Extensive reference has already been made to the joint judgment of the Supreme Court and Privy Council in *Jogee; Ruddock*. This section will consider why the Supreme Court concluded that the doctrine of 'parasitic accessory' or 'joint enterprise' liability constituted a legal wrong turn. As has already been explained, the Supreme Court attributed the development of parasitic accessory liability to the opinion of the Board in *Chan Wing-Siu*, in which Sir Robin Cooke stated:

In the typical case [of aiding and abetting] the same or the same type of offence is actually intended by all the parties acting in concert. In view of the terms of the directions to the jury here, the Crown does not seek to support the present convictions on that ground. The case must depend rather on the wider principle whereby a secondary party is criminally liable for acts by the primary offender of a type

---

[287] [1999] 1 AC 1, 13–16.

[288] Irrespective of whether it is completed. Simester argued that it was a fiction to say that D aids and abets crime B: see n 76. But the actus reus of aiding is D's participation in crime A despite D foreseeing that B might occur.

[289] *Rook* [1993] Crim LR 698.   [290] cf *Gnango* [2011] UKSC 59.

which the former foresees but does not necessarily intend. That there is such a principle is not in doubt. It turns on contemplation or, putting the same idea in other words, authorisation, which may be express but is more usually implied. It meets the case of a crime foreseen as a possible incident of the common unlawful enterprise. The criminal liability lies in participating in the venture with that foresight.

After an extensive review of the relevant authorities, the Supreme Court in *Jogee* concluded that the Privy Council in *Chan Wing-Siu* and the House of Lords in *Powell and Daniels, English* had in fact laid down a new principle. The authorities relied upon by the Privy Council and accepted by the House of Lords did not support the proposition that if two people set out to commit an offence (crime A), and in the course of it one of them commits another offence (crime B), the second person is guilty as an accessory to crime B if he foresaw it as a possibility, but did not necessarily intend it. The Supreme Court also stated that the Privy Council had made the error of eliding foresight with intention.

Although it confirmed that it was open to the courts to alter the common law in a way that made it more severe, the Supreme Court stated that judges must be cautious before doing so. Although the policy arguments relied upon in subsequent cases to justify the imposition of liability, specifically the problems of escalation associated with group violence, were important, the Supreme Court ultimately concluded that they were insufficient to justify making D guilty of murder as opposed to manslaughter. Of particular relevance to this issue was the fact there was no consideration in *Chan Wing-Siu* or in *Powell and Daniels, English* of the fundamental policy question of whether and why it was necessary and appropriate to reclassify such conduct as murder rather than manslaughter. It was held that such a discussion would necessarily have to entail the consideration of questions about fair labelling and fair discrimination in sentencing. The Supreme Court concluded that the principle enunciated in *Chan Wing-Siu* was based upon an incomplete, and in some respects, erroneous, reading of previous case law, coupled with generalized and questionable policy arguments. The court gave the following reasons for why it was right to correct the error and reverse a statement of principle despite it having been made and followed by the Privy Council and the House of Lords on a number of occasions:

- the court had the benefit of a much fuller analysis than on previous occasions when the topic had been considered;
- it could not be said that the law was now well established and working satisfactorily. Rather, it was highly controversial and a continuing source of difficulty for trial judges, leading to a large number of appeals;
- secondary liability is an important part of the common law, and if a wrong turn has been taken, it should be corrected;
- in the common law, foresight of what might happen is ordinarily no more than evidence from which a jury can infer the presence of the requisite intention. The court recognized that it may be strong evidence, but its adoption as a test for the mental element for murder in the case of a secondary party was a serious and anomalous departure from the basic rule, which resulted in over-extension of the law of murder and reduction of the law of manslaughter. The court noted that murder already has a relatively low mens rea threshold, because it is sufficient that D has an intention to cause serious injury, without intent to kill or to cause risk to life. The *Chan Wing-Siu* principle extended liability for murder to a secondary party on the basis of a still lesser degree of culpability, namely foresight only of the possibility that the principal may commit murder but without there being any need for there to exist an intention to assist him to do so;
- the rule brings what was characterized as 'the striking anomaly' of requiring a lower mental threshold for guilt in the case of the accessory than in the case of the principal.

919

The Supreme Court restated the principles that govern secondary liability and emphasized that nothing less than an intention to assist or encourage will suffice for D to be guilty as a secondary party. The mens rea for secondary liability was considered earlier in this chapter.

6.5.1.2 Evaluating *Jogee*

In correcting the 'wrong turn' that led to the development of parasitic accessory liability, the Supreme Court's judgment in *Jogee* simplifies the law.[291] The court also clarified that, in agreement with the previous editions of this work, 'there is no reason why ordinary principles of secondary liability should not be of general application'.[292] In concluding that nothing less than intention will suffice for D to be guilty as an accessory, the judgment also ensures that the threshold for imposing liability upon the accessory is no longer significantly lower than that of the principal. The judgment has, however, proved to be controversial for a number of reasons. First, it has been cogently argued that the Supreme Court's conclusion that *Chan Wing-Siu* introduced a 'new principle' that changed the common law in a way which made it more severe is highly suspect.[293] Stark argues that the Supreme Court cited selectively from the relevant case law, giving the most sympathetic view of history that it could. On his analysis of the case law relied upon by the Supreme Court, Stark argues that *Chan Wing-Siu* confirmed was what already beginning to become clear, namely that there was a 'wider principle' beyond standard aiding and abetting, 'whereby a secondary party is criminally liable for acts by the primary offender of a type which the former foresees but does not necessarily intend'.[294] Stark's analysis leads him to conclude, convincingly it is submitted, that the Supreme Court in *Jogee* engaged in substantive law reform. As he notes, there are clear constitutional issues that arise from the court undertaking such a significant change to the common law.

Secondly, the practical impact of *Jogee* is contestable. Whilst the Supreme Court held in emphatic terms that nothing less than intention will suffice for D to be guilty as an accessory, it confirmed that foresight is evidence of intention and that conditional intention will suffice for D to be guilty. Sir Brian Leveson P confirmed subsequently in *Anwar* that the same facts which would previously have been used to support the inference of mens rea before the decision in *Jogee* will equally be used post the judgment. His lordship stated that the evidential requirements justifying a decision that there is a case to answer are likely to be the same even if, applying the facts to the different directions in law, the jury might reach a different conclusion.[295] It could transpire, however, that juries are just as likely to convict after *Jogee* as they were before. Indeed, in *Chan Kam Shing* the Hong Kong Court of Final Appeal stated that the concept of conditional intent was interpreted in *Johnson* and *Anwar* in much the same way as the foresight requirement in *Chan Wing-Siu*. This 'drift back to joint criminal enterprise' led Ribeiro PJ to question the true extent of the changes effected by the Supreme Court's decision.[296]

Finally, the judgment has been subject to sustained criticism by courts in other common law jurisdictions. In *Chan Kam Shing*, the Hong Kong Court of Final Appeal declined to follow *Jogee* and held that parasitic accessory liability should continue to be applied in Hong Kong. Ribeiro PJ gave three reasons for this conclusion. First, that secondary parties

---

[291] cf R Buxton, '*Jogee*: Upheaval in Secondary Liability for Murder' [2016] Crim LR 324; M Dyson, 'Shorn-Off Complicity' (2016) 75 CLJ 196.

[292] *Jogee* [2016] UKSC 8, [76].

[293] F Stark, 'The Demise of "Parasitic Accessorial Liability": Substantive Judicial Law Reform, not Common Law Housekeeping' (2016) 75 CLJ 550.

[294] *Chan Wing-Siu* [1985] AC 168, 175.   [295] *Anwar* [2016] EWCA Crim 551, [22].

[296] [2016] HKCFA 87, [92]–[93].

to a joint criminal enterprise deserve 'to be regarded as gravely culpable'. Secondly, that the abolition of joint enterprise would 'deprive the law of a valuable principle for dealing with dynamic situations involving evidential and situational uncertainties which traditional accessorial liability rules are ill-adapted to addressing'. Finally, the court expressed concern about the introduction of the concept of conditional intent, on the basis that it 'gives rise to significant conceptual and practical problems'. Key to the court's decision to retain parasitic accessory liability was its conclusion that there are two distinct doctrines: basic joint enterprise or 'common purpose' liability, and parasitic accessory liability or 'extended joint criminal enterprise'. In reaching this conclusion, the court disagreed with *Jogee* in which the Supreme Court, citing with approval the previous edition of this work,[297] held that there is no reason why ordinary principles of secondary liability should not be of general application. Krebs argues that this difference in taxonomy means that the two judgments are at cross-purposes.[298]

The judgment in *Jogee* was also criticized by the High Court of Australia in *Miller v The Queen*. A majority of the High Court were not persuaded by the arguments of policy and principle that led the Supreme Court in *Jogee* to declare that *Chan Wing-Siu* constituted a 'legal wrong turn'. The High Court identified six broad reasons for retaining the doctrine of parasitic accessory liability. First, it rejected claims of over-criminalization as being unfounded. Secondly, it held that parasitic accessory liability is an independent type of secondary liability rather than a sub-species of accessory liability, so the differences between the two are not unprincipled. Thirdly, the court expressed concern about the practical difficulties in proving individual contributions in multi-handed situations. Fourthly, it expressed disagreement with the proposition that parasitic accessory liability makes trials unduly complex. Fifthly, it was considered 'undesirable' to alter parasitic accessory liability without reviewing the law of homicide and secondary liability generally. Finally, the court regarded judicial reform as being inappropriate against a background of legislative reform efforts in various Australian states. Krebs argues that the majority judgment in *Miller* does little more than reassert the well-rehearsed arguments in favour of parasitic accessory liability without engaging with the relevant counter-arguments.[299] Gageler J dissented and agreed with the view expressed by the Supreme Court in *Jogee* that escalating group violence does not, without more, provide support for parasitic accessory liability. In *Miller*, the majority were concerned that requiring intent on the part of the secondary party set the threshold of liability too high. Whilst foresight sets the threshold of liability too low, Krebs suggests that the decision in *Miller* could indicate that requiring full-blown intention is 'beginning to look a step too far in the opposite direction'.[300] She states that it may be necessary to find a middle ground between foresight and full-blown intention to deal with the phenomenon of incidental crimes.

The judgment in *Jogee* is clearly not a panacea.[301] As this section has demonstrated, the juridical foundation of the Supreme Court's decision is controversial and there are a number of matters that the courts still need to resolve. Not least of which is what to do about those defendants who were convicted on the basis of parasitic accessory liability. In *Jogee*, the Supreme Court stated that, 'the effect of putting the law right is not to render invalid all convictions which were arrived at over many years by faithfully applying the law as laid down in the *Chan Wing-Siu* case and in *R v Powell; R v English*'.[302] Where a conviction

---

[297] *Jogee* [2016] UKSC 8, [76].
[298] B Krebs, 'Hong Kong Court of Final Appeal: Divided by a Common Purpose' (2017) 81 J Crim L 271.
[299] B Krebs, 'Accessory Liability: Persisting in Error' (2017) 76 CLJ 7.   [300] ibid, 10.
[301] Judges still slip in directing juries, as demonstrated by *Noble and Johnson* [2016] EWCA Crim 2219.
[302] [2016] UKSC 8, [100].

921

has been arrived at by faithfully applying the law as it stood at the time, the court held that it can be set aside only by seeking exceptional leave to appeal to the Court of Appeal out of time. In the subsequent case of *Johnson* the Court of Appeal confirmed that it will be for the applicant for exceptional leave to appeal out of time to demonstrate that a substantial injustice would be done.[303] In determining whether that high threshold has been met, the court stated that it will primarily and ordinarily have regard to the strength of the case advanced that the change in the law would, in fact, have made a difference.[304] If the particular crime is a crime of violence which the jury concluded must have involved the use of a weapon, so that the inference of participation with an intention to cause really serious harm is strong, the court concluded that is likely to be very difficult. If, however, the crime did not involve intended violence or use of force, the court stated that it may well be easier to demonstrate substantial injustice. It is submitted that the approach adopted by the Court of Appeal will preclude most of those whose convictions are based upon the 'wrong turn' taken in *Chan Wing-Siu* from appealing their convictions. The impact of *Jogee* may therefore only be felt prospectively.[305] Many will feel disappointed by this state of affairs. This issue is compounded by the fact that the Court of Appeal confirmed in the subsequent case of *Garwood* that it has no jurisdiction to certify a point of law of general public importance in cases where leave to appeal has been refused. This means that an individual in such a case will be unable to challenge the Court of Appeal's conclusion that there was no substantial injustice before the Supreme Court.[306]

6.6 Secondary participation must be in 'an offence'

6.6.1 Can there be secondary liability in an inchoate offence?

It is an offence to do acts capable of assisting or encouraging,[307] or to conspire, or to attempt, to commit an offence.[308] It is *not* an offence to attempt[309] or, it is submitted, to conspire[310] to do an act which would involve no more than secondary liability for the offence if it were committed.

Secondary liability is triggered by the commission of the substantive principal offence. To demonstrate the operation of the rules, consider the following example. Knowing that P intends to drive his car, D2 urges D1 to 'lace' P's drink with so much alcohol that if P drives after consuming the drink he will inevitably commit an offence under s 5(1) of the Road Traffic Act 1988.[311] D1 agrees to do so and attempts to, or does, lace the drink. If P consumes

---

[303] [2016] EWCA Crim 1613.

[304] The same approach was adopted by the Northern Ireland Court of Appeal in *Skinner* [2016] NICA 40.

[305] For further discussion, see K Laird [2017] Crim LR 216. At the time of writing, the Court of Appeal has quashed a conviction and ordered a retrial in only one case. See *Crilly* [2018] EWCA Crim 168.

[306] There are now numerous cases on which the Court of Appeal has rejected the submission of substantial injustice. See *Grant-Murray* [2017] EWCA Crim 1228; *Agera* [2017] EWCA Crim 740; *Varley* [2017] EWCA Crim 268. In all these cases, the court concluded that even if the jury had been directed in accordance with *Jogee*, it would have 'made no difference'.

[307] The SCA 2007 replaced common law incitement with three statutory inchoate offences of assisting or encouraging in ss 44–46.

[308] See Ch 11.

[309] Criminal Attempts Act 1981, s 1(4)(b); *Dunnington* [1984] QB 472, [1984] Crim LR 98, CA. Cf *Chief Constable of Hampshire v Mace* (1986) 84 Cr App R 40, [1986] Crim LR 752. See the debate between M Bohlander and J Child in [2009] Crim LR, discussed in Ch 11, p 432.

[310] *Kenning* [2008] EWCA Crim 1534; *Hollinshead* [1985] 1 All ER 850 at 857–858, CA. The House of Lords left the question open: [1985] AC 975. See JC Smith, 'Secondary Participation and Inchoate Offences' in *Crime, Proof and Punishment*, 21.

[311] Driving or being in charge of a motor vehicle with an alcohol concentration above a prescribed limit.

the drink, drives his car and thus commits the offence under the Road Traffic Act 1988, D2 and D1 will be guilty as secondary parties;[312] but if P declines the drink, or does not drive the car, D2 is not guilty of conspiracy and D1 is guilty neither of conspiracy nor of attempt to commit the offence. The act encouraged, agreed upon, attempted and indeed done, lacing the drink, is not the offence.[313] D may be liable under s 44 of the SCA 2007.[314]

Assuming that P consumes the laced drink and drives, P could be guilty as the principal offender, notwithstanding his lack of mens rea, on the ground that the offence is one of strict liability. Where the offence is one requiring mens rea, which the actual perpetrator of the actus reus lacks, then those who procured him to act will be liable because they, or one of them, will be principal offenders.

In the case of conspiracy, one who abets or counsels the commission of the crime appears to be a principal offender in the conspiracy. It is also possible to abet or counsel an attempt.[315]

For the scope of D's liability for assisting or encouraging P to assist or encourage P2, see Ch 11.

6.7 The relationship between the liability of the principal and secondary party

6.7.1 Procedural issues

Even if the alleged principal offender has been acquitted, a conviction of another person as an accessory may be logical. This is so even if it is assumed[316] that an accessory may be convicted only when the principal offender himself is guilty. The acquittal of the alleged principal offender, far from being conclusive that no crime was committed, is not generally admissible in evidence at a subsequent trial of the secondary parties.[317] A second jury may be satisfied beyond reasonable doubt that the crime was committed upon evidence which the first jury found unconvincing; evidence may be admissible against D which was not admissible against P, or fresh evidence may have come to light or P may have been acquitted because the prosecution offered no evidence against him.

The position would seem to be the same where D is tried first and convicted and P is subsequently acquitted[318] and when the parties are jointly indicted.[319] In *Hughes*,[320] after the prosecution had offered no evidence against P, he was acquitted and called as a witness for the Crown, with the result that D was convicted by the same jury as an accessory to P's alleged crime. Where principal and secondary parties are tried separately, this result is supported by the analogous rule laid down in *DPP v Shannon*[321] that the acquittal of one

---

[312] *A-G's Reference (No 1 of 1975)*, p 186.

[313] The adulteration of the drink might possibly amount to the administration of a noxious thing, contrary to the OAPA 1861, s 24, see Ch 16.

[314] Virgo argues that the inchoate offences could in future be deployed to avoid the Supreme Court's restrictive interpretation of accessorial liability in *Jogee*. See G Virgo, 'The Relationship Between Inchoate and Accessorial Liability after *Jogee*' [2016] 9 Arch Rev 6. Given the complexity of the offences in the SCA 2007, this seems unlikely.

[315] *Hapgood and Wyatt* (1870) LR 1 CCR 221, CCR; *S v Robinson* 1968 (1) SA 666.

[316] Contrary to the view expressed, see p 222.

[317] *Hui Chi-ming v R* [1991] 3 All ER 897, PC. Under the Police and Criminal Evidence Act 1984, s 74, a conviction is now admissible to prove the commission of the offence by the principal: *Turner* [1991] Crim LR 57.

[318] In *Rowley* [1948] 1 All ER 570, D's conviction was quashed when, after he had pleaded guilty as an accessory, the alleged principals were acquitted by the jury. But the decision is criticized in *Shannon* [1974] 2 All ER 1009 at 1020 and 1049. Cf *Zaman* [2010] EWCA Crim, on which see Ch 7, p 237.

[319] See also *Petch* [2005] 2 Cr App R 657.   [320] (1860) Bell CC 242.

[321] [1975] AC 717 HL; Ch 12.

party to a conspiracy does not invalidate the conviction of the only other party on an earlier or later occasion. *Shannon* left open the question whether one party may be convicted of conspiracy when the other is acquitted at the same trial;[322] and in *Anthony*[323] it was said, *obiter*, that a jury cannot acquit P and at the same time find D guilty of counselling him to commit the crime.

If P and D are tried together and the evidence tending to show that P committed the crime is the same against both, then it would be inconsistent to acquit P and convict D.[324] Where, however, there is evidence admissible against D but not against P that P committed the crime (eg a confession by D that he counselled P to commit the crime and saw him commit it), it would be perfectly logical to acquit P and convict D of counselling him (and of conspiring with him). In *Humphreys and Turner*,[325] which was just such a case, Chapman J held that D might be convicted as an accessory, distinguishing the *dicta* in *Anthony* as applicable only to felonies. It is submitted that, ever since the Criminal Law Act 1967 came into force, the rule stated in *Humphreys and Turner* is applicable to all offences.

It is one thing for a court which is trying D alone to reject or ignore the holding of another court that P was not a principal offender and to hold that he was; and that, therefore, D might be convicted as an accessory to P's crime. It is quite another thing for a court to hold at one and the same time: (a) that P was, in law, not guilty[326] and (b) that D was guilty, as a secondary party, of P's crime. These propositions seem, at first sight, to be inconsistent with the derivative nature of secondary liability.[327]

6.7.2 Secondary party guilty of a greater offence than the principal

Since secondary liability is said to derive from that of the principal, it may seem hard to see how the liability of the secondary party can properly be held to be greater than that of the principal offender. Historically,[328] distinctions were drawn based on the presence at the crime and it was thought that the liability of the accessory who was absent could never 'rise higher' than that of the principal offender. The distinctions depending on whether the accessory is present at, or absent from, the commission of the crime are no longer applicable.[329]

There are some cases where it seems obvious that a person who, at least, appears to be an accessory ought to be convicted of a greater offence than the immediate perpetrator of the actus reus. We have already noticed that offences may be committed through innocent agents and that if D, with intent to kill, sends a letter-bomb through the post to V who is killed by the explosion, D is guilty of murder as a principal offender and E, the postman, is an innocent agent. Suppose, however, that E notices some wires sticking out of the parcel and that he is aware that a number of letter-bombs have been sent by terrorists lately with fatal results. He thinks, 'This could be a letter-bomb—but it's not likely and I'm in a hurry, I'll risk it' and pushes the letter through V's letter box where it explodes and kills V. If these facts are proved, E behaved recklessly and is guilty of manslaughter. He is no longer an

---

[322] The point is now settled by the Criminal Law Act 1977, and *Longman and Cribben* (1981) 72 Cr App R 121, p 460; but *Shannon* is relevant to the common law governing secondary participation.

[323] [1965] 2 QB 189. Cf *Surujpaul v R* [1958] 1 WLR 1050.

[324] *Surujpaul v R* [1958] 1 WLR 1050.

[325] [1965] 3 All ER 689 (Liverpool Crown Court).Followed in *Sweetman v Industries and Commerce Department* [1970] NZLR 139. Cf *Davis* [1977] Crim LR 542, CA and commentary and *Fuller* [1998] Crim LR 61.

[326] Not merely that there was not enough evidence to convict him, but that there was evidence which established his innocence.

[327] See p 222.   [328] Hawkins, II PC, c 29, s 15.

[329] It depended on the distinction in the law of felonies between a principal in the second degree and an accessory which has been abolished.

innocent agent. But it would be absurd if D who sent the letter with intent to kill should escape liability for murder.

Alternative approaches have been advanced by academics. Glanville Williams suggests that a person like our postman should be regarded as a semi-innocent agent.[330] Professor Kadish[331] prefers to say that D can properly be said to have caused V's death. Because P's actions are not 'fully voluntary' they do not break the chain of causation.[332] His approach explains the following difficult example:

[D] hands a gun to [P] informing him that it is loaded with blank ammunition only and telling him to go and scare [V] by discharging it. The ammunition is in fact live (as [D] knows) and [V] is killed. [P] is convicted only of manslaughter....It would seem absurd that [D] should thereby escape conviction for murder.[333]

P's act would be regarded by Kadish as not 'fully voluntary' because, through his ignorance of material facts, he was not fully aware of what he was doing or its consequences; so D has caused the death, intending to kill and is a principal murderer.[334]

For many years English law seemed to accept that D could not be liable for a more serious offence than P. This flowed from *Richards*,[335] which the Court of Appeal and Lord Mackay (in *Howe*) considered to be wrongly decided. D, a woman, hired P1 and P2 to beat up her husband 'bad enough to put him in hospital for a month'. She signalled to P1 and P2 when V left the house. They inflicted a wound upon V, not amounting to a serious injury. D was convicted of wounding with intent to cause grievous bodily harm but P1 and P2 were acquitted of that offence and convicted of the lesser offence of unlawful wounding. D's conviction was quashed and a conviction for unlawful wounding substituted.[336]

Richards was heavily criticized and, in view of the disapproval expressed in *Burke* (conjoined with *Howe* on appeal), though only *obiter*, may not be followed in future. It has some academic supporters.[337]

The anomaly of holding D liable for the greater offence is emphasized if it is supposed that V, by some unforeseeable mischance, had died of the slight injury inflicted by P1 and P2. This would have been manslaughter by P1 and P2. If D was guilty of the s 18 offence, it would follow logically that she was guilty of murder. It may be argued that this would be wrong (though she had the necessary mens rea), because no act was ever done with *intent thereby* to kill or cause serious bodily harm—there was no 'murderous act'. If, however, P1 and P2 had acted with intent to do serious bodily harm but succeeded in inflicting only a slight injury it would have been murder by all three if V had died of that. But then the act would have been done in pursuance of a joint enterprise to cause serious bodily harm. In fact, there was no

---

[330] TBCL, 373.   [331] *Blame and Punishment* (1987) 183.

[332] eg P shoots at V, intending to kill but only wounds. D treats the wound recklessly and V dies of the maltreated wound. P and D have both caused V's death. P is guilty of murder and D of manslaughter. Both are principals.

[333] *Burke and Howe* [1986] QB 626 at 641–642, CA. Lord Mackay agreed with the Court of Appeal who found this example convincing: [1987] AC 417, HL.

[334] It is not so clear that the causation theory is a satisfactory explanation of the case where D intends the result and E is reckless whether he causes it—eg the postman case discussed earlier. It seems to be straining rather to say that the postman's act is not 'fully voluntary'.

[335] [1974] QB 776, CA.

[336] This followed Hawkins' view, n 328. It was assumed that under the old law of felonies, D would have been an accessory and not a principal in the second degree.

[337] Kadish ('Complicity and Causation' (1985) 73 Cal L Rev 323 at 329) supports the *Richards* view arguing (a) that D did not cause the actions of P1 and P2 because they were not her unwitting instruments but chose to act freely as they did and (b) she could not be held liable 'for an aggravated assault [ie an assault with intent to cause grievous bodily harm] that did not take place'.

GBH committed and no charges of such. For that reason, though not for the reasons given, it may be that the decision in *Richards* was right after all.

The position is more straightforward where D and P both have the mens rea for the greater offence but P's liability is reduced for some reason to that of a lesser offence. If P causes the actus reus in carrying out the agreed plan but his liability is reduced 'for some reason special to himself',[338] such as loss of self-control or diminished responsibility,[339] it seems clearly right that D should not be able to shelter behind P's personal exemption from liability for the greater offence.

In the case considered in *Burke* (conjoined with *Howe* on appeal), however, the reduction in P's liability did not depend on a personal consideration of this kind. P's defence was that he had agreed to shoot V out of fear of D, but that, when it came to the event, the gun went off accidentally. The killing was therefore unintentional and amounted to no more than manslaughter. The judge, following *Richards*, directed that if the jury found P guilty only of manslaughter, then D could at most be guilty of manslaughter. The implication of the decision of the House is that this was wrong. It is submitted that the true position is that if P has gone beyond a merely preparatory act and is attempting to commit the crime when he 'accidentally' kills, both D and P are guilty of murder; but, if P is doing only a preparatory act when he happens to kill—he is driving to V's house with intent to blow it up when the bomb in his car goes off and kills V who has unexpectedly gone out for a walk—P is liable only for manslaughter and so is D. The killing which occurs is not the killing he intended, though the victim happens to be the same.[340]

6.7.3 Where the 'principal' is not guilty

Here we are concerned with cases where the immediate perpetrator of the actus reus is not guilty of the offence alleged and the offence is one which is incapable of being committed by a person as a principal offender acting through an innocent agent. Examples include rape and other offences involving sexual intercourse, driving offences and bigamy (except where the bigamous marriage is by proxy). There are three possible situations:

(1) P has committed the actus reus of the offence with mens rea but has a defence;

(2) P has committed the actus reus but has no mens rea;

(3) P has not committed the actus reus.

The approach to these is best examined by analysis of a series of cases in which the issues have arisen.

6.7.3.1 P performs actus reus and mens rea but has a defence

In *Bourne*,[341] D by duress compelled his wife (P) to have sex with a dog. His conviction of abetting her to commit buggery was upheld although it was assumed that the wife, if she had been charged, would have been acquitted on the ground of coercion.[342] Sir Rupert Cross[343] argued that this was in accordance with principle because 'The wife committed the "*actus reus*" with the "*mens rea*" required by the definition of the crime in question and

---

[338] The phrase used by Lord Mackay in *Burke*, n 333.

[339] This case is covered by s 2(4) of the Homicide Act 1957. D's liability for murder is not affected by E's diminished responsibility. The Coroners and Justice Act 2009, s 54(8) applies the same rule to loss of self-control.

[340] See commentary [1987] Crim LR 481 at 484.

[341] (1952) 36 Cr App R 125. See JL Edwards, 'Duress and Aiding and Abetting' (1953) 69 LQR 297; R Cross, 'Duress and Aiding and Abetting (A Reply)' (1953) 69 LQR 354.

[342] See p 379.   [343] (1953) 68 LQR 354.

the husband participated in that *"mens rea"*.' The wife had mens rea in the sense that she knew exactly what she was doing, though she was to be excused for doing it. According to some theorists, where the defence relied upon by the principal is excusatory, that does not preclude the accessory from being convicted.

6.7.3.2 P performs the actus reus but lacks mens rea

In *Cogan and Leak*,[344] D terrorized his wife, V, into submitting to sexual intercourse with P. P was convicted of rape and D of abetting him but, on appeal, P's conviction had to be quashed because the jury had not been directed correctly, and it may have been that P lacked the mens rea as to V's consent. D's conviction was upheld but primarily on the ground that D was the principal offender acting through an innocent agent. The agency theory is misconceived. If it were right, a woman could be convicted of rape as the principal offender and it is plain that she cannot commit that offence; she does not have a penis. To suggest that D raped his wife V using P's penis is nonsense. The court's second reason was that D was rightly convicted as a procurer because V had been raped ('no one outside a court of law would say she had not been') and 'therefore the particulars of offence accurately stated what [D] had done, namely that he procured [P] to commit the offence'. But if P believed V was consenting, V had not, as a matter of law, been raped. If X's bike is taken from the place he left it by Y who owns an exactly similar model and thinks this is his, X, who has lost his bike forever, reasonably believes it has been stolen, but he is wrong. Y has not committed theft. The court's distinguishing of *Walters v Lunt*[345] (trike not stolen goods because taken by a seven-year-old) was erroneous. If the hypothetical bike and trike were not stolen, and plainly they were not, V was not raped by P in *Cogan*. The court's opinion that D had procured not merely the actus reus but the offence of rape is wrong.

If a conviction is to be upheld in such a case, and policy and justice seem to require it,[346] this could be on the ground that it is an offence to procure the commission of an actus reus; and the courts took this step in *Millward*.[347] D instructed his employee, P, to drive on a road a vehicle which D knew, but P did not know, was in a dangerous condition. It was assumed that the actus reus of reckless driving was committed simply by the driving of the vehicle on the road. The condition of the vehicle resulted in a collision causing death. P was charged with causing death by reckless driving and D of abetting him. P was acquitted, D was convicted and his conviction upheld on the ground that he had procured the actus reus. This approach was advocated in the first seven editions of this book and it seems the best available to the courts; but there is force in the opinion of Kadish[348] that it 'at least technically... amounts to creating a new crime'. As there is no principal offender, there is no question of participation in the guilt of another or of 'secondary liability' and it becomes, in effect, a substantive offence to procure the commission of the actus reus of any crime.

Bourne, *Cogan and Leak* and *Millward* were all cases of alleged procuring and it is not certain whether the principle of *Millward* extends to other modes of secondary participation.

---

[344] [1976] QB 217, [1975] Crim LR 584 and commentary. Discussed in *Watkins* [2010] EWCA Crim 2349.

[345] [1951] 2 All ER 645, p 1035.

[346] The conduct may well be caught by the offences in the SCA 2007, ss 44–46.

[347] [1994] Crim LR 527. See RD Taylor, 'Complicity, Legal Scholarship and the Law of Unintended Consequences' (2009) 29 LS 1. In *DPP v K and B* [1997] 1 Cr App R 36, [1997] Crim LR 121, DC, some teenage girls procured a boy to 'rape' V. He may have been *doli incapax* (ie at that time incapable of committing the crime). They were held guilty of rape. It was said that it would have been different if the unidentified boy had been, or may have been, under ten because then there would have been no actus reus of rape. It is submitted that that is wrong. The actus reus was the voluntary penetration of the vagina by the penis, whatever the age of the boy.

[348] *Essays in Criminal Law*, 180.

Procuring is narrower than the other modes in that (a) it must be the cause of the conduct or circumstance element of the actus reus and, perhaps, (b) it must be the procurer's purpose to bring about the result—'To procure means to produce by endeavour'[349]—but that may be too restrictive. Bourne and Leak were endeavouring to bring about the whole actus reus; but Millward, while he was 'endeavouring' to have the dangerous vehicle driven on the road, which was assumed to amount to reckless driving, was certainly not endeavouring to have anyone killed. If the driver had been guilty of reckless driving, then both he and Millward would have been guilty of causing death by reckless driving; but it does not necessarily follow that Millward should be guilty of that offence when the driver is not guilty. If 'procure' does imply purpose and if the principle is limited to procuring, then he ought to have been convicted only of reckless driving and not of causing death. The cases may also be approached in terms of justification and excuse, although it is doubtful that this assists greatly—the principal offender in each case was acquitted on the basis of an excusing factor (duress or lack of mens rea), and according to the theory this does not preclude secondary liability.[350] It is unclear what impact *Jogee* will have on these cases. Are they an exception to the rule that D must intend P to act with mens rea, or does *Jogee* implicitly overturn them? It is submitted that the former is the preferable approach.

6.7.3.3 No actus reus by P

In *Morris v Tolman*,[351] D was charged with abetting the owner of a vehicle in using that vehicle for a purpose for which the vehicle had not been licensed. The statute (the Roads Act 1920) was so phrased that the offence could be committed only by the licence-holder. It was held that, there being no evidence that the licence-holder, P, had used the vehicle for a purpose other than that for which it was licensed, D must be acquitted. Though he, in fact, had so used the vehicle, that was not an actus reus. Again, in *Thornton v Mitchell*,[352] D, a bus conductor, negligently signalled to the driver of his bus, P, to reverse. Two pedestrians, whom it was not possible for the driver to see, were knocked down and one of them killed. The driver having been acquitted of careless driving, it was held that the conductor must be acquitted of abetting. Again, there was no actus reus. The driver's acquittal shows that he committed no actus reus, for careless driving is a crime which requires no mens rea beyond an intention to drive and D could not be said to have driven the bus. There would have been no such obstacle in the way of convicting D for manslaughter. That would, at that time, simply have raised the question whether D's negligence was sufficiently great.[353]

Thornton and Mitchell was distinguished in *Millward* on the ground that there was no actus reus of careless driving in the former case. And in *Loukes*[354] where the facts were similar to those in *Millward*, D's conviction for procuring the offence of causing death by *dangerous* driving was quashed. The actus reus of dangerous driving[355] is more precisely defined and a condition of the liability of the driver, P, in this situation is that 'it would be obvious to a competent and careful driver that driving the vehicle in its current state would be dangerous'. The judge directed an acquittal of the driver on the ground that there was no evidence that the dangerous condition of the vehicle would have been obvious to a competent and careful driver. The conviction of Loukes, who was responsible for the maintenance

---

[349] See p 190.

[350] See JC Smith, *Justification and Excuse*; G Williams, 'Theory of Excuses' [1982] Crim LR 722, especially 735–738; Taylor [1983] Crim LR 656.

[351] [1923] 1 KB 166.   [352] [1940] 1 All ER 339. See Taylor [1983] Crim LR 656, and (2009) 29 LS 1.

[353] See Ch 14.

[354] [1996] Crim LR 341. See commentary doubting whether there was an actus reus in *Millward*. And cf *Roberts and George* [1997] Crim LR 209.

[355] See Ch 32. It seems that there is no room for procuring the actus reus as distinct from the offence because there is no actus reus unless the fault element is present—ie the full offence is committed: *Roberts and George* [1997] Crim LR 209 and commentary.

of the vehicle, for procuring the commission of the offence, was quashed. There being no actus reus, he could not be held to have procured one.[356]

6.8 Withdrawal by a secondary party

Where D has counselled P to commit a crime, or is present, aiding P in the commission of it, it may still be possible for him to escape liability by withdrawal before P goes on to commit the crime.[357] An effective withdrawal will not, however, affect any liability he may have already incurred for conspiracy, or, if the withdrawal took place after P had done a more than merely preparatory act,[358] attempting to commit the crime.[359] It is important also to note that the Serious Crime Act offences in ss 44 to 46 allow for D to be prosecuted where he has done acts *capable of* assisting or encouraging P, irrespective of whether P commits any offence. Liability arises once D performs the acts capable of assisting or encouraging, irrespective of whether the acts do in fact assist or encourage. There is no withdrawal defence.

Although the principle that 'a person who unequivocally withdraws before the moment of the actual commission of the crime by the principal offender should not be liable for that crime',[360] is clear, it is less easy to identify not only what is meant by 'unequivocal withdrawal' but also on what basis the defence operates. It is unclear whether it is designed primarily to serve as an incentive to D to withdraw or to reflect his diminished degree of blameworthiness.[361]

There are at least three bases on which a withdrawal defence might be constructed.

(1) The defence operates only where D brings to an end the actus reus of assisting or encouraging P. On this interpretation the defence would be relatively narrowly constructed.

(2) The defence may operate because D's withdrawal negates his mens rea of intention to assist or encourage. Such an approach would create an extremely broad defence, potentially D's unannounced unilateral decision to take no part would suffice. That would seem unworkable. It also seems to be unprincipled. If D does acts assisting or encouraging with the requisite mens rea, his subsequent withdrawal cannot negate his mens rea in relation to his completed actus reus.

(3) It is possible to construe the defence as a 'true' defence operating despite the presence of D's continuing actus reus and mens rea as a secondary party.[362]

---

[356] In *Pickford* [1995] 1 Cr App R 420, 429–430 it was held that it was not an offence to aid and abet a boy under the age of 14 (at that time presumed to be incapable of sexual intercourse) to commit incest with his mother. The act would not be an actus reus.

[357] See A Reed, 'Repentance and Forgiveness: Withdrawal from Participation and the Proportionality Test' in A Reed and M Bohlander (eds), *Participation in Crime: Domestic and Comparative Perspectives* (2013); KJM Smith, 'Withdrawal and Complicity' [2001] Crim LR 769; D Lanham, 'Accomplices and Withdrawal' (1981) 97 LQR 575; Williams, TBCL, 310–311.

[358] See p 422.   [359] Withdrawal does not affect liability for an attempt; see p 434.

[360] *O'Flaherty* [2004] EWCA Crim 526, [2004] Crim LR 751; applied in *Mitchell* [2008] EWCA Crim 2552; *Campbell* [2009] EWCA Crim 50; and *Rajakumar* [2013] EWCA Crim 1512.

[361] For a comprehensive discussion of these approaches, see KJM Smith [2001] Crim LR 769.

[362] This is the approach favoured by Reed, see n 357. He argues that withdrawal is not predicated upon the neutralization of actus reus or mens rea, but rather is a true defence that represents D's reduced level of culpable dangerousness. Unlike other defences, Reed suggests that withdrawal does not fit into the excuse/justification dichotomy, but is more analogous to consent.

English law has yet to address these issues in detail and they were not considered by the Supreme Court in *Jogee*. The Law Commission identifies the basis of the defence as 'negating the effect of the assistance, encouragement or agreement'[363] with the ultimate decision whether D has so managed being one for the jury.[364]

6.8.1 An effective withdrawal?

For any withdrawal to be effective, it must be voluntary, real and effective and communicated in some form in good time.[365] If D is arrested, he can hardly be said to have 'withdrawn'. His arrest does not necessarily demonstrate any repentance on his part, nor undo any aid, advice or encouragement he may have already given.[366] Of course, it usually precludes any future secondary participation by him;[367] but in this section we are concerned with absolution from the potential liability arising from D's past acts. Withdrawal has no part to play if D denies that he was involved in the offence in any way.[368]

In addition to a general voluntary awareness on D's part, a clear precondition for the defence to operate is an unequivocal communication of withdrawal.[369] This can be communication to the principal offender, and if more than one to all principal offenders, or by communication with the law enforcement agency.[370]

Mere repentance, without any action, is not a sufficient or necessary condition for the defence.[371] D's 'innocent' state of mind at the time of the commission of the crime is no answer if he had mens rea when he did the act of counselling or aiding. English courts are generally reluctant to inquire into questions of motive. D may have seen the error of his ways, or he may be acting out of malice against his accomplices or because of fear of detection or because he has decided that the risks outweigh the possible rewards. It is submitted that it should make no difference. It has been recognized, for example, that if D neutralizes the effect of any assistance or encouragement he has given, he is not liable, even if he did not intend to neutralize its effect.[372]

6.8.1.1 Preventing or attempting to prevent the crime

To be effective must D's withdrawal involve his taking all reasonable steps to prevent the crime? It is submitted that this is not a necessary, although clearly it should be a *sufficient*, basis for the defence. Where D gives timely warning to the police, the effect ought in most cases to be that the crime will be prevented; but this may not always be so and, even where it is, there remains D's potential liability for abetting P's attempt, if P has gone beyond mere preparation. Surely, however, efforts to prevent the commission of the crime by informing the police ought to be an effective withdrawal, whether D has or has not attempted to persuade P to desist. Apart from being the best evidence of repentance, it is conduct which the law should and does encourage.[373]

---

[363] LC 305, para 3.60.   [364] ibid, para 3.65.   [365] *Otway* [2011] EWCA Crim 3.

[366] *Johnson and Jones* (1841) Car & M 218. *Jackson* (1673) 1 Hale PC 464 at 465 appears *contra* but is an obscure and unsatisfactory case. See Lanham (1981) 97 LQR 575 at 577.

[367] For an infamous example where it did not, see *Craig and Bentley* (1952) The Times, 10–13 Dec.

[368] *Gallant* [2008] EWCA Crim 111.   [369] *O' Flaherty* [2004] EWCA Crim 526.

[370] cf the Law Commission's view that D ought not to be automatically denied the defence if he has not informed all parties: LC 305, para 3.65.

[371] Hale, I PC, 618; Stephen, *Digest* (4th edn) art 42; Williams, CLGP, s 127; *Croft* [1944] 1 KB 295; *Becerra*, n 379.

[372] *Rook* [1993] 2 All ER at 963. See the discussion in LC 305, para 3.126.

[373] cf the large 'discounts' on sentence which may be earned for information given after D has become liable for and been convicted of the offence.

6.8.1.2 Withdrawal by cancelling assistance provided

The question of withdrawal is usually approached by ascertaining whether D has 'neutralized' any input his assistance or encouragement might have had irrespective of whether that will in fact prevent the crime being committed. However, this is a difficult test to apply.[374] For example, where D has supplied information it may be impossible in any meaningful sense to cancel the effect of that assistance by merely communicating withdrawal to P and suggesting that D will have no further part to play. In such cases, D's communicated countermand must go further if it is to be effective in neutralizing *the effect* of the assistance. It may be that D in such cases would be obliged to inform the police or do some act to prevent the crime, but the courts have not insisted on this.

Although no clear test has evolved, what seems to be involved in these cases is an unarticulated proportionality test, assessing the exculpatory conduct (what was done or said, to whom, at what stage of the criminal conduct), and the mode of D's participation in the contemplated offence (supply of weapons or advice, mere encouragement, presence at the crime, having been the instigator[375]). In *O'Flaherty*, the court suggested that in evaluating the effectiveness of the withdrawal, account will be taken of 'the nature of the assistance and encouragement already given and how imminent the [principal offence] is, as well as the nature of the action said to constitute the withdrawal'.[376] The court emphasized that it is not necessary for D to have taken reasonable steps to prevent the crime in order to have successfully withdrawn.

If D's assistance consisted only in advising or encouraging P to commit the crime, it may be enough for him to tell P to desist.[377] If P then commits the crime he does so against D's advice and without his encouragement. It may be that P would never have committed the crime if D had not put it into his head in the first place; but then D may be properly and adequately dealt with by conviction under ss 44 to 46 of the SCA 2007. If D has counselled more than one person, then it seems that he must communicate his countermand to all of those who perpetrate the offence, for otherwise his counselling remains operative.[378] To be effective, the communication must be such as 'will serve unequivocal notice upon the other party to the common unlawful cause that if he proceeds upon it he does so without the further aid and assistance of those who withdraw'.[379] The position might be different where D has supplied P with the means of committing the crime. Aid may be no less easily neutralized than advice.

In *Grundy*,[380] D had supplied P, a burglar, with information which was presumably valuable to P in committing the crime; but, for two weeks before P did so, D had been trying to stop him breaking in. It was held that there was evidence of an effective withdrawal which should have been left to the jury. In *Whitefield*,[381] there was evidence that D had served unequivocal notice on P that if he proceeded with the burglary they had planned together,

---

[374] The Supreme Court of Canada, by a majority, held in *Gauthier* [2013] SCC 32 that an effective withdrawal requires D, in a manner proportional to his participation in the commission of the planned offence, to take reasonable steps in the circumstances either to neutralize or otherwise cancel out the effects of his participation or to prevent the commission of the offence. Dissenting, Fish J held that Canadian law had never required D to have taken steps to neutralize his participation and that such steps would strengthen the defence, but that they were not necessary.

[375] *Mitchell* [2008] EWCA Crim 2552 (D started fight, paused for short period while some others fetched weapons including a mace, and violence recommenced with D present. V killed. D guilty of murder).

[376] [2004] EWCA Crim 526, [60].   [377] *Saunders and Archer* (1573) 2 Plowd 473.

[378] *State v Kinchen* (1910) 52 So 185, quoted by Lanham, n 357.

[379] *Whitehouse* [1941] 1 WWR 112, per Sloan JA (Court of Appeal of British Columbia) approved in *Becerra* (1975) 62 Cr App R 212, CA. Cf *Fletcher* [1962] Crim LR 551; *Grundy* [1977] Crim LR 543, CA.

[380] [1977] Crim LR 543.   [381] (1984) 79 Cr App R 36.

he would do so without D's aid or assistance. The jury should have been told that if they accepted the evidence, that was a defence. D would now be liable for an offence under ss 44 to 46 of the SCA 2007.

If a rejected countermand may be an effective withdrawal, as in *Grundy*, it is arguable that an attempt to countermand should be the same. D has done all in his power to communicate his countermand to P but failed. In all these cases, the countermand has, *ex hypothesi*, failed; and, if the question is whether D has done his best to neutralize his input, the answer does not depend on the reasons for the failure.[382] It could be argued that where D has failed to communicate, he can escape only by going to the police; but this was not insisted on in *Grundy* when persuasion failed. This suggests that the basis for the defence lies not in neutralizing the actus reus of assisting so far performed by D, but on some broader principle operating to exculpate D despite his continuing actus reus.

An effective withdrawal may often be made more easily at the preparatory stage than where the crime is in the course of commission. Thus, in *Beccara* where D handed P a knife so that he could use it on anyone interfering in a burglary, D did not make a sufficient communication of withdrawal when, on the appearance of V, he said 'Come on, let's go', and got out through a window. Something 'vastly different and vastly more effective' was required and, possibly, nothing less than physical intervention to stop P committing the crime would be required.[383] In that case, the 'withdrawal' occurred at a very late stage. When the knife is about to descend, the only effective withdrawal may be physical intervention to prevent it reaching its target. This reasoning has been echoed in numerous cases.[384]

6.8.1.3 Spontaneous violence

In all the cases discussed above the offence was pre-planned. It was held in *Mitchell and King* that cases of spontaneous violence are different.[385] On this view, if A and B spontaneously attack V, they are aiding and abetting one another, so long as each is aware that he is being assisted and encouraged by the other; but, if B simply withdraws, his participation in the offence apparently ceases without the need for any express communication to A, so that he will not be liable for acts done by A thereafter. This was reiterated in *Rajakumar*[386] in which Davis LJ stated that:

Classically, as the authorities make clear, issues of withdrawal are a matter of fact and degree (and the authorities also make clear there can be some quite tight requirements if withdrawal is to be satisfied—albeit the burden of proving continuation of participation, and lack of withdrawal, remains on the Crown). Moreover, what may suffice to constitute withdrawal in spontaneous and unplanned group violence may not necessarily so suffice in pre-planned group violence.

The appropriateness of this test depends on which basis the defence rests. If it is regarded as a defence which operates by D neutralizing his actus reus, it can be seriously doubted: if P was encouraged by D's participation and was unaware that D had withdrawn, P continues to be encouraged. There is still an effective actus reus. As noted earlier, there are cases in which the defence has been successful where D has failed to neutralize the effect of his acts of assistance.

In the case of *Robinson*,[387] the Court of Appeal explained *Mitchell and King* as an exceptional case. Referring to the criticisms outlined earlier, the court stated that:

---

382 Lanham, n 357.   383 *Becerra*, n 379. Cf *Baker* [1994] Crim LR 444.

384 See *Campbell* [2009] EWCA Crim 50; *Mitchell* [2008] EWCA Crim 2552.

385 *Mitchell and King* (1998) 163 JP 75, [1999] Crim LR 496, DC. Reed is extremely critical of this distinction, characterizing it as 'nebulous'. See n 362.

386 [2013] EWCA Crim 1512, [42].

387 [2000] 5 Arch News 2, CA. See also *Mitchell* [2008] EWCA Crim 2552.

it can only be in exceptional circumstances that a person can withdraw from a crime he has initiated. Similarly in those rare circumstances communication of withdrawal must be given in order to give the principal offenders the opportunity to desist rather than complete the crime. This must be so even in situations of spontaneous violence unless it is not practicable or reasonable so to communicate as in the exceptional circumstances pertaining in *Mitchell* where the accused threw down his weapon and moved away before the final and fatal blows were inflicted.

More recently, however, in *O'Flaherty*, the court again followed the distinction between 'planned' and 'spontaneous' violence drawn in *Mitchell and King*. The Court of Appeal concluded that 'in a case of spontaneous violence such as this where there has been no prior agreement, the jury will usually have to make inferences as to the scope of the joint enterprise from the knowledge and actions of individual participants'.[388] The courts seem to avoid a more precise definition, favouring regarding the matter as one of fact and degree to be left to the jury.

The ambiguity surrounding the availability of the defence and its elements renders it all too easy for the courts to apply it in a confusing fashion. A good illustration of the confusion is the case of *Rafferty*.[389] D and his co-defendants, P1 and P2, attacked V. D punched V twice. He then left the scene with V's cash card heading for an ATM. Meanwhile, P1 and P2 continued the attack on V escalating the violence by kicking him in the head and, finally, drowning him in the sea. D returned to find V dead. The trial judge left to the jury the question whether D had withdrawn from the enterprise (and, if so, whether he was then liable for causing the death as a principal). The Court of Appeal concluded, rightly it is submitted, that D could not be guilty as a principal—he was not a cause of death. Nor, applying the joint enterprise doctrine then in place, was D necessarily a secondary party: the acts of P1 and P2 could have constituted what was then a 'fundamentally different act' and could now, post-*Jogee*, be seen as an overwhelming supervening event. It is submitted that there was no issue of withdrawal.

6.9 Victims as parties to crime

It has been noted[390] that when a statute creates a crime it does not generally provide that it shall be an offence to aid, abet, counsel or procure it. Such a provision is unnecessary, for it follows by implication of law. There is, however, one exception to this rule. Where the statute is designed for the protection of a certain class of persons it may be construed as excluding by implication the liability of any member of that class who is the victim of the offence, even though that member does in fact aid, abet, counsel or procure the offence.[391]

In *Tyrrell*,[392] D, a girl between the ages of 13 and 16, abetted P to have unlawful sexual intercourse with her. This was an offence by P under s 5 of the Criminal Law Amendment Act 1885.[393] It was held, however, that D could not be convicted of abetting because the Act 'was passed for the purpose of protecting women and girls against themselves'.[394] In

---

[388] [2004] EWCA Crim 526, [65].   [389] [2007] EWCA Crim 1846.   [390] See p 178.

[391] See LC 305, para 5.24. See also: B Hogan, 'Victims as Parties to Crime' [1962] Crim LR 683; G Williams, 'Victims as Parties to Crimes—A Further Comment' [1964] Crim LR 686; G Williams, 'Victims and Other Exempt Parties in Crime' (1990) 10 LS 245; Criminal Law Revision Committee, Fifteenth Report, *Sexual Offences* (1984) Cmnd 9213, Appendix B.

[392] [1894] 1 QB 710.   [393] See now Sexual Offences Act 2003, s 9; see p 805.

[394] Per Lord Coleridge CJ at 712. Both the Chief Justice and Mathew J pointed out that there was nothing in the Act to say that the girl should be guilty of aiding and abetting; but, it is submitted, no importance could be attached to that, for statutes hardly ever do.

Pickford,[395] the court held (though it was probably not necessary for the decision) that *Tyrrell* was applicable to the case of a woman committing incest with her 13-year-old son, but it is not obvious that s 11 of the Sexual Offences Act 1956 (which made it an offence for the woman to permit 'her grandfather, father, brother or son' to have intercourse with her) was intended for the protection of anyone. Under the Sexual Offences Act 2003, there is nothing to prevent the boy being treated as a principal offender.

It has been held that a woman who is not pregnant can be convicted of abetting the use upon herself by another of an instrument with intent to procure her miscarriage, although the clear implication of the statute[396] is that such a woman cannot be convicted of *using* an instrument on herself with that intent.[397] However, a pregnant woman can be convicted (under the same section) of using an instrument on herself so it cannot be argued that this section was passed for the protection of *women* and it would be curious that Parliament should have intended to protect non-pregnant women from themselves, but not pregnant women. How far the rule in *Tyrrell* extends has not been settled. The court referred to 'women' as well as girls and it may well be that it extends to the offences of procuration of women to be prostitutes and of brothel-keeping which were in the 1885 Act and then in the Sexual Offences Act 1956.[398] It was held that it applied to the prostitute who abets a man who is living off her earnings.[399]

In all these cases, it seems clear that the protection of the law extended only to a person of the class who is a *victim*. Thus, a child under 16 could be convicted of abetting P in having intercourse with another child under 16; a boy under 14 could be convicted, even before the Sexual Offences Act 1993, of abetting P in intercourse with another boy under 14; a prostitute could abet P in keeping a brothel in which she was not a participant, or of living on the earnings of another prostitute. There are many instances other than sexual offences where laws are passed for the protection of a particular class of persons.

The Supreme Court stated in *Gnango*[400] that the principle should only apply if the offence is one that is intended to protect a specified class. This means, for example, that it does not apply to murder or offences against the person. By way of example, Lord Phillips suggested that the sadomasochists in *Brown*[401] would not only be guilty of GBH for inflicting that harm on each other, but could also be guilty of aiding and abetting the infliction of those injuries upon themselves.[402]

The Law Commission propose to preserve the *Tyrell* principle. There will be no liability where the principal offence is for the protection of a particular category of persons and both (a) D falls within that category and (b) he is the victim.[403]

---

[395] [1995] 1 Cr App R 420, 428.   [396] OAPA 1861, s 58; see Ch 15.

[397] *Sockett* (1908) 72 JP 428; see p 646.

[398] Sections 22–24, 28 and 29. Repealed, see now Sexual Offences Act 2003, ss 52–55.

[399] *Congdon* [1990] NLJR 1221 (Judge Addison); Hogan [1962] Crim LR 683 at 692–693; Williams (1990) 10 LS 245 at 248–249. The offence is repealed by the Sexual Offences Act 2003, under which children are a protected class, but liable to conviction for participating in the sexual activity. *Tyrell* seems to be largely ignored in the 2003 Act. See the article developing this point and cataloguing the instances in which the Act deviates from the principle: M Bohlander, 'The Sexual Offences Act 2003—The *Tyrrell* Principle—Criminalising the Victims' [2005] Crim LR 701.

[400] [2011] UKSC 59, [44]–[53].   [401] [1994] 1 AC 212. See Ch 16.

[402] For criticism, see J Herring, 'Victims as Defendants: When Victims Participate in Crimes Against Themselves' in A Reed and M Bohlander (eds), *Participation in Crime: Domestic and Comparative Perspectives* (2013).

[403] LC 305, cl 16 of the Draft Bill.

6.10 Instigation for the purpose of entrapment

Police or other law enforcement officers or their agents sometimes do acts for the purpose of entrapping, or getting evidence against offenders, which would certainly amount to counselling or abetting an offence if they were not done for that purpose.[404] The difficult question is how far an officer may go without himself incurring liability for the offence. Law enforcement officers have no general licence to aid and abet crime.

Two separate questions are involved: (a) in what circumstances will the law enforcement agency official have committed a crime by his encouragement and (b) in what circumstances will the person encouraged by the officer be entitled to rely on such entrapment to excuse his conduct? We are concerned here only with the first of those questions, the second being a matter only of a procedural defence in terms of stay of proceedings.[405]

It should be noted that where charges are brought in these circumstances for offences under ss 44 to 46 of the SCA 2007, a defence is available under s 50 where D proves (a) that he knew[406] certain circumstances existed; and (b) that it was reasonable for him to act as he did in those circumstances.

6.10.1 Secondary liability for the agent provocateur

As long ago as 1929, the Royal Commission on Police Powers stated:[407]

As a general rule, the police should observe only, without participating in an offence, except in cases where an offence is habitually committed in circumstances in which observation by a third party is *ex hypothesi* impossible. Where participation is essential it should only be resorted to on the express and written authority of the Chief Constable.

In *Sang*,[408] Lord Salmon said:

I would now refer to what is, I believe and hope, the unusual case, in which a dishonest policeman, anxious to improve his detection record, tries very hard with the help of an agent provocateur to induce a young man with no criminal record to commit a serious crime; and ultimately the young man reluctantly succumbs to the inducement...The policeman and the informer who had acted together in inciting him to commit the crime should...both be prosecuted and suitably punished.

It is not clear that the word 'dishonest' adds anything to the postulated facts and it should make no difference that the policeman's motive is hatred of crime. It can hardly be necessary that the person induced to act should be 'young'; and it might be even more serious to induce a person with a bad record who was 'going straight', for the consequences for him would be worse. These matters go to sentence, not liability.

The essence of the *dictum* seems to be that a person who would not otherwise have committed a particular crime is induced to do so,[409] and the House of Lords in *Looseley* confirmed that this is the essential basis of the concept of entrapment in English law:

Whether the police conduct preceding the commission of the offence was no more than might be expected from others in the circumstances?[410]

---

404 Williams, CLGP, s 256.

405 See, generally, the decision of the House of Lords in *Looseley* [2001] UKHL 53, [2002] 1 Cr App R 360 and *Moore* [2013] EWCA Crim 85. A Ashworth, 'Redrawing the Boundaries of Entrapment' [2002] Crim LR 161; D Ormerod and A Roberts, 'The Trouble with *Teixeira*: Developing a Principled Approach to Entrapment' (2002) Int J E & P 38; A Ashworth, 'Testing Fidelity to Legal Values: Official Involvement in Criminal Justice' (2000) 63 MLR 633, 642–652.

406 Note that it is not enough that D believed they existed.   407 (1929) Cmd 3297, 116.

408 (1979) 69 Cr App R 282 at 296.   409 cf *Birtles* [1969] 1 WLR 1047.

410 Lord Nicholls, [23].

An officer who agrees, and intends, to participate in such an offence is guilty of conspiracy.[411] Merely to provide the opportunity for and temptation to commit an offence will be lawful,[412] as is participation in an offence which has already been 'laid on' and is going to be committed in any event, in order to trap the offenders.[413] In such a case it makes no difference that the police intervention may have affected the time or other circumstances of the commission of the offence.[414]

Where there is a continuing general conspiracy—for example, to supply drugs to anyone asking for them—it seems that a law enforcement officer commits no offence by inducing the general conspirators to enter into a particular conspiracy within the ambit of the general conspiracy, for example to supply him with specified drugs.

It cannot be the law that the police may properly participate in a crime to the point at which irreparable damage is done. A policeman who assists P to commit murder in order to entrap him must be guilty of murder. It is submitted that the same must be true of any injury to the person, unless it is trivial and V consents to it; and probably to any damage to property, unless the owner consents.

The Law Commission propose a new defence where D shows (on the balance of probabilities) that he was acting in order to prevent the commission of an offence or occurrence of harm and it was reasonable to act as he did.[415]

6.11 Reform of secondary liability

The recommendations in Law Commission Report No 305 would, if implemented, transform the scope of accessorial liability. Taken together with Part 2 of the SCA 2007, there will, in effect, be eight types of liability for conduct that assists or encourages crime or is capable of doing so. Only a very short overview can be offered here. The likelihood of them being enacted is very low particularly since the decision in *Jogee* has sought to deal with one of the most troubling issues—that of joint enterprise.

(1) First, D may be liable for an inchoate offence where he intentionally does acts capable of assisting or encouraging the commission of a crime by P. D must believe or be reckless as to whether P will act with the mens rea of the offence and D must intend or believe that any relevant consequences or circumstances of P's offence will be satisfied (SCA 2007, s 44). This offence can be charged whether or not P commits the full offence.

(2) Second, D may be liable for an inchoate offence where he does acts capable of assisting or encouraging the commission of a crime by P, and believes that the conduct element of the actus reus of the crime will be committed by P, believing or being reckless as to whether P will have the mens rea for the offence, and believing or being reckless as to whether any relevant consequences or circumstances of P's offence will be satisfied (SCA 2007, s 45). The offence can be charged whether or not P commits the full offence.

---

[411] *Yip Chiu-Cheung v R*, see p 459. See the Law Commission proposals on Conspiracy discussed at p 673.

[412] *Williams v DPP* (1993) 98 Cr App R 209, DC where the 'bait' was cartons of cigarettes left in a vulnerable position. The court said that the police had not aided, abetted, etc: but had they not procured the commission of the offence? They would have regarded the operation as a failure if no one had stolen the cartons.

[413] *McCann* (1971) 56 Cr App R 359.   [414] *McEvilly* (1973) 60 Cr App R 150.

[415] cf s 50 of the SCA 2007, discussed at p 483 in which Parliament corrupted the Law Commission's similar proposals in relation to incitement.

(3) Third, D may be liable for an inchoate offence where he does acts capable of assisting or encouraging the commission of one of a number of specified crimes by P, and believes that one of those crimes will be committed by P, believing or being reckless as to whether P will possess any mens rea required for one of the offences, and believing or being reckless as to whether any relevant consequences or circumstances of one of those offences will be satisfied (SCA 2007, s 46). This offence can be charged whether or not P commits the full offence.

In each of these offences under the SCA 2007, liability is inchoate. It is arguable that the scope of criminal liability has extended too far by allowing for conviction and sentence for serious offences where D's conduct is so remote from the harm of the full offence—P need not even have attempted the principal crime.

(4) Fourth,[416] D may be liable as an accessory[417] if D's conduct assists or encourages P in fact, whether directly or not, and whether the assistance or encouragement is substantial or not. The assistance or encouragement may be by acts (words or conduct), or omission if D is under a relevant duty (eg by contract or relationship), but not by failure to control P where D has a specific entitlement to do so. D must have a direct or oblique intent[418] that P commit the conduct element of the offence. This mens rea element is central to the Commission's proposals reflecting the need for parity of culpability between D and P[419] if D is to be prosecuted, labelled and sentenced in the same manner as P. It is not necessary that D intends P to commit the full offence. D must believe that the circumstances and consequences of P's offence will be satisfied, *or* D must himself have the mens rea for the full offence of which P commits the conduct element.[420]

(5) Fifth, D will be liable for a joint venture[421] where he agrees with P to commit an offence or shares a common intention with P and D intended (directly or obliquely) that P or another party to the venture should commit the conduct element of the principal offence or believed that P or another would or might commit the conduct element of the offence. D would not be liable if P's act is outside the scope[422] of the joint venture.[423] This would take the law back to the approach before *Jogee* in most respects.

It is significant that these fourth and fifth forms of liability replace aiding and abetting, counselling and procuring. They are considerably narrower than the present secondary liability presumably because there is no need to extend liability in view of the offences under ss 44 to 46 of the SCA 2007.

(6) Sixth, in the case of homicide,[424] a joint venture will be caught by the fifth category— D will be liable for murder[425] if D intended to assist or encourage P to commit the relevant offence or D engaged in a joint criminal venture with P and realized that P or another party to the venture might commit the relevant offence. D would be liable for

---

[416] LC 305, Part III, especially at paras 3.15 et seq.   [417] Neither term is defined.

[418] LC 305, para 3.88. Cf Wilson arguing that it should be purposive intent—[2008] Crim LR 16.

[419] LC 305, para 3.80.   [420] ibid, para 3.109.   [421] Which is undefined.

[422] Not defined.

[423] For criticism, see Sullivan [2008] Crim LR 19, commenting on the absence of definition, heavy reliance on the existing law and the undue complexity resulting, and Buxton [2009] Crim LR 230, n 14 who regards them as 'unreasonably and unnecessarily' extending the scope of criminal liability and being 'very burdensome' to apply, at 243.

[424] Special proposals for joint venture were made in LC 304, *Murder, Manslaughter and Infanticide* (2006) Part 4.

[425] As defined in the LC Report, see Ch 12.

manslaughter if D and P were parties to a joint venture, P committed murder in relation to the fulfilment of that venture and D intended or foresaw that non-serious harm
or the fear of harm might be caused by a party to the venture and a reasonable person
in D's position and with D's knowledge of the relevant facts would have foreseen an
obvious risk of death or serious injury being caused by a party to the venture.[426] Again
this would take the law back to the position before *Jogee*.

(7) Seventh, D may be liable under a new statutory form of innocent agency.[427] D will be
liable if he intentionally caused P to commit the conduct element of the offence, but,
although P does commit the conduct element, P is not guilty of the full offence because
he is under ten, insane or lacks mens rea.[428] D must also be proved to have the mens
rea element of the offence he intended to cause. In the case of strict liability offences,
D must know or believe that P would commit the offence (which he would even if he
lacked mens rea) in the circumstances and with the consequences it requires.[429] The
new offence will extend to cases where the offence committed by P is only capable of
being committed by a person of a particular description (eg a licensee), even if D is not
such a person. There is no requirement that D needs to believe that the full offence will
be committed or that it will be committed by P himself.[430]

(8) Eighth, D may be liable where he intentionally causes a 'no fault' offence[431] to be committed by P and D knew or believed that his conduct would cause the offence to be
committed.[432] It will be sufficient that D causes the circumstances of the no fault
offence to be committed, for example with drink-driving, it is enough that D laces P's
drinks causing the circumstance element (that P is over the limit) without causing the
conduct element (the driving of a motor vehicle).

The Law Commission also propose to preserve the *Tyrell* principle, and create a defence for
those acting in order to prevent the commission of an offence or occurrence of harm where
it was reasonable to act in that way.

The Law Commission's proposals for secondary liability as set out in its Report No 305[433]
were designed to represent a coherent scheme complementing the inchoate offences recommended by the Commission in Report No 300. However, the coherence has been lost. First,
Parliament enacted the inchoate liability provisions in the SCA 2007, but in doing so made
fundamental changes to the scope of those provisions. Secondly, although the SCA 2007 is
in force, the proposals in relation to secondary liability are not likely to be enacted. Finally,
and more worryingly, the government's amendment of the scheme for incitement proposed
in Report No 300 and enacted in the SCA 2007 led to wider offences and a change to the
scope of the defences available. To maintain coherence, it seems that the Law Commission
proposals on secondary parties will have to be similarly expanded. The logical conclusion is
that in its future proposals in this area the Commission is now forced to offer wider offences
to maintain consistency and coherence with the SCA 2007 provisions.[434]

---

[426] The proposal was supported by the government in its paper *Murder, Manslaughter and Infanticide*
(2008), 19/08 at paras 89–90. The proposals were not taken forward into the Coroners and Justice Act 2009.

[427] See LC 305, Part IV.

[428] It is not enough that P was under duress, etc.

[429] D aged ten tells P aged nine to have sex with V aged nine. D must know or believe that V will be under 13
(circumstances as to age being strict under s 5 of the Sexual Offences Act 2003).

[430] For critical comment, see RD Taylor [2008] Crim LR 19.

[431] ie a strict liability offence—where no proof of mens rea is required as to one or more elements of the
actus reus.

[432] LC 305, para 4.31.

[433] (2007) on which see Wilson [2008] Crim LR 3; Taylor [2008] Crim LR 32; Sullivan [2008] Crim LR 19;
J Horder, 'Joint Criminal Ventures and Murder' in J Horder, *Homicide and the Politics of Law Reform* (2012).

[434] See the proposals on conspiracy and attempts discussed in Ch 11.

21

Making off without payment

21.1 Making off under the Theft Act 1978

By s 3[1] of the Theft Act 1978 as amended:

(1) Subject to subsection (3) below, a person who, knowing that payment on the spot for any goods supplied or service done is required or expected from him, dishonestly makes off without having paid as required or expected and with intent to avoid payment of the amount due shall be guilty of an offence.

(2) For purposes of this section 'payment on the spot' includes payment at the time of collecting goods on which work has been done or in respect of which service has been provided.

(3) Subsection (1) above shall not apply where the supply of the goods or the doing of the service is contrary to law, or where the service done is such that payment is not legally enforceable.[2]

By s 4 the offence, which is triable either way, is punishable on summary conviction by imprisonment and/or an unlimited fine, and on indictment by imprisonment for a term not exceeding two years and/or a fine.

This offence aims to deal in a simple and straightforward way with a person who having consumed a meal in a restaurant, or filled the tank of the car with petrol, or reached their destination in a taxi, leaves without paying. Such cases were known as bilking. Although factually simple, difficulties arise in prosecuting such cases as theft.[3] There are no such difficulties under s 3. Under s 3, there is no requirement that D's conduct amounts to theft or fraud or that he has practised any deception at all. There is no requirement to prove that D was dishonest when he ordered the meal or began to fill his car; it is sufficient if the dishonesty occurs at the point of making off.

The offence may have been rendered redundant in many situations by the Fraud Act 2006. Before that Act, the old deception offences applied and D could only be liable for one of those if his deception occurred *before* the relevant property passed to him (or the service was provided etc depending on which type of deception offence was charged). In contrast, under s 2 of the Fraud Act 2006, D may be liable even if he makes a false representation *after* the entire proprietary interest has passed to him, provided that there is an intention to make

---

[1] See generally Ormerod and Williams, *Smith's Law of Theft*, Ch 6; Griew, *Theft*, Ch 13; Smith, *Property Offences*, Ch 20; J Spencer, 'The Theft Act 1978' [1979] Crim LR 24, 35; G Syrota, 'Annotations to Theft Act 1978' in *Current Law Statutes* 1978 and 'The Theft Act 1978' (1979) 42 MLR 301, 304.

[2] Section 3(4) was repealed by the Serious Organised Crime and Police Act 2005, Sch 17, Part 2, para 1.

[3] See eg *DPP v Ray* [1974] AC 370, [1973] 3 All ER 131, HL, p 944; *Edwards v Ddin* [1976] 3 All ER 705, [1976] 1 WLR 942.

a gain or cause a loss thereby. It follows that if, after D has transferred fuel to the tank in his vehicle and the entire proprietary interest in the fuel has passed to him, he then falsely represents to V (the cashier) that it will be paid for by D's firm, D commits fraud under s 2.[4] A prosecution under s 3 of the 1978 Act may nevertheless be preferable because it describes precisely what D did, and it does not involve proof of a false representation. Moreover, in some cases s 3 of the 1978 Act will be the necessary charge because the fraud offence is limited to cases of intending to gain or cause loss in terms of *property*.[5]

The s 3 offence creates an exception to the general principle that it is not an offence dishonestly to avoid the payment of a debt.[6] This might be thought to pose a potential problem of over-criminalizing[7] and has predictably generated academic interest. Green suggests that there are two ways of reconciling the making off offence with the general principle that it is not an offence to avoid payment of a debt. The first is to presume that D never intended to pay for the goods or services in question. The second approach is the one adopted in *DPP v Ray*,[8] namely that D *at some point* formed the intention never to pay for the goods or services. Green rejects these two theories as being artificial and concludes that the making off offence represents a compromise. The individual who falsely represents that he intends to pay is treated less harshly than he ought to be (had he been charged with fraud), while the individual who only formed the intention never to pay at some later point is treated more harshly than he deserves. It is the difficulty of recognizing which category a given case falls into that explains the existence of the offence.

In practical terms, the offence creates a desirable exception to the general principle. A dishonest debtor who can be traced can be coerced into payment via civil remedies without resort to criminal sanctions. In contrast, where someone makes off from the point of payment the person becomes difficult, if not impossible, to trace. Enforcement can usually only occur on the spot.[9]

21.1.1 Actus reus

21.1.1.1 Makes off

The term 'makes off' might be thought to have a pejorative connotation implying some requirement of stealth in the manner of the making off. Certainly, the offence extends to such cases (the diner who waits until the manager leaves the room or exits via the cloakroom window) but it cannot be confined to such cases. A diner who brazenly walks out of the restaurant after finishing his pudding is properly said to make off though his act is done openly and without stealth; so, too, a heavyweight boxer whose departure cannot be prevented by a timorous restaurant owner.[10]

'Makes off' appears to mean simply that D leaves one place (the place where the payment is required) for another place. The offence does not necessarily require that D should have 'made off' from V's premises. The spot from which D makes off is simply the place where

---

[4] cf under the old law *Collis-Smith* [1971] Crim LR 716, CA.   [5] See p 933.

[6] See further GH Treitel, 'Contract and Crime' in *Crime, Proof and Punishment*, 89.

[7] See Green, *13 Ways*, 89–90. One could also plausibly argue that the offence is not a compromise but simply reflects the fact that English law does not recognize the moral distinction between D who never intended to pay and D who only formed the intention later on.

[8] [1974] AC 370.

[9] Hence originally by s 3(4) a power of arrest was conferred which was necessary since the offence carries only a maximum two-year sentence and was not, before the Serious Organised Crime and Police Act 2005, automatically arrestable.

[10] See F Bennion, 'Letter to the Editor' [1980] Crim LR 670.

payment is required[11] and this may be a news vendor's stand or an ice-cream van on the highway. In the case of a taxi ride, it will be the agreed destination.[12] If D has not left the first place he has not made off, but if he is in the process of leaving there may be an attempt.[13] Presumably, this element of the actus reus continues for such time as D can be said to be in the process of 'making off'.[14]

If D leaves with V's consent it may be more difficult to say that D has made off. Suppose that D, having determined never to pay, gives his correct name and address to V and is allowed to go. It would be a strained reading of the section to say that D had made off; D has left without paying but the offence requires something more than that. A more difficult case is that where E, who also intends never to pay, gives a false name and address to V and is allowed to go. The two cases differ in that D can be traced and coerced into payment under the civil law while E cannot be traced at all. Spencer[15] argues that the difference between these cases is material. The mischief aimed at by this section, he argues, is the bilking customer who cannot be traced.[16]

Spencer's argument that the applicability of the offence turns on the traceability of the bilker has force, but is not easy to square with the language of s 3. It can lead to some illogical results. For example, assume that F is V's best customer of many years' standing. One day F determines not to pay and decamps from the premises via the toilet window. All the elements of the offence appear to be present unless it is to be said that F did not make off. It may puzzle us all to wonder why F should have thought that he could get away with his conduct but he seems clearly to have made off even though he is clearly traceable by the owner and he knows that at the time of leaving. A customer using a wheelchair would surely make off if he decamps without paying though he does not at all fancy his chances of outpacing the restaurateur.[17] If the untraceability of D was the touchstone of the offence, it is arguable that the offence would then fail to protect the proprietor (eg the restaurant owner) who knows who D is, but is unlikely to pursue D's small debt via the civil courts.[18] The CLRC[19] certainly regarded the purpose of the offence as to protect legitimate business.

Section 3 does not, on a natural interpretation, mean that D does not make off if he gives a correct identification but E does make off if he gives a false one. Suppose in the latter case that V orders a taxi for E and bids him a cheery farewell from the hotel lobby. Can it really be said that E has made off?[20]

---

[11] Payment may be legitimately required at more than one spot: *Moberly v Allsop* [1992] COD 190, 156 JP 514, DC. See also *Aziz* [1993] Crim LR 708.

[12] Although not necessarily at the moment the taxi arrives at its destination. If V, the taxi driver, permits D to leave the taxi with the purpose of getting money to pay the fare, the time at which payment is expected will be deferred. See *Morris* [2013] EWCA Crim, [2013] Crim LR 995. The *ex turpi causa* doctrine prevents the bilker recovering damages where the cab driver injures him in attempts to prevent the making off: *Beaumont v Ferrer* [2016] EWCA Civ 768 (those engaged in the commission of a crime should not be able to recover for the consequences of their criminal conduct).

[13] *Brooks and Brooks* (1982) 76 Cr App R 66, [1983] Crim LR 188, CA; making off, said the court, 'may be an exercise accompanied by the sound of trumpets or a silent stealing away after the folding of tents'.

[14] This was important for determining the lawfulness of arrests: *Drameh* [1983] Crim LR 322.

[15] [1983] Crim LR 573.

[16] He supported this argument by the fact that, as originally enacted, V had a power of arrest; it would be highly undesirable if V could arrest a customer of whose identity he is aware, that power being required for the unidentifiable bilker.

[17] For further views on this difficult aspect of the offence, see Williams, TBCL, 878; F Bennion, Letter, 'The Drafting of Section 3 of the Theft Act 1978' [1980] Crim LR 670 and Letters [1983] Crim LR 205, 574; Griew, *Theft*, paras 13–16.

[18] See Griew, paras 13–16.   [19] Thirteenth Report (1977) Cmnd 6733, para 19.

[20] cf *Hammond* [1982] Crim LR 611, n 32.

If, however, V permits D to leave the spot where payment is required for a purely temporary purpose (eg to answer a telephone call or to collect his wallet from his overcoat which he has deposited in the cloakroom) expecting him to return to settle up, it is submitted that D commits the offence if he then decamps. In such cases V has not consented to D leaving without paying; quite the contrary, in the latter example he has consented to D taking steps to facilitate payment. So where V, a taxi driver, permits D to leave so that D, as he claims, may go into his house to get the fare it would appear that D, if he then runs off, has made off within the meaning of this section.[21]

21.1.1.2 Goods supplied or service done

The offence requires that the goods[22] be *supplied* or that a service be *done*. Most obviously, goods are supplied where V delivers them to D but the offence cannot be limited only to cases of delivery by V. Petrol is clearly supplied to D at a self-service filling station though D supplies himself and, similarly, goods taken by D from the shelves in a supermarket are supplied.[23] 'Supplied' in this context suggests goods proffered by V and accordingly taken by D. Hence, it would not be an offence under this section, though it may be theft, for D to take goods in a shop which is not self-service; such goods are not proffered until tendered by V or his assistant. It is submitted that goods may be supplied for the purpose of s 3 even though D has a dishonest intent from the outset and therefore steals the goods. It can hardly have been intended that theft and making off should be mutually exclusive since the effect of that would create difficulties for prosecutors.

Where 'service' is concerned, the service must be 'done'. An obvious example of a service done is the provision of hotel accommodation, or a meal in a restaurant, but it will also apply to the collection of goods, such as clothes, shoes or cars, on which work (repair, etc) has been done. A service may be done (as goods may be supplied) though nothing is physically done by V other than proffering the service of which D takes advantage, as where D is permitted to park his car on V's parking lot.

There is no definition of 'service' in s 3. 'Service' is not the same as the extended meaning of 'services' which was contained in s 1 of the 1978 Act.[24]

21.1.1.3 Unenforceable debts

The offence under s 3, unlike the repealed offence under s 1 of the 1978 Act, cannot be committed where the supply of the goods or the doing of the service is contrary to law; or where the service done is such that payment is not legally enforceable.[25] Thus, it is no offence for D to make off from a brothel without paying.

Whether a supply of goods or services is contrary to law or whether payment for a service is not legally enforceable involves a consideration of the general law of contract and cannot be detailed here.[26] But the distinction that s 3 makes may be illustrated by reference

---

[21] This approach was approved in *Morris* [2013] EWCA Crim 436, [2013] Crim LR 995. The court may have gone further by stating that D simply failing to return is sufficient.

[22] As defined in s 34 of the 1968 Act, applicable to the 1978 Act by s 5(2).

[23] *Contra* ATH Smith, 'Shoplifting and the Theft Acts' [1981] Crim LR 586. Cf Griew, *Theft*, para 13.07; Ormerod and Williams, *Smith's Law of Theft*, para 6.12.

[24] See on that *Sofroniou* [2003] EWCA Crim 3681, and p 773 in the 11th edition of this work. Section 1 was repealed by the Fraud Act 2006.

[25] The reason for the distinction is that while the aim of s 1 was to punish fraud, the aim of s 3 is to protect legitimate business.

[26] For a general review of the relationship and consideration of s 3, see Treitel, 'Contract and Crime' in *Crime, Proof and Punishment*, 81.

to transactions entered into by a minor.[27] As a matter of civil law, the supply of unnecessary services to a minor will not create a legally enforceable contract. It is a question of law whether the items are necessary. To be necessary they must be of a nature suitable to the child's condition in life and actually required by him at the time and he must not already be otherwise sufficiently provided with them.[28] So, if a landlord of a pub supplies beer to a minor, the transaction is contrary to law and the minor commits no offence in making off without payment. If the minor has a service provided to him which is not a 'necessary' one (say, flying lessons) he commits no offence in making off since payment for that service is not legally enforceable. If the minor is supplied with non-necessary *goods* (say, 11 fancy waistcoats) and makes off he commits the offence; while payment for the waistcoats is not legally enforceable, the supply of these *goods* is not contrary to law.

The courts do not seem to have been troubled by defence claims that although performance of the contract was not contrary to law, some collateral aspect of V's conduct in the supply of the goods or services was contrary to law and therefore unprotected by s 3. It was anticipated by some that this would give rise to problems in cases such as D bilking on the unlicensed taxi driver.[29]

21.1.1.4 Without having paid as required or expected

It is implicit in the section that V requires or expects payment on the spot and that the payment is due in fact and law. If a taxi driver, in the course of a journey, commits a breach of contract entitling his passenger to rescind the contract, the passenger does not commit an offence by making off.[30] Where the money is due, does a person who gives a worthless cheque in 'payment' of the debt commit the offence? The question was previously of little importance because D would have been guilty of the more serious offence under s 2(1)(b) of the 1978 Act. The offence would now be one under s 2 of the Fraud Act 2006 as D makes a false representation that the cheque will be honoured.[31] In the one reported case (although only at first instance)[32] in which the matter has arisen the judge ruled that the s 3 offence was not committed because a worthless cheque was not the same as counterfeit money, and that D was not making off because he departed with V's consent. The true answer may well be that D is guilty because he has not paid 'as required or expected'. V requires and expects payment in legal tender or by a good cheque. Payment by a worthless cheque no more satisfies his requirement or expectation than payment in counterfeit money. In the rare cases in which payment by cheque nowadays occurs, it will inevitably be backed by a cheque guarantee card, and depending on the conditions of its issue, D may have paid as required or expected although his authority to use the card has been withdrawn or even if it has been stolen.[33] The same is true of payment by credit card.[34] V has been paid if the bank or card issuer is bound to honour the cheque or card, and that is a question of civil law. The offence is not committed if the supplier consents to D's leaving without payment, even if the consent was obtained by fraud, as where D deceives V into accepting postponement of payment.[35]

---

[27] cf P Rowlands, 'Minors: Can They Make Off Without Payment' (1981) 145 JP 410: cf Smith, *Property Offences*, para 20.69.

[28] *Bainbridge v Pickering* (1779) 2 Wm Bl 1325.   [29] See Griew, *Theft*, para 13.10.

[30] *Troughton v Metropolitan Police* [1987] Crim LR 138, DC.

[31] See G Syrota, 'Are Cheque Frauds Covered by Section 3 of the Theft Act 1978?' [1980] Crim LR 413.

[32] *Hammond* [1982] Crim LR 611 (Judge Morrison).

[33] cf *First Sport Ltd v Barclays Bank plc* [1993] 3 All ER 789, CA (Civ Div).

[34] cf *Re Charge Card Services Ltd* [1988] 3 All ER 702, [1988] 3 WLR 764, CA (Civ Div).

[35] *Vincent* [2001] Crim LR 488, [2001] 2 Cr App R 150, [2001] EWCA Crim 295, CA. See also *Evans v Lane* (1984) CO/137/84, CA.

Payment in such a case is not required or expected at *that* time. This may be an offence under s 2 of the Fraud Act 2006.

21.1.2 Mens rea

The offence requires that D should make off: (a) dishonestly; (b) knowing that payment on the spot is required or expected from him; and (c) with intent to avoid payment.

21.1.2.1 Dishonesty

Reference may be made to the general discussion of dishonesty.[36] It does not matter at what stage D decides to act dishonestly as long as he is dishonest when he makes off. Dishonesty is a question for the jury. If D genuinely believed that no payment was due at that time or that none was due owing to the poor standard or deficient goods, following *Ivey*[37] it would be for the jury to determine whether D was dishonest in refusing to pay for goods or a service. D's perception of how reasonable people would view his conduct is no longer fundamental since the *Ghosh* test was rejected.

21.1.2.2 Knowing that payment on the spot is required or expected of him

The offence is concerned only with cases where payment on the spot is required. Such transactions are difficult to define in abstract terms. They are usually easy enough to identify[38] by reference to normal trading practices, although these may in particular instances be modified by the course of dealing between the parties.[39] If D believes that the transaction is on credit terms, he cannot be convicted of this offence for he does not *know* the transaction to be a spot transaction. Where D believes that payment is to be made by another (eg where he believes that E will pay for the meal) he does not commit the offence because he does not know that payment is to be required of him.[40] Presumably D would not be liable if, having drunk too much alcohol with his meal, he staggers out of the restaurant without paying and is so intoxicated that he does not know what he is doing.

21.1.2.3 Intention to avoid payment

Section 3 does not explicitly require an intention to make permanent default, and commentators tended to favour the view that a dishonest intention temporarily to avoid payment would suffice. However, *Allen*[41] holds that the offence requires an intention to make permanent default. D had left an hotel without settling his bill and the trial judge directed the jury that all that was required was an intention to make default at the time payment was required. The Court of Appeal held, however, that an intention to make permanent default was required because s 3 required both (a) a making off without paying on the spot; and (b) an intention to avoid payment. In view of the requirement in (a), (b) made sense only if

---

[36] See p 873.   [37] [2017] UKSC 67, [74]. For discussion, see p 879.

[38] Section 3(2) provides that it includes 'payment at the time of collecting goods on which work has been done or in respect of which service has been provided'. But this seems to have been added *ex abundanti cautela* and adds nothing.

[39] It cannot be enough that V requires a payment to be made on the spot, eg seeing D who owes him £10 lent a month ago, V demands payment on the spot. The reference is to those transactions where payment *customarily* follows immediately upon the provision of the goods or service.

[40] *Brooks and Brooks* (1982) 76 Cr App R 66, [1983] Crim LR 188, CA.

[41] [1985] AC 1029, [1985] 2 All ER 641, [1985] Crim LR 739.

permanent default was intended. The House of Lords endorsed this view and drew further support for it by reference to the fact that the CLRC had intended permanent default to be necessary.[42]

The Home Office rejected a reform proposal suggested by garage owners[43] which would have extended the offence to include cases where D acts with intent to defer payment.

---

[42] Thirteenth Report (1977) Cmnd 6733, para 18.

[43] Home Office, *Fraud Law Reform: Consultation on Proposals for Legislation* (2004) para 45: http://webarchive.nationalarchives.gov.uk/+/http://www.homeoffice.gov.uk/documents/cons-fraud-law-reform/. Complaining of individuals who, having filled their cars with fuel, claimed to have left their wallets at home and promised to pay at a later date. That may be an offence under s 2 of the Fraud Act 2006.